Introduction to Forensic Psychology

Fifth Edition

D1122491

To the fabulous four:
Kai Arman, Madeleine Riley, Darya Alessandra, and Shannon Marie
and their equally fabulous parents:
Gina Marie, Ian Kurt, Soraya Elizabeth Moein, and James Riley

Introduction to Forensic Psychology

Research and Application

Fifth Edition

Curt R. Bartol

Anne M. Bartol

Los Angeles | London | New Delhi
Singapore | Washington DC | Melbourne

FOR INFORMATION:

SAGE Publications, Inc.
2455 Teller Road
Thousand Oaks, California 91320
E-mail: order@sagepub.com

SAGE Publications Ltd.
1 Oliver's Yard
55 City Road
London EC1Y 1SP
United Kingdom

SAGE Publications India Pvt. Ltd.
B 1/I 1 Mohan Cooperative Industrial Area
Mathura Road, New Delhi 110 044
India

SAGE Publications Asia-Pacific Pte. Ltd.
3 Church Street
#10-04 Samsung Hub
Singapore 049483

Printed in the United States of America

Library of Congress Cataloging-in-Publication Data

Names: Bartol, Curt R., author. | Bartol, Anne M., author.
Title: Introduction to forensic psychology: research and application / Curt R. Bartol, Anne M. Bartol.

Description: Fifth Edition. | Thousand Oaks: SAGE Publications, [2018] | Revised edition of the authors' Introduction to forensic psychology, [2015] | Includes bibliographical references and index.

Identifiers: LCCN 2017033026 | ISBN 9781506387246 (pbk.: alk. paper)

Subjects: LCSH: Forensic psychology.

Classification: LCC RA1148 .B37 2018 | DDC 614/.15—dc23 LC record available at https://lccn.loc.gov/2017033026

Acquisitions Editor: Jessica Miller
Content Developmental Editor: Neda Dallal
Editorial Assistant: Rebecca Lee
Production Editor: Laureen Gleason
Copy Editor: Diane DiMura
Typesetter: Hurix Digital
Proofreader: Susan Schon
Indexer: Terri Morrissey
Cover Designer: Scott Van Atta
Marketing Manager: Jillian Oelsen

This book is printed on acid-free paper.

SUSTAINABLE FORESTRY INITIATIVE
Certified Chain of Custody
Promoting Sustainable Forestry
www.sfiprogram.org
SFI-01268
SFI label applies to text stock

18 19 20 21 22 10 9 8 7 6 5 4 3 2 1

BRIEF CONTENTS

PART I • INTRODUCTION

PART II • POLICE AND INVESTIGATIVE PSYCHOLOGY

PART III • LEGAL PSYCHOLOGY

PART IV • CRIMINAL PSYCHOLOGY

PART V • VICTIMOLOGY AND VICTIM SERVICES

PART VI • CORRECTIONAL PSYCHOLOGY

DETAILED CONTENTS

PART II • POLICE AND INVESTIGATIVE PSYCHOLOGY

PART III · LEGAL PSYCHOLOGY

PART V · VICTIMOLOGY AND VICTIM SERVICES

PART VI • CORRECTIONAL PSYCHOLOGY

LIST OF BOXES, TABLES, AND FIGURES

FROM MY PERSPECTIVE BOXES

FOCUS BOXES

TABLES

FIGURES

PREFACE

This book is intended to be a core text in courses in forensic psychology, including those enrolling criminal justice majors and social work majors. However, the book is also addressed to general readers and mental health professionals seeking a basic overview of the field. Although many people associate forensic psychology with criminal profiling, crime scene investigations, and testifying in court, the field is much broader in scope. In fact, forensic psychology is an engaging yet difficult field to survey because of its topical diversity, wide range of application, and very rapid growth.

The spirited debate about how forensic psychology should be defined and who should be called a forensic psychologist has continued since the first edition of the book was published. We discuss this in Chapter 1, where we comment on developments over the past 25 years, including the adoption of "Specialty Guidelines for Forensic Psychology" (American Psychological Association [APA], 2013c) and certification of forensic psychologists. For our purposes, forensic psychology will refer *broadly* to the production of psychological knowledge and research findings and their application to the civil and criminal justice systems. Forensic psychologists may be involved in clinical practice, in consulting and research activities, and as academicians, and they work in many contexts. What they have in common is consultation with the legal system in some capacity.

The book is organized around five major subareas of the field, which often overlap: (1) police and investigative psychology; (2) legal psychology, sometimes referred to as psychology and law; (3) criminal psychology; (4) victimology and victim services; and (5) correctional psychology (including institutional and community corrections for both adults and juveniles). Victimology and victim services represent the newest areas in which forensic psychologists are beginning to participate in increasing numbers. We emphasize here and throughout the book that not all psychologists working in these areas are forensic psychologists—in fact, many do not consider themselves to be.

The text concentrates on the *application* side of the field, focusing on research-based forensic practice. Throughout the book, we emphasize the professional application of psychological knowledge, concepts, and principles to both the civil and criminal justice systems, including services to defendants, plaintiffs, offenders, and victims. The topics included in the text are largely dictated by what forensic psychologists and psychologists practicing in forensic settings do on a day-to-day basis. Their work, though, should rely heavily on the continuing research they or their professional colleagues are engaged in. For example, forensic psychologists conducting risk assessments must be aware of the evaluation research on the various methods and measures that they employ. Expert witnesses must be knowledgeable about latest findings in such areas as eyewitness identification or adolescent brain development. Research is relevant to child custody evaluations, risk assessments in many contexts, competency and sanity evaluations of criminal defendants, threat assessments for schools, counseling services to victims of crime, screening and selection of law enforcement applicants, assessment of various civil capacities, the assessment of posttraumatic stress disorder (PTSD), and assessment of juvenile comprehension of legal rights.

One of the major goals of the text is to expose readers to the many careers related to forensic psychology. During our years of college teaching, it became apparent that an overriding concern of many students was to discover what kinds of employment opportunities are available in their chosen major or favorite subject area as well as the stimulating challenges they will meet and the contributions they can make. In an effort to address this, we provide examples of forensic practice. And, as in the third and fourth editions, we include personal narratives written by professionals in the field. These "Perspectives" should provide readers with information about career choices as well as helpful advice about pursuing their goals. Often, students begin and sometimes end their undergraduate days not knowing exactly what they want to do career wise. As many of the essayists will indicate, this is not unusual. Common themes in the essays are to obtain varied experiences, find academic mentors, remain open to new possibilities, take time to enjoy your life, and persist.

Because students are often drawn to the word *forensic* without realizing the many branches of practice contained within the label, the book begins by covering the forensic sciences *in general*. It then moves on to the various levels of graduate training, internships, and fellowships relevant to forensic *psychology*. It will become very clear to aspiring forensic psychologists at the outset that they will have to pursue several years of graduate and even postgraduate education. Many of the Perspectives essays, though, emphasize the value of both undergraduate and graduate internships—which students can begin now—with experiential learning in their communities. Though the path to becoming a practicing psychologist may be a long one, this is an enormously rewarding career.

Another major goal of the text is to emphasize the multicultural perspective that is an integral part of the day-to-day work of all practicing and research psychologists. Well-trained forensic psychologists recognize that ethnic and racial sensitivity is critical to successful practice, and they know they must be constantly vigilant to the injustices that can result from a monocultural or isolationist perspective. Although this has always been important, it is especially crucial today. Researchers in the field also must pay attention to these issues. Recognizing the changing nature of relationships, including family relationships, is vital as well.

Some features of the text should make it accessible even to readers with a limited background in psychology. Key terms appear in boldface in the text narrative (their definitions can be found in the Glossary), and lists of key concepts and review questions appear at the end of each chapter. Every chapter begins with a list of objectives to help students obtain a sense of what is ahead. The text also includes an extensive list of references that will aid readers to find more material on the subject areas covered. Material in boxes (Perspectives and Focuses) not only provides more information about career options, but also should prompt discussion on contemporary issues relevant to the practice of forensic psychology. For example, there are Focus boxes relating to mental health courts, community-oriented policing, eyewitness identification, child abduction, hate crimes, the death penalty, human trafficking, and aid in dying. Focus boxes also contain discussion questions, some of which may engender fierce debates in a classroom setting.

NEW TO THIS EDITION

The fifth edition includes a number of changes, many of which were made at the recommendation of peer reviewers. We have retained the same structure of chapters, a structure that was changed between the third and fourth editions. Inevitably, some topics straddle one or more chapters. For example, although there is a final chapter on juvenile justice and delinquency, material related to juveniles can be found in many earlier chapters as well. Likewise, risk assessment—because it is a task highly relevant to forensic psychology—is introduced early in the book but reappears in most later chapters.

The new edition includes the following changes:

- Updated statistics, research, and case law

- New focus boxes, and updated material in those boxes that were retained from the 4th edition

- Expanded coverage of eyewitness identification and consultation with law enforcement on that issue

- More attention to immigration-related issues, such as competency evaluations of undocumented immigrants subject to deportation and serving immigrant populations

- Additional coverage of human trafficking and online sexual predators

- Recent research on violent video games and cyberbullying

- Focus on alternative police interviewing techniques, such as information gathering and cognitive interviewing

- Expanded coverage of investigative psychology and its many contributions to forensic psychology

- Attention to the important contributions of forensic neuropsychologists

- Additional coverage of female offending

- Increased coverage of the various forms of bias, including police bias

- Expanded viewpoint of victimology issues, particularly from a multicultural and ethnic framework

- Expanded attention paid to adolescent brain development as it pertains to the legal system

- Promising community-based treatment approaches for juveniles

Numerous topics in this book deserve far more attention than we have been able to give them here; other topics relevant to forensic practice, particularly in the civil context, are left uncovered. Fortunately, Perspective boxes often fill these gaps. In addition, discussion of cases, particularly Supreme Court cases, are not meant to be comprehensive but rather to illustrate important psychological concepts and considerations. Nevertheless, we hope that this introductory material will prompt readers to explore topics of interest in more depth. The text should serve as an overview of the field of forensic psychology and an invitation to learn more about this very attractive and exciting career option.

ACKNOWLEDGMENTS

The book is dedicated to our grandchildren and their parents, all the light of our lives. We are awed by their goodness, wit, resilience, beauty, and their accomplishments in so many realms. And, they provide much needed time out and the opportunity to laugh, play, and grumble together, even when a deadline is looming.

We thank the academic and professional colleagues who reviewed the fourth edition of the book and provided detailed, chapter-by-chapter commentary. Each one offered thoughtful suggestions for revision, and we hope we addressed most of them. The reviewers were Professors Michael Anderson, National University; Apryl Alexander, University of Denver; Kendell L. Coker, University of New Haven; Michael P. Hoff, Dalton State College, Marie Robbins, Grimsby Institute; and Albert Toh, University of Arkansas at Pine Bluff.

We are also grateful to the thirteen psychologists who wrote about their backgrounds and experiences and gave advice to students thinking of career opportunities in this field for our Perspectives boxes. This feature of the book is in some ways the most satisfying to produce; it captures the enthusiasm forensic psychologists have for their work, their continuing productivity, and their confidence in the professionals of tomorrow. We remain grateful as well to essayists from the third and fourth editions, many of whom recommended their colleagues for this new edition. We know that each essayist is a busy professional with multiple demands on his or her time—yet they were willing to help us out and communicate with students in this unique way. It has been a pleasure to work with them, and we know that readers will appreciate their insights. Finally, we also acknowledge the work of the numerous scholars whose research is cited throughout the book and in our rather massive list of references.

Readers of textbooks are usually not aware of the behind-the-scenes labor involved from the moment a book is signed to its final production. The authors prepare the content, but the editors, assistants, proofreaders, artists, designers, and production, marketing, and sales staffs, have a multitude of tasks that result in getting a book into your hands. Through all editions of this and other books, the SAGE family has been there for us, and we are truly grateful to them. Acquisitions Editor Jessica Miller and Editorial Assistants Jennifer Rubio and Rebecca Lee have been efficient and helpful from the outset. They advocated for us, contacted reviewers, provided photo samples, and responded quickly and patiently to our questions as the manuscript was being prepared. Production Editor Laureen Gleason seamlessly carried the manuscript on, including by bringing on board our meticulous copy editor, Diane DiMura. Thank you, Diane, for your patience, the friendly banter, and for giving such close attention to that mighty reference file. Thanks also to Susan Schon for proofreading the composed pages and to Terri Morrissey for creating the book's indexes. We know that Marketing Manager Jillian Oelsen and her staff have efficiently promoted the book, and that they and many sales representatives will continue to do that! We selected Scott Van Atta's cover design at a dining table with dear friends—it was an easy choice to make. We are grateful to have all of you on our team.

PUBLISHER'S ACKNOWLEDGMENTS

SAGE wishes to acknowledge the valuable contributions of the following reviewers: Apryl Alexander, University of Denver; Michael Anderson, National University; Kendell L. Coker, University of New Haven; Michael P. Hoff, Dalton State College; Marie Robbins; and Albert Toh, University of Arkansas at Pine Bluff.

DIGITAL RESOURCES

STUDENT STUDY SITE

SAGE edge for Students provides a personalized approach to help students accomplish their coursework goals in an easy-to-use learning environment.

Mobile-friendly **eFlashcards** strengthen understanding of key terms and concepts.

Mobile-friendly practice **quizzes** allow for independent assessment by students of their mastery of course material.

A customized online **action plan** includes tips and feedback on progress through the course and materials, which allows students to individualize their learning experience.

Access to full-text **SAGE journal articles** that have been carefully selected to support and expand on the concepts presented in each chapter is included.

INSTRUCTOR TEACHING SITE

Password-protected **Instructor Resources** include the following:

SAGE edge for Instructors supports your teaching by making it easy to integrate quality content and create a rich learning environment for students.

Microsoft® Word Test banks provide a diverse range of prewritten options as well as the opportunity to edit any question and/or insert your own personalized questions to effectively assess students' progress and understanding.

Sample course syllabi for semester and quarter courses provide suggested models for structuring your courses.

Editable, chapter-specific **PowerPoint® slides** offer complete flexibility for creating a multimedia presentation for your course.

Access to full-text **SAGE journal articles** that have been carefully selected to support and expand on the concepts presented in each chapter is included.

Lecture notes summarize key concepts by chapter to help you prepare for lectures and class discussions.

"From My Perspective" essays from the third and fourth editions are included and feature profiles of professionals who work in forensic psychology.

Sara Miller McCune founded SAGE Publishing in 1965 to support the dissemination of usable knowledge and educate a global community. SAGE publishes more than 1000 journals and over 800 new books each year, spanning a wide range of subject areas. Our growing selection of library products includes archives, data, case studies and video. SAGE remains majority owned by our founder and after her lifetime will become owned by a charitable trust that secures the company's continued independence.

Los Angeles | London | New Delhi | Singapore | Washington DC | Melbourne

INTRODUCTION

CHAPTER ONE

INTRODUCTION TO FORENSIC PSYCHOLOGY

Shortly before midnight on December 2, 2016, fire broke out during a rave party in a converted warehouse in Oakland, California, resulting in the death of about three dozen people. Forensic investigators were called in not only to identify the bodies, but also to determine the cause of the blaze. The warehouse, known as the "Ghost Ship," was an artists' collective in which various artists lived and shared work space. Federal investigators announced in late December that they had ruled out arson, but that electrical wiring could have caused the fire. The building also was said to have multiple building code violations.

Forensic experts of a different type came to the aid of the Target Corporation in late 2013, when it was learned that Target's databases had been hacked into, and credit card data of some 70 to 110 million shoppers had been compromised. These experts dug through firewall logs, web traffic logs, and e-mails to find the source of the problem.

When the space shuttle Columbia disintegrated upon reentry into the Earth's atmosphere in 2003 and when a bomb was detonated in New York's Times Square in 2010, these events were investigated by scientists representing various federal and state agencies. Likewise, when bombs disrupted the Boston Marathon in 2013, killing three and injuring more than 260 others, scientists examined the crime scene as well as the remnants of the incendiary materials.

Chapter Objectives

- Define forensic psychology and trace its historical development.
- Review career areas in the forensic sciences.
- Distinguish forensic psychology from other forensic sciences.
- Identify and describe major subareas of forensic psychology.
- Review the educational, training, and certification requirements to become a forensic psychologist.
- Illustrate roles and tasks performed by forensic psychologists.

As all of these examples indicate, the term forensic refers to anything pertaining or potentially pertaining to law, both civil and criminal. Forensic scientists participate in the investigation of major crimes—not necessarily violent ones—and are present at many accident scenes.

Investigations of this sort almost invariably occur whenever there are unexpected and unexplained events that are not obvious natural disasters. In these contexts, scientists can perform numerous functions. They may be able to determine whether human factors—for example, sabotage, negligence, or terrorist activities—caused the tragedies. The information they provide can help in identifying those responsible. In the case of the Oakland fire, scientists tried to determine not only its cause, but also whether there was indication that it had been deliberately set. They also worked to identify the remains of those who had perished. In the case of cyberhacking, experts search for digital footprints to determine how hackers get in and how to prevent further breaches of security.

Forensic science has become an all-encompassing professional activity and a popular career choice among students. Nearly every conceivable profession, including psychology, has a forensic specialization. Many people are confused about the various forensic areas and assume that professionals within these fields do largely the same thing. It will become clear in this book, however, that they do not. What they do have in common, in addition to their association with the law, is the fact that all of these fields are based on scientific principles. Although **forensic psychology** is the subject of this text, it is helpful to begin with illustrations of other forensic sciences for comparison purposes. In other words, it is important for readers to know at the outset what forensic psychology is not.

THE FORENSIC SCIENCES

Examples of the forensic fields, in addition to forensic psychology, include forensic engineering, forensic linguistics, forensic oceanography, forensic medicine, forensic digital investigation, forensic social work, forensic nursing, forensic pathology, forensic anthropology, and forensic archaeology. The focus of each discipline is evident from the terms. Forensic linguistics, for example, is concerned with the in-depth evaluation of language-related characteristics of text, such as grammar, syntax, spelling, vocabulary, and phraseology, either to profile an offender or to determine whether specific writing samples are from the same author (H. C. Black, 1990). Forensic anthropology refers to the identification of skeletal, badly decomposed, or otherwise unidentified human remains. Forensic pathology is that branch of medicine concerned with diseases and disorders of the body that relate to questions that might come before the court. The forensic pathologist—popularized in shows such as the *CSI* series, *Bones*, and *NCIS*, and in many crime novels—examines the bodies of crime victims for clues about the victim's demise. Forensic anthropologists and forensic pathologists often work in conjunction with homicide investigators to identify the person who died; discover evidence of foul play; and help establish the age, sex, height, ancestry, and other unique features of the decedent from skeletal remains. Forensic nurses, who often work in hospital emergency departments, are nurses with special training in the collection of evidence pertinent to a crime, such as a sexual assault.

Forensic laboratories are usually maintained or sponsored by governmental agencies specifically to examine physical evidence in criminal and civil matters. In 2014, there were 409 publicly funded forensic crime labs in the United States (Bureau of Justice Statistics, 2016). The scientists working in these laboratories are expected to prepare reports and provide courtroom testimony on the physical evidence if needed. Alternatively, private laboratories provide services to governmental agencies on a contractual basis or employ scientists who conduct independent research.

Scientists from both public and private laboratories may be asked to examine and testify about latent fingerprints, hair fibers, firearms and ballistics, blood spatter, explosives and fire debris, toxic material, and other pertinent evidence found at or near a crime scene or tragic accident. Some forensic labs are better at investigating certain types of evidence than others, and the news media occasionally uncover deficiencies in labs, such as the misuse of DNA evidence or the failure to process rape kits in a timely manner. On a more positive note, a lab maintained by the Food and Drug Administration (FDA) was instrumental in investigating a major product-tampering case that occurred in the United States in 1982. Seven persons in the Chicago area collapsed and died soon after taking Tylenol capsules. The capsules had been purchased in six different stores, and victims included a 12-year-old girl, a woman who had just returned from the hospital after giving birth, and three members of one family. Chemical investigation revealed that the capsules had been laced with potassium cyanide. FDA chemists developed fingerprinting-like techniques that allowed authorities to trace the cyanide back to the specific manufacturer and distributor (Stehlin, 1995). Unfortunately, despite the fact that the poison was identified and the source was traced, the perpetrator was never found, but the case did change the way we purchase and consume over-the-counter medications (Markel, 2014). Forensic examination indicated that the Tylenol bottles had been removed from drug store shelves, laced with cyanide, and returned to shelves to be purchased by unknowing victims. The FDA and the manufacturer of Tylenol introduced new tamperproof packaging, which included foil seals and other safeguards to indicate to the consumer if the package had been tampered with.

With increased threats of mass violence and events such as the anthrax scare that followed the September 11, 2001, terrorist attacks on the twin towers in New York and the Pentagon in Arlington, Virginia, quick forensic chemical-detection methods such as those described above have become especially crucial. In addition to terrorism-related concerns, also critical are forensic techniques that can address more common crimes, such as drug trafficking, computer crimes, and a wide variety of white-collar offenses that involve fraudulent documents.

Forensic laboratories also often employ scientists who specialize in **forensic entomology**, which is the study of insects (and their arthropod relatives) as it relates to legal issues. This specialty is becoming increasingly important in both civil and criminal investigations. For example, entomological investigations of termite infestation may be used to support civil litigation dealing with real estate, pest control, or landlord–tenant disputes. In another context, forensic entomology may be useful in investigations of food contamination. Scientists try to determine where an infestation occurred (e.g., which warehouse or store), when it occurred, and whether it was accidental or the possible result of human tampering. (Whether there actually was negligence or evil intent, though, is left to the courts to decide.)

In criminal investigations, forensic entomology is used to determine the time since death (postmortem interval), the location of the death, placement or movement of the body, and manner of death. Forensic entomology can also be applied to investigations of drug trafficking. Insects are sometimes found in drugs, and their identity can help in pinpointing where the drugs were produced or packed. In some cases, forensic entomologists can establish from the DNA of body or head lice whether two individuals had contact with each other (Mumcuoglu, Gallili, Reshef, Brauner, & Grant, 2004).

Still another science represented in forensic laboratories is forensic document examination. This science analyzes handwriting, print fonts, the authenticity of signatures, alterations in documents, charred or water-damaged paper, the significance of inks and papers, photocopying processes, writing instruments, sequence of writing, and other elements of a document to establish authorship and authenticity. The process is often called **questioned document examination or analysis**. The questioned document may be a check, a threatening letter, a hold-up note, a credit application or receipt, a will, an investment record, a tax form, or a medical record (R. Morris, 2000). Questioned document analysis can be applied to many types of investigations, including fraud, homicide, suicide, sexual offenses, blackmail, bombings, and arson. Questioned handwriting analysis, for example, may include the forensic examination of a signature, a handwritten letter, entries on a form, or even graffiti on a wall. A forensic document examiner (FDE) may be asked to examine and render opinions on the authorship of writing on building walls; recover engraved or obliterated writing on different types of surfaces; or determine the brand or model of typewriters or keyboards, printers, embossers, inks, and printing processes (R. Morris, 2000).

Another electronic forensic specialty is **digital investigative analysis** (DIA). Anyone who has experienced hard drive failure or other digital memory loss can recall the momentary panic it engenders. We now know that most "lost" data can actually be recovered. As embarrassed politicians, their staffs, and other high-profile professionals and public figures have learned, e-mail or text messages on computers, online voicemail systems, tablets, or smartphones do not inevitably disappear in cyberspace, even with the press of the delete key or the smash of a hammer. Shortly after two individuals killed 14 people in a terrorist attack in San Bernardino, California, in December 2015, digital analysts were able to find evidence that they had planned other attacks from equipment in their home that had been smashed. Today, with increases in mobile devices, e-mails and electronic data can exist in multiple locations, and a skillful forensic data recovery specialist can usually find them. A digital investigative analyst has the training to seize, search, and analyze electronic media originating from a variety of operating systems pursuant to the execution of a search warrant or subpoena. Without specialized training, though, a law enforcement officer armed with a search warrant would not be advised to open computer files from the office or home of a person suspected of bank fraud or one suspected of distributing child pornography. The major goal of the specialist or investigator is to recover the data or images without modifying them. These skills are used in a wide variety of investigations, such as fraud, embezzlement, sexual harassment, child pornography, program vandalism, identity theft, document forgery, software piracy, narcotics trafficking, money laundering, and terroristic activity.

With the creation of new technologies doubling about every 2 or 3 years (Friedman, 2016), the recovery of digital evidence becomes increasingly challenging, however. Today, forensic digital analysts examine everything digital "including desktop computers, laptops, mobile devices (cell phones and tablets), GPS navigation devices, vehicle computer systems, Internet of Things (IoT) devices, and much more" (Carroll, 2017, p. 25). Mobile phones have drawn the greatest amount of forensic scrutiny. As noted by Daniel Ogden (2017), "With mobile devices allowing consumers to communicate, socialize, bank, shop, navigate, start their car, track their health, and monitor their in-home surveillance cameras, a plethora of information is contained on these devices" (p. 11). And each year smartphones increase their security features, making them more challenging for digital investigators to decipher.

As is apparent from the above illustrations, forensic investigations usually require expertise in chemistry, biology, physics, or other sciences, including electronic technology. Although television, movies, and popular novels provide numerous graphic examples of forensic examinations of evidence, the extensive scientific preparation required to work in forensic laboratories is usually not emphasized. The scientists depicted typically have access to state-of-the-art equipment, and they are often glamorous or have complex emotional lives, a depiction that may be quite unrealistic. Many students express a keen interest in the forensic sciences and seriously consider pursuing a career in the field without fully understanding what it is or what is required to reach their goal.

The field of forensic psychology involves a very different type of preparation and is significantly different in content, but it, too, requires considerable preparation. Nonetheless, there are many different avenues to entering this field, as will become apparent in this text.

FORENSIC PSYCHOLOGY: AN OVERVIEW

For some time, the definition of forensic psychology has been in flux. As Otto and Ogloff (2014) observe, "Perhaps it is surprising, given the relatively long history and growth of forensic psychology over the past 40 years, that there is no uniform or consensual definition for this specialty area" (p. 35). In a similar way, John Brigham (1999) wrote that if a group of psychologists who interact with the legal system in some capacity are asked, "Are you a forensic psychologist?" many will say yes, some will say no, and a majority will probably admit they really do not know. Referring to his own testimony in court, Brigham noted that, when asked the question, his most accurate current response would be, "Well, it depends."

As Brigham (1999) and Otto and Ogloff (2014) point out, differences in definition revolve around how narrowly or broadly the field is defined. Some of the professional literature refers to forensic psychology broadly as the *research* and *application* of psychological knowledge to the legal system, whereas some of it prefers a more narrow approach, limiting forensic psychology to the *application* and *practice* of psychology as it pertains to the legal system. A while back, we (Bartol & Bartol, 1987) offered the following definition:

> We view forensic psychology broadly, as both (1) the research endeavor that examines aspects of human behavior directly related to the legal process . . . and (2) the professional practice of psychology within, or in consultation with, a legal system that embraces both civil and criminal law. (p. 3)

Ronald Roesch (cited in Brigham, 1999) suggested a narrow definition: "Most psychologists define the area more narrowly to refer to clinical psychologists who are engaged in clinical practice within the legal system" (p. 279).

The narrow definition may be too restrictive because it seems to imply a specialty called "forensic *clinical* psychology." Furthermore, it excludes—among others—clinicians who perform corrections-related tasks, such as assess inmates for parole decision-making purposes, or clinicians who offer consulting services to police departments. The broad definition, on the other hand, includes not only clinicians (also called practitioners), but also social, developmental, counseling, cognitive, experimental, industrial/organizational, and school psychologists—some but not all of whom are clinicians. The common link is their contribution to the legal system. We recognize, however, that only a small proportion of their work may be performed in this context, so they might not consider themselves forensic psychologists. So, Brigham was correct in answering, "It depends."

DeMatteo, Marczyk, Krauss, and Burl (2009) note that the lack of consensus for defining forensic psychology as well as the activities it comprises has continued: "[T]here is considerable disagreement over the scope of forensic psychology and what activities (i.e., research, assessment, and treatment) and roles should appropriately be considered the exclusive province of forensic psychology" (p. 185). They point out that increasing dissatisfaction with narrow conceptualizations led the American Psychology-Law Society to endorse a broad definition, particularly one that would embrace the contributions of researchers as well as clinicians. Most recently, following these recommendations, the **Specialty Guidelines for Forensic Psychology** (American Psychological Association [APA], 2013c) promoted a broad definition, which is one we endorse and illustrate throughout this text:

> Forensic psychology refers to professional practice by any psychologist working within any sub-discipline of psychology (e.g., clinical, developmental, social, cognitive) when applying the scientific, technical, or specialized knowledge of psychology to the law to assist in addressing legal, contractual, and administrative matters. (p. 7)

The above broad definition of forensic psychology focuses primarily on forensic practice, referring as it does to the application of psychology's specialized knowledge to the law. It is understood that this application must be based on solid research. The practice of forensic psychology, as it will be treated here, includes investigations, studies, evaluations, advice to attorneys, advisory opinions, and depositions or testimony to assist in the resolution of disputes relating to life or property in cases before the courts or other law tribunals. It can—and does—encompass situations before they reach the court as well as those situations following the court decision. It includes activities as varied as the following: courtroom testimony, child custody evaluations, screening and selection of law enforcement candidates, and clinical services to offenders and staff in correctional facilities. It also includes research and theory building in criminology; the design and implementation of intervention, prevention, and treatment for youth offenders; and counseling of victims of crime.

For organizational purposes, we divide forensic psychology into five subspecialties: (1) police and public safety psychology, (2) legal psychology, (3) psychology of crime and delinquency, (4) victimology and victim services, and (5) correctional psychology. It should be emphasized, however, that this is for purposes of organizing the text and is not necessarily the organizational schema that is universally accepted in the field. Other scholars have adopted various methods of addressing the many ways psychology can interact with the law (e.g., Melton, Petrila, Poythress, & Slobogin, 2007; Otto & Ogloff, 2014). Furthermore, we recognize and appreciate that some psychologists prefer to maintain a distinction between forensic psychology and their own specialty area, such as correctional psychology (Magaletta et al., 2013) or police and public safety psychology (Brewster et al., 2016) This is addressed in more detail below.

Each of our subdivisions has both research and applied aspects, and psychologists conducting research in one area of forensic psychology may consult with or train practitioners in other areas. Finally, a forensic psychologist may operate in more than one of the above subspecialties. Although we separate them for organizational purposes, we do not intend to isolate them or suggest that they have little in common with one another. We will discuss each subspecialty in more detail after briefly reviewing the history of the field.

BRIEF HISTORY OF FORENSIC PSYCHOLOGY

Although the growth of forensic psychology has been especially apparent since the 1970s, its history can be traced back at least to the end of the 19th century, when J. McKeen Cattell conducted a very simple psychological experiment on eyewitness testimony in a psychology class at Columbia University. Cattell merely asked his students questions such as what the weather was like exactly a week before. Surprised at the wide variation in responses—often given with absolute certainty, even though they were wrong—Cattell decided to explore in greater depth and with more sophistication both memory and the field of eyewitness identification. Numerous psychologists subsequently undertook similar research. Some, for example, staged exercises wherein an "intruder" would enter the classroom, "confront" the professor, and leave. Students would then be asked to describe the intruder and the events that followed. To this day, both memory and eyewitness research remain of high interest to many forensic psychologists, yielding a rich store of information.

Psychologists also studied other topics that eventually produced knowledge of great value to the legal system. Research on human cognition, child development, abnormal behavior, the detection of deception, and stress are but a few examples. In the 20th century, such psychological knowledge gradually was introduced into legal proceedings in the form of expert testimony, first in civil courts and later, as the century wore on, in criminal courts (Bartol & Bartol, 2014; Otto, Kay, & Hess, 2014). In the early part of that century, psychologists also began to consult with juvenile courts and offer treatment services to juvenile and adult correctional facilities. By the start of World War II, psychologists like Lewis Terman had brought intelligence and aptitude testing to the military and some civilian law enforcement agencies. By mid-century, it was not unusual to see psychologists consulting formally with law enforcement agencies, particularly by offering services for the screening of candidates for police positions.

In the 1960s and 1970s, psychologists began to testify in courts in increasing numbers. They also joined other mental health professions in submitting amicus curiae briefs to appeals courts, offering scientific information about topics that reached the courts, such as the effects of discrimination or research on human development. They sometimes consulted with lawyers in trial preparation and jury selection, and they began to offer predictions of dangerousness under limited circumstances. Each of these areas of involvement will be discussed in detail in the chapters ahead. Focus 1.1 provides selected benchmarks in the history of forensic psychology.

In 1981, Loh observed that the relationship between psychology and law had come of age. Board certification in forensic psychology, provided by the American Board of Forensic Psychology, had begun in 1978 (Otto & Heilbrun, 2002). Shortly thereafter, the American Psychological Association (APA) established Division 41, the American Psychology-Law Society (AP-LS), and that society was instrumental in prompting the APA to adopt forensic psychology guidelines in 1991 (subsequently revised in 2013). Forensic psychology was accepted by the APA as a specialty in 2001 and recertified in 2008. In 2010, Heilbrun and Brooks noted that forensic psychology had matured. They observed, "we are closer to identifying best practices across a range of legal contexts that are addressed by forensic psychology research and practice" (p. 227). The growth in the field is reflected in the development of professional organizations devoted to research and practice in forensic psychology, significant increases in the number of books and periodicals focusing on the topic, the development of undergraduate and graduate training programs, and the establishment of standards for practitioners working in the discipline (DeMatteo et al., 2009; DeMatteo, Burl, Filone, & Heilbrun, 2016; Heilbrun & Brooks, 2010; Weiner & Otto, 2014).

FOCUS 1.1. SELECTED HISTORICAL BENCHMARKS PERTINENT TO FORENSIC PSYCHOLOGY

1893—First psychological experiment on the psychology of testimony is conducted by J. McKeen Cattell of Columbia University.

1903—Louis William Stern of Germany establishes a periodical dealing with the psychology of testimony (*Beiträge zur Psychologie der Aussage* [Contributions to the Psychology of Testimony])

1906—Publication of a little-known work, *Psychology Applied to Legal Evidence and Other Constructions of Law,* by George Frederick Arnold.

1908—Publication of Hugo Münsterberg's *On the Witness Stand,* arguably one of the first professional books on forensic psychology. Some scholars consider the author, a Harvard professor of psychology, to be the father of forensic psychology.

1908—Social science brief submitted to an appellate court, the Oregon Supreme Court, in *Muller v. Oregon.*

1909—Clinic for juvenile offenders established by psychologist Grace M. Fernald and psychiatrist William Healy.

1911—J. Varendonck becomes one of the earliest psychologists to testify in a criminal trial, held in Belgium.

1913—First time that psychological services are offered within a U.S. correctional facility (a women's reformatory in New York State), by psychologist Eleanor Rowland.

1917—Psychologist-lawyer William Marston develops the first "polygraph." Shortly thereafter, his expert testimony on the polygraph is rejected by a federal court (*Frye v. United States,* 1923) because the polygraph, as then developed, lacked general acceptance by the scientific community.

1917—Louis Terman becomes the first American psychologist to use psychological tests in the screening of law enforcement personnel.

1918—First inmate classification system developed by psychologists, established by the New Jersey Department of Corrections. New Jersey also becomes the first state to hire full-time correctional psychologists on a regular basis.

1921—First time an American psychologist testifies in a courtroom as an expert witness (*State v. Driver,* 1921).

1922—Karl Marbe, a psychology professor at the University of Würzburg, Germany, becomes the first psychologist to testify at a civil trial.

1922—William Marston becomes the first to receive a faculty appointment in forensic psychology, as "professor of legal psychology" at American University.

1924—Wisconsin becomes the first state to provide comprehensive psychological examinations of all admissions to its prison system and all applications for parole.

1929—Psychologist Donald Slesinger is appointed associate professor at Yale Law School, qualifying him as the first psychologist granted faculty status in an American law school.

1931—Howard Burtt's *Legal Psychology* is published—the first *textbook* in the forensic area written by a psychologist.

(Continued)

(Continued)

1954—U.S. Supreme Court cites social science research, including that of psychologists Kenneth and Mamie Clark, in its landmark ruling, *Brown v. Board of Education.*

1961—Hans Toch edits one of the first texts on the psychology of crime, *Legal and Criminal Psychology.*

1962. Psychologists are recognized as experts on the issue of mental illness by D.C. Court of Appeals in *Jenkins v. United States.*

1964—Psychologist Hans J. Eysenck formulates a comprehensive and testable theory on criminal behavior in the book *Crime and Personality.*

1968—Martin Reiser, the first prominent full-time police psychologist in the United States, is hired by the Los Angeles Police Department. Reiser became instrumental in establishing police psychology as a profession.

1968—The first PsyD program is established at the University of Illinois.

1972—Under the guidance and leadership of the American Association for Correctional Psychology (AACP), Stanley Brodsky, Robert Levinson, and Asher Pacht, correctional psychology becomes recognized as a professional career.

1973—The first successful interdisciplinary psychology and law program is developed at the University of Nebraska–Lincoln.

1978—The American Board of Forensic Psychology provides board certification in forensic psychology.

1978—The American Psychological Association approves a clinical internship in corrections at the Wisconsin Department of Corrections.

1991—The American Academy of Forensic Psychology and American Psychology-Law Society (Division 41 of the APA) publishes *Specialty Guidelines for Forensic Psychologists.*

2001—The American Psychological Association recognizes forensic psychology as a specialty.

2006—The Committee on the Revision of the Specialty Guidelines for Forensic Psychologists recommends a broader definition that encompasses research as well as clinical practice.

2008—The American Psychological Association recertifies forensic psychology as a specialty.

2013—The *Specialty Guidelines for Forensic Psychology* are published. Forensic psychology is described as "professional practice by any psychologist working within any subdiscipline of psychology (e.g., clinical, developmental, social, cognitive) when applying the scientific, technical, or specialized knowledge of psychology to the law to assist in addressing legal, contractual, and administrative matters."

2013—Police and Public Safety Psychology (PPSP) is recognized by the American Psychological Association as a specialty.

FORENSIC PSYCHOLOGY TODAY

Today, the practice of forensic psychology is evident in numerous contexts. Here are just a few examples of things that forensic psychologists (depending on their specialty) may be asked to do, in addition to working in academic settings.

Police and Public Safety Psychology

- Assist police departments in determining optimal shift schedules for their employees.

- Establish reliable and valid screening procedures for public safety officer positions at various law enforcement, fire, first responder, fish and wildlife, police, and sheriff's departments.

- Perform fitness-for-duty evaluations of officers after a critical incident, such as a hostage-taking situation ending in multiple deaths.

- Train police officers on how to assist mentally ill persons.

- Provide counseling and debriefing services to officers after a shooting incident.

- Provide support services to the families of law enforcement officers.

- Inform police of the research evidence regarding the reliability of eyewitness identification.

- Help detectives solve crimes, such as by examining a crime scene.

Legal Psychology

- Conduct child custody evaluations, visitation risk assessments, and child abuse evaluations.

- Assist attorneys in jury selection through community surveys and other research methods.

- Perform evaluations of a defendant's competency to stand trial.

- Testify at a trial in which the defendant has pleaded not guilty by reason of insanity.

- Evaluate civil capacities, such as the capacity to make a will or consent to treatment.

- Testify before a legislative committee on relationships between aggression and violent video games.

- Provide outpatient psychotherapy to individuals who have been ordered to receive treatment by the court.

- Assess hardships suffered by individuals threatened with deportation during immigration proceedings.

Psychology of Crime and Delinquency

- Evaluate the effectiveness of intervention strategies designed to prevent violent behavior during adolescence.

- Conduct research on the development of psychopathy.

- Consult with legislators and governmental agencies as a research policy advisor on responses to stalking.

- Consult with school personnel on identifying troubled youth who are a potential threat to other students.

- Develop a psychological measure for assessing risk of harm to self or others among the mentally ill.

- Inform the legal community about research on decision making in adolescence.

Victimology and Victim Services

- Evaluate persons who are the victims of crime or witnesses to crime.

- Conduct psychological assessments for personal injury matters related to auto accidents, product liability, sexual harassment and discrimination, medical negligence, worker's compensation, or disability.

- Educate and train victim service providers on psychological reactions to criminal victimization, such as posttraumatic stress disorder.

- Conduct forensic assessments of victims of persecution and torture for evidence at immigration hearings.

- Assess, support, and counsel those who provide death notification services.
- Educate service providers on the impact of multiculturalism when victims seek mental health and support services.

Correctional Psychology

- Assess inmates entering jail or prison for both mental health needs and suitability for treatment and rehabilitation programs.
- Assess prisoners for risk in parole decision making.
- Assess violence risk in juveniles and adults.
- Evaluate the effectiveness of programs for juvenile and adult offenders, such as victim–offender reconciliation programs, sex offender treatment, violence prevention, or health education programs.
- Conduct sexually violent predator assessments.
- Establish reliable and valid screening procedures for correctional officer positions at correctional facilities.
- Offer mental health treatment to adults and juveniles in correctional settings.

It should be mentioned that the above list would be shortened considerably if we were to adopt a narrower, clinically based definition of forensic psychology or apply it only to contact with the court system. In addition to the above, forensic psychologists teach in colleges and universities and conduct research that is relevant to the legal system, such as research on eyewitness testimony, the comprehension of constitutional rights, and jury decision making.

The work settings in which forensic psychologists are found include, but are not limited to, the following:

- Private practice
- Family, drug, and mental health courts
- Child protection agencies
- Victim services
- Domestic violence courts and programs
- Forensic mental health units (governmental or private)
- Sex offender treatment programs
- Correctional institutions (including research programs)
- Law enforcement agencies (federal, state, or local)
- Research organizations (governmental or private)
- Colleges and universities (teaching or research)
- Juvenile delinquency treatment programs
- Legal advocacy centers (e.g., for immigrants, prisoners, the mentally ill or intellectually disabled)

Throughout this book, text boxes in most of the chapters will introduce you to professionals who are engaged in these activities and work in these settings. Although their experiences are varied, a common theme is their willingness to pursue different and sometimes unexpected paths and opportunities, leading them to their present careers.

In today's economic climate, many students are worried that they will not secure employment upon graduation from college or upon earning an advanced degree. It is a reality that government grants and positions are often cut, and these affect scientists at all levels, even more so than when the 4th edition of this book was published. In April 2017, nationwide and global Marches for Science were held to resist executive orders and planned cuts in scientific programs. Of equal concern are threatened cuts to many health and social programs that affect vulnerable populations. Forensic psychology has thus far not been extensively damaged, and the outlook for career opportunities in its many facets is bright (Griffin, 2011), as illustrated by research cited in the text and by the comments of many essayists. Keep in mind, though, that with greater competition for available dollars comes greater accountability in the provision of services. For example, in the treatment arena, treatment providers are asked to document that their services are effective—in other words, that they are based on research evidence. *Evidence-based treatment* has become an important term in the correctional lexicon as well as in other areas of human services. Likewise, evidence-based practice—whereby psychologists use methods and instruments that, if not perfect, have respectable reliability and validity—is crucial for professionals interacting with the legal system.

FORENSIC PSYCHOLOGY, FORENSIC PSYCHIATRY, AND FORENSIC SOCIAL WORK

Some of the tasks listed above are performed by mental health professionals who are not psychologists, most particularly psychiatrists or social workers. Increasingly, these three groups of professionals work in collaboration, but it is important to point out some of the differences among them.

Psychologists, particularly but not exclusively those with specialties in clinical, counseling, or forensic psychology, are often confused with psychiatrists by the public and the media. Today, the lines of separation between the two professions are becoming increasingly blurred. Clinical, counseling, and forensic psychologists, along with psychiatrists, are trained to provide direct assessment and treatment services to persons with emotional, cognitive, or behavioral problems and also consult with attorneys and testify in court proceedings.

Psychiatrists are medical doctors (MDs) (or, in some cases, doctors of osteopathy [DOs]), who specialize in the prevention, diagnosis, and treatment of mental, addictive, and emotional disorders. Psychologists do not hold a medical degree, although some may have earned related degrees, such as a master of public health (MPH). Another major distinction between the two has been the license to prescribe drugs, including psychoactive drugs. Traditionally, psychologists have not been permitted by law to prescribe any medication. Now, that is beginning to change. In 2002, New Mexico became the first state to allow properly trained psychologists to prescribe psychoactive drugs, or drugs intended to treat mental disorders or behavioral problems. In 2004, Louisiana became the second state to pass a law authorizing properly trained psychologists to prescribe certain medications for the treatment of mental health disorders. In that state, these practitioners are called "medical psychologists." In 2014, Illinois enacted legislation granting prescriptive authority to psychologists who have training in psychopharmacology, and Iowa and Idaho enacted similar legislation in 2016 and 2017, respectively. Other bills are pending in several other states, suggesting there may be an emerging trend in this direction. Psychologists in the military also have prescription privileges. Properly trained psychologists in the Department of Defense, the U.S. Public Health Service, and the Indian Health Service are able to prescribe (American Psychological Association [APA], 2016a).

Medical associations typically have resisted extending prescription privileges, maintaining that this will lead to abuses and decrease the quality of patient care. Nevertheless, even among clinical psychologists there is not universal support for prescription privileges or authority, although most surveys find at least a majority in favor (e.g., Baird, 2007; Sammons, Gorny, Zinner, & Allen, 2000).

Many psychiatrists, like psychologists, work in a variety of forensic settings, including the court, correctional facilities, and law enforcement, but especially the first. Psychiatrists who are closely associated with the law are often referred to as **forensic psychiatrists**. In some areas, such as issues relating to insanity determination by the courts, psychiatrists are more visible—and sometimes more preferred—than psychologists. As we will discuss in a later chapter, this reflects a greater comfort on the part of some judges with the medical model approach to mental disorder (Melton et al., 2007). Nevertheless, psychologists routinely carry out these pretrial evaluations. Psychologists and psychiatrists seem to be equally involved in pretrial assessments of juveniles, while psychologists are more likely to conduct custody evaluations, consult with law enforcement, and work within the correctional system. Forensic neuropsychologists, who have expertise in brain research, assessments, and the law, are frequently consulted in both criminal and civil matters. Law-related research tends to be the bailiwick of psychologists, although some psychiatrists are also engaged in conducting and publishing such research.

Forensic social workers also can be found in the same arenas as their psychological and psychiatric counterparts. They may counsel victims of crimes or families of victims and offenders and provide substance abuse and sex offender treatment to offenders, among other functions. In many correctional facilities, social workers are part of the treatment team. Forensic social workers may be found participating in child custody evaluations, termination of parental rights, spousal abuse cases, and juvenile justice and adult corrections.

Forensic social work is the application of social work principles to questions and issues relating to law and legal systems. A professional group, the National Organization of Forensic Social Work (NOFSW), publishes the *Journal of Forensic Social Work*, which addresses contemporary forensic practice issues for practitioners and social researchers. Although some have doctoral degrees, forensic social workers typically possess a master's degree in social work (MSW) with a forensic concentration and supervised field experience. In most states, they are not recognized as experts in criminal cases but do testify in civil cases.

In all areas of forensic work, collaboration among professionals is crucial. Therefore, although our text focuses on the work of psychologists, it is important to stress that contributions from other mental health professionals cannot be overlooked and that the disciplines often work in collaboration.

ETHICAL ISSUES

With the increasing opportunities available to forensic psychologists, numerous pragmatic and ethical issues also have been raised. Prescription authority, mentioned briefly above, is one example. Other ethical issues pertain to the dual relationships between the psychologist and the client, conflicts of interest, bias, participation in research, issues of confidentiality, and the tension between punishment and rehabilitation (A. Day & Casey, 2009; Murrie & Boccaccini, 2015; Neal & Brodsky, 2016; Ward & Birgden, 2009; Weiner & Hess, 2014). In recent years, contentious issues have revolved around psychologists participating in military interrogations, making recommendations in child custody cases, conducting violence risk assessments in death penalty cases, labeling juveniles as psychopathic, and establishing proper boundaries between assessment and treatment. A growing field of practice, working with undocumented immigrants subject to deportation proceedings or immigrants victimized by crime, carries with it many ethical implications, including culturally rooted misunderstandings and the applicability of psychological measures to diverse groups (Filone & King, 2015).

Like all psychologists, forensic psychologists are expected to practice in accordance with the "Ethical Principles of Psychologists and Code of Conduct" (APA, 2010a), which includes five general principles and ten standards. The latter are mandatory rules that psychologists are obliged to follow. In addition, the aforementioned *Specialty Guidelines* for *Forensic Psychology* (APA, 2013c), as well as a variety of other guidelines published by the American Psychological Association, should be consulted. We will visit these guidelines as they relate to material in the chapters ahead.

CAREERS IN PSYCHOLOGY

Since the 1970s, there has been an enormous expansion of the profession of psychology in general (Reed, Levant, Stout, Murphy, & Phelps, 2001) as well as forensic psychology specifically (Packer & Borum, 2013). Psychology encompasses a wide spectrum of topics ranging from engineering designs (human factors) to animal behavior, and it has a place in every imaginable setting. Psychologists can be found in "personnel selection and training, developing user-friendly computer software, the delivery of psychological services to victims of natural and man-made disasters, the profiling of serial killers, the creation of effective commercials that increase the sale of a product, and so on" (Ballie, 2001, p. 25).

In 2015, there were approximately 77,550 professional members of the **American Psychological Association** (APA) (APA, 2016b). If we include undergraduate students, high school students, teachers, international members, affiliates, and professional members, the total membership in the APA reaches approximately 134,000. Seventy-six percent of the membership are women. The APA, based in Washington, D.C., is the largest association of psychologists worldwide. As of 2016, approximately 26,000 psychologists from the United States and abroad, whose specialties span the entire spectrum of scientific, applied, and teaching areas, were members of the **Association for Psychological Science** (APS) (www.psychologicalscience.org), the second-largest psychological organization in the United States. The APS, also based in Washington, is a nonprofit organization dedicated to the advancement of scientific psychology.

In addition to the APA and APS, psychologists belong to many other professional organizations at the international, national, state, and local levels. In Canada, for example, there are approximately 7,000 members of the Canadian Psychological Association (CPA). It should be noted that the CPA groups psychologists who work in a variety of criminal justice and forensic psychology settings into a category called criminal justice psychology. This category includes corrections, law enforcement, the courts, hospitals, community mental health, and academic settings. In the United Kingdom, the British Psychological Society (BPS) had 49,678 members and subscribers in 2012.

Education and Training

The number of colleges and universities that offer at least one undergraduate course in forensic psychology has grown rapidly over the past decade in the United States, and many of these courses tend to be very popular (DeMatteo et al., 2016). A similar pattern exists in the United Kingdom and in Canada (Helmus, Babchishin, Camilleri, & Olver, 2011). While many colleges and universities offer undergraduate courses in forensic psychology or psychology and law, very few offer specific majors or concentrations in the field at the undergraduate level.

As most psychology undergraduates become quickly aware, the bachelor's degree provides a basic foundation in psychology, but it does not adequately prepare a person to be a professional psychologist. The minimum educational requirement for psychologists is the master's degree, but that degree is also limited. Psychology is a doctoral-level profession. In some states, graduates of master's degree programs in psychology—with the appropriate clinical training—may be eligible for licensure as a psychological associate (LPA) or as a masters-level psychologist (MacKain, Tedeschi, Durham, & Goldman, 2002).

Graduates with a master's degree in psychology may also qualify for positions in school or industrial/organizational (I/O) psychology, although most states prohibit them from using the professional title *psychologist*. This term is reserved for individuals with doctorate degrees. If the graduate with the master's degree obtains several years of experience in business or industry, he or she may be able to obtain a position in consulting or in market research. In some states, graduates with master's degrees in psychology may be licensed with *non-psychology* titles, such as licensed mental health counselor, marriage and family therapist, or psychotherapist (MacKain et al., 2002). The most common master's degrees in psychology are in clinical, counseling, or I/O psychology.

In addition to course work at the undergraduate and master's level, various types of internships provide students with valuable opportunities to learn more about the field. As you read through this text, you may note that quite a few of the essayists featured in the Perspectives boxes mention internships during their undergraduate or early graduate years. As they pursued doctoral-level training, the internships became more advanced and involved additional responsibilities.

In addition, specialization in psychology usually begins at the graduate or even postgraduate level, although many undergraduate programs offer concentrations in certain areas, such as social psychology, educational psychology, forensic psychology, or human development. Graduate programs in psychology usually offer graduate degrees in experimental, biopsychology, developmental, cognitive, clinical, counseling, school, and industrial/organizational psychology. The last four represent the more applied or practitioner's side of psychology. Recently, as we will see shortly, forensic psychology was recognized as another applied branch or specialty in the field, and in 2013, police and public safety psychology was recognized as still another specialty.

Graduate Training: Doctoral Level

At the doctoral level, clinical psychology attracts the largest number of students of all the applied specialties. A doctorate is considered the entry-level credential for the independent practice of psychology (Michalski, Kohout, Wicherski, & Hart, 2011). Interestingly, in a recent year (2008–2009), U.S. and Canadian graduate departments awarded slightly more PsyD doctorates than PhD doctorates—1,350 versus 1,222 (Kohout & Wicherski, 2010). Approximately 4,000 students earn doctorates in the many other fields of psychology (N. B. Anderson, 2010). In their 2008–2009 survey, Michalski, Kohout, Wicherski, and Hart discovered that 72% of the responding psychologists who earned their doctorate in 2009 said they obtained their first choice when looking for a job. A large majority indicated they had secured their first choice within 3 months of obtaining their doctorate.

The PhD degree (doctor of philosophy) requires a dissertation and is well accepted in the academic world as appropriate preparation for scientists and scholars in many fields across the globe (Donn, Routh, & Lunt, 2000). It is regarded primarily as a research-based degree. A dissertation refers to a substantial paper based on the PhD candidate's original research, which should make a significant contribution to the research literature. The PsyD (doctor of psychology) is a graduate degree designed primarily for students who wish to become practitioners or clinicians rather than researchers. The first PsyD program was established in 1968 at the University of Illinois (Peterson, 1968). Although many PhD psychologists have questioned the soundness of the PsyD since its beginnings, especially in light of its limited research focus, the degree has received increasing professional recognition in recent years and has attracted the interest of many students, especially those drawn to the intensive clinical focus of the PsyD programs. In summary, PsyD programs usually place strong emphasis on clinical training, while PhD programs place strong emphasis on understanding and engaging in scientific research. The line of demarcation between these degrees is somewhat blurred, however. Many psychologists who hold the PhD have also had clinical internships, and those who hold the PsyD have some research training. In summary, obtaining either a PhD or a PsyD requires motivation and persistence, but as many essayists throughout this book will indicate, it is well worth the toil. All requirements of the doctorate can usually be completed in 4 to 6 years (of full-time study beyond the undergraduate degree). If an internship is required, it usually takes a year or longer to complete the degree. The internship setting for students interested in forensic psychology can be at sites that provide a forensic experience, such as court clinics, forensic hospitals, or assessment centers. Forensic experiences in predoctoral internship programs are becoming increasingly common (Krauss & Sales, 2014).

Licensure

According to Tucillo, DeFilippis, Denny, and Dsurney (2002), by 1977, every U.S. state had laws relating to the licensure of psychologists, and in 1990, all Canadian provinces regulated the practice of psychology. In 1987, in an effort to encourage standardized licensing requirements, the APA developed a model act to serve as a prototype for drafting state legislation (Tucillo, DeFilippis, Denny, & Dsurney, 2002). One of the chief criteria to qualify for licensing is possession of the doctoral degree. In 2012, approximately 106,500 psychologists in the United States possessed current licenses (APA, 2014a). Professional psychologists are also ethically obligated to comply with the standards pertaining to their practice, as outlined by the **"Ethical Principles of Psychologists and Code of Conduct"** (EPPCC) (APA, 2002, 2010a).

Guidelines are also offered in a number of areas associated with research and clinical practice. A good example is the *Specialty Guidelines for Forensic Psychology* (SGFP; APA, 2013c) mentioned above. One distinction between standards and guidelines should be made. Psychologists are expected to comply with *standards*, and there is an enforcement mechanism in place in case they do not. For example, a violation of the standards outlined in the Code of Conduct could result in a complaint to the APA's Professional Conduct Board or a state's licensing board and, ultimately, loss of one's license to practice psychology. By contrast, the *guidelines* are aspirational; psychologists are strongly encouraged—but not required—to abide by them. However, the various guidelines offered to psychologists are extremely helpful to those working in clinical as well as research settings.

Employment

Surveys are periodically done to determine where psychologists with recent doctorates find employment. One such survey (D. Smith, 2002) found that about three quarters are employed in higher education or human service settings (such as schools or hospitals). The rest were working in business, government, or private practice. About 25% of those with new doctorates found employment in academic positions at 4-year colleges and universities. Morgan, Kuther, and Habben (2005) edited an interesting book in which new doctorates in psychology wrote about the rewards and challenges they faced at the entry level of their careers. Kuther and Morgan (2013) also published a work reviewing careers in psychology in a changing world. Another very helpful book is *Career Paths in Psychology: Where Your Degree Can Take You*, edited by Robert J. Sternberg (2017).

A survey conducted by the AP-LS (P. Griffin, 2011), one specifically related to forensic psychology, found that independent practice was the primary work setting of psychologists involved in psychology and law activities. Approximately 45% identified independent practice (e.g., conducting child custody evaluations or risk assessments) as their main setting. Another 25% worked primarily in university settings, 12% in hospital or other human service settings, and approximately 10% in government settings. It should be noted that, although psychologists will have a primary setting, many also overlap their work into other settings—as you will again find as you read the essays in this book. For example, a number of psychologists whose primary setting is a college or university also maintain private practices. A recent survey of individuals who identified themselves as forensic psychologists found that their average salary was $88,000, with a range of $37,664 to $105,907 (Payscale.com, 2016). Individuals who practice forensic psychology successfully for many years often earn between $200,000 and $400,000 annually, especially if their practice involves consultation with attorneys and court appearances (APA, 2014a).

Those with doctorates in psychology have a strong foundation in theory, research methodology, and analysis that allows them to work in a variety of occupations. "Rather than being stereotyped as a professor or therapist, more and more psychologists are being seen as applied scientists" (Ballie, 2001, p. 25). Again, Perspectives essays throughout the book will illustrate the many professional hats worn by these professionals.

The Applied Specialties

After obtaining their doctoral degrees, many psychologists seek to be certified as professionals in one of a number of areas of practice. Such certification typically follows years of experience as well as a demonstrated expertise. At present, 15 specialties of professional psychology have been recognized by the American Psychological Association (see Table 1.1). As should be apparent from the table, there can be considerable overlap in the knowledge and skills associated with various specialties, and many specialties are pertinent to forensic psychology, which is its own separate specialty. For example, specialists in clinical child psychology, family psychology, and clinical neuropsychology all may make contributions in the forensic realm. Thus, although these specialties may have distinct features, journals, associations, and interests, they also have many things in common.

In all of these practices, many psychologists find that their clients are often from cultural backgrounds, races, and ethnicities different from their own. Fortunately, this is changing as service providers themselves are more diverse. Although members of racial/ethnic minority groups accounted for less than one fifth of the psychology workforce in 2013, the profession has become more diverse, with the proportion of minority group growing from 8.9% to 16.4% in the early 21st century (APA Center for Workforce Studies, 2015). It should be noted, as well, that the APA has a minority fellowship program that provides assistance to members of racial/ethnic minorities to further their professional goals as well as serve diverse communities. Thus psychologists not only are encountering in their practices more persons of Latino, Asian, Native American, and Middle Eastern heritage, but they are themselves reflecting multicultural groups. In recognition of the need to be aware of diversity and a changing society, various guidelines have been adopted in recent years (e.g., APA, 2003b, 2012).

Also in recent years psychologists and other mental health professionals have become attuned to realities facing immigrant populations. It is interesting to note that the immigrant population in the United States tends to be at the highest and lowest ends of the educational and skills continuum (APA, 2012). For example, immigrants represent 25% of physicians and 47% of scientists with doctorates in the United States; they also gather in the agricultural, service, and construction industries. Seventy-five percent of all hired farm workers are immigrants (APA, 2012). Regardless of where they lie on this continuum, though, they may experience anxiety, depression, suicidal ideation, or serious mental illness. The 21st century has become a time when many immigrants groups are viewed with suspicion, targeted for selective prosecution, subjected to hate crimes, and in some cases threatened with deportation. Many fear for the safety of relatives and friends facing persecution or violence in another country.

Since the turn of the century, psychologists involved in assessing or treating members of immigrant groups have reported numerous issues in both adults and children, ranging from post-traumatic stress, anxiety disorders, language barriers, and problems with acculturation. Immigrants who are undocumented often fear reporting victimization—such as domestic violence, sexual

Table 1.1 Specialties in Professional Psychology and Year of Initial Recognition	
Clinical Neuropsychology	1996
Industrial/Organizational Psychology	1996
Clinical Health Psychology	1997
School Psychology	1998
Clinical Psychology	1998
Clinical Child Psychology	1998
Counseling Psychology	1998
Psychoanalysis in Psychology	1998
Behavioral and Cognitive Psychology	2000
Forensic Psychology	2001
Family Psychology	2002
Professional Geropsychology	2010
Police and Public Safety Psychology	2013
Sleep Psychology	2013
Rehabilitation Psychology	2015

assault, sex trafficking—so as not to bring attention to themselves. There are also social and cultural barriers to seeking mental health services. Many psychological assessment tools (e.g., certain standardized tests) were not normed on these groups and thereby lack reliability (APA, 2012). Finally, psychologists who are not themselves recent immigrants must be attuned to the possibility that they are subject to a negative worldview about immigrants that they have derived from political figures and media (Bemak & Chi-Ying Chung, 2014). We will return to some of these topics in later chapters.

FORENSIC PSYCHOLOGY AS A SPECIALTY

Educational and Training Requirements

Regardless of the debate over how broadly or narrowly forensic psychology should be defined, the growth in the field is demonstrated by the continuing development of graduate programs throughout the world, particularly in Canada, the United States, the United Kingdom, and Australia. As of 2017, there were about 80 forensic psychology graduate programs, at both the MA and PhD or PsyD levels across the globe. Some were campus based and others were online programs. In the United States and Canada alone, it is estimated that 41 institutions offer 68 programs in forensic psychology, "including 15 clinical PhD programs, 10 PsyD programs, 15 nonclinical PhD programs, 12 joint-degree programs . . . and 16 master's programs" (Burl, Shah, Filone, Foster, & DeMatteo, 2012, p. 49). (See Table 1.2 for a current list of graduate programs in the United States.)

One interesting path is that taken by individuals who pursue joint degree training—they earn both a PhD and a Juris Doctor degree in law (JD) at the same or associated institution. Some decide on a PhD and a master's degree in legal studies (MLS). The joint degree, though not necessary for forensic psychologists, is a good option for graduate students feeling a strong pull toward both psychology and law. (See Perspective 1.1, in which Dr. David DeMatteo discusses the utility of a joint degree.)

It is a mistake to believe you need a degree specifically in forensic psychology to work in the field, however. Many graduate programs in clinical psychology, counseling psychology, and criminal justice, among others, have forensic concentrations that provide students with academic and training opportunities in forensic psychology, whether through specific course work or internships. Furthermore, many psychologists recommend a broad background in psychology, such as would be obtained by a clinical or counseling degree, rather than a degree in forensic psychology. The choice one makes can depend upon numerous factors: the availability of a mentor, the content of courses offered, the opportunity for internships, funding, the geographic area, and the reputation of the program, among many considerations. In reality, there are different avenues through which to work in forensic psychology.

Most of the graduate programs in the United States concentrate on either clinical or counseling psychology or on social psychology as it relates to legal psychology or psychology and law. Formal programs offering specific degrees in police psychology are virtually nonexistent in the United States and Canada, although there are several programs called "investigative psychology" in the United Kingdom. Furthermore, now that police and public safety psychology has been recognized as a specialty, it is likely that more academic concentrations in this area will be developed. In anticipation of this happening, the Council of Organizations in Police Psychology (COPP) has proposed educational and training guidelines (Brewster et al., 2016), which will be mentioned again in Chapter 2. Academic and research institutions in Canada have long supported research in correctional psychology, and the curricula in Canadian forensic programs reflect this strong research or empirical emphasis. Interestingly, forensic programs in the United States have been slow in giving sufficient attention to corrections and the skills needed to practice in that area (Magaletta et al., 2013).

Table 1.2 Colleges and Universities Offering Graduate Programs in Forensic and/or Legal Psychology

Programs Offering a PhD	University of Alabama, University of Arizona, University of California–Irvine, Drexel University, Fairleigh Dickinson University, Florida International University, Fordham University, John Jay College of Criminal Justice, University of Massachusetts–Lowell, University of Nevada–Reno, University of North Texas, University of Texas–El Paso, Nova Southeastern University, Palo Alto University, Sam Houston State University, Simon Fraser University, Texas A & M University, Texas Tech University, University of Wyoming, West Virginia University
Programs Offering a PsyD	Nova Southeastern University, Pacific University School of Professional Psychology, Spalding University, Chicago School of Professional Psychology, William James College, Widener University
Programs Offering Joint Degrees in Psychology and Law or Legal Studies	Arizona State University, Cornell University, Drexel University, Palo Alto University, University of California–Irvine, University of Florida, University of Minnesota, University of Nebraska–Lincoln.
Programs Offering a Master's Degree	America International College, Adler School of Professional Psychology, California State University, The Chicago School of Professional Psychology, College of Saint Elizabeth, Fairleigh Dickinson University, Holy Names University, John Jay College of Criminal Justice, Marymount University, Nova Southeastern University, Palo Alto University, Roger Williams University, The Sage Colleges, University of California–Irvine, University of Colorado–Colorado Springs, University of Denver, University of Houston–Victoria, University of Leicester, University of Nevada–Reno, University of North Dakota, William James College.

Source: Created using data from *Guide to Graduate Programs in Forensic and Legal Psychology 2016-2017*, Developed in collaboration with the Teaching, Training, and Careers Committee of the American Psychology-Law Society, Division 41 of the American Psychological Association. Updated by Apryl Alexander, PsyD, University of Denver.

In both the United States and Canada, however, more aggressive efforts are now made to recruit graduate students into practica that will be of benefit to both their future careers and the institutions they serve during these internship experiences (Magaletta, Patry, Cermak, & McLearen, 2017; Olver, Preston, Camilleri, Helmus, & Starzomski, 2011). It is important to mention, also, that students with psychology backgrounds often enroll in doctoral programs that confer degrees in criminal justice, criminology, sociology, and social work, such as the distinguished programs at the State University of New York at Albany, the University of Cincinnati, and the University of Maryland. Although they are not psychologists, the professors, practitioners, and researchers with such doctoral degrees make significant contributions to this field. Moreover, these graduate programs often include PhD or PsyD psychologists on their faculty.

In addition to obtaining a doctorate, some clinicians become certified or become diplomates in forensic psychology. A **diplomate** is a professional designation signifying that a person has been certified as having advanced knowledge, skills, and competence in a particular

The Utility of Joint-Degree Training

David DeMatteo, JD, PhD, ABPP (Forensic)

Courtesy of David DeMatteo.

One of the more common questions I get asked by prospective students is whether they should pursue joint-degree training or instead focus on one degree. Despite having a JD and a PhD and directing a joint-degree program, my answer to this important question is, "It depends." This answer seems to surprise many, who apparently expect me to blindly endorse joint-degree training for all students. The reality, though, is that joint-degree training, like any specialized training, is not for everyone. Whether joint-degree training is the right choice for someone depends on several considerations. Before describing those considerations, I will explain why I pursued joint-degree training, what I have done with my degrees, and the benefits of such training.

As a freshman in college, I knew with absolute certainty that I wanted to become a lawyer and practice law . . . until I started taking psychology courses. Despite my long-standing interest in pursuing a legal career, I fell in love with psychology. I loved its utility and broad scope. I loved the idea of helping people and society through psychological research and practice. A few short months after entering college, the pendulum of my career interests had swung from one side (law) to the other (psychology), and I decided to pursue a career in psychology. Admittedly, I was lucky; many people change majors multiple times before settling on a career choice.

Eventually, however, I realized that my true interests were not entirely in psychology or in law, but at the intersection of psychology and law. Throughout college, my interests evolved and matured, and I became interested in conducting methodologically rigorous research aimed at helping legal decision makers and policy makers make better informed decisions, and evaluating criminal offenders and civil litigants so that attorneys and courts could make better decisions. Given these interests, I found myself gravitating toward a career in psychology because lawyers do not typically conduct research and certainly do not perform clinical evaluations. I found myself in a quandary. I no longer wanted

to practice law, but I still wanted to learn about the law. I also wanted to be able to think like a lawyer and have the analytical skills of a lawyer, and I wanted to use those attributes to enhance my work in the psychology field. Fortunately, I found out about a joint-degree program offered by MCP-Hahnemann University and Villanova Law School—one of only a few joint-degree programs in the United States at that time—that would enable me to pursue advanced training in both psychology (PhD) and law (JD).

If we fast-forward to when I was approaching graduation from the 7-year joint-degree program, the next major question I faced was how to use both degrees in a meaningful way that satisfied my career interests. My main interests—conducting policy-relevant psycho-legal research and working with offenders and litigants—remained intact, and other interests, such as teaching and consulting, had emerged. I wanted to find a job that satisfied these diverse interests. As many people find out, getting the right job is an iterative process—that is, your first job will likely not be your final professional stop. The goal should be that each successive job satisfies more of your career interests. I first obtained a position as a research scientist at the Treatment Research Institute (TRI), which is a nonprofit research institute that works closely with the University of Pennsylvania, where I satisfied my interest in conducting sophisticated and policy-relevant drug-policy research. My work at TRI focused on drug-involved criminal offenders, and our research examined the effectiveness of drug courts, the ethics of obtaining consent from individuals to participate in drug abuse research, and the development of interventions for offenders with less severe substance use problems. However, I had little opportunity to teach or consult, and I wanted to use my clinical-forensic skills and work more closely with students. After 4 rewarding years at TRI, I was hired as a faculty member in the Department of Psychology at Drexel University.

Over the past 10 years in academics, I have been able to put both of my degrees to good use. I spend my time conducting research aimed at influencing policy and practice in several areas; teaching courses

(Continued)

to undergraduate, graduate, and law students; mentoring undergraduate and graduate students; conducting forensic mental health assessments of juveniles and adults; consulting with attorneys, courts, and other agencies; sitting on various committees and editorial boards; and publishing and presenting my research. Moreover, as director of Drexel's JD/PhD program, I helped develop a law–psychology training curriculum and serve as a mentor to the next generation of law–psychology professionals. My days are professionally fulfilling and not always predictable. Depending on the day, I might be in my office, in the classroom, in a jail, or in a courtroom. I might be developing a new course, writing a book, conducting research, working on a forensic report, or meeting with students to advance their education and training. The varied nature of my job is something I truly enjoy.

Before returning to the original question of whether joint-degree training is a good idea, let me address the other question I routinely get asked—that is, whether my joint-degree training has helped me in my career. Fortunately, the answer to this question is an unequivocal "yes." To my knowledge, no jobs *require* having both degrees (perhaps with the exception of being director of a joint-degree program), but having both degrees provides a unique skill set, increased marketability, and a multitude of professional options. Although I initially believed that having a law degree would be most beneficial in terms of my forensic assessment work, which requires interacting with attorneys and having some amount of legal knowledge, it has actually proved more beneficial in my research. Much of my research is conducted with justice-involved individuals, and having a law degree has enhanced my credibility with those from whom we need permission to conduct such research (e.g., judges, attorneys, court administrators). Further, having both degrees enabled me to be appointed to the American Psychological Association's Committee on Legal Issues (COLI). As Chair of COLI in 2011, I assisted in drafting three amicus curiae briefs submitted to the Supreme Court of the United States. These amicus briefs focused on psychological research that was relevant to the issue the Supreme Court was addressing in each case. Two of the Supreme Court cases dealt with the reliability of eyewitness identification, and the third case focused on predicting future dangerousness in death penalty cases.

So, let's return to the original question of whether joint-degree training is a good idea if you have interests in both psychology and law. It depends on several factors, including the availability of joint-degree programs (6 to 8 at this time), the level of funding being offered, how much time one has for education and training (with most joint-degree programs taking 5–9 years to complete), and professional goals. Focusing on professional goals deserves additional comment. Students should ask themselves how they want to spend their professional time and then carefully consider whether having both degrees will help them obtain a position that is consistent with their professional goals.

Most people who receive joint-degree training work either in law or psychology, and then use the "other" degree to enhance their primary work. For example, some are practicing lawyers—they need a law degree to practice law but of course are not required to have a doctoral degree in psychology—and they practice in areas of law in which having psychology training can be particularly helpful (e.g., family law, mental health law, litigation). Some individuals with joint-degree training mainly use their doctoral degree in psychology (e.g., academics, research, forensic assessment work), and they use their law degree to enhance their functioning in these areas. In essence, joint-degree training may be right for you if you are interested in becoming a scientist–practitioner who will produce legally sophisticated social science research to aid the legal system to make empirically based decisions; a lawyer–psychologist who will participate in the development of more empirically and theoretically sophisticated mental health policy and law; or a clinician who can contribute to the advancement of forensic psychology in areas such as criminal law, civil law, family law, and mental health law. Joint-degree training is a long but rewarding journey, and it is of great benefit to those whose goals are consistent with such training.

Dr. DeMatteo is an Associate Professor of Psychology and Law at Drexel University, where he is also Director of the JD/PhD Program in Law and Psychology. His research interests include psychopathy, forensic mental health assessment, drug policy, and diversion, and he also maintains a private forensic assessment practice. He is board certified in forensic psychology by the American Board of Professional Psychology, and he is currently President of the American Psychology-Law Society (AP-LS; Div. 41 of the American Psychological Association). He enjoys reading, running, traveling, and spending time with his wife and two children.

specialty. Diplomate certification in forensic psychology attests to the fact that an established organization of peers has examined and accepted the psychologist as being at the highest level of excellence in his or her field of forensic practice. The psychologist must be licensed to qualify for diplomate status.

In approximately 17 states, forensic psychologists must obtain licenses or state-issued certificates in order to engage in forensic practice, such as conducting competency evaluations for the courts or assessing sexually violent offenders who may be subjected to civil commitment proceedings. Virtually all of the laws relating to certification in various states were passed after the year 2000, which is testament to the growth in this field. Heilbrun and Brooks (2010) have published a helpful table summarizing these statutes.

Another level of certification is "board certification," which can add stature to an individual's credentials if he or she is called to testify in court. On a national level, the predominant organization that provides board certification in forensic psychology (as well as 12 other specialty areas) is the American Board of Professional Psychology (ABPP). In addition, the American Board of Forensic Psychology (ABFP) has provided board certification since 1978 and is now affiliated with the ABPP (Heilbrun & Brooks, 2010). Another certifying body is the American Board of Psychological Specialties (ABPS), which is affiliated with the American College of Forensic Examiners (ACFE). Criteria used by the various boards and organizations to grant credentials or titles vary widely (Otto & Heilbrun, 2002). According to Heilbrun and Brooks (2010), with regard to board certification, the ABFP "appears to be the most rigorous, requiring a credentials review, a work sample review, and the passing of both a written and an oral examination for all candidates" (p. 229).

RESEARCH AND PRACTICE CAREERS IN FORENSIC PSYCHOLOGY

We now discuss briefly the five major areas in the research and practice of forensic psychology to be covered throughout the text, along with two related "subareas," family forensic and forensic school psychology. Although examples of what psychologists do in each of these areas were listed earlier in the chapter, this section offers additional details.

Police and Public Safety Psychology

Police and public safety psychology (PPSP) is the research and application of psychological principles and clinical skills to law enforcement and public safety (Bartol, 1996). The goal of this specialty is to assist law enforcement and other public safety personnel and agencies in carrying out their mission and societal functions with effectiveness and safety. Psychologists who work in law enforcement and public safety are involved in the following four areas: (1) assessment (e.g., screening and selection of personnel, fitness-for-duty evaluations [FFDEs]; special unit evaluations); (2) clinical intervention (post-shooting incidents, line-of-duty deaths counseling, deep undercover stress reactions); (3) operational support (e.g., hostage negotiation; criminal activity analyses); and (4) organization consultation (e.g., gender and ethnic/minority issues; excessive force concerns, police corruption problems, workplace stressors).

Police psychologists are sometimes left out of the umbrella category of forensic psychologist, and as noted above, some do not consider themselves such. This field also has grown dramatically, embracing a number of national organizations, and it has achieved APA recognition as a specialty of its own. However, because of the overlap between forensic and police psychology, we continue to treat it as a branch of forensic psychology for organizational purposes.

In the early years, the term *police psychology* was used, but this has given way to the broader term, which encompasses the many professions that are associated with public safety concerns, such as deputy sheriffs, fish and wildlife agents, airport security, immigration agents, marshals, constables, and many other types of state and federal agents. It also includes military personnel and private contractors.

Scholars often mark the beginning of the psychology and police relationship at 1917, when Lewis Terman began testing applicants for police positions (Brewster et al., 2016). The relationship between psychology and law enforcement has waxed and waned over the years, though, with considerable forensic psychology involvement—such as in candidate screening—followed by a period of quiescence. The police community has been characterized as "tight-knit, para-military, and rigid and . . . not given to innovation" (Scrivner, Corey, & Greene, 2014, p. 444). Scrivner, Corey, and Greene add that "Initially, the tradition-clad agencies were uncertain about the need for psychological services, and psychologists had an uphill battle to gain credibility and develop an understanding of the law enforcement culture." Overall, though, as law enforcement agencies have become more professional and psychologists more appreciative of the demands of law enforcement work, relations between the two professions have improved and become mutually respectful. "There is little question today that psychologists have made a difference and have had an impact on the delivery of law enforcement services across the country" (Scrivner et al., 2014, p. 444).

As noted earlier, they perform preemployment psychological assessments, fitness-for-duty evaluations, special unit evaluations, hostage team negotiations, and deadly force incident evaluations. As of 2016, 98.5% of all law enforcement agencies used psychologists to evaluate the psychological suitability of persons to perform the functions required of a police officer before they were hired (Corey, 2017). Psychologists also may be asked to do investigative-type activities, such as criminal profiling, psychological autopsies, handwriting analysis, and eyewitness (or earwitness) hypnosis. "Cop docs," as they are sometimes called, also provide support services to officers and their families. Larger police departments usually hire full-time, in-house police psychologists, whereas the smaller departments typically use psychological consultants.

Currently, there are no formal graduate programs in the United States specifically focused on police psychology, but as mentioned above, with recent recognition as a specialty, this may happen soon. It is best for students entering the field to earn a doctorate in psychology (especially clinical, counseling, or industrial/organizational) and, while in the graduate program, to work with a faculty member who is involved in police psychology and has worked with the law enforcement community if possible. It is also advisable to complete a doctoral or postdoctoral internship in an agency or organization that deals directly with police organizations. Regardless of the career path taken, it is critical that a person interested in police psychology become highly familiar with the nature of police work, its policies and procedures, and gain an understanding of law enforcement culture, which we discuss in more detail in the following chapter.

Legal Psychology

Legal psychology is an umbrella term for the scientific study of a wide assortment of topics reflecting the close relationship between psychology and the law, particularly but not exclusively the courts. These topics include—but again are not limited to— comprehension of one's legal rights, criminal responsibility (insanity defense), civil commitment, jury selection, jury and judicial decision making, child custody determinations, family law issues, eyewitness identification, and the effects of pretrial publicity on court proceedings. As treated here, legal psychology includes both research and application of behavioral and social science to criminal and civil courts.

Once they have earned their PhD or PsyD degree (or a joint JD/PhD), people with a background in legal psychology often go directly into academe or private practice, or they obtain postdoctoral positions in various agencies and research facilities like the Federal Judicial Center, the National Center for State Courts, the FBI, the National Institute of Justice, or the National Institute of Mental Health.

A caveat is in order, however. It is not unusual to see the terms *legal psychology*, *psychology and law*, and *forensic psychology* used interchangeably in academic and professional literature. Although we use *legal psychology* here as a subarea of forensic psychology, we recognize that this is not a universal approach. We also recognize the considerable overlap between legal psychology and the other subareas we have carved out. Eyewitness identification, for example, a rich research area for legal psychology, is of intense interest to police and public safety psychologists, who might be advising the law enforcement community on lineup procedures or the reliability of eyewitness testimony. In fact, we discuss these topics in Chapter 3, which deals with police investigative procedures. The legal psychologist is more likely than the police and public safety psychologist to be conducting *research* in these areas, however. Likewise, legal psychology and victimology intersect when psychologists perform risk assessments and some custody evaluations. The point here is that the various subareas of forensic psychology are not mutually exclusive.

One of the numerous topics holding considerable interest for legal psychologists is the psychology of false confessions, a topic we also discuss in Chapter 3. Most people are aware that suspects—for a wide variety of reasons—sometimes confess to crimes they did not commit. A suspect may be afraid, may be coerced into confessing, may desire to protect the real perpetrator, may think that no one will believe in his or her innocence, or may even want the notoriety associated with being blamed for the crime. What surprises many people, however, is this: Some suspects who are truly innocent come to believe they are truly guilty. Research strongly suggests that skillful manipulation by law enforcement officers can lead to this form of false confession (Kassin, 1997, 2008; Kassin, Goldstein, & Savitsky, 2003; Kassin & Kiechel, 1996; Loftus, 2004). Loftus observes that "we have every reason to believe that some people who are presented with false evidence that they committed a crime might actually come to believe that they did" (p. i). Legal psychologists have been at the forefront of studying this bizarre phenomenon.

Family Forensic Psychology

Many forensic psychologists are becoming increasingly involved in family law, so much so that specializing in **family forensic psychology** is a good career option. Note from Table 1.1 that family psychology itself is a specialty area, recognized by the APA in 2002. The family has changed dramatically, even over the past 20 years. The 2000 census indicated a major increase of cohabitating, single-parent, and grandparent-led families as well as increases in families formed by gay and lesbian parents and their children (Grossman & Okun, 2003). In 2007, the Centers for Disease Control and Prevention (CDC) reported that 39.7% of all births in the United States were to unmarried women. In 2012, this figure rose to half of all births (Adam & Brady, 2013). In 2013, the U.S. Supreme Court affirmed that legally married gay couples were entitled to federal benefits (*United States v. Windsor*, 2013) and also supported gay marriage in a different case (*Hollingsworth v. Perry*, 2013) by refusing to overturn a California court's decision to strike down a law that would have prohibited it. Finally, in 2015, the U.S. Supreme Court ruled in *Obergefell v. Hodges* that same-sex couples have the constitutional right to marry, a landmark ruling that applies nationwide.

These social changes and changes in the law affect the formation of families; family maintenance and dissolution; and numerous legal issues relating to children, medical and employment benefits, and even end-of-life decisions. Family forensic psychologists, then, are concerned with adoption; families in all their iterations; child support; divorce, including custody, relocation, and conflict resolution; abuse; elder law, including estate planning; family business; guardianship; juvenile justice; paternity; reproductive and genetic technologies; and other areas such as termination of parental rights. Family forensic psychology is involved in civil and criminal cases when the understanding of family dynamics and family systems is essential—for example, in cases involving visitation to prisons, release programs, and the impact of sentencing on family members (Grossman & Okun, 2003, p. 166). The best known areas of family forensic psychology involve child custody, family violence, and the assessment and treatment of juveniles, all topics that will be covered in some detail later in the book.

Psychology of Crime and Delinquency

The **psychology of crime and delinquency** is the *science* of the behavioral and mental processes of the adult and juvenile offender. It is primarily concerned with how antisocial behavior is acquired, evoked, maintained, and modified. Recent psychological research has focused on a person's cognitive versions of the world, especially his or her thoughts, beliefs, and values and how those that are inconsistent with leading a lawful life can be modified. It assumes that various criminal behaviors are acquired by daily living experiences, in accordance with the principles of learning, and are perceived, coded, processed, and stored in memory in a unique fashion for each individual.

Criminal psychology examines and evaluates prevention, intervention, and treatment strategies directed at reducing criminal or antisocial behavior. Research in crime and delinquency has discovered, for example, that chronic violence usually develops when children do poorly in school, do not get along with peers, have abusive parents, and attend schools that do not control disruptive and violent behavior (Crawford, 2002). Research has also found that social rejection by peers and others can lead to serious, violent offending: "A great deal of psychological functioning is predicated on belonging to the group and enjoying the benefits, both direct and indirect, of that belongingness" (Benson, 2002, p. 25). When this sense of belongingness is removed or restricted, a feeling of isolation and social exclusion occurs that tends to produce significant changes in behavior, such as an increase in aggression, violence, and other maladaptive behaviors. Under these conditions, human behavior may become impulsive, chaotic, selfish, disorganized, and even destructive. School shooters, for example, frequently express a sense of social isolation and rejection.

Researchers have also found, however, that well-designed and carefully executed prevention programs can prevent violence and a lifelong career path of crime. For example, the Fast Track Prevention Program, developed by researchers at Duke University, Pennsylvania State University, Vanderbilt University, and the University of Washington, has shown highly promising results in reducing juvenile crime. We will further discuss such programs in the chapters on crime and delinquency. Of late, applied psychologists working in school settings have found an increased need for their services, as we noted above. This has led to a keen interest in a new subdivision of school psychology.

Forensic School Psychology

A major area of research interest and practice today is **forensic school psychology**, which relates to the intersection of psychology, the educational system, and the legal system. Forensic school psychologists may not call themselves such—they may think of themselves simply as psychologists or school psychologists. Recall from Table 1.1 that school psychology was recognized as a specialty by the APA in 1998. If school psychologists routinely interact with a multitude of legal issues, we would consider them deserving of that additional title. Forensic school psychologists may work with local schools concerning school suspensions and expulsions, as well as possible placement of a youth into a residential school program and its concomitant implications for the youngster's home school district. They also perform a wide variety of assessment services, including assessing gifted students or those with special needs, such as intellectual, developmental, or emotional difficulties.

Educational programs are required for young people in correctional and psychiatric facilities throughout the country, and some states have established special school districts within these facilities (Crespi, 1990). The challenges for forensic school psychologists within these contexts are considerable. Although the primary focus of public and private schools in the community is obviously education, such education in most correctional or psychiatric settings may be secondary to the reasons for confinement.

Rehabilitation of the juveniles—which includes but is not limited to education—is crucial. Consequently, assessment and counseling services are critical roles for the school psychologist within these settings. Although many forensic school psychologists primarily work with mentally disordered offenders and youth in correctional facilities, they also work with public and private schools on issues that potentially relate to the legal system. For example, a psychologist in a public school setting might be asked to assess a student's potential for violence after being suspended from school temporarily as a result of sending threatening letters to his teacher.

The need for additional consultation with school psychologists within the public and private school systems across the United States took on chilling urgency in the late 1990s when a rash of school shootings made headlines. Communities across the nation that had previously had a low profile—West Paducah, Kentucky; Jonesboro, Arkansas; Pearl, Mississippi; Springfield, Oregon—suddenly became well known because of the violence that erupted within their schools. Since then, sporadic episodes of a student taking a gun to school or a student killing a school principal have been publicized.

The December 2012 school shooting in Newtown, Connecticut, where 20 first graders and six adults were killed was horrifying but an unusual instance of someone outside the school entering the premises. Other school shootings have involved a student opening fire on fellow students, teachers, or administrators. The most striking of such cases was the killing of 12 students and one teacher at Columbine High School in Littleton, Colorado, in April 1999. Twenty other students were injured, some seriously, during that incident. The two teenage boys who were responsible for the shootings also died. To the public and news media, the shooters appeared to be two ordinary boys from normal middle-class families living in a suburb of Denver. As more information became public, however, the shooters were described as isolated teenagers who were fascinated by weapons and often ridiculed by other students. Although there had been a number of school shootings prior to Columbine (at least 10 school shootings between 1996 and 1999), the Columbine incident prompted a great deal of alarm and concern from parents across the United States. The person responsible for the Newtown shooting was said to have been fascinated with the Columbine case, and other subsequent shooters apparently were as well. In one case, the shooter had traveled to Colorado to interview the principal of Columbine.

In light of the increasing attention paid to school violence, threat assessments to identify youth who are potentially dangerous have become more common. Such an assessment would occur, for example, when a student makes a spoken or written threat to harm classmates or teachers. Once a youth has been assessed, he or she may then be counseled in the school setting or in the community or may even be expelled. As noted above, that assessment task often falls to the school psychologist. We discuss threat assessments in more detail in Chapter 8.

Despite the media attention directed to Columbine, Newtown, and the other school tragedies, it is important to keep school violence in perspective. The school shootings described occurred during a time when juvenile violent crime was decreasing nationwide, and it has continued to decline. Nonetheless, additional incidences of violence have occurred, usually involving one student who brings a weapon to school and threatens or shoots one or two people. In an incident in April 2014, a 16-year-old student in Pennsylvania allegedly stabbed or slashed 19 high school students and one adult; he was initially charged with four counts of attempted homicide and 21 counts of aggravated assault. Whenever the news media highlight certain events and dramatize their significance, the events seem to be more widespread and frequent to people than they really are. This phenomenon is called the **availability heuristic**. In reality, although these shootings and stabbings are terrible and tragic, they are not representative of the juvenile crime picture as a whole.

Victimology and Victim Services

Victimology refers to the study of persons who have experienced either actual or threatened physical, psychological, social, or financial harm as the result of the commission or attempted commission of crime against them. The harm may be direct or primary (experienced firsthand) or indirect or secondary (experienced by family members, relatives, survivors, or friends because of their closeness to the victim) (Karmen, 2013).

Violent victimization of children, such as terrifying abductions, school shootings, and sexual attacks, can disrupt the course of child development in very fundamental ways and can be associated with emotional and cognitive problems over the course of the life span (Boney-McCoy & Finkelhor, 1995). In adults, there is strong evidence that the effects of criminal victimization—such as assault, robbery, and burglary—are both pervasive and persistent (Norris & Kaniasty, 1994). Until recently, psychological services were received by a very small fraction of crime victims (2%–7%) (Norris, Kaniasty, & Scheer, 1990). In fact, it has only been within approximately the past 40 years that criminal victimology has become recognized as a scientific and professional field of study (Karmen, 2013). Increasingly, psychologists are beginning to play major roles in the research, evaluation, and treatment of crime victims from diverse cultural contexts and age groups. These activities will be covered in greater depth in Chapters 10, 11, and 12.

Colleges and universities now routinely offer courses, majors, and concentrations in victimology. Students wishing to pursue a research career in victimology probably should obtain a research doctorate in psychology, criminal justice, social work, or sociology. Those desiring careers as practitioners in the field would be advised to obtain a doctorate in clinical or counseling psychology or an MSW (master of social work). However, there are other training opportunities and career paths as well.

Over the past 30 years, for example, the field of victim services has become a rapidly growing profession, and not all of these services are given directly to crime victims. Today, there is greater understanding of victims' issues due to legislation enacted to support victims' rights, increased funding for victim services, efforts by victim advocates, and active research in victimology. Victim services concentrating on victims of sexual assault; domestic violence; and partner, child, and elder abuse have especially grown in recent years, and federal and state legislation has broadened the scope of understanding and services for victims, though there is concern that federal funds will be reduced in the current political climate.

Correctional Psychology

Correctional psychology is a vibrant branch of forensic psychology, broadly defined, and one in which multiple career opportunities are available. However, like police and public service psychologists, many psychologists working in corrections prefer to not call themselves forensic psychologists. Rather, they are *correctional* psychologists. Some are also concerned that PhD programs in forensic psychology or those with forensic psychology concentrations do not adequately prepare people for the many varied responsibilities they must assume in both institutional and community corrections. According to a recent publication, "Among the leading scholars in the field [of correctional psychology] . . . the distinction between corrections practice and psychology-law or forensic training has been consistently observed, increasingly noted, and unfortunately, ignored" (Magaletta et al., 2013, p. 293). This criticism is not directed only at forensic programs, but at doctoral-level programs in psychology in general. Magaletta et al. also note,

Few empirical studies allow us to know specifically how graduate programs introduce corrections as an area of study or a venue for practice, making it difficult to understand the link between academic programs and a psychology services workforce in corrections. (p. 292)

In their own study of 170 training directors of APA-accredited doctoral programs, Magaletta et al. found that only 1 in 3 programs reported they had one or more faculty members interested in corrections, and only 6% of the programs offered a corrections course. This is a valid point that should be taken into consideration by all directors of doctoral programs.

At the end of 2015, there were 6,741,400 adults under correctional supervision in the United States (Kaeble & Glaze, 2016). This includes adults who were in prison, in jail, or supervised in the community, as on probation or parole. The overall figure represents a decline since 2009, when a decrease in the population was first noted, but declines in recent years have been very small—1.7% in 2013 and 2% in 2010. Placed in a different context, the official statistics indicate that 1 in 37 adults is under some form of correctional supervision. Despite the fact that the overall crime rate in the United States is decreasing, the rate of persons under correctional supervision is decreasing, but not comparably.

Virtually every detainee, prisoner, or offender serving time in the community requires or could benefit from one or more of the services offered by correctional psychologists, including assessment, crisis intervention, substance abuse treatment, or reentry planning, to name but a few. Recent meta-analyses of studies also indicate that mental health treatment results in improved mental health functioning as well as better adjustments and coping skills of offenders (R. D. Morgan et al., 2012). In addition, the large number of mentally disordered persons in the nation's jails and prisons is of increasing concern to psychologists as well as other mental health professionals. Among the developments in corrections that should be watched closely is the possible renewal of support for private prisons, which had received considerable scrutiny in past years. Privately operated prisons have been controversial on a number of fronts, and research does not support their effectiveness at reducing recidivism. We discuss this issue in its many facets in Chapter 12.

As the number of opportunities for psychologists in corrections has proliferated, correctional psychology has emerged as an exciting, rewarding, and challenging field. Yet, according to Magaletta et al. (2013), many positions remain unfilled, again partly because graduate schools have not adequately promoted this career option or sufficiently prepared doctoral students through relevant coursework.

Research psychologists who are not necessarily working within the correctional system often study the psychological effects of correctional systems on prisoner behavior. Topics include the general effect of imprisonment on special populations of offenders, such as the mentally disordered or the elderly, the effects of crowding, the effects of isolation, and the outcome of various rehabilitative programs.

Juvenile corrections is a related but also distinct area in which psychologists play important roles, as we discuss in the last chapter of the book. Juvenile corrections, both in institutions and in the community, should focus on rehabilitation—thus, assessment and treatment strategies are paramount. However, juvenile corrections also raises some of the same concerns as adult corrections, specifically, the assessment of risk; the effects of crowding and isolation; substance abuse programs; and work with special populations of offenders, such as juvenile sex offenders and juveniles with mental disorders and intellectual deficiencies.

Interestingly, psychologists who practice in adult as well as juvenile correctional settings are sometimes criticized for aligning themselves with prison administrators, and they may be confronted with ethical quandaries, such as when asked to perform custody-related functions like supervising or restraining inmates. In death penalty states, psychologists may be asked to assess the risk of future dangerousness of a person facing a potential death sentence. Lawyers representing prisoners on death row also may argue that they are not competent to be executed because they are either seriously mentally ill or intellectually disabled. These determinations require input from mental health professionals. Psychologists in recent years also have been asked to perform evaluations of sexual offenders at the end of their sentences, to determine whether they are eligible for civil commitment under sexually violent predator laws. The above are all controversial topics that will be covered in later chapters.

Psychologists working in and as consultants to correctional facilities often join associations representing their common interests. Examples are the American Correctional Association (ACA) and the International Association for Correctional and Forensic Psychologists (IACFP). The latter is guided by a series of standards (Althouse, 2010) that provide the minimum acceptable levels for psychological services offered to offenders, whether they are adults or juveniles held in local, state, or federal facilities, as well as in the community. The standards cover a wide range of principles as well as services, including staffing requirements, confidentiality issues, mental health screening, professional development, informed consent, segregation, and a host of other topics relating to this work.

SUMMARY AND CONCLUSIONS

As recently as 35 years ago, the term *forensic psychology* had barely been introduced into psychological or legal literature. Today, as we have seen, it is a commonly encountered term, but it still defies definition. It is often used interchangeably with legal psychology and psychology and law. Although some favor a narrow definition limiting it to clinical practice offered to the legal system, particularly the courts, the contributions of research psychologists may be undermined by such an approach. The most recently adopted *Specialty Guidelines for Forensic Psychology* (APA, 2013c), as well as the writings of prominent forensic psychologists (e.g., DeMatteo et al., 2009; Heilbrun & Brooks, 2010), recognize the importance of contributions from researchers, although there continues to be emphasis placed on practice. In other words, the researcher is not a forensic psychologist if he or she does not interact with the legal community. Furthermore, in some jurisdictions one must be certified as a forensic psychologist to practice in certain arenas, such as court settings.

In addition, though, it is important to consider the context in which psychology is practiced. Limiting forensic psychology to work with civil and criminal courts does not recognize well enough the law-related functions performed by psychologists working with law enforcement, corrections, or victims. Finally, the many contributions of psychologists who study the psychology of crime and delinquency deserve to be included in this field, as long as their findings are available to the legal system. The law surely can benefit, for example, from research on adolescent development and decision making or research on the prevention and control of sex offending. As we note throughout the book, and as illustrated in many of the Perspective boxes, researchers on such topics often testify in court as expert witnesses and consult with lawyers and judges on a regular basis.

We have persisted, then, in advocating for a broad definition of forensic psychology, one that might divide it into the five subareas covered in this chapter, although other organizational divisions are possible. In each of the areas discussed, numerous career opportunities exist. Both undergraduate and graduate programs have rapidly seen the need for preparation for careers in forensic psychology, whether by offering degree programs in the field or by offering concentrations within a broader program, such as a doctorate in clinical, counseling, or developmental psychology. Furthermore, professionals themselves are regularly offered opportunities for licensing, certification, and continuing education as well as guidelines for practicing their profession.

In sum, the field of forensic psychology, as we define it broadly, provides ample opportunities for psychologists interested in interacting with some aspect of the law. It is an area of specialization that has developed rapidly and shows no signs of stagnation. Many of the scholars who are cited and featured in this book began their studies at a time when forensic psychology was not prominent and was not widely considered a career choice. Moreover, as recently as the turn of the 21st century, a relatively small group of forensic specialists devoted themselves full-time to this field, whereas a much larger group of psychologists provided occasional forensic services or provided such services only within a circumscribed area, such as child custody evaluations (Otto & Heilbrun, 2002). Otto and Heilbrun predicted then that the field would grow, and they argued that the field must develop a plan to ensure that forensic practice overall was well-informed and competent. This plan was especially needed in the area of forensic testing and assessment.

More recently, Heilbrun and Brooks (2010) commented on the remarkable expansion of the field noting that there has been substantial progress. In proposing an agenda for the future, they emphasize the need for interdisciplinary and intercultural collaboration; continuing improvement in the quality of forensic mental health assessments; a better integration of science and practice; and better outreach to a variety of settings, many of which are covered in this text.

KEY CONCEPTS

American Psychological Association (APA) 15

Association for Psychological Science (APS) 15

Availability heuristic 28

Correctional psychology 28

Digital investigative analysis 5

Diplomate 20

Ethical Principles of Psychologists and Code of Conduct (EPPCC) 17

Family forensic psychology 25

Forensic entomology 5

Forensic psychiatrists 14

Forensic psychology 4

Forensic school psychology 26

Forensic social workers 14

Legal psychology 24

Police and public safety psychology (PPSP) 23

Psychology of crime and delinquency 26

Questioned document examination or analysis 5

Specialty Guidelines for Forensic Psychology 7

Victimology 28

QUESTIONS FOR REVIEW

1. Contrast the narrow and broad definitions of forensic psychology.

2. Contrast forensic psychology with other forensic sciences.

3. Identify the five subspecialties of forensic psychology covered in this text, and provide illustrations of the contributions of forensic psychologists in each one.

4. Explain the difference between the PhD and the PsyD degrees.

5. What are the pros and cons of obtaining a joint degree in psychology and law?

6. Give examples of any four ethical issues that might be faced by psychologists practicing forensic psychology.

7. What is meant by the term *prescription privileges* when applied to psychologists? Briefly discuss the progress psychologists have made in obtaining these privileges and discuss possible objections that might be raised.

POLICE AND INVESTIGATIVE PSYCHOLOGY

CHAPTER TWO

POLICE AND PUBLIC SAFETY PSYCHOLOGY

In 2015, a police officer in South Carolina shot an unarmed man in the back following a traffic stop. A first trial ended with a hung jury, and he later pleaded guilty in federal court to violating the man's civil rights.

In 2016, police officers across the United States acted calmly and professionally while citizens exercised their constitutional rights by peacefully marching in protest of controversial government policies. When some protests turned violent, law enforcement acted with restraint, but some officers abused their power and remonstrated by using excessive force.

In 2017, a police officer saved a woman from a burning car by punching out the car windows with his night stick. In another state, an off-duty officer rescued a half-blind dog from a ravine.

In 2017, after a presidential order to crack down on immigration, a border patrol agent said he was looking forward to having "fun" rounding up undocumented immigrants. In the same year, police departments across the country refused to participate in the ethnic targeting of individuals whose immigration status might have been questioned.

Law enforcement is a very large enterprise in the United States, and—perhaps like most other occupations—it attracts a range of personalities. Some students who hope to go into law enforcement can't wait to be the first to break down the door; others want to help people or protect child victims. Students who aspire to be police and public safety psychologists are always well advised to recognize not only the variety in police work but also the backgrounds, motivations, biases, and strengths of those who do become police and public safety professionals.

There are roughly 16,000 state and local law enforcement agencies employing 705,000 full-time sworn personnel (Reaves, 2012b). These numbers include about 477,000 sworn officers with general arrest powers working in 12,000 local departments, 189,000 sworn officers working for

Chapter Objectives

- Define and describe the common activities and tasks of police psychologists.

- Discuss police culture, and emphasize that it is not necessarily homogeneous.

- Provide an overview of job analysis and various types of validity as they relate to the assessment of police applicants.

- Describe various psychological tests and inventories used in the assessment of candidates for law enforcement positions.

- Examine police suicide.

- Describe the roles of psychologists and mental health professionals in assessing and treating officers after critical incidents, such as hostage taking, mass casualties, and shootings.

- Review research findings on police bias and the use of excessive force by police.

3,012 sheriff's departments (Burcham, 2016), and 61,000 state police officers employed by all 50 states (Reaves, 2012b). At the federal level, there are approximately 120,000 full-time law enforcement officers with authority to make arrests and carry a firearm (Reeves, 2012a). These data do not include territorial and tribal law enforcement, game wardens, or conservation officers. These figures, of course, vacillate over time in accordance with local, state, and federal budgets and priorities. For example, the federal government has recently announced the hiring of more border patrol agents.

In addition, there is a wide range of private and public safety agencies. Some are private security agencies, and others are supported by public funding, such as campus police departments on public university and college campuses. Virtually every university and college campus, public or private, has a public safety department, whose officers may or may not be armed and may or may not be invested with police powers. Two thirds of public colleges and universities employ armed officers, which is more than double the number of private colleges that employ armed officers (Reaves, 2015). Private security personnel, some armed, also are found in hospitals, schools, corporate offices, and large retail establishments.

In the past two decades, the composition of law enforcement officers across the nation has become more diverse, proportionally more female, more educated, and specialized (Bureau of Justice Statistics, 2015). Law enforcement agencies also have expanded significantly in size during this time, exceeding even the annual increase in the U.S. population (Reaves, 2012b). At the same time, officer retention has continued to be a problem, with people leaving the field or being forced to resign (2012b). Furthermore, in many communities across the United States, relationships between police and the public have been strained because of shootings, perceived increases in violence, fear, and the national political climate. All of these issues provide professional challenges for psychologists working with law enforcement.

Police and public safety psychology (PPSP) is the research and application of psychological knowledge and clinical skills to law enforcement and public safety. As we noted in Chapter 1, the degree of interaction between psychology and law enforcement has waxed and waned over the years. We have now reached the point, however, where psychologists play a vital and expanding role in many police and public safety agencies, as both in-house employees and community consultants (Scrivner, Corey, & Greene, 2014).

POLICE PSYCHOLOGY: A DEVELOPING PROFESSION

Precisely when a partnership between law enforcement and psychology first began is unclear. To a certain extent, community psychologists offered some type of consulting service to police, usually on an "as needed" basis, throughout the 20th century. Their earliest contributions were in the form of cognitive and aptitude testing of applicants for police positions, with psychologist Louis Terman being the first to use these methods in 1917.

Police psychology probably began in the United States as a viable profession in 1968, however, when Martin Reiser was hired as a full-time in-house psychologist by the Los Angeles Police Department (LAPD). Reiser (1982) himself modestly claimed that he was not altogether certain he was the first "cop doc." However, there is little doubt that Reiser was the most prolific writer on police psychology in the United States throughout the 1970s. He also established the first graduate student internship in police psychology at the LAPD, in conjunction with the California School of Professional Psychology. By 1977, at least six other law enforcement agencies in the United States employed full-time psychologists (Reese, 1986, 1987).

In the years spanning the 20th and 21st centuries, numerous books and journal articles on police psychology were published in the academic literature. They included works on screening candidates for law enforcement positions, coping with stress in policing, police culture, police corruption, police suicide and relationship problems, the legitimate use of force, and women in policing, among many other topics. Notable contributions were made by Blau (1994), Kurke and Scrivner (1995), Niederhoffer and Niederhoffer (1977), Scrivner (1994), and Toch (2002). Most recently, books by Toch (2012) and Kitaeff (2011) have focused on psychological aspects of police work.

Recognition of police and public safety psychology as a growing profession has expanded greatly in other ways during the past decade as well. On July 31, 2013, police and public safety psychology was officially recognized by the American Psychological Association as a professional specialty. This has encouraged APA-accredited doctoral programs in clinical psychology to offer degree concentrations in police and public safety psychology. In addition, some organizations have developed graduate, postdoctoral, and continuing education standards and opportunities for persons planning careers in police and public safety psychology (Gallo & Halgin, 2011).

Currently, there are five national police psychology organizations in the United States: (1) the Police Psychological Services Section of the International Association of Chiefs of Police (IACP-PPSS), (2) Division 18 (Police and Public Safety Section) of the APA, (3) the Society of Police and Criminal Psychology (SPCP), (4) the American Academy of Police & Public Safety Psychology (AAPPSP), and (5) the American Board of Police & Public Safety Psychology (ABPP) (Corey, 2013). In Canada, which has its own parallel history of police psychology, the major organization for police and forensic psychology is the Criminal Justice Psychology Section of the Canadian Psychological Association (CPA). This section is divided into several subsections, including police psychology and psychology in the courts.

As reflected in the name of the IACP, police agencies across the world share goals and cooperate in training. Specifically related to psychology, the IACP-PPSS has established guidelines for police psychological service (e.g., International Association of Chiefs of Police [IACP], 2002). The guidelines were updated four times over 27 years (Ben-Porath et al., 2011) and were again most recently updated in 2014 (Steiner, 2017). The guidelines cover preemployment psychological evaluations, psychological fitness-for-duty evaluations, officer-involved shootings, and peer emotional support during times of personal or professional crises. It should be noted that the Canadian Psychological Association also passed guidelines in 2013 for Canadian psychologists who conduct preemployment psychological assessments of police candidates.

In 2011, the American Board of Professional Psychology (ABPP) established a separate board, the American Board of Police and Public Safety Psychology, to serve as an avenue for psychologists to become certified in this field (Corey, Cuttler, Cox, & Brower, 2011). Scrivner, Corey, and Greene (2014) heralded this as the "most significant event in the history of the field" (p. 447). Approximately 60 psychologists in the United States now hold this certification.

There is a vast and ever-expanding literature on police and public safety psychology. To help organize the material in this chapter, we adopt the approach of Aumiller and Corey (2007), who divide police psychology into four general and overlapping domains of practice: (1) assessment, (2) intervention, (3) operational support, and (4) organizational/management consultation. (Table 2.1 shows some of the more common activities associated with each domain.) Aumiller and Corey were able to identify over 50 activities or services that police psychologists may be expected to provide. These categories are virtually identical to those identified in publications of the PPSP specialty: assessment, clinical intervention, operational support, and organizational consulting (Brewster et al., 2016).

Table 2.1 Common Activities and Tasks of a Police Psychologist

Assessment	Intervention	Operational	Consulting and Research
Job analysis	Individual therapy and counseling	Crisis and hostage negotiations	Research activities pertaining to law enforcement issues
Psychological evaluations of police applicants	Group, couple, and family therapy and counseling	Police academy education and training	Management and organizational consultation
Fitness-for-duty evaluations	Critical incident early intervention and debriefing	Threat assessments	Supervisory consultation
Psychological evaluations of specialty police units	Critical incident stress management and therapy	Criminal activity assessment and offender profiling	Development of performance standards for agency personnel
Emergency consultations concerning the seriously mentally disordered	Substance abuse and alcohol treatment	Operations-related consultation and research	Mediation

FORENSIC ASSESSMENT IN POLICE AND PUBLIC SAFETY PSYCHOLOGY

"Psychological assessment is considered a core competency for psychologists specializing in police and public safety" (Corey & Borum, 2013, p. 246). The two categories of assessments most commonly done in police psychology are preemployment psychological screening and fitness-for-duty evaluations. **Preemployment psychological screening** occurs when psychologists evaluate a person's psychological suitability for police work prior to being hired. Cochrane, Tett, and Vandecreek (2003) conducted a survey of police agencies across the nation and reported that nearly 90% used psychological testing for preemployment selection. Psychological screening of candidates for police positions is mandated by law in at least 38 states (Corey & Borum, 2013). It is estimated that 100,000 preemployment assessments of law enforcement applicants are conducted by 4,500 psychologists each year in the United States (Mitchell, 2017). In **fitness-for-duty evaluations (FFDEs)**, psychologists evaluate an employed police officer's ability to perform the job. This often occurs after the officer has been through a personally stressful experience, either in his or her personal life or on the job (e.g., sudden death of a spouse, being taken hostage, or involvement in a shooting incident).

We discuss both candidate screening and FFDEs below. As Corey and Borum (2013) note, these psychological assessments should be conducted by psychologists who have a fundamental and reasonable level of understanding and who are knowledgeable about police work. This brings us to the important topics of police culture and job analysis.

Police Culture

A police psychologist does not have to be a former police officer to be an effective service provider to law enforcement agencies. However, the police psychologist must be highly familiar with and knowledgeable about what policing involves, as well as the **police culture**, defined as the rules, attitudes, beliefs, and practices that are thought to be accepted among law enforcement officers as an occupational group. Woody (2005) notes that one of the clear requirements to be a successful police psychologist is to recognize and understand this culture, and he adds that the psychologist should reasonably accommodate it as long as it does not endanger the public safety; police ethics; or the mental, physical, or behavioral health of the officer.

Nearly all occupations have a "culture," and persons who enter them become socialized, or learn these cultures as they progress on the job. Manning (1995) describes occupational cultures as having "accepted practices, rules, and principles of conduct that are situationally applied, and generalized rationales and beliefs" (p. 472). The occupation of law enforcement is unique in that the working environment is not only potentially very hostile or dangerous, but officers have also been granted the legitimate power to create, display, and maintain their authority over the public (Paoline, 2003). Consequently, police officers work together to develop and maintain a unique occupational culture that values control, authority, solidarity, and isolation (L. B. Johnson, Todd, & Subramanian, 2005). As Scrivner et al. (2014) noted, the profession has often been characterized as highly structured, paramilitary, tight knit, and bureaucratic. The coping mechanisms prescribed by the police culture are often critical to handling the many stresses that this work environment entails (Paoline, 2003). Officers, perhaps more than people in other occupations, depend on one another for the protection and social and emotional support they need to do their jobs. This can be particularly important at times when police actions come under intense public scrutiny. Most scholars and practitioners in the field (e.g., Kirschman, 2007; Kitaeff, 2011; Scrivner et al., 2014; Toch, 2012) note that it is crucial for police psychologists to understand this about police work.

Paoline (2003) perceptively observes, though, that researchers, scholars, and practitioners (including psychologists) often make the mistake of assuming that there is a single, homogenous police culture. He emphasizes that police cultures may vary in terms of the style, values, purpose, and mission of the organization itself, starting from the top down. The culture of a federal agency, for instance, is likely to be different from that of a county sheriff's department. The culture may also vary according to rank. The street cop culture is apt to be quite different from the cultures in administration and supervision. In addition, there may be "subcultures" within the ranks, with some officers adopting a different style of policing from that of others. Some supervisors may play strictly by the book, whereas others may be flexible in interpreting departmental procedures and policies. Finally, the changing face of law enforcement as a result of recruitment of women and ethnic and racial minorities has certainly affected the concept of police culture. Paoline notes,

> As police forces have become more heterogeneous, one would expect a single cohesive police culture to give way to a more fragmented occupational group. The modal officer of the past . . . is continually changing as the selection and recruitment of officers has diversified. (p. 208)

In short, claiming to be an expert without understanding and earning the acceptance and respect of a police agency, and without acknowledging the many facets of police culture, will likely lead to limited success for a new or inexperienced psychologist. Interestingly, although law enforcement experience is not necessary, some police and public safety psychologists choose that path after spending some years as police officers (e.g., Fay, 2015). For those without prior police experience—the majority—entry into the field of police psychology usually begins with providing limited consulting services to police agencies, such as screening and selection, or psychotherapy or counseling of police officers and their families. Ride-along programs, in which the psychologist accompanies police officers in patrol cars, are usually helpful in educating psychologists about the realities of the police experience (Hatcher, Mohandie, Turner, & Gelles, 1998). As experience accumulates and the agency becomes more familiar with the psychologist and his or her work, the psychologist may be asked to do many other things, such as perform FFDEs or become a member of the hostage/crisis negotiation team.

The invitation to the psychologist to participate in the hostage/crisis negotiation team appears to depend upon three factors: (1) mutual acceptance, (2) professional credibility (timely provision of critical information and behavioral analysis), and (3) an ability to function in the field setting. (Hatcher et al., 1998, p. 462)

We will discuss the role of the police psychologist as an integral member of the hostage/crisis negotiation team later in the chapter.

Job Analysis

The psychologist conducting assessment procedures should have a good understanding of what the job involves. The tasks required go far beyond those reflected in media and popular culture. Although some tasks are similar regardless of the agencies, others are specific to the nature of the job or the setting. In order to evaluate whether someone is a good candidate for law enforcement, one must first understand what the job entails. In order to assess whether someone is fit to return to duty, one must understand what that duty involves. Job analysis, then, is the process of identifying and analyzing how, where, and why a particular job is done. In the context of this chapter, **job analysis** is a systematic procedure for identifying the skills, abilities, knowledge, and psychological characteristics that are needed to do public safety work successfully. A comprehensive job analysis of a particular law enforcement agency should reveal the essential functions of the personnel,

the working conditions unique to their respective ranks and assignments, the common and novel stressors inherent in public safety work, the normal and abnormal adaptation to occupational stress and trauma, [and] the research pertinent to resilience and recovery in public safety. (Trompetter, 2011, p. 52)

▶ **Photo 2.1** A police officer speaks with a woman at the scene of a crime. Even as the officer is comforting the woman, he is obtaining information about the incident she has witnessed.
Source: Jupiterimages/Thinkstock.

The first step is to understand what officers working within a particular agency do on a day-to-day basis. In the past, many law enforcement screening procedures have been based on intuition and "gut feelings" rather than a comprehensive analysis of job requirements. However, without a job analysis to justify the choice of psychological measures, it is extremely difficult for the psychologist doing the screening to know what he or she is looking for—let alone measure it (Aumiller & Corey, 2007).

Job analyses have revealed characteristics that are desirable, and sometimes necessary, for all successful police officers. For example, successful candidates need to have good judgment and common sense, appropriate decision-making skills, interpersonal skills, a solid memory, good observation talents, and communication skills (both oral and written) (Spielberger, 1979). (See Photos 2.1 and 2.2, in which officers are obtaining information from and comforting witnesses.) Integrity and trustworthiness are certainly other important traits. Overall emotional stability and the ability to remain steady under stress are also considered critical traits for successful and competent police officers (Detrick & Chibnall, 2006, 2013). Although the emphasis that each agency places on the above characteristics may differ slightly, they tend to be universal psychological requirements for law enforcement work.

Police psychologists who assess candidates for hire, fitness for duty, promotion, or special assignments should be familiar not only with the general literature on job analysis, but also with how to conduct their own analysis. An agency may require psychological strengths in addition to the general requirements listed above, such as the ability to work in special units with victims of sexual abuse, searching for missing children, or hostage negotiation. In addition, a job analysis must be carefully done and the assessment measures used should comport with the analysis. Data may be subjected to legal scrutiny concerning gender, racial, salary, promotional, selection, and—more generally—psychological testing issues. For example, a police applicant who

▶ **Photo 2.2** Police officers obtain information from eyewitnesses at the scene of a crime. Calm, efficient interaction with the public is essential to good police work.
Source: iStock/JayLazarin.

feels he has been unfairly evaluated may challenge the entrance exam used by the agency on the grounds that the test is not valid or is discriminatory.

There are various procedures for doing a comprehensive job analysis, but most are done through interviews and questionnaires. Psychologists possessing well-founded research skills are often asked to conduct and update the job analysis. In some cases, observations of job behavior may be necessary. In police work, for example, officers and supervisors are asked what is done on a daily basis; what skills and training they believe are necessary; and what temperament, personality, and intellectual capacities best fit particular tasks or responsibilities. The information gathered from a well-done job analysis is summarized as a job description that details what is done, how, and why (McCormick, 1979; Siegel & Lane, 1987).

Preemployment and Post-Offer Psychological Evaluations

Nearly all law enforcement agencies are subject to law, regulations, or accreditation standards that require psychological evaluations of public safety candidates (Aumiller & Corey, 2007; Mitchell, 2017). As noted above, at least 38 states mandate psychological evaluations for police officers. These psychological evaluations—usually in the form of personality measures—help to ensure that the candidates are free of mental or emotional impairments that would interfere with effective, responsible, and ethical job performance as a police officer. A candidate who is severely depressed, or one who has strong paranoid tendencies or is prone to aggressive behavior with minimal provocation, is unlikely to perform well as a law enforcement officer. Consequently, psychological evaluations are necessary to identify any job-relevant risk behaviors and the presence of job-critical personal and interpersonal qualities that are likely to endanger public safety.

Also as mentioned above, the IACP Police Psychological Services Section (2010) has developed guidelines for police psychologists who conduct preemployment psychological evaluations. The guidelines spell out recommended standards for examiner qualifications, conflict-of-interest issues, and informed consent recommendations for those police candidates who undergo the examination. The guidelines also offer advice on what should be included in the psychological report and what procedures and psychological measures should be included in the evaluation.

The measures used to evaluate officers have never been consistent across the United States. In the mid-20th century, psychologists often administered intelligence tests, and agencies used scores on these tests to help in their hiring decisions. However, over the years it became clear that intelligence tests per se were not effective measures of how an officer is likely to perform on the street. Although some psychologists continue to use these tests as a standard practice in other contexts (e.g., various court-ordered evaluations, educational assessments, and prisoner intakes), intelligence tests are not commonly used in psychological screening of law enforcement applicants. However, it should be emphasized that a majority of police agencies and police academies still require a written or aptitude test. Interestingly, it has been documented that neither high intelligence nor a college education necessarily means that an individual will be a good police officer (Henderson, 1979; Spielberger, Ward, & Spaulding, 1979). Nevertheless, college-educated officers have been shown to have better communication skills, and they have earned promotions at a higher rate than non–college-educated officers (Cole & Smith, 2001). Furthermore, officers with a college education also have an effect on changes in the police culture (Paoline, 2003). Most federal and state agencies, and many local ones, now require a minimum of 2 years of education beyond high school for entry into police work, and some require a 4-year college degree.

In most cases, only licensed or certified psychologists or psychiatrists who are trained and experienced in psychological assessment instruments and their interpretation should conduct candidate evaluations. As mentioned previously, it is also important that the examiners be knowledgeable about what law enforcement demands as well as the research literature on public safety. The examining psychologist should also be familiar with ethnic and cultural differences in the various minority applicants applying for law enforcement or public safety positions, although such information is not always available, particularly in paper-and-pencil measures. Some minority applicants may interpret questions differently than other cultural groups, and their responses may be outside the norms, but they should not be disqualified on that basis. Finally, the examiner must be aware of developments in the law relating to the hiring of candidates. For example, one of the most relevant laws is the Americans with Disabilities Act of 1990.

Americans with Disabilities Act of 1990 and Beyond

The **Americans with Disabilities Act (ADA)** is a far-reaching civil rights law that prohibits discrimination and mandates equal treatment of all individuals regardless of physical or mental disabilities. Its sections on employment prohibit public employers and private employers with 15 or more employees from discriminating against any qualified person with a disability who can perform the essential (as opposed to marginal or incidental) functions of the job he or she holds or seeks. A qualified individual with a disability is an employee or job applicant who meets the legitimate skill, experience, education, or other requirements of a job. As such, the law has a significant effect on day-to-day police practices and—for our purposes here—on screening procedures used in law enforcement. The police psychologist who designs employment screening, selection, and promotional procedures for police agencies must be familiar with all the nuances of the act as well as any case law that has emerged from its interpretation.

At the turn of the 21st century, several U.S. Supreme Court decisions limited the scope of the ADA, to the point that critics estimated that it went from protecting 43 million Americans when it was first passed to protecting 13.5 million (Rozalski, Katsiyannis, Ryan, Collins, & Stewart, 2010). In 2008, Congress amended the act to attempt to restore more protection, in the Americans with Disabilities Act Amendments Act (ADAAA). Congress also passed another law, the Genetics Information Nondiscrimination Act (GINA), which placed limits on the type of information law enforcement agencies could use in screening applicants (Scrivner et al., 2014). Although both the ADA (and ADAAA) and GINA are pertinent to a wide variety of employment situations—not just law enforcement—it is obviously crucial for police and public safety psychologists to remain up to date with changes to and requirements of these laws.

In balancing individual rights and an organization's right to know of an applicant's physical and mental fitness, the Equal Employment Opportunity Commission (EEOC) has divided disability inquiries into two stages: (1) pre-offer of employment and (2) post-offer/pre-hire. At the pre-offer stage, a police agency, for example, must not ask applicants any health or fitness questions that elicit information about disabilities. The agency *may* ask general "job performance" questions, such as presenting a scenario and asking the candidate how he or she would handle it. At the post-offer/pre-hire stage, a police department may make direct inquiries about disabilities and may require applicants to undergo medical and psychological examinations. Such post-offer inquiries are allowed because the employer, by making a conditional offer of employment, can rescind that offer if it can be shown that the person is unable to perform the essential functions of the job, even with reasonable accommodation.

These laws affect law enforcement agencies beyond accommodating and providing for equal opportunity for employment within the agency. They also affect the agency's dealing with the public. The ADA in particular is relevant to receiving citizen complaints; interviewing witnesses; arresting, booking, and holding suspects; operating 911 emergency centers; providing emergency medical services; and enforcing the laws. In all these activities, the agency must try to make reasonable accommodations in its services to people who are disabled. In one noteworthy case, police were sued after they arrested a wheelchair-bound suspect and transported him to the police station without his wheelchair. They apparently thought the chair was a prop, but it was not.

Screening Out and Screening In

One of the more challenging tasks for the police psychologist is the process of screening out compared to screening in police officer candidates, usually through the use of personality measures. **Screening-out procedures** try to eliminate those applicants who appear to be poorly suited for work in law enforcement. For example, the candidate may be evaluated as showing signs of poor judgment and common sense or poor stress tolerance. The screening procedure may also reveal that the candidate shows an unwillingness to follow rules, exhibits difficulty working within a chain-of-command work environment, or demonstrates a lack of *basic* ability or mental acuity to perform the job in a safe and responsible manner. Screening-out procedures are those most commonly used by police psychologists when screening police candidates (Varela, Boccaccini, Scogin, Stump, & Caputo, 2004). **Screening-in procedures**, on the other hand, are intended to identify those attributes that distinguish one job applicant as being potentially a more effective officer than another. Implicit in this approach is the ability to rank-order applicants, allowing agencies to select the top candidates from a pool that passed the initial screening procedures. This approach assumes that there are traits, habits, reactions, and attitudes that distinguish an outstanding officer from a satisfactory one. Scrivner et al. (2014) observe that the development of screening-in measures has progressed in recent years. To date, though, there is little evidence that psychologists have reached the goal of establishing valid measures for ranking applicants in some hierarchical order of suitability, although some tests are more useful than others.

Before discussing some of the instruments commonly used in police screening, it is helpful to review the importance of validity in psychological testing. Validity addresses the question, "Does the test or inventory measure what it is designed to measure?" Although psychologists discuss many types of validity, three are of particular relevance here: concurrent validity, predictive validity, and face or content validity.

Concurrent validity is the degree to which a test or an inventory identifies a person's *current* performance on the dimensions and tasks the test is supposed to measure. Many personality measures are called inventories rather than tests. An *inventory*, which is typically self-administered, is a list of items, often in question form, used in describing or investigating behavior, interests, and attitudes. A *test* is a standardized set of questions or other items designed to evaluate knowledge or skills.

To develop a concurrently valid inventory (or to consider using an established inventory), the psychologist should assess the personality, interests, or attitudinal characteristics of already-employed police officers to establish predictors of good performance. Typically, the inventory is administered to officers representing varying degrees of success in law enforcement work, with "success" determined by supervisor evaluations, peer ratings, or both. For example, if a high percentage of officers evaluated by supervisors as "successful" respond differently to certain questions on a scale from a group of "unsuccessful" officers, the scale is considered a good evaluator of *current* on-the-job performance. Applicants who subsequently take the inventory should obtain results that are similar to those of the successful officers in order to be assessed as suitable candidates for employment.

Research that examines the current performance of individuals already on the force has a critical limitation, however, because it ignores the important psychological characteristics of those officers who were hired but dropped out because of various problems during the course of their career path. Thus, significant segments of the population are missed. One of the primary reasons for using any screening instrument is to discover the potential dropouts or failures as early as possible in their careers, which could save both time and money for the department.

Predictive validity is the degree to which an inventory or test *predicts* a person's subsequent performance on the dimensions or attributes the inventory (or test) is designed to measure. In other words, an instrument has predictive validity if it is able to identify which candidates will and will not succeed at law enforcement work. As a research procedure, predictive validation is more useful and rigorous than concurrent validation, but it is rarely implemented because it requires a longitudinal design in which officers must be evaluated over an extended period of time, usually several years. Candidates are tested during a pre-employment stage and then followed over their careers to see how the initial testing results could have predicted eventual problems and successes. If a test or inventory is able to distinguish those who eventually perform well from those who do not, it has high predictive validity and is considered a powerful device for the screening and selection of candidates prior to entry into law enforcement.

A test or inventory has **face (or content) validity** if its questions appear relevant to the tasks needed in law enforcement—in other words, someone looking at the inventory will attest that it seems relevant, regardless of whether it really is. Face validity refers not to what the test actually measures, but to what it superficially *appears* to measure (VandenBos, 2007). In reality, there may be no empirical support for these assumptions. However, face validity has value because examinees believe the exam is at least pertinent to the job for which they are applying. In addition, Otto et al. (1998) emphasize the importance of face validity for application in the legal context because any measuring instrument should look pertinent and relevant to the legal questions at hand. Judges, lawyers, and jurors may have more faith in a test or inventory with face validity. Psychologists know, though, that unless other types of validity are also ensured, the fact that a test has high face validity has little overall bearing on whether it measures what it is supposed to.

In summary, of the above three forms of validity, predictive validity is the most desirable to achieve but also the most challenging to establish. Face validity is probably the easiest to establish and is also desirable, particularly if we must persuade non-psychologists of the value of an inventory. However, face validity alone is not sufficient to establish a test or inventory's ability to measure what it is designed to.

Commonly Used Inventories in Police Screening

There is a lack of consensus concerning which personality inventory or measure is most useful in the screening and selection process. Research on law enforcement screening (e.g., Cochrane, Tett, & Vandecreek, 2003) indicates that the following six personality measures are the most commonly used:

- The Minnesota Multiphasic Personality Inventory–Revised (MMPI-2)

- The Inwald Personality Inventory (IPI)

- The California Psychological Inventory (CPI)

- The Personality Assessment Inventory (PAI)

- The NEO Personality Inventory–Revised (NEO PI-R)

- The Sixteen Personality Factor Questionnaire–Fifth Edition (16-PF)

In addition to these six, a restructured version of the MMPI—the Minnesota Multiphasic Personality Inventory-Revised-Restructured Form (MMPI-2-RF)—is increasingly being used.

To say these measures are commonly used is not to say they are necessarily the best measures, however. As we note below in discussing each, the jury is still out as to which is most deserving of continued use. Furthermore, many agencies make use of alternative approaches, particularly measures designed specifically for preemployment screening of police candidates (Scrivner et al., 2014). One recently developed example of these alternative measures is the Matrix-Predictive Uniform Law Enforcement Selection Evaluation (M-PULSE; Davis & Rostow, 2008). However, it is critically important for alternative tests to be validated for use in police officer selection procedures.

Minnesota Multiphasic Personality Inventory–Revised (MMPI-2)

For over six decades, the most commonly used psychological instrument for police and public safety preselection screening has been the **Minnesota Multiphasic Personality Inventory-Revised (MMPI-2)** (Ben-Porath, Corey, & Tarescavage, 2017). Police officer candidates often know it by its length ("that endless test"—it has 557 questions!). The MMPI-2 is a revision of the MMPI, and both were originally designed to measure psychopathology or behavioral disorders. In recent years, however, psychologists have modified the scoring of the MMPI-2 to measure positive personality traits, such as stress tolerance, emotional maturity, self-control, and judgement.

Cochrane et al. (2003) discovered that the MMPI-2 was used in 70% of all surveyed police departments in the United States in preemployment screenings. This is probably a good thing, because a large amount of research has demonstrated that the MMPI-2 is a useful predictor of police officer job performance (Ben-Porath et al., 2017; Caillouet, Boccaccini, Varela, Davis, & Rostow, 2010; Detrick, Chibnall, & Rosso, 2001; Sellbom, Fischler, & Ben-Porath, 2007; P. A. Weiss, Vivian, Weiss, Davis, & Rostow, 2013). Nevertheless, it should be emphasized that performance on the MMPI-2 should be only one factor to be considered in the overall screening or evaluation process. Other sources of information—such as background checks, performance on oral board examinations, and prior law enforcement experience—are all pertinent.

In 2008, the **Minnesota Multiphasic Personality Inventory-Revised-Restructured Form (MMPI-2-RF)** was published (Ben-Porath & Tellegen, 2008). Although this inventory used 60% of the items from the MMPI-2, it should not be considered a revision of the MMPI-2 (Butcher, Hass, Greene, & Nelson, 2015). "Rather, it is a new test, made from MMPI-2 items, that has to be researched and validated to establish its own merits and not just accepted as a newer version of the MMPI-2" (Butcher et al., 2015, p. 251).

The MMPI-2-RF has 338 items and 51 scales, compared with 10 clinical and 4 validity scales on the MMPI-2. Preliminary research suggests that it appears to be a somewhat stronger measure than the MMPI-2 for predicting law enforcement officer performance (Sellbom et al., 2007; Tarescavage, Corey, & Ben-Porath, 2015, 2016). As noted by Ben-Porath et al. (2017), the MMPI-2-RF builds on the power of the MMPI-2 with "a comprehensive, modern literature documenting associations between pre-hire scores and a broad range of job-relevant variables" (p. 69). To date, however, practicing psychologists prefer the MMPI-2 to the MMPI-2-RF by a 3 to 1 margin (Butcher et al., 2015).

The Inwald Personality Inventory (IPI)

The **Inwald Personality Inventory (IPI)** is a 310-item, true/false questionnaire that has 26 scales. The IPI was specifically designed to measure the suitability of law enforcement and public safety candidates based on a variety of personality traits and behavioral patterns (Inwald, 1992). It was developed to measure both positive personality traits and problematic behavioral patterns, such as job difficulties, substance abuse, driving violations, absence abuse (missing excessive days of work), and antisocial attitudes. The IPI also contains a 19-item validity scale called "Guardedness," which is intended to identify those individuals resistant to revealing negative information about themselves (the MMPI-2 has a similar "Lie" scale). As Inwald states, "When a candidate denies such items, a strong need to appear unusually virtuous is indicated" (p. 4). If the guardedness score is problematic, the other scale scores may be affected due to socially desirable responses from the respondent.

The IPI is also known as the Hilson Personnel Profile/Success Quotient (Inwald & Brobst, 1988). In *some* situations, the IPI does slightly better than the MMPI-2 in predicting the performance of public safety personnel and probably is a useful instrument when used in combination with other screening instruments. One strength of the IPI is that it has good face validity. A 2003 survey (Cochrane et al., 2003) found that the IPI was used in the preemployment screening process by about 12% of all municipal police departments across the country. Since that time, however, little research has been conducted on the instrument, and it is unknown to what extent it is in use.

The California Psychological Inventory (CPI)

The **California Psychological Inventory (CPI)** (Gough, 1987) contains 462 true-or-false questions designed to measure various personality features that are considered positive. An earlier version, called Version I, has 480 questions. The inventory is to be used with both adolescents and adults to predict how individuals will behave and react in a variety of interpersonal situations. The items are grouped into 20 scales developed to measure attributes of personality involved in interpersonal behavior and social interaction (K. R. Murphy & Davidshofer, 1998). Norms of law enforcement applicants are available from the publisher (Consulting Psychologists Press, Inc.). The nationwide survey conducted by Cochrane et al. (2003) revealed that approximately 25% of the departments responding indicated that they used the CPI in their screening procedure.

Some success has been reported for the ability of the CPI to predict performance, both during training and in the field. Topp and Kardash (1986) compared the CPI scores of police recruits who passed academy training with the scores of those who failed or resigned from the academy prior to graduation. Based on CPI score patterns, the researchers described those who graduated as more outgoing, stable, venturesome, confident, controlled, and relaxed. In a comprehensive meta-analysis assessing the overall validity of personality measures as predictors of the job performance of law enforcement officers, Varela et al. (2004) discovered that prediction was strongest for the CPI compared to the MMPI or IPI. Varela and his coauthors reasoned that one possible explanation for the superior performance of the CPI is that it is designed to measure *positive* and hopefully normal personality traits, in contrast to the MMPI-2, which—as we mentioned previously—was originally designed to measure psychopathology. They write,

> personality measures that are designed to assess normal personality traits, such as the CPI, may be more useful in this context because they provide information that is not obtained during the initial screening process. For instance, the CPI was designed to provide information about consistent styles of interpersonal behavior. Because being a successful police officer requires effective interpersonal skills . . . the CPI may be a useful measure for predicting this important aspect of officer performance. (p. 666)

The Personality Assessment Inventory (PAI)

The **Personality Assessment Inventory (PAI)** (Morey, 1991, 2007) is a self-administered, objective inventory of adult personality that provides information on "critical clinical variables."

The PAI contains 344 statements. Respondents are asked to rate the degree each statement is true of themselves on a 4-point scale (1 *very true*, 2 *mainly true*, 3 *slightly true*, 4 *false*). Responses to statements determine scores on 4 validity scales, 11 clinical scales, 5 treatment scales, and 2 interpersonal scales. Research suggests that the PAI may be a decent predictor of violence, suicide, aggression, and substance abuse and may be a reasonable instrument to use in the selection of police officers. However, it is currently used mostly in corrections to predict criminal reoffending, inmate misconduct, and violence (Gardner, Boccaccini, Bitting, & Edens, 2015; Reidy, Sorensen, & Davidson, 2016; Ruiz, Cox, Magyar, & Edens, 2014).

The NEO Personality Inventory–Revised (NEO PI-R)

The **NEO Personality Inventory–Revised (NEO PI-R)** (Costa & McCrae, 1992; Detrick & Chibnall, 2013, 2017) is specifically designed to measure the five major domains of personality, called the "Big Five" and often remembered with the acronym OCEAN. They are (1) openness to experience, (2) conscientiousness, (3) extraversion, (4) agreeableness, and (5) emotional stability (which taps neuroticism). The NEO PI-R contains six trait or facet measures that define each of the five personality domains. Taken together, the five domain scales and 30 facet scales of the NEO PI-R facilitate a comprehensive and detailed assessment of healthy adult personality.

At first, the five-factor model of personality as measured by the NEO was thought to be the answer to the ongoing search for a comprehensive and valid measure of personality and was met with enthusiasm by those involved in personnel selection. So far, though, the NEO has had mixed success. In a meta-analytic study, Barrick and Mount (1991) found that, except for openness to experience, the other four Big Five domains correlated significantly but only moderately with police performance. In a later study, Barrick and Mount (2005) report that the personality traits of extraversion, agreeableness, and openness to experience are valid predictors of performance but only for specific occupations. For instance, extraversion appears to be related to job performance in occupations "where a significant portion of the job involves interacting with others, particularly when that interaction is focused on influencing others and obtaining status and power" (Barrick & Mount, 2005, p. 360). Jonathan Black (2000) investigated the predictive validity of the NEO PI-R in screening police officers in New Zealand. He administered the NEO PI-R to recruits at the beginning of training and then analyzed how well the scales predicted outcomes at the end of training. He found significant relationships between the conscientiousness, extraversion, and neuroticism domains and several performance measures conducted during the training. Similarly, Detrick, Chibnall, and Luebbert (2004) examined the predictive validity of the NEO PI-R in relation to police academy performance in a large metropolitan area of the midwestern United States. They found that high scores on three facets of the neuroticism domain, and lower scores on one facet scale of the conscientiousness domain, were related to performance during academy training. Disciplinary and absenteeism factors were predicted by multiple facets. The vulnerability facet scale also emerged as a significant predictor of non-graduation. Overall, the authors concluded that the study provided support for the validity of the NEO PI-R as a predictor of police academy performance.

In another study, Detrick and Chibnall (2006) found that the NEO PI-R may also be a powerful tool for predicting officer performance in the field, rather than simply police academy or training performance. Based on NEO PI-R test data, the best entry-level police officers were described as "emotionally controlled, slow to anger, and steady under stress; socially assertive with high need for stimulation; guarded regarding others' motives and strategic in social exchange; and highly conscientious, goal-oriented, and disciplined" (p. 282). According to Detrick and Chibnall, these characteristics represent a very useful benchmark for psychologists to consider in evaluating law enforcement applicants. Another recent development is the establishment of police applicant norms for the NEO PI-R, which makes it more attractive as a measure of positive personality characteristics of successful police officers (Detrick & Chibnall, 2017).

The Sixteen Personality Factor Questionnaire (16-PF)

The **Sixteen Personality Factor Questionnaire (16-PF)** is another instrument designed to measure adult personality traits. The questionnaire contains 185 items that require a person to answer along a 3-point Likert-type scale. A Likert scale usually requires respondents to indicate their reactions to various statements on a response scale, typically with seven responses, ranging from "strongly agree" to "strongly disagree." The items on the 16-PF are grouped into 16 primary-factor scales representing the dimensions of personality initially identified by Raymond Catell (cited in K. R. Murphy & Davidshofer, 1998). The questionnaire was based on a series of factor-analytic studies of items that contained personality dimensions that differentiate presumably well-adjusted individuals from those with significant behavior problems. The 16-PF has been heavily researched and consistently demonstrates solid reliability and validity on normal personality traits (Butcher, Bubany, & Mason, 2013). The Cochrane et al. (2003) survey reported that the 16-PF was used by about 19% of the police departments in their pre-employment screening procedures. Only a very limited amount of research has been done on its ability as a valid predictor of law enforcement performance and success, however.

Fitness-for-Duty Evaluation (FFDE)

Police officers, emergency personnel, crisis team members, and firefighters who witness an especially disturbing event—such as the bodies of young children, terrorist attacks, victims of child sexual abuse or sex trafficking, plane crashes, the devastation following natural disasters, or catastrophes involving fellow officers—may exhibit intense emotional or psychological reactions. In addition, officers may experience personal crises, such as the death of someone close to them or the shooting of a suspect later found not to be armed. In these situations, they may take a leave of absence or be placed on administrative leave. Following such leaves, a fitness-for-duty evaluation (FFDE) may be required. In other situations, the officer may have displayed behavior that is of concern, such as harassing or abusing a citizen with a firearm, displaying wide variations in mood and irritability while on duty, talk of committing suicide, or being unreliable in completing assigned tasks. In any one of these situations, the FFDE may be needed to determine whether the officer has the mental and psychological stability to continue as an effective officer on the street, at least for the foreseeable future. This requires a much more extensive assessment than the psychological screening evaluation for initial employment positions.

Psychologists are often asked to perform FFDEs for organizations in addition to law enforcement agencies. Large private corporations, federal agencies, universities, hospitals and other health care agencies, and licensure bureaus often ask them to do FFDEs (Bresler, 2010). The basic goal of any FFDE is "to ascertain to what extent an employee is, or is not, able to meet job expectations" (p. 1). However, our focus here is on FFDEs designed to serve law enforcement agencies. In addition, we will focus on psychological issues instead of physical impairments where the examination usually requires medical personnel, such as a physician, nurse practitioner, or other qualified professional.

The order or request for the FFDE for law enforcement comes from the department supervisor or head, and the evaluation is usually conducted by a police psychologist or qualified licensed psychologist who is highly familiar with police psychology issues and research. It may be ordered or requested when an officer displays behavior that raises serious questions as to whether he or she is fit to carry out public safety duties. For example, Anthony V. Stone (1995) estimated that the alleged use of excessive force accounted for 19% of FFDE referrals. Some FFDEs are ordered because the officer displays change of behavior on the job that presumably arises from personal or job-induced stress. However, some agencies *require* these evaluations as standard procedure after a critical incident (such as a fatal shooting), whether or not an officer displays problematic behavior. (See Focus 2.4 later in chapter for more information on fatal shootings.) Therefore, it should not be assumed that a request for an FFDE occurs only when there are signs that an officer is facing problems on the job. In addition to carrying out the evaluation, the examining psychologist should recommend intervention methods or reasonable accommodations that would help improve the officer's effectiveness. These may involve counseling, retraining, or treatment. Scrivner et al. (2014) note that many police departments, including those that have had a pattern of inappropriate police behavior in the past, have developed an **early intervention system (EIS)** "wherein supervisors learn to recognize certain types of behavior and help the employee get assistance before a problem develops to a level that a mandatory evaluation is required" (p. 450). FFDEs are sensitive areas for the police psychologist, and they raise ethical issues revolving around confidentiality and treatment. The psychologist conducting an FFDE should not be the one providing treatment to the officer being evaluated, because this would constitute a dual relationship (assessor and treatment provider), which is frowned upon by the Ethical Standards and Code of Conduct.

Psychologists conducting the FFDE are advised to employ a variety of methods in their assessments, including psychological tests or inventories and a standard clinical interview that assesses mental status. They should obtain background information from files, the officers themselves, and other significant parties if possible. The evaluations must be done with the informed consent of the officer, but the examiner is under no obligation to explain the results to the officer. The "owner" of the FFDE is essentially the agency requesting the evaluation. On the other hand, the agency is not entitled to any more psychological information regarding an employee than is necessary to document the presence or absence of job-related personality traits, characteristics, disorders, propensities, or conditions that would interfere with the performance of essential job functions (IACP Police Psychological Services Section, 2010). Mayer and Corey (2015) emphasize that "Psychological FFDEs are often contentious examinations in which the employee being evaluated has much to lose, public and officer safety is at risk, and the likelihood of an administrative grievance, arbitration or litigation is high, particularly when the officer is deemed to be unfit for duty and the results are contested" (pp. 110–111).

The FFDE report usually includes the psychological measures used, a conclusion regarding the determination of fitness for duty, and a description of the functional limitations of the officer. In most instances, the FFDE report is provided to the department as a confidential personnel record. Periodic evaluations of the officer may also be necessary. The IACP (2010) recommends that the psychologist conducting the FFDE include performance evaluations, commendations, testimonials, reports of any internal affairs investigation, preemployment psychological screening, formal citizen/public complaints, use-of-force incidents, officer-involved shootings, civil claims, disciplinary actions, incident reports of any triggering events, medical/psychological treatment records, or other supporting or relevant documentation related to the officer's psychological fitness for duty. The IACP further recommends that only personality, psychopathology, cognitive, and specialized tests that have been validated be used in the assessment process.

Special Unit Evaluations

Psychological assessments are also done as standard procedure for members of special teams, such as special weapons and tactics teams (SWATs) and tactical response teams (TRTs); undercover agents; and narcotics, internal affairs, and crisis/hostage negotiation teams, to determine if they are psychologically fit to undergo the pressures and possess the judgment requirements of high-stress positions. These evaluations are usually referred to as psychological evaluations for police special assignments (PEPSA) (Trompetter, 2017). Successful members of SWAT teams, for example, tend to be "self-disciplined, conscientious, adherent to rules, comfortable accepting rules, conforming, and helpful" (Super, 1999, p. 422). Special units usually deal with the execution of high-risk search warrants or high-risk arrest warrants, barricaded persons, hostage situations, heavily armed offenders, terrorist acts, and suicidal persons.

It is not unusual for team members to be reevaluated periodically to identify problems before they develop into more serious behavioral patterns that would interfere with effective job performance. However, very little research has focused on the validity of assessment procedures used to aid in special team selection. As concluded by Super, "There is a serious need for rigorous research regarding psychological assessment and special unit appointments" (p. 422). Although the National Tactical Officers Association in conjunction with the International Association of Police Chiefs (2015a, 2015b), has proposed standards for tactical police teams, Super's statement about research still rings true today.

Conclusions on Psychological Testing for Police and Public Safety Personnel

Although many different assessment techniques and personality inventories have been used in the screening, selection, and promotion of law enforcement officers, only a few have emerged as reasonably valid predictors of effective on-the-job law enforcement performance. Police officer candidates are usually administered two self-report inventories that measure abnormal and normal behaviors, a practice that is quite common for many law enforcement officer evaluations. In some cases, the revised MMPI-2 and the relatively new MMPI-2-RF can serve as both measures.

There is increasing work on validating the various tests used for both pre-screening and later assessment, and some tests have performed better than others in both of these domains (Corey & Borum, 2013). As Scrivner et al. (2014) write, "Irrespective of the tests selected for a suitable battery, it is very clear that the research component of this domain has expanded considerably, and today there is a rich literature available on assessing police candidates for psychological suitability" (p. 449). Empirical investigations evaluating relationships between initial selection standards (predictors) and the actual job performance of law enforcement officers must continually be undertaken. The two most promising and validated psychological inventories to date are the MMPI-2 and the MMPI-2-RF. The MMPI-2 has accumulated extensive research data over the past six decades, and the MMPI-2-RF is showing very promising data pertaining to the selection of law enforcement personnel.

Psychologists using any of these measures also must be aware of any research relating to how they apply to diverse populations, such as women compared with men or various ethnicities. For example, ethnic diversity sometimes does have a very small effect on MMPI-2 or other personality inventory scores, a factor that must be taken into account by the evaluating psychologist. For example, some ethnic groups tend to respond in ways that present themselves more favorably than other applicants. The Civil Rights Acts of 1964 and 1991 prohibit discrimination in the workplace on the basis of race, color, religion, sex, or national origin (Ben-Porath et al., 2017). The 1991 update of the Civil Rights Act (CRA) also makes it illegal to alter the results of employment related tests or inventories on the basis of race, color, religion, sex, or national origin. In recent years, there has been a concerted effort to adjust but not alter testing administration, scoring, and interpretation of police officer selection procedures to abide by the spirit of the CRA of 1991.

The psychologist working with a police agency for screening and selection purposes should have a strong background in and solid knowledge of psychological testing, including experience with the specific tests used. The selected test or personality inventories should also meet the criteria recommended by the "Standards for Psychological and Educational Testing," which were developed by the Joint Committee for the Revision of the Standards for Educational and Psychological Testing of the American Educational Research Association, the American Psychological Association, and the National Council on Measurement in Education. The intent of the Standards is to encourage the sound and ethical use of tests and to provide criteria for their evaluation.

Single psychological tests as predictors of effective law enforcement performance take considerable and carefully designed research. This is partly due to the diversity and complexity of behaviors required of law enforcement officers, but it is also due to varying work situations across departments. Police duties range from preventing and detecting crime to investigating accidents, intervening in disputes, handling domestic disturbances, and responding to a wide range of requests from the public. The smaller the department, the more varied the responsibilities of individual officers are. It is not unusual to find a local, small-town law enforcement officer offering safety tips to an elementary school class and, on the same day, dealing with a violent domestic altercation. Because specialization is a luxury very small departments cannot afford, it is very difficult to establish objective performance criteria on which to base predictions. Some officers may perform very competently on certain tasks while failing at others. The officer who relates exceptionally well to fun-loving teenagers may perform poorly in crisis situations involving difficult adults.

To tap the heterogeneity of law enforcement activities, screening devices should contain a number of predictors based on a multitude of behaviors, but few psychological measures are able to do this. In addition, because law enforcement work often differs from one jurisdiction to another, a test may be adequate for a given department but may not suffice elsewhere. Rural or small-town law enforcement may require different behaviors and talents from metropolitan or urban law enforcement work.

The broad scope of law enforcement, together with the urgent need for more vigorous and sophisticated methods of study, warn us that we should expect few solid conclusions in the research literature as to what are adequate predictors of success or failure in law enforcement work. As expected, the literature is littered with inconclusive or mixed results. This does not mean that reliable and valid psychological assessment is beyond reach. It may mean, though, that a successful testing program may have to be tailor-made to reflect the needs of a particular agency. In addition, it is certainly acceptable to "screen out" those candidates who exhibit gross indicators of problems, such as mental disorder, highly aggressive or antisocial behaviors, or poor judgment.

PSYCHOLOGICAL INTERVENTION RESPONSIBILITIES

The second major category of tasks performed by police and public safety psychologists, according to Aumiller and Corey (2007) includes a variety of services that provide support to individual officers, their colleagues and families, and the police organization itself. Primary examples are stress management, dealing with posttraumatic stress from shooting incidents, and preventing police suicide.

Stress Management

The management of stress became a dominant theme in police psychology from the mid-1970s to the early 1980s and remains an important consideration today. The earliest full-time police psychologists, as well as community consultants, were called on to identify and dissipate stress, which, if left unmanaged or untreated, could result in an array of psychological and physical health problems for the officer and potentially put the public at risk due to faulty judgment and decision making. *Stressors, burnout, posttraumatic stress disorder* (PTSD), and *critical incident trauma* became standard terms in the police psychologist's vocabulary. The focus on stress was significant because it moved police psychologists away from their traditional assessment functions and into a much larger realm of opportunity and services. Consequently, psychologists began to offer not only stress management but also crisis intervention training, hostage negotiation training, domestic violence workshops, and substance abuse and alcohol treatment.

Many researchers, as well as officers and their families, consider law enforcement to be one of the most stressful of all occupations, with correspondingly reported high rates of divorce, alcoholism, suicide, and other emotional and health problems (Finn & Tomz, 1997). Persons in many occupations may argue that they face more physical danger than law enforcement officers. Construction workers, miners, stunt pilots, firefighters, and demolition workers are all exposed to potential death or physical injury. However, perhaps few occupations encounter the wide variety of stressors, ranging from organizational demands (e.g., shift work) to the nature of police work itself (e.g., exposure to violence, suffering, and tragedy at all levels), as consistently as law enforcement. An additional source of stress in the current political climate is the tension between police and the community they serve in communities across the country, where shootings by police have resulted in citizen distrust and, in some cases, federal investigations. We discuss this again later in the chapter, when we cover police bias and the use of excessive force. (See also Focus 2.1 regarding research on the so-called "Ferguson Effect.")

FOCUS 2.1. BEFORE AND BEYOND FERGUSON: IS THERE A "FERGUSON EFFECT"?

Ferguson, a small city in Missouri, gained national attention in 2014 after a fatal police shooting of an unarmed black man, 18-year-old Michael Brown, by a white police officer, Darren Wilson. According to Wilson, Brown reached into his patrol car and tried to grab his gun. Witnesses varied in their accounts of the scene, with some saying Brown approached the car with his hands up while others said he was confrontational. There was unrest in the community both before and after the case went to a grand jury. The grand jury did not indict Wilson, an outcome that led to some peaceful protests and demonstrations nationwide, but also to violence such as cars being set afire and bricks thrown.

Controversial actions taken by police against racial or ethnic minorities are not new and not unique to Ferguson. In an infamous episode in 1991, Rodney King was beaten by Los Angeles police officers, a beating captured by a bystander with a video camera. The four officers charged with aggravated assault were found not guilty, but two of the four were later found in a federal court to have violated King's civil rights and were sentenced to prison terms. In 1999, Amadou Diallo was shot to death by police when he pulled out his wallet to show identification. Shortly before and after Ferguson, racially tinged incidents occurred in other cities, including Staten Island, Baltimore, North Charleston, and Cleveland. Each of these incidents, and more, spread on social media and were covered extensively by traditional news outlets.

It has been suggested that negative public reactions to police use of force has produced a Ferguson Effect.

Specifically, law enforcement officers are so concerned about public criticism and scrutiny of their work, of being captured on video, or of being accused of racial bias, that they are demoralized, unmotivated to do their job, and less likely to use aggressive tactics when these tactics are called for. Put another way, they engage in "de-policing," and this de-policing leads to increases in crime. The speculations are fueled by increases in violent crime in some cities, even while crime rates overall have decreased in the 21st century. There is no empirical evidence that a Ferguson Effect has indeed occurred, and criminologists consider it highly unlikely that— even if police are demoralized—this explains scattered upticks in the crime rate (Wolfe & Nix, 2016).

Wolfe and Nix raised an additional question about the alleged Ferguson Effect, however. They wondered whether police may be less likely to work hand in hand with the public or engage in community partnerships if they perceived that the public was critical of the work they are doing. "[T]he relentless negative coverage of incidents such as Ferguson in news outlets and on social media presents a social climate whereby the legitimacy of law enforcement . . . is being challenged. It is likely that such a situation may make it difficult for some officers to be motivated to work in law enforcement and, as a consequence, be less willing to engage in community partnership" (p. 1).

Wolfe and Nix administered a survey to 567 deputy sheriffs in a southeastern law enforcement agency and found little indication that they engaged in de-policing. Respondents were aware of and concerned about public perceptions of police, and there was some indication that negative publicity affected their motivation. However, they were not less likely to do their jobs. In addition, deputies who were confident in their own authority and who perceived their supervisors as fair and supportive were more likely to be receptive to engage in community partnership. In sum, the Ferguson Effect *may* be a reality insofar as it affects officer morale, but its impact on crime rates thus far is undocumented. Furthermore, if it does exist, it can be dampened by fellow officers and supervisors who promote fairness and legitimacy within the department.

Questions for Discussion

1. Define the *Ferguson Effect* and discuss whether it is intuitively logical.

2. The Michael Brown case and others like it (e.g., Trayvon Martin, Eric Garner, Freddie Gray, Walter Scott, Tamir Rice) spurred the growth of Black Lives Matter, a social movement meant to bring attention to the treatment of blacks by the criminal justice system. In response to the movement, a contrapuntal movement—Blue Lives Matter—was created to support police. Is it reasonable to be a strong supporter of both of these movements? Agree or disagree with the following statement: Those who started Blue Lives Matter are missing the point.

3. What is meant by a law enforcement officer being confident in his or her own authority? Is this a good thing or a bad thing?

A common strategy employed in the police stress literature is to divide the occupational stressors identified by police officers into four major categories: (1) organizational, (2) task related, (3) external, and (4) personal.

Organizational Stress

Organizational stress refers to the emotional and stressful effects that the policies and practices of the police department have on the individual officer. These stressors may include poor pay, excessive paperwork, insufficient training, inadequate equipment, weekend duty, shift work, inconsistent discipline or rigid enforcement of rules and policies, limited promotional opportunities, poor supervision and administrative support, and poor relationships with supervisors or colleagues. Rural police officers and sheriff's deputies often deal with limited training, old equipment, lack of proper resources, and outdated technology (Page & Jacobs, 2011). Organizational stressors in major departments may also include antagonistic subcultures within the department, such as intense competition between specialized units, precincts, or even shifts. Being investigated by the internal affairs division is another troubling stressor.

One study from the early 2000s reveals that excessive shift work contributes to more errors in judgment and greater increases in stress than perhaps any other factor in the police environment (Vila & Kenney, 2002). Some officers work more than 14 hours a day on a regular basis, and some "moonlight" for extra income. Excessive hours on the job not only interfere with sleep and eating habits but also wreak havoc with family life and responsibilities. Furthermore, irregular hours often interfere with social get-togethers and family activities, isolating the officer even more from social support systems. Also, the organizational structure of large police departments often promotes office politics, lack of effective consultation, nonparticipation in decision making, and restrictions on behavior. In fact, organizational stressors have been considered to be the most prevalent and frustrating source of stress for law enforcement personnel (Bakker & Heuven, 2006; Finn & Tomz, 1997).

Task-Related Stress

Task-related stress is generated by the nature of police work itself. These stressors include inactivity and boredom; situations requiring the use of force; responsibility of protecting others;

the use of discretion; the fear that accompanies danger to oneself and colleagues; dealing with violent or disrespectful, uncivil individuals; making critical decisions; frequent exposure to death; continual exposure to people in pain or distress; and the constant need to keep one's emotions under close control. In many rural police or sheriff's departments, the officer must deal with the situation alone or without immediate backup.

Law enforcement is frequently confronted with interpersonal violence, confrontational interactions with individuals, and emotionally charged encounters with victims of crimes and accidents (Bakker & Heuven, 2006). Police are expected to keep their emotions under control, a process that has been referred to as "emotional labor" (G. A. Adams & Buck, 2010; Grandey, 2000). Furthermore, they must regulate their emotional *expressions* to conform to societal norms and expectations. Although this is expected to some degree in many other occupations (e.g., lawyers, physicians, health care workers), this is especially expected of police officers on a day-to-day basis. Police officers are expected to regulate their emotions to display a facial and physical expression that is neutral, solid, and controlled. Moreover, police officers are expected to master the art of constantly switching between a more human response and the control of emotional expression (Bakker & Heuven, 2006) because sometimes a more "human" response is desired, as when an officer must inform people of the death of a loved one. Grandey calls this emotional regulation "surface acting," which is accomplished by suppressing the emotion that is actually felt (e.g., anger or sadness) and faking the appropriate emotion that the situation (or job) demands. Some researchers refer to this response as *emotional dissonance* (G. A. Adams & Buck, 2010). In essence, "emotional dissonance is the discrepancy between authentic and displayed emotions as part of the job" (Bakker & Heuven, 2006, p. 426). Increasing evidence supports the view that emotional dissonance has detrimental effects on health and well-being (Heuven & Bakker, 2003).

Stressful assignments, such as undercover duty or drug raids, also play a role in the stress equation. Police officers also fear air- or blood-borne diseases, either intentional (e.g., spread by terrorists) or accidental, and exposure to toxic or hazardous materials (Dowling, Moynihan, Genet, & Lewis, 2006). More recently, budget cutbacks and fiscal uncertainty due to the economy have resulted in concerns about job security and opportunity for advancement.

Task-related stress also occurs when officers experience role conflict, such as being at once an enforcer of the law, a social worker, a counselor, and a public servant (Finn & Tomz, 1997). For reasons to be discussed in later chapters, there is also increasing police interaction with mentally ill individuals, for example, which requires special skills on the part of the officer. Community-oriented policing (COP), an approach whereby police and citizens work more closely together in positive endeavors, has added new pressures, but supporters see it as a better approach than "law and order" policing. (See Focus 2.2.) It requires that officers "give up" a certain amount of control by "walking the beat," meeting with citizens, and adopting a service orientation more than a crime-fighting orientation. COP does not ignore crime or public safety, but it encourages police to form partnerships with citizens to prevent crime and improve safety for the public. Although its benefits are apparent, some officers find it difficult to adapt to its accompanying changes in strategies and policies.

Perhaps the most troubling task-related stress in police work is dealing with **critical incidents.** These are emergencies and disasters that are nonroutine and unanticipated, such as a shooter on the loose on a college campus or a family hostage-taking situation involving young children. These events tend to be very stressful primarily because they threaten the perceived control of the police officers (Paton, 2006) and have the potential to cause many deaths and injuries. Critical incidents can produce a number of psychological, neurological, and physical symptoms in responding officers, including confusion, disorientation, chest pain, sweating, rapid heart rate, and loss of memory. These symptoms may occur during or shortly after the critical incident. However, delayed post-incident stress symptoms may occur weeks or months

FOCUS 2.2. COMMUNITY-ORIENTED POLICING AND LAW AND ORDER POLICING: CAN THEY COEXIST?

Community-oriented policing (COP), an approach whereby citizens and police work as partners to improve the community, has received positive reviews from members of the public, politicians, researchers, and many law enforcement officials. As indicated in the text, COP is not always easy to implement, particularly because it seems to require that police give up some of their legitimate authority. At its best, though, COP lets police maintain their authority and fight crime, while also gaining more respect from the public they are sworn to serve and protect.

In the early 21st century, after a number of high-profile incidents in which police shot and sometimes killed young black males, the U.S. Justice Department initiated investigations into discriminatory practices in law enforcement. Subsequently, the Justice Department entered into agreements with cities (e.g., Baltimore, Chicago, Seattle, Ferguson) to modify their policing practices. In Spring 2017, a new Justice Department under Attorney General Jeff Sessions announced these agreements would be revisited, with an eye to protecting the law-and-order emphasis supported by the present administration.

Law and order policing is reflected in such practices as "stop-and-frisk" and in such philosophies as police militarization. Stop-and-frisk refers to stopping people temporarily, asking questions, and possibly doing a brief pat-down. Militarization refers to putting emphasis on the command and control functions of police, and de-emphasizing the need for citizen input on services or representation on review boards.

The American Psychological Association in late 2014 submitted testimony to a U.S. Senate committee charged with overseeing federal programs for equipping state and local law enforcement with surplus military equipment (Keita, 2014). Basically, the testimony was concerned with the possible increasing militarization of police, to the detriment of community policing strategies. In the testimony, psychologist Gwendolyn P. Keita cited important psychological research. This includes research on (a) effective ways to reduce ethnic and racial bias, (b) improve community relations, and (c) de-escalate confrontations and reduce the potential for violence. She noted that the growing militarization of police, particularly in communities heavily populated by minority groups, has resulted in community fears of law enforcement officers and a reduction of trust on both sides.

Several recommendations were made in her testimony:

- Implement community-based policing nationwide and train law enforcement personnel on how their implicit biases affect perceptions and decisions.
- For those departments that receive surplus military equipment, *require* education on community policing and *require* bias-free police training.
- Provide additional funding for community-based policing initiatives.
- Encourage the development of community-driven responses that empower communities with limited resources.
- Collect national-level data on police shootings and the racial/ethnic makeup of citizens involved in incidents such as stop-and-frisk.

Questions for Discussion

1. As noted, the above testimony occurred at the end of 2014. Have these recommendations been carried out? Why or why not?
2. Is it possible for community-oriented policing and law and order policing to coexist? Do you favor one approach over the other?
3. What are examples of community-driven responses that empower communities with limited resources?

after the incident. These delayed symptoms include restlessness, chronic fatigue, sleep disturbances, nightmares, irritability, depression, problems in concentration, and misuse of alcohol or illegal substances. In addition, officers are often concerned about how they reacted in critical incidents, and they want to know whether their psychological reactions were normal and appropriate (Trompetter, Corey, Schmidt, & Tracy, 2011). Police encounters with deadly-force confrontations are rapidly unfolding, ambiguous, and highly dangerous situations, and after the incident the officer is often unsure whether he or she performed adequately (Trompetter et al., 2011).

Considerable research strongly supports the effectiveness of immediate intervention after traumatic events (Trompetter et al., 2011; A. T. Young, Fuller, & Riley, 2008). Moreover, it appears that this intervention is especially effective if it occurs at or near the location of the crisis (Everly, Flannery, Eyler, & Mitchell, 2001; A. T. Young et al., 2008). Some psychologists work as members, advisors, or consultants on critical incident stress management (CISM) teams or critical incident stress debriefing (CISD) teams. They are sometimes called crisis intervention teams (CITs). The primary focus of these teams is to minimize the harmful effects of job stress as a result of very unusual crisis or emergency situations. As we will note below, however, the value of this immediate debriefing and its impact on preventing further symptoms down the line (e.g., symptoms of PTSD) is debated in the literature (Scrivner et al., 2014).

Many departments do not wait for an officer to be confronted with a critical incident. Rather, as part of candidate training, officers are provided with pre-incident education, which helps to psychologically immunize them by teaching them to anticipate and understand how traumatic events may affect them. Furthermore, with experience on the job, police officers usually go through a desensitization process whereby they become accustomed to many taxing events that can be expected to occur within the normal routine of policing. However, some traumatic events may be considered extraordinary and beyond preparation. Critical incidents most likely to cause high levels of stress include the following: the suicide or fatal shooting of a colleague; the accidental killing or wounding of a citizen by the police officer; death or serious injury to a child or multiple children; events that draw high media coverage; and events involving a number of deaths, such as major fires, terrorist bombings, or far-reaching natural disasters such as hurricanes, earthquakes, or tornadoes.

External Stress

External stress refers to an officer's ongoing frustration with the courts, the prosecutor's office, the criminal justice process, the correctional system, the media, or public attitudes. Available data suggest that for every 100 felony arrests, 43 are typically dismissed or not prosecuted (Finn & Tomz, 1997). Although this is not necessarily a bad thing, police often find it troubling. Moreover, many law enforcement officers feel court appearances are excessively time consuming, and they are often frustrated over what they perceive as inefficiency and "unjust" court decisions.

Another example of stress from external sources is that arising from police–citizen relationships, particularly when tied to various encounters. Since 1991, when the infamous incident involving the arrest of Rodney King was captured on a video recording, many other police–citizen or police–suspect encounters have been recorded on cell phones, street cameras, and police body cameras. Videos taken by members of the public are often circulated on the Internet—as one was when then North Charleston, South Carolina, police officer Michael Slager shot Walter J. Scott in the back as he ran away after a routine traffic stop. Slager was charged soon after the incident. A jury deliberated 4 days but could not reach a verdict, and a mistrial was declared in December 2016. Although a new trial was scheduled, the case ended when Slager pleaded guilty in federal court in May 2017 to violating Scott's civil rights.

Tactics other than force also have come under scrutiny in recent years and have undoubtedly produced stress among the law enforcement ranks. In the years following the events of September 11, 2001, police in New York City took an aggressive approach to encounters with people on the streets. This took the form of a stop-and-frisk program, which was widely condemned as illustrating racial/ethnic profiling. Data indicated that police were disproportionately stopping and questioning—if not searching—nonwhite individuals, particularly African Americans and Hispanics, and that they were more likely to use force with these groups. Lawsuits were filed, including by the U.S. Justice Department, and stop-and-frisk was curtailed.

A new mayor, William de Blasio, said that he hoped to return the city to focus more on the COP discussed above in order to restore the trust of citizens in their police force. One would hope that this approach would ultimately result in stress reduction for individual officers as well as better police–community relations. However, stop-and-frisk policies have been praised by the current presidential administration, and it is unclear whether the Department of Justice under different leadership will encourage these approaches.

Personal Stress

Personal stress refers to stressors involving marital relationships, health problems, addictions, peer group pressures, feelings of helplessness and depression, discrimination, sexual harassment, and lack of accomplishment. Some officers worry about their competency to do the job well or worry about doing something against regulations. Many police officers feel that the nature of their work has an adverse effect on their home life and social life. Older officers, because of their long, stressful careers, are especially vulnerable to serious physical and mental health problems (Gershon, Lin, & Li, 2002). In addition, female officers appear to be more prone to depressive symptoms and suicide due to stress factors than male officers (Violanti et al., 2009). This finding does not imply a weakness on the part of the officer; rather, it is more likely a symptom of the traditionally male environment in which the female officer works. We will discuss this in more detail shortly.

Although criminal justice literature frequently mentions exceedingly high divorce rates and general marital unhappiness among law enforcement officers, documentation is very difficult to obtain. Borum and Philpot (1993), in their study, found that divorce rates among police families were no higher than those found in the general population. Similar results are reported by Aamodt (2008). Yet, there is little doubt that the whole family suffers the stressors inherent in law enforcement. In one study of 479 spouses of police officers, 77% reported experiencing unusually high amounts of stress from the officers' job (Finn & Tomz, 1997). According to Finn and Tomz, the most common sources of spousal stress include the following:

- Shift work and overtime

- An officer's cynicism, need to feel in control at home, or inability or unwillingness to express feelings

- The fear that the officer will be hurt or killed

- The officer's and other people's excessively high expectations of their children

- Avoidance, teasing, or harassment of children because of their parent's job

- The presence of a gun in the home

In light of the above data, it is not surprising that police departments are increasingly hiring either full-time police psychologists or psychological, counseling, or mental health consultants who are available to consult on cases as well as offer their services to individual officers and their families. Delprino and Bahn (1988) reported that 53% of police agencies in their sample used counseling services for job-related stress. Since that survey, police psychologists have moved from providing counseling services for stress to a broad range of law enforcement-related activities (Dietz, 2000). About one third of these agencies also hired psychologists to provide relevant workshops and seminars. In addition, many support groups for families of police officers are appearing throughout the United States, frequently at the instigation of police spouses who band together to discuss and solve common problems. In some cases, police psychologists provide therapy or group counseling sessions to spouses or other family members of law enforcement officers without the participation of the officers themselves (Trompetter, 2017).

Peer counseling programs are available in a number of departments, but many police officers prefer to work with mental health professionals who are knowledgeable about police work but who are *not* police officers themselves. Officers are often resistant to discussing with other police officers the problems that are generally unacceptable within the police culture, such as sexual dysfunction, fear of getting hurt, or inability to use force when perceived to be necessary in the line of duty. This varies, though, because other officers distrust clinicians whom they may see as working for the police administration. In any case, it seems that psychologists must be careful *not* to try to act and talk like police officers as a means of gaining acceptance, or they may be labeled as "cop wannabes."

It is probably fair to speculate that most law enforcement officers have experienced one or more highly stressful situations, though they have not necessarily sought professional help in dealing with them. It is the atypical officer, for example, who has *never* been worried about getting hurt, *never* experienced marital or relationship problems, *never* been devastated after seeing a dead child, and *never* had sleep problems. At least one of these must have been experienced. In the following sections, we will cover two situations that are less common and thus perhaps far more problematic to the individual officer who experiences them.

Post-Shooting Traumatic Reactions

A **post-shooting traumatic reaction (PSTR)** represents a collection of emotions and psychological response patterns that may occur after a law enforcement officer shoots a person in the line of duty—which in itself is usually considered a critical incident. The traumatic reaction is especially likely when the victim dies. Fortunately, in contrast to what is depicted in so many media portrayals of police work, most law enforcement officers complete their career without ever firing a weapon in the line of duty. About 350 to 400 individuals are shot and killed by law enforcement officers each year, and another 200 are wounded (Federal Bureau of Investigation [FBI], 2008). Laurence Miller (1995) estimates that in the United States, two thirds of the officers involved in shootings demonstrate moderate to severe psychological problems after the shooting, and about 70% leave the force within 7 years after the incident. The most common psychological problem after a serious critical incident is posttraumatic stress disorder (PTSD). According to Brucia, Cordova, and Ruzek (2017), "Duty-related critical incidents most strongly associated with PTSD are killing someone in the line of duty, the death of a fellow officer, and physical assaults" (p. 121). In 2015, 86 law enforcement officers were killed in line-of-duty incidents (FBI, 2016c). Of these, 41 were killed as a result of felonious acts, and 45 died in accidents. Approximately 50,000 officers were victims of line-of-duty assaults. Prevalence rates of PTSD among police officers after a serious critical incident range from 7% to 19% (Brucia, Cordova, & Ruzek, 2017).

As suggested above, the number of individuals killed by police each year outnumber the number of officers who are killed, by a ratio of approximately 4:1. If we exclude accidents, the ratio is closer to 8:1. Interestingly, persons who are fatally shot by police are not typically the most violent repeat offenders. Rather, they tend to be petty criminals, the mentally ill, persons encountered by police in domestic altercations, and juveniles (L. Miller, 2015). In one recent incident, for example, a young boy was shot by police as he played with a toy gun in a city park. In another, a person with a history of depression was killed by police as he emerged from his home, running at officers and brandishing a knife.

The standard operating procedure in large agencies after a critical incident—such as a shooting—is to immediately contact the on-duty post-shooting peer support team members and the police psychologist. The psychologist will consult with supervisors to determine whether he or she should arrange to meet with the involved officers at that time or see the officer at a later time. Police psychologists generally realize that many police officers have a reputation for shunning mental health services under a wide range of circumstances. Laurence Miller (1995) writes that some officers have a notion of the psychotherapy experience as akin to brainwashing or as a humiliating, infantilizing experience. More commonly, the idea of needing "mental help" implies weakness, cowardice, and lack of ability to do the job.

These attitudes may be changing, however, and Miller himself later noted (2015) that the vast majority of officers who were involved in justified deadly force encounters return to the job quite soon afterward. Despite cynicism toward mental health professionals, many agencies require that the involved officer or officers receive immediate attention from both the peer support group and the police psychologist, regardless of the circumstances. Some agencies provide a "companion officer" as soon as possible, preferably a trusted colleague who has been through an officer-involved shooting himself or herself (Trompetter et al., 2011). Some researchers (e.g., Kamena, Gentz, Hays, Bohl-Penrod, & Greene, 2011) note that psychologists have a valuable role to play in training peer support teams. If the officers see a mental health professional after the incident, Trompetter, Corey, Schmidt, and Tracy (2011) assert that—if possible—the most effective post-shooting intervention occurs if the officer is offered privileged communication while working with the mental health professional. Nevertheless, in reality, some officers prefer to go to a respected mental health professional than to a peer support group. Both options—the professional psychologist and the peer team—should be available. (See Focus 2.3 for related topic.)

It is also standard procedure at most agencies for the involved officer to immediately be placed on administrative leave for 3 days or longer. During that leave, it is usually common practice to recommend that the officer see the police psychologist for critical incident stress debriefings (CISDs). Usually, the CISD takes place within 24 to 72 hours after the critical incident and consists of a single group meeting that lasts approximately 2 to 3 hours (L. Miller, 1995).

FOCUS 2.3. FIREFIGHTERS, EMTs, AND MORE

The term *public safety personnel* encompasses numerous individuals other than those engaged in law enforcement. Firefighters, emergency medical technicians (EMTs), paramedics, search and rescue workers, emergency dispatchers, and other first responders all keep the public safe and may come into contact with forensic psychologists. These professionals are routinely exposed to crises, disasters, danger, and life-threatening situations. They are often responsible for the recovery of the seriously injured and the dead, and in many cases they are expected to console the family and acquaintances of victims at the scene of the tragedy.

As a result of their frequent encounters with trauma, shock, and grief, these public safety professionals—like law enforcement officers—often exhibit trauma-related symptoms of PTSD, depression, and drug and alcohol problems (Kleim & Westphal, 2011). Research reveals, for example, that 8% to 32% of first responders show signs of PTSD, usually at moderate levels (Haugen, Evces, & Weiss, 2012).

PTSD and depression, if left unrecognized and untreated, result in significant impairment and inability of public safety personnel to do their jobs effectively. Increasingly, clinical forensic psychologists and police psychologists are used in the screening, selection, training, and treatment of public safety personnel at all levels. At this point, however, while there is growing research literature on the screening and selection of law enforcement applicants, there is very little research on these topics for first responders. Furthermore, effective treatment methods for helping public safety professionals deal with consistent encounters with trauma and tragedy are also heavily weighted toward law enforcement, and very little is directed at other public safety professionals beyond the importance of social and peer support (Haugen et al., 2012; Kirby, Shakespeare-Finch, & Palk, 2011; Kleim & Westphal, 2011). "The literature is startlingly sparse and is not sufficient for evidence-based recommendations for first responders" (Haugen et al., 2012, p. 370).

Questions for Discussion

1. In many communities across the United States, firefighters, EMTs, and other first responders work part time or as community volunteers. Is this part-time or volunteer status likely to affect the likelihood that they will develop task-related adjustment problems?

2. Compare and contrast the work of a firefighter and a law enforcement officer. To what extent are the topics discussed in this chapter relevant to both professions?

Thereafter, affected personnel may be seen individually or in groups. Interestingly, some research indicates that debriefing of this sort may be harmful, does not prevent PTSD, and should not be mandatory (Choe, 2005; McNally, Bryant, & Ehlers, 2003). Commenting on this research, Scrivner et al. (2014) say it is clear that further study is needed to resolve some of these issues.

Police Suicide

Data on the prevalence or frequency of police suicide are extremely difficult to obtain. Law enforcement agencies are often reluctant to allow researchers access to police officer suicide data (O'Hara, Violanti, Levenson, & Clark, 2013). The common assumption is that the rate of suicide among police officers is one of the highest of any occupational group in the United States (Violanti, 1996). It is estimated that twice as many officers die by their own hand as are killed in the line of duty (Violanti et al., 2009). Moreover, most victims are young patrol officers with no record of misconduct, and most shoot themselves while off duty (L. Miller, 1995). A study of police suicide conducted by Aamodt and Stalnaker (2001), however, indicated that the suicide rate among police officers is significantly well below the rate of suicide in the sector of the population comparable to police officers in age, gender, ethnic/minority, and racial group. Similar results were found in later studies (Aamodt, Stalnaker, & Smith, 2015; O'Hara & Violanti, 2009; O'Hara et al., 2013).

The study by O'Hara, Violanti, Levenson, and Clark (2013) documented that only 126 police suicides occurred in 2012, a decrease from earlier studies by the researchers in 2008 and 2009. In 2012, suicides clustered around the police group of 40 to 44 years of age with 15 to 19 years of experience. O'Hara et al. also discovered that police departments apparently did not notice warning signs of the impending suicide. Ninety-six percent of the officers seemed to slip completely "under the radar" by hiding their symptoms of distress before taking their lives. The authors write, "Law enforcement does have its own code of conduct and subculture and many officers still feel a need to disguise signs of psychological distress for fear of being perceived as 'soft' or weak" (p. 35).

Even though suicide rates among police officers are not higher than found in a comparable population, suicide is still a serious and devastating problem. Each public safety officer who commits suicide leaves behind family, partners, supervisors, friends, and a depressing void within the department (D. W. Clark, White, & Violanti, 2012). Police suicide may result from a number of factors, including psychological reactions to critical incidents, relationship difficulties, internal investigations, financial difficulties, frustration and discouragement, and easy access to weapons (Clark & White, 2017; Herndon, 2001). The strongest reason for police suicide, however, appears to be difficulties in marital or intimate partner relationships, followed by legal problems and internal investigations (Aamodt & Stalnaker, 2001).

If suicide rates for law enforcement personnel are lower than previously believed, this might be explained by several factors. These include the sophisticated screening procedures and rigorous evaluations at the time of hiring, increased use of stress awareness training, better police training, increased counseling opportunities, and the many services provided by police psychologists and other psychologists working closely with police agencies. A recent study by Conn and Butterfield (2013) reported that a large segment (80%) of the new generation of police officers expressed a desire for access to mental health resources, including counseling and psychotherapy. This finding suggests that the police cultural resistance toward mental health issues may be changing.

OPERATIONAL RESPONSIBILITIES

The biggest shift in the role of police psychology in recent years has been in the area of operational support (Dietz, 2000). As police departments have become more specialized, psychological input has become important in many areas. A few, listed by Scrivner et al. (2014), include liability mitigation (minimizing the likelihood of being sued), program evaluation, conflict management within the agency, training to reduce the effects of racial bias, and training to improve police performance in specific skills. Operational support also may include assisting in hostage-taking incidents, crisis negotiations, criminal investigations, and threat assessments. Investigation will be covered in Chapter 3 and threat assessment in Chapter 8. We will discuss hostage taking and crisis negotiation in some detail in this chapter.

Hostage-Taking Incidents

Police and public safety psychologists often serve as consultants, either training for hostage-taking incidents or assisting during the incident itself. A *hostage situation* is characterized by a person (or persons) holding victims against their will who are used to obtain material gain, deliver a sociopolitical message, or achieve personal advantage. Typically, the hostage taker threatens to take the lives of victims if certain demands are not met within a specified time period. A *barricade situation* is one in which an individual has fortified or barricaded himself or herself in a residence or public building or structure and threatens violence either to the self or to others. Barricade situations may or may not include the taking of hostages. Included in the broad hostage-taking category are abductions and kidnappings, vehicle abductions (including aircraft or other forms of public transportation), school captive takings, and some acts of terrorism. Nearly 80% of all hostage situations are "relationship driven" in that perceived relationship difficulties and resentment seem to be the precipitating factor (Van Hasselt et al., 2005).

Police experts have classified hostage takers into four very broad categories: (1) political activists or terrorists, (2) individuals who have committed a crime, (3) prisoners, and (4) individuals with mental disorders (Fuselier, 1988; Fuselier & Noesner, 1990). Political terrorists, who take hostages primarily to gain publicity for their cause, are considered the most difficult to deal with. Their demands often go beyond the authority of the local police departments and usually require the involvement of federal officials. According to Fuselier, political terrorists take hostages for four basic reasons:

> (a) to show the public that the government cannot protect its own citizens; (b) to virtually guarantee immediate coverage and publicity for their cause; (c) to support their hope that after repeated incidents the government will overreact and place excessive restrictions on its citizens; and (d) to demand the release of members of their group who have been incarcerated. (p. 176)

The hostage taker who committed a crime is usually trapped while committing the crime, such as robbery or domestic violence, and is trying to negotiate some form of escape. Prisoners, on the other hand, usually take hostages (typically correctional personnel) to protest conditions within the correctional facility. Persons with mental disorders take hostages for a variety of reasons but primarily to establish their sense of control over their life situations. Research suggests that more than 50% of all hostage-taking incidents are perpetrated by individuals with mental disorders (Borum & Strentz, 1993; Grubb, 2010). Consequently, the need for well-trained psychologists as part of the crisis negotiation team is becoming increasingly apparent to many police agencies.

Hostage negotiation is essentially a tactical team endeavor, which may or may not involve the assistance of a psychologist (Palarea, Gelles, & Rowe, 2012). The hostage taker (or takers) holds and threatens others under his or her control, and the negotiation team may defuse the situation without other assistance. Or, hostage taking may require a tactical response, such as a SWAT team or other specialized unit, when—despite negotiation efforts—a peaceful resolution appears unlikely (Vecchi, Van Hasselt, & Romano, 2005).

Research by W. M. Butler, Leitenberg, and Fuselier (1993) discovered that police agencies that used a psychologist on the scene or in some other capacity (e.g., phone conversation) to assess suspects reported significantly fewer incidents in which the hostage taker killed or seriously injured a hostage. More specifically, police agencies that used a psychologist reported more hostage incidents ending by negotiated surrender and fewer incidents resulting in the serious injury or death of a hostage. The data confirmed the observation that psychologists can make valuable contributions in resolving hostage incidents with a lessened chance of injury or death. Research data reveal that in about 83% of the cases, hostages are released without serious injury (Daniels, Royster, Vecchi, & Pshenishny, 2010; McMains & Mullins, 2013).

Crisis Negotiation

Crisis negotiation is very similar to hostage negotiation, except crisis negotiation is a more general term, involving a broad range of situations and strategies. All hostage taking is a crisis, but not all crises are hostage-taking incidents. For example, a jumper situation is a special crisis involving thoughts of suicide by a depressed or highly emotionally upset person, requiring empathy, understanding, and considerable psychological skill. Police psychologists are more directly involved in crisis than in hostage situations.

Law enforcement and public safety personnel are often present in crisis situations that do not involve hostage taking. "Crisis negotiation is closely linked to the behavioral sciences and, more specifically, to psychology" (Palarea et al., 2012, p. 281). These authors note that the knowledge, skills, and training possessed by psychologists are well suited for operational application to crisis negotiations. The negotiation task, for example, may involve talking a suicidal person down from jumping off a bridge or ledge of a high office building, where a tactical response is uncalled for. You do not usually send a SWAT team in to prevent someone from committing suicide, although there are exceptions. However, law enforcement officers can be trained by psychologists to effectively negotiate in a crisis situation, and the crisis negotiation team may comprise both law enforcement officers and psychologists. As noted by Andrew T. Young (2016), "A primary negotiator endeavors to understand and have empathy for the individuals involved, allow for emotional expression, establish a relationship of trust, develop rapport, and then tries to problem solve and find solutions for the situation at hand" (p. 310). The perpetrators may be highly emotional, under the influence of drugs or alcohol, suicidal, violent, stressed, or struggling with psychological disorders (A. T. Young, 2016).

M. G. Gelles and Palarea (2011) and Palarea, Gelles, and Rowe (2012) point out that police psychologists have several important roles during each of three phases of crisis negotiations. They are (1) pre-incident duties, (2) intra-incident duties, and (3) post-incident duties. During the pre-incident phase, psychologists may provide psychological screening and selection of negotiators; deliver training to negotiators on the psychological aspects that are pertinent to crisis negotiations, such as active listening and persuasion techniques; and suggest strategies for a quick threat and violence risk assessment. (This should be distinguished from threat and violence risk assessments performed by psychologists in other contexts, which are complex and will be discussed in later chapters.)

During the intra-incident phases, the psychologist on the premises may monitor the negotiations, offer advice on the emotional state and behavior of the individual in crisis, and assist negotiators in influencing the person's behaviors and intentions. During the post-incident phase, the psychologist may provide stress management strategies, debriefing, and counseling services to the crisis management team. This may be especially needed if the crisis was not resolved successfully but is still relevant even if the worst possible situation was successfully averted.

Palarea et al. (2012) recommend that the psychologist involved in the intra-incident phase of the operation not be the psychologist to offer post-incident debriefing or counseling to the crisis team. He or she is a member of the crisis team and may be unable to maintain the necessary objectivity during the post-incident phase.

Individuals aspiring to be on the crisis/negotiation teams as psychologists, however, should realize that multiyear training—as expected of all crisis/negotiation team members—is necessary to become an effective member of the team. This includes not only crisis negotiation training but also the appropriate level of operational experience and training (M. G. Gelles & Palarea, 2011). Part of that training may require some "street experience" such as ride-alongs with experienced officers and observations of seasoned officers in hostage/crisis situations. "The chaos of the field or street situation, the military-like police command structure, and presence of real personal risk can come as quite a shock, no matter how professionally well trained one is" (Hatcher et al., 1998, p. 463). The negotiator should have interview and listening skills; the ability to deal with stressful situations; and an easygoing, nonconfrontational personality style (Terestre, 2005). He or she should be ready to be called, 24 hours a day.

In addition, psychologists aspiring to be involved in crisis negotiation should remain mindful of how individuals within various cultures and ethnicities differ (M. G. Gelles & Palarea, 2011). In recent years, there has been a discernible shift in the cultural diversity of hostage takers and other crisis situations (Giebels & Noelanders, 2004). This trend demands that psychologists increase their efforts to study and identify cultural differences in approaches to social interaction and understand how violent individuals from various cultures are likely to react to efforts to dissuade them from causing harm to their victims or themselves (Giebels & Taylor, 2009). According to Giebels and Taylor, "a more sophisticated understanding of cross-cultural communication will help police formulate culturally sensitive negotiation strategies and enhance their appreciation of why perpetrators react the way they do" (p. 5). In addition, forensic psychologists and other mental health personnel can play a critical role in the training of negotiators and police officers by providing workshops and training sessions in cultural differences in persuasive arguments during crisis negotiations.

In years past, an estimated 30% to 58% of law enforcement agencies with a crisis/hostage negotiation team used a mental health professional in some capacity, of which 88% were psychologists as opposed to psychiatrists, social workers, and other professionals (W. M. Butler et al., 1993; Hatcher et al., 1998). More recently, the use of psychologists on crisis/hostage negotiation teams appears to be on the increase (Call, 2008; Van Hasselt et al., 2005; Scrivner et al., 2014).

CONSULTING AND RESEARCH ACTIVITIES

In describing the roles of the consulting police psychologist, Aumiller and Corey (2007) mention the development of performance appraisal systems, which "involves the design and development of organizational policies, processes and instruments for measurement and feedback of individual job performance" (p. 75). These activities are intended to increase performance improvement and help in the career development of the individual officer. In some cases, they may be used in promotional considerations. Consulting psychologists may also be expected to participate in the resolution of interpersonal conflict among individuals within the organization or between the department and the community.

Consulting psychologists often do some training and education to assist agency personnel in optimizing their leader, management, and supervisory effectiveness (Aumiller & Corey, 2007). In recent years, many departments in the United States, the United Kingdom, and Canada have asked psychologists for assistance in training officers in such areas as interviewing witnesses and suspects (Brewster et al., 2016; Eastwood, Snook, & Luther, in preparation). (See Perspective 2.1 in this chapter, and 3.2 in the following chapter, in which Dr. Kirk Luther and Dr. Joseph Eastwood refer to their work with law enforcement agencies.) In general, consulting and in-house psychologists are frequently shifting their roles to meet the crisis or problems that must be dealt with on an ongoing basis. In this section, we discuss a few of the concerns police administrators might have, including creating opportunities for women and ethnic minorities on the force and confronting problems involving excessive force and corruption.

Gender and Ethnic Minority Issues

Before the 1970s, many police departments did not hire non-Caucasians (Cole & Smith, 2001), and female officers, few in number, were often restricted to specified duties, such as processing

---

FROM MY PERSPECTIVE 2.1

The Indirect Path to Academe

Kirk Luther, PhD

Courtesy of Kirk Luther.

When I was finishing high school, I wasn't completely sure what I wanted to pursue for a career. Since one of my hobbies involved tinkering with computers, I decided to attend a technical college and study information technology (IT). However, after finishing the program, I felt as though a career in IT wasn't the perfect fit for me. I liked the program and still enjoyed working with computers, but this career choice wasn't something that interested me as much as I thought it would. In order to reevaluate my personal and career goals, I took some time off to think about the direction I wanted to take my life.

It was important to me that my break be meaningful, so I decided to volunteer with an organisation called Canada World Youth—an international volunteer program that provides young people with the opportunity to travel overseas and gain leadership experience. The program pairs a Canadian youth with one from the partner country, and each pair spends 3 months in Canada and 3 months overseas. In my year, the partner country was Kenya. My group lived with host families and spent time volunteering with various local organisations doing work on social justice issues and environmental stewardship. Joining this volunteering program was one of the best decisions I ever made as I could take time to figure out the career I wanted for myself, gain leadership experience, and learn more about the world in general (which was helpful to me since I grew up in a small town in Canada and this was my first experience abroad). In addition to the new skills and perspective I gained, one of the most life-changing parts of this experience was

that I met my wife! As I said, one of the best decisions I ever made.

After completing the volunteer program, I was still struggling with the type of career that I wanted to pursue. I now knew that I wanted to do something where I could help people and make a difference. I had always been interested in the study of human behaviour, and I thought the best way to pair that interest with a career in helping people would be to study clinical psychology. That led me to enroll at Memorial University of Newfoundland (MUN) and to complete a BSc (Hons.) in psychology. I have to admit to some apprehension about attending university as I was a bit older than the majority of my classmates. However, I decided to push forward and stick with it.

During my undergraduate degree, I wanted to obtain research experience. Fortunately, I came across Dr. Brent Snook's lab. He studies human behaviour within the criminal justice system and is an expert in the field of investigative interviewing. Volunteering in the lab and working with Dr. Snook opened up another career option for me—experimental psychology. Prior to this, I had never really considered being an experimental psychologist. In fact, at the time I knew very little about what an experimental psychologist's job entailed. I quickly learned that this career is quite unique; every day presents itself with a different challenge or question to answer. While there is no set day-to-day routine, typical tasks involve designing research projects to answer theoretical and/or applied questions, delivering lectures, supervising and mentoring students, publishing your research in journals and books, and presenting your research to practitioners and academics at conferences around the world. All of this appealed to me.

Fortunately, Dr. Snook agreed to supervise me for my MSc and PhD degrees (I think mainly because I kept him caffeinated).

During my PhD, my research revolved around two main themes. The first theme was safeguarding legal rights for both adults and youth. Whenever someone is arrested, they are permitted certain legal rights (e.g., right to silence). It turns out that people don't understand much of their legal rights (less than 50% in many cases). My colleagues and I have been working on ways to improve people's comprehension of their legal rights through various theories from psychological science and digital technologies (which allows me to incorporate my IT education).

My second research interest is investigative interviewing. Being able to conduct effective interviews with witnesses, victims, and suspects is a key role for police officers and security professionals. As researchers, our goal is to provide these practitioners with tools that are ethical and based on the best empirical evidence to help them do their jobs. I've had the pleasure of working directly with police officers and other practitioners, and it is extremely rewarding to see findings from our research be incorporated into practice.

As my PhD studies came to a close, I began looking for a job and saw an amazing opportunity at Lancaster University in the United Kingdom. It was a permanent lectureship position, equivalent to assistant professor in North America, and it provided me the opportunity to work alongside Professor Paul Taylor (an expert in cooperation and negotiation). I plan to continue my themes of research on legal rights comprehension and investigative interviewing here in the United Kingdom.

While I am still early in my career, my advice for you is to take advantage of every opportunity possible. I can't stress this enough. Whether it's taking part in research communication contests (e.g., Three-Minute Thesis), applying for funding, delivering a guest lecture, or presenting your research at a conference—all of these activities will provide you with invaluable learning experiences that will not only help you to practice important skills, but also develop a strong and competitive curriculum vitae (CV). Also, make sure that you find a supervisor who you work well with—I wouldn't be where I am today without Dr. Snook's mentorship. Most importantly, don't worry if your career path isn't quite set out yet—the indirect path can be much more fun.

As noted, Dr. Luther is a lecturer at Lancaster University. He enjoys traveling with his wife, Elisabeth, and their son, Noah. He also enjoys the sunny days in the United Kingdom by going on hikes or playing golf (albeit [he says] poorly).

female arrestees or interviewing child witnesses. However, the makeup of departments and assigning women to limited duties changed beginning in that decade.

A survey of the nation's 50 largest cities discovered that, between 1983 and 1992, approximately 29% of the departments reported an increase of 50% or more in the number of African American officers, and 20% reported a similar increase in the number of Latino officers (Cole & Smith, 2001). These percentage increases are not significant if the original numbers were low to begin with, however. Nevertheless, improvements in racial and ethnic diversity nationwide have been noted over the past 20 years. In 2013, 27% of police officers were members of racial or ethnic minority groups, compared to 15% in 1987 (Bureau of Justice Statistics, 2015). The largest increase in recent years has been Hispanics or Latinos. In the federal system, across many law enforcement agencies, racial and ethnic minorities made up one third of officers with arrest and firearm authority in 2008 (Reaves, 2012a). In the same year, about 1 in 4 police officers in local and state police agencies in the United States were members of a racial or ethnic minority (Reaves, 2012b). More significantly, though, the racial and ethnic makeup of police departments rarely reflect the makeup of the community they serve.

On the whole, ethnic and racial minorities are better represented in law enforcement than are women. At the turn of the 21st century, women still remained a small minority in law enforcement nationwide, comprising only 11.5% of active duty police officers in the United States (Federal Bureau of Investigation, 2016a), a figure that is about 3 percentage points higher than in 1990. In large departments, women account for 12.7% of the sworn officers. In small and rural departments (fewer than 100 police officers), women comprise an even smaller number—8.1% of the officers. Although women gained about 0.5% per year from 1972 to 1999, there has been little movement since. Ten years into the 21st century, women still comprised less than 15% of all sworn police officers in the United States in federal, state, and local law enforcement agencies (Bergman, Walker, & Jean, 2016; Langton, 2010). In major metropolitan areas and in cities where a few women are chiefs, the percentages may be higher. In the federal system, one sixth of officers with arrest and firearm authority in 2008 were women (Reaves, 2012a).

The major impediment to women gaining a greater proportion of representation in law enforcement agencies across the country is the common perception that policing is a male-oriented profession, requiring physical strength and a display of physical prowess for many of the tasks. This perception seems to hold even though women are as capable at police work as men. Moreover, female police officers are far less likely than male officers to use excessive force, while maintaining effective policing strategies (Bergman et al., 2016). However, women who might be attracted to law enforcement work may be reluctant to apply when a department has the reputation of being hostile toward women or has a high female officer turnover rate.

Researchers also have found that women are making some progress in acquiring promotions and administrative positions, although they have traditionally encountered resistance from police managers, supervisors, and administrators (S. E. Martin, 1989, 1992). At the turn of the century, less than 4% of supervisory positions were held by female officers, though the percentages were higher in larger departments (National Center for Women & Policing, 2012). The National Center for Women & Policing's website indicated that there were 232 female chiefs of police across the United States in 2010. During about the same period, Langton (2010) reported there were 219 chiefs in a total of approximately 14,000 police agencies. On a more positive note, in 2013, women headed seven major law enforcement agencies in Washington: the D.C. Metropolitan Police, the U.S. Park Police, the U.S. Marshal's Service, the Secret Service, the FBI Washington field office, Amtrak police department, and the Drug Enforcement Administration (DEA).In 2017, Carla Provost was named the first female head of the U.S. Border Patrol in its 93-year history. At the same time, however, women held only 5% of all agent positions. In a recent address, Director Provost indicated the agency would try to do a better job at female recruitment.

Worden (1993) found very few differences between male and female officers in their *attitudes* toward policing. She wrote,

> Overall, female as well as male police officers were predictably ambivalent about restrictions on their autonomy and the definition of their role, only mildly positive about their public clientele, complimentary of their colleagues, and unenthusiastic about working conditions and supervisors. (p. 229)

She suggested that much of this gender similarity in policing may be due to occupational socialization, a process that seems to wash out many of the major differences in gender roles. *Occupational socialization* refers to the learning of attitudes, values, and beliefs of a particular occupational group (Van Maanen, 1975). Recall that earlier in the chapter we discussed the concept of an occupational culture as it relates to police. In general, women have the ability to become socialized into the police culture as successfully as men. An increase in their numbers, however, can also have a positive effect on that culture.

Anne Morris (1996) reports that among New York Police Department (NYPD) officers, women as well as ethnic minorities received substantial social and psychological support from their police colleagues, and the women officers described mostly positive professional and social interactions while on the job. The one major gender difference identified by Morris was that female officers, compared to their male colleagues, were less likely to socialize off the job with other police officers. Their closest personal friends also tended to be outside the police community. This observation is not surprising if we consider that women police officers are likely to have families, including dependent children, to whom they prefer to give their off-duty attention. However, women officers also may feel more isolated in the male-dominated police work environment; consequently, family life becomes a stronger source of social support (Violanti et al., 2009).

Accumulating research, both in the United States and internationally, indicates that the style of law enforcement used by women as a group may be more effective than the policing styles employed by men as a group (Bergman et al., 2016; Bureau of Justice Assistance, 2001). For example, many law enforcement administrators, peer officers, and members of the public are convinced that female officers are more skillful at defusing potentially dangerous, difficult, or violent situations (Balkin, 1988; Seklecki & Paynich, 2007; Weisheit & Mahan, 1988). They are also less likely to become involved in incidents of excessive force (Bureau of Justice Assistance, 2001). Worden (1993) found that female police officers seem to be guided more by altruistic and social motives than men, who tended to be more motivated toward the financial rewards of the occupation.

Female officers *as a group* generally possess better communication and social skills than their male colleagues and are better able to facilitate the cooperation and trust required to implement a community policing model (Bergman et al., 2016; Bureau of Justice Assistance, 2001). It is important to stress group rather than individual differences, because many male officers also possess communication and social skills and can adapt well to a community policing model. Women also may respond more effectively than men in situations involving violence against women (such as domestic abuse or sexual assault), although more research is needed in the area. Some research (e.g., Rabe-Hemp & Schuck, 2007) suggests that female officers may be at greater risk of being assaulted in domestic violence situations, especially when the assailant is drug or alcohol impaired. Nevertheless, hiring more women is likely to be an effective way of addressing the problems of excessive force and citizen complaints and also of improving community policing in general. It should also reduce the problem of sex discrimination and sexual harassment by changing the climate of the agency.

Police Bias and Excessive Force

As indicated at various points throughout the chapter, law enforcement agents today are under considerable public scrutiny. Both the entertainment and the news media, along with social media, are not hesitant to portray bad cops, particularly those who use excessive force in carrying out their duties. Examples are not difficult to find. Moreover, and as noted above, with the help of portable video equipment such as smartphones, police–citizen encounters are often recorded and circulated on the Internet. In the summer of 2014, Eric Garner, a black man allegedly selling cigarettes illegally on a street corner was placed in a chokehold by a white police officer and died. Subsequently, a grand jury refused to indict the officer in Garner's death. "I can't breathe," the words uttered by Garner, became a rallying cry during nationwide protests of police brutality following that incident.

Police bias against minority groups has been a major area of concern. At its worst, bias leads to excessive or fatal force. Bias against groups—commonly thought of as holding racial stereotypes—is culturally ingrained, and law enforcement officers are no more or no less likely than others to hold stereotypical views (Kahn & McMahon, 2015, and references within). It is important to recognize that even well-intentioned people have implicit biases, which are outside their sphere of awareness. The biases themselves do not lead to "bad" action; that is, if we recognize that we have biases and take steps to reduce them, we can temper our actions accordingly. Unfortunately, a long line of research indicates that police as a group exhibit racial bias in their treatment of minority groups, particularly black individuals. They are stopped, questioned, and frisked on streets, and they are disproportionately pulled over for traffic violations on the nation's highways. Police appear to use greater force with black than white suspects (Hyland, Langton, & Davis, 2015) and black suspects are more likely to die at the hands of police than white suspects

(Correll et al., 2007). Some research also indicates that black youth are more likely than youth of other races to be perceived as older and less innocent than white youth (Goff, Jackson, DiLeone, Culotta, & DiTomasso, 2014). In Cleveland in 2014, 12-year-old Tamir Rice was playing in a park with a pellet gun when he was shot to death by a police officer. A grand jury refused to indict the officer (who was subsequently fired in 2017, not because of the shooting, but for lying on his police application). Would Tamir Rice have been shot had he not been a black youth? Adequate training can encourage officers to recognize their implicit biases and keep them in check when carrying out their duties. (See Focus 2.4 for a review of research on police bias.)

When the level of force exceeds what is considered justifiable under the circumstances, it is called **excessive force**. Excessive force is unacceptable and illegal behavior demonstrated by an individual officer or group of officers, or it might be a pattern and practice of an entire law enforcement agency. In many instances, excessive force probably reflects some combination of both.

Prior to the 1970s, the police had wide discretion in the use of force, including deadly force (Blumberg, 1997). Police agencies often had poorly defined or nonexistent policies regarding the use of force generally. Blumberg writes that, prior to 1970,

> Investigations into police shootings were sometimes conducted in a half-hearted manner, and police agencies often did not keep records of all firearm discharges by officers. In addition, social science research on this topic was practically nonexistent and no meaningful attempt to measure the incidence of police killings on a national basis had been undertaken. (p. 507)

There is ample anecdotal evidence of force, including lethal force, used by law enforcement officers today. Empirical evidence is harder to come by. How common is the use of force by police officers today? And under what circumstances or in what contexts does it occur? A report released by the Department of Justice in 2006 revealed that there were 26,556 citizen complaints about police use of force involving large state and local law enforcement agencies (Hickman, 2006). About 8% of these complaints were supported by investigations and were sufficient enough to justify disciplinary action against the officer or officers. The remainder of the complaints were not supported or were unfounded. The National Institute of Justice (NIJ) (K. Adams et al., 1999) released an earlier report summarizing what is known about police use of force. The report found the following:

- Police use force infrequently.

- Police use of force typically occurs at the lower end of the force spectrum, involving grabbing, pushing, or shoving.

- Use of force typically occurs when police are trying to make an arrest and the suspect is resisting.

A recent source of information about police use of force is the Bureau of Justice Statistics (Hyland et al., 2015). This is a survey of police and public contacts based on interviews with residents rather than on police records. According to this report, an annual average of 44 million persons, age 16 or older, had one or more face-to-face contacts with police over a 10-year period (2002–2012). Of those persons who had contact, 1.6% experienced the threat or the use of nonfatal force by the officer during their most recent contact. "About 75% of those with force (1.2% of persons with police contact) perceived the force as excessive" (Hyland et al., 2015, p. 1). A greater percentage of blacks experienced force than those from other racial groups (see Table 2.2).

FOCUS 2.4. RACIAL BIAS AND DECISIONS TO SHOOT

It is well-documented that police officers rarely discharge their weapons in the line of duty. "[T]he discharging of one's weapon in the line of duty is a rare and profound event that almost always leaves a psychological trace on the officer involved" (L. Miller, 2015, p. 107, citing multiple references). Firing a gun does not always result in a death, but when it does an investigation of this "officer-involved shooting" invariably follows. The majority of these incidents of deadly force are found to be justified, but in some, officers are charged with crime. Both indictments and convictions are rare.

Extensive publicity in recent years has focused on lethal shootings of minorities, particularly black men and youth. Victims like Michael Brown, Walter Scott, and Tamir Rice have become symbols of what is perceived as racial bias displayed by members of the law enforcement community. It is widely recognized that racial bias exists throughout society, sometimes explicitly but more often implicitly. Forensic psychologists are not immune to implicit bias, a point made in Chapter 1. When bias produces discriminatory behavior, this becomes a problem. Is bias at the root of decisions to use force, including shooting members of a minority group? Not surprisingly, a number of psychologists and criminologists have conducted research examining the decision to shoot.

Following are highlights of some of this research. You will note that some findings seem to be contradictory.

- Officers of any race or ethnicity are equally likely to be involved in a deadly force incident (McElvain & Kposowa, 2008).
- Personal philosophies of chiefs and other supervisory personnel, not the level of crime in the community, are determinants of police shootings (Fyfe, 1988; H. Lee & Vaughn, 2010)
- Training and experience are effective in minimizing the effect of implicit bias (Correll et al., 2007; Sim, Correll, & Sadler, 2013).
- In simulated experiments, police demonstrate less bias in shooting than community samples, including college students (Correll et al., 2007).
- Racial bias tends to be demonstrated more in response time (i.e., how long it takes to make a

decision) than in the ultimate decision to shoot (Cox, Devine, Plant, & Schwartz, 2014).
- Officers use more deadly force against blacks than whites (Goff & Kahn, 2012).
- Contextual factors, such as neighborhood race, rather than suspect race, explain police decisions (Terrill & Reisig, 2003).
- Black and Latino suspects were subjected to force earlier during police interaction, while white suspects were subjected later during the interaction (Kahn, Steele, McMahon, & Stewart, 2017).

In general, the literature on police bias and shooting shows mixed results, with some indicating little overall bias when other factors are controlled, while other research suggesting strong racial stereotyping. What are we to make of these different and sometimes divergent findings? Although research on the extent of disparate treatment must continue, it is clear that effective training of police to recognize their implicit biases and to exercise cognitive control in making decisions is essential (Kahn & McMahon, 2015).

Questions for Discussion

1. Although we focus here on lethal shootings, research indicates that force in general is used disproportionately more against blacks than suspects of other races. Discuss reasons why this might occur.
2. The above are just a few conclusions from research relating to bias in policing. Find and discuss results of a recent study on this topic. Is it consistent with the research highlighted above?
3. Laurence Miller (2015, p. 104), notes that most actual shooting scenarios involve "petty criminals, mentally disordered subjects, domestic violence escalations, or the posturings of young-and-dumb juveniles." Does this square with how the entertainment media portray police use of lethal force? Assuming Miller is correct, how might this affect the officer who shot?
4. How do you respond to the phrase "the posturings of young-and-dumb juveniles"?

Table 2.2	Residents With Police Contact Who Experienced Threat or Use of Force, by Race or Hispanic Origin, 2002–2011		
	Face-to-Face Contact	Force Threatened or Used	Excessive Force
All races	43.9 million	715,500 (1.6%)	35,300 (1.2%)
White	32.9 million	445,500 (1.4%)	329,500 (1.0%)
Black	4.6 million	159,100 (3.5%)	128,400 (2.8%)
Hispanic	4.4 million	90,100 (2.1%)	59,600 (1.4%)

Source: Hyland et al., 2015.

The BJS report divided the police contacts into two categories: traffic stops and street stops. Blacks were more likely than whites or Hispanics to experience force during street or non-traffic stops (14% compared with 6.9% for both whites and Hispanics) as well as during traffic stops. The use of force was more frequent during all stops in which the police suspected the person of wrong doing compared to other types of contact, such as during investigation of a crime where police were seeking information. Males and younger persons (ages 16 to 25) were more likely to experience police contact and use of force than females and persons ages 26 or older.

Police psychologist Ellen Scrivner (1994), in a report sponsored by the National Institute of Justice (NIJ), investigated some of the psychological attributes characteristic of officers who engage in excessive force. Police psychologists assigned to conduct fitness-for-duty evaluations should be knowledgeable about the behaviors outlined in the report. Scrivner identified five different officer profiles that are prone to excessive force complaints or charges:

1. Officers with personality patterns that reflect a lack of empathy for others and antisocial, narcissistic, and abusive tendencies

2. Officers with previous job-related experiences such as involvement in justifiable police shootings

3. Officers who experienced early career-stage problems having to do with their impressionability, impulsiveness, low tolerance for frustration, and general need for strong supervision

4. Officers who had a dominant, heavy-handed patrol style that is particularly sensitive to challenge and provocation

5. Officers who had personal problems such as separation, divorce, or perceived loss of status that caused extreme anxiety and destabilized job functioning

The Scrivner (1994) study focused primarily on the psychological profiles of individual police officers. It was not intended to give attention to the properties of entire police organizations that may implicitly (or explicitly) promote or condone excessive force within their ranks. For example, an agency may have an aggressive policing policy that encourages confrontational tactics that increase the probability of violence on the part of officers as well as members of the public. As K. Adams et al. (1999) state, "A major gap in our knowledge about excessive force by police concerns characteristics of police agencies that facilitate or impede this conduct" (p. 11). Adams and his colleagues further assert that many formal aspects of the organization—such as hiring criteria, recruit training, in-service programs, supervision of field officers, disciplinary mechanisms, operations of internal affairs, specialized units dealing with ethics and integrity, labor unions, and civilian oversight mechanisms—plausibly are related to the levels of officer misconduct. (p. 11)

As suggested above, knowledgeable police psychologists should realize that, in some cases, the law enforcement agency itself might be a major factor in implicitly encouraging the use of excessive force by its officers. Possibly, agencies may be placed on a continuum signifying the degree of aggressive policing they advocate in the community, especially in areas that have high crime rates. At one pole, the agency advocates that minimum force be applied when dealing with suspects, but at the other pole, the agency encourages force—and, if necessary, something approaching excessive force—in dealing with the suspects.

In summary, research data consistently show that only a small minority of police officers engage in excessive force in dealing with the public. Fortunately, an "early warning system," used by an increasing number of departments, can help supervisors identify problem officers early and intervene through counseling or training to correct problem behaviors (S. Walker, Alpert, & Kenney, 2001), not only those related to the use of force. **Early warning systems** are data-based management tools, usually consisting of three basic phases: (1) selection, (2) intervention, and (3) post-intervention monitoring (Bartol & Bartol, 2004). The criteria by which officers are selected vary from agency to agency but usually include some threshold combination of citizen complaints, civil litigation, firearms discharge or use-of-force reports, high-speed pursuits, and resisting-arrest incidents (S. Walker et al., 2001). Early warning systems of various types are increasingly being introduced into police agencies nationwide (Scrivner et al., 2014). Preliminary research on the effectiveness of early warning systems suggests that they are effective, especially if used in combination with department-wide attempts to raise standards of performance and improve the quality of police services.

Police Corruption

The term *police corruption* covers a wide range of illegal behaviors that represent a violation of the public trust. Accepting bribes, confiscating drugs or drug money, planting evidence, and soliciting sexual activity in exchange for giving a suspect a "break" are all illustrations. Can police psychologists assist departments in selecting out candidates who are likely to be engaged in corrupt activities?

The Defense Personnel Security Research Center (PERSEREC) conducted one of the most extensive studies on the ability of personality measures to predict police corruption and misconduct. The PERSEREC began the Police Integrity Study in 1992, using four commonly used personality inventories in law enforcement: the MMPI-2, IPI, 16-PF, and CPI, each of which was discussed earlier in the chapter. Sixty-nine departments met all the prerequisites for participation and supplied personality test data on 878 officers, 439 of whom demonstrated misconduct and 439 of whom did not. (The departments were asked to identify equal numbers from each group.) The preemployment personality inventories most frequently administered to those officers when they originally applied to their respective departments was the MMPI-2 (92.7%), followed by the CPI (41.0%), 16-PF (11.2%), and IPI (11.0%). (These percentages will total more than 100% because many departments administered more than one personality inventory during the screening and selection stage.)

Overall, the study concluded that the personality data could only modestly identify later misconduct or corruption. The few personality inventories that had any success tended to indicate that those officers who engaged in misconduct or corruption during their careers not surprisingly had more of the following characteristics:

- Difficulty getting along with others

- Delinquent or problem histories in their police careers

- Indications of maladjustment, immaturity, irresponsibility, or unreliability

Basically, the study found that the *single* best predictor of corruption was not a personality measure administered prior to hire, but rather misconduct on the job after employment had begun and usually relatively early in the officer's career.

In other words, none of the preemployment psychological tests currently being used by law enforcement departments appears to offer a general scale or dimension that can reliably and validly differentiate officers at the beginning of their career who are likely to violate the public trust later in their career (Boes, Chandler, & Timm, 2001). Rather, the *strongest* predictor was post-hire misconduct. Officers who got into trouble for misconduct early in their careers were most likely to be punished for later acts of corruption. Furthermore, the study found that the decision of whether or not to engage in acts of corruption is largely shaped by environmental factors, such as opportunity combined with the values particular police subcultures allowed or that were condoned by certain departments.

SUMMARY AND CONCLUSIONS

Individual psychologists have likely consulted with various law enforcement agencies in the United States throughout the 20th century, but police psychology as a subfield of applied psychology was not officially recognized until the late 1960s or early 1970s. Since then, it has expanded rapidly and is more commonly referred to as police and public safety psychology. It was recognized by the APA as a specialty in 2013. The many professional organizations devoted to this work and the increasing number of publications in the professional literature attest to the fact that police and public safety psychology is thriving.

Police psychologists today participate in the screening and selection of law enforcement candidates, conduct promotional exams and fitness-for-duty evaluations, provide counseling services to officers and their families, offer workshops in stress management, and assist in hostage negotiation training, among many tasks. They are also increasingly more involved in consulting with administrators in areas like optimal shift schedules, training for special operations, program evaluation, or conflict management within the agency. In addition, there is a rich store of psychological research on topics relating to law enforcement work, most of which is conducted by academic or legal psychologists. Examples of such research topics include police handling of those with mental disorders, excessive force, adaptations to stress, gender differences in policing, police response to crisis situations, racial bias, police interrogations, and

reliability and validity of various instruments for use in screening. Police and public safety psychologists can bring this research to the attention of the police agency.

The screening and selection of police candidates has been a fundamental task of police and public safety psychologists. The great majority of agencies administer psychological evaluations to police candidates, and 38 states require this by law. Psychologists typically administer and evaluate psychological tests designed to identify desirable characteristics (screening in) or detect problem behaviors (screening out). Before deciding on how to perform this task, the psychologist must have a thorough understanding, not only of police culture, which may be variable, but also of the requirements of the specific job at hand. Some qualities are common to all good officers—for example, compassion, remaining calm in the face of danger. In other situations, such as assessments for work in special units, specific competencies may be required.

We reviewed the most common tests used in the screening and selection of law enforcement but stressed that other measures are available as well. It is important, though, that the approach taken be empirically validated and that the tests conform to federal laws such as the Americans with Disabilities Act and its revision. Candidate screening has traditionally focused more on detecting problems or pathology than on identifying positive features that predict success in law enforcement. In recent years, more tests have been developed with a goal of identifying the positive features. These must be continually subjected to validation, however.

Police work ranks high among stressful occupations. We discussed a number of occupational stressors that officers encounter, including those that are organizational, external, task related, and personal. Police psychologists not only study the effects of stress, but also provide direct service to officers and their families. Critical incidents—such as hostage-taking situations, mass casualties, or police shootings—are good examples of task-related stress. Psychologists are often on the scene to respond to police who have experienced a critical incident. When unaddressed stress reaches high levels, there is danger of major dysfunction in personal relationships or police suicide. Although research does not support a higher incidence of suicide among police than among the general population, when suicide occurs, it has a major impact on the police community.

Racial bias among police has received increasing attention in recent years, particularly in relation to highly publicized shootings of unarmed black suspects. Implicit bias is not unique to law enforcement officers; it is a characteristic shared by many if not most individuals as a result of cultural indoctrination. In public safety officers,

however, bias that is reflected in discriminatory actions is unacceptable. A substantial amount of research has been done on this topic. Research indicates that police as a group do treat minority individuals, particularly blacks, more harshly than other racial groups. This is demonstrated in police stops, arrests, use of force, and even in lethal actions. However, studies also indicate that training can attenuate the effects of implicit bias.

Research suggests that officers who received excessive force complaints were more likely to have displayed personality factors like lack of empathy or narcissism, showed evidence of behavior problems early in their careers, had heavy-handed patrol styles, and experienced marital or other relationship problems. Many departments have now adopted early warning systems to offer peer and professional support to officers who may be showing signs of problem behaviors.

Like excessive force, corruption is unlikely to be predicted before a candidate is hired. Research on police corruption indicates that it is often related to the environment of the department—it is not typically a problem of one officer. Assessment measures given by psychologists can only modestly predict eventual corruption or a pattern of misconduct.

KEY CONCEPTS

QUESTIONS FOR REVIEW

1. What has job analysis revealed about police work?

2. List and describe briefly the six personality measures currently most used in police screening.

3. Give examples of each of the four types of stressors that are common in law enforcement.

4. Provide examples of five minority or gender issues relating to law enforcement.

5. Other than candidate screening, describe any three special evaluations that might be conducted by a police psychologist.

6. List at least five findings of the research on racial bias in policing.

7. Discuss the common psychological reactions police may have to a shooting incident.

8. In the Scrivner study, what five different officer profiles were prone to excessive force complaints?

 SAGE edge™

Want a better grade? Go to **edge.sagepub.com/bartol5e** for the tools you need to sharpen your study skills. Access practice quizzes, eFlashcards, an action plan, and SAGE journal articles for enhanced learning.

CHAPTER THREE

PSYCHOLOGY OF INVESTIGATIONS

In an episode of a popular cable network show, police called in a self-described profiler to aid them in the investigation of a series of rapes that had stymied them for several months. The profiler rapidly reviewed reports of the crime scenes, looked at the evidence that had been left behind, and read reports of interviews with the victims. Within a few hours, the profiler was able to pinpoint where the perpetrator likely lived, how old he likely was, and when he was likely to strike again. Police then found and arrested a suspect, who was subsequently charged with four rapes and convicted.

This may make for good media entertainment, but it is unrealistic. Whether we use the term *profiling*, *behavioral analysis*, *psychological assistance to police*, or any variants of these terms, the process by which forensic psychologists participate in criminal investigation is complex, and it is often controversial.

The investigation of crime offers a multitude of both research and practical activities for the forensic psychologist. Some of these activities relate directly to identifying the perpetrator, such as in the illustration above, or helping police understand the behavioral aspects associated with the crime, such as how victims are targeted. Other activities relate to the methods police use once a suspect or suspects have been apprehended. In the previous chapter, we focused on services psychologists and other mental health professionals offer to the police agency itself, such as training, candidate screening, or stress management. In this chapter, we focus on the various methods law enforcement employs to solve crimes where psychology can make important contributions. A rapidly growing psychological contribution to law enforcement is the scientific area of study called **investigative psychology**. It is an umbrella term that can apply to all of the activities covered in this chapter.

Chapter Objectives

- Explore the many ways psychology contributes to investigations of crime.
- Define and distinguish among five types of profiling.
- Examine the history, methods, limitations, and problems of profiling.
- Review methods of police interviewing and interrogation.
- Discuss types and incidents of false confessions.
- Review the psychology of detecting deception through the polygraph and other methods.
- Assess the usefulness of forensic hypnosis.
- Review research on eyewitness identification.
- Examine the psychology of pretrial identification methods, such as lineups and show-ups.

INVESTIGATIVE PSYCHOLOGY

The term *investigative psychology* was minted by Professor David Canter, the director of the International Centre for Investigative Psychology at the University of Liverpool. Canter and his colleagues believed that there was "a wealth of psychological literature that can be drawn upon to aid in the contribution to the psychology of investigations" (Alison & Canter, 1999, p. 9). Basically, investigative psychology (IP) refers to a new scientific approach designed to improve our understanding of criminal behavior and the investigative process (Taylor, Snook, Bennell, & Porter, 2015).

To date, the majority of IP studies fall into three broad categories: (1) the nature of offender behavior, (2) the social psychology of group crime and terrorism, and (3) the cognitive psychology of investigative decision making by law enforcement investigators (Taylor et al., 2015). In this chapter, we will focus on two of these three—the nature of offender behavior, especially as examined through profiling, and the investigative process used by law enforcement. It should be emphasized at the outset that IP includes much more than profiling serial killers and rapists. Rather, IP "provides a framework for the integration of many aspects of psychology into all areas of police and other investigation, covering all forms of crime that may be examined by the police as well as areas of activity that require investigation that may not always be considered by police investigators, such as insurance fraud, malicious fire setting, tax evasion, or customs and excise violations and even terrorism" (Canter & Youngs, 2009).

From a psychological perspective, three fundamental questions characterize all criminal investigations (Canter & Alison, 2000), assuming that an individual has not been caught in the act of committing a crime. The questions are as follows: (1) What are the important behavioral features associated with the crime that may help identify and successfully prosecute the perpetrator? (2) What inferences can be made about the characteristics of the offender that may help identify him or her? (3) Are there any other crimes that are likely to have been committed by the same person? These questions are central to the psychology of investigations in their early stages, when the perpetrator of a crime is unknown. Answering these questions may or may not involve the task of profiling, which is so fascinating to the public, the media, and many students of forensic psychology. Profiling in its various forms also has gained popularity in law enforcement circles since first used by the Federal Bureau of Investigation in 1971 (Pinizzotto & Finkel, 1990). Canter himself disavows the term *offender profiling*, however, both because it suggests that psychologists possess abilities beyond what is realistic and because it is not broad enough to encompass the realm of investigative psychology. (See Perspective 3.1 in which Professor Canter writes about his life's work.)

Today, virtually every form of entertainment media offers its version of a profiling show, and profilers make regular appearances in the news, particularly when serious crimes occur. Despite the media attention and popular TV and movie depictions of highly successful and probing profilers employing sophisticated techniques to identify the offender, reality is far from that picture. If the number of actual success stories in profiling were compared to the total number of misses or failures, the ratio of hits to misses might be close to chance. Over the past decade, however, some techniques associated with profiling have become more scientifically based, as we will note shortly. In addition, although there are few limitations on who can call themselves profilers, training in *behavioral analysis*—a term often preferred to profiling—has become more extensive and rigorous. Therefore, although many psychologists and other scholars are skeptical of the profiling endeavor, it should not be rejected outright as having no value.

We begin the chapter by focusing on profiling and summarize some of the research on its validity. Is profiling useful? Successful? How exactly is it done? Are some profiling techniques more acceptable than others, and how does one distinguish a "good profiler" from one who might be seeking media attention? Later in the chapter, we discuss other topics that are equally relevant (and in many ways more relevant) to the psychology of investigations—such as the interviewing and interrogation of witnesses and suspects, the detection of deception, and evaluating the accuracy of eyewitness testimony. Psychological research in these areas applies psychological concepts to principles of criminal investigation. As we will see, properly applied, findings from research in these areas can help police solve crimes as well as discourage them from focusing their attention on innocent people.

The Emergence of Investigative Psychology

David Canter, PhD

Courtesy of David Canter.

Sometimes an event occurs in your professional career which, at the time, does not seem very significant but later turns out to have changed who you are and what you do. That happened to me in 1986. Having had no previous contact with police investigations, almost by accident I was asked if I could help a major police enquiry into a series of rapes and murders around London. As it turned out, the police said my subsequent report was extremely helpful. This opened doors to many other investigations and, crucially, enabled me to gain access to data on which to base systematic research. It was out of this research that I realised a broad based discipline was emerging that I called *Investigative Psychology*.

Looking back on my contribution to the solving of the series of serious crimes and the emergence of the new area of psychology, I think I was fortunate in the timing within my own professional development as well as the evolution of police investigations within the United Kingdom. Although I had specialised in science at high school and had a conventional, laboratory-experiment-oriented training in my undergraduate degree at Liverpool University, my interests in the arts led me to want to pursue psychology outside of the laboratory. Consequently my PhD work was based in a Department of Building Science, studying the impact of open-plan office design on worker performance.

The focus of my doctorate, awarded in 1968, drew me into research and teaching in a school of architecture, at Strathclyde University in Glasgow. This enabled me to help develop what was initially called Architectural Psychology, but later became known more generally as Environmental Psychology. I published widely in that area and set up the first academic *Journal of Environmental Psychology*, becoming aware through these activities of the processes out of which new academic disciplines emerge.

A further fortunate success was my being awarded a yearlong fellowship, derived from my involvement in architectural research, to the Tokyo Building Research Station. The threat of earthquakes made the Japanese very concerned with building evacuations. Therefore, I became aware of the importance of designing buildings not only in preparation for earthquakes, but also for fires and other emergencies. Understanding human behavior in these contexts was crucial. Consequently, starting in the mid-1970s, I carried out a decade of research studying what people did when caught in a building on fire. This had important professional consequences for me, requiring me to interact with policy makers and senior management. I was called to give evidence to government enquiries into disasters and provide consultancy to major industries on how to reduce accidents in potentially very dangerous factories.

As a result of these experiences, when asked by a senior police officer in 1986 if I could "help catch the man before he killed again," I had the professional and academic experience to be able to indicate how I could work with the police to help them. I subsequently described this in my award-winning book, *Criminal Shadows* (Canter, 2000). I tackled the task given me as a consultancy task, not as an academic research project. But I brought to it an approach to examining what actually happens, what people do in their daily lives, which had been honed in the School of Architecture and studying emergencies and accidents in industry.

This was rather different from the usual approach that psychologists took to criminals a quarter of a century ago. Then, most psychologists who had contact with criminals did so through their clinical practice. Consequently, their approach was to treat criminals as patients who dealt with the world in somewhat bizarre ways. My view was that—although the psychological reasons for the crimes may be somewhat imponderable—their behavioral processes were open to study as was any other activity outside the laboratory.

In the initial case of the London rapist and murderer, the police only made available the details of those crimes. But once my contribution was regarded as a success, they gave me access to more information in police records. Analyses of this material showed there were recurring patterns within it. This led me to realize that there were many aspects to the ways in which

(Continued)

psychology could contribute to investigations. It was clear these ways included improving how information is collected by the police. After all, analyses of police documents were useless if those documents were full of errors. Such improvements of police data encompassed the organization of the material they collect as well as issues such as detecting deception, false confessions, and false allegations.

Thus my work challenged the popular view of the psychologist contributing to an investigation as a lone genius with brilliant insights. This notion is derived from crime fiction, owing more to the exploits of Sherlock Holmes than to any real life input. I became aware that there was a systematic discipline growing out of scientific psychology that had much to offer. This was very different from the notion of "offender profiling," which has been given an almost mythical status because of its fictional representations. These were strongly influenced by FBI Special Agents claiming unique skills in determining the characteristics of offenders from the details of the crime scene. They therefore came up with assertions, like the often reported one that it was useful to distinguish between 'organized' and 'disorganized' serial killers, when they did not really know how to test those assertions. So when they were tested, it was no surprise that their distinction was not supported.

The insights of special agents that the way a crime is committed can tell us something about the criminal are valuable, but their lack of understanding that this relationship was central to many areas of psychology led them to make some inappropriate claims. For example, the claim that their insights were only relevant to bizarre crimes or those with some significant "psychological" component does not have any scientific basis. A moment's thought reveals that, to take just one type of general crime, how a person commits a burglary tells us something about that person. Establishing the relationship between a person's actions and their characteristics is really a problem of developing empirically sound inferences.

It was these considerations that led me to become aware that a new discipline should be clearly identified to bring together the interrelated aspects of psychological contributions to investigations. From my background working with architects and decision makers, I knew that such a discipline should connect directly with what actually happens in investigations. Consequently, as well as incorporating investigative information and the development of inference processes, it was essential that consideration was given to how the possibilities derived from psychological analyses could actually support investigative decision making. These three interrelated components of (a) information retrieval and evaluation, (b) inference development around the notion of a "profiling equation," and (c) decision support became the formal definition of the new area of *Investigative Psychology*. Masters and doctoral programs as well as a textbook and journal all helped to establish this as a fruitful new area of psychology.

Looking back on all this, I see that in fact I've always been an investigative psychologist in a broad sense, taking the idea of investigation as a form of problem-solving psychology, not only concerned with the investigation of crimes. Studying how people coped with working in vast open offices, actions in a building on fire, increasing safety in dangerous industries, are all aspects of problem solving in real-world contexts. They all require an investigation into ongoing issues of what people do and the sense that can be made of that. In my grander moments, therefore, I like to think that what has emerged out of all this research is a new way of doing psychology that is relevant to challenges outside of academia.

Dr. Canter is Emeritus Professor at the University of Liverpool, U.K., and directs the International Research Centre for Investigative Psychology at the University of Huddersfield, U.K. He was awarded an Honorary Fellowship of the British Psychological Society and is a Fellow of the American Psychological Association and The Academy of Social Sciences, whose journal Contemporary Social Science *he edits. Besides continuing to publish widely in many areas of the application of psychology he composes music in a contemporary classical idiom, having recently completed an MA in music composition and is currently studying for a PhD in composition.*

PROFILING

Profiling is a technique that attempts to identify the behavioral, cognitive, emotional, and demographic characteristics of a person based on information gathered from a wide range of sources. In a majority of cases, profiling attempts to describe an *unknown* person, but in some cases it is used to chronicle the behavioral patterns, thought features, and emotional characteristics of a *known* person. Many professionals who are engaged in this activity today prefer to call themselves behavioral analysts rather than profilers. Behavioral analysis connotes a more scientific activity, and in some agencies, a behavioral analyst is given more credence than a profiler. In reality, they may or may not have been trained in the same way. We continue to use the more common term, but we emphasize that continuing efforts are needed to render profiling a scientific enterprise.

Broadly speaking, we can divide profiling into five categories: (1) crime scene profiling (often called criminal profiling, offender profiling, or criminal investigative analysis), (2) geographical profiling, (3) suspect-based profiling, (4) psychological profiling, and (5) equivocal death analysis (also called the psychological autopsy). Although there is some overlap among the types—such as with crime scene profiling and geographical profiling—we believe the division helps in understanding the various and complex distinctions among the different methods (Bartol & Bartol, 2013).

Crime Scene Profiling

Crime scene profiling is assumed to have been developed by the FBI in the early 1970s to provide investigative assistance to law enforcement in cases of serial homicide or serial rape (Homant & Kennedy, 1998). At that time, the FBI opened its training academy in Quantico, Virginia, and established its Behavioral Science Unit (BSU), which is now called the Behavioral Analysis Unit (BAU). Even earlier than that, police investigators occasionally consulted behavioral scientists for help in hard-to-solve crimes—such as the case of New York's Mad Bomber in the 1950s and the Boston Strangler in the 1960s (Bartol & Bartol, 2013; Greenburg, 2011). The FBI's approach, however, was the first systematic effort in the United States to make profiling a normal part of law enforcement investigations. Profiling developed rapidly in the United Kingdom during the same time period, chiefly as a result of the work of social psychologist David Canter, who as mentioned above ultimately established a Centre for Investigative Psychology. Also as mentioned, Canter avoided the term *profiling*, and he steered away from the clinically based approach that was emphasized by the FBI at that time. He chose, rather, to focus on a data-based method for investigating criminal activity (see again Perspective 3.1). Today, crime scene profiling has expanded to various countries across the globe (Goodwill, Lehmann, Beauregard, & Andrei, 2016).

Regardless of whether it is clinically or statistically based, **crime scene profiling** requires describing some of the significant behavioral, cognitive, emotional, lifestyle, and demographic features of an unknown person believed to be responsible for a series of crimes. In other words, the crime scene characteristics at best should link up with who the offender is in general; at least, they should help police understand something about the crime. In most cases, the profile sketch is based on characteristics and evidence gathered at the crime scene as well as reports from victims or witnesses, if there are any. Based on this information, the profiler tries to predict characteristics and habits of the offender and where and how his next crime may occur.

Crime scene profiling, at its best, is not about entering "the evil mind of the serial killer" but has more to do with discovering how victims are chosen, how they are treated, and what forensic evidence is left at the crime scene or on the victim that will assist in apprehending the offender. One of the most common misconceptions about crime scene profiling is that profilers make predictions or assumptions about an offender's personality (Rainbow & Gregory, 2011). However, conclusions and descriptions of an unknown offender's personality not only lack reliability and validity, but the statements also often do not help police identify potential suspects. It does not help to tell police that the perpetrator is likely to be masochistic, for example; telling them of possible behaviors *associated* with masochism is more helpful. Another common misconception is that crime scene profiling is an established scientific enterprise. This probably springs from information found in the entertainment media, especially popular TV programs such as the *CSI* series. Although profilers are expected to offer advice that is methodologically sound and based on empirical research and psychological principles, profiling, at this stage of its development, has not achieved established scientific status (Kocsis, 2009; Rainbow & Gregory, 2011; Snook, Cullen, Bennell, Taylor, & Gendreau, 2008).

Crime scene profiling is most often undertaken when investigators have few clues that could help solve the case and they are making little headway in identifying potential suspects. To a very large extent, the profiling process is dictated by the quality of the data collected on previous offenders who have committed similar offenses. For example, if the profiler believes, on the basis of research, that most burglars are male, are under 30, and commit their burglaries within a 20-mile radius of where they live, these are helpful clues in searching for suspects. Based on previous data, the profiler also may suggest that the person is likely to be a young, unmarried, male, blue-collar worker with highly aggressive tendencies who makes frequent appearances on the bar scene, or a female, semiskilled worker who is a substance abuser. Perhaps the perpetrator is even more likely to be a middle-aged loner with a steady income who seldom draws attention to himself. Note the importance of the word *likely* in each of these speculative comments. Crime scene profiling—even in its most sophisticated form—rarely can point *directly* to the person who committed the crime. Instead, the process helps develop a reasonable set of hypotheses for identifying the persons who might have been responsible for a crime or series of crimes. It may be very helpful during the investigative process, but the eventual identification of the primary suspect is accomplished through competent police work.

Furthermore, contrary to popular belief, crime scene profiling is not and should not be restricted to serial murder or serial sexual assaults. It has considerable *potential* value when applied successfully to crimes such as arson, terrorist acts, burglary, shoplifting and robbery, Internet crimes, computer hacking, and white-collar crimes such as bank fraud or embezzlement.

In most instances, a series of crimes thought to be committed by the same person or persons is most likely to draw an attempt at profiling, especially if law enforcement investigators are baffled concerning potential suspects. If done correctly, the profile should at least eliminate very large segments of the population as suspects. If done incorrectly, it can lead investigators far astray. If the profile proves helpful to investigators, it can often suggest that a series of crimes has been committed by the same person, a process called linkage analysis. **Linkage analysis** is a method of identifying crimes that are likely to have been committed by the same offender because of similarities across the crimes (Woodhams, Bull, & Hollin, 2010). Like crime scene profiling in general, however, linkage analysis has its supporters as well as its detractors (Risinger & Loop, 2002).

Nevertheless, despite its enormous public and media interest—including depictions of profilers in the entertainment media—profiling is not a *frequent* investigative activity of the police and public safety psychologists discussed in Chapter 2. In fact, many police psychologists question the use of this technique. In a nationwide survey of police psychologists by Bartol (1996), for example, 70% said they did not feel comfortable profiling and seriously questioned its validity and usefulness. Ten years later, Torres, Boccaccini, and Miller (2006) found that less than 25% of trained psychologists and psychiatrists thought profiling was scientifically reliable and valid.

Interestingly, though, there may be a tendency to embrace crime scene profiling under different names, such as behavioral analysis, investigative psychology, or **criminal investigative analysis**. The Torres et al. (2006) survey discovered that forensic professionals who were asked to evaluate the term *criminal investigative analysis* believed the procedure was significantly more reliable and valid than those professionals asked to rate the term *profiling*. The authors' findings support the position that when we attach a more scientific-sounding name to this practice, profiling is viewed more favorably. A similar view appears to be held by the courts (Cooley,

2012; Risinger & Loop, 2002). According to Torres et al., "Many professionals who engage in profiling work believe that profiling testimony is more likely to be admitted into court when it is called something other than profiling" (p. 53).

Moreover, it appears that a majority of *police investigators* believe that profiling, broadly defined, is useful (Snook et al., 2008). For example, J. L. Jackson, van Koppen, and Herbrink (1993) surveyed police officers in the Netherlands and found that 5 out of 6 thought that criminal profiling had some usefulness. In the United Kingdom, Copson (1995) found that about 83% of police officers believed that criminal profiling was operationally useful, and 92% said they would seek criminal profiling advice again. Many years ago, Pinizzotto (1984) discovered that only 17% of police officers thought profiles were useful. There continues to be extensive debate on the effectiveness of the profiling endeavor, whether or not it is cloaked in scientific terminology. Therefore, an area desperately in need of attention from forensic psychologists is profiling *research*. In other words, it is critical that we learn how reliable or valid the various profiling procedures and methods currently being used are, and how (or if) they can be improved to allow meaningful application to law enforcement and other forensic realms. (See Table 3.1 for a summary of the various types of profiling.)

Geographical Profiling and Crime Mapping

Offending patterns often occur or cluster within certain geographical areas, such as a specific area of a city. There are two major ways these crime patterns may be analyzed: geographical profiling and geographical mapping. **Geographical profiling** refers to the analysis

Table 3.1 Forms of Profiling and Key Weaknesses of Each

Form	Brief Definition	Key Weaknesses
Crime Scene Profiling	Examines features of the crime scene to infer or deduct characteristics or motivations of offender	Often based on unvalidated assumptions—such as organized versus disorganized crime scenes; subject to investigator biases, especially commitment bias; insensitive to manipulation by offenders and changes in their behavior
Geographical Profiling and Mapping	Analyzes locations associated with an unknown usually serial offender; analyzes hot spots of crime	Not helpful if offenders move out of area; does not consider psychological characteristics other than an offender's comfort zone
Suspect-Based Profiling	Systematic collection of data on previous offenders to identify additional offenders	Lends itself to illegal or biased profiling, based on characteristics such as race, religion, ethnicity
Psychological Profiling	Detailed description of psychological characteristics of one known individual, not necessarily criminal; used in threat or risk assessment	Descriptive, may be speculative and dependent upon unreliable source material; in threat and risk assessment, type of measures used may not be valid
Psychological Autopsy	Detailed description of psychological and background characteristics of deceased individual, with intent to determine the manner of death	No accepted guidelines on how to conduct. When raised in court, highly subject to not being admitted, or to being refuted

of geographical locations associated with the spatial movements of a *single* serial offender, whereas **geographical mapping** is concerned with analyzing the spatial patterns of crimes committed by numerous offenders over a period of time. We should emphasize, though, that both procedures may be used in tandem or together. In a sense, geographical mapping focuses on identifying the "hot spots" of certain types of crime. The procedure has been used in Europe since the first half of the 19th century and began to be used in the United States during the early 1900s. It continues today in more sophisticated fashion and is often demonstrated in popular law enforcement TV shows like *NCIS* and its spin-offs. It is not unusual for urban police departments to train some officers as geographical mappers or to hire someone who specializes in that task, either full time or as a consultant. Geographical profiling—as opposed to mapping—focuses on the offender rather than only on spatial crime patterns. It is a method of identifying the area of probable residence or the likely area of the next crime of an unknown offender, based on the location and spatial relationships among various crime sites (Guerette, 2002). Whereas a *crime scene profiler* hypothesizes about the demographic, motivational, and psychological features of the offender, the *geoprofiler* concentrates on developing hypotheses on the approximate location of the offender's residence, his base of operations, and where the next crime may occur. It is usually used when a series of crimes are occurring—such as burglaries, car thefts, arsons, sexual assaults, bombings, bank robberies, child abductions, or murders—and the primary suspect is believed to be one person or a small group.

Although it may not seem that geographical profiling has much to do with psychology, the enterprise can be tied to psychological principles, such as the need to operate within one's comfort zone or the desire to commit crime as far away from one's home as possible. A good example of a psychological connection with geographical profiling is the "hunting patterns" theory proposed by Rossmo (1997). From a large database of criminal offenders, Rossmo suspected that offenders often have known movement patterns or comfort zones in which they operate. Rossmo developed a computer program called *Criminal Geographic Targeting* (CGT), which created a topographical map assigning different statistical probabilities to areas that fall within an offender's territory. From that information, the offender's residence or base of operations may be estimated. Rossmo's theory is most relevant to serial offenders, particularly violent offenders like those who rob or sexually assault. We will return to Rossmo's approach in Chapter 9.

Rossmo (1997) recommends that geographical profiling be combined with criminal or crime scene profiling for maximum effectiveness in developing probabilities for offender identification. In addition, he admonishes that geographical profiling is essentially an investigative tool that does not necessarily solve crimes but should help in the surveillance or monitoring of specific locations.

Suspect-Based Profiling

Whereas crime scene and geographical profiling examine features of a current unsolved crime, **suspect-based profiling** is derived from the systematic collection of behavioral, personality, cognitive, and demographic data on previous offenders. In most instances, the suspect-based profile summarizes the psychological features of persons who *may* commit a crime, such as drug trafficking, detonating a bomb, or hijacking a plane, based on features of past individuals who have committed similar crimes. The end product of suspect-based profiling should describe people from various offender groups. "For example, someone driving at a certain speed, at a certain time of day, in a certain type of car, and of a certain general appearance may fit the profile of a drug courier and be stopped for a search" (Homant & Kennedy, 1998, p. 325). "General appearance," as used in the above quote, may refer to patterns of suspicious behavior, age, or manner of dress, but it also unfortunately has referred to race or ethnicity.

Probably the best-known and most controversial type of suspect-based profiling is **racial profiling**, which refers to

police-initiated action that *relies on* the race, ethnicity, or national origin rather than the behavior of an individual or information that leads the police to a particular individual who has been identified as being, or having been, engaged in criminal activity. (Ramirez, McDevitt, & Farrell, 2000, p. 53, emphasis added)

Profiling of this type is illegal—courts have determined that police action cannot be taken against a person just because that person is black or Hispanic, for example. As we noted in Chapter 2, a federal judge in 2013 ruled the stop-and-frisk policy of the New York Police Department was unconstitutional because the policy encouraged police to rely on race or ethnicity in stopping and questioning citizens rather than on suspicious behavior. Since then, stop-and-frisk programs across the United States have been scrutinized by civil liberties groups, citizens, public officials, and courts for their possible infringement on constitutional rights.

In the 21st century, immigration has emerged as a hot-button political issue, particularly but not exclusively in states bordering Mexico. The combination of high unemployment rates and concerns about drug trafficking led to a desire among some for a "crackdown" on people entering the United States illegally or remaining here after temporary visas have expired. Note that two separate problems are identified here: (1) cross-border transportation of illegal drugs and (2) immigration status that is not documented. It is obvious that, though drug trafficking is a problem, people who seek to enter the United States are not typically drug dealers—they are doing so in search of a better way of life. Many also are refugees seeking asylum from repressive regimes or safety after suffering from environmental disasters. (See Focus 10.1 in Chapter 10 for discussion of ways in which psychologists assess and work with immigrants.)

Ethnic and racial profiling has been used beyond the detection of drug couriers or undocumented immigrants, and profiling also has been extended to religious groups, most particularly Muslims. Since the terrorist attacks of September 11, 2001, and subsequent crimes (e.g., Boston Marathon bombing in 2013, San Bernardino attack of 2015), ethnic, racial, or religious groups who fit the "profile" of terrorists have been subjected to more scrutiny by law enforcement officers and more extensive security screenings in airports or at immigration checkpoints. The discovery of explosive devices in shoes, underwear, and cargo led the Transportation Security Administration (TSA) to initiate full-body scans or pat-downs of all air travelers in many airports across the United States in 2010. Public outrage at the scans—as well as threatened and actual legal action—led the TSA to modify some of its procedures in recent years. The intrusive full body scans are not as extensively used, and travelers who are asked to undergo them—but who object—may request a pat-down search instead. Critics of these security measures believe that, even if all passengers are subjected to searches of their baggage and possessions, persons of Middle Eastern descent are more likely to be taken aside for more invasive body scans or pat-downs. Moreover, some convicted individuals—including the so-called Shoe Bomber, Richard Reeve, and Colleen R. LaRose, otherwise known as "Jihad Jane"—did not conform to the profile. Both were convicted of terrorist activities and sentenced to federal prisons.

After 2001, the TSA trained more than 2,000 airport security personnel in various methods of identifying suspicious behavior and facial expressions that suggest terrorist or destructive intentions (Bradshaw, 2008). The training in passenger profiling is partly based on the research of psychologist Paul Ekman (2009) and the success of a 2002 pilot program at Boston's Logan International Airport (Bradshaw, 2008). However, the technique developed by Ekman is far from foolproof. Ekman admits that 9 out of every 10 persons detected have perfectly innocent reasons for their suspicious behavior. This hit-to-miss ratio is of concern to many civil libertarians. "Many travelers may be subjected to undue attention simply because they have a fear of flying, feel intimidated by being scrutinized by uniformed screeners or are carrying items that cause them shame, such as legal but erotic literature" (Bradshaw, 2008, p. 10). We will discuss research on the detection of deception more fully later in the chapter.

Psychological Profiling

In the psychology of investigation, **psychological profiling** refers primarily to the gathering of information—usually on a *known* individual or individuals who pose a threat or who are believed to be dangerous. In some cases, the identity of the individual is unknown, but he or she has made a clear threat to do harm to some specified target, such as by sending an anonymous letter. The target may be a person, a group, an organization, or an institution. Psychological profiling in this context is also used to assess the risk that someone will be violent in the future, even though he or she may not have made an explicit threat.

There are two primary and overlapping procedures used in psychological profiling: threat assessment and risk assessment. Threat assessment is used to determine if an actual, expressed threat is likely to be carried out; risk assessment is used to determine if a person is dangerous to self or to others. Both of these assessments are accomplished through various evaluation measures, background checks, observations, and interviews. It is important to stress that forensic psychologists conduct risk and threat assessments for purposes other than investigation, and there is a rich store of research in both areas. We will discuss them in more detail in the chapters ahead. Risk assessment will be covered in the next chapter, where the most common tasks of forensic psychologists are discussed. Threat assessment, a related but separate enterprise, will be discussed in Chapter 8.

Psychological profiling also occurs outside the psychology of investigations, although it still may be useful to those investigating crime. This occurs when researchers prepare profiles of a specific group of offenders—e.g., the spouse abuser, the child molester, the firesetter, or the stalker. Some psychologists, particularly those who are more clinically based, are highly engaged in preparing these types of profiles, with varying degrees of success. Investigators may make use of these profiles in deciding whether a particular suspect "fits the profile" of a certain type of stalker or a certain type of sex offender. Although profiles of this type may be helpful, they also may mislead investigators and must be approached cautiously. We will discuss profiles of this type in chapters where specific crimes are covered, such as stalking, sex offending, and domestic assault.

Finally, a more clinical enterprise must be mentioned. Mental health practitioners, such as psychologists or psychiatrists, sometimes prepare an extensive report on the psychological characteristics of one known individual. This is a speculative process, based on available documents as well as interviews, including at times interviews with the subject, although such personal interviews are rare. Psychological profiling of this type has a long history of use by military and intelligence organizations (Ault & Reese, 1980; Omestad, 1994). Profiles have been prepared of individuals as varied as Adolf Hitler, Osama Bin Laden, international leaders, and U.S. presidents as well as lesser political figures. Although these profiles may make for interesting reading, they have very little scientific validity and are not the type of profiles we give attention to in this text.

The Psychological Autopsy

The final category of profiling discussed herein is the **psychological autopsy**, which refers to a procedure that is done following a person's death in order to determine his or her mental state prior to the death. For instance, determining whether a death is due to autoerotic stimulation or suicide is extremely important, especially for parents and other family members and friends. Likewise, survivors often want to know whether a loved one's death was an accidental drug overdose or a suicide. In other cases, what appears to be a suicide might actually be a homicide.

The psychological autopsy was originally devised to assist certifying officials in clarifying deaths that were initially ambiguous, uncertain, or equivocal as to the *manner* of death (Shneidman, 1994). The method was first used in 1958, when the Los Angeles medical examiner/coroner Theodore J. Murphy consulted Edwin S. Shneidman, director of the LA Suicide Prevention Center, for assistance in determining the cause of an unusually high number of equivocal, or unexplained, deaths. Shneidman is generally credited with first using the term *psychological autopsy*.

The postmortem psychological analysis is also called the **reconstructive psychological evaluation (RPE)**, or **equivocal death analysis (EDA)** (Poythress, Otto, Darnes, & Starr, 1993), but *psychological autopsy* is the more common term (Brent, 1989; Ebert, 1987; Selkin, 1987). The EDA, or the equivocal death psychological autopsy (EDPA), is usually reserved for those investigations conducted by law enforcement officials, especially the FBI, who primarily examine the crime scene material and other information directly available to the police (Canter, 1999; Poythress et al., 1993). Psychological autopsies may also be important in determining insurance payments as well as national security issues (Ebert, 1987). For example, the autopsy may reveal that the deceased individual committed suicide after violating a code that forbade divulging classified information to others (Ritchie & Gelles, 2002).

An *equivocal death* is one where the manner of death is unknown or undetermined, and it is believed that about 5% to 20% of all deaths are equivocal (Shneidman, 1981; T. J. Young, 1992). The term *manner* has special significance in any death investigation. Basically, "the manner of death refers to specific circumstances by which a death results" (La Fon, 2008, p. 420). There are five generally accepted manners of death: natural, accident, suicide, homicide, and undetermined (La Fon, 2008).

Today, the psychological autopsy is primarily undertaken in an effort to make a reasonable determination of what may have been in the mind of the deceased person leading up to and at the time of death—particularly if the death appears to be a suicide. La Fon (2008) identifies two basic types of psychological autopsy: suicide psychological autopsy (SPA) and equivocal death psychological autopsy (EDPA). The goal of the SPA is to identify and understand the psychosocial factors that contributed to the suicide. In this case, suicide has been established (e.g., witnesses may have seen the person shooting himself), but the person conducting the autopsy must try to discern the reasons why he did this. The goal of the EDPA, on the other hand, is to clarify the manner (or mode) of death and to determine the reasons for the death. It may not be a suicide. Although the cause of death is generally clear, the manner is often unclear (T. J. Young, 1992). For example, T. J. Young gives the example of a parachutist who falls to the ground from an altitude of 5,000 feet and dies as the result of multiple injuries. In this case, an investigator cannot immediately ascertain whether the parachute malfunctioned (accident), or whether the parachutist intentionally jumped with a bad parachute (suicide). Alternatively, the parachute may have been tampered with by someone else (homicide), or the parachutist may have suffered a heart attack during the jump (natural).

In most instances, the psychological autopsy is done for insurance purposes. Although some insurance policies do compensate the family if the death is determined to be suicide, many policies do not. Consequently, if the manner of death is equivocal, it is in the best financial interest of the insurance company to hire a forensic psychologist to do a complete psychological autopsy to determine whether the death was more likely the result of suicide or some other cause. A vast majority of the psychological assessments to uncover a person's thoughts and feelings prior to his or her death have been done in the United States, usually in civil or criminal litigation (Canter, 1999). In recent years, many product-liability lawsuits have revolved around whether certain drugs can be blamed for suicides of both adults and juveniles. According to the U.S. Food and Drug Administration (FDA), at least 130 prescription drugs can produce suicidal thoughts or actions (Lavigne, McCarthy, Chapman, Petrilla, & Knox, 2012), but this does not mean that a court will agree that a particular drug was directly responsible for a person's suicide. Nevertheless, some plaintiffs have been successful in winning suits or have arrived at settlements based on the results of psychological autopsies.

According to La Fon (2008), the U.S. military is one of the major consumers of psychological autopsies: "Each branch of the Armed Forces, including the Navy, Army, and Air Force, [has] the task of conducting an EDPA for every equivocal death that occurs either on base property or to military personnel" (p. 422). Both civilian and military forensic psychologists conduct these autopsies, and they are conducted both in cases of equivocal death and suspected suicide. In most cases, the beneficiaries of the deceased military personnel receive remuneration regardless of the cause of death. Interestingly, there is evidence that the suicide rate among military personnel during and after deployment in Iraq and Afghanistan was higher than during any other war or occupation. Increasing numbers of suicides by military personnel both during and after deployment prompted mental health advocates and some military leaders and politicians to call for more support and treatment programs for military personnel and veterans.

In legal contexts, the psychological autopsy is frequently conducted to reconstruct the possible reasons for a suicide and ultimately to establish legal culpability on the part of other persons or organizations. For example, if a police officer shoots himself on the steps of the state capitol building, the message he was trying to send to all those concerned may be unclear. Family members of the deceased, convinced the department had poor stress-management techniques or nonexistent early-detection procedures for identifying emotional problems in its officers, may sue the department for emotional and financial damages. Under these conditions, a mental health professional may be retained to reconstruct the victim's mental state during and before the incident. Psychological autopsies have also been part of civil proceedings in the private sector, where it was necessary to ascertain whether certain events on the job affected the person—such as various kinds of harassment by fellow workers or supervisors—or whether certain job-related accidents prompted the eventual suicide. Failure of the company or organization to have adequate policies and procedures in place for handling problems of this sort may be sufficient reason to find the company liable. Another purpose of psychological autopsy is as a research tool to collect data that are likely to be useful in the prediction and prevention of suicide (T. J. Young, 1992). For example, research indicates that a majority of suicide victims communicate their intentions to at least one person before killing themselves. Many victims also leave suicide notes. Research further indicates that psychological autopsies can be of therapeutic value to survivors (Ebert, 1987; Henry & Greenfield, 2009).

Although some progress has been made in determining the reliability and validity of the psychological autopsy, much work still needs to be done, and even psychologists who conduct such autopsies are concerned about this issue (Snider, Hane, & Berman, 2006). Some research reveals that the psychological autopsy shows considerable promise for determining suicide intentions of the deceased (Portzky, Audenaert, & van Heeringen, 2009). Of course, the quality of the psychological autopsy will depend significantly on the training, knowledge, experience, and clinical acumen of the investigator (J. L. Knoll, 2008). Poythress et al. (1993) further warn that

> persons who conduct reconstructive psychological evaluations should not assert categorical conclusions about the precise mental state or actions suspected of the actor at the time of his or her demise. The conclusions and inferences drawn in psychological reconstructions are, at best, informed speculations or theoretical formulations and should be labeled as such. (p. 12)

PROBLEMS WITH PROFILING

Contemporary scholars (Alison, Bennell, Ormerod, & Mokros, 2002; Alison & Canter, 1999; Goodwill et al., 2016; Snook et al., 2008; Taylor et al., 2015) identify many flaws with profiling, particularly with crime scene profiling. One major flaw is the assumption that human behavior is consistent across a variety of situations; another is the assumption that offense style or crime scene evidence is related to specific psychological characteristics. The second point refers to the tendency of profilers to believe that specific clues gathered at the crime scene reveal certain generalizable psychological characteristics and thought patterns of certain types of offenders. Recall that Table 3.1 summarizes the key weaknesses of each form of profiling. Below we focus on these specific limitations, while also recognizing that some weaknesses pertain to more than one form.

Crime-Scene Profiling Limitations

In summarizing problems associated with profiling, Alison, Bennell, Ormerod, and Mokros (2002) underscore the fact that many professional profilers, especially those who rely on crime scene information, tend to have unsubstantiated assumptions about personality theory, the power of that personality or disposition to virtually override the influence of all situations, and the validity and accuracy of the profiling process itself. Profilers often rely too heavily on "gut feelings," believing they have special knowledge and experience to put the pieces of the puzzle together, and too little on science.

The tendency to rely heavily or exclusively on gut feelings, intuition, hunches, subjective experiences, or whatever nonscientific approaches a profiler may take in forming his or her opinion, puts offender profiling in serious jeopardy in the eyes of the judicial system. Consequently, courts in the United States, Canada, Australia, and the United Kingdom are requiring criminal profiling to meet a rigorous standard in order to be admitted as valid scientific evidence (see, generally, Bosco, Zappalà, & Santtila, 2010, for a review of this important issue). For example, profiling has very rarely been admissible in the British legal system as expert evidence because of its lack of established reliability and validity (Gregory, 2005). In the United States, the situation varies, often depending upon the credentials of the profiler or the degree to which the profiler can persuade the court that his or her testimony is based on reliable and valid scientific principles (Bartol & Bartol, 2013; J. A. George, 2008; Risinger & Loop, 2002).

A common error by some profilers is the failure to consider the power of the situation to influence behavior. Part of the situation is the victim and all the characteristics brought to the incident by that individual or individuals. As noted by Jenkins (1993), "The failure to consider victim-oriented factors often leads researchers to misunderstand the nature of such activity" (p. 462). Considering these factors is not equivalent to blaming the victim for the crime; rather, the focus is more on what type of victim is likely to be chosen by an offender or where victims might reside. The lack of a victimology perspective generates confusion and often leads to further flaws in the development of offender profiles. Jenkins strongly asserts that an overlooked tool available to profilers is examining characteristics of the victim, because "offenders and victim comprise a common and interdependent ecology" (p. 463). Cromwell, Olson, and Avary (1991) also discuss the importance of the victim perspective in their study of burglary. Cromwell and his colleagues contend that the activities of the victim play a critical role in how burglars pick a home to burglarize, how they enter, and how long they remain. The authors believe that "most burglaries in the jurisdictions studied appeared to result from a propitious juxtaposition of target, offender, and situations" (p. 47).

Profiling is ultimately based on the assumption that human behavior is consistent across time (**trans-temporal consistency**) and place (**trans-situational consistency**). The profile process, by its very nature, presupposes that crime scene clues provide the skillful investigator with clues of the perpetrator's personality traits, habits, and even thought processes. Furthermore, there is an assumption that key factors of the personality identified at the crime scene should generalize to other situations, including future crimes.

The ability to predict the behavior and tendencies of individuals across different situations (trans-situational consistency) is very much open to debate. For example, some earlier researchers (e.g., Mischel, 1968; Mischel & Peake, 1982) argued that human behavior across different situations is inconsistent and that notions of stable behavioral dispositions or personality traits are largely unsupported. Research by Merry and Harsent (2000) cogently illustrates that most criminal behavior, such as burglary, changes as the dynamics of the situation change. Consequently, crime scene activity is likely to be different from crime to crime. Although trans-situational consistency remains highly questionable, consistency across time, or temporal consistency, is acknowledged. As long as situations are similar, people will likely respond the same way over their life spans. But when situations change, behavior is apt to change. Therefore, criminal behavior that has been reinforced in a particular context is more apt to recur in a similar context than across a wide variety of different settings. A person who had engaged in a lifetime of burglary, for instance, is more likely to burglarize again if surrounded by similar psychosocial situations that have a perceived reward value. Therefore, there is trans-temporal consistency in behavior if the perceived situation is the same. On the other hand, if his or her environment has changed substantially (e.g., longtime partner in crime has died, or the person has aged to the point where physical agility or mental ability has substantially deteriorated), the burglarizing is less likely to continue.

In addition, if the offender has learned that some behavioral patterns do not work well, he or she is likely to modify this approach. These offenders, whether rapists, burglars, arsonists, killers, or child sexual offenders, often change their **modus operandi (MO)** as they become more proficient at their crime. Or, as Turvey (2002) points out, the MO may change due to an offender's deteriorating mental state, the increased use of drugs or alcohol, or changes in lifestyle and habits. There may also be developmental and maturation changes in offenders, especially as these pertain to the brain.

The MO refers to the actions and procedures an offender uses to commit a crime successfully. It is a behavioral pattern that the offender learns as he or she gains experience in committing the offense. However, it is subject to change. For example, burglars are continually changing their procedures and techniques to better accomplish their goals, and serial killers often become more daring and risky in their selection of victims. Because the offender generally changes the MO until he or she learns which method is most effective, investigators may make a serious error if they place too much significance on the MO when linking crimes.

Investigators may make another serious error if they believe offenders lack intellectual skills. Turvey (2002) suggests that some offenders improve their MO through educational and technical materials: "Professional journals, college courses, textbooks, and other educationally oriented media available at a public library, or now via the Internet, can provide offenders with knowledge that is useful toward refining their particular MO" (p. 232). Turvey further writes, "arsonists may read *Kirk's Fire Investigation* . . . rapists may read *Practical Aspects of Rape Investigation* . . . murderers may read *Practical Homicide Investigation* . . . and bank robbers may subscribe to security magazines" (p. 232). In addition, many offenders read newspaper, magazine, and television accounts of their crimes, which sometimes provide clues that the police have identified concerning the MO. Such accounts may prompt the offender to alter his or her methods of operation. In some instances, the offender may perfect the MO by engaging in a career or profession that enhances the methods used, such as an arsonist joining a volunteer fire department or even becoming a fire investigator.

The above discussion emphasizes that accurate assessment and prediction require not only an evaluation of the person, but also an evaluation of the psychosocial environment within which the behaviors we are trying to predict occur. Failure to consider the context of the behavior is destined to produce disappointing results.

Suspect-Based Profiling Limitations

The limitations mentioned above pertain particularly to crime scene profiling. Suspect-based profiling has its own shortcomings. It is (or should be) a *nomothetic* enterprise in that it tries to make *general* predictions about offenders based on clusters of data gathered from previous offenders. A **nomothetic approach** refers to the search for general principles, relationships, and patterns by examining and combining data from *many* individuals. Research psychology is largely nomothetic as opposed to *idiographic* in scope. The **idiographic approach** emphasizes the intensive study of *one* individual, usually called the case study. A case study of the coping behaviors of an individual or the biography of a famous person is an example of the idiographic approach.

Unfortunately, some profilers take the idiographic approach rather than the nomothetic and consequently are in danger of missing the mark. This is especially so if taking the nomothetic approach would emphasize situational variables. For example, data gathered on many offenders might reveal that the late afternoon hours are a prime time for burglaries in a particular geographical area, yet a certain clinician might have had four burglars on her caseload over several years of personal experience in dealing with offenders, each of whom committed the crime in the early morning hours. She might then infer that early morning hours are the time most burglaries will likely occur. Too many profilers and clinicians prefer exclusive use of the idiographic approach, even though research has continually revealed that predictions based on statistical probability, calculated from research on clusters of offenders under various conditions, are far more accurate. Predictions based on statistical probability and data are called **actuarial predictions**, as opposed to **clinical predictions**, which are based on subjective experience.

Psychological Autopsy Limitations

As described earlier, the conclusions and inferences drawn from psychological autopsies are far too often informed speculations that lack standardized protocol backed by systematic research. In addition, considerable systematic research needs to be conducted to establish the reliability and validity of psychological autopsies. However, as mentioned, strides are being made in that direction as researchers are suggesting standard protocols.

Psychological Profiling Limitations

Psychological profiling has many of the same limitations as the other forms of profiling, but considerable progress has been made in this area during the past 25 years (Hanson, 2005, 2009). As we will note in later chapters, research on the predictive accuracy of current risk and threat assessment instruments is extremely robust. Most of these instruments demonstrate levels of predictive accuracy superior to that of professional opinion (Hanson, 2009). This is because the instruments are largely based on actuarial prediction rather than strictly on clinical prediction. Nonetheless, actuarial prediction combined with structured clinical judgment is a worthy approach. Structured clinical judgment—also known as structured professional judgment—refers to a trained clinician's judgment coupled with empirically based guidelines. We will return to this topic in the next chapter.

Overall Limitations

There are other general problems with profiling, in addition to those mentioned above. Some recent studies reveal that a large proportion of the conclusions and predictions contained within profile reports are both ambiguous and unverifiable (Alison, Smith, Eastman, & Rainbow, 2003; Alison, Smith, & Morgan, 2003). That is to say, statements are so vague that they are open to a wide range of interpretations. For example, what does it mean that someone is "a loner" or "goes to church regularly"?

Moreover, there seems to be a tendency for some police investigators to "creatively interpret" the ambiguous information contained within profiles to fit their own biases about the case or the suspect. They select those aspects of the profile that they perceive as fitting the suspect while ignoring the many conclusions and predictions that do not seem to fit.

> If a suspect does arise during the investigation, officers may wish to actively ignore the information that does not fit the suspect, or perhaps unwittingly exaggerate the merits of the information that might fit and not appreciate the extent to which the information could fit a wide range of individuals. (Alison, Smith, & Morgan, 2003, p. 193)

The strong preference to have one's views confirmed is known as **confirmation bias**. "When it operates, it places us in a kind of closed cognitive system in which only evidence that confirms our existing views and beliefs gets inside; other information is sometimes noticed but is quickly rejected as false" (Baron & Byrne, 2000, p. 8). In short, confirmation bias is the tendency to notice and remember information that lends support to our views on something, such as a suspect. It is a tendency that might be prevalent not only in the subjective interpretations of a profile but also in its creation.

Although there are many flaws in current profiling methods, if conducted appropriately, profiling could have a promising and extremely useful future. Despite the concerns of many critics, some psychologists who engage in this practice defend it vigorously (see, e.g., Dern, Dern, Horn, & Horn, 2009). If profilers take into account the interaction between the person and the situations (and the influence of the victim), the science of profiling can lead to more accurate and helpful sketches of the offender. In addition, profilers should be cautious about relying exclusively on trait or personality theory and rely more on contemporary psychological theory and research on human behavior. They should look for the conditional probability of certain behaviors occurring under certain situations instead of assuming that behavior remains consistent across all situations. All of this will require greater reliance on and involvement in well-executed scientific research.

POLICE INTERVIEWING AND INTERROGATION

The interviewing of witnesses or other persons with possible information about a crime is fundamental to law enforcement work. When questioning a person who is suspected of the crime and who is in custody, the process is an accusatory one and is properly called an interrogation. However, persons who eventually become suspects may first be simply interviewed—thus, an interview often turns into an interrogation. When that point is reached, though, the individual must be advised of his or her legal rights.

The primary aim of police interrogation is to obtain a confession from a suspect or to gain information (usually incriminating evidence) that may lead to a conviction. Approximately 80% of criminal cases are solved by less than a full confession (O'Connor & Maher, 2009). Interrogation is most often initiated when there is weak evidence against the suspect. Once interrogation is used, it is successful in gaining at least some incriminating evidence about 64% of the time (Blair, 2005; Leo, 1996).

Experienced police interrogators use a wide variety of methods and techniques that are tailored to their personality and style. Recent research has identified 71 unique interrogative techniques used by law enforcement that fall under six major headings (Kelly, Miller, Redlich, & Kleinman, 2013). (See Table 3.2.) Nevertheless, most have been trained in a dominant method—the **Reid method**—which is taught in police academies across the United States (Inbau, Reid, Buckley, & Jayne, 2004, 2013). Available research indicates that approximately one half of all police investigators in the United States have been trained in the Reid method (Cleary & Warner, 2016; Kostelnik & Reppucci, 2009). Skillful and legally useful interrogation involves the application of psychological principles and concepts. Although we cover

Table 3.2 Categories and Examples of Major Interrogation Techniques	
Technique Category	**Technique Example**
Rapport and Relationship Building	Show kindness and respect
Context Manipulation	Conduct the interrogation in a small room
Emotion Provocation	Interrogate suspect while very stressed
Confrontation and Competition	Threaten suspect with consequences for non-cooperation
Collaboration	Make bargain with suspect
Presentation of Evidence	Bluff or bait suspect about supposed evidence of involvement in crime

Source: Table adapted from Kelly, Miller, Redlich, & Kleinman, 2013.

this topic in this chapter, it should be emphasized that police psychologists are less likely to be conducting research on interrogation-related issues than are psychologists associated with academic institutions who are conducting research in legal psychology (e.g., Crozier, Strange, & Loftus, 2017; Kassin et al., 2010; Rogers et al., 2009; Rogers et al., 2010). However, police and public safety psychologists may serve as consultants, training officers in methods of interview and interrogation. In addition, they should be very aware of the pitfalls and myths surrounding the process.

Accusatorial Versus Information Gathering Approaches

Research on police interrogations has focused on the effectiveness of two different approaches: the **accusatorial approach** (primarily used in the United States) and the **information-gathering approach** (developed in the United Kingdom) (J. R. Evans et al., 2013; Meissner, Redlich, Bhatt, & Brandon, 2012). The accusatorial approach is best represented by the Reid method mentioned above. However, numerous researchers have criticized the Reid method for a variety of reasons, but especially because of its strict accusatorial tone (Kassin et al., 2010; L. King & Snook, 2009). As stated by Kassin et al., "the modern American police interrogation is, by definition, a guilt-presumptive and confrontational process—aspects of which put innocent people at risk" (p. 27).

As practiced, the Reid method is basically highly confrontational, pitting police interrogators against the suspect who is typically placed under stressful conditions, even though it may begin with an interview approach (e.g., inviting a person to come to the police station or questioning the person in a nonconfrontational style). Its overall direct purpose is to obtain a confession from the suspect if at all possible, rather than acquiring information. In this approach, the interrogator is instructed to maintain psychological control, use psychological manipulation whenever possible, and ask straightforward "yes" or "no" questions. It requires several steps that include (a) custody and isolation, (b) confrontation, and (c) minimization. In the custody and isolation step, the suspect is detained in a small interrogation room and left long enough to experience the uncertainty, the stress, and the usual insecurity associated with police custody and interrogation. We have all seen this approach, with the suspect sitting alone in a small room, observed through a one-way mirror, waiting tensely for a detective to enter and begin the questioning. The confrontation step focuses on the interrogator accusing the suspect of the crime, expressing certainty in that accusation, citing real or manufactured evidence, and preventing the suspect from denying the accusations as much as possible. Minimization—which may come into play at any time—involves a "sympathetic" second interrogator morally justifying the crime to the suspect, saying anyone else in that situation would probably do the same, and expressing sympathy with the suspect's understandable predicament. The presumption here is that the suspect is likely to believe that more lenient and understanding treatment will be given once he or she confesses.

This approach is strongly advocated by Inbau et al. (2013) in their extensively used police manual on interviewing and interrogation. (Note that interviewing is included in the manual.) "Conceptually, this [interrogation] procedure is designed to get suspects to incriminate themselves by increasing the anxiety associated with denial, plunging them into a state of despair, and minimizing the perceived consequences of confession" (Kassin & Gudjonsson, 2004, p. 43). However, although the approach frequently results in obtaining confessions, the method can also lead to false confessions, a topic we will cover below. In addition, Reid-like, confrontation methods are often used by police in questioning children and adolescents suspected of committing crimes, a practice that has been criticized because of the vulnerability of this age group (Cleary, 2017; Cleary & Warner, 2016; Reppucci, Meyer, & Kostelnik, 2010).

Canada and Western European countries, by contrast, often use less confrontational "interrogation," which many prefer to call investigative interviewing. Those asking the questions may believe the individual they are questioning is guilty, but they avoid confrontational behavior. The tenor of the interrogator or investigative interviewer focuses on gathering information about the crime (Beune, Giebels, & Taylor, 2010; Bull & Milne, 2004). This approach is designed for investigators to take a more neutral role by probing the suspect's knowledge through open-ended questions (in contrast to the yes/no questions) and a more informal conversational style. Unlike the accusatorial style, the information-gathering approach avoids trickery and deceit as much as possible. The "bait question," through which police tell a suspect that they have evidence they really do not have, is often expressly forbidden. This type of questioning has been found to produce misinformation (Luke, Crozier, & Strange, 2017). The nonconfrontational, information-gathering technique emphasizes rational arguments and being kind as methods of persuading the interviewee to provide information. The Reid method has some aspects of this—for example, it begins with an "interview" and moves on to the "interrogation" stage if enough information has been derived from the person to consider him or her a suspect. In one of the very few studies examining the two methods to date, J. R. Evans et al. (2013) found that the information-gathering approach yields more relevant and useful information than the accusatorial approach. In addition, some researchers (e.g., Meissner et al., 2012) believe that the information-gathering approach will lead to substantially fewer false confessions.

One illustration of the information-gathering approach is the PEACE model, which was developed in the United Kingdom in the early 1990s and is gaining acceptance in Europe, Canada, Australia, New Zealand, and some parts of the United States (Starr, 2013). The acronym PEACE stands for Planning and Preparation; Engage and Explain; Account; Closure; and Evaluation. According to Starr, "By 2001, every police officer in England and Wales had received a basic level of instruction in the method" (p. 48). Cleary and Warner (2016) note that "the PEACE model is considered a successful alternative to accusatory interviewing and has . . . expanded to additional nations and organizations" (p. 271).

In this approach, police use the interview to gather evidence and information rather than to obtain a confession. They are told not to focus on the nonverbal behavior of the person being interviewed—such as signs of anxiety. Interestingly, they are not allowed to bluff or suggest that they have evidence that they do not have—which is very different from what the Reid method allows.

In the PEACE model, the interviewers are encouraged to establish rapport, use open-ended questions, and "address contradictions via the strategic presentation of evidence" (Swanner, Meissner, Atkinson, & Dianiska, 2016, p. 296). The research literature strongly indicates that the PEACE model and similar information-gathering approaches are effective methods for eliciting more useful information from both cooperative and reluctant individuals (Swanner et al., 2016).

HUMINT Interrogation

During the past two decades, a vast amount of psychological research has been directed at forensic interrogation. More recently, however, a growing interest has shifted toward the psychological aspects of military intelligence interviewing and interrogation, or **HUMINT (HUManINTelligence) interrogation**. Part of the shift in interest was prompted by interrogation practices in Guantanamo Bay, Iraq, and Afghanistan (Evans, Meissner, Brandon, Russano, & Kleinman, 2010), and the threat of terror worldwide (Granhag, Vrij, & Meissner, 2014). It is critical to emphasize here that we do not refer to the controversial interrogation measures that were denounced by the American Psychological Association in 2009 and again in 2015.

HUMINT interrogations are intended to be humane, but they differ in important ways from the forensic interrogation associated with civilian law enforcement agencies. The goal of forensic interrogation is to acquire admissions and evidence of past behavior that will lead to a conviction at trial. "The goal of a HUMINT interrogation is to obtain reliable information from a source about the past, present, or future, which can be used to improve national security and/or further national interests" (Evans et al., 2014, p. 867). In other words, forensic interrogation seeks identifying who is responsible for a crime, whereas HUMINT interrogations seek knowledge for security purposes and in so doing prevent crime, including terrorist activities.

A second major difference is that forensic interrogation primarily utilizes one or two interrogators, whereas HUMINT usually relies on a team approach that includes an interrogator, interpreter, and analyst (Russano, Narchet, & Kleinman, 2014). The interpreter is responsible for facilitating communication and building relationships during the interrogation. In cross-cultural interrogations, the interpreter not only speaks the national language, but often will represent the cultural bridge to help the interrogator relate to the person being interrogated. The analyst prepares the interrogator with information about the person being interviewed and interrogated and helps to make sense of the information elicited. In a sense, the analyst is the "fact checker." Experienced interrogators recognized that competent interpreters and analysts are indispensable team members in the HUMINT process.

A third difference is that the interrogation practices of HUMINT are governed by international policies. In 2009, for example, then-president Obama stated that all HUMINT interrogations must conform to the Geneva Convention (Evans et al., 2014). This of course prohibits any techniques of interrogation that are deemed to be torturous, such as simulated drowning.

Most experienced HUMINT interrogators firmly believe that rapport and relationship building are the most effective at eliciting reliable information, whereas interrogative practices that rely on confrontational approaches are significantly less effective (Brandon, 2014; Russano et al., 2014). Research from around the world resonates with growing conclusions that forensic or HUMINT interviewing or interrogations that treat people who are interrogated with respect and recognition of a shared humanity are the most successful at obtaining reliable information (Brandon, 2014). Accusatorial, confrontational forms of interrogation, and the presentation of false evidence or bluffing about evidence can be very problematic (Evans et al., 2014).

One approach that has been shown to be especially effective in eliciting reliable information from cooperative respondents, and even from criminal suspects, is the **cognitive interview (CI)** (Fisher & Geiselman, 1992; Rivard, Fisher, Robertson, & Mueller, 2014). The CI is a method that utilizes memory retrieval and communication techniques aimed at increasing the amount of accurate information from witnesses, informants, victims, or suspects. We cover the CI in more detail in the later section of this chapter discussing eyewitness testimony. However, the CI has shown to be of significant value in gaining information in both forensic interrogation and intelligence gathering (Swanner et al., 2016).

In summary, though, the confrontational Reid and similar models are so firmly established in police procedure that they are unlikely to disappear or even be modified substantially anytime soon. Many police are resistant to giving up this cherished approach. Furthermore, courts—including the U.S. Supreme Court—have by and large been supportive of police interrogation methods, unless they involve the most flagrant violations. Nevertheless, with more exposure to alternative, information-gathering methods, and with more evidence of the incidence of false confessions resulting from accusatorial interrogation strategies, future modifications may occur.

The U.S. Supreme Court, as suggested above, has granted law enforcement wide latitude in trying to obtain confessions from suspects (see, generally, Leo, 1996). Despite the landmark ruling in *Miranda v. Arizona* (1966) establishing the basic rule that suspects in custody must be informed of their right to remain silent and their right to an attorney prior to being questioned, many criminal suspects do not understand these rights and often waive them. Courts have allowed police to lie or trick suspects, such as by pretending they have eyewitness testimony or evidence that does not exist. This is sometimes referred to as bait questioning—and as noted earlier, such questioning is not allowed in PEACE model versions of investigative interviewing. Research on bait questioning indicates that it is psychologically coercive (Kassin et al., 2010) and even affects how juries respond to evidence down the line (Luke, Crozier, & Strange, 2017). The boundaries of such deception—that is, just how far can police go?—continue to be challenged in the courts. In New York, for example, the court of appeals (the highest appellate court in the state) considered a case involving police deception during interrogation and concluded that police went over the line in their questioning (see Focus 3.1). They told the suspect that the child he was accused of harming was still alive, when the child had actually died. The suspect confessed to battering the child, but his attorney argued that this confession was psychologically coerced. The defense attorney sought to put on the stand a psychological expert on coerced confessions but was denied that opportunity at the trial level.

A confession must be freely and voluntarily given if it is to be used as evidence; it cannot be coerced. A waiver of one's rights must be voluntary, knowledgeable, and intelligent—and many police agencies require a signed waiver before allowing the interrogation of a suspect in custody without a lawyer's presence. Even so, many legal psychologists are concerned about the potential for psychological coercion, and they have explored whether suspects truly understand the significance of their *Miranda* rights. A long line of research in developmental and legal psychology (e.g., Grisso, 1981, 1998; Rogers, Harrison, Shuman, Sewell, & Hazelwood, 2007; Rogers et al., 2009, 2010) indicates that many individuals, including but not limited to juveniles and persons with mental disorders or deficiencies, have difficulty understanding the significance of the *Miranda* warning that is routinely given in the United States. Researchers in Canada have reached similar conclusions with respect to police cautions (Eastwood & Snook, 2010; Eastwood, Snook, Luther, & Freedman, 2016). Even words that are typically used in these warnings—words like *consult, entitled, interrogation*—are unfamiliar to many suspects, and the role of the lawyer is often not understood. (See Perspective 3.2, in which Dr. Eastwood discusses research on comprehension of rights as well as training police officers in interrogation techniques.)

Interrogation of Juveniles

Interestingly, recent research has revealed that interrogators use the same tactics to interrogate adolescents as they do for adults (Cleary & Warner, 2016; Feld, 2013; Meyer & Reppucci, 2007; Reppucci, Meyer, & Kostelnik, 2010). However, developmental and forensic psychologists have long known that adolescents are fundamentally different from adults biologically, cognitively, and psychologically (Cleary, 2017). Cleary writes, "These developmental changes that all youth—regardless of legal involvement—experience during adolescence hold the potential to powerfully impact youth perception, behavior, and decision making inside the interrogation

FOCUS 3.1. PSYCHOLOGICAL COERCION: A CASE EXAMPLE

In 2009, Adrian Thomas was convicted of murder in the death of his 4-month-old son and sentenced to 25 years to life in prison. Thomas, who is tall and large, had confessed to throwing the infant, who had been born prematurely, forcefully onto a low-lying mattress, but the New York Court of Appeals—that state's highest court—ruled unanimously in 2014 that the confession was not a valid one; it was psychologically coerced in violation of the man's constitutional rights (*Thomas v. New York*, 2014).

When Thomas was questioned by police, he knew that his son had suffered a brain injury but did not know that the baby had been declared brain dead. His 9.5-hour interrogation was divided into two segments, because after 2 hours, Thomas demonstrated suicidal tendencies. He was hospitalized for 15 hours, then returned for another round of questioning.

Detectives used a variety of psychological tactics to obtain a confession. They threatened to arrest his wife if he did not confess to harming the child; they told him the baby was still alive; they told him he would not be charged with a crime if he confessed to throwing the baby down, because it had been an accident; they told him his son might be saved if he would tell them exactly what he did to cause the brain injury. "Do you want to save your baby's life, or do you want your baby to die tonight?" he was asked. After the lengthy interrogation, he admitted to having thrown the baby on at least three separate occasions in the week preceding the baby's death, and he demonstrated the force with a clipboard that police had provided. The court of appeals later ruled that, taken together, these tactics amounted to psychological coercion that rendered his confession involuntary.

Chief Judge Jonathan Lippman, who wrote the opinion of the seven-member court, noted that the record was replete with false assurances made to the suspect, and that his will was overborne. In other words, even if Thomas had indeed thrown the infant down, this was an invalid confession.

As we note in the text, police in the United States are allowed to mislead suspects and to lie in order to obtain a confession, but they may not force a confession. In cases involving psychological trickery, the line between acceptable deceit and coercion is often blurry. Like many courts before it, the New York court did not set a hard and fast rule. Looking at the facts of this particular case, they concluded that police used trickery to an extreme, and it violated the defendant's right against self-incrimination. The court ordered Thomas to be retried without the evidence of the confession.

At the second trial, jurors did not hear the confession. Although the prosecution offered medical testimony, the defense called a nationally known pediatric neuroradiologist who testified that swelling and bleeding in the infant's brain could have occurred as early as birth. In this expert's opinion, the infant died because of the resulting aggressive bacterial infection, not at the hands of the father. Thomas was found not guilty.

Questions for Discussion

1. Should police be allowed to deceive suspects in order to obtain a confession? If yes, how can they know where to draw the line? If no, why not?
2. There are many additional facts associated with this case, but based on the above information alone, which interrogation tactics used by the police, if any, do you believe were unacceptable?

room" (p. 119). Adolescents, Cleary goes on to say, are basically ill-equipped to withstand the pressures and stresses of interrogation. Moreover, they often fail to adequately comprehend their constitutional rights, including those protected by the Miranda warnings.

Neurodevelopmental research has demonstrated that the adolescent brain is not fully developed until the early to mid-20s. These findings have significant implications for how the tactics of interrogators should be applied when dealing with juveniles. Researchers have both suggested ways of making these rights more understandable to juveniles (Eastwood et al., 2016) and developed specific instruments for measuring both adult and juvenile comprehension of their rights (Rogers et al., 2007, 2009, 2010).

Forensic Psychology: Using Research to Answer Real-World Questions

Joseph Eastwood, PhD

Courtesy of Joseph Eastwood.

During the third year of my undergraduate degree at the University of New Brunswick, I happened to notice a handwritten leaflet posted on the bulletin board in the psychology department. The leaflet asked any students interested in joining a forensic psychology research group to contact Dr. Brent Snook. Despite having no concept of what the field of forensic psychology entailed, or what being part of a research group meant for that matter, I decided to e-mail Brent and express my interest. And the rest, as they say, is history.

After my undergraduate degree was completed, my wife Joanna and I tossed all our earthly possessions into our 10-year-old Toyota Tercel and headed to Memorial University in Newfoundland where Brent now worked. I spent the next 6 years completing my MSc and PhD in experimental social psychology under Brent's supervision. Then, in 2013, after a 2-year stint teaching at Bishop's University in Quebec, I took an Assistant Professor position within the Forensic Psychology program at the University of Ontario Institute of Technology (UOIT), where I remain.

As a reader of this textbook, you likely have, or are developing, an interest in the field of forensic psychology. And the question that I've often asked myself is, out of all the possible academic disciplines and areas of interest, why did I choose this field? To me, the attraction of conducting research within forensic psychology is that it allows us to ask fascinating and relevant questions about human behaviour while also providing the means to answer them systematically. For example, during my doctoral thesis I began one of my current streams of research with the simple question—Do people understand their legal rights when being questioned by the police? The answer, as revealed through a series of studies using samples of both adults and youths, was a resounding "no" (Eastwood & Snook, 2010; Freedman, Eastwood, Snook, & Luther, 2014). This led to further studies identifying ways to increase the comprehension of interrogation rights—and thereby increasing the ability of these rights to protect interviewees—by modifying the structure and wording of the rights and

the way in which they were delivered by interviewers (Eastwood & Snook, 2012; Eastwood, Snook, Luther, & Freedman, 2016).

Along with measuring the comprehension of interrogation rights, my two other major streams of research are focused on (1) how alibis are generated and assessed within criminal investigations, and (2) identifying practical tools to facilitate recall from interviewees. For example, in my current alibi research I am trying to answer the question—"What factors do people consider when attempting to judge the truthfulness of an alibi?" Results thus far have suggested that in order to be rated as highly believable, alibis should contain corroborating testimony from several people unrelated to the suspect—which is problematic given that many innocent suspects are unlikely to be able to generate this level of corroborating evidence (Eastwood, Snook, & Au, 2016).

With regard to the final stream, my colleagues and I have recently completed a series of studies measuring the ability of sketching (i.e., drawing out an event on paper) to boost the amount of information recalled by interviewees versus just asking them to recall the event verbally (Eastwood, Snook, & Luther, in preparation). Results from these studies suggest that using the sketch procedure leads interviewees to generate more substantial information than a standard interviewing approach, and therefore sketching may be an effective tool for officers to use when interviewing victims and witnesses of crimes.

Outside of the laboratory, I have worked with law enforcement organizations across Canada to provide science-based investigative interviewing training to their members. Most recently, this has included designing and delivering courses on victim, witness, and suspect interviewing to officers with the Durham Regional Police Service. These training experiences have led to many of the real-world research questions that I pursue. In turn, I continually update the content of my training based on the results of my research. I have found this opportunity to conduct systematic psychological research, and then integrate those findings into applied practice to improve the workings of the criminal justice system, to be among the most gratifying aspects of my job. It is matched only by the opportunity to meet and interact with many excellent police officers.

My primary advice to anyone interested in this area is to never lose your sense of curiosity about human behaviour and fascination with how psychological science can help to better understand it. The pages of this textbook are filled with new insights into how people think and behave within the justice system. These insights only exist because of the efforts of forensic psychological researchers to ask and answer questions effectively—a body of knowledge that I hope many of the readers will one day contribute to as well!

On that note, I want to highlight the impact of Brent Snook on my academic career. His passion for psychological research, his desire to see the resulting findings be implemented in practice, and his willingness to put the success of his students above his own continue to inspire and motivate me as a scholar. Any success that I have had, or will have, is a direct result of his mentorship. So regardless of whether you are just beginning your journey in the study of forensic psychology or almost finishing it, I trust that you enjoy your time in this fascinating field of study as much as I have.

Dr. Eastwood teaches and conducts research at the University of Ontario Institute of Technology. He lives in Oshawa with his wife Joanna and their three young children— Chloe, Alex, and Lyla. In his free time, he enjoys watching sports and engaging in rousing theological discussions with his seven siblings whenever possible.

In addition, there is growing evidence that because of their neurological and psychosocial immaturity, adolescents are more prone to giving false confessions (Steinberg, 2014a), a topic to be discussed below. They appear to be especially prone to fall for the interrogative strategy of "minimization," in which the alleged behavior is downplayed by the interrogator. ("If I were in your shoes, I probably would have done the same thing.") The juvenile is led to believe that the interrogator will be more lenient and release him or her from custody sooner if he or she cooperates and admits to the alleged behavior. A sobering example is the real life case of the Central Park 5, five teenagers who were convicted of attacking and raping a jogger in 1989. They were later exonerated, but not before one had served 11 years and four had served 7 years in prison. Defense lawyers argued unsuccessfully that their confessions were false, produced by coercive interrogation techniques. Thirteen years after the crime, a prisoner serving a sentence for three rapes and a murder confessed to the attack. His unique knowledge of the crime and a DNA match on the samples recovered from the victim resulted in the original convictions of the teenagers being vacated.

Cleary (2017), following the work of Laurence Steinberg, outlines three interrelated factors that are important in understanding the differences between adolescents and adults during interrogation: (1) reward sensitivity, (2) self-regulation, and (3) future orientation. In reference to *reward sensitivity*, adolescents are far more sensitive to immediate rewards than adults are. They are more attentive to the good things and more willing to take risks to get them immediately. During the long and stressful experience of interrogation, the immediate reward of getting to go home is a powerful one for the adolescent. Research by Drizin and Leo (2004), for example, found that "getting to go home" was one of the most frequent reasons cited for adolescents to falsely confess to a crime they had not committed. Lack of *self-regulation* (self-control) will likely allow the adolescent to take the immediate reward to go home in place of maintaining innocence in the face of the unpleasant confrontation of interrogation. The lack of *future orientation* allows the adolescent to prefer going home immediately without considering the future consequences of admitting guilt. Adolescents "tend to be focused myopically on short-term gains and losses rather than the longer-term consequences for their actions" (Kassin, Perillo, Appleby, & Kukucka, 2015, p. 253). To a large extent, the reward sensitivity aspect of adolescent development appears to override the ability to suppress immediate inappropriate actions in favor of long-term appropriate ones (Casey & Caudle, 2013).

False Confessions

In recent years, a Sundance channel series, *Rectify*, followed the life of a man who confessed to and was convicted of the murder of a young girl when he was 18 and then sentenced to death. He had spent 19 years on death row before being exonerated based on DNA evidence. The series depicts his adjustment to freedom and struggles to cope with his experiences, build new relationships, and repair relationships with his family. It also depicts, in flashbacks, his life on death row. But viewers of the series sometimes wondered, why would he have confessed to something he did not do?

Rectify is a fictional account, but it is not an unrealistic one. As a result of recent DNA exonerations, it has become increasingly clear that a disturbing number of convictions were the result of such false confessions gained through questionable procedures or illegal tactics (Kassin et al., 2007; Kassin et al., 2015). A false confession "is an admission to a criminal act—usually accompanied by a narrative of how and why the crime occurred—that the confessor did not commit" (Kassin et al., 2010, p. 5). These DNA exonerations and other high-profile cases leading to the convictions of innocent people have prompted increased scrutiny of police interviewing and interrogation methods and strategies (DeClue & Rogers, 2012). We must emphasize that only a percentage of DNA exonerations involved false confessions, however. Studies have suggested that about 16% to 25% of the DNA exonerations have involved false confessions (Garrett, 2011; Kassin et al., 2015; O'Connor & Maher, 2009), while a majority have involved inaccurate eyewitness testimony (which also may be a significant factor in false confessions, because suspects confess falsely after having been told that an eyewitness identified them). We discuss eyewitness identification later in the chapter.

Numerous individuals cleared by DNA evidence never confessed to their crimes; on the contrary, they maintained their innocence from the moment of their arrest. (Focus 3.2 highlights the work of the Innocence Project, a research and advocacy group for prisoners believed to have been wrongfully convicted.) However, as the DNA exonerations came rolling in, many stories did involve false confessions and how they were obtained. "Many of these stories recount horrific tales of psychologically—and, in some cases, physically—abusive interrogations of children and adults, including many who were cognitively impaired" (Kassin et al., 2007, p. 382). These stories and the other high-profile cases have underscored the enormous role that psychologists can play in the research, investigation, and prevention of wrongful convictions (Kassin et al., 2010). Kassin (2008) contends that throughout the criminal justice system, confessions are met with naïve and uncritical acceptance. He finds that this naïveté is strongly buttressed by five myths: (1) Innocent people cannot be induced to confess through the use of legal and noncoercive interrogation tactics; (2) police investigators are often convinced they can identify truth tellers from liars during interviews, and consequently feel they are able to determine who should be interrogated; (3) relying on some combination of intuition and corroboration, police officers and other criminal justice personnel can distinguish between true and false confessions; (4) people facing interrogation are protected by their constitutional rights to silence and to counsel; and (5) if the confession was coerced and is erroneously admitted at trial, appellate courts can reasonably determine whether the error was harmless. We reiterate that Kassin stresses that the above are myths, not facts.

At this point, no one can accurately estimate the rate of police-induced false confessions across the United States or the number of wrongful convictions caused by false confessions (Kassin et al., 2010; Leo & Ofshe, 1998), but the research clearly indicates that people can be induced to confess. As mentioned previously, though, it should be understood at the outset that most convictions are the result of the evidence acquired at the crime scene or through witness reports rather than through interrogations and a confession from the suspect.

Nevertheless, when a suspect does confess, the confession is universally treated as damning and compelling evidence of guilt; it is likely to dominate all other case evidence and lead to a defendant's conviction (Leo & Ofshe, 1998). As a society, then, we should be particularly wary of the false confession, as well as the confession that is coerced. According to Leo and Ofshe, American police are poorly trained about the dangers of interrogation and false confession. "Rarely are police officers instructed in how to avoid eliciting confessions, how to understand what causes false confessions, or how to recognize the forms false confessions take or their distinguishing characteristics" (p. 437). This is one important training service that police psychologists should be able to provide, and there is considerable evidence that they are beginning to do that (DeClue & Rogers, 2012; Lassiter & Meissner, 2010; Malloy, Shulman, & Cauffman, 2014). In addition, psychologists have been very active in researching what factors influence false confessions (Meissner et al., 2012; Redlich, 2010).

Most American police are exposed to only a cursory review of interviews and interrogation at the police academy and receive more extensive training when they become detectives or interrogation specialists at the police agency. However, police investigators are often convinced of their ability to tell who is lying and who is not during interviews and interrogations. This confidence stems from some combination of on-the-job experience and police training programs that promise increased accuracy in deception detection (Kassin et al., 2007). Some programs claim an 85% accuracy rate after the training. Unfortunately, research continually reveals that training does not produce reliable improvement. In a majority of research findings, the accuracy rate of police investigators and other professionals improved only slightly better than chance after the training (Kassin et al., 2010).

Interrogation of suspects usually is undertaken after the police investigator(s), on the basis of an interview or investigation, determine or "feel" that the suspect is culpable. Consequently, in many instances, the interrogation process begins with an assumption of guilt, and the tactics employed in the interrogation are intended to break down the anticipated resistance of the suspect.

We must emphasize that estimates of *false* confessions are not high; the great majority of individuals who confess to crimes are probably guilty. In Europe, 12% of prisoners report that they have confessed to crimes they did not commit (Gudjonsson, 2003). In North America, police investigators estimate that about 5% of innocent people confess to crimes during interrogation (Kassin, 2008). Some experts suggest the percentage might be higher (O'Connor & Maher, 2009). But why does even this relatively small number confess? People confess to crimes they did not commit because they are promised lighter sentences, to protect others, because they are mentally ill, because they want to become "celebrities," because they are exhausted after an extensive interrogation process, because they have little faith that they will be believed, as well as other reasons. In addition, some innocent people confess to a crime they did not commit because they come to believe (usually through persuasion) that they actually did do it.

In a summary of the research literature, Kassin and Wrightsman (1985) identified three types of **false confessions**: (1) voluntary, (2) coerced-compliant, and (3) coerced-internalized. The first type, **voluntary false confessions**, refers to a self-incriminating statement made without any external pressure from law enforcement. A well-known example of this type of voluntary false confession, Kassin (1997) notes, is when more than 200 people came forward and confessed to kidnapping the Charles Lindbergh baby, the most famous kidnapping case in U.S. history. Charles Lindbergh was an American hero, the first man to fly solo over the Atlantic Ocean. On March 1, 1932, the first-born child of Lindbergh and his wife, Anne, was kidnapped for ransom and later was found dead. The child was 20 months old. Although Bruno Richard Hauptmann was convicted and executed for the crime, doubts about his guilt have persisted around the case for years. As Kassin notes above, a large number of other individuals confessed to the crime, ostensibly in an effort to receive recognition or fame.

The coerced-compliant and the coerced-internalized false confessions, as their names imply, involve pressure from police officers and sometimes from other persons as well. Research has indicated that skillful manipulation, deception, or suggestive tactics under stressful conditions may lead to false confessions (Gudjonsson, 1992; Kassin, 1997). Persons who are mentally disordered or intellectually disabled are often asked more questions during the interrogation

FOCUS 3.2. THE INNOCENCE PROJECT

It is now clear that some people who are serving time in prisons have been wrongfully convicted. The Innocence Project is an independent nonprofit organization whose mission is to free these individuals and to reform the system that is responsible for their imprisonment. In some cases, the convictions are partly attributable to "false confessions" or to other incriminating statements made to police, but in the majority of cases the individuals have consistently maintained their innocence.

The Innocence Project was founded in 1992 by Barry Scheck and Peter Neufeld at the Benjamin N. Cardozo School of Law at Yeshiva University. DNA testing is the primary means the Project has employed, and by 2017, a total of 350 people in the United States had been exonerated. At least 18 of these individuals had been sentenced to death.

According to the project's website (www.inno cenceproject.org), eyewitness misidentification played a role in over 70% of convictions that were ultimately overturned. Judges and juries had weighed this eyewitness testimony heavily at their trials. Invalidated or improper forensic science, inadequate defense, government misconduct, false confessions, and the testimony of informants also play a role in DNA cases that are ultimately overturned. Daniel Gristwood, the father of five children, was submitted to 15 hours of interrogation, and had no sleep for 34 hours before he provided false statements to police that resulted in his conviction for killing his wife. He spent 10 years in prison before being exonerated (R. J. Norris & Redlich, 2010). The true perpetrator ultimately confessed. Similarly, in the case of the Central Park Five, all of whom spent years in prison, another individual ultimately admitted to the rape. In another example, a man who was mentally disordered, was led to believe he was helping police "smoke out" the real killer of a 16-year-old girl by confessing falsely that he had killed her. As noted in the text, research has found that the mentally disordered are more likely than those who are not to give false confessions.

What happens to individuals who are exonerated? The answer is not clear, and there is likely wide variation in their success at rebuilding their lives. Furthermore, not all states provide financial compensation for the years they have been imprisoned. According to R. J. Norris and Redlich (2010), only 27 states, the District of Columbia, and the federal government do provide for such postexoneration reparation, and only 60% of 250 exonerated individuals have been compensated.

Questions for Discussion

1. Go to the website of the Innocence Project and discuss any two recent cases highlighted there.
2. Should persons wrongly convicted of crime be compensated for the time they have spent in prison? If so, what is the best form of compensation?
3. What role or roles do forensic psychologists have in preventing false confessions?

process and are not surprisingly more confused by the experience (Redlich, Kulich, & Steadman, 2011). They are also more likely to give false confessions than those not disordered or disabled (Redlich, Summers, & Hoover, 2010). Under the stressful circumstances associated with interrogations, even an innocent person may come to believe that he or she is guilty of the crime. Kassin attributes much of the coerced false confession phenomenon to such psychological concepts as compliance and internalization, processes first identified by Kelman (1958). *Compliance* is a form of conformity in which we change our public behavior—but not our private beliefs or attitudes—to appease other people or reduce social pressure or threats from others. *Internalization*, on the other hand, refers to changes in our private thoughts or beliefs that occur because we sincerely believe in the issue or perspective.

Coerced-compliant false confessions, Kassin (1997) concludes, are most likely to occur after prolonged and intense interrogation experiences, especially in situations when sleep deprivation is a feature. The suspect, desperate to avoid further discomfort, admits to the crime even though this person knows he or she is innocent. Some of the original suspects in the

Central Park case apparently confessed at the urging of a parent or because they believed they would then be free to go home after being held at the police station for many hours. Other suspects have confessed to a crime after being told police had incriminating evidence against them, such as that a witness had identified them or their fingerprints were at the scene of the crime. These are examples of compliance without internalization.

Coerced-internalized false confessions, on the other hand, occur when innocent persons—who are tired, confused, and highly psychologically vulnerable—come to believe that they actually committed the crime (Kassin, 1997; Kassin & Kiechel, 1996). This is an example of compliance eventually developing into an internalization of the belief. In addition, the pressures to confess may not necessarily originate from police officers but may come from family members, friends, religious figures, and colleagues who communicate to the suspect that he or she will feel better by doing the right thing and admitting to the offense (or atoning for his or her sins) (McCann, 1998).

Summary

The spate of prisoners who have been cleared in recent years as a result of DNA evidence suggests that something went wrong as they were processed through the criminal justice system. Although many things could have gone wrong (e.g., inadequate assistance of counsel, misidentification by eyewitnesses), we have focused thus far on the interrogation process, which may have resulted in a false confession. However, even a "true" confession can be overturned by the courts if it is illegally obtained, in violation of the suspect's constitutional rights. Law enforcement agents must learn to "do it right." A confession must not be coerced, either physically or psychologically. Determining what, exactly, is psychological coercion can be very difficult, however.

Meissner, Hartwig, and Russano (2010) recommend that, given the number of training manuals and training programs that promote flawed interrogation methods, the ability to offer more effective and sound alternatives is of critical importance. These researchers call for a systematic research-based approach that identifies promising interrogation techniques with which "truth" can be established (Meissner, Russano, & Narchet, 2010). Their proposal urges police psychologists and other researchers to seek opportunities to partner with police investigators in developing interrogation techniques. This integrative approach has proved very successful in the United Kingdom and Canada, as we noted above in discussing the PEACE model (see also Bull & Soukara, 2010).

Meissner and Lassiter (2010) propose five recommendations for reforming police interrogations:

1. Record, preferably on video, all interrogations from beginning to end.

2. Prohibit the use of psychologically manipulative interrogation tactics that have been shown to produce false confessions.

3. Protect vulnerable persons (e.g., juveniles, intellectually disabled persons) in the interrogation room.

4. Ensure the appropriate administration (knowing and intelligent waiver) of *Miranda* rights prior to interviewing a suspect.

5. Train law enforcement investigators regarding factors that contribute to false confessions.

Taking such preventive measures would not only increase public confidence in police, but would also make it far less likely that evidence, including confessions, obtained during the interrogation or interview process will be disallowed from the final trial proceeding.

DETECTION OF DECEPTION

Entertainment media often portray police interviewing witnesses or suspects as being able to tell when they are telling the truth, often through their nonverbal behaviors. As in portrayals of profiling, the media presentation does not mesh with reality. Most forensic psychologists urge caution in dealing with nonverbal behaviors; although some behaviors may suggest that an individual is not telling the truth, there is no sure way to ascertain this. Licking one's lips may indicate nothing more than the fact that one is nervous or thirsty, and it is not unusual to be nervous if one is being interviewed or questioned by law enforcement officials.

This section will be focused on the detection of deception. Deception is behavior that is intended to conceal, misrepresent, or distort the truth or information for the purpose of misleading others. Obviously, the ability or procedure to detect deception would be an invaluable tool for any investigation. Furthermore, the global threat of terrorism "has led to an increased emphasis on the detection of deception in public places, including country borders, security checkpoints, airports, bus terminals, train stations, shopping malls, and sport venues" (Vrij & Granhag, 2014, p. 936).

The detection of deception or lying is an area of psychological research that has the potential to make highly meaningful contributions to investigations ranging from intelligence gathering and criminal interrogations to insurance fraud. However, the research so far has not been particularly promising. Attempts to identify reliable deception techniques have shown an accuracy level of barely above chance (54% to 57%) (Logue, Book, Frosina, Huizinga, & Amos, 2015). In addition, professionals—such as police officers and psychologists—are often no more accurate than laypersons (Gongola, Scurich, & Quas, 2017). More surprising, adults do not appear any better at detecting deception in children than they are at detecting deception in adults (Gongola et al., 2017). And the age of the child did not matter.

Research psychologists have identified three basic processes involved in deception: (1) emotion, (2) behavioral control, and (3) cognitive load (Vrij, 2008; Vrij, Granhag, & Mann, 2010; Zhang, Frumkin, Stedmon, & Lawson, 2013). For many years, it was assumed that emotions were the best indicator of deception. A lie has traditionally been associated with two different types of emotion: guilt and fear of detection (Vrij et al., 2010). It is commonly believed that deception is indicated if a person is nervous and anxious, especially during questioning. For instance, eye contact avoidance, excessive eye blinking, profuse sweating, unusual amount of face touching and rubbing, shaking hands or twitching legs, and nail biting are often assumed to be physical, emotional signs of fear or guilt. However, in recent years, research studies have consistently found that these behavioral patterns are not reliable cues for deception. For example, researchers have found that, rather than avoiding eye contact, liars tend to display more deliberate eye contact than truth tellers (Mann et al., 2013). Furthermore, one of the most important findings reported during the past decade is that very few people—whether professional experts or laypersons—are able to detect deception (or honesty) with much accuracy when relying on emotion-based cues (van Koppen, 2012).

Still, most people—including police investigators—are convinced that they are able to tell who is lying and who is not (Vrij, Akehurst, & Knight, 2006), if not on emotion-based cues, then certainly on nonverbal or behavioral ones. The results here are not impressive either.

According to Vrij et al. (2010), one of the reasons why people make errors in lie detection is that they fail to take into consideration the full complexity of deception. The research on behavioral control cues has generally focused on what attributes make a good liar. Vrij and his colleagues note that good liars possess at least 18 attributes that render deception difficult to identify. These attributes include lack of guilt or fearful feelings, self-confidence, and good acting ability. In addition, this area of research contends that not only do good liars try to continually monitor their own behavior, but they also monitor the interviewer's reactions to their answers to the questions asked (Burgoon, Blair, & Strom, 2008; Vrij et al., 2010; Zhang et al., 2013). Therefore, studies suggest that good liars are fully aware of the common belief that nonverbal cues may signify deceit and thus concentrate on controlling them, such as controlling their own bodily indicators of guilt and nervousness. In summary, the research to date strongly suggests that neither emotions nor nonverbal cues are decent guides for identifying deception.

Vrij and Granhag (2007, 2012) argue that verbal cues may well be better guides. They believe that (1) concentrating on the verbal patterns of the suspect and (2) analyzing the manner in which the interviewer handles the questions will lead to improved deception detection. Vrij and Granhag further maintain that interviewers should create a **cognitive load** on the person being interviewed. In other words, interviewers and interrogators should try to increase the work load of the suspect when answering questions. This is because lying requires considerable cognitive effort, as the deceptive person must actively suppress truthful information and construct and remember false information (Carrión, Keenan, & Sebanz, 2010; Vrij et al., 2008; Vrij, Granhag, Mann, & Leal, 2011). Moreover, liars usually find it very difficult to provide much additional detail to their story, whereas truth tellers usually do not. Essentially, liars often try very hard to keep their story as simple as possible (Granhag & Strömwall, 2002). An effective approach for increasing cognitive load is to ask questions that the suspect does not anticipate, or to ask for more detail to the story (Lancaster, Vrij, Hope, & Waller, 2013). Another approach might be to ask the suspect to tell the story in reverse order (Vrij & Granhag, 2012). This approach increases cognitive load because it runs counter to the usual sequence of telling stories and is therefore more challenging for the suspect. This verbal approach is referred to as **cognitive lie detection** (Vrij, Fisher, & Blank, 2017).

Recent research has demonstrated that the cognitive lie detection approach produces superior results in accuracy detection (67%), lie detection (67%), and total detection (truth and lie detection together of 71%) compared to the usual methods of detection of truth detection (57%) lie detection (47%), and total detection (56%) (Vrij et al., 2017). The results indicate that using the cognitive lie detection method increases the chances of classifying individuals correctly as being either truth tellers or liars.

The Polygraph

Perhaps a more scientific method of attempting to detect truthfulness is the polygraph, commonly called the "lie detector." It is important to emphasize, though, that the polygraph does not really detect lies or deception, but only the neurophysiological responses that accompany emotional reactions to guilt, shame, and anxiety. The instrument usually records heart rate, blood pressure, breathing rate, and skin conductance. *Skin conductance* refers to how well the skin conducts a small, imperceptible electrical current that is affected by slight changes in perspiration. One of the assumed telltale indicators of lying is increased perspiration. Presumably, when one tries to deceive, there are telltale bodily or physiological reactions that can be measured with sophisticated equipment and detected by a trained examiner called a polygrapher. In addition to observing the physiological measures, the skillful polygrapher makes behavioral observations and notations to infer truth or deception in the subject being examined. There is little doubt that the polygraph can accurately measure and record the physiological responses of the peripheral nervous system. Whether it can detect actual lying and deception is another matter. As William Iacono (2008), one of the foremost researchers in this area, notes, "It is generally recognized that there is no physiological response that is uniquely associated with lying" (p. 1295).

The first, crude lie-detection machine was invented by the psychologist William Marston, who also rather astonishingly created the character of Wonder Woman. During its early beginnings in the United States, Marston's polygraph and others like it were used almost exclusively in criminal investigations. As noted by Iacono and Patrick (2014), polygraph testing was commonly used when the question at hand could not be resolved by the available evidence. However, as criminal suspects became more aware of their right not to incriminate themselves, and as civil libertarians challenged the instrument's validity, the use of the polygraph became less common. Furthermore, Congress severely limited the extent to which private employers can use the polygraph with the passage of the Employee Polygraph Protection Act (EPPA), enacted in 1988. This law has, in effect, ended preemployment polygraph screening by *private* employers as well as the periodic testing of employees to verify their good behavior (Iacono & Patrick, 1999). However, we still see examples of suspects volunteering to take a polygraph to clear their names or use of the polygraph in counterintelligence investigations.

One of the problems with the polygraph is the weight that juries are likely to attach to polygraph evidence (Iacono & Patrick, 2014), although some research has questioned this assumption (Myers, Latter, & Abdollahi-Arena, 2006). That is, if the polygraph evidence shows the defendant may be lying, there is a strong tendency for the jury to assume he or she is guilty. "Unlike other types of evidence a jury may hear, polygraph evidence has the potential to usurp the jury's constitutionally mandated task of deciding guilt" (Iacono & Patrick, 2014, p. 649). Consequently, criminal courts normally have excluded polygraph testimony on the grounds that it may unduly influence jury decision making. For example in *United States v. Alexander*, 1975, the court, in reference to admitting polygraph evidence wrote,

> Based upon presentation of this particular form of scientific evidence, present-day jurors, despite their sophistication and increased educational levels and intellectual capacities, are still likely to give significant, if not conclusive, weight to a polygraphist's opinion as to whether the defendant is being truthful or deceitful in his response to a question bearing on a dispositive issue in a criminal case. (p. 168)

However, in some cases, polygraph evidence can be admitted in a criminal hearing or trial in one of two ways. Basically, since a defendant cannot be forced to take a polygraph (*United States v. Piccinonna*, 1989), the defense must introduce it. In one situation, polygraph evidence can be introduced with prior stipulation of both the prosecution and the defense (Myers et al., 2006). Typically, under this condition, "the defendant may take a polygraph test with the agreement that the prosecutor will drop the charges if the test is passed, but may enter the test results into evidence without objection if the test is failed" (Myers et al., 2006, p. 509). About half the states allow this stipulation. The second way polygraph evidence may be introduced in a trial is when the defense asks to include the polygraph test results in the trial over the objection of the prosecution. Under these conditions, a pretrial hearing is normally held to determine if the judge will allow the results to be admitted into evidence. In these cases, the defense believes that polygraph evidence that demonstrates the defendant is not lying improves its case for a not-guilty verdict. Interestingly, despite the ongoing refusal by the courts to allow polygraph results into evidence except under unusual circumstances, the study by Myers et al., referenced above, reveals that jury-eligible adults did not find polygraph evidence to be persuasive in influencing their verdicts.

For the most part, however, the major uses of polygraph testing are in personnel selection or screening by government agencies and certain strategic industries, such as nuclear energy. The government exempted itself from coverage of the EPPA and has expanded the use of polygraph testing because of recent concerns about terrorism and national security (Iacono & Patrick, 2014). Currently, two dozen federal agencies routinely use polygraph screening, including the Departments of Defense, Energy, Homeland Security, and Treasury (Iacono & Patrick, 2014). U.S. governmental counterintelligence polygraph tests far outnumber the tests given at other organizations and at all other agencies (Krapohl, 2002). Furthermore, polygraph screening of police, law enforcement, and governmental security applicants has either remained at the same level or increased in recent years. Twenty years ago, Meesig and Horvath (1995) reported that approximately 99% of the large police agencies and 95% of the small police departments in the United States required the polygraph as an integral and indispensable part of their preemployment screening procedures. There is little reason to believe that this observation is any less true today.

It should be mentioned that the typical polygraph examiner in the United States today does not have graduate psychological or research training, nor are all polygraph examiners licensed or graduates of accredited schools. As posited by Iacono and Patrick (2014), "it is unlikely that a forensic psychologist has administered a polygraph" (p. 613). They go on to emphasize that "polygraphs are administered by polygraphers who work in a profession that is largely disconnected from psychology and informed little by psychological science" (p. 613).

Research on the Polygraph

Many researchers continue to be very wary of the polygraph and its overall accuracy. Historically, professional field polygraphers have claimed extraordinary accuracy rates, ranging from 92% to 100% (Bartol & Bartol, 2004). Most biopsychologists and research psychologists find these statistics to be highly questionable. In addition to occasional arithmetic errors, none of the published reports gave any details of the methods and procedures used or of the criteria used to decide accuracy rates. Currently, the research conducted under laboratory or controlled conditions indicates that the correct classification of truthful and deceptive examinees ranges between 70% and 80% (Krapohl, 2002; Vrij & Fisher, 2016). However, the accuracy can be increased slightly through careful and intensive training of the examiner. Furthermore, in lab studies, computerized polygraph systems, in contrast to human evaluations, are slightly more accurate for detecting both truthful and deceptive respondents (Kircher & Raskin, 2002). Although many polygraphic research studies are available, they are subject to debate when conducted by polygraphers themselves rather than independent researchers (National Research Council, 2003).

The accuracy of the polygraph in detecting who is telling the truth and who is being deceptive is a highly complicated issue.

> A number of factors—such as the specific technique used, the nature of the population tested, the issues to be resolved, the context of the examination, whether one is trying to detect truth or deception, the training of the examiner, what cues the examiner considers besides the polygraphic data, or even whether one is examining the victim or the suspect—all must be carefully considered before any tentative conclusions can be advanced. (Bartol & Bartol, 2004, p. 285)

The specific technique used has come under extensive research scrutiny. Several dominant approaches are used, the most widely adopted being the **Control Question Technique (CQT)**, also referred to as the Comparison Question Test. According to Iacono (2009, p. 229), "Almost all practicing polygraph examiners assert that [the CQT] is nearly infallible." Interestingly, polygraph researchers who are not affiliated with the polygraph profession are generally nonsupportive of the CQT (Iacono & Patrick, 2014). The CQT juxtaposes questions that are relevant to the crime with "control" questions—or questions whose truthful answers are known to the examiner. Physiological responses that differ from responses on control questions are then regarded suspiciously. Although the actual CQT is, of course, far more complex than we present here, its essential feature is the comparison of physiological responses, which only a trained examiner is able to interpret. However, critics of the CQT argue that its reliability and validity have not been sufficiently established through independently conducted research that is separate from the research conducted by the polygraphers themselves.

Researchers are more favorably disposed toward the **Guilty Knowledge Test (GKT)**, one developed by the polygraph expert David Lykken (1959). Although this test is not widely used in the United States, it is used in other countries and is strongly endorsed by researchers

(Ben-Shakhar, 2002; Iacono & Patrick, 2014). The GKT requires that the polygrapher have access to information about the crime that would be known only to the perpetrator and has not been reported to the public. For this reason, it is best at "clearing" innocent suspects, because they are unlikely to exhibit damaging physiological responses to questions revealing details of the crime (Iacono, 2009). The test is impractical, however, because it is often difficult for examiners to obtain details that have not yet been widely circulated. Despite its strong research support, polygraphers do not generally get trained in the GKT and almost invariably use the CQT in conducting their examinations.

In recent years, there has been growing interest in the use of the polygraph in the supervision and treatment of sex offenders (Grubin, 2002, 2008; Iacono & Patrick, 2014). It is believed that the polygraph—compared with case records or offender self-reports—provides more complete and accurate information about an offender's history, sexual interests, and offense behavior, thereby enabling more effective and targeted treatment strategies (Grubin, 2008). Some mental health and criminal justice professionals also think the polygraph is helpful in monitoring behavior and achieving adherence to prevention goals. One survey estimated that in the United States, polygraph examinations were used with 70% of community sex offenders in 2002 (R. J. McGrath, Cumming, & Burchard, 2003). In England, legislation was passed in 2007 that mandated polygraphic testing of sex offenders by the probation service on a trial basis (Ben-Shakhar, 2008; Grubin, 2008).

The use of polygraph testing for sex offenders has been criticized, however. As pointed out by Grubin (2008), the criticism has centered on three main issues: (1) concerns regarding how the polygraphic examinations are conducted, (2) the lack of scientific validity of the procedure, and (3) ethical concerns. Ben-Shakhar (2008) asserts that there are many major flaws in the reliability as well as other scientific shortcomings in polygraph examinations of sex offenders. Some forensic clinicians, however, continue to argue that the polygraph is highly useful in the management and treatment of convicted sex offenders.

FORENSIC HYPNOSIS

Compared with efforts to detect deception, efforts to obtain information by means of hypnosis are quite rare. Nevertheless, they do occur, but typically more with victims of crimes than with suspects. For example, a victim of an aggravated assault who seems to have "blocked out" the appearance of his or her assailant might be hypnotized in an effort to help the victim recall features that would help in identifying the perpetrator. However, this is a procedure that should be used only by highly trained and properly credentialed professionals.

In hypnosis, a mental health, general health, or forensic professional suggests to the participant that he or she try to experience particular changes in sensations, perceptions, thoughts, and behavior. Hypnosis is usually established by what is commonly referred to as an *induction procedure*. Although there are many different induction procedures, most center on suggestions for relaxation, calmness, and well-being. Induction instructions usually include asking the participant to imagine or think about pleasant experiences or things. During the induction, the participant may be sitting comfortably or lying down while concentrating on a "target" (such as a lit candle) and listening to the hypnotist's voice. The participant is usually encouraged to drift into a sleep-like state while always hearing the hypnotist's voice. Overall, most people who do become hypnotized find the experience very pleasant and relaxing.

People differ widely in their responses and susceptibility to hypnosis. "Some people cannot be hypnotized, a few are extremely hypnotizable, and the majority of the population has some moderate capacity to experience hypnosis" (Scheflin, 2014, p. 661). The ability to be hypnotized is believed to be an enduring and stable attribute, which peaks during the life cycle in late childhood and declines gradually thereafter (Spiegel & Spiegel, 1987). Among the factors that are important in inducing hypnosis are the following: (1) the level of trust the participant has in the hypnotist, (2) the participant's motivation and desire to cooperate, (3) preconceived notions the participant has about hypnosis, and (4) the context and reasons for the hypnosis (e.g., entertainment or critical information gathering). Trust, motivation, a strong belief in hypnotism's powers, and a serious context (such as a criminal investigation) inspire most people to become hypnotized, but this does not mean that they will accurately recall events. Apparently, what distinguishes truly being hypnotized from simple behavioral compliance is the person's ability to experience suggested alterations in perception, memory, and mood (Orne, Whitehouse, Dinges, & Orne, 1988).

A person's ability to experience hypnotic suggestions is most often inhibited by fears and concerns arising from some common misconceptions. Contrary to some depictions of hypnosis in books, movies, or other media, people who have been hypnotized do not lose control over their behavior. Hypnotized individuals remain aware of who and where they are, and unless some form of temporary forgetfulness is specifically suggested, they usually remember what transpired during the hypnosis. It has long been known that all the experiences and responses that are elicited during hypnosis can also be produced in a normal state without hypnotic induction (Braffman & Kirsch, 1999). Hypnosis does, however, increase suggestibility. As noted by Braffman and Kirsch, "The only thing which characterizes hypnosis as such and which gives any justification for calling it a 'state' is its generalized hypersuggestibility" (p. 578). The hypersuggestibility aspect, however, is the one feature that is most troubling to forensic investigators and researchers concerned with recollections of witnesses or victims of crime incidents. In fact, "[t]he subject's willingness to accept fantasy as reality during the hypnotic experience, together with the often dramatic vividness of recollections in hypnosis, may inspire great confidence that the recalled material is true to fact" (Orne et al., 1988, p. 25). This *induced* confidence, for example, may soundly convince the witness that his or her ambiguous view of the offender was much clearer than it really was.

Hypnosis has long been used in a variety of ways: as a form of entertainment (getting some people in an audience to do humorous things, presumably without their awareness), as a method to encourage people to give up smoking or lose weight, as a procedure in several branches of medicine for pain reduction, and as a means of enhancing the memory of eyewitnesses and victims in the criminal justice system. A common belief among some practitioners is that hypnosis can exhume long-forgotten or buried memories, such as repressed memories of sexual abuse. This belief has frequently been bolstered by anecdotal or clinical claims describing cases in which previously inaccessible memories have been brought to light by the mysterious hypnotic trance. (We will discuss this topic in more detail in Chapter 11.) Enhancement or revival of memory through hypnosis is known as **hypnotic hypermnesia**. Enhancement or recovery of memory through *non-hypnotic* methods, such as free association, fantasy, or recall technique, is called **non-hypnotic hypermnesia**.

Despite its long and varied history, we do not know precisely how hypnosis works, nor do we understand why some persons are readily susceptible to its influence but others are impervious. We do know that hypnosis seems to trigger few significant changes in bodily function other than those that occur in normal relaxation. We know also that hypnosis is not the same as sleep or a form of sleepwalking.

Hypnotic Trance Theory

Currently, two major theoretical perspectives exist for explaining the mechanisms behind the effects of hypnosis. One perspective, known as the **hypnotic trance theory**, assumes that hypnosis represents a *special state of consciousness* that promotes a high level of suggestibility and changes in bodily experiences. Under this special state, the theory maintains, the hypnotized person may be able to do things that he or she could not do under a normal state of consciousness. For example, the person might regress to childhood and vividly remember or act out events that have been repressed or put out of consciousness for an extended period of time. While in the trance, participants may be instructed to feel little or no pain or to perform acts that they are unable to do when not hypnotized. The hypnotic trance theory holds that individuals can be instructed or trained to sense, feel, smell, see, or hear things that are not possible during normal consciousness. For some individuals, hypnosis can substantially improve their ability to remember things. Generally, trance theory contends that the deeper the "hypnotic trance," the more intense, detailed, and vivid a scene becomes to the participant. Historically, the most influential perspective on hypnotic trance theory was from Ernest Hilgard (1986). The research evidence supporting this position, however, is very slim and overall not very convincing.

Cognitive-Behavioral Viewpoint

The second major theory is referred to as the **cognitive-behavioral viewpoint**, which contends that respondents are not in a special state of consciousness when they *appear* hypnotized. Rather, hypnosis is a product of certain attitudes, motivations, and expectancies toward the "hypnotic state"—not a "true" alteration of consciousness. According to the cognitive-behavioral viewpoint, people who have a positive attitude toward hypnosis and are highly motivated to be hypnotized actually role-play the "trance" by closely following many of the suggestions provided by the hypnotist. For example, when the hypnotist suggests to them that they feel relaxed, they will try to—and probably will—feel relaxed. Or, when the hypnotist suggests their eyes will tear up from staring so long at the target, their eyes will begin to tear.

Theodore X. Barber, one of the chief spokespersons for the cognitive-behavioral perspective (T. X. Barber, Spanos, & Chaves, 1974), hypothesized that the good hypnotic respondent is one who not only has the proper mixture of attitude, motivation, and expectancy, but also has the ability to think and imagine with the hypnotist. According to Barber, the good hypnotic respondent is similar to a person watching a captivating video or movie. This person experiences—sometimes intensely—the emotions and actions portrayed by the actors on the screen. In this sense, the "hypnotized" person is mesmerized by the imagery created in his or her mind.

Martin Orne (1970; Orne, Dinges, & Orne, 1984), who was one of the 20th century's foremost authorities on hypnosis, hypothesized a similar viewpoint to the cognitive-behavioral theory, arguing that role-playing accounts for much of the so-called hypnotic phenomenon. That is, participants act the way they *think* a truly hypnotized individual would act. Orne believed that "a prerequisite for hypnosis is the willingness to adopt the role of the 'hypnotic subject,' with its implicit social contract for uncritical acceptance of appropriate suggestions administered by the hypnotist" (Orne et al., 1988, p. 23). The "hypnotic subject" is willing to relinquish his or her sense of reality temporarily, hold any critical thinking in abeyance, and concentrate on what the hypnotist says. He called this state "trance logic" to describe the behavior of hypnotized participants who appeared to display a "peaceful coexistence between illusion and reality" (Kihlstrom, 2001, p. 754). Orne had found in his research that the material described under so-called hypnotic trances is often inaccurate and embellished with many intervening events that occur between the initial incident and the hypnotic session. It appears that some hypnotic participants are highly susceptible to distortions, suggestions, and leading questions posed by the hypnotist. Particularly if the interrogator is a police officer convinced of the powers of hypnosis, he or she is apt to inadvertently suggest events, details, or behaviors that were not present during the crime. The hypnotized witness or victim, eager to please the interviewer, can easily imagine a scene decorated with subjective fantasies and thoughts in line with the suggestions of the questioner. Under these suggestible conditions, the hypnotized participant may begin to be convinced of the accuracy and power of hypnosis to the same degree as the hypnotist. Furthermore, the participant also may become increasingly convinced of the accuracy of his or her revised account of the imagined scene, in contrast to the original (pre-hypnotic) account.

Hypnosis in Forensic Settings

Orne became well-known as a result of his skillful evaluation of Kenneth Bianchi, the accused "Hillside Strangler" who killed women and girls in the Greater Los Angeles area in the late 1970s. Bianchi maintained under hypnosis that his alter personality, "Steve Walker," had committed the murders. Bianchi's lawyer then argued that because Bianchi was suffering from a multiple personality disorder, he should not be held responsible for the serial murders. Ultimately, he was hoping for a successful insanity defense. Orne, however, was able to convince the court that Bianchi was merely playacting the different personalities while pretending to be hypnotized. Bianchi, because of Orne's testimony, dropped the multiple personality act and agreed to testify against his co-murderer, Angelo Buono, and to accept a life sentence without the possibility of parole. Orne's critical perspective on forensic hypnosis influenced more than 30 state Supreme Court decisions as well as the U.S. Supreme Court. He also developed guidelines for forensic hypnosis that were adopted by the Federal Bureau of Investigation (Kihlstrom, 2001).

When forensic hypnosis is used as a method to recall events that may be anywhere from several hours to several years old, the fundamental assumption is that human memory functions like a videotape: All the events and details are stored completely and accurately and, with the proper procedure, can be recalled or brought to consciousness intact. This assumption, however, is without much research support (Bartol & Bartol, 2004). Human perception and memory are flawed and permeated with inaccuracies and distortions. The frailties of perception and memory, combined with the highly suggestive medium under which hypnosis is conducted, provide a situation in which critical inaccuracies have a high probability of occurring. Memory recall under hypnosis is extremely malleable and manipulatable, especially in highly suggestible respondents (Haber & Haber, 2000). Therefore, leading or suggestive questions may have a substantial effect on the respondents' recall of events after they are hypnotized (Kebbell & Wagstaff, 1998). The danger is particularly high when the forensic examiner is untrained or uninformed about the power of questioning suggestible respondents. In addition, the tendency to make up things to fill the gaps in memory appears to be greater under hypnosis (Orne et al., 1988).

Despite the above findings, some recent research is more favorable toward the use of hypnotic techniques, particularly in the investigative phases of a case. Scheflin (2014) maintains that police have documented many cases in which hypnosis was crucial to the solving of criminal cases. Wagstaff (2008) notes that in some situations, hypnosis can enhance one's memory, and Webster and Hammon (2011) note that enhanced memory recall is particularly likely to occur for material that is personally meaningful. On the other hand, hypnosis also may bring about an increase in false recollections and misinformation.

It is important, therefore, that the forensic psychologist be aware of the research and the many dangers of poorly conducted interrogations or interviews when hypnosis is used, as well as the possible benefits of conducting interviews that retain some elements of hypnosis—such as relaxation techniques or allowing witnesses and victims to give their account of an incident freely and without interruption. Scheflin, Spiegel, and Spiegel (1999) emphasize that "When hypnosis is used for forensic purposes, strict guidelines must be scrupulously followed" (p. 491). As pointed out by some experts in the field, "few would contest the claim that hypnosis produces an admixture of accurate memories, and that any increase in memories is typically accompanied by inaccurate memories that equal or surpass the volume of accurate memories" (Lynn, Boycheva, Deming, Lilienfeld, & Hallquist, 2009, p. 94). Moreover, hypnosis can enhance the confidence in inaccurate memories as well as accurate ones (Lynn et al., 2009). The danger in forensic settings is that witness confidence, pertaining to inaccurate memories, can potentially lead to wrongful convictions.

In sum, hypnosis can be a useful tool if used properly and with the understanding that it is no shortcut or replacement for standard investigative procedures (Scheflin, 2014;

Scheflin et al., 1999). After extensively reviewing the literature on the topic, Wagstaff (2008) concluded that, despite many misconceptions about hypnosis, it should not be banned outright as an *investigative* technique. Indeed, some of the procedures associated with hypnosis, like meditation, relaxation, and eye closure, can yield useful information. It can help, for instance, when trauma has occurred, and it is difficult for the person to mentally or physically revisit the scene without the relaxation and concentration states that can be accomplished through this procedure.

EYEWITNESS EVIDENCE

Police officers routinely interview witnesses to a criminal incident. Typically, this task requires attempts at some form of identification of the offender, especially the facial and other physical features, but also of the events that transpired before, during, and after the incident. These tasks require the accurate recall and recognition of something or someone the witness has observed, often for the first time and often under stress.

The identification of suspects by witnesses begins as soon after the offense as possible. Police investigators usually obtain verbal descriptions of the perpetrators from witnesses or show them photographs to obtain a preliminary identification. In some instances, the police will have witnesses look over photos of individuals with previous criminal records, either to identify the specific offender or to obtain an approximation of the offender's appearance. Police agencies routinely ask witnesses to examine a group of photographs (photo boards, photo spreads, photo arrays, mug shots) that are fairly well matched to the physical characteristics described by the witnesses, including the person the police suspect to be the guilty party if they have a suspect in mind or in custody.

Eyewitness Testimony

Before we proceed, it is important to realize that eyewitness testimony is one of the most influential pieces of evidence admitted into the courtroom, especially if the witness claims to have actually seen an offender committing a crime. Jurors appear to have a strong tendency to accept eyewitness testimony at face value, even if the testimony is contradicted by other types of forensic evidence (e.g., fingerprints, blood type, DNA). "Few categories of evidence are as compelling to members of a jury as eyewitness evidence, a fact long acknowledged by judges" (Semmler, Brewer, & Douglass, 2012, p. 185).

Importantly, eyewitness perception and memory are among the most heavily studied processes in experimental psychology and are extremely relevant to the practice of forensic psychology. For over 100 years, psychological research has continually underscored the fact that memory and recall of past events are at least partially unreliable and highly susceptible to numerous influences. In reference to eyewitness testimony in forensic settings, Frenda, Nichols, and Loftus (2011) write, "In the wake of more than 30 years of research, an ever-growing literature continues to demonstrate the distorting effects of misleading postevent information on memory for words, faces, and details of witnessed events" (pp. 20–21). Today's researchers continue to find new paradigms for studying the limitations on memory as well as methods for improving it (e.g., Luke, Crozier, & Strange, 2017; Strange & Takarangi, 2012). (See Perspective 4.1 in Chapter 4, in which Dr. Strange describes her memory research.)

In two surveys conducted by Simons and Chabris (2011), nearly 40% of those surveyed believed that the testimony of a single confident eyewitness should be enough to convict a criminal defendant. Simons and Chabris conclude, "This discrepancy between science and popular beliefs confirms the danger of relying on intuition or common sense when evaluating claims about psychology and the mind" (p. 6). Other studies find that U.S. law students and undergraduate students have very limited knowledge about factors that affect the reliability of eyewitness memory (Wise & Safer, 2010). These findings strongly suggest that the same misconceptions also exist in jurors and perhaps many court officials. In a study by Loftus (2013), she found that potential jurors held many beliefs that are contradicted by psychological science. Interestingly, it appears that U.S. defense attorneys are more knowledgeable about eyewitness memory than prosecuting attorneys or judicial personnel, and their knowledge corresponds well with that held by memory experts (Magnussen & Melinder, 2012; Wise, Pawlenko, Meyer, & Safer, 2007; Wise, Pawlenko, Safer, & Meyer, 2009).

In recent years, Loftus (2013) identified a shift in research on eyewitness memory. She writes that the contemporary research is not so much about the factors that affect the accuracy of eyewitness testimony anymore, but rather "about whether people in general and jurors in particular are knowledgeable about those factors" (p. 557).

Eyewitness research also has shown that suggestive questioning and suggestive lineup procedures can have enormous effects on eyewitness testimony (Wells & Loftus, 2013). In many cases, the eyewitness is highly inaccurate about what he or she saw and heard. "Memories for events that never occurred are readily confused with memories for actual events, and mistaken eyewitness identifications are readily confused with accurate eyewitness identifications" (Wells & Loftus, 2013, p. 627). Unfortunately, law enforcement, prosecutors, and the courts have been reluctant to utilize the rapidly emerging eyewitness research by forensic and research psychologists. Law enforcement officers, for example, often do not know how to interview eyewitnesses without contaminating their observations by asking leading and highly suggestive questions.

Loftus (2013) notes, however, that things are beginning to change, with the biggest boost to public appreciation of eyewitness research coming through forensic DNA testing, as indicated earlier in the chapter. Courts also are increasingly more willing to allow experts on eyewitness research to testify in criminal cases, although typically only if the defendants are able to afford them (see, for example, Focus 3.3).

Cognitive Interview

The cognitive interview (CI), described briefly earlier in the chapter, represents a significant improvement in eliciting relevant information from witnesses or victims. In the typical (noncognitive) interview, the police interviewer dominates the conversation and the interviewee plays a subordinate role. The police will ask a number of specific, short-answer, true or false questions until the interviewer has exhausted his or her list (Fisher & Geiselman, 2010). In addition, the interviewer will often interrupt to ask follow-up questions which are usually leading or suggestive. In many cases, the interviewer is focused on completing the predetermined written checklist required by the department.

In order to obtain as much pertinent information about the incident as possible, the CI takes a very different approach. For example, the interviewer is encouraged to allow the witness to dominate the narrative as much as possible. In CI, the investigative interviewer skillfully and gently guides the witness (or victim) through a number of steps (Fisher & Geiselman, 2010). During the early stages of the interview, the interviewer tries to build rapport with the witness and allows and encourages him or her to describe their emotional feelings at the time of the incident. The interviewer then uses four retrieval prompts designed to restore the original state of the experience. The first prompt is to ask an open ended question of what happened, without interruptions. In the second prompt, the witness or victim is asked to close his or her eyes and try to recount the incident again. Studies of the CI have revealed that eye closure leads to more focused concentration and better accuracy (Vrij, Mann, Jundi, Hillman, & Hope, 2014). Vrij et al. write, "eye closure frees up cognitive resources that would otherwise have been involved in monitoring the environment and subsequently improves memory" (p. 861). The third prompt requires the witness to retell the story in reverse order, from the end to the beginning. The reverse order helps improve the memory of the incident as well as correct errors

FOCUS 3.3. EYEWITNESS IDENTIFICATION: COURTS IN VIRGINIA WEIGH IN (*PAYNE V. COMMONWEALTH*, 2016)

Deante Payne was convicted of two counts of robbery and the use of a firearm during a felony. His conviction was based solely on the testimony of the victim, who was accosted in an apartment laundry room by two men after arranging to buy a laptop computer. One man held a gun, the other held a knife to the victim's side. Payne was charged by prosecutors as having the gun, but he denied being involved in the crime and suggested that a third person might be involved. (Police interviewed the third person, and one detective mentioned in an e-mail that this individual looked like Payne, but the e-mail was not allowed into evidence.)

Because Payne was indigent, his defense counsel requested funds to pay for an expert to testify on the unreliability of eyewitness testimony. That request was denied by the trial judge. Before the case went to the jury, Payne's lawyer asked that the judge instruct jurors that they could consider such factors as the effect of lighting or the stress on the victim and how that might influence his identification of the perpetrator. The judge refused to do that, saying such information would only confuse the jury.

As noted in the chapter, eyewitness testimony can be very fallible, which is not to say that eyewitnesses are wrong. An eyewitness, including the direct victim of a crime, can be credible, and they may think they are accurate, but they are not necessarily reliable. A long line of psychological research makes this clear.

Payne was convicted and sentenced to 9 years imprisonment. His lawyers appealed to an intermediate appellate court, lost there, and then to the Virginia Supreme Court. The American Psychological Association submitted an amicus brief on Payne's behalf, urging the Virginia Supreme Court to rule that the requested jury instructions should have been given. The brief also indicated that psychological research in the area of eyewitness testimony was highly reliable. The Court in December 2016 upheld the lower courts, saying there was no indication of errors made by the courts below.

Questions for Discussion

1. *Payne v. Commonwealth of Virginia* has been appealed to the U.S. Supreme Court, but at this writing it is unknown whether the Court will agree to hear it. Discuss why the Court should or should not hear this case.
2. Is it reasonable for trial judges to refuse to instruct a jury on a matter because it might be too confusing?
3. Payne was unable to afford an expert testifying on his behalf. Based on the facts mentioned above as well as material in this chapter, do you think an expert witness would have made a difference in this case?

of omission. The fourth prompt asks the witness to describe the event from the perspective of others (Memon, Meissner, & Fraser, 2010).

According to Fisher and Geiselman (2010), the CI has demonstrated effectiveness in improving witness memory in many studies in the United States, England, Germany, and Australia. It has been shown to be effective across cultures, types of witnesses (young, elderly, cognitively impaired) and kind of event to be recalled (crime, accident, daily activities).

Identifying the Face

As described above, courts—particularly criminal courts—rely heavily on eyewitness recognition as critical evidence either for or against the defendant. An accumulation of scientific studies, however, demonstrates that the accurate recognition of a relatively unfamiliar face is an extremely complex and error-ridden task (Bartol & Bartol, 2004, 2013). Research also reveals that the accuracy of facial recognition depends greatly on the type of face being recalled. For reasons unknown, some faces are easier to identify than others. Highly unique faces, for example, are better recognized than plain or average faces (Chiroro & Valentine, 1995;

M. E. Cohen & Carr, 1975; MacLin & Malpass, 2001). Faces that are high and low in attractiveness also are easier to recognize than faces judged to be of medium attractiveness (Shepherd & Ellis, 1973). Because attractiveness is subjective, this may not be a helpful finding. Not surprisingly, the longer a person views a face, the better its recognition at a later time (MacLin, MacLin, & Malpass, 2001).

In some cases, computerized or artist drawings of the face from descriptions supplied by the eyewitnesses or victims are done to help identification—these are called **facial composites**. However, studies have shown that constructing and viewing facial composites may hinder identification accuracy and one's memory for the suspect's face (Topp-Manriquez, McQuiston, & Malpass, 2016).

Unconscious Transference

On occasion, witnesses identify persons they have seen at some other time and place as the perpetrators of a more recent crime. This phenomenon, called **unconscious transference**, occurs when a person seen in one situation is confused with or recalled as a person seen in another situation. It is called "unconscious" because people do not realize they are doing it. A witness may have had limited exposure to a face (e.g., in a grocery store) and, on seeing the face at a later time, may conclude that it is the offender's. Loftus (1979) believes that unconscious transference is another feature of the fallible and malleable nature of human memory, where earlier input becomes "tangled" with later input. As we noted above, research has continually shown that human memory is not like a videotape or smartphone that stores things exactly as seen. Rather, memory is continually changing or being revised in line with our cognitive beliefs and versions of the world. Most psychologists would agree that "memory is a risky route to figuring out the past" (Turtle & Want, 2008, p. 1245).

The phenomenon of unconscious transference illustrates that it is highly possible that a fast-food worker who is witness to a robbery of the restaurant might incorrectly identify as the perpetrator an occasional customer who may have some of the features of the actual culprit. However, for unconscious transference to occur, the previous encounters with the innocent face must have been relatively brief. *Frequent* encounters with customers by the witness are unlikely to trigger unconscious transference involving those particular customers.

Own-Race Bias (ORB)

There is now considerable evidence that people are much better at discriminating between faces of their own race or ethnic group than faces of other races or ethnic groups (Bartol & Bartol, 2015). Researchers call this phenomenon **own-race bias (ORB)**, or it is sometimes referred to as "own-race effect" or "cross-race effect." Scientific research across a wide band of cultures and countries has documented ORB, and it exists across diverse ethnic groups (Hugenberg, Young, Bernstein, & Sacco, 2010; Meissner & Brigham, 2001; Sporer, 2001). Unfortunately, ORB accounts for many identification errors, or false alarms. *False alarms* refer to any situation where a witness identifies the wrong person as the offender. Although the frequency of false alarms seems to be increasing in our society, racial attitudes or prejudices do not seem to account for this phenomenon in a majority of cases (Meissner & Brigham, 2001). Nonetheless, it is disturbing that such a high number of DNA exonerations based on mistaken identification involved that of black suspects (Innocence Project, 2014).

Although there are several possible explanations for ORB, the most popular is called the **differential experience hypothesis**. The hypothesis states that individuals will have greater familiarity or experience with members of their own race and will thus be better able to discern differences among its members. Furthermore, it is the frequency of meaningful and positive contacts with other races that develops the skill to differentiate among racial or ethnic faces (MacLin & Malpass, 2001; Yarmey, 1979). For example, having close friends of other races or ethnicities is more likely to promote better facial recognition than having frequent but casual exposure. Furthermore, additional support for the differential experience hypothesis is provided by studies that show that training in face familiarization significantly reduces the other-race effect (Hancock & Rhodes, 2008; Sangrigoli, Pallier, Argenti, Ventureyra, & de Schonen, 2005; Tanaka & Pierce, 2009). The typical witness to a crime has not had such training, however.

In summary, the research literature is consistent in concluding that people have difficulty recognizing unfamiliar persons of other races. Moreover, this phenomenon may be far too often responsible for the misidentification of numerous suspects who were later convicted but ultimately cleared by DNA evidence.

PRETRIAL IDENTIFICATION METHODS

Forensic psychologists have long known that pretrial identification methods are especially vulnerable to biases and error, and many forensic researchers emphasize that mistakes made by victims or witnesses are honest ones. They truly believe that the individuals they are identifying are the culprits or that the events they are recalling are accurate. However, researchers have discovered that the exact methods used by police, ranging from very blatant practices to more subtle innuendo, can influence the witness's identification. One of the most heavily studied topics is the suspect lineup.

Lineups and Photo Spreads

When police have a suspect in custody, it is not unusual to place the suspect in a lineup with typically two to five other individuals, in the hope that a victim or other witness will be able to identify the suspect as the perpetrator. (See Photo 3.1.) This is called a **simultaneous lineup**. The individuals also may be shown to the witness one by one, a procedure called a **sequential lineup**. Which lineup procedure is more accurate? As noted by Moreland and Clark (2016), early studies indicated that the sequential lineup demonstrated a large accuracy advantage over the simultaneous lineup. However, later studies, beginning in 2012, began to show that simultaneous lineups may be more accurate (e.g., Dobolyi & Dodson, 2013; Mickes, Flowe, & Wixted, 2012). At this point, "the simultaneous-sequential debate is far from settled" (Moreland & Clark, 2016, p. 280). Even more commonly, though, with or without someone in custody, police show photos or video clips of each individual, simultaneously or sequentially. As just noted, legal psychologists have traditionally recommended greater use of the sequential approach, and it is becoming more common, particularly for photo arrays (Police Executive Research Forum [PERF], 2013). Interestingly, law enforcement agencies report their most commonly used methods for eyewitness identification are the photo lineup or photo array (94.1%); show-ups (61.8%—to be discussed below); composite sketches (35.5%); mugshot books (28.8%); and the live lineup (21.4%) (PERF, 2013). Regardless of which method is used, we must keep in mind all of the previously mentioned problems with eyewitness identification (e.g., identifying a face, the fallibility of memory, own-race bias).

▶ **Photo 3.1** A woman points her finger at the person she believes she saw committing a crime. The woman also will have to verbally identify the person by number.
Source: © iStock.com/ RichLegg.

Legal psychologists have been particularly interested in research on the live lineup, because this is where mistaken identification seems more likely to occur. In the live lineup, the witness or victim may be influenced by the comments or behavior of police or by the construction of the lineup itself. Interestingly, courts do not necessarily rule for a defendant, even if the lineup was a suggestive one. Other factors are taken into account, such as whether the witness was confident, how much time had elapsed between the crime and the identification, and whether the witness's description of the perpetrator was consistent over time. However, the U.S. Supreme Court, in a number of cases, has ruled that a lineup may not be *impermissibly* suggestive.

Live lineup members in particular should fit the description the witness gave police. In other words, they should have similar characteristics—such as age, height, physical stature, race, hairstyle, and facial hair—that were included in the original witness description. It is also well-known that, before appearing in lineups, many suspects will try to change their appearance to mislead eyewitnesses, if they have the opportunity to do so (Cutler, Penrod, & Martens, 1987). If the witness remembered the offender as a 6-foot, 6-inch individual with black, curly hair and a beard, the lineup is obviously biased if only one person in five fits that description. This would be an example of **composition bias**.

Another area of pretrial identification that must be closely monitored is that of **commitment bias**. This is the concept that, when a witness has initially identified a face, even an incorrect one, he or she will be more likely to choose that face again. Commitment bias is most likely to occur when witnesses are eager to please police investigators and when they further assume that the police have good evidence against someone in the pretrial identification process. Because of commitment bias, a witness who initially identifies a suspect, but who has some doubt, is more likely to identify the suspect in subsequent exposures with greater conviction. In other words, each time the witness identifies the suspect as the perpetrator of the crime, the witness becomes more convinced that this was indeed the person who committed the crime.

The tactics taken by police during the lineup proceeding also may influence the witness or victim. For example, an officer may subtly nod or may ask, "Are you sure?" This behavior communicates approval or disapproval of the choice made. To avoid this possible influence, legal psychologists (e.g., Steblay, Dysart, & Wells, 2011; Wells, 1993) advocate that the person conducting the lineup not be aware of the identity of the suspect—an approach called the double-blind lineup. If the lineup conductor is not aware of the identity of the suspect, he or she cannot give subtle cues to the witness or victim.

One controversial pretrial identification procedure is called the **show-up**. "This is an identification procedure in which police present a single suspect to the eyewitness(es) to see if the eyewitness(es) will identify that person as the perpetrator" (Wells, 2001, p. 795). Unlike the lineup, there are no distractors or foils in a show-up procedure. A *distractor* or *foil* is anyone in the lineup who is not the suspect. A show-up is legal in the United States as long as it occurs soon after the offense (within hours) or under circumstances that would make a lineup impracticable or impossible. For example, if a crime victim is hospitalized and not likely to live, police may bring in a suspect for identification (*Stovall v. Denno*, 1967). This is not a frequent scenario, though. Show-ups are more likely to occur when police drive a victim by someone on the street and ask whether he or she is the perpetrator, or when they interview a witness and point out another person with whom police are talking. In 2012, the U.S. Supreme Court heard a case (*Perry v. New Hampshire*) in which a witness identified a suspect from her apartment window, while he was handcuffed by police. In an 8–1 decision, the Court ruled that this was not inappropriately set up by police. We highlight this case again in Chapter 4. As noted above, the PERF (2013) survey indicates that show-ups are a very common method of securing eyewitness identification nationwide. Research indicates that show-ups are far more likely to lead to mistaken identification than lineups (Wells, 2001). This is because in a lineup, the error of mistakenly identifying a suspect is spread out among the foils and distractors. Even in a sequential lineup, the witness is aware that other possibilities will be presented. In the show-up situation, on the other hand, there is only one choice, right or wrong. To confirm and formalize the identification, show-ups are often followed by a live lineup once the suspect is in custody. Although this is a reasonable precaution, confirmation bias is likely to be at work. The victim or witness has already identified an individual as the perpetrator and is unlikely to change his or her identification at a later time. Interestingly, in the New Hampshire case mentioned above, the witness who identified the suspect from her apartment window was unable to pick him out of a photo array later at the station. Nonetheless, the initial identification was allowed into evidence.

In 2001, the American Psychology-Law Society, in an effort to make certain that forensic psychologists and personnel in the criminal justice system were aware of ways to improve lineup procedures, published a comprehensive document known as the "Police Lineups" white paper (Wells, 2001). To protect the rights of everyone accused of crime, the white paper made four recommendations for implementing valid procedures in conducting lineups or photo spreads (see Wells et al., 1998). First, the panel recommended that the person *putting together* the lineup or photo spread know which member is the suspect; however, the person *administering or conducting* the lineup should *not* know. In addition, the eyewitness should be informed that the person administering the lineup does not know which person is the suspect in the case. This recommendation is designed to prevent the witness from looking for subtle clues or identifying information from the officer administering the lineup. This has come to be called the **double-blind lineup**, mentioned above. It indicates that neither the witness nor the officer administering it is aware of the true suspect. Second, eyewitnesses should be clearly told that the suspect might *not* be in the lineup or photo spread. Under these conditions, the witness will not feel compelled to make an identification if he or she does not believe the suspect is in the lineup. Third, the suspect should not stand out in the lineup or photo spread as being clearly different from the distractors, based on the eyewitness's (or eyewitnesses') previous description. Fourth, a clear statement should be taken from the eyewitness at the time of identification, prior to any feedback from the police that would inform the witness whether he or she had chosen the "right" suspect. This last recommendation is based on the observation that witnesses are often susceptible to inadvertent or intentional communication about the suspect during the lineup or immediately after it occurs. Findings from the white paper were incorporated into a 44-page government guide for law enforcement officers working with eyewitness identification (Reno, 1999).

Since these recommendations were made, numerous forensic psychologists, legal scholars, and prisoner advocacy groups have pushed for changes in the procedures used in police lineups. The sequential lineup is preferred by many, but other researchers are concerned that it may result in guilty persons not being identified because the witness may believe a better match will appear (S. E. Clark, 2012). Many agencies thus allow the witness to go through the photo array or view the live sequential lineup more than once. However, some research suggests that care must be taken with allowing multiple laps through the choices because these multiple viewings (more than two) lead to guessing and placing innocent suspects at risk (Horry, Memon, Wright, & Milne, 2012; Steblay, Dietrich, Ryan, Raczynski, & James, 2011).

Supporters of sequential lineups also assert that the double-blind procedure, whether the lineup is sequential or simultaneous, has the greatest likelihood of avoiding misidentification and protecting suspects who are truly innocent. As noted previously, if the person conducting the lineup is unaware of the identity of the suspect, he or she cannot give even subtle cues to the witness. At least two states (New Jersey and North Carolina) and several jurisdictions (e.g., Madison, Wisconsin; Boston, Massachusetts; Virginia Beach, Virginia) have implemented the sequential double-blind as standard procedure in lineups (Innocence Project, 2010). Approximately one third of jurisdictions that use photo or live lineups now use a sequential procedure (PERF, 2013), but most of these do not use the double-blind approach, apparently because it is difficult to find an officer who does not know the identity of the suspect. Interestingly, most agencies have no written policies for conducting eyewitness identification procedures, although large agencies (with 500 or more sworn officers) are more likely to have such a written policy (PERF, 2013).

SUMMARY AND CONCLUSIONS

The psychology of investigations is a fertile area for research and practice. It began officially in the United States with the work of the FBI's Behavioral Science Unit and in the United Kingdom with the investigative psychology propounded by psychologist David Canter. It focuses on identifying features of a crime and likely characteristics of its perpetrator. The generic term *profiling*, as used in this chapter, is subsumed under this topic, but many psychologists who consult with police during the crime-solving process prefer not to be called "profilers." We discussed five overlapping forms: crime scene profiling (often called criminal or offender profiling), suspect-based profiling, geographical profiling, psychological profiling, and the psychological autopsy. It is important to realize, though, that these terms are very often used interchangeably in the literature. In addition, profiling may be used in areas that do not involve criminal investigation, particularly in the case of psychological profiling and psychological autopsies.

Crime scene profiling, though not a dominant activity performed by most forensic psychologists, has gained considerable media attention. If done correctly, it can provide statistical probabilities of features of an individual, including an offender, but it is far from a foolproof procedure. Again, many if not most forensic psychologists who engage in this endeavor prefer to call themselves behavioral analysts, and there is continuing interest in promoting a more scientific approach to the procedures they employ. The global term "investigative psychology" is often used to emphasize this.

Suspect-based profiling—which gathers together characteristics most likely to be possessed by someone committing a certain crime—is extremely controversial because the characteristics used have included race, ethnicity, and religious affiliation. When these characteristics are at the forefront of the profiling activity, they are illegal.

Geographical profiling analyzes spatial characteristics to yield probabilities of a perpetrator residing or offending in a particular location. It is used primarily to solve serial crimes, in which a pattern of offending occurs over time. It is more likely to yield positive results when combined with criminal profiling, although we must caution that the scientific status of the latter remains in question.

Psychological profiling focuses on describing the characteristics of a known individual or individuals, and it may or may not have anything to do with crime. A psychological profile may be extensive, based on a multitude of documents, reports, psychological measures, and interviews with the person or others who know the person, or it may

be quite simple, based on just a few measures. Mental health professionals have offered psychological profiles of individuals ranging from American presidents to notorious serial killers. These profiles may be interesting to read, but they are rarely submitted to empirical scrutiny.

Psychological autopsies—more formally called reconstructive psychological evaluations—are performed after a person has died and the manner of death is uncertain or equivocal. The psychologist conducting the autopsy tries to reconstruct the victim's behavior and thought processes leading up to the death. This procedure is often used in cases of apparent but questionable suicide. As yet, there is no established, standard method for conducting a psychological autopsy, and its validity has yet to be demonstrated.

We discussed some of the reasons profiling is difficult. Chief among these is the fact that much of human behavior is not consistent across different situations. Dynamic risk factors of an individual, particularly those that are acute—such as mood swings and drug-induced effects—contribute to this lack of consistency. In addition, crime scene evidence does not necessarily relate to specific psychological characteristics of the perpetrator. Although some professional profilers are cautious about the power of their predictions, others are too ready to rely on unsubstantiated assumptions, some of which are based on outdated interpretations of personality theory. In sum, profiling—though fascinating to the public— is an enterprise that must be approached with extreme caution, at least until research demonstrates that it has greater predictive validity.

The psychology of investigations also includes research and practice in broader areas, such as interviewing and interrogation, the detection of deception, polygraphy, forensic hypnosis, facial recognition, eyewitness identification, and lineups. Essentially, we have included in this chapter a variety of areas in which practicing and research psychologists have much to offer law enforcement agencies in their investigations of crimes.

The methods used by police in interviewing and interrogating witnesses and suspects have received considerable attention in forensic psychology. Three main problems can be identified: Many people, including juveniles, do not understand their constitutional rights, many confess to crimes because they are coerced, and some people confess to crimes they have not actually committed. Legal psychologists have been critical of the dominant method of interrogation advocated in the United States, and many are recommending a shift to a less confrontational form of questioning in order to lessen the likelihood of coercion and false confession. Researchers and practitioners in other Western nations (e.g., Canada, the United Kingdom, Australia) have been prominent in developing methods of interviewing that emphasize interaction rather than confrontation and encourage interviewees to tell a story rather than respond to forceful questioning. The PEACE model, HUMINT interrogations, and the cognitive interview are illustrations of these alternative methods.

Researchers also have looked carefully at the ability of anyone—including police officers—to detect deception in others. Traditional beliefs about nonverbal behavior have given way to beliefs that other methods are more fruitful. For example, rather than focusing on a suspect's fidgeting behavior, interviewers could increase the cognitive load placed on him, such as by asking him to review his actions on a given day in backward sequence. Some legal psychologists also note that encouraging someone to tell his or her story in an open-ended manner provides more information that can then be reviewed for accuracy.

The polygraph, as a method of detecting deception, is used in a wide variety of criminal and civil contexts. In law enforcement, it is used primarily in the selection of candidates for law enforcement positions and much less in criminal investigation because courts have generally found its results inadmissible. Police may still administer polygraphs if suspects willingly take them, however. The dominant method is apparently the CQT, though questions are raised about its validity. Many researchers favor the GKT, but it is an impractical tool because it requires that the polygrapher know details of the crime that are not generally known to the public. Results from polygraph tests are not admitted into courts against the wishes of criminal defendants, but they have been allowed in some courts to support a defendant's contention that he or she did *not* commit the crime. It appears that the polygraph is also being used more extensively in counterintelligence and by federal agencies than it has been in the past. Polygraphs are also used to monitor offenders in the community who are on probation or parole; this is particularly the case for sex offenders. Like the other techniques discussed in this chapter, the polygraph has not garnered impressive research results with respect to reliability and validity. Nevertheless, some researchers do support its use in limited situations and when administered by highly trained polygraphers.

We ended the chapter with a discussion of forensic hypnosis, eyewitness identification, and the construction of police lineups. Hypnosis is a controversial topic, particularly when used to elicit repressed memories of traumatic events in victims of crime. It may also be used to enhance recall of nonvictim eyewitnesses to a crime. Although the weight of the scientific evidence is still very much against its use, research over the past decade has begun to challenge early assumptions.

One of the most consistent findings in experimental psychology is the fallibility of memory and its impact on eyewitness recollection of events. For over 100 years, researchers have documented that the testimony of eyewitnesses, especially witnesses to traumatic events, may be believable, but it is often not reliable. Multiple witnesses to one event often report different versions of the event, even when they firmly believe their own version is the accurate one. In the criminal justice area, errors in eyewitness recall have led to false confessions and to wrongful convictions. Continuing research in this area is gradually brought to the attention of the courts, and police are sometimes trained in more effective interviewing skills to minimize the problems in eyewitness identification.

In recent years, psychologists have made significant research contributions relating to the construction and administration of police lineups, but some of that research is equivocal. For example, while a long line of research initially supported the sequential lineup over the simultaneous lineup, recent research has challenged that, and the matter of which method is better remains unsettled. Double-blind lineups—where neither the witness nor the officer conducting the lineup is aware of the identity of the suspect—are highly recommended, though. Some research recommendations have been incorporated into government guidelines used by law enforcement officers nationwide, but many agencies do not have written policies for conducting lineups.

KEY CONCEPTS

Accusatorial approach   91
Actuarial predictions   89
Clinical predictions   89
Coerced-internalized false
    confessions   101

Coerced-compliant false
    confessions   100
Cognitive interview (CI)   93
Cognitive lie detection   103
Cognitive load   103

Cognitive-behavioral
    viewpoint   108
Commitment bias   115
Composition bias   115
Confirmation bias   90

QUESTIONS FOR REVIEW

1. What three questions are central to the process of investigative psychology?

2. Distinguish among the five types of profiling covered in the chapter.

3. Distinguish between geographical profiling and geographical mapping.

4. What are the three types of false confessions?

5. What suggestions have psychologists offered for improving the police interviewing and interrogation process?

6. In light of research findings on deception, how can investigators best detect deception on the part of persons being interviewed?

7. List any five findings from the research on (a) the polygraph and (b) hypnosis.

8. List five findings from the research on eyewitness identification.

9. What recommendations were made by researchers regarding lineups and photo spreads in the "Police Lineups" white paper to increase the reliability of identifications made in these lineups?

SAGE edge™

Want a better grade? Go to **edge.sagepub.com/bartol5e** for the tools you need to sharpen your study skills. Access practice quizzes, eFlashcards, an action plan, and SAGE journal articles for enhanced learning.

LEGAL PSYCHOLOGY

CHAPTER FOUR

CONSULTING AND TESTIFYING

"The cross-examining attorney had just asked the psychologist on the witness stand how much she was getting paid. After she answered, the attorney moved a little closer to the witness stand, just barely visibly wet his lips with his tongue, and then, in a booming voice, demanded,

'That's a great deal of money, isn't it, doctor?'

The psychologist paused before answering. Then she leaned forward a little, and in a quiet, assured voice, answered,

'Not at all. It is exactly the right amount of money, given how much time I have worked on this evaluation and given my training.'" (Brodsky, 2012, p. 138)

Chapter Objectives

- Introduce the reader to the court system.
- Describe the judicial process.
- Define and describe what is meant by expert testimony.
- Discuss the legal standards for the admission of scientific evidence in the courtroom.
- Provide a brief overview of forensic risk assessment.
- Describe and discuss the duty to warn and duty to protect.
- Discuss confidentiality and ultimate issue testimony as they relate to expert witnesses.

The psychologist is a common sight in the courtroom today, both on the witness stand and, less frequently, sitting at the defense or prosecution table as a jury or trial consultant. Even when psychologists are not actually in the courtroom, their presence may be felt in the reports they have prepared or sworn statements they have made that are entered into the court record. As another example, in a criminal case, the judge at a sentencing hearing may have access to a psychological report detailing an offender's mental status or assessing the likelihood that he would benefit from substance abuse treatment in a community setting.

Very early in the case, when attorneys are gathering information and preparing their trial strategy, a psychologist may be called to testify during a deposition. **Deposition** refers to proceedings during which potential witnesses are questioned by attorneys for the opposing side, under oath and in the presence of a court recorder, although typically away from the courtroom. For example, lawyers for a plaintiff in an employment-discrimination suit may depose the psychologist who administered and evaluated promotional exams.

Psychology's entry into the courtroom did not come easily. Until the 1960s, psychiatrists were the only mental health experts recognized in many courts. Those courts that *did* welcome psychologists tended to limit their tasks to very specific areas, such as reporting on the results of intelligence tests or personality inventories. Criminal courts were particularly reluctant to accept expert testimony from a nonmedical professional when a defendant's criminal responsibility or sanity was in question. Because mental disorder was considered a disease, the professional with a medical degree—the psychiatrist—was believed to be the appropriate expert. Although there were exceptions, for the most part, the courtroom was the province of the psychiatrist in such cases, not the psychologist.

In 1962, however, a federal appeals court in *Jenkins v. United States* ruled that the lack of a medical degree did not automatically disqualify psychologists from providing expert testimony on the issue of mental disorder. Jenkins had pleaded not guilty by reason of insanity to sexual assault charges. Interestingly, the judge at his trial had allowed psychologists to testify that he did not have the required mental state to be found responsible, but the judge then told the jury to disregard the psychologists' testimony. "A psychologist is not competent to give a medical opinion as to a mental disease or defect," the judge said. Jenkins was convicted, but he appealed his conviction, claiming that the judge's instruction to the jury violated his right to due process. The federal appeals court agreed and ruled that a psychologist with proper credentials could indeed provide expert testimony on the issue of mental disorder. Gradually, after the *Jenkins* case, psychologists began to testify not only on issues relating to mental disorder, but also on a wide range of issues about which they were conducting research. To some extent, they had done that in the past, but the decision in the *Jenkins* case opened the door even wider. Thus, they testified and provided data on subjects as diverse as the influence of pretrial publicity on juries, memory, the reliability of eyewitness identification, stereotyping, and the influence of advertisements on consumers.

This chapter will offer many additional examples of psychologists working directly in courtroom settings, testifying, or consulting with lawyers at tasks relevant to the judicial process. Although most of us are familiar with the appearance of a courtroom either from personal experience or from media portrayals, knowledge of how courts are set up and how a case proceeds through various stages is less common. Therefore, the chapter begins with a brief overview of the structure and process in both criminal and civil courts along with illustrations of how psychologists may interact with the legal system at each phase of this process.

COURT STRUCTURE AND JURISDICTION

In the United States, federal and state courts exist side by side, independently of one another, sometimes in the same geographical location. In most sizable cities, one can find municipal or county courts in one building and the federal court building not too far away. This **dual-court system** exists to recognize the unity of the nation as a whole, on one hand, and the sovereignty of the 50 individual states on the other. Among their many functions, federal courts interpret and apply the U.S. Constitution and acts of Congress; settle disputes between states or citizens of different states; and deal with such specialized matters as bankruptcies, copyrights, and patents. Persons accused of violating federal criminal laws are also processed in federal courts. State courts interpret and apply state constitutions and laws passed by state legislatures. They also settle disputes between citizens or between the government and citizens within the state.

All courts, federal and state, are either established under the U.S. Constitution or the constitutions of the various states, or are created as needed by Congress or state legislatures. In the federal system, some judges—those appointed under Article III of the Constitution—have lifetime appointments, contingent on good behavior, making theirs a highly desirable position. Judges in legislative courts—those appointed under Article I of the Constitution—have time-limited rather than lifetime appointments. A good example of Article 1 judges is the approximately 300 judges who serve in the nation's 58 immigration courts. Among other immigration-related matters, these courts have the important role of deciding whether persons charged by the Department of Homeland Security with violating immigration laws or persons seeking asylum should be deported or allowed to remain in the United States.

History, including very recently, has numerous examples of vacancies on the federal bench because of political delays in confirming appointments of Article III judges nominated by the sitting president (Bartol & Bartol, 2015). Vacancies contribute to what is widely recognized today as an overwhelming workload for many federal courts. As of early April 2017, for example, there were 126 vacancies on federal courts. In 2015 and 2016, the vacancy on the U.S. Supreme Court created in 2016 by the death of Justice Antonin Scalia became a major political issue. The Republican-controlled U.S. Senate refused to consider the candidate proposed by then President Barack Obama, and the Court worked with eight rather than nine Justices until April 2017, when Justice Neil Gorsuch was confirmed by a Senate that split sharply along political party lines. In order to confirm Justice Gorsuch, the Senate changed its rules to allow a simple majority vote to confirm a Justice to the U.S. Supreme Court. The vote was 54 to 45.

The constitution or the legislative enactment also specifies the court's jurisdiction, or authority. All courts have **subject matter jurisdiction** and **geographical jurisdiction** as outlined in the law. For example, a family court may have authority over divorce, custody, adoption, and delinquency matters (subject matter jurisdiction) in a given county within the state (geographical jurisdiction). Many courts have only **limited jurisdiction,** or limited authority, meaning that they can only settle small disputes or deal with preliminary issues in a major case. By contrast, courts of **general jurisdiction** have broad authority over a vast array of both simple and complex cases, both civil and criminal. **Appellate jurisdiction** refers to a court's authority to hear appeals regarding decisions of lower courts.

Courts present an often-confusing array of physical structures, terminology, and individuals with an equally confusing array of titles and roles. Some court proceedings are conducted at a table in the basement of a town hall at 10 p.m., whereas others are conducted in dignified, velvet-curtained surroundings. Increasingly today, court proceedings— particularly at the early stages of a case—are conducted via closed-circuit television. A person being detained in jail, for example, may "appear" before a judge for a bail-reduction hearing. However, the individual who was charged with a crime is in the jail, and the judge is in his or her courtroom 5 miles away. Via closed-circuit television, the judge may reduce the bail and communicate to the person the conditions under which he or she is being released.

The structure of the federal court system is actually quite simple, especially at the appellate level, with one Supreme Court—the court of last resort—and thirteen Circuit Courts of Appeal. (See Table 4.1.) At the trial court levels are courts of general jurisdiction (U.S. district courts) and limited jurisdiction (e.g., magistrate judge's courts, bankruptcy courts).

By contrast, state court structures can be quite complicated. No two state court systems are identical, leading to the often-made comment that we have 51 very different court systems in the United States: the federal system and the systems of each of the 50 states. Nonetheless, common features exist. Like the federal system, all states have trial and appellate courts, with the trial courts being divided into those of limited

▶ **Photo 4.1** A judge presiding over a drug court addresses a defendant.
Source: Daniel Acker/Bloomberg via Getty Images.

Table 4.1 Structure of the Federal Court System
Highest Appellate Court
U.S. Supreme Court
Intermediate Appellate Courts
U.S. Courts of Appeals
12 Regional Circuit Courts of Appeals
1 U.S. Court of Appeals for the Federal Circuit
Trial Courts
U.S. District Courts
94 judicial courts
U.S. Bankruptcy Court
U.S. Court of International Trade
U.S. Court of Federal Claims
Federal Courts and Other Entities Outside the Judicial Branch (e.g., immigration courts)
Military Courts (trial and appellate)
Court of Veterans' Appeals
U.S. Tax Court
Federal Administrative Court
Tribal Courts

very lowest level are courts overseen by a justice of the peace or a magistrate who presides over minor civil and criminal matters. This level also may include municipal courts—sometimes called traffic courts, night courts, or city courts. These lower courts are courts of limited jurisdiction and typically cannot conduct major civil trials or felony trials.

At the next level are county courts, which have been called the "workhorse of the average judiciary" (Abraham, 1998, p. 155). County courts are courts of general jurisdiction, handling a wide range of both civil and criminal cases. Every state also has a court of last resort, which is the highest appellate court in that state, and some states have two, one for criminal appeals and one for civil appeals. Not all have *intermediate* appeals courts, though. In addition, states often have a variety of specialized courts, which deal only with particular matters. Examples include family, drug, mental health, veterans', and domestic violence courts (see Photo 4.1). Most recently, some large urban areas around the country are seeing the establishment of girls' courts, which are intended primarily to provide counseling and support services to girls and young women who have been arrested for prostitution or are at risk of being victimized by the sex-trafficking industry (P. L. Brown, 2014). Specialized courts are often of particular interest to psychologists because of the subject matter with which they deal. A primary example is the mental health court (see Focus 4.1).

The federal and state systems intersect when a case moves—or attempts to move—from the state court to the federal courts. Although there are a variety of ways in which this can happen, perhaps the most common is when an individual has lost his or her case after having exhausted all appeals in state courts. If a substantial federal question has been raised, the case may be heard in the federal courts. For example, when a state law is said to violate the U.S. Constitution or to otherwise impinge on federal law, the federal courts may ultimately decide whether it truly does. A recent example of this was *Obergefell v. Hodges* (2015), the ruling that declared that state bans against same-sex marriage violated the Fourteenth Amendment due process and equal protection clauses. It should be noted that the Supreme Court has virtually unlimited discretion as to whether it will accept a case for review. The U.S. Supreme Court decides to hear about 80 cases of the 7,000 requests that are submitted to the Court each year. Generally, the Justices decide another 50 cases without hearing arguments—that is, on reviewing documents alone. The cases they select to hear usually address constitutional issues or federal law, particularly when federal courts of appeal have come to different conclusions.

Civil and Criminal Courts

The distinction between criminal and civil courts essentially refers to the type of case being heard. In large courthouses, specific rooms are set aside for criminal proceedings and others for civil cases. In small communities, the same courtroom may be used for a criminal trial one week and civil proceedings the next. Furthermore, the same judge may be presiding over all.

Civil and criminal cases can be distinguished according to who brings the action and, to a lesser extent, the disputative versus punitive nature of the proceedings. In a civil case, two or more parties (litigants) approach the legal system, often seeking resolution of a dispute. In the most common of civil actions, the plaintiff seeks relief or a remedy from the defendant (who may also be called the respondent), maintaining that he or she has been personally harmed. This relief or remedy could come in the form of a court injunction (an order to stop some practice), a protective order (such as an order to remain beyond a certain distance from an individual), or damages (a money award) for losses suffered. Although civil cases are normally between private

FOCUS 4.1. MENTAL HEALTH AND OTHER PROBLEM-SOLVING COURTS

Mental health courts are a possible solution to the vexing problem of crime—typically minor crimes—committed by individuals with mental disorders. While serious crimes allegedly committed by persons with mental illness gain media attention, these are not the usual offense. Crimes committed by the mentally disordered are more typically trespassing, burglary, public intoxication, petty larceny (e.g., shoplifting), or simple assault (e.g., shoving or hitting).

Although mental health courts operate in different ways, most involve an immediate screening by a mental health clinician or team, which then makes a treatment recommendation to the presiding judge. Defendants or their guardians may have to consent to go to this specialized court, but avoiding placement in a traditional jail setting is a strong incentive for doing so. Some mental health courts accept defendants only after they have pleaded guilty to a criminal offense. In that case, the judge orders mental health treatment as a condition of probation and supervises the progress of this treatment. Ideally, psychologists or other mental health professionals associated with the court work cooperatively with the judge to follow the individual through the course of treatment.

When mental health courts first came on the scene, observers expressed a range of concerns (Hasselbrack, 2001; Goldkamp & Irons-Guynn, 2000; Steadman, Davidson, & Brown, 2001). It was feared that judges had too much power over decisions that should be made by clinicians, that there was not sufficient time for mental health professionals to conduct comprehensive assessments, and that resources were not available to provide recommended treatment. In recent years, however, mental health courts have been evaluated and received good reviews, presumably appeasing some of the earlier fears (Heilbrun et al., 2012; Luskin, 2013).

Interestingly, media accounts have sometimes prompted needed changes in the operations of mental health courts. For example, investigative reporters in Broward County, Florida, found a backlog of more than 1,200 cases and also found that the average defendant in mental health court waited 3 years for his or her case to be heard, compared with 6 months in regular court. Procedures changed quickly as a result, with more rapid screening of defendants and diversion to treatment of those seriously mentally ill ("Mental Health Court," 2017).

Mental health courts and other problem-solving courts (e.g., drug courts, domestic violence courts) continue to face numerous challenges, including adequate funding, and they require continuing research attention. Like the mental health courts, drug courts have been subjected to many evaluation studies and meta-analyses and have received positive reviews (Hiller et al., 2010), but mixed reviews are not uncommon (Morgan et al., 2016; Shannon, Jones, Perkins, Newell, & Neal, 2016). It is obvious that continuing research is needed to judge their effectiveness as well as that of newer problem-solving courts, such as the girls' courts and veterans' courts mentioned in the text.

Questions for Discussion

1. What are the advantages and disadvantages of having courts that specialize in certain groups of individuals, like the mentally disordered, substance abusers, or veterans charged with crimes?
2. Are some groups of individuals more deserving or more needful of special courts than others? Offer arguments and cite research in support of your answer.

individuals or organizations, governments also may be involved. For example, a state may file a civil action against an employer for allegedly discriminatory hiring practices, in violation of the state's antidiscrimination laws. A criminal case, on the other hand, involves an alleged violation of rules deemed so important that the breaking of them incurs society's formal punishment, which must be imposed by the criminal courts. In a criminal case, the government, represented by the prosecutor, brings the action against the individual, called the defendant.

Sometimes, the lines between civil and criminal cases are blurred. In most states, for example, if a juvenile is accused of committing a crime, he or she will most likely be brought to a juvenile or family court, which is considered a civil rather than a criminal setting. Juvenile courts are more informal and are typically closed to the public. However, they include aspects of criminal proceedings. For example, the juvenile has a right to a lawyer and the opportunity to confront and cross-examine his accuser and other witnesses.

Disputes between private persons or organizations, such as breaches of contract, libel suits, or divorce actions, are clearly civil cases. Certain actions, however, can incur both civil and criminal penalties. This often happens in cases involving corporate malfeasance: for example, the offshore oil spill in the Gulf of Mexico, which cost the lives of 11 oil workers and is now recognized as the worst environmental disaster in U.S. history; and civil and criminal charges filed against major banks and credit card companies. Furthermore, persons charged with crimes are sometimes sued in civil courts by victims of their families, even if their criminal case ends in acquittal. An oft-cited example is the infamous O. J. Simpson case, wherein Simpson was found not guilty in 1995 of the murders of Nicole Brown Simpson and Ronald Goldman but was later found responsible for their deaths in a civil proceeding. Simpson was later found guilty of a different crime, armed robbery, and spent 9 years in prison. He was granted parole in July 2017 and was released in October of that year.

Despite media coverage suggesting the opposite, most cases reaching the courts are civil rather than criminal, and civil cases are often more complex. The backlog of civil disputes is very high, and the process of achieving settlement can be tedious. In addition, civil courts deal with extremely emotionally wrenching issues, including the personal disputes that occur among family members and intensely personal matters such as those requiring end-of-life and other medical decisions.

THE JUDICIAL PROCESS

The judicial process consists of a series of steps or stages through which litigants proceed. In high-profile or complex cases, the process can be very lengthy, sometimes taking years to complete, especially in civil cases. In the 1990s, tobacco and asbestos litigation cases threatened to immobilize the courts. Even relatively simple cases can get bogged down in the courts, however. These delays can be problematic in both criminal and civil cases, for all parties involved and for many different reasons. For example, in criminal cases, evidence deteriorates, and crime victims, as well as defendants, are held in abeyance. The defendant also may be confined in jail, unable to post bail. In civil cases, both plaintiffs and defendants have their lives on hold until the court proceedings have been terminated. On the other hand, delays also can be functional, such as when they encourage a settlement, allow more extensive investigation, or uncover new witnesses who may come forward and help absolve an innocent defendant.

It is helpful for our purposes to divide the judicial or court process in both criminal and civil cases into four broad stages: (1) pretrial, (2) trial, (3) disposition, and (4) appeals. Various court appearances and hearings can occur at each of these stages, and there are many illustrations of what psychologists can contribute. In the discussion below, we will emphasize those proceedings at each stage that are most likely to involve the assistance of the forensic psychologist. Unless otherwise specified, the discussion relates to both civil and criminal cases. In addition, although we describe a process that is typical in courts across the United States, the proceedings and what they are called may vary across jurisdictions.

The Pretrial Stage

The courts can become involved in a *criminal* case very early, when police contact a judge or a magistrate to obtain a *warrant* to search or to arrest a suspect. Most arrests and many searches do not require warrants, however. For example, an officer does not need a warrant to arrest someone who is observed committing a crime, and courts have allowed a variety of "warrantless" searches of persons, homes, and possessions (e.g., during a lawful arrest; in exigent circumstances; to prevent the destruction of evidence). Police cannot search a person's cellphone without a warrant, however (*Riley v. California*, 2014), nor may they place a GPS tracking device on a vehicle without first obtaining a warrant (*U.S. v. Jones*, 2012). In a case to be decided during the 2017–2018 term, *Carpenter v. U.S.*, the Court will rule on whether investigators may obtain cell phone records from a third party, such as a service provider, without a warrant. In general, though, a court's first contact with a criminal case is either at the initial appearance or the arraignment. However, in the federal system and some states, the prosecutor must obtain an indictment from a grand jury very early in the process. The **grand jury** is a body of citizens that reviews the evidence provided by the prosecutor and decides whether there is sufficient evidence to indict (formally accuse) the individual. Although grand juries rarely come to public attention, this changes when a grand jury decides not to indict an individual in a controversial case, such as a police shooting.

Someone arrested must be given an **initial appearance**—typically within 24 hours—if he or she is held in jail rather than released or cited to appear in court at a later date. At this initial appearance, a judge or magistrate must ensure that there are legal grounds to hold the individual, such as probable cause to believe the person committed the crime with which he or she is charged. Because jail detention can be an extremely stressful occurrence, detainees may be screened for evidence of mental disorder or psychological crisis. Although jail officers or social caseworkers can perform this initial screening, a consulting psychologist or psychiatrist may be called in if a detainee appears to be in major psychological crisis. Some large jails have psychologists, psychiatrists, or other mental health professionals on staff, but the typical jail setting employs them on a contract or as-needed basis. As indicated above, communities across the United States are experimenting with mental health and other problem-solving courts to divert some defendants away from traditional criminal courts.

The next pretrial step relevant to psychological practice is the **arraignment**, an open proceeding at which formal charges are read. The arraignment can occur very soon after the arrest or even months later. At the arraignment, the presiding judge asks defendants if they understand the charges, informs them of their right to counsel, and asks them to enter pleas. At this point, it is not unusual for persons charged with minor offenses and even many felonies to plead guilty and receive an immediate fine or sentence. Others plead *nolo contendere*, indicating that they will not contest the charges but are not admitting their guilt. For purposes of the criminal law, a nolo contendere plea has the same effect as a guilty plea; that is, a conviction is entered on the record.

Since the 1990s, forensic psychologists and psychiatrists have given considerable attention to the issue of a person's competency to plead guilty (Grisso, 2003; Melton, Petrila, Poythress, & Slobogin, 2007). This is an important matter because approximately 90% to 95% of criminal defendants plead guilty at arraignment or change their not-guilty plea to guilty before a trial date (Neubauer, 2002; Redlich, Bibas, Edkins, & Madon, 2017). Another possible plea—one highly relevant to forensic psychology—is not guilty by reason of insanity (NGRI), which is actually a not-guilty plea accompanied by notice that insanity will be used as a *defense*. When an NGRI plea is being considered, the forensic psychologist or psychiatrist is typically asked to examine the defendant and determine whether an insanity defense could be supported. This evaluation—called a criminal responsibility (CR) or mental state at the time of the offense (MSO) evaluation—is usually requested or arranged by the defense lawyer. A separate inquiry, to determine whether the defendant is competent to stand trial, may be conducted at the request of the defense lawyer, the prosecutor, or the presiding judge. Criminal responsibility and competency examinations will be covered in detail in Chapter 5.

The not-guilty plea sets the trial process in motion. The next step is one or more pretrial hearings, during which witnesses, arresting officers, and other parties may present evidence. Numerous decisions may be made during these hearings. They include whether evidence (e.g., an eyewitness identification or a confession) is admissible, whether a trial should be moved because of extensive pretrial publicity, whether a youth should be transferred to juvenile court (or to criminal court), whether a defendant is competent to stand trial, and whether bail should be denied because of the alleged dangerousness of a defendant.

Forensic psychologists are involved extensively during the pretrial stage in both juvenile and adult criminal cases. In cases where a judge must decide whether a juvenile's case should be heard in criminal court or in juvenile court, psychologists frequently assess the juvenile and file a report (or testify) as to the juvenile's level of development and ability to be rehabilitated. As noted above, when the mental health of a defendant is in question, the psychologist is again called on to perform an assessment. If a defendant is subsequently determined not competent to stand trial, psychologists may be involved in treating the defendant to restore competency—although the psychologist treating the defendant should not be the forensic psychologist who evaluates the defendant's competency. Defendants also may be evaluated with reference to their potential dangerousness or risk to the community if allowed free on bail pending their next court appearance.

The pretrial process in *civil* cases has parallels to the above but many differences as well. The plaintiff's lawyer files a complaint outlining the alleged wrong and the desired remedy. The defendant (or respondent) is served with the complaint and is given a time limit in which to respond. As in criminal cases, there may be extensive negotiation between parties. In addition, there are depositions and pretrial conferences with the judge in an attempt to facilitate a settlement. In civil cases, forensic psychologists are more likely to be involved behind the scenes, consulting with one or the other attorney in the preparation of a case. A neuropsychologist, for example, may be asked to conduct a variety of tests on a plaintiff who is suing her employer alleging that hazardous work conditions resulted in a near-fatal accident and substantial injury to the brain.

The **discovery process** is an important component of the pretrial process in both criminal and civil cases. This requires each side to make information at its disposal available to the other side in the preparation of its case. The exact type of information to be made known to the other side is regulated by statute. However, there is a constitutional requirement, established in the U.S. Supreme Court case *Brady v. Maryland* (1963), that prosecutors inform defense lawyers about information that might *exculpate* (or help clear) the defendant. Unfortunately, there is anecdotal evidence and case law from many jurisdictions that the *Brady* decision has been interpreted in different ways, and that the obligation is often not honored. For example, prosecutors may say the source of the exculpatory evidence is not reliable and therefore the evidence does not have to be turned over. Some prosecutors have also waited until the last possible moment before turning over the information, placing the defense lawyer at a disadvantage. The defense lawyer is not bound to inform the prosecutor of evidence that might *inculpate* (or work to the detriment of) his or her client. However, if the defendant plans to raise a defense based on mental state (e.g., insanity or duress), the defense lawyer is expected to share the contents of a *court-ordered* psychological evaluation with the prosecutor.

As part of the discovery process, depositions (defined earlier in the chapter) may be required. The deposition is part of the court record, and information therein may well reappear at the trial. Recall that potential witnesses are questioned under oath and in the presence of a court reporter. Forensic psychologists who are deposed are advised to review the transcript of a deposition very carefully, in the event that clerical errors might have been made (Otto, Kay, & Hess, 2014).

The Trial Stage

In both criminal and civil cases, trials follow a similar pattern of stages. If it is to be a trial by jury (as opposed to a trial before only a judge, called a **bench trial/court trial**), the first step is to select jurors from a jury pool that is representative of the community. The process of selecting jurors from a pool for a particular trial is relevant to those forensic psychologists who serve as trial consultants to lawyers. In all jury trials, potential jurors are questioned by lawyers and sometimes by the presiding judge. This process, formally called the **voir dire**, is done to uncover bias and to attempt to produce an objective jury. Most states do not allow extensive questioning of potential jurors regarding their backgrounds and attitudes, however (Lieberman, 2011). Therefore, although the voir dire allows lawyers to select individuals whom they believe will be sympathetic to their case, there are limits to what it can uncover. When jury consultants are involved, they have often gathered information about potential jurors from public records or even from interviews with their acquaintances. The lawyer can then use this information in forming questions to ask of a potential juror, but the judge will not necessarily allow them. The consultant also may sit at the defense or prosecution table and make inferences based on a potential juror's nonverbal behavior or reaction to questions. These inferences are then communicated to the lawyer who has hired the consultant, and the lawyer must decide whether to "strike" the individual from the jury.

Lawyers have two avenues by which to strike or remove a potential juror. One, the **peremptory challenge**, allows the lawyer to reject a potential juror without stating a reason. Based on a "gut feeling" or on the recommendations of a consultant, a lawyer may decide that a given individual would not be receptive to the lawyer's side. The U.S. Supreme Court has placed some limitation on these challenges, ruling that they may not be exercised on the basis of race or gender (*Batson v. Kentucky*, 1986; *J. E. B. v. Alabama*, 1994). For example, a lawyer cannot remove all women from a jury because the lawyer believes women would not be sympathetic to his client. If the presiding judge suspects that this is being done, the judge must inquire into the lawyer's reasons to ensure that the peremptory challenge is not being used in a discriminatory fashion. In the most recent U.S. Supreme Court case on this issue, *Foster v. Chatman* (2016), the Court by a 6–2 majority affirmed the importance of avoiding discrimination in the jury selection process. Foster was convicted of capital murder and sentenced to death. Prior to selecting jurors, however, prosecutors had made a list of potential jurors and clearly highlighted the race of black individuals—they then successfully removed four black persons whom they had targeted by using their peremptory challenges. Records also indicated how they had prepared to justify their removal by citing other reasons, which the Court found were nonpersuasive. Although lower courts of appeals had rejected Foster's claims, the Supreme Court sent the case back to the state for a new trial.

The second avenue for striking a potential juror is the **challenge for cause**. Here, a specific reason for removing the individual is offered. For example, the potential juror may have had a past relationship with one of the parties or may even be an outspoken advocate on a matter that is crucial to the case at hand. A potential juror who has already formed a strong opinion of the case is also apt to be removed "for cause."

During the opening arguments, the presentation of evidence, the cross-examination of witnesses, and the closing arguments, forensic psychologists who serve as trial consultants may continue to sit near the defense or prosecution table, conducting tasks similar to those performed during jury selection. Alternately, they may be working behind the scenes helping an attorney in ongoing case preparation, including the preparation of witnesses. The most visible role for psychologists during the trial as well as the pretrial is that of expert witness. These topics will be covered in some detail in the pages ahead.

The Disposition Stage

In a criminal case, when a judge or jury renders a verdict of not guilty, the case is over and the defendant is free to go, unless he has been found not guilty by reason of insanity, which will be discussed in the next chapter. If the defendant is convicted, however, a decision must be made whether to incarcerate the individual and, if so, for how long. In death penalty cases, a separate proceeding occurs during which the jury must decide whether to impose the ultimate penalty or an alternative life sentence.

At sentencing, judges may order convicted offenders to undergo treatment, such as substance abuse treatment for addicts or psychological treatment for sex offenders. The role of the forensic psychologist at sentencing can be a critical one. He or she may be asked to evaluate a defendant's potential for responding favorably to such treatment. The psychologist also may be asked to assess the risk for violent behavior, a topic to be discussed shortly.

In civil cases, when a verdict favors the plaintiff, a judgment is handed down, specifying the remedy to be borne by the defendant or respondent. In deciding on a remedy, judges and juries often consider testimony relating to the psychological harm a plaintiff may have suffered. This is not unusual in cases involving work injuries, sexual harassment, or harm suffered from defective products, to give just a few examples. It should be noted that the juvenile process—which is civil—also might involve a "sentence," which is called a **disposition** in juvenile courts. Here, psychologists may be asked to offer opinions on the type of rehabilitative strategies that could be used for a particular juvenile.

In many felony cases, sentencing judges will have obtained a **presentence investigation (PSI)** report. This is a document that has been prepared by an agent of the criminal justice system (typically a probation officer) or by a private firm. The PSI is a social history that includes information about the offender's family background, employment history, level of education, substance abuse, criminal history, medical needs, and mental health history, among other factors. PSI reports often include a *victim impact statement*, which is a summary of what the victim suffered—both physically and emotionally—as a result of the crime. Victims themselves as well as people close to them also have the right to speak out at sentencing. Psychologists who have examined the offender or the victim may submit a report that is appended to the PSI report. Alternatively, information obtained by psychologists may be included within the document itself.

The Appellate Stage

Neither civil nor criminal cases necessarily end with the trial and disposition stages. Defendants who are losing parties have a variety of options for appealing their convictions, their sentences, or the judgments against them. A person convicted of a crime may appeal his or her conviction on a number of grounds, including police errors, mistakes made by judges or attorneys during the pretrial or trial stages, faulty instructions given to the jury, or inadequate assistance of counsel. Likewise, sentences may be appealed for being disproportionate to the crime committed or on the basis of errors made during the sentencing hearing. The vast majority of criminal appeals are unsuccessful; roughly 1 out of 8 criminal appellants wins on appeal (Neubauer, 2002). A "win" does not mean that the convicted person will be free, however. When appeals courts rule in favor of convicted offenders, they almost always order new trials, a resentencing, or a lower court review of the case consistent with the appellate court's decision.

It should be noted that a prosecutor cannot appeal a not-guilty verdict (this would violate the Constitution's prohibition against double jeopardy), but he or she can appeal a sentence that is considered too lenient, though this is very rarely done. Death sentences must be appealed at least once, by law. If the first appeal is unsuccessful, public defense lawyers and groups who oppose the death penalty often continue seeking grounds for appeal until the moment of execution. The grounds do not necessarily involve irregularities in sentencing, though. They may involve new evidence, the death row inmate's mental state, or the manner in which the execution will be carried out.

Today, one common area of appeal in death penalty states is the lethal injection drug protocol used to put prisoners to death. Interestingly, some companies manufacturing the common drugs used have been reluctant to market them for that purpose and they have been less readily available. In 2017, the state of Arkansas attempted to execute in rapid succession eight death row inmates before the drug supply ran out—and it succeeded in executing four over a two-week period. Opponents of the death penalty have argued that one drug in particular—midazolam—commonly administered as the first drug in a three-drug protocol—did not sufficiently dull the senses and constituted cruel and unusual punishment in violation of the Eighth Amendment. A widely publicized botched execution in Oklahoma in 2014 and other midazolam-related executions in Florida, Ohio, and Arizona led some judges to stay executions, and in Ohio, Governor John Kasich delayed scheduled executions until a suitable drug protocol could be found. In 2015, however, the U.S. Supreme Court ruled 5–4 that Oklahoma's drug protocol did not violate the Constitution (*Glossip v. Gross*, 2015).

Appeals of civil cases often revolve around a defendant's appeal of a judgment or a jury award. Jury awards may be compensatory or punitive; compensatory damages are based on the actual harm the plaintiff suffered, while punitive damages are intended to place extra punishment on the person responsible. Defendants have often appealed large damage awards—particularly punitive awards—and some judges have reduced these awards. Legal psychologists have been very involved in studying how jurors arrive at these awards and the factors that lead to excessive awards that are later reduced. Interestingly, however, research reveals that "overall, jurors perform relatively well in determining liability and damages" (Robbennolt, Groscup, & Penrod, 2014, p. 468). Citing a number of studies on this issue, Robbennolt et al. also note that punitive damages are "infrequently sought, infrequently awarded, typically not extremely large, and rarely collected in the amounts awarded" (p. 471). Judgments in civil cases also are notoriously difficult to enforce, and when defendants do not comply, plaintiffs must initiate further legal action. "The arduous process of litigation may prove to be only a preliminary step to the equally protracted travail of collecting the award" (Neubauer, 1997, p. 331).

Although researchers are avidly interested in this area, the appellate stage is not one in which forensic psychologists frequently consult or operate. Nevertheless, the individual forensic psychologist may have considerable stake in the outcome. In some cases, the psychologist's role during the earlier stages of the case may itself be in question. During the 1980s, for example, many individuals convicted of child sexual abuse appealed their convictions on the basis that psychologists who had interviewed alleged victims unduly influenced their testimony. In other cases, convictions have been overturned and individuals granted a new trial because of questionable credentials or testimony presented by a mental health expert. Perhaps the most direct connection between the forensic psychologist and the appellate stage is the filing of **amicus curiae** (friend of the court) **briefs**. An amicus brief is a document filed by interested parties who did not participate directly in the trial but either have a stake in the outcome or have research knowledge to offer the appellate court (Saks, 1993). Amicus briefs are typically filed by organizations on behalf of their members. The American Psychological Association, for example, has filed numerous briefs with state and federal appellate courts on topics such as involuntary civil commitment, marriage equality, sexual orientation, affirmative action, false confessions, professional licensing, child testimony in sexual assault cases, the forced medication of inmates, and the effects of employment discrimination. (Briefs are often filed in cases that involve eyewitness testimony, as illustrated in the previous chapter. Focus 4.2 includes information from another such amicus curiae brief on that topic.)

Appellate courts do not necessarily rule in accordance with the weight of the social science evidence. Even when they seem to weigh such evidence heavily, additional clarification may be needed. A good case in point is *Atkins v. Virginia* (2002), which involved the execution of individuals who are intellectually disabled. The brief writers argued that, considering the decision-making abilities of persons whose intellectual development is below the normal range, it violated common standards of decency to put these individuals to death. In a 6–3 decision, the Supreme Court agreed, ruling that persons who were so intellectually disabled that they could not perform for themselves the daily tasks of living could not be put to death. However, the Court did not make it clear how this disability would be assessed and left it to states to make this determination. In 2014, the Supreme Court revisited this issue in *Hall v. Florida* and revisited it still again in 2017, in *Moore v. Texas*.

Both before and after the *Atkins* case, some death penalty states adopted a specific IQ cutoff point (e.g., 70); if a person reached that IQ level, he or she was considered eligible for death,

FOCUS 4.2. *PERRY V. NEW HAMPSHIRE*: A CASE THAT CENTERED ON EYEWITNESS IDENTIFICATION

The topic of eyewitness identification has intrigued psychologists for at least a century, but a strong, consistent line of research since the 1970s has documented that eyewitness identifications must be viewed very guardedly. Although an eyewitness may firmly believe he or she is right—and he or she may well be—many factors influence what one observes and recalls.

Brian Perry was imprisoned after being convicted of burglary of a parked car. A witness noticed a man taking something out of a car from her apartment window. When police arrived and began questioning apartment dwellers, including this woman, she looked out her window and identified Perry while he was standing by the police car, handcuffed by police. Later, this same witness was unable to pick him out from a photospread display. Perry's lawyers argued unsuccessfully that the first identification should be kept out of court because it was unnecessarily suggestive and violated his due process rights. Prosecution lawyers said police had not created an unduly suggestive identification procedure—the witness merely looked out the window, saw Perry standing with police, and pinpointed him as the burglar. The identification was allowed, and Perry was convicted.

When the case reached the U.S. Supreme Court (after Perry again lost at the state court appellate level), his lawyers made the argument that, even if police had not set up an unduly suggestive identification procedure, eyewitness testimony was extremely unreliable and that should have been taken into account during pretrial proceedings. The witness's identification, they said, should have been suppressed.

The American Psychological Association submitted a lengthy amicus brief that summarized a long line of research on eyewitness testimony. The brief outlined a number of factors that could influence the accuracy of such testimony, independent of any procedures used by the police. In other words, even if police did not influence the identification, other things might. These included the passage of time between the observation and the identification, the level of stress experienced by the witness, the duration of exposure, the distance between the witness and the perpetrator, the presence of a weapon, and the race of the witness and the perpetrator.

In deciding the case, the U.S. Supreme Court ruled 8–1 that because there was no effort by police to create an unduly suggestive procedure, the lower courts had not erred by allowing the identification. The Justices did say, though, that judges could caution jurors not to place undue weight on eyewitness testimony that might have questionable validity.

Questions for Discussion

1. This case is used to illustrate a recent amicus curiae brief. Does it also illustrate that the U.S. Supreme Court does not always rule in keeping with social science research? Consider this carefully and explain your answer.

2. The brief outlined a number of things that can influence the accuracy of eyewitness testimony. Given the facts as described above, which if any of these factors might have influenced the witness's identification? What other facts would you want to know?

even if the score was just one or two points above the cutoff. Florida, for example, set 70 as the threshold level for determining intellectual disability. Under that state's law, a person would have to score 70 or below on an IQ test before being allowed to present additional evidence that he or she was intellectually disabled and should not be put to death. Freddie Lee Hall was convicted of a 1978 murder and has been on death row in Florida since that time—some 35 years. He has obtained scores as low as 60 and as high as 80 on IQ tests and has often been described as "mentally retarded" by both courts and examining psychologists. (Although the term *intellectual disability* is now preferred, many statutes as well as much professional literature continue to use the old term.) Florida kept Hall on death row because the scores were above its statutory cutoff point.

When his case (*Hall v. Florida*, 2014) reached the U.S. Supreme Court, amicus curiae briefs on his behalf—reflecting contemporary professional standards—emphasized that results of IQ tests should be interpreted cautiously and that a rigid cutoff point of 70 was inappropriate. Furthermore, other factors besides the test score should be taken into account in determining that the inmate was intellectually disabled. Accepting these and other arguments, the U.S. Supreme Court ruled against the state in a 5–4 decision. In a majority opinion written by Justice Kennedy, the Court said that the Florida law violated the Eighth and Fourteenth Amendments of the U.S. Constitution. Interestingly, the dissent, written by Justice Samuel Alito, chastised the majority for paying too much attention to professional organizations, such as the American Psychiatric Association, the American Psychological Association, and other groups advocating for the intellectually disabled.

From these two cases—*Atkins v. Virginia* and *Hall v. Florida*—it was still not clear what standard for determining intellectual disability would be acceptable or not acceptable to the Court. In *Moore v. Texas* (2017) the Court clarified to some extent, ruling 5–3 that the system used by Texas would not suffice. (See Focus 12.4 in Chapter 12 for further discussion. And, for a list of key cases cited in this chapter, see Table 4.4 on page 155.)

In this and the following two chapters, we will turn our attention to a discussion of specific tasks assumed by psychologists in their interaction with the civil and criminal courts. In this chapter, we discuss psychologists' important task of conducting risk assessments; their work as trial consultants, both in preparation for the trial and during the trial itself; and their participation as expert witnesses.

THE ASSESSMENT OF RISK

Forensic psychologists are very often asked to predict the likelihood that a particular individual will be "dangerous" to himself or herself or to others. In contemporary psychology, this enterprise is referred to as **risk assessment**, most commonly *violence* risk assessment (K. S. Douglas, Hart, Groscup, & Litwack, 2014). Risk assessment is often used in evaluating "individuals who have violated social norms or displayed bizarre behavior, particularly when they appear menacing or unpredictable" (Hanson, 2009, p. 172). In the context of this chapter, risk assessment can happen at several points in the judicial process, including very early in the proceedings, when a court is deciding to detain a suspect or release him on bail. It can also occur at the sentencing phase, when a judge is deciding between incarceration and probation. Risk assessment is crucial in the sentencing process in at least two death penalty states, where the sentencer must take into account the "dangerousness" of the individual being sentenced.

Violence risk assessment will be relevant in many later chapters as well. Thus, the populations on which violence risk assessments are done vary across several legal contexts and situations (K. S. Douglas et al., 2014; Hanson, 2005, 2009; Skeem & Monahan, 2011). For example, in the criminal and juvenile justice systems, the results of risk assessment often play a significant role—as mentioned above—in decisions made by the courts regarding bail and sentencing. Dangerousness also becomes an issue in deciding whether someone should be held in a psychiatric hospital or other confined setting against his or her will; in that case dangerousness to self as well as to others are important considerations. Skeem and Monahan note that "risk assessments for workplace violence and violent terrorism are also becoming increasingly common" (p. 38). Finally, risk assessments are conducted on a regular basis in correctional institutions, a process that may focus on whether the individual is dangerous to himself or herself or others at the facility. Parole boards often want to know the probability that an inmate will reoffend if released, and probation officers make use of risk assessment to try to judge the likelihood of recidivism (Ricks, Louden, & Kennealy, 2016).

Can Violence Be Predicted?

Can psychologists or any other clinicians predict violent behavior with any degree of confidence? Some clinicians who were called to testify in criminal and juvenile courts during the last quarter of the 20th century were quick to say that they could make such predictions. "On a scale of 1 to 10, with 10 being the most dangerous, this person is an 11," one psychiatrist who testified in many capital punishment trials was fond of saying. Others made statements such as, "For his own good, this juvenile must be locked up; he will definitely commit more crimes if not institutionalized." These types of predictions were cited in court cases (e.g., *Barefoot v. Estelle*, 1983) in which individuals challenged their bail denials, their sentences, or their confinements. For the most part, courts have allowed clinicians to make predictions but have also acknowledged their fallibility. In a juvenile case, *Schall v. Martin* (1984), for example, the U.S. Supreme Court recognized that predictions of behavior were imperfect and fraught with error but ruled nevertheless that they had a place in the law. The case involved juveniles who were held in secure detention prior to their delinquency hearings, even if they were not accused of committing violent acts, partly because there was a serious risk that they would commit more illegal activity if allowed to remain free.

Today, forensic psychologists are careful to point out the fallibility of behavioral prediction. Although they acknowledge that prediction is an important aspect of the services they provide to courts and other institutions, they are carefully guarded in their conclusions. When it comes to predicting violence, virtually everyone now prefers the terms *risk assessment* or the *assessment of dangerousness potential* rather than prediction of dangerousness. The words *risk* and *potential* communicate the important point that in their evaluation, psychologists are providing courts or other agencies with a probability statement that a given individual will behave in an inappropriate manner. The probability assessment may be based on clinical judgment or on certain "predictor variables" that are in the individual's background. For example, past violent behavior, age, lack of an adequate system of social supports, alcohol or other substance abuse, and a history of serious mental disorder together are good indicators that a person is likely to be violent once again (Monahan, 1996).

In addition, Borum, Fein, Vossekuil, and Berglund (1999) point out that dangerousness is not viewed as a personality trait that cannot change. More sophisticated models of risk assessment view dangerousness as highly dependent on situations and circumstances, constantly subject to change, and varying along a continuum of probability. Someone who was considered potentially dangerous at one point in his life may have experienced life changes that make it unlikely he will continue to be a danger to himself or others.

Clinical Versus Actuarial Prediction

There has been long-standing debate about the relative merits of clinical and statistical (actuarial) risk assessment (K. S. Douglas & Ogloff, 2003; McEwan, Pathé, Ogloff, 2011; McGowan, Horn, & Mellott, 2011; Melton et al., 2007). Predictions of violence based on clinical assessments—which rely on clinical experience and professional judgment—have not fared well compared to actuarial assessments. For over 50 years, statistical models that rely on measurable, valid risk factors have been, in a majority of cases, superior to clinical judgment or professional opinion (Hanson, 2005, 2009; Meehl, 1954). Early research almost invariably supported the use of actuarial prediction over clinical. However, actuarial instruments had shortcomings, which were often noted by mental health practitioners who wanted to retain some aspect of clinical judgment in their assessments. Heilbrun, Marczyk, and DeMatteo (2002) summarized their concerns as follows. Actuarial instruments, they say,

- Focus on a small number of factors and may ignore important factors that are idiosyncratic to the case at hand (e.g., recent legal or medical problems);

- Are passive predictors, focusing primarily on relatively static variables, such as demographics and criminal history;

- May include risk factors that are unacceptable on legal grounds, such as race or sex, and may ignore risk factors that have unknown validity but are logical to consider (such as threats of violence);

- Have been developed to predict a specific outcome over a specific period of time in a specific population, and they may not generalize to other contexts;

- Have a restricted definition of violence risk and cannot address the nature of the violence, its duration, its severity or frequency, or how soon it may occur. (p. 478)

Heilbrun et al. add that clinicians themselves—unless they are sufficiently schooled in psychometric theory and research—may tend to overuse or underuse the actuarial instruments. Although the authors acknowledge the value of risk assessment instruments, they also caution forensic psychologists not to undermine the role of clinical judgment in their assessments of risk. Nevertheless, they conclude, "the problem with the judgment-based approaches is that they are inherently speculative" (p. 478).

Even so, many clinicians today argue very persuasively that these statistical measures must be balanced with sound, clinical judgment developed through years of experience and training. Furthermore, after reviewing recent risk assessment research, including a number of meta-analyses conducted over the last decade, K. S. Douglas et al. (2014) question the long-standing assumption about the superiority of actuarial data, noting that in some situations, *structured* clinical judgment—more commonly termed **structured professional judgment (SPJ)**—may be a better alternative. Clinicians who use an SPJ approach generally abide by various guidelines for conducting a comprehensive clinical evaluation of violence risk for a particular individual in a particular context (K. S. Douglas et al., 2014). SPJ guidelines include gathering critical information, identifying the presence of risk factors, evaluating their relevance, and developing scenarios in which the person being evaluated might or might not be violent. As K. S. Douglas et al. phrase it, "evaluators need to consider what kinds of violence the examinee might perpetrate, for which motivations, against which victims, with what kinds of consequences, and at which times" (p. 415). This gives some weight to the above comment that clinical judgment is inherently speculative. SPJ-oriented clinicians also develop and recommend management plans for preventing potential violence and communicate these to whoever requested the evaluation. This is not to say that clinicians using a more actuarial approach do not offer such recommendations, however.

Dynamic and Static Risk Factors

An important concept in risk assessment is the distinction between dynamic risk factors and static risk factors (Andrews & Bonta, 1998; Andrews, Bonta, & Hoge, 1990; Beech & Craig, 2012; A. McGrath & Thompson, 2012). Risk factors are individual characteristics believed—to varying degrees—to be associated with or predictive of antisocial behavior. **Dynamic risk factors** are those that change over time and situation. For example, substance abuse and negative attitudes toward women have potential for change, in contrast to **static risk factors**—like one's age at the onset of antisocial behavior. Static risk factors are historical factors that have been demonstrated to relate to offending potential. In short, dynamic factors can change, whereas static factors cannot. Researchers who support SPJ note that actuarial risk instruments focus more on static factors and tend not to include dynamic factors, while SPJ encourages evaluators to consider them. "The SPJ model helps clinicians decide how often to reevaluate risk factors and how to link risk assessment to risk management" (K. S. Douglas et al., 2014, p. 397).

Dynamic factors can be subdivided into stable and acute (Hanson & Harris, 2000). (See Table 4.2 for examples.) **Stable dynamic factors**, although they are changeable, usually change slowly and may take months or even years, if they change at all. Consider, for example, one's attitudes about violent pornography or one's long-time association with deviant peers. **Acute dynamic factors**, on the other hand, change rapidly (within days, hours, or even minutes), sometimes dependent upon mood swings, emotional arousal, and alcohol or other drug-induced effects. Hanson and Harris found that acute dynamic factors, such as anger and subjective distress, were better predictors of the tendency of sex offenders to reoffend than were the more stable dynamic factors, such as the sex offender's attitudes about women. Nonetheless, both are risk factors to be addressed not only in prediction of future offenses, but also in the treatment of sex offenders.

Risk Assessment Instruments

Risk assessments should only be conducted by psychologists or other mental health professionals who have been trained to administer various measures and perform a comprehensive assessment of the behavioral, emotional, and cognitive features of the person in question. Today, many instruments are available to psychologists engaged in the risk assessment enterprise, and the research literature now contains numerous studies evaluating them (e.g., Churcher, Mills, & Forth, 2016; K. S. Douglas et al., 2014; Quinsey, Harris, Rice, & Cormier, 2006; Viljoen, Shaffer, Gray, & Douglas, 2017). Although some who perform these assessments may not use the instruments that are available for this purpose, not doing so may leave an examiner open to criticism if the results of his or her assessment are challenged. By the same token, however, examiners should be certain that the instruments they choose have empirical support in the research literature.

The instruments are typically designed by gathering information on a large group of individuals within a target population (e.g., violent offenders, paroled offenders, youths in detention, or patients in a mental institution). On the basis of data from that group, the researcher identifies key variables (e.g., age of onset of antisocial behavior, history of violence) that are associated with the behavior of concern. People are then rated on the number of these variables

Table 4.2 Some Examples of Static and Dynamic Risk Factors		
Dynamic Risk Factors (change over time and across situations)	Stable dynamic (change slowly) Attitudes Deviant peers	Acute dynamic Mood swings Anger Effects of alcohol or drugs
Static Risk Factors (embedded in background—do not change)	Early onset of criminal behavior Criminality in family background Certain child diagnoses (e.g., conduct disorder [CD]) Neurological issues (e.g., traumatic brain injury [TBI]) History of violence	

they have in their present lives or backgrounds, with some factors being weighted more heavily than others. An individual with a score below the cutoff for a particular risk assessment instrument would be judged as being at a high risk of offending.

As noted above, the empirical literature has consistently supported the superiority of actuarial or statistical data over clinical data in the prediction of human behavior, particularly if the clinical data are unstructured. In this context, unstructured means that the clinician is not using research-based guidelines in the assessment but is instead relying heavily on personal experience. Some studies have suggested that psychologists who rely on unstructured clinical judgment were incorrect 2 out of every 3 times when trying to predict an individual's violent behavior (Vitacco, Erickson, Kurus, & Apple, 2012). However, actuarial instruments are not perfect, and some forensic psychologists were not comfortable with the use of risk assessments that were based heavily on static factors and did not incorporate professional judgment sufficiently. This led to the development of instruments that included some clinical judgment. Risk assessment now exists on a continuum, with completely unstructured clinical judgment on one end and completely structured assessment on the other; in between are partially structured assessment instruments (Skeem & Monahan, 2011). (See Table 4.3 for a representative list of both actuarial and SPJ instruments.)

Today, in light of stalking laws, restraining orders, hate crime laws, and increased concerns about workplace and school violence, mental health professionals have been asked to provide forensic assessments of potential violence in a wide variety of settings. Moreover, professionals are not being asked simply to assess risk for general violent behavior, but rather to assess risk for specific types of violence, such as domestic and sexual violence. Two of the more popular and well-researched instruments for assessing the risk of domestic violence are the Ontario Domestic Assault Risk Assessment (ODARA) and the Domestic Violence Risk Appraisal Guide (DVRAG) (see Hilton, Harris, & Rice, 2010a, 2010b). The ODARA will be discussed again in Chapter 8. Instruments for assessing sex offender risk include the Static-99 and the SORAG, both actuarial instruments, and ERASOR, a structured instrument intended for use with adolescents with histories of sexual violence.

In summary, forensic psychologists need to remain alert to the ongoing debate and research literature on the various types of risk assessment instruments, their strengths and their weaknesses. Virtually all research is nonsupportive of *unstructured* clinical judgment, but structured professional judgment is gaining more adherents. K. S. Douglas et al. (2014) maintain that, contrary to previous opinion, "clinical judgments of risk—*so long as they are derived in a structured context, such as that provided by the SPJ model*—are as or more accurate compared to actuarial predictions of violence" (p. 426; emphasis added). Calling this a "liberating finding" (p. 426), they note that this allows risk assessment research to develop more expansively, such as determining how clinicians decide which risk factors are most relevant in a given case; how dynamic factors can change over time; the role of protective factors (e.g., individual resilience, family support); and whether risk factors can be applied equally across gender, racial, and ethnic backgrounds.

Risk assessment—particularly violence risk assessment—is a heavily researched and highly practiced activity in forensic psychology. Debates about the form it should take continue to occur with great frequency in the professional literature. The topic is introduced in this chapter because it is an enterprise so commonly performed by forensic psychologists in consulting with courts. However, it appears in many contexts and in both civil and criminal situations. We will revisit it in chapters ahead, as it pertains to these various contexts.

TRIAL AND LITIGATION CONSULTATION

Psychologists often consult with key players in the judicial process, particularly lawyers. There appears to be no shortage of tasks to perform, both before the trial and during the trial itself, and the work can be quite lucrative. Although members of other professions can and do serve as trial consultants (e.g., sociologists, economists, political scientists), the majority of them are psychologists (Strier, 1999). They do not necessarily consider themselves "forensic psychologists," however, despite the fact that they work in the forensic arena. Furthermore, trial consultants are often associated with major, nationwide consulting firms based in metropolitan areas. Many trial consultants also are themselves lawyers.

Trial or jury consultants often have backgrounds in industrial psychology or social psychology, but this is not a requirement. The two main areas in which they work are jury selection and assisting the lawyer during the trial process. Increasingly, consultants help attorneys at a variety of trial-preparation tasks, such as preparing witnesses and making decisions about particular trial strategies (Boccaccini, 2002; B. Myers & Arena, 2001). As an example, a lawyer might

Table 4.3   Representative Violence Risk Assessment Instruments and Populations for Which They Are Intended

Assessment Instrument	Intended Population	Developer
Actuarial		
COVR (Classification of Violence Risk)	Psychiatric patients being discharged to community	Monahan et al. (2005)
J-SORRAT-II (Juvenile Sexual Offense Recidivism Risk Assessment Tool–II)	Juvenile sex offenders	Epperson, Ralston, Fowers, DeWitt, and Gore (2006)
LS/CMI (Level of Service/Case Management Inventory)	Adult offenders	Andrews, Bonta, and Wormith (2004a)
LSI-R (Level of Service Inventory–Revised)	Adult offenders	Andrews and Bonta (1995)
ODARA (Ontario Domestic Assault Risk Assessment)	Adult males with police record for domestic assault	Hilton et al. (2004)
SORAG (Sex Offender Risk Appraisal Guide)	Sex offenders	Quinsey et al. (2006)
Static-99	Adult male sex offenders	Hanson and Thornton (1999)
VRAG (Violence Risk Appraisal Guide)	Adult male offenders; forensic patients	Harris, Rice, and Quinsey (1993)
Structured Professional Judgment		
ERASOR (Estimate of Risk of Adolescent Sexual Offense Recidivism, Version 2.0)	Adolescents with history of sexual violence	Worling and Curwen (2001)
HCR-20 Version 2 (Historical-Clinical-Risk Management-20)	Adult males and females	Webster, Douglas, Eaves, and Hart (1997)
SARA (Spousal Assault Risk Assessment Guide)	Men or women with current or former intimate partners	Kropp, Hart, Webster, and Eaves (1998)
SAVRY (Structured Assessment of Violence Risk Among Youth)	Adolescents	Borum, Bartel, and Forth (2006)
SVR-20 (Sexual Violence Risk-20)	Male adults with histories of sexual violence	Boer, Hart, Kropp, and Webster (1997)

wonder what type of mental health professional to contact for the purpose of testifying about the effects of posttraumatic stress disorder. In his or her role as trial consultant, the psychologist would offer suggestions. The psychologist also might help to prepare these experts for the trial or help the attorney interpret clinical reports provided by mental health practitioners. In addition, once a jury has been seated, the consultant may inform the lawyer about existing jury research. One noted trial consultant firm advertises its success at helping lawyers get into the minds of jurors.

Again, though, the case that actually goes to trial is the exception. The great majority of both civil and criminal cases (often as much as 90%) are resolved through negotiation or mediation. The cases that do go to trial are often high-profile cases in which the defendants (both criminal and civil) have a good deal to lose if the verdict does not come out in their favor. In the criminal context, they may be cases in which the defendant is truly innocent, despite the fact that probable cause to believe he or she committed the crime has been established. They may be death penalty cases or cases that would incur a long prison sentence. In the civil context, cases that go to trial may involve highly emotional situations in which one or both sides do not wish to compromise, such as litigation over custody of dependent children or the contesting of a will. They also may be those in which a corporate defendant stands to lose millions of dollars or even faces corporate dissolution if found to be at fault. The highly litigated cases against BP and Haliburton after the oil spill in the Gulf of Mexico are examples. Other examples are product liability suits, where plaintiffs have received high awards, although, as mentioned, research suggests that excessive awards are not the norm (Robbennolt et al., 2014). Nevertheless, when stakes are high, defendants (and occasionally prosecutors) with the financial means to do so are willing to assume considerable expense to hire experts to assist them in their jury selection and other trial-preparation work.

Scientific Jury Selection

In 2016, a major network premiered a television show—*Bull*—whose main fictional character was a trial consultant. His firm included a variety of assistants, including lawyers, psychologists, neurologists, and former detectives—all of whom contributed to mostly successful outcomes for the litigants who had hired them. Many real trial consultants criticized the show, indicating that it did not realistically represent the work they did or the reality that successes were not guaranteed. Bull's work often involved helping lawyers select jurors who would most likely decide cases in their favor.

Although a good deal of Bull's work was based on "gut feelings," the firm also made some use of **scientific jury selection (SJS)**. This is the application of social science techniques in an effort to find a jury that will be favorably disposed toward one's case. This process may include attitude surveys within the community in an attempt to determine representative views on matters dealing with the upcoming case. For example, defense lawyers representing a corporate client being sued for illegally dumping hazardous wastes might want to know how members of the community in general view corporate crime. More important, what are the demographic profiles of persons who are friendly toward corporations? And what of the anticorporation individual? What type of individual is most likely to be favorably disposed toward someone suing a large corporation? Those who practice SJS try to answer such questions by reviewing relevant research, studying the makeup of the community from which jurors are drawn, and observing the behavior of potential jurors, among other techniques. SJS is an expensive and time-consuming process. Trial consultants who engage in it often conduct surveys, set up focus groups, interview community members, and employ other research strategies to try to help predict who will likely be a good juror for their client.

At the pretrial stage, lawyers are also concerned about the effect of publicity that could be prejudicial to their client's case. Thus, trial consultants may be asked to conduct surveys of the community and collect evidence of negative publicity, which would support a motion for a change of venue (change in the location of the trial). During the trial itself, consultants sometimes also use **shadow juries**—groups of people similar to the jurors in demographic characteristics and possibly attitudes. Shadow jurors are consulted on a regular basis to see how they are reacting to various aspects of the proceedings. Once the trial is over, consultants may be asked to conduct posttrial interviews with members of the jury who agree to be interviewed. This allows insight not only into the decision making of the jurors, but also into the effectiveness of the strategies engaged in by attorneys during the trial itself.

Interestingly, it is believed that consultants who are knowledgeable about SJS techniques are used in all major trials (Lieberman, 2011). Examples of major trials are those that attract extensive publicity—such as high-profile criminal cases—or pit individuals against corporations. Most criminal trials, even though a life sentence may be at stake, are not likely to see the involvement of a trial consultant unless the defendant is a recognized public figure or the crime was especially heinous, such as the Boston Marathon bombing in April 2013.

For those trials that do involve SJS techniques, it is not clear precisely which of the techniques is being employed. That is, researchers have not examined the extent of use of surveys as opposed to shadow juries or interviews, or in some cases a combination of many different methods. In the Boston Marathon case, the defense commissioned geographical studies in an attempt to show that jurors were not being randomly chosen from communities within and surrounding the city. Based on these studies, they argued that the trial should be moved to a different location—but it was not. The defendant was ultimately convicted and sentenced to death.

The complexity of the SJS process in any one case is obviously dependent upon the resources of the client. It is also unclear what determines "success" when SJS is used. Because no two trials are equivalent with respect to the facts of the cases, the performance of the attorneys, the makeup of the jury, the rulings of the trial judge, or the quality of the evidence, it is impossible to conclude that SJS was a determining factor in the outcome of any given trial. It should be recognized as well that a history of research on juries indicates that the strength of the evidence presented to them is the main variable that affects their decision.

Witness Preparation

Trial consultants also help attorneys prepare witnesses and determine effective strategies for presenting evidence and persuading jurors (B. Myers & Arena, 2001). In preparing for the trial date, attorneys on each side of the conflict often meet with the witnesses they will be calling to the stand. This is done "to review, discuss, and sometimes modify the substance and delivery of their anticipated testimony" (Boccaccini, 2002, p. 161). In the case of lay witnesses who are not accustomed to a courtroom appearance, this prior meeting with lawyers (or sometimes with trial consultants) is considered an important step to avoid "surprises" in the testimony and to lessen the courtroom-related stress that witnesses may experience. Although attorneys are obviously concerned about the substance of a witness's testimony, they also are concerned about the presentation. The task of preparing witnesses may be shared with a trial consultant, part of whose task is to coach an individual in how to be a persuasive, confident witness. Finkelman (2010) emphasizes that "ethics require that preparation is limited to presentation techniques, rather than attempting to alter factual circumstances" (p. 14). Even psychologists serving as expert witnesses may benefit from being coached.

Certain aspects of witness preparation are controversial because they may reinforce in the witness a memory that is actually quite weak. Recall the discussion about commitment bias in Chapter 3. An initially uncertain witness can be led to be very certain by police statements that imply approval of his or her lineup identification. In a similar fashion, rehearsal of one's testimony during witness preparation is likely to increase one's confidence in that testimony. Research on eyewitness testimony indicates that jurors are more likely to believe or find credible a witness who speaks clearly and appears highly confident (Penrod & Cutler, 1995).

Suggestive questioning by attorneys or trial consultants also might lead witnesses to recall details that they did not initially remember. "Objectively false but subjectively true testimony can be created when a witness's memory of an event is distorted during the course of witness preparation, leading them to give unknowingly false or misleading testimony" (Boccaccini, 2002, p. 166). In fact, as emphasized in Chapter 3, eyewitness memory itself, even without the benefit of witness preparation, is extremely fallible. Such information has been a principal source of evidence in both criminal and civil cases. The expanding psychological research in the area, however, indicates that the judicial system should carefully examine some of its assumptions about eyewitness testimony. As noted above, psychological research has strongly suggested that evidence gained through eyewitness questioning and testimony is often teeming with inaccuracies and misconceptions, regardless of how certain the eyewitness claims to be (Loftus, 2013; Strange & Takarangi, 2012, 2015). (See Perspective 4.1, in which Dr. Strange writes about her research on memory and the fallibility of eyewitness identification.)

The Voir Dire

During the trial itself, trial consultants perform a different group of tasks. The first stage of the trial is the jury selection process, technically called the *voir dire*. This involves the questioning of potential jurors to best ensure a nonbiased jury. Here, the pretrial research done by the trial consultant—if it was done—is put to practical use, as lawyers use their allowable challenges and try to remove from the jury persons who will not likely be sympathetic to their side and select those who would be. The consultant may suggest voir dire questions to lawyers and

FROM MY PERSPECTIVE 4.1

Memory: Elusive, Fallible, and Fascinating

Deryn Strange, PhD

Courtesy of Deryn Strange.

I do not remember deciding to do a PhD. I remember studying, designing experiments, collecting data and writing . . . lots of writing. But I do not remember making the decision. And that amuses me: It is an example of the memory failures I have spent my career examining.

What I do remember is sitting in class in the third year of my undergraduate degree. The topics kept getting more interesting: eyewitness memory errors, false confessions, and false memories. For the first time, I was motivated to learn *more*. I'd always done my class readings, but I'd never sought out additional journal articles on a topic because the material covered in class so surprised me. I'd always gone to my required labs, but I'd never sought out additional research opportunities because I wanted to contribute to what we knew. How nerve-wracking to ask Professors if they needed help in their labs! What could I possibly contribute? But I did do those things, and those efforts resulted in me joining Dr. Maryanne Garry's lab at Victoria University of Wellington in New Zealand. Six years later, I left her lab with a PhD. After a postdoctoral fellowship at the University of Otago, I moved to the other side of the world to take up an Assistant Professorship at John Jay College of Criminal Justice, New York, in a department with many of the people whose research had so fascinated me. I am still at John Jay, but now I'm a tenured Associate Professor.

Broadly speaking, I study failures of memory with consequences ranging from the relatively benign (forgetting to pick up milk when you go shopping *specifically*

(*Continued*)

(Continued)

for milk) to the catastrophic (mis-remembering the face of an assailant and an innocent person goes to prison). Since I began at John Jay, my research has focused on the causes and consequences of traumatic memory distortions and memory distortions in the justice system.

Memory plays an integral role in the diagnosis of posttraumatic stress disorder (PTSD): People experience flashbacks, intrusive recollections, and often complain that they have an "incomplete" memory for the event. But how accurately people remember the precipitating traumatic event—and the role that (in)accuracy plays in their subsequent psychological maladjustment—is only just starting to receive empirical attention. For example, how *accurately* does the soldier remember the details of the RPG attack that left his good friend dead? This gap in the literature is practically and theoretically significant for several reasons. Under the current diagnostic criteria for PTSD, a person's symptomatic response after a trauma is assumed to be directly attributable to that trauma (and any predispositions). Therefore, the diagnosis relies on a person's report—their memory—of the event. Yet people's memories for traumatic events are—like their memories for more mundane events—easily distorted. Indeed, evidence from both field and lab studies reveals a specific pattern to traumatic memory distortion: People tend to remember more trauma then they experienced and those who do tend to exhibit more PTSD symptoms.

Dr. Melanie Takarangi (Flinders University, Australia) and I—along with our students—have worked to fill that gap in the literature by answering two overarching questions: How and why do we misremember trauma? We developed a paradigm that reliably demonstrates memory distortion for an analogue trauma. People watch a highly emotional film of a fatal car accident. The film appears as a series of short segments with brief black buffers between segments; the twist is that some critical aspects of the film are missing. And those critical aspects are either traumatic scenes (a child screaming for her parents) or nontraumatic (the arrival of the rescue helicopter). The next day, we give people a test showing them a series of scenes and asking them to choose whether or not they saw that scene the day before. The experiment is more complex than I can describe here, but the bottom line is that people falsely remembered seeing 26% of the missing scenes, or an additional 13.5 seconds (7%) more of the event than they actually did see and people were more likely to falsely remember the more traumatic scenes compared to the less traumatic scenes. We also found that people who reported getting "flashes" of memory—seeing a scene from the film "replaying" in their mind—reported more false memories. Thus we had preliminary evidence that memory distortion may play a critical role in people's responses to trauma (Strange & Takarangi, 2012). We have added evidence to this over the last few years with a variety of different approaches (Strange & Takarangi, 2015; Takarangi, Strange, & Lindsay, 2014).

To date, Melanie and I have collaborated on 17 empirical papers and we have more in the pipeline. Which brings me to my primary piece of advice for graduate students: Find a great collaborator, someone whom you work with *really* well. It will still be work but it will be much more fun. Melanie and I complement each other's skill set. We work similarly, which turns out to be critical to a successful, long-term, collaboration. Most importantly, we enjoy each other's company. We have worked through experimental designs while shopping for shoes, walking the perimeter of Manhattan, and tasting wines in the Barossa Valley. We have worked on grant applications on the beaches of Hawaii and in fantastic restaurants. We have the confidence to offer our most outlandish explanations for data patterns and use each other as sounding boards to try and make sense out of what does not make sense. It works. So, my advice is find your own Melanie.

My second line of research focuses on memory distortions in the legal system. And there, there are simply too many opportunities for memory failures to have truly devastating consequences. Many of those avenues have been studied for decades by the preeminent researchers in psychology and law: For example, we know a lot about why people can misidentify an innocent person as the perpetrator of a crime and what factors can contribute to false confessions. My students and I have focused on some of the less well understood and emerging areas in psychology and law: alibis, source monitoring failures in the courtroom, the implications of bait questions, and how people remember and interpret body camera footage.

For example, the same processes that cause us to forget where we placed our keys or to pick up the milk from the market on the way home can directly result in an innocent person appearing guilty to police officers, prosecutors, and jurors. A simple memory error—getting your weekends mixed up, or mistaking one Tuesday for another—can have devastating consequences. In fact, what starts out as a normal memory error can have cascading effects throughout the entire legal process: altering the course of an investigation, increasing the chance a suspect pleads guilty, or negatively influencing how a juror views a defendant making it more likely that an innocent person will be convicted. To try and prevent these kinds of errors, we are working on different approaches investigators can use when enquiring about an alibi (Crozier, Strange, & Loftus, 2017).

In other work, we have examined the impact of the bait question, a hypothetically phrased question that asks a suspect to explain incriminating evidence that may or may not exist. Police often use this approach. For example, they may ask, "You say that you were not involved in the crime . . . is there any reason that we would find your fingerprints on the murder weapon?" The police may not have the murder weapon, let alone the suspect's fingerprints. But the question is designed to "bait" the suspect into changing their story and offering an explanation for why their fingerprints might appear on the gun. If the suspect does take the bait, the technique teaches that the suspect is probably guilty. Our interest is in the memorial side effects of using bait questions: Can these bait questions cause jurors, interrogators, and suspects to believe that the hypothetical evidence exists, thereby altering the investigation of the case and putting innocent people at risk for a wrongful conviction? It turns out that mock jurors certainly get confused and think the hypothetical evidence actually exists, even when they are explicitly taught what a bait question is and why it is used (Luke, Crozier & Strange, 2017). Whether these errors extend to the people asking the questions (interrogators) and the people answering the questions (suspects) is the focus of our current work.

In summary, my work is diverse, but every question I examine falls under the umbrella of "memory distortions." I have learned that it is important to have a variety of projects going at any one moment: If you get stuck on one, there is always another to focus on and your pipeline of research keeps moving. So, what can I offer as my final piece of advice? Read widely, go to talks outside your narrow interest area at conferences, and talk to people whose work interests you. Research ideas are everywhere.

As noted above, Dr. Strange is an Associate Professor of Psychology at John Jay College of Criminal Justice in Manhattan. She currently serves as the President of the Society for Applied Research in Memory and Cognition and regularly testifies as an expert witness. She also likes wine.

make inferences about prospective jurors based on their responses or even on their nonverbal behavior (Strier, 1999).

One crucial aspect is the question of whether potential jurors may be biased against a racial, ethnic, religious, or gender group to which the defendant belongs. How likely is it that such bias will be detected during the voir dire? Additionally, can a juror set aside such a bias and decide the case based solely on the evidence? If bias is voiced in the jury room, the defendant's constitutional guarantee of a fair trial by an impartial jury is compromised. Indeed, in 2017, the U.S. Supreme Court issued a crucial decision that highlights the importance of selecting unbiased jurors (*Pena-Rodriguez v. Colorado*, 2017). Pena-Rodriguez was charged with harassment and attempted groping of two teenaged girls. During jury deliberations, a juror described as a former law enforcement officer commented that the defendant obviously committed the crime because he was Mexican, and Mexicans took what they wanted. The juror also stated that one of the witnesses on Pena-Rodriguez's behalf was an "illegal," despite the fact that the witness was a U.S. citizen who traveled to Mexico. After the defendant was convicted, two jurors reported the comments, and Pena-Rodriguez requested, but was denied, a new trial. Appellate courts denied his request, noting that jury deliberations were secretive, and inquiry into verdicts was unacceptable. Past cases also had allowed jury verdicts to stand despite evidence that some juries had displayed inappropriate behavior (e.g., drinking beer during lunch, using illegal drugs, or falling asleep in court).

However, the U.S. Supreme Court did not agree with the lower courts. By a vote of 5–3, the Court ruled that racial or ethnic bias in the jury room was a different matter. In that case, the bias was extreme, so the guarantee of a fair trial superseded the tradition of secrecy in jury deliberations. Presumably, had the trial judge been informed of the juror's comments before the verdict was announced, an inquiry into their deliberations would have been warranted. After the conviction, Pena-Rodriguez should have been granted a new trial. Thus, although bias may not be easy to detect in *choosing* jurors, it appears that efforts should be made to continue to do just that.

Trial Consultation: The Main Concerns

Research psychologists tend to be very skeptical of trial consulting, particularly the aspect of attempting to select jurors sympathetic to one's case. As mentioned above, some aspects of witness preparation also raise concern. With respect to scientific jury selection, comments by Ellsworth and Reifman (2000) are representative: "Jury researchers have searched in vain for individual differences—race, gender, class, attitudes, or personality—that reliably predict a person's verdict and have almost always come up empty handed" (p. 795). In a similar vein, law professor John Conley (2000) expressed wonderment "at the vast sums of money that lawyers and clients expend on jury-selection 'experts' who purport to produce psychological profiles of 'ideal' jurors for particular cases" (p. 823).

The lack of oversight of trial consulting has also been noted. As Strier (1999) observed, both for-profit and nonprofit trial consulting can now be found online, but whether online or not, it is largely unregulated: "There are no state licensing requirements, nor is there any binding or meaningful code of professional ethics" (p. 96). Others have observed that there are no qualifications or education requirements, so trial consultants work with few restrictions (Griffith, Hart, Kessler, & Goodling, 2007). B. Myers and Arena (2001), acknowledging the legitimacy of such concerns, nevertheless are supportive of trial consultation. Psychologists, they believe, can help to restore the balance in the presently unbalanced scales of justice. They agree, though, that better standards in training and methodology are needed if the field is to advance.

There is indication, too, that jurors might be leery of trial consultation, although the research on this issue is very sparse. Griffith et al. (2007) surveyed jury-eligible individuals in two states on their perceptions of trial consultants. Although there were wide individual differences influenced by income, ethnicity, age, gender, and belief in the fairness of the system, overall, 18% of those surveyed said they would be biased *against* the side using a trial consultant, while less than 0.25% said they would be biased *in favor* of the side that used a trial consultant. The researchers remarked that the side using a trial consultant might want to downplay this use, such as by limiting "face time" with the jury, while the side not using a consultant might want to be sure that the jury is aware of this use. According to Griffith et al., the public might have a more favorable view of trial consultants if they could be persuaded that they did not compromise the fairness of the system. This might be done by having trial consultants provide more pro bono work and by educating the public better about the services they provide.

EXPERT TESTIMONY

In addition to working behind the scenes or sitting in the courtroom as trial consultants, psychologists also may be found on the witness stand, testifying as expert witnesses in a wide range of cases (see Photo 4.2). This very visible role has produced extensive research and commentary and has been the subject of three significant Supreme Court decisions directly on the matter and a multitude of cases in lower federal and state courts. Together, the three U.S. Supreme Court decisions (*Daubert v. Merrill Dow Pharmaceuticals, Inc.*, 1993; *General Electric Co. v. Joiner*, 1997; *Kumho Tire Co. Ltd. v. Carmichael*, 1999)—collectively referred to as the *Daubert* trilogy—articulate the standard to be applied by federal courts in deciding whether expert testimony should be admitted if it is challenged by the opposing lawyer. Many states—over half—have adopted a standard identical to or closely related to *Daubert* (Fournier, 2016; Parry & Drogan, 2000). We will discuss *Daubert* in more detail shortly.

Expert testimony may occur in a variety of pretrial hearings, during both civil and criminal trials or delinquency proceedings, or during sentencing or disposition hearings. In each of these contexts, the role of the expert witness is to help the judge or the jury in making decisions about matters that are beyond the knowledge of the typical layperson. Most jurors and judges, for example, are not versed in neurology and the fine workings of the brain. Thus, a neuropsychologist may be called to testify about the effects of physical trauma—such as a severe head injury—on brain functioning. Likewise, most jurors and judges are unfamiliar with the psychological effects of ongoing physical abuse or experiencing a highly traumatic event such as a rape or a kidnapping; in such cases, experts on child abuse or on posttraumatic stress disorder (PTSD) might be called to the stand. Psychologists also have valuable information to convey to courts relative to eyewitness identification, human perception and memory, the credibility of child witnesses, and the effect of divorce on children.

▶ Photo 4.2
A psychologist testifies at a pretrial hearing in 2005, illustrating research findings via a bar graph.
Source: Douglas C. Pizac-Pool/Getty Images.

Eyewitness testimony and the role of memory in many contexts has seen a very strong line of research. As emphasized at several points in this and the previous chapter, the fallibility of eyewitness accounts is well recognized (Cutler, 2015; Loftus, 2013; Strange & Takarangi, 2015; Zajac, Dickson, Munn, & O'Neill, 2016). Recall that in Chapter 3 we covered pretrial identification procedures that police use to charge a suspect. Once a witness or victim has identified a suspect, they are typically committed to this identification, even with some doubt that this was the person they did indeed see. Many social and experimental psychologists have studied how memory works and ways to promote its accuracy. The knowledge they have obtained can be used, not only in training law enforcement as we discussed in the previous chapter, but also in consulting with attorneys and testifying as experts in the courts. For many years, though, courts were reluctant to accept this social science evidence. However, persistent efforts by eyewitness researchers as well as mounting evidence of wrongful convictions based on misidentifications suggests that these legal obstacles to the admission of social science evidence in this area may be diminishing (Newirth, 2016).

Clinical psychologists are also frequently called to testify about the results of evaluations they have conducted. In the criminal context, for example, psychologists often conduct court-ordered evaluations of a defendant's competency to stand trial or of his or her mental state at the time of the crime. In these situations, the psychologist will submit a written report to the judge and the attorneys. If the parties do not agree with the psychologist's conclusions, or if the judge wishes additional information or clarification, the psychologist may then be called to testify. In highly litigated cases—such as in a serious violent crime or a custody dispute—another clinician may be called to testify as well. This sometimes sets up the so-called "battle of the experts," where experts for each side report different findings or even reach opposing conclusions.

Research with mock juries suggests that the response to expert testimony is lukewarm or guarded, rather than wholeheartedly supportive (Nietzel, McCarthy, & Kerr, 1999), and that clinical testimony is favored more than the research-based testimony provided by academicians (Krauss & Sales, 2001). In a survey of 488 adult residents in one state, Boccaccini and Brodsky (2002) found that the public was far more likely to believe expert witnesses who worked with patients rather than those who engaged in academic activities. Respondents also were more likely to believe experts who received no payment for testifying. Recall the anecdote at the opening of this chapter, in which the cross-examining attorney emphasized the amount of money the psychologist was being paid. The survey also found there was some preference for those who came from the community, rather than flown in from afar. Expert testimony will be covered again in the chapters ahead, as we cover specific topics. For the present, it is important to look at issues that are common to all such testimony.

Expert Certification

To qualify as an expert witness, a psychologist must first establish his or her credentials, including the requisite advanced degree, licensing or certification if relevant, and research or practical experience in areas about which he or she is testifying. In each case, it is left to the discretion of the trial judge to accept or reject an individual's qualifications as an expert, subject to review by appellate courts. However, laws in some states require specific credentials or licensing to perform some of the evaluations and subsequently testify in court proceedings (Heilbrun & Brooks, 2010).

Legal Standards for the Admission of Scientific Evidence

Even though an expert has the professional background to qualify for certification as an expert witness, it is possible that the presiding judge will not allow the evidence the expert has to offer. Under federal law and the laws of the states that have adopted similar standards, if the opposing lawyer challenges the introduction of the evidence, the judge must decide whether the evidence is reliable, legally sufficient, and relevant to the case at hand. This was the standard for federal courts announced by the U.S. Supreme Court in its 1993 decision, *Daubert v. Merrill Dow Pharmaceuticals, Inc.* The **Daubert standard** replaced an earlier standard (announced in *Frye v. United States*, 1923), which was loosely known as the **general acceptance rule**. According to that earlier standard, the expert's evidence must have been gathered using scientific techniques that had reached a general acceptance in the science field. Once that standard had been met, all relevant testimony would be admissible.

Over the years, the *Frye* standard lost favor because—among other things—it was considered too stringent, presenting an obstacle to the introduction of evidence that had not yet reached "general acceptance." On the other hand, there was also concern from those who believed that the *Frye* standard was not scientific enough. In the Federal Rules of Evidence, adopted in 1975, Congress provided a different standard. The pertinent rule, Rule 702, did not require general acceptance, but it did require that evidence be relevant and reliable. Even relevant information could be excluded, however, if it would serve to prejudice the jury. In the *Daubert* case, the Supreme Court supported the standard set by the Rules of Evidence. It ruled that expert evidence must be relevant, reliable, and legally sufficient and that its probative value must outweigh its prejudicial value. In essence, the Court required that federal judges act as gatekeepers, scrutinizing expert evidence very carefully before admitting it into court. It did not completely denigrate the "general acceptance" criterion, however. Rather, it announced that general acceptance by the scientific community could be taken into consideration in deciding whether evidence was reliable. General acceptance should not, however, be a *necessary* condition. Some commentators have described the *Daubert* guidelines more succinctly, suggesting that they focus on testability, peer review, error rate, and general acceptance (Fournier, 2016).

The *Daubert* case and the federal rules of evidence apply to federal courts. State courts are free to adopt their own rules of evidence, but in practice many use federal rules as a model. Approximately 30 states use *Daubert*-like criteria for the admission of scientific evidence. Approximately 14 states still use a general acceptance standard, however (J. W. Hunt, 2010). Interestingly, research also indicates that many judges, even after *Daubert*, rely heavily on general acceptance in deciding whether to admit evidence, even if they give some attention to the other scientific criteria. Other courts, though, have moved away from the general acceptance standard and are giving close scrutiny to the scientific foundation of the evidence that is offered (Ogloff & Douglas, 2013). In the first instance, if the expert is professionally qualified, the judge is influenced by whether or not the method or information the expert is offering (e.g., a particular risk assessment instrument) has general acceptance in the scientific community. In the second instance, even if the expert is professionally qualified, the judge expects he or she will demonstrate that the risk assessment measure is relevant and reliable.

Despite the above discussion, it is important to emphasize that a judge will not conduct a review of the relevance and reliability of the expert's testimony in all cases. Judges typically apply the *Daubert* standard only when an attorney challenges the *introduction* of the evidence. Shuman and Sales (2001) write that

> like most other rules of evidence, *Daubert* relies on trial lawyers to identify issues of admissibility (e.g., the reliability of the expert testimony) and choose whether to raise them before the trial judge, to present on issues of credibility to the jury, or to ignore these issues. (p. 71)

Shuman and Sales add that a lawyer may not recognize that certain expert testimony is based on unreliable methods; alternatively, the methods used by the lawyer's own expert may be just as faulty. In neither case would the lawyer be likely to challenge the opposing expert. In still another scenario, the lawyer may wait until the opposing expert is on the witness stand and within view of the jury before questioning the credibility of the information. Finally, pretrial *Daubert* motions cost money, take up court time, and require judges and lawyers to master science as well as the law. For all of the above reasons, Shuman and Sales state, motions to exclude scientific evidence are not likely to become enthusiastically embraced in the nation's courtrooms.

Despite these predictions, judges on the whole do seem to be excluding more evidence than before *Daubert* (McAuliff & Groscup, 2009). However, McAuliff and Groscup (2009) emphasized that, though judges are more likely to exclude evidence now than they did before *Daubert*, this careful scrutiny did not mean judges were admitting valid evidence or excluding "junk science." "The past 15 years of social scientific research and legal commentary have revealed critical limitations in the ability of legal professionals and laypeople to identify flawed psychological science in court" (p. 48).

In the years since the *Daubert* decision, considerable research and commentary has addressed the Court's assumption that judges, who rarely have a scientific background, would be able to evaluate scientific evidence. Kovera, Russano, and McAuliff (2002) maintain that most judges and jurors are similar in their ability to identify flawed expert evidence because neither has received formal training in the scientific method. They further maintain that such individuals cannot differentiate between valid and flawed research. Jurors, as the research has consistently indicated, are highly unlikely to be able to distinguish the flawed research, even when an opposing expert highlights these flaws (Cutler & Penrod, 1995; Cutler, Penrod, & Dexter, 1989). Neither jurors nor judges nor lawyers typically can understand the importance of control groups or appreciate the relative merits of small and large sample sizes (Kovera, Russano, & McAuliff, 2002).

Kovera and her colleagues (Kovera & McAuliff, 2000; Kovera et al., 2002) asked judges and attorneys to evaluate studies that represented four methodological variations: a valid study, a study that was missing a control group, a study that contained a confound, and a study that used a non-blind confederate. Judges were asked whether they would admit the evidence; lawyers were asked whether they would file a motion to exclude it. Judges admitted flawed research at the same rates as they admitted valid testimony. When attorneys wanted evidence excluded (which was almost invariably), it had no relationship to their perceptions of its scientific reliability. Kovera and her colleagues concluded that it remains likely that some "junk science" will make its way into the courtroom and that some valid evidence will be excluded.

Other research produces more positive findings, including research indicating that federal judges are more likely than state judges to understand the confusing aspects of the *Daubert* standard (e.g., the error rate). On the whole, however, there is wide variability in application of *Daubert* in both federal and state courts, and in both, some judges appear to ignore the standard altogether, even when mandated to apply it (Fournier, 2016).

Although the fallout from the *Daubert* decision continues to be investigated, expert witnesses face additional challenges in the courtroom. As many commentators have remarked, testifying in court is not an exercise for the faint of heart. Expert witnesses—just like lay witnesses—face the possibility of being subjected to grueling cross-examination. Even very low-profile trials or pretrial proceedings can produce anxiety for the expert being subjected to sharp cross-examination. Some experts also struggle with their concerns about confidentiality and "ultimate opinion" testimony.

The Confidentiality Issue

The obligation to maintain confidentiality in the patient–therapist relationship is fundamental. In the courtroom setting, though, confidentiality is not absolute. When clinicians have been asked by the court to evaluate a defendant, the results of that evaluation are shared among the judge and the lawyers. In these situations, the clinician's client is the court, not the individual being examined. The evaluation also may be discussed in the open courtroom if the clinician is called to the stand. In such cases, persons who have been evaluated have been warned of the limits of confidentiality at the outset of the evaluation. Even the confidentiality of test data is not guaranteed if the client signs a release or if the court orders that it be released. It is not unusual, though, for the written psychological report to be redacted (certain portions blacked out) or sealed so that it does not appear in the final case record.

Under both the "Ethical Principles of Psychologists and Code of Conduct" (EPPCC) and the "Specialty Guidelines for Forensic Psychology" (American Psychological Association [APA], 2013c), clinicians are expected to inform the individual of the nature and purpose of an evaluation, as well as who will be receiving a report. They also should ensure that the individual is informed of his or her legal rights. In many cases, however, the person has been ordered to undergo an examination by the court. As Ogloff (1999) notes,

> If the person [being assessed] is not the client, the psychologist owes no duty of confidentiality to that person, but, because of the requirement of informed consent, must make the fact known to the person being assessed that the information to be obtained is not confidential. (p. 411)

Nonetheless, even if notified of the limits of confidentiality, the individual in reality has little choice in submitting to the evaluation ordered by the court if he or she has not requested it. In addition, the individual may suffer harm as a result of the psychologist's participation in the evaluation process (Perlin, 1991). However, the mental health practitioner can conduct the examination over the client's objection, without obtaining consent.

When it is not evaluation but rather psychotherapy or treatment that is at issue, all courts recognize the patient–therapist privilege, although it is not absolute. The U.S. Supreme Court, for example, has firmly endorsed confidentiality in federal courts (*Jaffe v. Redmond*, 1996). Redmond was a police officer who shot and killed an allegedly armed suspect who she believed was about to kill another individual. The suspect's family sued, maintaining that he was not armed and that Officer Redmond had used excessive force, a civil rights violation. When the plaintiffs learned that Redmond had attended counseling sessions with a psychiatric social worker after the shooting, they subpoenaed the social worker, who confirmed that the officer had been a patient. However, the social worker refused to answer specific questions about treatment. The judge in the case refused to recognize a therapist–patient privilege and informed the jury that they were entitled to presume that the testimony would have been damaging to Redmond's case. The jury found for the plaintiffs, but the Seventh Circuit Court of Appeals threw out the verdict.

In its 7–3 decision, the U.S. Supreme Court affirmed the appeals court's decision. The Justices not only recognized the importance of the psychotherapist–patient privileged communication but also placed licensed social workers under this protective cloak. The Court did not consider the privilege absolute—or totally protected under all conditions—but it also did not specify when it would *not* apply. It is likely, however, that restrictions of the psychotherapist–patient privilege in federal courts would be similar to those in the states. For example, the privilege generally does not apply when patients voluntarily introduce their mental health into evidence. Confidentiality also is not protected when a patient sues the therapist, because the therapist is entitled to use otherwise privileged information to defend himself or herself (Ogloff, 1999).

Duty to Warn or Protect

An issue closely related to confidentiality is the obligation of mental health practitioners in some states to warn or protect third parties who might be in danger from a patient who has threatened their lives. The **duty to warn or protect** is referred to as the *Tarasoff* requirement, named after a court ruling (see Focus 4.3). The specific requirements vary by state, which is why it is alternatively called a duty to warn and a duty to protect. In some states, for example, therapists are expected to notify the threatened individual directly (warn), whereas in other states, therapists can meet the requirement by contacting law enforcement authorities or by taking active steps to have their patient institutionalized (protect). In those states with duty to warn or duty to protect legislation, psychologists who fail in this duty are subject to being sued in civil court by victims who suffer harm at the hands of their (psychologists) clients. In all states, practitioners also are required by law to report evidence of child abuse (and, in some cases, elder or other abuse) encountered in their practice to appropriate parties, which may include law enforcement or social service agencies. Although many clinicians say they can live within the spirit of *Tarasoff* and other reporting requirements, others have been critical of the violation of trust that these requirements engender.

Ultimate Issue or Ultimate Opinion Testimony

The testimony provided by expert witnesses is different from that provided by lay witnesses. Recall that a main role of the expert is to assist triers of fact (judges and juries) in matters about which they would not otherwise be knowledgeable. In most jurisdictions, *lay* witnesses can testify only to events that they have actually seen or heard firsthand. Their opinions and

FOCUS 4.3. *TARASOFF*'S DUTY TO PROTECT—AND MORE

In some jurisdictions, mental health professionals can be held liable for not warning potential victims of violence or physical harm at the hands of their patients. In late 1969, a young California woman was murdered by a man who 2 months earlier had confided to his psychologist his intention to kill her. Although the psychologist, who was employed by the University of California, had notified campus police of the death threat, he informed no one else except his supervisor. After the murder, the woman's parents sued the university, the psychologist, and the police for failing to warn the family and take action against the offender. This case established

(Continued)

(Continued)

the well-known *Tarasoff v. Regents of the University of California* (1974, 1976) ruling.

In *Tarasoff*, the California Supreme Court first held that, in certain circumstances, when a mental health professional determines that a patient or client is a serious danger to another, the professional has a duty to warn the intended victim that he or she may be in danger. Two years later, the court redefined the clinician's responsibility as a duty to protect. This difference is an important one, because protection need not require notification to the intended victim, but it does require *active* steps on the part of the mental health professional. This might mean contacting law enforcement officials or initiating steps to have a patient hospitalized. The court believed that the need to protect persons from serious harm takes precedence over the confidentiality of the therapist–patient relationship.

The duty to protect doctrine has since been adopted via statute or common law by a majority of states (DeMatteo, 2005a; Reisner, Slobogin, & Rai, 2004). Some states have explicitly rejected the doctrine (DeMatteo, 2005a). Many states have also made modifications to the doctrine since the California cases and since very recent tragic events. In California, the state's court of appeals expanded *Tarasoff* by asserting that a communication from a third party, such as a patient's *family member* may trigger a therapist's duty to protect (*Ewing v. Goldstein*, 2004). For example, if an individual tells a therapist that his brother—the therapist's patient—has threatened to harm his mother, the therapist might have a duty to protect the mother by alerting law enforcement officials or by taking steps to have the brother hospitalized, even though the patient himself never expressed that thought to the therapist. *Tarasoff*-like requirements have been in the news in recent years because of mass shootings such as those that occurred at Virginia Tech (2007); Newtown, Connecticut (2012); and Aurora, Colorado (2012), as well as less highly publicized events. In each of these cases, therapists apparently had had contacts with the shooters. The cases have led to more legislation requiring mental health practitioners to report their concerns if

in their professional judgment they consider a patient in imminent danger of harming others.

In some jurisdictions, imminence is not required, thus producing a very vague requirement that could be quite difficult to interpret. In addition, the newer laws do not require a potential threat to a specific individual. In the most recent expansion of *Tarasoff*, for example, the Washington State Supreme Court said mental health professionals had a duty to protect and warn potential victims of violence even when no potential victims were named by the patient. In other words, mental health professionals were charged with protecting the society at large (*Volk v. DeMeerleer*, 2016).

Questions for Discussion

1. To what extent should psychologists and other mental health professionals be required to report concerns about their clients to local authorities? Should they be required to warn potential victims directly?
2. Commentators have remarked that even without these laws, or even in jurisdictions where the *Tarasoff* doctrine has been explicitly rejected, mental health practitioners typically abide by the spirit of *Tarasoff*. Discuss how this might be done.
3. Assuming that a mental health professional should be obliged to report a specific threat to law enforcement, should the threat be (a) against a specific person, (b) against a group, or (c) against society at large?
4. In the Washington State case mentioned above, a man fatally shot a woman and her 9-year-old son and attempted to kill another son, before committing suicide. The shooter had been in therapy for 9 years and had expressed suicidal and homicidal ideations to his psychiatrist, but had not named potential victims. Do you agree with the Washington court that the psychiatrist had an obligation to protect society, even if the patient had not named a potential victim? If you are unsure, what facts would you want to know before giving an answer?

inferences are generally not admissible. *Expert* witnesses, on the other hand, testify to facts they have observed directly, to tests they may have conducted, and to the research evidence in their field. Moreover, the opinions and inferences of experts not only are admissible but are also often sought by the courts.

However, there is considerable debate among mental health professionals about the wisdom of offering an opinion on the "ultimate issue." The ultimate issue is the final question that must be decided by the court. For example, should the expert provide an opinion about whether the defendant was indeed insane (and therefore not responsible) at the time of his crime? Should the expert recommend which parent should be awarded custody? Should the expert declare that a defendant is competent to be executed? Should the expert recommend that a juvenile's case be transferred to criminal court? It is quite clear that courts frequently request and hope for such opinions (Melton, Petrila, Poythress, & Slobogin, 1997, 2007; Redding, Floyd, & Hawk, 2001; Slobogin, 1999). In one study, even despite a statutory prohibition on ultimate opinion testimony in insanity cases, judges and prosecutors said they had a strong desire for clinical opinion (Redding et al., 2001). Defense attorneys were less likely to support this.

Those who oppose ultimate issue testimony (e.g., Melton et al., 1997, 2007) believe—among other things—that it is highly subject to error. The expert may misunderstand the law; may apply hidden value judgments; or may believe a particular outcome is best for an individual, even if legal criteria are not met. A clinical psychologist, for example, may truly believe that an individual needs to be placed in a secure mental health facility and treated for a serious mental disorder, even if the person does not technically meet the criteria for institutionalization. Thus, the psychologist might offer the opinion that the individual is not competent to stand trial, knowing that if the individual is ruled incompetent, he or she will most likely be sent to a mental hospital and will receive some treatment. This is not to say that the psychologist is trying to evade the law; he or she may truly believe the person is incompetent in a clinical sense, without fully understanding the legal criteria for incompetency.

A related issue is that of possible bias on the part of the expert, a bias that may be subconscious, but that may nonetheless influence the expert's own conclusions. Murrie and his colleagues (e.g., Murrie & Boccaccini, 2015; Murrie, Boccaccini, Guarnera, & Rufino, 2013) have conducted research that suggests an "adversarial allegiance," or the fact that experts can be biased in favor of the side that has hired them, even without intending to be. (See Perspective 5.1 in Chapter 5, in which Dr. Murrie discusses this research.) In a similar fashion, Neal and Brodsky (2016) refer to the "bias blind-spot" to which all mental health professionals are subject. Such biases and allegiances may affect not only ultimate issue testimony, but also assessments of risk.

Opponents of ultimate issue testimony also fear the undue influence of the expert on the fact finder. They stress that decisions such as whether an individual was insane at the time of the crime or whether a father or a mother should be awarded custody of a minor child are legal decisions. Asking the expert to express his or her opinion suggests that great weight will be placed on that opinion, when in fact the decision must be made by a judge or a jury and must be based on legal factors.

There is partial research support for the assumption of undue influence. Research suggests that the expert's opinion heavily influences judges in *pretrial* situations but not judges or juries at the *trial* stage. On issues such as competency to stand trial or the dangerousness of a defendant (warranting a denial of bail), the influence of the expert is substantial (Melton et al., 1997, 2007). This may be one reason why opposing experts are important, to offset an advantage gained by one side; in many pretrial situations, however, only one expert is called upon, typically at the request of the court. In other words, in pretrial situations the opposing attorneys may agree to have a court-appointed clinician examine the defendant. Trial jurors, however, do not seem to be unduly swayed by the opinions of experts (Nietzel et al., 1999). This may be because opposing experts and aggressive cross-examination are more likely in a trial situation than in a pretrial hearing. Furthermore, jurors perceive experts as "hired guns" who would not be placed on the stand if their opinions did not support the side that called them. Jurors do listen to expert testimony, but "the effect is modest and leaves opportunity for both foes and fans of ultimate opinion testimony to find support for their positions" (Nietzel et al., 1999, p. 41).

Those who favor testimony on the ultimate issue (e.g., Rogers & Ewing, 1989) argue that judges often depend on it and that such testimony can be carefully controlled, particularly by means of effective cross-examination. They note also that judges and lawyers are becoming increasingly sophisticated about possible sources of error in an expert's opinion; to believe otherwise is to insult their intelligence. Furthermore, in pretrial proceedings in both criminal and civil cases, judges typically ask an opinion of the clinician who has been appointed by the court and who is acceptable to both parties. These court officers have come to value and trust the professional's opinion as a result of having him or her involved in past cases. Finally, forensic psychology has developed rapidly, and many graduate and postgraduate programs now offer internships, specialized training, and other opportunities for psychologists and other clinicians to learn the laws. As a result, the quality of evaluations has improved significantly over the past decade.

Nevertheless, reflecting the lack of consensus on the matter of ultimate issue testimony, the American Psychological Association has not taken a stand on whether it should be provided, even when courts request it. The 2010 "Guidelines for Child Custody Evaluations in Family Law Proceedings" (APA, 2010b), for example, specifically refer to the lack of consensus. Guideline 13 notes that psychologists "seek to remain aware of the arguments on both sides of this issue . . . and are able to articulate the logic of their positions on this issue." The guideline also states that, if they choose to make child custody recommendations, these recommendations are derived from sound psychological data and address the psychological best interests of the child. In addition, they should "seek to avoid relying upon personal biases or unsupported beliefs." Interestingly, the "Specialty Guidelines for Forensic Psychology" (APA, 2013c) neither encourage nor discourage ultimate issue testimony. Whereas an earlier version of the guidelines noted that professional observations, inferences, and conclusions must be distinguished from *legal* facts, opinions, and conclusions, the 2013 version emphasizes that psychologists strive to provide the basis and reasoning underlying their opinions as well as the salient data or other information that was considered in forming them (Guideline 11.04). This change may be in recognition of a developing trend for courts to require clinicians to identify the factual bases for conclusions and opinions they offer (Zapf, Roesch, & Pirelli, 2014).

SURVIVING THE WITNESS STAND

It is important to emphasize that many forensic psychologists never testify in court proceedings. Those who do, either occasionally or on a regular basis, learn to do so with aplomb and leave with their own mental health intact. Yet, as noted above, courtroom testimony can be a stressful experience. Cross-examination by an opposing attorney is particularly discomfiting. In one trial, the defense attorney asked the prosecution's expert witness if she could call him by his first name. When he said she could, the attorney continually used the first name rather than "Doctor," thereby diminishing his status in the eyes of the jury. Tactics such as this may seem inconsequential, but they can affect the jury's perceptions of the expert. Forensic psychologists, like other expert witnesses, may enter the courtroom totally confident in their professional knowledge and the evidence they are about to present. However, faced with the grueling questions of a legal adversary and frustrated with legal rules of evidence that limit their testimony, they may wish for a very quick end to a painful experience.

Despite the pitfalls, numerous forensic psychologists have learned to navigate the landscape of the courtroom and have developed the skills needed both to provide the court with specialized knowledge and to respond to cross-examination in a calm, professional manner. This is crucial, because it is not unusual for cross-examining attorneys to berate or insult experts, their field of study, or methods used in their research. The professional literature contains ample advice for psychologists preparing to testify as expert witnesses (e.g., Brodsky, 1999, 2004; Otto et al., 2014). Today, most graduate programs with specializations in forensic psychology offer courses or workshops on testifying in court.

Table 4.4 Key Cases Cited in This Chapter

Case Name	Year	Topic
Jenkins v. U.S.	1962	Psychologists' qualifications to testify as experts on mental health issues
Batson v. Kentucky *J.E.B. v. Alabama* *Foster v. Chatman*	1986 1994 2016	Race, gender, and peremptory challenges
Perry v. New Hampshire	2012	Eyewitness testimony
Glossip v. Gross	2015	Drug protocol in executions
Atkins v. Virginia *Hall v. Florida* *Moore v. Texas*	2002 2014 2017	Intellectual disability and capital punishment
Pena-Rodriguez v. Colorado	2017	Secrecy of jury deliberations
Frye v. United States *Daubert v. Merrill Dow Pharmaceuticals*	1923 1993	Expert testimony in federal courts
Jaffe v. Redmond	1996	Psychotherapist-patient privilege
Tarasoff v. Regents of the University of California	1974, 1976	Duty to warn and protect

Other scholars have offered advice not only for the witness stand, but also for a wide range of meetings and proceedings that are part of the trial preparation process (e.g., Heilbrun, 2001; Heilbrun et al., 2002; A. K. Hess, 2006). Expert witnesses are urged to establish a communicative relationship with the attorney who has called them early in the legal process so that each side will know what can realistically be expected from the other. Experts are also advised to answer only the question addressed to them and to see their role as an educator. "Thus, the expert witness's goal should be to communicate what he or she did, learned, and concluded—all using language and concepts that the decision maker can understand" (Otto et al., 2014, p. 739).

Pretrial *preparation* is essential, and psychologists should not allow themselves to be persuaded to enter the courtroom without advance notice and sufficient preparation time (Otto et al., 2014; Singer & Nievod, 1987). They are advised to gather information carefully; pay attention to details of the case and the legal issues involved; remain impartial; and keep clear, organized notes (Chappelle & Rosengren, 2001). Many expert witnesses today maintain that well-prepared PowerPoint exhibits are helpful if not essential, although these can have the effect of dulling the attention of the fact finder, particularly the jury, if they are not visually appealing. Experts also should be aware that their notes, correspondence, and tape recordings may be made available to attorneys for both sides under the rules of discovery. At some point in the proceedings, considering *Daubert* and other relevant cases, either the judge or the opposing attorney may inquire whether the techniques or theories on which the expert is relying have been scientifically evaluated. Although judges seem to be particularly concerned about the expert's credentials and whether the information would assist the trier of fact, many judges and attorneys also will carefully quiz the experts on such matters as error rates and reliability, as well as general acceptance. Thus, in the process of preparing his or her testimony, the expert witness must take care to address these questions.

Expert witnesses are also advised to pay particular attention to their nonverbal behavior in the courtroom. Any behaviors that suggest arrogance, confusion, hostility, or anxiety are to be avoided. Chappelle and Rosengren (2001), reviewing the literature on expert testimony, remarked that the need to maintain composure is a theme in this literature. The knowledge offered by the expert is more likely to be accepted by judge and jury if the expert projects a professional, confident, and respectful persona. As Otto et al., 2014, observe, he or she should never exhibit frustration or anger.

SUMMARY AND CONCLUSIONS

The main purpose of this chapter has been to introduce the structure and process in criminal and civil courts along with some of the specific tasks performed by forensic psychologists in those settings. We reviewed court structure, discussed basic concepts relating to criminal and civil cases, and provided illustrations of the work psychologists do at each of the major stages of the court process. In the chapters ahead, these court-related tasks will be described in greater detail.

A major undertaking for forensic psychologists is to conduct risk assessments—more specifically violence risk assessments—which are then communicated to representatives of the legal system. Although these assessments are loosely called predictions of dangerousness, most psychologists emphasize that they cannot truly predict human behavior. They can, however, offer probabilities that certain behavior will occur. Methods to assess risk have developed rapidly over the past 30 years. Whereas the use of unstructured clinical judgment was common in the past, this was replaced by the development of risk assessment instruments that were actuarial, or statistically based. Actuarial instruments identify risk factors (e.g., age of onset of antisocial behavior) that clinicians take into account in deciding on the probability that a given individual will engage in violent behavior in the future.

Actuarial assessments were almost universally viewed in the research literature as superior to unstructured clinical judgment, but they had shortcomings, as noted in the chapter. Many psychologists sought a combination of the best aspects of both actuarial and clinical assessments of risk, while avoiding the weaknesses of both. Over the past decade, instruments based on structured professional judgment were developed. These instruments provide guidelines to the clinician to incorporate risk factors while also allowing for his or her professional judgment of the individual being assessed in light of the particular circumstances of the case. Today, forensic psychologists have a range of risk assessment instruments from which

to choose. We stressed the importance of being aware of the research literature on which method of risk assessment is used. This is not only professionally responsible but is also crucial if the forensic psychologist expects to testify in a court proceeding. The instruments used may be scrutinized by a court in keeping with *Daubert* guidelines. Many psychologists also indicate that the assessment of risk should be accompanied by suggestions for managing that risk whenever possible.

Some psychologists are actively involved in trial or litigation consultation. In this capacity, they assist lawyers in tasks as varied as preparing witnesses for trial, identifying effective tactics for cross-examination, or helping to select jurors who are most likely to be sympathetic to the lawyer's side. This last process, referred to as scientific jury selection, is used in some form in major trials, particularly those that attract heavy media publicity. The success of scientific jury selection is undetermined, primarily because its effects are difficult if not impossible to measure. Most research has determined that juror behavior cannot be predicted.

Although many forensic psychologists are not called to testify in court proceedings, many others serve as expert witnesses in both criminal and civil courts, not only at trial, but also at a variety of pretrial and posttrial proceedings (e.g., a bail hearing, a sanity hearing, a sentencing hearing). It is now clear that all experts—from the physical, behavioral, and social sciences, as well as those representing medicine and law—fall under the mantle of science identified in the *Daubert* case, at least in federal courts. Courts in most states also have adopted *Daubert* or highly similar standards as well. Since *Daubert*, many judges are scrutinizing and rejecting expert testimony more than before, although some are more likely to focus on whether the evidence will assist the trier of fact and whether it has general acceptance in the scientific community.

The present chapter also covered issues that cause some psychologists to pause before agreeing to participate in court proceedings. Some psychologists are not comfortable divulging information that in other contexts would be confidential, even though they are allowed (and sometimes required) to do so by law. Related to this is the duty to warn or to protect persons who might be harmed by a psychologist's client. However, when psychologists are asked to conduct an evaluation, the client is often not the individual being evaluated but the court. In that case, copies of the psychologist's report are sent to the court as well as to attorneys on both sides of the case. The patient–therapist relationship is different from the relationship between the examiner and the person being evaluated. Courts have respected patient–therapist confidentiality, but even that may give way in certain situations when balanced against other interests. In many jurisdictions, for example, therapists have a duty to warn

or protect when their clients have made serious physical threats against an identified third party.

Some forensic psychologists also resist being pressed for an opinion on legal matters or being subjected to grueling cross-examination by an opposing lawyer. Yet each of these is a routine occurrence in courtroom appearances. Judges often want to know the psychologist's conclusion as to whether an individual is competent to stand trial, whether someone is insane, or who would be the better of two parents in a custody battle. Technically, these are legal issues—the "ultimate issues" to be decided by the court, not the psychologist. Although some forensic psychologists are willing to express these opinions, others find them out of their purview. Nevertheless, the trend today appears to be to offer such an opinion if requested, as long as one is ready to carefully explain the facts on which that opinion is based.

KEY CONCEPTS

Acute dynamic factors   138

Amicus curiae briefs   133

Appellate jurisdiction   125

Arraignment   129

Bench trial/court trial   131

Challenge for cause   131

Daubert standard   148

Deposition   123

Discovery process   130

Disposition   132

Dual-court system   124

Duty to warn or protect   151

Dynamic risk factors   138

General acceptance rule   148

General jurisdiction   125

Geographical jurisdiction   125

Grand jury   129

Initial appearance   129

Limited jurisdiction   125

Peremptory challenge   131

Presentence investigation (PSI)   132

Risk assessment   135

Scientific jury selection (SJS)   141

Shadow juries   142

Specialized courts   126

Stable dynamic factors   138

Static risk factors   138

Structured professional judgment (SPJ)   137

Subject matter jurisdiction   125

Tarasoff requirement (duty to warn or protect)   151

Trial consultants   140

Ultimate issue   153

Voir dire   131

QUESTIONS FOR REVIEW

1. What is the significance of *Jenkins v. United States* to forensic psychology?

2. Review the main steps or stages of the judicial process and provide illustrations of tasks forensic psychologists might perform at each one.

3. Explain the differences between actuarial predictions, clinical predictions, and structured professional judgment as they relate to assessments of risk.

4. What are amicus curiae briefs, and why would a psychological association or organization want to file them?

5. Scientific jury selection is used in major cases but is not prevalent in the typical criminal or civil case. Give at least three reasons why this might be so.

6. Discuss the tasks psychologists perform in witness preparation. What are the pros and cons of psychologists participating in these tasks, particularly as they relate to lay witnesses?

7. Briefly explain the difference between the *Frye* general acceptance standard and the *Daubert* standard for evaluating expert testimony.

8. Summarize each side of the argument as to whether an expert should provide an opinion on the "ultimate issue."

SAGE edge™

Want a better grade? Go to **edge.sagepub.com/bartol5e** for the tools you need to sharpen your study skills. Access practice quizzes, eFlashcards, an action plan, and SAGE journal articles for enhanced learning.

CHAPTER FIVE

CONSULTING WITH CRIMINAL COURTS

Jared Loughner pleaded guilty to 19 charges of murder and attempted murder in the Arizona case in which U.S. Representative Gabrielle Giffords was shot during a "meet and greet" with her constituents in January 2011. Six people were killed in the incident. Loughner was initially found incompetent to stand trial and was hospitalized and treated with antipsychotic medication against his will. He was then brought back to court and found competent. After pleading guilty, he was sentenced to life in prison without parole.

James Holmes opened fire in a crowded theater during a midnight showing of a Batman film in 2012. Twelve people were killed and dozens injured. Holmes displayed bizarre behavior prior to the crime as well as in court. Diaries he kept included disjointed meanderings and disturbing drawings, and he had a vacant facial expression in the courtroom. He pleaded not guilty by reason of insanity, but a jury found him guilty. He was given 12 life sentences without the possibility of parole.

Lucille L., a 54-year-old woman with no prior arrests but a history of neurological problems, drove her car onto a city sidewalk and into a group of people, killing one man and injuring several others. Devastated by the incident, she pleaded guilty to careless and negligent driving, death resulting. Prior to her sentencing, she was evaluated by a neuropsychologist who confirmed to the court that she had suffered a traumatic brain injury in her early forties, which likely had residual effects on her coordination. The judge considered this a mitigating factor and gave her the minimum sentence allowed under the law.

The above scenarios, reporting on actual court cases, illustrate some of the most common roles performed by psychologists and psychiatrists consulting with criminal courts: competency evaluations, assessment of mental state at the time of the offense (sanity evaluations), and presentencing evaluations. In these roles, the clinicians conduct **forensic mental health assessments (FMHAs)**.

By far, the most common FMHAs are those assessing competency to stand trial, also referred to as fitness to stand trial. At the end of the 20th century, it was estimated that some 60,000 criminal defendants were evaluated for this purpose every year (Bonnie & Grisso, 2000); since then,

Chapter Objectives

- Describe typical roles of psychologists consulting with the criminal courts.

- Describe the legal standards for competency and criminal responsibility.

- Provide an overview of psychological inventories and testing instruments used in evaluating criminal competency and criminal responsibility.

- Review research on insanity and its outcome.

- Provide an overview of the role of forensic psychologists at the sentencing stage of criminal cases.

- Outline the roles and dilemmas for psychologists in capital sentencing.

- Outline the roles and dilemmas for psychologists in assessing sex offenders.

the number has increased steadily (Zapf & Roesch, 2006; Zapf, Roesch, & Pirelli, 2014). Zapf, Roesch, and Pirelli also observed that—when considering both community and institutional evaluations—the typical cost of a competency evaluation for one defendant is $5,000. When found not competent, efforts are made to restore defendants to competency. A conservative estimate of restoration costs in an institution is $36,250 for a 3-month period. Considering the estimated number of defendants evaluated nationwide, Zapf et al. (2014) estimate upward of $700 million annually is spent for both evaluation and restoration costs in the United States (p. 286). **Competency to stand trial** is only one of several legal competencies that are evaluated by forensic psychologists—as a group they are often called "adjudicative competencies." These include competency to waive one's rights, competency to serve as one's own lawyer, and competency to plea bargain, among others.

Sanity evaluations are different and are thought to occur far less frequently, though the exact number is difficult to determine. Sanity evaluations are also called criminal responsibility (CR) or mental state at the time of the offense (MSO) evaluations. Many defendants indicate they will use the insanity defense but ultimately do not, presumably after evaluations do not support it. However, even if the evaluations do support an insanity defense, defendants may decide not to use it for many reasons that will be mentioned later in the chapter. CR evaluations also are often combined with evaluations of competency to stand trial. That is, some jurisdictions allow the examiner to evaluate both competency and sanity, although in other jurisdictions this is frowned upon or even forbidden. Scholarly experts usually warn clinicians not to conduct dual-purpose evaluations of this nature because the two concepts are legally distinct (Melton et al., 2007; Zapf et al., 2014).

At sentencing, psychological and psychiatric input is the exception rather than the rule, but it is becoming more common, particularly if the sentencing judge is interested in knowing an offender's amenability to substance abuse treatment or sex offender treatment. Psychologists and psychiatrists also may be asked to assess psychoneurological factors that could mitigate the degree of responsibility of the defendant, as in the example of Lucille L. at the beginning of the chapter. Clinical input also may be sought in death penalty cases, particularly when statutes require that the jury take into account the future dangerousness of the person being sentenced, as is the case in at least two death penalty states.

This chapter will be devoted primarily to these three areas: competency, insanity, and sentencing. Throughout the chapter, we will be referring to the forensic psychologist, but it is important to remind readers that forensic examiners are often psychiatrists or psychiatric social workers. The role of mental health professionals in criminal court settings is crucial. The U.S. Supreme Court has made it clear that, along with a right to legal representation, criminal defendants have a constitutional right to mental health assistance if they cannot afford it (*Ake v. Oklahoma*, 1985). Most recently, the Court clarified that that assistance must be independent of the prosecution—that is, not a mental health practitioner shared by the two sides (*McWilliams v. Dunn*, 2017). In addition, we will cover in this chapter the controversy surrounding the civil commitment of some sexual offenders after they have served their criminal sentences, a topic that reminds us of the interrelationship between criminal and civil courts. Treatment of sex offenders in prison and community settings will be covered in Chapter 12.

COMPETENCY TO STAND TRIAL

Of the many defendants who are evaluated for competency to stand trial, approximately 20% are initially ruled not competent by the presiding judge. Like Jared Loughner, however, most incompetent defendants are eventually restored to competency. It should be noted that although courts and statutes continue to use the term *competency to stand trial*, the psychological research literature is increasingly replacing the term with *adjudicative competence* (e.g.,

Mumley, Tillbrook, & Grisso, 2003; Nicholson & Norwood, 2000). This is in response to the theory proposed by Richard Bonnie (1992), who suggested that competency to stand trial must involve both "competency to proceed" and "decisional competency." As Bonnie stated, courts to that point had focused almost exclusively on the competency to proceed without thoroughly taking into account the complex decisional abilities that are required of defendants in a wide variety of contexts—for example, competency to plead guilty, to represent themselves, and to engage in plea bargaining. Since that time, the U.S. Supreme Court weighed in on competency in a few other areas, as we note shortly. The term **adjudicative competence** also is broad enough to subsume a wide range of abilities defendants are expected to possess. For example, if defendants want to waive their rights to lawyers, the law says they must be competent to do so. If they plead guilty to a crime—and thereby waive their right to a trial with all of the due process protections that a trial entails—they must be competent to do so. As noted in the previous chapter, it is estimated that 90% to 95% of criminal defendants plead guilty rather than going to trial.

Criminal defendants have much to lose in the face of criminal prosecution (e.g., their freedom and sometimes their lives). Therefore, the law guarantees them a number of substantive and due process protections, including the right to a lawyer during custodial interrogation, the right to a lawyer at every critical stage of the criminal proceedings, and the right to a jury trial in most felony and some misdemeanor cases. Again, if they waive these rights, they are supposed to be competent to do so. As we learned in Chapter 3—in discussing police interrogation—a confession (which is a waiver of one's right to remain silent) is not valid if it is not made voluntarily. The Supreme Court has often reiterated that a waiver of constitutional rights must be knowing, intelligent, and valid (e.g., *Fare v. Michael C.*, 1979).

Legal Standard for Competency

The standard for competency to stand trial was announced by the Supreme Court in the 1960 case *Dusky v. United States* and has been adopted in most states. A similar standard exists in Canadian courts and in the United Kingdom, based on court cases in those countries (Ramos-Gonzalez, Weiss, Schweizer, & Rosinski, 2016). In the *Dusky* case, the Court ruled that defendants are competent to stand trial if they have "sufficient present ability to consult with [their] lawyer with reasonable degrees of rational understanding . . . and a rational as well as a factual understanding of the proceedings" (p. 402). Competency requires not only that defendants understand what is happening, but also that they be able to assist their attorneys in the preparation of their defense. This has become known as the two-pronged *Dusky* standard. Many scholars have pointed out that the Supreme Court did not give enough attention to the *level* of competency required in a particular case (e.g., Brakel, 2003; Roesch, Zapf, Golding, & Skeem, 1999). For instance, a defendant might meet the standard for competency if charged with retail theft in a straightforward case. However, the same defendant, charged with manslaughter and facing what is expected to be a protracted trial, might not meet the standard. Therefore, the clinician assessing a defendant's competency to stand trial must not only consider a person's overall ability to understand charges and help his or her attorney, but must also consider the complexity of the specific case. (See Table 5.1 for list of *Dusky* and other competency-related cases.)

The Supreme Court has ruled (*Godinez v. Moran*, 1993) that the *Dusky* standards apply to other competencies as well, such as the competency to waive one's *Miranda* rights, plead guilty, or engage in plea bargaining. Again, some mental health professionals believe that this one-size-fits-all approach leaves much to be desired. Guilty pleas, they argue, should be scrutinized very carefully because of their implications. The waiver of a number of constitutional rights that a guilty plea entails requires decisional competence that many defendants simply do not have.

Table 5.1 Representative U.S. Supreme Court Cases Relevant to Competency to Stand Trial	
Dusky v. U.S. (1960)	Established two-pronged standard
Jackson v. Indiana (1972)	Incompetent defendant cannot be institutionalized indefinitely if no progress is made to restore to competency
Godinez v. Moran (1993)	Dusky standard applies to other pretrial competencies
Cooper v. Oklahoma (1996)	Burden of proving incompetence must not be higher than preponderance of evidence
Sell v. U.S. (2003)	Forced medication to restore competency is subject to stringent review; nonviolent/nondangerous defendant should not be medicated against his will
Indiana v. Edwards (2008)	State can deny the right of self-representation to a defendant who is mentally disordered but still competent to stand trial

Immigration Proceedings

Recently, the question of adjudicative competency in immigration deportation or removal proceedings has been raised by immigration lawyers and legal and behavioral scholars and researchers (e.g., American Bar Association, 2009; Filone & King, 2015; Ochoa, Pleasants, Penn, & Stone, 2010; Ramos-Gonzalez et al., 2016; Wilson, Prokop, & Robins, 2015). It is important to emphasize that these proceedings are civil, not criminal in nature, and are not identical to the competency discussed above. Nevertheless, they are highly relevant to our discussion. Virtually every scholarly article on this topic includes four dominant themes: (1) the extent of mental health problems that immigrants face (e.g., depression, PTSD), (2) the complex and changing nature of immigration law, (3) the special challenges that face the mental health professional (e.g., language barriers, importance of appreciating cultural differences), and (4) the likelihood that mental health practitioners will be conducting increasingly more assessments of immigrants. Recall that in Chapter 4, we referred to the increase in immigration judges in recent years to handle growing caseloads of deportation cases.

Immigrants obviously have a lot to lose in deportation proceedings, including separation from their families, and some are at risk of being returned to places where they face severe hardships. Those who seek asylum and fear being denied are subject to persecution, including torture, in the country they sought to escape. In reality, immigrants often do not show up for court hearings because they did not understand how to connect with lawyers, or out of fear of being immediately deported (Preston, 2017). It is humane to recognize, then, that those immigrants who do appear have a need to understand proceedings and help attorneys. (See Photo 5.1.)

As stated above, removal proceedings are deemed civil, not criminal, and therefore immigrants are not granted the same constitutional rights as criminal defendants in this context (Filone & King, 2015). Nevertheless, as a matter of fairness, courts have recognized the need for competence in removal proceedings. For example, a three-pronged test was announced in the case *In Re M-A-M* (2011) (Ramos-Gonzales et al., 2016), and a later case, *Franco-Gonzalez v. Holder* (2013), articulated the following standard:

> The test for determining whether an alien (sic) is competent to participate in immigration proceedings is whether he or she has a rational and factual understanding of the

nature and object of the proceedings, can consult with the attorney or representative if there is one, and has a reasonable opportunity to examine and present evidence and cross-examine witnesses. (p. 479)

As noted by Ramos-Gonzales et al. (2016, p. 286), "the legal standard for immigration proceedings in the United States addresses the additional responsibilities faced by claimants, and therefore requires a higher level of competence than is required by the criminal standard in either Canada or the United States."

Note that the standard does not require that a lawyer be appointed. At about the same time of the court ruling, the U.S. Justice Department (DOJ) and Department of Homeland Security (DHS) issued guidelines that required immigration judges to be more alert to possible mental health problems in persons subject to deportation, most particularly those who were unrepresented. The guidelines also offered protections, including mental health screening, independent forensic mental health assessments by certified and trained psychiatrists and psychologists, and qualified representatives for those who were incompetent, to list a few of these protections (Filone & King, 2015).

▸ **Photo 5.1** People outside an immigration court express support for immigrant families. *Source:* © iStockphoto.com/AAraujo.

Because the guidelines are new, little research has been conducted on their implementation. Relevant research indicates that immigration lawyers or appropriate representatives are unlikely to question the competence of their clients unless signs of severe intellectual disability or mental disorder were present (Becker, 2014). Furthermore, agency officials and immigration judges are faced with crowded dockets and are not equipped to see signs of psychological problems; as a group, judges in criminal courts are more familiar with issues surrounding competency to stand trial. Finally, law and policy with respect to immigration issues is changing rapidly. For these reasons, there may be far fewer referrals made for assessments by forensic mental health professionals than are truly warranted.

Self-Representation in Criminal Cases

Criminal defendants have the right to be represented by lawyers in all criminal prosecutions if there is the possibility of even one day incarcerated (*Gideon v. Wainwright, 1963*; *Argersinger v. Hamlin*, 1972). This means that if a criminal defendant cannot afford a lawyer, one will be assigned. Note that adequate representation, not perfect representation, is what is guaranteed.

In some criminal cases, defendants choose to waive the right to an attorney and to represent themselves. This, too, is a right guaranteed under the U.S. Constitution (*Faretta v. California*, 1975) but one which is exercised by very few criminal defendants. To paraphrase a well-worn but perhaps too cynical bromide, "The man who chooses to defend himself has a fool for a lawyer." Alternatively, some defendants choose to ignore the advice of their attorneys and proceed with a defense that the attorney believes is not in their best interest.

There are many high-profile criminal cases that lead scholars to question the wisdom of allowing criminal defendants who are presumably mentally disordered to take such an approach. Theodore Kaczynski (the Unabomber) was an apparently delusional defendant who rejected the advice of his attorney to plead not guilty by reason of insanity. He subsequently pleaded guilty and avoided a death sentence, but had he taken his attorney's advice, he *might* not have been convicted (though he almost certainly would have been institutionalized). Colin Ferguson, who opened fire on a Long Island commuter train, killing six people and injuring many others, was allowed to waive his right to a lawyer and represent himself during his trial. Ferguson suffered from a paranoid personality disorder but was nonetheless competent to stand trial. Ferguson rejected the advice of his attorney that he plead not guilty by reason of insanity, then insisted on defending himself, and was allowed to do so. He was convicted and remains imprisoned to this day, serving life sentences, and he is often sent to isolation for violating prison rules. However, many scholars and observers believe that the trial of Colin Ferguson was an embarrassment to our system of justice (Perlin, 1996). "Ferguson proceeded to represent himself in a fashion that observers unanimously considered bizarre" (Slobogin & Mashburn, 2000, p. 1608). During the trial, he made rambling statements, proposed conspiracy theories, and tried to call then-President Clinton as a witness. Over 10 years after the Ferguson case, the Supreme Court ruled that a defendant who was competent to stand trial was not necessarily competent to serve as his own lawyer (*Indiana v. Edwards*, 2008—see Focus 4.1). In other words, a judge can deny the request of a defendant who wants to serve as is own lawyer, but who is clearly mentally disordered but still competent to stand trial. Had the Ferguson case occurred after *Indiana v. Edwards*, would a judge have been inclined to override Ferguson's decision to serve as his own lawyer?

In a later case, Zacarias Moussaoui, the man known as "the 20th 9/11 hijacker," spent over 4 years in jail before finally pleading guilty to a variety of conspiracy charges. During those years of pretrial detention, he refused to enter pleas, fired his attorney, was ordered to undergo psychological evaluations, was found competent, and was given permission to represent himself (a permission the judge later withdrew), among many other pretrial machinations. Moussaoui eventually decided to plead guilty. After doing so, he gave testimony detrimental to his own interests at his sentencing hearing, against the advice of his attorney.

Most recently, Dylann Roof, convicted in the 2015 Mother Emanuel church killings, initially wanted to represent himself during his trial, after having gone through several competency hearings and ultimately being found competent. He changed his mind, had lawyers during the trial, but represented himself during the capital sentencing phase. He rejected the advice of stand-by lawyers that he introduce evidence of his mental state. (A stand-by lawyer is one appointed by the judge to offer advice on as needed basis to defendants who choose to represent themselves in criminal proceedings.) Instead, Roof told the jury to disregard anything they heard from his lawyers about his mental state during his trial, said he did not have psychological problems, and pontificated about the need to keep the white race pure. Roof was sentenced to death. In April 2017, he pleaded guilty to the nine murders in state court and was sentenced to consecutive life sentences. It is possible that Roof will never be executed—no federal inmate has been put to death since Timothy McVeigh, the Oklahoma City bomber—but he almost assuredly will spend the rest of his life in prison.

Finally, it must be mentioned that—in the immigration-related proceedings discussed above—immigrants who appear in court have little choice other than to represent themselves or be represented by an advocate who may not be proficient in immigration law. There is a shortage of lawyers who specialize in immigration law (Filone & King, 2015). Because immigration proceedings are civil in nature, they do not carry a right to legal representation, and there is as of yet no incentive for a judge to deny self-representation—in fact, self-representation may be the norm. It is crucial that, in assessing competency to participate in removal proceedings, a forensic examiner carefully assess the individual's understanding of this court process and how he or she will present a case to the presiding judge (Filone & King, 2015).

There are several reasons why competency evaluations are so common. First, questions about a defendant's adjudicative competence can arise at many different stages of the criminal process, and defendants get evaluated and reevaluated. In a case to be discussed again below (*Cooper v. Oklahoma*, 1996), questions about competence were raised five different times, the

FOCUS 5.1. *INDIANA V. EDWARDS*: COMPETENCY TO STAND TRIAL AND COMPETENCY TO REPRESENT ONESELF

Ahmad Edwards, an individual with schizophrenia, had a lengthy psychiatric history. In relation to the present case, Edwards had tried to steal a pair of shoes from a department store. In the process, he fired at a security officer and wounded a bystander. He was charged with attempted murder, battery with a deadly weapon, criminal recklessness, and theft.

Edwards's case illustrates the circuitous route criminal cases can take on the road to the actual trial. The defendant had three different competency hearings; he was found incompetent in the first and was hospitalized for competency restoration. In a second hearing, he was found competent, but his lawyer soon asked for another competency evaluation; in a third hearing, he was found incompetent, was rehospitalized, and subsequently was found competent to stand trial. He then asked to represent himself but was denied the request, was appointed a lawyer, and was ultimately convicted. Edwards appealed to the Indiana Court of Appeals, arguing that his right to represent himself had been violated. The court agreed with Edwards and ordered a new trial. The state then appealed to the Indiana Supreme Court, and that court also agreed with Edwards. As a last resort, the state of Indiana asked the U.S. Supreme Court to review the decision, which it agreed to do.

The Court (*Indiana v. Edwards*, 2008) ruled that a judge could *insist* that a seriously mentally ill defendant be represented by a lawyer, even if he was found competent to stand trial; in other words, just because a defendant was competent to stand trial, it did not necessarily mean he was competent to represent himself. It is interesting to note, though, that Indiana also asked the Court to issue a general rule that would deny criminal defendants the right to represent themselves at trial if they could not communicate coherently with the court or a jury. The Supreme Court rejected that universal rule, preferring to have judges make the determination on a case-by-case basis, based on their information and observations of the defendant.

Like most cases that reach the level of the U.S. Supreme Court, the *Edwards* case is obviously more complex than what we can present here. However, it is now clear that, although defendants still have a constitutional right to self-representation in keeping with *Faretta v. California* (1975), states can allow judges to deny that right to seriously mentally ill defendants.

Questions for Discussion

1. Should judges be allowed to deny someone other than one who is seriously mentally ill the right to represent himself or herself in a criminal proceeding?
2. Why would someone want to serve as his or her own lawyer in a criminal case?

---

last time at Cooper's sentencing hearing. The defendant in the *Edwards* case discussed above had had three competency hearings and two hearings on whether he could represent himself at trial. Both Loughner and Roof had several competency evaluations and hearings before their cases reached the trial stage.

Second, an unknown number of criminal defendants are reevaluated over a period of years after their first cases have been resolved because they are charged with additional crimes. Although our examples thus far have been of serious cases, competency evaluations routinely involve defendants charged with relatively minor crimes (Pirelli, Gottdiener, & Zapf, 2011). In virtually every state, certain defendants charged with misdemeanors or lesser felonies are well known to police, the judicial system, and the mental health system. They continually appear before the court, are sent for competency evaluation, are found incompetent (or competent), are hospitalized (or not), have charges dropped (or plead guilty), spend time on probation (or in jail), and go forth into the community until their next criminal charge. The mental health courts mentioned in Chapter 4 are intended to prevent the perpetuation of this revolving-door process by diverting primarily nonviolent, mentally disordered individuals from the criminal process and providing community supervision and meaningful treatment.

Finally, developments in forensic psychology itself may explain the frequency of competency evaluations. As we will discuss later in the chapter, the evaluation process has been made considerably simpler with the development of competency assessment instruments and the training of graduate and postgraduate students in making these assessments. Despite this, there is also evidence that lawyers do not always seek competency evaluations for their clients, even when they suspect incompetency (Hoge, Bonnie, Poythress, & Monahan, 1992; Murrie & Zelle, 2015). This is particularly likely to occur in less serious cases, and several reasons may account for it, including a lawyer's resistance to having the client institutionalized, the time and cost involved, or a genuine belief that the client is better served if his or her case is disposed of quickly through a plea bargain. Finally, lawyers also may fail to recognize that a deficit such as intellectual disability may render a defendant not competent to participate in the court proceedings (Murrie & Zelle, 2015). (See Perspective 5.1 later in the chapter, in which Dr. Murrie discusses his career and his wide-ranging research interests.)

Evaluating Adjudicative Competence

Forensic psychologists evaluate defendants for adjudicative competence in a number of different settings. For example, a brief competency screening may be carried out very early in criminal processing while the defendant is being held in jail. Defendants also may be evaluated in the community, on an outpatient basis, while on pretrial release. Additionally, as noted above, questions about the competency of individuals at risk of deportation are often raised. Although these are not criminal proceedings, standards for assessing competence still apply. However, immigration evaluations almost invariably occur in detention facilities rather than in hospital or community settings.

Although outpatient evaluations are on the increase, partly because of the cost factor (Zapf, Roesch, et al., 2014), many defendants are still evaluated while hospitalized in a public mental facility. Outpatient *evaluation* is far more common than outpatient *treatment*, however. In other words, the estimated 20% of defendants who are found incompetent to stand trial are usually hospitalized for treatment, whether or not they were evaluated in the community. This is beginning to change, with more treatment options available in the community, as we will note shortly.

Despite a large body of research on competency, Golding (2016) concludes that to date, very little research tells us why defendants are evaluated or adjudicated as incompetent. We do know, though, that persons referred for competency evaluations tend to be those with a past history of mental disorder or those presenting signs of current mental disorders. The typical evaluation is conducted when defendants are deemed mentally disordered, such as suffering from schizophrenia or psychosis (Mumley et al., 2003). Therefore, competency evaluations often are prompted by a defendant's past history of psychiatric care, institutionalization, bizarre behavior at arrest, or attempt to commit suicide while held in detention. On the other hand, intellectual disability, emotional distress, or even advancing age might also lead to questions about a defendant's competence. For example, a defendant charged with vehicular homicide might be so distraught over the incident that she is unable to meet the standard for adjudicative competence. In such situations, the individual is less likely to require hospitalization in a mental health facility during the evaluation process.

The request for an evaluation may come directly from the defense attorney or from any officer of the court, including the prosecuting attorney or the judge. It is important for psychologists to note the difference. When the defense requests and pays for the evaluation, the client is the person being examined and the report goes to his or her representative, the defense attorney. Depending on the evaluation's results, the attorney may or may not share the report with the prosecutor. When the evaluation is court ordered, even if ordered at the request of the defense attorney, the client is the court. Motions for court-ordered examinations may be made by the defense attorney (whose client is unable to pay for a private evaluation), the prosecutor, or the judge. The examiner should expect that the report of a court-ordered evaluation will be shared among all parties.

Research indicates that most competency evaluations are court ordered and that no more than one evaluation is performed (Melton et al., 2007). "Competing" evaluations are not the norm. In high-profile cases, such as those that might involve a life sentence or the death penalty, competing evaluations are more likely. When there are no opposing experts, though, judges almost always accept the recommendation of the clinician conducting the evaluation (Cochrane, Herbel, Reardon, & Lloyd, 2013; Cruise & Rogers, 1998; Melton et al., 2007). Some researchers report agreement rates that are well over 90% (Cruise & Rogers, 1998; Zapf, Hubbard, Galloway, Cox, & Ronan, 2002). In at least this pretrial context, therefore, clinicians seem to have considerable influence on the courts. When evaluators disagree as to whether the defendant is competent, the judge is more likely to find the defendant incompetent (Gowensmith, Murrie, & Boccaccini, 2012). This is likely because, when there is doubt, the judge prefers to err on the side of caution.

As in all forensic mental health evaluations, the assessment of adjudicative competence should begin with a notice to the person being evaluated of the limits of confidentiality and the purpose of the evaluation (see Focus 5.2 for a list of factors common to all evaluations; see also Heilbrun, Grisso, & Goldstein, 2009). As noted above, unless the psychologist is hired directly by the defense attorney for an appraisal of his or her client's competency and general mental status, the competency report will be shared among the attorneys and the presiding judge. For this reason, examiners are often reminded to carefully limit the report to the defendant's present status and not to include information that might provide details about the crime itself (Grisso, 1988; Roesch et al., 1999; Zapf et al., 2014).

The examination process itself varies widely according to the examiner's training and theoretical orientation. As Cruise and Rogers (1998) stated, "There is no clear consensus on a standard of practice for competency evaluations" (p. 44). Likewise, Golding (2016) points out that no one approach or assessment procedure suffices for assessments when it comes to competency evaluations, "so in supervision, I encourage professionals to develop their own professional identity by crafting a methodology that reflects both professional practice standard and their own views" (p. 75). Some examiners conduct only a clinical interview, whereas others conduct an interview and administer a variety of objective or projective measures—such as standard psychological tests of intelligence or measures of personality. Other examiners file a generic report that includes behavioral observations of the defendant and extensive background information. Traditionally, though, competency evaluations tended to include a good deal of information that was irrelevant to the issue of whether the defendant was competent to stand trial (Grisso, 1988). Later, with more guidance provided to clinicians, misconceptions about competency evaluations lessened and reports improved in quality (Roesch et al., 1999). Moreover, more courts began to require that examining clinicians cut to the chase and provide a basis for any of their conclusions. Nevertheless, despite the suggestion that the quality of reports is improving, a study of reports submitted to judges in one state found that only 25% were of high quality (Robinson & Acklin, 2010).

Guidelines and suggestions for evaluating competencies are widely available to clinicians (e.g., American Psychological Association [APA], 2012; Golding, 2016; Grisso, 2003; Murrie & Zelle, 2015; Zapf, Roesch, et al., 2014). For example, examiners should review the case records available before proceeding with the evaluation and consider the context in which they are evaluating the defendant. Mental status is not the only consideration because a person with a mental disorder may be perfectly competent to understand the legal process and assist his or her attorney. As Zapf, Roesch, et al. observe, "it is quite possible that too many evaluators inappropriately

FOCUS 5.2. FACTORS COMMON TO FMHAs

Although forensic mental health assessments (FMHAs) are conducted for a wide variety of reasons, they should have at least the following features in common:

Before meeting with the person being assessed, the examiner should

- Understand the purpose of the referral;
- Decline to conduct the evaluation if there is a conflict of interest or if the examiner has ethical or moral objections to participating;
- Gather background information and records when available;
- Be knowledgeable about the law relative to the assessment;
- Clarify and agree on the method of payment and when it will be made;
- Clarify when a report is needed and to whom it should be submitted.

Before conducting the evaluation, the examiner should

- Explain its purpose to the person being evaluated;
- Stress that this is not a treatment relationship;
- Explain the limits to confidentiality;
- Warn the examinee of the possible uses of the examination;

- Tell the examinee who will be getting copies of the report;
- Obtain the examinee's written consent, if consent is needed.

The examiner's written report should

- Be clearly written and free of slang or excessive jargon;
- Be submitted within a reasonable time after the evaluation has been completed;
- State the purpose of the report, identify the legal issues, and note who requested the report;
- Specify documents reviewed and any tests/inventories that were administered;
- State clearly the basis for any conclusions reached;
- Be submitted with an awareness that a variety of individuals will see the report.

Questions for Discussion

1. All of the above factors are important, but could some be considered more important than others? If so, which ones and why?
2. Discuss any problems that may arise in addressing the factors listed as "before conducting the evaluation."

rely on traditional mental status issues without considering the functional aspects of a particular defendant's case" (p. 291).

Competency Assessment Instruments

Over the past 40 years, researchers have developed and tried to validate a variety of instruments for the assessment of competency to stand trial. Pirelli et al. (2011) identified at least 12 such instruments. Unfortunately, there is "scant scientific evidence for the reliability and validity of many of the adjudicative competence measures" (Poythress & Zapf, 2009, p. 320). As with risk assessment instruments, practitioners should be aware of the research evidence pertaining to any competency assessment instrument they use. Moreover, "all existing forensic assessment instruments are 'tools' in the sense that none are meant to be solely relied upon" (Golding, 2016, p. 75).

Some are screening instruments generally taking under 30 minutes to administer, whereas others are more elaborate instruments based on both interviewing and test administration. Screening instruments serve as quick appraisals to determine if someone is potentially incompetent; if so, they are then referred for a more extensive examination. Also available is a computer-assisted tool—the CADCOMP (Computer-Assisted Determination of Competency to Proceed), which is heavily based on the defendant's self-reports of his or her background, legal knowledge, and behaviors (Barnard et al., 1991). A number of reviews of these assessment instruments are available (e.g., Pirelli et al., 2011; Zapf, Roesch, et al., 2014; Zapf & Viljoen, 2003). Although we do not provide a comprehensive review here, we will discuss a few of the instruments for illustrative purposes.

The Competency Screening Test (CST)

The **Competency Screening Test (CST)** (Lipsitt, Lelos, & McGarry, 1971) is a sentence-completion test that is intended to provide a quick assessment of a defendant's competency to stand trial. The test taps the defendant's knowledge about the role of the lawyer and the rudiments of the court process. For example, defendants are asked to complete the following: "When a jury hears my case, they will. . . ." If defendants score below a certain level, they are evaluated more completely. The test's main advantage is the ability to screen out quickly the obviously competent defendants. According to Roesch, Zapf, Golding, & Skeem (1999), the test has a high false-positive rate (53.3%), identifying many competent defendants as incompetent. Because persons so identified in a screening test are likely to be hospitalized for further evaluation, this presents a significant deprivation of liberty for the defendant who would otherwise be free on bail. Based on its potential for misclassifying defendants, scholars are wary of recommending the CST as the sole method of screening (Zapf, Roesch, et al., 2014).

The MacArthur Competency Assessment Tool–Criminal Adjudication (MacCAT-CA)

The MacArthur Foundation Research Network on Mental Health and the Law initially developed the MacArthur Structured Assessment of the Competencies of Criminal Defendants (MacSAC-CD) (Hoge et al., 1997). This was a rather cumbersome research tool that led to a shorter instrument, the **MacArthur Competency Assessment Tool—Criminal Adjudication (MacCAT-CA)**, containing 22 items. Defendants are provided with a vignette describing a situation in which a person is charged with a crime and are asked questions about it. They are also asked questions about their own situation. Shortly after its introduction, the MacCAT-CA began to receive good reviews as being superior to other assessment instruments (Cruise & Rogers, 1998; Nicholson, 1999; Zapf & Viljoen, 2003).

Evaluation of Competency to Stand Trial—Revised

The ECST-R was developed by Rogers, Tillbrook, and Sewell (2004). It is an interview-based instrument that focuses on the *Dusky* standard, such as by inquiring into the degree to which defendants understand the role of their lawyers. A main feature of this instrument is its ability to detect malingering (faking) in defendants who want to be found not competent. The ECST-R represents "the first formal competency assessment instrument created specifically to serve, in part, as a screener of feigned incompetency" (Zapf, Roesch, et al., 2014, p. 299). The instrument has high interrater reliability and is likely to remain an important tool in the competency evaluator's armory.

Other Measures of Competency

Several measures also receiving positive research attention are actually revisions of earlier tests. The **Interdisciplinary Fitness Interview–Revised (IFI-R)** (Golding, 1993) reflects both research on competency instruments and holdings in various competency-related court cases. Interestingly, the IFI-R demonstrated high reliability among examiners as well as attorneys (Zapf, Roesch, et al., 2014). For screening purposes, another instrument, the Fitness Interview Test–Revised (FIT-R) (Roesch, Zapf, & Eaves, 2006) has also been highly rated. The IFI-R and the FIT-R are basically semi-structured interviews intended to help examiners explore the broad spectrum of psychological abilities associated with competency (Golding, 2016). Although earlier versions of each of these measures did not receive favorable results, the revisions have demonstrated more promise.

Despite the continuing development of forensic assessment instruments, and despite the fact that some now have good research support, they do not appear to be widely used in forensic practice, particularly by practitioners who serve as only occasional experts (Skeem, Golding, Berge, & Cohn, 1998). This may be partly due to the fact that there is not sufficient scientific reliability or validity for many of these instruments (Poythress & Zapf, 2009). A study by Borum and Grisso (1995) indicated that 36% of psychologists in their sample never used such forensic assessment instruments, whereas 40% used them almost always or frequently, a finding that—according to Zapf and Roesch (2006)—indicated a slow increase. "Unfortunately, little research on the comparative validity of various competency assessment approaches is available to guide forensic examiners in their selection of assessment tools" (Golding, 2016, p. 77).

Assessment of Malingering

Virtually every type of forensic mental health assessment requires some appraisal of possible **malingering** on the part of the person being evaluated. With respect to competency evaluations, criminal defendants may pretend they have symptoms of a serious disorder for a variety of reasons (e.g., delay proceedings, get a case dismissed, avoid a trial altogether). Rogers (1997) has described malingering as a response style in which the individual consciously fabricates or grossly exaggerates his or her symptoms. He observes that this is understandable in the light of the individual's situation. The obvious example is the offender who pretends to be mentally ill, believing that the judge is less likely to sentence him to prison. In the competency context, a defendant may pretend to have symptoms of a mental disorder to postpone the trial or avoid going to trial altogether—unaware that symptoms of a mental disorder do not equate with incompetency. Although we discuss malingering in this chapter, it should not be assumed that this problem is limited to the criminal context. As we will note in Chapter 6, individuals being assessed in civil cases may be equally motivated to feign symptoms.

Forensic psychologists have at their disposal a variety of validated tests for detecting malingering. The Structured Interview of Reported Symptoms (SIRS; Rogers, 1992, 2012) is a well-regarded instrument for detecting the malingering of psychotic symptoms. As noted above, Rogers and his colleagues (Rogers, Tillbrook, & Sewell, 2004) later developed a competency assessment instrument that includes screening for malingering. Another example is the Test of Memory Malingering (Tombaugh, 1997). In addition, some commonly used psychological tests, such as the Minnesota Multiphasic Personality Inventory (MMPI-2) and the Millon Clinical Multiaxial Inventory–III (Millon, 1994), as well as some forensic assessment instruments (e.g., the Rogers Criminal Responsibility Assessment Scales [R-CRAS]), also have power to detect malingering. There is, though, no foolproof way to detect malingering (Butcher & Miller, 1999). As Heilbrun, Marczyk, & DeMatteo (2002) assert, it is important for the clinician to use multiple measures rather than one or two tests to assess this.

Restoration to Competency

Research indicates that approximately 20% of defendants referred for competency evaluations nationwide are initially found incompetent. However, these percentages vary widely across jurisdictions, as well as across the setting of the evaluation. Pirelli et al. (2011), in their meta-analysis, found incompetency determinations as low as 7% and as high as 60%. These differences can be attributed to a number of factors, including variations in examiner training, the extent to which judges scrutinize requests for evaluations, and the availability of pretrial mental health services, to name but a few (Zapf, Roesch, et al., 2014).

Another reason for the jurisdictional differences may be the burden of proof—in some jurisdictions, defendants bear the burden of proving their incompetency, while in others the prosecutor must prove the defendant is competent (see Focus 5.3 for a review of the burdens of proof). This subtle distinction suggests that, where burden is on the defendant, it may be more difficult to be found incompetent, assuming that is what the defendant wishes. Fortunately for these defendants, the Supreme Court has ruled that the burden of proof cannot be greater than a **preponderance of the evidence** (*Cooper v. Oklahoma*, 1996). Charged with the murder of an elderly man, Cooper was originally ruled incompetent to stand trial (IST). He was subsequently treated in a mental institution for 3 months and then was found competent. His behavior during the competency hearing and the trial was bizarre at best. He refused to wear civilian clothes during his trial, claiming that these clothes were burning him, so he wore prison overalls. He crouched in a fetal position and talked to himself during much of the trial. However, the state of Oklahoma at the time required **clear and convincing evidence** of a defendant's incompetence, and the judge in the case concluded that Cooper had not met that burden. The Supreme Court emphasized that though states could require defendants to establish their incompetence, Oklahoma's clear and convincing evidence requirement was too high a burden for the defendant to bear. Put another way, Cooper's behavior may not have demonstrated his incompetence by clear and convincing evidence, but it would be difficult to argue that it was not demonstrated by a preponderance of the evidence. In other words, it was more likely than not (the preponderance standard) that Cooper was incompetent to stand trial. Obviously, a state could not require a defendant to prove incompetence **beyond a reasonable doubt**, the most stringent standard of proof.

FOCUS 5.3. LEGAL BURDENS OF PROOF

In adversary proceedings, legal decisions require that proof be established at a specified level.

Beyond a Reasonable Doubt

This is the standard of proof required in all criminal proceedings as well as delinquency proceedings when a juvenile is charged with a crime. It is proof that is just short of absolute certainty. "In evidence [it] means fully satisfied, entirely convinced, satisfied to a moral certainty" (H. C. Black, 1990).

Clear and Convincing Evidence

This is the standard required in some civil proceedings, such as when the state wishes to commit an individual to a psychiatric hospital against his or her will. It is an intermediate standard, resulting in "reasonable certainty of the truth of the ultimate fact in controversy. Clear and convincing proof will be shown where the truth of the facts asserted is highly probable" (H. C. Black, 1990).

Preponderance of the Evidence

This is proof that one side has more evidence in its favor than the other. It is "evidence which is of greater weight or more convincing than the evidence which is offered in opposition to it; that is, evidence which as a whole shows that the fact sought to be proved is more probable than not" (H. C. Black, 1990). It is the standard required in most civil suits and may be relevant to criminal proceedings as well. For example, when states require criminal defendants to prove they are incompetent to stand trial, they cannot require this by a standard more demanding than a preponderance of the evidence.

Questions for Discussion

1. Think of a jury deliberating a criminal case, where the prosecution must prove the defendant is guilty beyond a reasonable doubt. Why is this such a difficult standard to meet, and why is the standard so high?
2. Should a criminal defendant raising an insanity defense have to prove he or she was insane (by definition, at the time of the crime), or should the prosecutor be required to prove that the defendant was *not* insane? Why is the distinction important?
3. What about a defendant who claims he or she is incompetent to stand trial? Should that defendant be required to prove incompetence or should the prosecutor be required to prove the defendant is competent?

Persons found incompetent tend to be those with a history of institutional treatment or diagnosis of a serious mental disorder. The majority of persons found incompetent to stand trial are those suffering from schizophrenia and psychotic symptoms (Morse, 2003). Although mental disorder seems to be a requirement for most incompetency determinations, mental disorder itself—even serious mental disorder—is not *sufficient*. However, research also suggests that a clinical diagnosis, when included in a competency evaluation report, is a strong predictor of a finding of incompetence (Cochrane, Grisso, & Frederick, 2001).

Forensic psychologists are often advised not to include diagnoses in their reports (APA, 2012; Golding, 2016; Golding & Roesch, 1987; Grisso, 1986). This is because diagnoses are often subjective, and they are labels that can carry undue weight with persons who are not mental health professionals. In the case of competency evaluations, courts need to be made aware of the functional abilities of the defendants, and as noted above, the reports should be crafted to the requirements of that particular case. Even with an established and valid diagnosis, a defendant may understand the legal process and be able to help her attorney, while other individuals *without* an established diagnosis, who do not have a mental disorder, may not be able to understand the process or help their attorneys. Put another way, they may not be able to function as defendants. Consider, for example, the case of a person who is significantly intellectually deficient, or the defendant who is temporarily cognitively impaired due to depression because the car he was driving killed a child. However, some courts continue to be swayed by a mental disorder diagnosis alone, while others rule defendants competent *despite* a serious mental disorder.

Once an individual has been found incompetent to stand trial (IST), efforts are made to restore the person to competence so as to bring him or her to trial. This is usually achieved through the administration of psychotropic medication, to be discussed below. Clinicians typically are asked to make some assessment of the likelihood that an individual will be restored to competency or even estimate how long this will take. As Murrie & Zelle (2015) observed, though, this is asking quite a bit. "Historically . . . most authorities have concluded that clinicians are not particularly skilled at making predictions about an individual's restorability . . ." (p. 147). If restoration is highly unlikely, the state must decide whether to drop the criminal charges and, if necessary, initiate involuntary civil commitment proceedings, which might mean the person is sent to a psychiatric hospital or mandated to receive treatment on an outpatient basis.

We should note that the vast majority of individuals initially found incompetent are restored to competency in a relatively short period of time, usually within 3 to 6 months (Colwell & Gianesini, 2011).

Nevertheless, there are many examples of defendants who were found incompetent to stand trial and who are held in institutions for seemingly lengthy periods. In some states, civil liberties groups such as the ACLU have sued on behalf of incompetent defendants whose treatment was delayed due to waiting lists in state psychiatric facilities. In early 2016, for example, Pennsylvania reached a settlement with the ACLU both to create new treatment spots and to allocate funds for housing for outpatient restoration (National Psychologist, 2017).

In a 1972 case, *Jackson v. Indiana*, the U.S. Supreme Court placed a limit on the confinement of defendants found incompetent to stand trial, ruling that they could not be held indefinitely if there was no likelihood that they would be restored. However, they can be subjected to civil commitment, as mentioned above. In most states, periodic hearings are held to assess an incompetent defendant's status; defendants are kept institutionalized as long as some progress is being made. Some states do not allow incompetent defendants to be held for longer than the maximum sentence they would have served had they been convicted. On the other hand, there is resistance in some states to releasing individuals who were found incompetent to stand trial but are deemed unrestorable, even if they do not strictly meet the requirements for continued civil commitment (Hoge, 2010).

Competency restoration need not be done in an institution, although in some states the law requires this. Furthermore, some states have time limits on the hospitalization

(Miller, 2003). Like competency evaluations, treatment for incompetent defendants can be provided in community settings, and this is occurring in increasingly more cases. Recent research suggests that competency restoration in the community is effective, cost efficient, and less likely to fail compared to inpatient restoration (Gowensmith, Frost, Speelman, & Thersen, 2016).

Current research is beginning to address specific factors that predict success at competency restoration (Gay, Vitacco, & Ragatz, 2017). Gay, Vitacco, and Ragatz, for example, found certain psychotic and neuropsychological symptoms predicted nonrestoration. A diagnosis of intellectual disability and a greater number of psychotic and manic symptoms made it unlikely that competency would be restored (Mossman, 2007). What appears most troublesome, however, is the lack of information about how incompetent defendants are restored to competency, either in institutional settings or in the community.

According to Roesch et al. (1999), "The disposition of incompetent defendants is perhaps the most problematic area of the competency procedures" (p. 333). In the late 20th century, prominent researchers observed that IST defendants were rarely treated differently from other hospitalized populations (Roesch et al., 1999; Siegel & Elwork, 1990). Indeed, the predominant method still seems to be through medication for the underlying mental disorder (Murrie & Zelle, 2015; Zapf & Roesch, 2011). However, Murrie and Zelle note that informal surveys suggest that larger facilities serving IST defendants, also involve education on legal concepts and the trial process. Nevertheless, they add, "our field knows surprisingly little about where, how, and how effectively competence restoration services are delivered" (p. 148). (Dr. Murrie discusses his career and many research interests in the Perspective 5.1.)

In recent years, much attention has been given to the plight of individuals with intellectual disabilities who are arrested and processed by the criminal justice system. Intellectual disability does not guarantee that an individual will not be held responsible for a crime; indeed, prisons and jails in the United States are believed to hold a substantial number of convicted offenders with intellectual deficits, and some are on death row. Furthermore, as Zapf, Roesch, et al. (2014) have noted, persons with a mild intellectual disability may try to "hide" this disability, even from their lawyers. Thus, the issue is not raised either in pretrial evaluations or in mitigation for the offense, if the individual is convicted.

However, when individuals with intellectual disabilities are found incompetent to stand trial, restoration is unlikely to occur because of the chronicity of their condition. S. D. Anderson and Hewitt (2002) reported on an education program in Missouri that specifically addressed the restoration needs of these defendants. The program consisted of a series of classes in which defendants learned about the legal system and participated in role-playing activities. The competency training had very little success, with only one third of all defendants restored to competency. The defendant's IQ contributed to the outcome, but the IQ score was just short of reaching statistical significance. According to the researchers,

> Persons with certain levels of MR [mental retardation] may inherently lack the skills needed to actively participate in trial proceedings. Abilities such as abstract reasoning, decision-making, and so forth are not only difficult to teach but are extremely difficult to learn. (p. 349)

Once again, this speaks to the importance of mental health courts and their ability to divert some individuals from the criminal process.

Drugs and the Incompetent Defendant

As noted above, medication is the primary approach taken to restore incompetent defendants to competency. Antipsychotic or psychoactive drugs have improved significantly in effectiveness, but they still may produce unwanted side effects including nausea, headaches, loss of creativity,

Finding a Career in Forensic Assessment, and More

Daniel Murrie, PhD

Courtesy of Daniel Murrie.

As an undergraduate, I knew little about forensic psychology—certainly less than the sophisticated undergraduates I meet today. But being raised in a family that housed many foster children and was active in volunteer service, I wanted to work with people on the margins. So I pursued undergraduate degrees in psychology and social work. The classes were pleasant enough, but I really enjoyed the summer internships I sought out: in a group home for troubled youth, a wilderness program for first-time juvenile offenders, and even the FBI headquarters in Washington, DC.

These experiences left me certain that I wanted to do *something* with psychology—perhaps in the justice system—but I knew nothing about graduate school. I attended a small college that did not provide the research experience or guidance that seemed necessary for grad-school admission. So I spent my first year out of college doing volunteer work in the housing projects of urban Houston and in a psychology research lab; to pay rent, I waited tables and tended bar at night. (Tip: All of these turn out to be relevant to a psychology career.) Still not quite sure what kind of career I wanted, I applied to a variety of clinical psychology doctoral programs, with vague goals to work with troubled youth.

I was delighted to enter a clinical psychology doctoral program at the University of Virginia (UVA), under the mentorship of Dr. Dewey Cornell, a skilled forensic psychologist and national authority on school violence. At UVA, I also had the opportunity to work at the Institute of Law, Psychiatry, and Public Policy (ILPPP), an interdisciplinary center for forensic research and training. Although I had known *nothing* about psychological assessment prior to graduate school, generous supervisors convinced me I had a knack for the work. Meanwhile, my wife and I had our first child, and I became sure that providing therapy was too emotionally draining for me to be the kind of husband and father I wanted to be. (Tip: Grad school is a surprisingly feasible time to be a stay-at-home dad, and dissertations can be written during baby naps.) So forensic assessment became my focus, and after completing graduate school, I returned to the ILPPP as a postdoctoral fellow in forensic psychology.

The more my work focused on forensic assessment, the more I heard pesky questions from my friends in other disciplines: "Can't attorneys just find an expert witness to say whatever they want?" or "Don't experts just find whatever they are asked to find?" As a rookie in the field, I adamantly argued against these misperceptions. Our ethical code, I explained, forbade bias and demanded neutrality. I perceived most of my forensic mentors to be conscientious, scrupulous, and objective. I personally saw little evidence of bias in the field; but those questions about bias still nagged me. When I looked to research for clarity, I found there was none. The few studies that were routinely cited as evidence of reliable and objective forensic assessments did not *actually* provide that evidence upon careful review. Furthermore, basic research in cognitive psychology underscored my growing concerns about expert bias, suggesting that people generally see what they expect to see and find what they are motivated to find.

I continued to mull over these questions about bias as I entered a faculty position at Sam Houston State University, in a doctoral program emphasizing forensic applications of clinical psychology. The job was ideal: I was able to teach students about forensic assessment, research forensic topics, and maintain a private practice in forensic assessment. I also developed an enduring research collaboration with my friend Marc Boccaccini, an expert in statistics and research methods. (Tip: It helps to find a professional collaborator who complements your weaknesses.) We addressed a variety of research questions together, but one highlight was finally finding a way to systematically explore some of my concerns about bias. For example, in studies of Texas "sexually violent predator" proceedings, we found that opposing forensic experts administering the same risk instruments to the same offenders tended to assign very different scores, in ways that supported the side for whom they worked . . . strongly suggesting bias.

After about five years in Texas, I was invited to return to the University of Virginia's Institute of Law, Psychiatry, and Public Policy, in a position that had been my dream job when I was a UVA doctoral student and postdoc. In my last 10 years at ILPPP, most of my days have been devoted to forensic assessments in our clinic (e.g., competence, sanity, death penalty cases, threat assessments). But I also oversee a statewide training program for forensic evaluators, supervise postdoctoral fellows, teach in the law school, and continue research.

My research has increasingly focused on those nagging concerns about expert bias. After several years of field studies, Marc and I received support from the National Science Foundation to conduct a true experiment. We asked over 100 forensic psychologists and psychiatrists to review case records and score risk instruments, but led half to believe they were working for the defense and half to believe they were working for the prosecution (Murrie, Boccaccini, Guarnera, & Rufino, 2013). Sure enough, those working for the defense tended to assign lower risk scores, and those working for the prosecution tended to assign higher risk scores, providing strong evidence of a bias that we now call *adversarial allegiance* (Murrie & Boccaccini, 2015). Admittedly, this research has not been *entirely* popular; one senior colleague warned me that pursuing these research questions would ruin my career. (Tip: Don't take *all* the career advice you get!) But far more colleagues have been interested and supportive of this work, understanding that identifying our field's weaknesses is a necessary first step toward overcoming them. Most of us understand the gravity of the forensic evaluations we perform, and we want our work to be as objective and accurate as possible.

Most recently, our bias research has expanded from forensic psychology to the broader forensic science community. In response to mounting concerns that strong biases influence even the "hard" forensic sciences (e.g., fingerprints, ballistics [NRC, 2009]), I have become involved in a federally funded center devoted to improving the forensic sciences. So my professional duties now include applying psychological research on expert bias to other forensic sciences and exploring vulnerabilities like those we found in forensic psychology—a turn of events I could not have foreseen even a few years ago. Entering a new line of research—even a new discipline—after 15 years in the field underscores one lesson I've learned throughout this process: that following your interests and curiosity (with help from kind colleagues and mentors) can make for a challenging and satisfying career.

Dr. Murrie works as the Director of Psychology at the University of Virginia's (UVA's) Institute of Law, Psychiatry, and Public Policy. He is a Professor of Psychiatry and Neurobehavioral Sciences in the UVA School of Medicine and an instructor in the UVA School of Law. His duties involve conducting, teaching, and researching forensic assessment. Outside work, he enjoys athletics and good food with his wife and three children in Charlottesville, Virginia.

inability to express emotions, and lethargy in some individuals. Therefore, because of these feared side effects, some individuals found incompetent to stand trial may challenge the government's right to give them this medication. In other cases, this may be a defense strategy to buy time to prepare a defense or delay taking the case to trial.

In recent years, the involuntary administration of these drugs has received considerable national attention. A high-profile case in 1998 involving the alleged shooter of Capitol police officers (the Weston case); a U.S. Supreme Court case, *Sell v. United States* (2003); and many lower-court cases have revolved around this issue. As mentioned at the beginning of the chapter, Jared Loughner, the man who shot U.S. Representative Gabrielle Giffords and others in Arizona in January 2011, was unsuccessful in his attempt to refuse medication to restore him to competency.

Sell v. United States (2003) involved a defendant found incompetent to stand trial who refused to take antipsychotic medication during his hospitalization for competency restoration. Sell was a former dentist who was charged with fraud, and he had a history of mental disorder and bizarre behavior, including once calling police to report that a leopard was boarding a bus. During an earlier period of hospitalization, he had taken antipsychotic medication and claimed to have suffered negative side-effects. Sell's case proceeded through a number of administrative and court hearings. Staff at the federal medical facility, as well as a federal magistrate, determined that he was dangerous to others and therefore required involuntary medication. He had apparently become infatuated with a nurse and had inappropriately accosted her, though he had not physically harmed her. A district court judge and the 8th Circuit Court of Appeals both ordered the medication on different grounds. These courts did not consider him dangerous, but they did approve the forced medication to render him competent to stand trial.

In 2003, the Supreme Court sent the case back for further inquiry (*Sell v. United States*, 2003). According to the Justices, Sell's dangerousness had not been established, a fact that had been noted by the federal district court and the court of appeals. Moreover, those courts had not sufficiently reviewed the possible trial-related risks and side effects of the medication. The Court stated,

> Whether a particular drug will tend to sedate a defendant, interfere with communication with counsel, prevent rapid reaction to trial developments, or diminish the ability to express emotions are matters important in determining the permissibility of medication to restore competence.

Therefore, the Court allowed medication to restore a defendant to competency against his will, but not until a hearing was held to determine the need for that medication. The Court did not specify that this should be a *court* hearing, however, which was a critical issue in Jared Loughner's case.

After he was found incompetent to stand trial for the Arizona shootings, Loughner was institutionalized to be restored to competency. His lawyers argued that he should not be forced to take medication. Furthermore, they argued that the decision regarding whether he could be medicated against his will should be made in a court proceeding, not an administrative hearing held in the psychiatric facility. Loughner lost this fight. He was medicated, presumably against his will, and was restored to competency. In August 2012, after having been ruled competent to stand trial, he pleaded guilty and was sentenced to life without the possibility of parole. In similar fashion, Dylann Roof—the Charleston church shooter--was unsuccessful in his attempt to avoid medication.

Sell's alleged crimes (Medicaid fraud, mail fraud, and money laundering) were not violent. However, the crimes committed by Loughner and Roof were. The crimes allegedly committed by Eugene Russell Weston, the shooting death of two Capitol police officers and the wounding of two others in the summer of 1998, were violent as well. Like Sell, Weston had a history of mental disorder that included serious delusional symptoms, and he was found incompetent to stand trial. Also like Sell, he resisted taking the medication that was intended to restore him to competence. He languished in federal detention for 3 years, unmedicated, while his lawyers argued before various courts that he should not be forced to take medication against his will. In July 2001, a federal court of appeals carefully reviewed his claims and ultimately ruled that the government's strong interest in bringing this defendant to trial overrode his right to remain free of psychoactive drugs and therefore allowed the medication. The Supreme Court refused to hear the case, leaving the decision of the lower court standing.

Weston's case differs from Loughner's and Roof's cases in that he was never brought to trial. Forced medication did not restore him to competency. Six years after the offense, in 2004, a court suspended his criminal case because he was not making progress toward competency, but the court did not dismiss the charges, and he remained hospitalized. Ten years after the offense, in 2008, Weston asked for a judicial hearing on his mental state; he appeared via teleconference before a judge, but was denied his request to be released. Nearly 20 years after the offense, Weston has never been brought to trial and apparently remains hospitalized in a federal medical facility.

The medication controversy extends to the trial process itself. Although defendants often respond well enough to medication to render them competent to stand trial, continual medication during the trial itself (if their case goes to trial) may be warranted. In other words, to remain competent, the defendant must continue to be medicated. Yet the medication itself may affect the defendant's ability to participate in the proceedings, as the Supreme Court observed in the *Sell* case. Medication also creates an interesting conundrum for defendants who have raised an insanity defense. We will return to this issue below, after introducing the concept of insanity and its assessment.

INSANITY

A person cannot be held responsible for a crime if he or she did not possess the "guilty mind" that is required at the time the criminal act was committed. The law recognizes a number of situations under which the guilty mind is absent. For example, if a person acts in self-defense, believing he or she is in imminent danger of grave bodily harm, that person will not be held responsible provided a judge or jury agrees with the individual's perceptions. If a person commits a crime under duress, such as being forced to rob a convenience store while a loved one is being held hostage, the guilty mind is absent. When it is a mental disorder that robs the individual of a guilty mind, the law refers to this as **insanity**.

The distinction between insanity and competency to stand trial is crucial. Competency refers to one's mental state *at the time of the criminal justice proceedings* (e.g., when waiving the right to a lawyer, pleading guilty, standing trial). Sanity (or criminal responsibility) refers to mental state *at the time of the crime*. It is possible for a person to be insane yet competent to stand trial or sane but incompetent. Obviously, it is also possible for people to be both insane and incompetent or sane and competent. Furthermore, in contrast to competency to stand trial, where the *Dusky* standard is universal, there is no uniform standard for determining insanity.

Insanity Standards

Federal and state courts use a variety of "tests" for this purpose, a common one being knowledge of the difference between right and wrong. The tests are typically named after court cases, e.g., *Durham v. United States* (1954) and *Regina v. M'Naughten* (1843), but they have been modified to such an extent over the years that it is best to describe them according to their main elements. In federal law, the **Insanity Defense Reform Act (IDRA)** sets the standard for the small number of insanity cases in federal courts (see Table 5.2 for examples of insanity tests; relevant insanity court cases are listed in Table 5.3). All tests require that a documented mental disorder first be shown.

In some states, even if a person knew the difference between right and wrong, evidence of an inability to control his or her behavior satisfies the standard. This is sometimes referred to as the *volitional prong*, and it acknowledges that, by virtue of a serious disorder, the individual was unable to conform his conduct to the requirements of the law. For example, in these states a person who—as the result of a mental disorder—is compelled by "voices" to kill his victim could be excused. These states are in the minority, with only 16 accepting a volitional prong (A. M. Goldstein, Morse, & Packer, 2013). The U.S. Supreme Court has given wide latitude to

Table 5.2 Representative Insanity Tests in State and Federal Law

Test	Question Asked
Right/Wrong Test	Did the person know the difference between right and wrong?
Right/Wrong Test With Volitional Prong	If the person knew the difference, was he unable to appreciate the criminality of his actions or control his conduct to conform to the requirements of the law?
Product Rule	Was the person's behavior a product of mental illness?
Model Penal Code	Did the person lack the substantial capacity to appreciate the wrongfulness of his actions or to conform his conduct to the requirements of the law?
IDRA (federal)	Did the person lack the capacity to appreciate the wrongfulness of his actions?

Table 5.3 Representative Insanity Cases

Case Name	Ruling
Regina v. M'Naughten (1843)	Established the right/wrong test
Durham v. U.S. (1972)	Established product rule for federal courts
U.S. v. Brawner (1972)	Ends product rule; adopts ALI test for insanity
Riggins v. Nevada (1992)	Persons raising insanity defense have right to be seen in a nonmedicated state
Foucha v. Louisiana (1992)	Persons found NGRI and institutionalized cannot be held once they are no longer mentally ill and dangerous
Shannon v. U.S. (1994)	Persons pleading NGRI do not have right to have jury informed of consequences of an insanity verdict
Delling v. Idaho (cert. denied) (2012)	Court refuses to say insanity defense is required under the Constitution
Clark v. Arizona (2006)	States have wide leeway to craft their own insanity standards

states to decide their own insanity standards, upholding a state's very rigid approach (*Clark v. Arizona*, 2006). The Court also has refused to say that the insanity defense is required under the U.S. Constitution (*Delling v. Idaho*, cert. denied, 2012). Idaho, Montana, Utah, and Kansas do not allow the insanity defense, although they still allow defendants to demonstrate that a severe mental illness deprived them of the guilty mind **(mens rea)** needed to commit a crime.

Over the past 30 years, changes in the federal law as well as numerous state laws have made it more difficult for defendants pleading not guilty by reason of insanity to win acquittal. The federal law was modified after the high-profile case of John Hinckley, to be discussed below. Hinckley was found not guilty by reason of insanity, an outcome that prompted Congress to adopt the IDRA. The following are a few reasons why it is harder for defendants today to be acquitted:

- The federal government and most states now no longer allow defendants to claim they could not control their behavior; if they knew the difference between right and wrong, they can still be held responsible.

- The federal government and most states now require defendants to prove their insanity, either by clear and convincing evidence or a preponderance of the evidence. (Recall that defendants arguing they are *incompetent to stand trial* cannot be required to prove this by clear and convincing evidence.)

- As noted above, a minority of states (Idaho, Montana, Utah, and Kansas) have abolished the insanity defense. In Nevada, the defense was abolished, but the supreme court of that state later ruled that the state constitution required it (*Finger v. State*, 2001).

- In federal courts and in some states, forensic examiners are not allowed to express an ultimate opinion on whether the defendant was insane.

- Public opinion polls indicate that members of the public have little sympathy for the defense, often believing that defendants get off too easily. This is especially the case when they are charged with serious violent crimes.

Interestingly, research indicates that juries sitting on cases involving the insanity defense rarely apply the tests for insanity, so changes in these tests may not be that significant. As Zapf, Golding, Roesch, and Pirelli (2014) observe, "researchers have found that it is typically inconsequential whether jurors are given *any* test or standard" (p. 339). Rather, insanity cases appear to be decided more on moral grounds or on what jurors believe is the "right" decision rather than on correct legal grounds. Put another way, "their own implicit theories of insanity and responsibility guide their interpretation of the admittedly vague and nonspecific linguistic terms of insanity standards" (Zapf, Golding, et al., p. 339). A good illustration may be the Colorado theater shooting in 2012 in which the perpetrator killed 12 people and injured many others. There was considerable evidence that James Holmes had a serious mental illness. He kept notebooks of his bizarre fantasies; was diagnosed with a schizoid personality disorder, depression, and a social anxiety disorder, among other problems; and had vacant looks during his court appearances. He pleaded not guilty by reason of insanity, but was convicted. Another example is Andrea Yates, the woman who drowned her five children in a bathtub in 2001. Although she had a long history of mental illness, a jury convicted her. Years later, in a second trial before a judge, she was acquitted and was subsequently sent to a mental hospital, where she remains to this day.

Anecdotal reports also suggest that juries have difficulty with the insanity defense, but other anecdotes differ. In a recent case in which a psychologist was killed in her office, the jury apparently debated the insanity issue for about 10 days and ultimately could not decide on a verdict. In the defendant's second trial, a new jury found him guilty. In a high profile case involving the 1979 abduction and murder of a 6-year-old boy, Etan Patz, an arrest was made 33 years after the event occurred. The defendant, who had a history of intellectual disability and mental illness, had confessed to police. Although lawyers argued that the confession was coerced, they also raised the insanity defense. The jury deliberated 18 days (although it is unknown how much of this deliberation focused on the insanity issue) and could not reach a unanimous decision. The judge declared a mistrial. In a second trial, the defendant was convicted. (See Focus 5.4 for more information about this case.) In a different scenario, a 19-year-old woman was acquitted in a brutal stabbing of a taxi driver after a psychologist testified that she had suffered from delusions and hearing voices for many years; he called her the face of mental illness. A jury found her not guilty by reason of insanity after little deliberation.

Incidence of Insanity Defense

Cases in which defendants actually plead not guilty by reason of insanity (NGRI) are rare, comprising a mere 1% to 3% of all felony criminal cases (Golding, Skeem, Roesch, & Zapf, 1999). In high-profile cases, defendants may indicate that they will use the insanity defense but decide not to do it later in the process. Furthermore, despite media publicity surrounding the insanity defense—one commentator (Perlin, 2003) has referred to it as the "media darling"—the defense is usually not successful. Most defendants who argue that they were not criminally responsible are found guilty, which may be one reason why individuals who initially indicate they will use the defense change their mind. Another reason is that defendants who are acquitted on this basis do not go free, as we will discuss shortly.

The rates of acquittal vary widely by jurisdiction, though. Some multistate surveys have found acquittal rates of 20% to 25% (Cirincione, Steadman, & McGreevy, 1995). Although a "success" rate of 1 in 4 may surprise some observers, acquittal does not bring freedom to NGRI defendants. The defense may be used in both misdemeanor and felony cases, and it is sometimes used to obtain treatment for an individual who might not otherwise qualify for civil commitment. Consider the following example, based on facts from an actual case.

A person who is mentally disordered breaks into a vacant home to obtain shelter for the night (breaking and entering). Because he is not a danger to himself or others, nor is he gravely disabled, he would not be eligible for involuntary hospitalization. Charged with a crime, though,

FOCUS 5.4. A LONG-UNSOLVED CHILD ABDUCTION

On May 24, 1979, 6-year-old Etan Patz left his home in the SoHo District of New York City to walk to the school bus, carrying a small tote bag decorated with elephants. He never got to school or returned home. The case drew national attention. Flyers with his picture were pasted on poles, and Etan became one of the first missing children to have his face displayed on a milk carton. Neither the tote bag nor his body was ever found. Some 36 years later, 54-year-old year old Pedro Hernandez went on trial for his abduction and murder. The trial was declared a mistrial, and Hernandez was tried again in October 2016 and convicted four months later. The case presents numerous issues relevant to the work of forensic psychologists.

Hernandez was an 18-year old high school dropout at the time of the boy's disappearance. He worked at a bodega in Etan's neighborhood, a store the child passed every day on his way to the school. Although he was usually accompanied by an adult, the day he disappeared he had pleaded with his mother to allow him to walk to the bus by himself—something that was not unusual for children at that time. Police interviewed hundreds of individuals, including Hernandez, and they even pursued one suspect who was acquainted with the family indirectly through a babysitter. That suspect, Jose Ramos, was eventually convicted and imprisoned for child molestation in a separate case, but police could not tie him to Etan's disappearance. Etan was declared legally dead in 2001.

Hernandez moved to New Jersey shortly after Etan disappeared. Over the years, he told a number of people, including his fiancée and members of a church group, that he had killed a child while in New York, but there were differences in the accounts he gave them. He was married and divorced, and then remarried. He appeared to lead a simple life and was apparently never in trouble with the law. He did, though, have mental issues, including intellectual disability and diagnosed personality disorders.

In about 2012, Hernandez's brother-in-law contacted police and said he thought Hernandez had committed the crime over 30 years ago. Detectives interviewed and interrogated Hernandez for several hours. He told them he had lured Etan into the bodega by offering a soda, had taken him to the store basement, choked him, placed his body in a plastic bag and a box, and disposed of the box in garbage. He denied sexually assaulting the child and said Etan was alive when he was placed in the bag. In addition, Hernandez said he hid the tote bag Etan carried behind a refrigerator. Neither the boy's body nor any of these items were ever found. Hernandez's prosecution in 2013 was based on his confession to police and the statements he had made to relatives and acquaintances.

Defense attorneys tried unsuccessfully to suppress the confession, saying that it was not freely given. They focused on both his intellectual deficiencies and his mental disorder. A personality disorder made it difficult for him to separate reality from fiction, so he may have come to believe he had indeed killed Etan, the defense said. Defense lawyers also advanced an opposing theory: Ramos, the convicted child molester, who was then in prison, had actually committed the crime. This man had supposedly admitted to killing a boy who could have been Etan; defense attorneys were not allowed to call him as a witness, but they were allowed to present this alternative theory to the jury.

The jury deliberated for 18 days but could not reach a verdict. One juror believed his fellow jurors were not open to considering the defendant's fragile mental state or that someone else might have committed the crime. The juror also believed police had coerced the confession from a vulnerable individual, and that other witnesses to the defendant's confessions had not been credible. The judge declared a mistrial.

Hernandez was once again tried in October 2016. Jury deliberations in this second trial began almost four months later, in early February 2017. After deliberating for 9 days, the jury convicted Hernandez of kidnapping and murder. In April 2017, he was sentenced to 25 years to life in prison. Defense attorneys said they would appeal the conviction.

Questions for Discussion

1. Review the material on false confessions in Chapter 3. It is of course possible that Hernandez's confession was false. Is it likely? Why or why not?
2. Why do you think people who first heard the claims made by Hernandez apparently did not come forward years ago?
3. Hernandez at one point pleaded not guilty by reason of insanity. The disappearance occurred in 1979, and the first trial was held over 30 years later. What problems would that present for an NGRI defense? How would the time lapse affect a criminal responsibility evaluation?

he may be referred for a competency evaluation. The evaluation allows his hospitalization for at least a temporary period, which may be sufficient to stabilize his mental disorder. Returned to court, he is found competent, but his attorney wonders whether a defense of not guilty by reason of insanity could be supported. The defendant is returned to the hospital for another evaluation, which concludes that such a defense could indeed be supported. The prosecutor and defense attorney stipulate to the report (accept its findings), and the judge enters a not-guilty verdict. The acquitted individual then may be returned to the hospital for more treatment. Such "backdoor" commitments are believed to be common in many places where community mental health services and resources for the mentally disordered are not available.

In approximately 20 states, an alternative verdict of **guilty but mentally ill (GBMI)** or guilty *and* mentally ill can be returned. This interesting but troubling verdict form allows judges and jurors a middle ground, supposedly reconciling their belief that the defendant "did it" with their belief that he or she "needs help." It makes little difference in the life of the person who obtains this verdict, however. Defendants found guilty but mentally ill are still sent to prison and—on the whole—are no more likely to receive specialized treatment for their disorder than other imprisoned offenders (Borum & Fulero, 1999; Bumby, 1993; Zapf, Golding, & Roesch, 2006). Some states (e.g., Pennsylvania) are more likely to offer treatment for GBMI prisoners, however. Nevertheless, "Virtually all commentary concerning the GBMI verdict has been scathingly negative for the reasons suggested: The verdict is unrelated to criminal responsibility, and it does not guarantee any special psychiatric treatment" (A. M. Goldstein et al., 2013, p. 458).

ASSESSMENT OF CRIMINAL RESPONSIBILITY

The evaluation of a defendant's criminal responsibility at the time of the crime is widely recognized by clinicians as an extremely complex one. Rogers (2016) writes that assessments of criminal responsibility "represent the most challenging forensic assessments within the criminal domain" (p. 112). Furthermore, forensic psychologists intending to carry out these evaluations must be "solidly grounded in the relevant case law, legal formulations, and specialized methods" (p. 97). Note that these assessments are, by definition, retrospective. The clinician must look back and attempt to gain some understanding of the defendant's state of mind at the crucial point in the past when the crime was committed. This may be weeks or even months after the event itself. According to Golding et al. (1999), the clinician must determine whether and what sort of disturbances existed at the behavioral, volitional, and cognitive levels and clarify how those disturbances relate to the criminal act. Melton et al. (2007) have likened the clinician's role to that of an investigative reporter, who gathers information and documents from a wide variety of sources. Likewise, Shapiro (1999) notes that in addition to a clinical interview, the evaluator should obtain copies of police reports, hospital records, statements of witnesses, any past psychological tests, and employment records, if possible.

All of the cautions mentioned in our discussion of competency evaluations (and the principles in Focus 5.2) apply here as well. One point on which clinicians seem to lack consensus, though, is the appropriateness of conducting **dual-purpose evaluations**. It is not unusual for clinicians to conduct evaluations of a defendant's competency to stand trial and criminal responsibility at the same time. In fact, statutes in many states encourage this practice. Judges will frequently order both a competency evaluation and a **criminal responsibility evaluation** "to see whether an insanity defense could be supported." In one study (Warren, Fitch, Dietz, & Rosenfeld, 1991), 47% of competency evaluations also addressed questions of sanity. Although this seems like an efficient and cost-saving practice, it poses problems, and, as noted earlier in the chapter, some scholars have been extremely critical of the process (e.g., Melton et al., 2007; Roesch et al., 1999; Zapf, Roesch, et al., 2014), emphasizing that competency and criminal responsibility are very separate issues requiring separate determinations. According to Roesch et al., it is "cognitively almost impossible" for a judge to keep them distinct when the reports are combined. In addition, an evaluation of criminal responsibility is likely to include a good amount of background information that should be irrelevant to the limited question of whether the defendant is competent to stand trial.

These criticisms voiced by scholars—as well as the increasing availability of instruments for the purpose of assessing competency may lower the frequency of dual purpose evaluations, but not substantially. Very recent research suggests that they are still the norm (Kois, Wellbeloved-Stone, Chauhan, & Warren, 2017). However, the message may be getting out to the judicial community, particularly when very serious cases are involved. The judge who ordered a competency evaluation of Jared Loughner, for example, made it very clear that the evaluation was to be limited to the issue of competency and not include an appraisal of his sanity.

Instruments for Evaluation

Clinicians have access to forensic assessment instruments similar to those discussed in the competency evaluation process to help in their CR evaluations. They are not intended to be used exclusively, but rather to be incorporated into a broader assessment of criminal responsibility. Scholars recommend that evaluators use multiple sources of data, such as information from third parties, interviews with the defendants, and more traditional psychological tests (Goldstein et al., 2013; Zapf, Golding, et al., 2014).

By far, the most dominant forensic instruments related to insanity are the **Rogers Criminal Responsibility Assessment Scales (R-CRAS)**, developed by Richard Rogers (1984). Defendants are rated on a number of characteristics, including psychopathology, reliability of their report of the crime, organicity, cognitive control, and behavioral control. Rogers has used a quantitative approach and notes that the R-CRAS has been validated through a series of empirical studies (Packer, 2009; Rogers & Sewell, 1999; Rogers & Shuman, 1999).

Another instrument, the **Mental State at the Time of the Offense Screening Evaluation (MSE)** (Slobogin, Melton, & Showalter, 1984), is, as its name implies, a way of both screening out the clearly not insane and screening in the "obviously insane" (Zapf, Golding, et al., 2014). The MSE encourages "an observation of the person's appearance and grooming, and an assessment of orientation according to person, place, time, and situation" (Foote, 2016, p. 417). The forensic psychologist should also take note of the person's psychomotor activity, behavior, attitude, and emotional responses during the examination. The psychologist may also test short-term and long-term memory. The subject's history should be included in the examination.

Compared with the R-CRAS, the MSE has received less research attention. Zapf, Golding, et al. (2014) report that there have not been any published studies of its reliability, although its validity was established by Slobogin et al. However, "given the lack of research on its reliability and the limited validity data available, the MSE should be viewed as a guide for evaluators to ensure that relevant areas of inquiry are addressed" (Zapf, Golding, et al., 2014, p. 327) and used as only one of many sources of data.

Research is sparse about the extent to which any of the above instruments are used. Most experts agree that these evaluations are complex and require the review of archival data, police reports, interviews with the defendant and relevant acquaintances, and multiple other sources of information (Melton et al., 2007; Zapf, Golding, et al., 2014). Partly due to their complexity, these assessments are often requested of only one clinician. In the typical insanity case, the court appoints an evaluator and both defense and prosecution agree to accept that person's findings. In high-profile cases, both defense and prosecution are more likely to want a separate assessment. However, although quality of the evaluations was not at issue, a recent study (Gowensmith, Murrie, & Boccaccini, 2013) found reason to question the reliability of sanity evaluations. The researchers studied actual evaluations performed by panels of psychologists and psychiatrists and found that they were unanimous in their recommendation in only 55.1% of the cases.

Insanity Trials

Once a defense attorney has received a clinician's report suggesting that an insanity defense could be supported, the attorney hopes for a verdict that his or her client is not guilty by reason of insanity. As in the competency context, this is a legal decision, not a clinical decision, and it is one that must be rendered by a judge or a jury. Research indicates that judges are far more sympathetic to the insanity defense than are juries, so a bench trial is more likely to result in a not-guilty verdict than a jury trial (Callahan, Steadman, McGreevy, & Robbins, 1991), as happened in the second trial of Andrea Yates. Juries also have been found to have many negative attitudes toward, as well as misconceptions about, the insanity defense (Golding et al., 1999; Perlin, 1994; Skeem, Eno Louden, & Evans, 2004). They often do not realize, for example, that defendants found NGRI do not often "go free," but are subject to civil commitment and hospitalization.

In 1994, the U.S. Supreme Court ruled that defendants using the insanity defense in federal courts did not have a right to have the jury told of the outcome should they be found not guilty (*Shannon v. United States*, 1994). Shannon, who had a felony record, was stopped by a police officer and asked to accompany the officer to the police station. After telling the officer he no longer wanted to live, Shannon crossed a street and shot himself in the chest. He survived this suicide attempt but was then charged with unlawful possession of a weapon by a felon. He pleaded not guilty by reason of insanity.

Under federal law (the IDRA), the jury had three options: guilty, not guilty, or not guilty only by reason of insanity. Also under federal law, a NGRI verdict required that the individual be given a commitment hearing within 14 days, to determine whether he should be hospitalized. Between the verdict and the hearing, the individual is detained. Shannon's lawyer asked that the jury be told of these consequences of an NGRI verdict prior to their deliberation, presumably so they would not assume he would automatically go free, but the judge denied the request, and an appellate court affirmed the denial. The Supreme Court ruled that persons using an insanity defense did *not* have a right to the jury instruction, although it acknowledged that in some circumstances informing the jury might be warranted. This would be left to the judge's discretion.

A critical issue pertains to the case of the medicated defendant. As we noted earlier, defendants found incompetent to stand trial are typically given psychoactive medications to restore them to competency. However, to maintain trial competency, defendants may need continued medication. Thus, during their trials, juries see them in a calm, often emotionless state that is far different from the mental state they claim they were in at the time of the crime. In *Riggins v. Nevada*, 1992, the Supreme Court ruled that defendants using an insanity defense have a right to be seen by a judge or jury in their natural, nonmedicated state. Yet, as noted in the section on restoring individuals to competency, medication is the primary method used, and continued medication may be needed to maintain the person's stability during the trial.

Treatment of Defendants Found Not Guilty by Reason of Insanity

When a defendant is found not guilty by reason of insanity, he or she will rarely be free to go. All states and the federal government allow a period of civil commitment in a mental institution or, less frequently, on an outpatient basis. Some states along with the federal government do require that the person be evaluated for possible hospitalization within a 2-week period, and that the evaluation be conducted in a secure setting. In practice, hospitalization is the most common outcome of a finding of not guilty by reason of insanity, and also in practice, numerous individuals found NGRI are hospitalized for longer than the time they would have served had they been convicted (Golding et al., 1999). John Hinckley, who was acquitted after shooting President Ronald Reagan and seriously wounding Press Secretary James Brady and two law enforcement officers, remained hospitalized for over 30 years, although he was eventually allowed visits to his mother's home in nearby Virginia. In 2016, Hinckley was released permanently. Brady, who was brain damaged as a result of the shooting, was a strong advocate of gun control legislation along with his wife Sarah for the remainder of his life. He died in August 2014 at the age of 73; Sarah Brady died less than a year later, in April 2015.

Civil commitment of a person found not guilty by reason of insanity cannot be automatic, however. A hearing must be held to document that the individual continues to be mentally disordered, in need of treatment, and a danger to the self or others. Commitment also cannot be indeterminate, without periodic reviews of the need for commitment. Most states require NGRI patients to prove they are no longer mentally ill and dangerous in order to be released, and this is not easy to do, particularly when the individual was originally charged with a violent crime. However, an individual cannot be held solely based on dangerousness if there is no longer evidence of mental illness (*Foucha v. Louisiana*, 1992). The exception may be the case of sexually violent predators, whom we will discuss later in the chapter.

Recall that persons found incompetent to stand trial are hospitalized with the goal of being restored to competency, so that the legal process may continue. Especially in serious cases—usually those involving the deaths of victims—the state has a strong interest in bringing them to trial. In the case of persons found NGRI, the state cannot retry them—this would be an example of double jeopardy, which is in violation of the Constitution. Thus, if they are institutionalized, they receive treatment that is usually indistinguishable from the treatment received by other hospitalized patients. In recent years, some states have crafted programs that are particularly directed at persons found NGRI, both in psychiatric hospitals and in community settings. Furthermore, aware that many insanity acquittees have "significant lifelong psychopathological difficulties" (Golding et al., 1999, p. 397), some states discharge individuals on a conditional basis and provide follow-up and monitoring services in the community.

Many researchers have studied **conditional release** (e.g., Callahan & Silver, 1998; Dirks-Linhorst & Kondrat, 2012; Manguno-Mire et al., 2007; Stredny, Parker, & Dibble, 2012; Wilson, Nicholls, Charette, Seto, & Crocker, 2016). Two recent, longitudinal studies of large numbers of insanity acquittees in two separate states, Connecticut and Oregon, have found that conditional release was an effective approach, and recidivism was low, providing adequate community supervision occurred (Norko et al., 2016; Novosad, Banfe, Britton, & Bloom, 2016). There are indications, not surprisingly, that the nature of the crime affects the likelihood that a person found NGRI will be released. For example, persons acquitted of homicide were found less likely to be released than those acquitted of other offenses (Dirks-Linhorst & Kondrat, 2012). Callahan and Silver (1998) studied conditional release in four states and found variations in crime seriousness; diagnoses; and, interestingly, in demographics, depending on the state. In general, the research indicates that persons who are conditionally released are less likely than convicted offenders to commit new crimes, and they are more likely to have their conditional releases revoked and be rehospitalized than to be incarcerated (A. M. Goldstein et al., 2013).

OTHER PSYCHOLOGICAL DEFENSES PERTAINING TO CRIMINAL CONDUCT

Although we have covered in detail the insanity defense, it is important to stress that criminal defendants may raise other defenses that are relevant to forensic psychology. For example, particularly in states that have abolished the insanity defense, defendants may maintain that certain psychological disorders robbed them of the mens rea (guilty mind) required to be held responsible for their crimes (A. M. Goldstein et al., 2013). In some cases, defendants maintain that they can be held only partially responsible—in other words, they had diminished capacity as the result of a mental disorder. Some specific, mental health–related defenses that have been raised include PTSD, automatism (e.g., sleepwalking), substance abuse disorders, dissociative disorders, duress, and extreme emotional disturbance, to name but a few.

The extent to which judges and juries are receptive to these claims varies extensively from jurisdiction to jurisdiction. In recent years, PTSD has become more acceptable as a defense, particularly in the case of veterans, with growing awareness of the problems associated with military service and multiple deployments (Gates et al., 2012; J. K. Wilson, Brodsky, Neal, & Cramer, 2011). Any of the above conditions may involve assessments from forensic psychologists and may result in very early diversion from court processing (e.g., referral to mental health or other specialized courts), acquittal, or favorable consideration at the sentencing stage.

SENTENCING EVALUATIONS

Criminal sentencing in the United States went through a period of reform during the last quarter of the 20th century. Until that time, sentencing was primarily indeterminate, with offenders being sent to prison for a range of years (e.g., 5 to 10). Indeterminate sentencing was based on a rehabilitative model of corrections; it was assumed that prisoners would be provided with rehabilitative services while in prison and that they would be released when they had made sufficient progress. Alternatively, offenders could be placed on probation to serve their sentences in the community, but again with the assumption that rehabilitation would be offered. The psychologist or psychiatrist might be asked to evaluate the offender and offer a recommendation for treatment, which would then be forwarded to correctional officials.

Although rehabilitation remains an important consideration, and although offenders in most states are still given a sentence range, rehabilitation is no longer the dominant consideration in the sentencing schemes of the federal government and approximately 15 states today. These jurisdictions have adopted determinate sentencing, which attempts to make the punishment fit the crime and have an offender serve the sentence he or she supposedly deserves, regardless of individual characteristics and the extent to which rehabilitation is accomplished. The sentencing discretion provided to the judge in these states is usually quite limited; judges are generally given guidelines that look primarily at the seriousness of the crime and the individual's prior record in determining the appropriate sentence. A major criticism of determinate sentencing focused on harsh penalties doled out to drug offenders, which contributed to overcrowding in many of the nation's prisons. In recent years, prison systems in some states have been so crowded that courts have stepped in and ordered states to reduce their prison populations (e.g., *Brown v. Plata*, 2011). We will discuss this again in Chapter 12. In states with determinate sentencing, courts may still consider evidence of diminished mental capacity or extreme emotional distress and may reduce the sentence that would otherwise be imposed. In addition, psychologists may be called on to assess risk or to testify as to whether the individual might benefit from specific types of treatment, such as substance abuse, anger management, or sex offender treatment. In short, sentencing evaluations may focus on treatment needs, the offender's culpability, or future dangerousness (Melton et al., 2007).

Regardless of whether the jurisdiction has determinate or indeterminate sentencing, however, the forensic psychologist might be called in to assess an offender's *competency* to be sentenced. There is very little literature on this as a separate competency assessment, and we have virtually no information on how often it occurs.

In those states where indeterminate sentencing is still in effect, the psychologist may play an especially crucial role. The defense attorney is the legal practitioner who is most likely to contact the clinician. The attorney is attempting, in this context, to craft the best sentencing package for his or her client. Thus, a lawyer trying to keep his or her client in the community rather than imprisoned might offer to the court a report from a forensic psychologist suggesting that the client would likely benefit from substance abuse treatment, which is only intermittently available in the state prison system.

Risk Assessment

Recall that we covered risk assessment in some detail in the previous chapter. Clinicians are now being called in frequently to assess the offender's dangerousness to society, including at the sentencing phase of criminal cases. As noted in Chapter 4, many clinicians today see their task as one of assessing risk rather than predicting dangerousness. This is to emphasize that human behavior, including that which is violent, cannot be comfortably predicted. Rather, the best a clinician can do is assess probabilities based on a variety of factors in the individual's unique situation. Risk assessments are useful to the courts in deciding whether an individual should remain in the community.

Heilbrun et al. (2002) emphasize the importance of clarifying the purpose of the risk assessment, as in all forensic mental health assessments. They note that the clinician must ascertain "whether the purpose . . . is to predict future behavior (e.g., provide a classification of risk or a probability of the likelihood of future violence), to identify risk factors and include recommendations for reducing risk, or both" (p. 461). They add that if the purpose is one but not the other, it may not be appropriate to address the other. We might illustrate this with the following example: A lawyer requesting a risk assessment prior to representing his or her client at a sentencing hearing may be interested only in an identification of risk factors and strategies for reducing risk, such as referring the client to an anger management program, in the hope that the judge will agree to place the convicted individual on probation. To include a statement that the individual has an extremely high probability of reoffending would be problematic for the client.

Capital Sentencing

Just over half the states, along with the federal government, currently authorize the death penalty, and public opinion for it is declining, although gradually. (See Photo 5.2.) In the last decade alone, approximately eight states have banned this option as a punishment for murder. Most recently, Maryland became the 18th state to abolish the penalty in 2013; in February 2014, the governor of Washington suspended the use of capital punishment in that state. The reasons are multiple, ranging from awareness of wrongful executions to the cost of carrying out this ultimate penalty. And, most recently, the drug protocol used in many states has been questioned, with some executions postponed until courts weighed in on its use. (See Focus 12.5 in Chapter 12 for additional discussion of the death penalty.) In those states that continue to sentence offenders to death, future dangerousness may or may not be a consideration. Where future dangerousness is relevant, some psychologists have provided opinions as to whether the person is likely to be a risk to society.

▶ **Photo 5.2** Citizens advocate for repeal of the death penalty in Maryland, 2013.

Source: © iStockphoto.com/ EyeJoy.

In cases in which offenders face a potential death sentence, forensic psychologists and other forensic professionals also may work with the defense team to present arguments for mitigation, a process known as **death penalty mitigation**. *Mitigation* in this sense means to reduce the sentence by avoiding the death penalty. In a recent Supreme Court case (*Cone v. Bell*, 2009), a Vietnam-era veteran went on a crime spree during which he killed an elderly couple; he was ultimately convicted and sentenced to death. The Supreme Court vacated the death sentence, stating that the veteran's drug addiction and his diagnosed PTSD should have been considered as mitigating circumstances by the sentencing jury.

Death penalty mitigation investigations are comprehensive psychobiological evaluations of potential neuropsychological deficits, mental disabilities, mental disorders, and conditions that may have affected a defendant's criminal actions. The psychologist also may be asked to provide a more general evaluation of the offender's psychological functioning to learn whether there is anything that might lessen the offender's culpability for the crime.

Some clinicians, however, also work with the prosecutor who seeks evidence *against* mitigation or evidence of **aggravating factors** associated with the crime. Thus, if a psychologist or psychiatrist gives the opinion that the individual is not intellectually disabled or is likely to engage in serious violent behavior, this would bolster the prosecutor's argument against mitigation. This aspect of capital sentencing is particularly controversial, and it may create ethical problems for some psychologists. Some researchers have suggested that the psychopath designation should not be used at this phase of the criminal process. Psychopaths are widely believed to be cold, unfeeling, nonresponsive to treatment, and—of course—dangerous. More recent research suggests that these assumptions are not necessarily valid, as we will discuss in later chapters.

After the reinstitution of the death penalty in the United States in 1976, the first case to consider mitigating evidence in capital cases was *Lockett v. Ohio* (1978) (R. King & Norgard, 1999). Sandra Lockett was convicted of felony murder as an accomplice in the robbery of a pawnshop during which the owner was killed. (She encouraged the robbery and drove the getaway car.) In 1978, Ohio passed a statute that *required* individuals convicted of aggravated murder to be given a death sentence. The defense argued that the Ohio statute was unconstitutional because it does not allow the sentencing judge to consider mitigating factors in capital cases, which is required by the Eighth and Fourteenth Amendments. At sentencing, Lockett offered evidence from a psychologist who reported that she had a favorable prognosis for rehabilitation. Among other things, she was only 21 years old at the time of the offense and had committed no other major offenses. The U.S. Supreme Court agreed and stated,

> We conclude that the Eighth and Fourteenth Amendments require that the sentencer, in all but the rarest kind of capital case, not be precluded from considering, as a mitigating factor, any aspect of a defendant's character or record and any of the circumstances of the offense that the defendant proffers as a basis for sentence less than death. (pp. 604–605)

The Court overturned the Lockett sentence and asserted that a law which prohibits one from considering mitigating circumstances is unreasonable and unconstitutional. Although mitigating factors vary among jurisdictions, most mitigators are phrased in legislation in terms that invite the participation of forensic practitioners (Melton et al., 2007). For example, many jurisdictions allow mitigation circumstances to include intellectual disability or mental or emotional distress. A childhood marred by extensive abuse, neuropsychological deficits, and—as noted above—PTSD are other examples of mitigating factors that should be taken into account (*Ring v. Arizona*, 2002).

The Court also ruled in several cases that a death sentence cannot be carried out against two groups of convicted offenders: those who are severely mentally ill (*Ford v. Wainwright*, 1986) and those who are severely intellectually disabled (*Atkins v. Virginia*, 2002). These cases—and the cases that followed them—warrant further discussion, because determining the extent of mental illness or intellectual disability requires the input of forensic psychologists and other mental health professionals.

In the *Atkins* case, the Court gave little direction to states as to how to determine intellectual disability that would spare a person being sentenced to death (or executed after sentencing if the matter had not been taken up earlier). Questions about an offender's intellectual disability often arise after he or she has spent many years on death row, as part of the appeals process. In 2014, the Court ruled that intellectual disability should not be determined solely on the basis of an IQ score (*Hall v. Florida*, 2014). In 2017, the Court waded further into this issue by ruling that a state's method of determining intellectual disability must be in keeping with current professional standards (*Moore v. Texas*, 2017). Texas relied on a system that looked at both IQ cut-offs and such criteria as whether the local community considered the individual mentally deficient. In Moore's case, although he had received IQ scores ranging substantially below 70 as well as above that cut-off, he played pool and held jobs to earn money. Courts in Texas considered him sufficiently astute to be put to death, even though he met the criteria for intellectual disability by current professional standards. The Supreme Court did not approve of Texas' approach.

The U.S. Supreme Court abolished capital punishment for offenders who were under the age of 16 at the time of their crime in *Thompson v. Oklahoma* (1988), and in 2005, in *Roper v. Simmons*, it struck down the death penalty for all juveniles up to age 18. Thus, if a 16- or 17-year-old commits a capital murder, he is not eligible for the death penalty, regardless of his age at the time of the trial. (These and other juvenile sentencing cases will be revisited in Chapter 13.) Finally, persons who commit rape (*Coker v. Georgia*, 1977), including rape of a child (*Kennedy v. Louisiana*, 2008), cannot be sentenced to death if their victims lived. Regardless of the heinous nature of the offense, the death penalty is to be limited to situations resulting in the victim's death.

According to Heilbrun et al. (2002), "Capital sentencing evaluations are among the most detailed and demanding forensic assessments that are performed" (p. 116). The clinician is asked to provide a broad-based report that will presumably assist in determining whether a person convicted of a capital crime should be sentenced to death. Some psychologists have strong moral objections to participating in any phase of a death penalty case, with particular antipathy toward assessing risk at the sentencing stage. Many also do not choose to participate in assessments of competency for execution, which occur later in the criminal process, as the execution date is approaching. Evaluations of competency to be executed will be discussed in Chapter 12.

In light of a long line of research documenting the deficiencies of clinical predictions of dangerousness, many forensic examiners are reluctant to rely on clinical impressions alone (Heilbrun et al., 2002). Nevertheless, as we noted in this and earlier chapters, actuarial or statistical data are not foolproof either. In the death penalty context, actuarial data may be especially suspect. Cunningham and Reidy (1998, 1999) have brought attention to an issue dealing with the base rate. In risk assessment, the base rate refers to the proportion or percentage of individuals within a given population who can be expected to engage in dangerous, violent behavior. Cunningham and Reidy contend that the base rate of murderers does not justify predicting dangerousness in death penalty cases. As a group, convicted murderers are neither violent in prison nor violent if released on parole (Bohm, 1999; Cunningham, Sorensen, Vigen, & Woods, 2011).

In sum, the role of the forensic psychologist at capital sentencing is both crucial for obtaining possible evidence in mitigation and controversial for its contribution to the jury's prediction of dangerousness. In at least two death penalty states, sentencing juries are asked to consider the risk of future dangerousness in their decision making. Cases in which the death penalty is a possible outcome are unique. As the Supreme Court has so frequently observed in its death penalty opinions, death is different, and there is a bright line separating capital from noncapital cases. In *Furman v. Georgia* (1972), where the death-is-different principle was first expressed, the Court noted that death is "an unusually severe punishment, unusual in its pain, in its finality, and in its enormity." The bright line that separates death penalty cases from those in which death is not a possible outcome is one that many psychologists prefer not to cross. Yet, others believe that they are in a unique position to document the existence of mitigating factors that may spare a convicted offender the death sentence.

Sex Offender Sentencing

Psychologists have conducted extensive research on the nature, causes, and treatment of sexual offending. Because of their expertise, psychologists are often asked to provide assessments of convicted sex offenders to help courts decide on a just punishment. In many jurisdictions, these evaluations are known as "psychosexual assessments." They are typically very broad based, with the psychologist providing a wealth of background information, test results, observations, and—in some cases—risk assessments. Psychosexual assessments also typically include recommendations for treatment and for managing any risk believed to be posed by the offender. For example, if an offender will almost assuredly be sent to prison, the evaluator may indicate that he is a good candidate for a sex offender treatment program known to be available in the prison system. For an offender who may be placed on probation, the evaluator might suggest that the supervising probation officer pay close attention to his employment status because he was particularly vulnerable to committing offenses during periods in which he was not working.

Heilbrun et al. (2002) warn clinicians to be very careful in using some of the typologies to classify sex offenders in their reports to the courts. Although the typologies may be useful in clinical practice and may be intuitively appealing, few have received empirical support. Typologies also offer convenient and catchy "labels" that may follow an offender throughout his prison career, again with little validity. An offender tagged by professionals as a "sadistic rapist" or a "fixated child molester" may encounter adjustment problems in prison over and above the problems faced by inmates with more innocuous or "normal" labels—burglar, killer, or even rapist. In addition, the typologies may unjustly confine an offender to a higher security level than is warranted or limit his opportunity for participation in work programs or for early release.

According to Heilbrun et al. (2002), more promising than typologies are the risk assessment scales that have been developed specifically for sex offenders (see Table 4.2 in Chapter 4). As with other risk assessment instruments, though, care must be taken to choose the appropriate instrument and to be sure it is used in combination with other methods of assessment. It should be emphasized that both the ethical code of the American Psychological Association (1992, 2002) and the *Specialty Guidelines for Forensic Psychology* (APA, 2013c) make it clear that psychologists should use validated instruments. Furthermore, they should acknowledge the limitations of the instruments they do use. Finally, they should communicate their findings in a manner that will promote understanding and avoid misleading comments that will lead the sentencing judge to draw unwarranted conclusions about the offender.

CIVIL COMMITMENT OF SEXUALLY VIOLENT PREDATORS

In the 1980s and 1990s, Congress as well as many state legislatures passed laws and funded programs that were designed to address the many problems associated with sex offending. Most of us are familiar with variants of these laws or programs that are named after the victims of heinous offenses (e.g., Sex Offender Registration and Notification Act [SORNA], Juvenile Sex Offender Registration and Notification [JSORN], Megan's Law, the Adam Walsh Child Protection and Safety Act, the Amber Alert in the case of missing children). As a group, these legislative enactments provide resources for police in the prevention of sex offending as well as services for victims and their relatives. Many of the laws also provide for registration of sex offenders after they have been released from prison and, in some instances, community notification. Today, names of registered sex offenders along with their addresses, are widely dispersed on the Internet.

In the early part of the 21st century, the U.S. government increasingly placed mandates on states to revise their systems pertaining to the classification of sex offenders, thereby presumably making registration and notification laws more consistent across the country (A. J. Harris, Lobanov-Rostovsky, & Levenson, 2010). Researchers are just beginning to assess the effects of these mandates (e.g., Freeman & Sandler, 2009; A. J. Harris et al., 2010), and some question the efficiency of these procedures as well as the effect on those sex offenders who, based on sex offender research (e.g., Hanson & Morton-Bourgon, 2005), are unlikely to recidivate (see A. J. Harris & Lurigio, 2010, for a comprehensive review). In addition, the monitoring of sex offenders living in the community—such as community notification and residency restrictions—is believed to conflict with or interfere with treatment goals, particularly for those who are mentally ill (A. J. Harris, Fisher, Veysey, Ragusa, & Lurigio, 2010). Questions have been raised about the efficacy of extending these laws to juvenile sex offenders (JSORN) as well. A recent study found no evidence that recidivism was lower among juveniles in jurisdictions with these laws than jurisdictions without them (Sandler, Letourneau, Vandiver, Shields & Chaffin, 2017).

Nevertheless, the public as a whole favors registration and monitoring, at least of adult offenders, likely because they provide a feeling of safety—despite the fact that they also create anxiety among neighborhood residents. Interestingly, a recent U.S. Supreme Court decision found unconstitutional a North Carolina law that prohibited registered sex offenders from using sites such as Facebook and Twitter (but did not prohibit other sites) as a restriction of their First Amendment rights (*Packingham v. North Carolina*, 2017).

The policy issues relating to sex offenders and former sex offenders living in the community are important. Less widely publicized is the commitment of violent sex offenders to mental institutions for indeterminate periods, against their will, after they have completed their prison sentences. Approximately 20 states and the federal government have such provisions, cumulatively known as **sexually violent predator (SVP)** statutes. "All 50 states have sex offender registries, but only 21 jurisdictions have taken the additional step of creating civil commitment laws especially designed for sex offenders" (Phenix & Jackson, 2016, pp. 162–163). The first estimates of the number of individuals detained or committed under these laws ranged from 1,300 to 2,209 (La Fond, 2003), but are now believed to be in the vicinity of 4,500 (Aviv, 2013). Janus and Walbek (2000) report that these commitment schemes are exceedingly expensive, with the annual cost per patient ranging from $60,000 to $180,000. This does not include the cost of commitment proceedings or capital costs for constructing needed facilities. Numerous legal, ethical, and practical issues have been raised about this practice. However, the U.S. Supreme Court has allowed it, provided the offender has a history of sexually violent conduct, a current mental disorder or abnormality, a risk of future sexually violent conduct, and a mental disorder or abnormality that is connected to the conduct (*Kansas v. Hendricks*, 1997). In *Kansas v. Hendricks*, the Court held that dangerous sexual predators may be civilly committed against their will upon expiration of their prison sentences. In *Kansas v. Crane* (2002), the Court added that the state also has to prove that the individual has *some inability* to control his behavior. (The Kansas Supreme Court had ruled that the individual had to be found *unable to control* his dangerous behavior; the federal Court ruled that this was too heavy a burden for the state to bear.) In its most recent ruling on the civil commitment of sex offenders (*United States v. Comstock*, 2010), the Court allowed the *federal* government also to hold violent sexual offenders beyond their prison sentence if they were mentally ill. The government could either keep them in federal facilities or transfer them to state mental institutions, with a state's permission. They are, however, entitled to periodic reviews of their mental status. The forensic psychologist or psychiatrist may be called in to assess this status. As a result of these and other developments, training sessions, workshops, and publications are now available to offer guidance to psychologists conducting evaluations of individuals thought to be sexually violent predators (e.g., Heilbrun et al., 2009). (Recall that in Perspective 5.1, Dr. Murrie mentions his research on adversarial allegiance in SVP evaluations.) Interestingly, the American *Psychiatric* Association has publicly denounced the practice of civil commitment for sex offenders and refuses to provide guidance for psychiatrists who are involved in these evaluations (Phenix & Jackson, 2016). To date, the American *Psychological* Association has neither denounced nor strongly advocated the practice and evaluations of civil involuntary commitments of sex offenders.

Although the involuntary civil commitment of SVPs technically comes under the purview of civil law, it is so closely related to the criminal justice process and to the violence risk assessment enterprise discussed above and in Chapter 4 that we cover the topic here. In Chapter 12, we will cover treatment of sex offenders in the correctional system.

Forensic psychologists may face a number of dilemmas relative to the assessment of sexually violent predators both when they are initially committed and when their continuing status is assessed. The usual concerns about the assessment of risk, including the use of specialized instruments with sexual offenders, must be considered. Although progress has been made on risk assessment in a number of contexts, the enterprise is by no means on solid empirical ground. This is an important point to make in all legal contexts, but when it comes to sexually violent predators, there are additional ethical considerations. Because of the nature of this type of crime, courts are highly likely to err on the side of caution and to accept any documentation provided by the clinician; the high numbers of offenders who have been committed under these statutes suggest that commitment is not difficult to achieve. "[T]he operative rule in sex offender commitments seems to be that if at least one expert says that the respondent is dangerous, then a finding to that effect will be made by the court" (Janus & Meehl, 1997). In both the federal system and in a number of states, risk assessment of sexual offenders is a busy and sometimes lucrative enterprise for some forensic psychologists.

It is also important to note that commitment does not require evidence of a recognized mental disorder; mental "abnormality" is sufficient. Researchers have found that many sex offenders do not suffer from mental disorder or mental illness, despite the fact that many if not most mental health practitioners believe all sex offenders need treatment (W. L. Marshall, Boer, & Marshall, 2014). In an analysis of sex offender commitment in Minnesota, Janus and Walbek (2000) learned that more than half of the 99 men in the study for whom diagnostic information was available had not been diagnosed with a sexual deviation disorder. Although other diagnoses were present (e.g., dementia, 2%; antisocial personality disorder, 26%; substance abuse or dependency, 52%), 10% had no diagnosis other than substance abuse or dependency. It should be noted that the civil commitment of persons other than SVPs requires a diagnosis of mental disorder or illness; a substance abuse or dependency diagnosis would not qualify. Under *United States v. Comstock* (2010), civil commitment in the federal system also requires the finding of a mental disorder. Interestingly, in a review of available research from various jurisdictions, McLawsen, Scalora, and Darrow (2012) found that persons who are civilly committed under SVP laws have lower proportions of serious mental illnesses than other civilly committed groups.

Minnesota's sex offender program, which is approximately 20 years old, was upheld in 2017 by a federal appeals court after a lower court had ruled it unconstitutional. It is apparently rare for sex offenders in Minnesota to be released from the program—only one person has ever been permanently discharged, and only seven were given conditional releases in recent years. Altogether, 721 people were held in the program as of 2017.

An additional concern expressed in the literature is the possible lack of treatment that accompanies SVP commitment (Janus, 2000; McLawsen et al., 2012; Wood, Grossman, & Fichtner, 2000). Although the statutes typically include a provision that treatment will be offered if available, most statutes do not guarantee that this will occur. "Nevertheless, many states claim that sex offender commitments are aimed at treatment, and that they are providing effective—or at least state of the art—treatment" (Janus & Walbek, 2000, p. 347). Minnesota and Florida, both of which have many treatment beds, are among them. Critics of these commitment statutes maintain that they are really being used to extend punishment rather than provide treatment (La Fond, 2000). In other words, treatment is a secondary purpose.

Still another concern is that sex offender commitment seems to result in very lengthy confinement. Janus and Walbek (2000) observed that committed sex offenders almost never get released. They note that, "[a]s a practical matter, the burden of proof to support discharge is a heavy one" (p. 346).

The above are only some of the many issues that have been raised about the wisdom and ethics of involuntary civil commitment for sexually violent predators. Psychologists are likely to be involved in both the assessment and the treatment (if provided) of sexual offenders. Some evaluators may assume, when conducting risk assessments, that treatment will be provided once the individual is civilly committed. As we have seen, this is not necessarily the case. In addition, as we will discuss again in Chapter 12, the *effectiveness* of sex offender treatment programs is still very much in question, even though there is positive movement in this area. Although the forensic psychologist does not set social policy, he or she should be aware of the research and the continuing controversy regarding this matter.

SUMMARY AND CONCLUSIONS

This chapter has reviewed a wide variety of tasks performed by forensic psychologists in their interaction with criminal courts. The available research suggests that the dominant tasks revolve around the various competencies that criminal defendants must possess to participate in criminal proceedings. Competency to stand trial, competency to waive the right to a lawyer, competency to plead guilty, and competency to be sentenced are examples. We also covered the topic of competency in immigration proceedings, even though these come under the rubric of civil rather than criminal law. However, in light of what is at stake for immigrants facing deportation, or those seeking asylum, their ability to participate in the legal environment is similar. Courts have recognized that undocumented immigrants do have due process protections, though they differ from those of criminal defendants. As but one example, they do not have the *right* to be represented by a lawyer as criminal defendants do, though lawyers or advocates can represent them in immigration proceedings.

There appears to be no consensus about how competency evaluations should be conducted, but most guidelines and publications indicate that the traditional clinical interview by itself does not suffice. Although some psychologists administer traditional psychological tests, instruments specifically designed to measure competency are now widely available. Some are designed as screening instruments to identify quickly persons who are obviously competent, while others are more extensive measures to identify the specific functional abilities that are lacking. Among the most promising are the MacCAT-CA, developed by researchers from the MacArthur Foundation, and the ECST-R, which was designed to assess malingering as well as competency. The results of the competency evaluation appear to have a significant effect on a judge's decision, with judges almost always agreeing with recommendations offered by the examiner. If there is more than one examiner and they do not agree, judges are most likely to find the defendant not competent.

Psychologists also conduct sanity evaluations, more formally known as assessments of criminal responsibility or of mental state at the time of the offense. These evaluations are far more complex than most evaluations of adjudicative competence—but there are exceptions. The assessment of criminal responsibility requires the collection of a large amount of background data, interviews with the defendant, and contacts with other individuals who may be able to provide insight into the defendant's state of mind when the crime was committed. The Rogers Criminal Responsibility Scale (R-CRAS) and the Mental State at the Time of the Offense Screening Evaluation (MSE) are the dominant instruments available for this purpose, though research suggests they are less likely to be used than are competency assessment instruments.

The decision as to whether a defendant was sane at the time of the offense—and therefore can be held responsible—may be made by a judge or a jury, applying a variety of rules adopted by states and under federal law. Over the last quarter century, both states and the federal government have made it increasingly difficult for defendants to mount a successful insanity defense, such as by narrowing the rules or placing the burden on the defendant to prove his or her insanity by clear and convincing evidence. Four states have abolished the insanity defense, and the Supreme Court has refused to say whether such a defense is required under the U.S. Constitution.

A controversial topic relating to both competency and insanity is the administration of psychoactive medication against an individual's will. Medication is the dominant way of treating incompetent defendants to render them competent to stand trial. However, medicated defendants may suffer a variety of side effects, some of which may interfere with their capacity to participate in the trial process. The U.S. Supreme Court has indicated that extreme care must be taken before medicating defendants against their will to restore them to competency. When defendants are charged with very serious crimes and the state has a strong interest in pursuing the case, however, forced medication is allowed as long as the court has carefully considered the merits of the argument. The Court has ruled, though, that defendants have a right not to be medicated during their trials if they are pleading not guilty by reason of insanity and want jurors to see them in their natural, nonmedicated state.

Psychologists also consult with criminal courts as judges are preparing to sentence an offender. These sentencing evaluations are conducted primarily to determine whether the offender would be a good candidate for a particular rehabilitative approach, such as substance abuse treatment or a violent offender program. Sentencing evaluations also may involve assessments of risk, however, because courts are often interested in an appraisal of the convicted offender's dangerousness. Risk assessment remains an imperfect enterprise, but a variety of valid instruments are available for this purpose. In this chapter, we reviewed some of the major concerns surrounding risk assessment of special populations, such as sex offenders and defendants convicted of a capital crime and facing a possible death sentence.

The chapter ended with a discussion of "sexually violent predators" and their indeterminate commitment to civil mental institutions. About half the states and the federal government now allow such a commitment, provided that the offender is dangerous and has a mental disorder or some mental abnormality—a very broad term that has been criticized by many scholars. Although statutes often indicate that treatment will be provided, it is widely suspected that the primary intention of these statutes is to keep certain sexual offenders incapacitated. And, although some states and the federal government do provide intensive treatment for sex offenders committed under these statutes, the reality is that it is very difficult for a sex offender under such civil commitment to be released. The civil commitment of sexual offenders after their prison terms have expired remains a controversial topic to many mental health professionals, including forensic psychologists.

KEY CONCEPTS

Adjudicative competence   161
Aggravating factors   187
Beyond a reasonable doubt   171
Clear and convincing evidence   171
Competency restoration   172
Competency Screening Test
    (CST)   169
Competency to stand trial   160
Conditional release   184
Criminal responsibility
    evaluation   181
Death penalty mitigation   186
Dual-purpose evaluations   181

Dusky standard   161
Forensic mental health assessments
    (FMHAs)   159
Guilty but mentally ill (GBMI)   181
Insanity   177
Insanity Defense Reform Act
    (IDRA)   177
Interdisciplinary Fitness Interview–
    Revised (IFI-R)   169
MacArthur Competency Assessment
    Tool–Criminal Adjudication
    (MacCAT-CA)   169
Malingering   170

Mens rea   178
Mental State at the Time of the
    Offense Screening Evaluation
    (MSE)   182
Preponderance of the
    evidence   171
Rogers Criminal Responsibility
    Assessment Scales
    (R-CRAS)   182
Sexually violent predator
    (SVP)   190

QUESTIONS FOR REVIEW

1. List at least five competencies in criminal suspects and defendants that might have to be assessed by forensic psychologists.

2. List at least five aspects that are common to all FMHAs.

3. Why are the following cases significant to forensic psychology: *Riggins v. Nevada, Jackson v. Indiana,* and *Foucha v. Louisiana?* What are any three other significant cases covered in this chapter?

4. Provide illustrations of how changes in federal and state statutes have made it more difficult for defendants pleading not guilty by reason of insanity.

5. Compare the assessment of competence to stand trial and that of sanity/criminal responsibility.

6. What is the role of the forensic psychologist in (a) capital sentencing and (b) sexually violent predator proceedings?

7. What arguments can be made for and against the involuntary civil commitment of sex offenders at the conclusion of their prison sentences?

SAGE edge™

Want a better grade? Go to **edge.sagepub.com/bartol5e** for the tools you need to sharpen your study skills. Access practice quizzes, eFlashcards, an action plan, and SAGE journal articles for enhanced learning.

CHAPTER SIX

FAMILY LAW AND OTHER FORMS OF CIVIL LITIGATION

Monica and Boris had been married for 9 years when they decided to end their marriage after many counseling sessions. It was to be a no-fault, amicable divorce, except for the fact that each wanted sole custody of their three children, ages 3, 6, and 7. Monica and Boris were both good parents who had been very involved in the children's lives, but they felt strongly that joint custody was not a good alternative. Each parent had a professional career, and each believed he or she could provide more stability for the children, with liberal visitation rights given to the other person. What was intended to be an amicable divorce turned into a bitter custody battle, with a family court obliged to make the ultimate custody decision.

Anyone wanting to become a forensic psychologist will likely spend a good part of his or her professional time dealing with family and civil law issues—for some forensic psychologists, civil law, rather than criminal law, is their main interest. Working within the family court system, for example, is an exciting and dynamic process, full of intellectual challenge (Kaufman, 2011). It can also be emotionally draining, such as when psychologists are asked to conduct parenting evaluations, as they were in the situation referred to above. With increasing frequency, psychologists and other mental health professionals (MHPs) are providing an array of services in family law cases, serving as psychological experts, consultants, mediators, review experts, and coaches (S. M. Lee & Nachlis, 2011). These various roles will be explained shortly.

Other civil cases are equally challenging, though perhaps less emotionally exhausting, to the forensic psychologist. They include but are not limited to assessing individuals applying for unemployment benefits, filing disability claims or malpractice claims, or suing employers and individuals for discrimination, such as gender bias or sexual harassment. These topics and more are addressed in the present chapter.

The chapter focuses on the civil courts in state systems that most often work with psychologists and other mental health practitioners (MHPs) in many different contexts, particularly family courts and probate courts. Nonspecialized courts of general jurisdiction, like county or district courts, also hear cases pertinent to this chapter (e.g., negligence suits). In addition, we cover areas where federal courts are likely to be involved, such as discrimination cases that involve alleged violations of federal laws like the Americans with Disabilities Act (ADA) or the Civil Rights Act of 1991.

Chapter Objectives

- Describe the roles and responsibilities of psychologists working with civil courts.

- Examine the roles of psychologists and other mental health professionals in family and probate courts, including child custody evaluations, visitation arrangements, and relocation requests.

- Describe the roles of psychologists and neuropsychologists in evaluating civil capacities.

- Review the many facets of personal injury claims, particularly those relating to employment.

- Introduce issues involving competence to consent to treatment.

- Examine the many questions and problems concerning involuntary civil commitment.

- Explore the challenges of psychologists and other mental health professionals in evaluating the effects of sexual and gender harassment.

Because no two state systems are exactly alike, there are variations in both the structure and the process of these courts on a nationwide basis, but we address in this chapter how they generally operate. **Family courts** hear cases involving family law, such as divorce, child custody and support, visitation rights, relocation, and domestic abuse such as restraining orders or orders of protections. (These orders also may be issued by criminal courts, however.) Juvenile delinquency proceedings are held in some family courts, while in other states, a separate juvenile court is charged with this function. In some jurisdictions, family courts also handle guardianship and civil capacity or incompetence hearings, while other jurisdictions leave these matters to probate courts.

Probate courts usually handle such legal matters as wills, decedents' estates, trusts, conservatorships, and guardianships. Among other things, the probate court administers and ensures the appropriate distribution of the assets of a decedent, evaluates the validity of wills, and enforces the provisions of a valid will. The probate court's responsibility for enforcement and compliance "varies from jurisdiction to jurisdiction, program to program, case to case, and event to event" (National College of Probate Judges, 2013, p. 14).

As mentioned in Chapter 4, courts of general jurisdiction are the workhorse of the judicial system, so many criminal and civil matters are dealt with in these forums. However, states are increasingly establishing specialized courts to deal with a very wide range of civil and criminal matters. Cases that formerly may have been the province of a more "typical" criminal or civil court are now heard in a drug court, a mental health court, a girls' court, or a veterans' court. These specialized courts may operate independently or may be attached to a broader court—for example, the drug court may be attached to the criminal court, or the girls' court may be attached to the family court. Forensic psychologists must of course be familiar with the structure and procedures relevant to the state and local jurisdictions with which they come in contact.

In this chapter, we will not deal with juvenile delinquency issues, even though they are handled by family courts in some states. Delinquency, and the juvenile justice process in general, will be separate topics covered in Chapter 13. Juvenile courts came on the scene long before family courts, specifically at the turn of the 20th century. Although there were some early attempts in the 1900s to create a family court separate from juvenile court, it was not until the 1970s that the movement for a court specifically to handle family law issues began to take hold across the United States (Adam & Brady, 2013). Today, family courts do not usually deal with juvenile delinquency cases (although, as noted above, some still do).

FAMILY OR DOMESTIC COURTS

Modern family courts—sometimes called domestic courts—are the venue for litigating divorce proceedings and making custody decisions, although these proceedings also may occur in courts of general jurisdiction (e.g., superior courts or district courts, depending on the state). Family courts also have the power to remove neglected and abused children from their homes and place them into temporary custody of the state, such as in foster homes, as well as the power to revoke parental rights permanently. Some juveniles themselves approach a family court with a request to be declared an emancipated minor. In states where minors must notify a parent and obtain parental consent before obtaining an abortion, family courts can override that requirement in the best interest of the girl seeking the abortion. In domestic violence situations, family court may be the place where a victim seeks a temporary or permanent restraining order against an abuser. Adoptions are finalized in family or probate courts. Similarly, contested wills, decisions about competency to make medical decisions, and involuntary commitments to mental institutions come under the jurisdiction of some—but not all—family or probate courts. In light of the powers listed above, it is not surprising that psychologists and other MHPs play a significant role in the day-to-day operation of these courts and that family forensic psychology is a rapidly developing specialization (see Focus 6.1).

S. M. Lee and Nachlis (2011) provide a handy summary of the roles played by psychologists and other mental health professionals in family courts. They include coaches, review experts, consultants, and mediators, in addition to their roles as expert witnesses and evaluators. (See Table 6.1 for a summary.) These roles are becoming increasingly complex, and skillful forensic psychologists must remain highly knowledgeable about the legal standards, precedents, and rulings that apply to the specialty area in which they practice. They must also keep fully informed about the research and clinical literature on child and adolescent development, forensic psychology, and relevant family dynamics.

Family courts can be dangerous places for court officers, other court personnel, and participants, because of the high emotion and occasional anger and dissatisfaction of the litigants. Unfamiliarity with the court proceeding can create highly stressful situations, which is one reason why the coaching role is so important. In addition, many litigants in family courts today are not represented by attorneys (Adam & Brady, 2013). Partly because of the high emotion, family courts—like criminal courts—have increased security measures, including metal detectors and scanners at entry points. Even so, verbal clashes and minor physical altercations are not uncommon. There may be high conflict between parents and sometimes between attorneys (Ackerman & Gould, 2015). Because of the heated arguments and tensions, MHPs—some of whom have their offices within or adjacent to family courts—are invaluable in offering assistance to the court judges, lawyers, litigants, and even the children of the involved families.

Table 6.1 Roles and Sample Tasks of Psychologists and Other Mental Health Professionals in Family Courts	
Role	**Examples of Tasks**
Expert witness	Testify about findings of assessments Testify about research on relevant issues (e.g., effects of separation/divorce/relocation on children)
Evaluator	Assess individuals through interviews, tests
Coach	Offer support to parent or child during custody proceedings Educate litigants about the process
Review expert	Examine work of other MHPs; offer appraisal of quality Highlight deficiencies in work of other professionals Provide opinion about data, studies cited
Consultant	Inform attorneys of research findings relevant to issue at hand Assist in trial strategy Help attorneys develop questions for expert witnesses
Mediator	Help manage distraught clients Help negotiate settlements to avoid costly trials

Source: Adapted from Lee and Nachlis, 2011; Kauffman, 2011; and Zapf, 2015.

FOCUS 6.1. FAMILY FORENSIC PSYCHOLOGY

In June 2003, the *Journal of Family Psychology* published a special issue devoted to the intersection of family psychology and family law. According to the editors of this special issue, its primary goal was "to introduce readers to new and emerging opportunities for research and practice in the areas where family psychology and family law overlap" (Grossman & Okun, 2003, p. 163). Since that time, family practice in forensic psychology has increased dramatically. Furthermore, the fact that courts now scrutinize scientific evidence in such matters as the effect of divorce on children or the quality of custody evaluations has raised the bar for expert testimony (Ackerman & Gould, 2015).

Family psychologists—whether clinicians or researchers—have extensive knowledge about human development and systems theories. Forensic psychologists have knowledge and expertise in assessment and consultation with courts and legal professionals. They also know legal theories and procedures that relate to clinical practice and have experience at providing expert testimony. Family forensic psychologists, then, represent a combination of the knowledge and skills of forensic psychologists and family psychologists.

Grossman and Okun (2003) define family forensic psychology as the study of families, members of family units, organizations, and larger systems from a family systems perspective in assessment and intervention regarding interaction with the legal system. Among the areas that assessment and intervention include are prevention, education, evaluation, various forms of conflict resolution, treatment, and outcome assessment. Family forensic psychologists provide expertise to the legal system (p. 166).

Family forensic psychologists also are of assistance to judges and other court officers by acquainting them with research on the changing nature and changing face of the family. (See Photos 6.1 and 6.2.) Some family court judges admit to being unprepared though not unwilling to deal with this (Bridge, 2006). They benefit from learning, for example, that extended family members on the premises are often beneficial to a child's stability, and that children of same-sex partners are at least as well adjusted as children of heterosexual partners.

In sum, family forensic psychology can make contributions in all of the following areas: adoption; divorce, child custody, and visitation; conflict resolution and mediation; juvenile justice; assessment of parental fitness; termination of parental rights; elder law and estate planning; child–parent relationships when parents are imprisoned; guardianship; reproductive rights and technologies; and family violence. Because all of these issues are increasingly being adjudicated in family courts and other specialized courts, family forensic psychologists should continue to be in high demand.

Questions for Discussion

1. What is meant by the changing nature and face of the family? Give examples.
2. Many different definitions of *family* are used in psychological and social science literature. Which of the following should be considered "family": (a) a divorced man, his three children, and his elderly mother; (b) a widower, his female partner, and his three children; (c) a widower, his male partner, and his three children; (d) a small, tight-knit group of young adults living on the streets; (e) three roommates; or (f) members of a fraternity living in a fraternity house? Are there limits to how family should be defined, and if so, what are they?

▶ **Photo 6.1 and 6.2** Parents and their children.
Source: © iStockphoto.com/funky-data; © iStockphoto.com/kali9.

CHILD CUSTODY EVALUATIONS

In the United States today, about half of all first marriages end in divorce within 15 years (U.S. Census Bureau, 2011). Second marriages have higher rates of separation or divorce than first marriages (U.S. Department of Health and Human Services, 2012). This country has one of the highest divorce rates in the industrialized world (Kourlis, 2012), perhaps because a divorce is relatively easy to obtain. In the past, grounds for divorce primarily centered on one party being at fault (e.g., adultery, physical or mental cruelty, desertion) or incapable of performing marital duties (e.g., imprisoned). Today the two parties typically agree that their differences are irreconcilable, and divorces are granted with no fault placed on one or the other. Rules for obtaining a divorce are governed by state laws. When children are involved, state laws also require that custody be determined for all dependent children under the age of 18 (Symons, 2013).

It is generally agreed among lawyers, judges, psychologists, and other mental health professionals that the most contentious areas faced by family courts are those involving divorce and child custody, most particularly when custody is contested, and typically, it is not. Although it is estimated that children are involved in about 40% of divorces (L. S. Horvath, Logan, & Walker, 2002; Krauss & Sales, 2000), the majority of these do not require a judge to make the custody decision. Custody is not contested because parents, alone or with the help of a mediator, have agreed on a mutually satisfactory custody arrangement. Studies suggest that courts make decisions in 6% to 20% of all divorce cases (Melton et al., 2007). Some recent data suggest that over 90% of divorce custody cases are settled without formal court involvement (Symons, 2013).

When the divorcing parents cannot come to a reasonable agreement concerning the custodial arrangement for the children, a court will order a **parenting evaluation** or assessment of parenting plans. The term *parenting* is gradually replacing *custody* in legal and clinical literature, but we use them interchangeably in this chapter. When parenting plans are needed, the courts usually turn to MHPs to conduct the evaluation. Research suggests that psychologists are, by far, the most preferred professional for **child custody evaluations (CCEs)** (Bow, Gottlieb, & Gould-Saltman, 2011; Bow & Quinnell, 2001; Mason & Quirk, 1997). However, many courts use mental health practitioners who are associated with public court service agencies, such as master's-level psychologists or clinical social workers (L. S. Horvath et al., 2002). Bow, Gottlieb, and Gould-Saltman (2011) continue to find that family law attorneys prefer doctorate-level psychologists who assume an objective and neutral position in their evaluations to do the CCEs. They also prefer psychologists who possess good communication skills, have had several years of child custody evaluation experience, and demonstrate solid presentation skills on the witness stand.

Psychologists have access to many professional articles and books on the topic of child custody evaluations (Stahl, 2014). In addition, the American Psychological Association (APA) (2010b) "Guidelines for Child Custody Evaluations in Family Law Proceedings" is a valuable resource. The Guidelines strongly emphasize that psychologists should remain familiar with specific laws and court rulings governing the practice and nature of child custody adjudication within the locality where they administer the evaluation. Equally important, the Guidelines urge forensic psychologists to maintain an up-to-date understanding of child development and family dynamics, child and family psychopathology, the impact of divorce on children, and the specialized child custody research literature. Zibbell and Fuhrmann (2016) summarize well the Guidelines and professional requirements when they write,

> Child custody evaluators require specialized skills in interviewing adults and children, an understanding of child/adolescent development and family dynamics, current knowledge of research in areas relevant to the questions asked by the court, and familiarity with the relevant family law statutes and cases in the jurisdiction in which they practice. (p. 401)

Interestingly, Bow et al. (2011) discovered that lawyers specializing in family law believe that the least important component of CCEs is the psychological testing of the parents and the child, even though psychological testing of the child and parenting questionnaires are commonly administered (Stahl, 2014). However, psychological tests are only one component of the assessment process, which also includes interviews with children and parents, observations, and a review of information from collateral sources (e.g., school records; criminal court records, if relevant). If psychological tests are used, the attorneys expect the psychologists to be clear concerning the limits of psychological testing in forensic contexts and to limit their use to that of making hypotheses or as supportive data of their overall findings. In addition, a majority of the attorneys (64%) want the psychologist to make recommendations about who should get custody, and an overwhelming majority (79%) believe that recommendations should be offered concerning the custodial arrangements following the divorce. Family law attorneys also had some advice for forensic psychologists conducting CCEs. They urged psychologists to follow child custody evaluation guideline standards closely and to draw conclusions and make recommendations that are logical, pragmatic, and based on the best interest of the child standard (to be discussed below).

Sometimes, individuals other than the child's biological or adoptive parents seek custody. In fact, family courts have seen an unprecedented explosion in both custody and visitation requests from stepparents, grandparents, other relatives, gay and lesbian partners of deceased biological or adoptive parents, cohabiting but non-married parents who have split up, family friends, and surrogate mothers (Grossman & Okun, 2003; Stahl, 2014). Although legal parents clearly have both constitutional and statutory rights to be involved in their children's lives, the rights of other individuals, including grandparents, are not universally well defined. The U.S. Supreme Court has denied grandparents a *constitutional* right to see their grandchild over the objection of the child's competent mother (*Troxel v. Granville*, 2000), but statutes in many states have recognized that grandparents should not completely be barred from their grandchildren, except under rare circumstances (e.g., grandparent has abused the grandchild). Moreover, in the *Granville* case, the mother had not totally deprived the grandparents of visitation privileges but had refused to allow more than one visit every month. Thus, although the decision did not represent a victory for grandparents, it is unclear what would have been decided had the mother refused to allow *any* visits.

The decision concerning who should have custody of the children does not just arise in divorce cases. For instance, parents or other relatives of the child may be involved in a custody dispute following the death of one or both parents. In addition, a state agency, such as a child protective or child welfare agency, may request a temporary or permanent custody determination when it believes the parents have been abusive or neglectful. It should be noted that child welfare agencies typically have very broad powers to place children in foster homes. Their decisions to do that—made by child welfare caseworkers who sometimes employ subjective criteria in concluding there was neglect—are rarely challenged successfully in court. Forensic psychologists are not typically involved, although the psychologist may be asked to assess the child's emotional and intellectual functioning.

Courts exercise greater oversight in the case of a decision to remove children permanently from the care of their parents. This requires first a **termination of parental rights**, then a decision as to who should have custody of the child or children (e.g., an agency, which places the children in a foster home, or an adoptive couple). Such terminations are rare and should occur only in cases of gross physical or emotional abuse. Parental rights have also been terminated when the custodial parent is a substance abuser, the child or children are at risk of being grossly neglected, and the parent makes no progress toward rehabilitation. Parental rights are not terminated when parents of young children are incarcerated, however. In such cases, dependent children are placed in foster care, preferably with relatives or friends of the incarcerated parent if the other parent is absent, imprisoned, or deceased.

Surrogate parents, unwed fathers, domestic partners, or friends also may seek to gain custody. In each of these situations, psychologists are often asked by the court to evaluate the needs of the child and the suitability of contesting parties to meet those needs.

Child Custody Standards

Historically, courts have relied on a number of different standards for determining child custody, but today the dominant one in all states and the District of Columbia is the **best interest of the child (BIC) standard**. The primary legal standard introduced over a century ago was the **tender years doctrine**, in which it was presumed that the children, particularly girls and very young children, were best left in the care of the mother. An early appellate case (*People v. Hickey*, 1889) suggested that even if the father was without blame, he had an "inability to bestow on [the child] that tender care which nature requires, and which it is the peculiar province of the mother to supply" (Einhorn, 1986, p. 128). Today, the tender years doctrine has given way to the BIC standard, which does not presume that either parent is naturally better than the other. Nevertheless, in the vast majority of custody cases, the mother receives primary custody (Gould & Martindale, 2013).

The BIC standard has been criticized in much of the literature as too vague and too likely to lend itself to subjectivity on the part of the decision maker. Efforts to limit this subjectivity have been made both by state legislatures and through court decisions. For example, Ackerman and Gould (2015) note that in 40 states, the statutes list particular factors to be considered in deciding what is in the child's best interest; in six states, court decisions have listed factors; in four states, it is left to the judge to consider which factors to take into consideration. In general, though, there is lack of consensus about what is meant by best interest of the child. This lack of consensus has led some commentators—and some courts—to propose additional measures or even standards to either expound on best interest or replace it completely. Krauss and Sales (2000) proposed a slightly different standard, the **least detrimental alternative standard**. They argued that psychological knowledge cannot determine which custody arrangement is truly in the child's best interest. At best, psychological knowledge can help in identifying which arrangement would do the least harm. Psychological assessment instruments, according to Krauss and Sales, tend to be pathology focused, identifying deficits more than strengths. In that sense, a custody evaluation would be more efficient at "screening out" the custody arrangement that would create problems for the child rather than making a determination that one parent would be better than the other. Interestingly, representatives of family forensic psychology suggest that the legal principle should be the best interest of the child *in relation to the family* (Grossman & Okun, 2003).

Still other modifications that have been proposed and have sometimes surfaced in court decisions are the approximation rule and the friendly-parent rule. The **approximation rule** encourages the court to look at how much caretaking has occurred in the past from each parent and to make a decision which most closely approximates that past involvement. Although this may seem sensible, it does not take into consideration a child's changing developmental needs. The **friendly-parent rule** presumes that it is best for children of divorce to remain in touch with both parents. For that reason, custody is weighed toward the parent who is most likely to encourage contact with the noncustodial parent, rather than to try to limit that contact. In some states, judges are expected to abide by the rule either because of precedent (past court decisions) or because this is called for in the state statutes. Judges and mental health practitioners who try to abide by a friendly-parent rule do so out of concern about the child's alienation from the noncustodial parent. However, this may overlook the fact that, in some cases, continuing contact with the noncustodial parent might not be in the child's best interest. In other words, the more inappropriate parent may present a veneer of being friendly toward the other parent in an effort to gain custody, while the more appropriate parent will not display friendliness toward the parent he or she believes is not a good influence on the child.

It is becoming increasingly apparent, though, that children themselves would like some input into the custody decision, although they generally do not want to be the ultimate decision makers (Parkinson & Cashmore, 2008). Even if the decision is not ultimately what they hoped it would be, if they perceive the process as being a fair one and if their wishes were taken into consideration, they are more likely to be better adjusted to the placement decision (Ackerman & Gould, 2015; Parkinson & Cashmore, 2008).

Another consideration in deciding what is in the best interest of the child centers around race, ethnicity, and culture in custody disputes. As noted by Maldonado (2017), "Custody statutes generally do not expressly authorize courts to consider the parents' racial, ethnic, or cultural background" (p. 213). However, Maldonado emphasizes that often judges do consider these in making their decisions regarding custody determinations. This observation includes a parent's language ability or immigrant status. "However, there is a risk that judges, custody evaluators, and practitioners will assess parenting attitudes and behaviors in accordance with dominant, predominantly White middle class norms" (Maldonado, 2017, p. 214). Maldonado further points out that many judges and custody evaluators have implicit biases they do not recognize, despite genuine efforts to be impartial and fair. Like all human beings, professionals in making custody decision and recommendations of what is the best interest of the child look for and process information that is consistent with their cognitive preferences. For example, any of the following might lead some evaluators to look less favorably on a parent: the parent has a multitude of tattoos and piercings; the parent is an atheist; the parent is vegan; the parent wants the child to be home schooled; the parent uses poor grammar; the parent is partially blind; the parent works at night; the parent is bisexual; the parent has limited education. None of these factors is relevant to the custody decision without further evidence that the child would be harmed as a result (e.g., if the parent works at night and the child is left alone.)

The American Psychological Association's Guidelines for Child Custody Evaluations (2010b) advise psychologists to be "aware of their own biases, and those of others, regarding race, gender, gender identity, ethnicity, national origin, religion, sexual orientation, disability, language, culture, and socioeconomic status" (p. 865). However, implicit biases are biases that individuals are not consciously aware of, and they may creep into custody evaluations unless evaluators carefully scrutinize their own internal standards and beliefs. It is not enough to recognize one's biases, however. Mental health practitioners must adopt concrete strategies to overcome these biases, such as by participating in training about the importance of objectivity or by critically examining their own conclusions (Neal & Brodsky, 2016).

In summary, no unitary standard for granting custody is a perfect one. Deciding what is in the best interest of the child sounds sensible, but the process of arriving at that determination remains highly subjective, vague, and controversial (Gould & Martindale, 2013). A number of researchers have noted that custody evaluations—compared with other psychological services—are disproportionately associated with ethical problems and complaints to state licensing boards (Bow & Quinnell, 2001; Kirkland & Kirkland, 2001). Ackerman and Pritzl (2011) found that close to 60% of the psychologists in their sample had received board or ethics complaints relating to child custody evaluations, 17% had been threatened with violence, and 11.1% had had property destroyed.

In reference to court acceptance of psychological evaluations, the American Psychological Association (2010b) states in its Guidelines, "The acceptance and thus the overall utility of psychologists' child custody evaluations are augmented by demonstrably competent forensic practice and by consistent adherence to codified ethical standards" (p. 863). Standards of good or best practice are also important to psychologists providing services to the family or probate court. Standards of good practice include such things as obtaining the necessary consents from all involved parties, communicating what the process of evaluation will entail, clarifying payment arrangements and limits of confidentiality, and making clear to the parties how the final report will be disseminated. Many of these points can be communicated by a written document given to the lawyers and parents at the outset (Symons, 2013).

The Ultimate Issue Question

Like the psychological evaluations discussed in the previous chapter (e.g., competency, criminal responsibility), custody evaluations also raise the "ultimate issue" question. Should examiners make recommendations as to which parent should be given custody of the child or as to whether a custodial parent should be allowed to relocate to a distant state? The aforementioned Guidelines (APA, 2010b) do not take a position on this beyond advising psychologists to be aware of both sides of the ultimate issue controversy and their own biases in making custody recommendations. This caveat is particularly relevant when we consider the changing definitions of family that go beyond the traditional definition of individuals related by blood or marriage. Some scholars (e.g., Melton et al., 2007; Tippins & Wittmann, 2005) argue that the ultimate issue should be decided by the judge and not the psychologist. Others (e.g., Rogers & Ewing, 2003) maintain that psychologists should be able to offer recommendations about the ultimate issue as long as their conclusions are based on sound, acceptable data.

Despite the debate, how do forensic psychologists in the field actually handle recommendations concerning the ultimate issue in child custody situations? In a survey conducted by Ackerman and Pritzl (2011), it was found that the majority of forensic psychologists (59%) were in favor of testifying on the ultimate issue. However, the survey also revealed that this percentage was a *slight* decline from the previous survey conducted in 1997 (66%). Ackerman and Pritzl concluded that, "As time progresses, it appears as if more and more psychologists are moving away from testifying to the ultimate issue" (p. 626). Nonetheless, it was also noted that, in many cases, the judge will insist on the psychologist answering the ultimate issue question, sometimes even under the threat of contempt. In some jurisdictions, recommendations regarding the ultimate issue are expected, and failure to offer them will lead to a substantial reduction in future court appointments for CCEs (Bow et al., 2011). Since the American Psychological Association (2002) ethical code advises psychologists not to make recommendations beyond their assessment data, Bow and his colleagues find that the ultimate issue may create "a significant ethical dilemma for conscientious evaluators who wish to adhere to their ethical standards and want to help families resolve their differences" (p. 309).

Methods of Evaluation in Child Custody Cases

The court order that starts the process of custody evaluation is frequently vague and open ended (Zervopoulos, 2010). "Often, the order is barely specific, citing only the parties to be evaluated, the psychologist appointed to conduct the evaluation, and the evaluation's general purpose— at times, the purpose, unwritten, is only implied" (Zervopoulos, 2010, p. 480). Although the psychologist may be allowed considerable latitude on how to proceed and what information and data to collect, it is recommended that the psychologist seek clarification from the court or from attorneys for further information and relevant documents if clarification is needed (Zibble & Fuhrmann, 2016). What's more, the psychologist's report is often the most important document the court considers when making a decision on what is in the best interest of the child. In some cases, however, the court order does ask the psychologist to evaluate situations of specific concern, such as allegations of sexual or physical abuse, intimate partner violence, or possible mental disorder in one of the parents. In these legal contexts, the courts are best served when the evaluating psychologists focus their assessments on matters before the court. In sexual abuse cases, for example, the psychologist would likely interview the alleged victim as the most important beginning in the evaluation, followed by interviews and assessments of the alleged perpetrator and a careful review of the records, including arrest records, medical records, and child welfare reports. Likewise, if intimate partner or other domestic violence is alleged, the examiner would conduct careful interviews and review official records, such as available police reports and restraining orders.

The APA Guidelines (2010b) emphasize, "Multiple methods of data gathering enhance the reliability and validity of psychologists' eventual conclusions, opinions, and recommendations" (p. 866). In conducting child custody evaluations, psychologists often use a variety of psychological inventories, interview questionnaires, and tests to evaluate parents, guardians, and children. Standard practice also calls for multiple sources of information, including electronic records, face-to-face contact and observation of family interactions, interviews with the parents and child, and the collection of collateral information from people knowledgeable about the family. Relevant documents and records, such as medical, mental health, legal proceedings, and educational records are frequently collected. This information forms the basis of the psychologist's report, conclusions, and recommendations. The psychologist, for example, may come to the conclusion that one or the other parent is depressed, and the depression is serious enough to hamper parenting abilities. Zervopoulos (2010) aptly summarizes the APA Guidelines for the psychologist facing this situation when he writes that they "require that psychologists focus their parenting evaluation conclusions on parenting capacity, the psychological and developmental needs of the child, and the resulting fit" (p. 482). In other words, the psychologist would best serve the family if he or she considers all factors, including—most importantly—the needs of the child.

Eve, Byrne, and Gagliardi (2014) asked judges, lawyers, social workers, psychologists, and other professionals experienced in parenting assessments what they thought constituted "good parenting." Based on the results of their surveys, the researchers were able to identify six broad categories to help define good parenting that may be useful in custody, visitation, and relocation proceedings. The categories are (1) insight, (2) willingness and ability, (3) day-to-day versus long-term needs, (4) child's needs before own, (5) fostering attachment, and (6) consistency as well as flexibility. Insight refers to understanding one's role as a parent. Willingness and ability emphasizes that good parenting requires the motivation and skills to provide adequately for the basic needs of the child. In assessing the day-to-day factor, one considers whether the parent tries daily to meet the child's physical, emotional, and cognitive needs. However, the parent also must support and encourage the child to become an independent person in the long term. Putting the child's needs before one's own means the parent must be able to sacrifice personal needs for the overall welfare of the child. Fostering attachment refers to developing an interactive attachment between the parent and the child on an ongoing basis. Consistency represents setting healthy limits and boundaries for the child on a consistent basis, while flexibility signifies the ability of the parent to adapt to the changing developmental needs of a child. Good parents, according to many professionals, achieve a balance between consistency and flexibility. Not all the professional literature agrees that these six categories are the best signs of good parenting, but Eve et al. (2014) do offer a beginning base for further research.

Assessment Measures

Psychological testing can have a profound effect on how psychologists arrive at their final assessments and recommendations. The instruments used may measure intelligence, personality, attitudes, cognitive impairment, and psychopathology. As noted by Erickson, Lilienfeld, and Vitacco (2007), these measures vary substantially in their ability to evaluate the suitability of the parents and the needs of the children. Erickson et al. warn that some are inappropriate for the assessment of adults or children involved in family court litigation.

Several studies have examined the methods used by psychologists in conducting custody evaluations as well as the professional time allocated to the process (e.g., Ackerman & Ackerman, 1997; Bow & Quinnell, 2001; Keilin & Bloom, 1986; LaFortune & Carpenter, 1998). These studies suggest that evaluators progressed from relying almost exclusively on interview data (Keilin & Bloom, 1986) to using a wide range of assessment measures, including tests developed specifically for custody evaluations (Bow & Quinnell, 2001). However, these tests and methods themselves have been criticized by some psychologists for not being grounded in sufficient research before being used in practice (Erickson et al., 2007; Krauss & Sales, 2000; Otto & Heilbrun, 2002).

Over the past decade, however, some agreement seems to have been reached as to how to approach an evaluation. "There are fewer and fewer areas of professional disagreement in the literature addressing how to conduct a child custody assessment. In fact, there is an emerging consensus about how evaluations should be conducted" (Ackerman & Gould, 2015, p. 427). What appears in the literature is not necessarily translated into practice, however, and there continues to be wide variability in the quality of custody or parenting evaluations, leading to frustration on the part of judges and attorneys (Ackerman & Gould, 2015).

Ackerman and Pritzl (2011), reporting on a 2008 survey, found some differences in the extent to which commonly administered measures were used, compared with the 1997 Ackerman and Ackerman study. The dominant instruments used were the same in the two time periods, but the percentages of psychologists using them were higher. These included personality measures (e.g., MMPI-2 for adults and MMPI-A for adolescents), intelligence tests, the Achenbach Child Behavior Checklist (CBCL), sentence completion test, and achievement tests. Measures whose use increased significantly between the two time periods included the Conners Rating Scale and the Children's Depression Inventory—in the case of children—and the Beck Depression Inventory and Michigan Alcohol Screen Test in the case of adults.

Surprisingly, the use of **projective instruments** (e.g., projective drawings, the Rorschach) had significantly increased since 1997, with over half of the psychologists utilizing them. Projectives are psychological tests designed under the assumption that personality traits and attributes are best revealed when a person responds to ambiguous stimuli, such as inkblots or pictures that can be interpreted in multiple ways. Projectives are very controversial. Some psychologists believe that personality assessment is incomplete without data from this technique. Other psychologists contend that the projectives lack reliability and have yet to be scientifically demonstrated as a valid measurement of personality. Furthermore, most research psychologists and many clinical psychologists do not believe projectives meet the *Daubert* standard for scientific acceptance. Most states adhere to the *Daubert* standard or something very similar to it in their court system.

Visitation Risk Assessments

Closely related to custody is the issue of visitation, and visitation recommendations are almost invariably included in custody assessments. Ideally, children should have access to both parents, and each parent also has the right to be involved in his or her child's life. However, it is not uncommon for a custodial parent to challenge or request a change in the visitation rights of the noncustodial parent. This usually occurs under the premise that the noncustodial parent is emotionally or physically damaging the child—or presents a strong risk of inflicting such harm. In some high-profile media cases, the custodial or noncustodial parent has absconded with the child or children, claiming that this was done to protect the child from abuse by the other parent. More than a few such cases have landed the child or children on a federal registry of missing children.

Consequently—in addition to custody evaluations—psychologists and other mental health practitioners are sometimes asked to conduct **visitation risk assessments** to help courts decide whether visitation rights should be limited or abrogated completely. For example, on the basis of such an assessment, the family court judge may decide to require that all visits be supervised by the child's social service caseworker or by a court-appointed guardian.

The psychologist conducting the visitation risk assessment ideally interviews both parents and, depending on the circumstances and the child's age, may also interview the child. The psychologist's role is to determine whether there is evidence of a psychological problem or behavior pattern that would likely lead to inappropriate and potentially harmful interactions between parent and child. Like the custody evaluations discussed above, there is no "standard of practice" for visitation risk assessments. However, there is more research available on custody evaluations than on visitation risk assessments. Moreover, there is considerable debate about what constitutes "good parenting" in many visitation proceedings (Eve et al., 2014).

Parental Relocation

Another important role involving forensic psychologists encompasses the issue of **parental relocation**. Cases involving relocation represent one of the most difficult types in all of family law (Atkinson, 2010). Often, the custodial parent wishes to move with his or her children to a new location following separation or divorce. When the noncustodial parent challenges this move, a court battle may follow. Parents who want to move usually have good reasons for doing so, such as better employment opportunities, a desire to be near their extended family, or to be near a new partner who needs to locate elsewhere (Atkinson, 2010). On the other hand, a custodial parent may want to move to punish the other parent and alienate him or her from the child or children. In a majority of cases in which relocation is challenged, the other parent is still involved with the child (or children) in some capacity, even if it is only occasional visitation.

Generally, the *noncustodial* parent may move or change jobs without asking permission from the court or from the custodial parent. It is another matter when the custodial parent's planned relocation is some distance away from the noncustodial parent. In these situations, the custodial parent may do so only with the consent of the former spouse (or partner) or with the express approval of the court, or both. "Twenty-five of the 37 states with relocation statutes explicitly require that the parent seeking relocation give notice to the other parent, usually by certified mail with return receipt requested" (Atkinson, 2010, p. 565). If the noncustodial parent opposes the move, it creates a conflict between the custodial parent's need for self-determination and the noncustodial parent's interest in maintaining meaningful contact with the child.

Relocation becomes especially problematic when the court has previously granted a joint custody arrangement during the divorce process, because the court now must decide whether to institute another arrangement. More important, the court must also decide on the potential damage to the relationship between the nonrelocating parent and the children involved (Austin, 2008a). Frequently, the psychologist or MHP is requested by the court to do a relocation evaluation. In these cases, the evaluator must be familiar with specific statutory requirements and case law precedent pertaining to relocation (Gould & Martindale, 2013; Stahl, 2010). For example, most states have statutes and case law that instruct what factors are to be considered before their courts decide whether a child may relocate with his or her parent. (See Focus 6.2 for a case illustration and example.) Unfortunately, many of these statutes do not take into account the potential harmful effects that can occur if a child is separated by distance from the other parent (Kreeger, 2003).

Developmental psychologists are beginning to recognize that a relocation move is only one factor in a long line of events, experiences, and changes that are likely to have significant impacts on a child's life. The developmental age of the child, the distance of the proposed move, the extent of the noncustodial parent's involvement in the child's daily activities, and the nature of the parents' conflict that resulted in a divorce are all key factors that require careful scrutiny in the relocation evaluation (Austin, 2008a, 2008b). The evaluating psychologist must carefully consider the likely impact the change in principal residence of the child will have on the child's physical, educational, and emotional development. These factors become especially critical if the child has special needs. In addition, the extent to which custody and visitation rights have been allowed and exercised in the past must be reported.

The evaluating psychologist is expected to pay close attention to the developmental age of the relocating child. Very young children may appear not to be negatively affected by the move, but as they grow older they may be confused as to why it occurred and, depending upon their relationship with the custodial parent, may strongly resent that it happened. Children between the ages of 8 and 12 years are more likely to show better adjustments to the move, primarily because they are better equipped with the cognitive and language skills necessary to maintain a long-distance relationship with the other parent and understand the dynamics of divorcing parents (J. B. Kelly & Lamb, 2003). Adolescents, on the other hand, often strongly resist the move, usually because they have strong ties to school, their peers, and athletic teams or clubs.

FOCUS 6.2. RELOCATION DECISION MAKING

As noted in the text, it is not unusual for one party in a divorce to want to relocate, often far away from the other party. Whatever form of custody the parents may have, it is also not unusual for the party who would be left behind to want to challenge the move. If the parents are unable to reach a satisfactory agreement, the courts may be left to approve or disapprove the relocation.

A noteworthy Pennsylvania case (*Gruber v. Gruber*, 1990), brought relocation issues to the forefront. The mother had been awarded primary custody of the children, but the father had liberal visitation rights. When the mother wished to move to Illinois where she would receive support from her family, the father challenged this. A district court did not allow the move, but an appellate court allowed it, but not before considering three specific factors, which came to be known as the Gruber three-part test. Essentially, that court reviewed whether the move would improve the mother's quality of life, what the motives for the move were, and the extent to which visitation for the noncustodial parent would still be possible. The court also indicated that the best-interest of the child standard was too vague to use in relocation decisions.

The case began a trend in other states to adopt similar or more extended standards. Many courts in other states believed the Gruber three-part-test was itself too vague and simplistic, so they added additional criteria. Moreover, the Pennsylvania legislature itself—in its Child Custody Act—later modified the test to one that included 10 factors, which are summarized below:

a. Assess the child's relationship with the custodial parent as well as the noncustodial parent and other significant persons in the child's life;
b. Consider the child's age, developmental stage, needs, and likely impact of the relocation;
c. Consider the feasibility of preserving the relationship between the child and the nonrelocating party, in light of logistics and financial circumstances of the parties;
d. Take into account the child's preference, considering his or her age and maturity;
e. Determine whether there is an established pattern of conduct of either party to promote or thwart the relationship of the child to the other party;
f. Assess whether the relocation will enhance the general quality of life for the party seeking the relocation;
g. Assess whether the relocation will enhance the general quality of life for the child;
h. Assess the reasons and motivation of each party for seeking or opposing the relocation;
i. Consider any present and past abuse committed by either party or anyone in the party's household, and consider whether there is a continued risk of harm to the child or an abused party;
j. Consider any other factor affecting the best interest of the child.

It is apparent that relocation requests can result in complex decision making that often calls for input from persons other than the presiding judge. When divorced parents are unable to craft a reasonable plan on their own, children are left to the mercy of the family court system.

Questions for Discussion

1. Other than the number of factors (3 versus 10), what is the essential difference between the 3-factor *Gruber* test and the 10-factor test in the Child Custody Act?
2. The last of the 10 factors listed above encourages a judge to consider any other factor affecting the best interest of the child. What would be an example of such a factor?
3. Which of the above factors are likely to require the input of a mental health professional?
4. Is there something similar to a *Gruber* relocation test in child custody statutes in your state?

In summary, the resolution of a dispute over relocation of a child requires a comprehensive evaluation of multiple factors. Although some relocation cases are easy to resolve, many are much more difficult (Atkinson, 2010). If the case is to be resolved according to the best interest of the child, each factor must be weighed in detail, and the courts rely heavily on psychologists and other MHPs to help them make these decisions.

Research on Custody Arrangements

Custody arrangements tend to fall into one of four patterns: (1) sole custody, (2) divided custody, (3) split custody, and (4) joint custody. These four arrangements are based on two fundamental categories of parental or caregiver's decision-making authority: legal and physical. **Legal parental authority** refers to decisions about the child's long-term welfare, education, medical care, religious upbringing, and other matters significantly affecting his or her life. **Physical parental authority** denotes the authority to make decisions affecting only the child's daily activities, such as decisions concerning whether the child can have an overnight at a friend's house, play baseball or softball, attend a birthday party, or have access to the parent's car. (See Table 6.2.)

Of the four custody arrangements, *sole custody* is the most common. It is when one parent has both legal and physical authority and the other parent does not, although the noncustodial parent usually retains visitation rights. In the United States, as noted above, mothers are overwhelmingly granted sole custody. In 2009, for example, 82% of custodial parents were mothers with sole custody (U.S. Census Bureau, 2011b).

Divided custody refers to arrangements where each parent is granted legal and physical parental authority on a rotating basis. For example, the arrangement may have the child or children living with one parent for 6 months of the year, and the other parent for the next 6 months, as long as the same school system is involved. When the two parents live in different geographical locations, the division of custody is typically made in accordance with the school year or vacations. If the parents live geographically close to one another, the alternating periods may have short time spans (e.g., Dad on weekends, Mom weekdays). *Split custody* refers to an arrangement where one or more children go with one parent, and other children go to the second parent. This is most likely to occur when the children are far apart in ages, such as adolescents and grade or preschoolers. *Joint custody* is where both parents share legal and physical

Table 6.2 Definitions and Characteristics of Four Basic Custody Arrangements*

Custody Arrangement	Definition	Features
Sole Custody	One parent has both physical and legal authority.	Most common; typically mother Noncustodial parent usually has liberal visitation privileges if desired. Court must be informed of major relocation plans; court must approve.
Joint Custody	Two parents share physical and legal authority equally.	Children may or may not alternate living with both parents; decisions made jointly. Is best when conflict between parents is at a minimum, but positive parent–child relationship is most important.
Divided Custody	Each parent has sole custody, both legal and physical authority, but on rotating basis.	Custodial period usually revolves around school year.
Limited Joint Custody	Parents share legal authority, but only one parent has physical authority.	Conflict between parents or between a parent and child make joint physical custody problematic. Also may occur when one parent is unable to assume physical authority but wants shared authority with respect to legal issues.

*Although these are basic custody arrangements, family courts and parents fashion variants in attempts to meet needs of children, particularly as these may change with age. Not mentioned above is split custody, where the decision is different for different children.

decision authority, but the children live predominately with one parent who will have physical authority to make the day-to-day decisions. In some joint custody arrangements, disagreement and conflict between the parents emerges, often over the physical authority issue. In these situations, the court may grant *limited joint custody*, where both parents share legal authority, but one parent is awarded exclusive physical authority and the other is granted liberal visitation rights. Family courts usually try to recognize some variant of joint or shared parenting that encourages frequent and continuing contact of the child with both parents (Connell, 2010).

Forensic psychologists and legal professionals are beginning to recognize the value of having children participate in the decision-making process that directly affects their own lives and welfare (Lehrmann, 2010). This is especially important for older children who are capable of reasoned judgment. The forensic psychologist should be cognizant of this consideration, but he or she must also realize that the legal perspective is different in these matters from the psychological one. "From a legal perspective, children lack decision-making power in most respects, although children's choices carry legal weight in various contexts" (Lehrmann, 2010, p. 474). In some legal contexts, the appointment of a legal counsel to protect the rights and wishes of the child may be necessary.

Psychologists and other mental health practitioners conducting custody evaluations also should be aware of the vast store of research on the effects of divorce and custody arrangements (e.g., Bricklin & Elliot, 1995; Johnston, 1995; Maccoby, Buchanan, Mnookin, & Dornsbusch, 1993; Wallerstein, 1989). Much of this research is dated, however, and today's rapid changes in economic opportunities, ethnic and cultural considerations, mobility, and social services suggest caution in relying on past studies. Moreover, sifting through this research can become an exercise in frustration because—as Krauss and Sales (2000) have observed—methodologically sound studies have reached different conclusions. Particularly equivocal has been research comparing joint custody to sole custody arrangements (e.g., Bauserman, 2002, 2012; Gunnoe & Braver, 2001), leading to conclusions that no one arrangement is clearly superior to the other.

Numerous factors have been found to play a part in a child's adjustment to divorce (see K. D. Hess, 2006, for a review) and custody arrangements, including—but not limited to—the child's age and gender, hostility between parents, parenting skills, the quality of the parent–child relationship, and the emotional and physical health of the parents. These factors should be taken into consideration when performing custody evaluations, but examiners should be careful not to generalize from the group data reported to what is in the best interest of the particular child or children involved in the presenting case. Moreover, as noted above, research on custody arrangements is not unequivocal.

In an important recent article addressing much of that research, Nielsen (2017) focuses on the decades-long assumption that joint custody is not warranted if there is conflict between the parents. Reexamining the research in this area, she concludes that the quality of relationship between the child and the parents is a better predictor of positive outcomes than a conflict-ridden relationship between the parents, unless the conflict is major. Put another way, if the child has a healthy relationship with each parent, joint custody can work even if the parents are not "amicable." It is obvious that conducting a competent child custody evaluation requires the skillful integration of both scientific knowledge and clinical acumen (Gould & Martindale, 2013).

Impact of Divorce on Children

In their review of the research literature, Gould and Martindale (2013) conclude, not surprisingly, that "Research findings have generally indicated that children are best served when they have strong and healthy relationships with both parents" (p. 123). As noted above, these can occur even when parents are separated or divorced, however. Some children of divorce are highly resilient and adjust quickly to the separation, even though it may be psychologically painful to them. Other children react very negatively to the divorce of their parents. In general, though, a considerable body of research suggests that divorce is likely to have negative effects on most children, at least in the short term (Krauss & Sales, 2000; M. E. Lamb & Malloy, 2013). Some studies indicate that many children who experience divorce are more likely to demonstrate poorer academic performance, delayed psychological development, difficulties in cognitive skills, and mental health problems compared to children of intact two-parent homes (Amato, 2000, 2001, 2010; H. S. Kim, 2011; Uphold-Carrier & Utz, 2012). Furthermore, some of these problems, especially depression and anxiety disorders, extend into adulthood for many of these children and adolescents. Paul Amato (2010) observes that adult children of divorced parents tend to display lower levels of psychological well-being and adjustment, and report more problems in their own marriages. They also feel less close to their parents and are at greater risk of having their own marriages end in divorce.

The Forensic Psychologist as a Case-Blind Consultant

An additional important role that many forensic psychologists play in child custody and divorce cases is that of case-blind consultant. The **case-blind consultant** is appointed by the court to provide some up-to-date knowledge about the research on family dynamics and child/adolescent development. The family and developmental research is expanding very rapidly, and judges and other legal professionals realize that they need to be frequently updated before making decisions on custody cases. Usually, the court is interested in a specific issue or topic—e.g., research on children with special needs or research on individuals with certain psychological disorders—and asks the psychologist to provide the information to aid in the decision process. By definition, the case-blind consultant has little or no knowledge about the details of the case. The consultant in these cases may provide this information in the judge's chambers or in open court, as an expert witness.

FORENSIC PSYCHOLOGY AND CIVIL LITIGATION

It has become commonplace to state that we are a litigious society, seeking redress through the courts for a wide range of alleged wrongs done to us by others. There are a variety of ways in which we may approach the civil courts, including—but not limited to—a civil rights claim, a claim of a breach of contract, intellectual property claim (e.g., a patent case), a prisoner case, or a labor case (e.g., unfair labor practices). Courts also consider alleged wrongs on such matters as defamation, invasion of privacy, toxic harm, and personal injury, to name but a few. As we shall learn in this section, the redress sought is typically some form of financial compensation.

In civil cases, the person filing the lawsuit is called the **plaintiff**, and the person or organization that he or she alleges caused the harm is called the defendant or **respondent**. In order to get some form of relief, the plaintiff would file a civil lawsuit. A plaintiff alleging emotional distress is subject to being evaluated not only by a clinician contacted by his or her lawyer, but also by a clinician hired by the defendant. In the usual case, the plaintiff hires the psychologist.

The most common civil suit is the **tort**, which is the legal term for a civil wrong in which a plaintiff alleges some negligence on the part of the defendant. A tort exists when certain elements are proven in court. Consequently, a tort is a proven wrongful act that may be subject to recoverable damages in a civil lawsuit (Foote & Lareau, 2013). As Drogin, Hagan, Guilmette, and Piechowski (2015) summarize, a plaintiff must prove four elements:

1. Duty—that the defendant had an affirmative responsibility to do something or not to do something,

2. Breach—that the defendant failed to meet that responsibility,

3. Harm—that something bad—some identifiable injury—must have happened to the plaintiff, and

4. Causality—that the defendant's wrongful behavior was the source of the injury (p. 472).

In most civil cases, forensic psychologists retained by attorneys would be expected to evaluate (a) whether the plaintiff was harmed by the defendant and (b) if the plaintiff was harmed, the type and degree of harm the plaintiff suffered (Foote & Lareau, 2013). In a majority of cases, the forensic psychologist focuses the evaluations on the type and extent of functional impairment suffered by the plaintiff. This approach is considered a more productive strategy than rendering, for example, a psychiatric diagnosis based on the *DSM-5* (*Diagnostic and Statistical Manual of Mental Disorders*, fifth edition) criteria, such as a generalized anxiety disorder or a major depressive disorder. This is because a psychiatric diagnosis is usually not legally effective in establishing compensable damages. Furthermore, as pointed out by Drogin et al. (2015, p. 496), the *DSM-5* itself stresses that the diagnoses are intended for clinicians, public health professionals, and researchers, and cautions against using them to meet the needs of the courts. Functional impairment, on the other hand, relates to what a person can and cannot do in his or her basic daily home and employment requirements. More important, functional impairment not only affects the plaintiff's quality of life, but may also prevent the plaintiff from performing the job he or she held prior to the damage.

The types of relief sought by plaintiffs generally fall into one of three categories: (1) an injunction, (2) a specific performance requirement, or (3) monetary compensation (Foote & Lareau, 2013). An **injunction** request is where the plaintiff desires the ongoing harmful behavior to stop. In the specific performance requirement request, the plaintiff desires the defendant to do something he or she is supposed to or required to do, such as provide reasonable accommodation in the workplace for a person with a documented disability. In most civil cases, however, the plaintiff pursues some form of financial compensation for alleged harm suffered.

Damages fall into two principal classifications: compensatory and punitive. **Compensatory damages** are intended to make up for the harm suffered by the plaintiff. **Punitive damages** are assessed when the harm done is so grave that the judge or jury believes the defendant should receive extra punishment. The main goal of punitive damages is to deter the defendant from further harmful action and to discourage others from committing similar harmful acts in the future (Lenton, 2007). In order to receive a damages award, the plaintiff must first be able to show some physical, emotional, or mental injury as a result of the actions of the respondent. Furthermore, the plaintiff must also prove that the defendant either committed the harmful act intentionally or at least was negligent. Similar to family and custody cases, a vast majority of other civil cases are settled out of court, before they would go to trial. Many claims by plaintiffs that are disputed by defendants assert that they suffered cognitive injuries or emotional harms as a result of the defendant's actions (Foote & Lareau, 2013), and these are cases where forensic psychologists usually are retained.

Forensic psychologists may participate in the early stages of a civil case by guiding the mediation process, evaluating plaintiffs and defendants, or consulting with attorneys. Later, if the case goes to trial, the psychologist may testify as an expert witness.

Psychologists also may be called as expert witnesses in these civil suits to testify more generally on the effects of the alleged wrong, without examining the plaintiff. For example, in a civil suit alleging discrimination on the basis of gender—a civil rights violation—a psychologist with research expertise on gender stereotyping may be called as an expert witness. As we noted in Chapter 4, researchers continue to examine the effects of the *Daubert* standard with regard to the admission of expert testimony in the courtroom. Thus far, it appears that lawyers are questioning expert testimony, and judges are scrutinizing it more carefully and rejecting more such testimony than they were in the years before the *Daubert* decision (McAuliff & Groscup, 2009).

How well judges are performing this gatekeeping function has yet to be determined, however (Dixon & Gill, 2002). And, as McAuliff and Groscup write,

> The fact that judges are scrutinizing expert testimony more carefully and excluding it more frequently after *Daubert* says nothing about the accuracy of their decisions. None of the research we have reviewed has provided any evidence that judges are admitting valid science and excluding junk science. (p. 28)

In the remainder of the chapter, we will cover other civil law areas where forensic psychology plays an important role. These areas encompass personal injury claims that include a psychological component; civil capacities, which covers the capability to make a will or take care of oneself; evaluations concerning competence to consent to treatment or to refuse treatment; and evaluations involving involuntary civil commitment. We will also cover the increasingly important topic of evaluating sexual and gender harassment, especially in the workplace. We begin with personal injury claims.

Employment Compensation, Disability, and Personal Injury Claims

Employment compensation laws were passed to avoid extensive tort actions on the part of employees who were injured in the course of their work. The legal framework of personal injury cases is defined largely by the law of torts. "Tort law recognizes a claim for monetary damages when one breaches duty of care owed to another and proximately causes them harm" (Greenberg, Otto, & Long, 2003, p. 412). In passing these employment compensation laws, Congress and state legislatures also recognized the formidable task faced by the injured worker pitted against his or her powerful employer. Under tort law, the employee would have to prove some fault on the part of the employer. This was a long, involved process that rarely resulted in a successful claim and often left the worker and his or her family in poverty (Melton et al., 2007).

Although **employment compensation claims** involve physical injuries, psychological injury or emotional distress is also typically asserted. To use a hypothetical example, Jason is employed by a roofing company that often repairs roofs that were damaged by severe weather conditions. While replacing shingles on a roof that is three stories high, Jason is caught by a wind gust and swept off, suffering extensive back injuries. In addition to this physical injury, Jason claims extreme emotional distress that includes fear of heights manifested in an inability to climb ladders, take escalators, or accompany his 10-year-old son on a chairlift at a ski area. Note that Jason is not claiming that his employer was at fault for dispatching him to repair the roof on a high-wind day. He is merely stating that he should be compensated for his lost wages, the physical and neurological effects of the fall (e.g., debilitating back pain, recurring headaches), and the life changes necessitated by his fear of heights.

On the other hand, an employer may be responsible for the harm suffered by employees, in which a civil suit might ensue. In the above scenario, for example, if Jason was equipped with inadequate safety gear and was dispatched to repair the roof on an exceptionally windy day, it could be argued that his employer breached an affirmative duty to protect his employee and was the cause of his painful injury. In that case, the issue might reach the tort stage rather than be settled as an employment compensation case.

Evaluations of mental injury—both psychological and neurological harm—also occur in a wide variety of personal-injury litigation that is not necessarily employment related. On an increasing basis, attorneys and judges look to psychologists and other MHPs for assistance in better understanding the claims of plaintiffs who allege that they have suffered emotional damage in situations outside of their place of employment (Greenberg et al., 2003). For example, mental health is included in "pain and suffering" and "emotional distress" claims by individuals who were injured in car accidents or in a fall in a neighbor's yard. Plaintiffs also claim psychological and neurological harm from exposure to environmental contaminants or from defective products. In these cases, "the court seeks the assistance of mental health professionals in such personal injury cases based on the assumption that the plaintiff's psychological functioning and adjustment is a complicated matter that is beyond the understanding of attorneys, judges, and juries" (Greenberg et al., 2003, p. 411).

Regardless of whether the assessment involves psychological or neurological harm—and often both—the assessment of disability conducted by the forensic psychologist is crucial and complex (Drogin, Hagan, Guilmette, & Piechowski, 2015; Piechowski, 2011). (See Perspective 6.1, in which Dr. Piechowski discusses her work in this area.) It involves not only identifying mental or neurological disorders, but also identifying the legally relevant functional abilities that have been affected.

FROM MY PERSPECTIVE 6.1

Specializing in Civil Litigation: An Often Overlooked Career Choice

Lisa Drago Piechowski, PhD, ABPP

Courtesy of Lisa Drago Piechowski.

One of my favorite ways to relax on a weekend morning is with a cup of coffee and the *New York Times* Sunday Crossword. You see, I've always loved solving puzzles. It's the process of discovering pieces of information that then become hunches and finally arrange themselves into a pattern to form a solution. It is especially gratifying when the problem at first seems incomprehensible, and then gradually, with much trial and error, begins to make sense. It's solving the most challenging problem that is the most rewarding.

I have been a forensic psychologist for more than 20 years now. Like solving puzzles, forensic psychology involves collecting disparate pieces of data in an attempt to discern a meaningful pattern. It is a field that I continue to find exciting and intellectually challenging. However, the road I took to reach this point was far from direct.

When I went off to college, I had no clear sense of what I wanted to do. I had thoughts of going to law school, but I didn't enjoy the political science courses I had been advised to take. I had three different majors over the course of my undergraduate career. After graduation, I went to work as a special education teacher. Although I enjoyed many aspects of this work, I knew it wasn't the right fit for me. I was still interested in law, but I was also very interested in understanding how people thought and behaved. I spent several years exploring different options. I earned a master's degree in counseling and worked as a

family therapist and then in a college counseling center. I was beginning to feel that I was on the right track, but I realized my career options would be limited without a doctoral degree. As a result, I made the decision to return to school to become a psychologist. I applied to a PhD program at the University of Massachusetts and received my letter of acceptance on my 33rd birthday. I knew immediately I had made the right choice.

After earning the PhD, I spent the early years of my career as a clinical psychologist working in various private practices. One of my supervisors during graduate school had been a forensic psychologist, and I developed an interest in exploring this area. I began to pursue training in forensic psychology through continuing education courses and reading. I was subsequently offered the opportunity to work as a consultant for a disability insurance company that was looking for assistance with mental health disability claims.

As I became immersed in this work, I discovered that very little had been written about forensic evaluation of disability. In order to fill that gap, I began thinking about how to apply the principles and practices of forensic psychology that I had been learning about to this specific type of work. I was influenced by Grisso's conceptual model of legal competencies which consists of five components (functional, causal, interactive, judgmental, and dispositional) and began to think about how this model could be applied to disability evaluations. I started writing about these ideas and ultimately published a book on best practices in forensic disability evaluation (Piechowski, 2011). From

(Continued)

(Continued)

disability, my interests expanded to include other types of employment-related cases, such as fitness for duty evaluations and cases involving the Americans with Disabilities Act (ADA), as well as more general civil litigation. Although I now do some criminal and family cases, I am among a minority of forensic psychologists who specialize in civil litigation.

I became board certified in forensic psychology by the American Board of Forensic Psychology in 2004. Since then, I have been actively involved in this organization, serving on the board of directors and as a member of the examination faculty. I have also been active in the American Psychological Association and have served as chair of the Committee on Professional Practice and Standards and the Committee on Legal Issues. I present continuing education courses in disability and employment evaluations for the American Academy of Forensic Psychology. These activities have given me the opportunity to know and work with some of the brightest and most knowledgeable forensic psychologists in the country.

Today I have a varied practice that includes civil, family, and criminal cases. I teach courses in forensic psychology, psychological assessment, and ethics for a doctoral program in clinical psychology. I write and do research. On a given day I might drive to a detention facility to evaluate a defendant's competency to stand trial, appear in court as an expert witness in a personal injury case, consult with an attorney about upcoming litigation, or meet with a student to discuss her research. I spend a great deal of time at my desk writing reports, reviewing records, and returning phone calls. Since I have a private practice, I also spend time doing less-than-glamorous tasks such as sending out invoices and picking up office supplies.

Much of my practice involves conducting evaluations of persons involved in some type of civil litigation. This process entails consulting with the attorney or other referral source about the specific issues in the case, deciding on a strategy for the evaluation, selecting appropriate psychological tests, obtaining pertinent records to review, and then meeting with the examinee to conduct the evaluation. Afterward, I score and interpret the tests, review all the material I have collected, and organize the data to address the questions I am trying to answer. Typically, I produce a written report summarizing the data and my opinions. If the case is going to trial, I meet with the attorney to discuss the scope of my testimony. To prepare for testimony, I review all of the material I have collected so that I am very familiar with my findings and can explain how I arrived at my opinions. Once in court, I describe my findings during direct examination (the easy part) and then respond to challenges by the opposing attorney during cross examination (the not so easy part).

I cannot imagine a career that would suit me better than forensic psychology. My work is never boring. No two days are the same and each case brings a fresh challenge. As with crossword puzzles, my work involves collecting pieces of data, forming hypotheses, and drawing inferences. And, as I said before, it's solving the most challenging problem that is the most rewarding.

Dr. Piechowski is an Associate Professor of clinical psychology at the American School of Professional Psychology at Argosy University Northern Virginia and maintains a private forensic psychology practice in Silver Spring, Maryland. She is the author of the book Best Practices in Forensic Mental Health Assessment: Evaluation of Workplace Disability. *Dr. Piechowski was the 2016 president of the American Board of Forensic Psychology.*

Neuropsychological Damages

In cases where specific neuropsychological damages are alleged, a neuropsychologist or a forensic psychologist specializing in neuropsychology may be retained. In fact, the area within clinical neuropsychology that has shown the greatest growth explosion is **forensic neuropsychology** (Bush, 2017; Otero, Podell, DeFina, & Goldberg, 2013). (See Focus 6.3 for careers in forensic neuropsychology.) This explosion is due partly to the increased demand by the legal system for expert testimony capable of identifying neuropsychological deficits. In civil litigation, the greatest growth has occurred in cases that involve traumatic brain injuries (TBIs), such as those suffered in motor vehicle accidents (Otero et al., 2013) and concussions in sports-related events. Considerable monetary compensation is often sought by the plaintiffs in these cases. Interestingly, a recent study in the *Journal of the American Medical Association* (Mez et al., 2017), reported that brain damage was found in 87% of donated brains of 202 deceased football players, including 110 of 111 brains of professional football players. The study concluded that the more professionally the person played, the more severe the brain injury.

In forensic settings, a neuropsychologist may be retained by an attorney, the court, or other public or private parties, such as insurance companies (Leonard, 2015). In criminal matters, they may be retained by prosecution or defense attorneys. The forensic neuropsychologist is expected to be objective and show no allegiance or responsibility to any one side or individual. Unlike clinical settings, "no psychologist-patient relationship is assumed to exist in most forensic work" (Leonard, 2015, p. 178). (Recall, however, Dr. Daniel Murrie's discussion of adversarial allegiance in Perspective 5.1 in the previous chapter.) All mental health professionals must guard against implicit bias and the bias blind-spot (Neal & Brodsky, 2016). In civil proceedings, forensic neuropsychologists assess people of a wide range of ages, from preschoolers to the elderly. The issues range from evaluating parenting capacity in child custody cases to fitness-for-duty evaluations for police officers. In some situations, they are asked to evaluate pediatric brain injury in tort cases (Leonard, 2015).

A variety of standardized tests and inventories may be used by the forensic neuropsychologist to collect information and make inferences concerning brain and behavior relationships. This comprehensive evaluation is usually undertaken when the TBI or other neurological damages appear serious and complicated in scope. A comprehensive evaluation may entail "objective measures of cognitive performance with historical, neurological, psychiatric, medical, and other diagnostic information by a clinician with competence in neuropsychological assessment" (APA, 2014d, p. 48). In some cases, however, the examination may not require a comprehensive evaluation. "The nature of the examination may range from a relatively brief clinical interview to a comprehensive examination that includes extensive psychological test administration" (Otero et al., 2013, p. 507). Otero et al. further report that modern technology, such as magnetic resonance imaging (MRI), fMRI, positron emission tomography (PET), computerized tomography (CT), and diffusion tensor imaging, has reduced much of the standardized testing relied on in the past to *localize* the brain damage. However, when it comes to identifying neurocognitive processes or ability, standardized neuropsychological tests are usually heavily utilized. This is because the testing and other assessment techniques applied during the assessment enable the forensic psychologists to provide supporting evidence or to refute the claims made by the plaintiff that he or she is suffering from brain or other neurological damage.

Before the psychologist or neuropsychologist even begins the forensic evaluation, however, he or she must fully understand the relevant law in order to identify those issues before the court that are psychological in nature and about which he or she can offer expert opinion (Greenberg et al., 2003; Grisso, 2003). Furthermore, forensic evaluations for mental and neurological damages and the accompanying report usually must be both retrospective and prospective in nature. These reports are retrospective in that the evaluator tries to determine how much damage (if any) was done and the specific cause; they are prospective in the sense that the evaluator must make some judgment about the plaintiff's future functioning: Will the plaintiff be able to function as he or she did prior to the claim? In the case of employment compensation claims, what is the extent of the loss in earning capacity suffered by the plaintiff? If the injury is work related, all information pertinent to the workplace is relevant to the inquiry.

Psychological Tests Used for Personal Injury Claims

As emphasized by Greenberg et al. (2003), not all personal injury examinations require the same assessment instruments. Neuropsychologists generally use neuropsychological measures, but they may depend on other standardized tests as well. Melton et al. (1997, 2007) point out that personality inventories are helpful, particularly if they can be compared with inventories taken before the injury occurred. In addition, they remind the psychologist to investigate the extent of physical injury, using neurological tests if needed, in addition to mental injury. Furthermore, the evaluator should be attuned to the possibility of posttraumatic stress disorder.

FOCUS 6.3. FORENSIC NEUROPSYCHOLOGY

The term *forensic neuropsychology* refers to the application of knowledge from the neuropsychological profession to legal matters. Neuropsychology is the study of the psychological effects of brain and neurological damage and dysfunction on human behavior. Clinical neuropsychology is the applied branch of the field that focuses on the assessment and diagnosis of neurological damage, along with treatment recommendations. It was the first specialty in professional psychology to be recognized by the APA, in 1996. Forensic neuropsychological testimony is often requested in both civil and criminal cases (Quickel & Demakis, 2017).

Forensic neuropsychologists provide information in legal cases on such matters as dementia, brain damage, and intellectual functioning. They are very frequently consulted in disability cases, including those in which plaintiffs allege that a defendant's action or failure to act resulted in harm. The neuropsychologist may be asked to testify as to the extent of a person's impairment and be expected to answer questions relating to employment fitness, the need for a guardian or health care provider, chances of full recovery, or the extent of rehabilitation needed. In criminal cases the neuropsychologist may be asked neurological questions about competency to stand trial, criminal responsibility, competency to waive Miranda rights, and competency to be executed (Quickel & Demakis, 2017).

Many veterans of conflicts in Iraq and Afghanistan have suffered traumatic brain injuries (TBIs) as a result of encountering improvised explosive devices (IEDs) in the course of their military duty. Likewise, children who were victims of child abuse or adult victims of domestic violence may also suffer TBI. With increasing awareness of the extent of these injuries, it is clear that military veterans and victims of crime are in need of assessment from neuropsychologists. Today, neuropsychologists are often consulted for evaluations of concussive sports-related injuries, even mild or moderate ones, especially if the concussions have been multiple. Neuropsychological assessment procedures and tests include measures that evaluate general intelligence, language, memory, attention, thought processes, perceptual-motor functioning, emotional status, and malingering. The field is also moving into assessments of decision making, impulsivity, judgment, and aggression (Leonard, 2015).

It is important to realize that the forensic neuropsychologist has different professional challenges from the clinical neuropsychologist who does not interact with the courts or the legal system (Leonard, 2015). The forensic neuropsychologist must inform legal decision making in an adversarial system "where diagnosis and treatment considerations are secondary to informing the fact finder about the psycholegal question of interest" (p. 178). The forensic neuropsychologist applies the same principles used in traditional practice and may also have a practice as a clinical neuropsychologist. However, in her or his capacity as a *forensic* neuropsychologist, she or he must understand how the legal system operates and how decisions are reached based on evidence.

Questions for Discussion

1. Neuropsychological evaluations are relevant to both civil and criminal cases. Give examples of when a forensic neuropsychologist might be consulted in a criminal case.
2. Does one need to become a medical doctor (MD) before becoming a neuropsychologist? Do research to answer this question, and then explain why or why not.

As we noted in Chapter 5, malingering and the exaggeration of symptoms have received considerable attention in the research literature (e.g., Gothard, Rogers, & Sewell, 1995; Mossman, 2003; Rogers, 1997). In all mental injury evaluations, psychologists and other clinicians must be concerned about the possibility that the individual being evaluated is "faking" the symptoms he or she is claiming, or presenting them as being much worse than they are. More comprehensively, malingering is "the intentional production of false or grossly exaggerated physical or psychological symptoms that are motivated by external incentives such as financial compensation" (Drogin et al., 2015, p. 477). Put more simply, plaintiffs making personal injury claims may exaggerate their symptoms in order to win their suit against an employer, a business, a neighbor, or a physician who allegedly harmed them. Malingering and deception is especially prevalent in disability claims where individuals seek compensation for work-related injuries (Piechowski & Drukteinis, 2011), and much of the research on malingering detections has been done by neuropsychologists (Drogin et al., 2015). Recall also that this topic was discussed in the context of malingering during competency and criminal responsibility evaluations in Chapter 5, specifically with the research of Rogers and his colleagues.

Detection of malingering thus becomes an important function of the forensic psychologist. Butcher and Miller (1999) emphasize that there is no foolproof way to assess malingering, although the MMPI-2 appears to have valid indicators. Many commentators have noted that clinical judgment alone cannot detect malingering and that a variety of measures must be considered, depending upon the alleged impairment (Carone & Bush, 2013; Guilmette, 2013; Heilbronner, Sweet, Morgan, Larrabee, & Millis, 2009).

Butcher and Miller (1999) also advise the evaluator to be extremely conscious of the role of the individual's lawyer: "One of the most problematic factors encountered in forensic assessment is the tendency of many attorneys to guide their clients through a desired strategy for responding to psychological test items" (p. 110). They advise clinicians to try to determine whether the individual has been "coached" by the lawyer and the extent and nature of the coaching. Basically, the individual should be asked what he or she has been told. The final report should reflect how this coaching might have affected the results of the examination. In addition, lawyers today often want to be in the examination room along with their client. "This tactic raises important practice and policy concerns as well as personal discomfort and logistical complications for the evaluator" (Drogin et al., 2015, p. 499). As Drogin et al. indicate, there are two sides to this argument. For example, having an observer may interfere with the evaluation process, but it also may protect the evaluator from complaints.

After a comprehensive discussion of mental injury evaluations, Melton et al. (1997) conclude with three general points about communicating with the courts relevant to these assessments. First—and as mentioned previously—they urge clinicians to not rely overly on diagnoses because these will not explain why a particular individual reacted in a particular way to the particular events. Second, they emphasize that a longitudinal history of the impairment, its treatments, and efforts at rehabilitation is necessary. Third, they maintain that conclusory information should be avoided. Clinicians should provide descriptive reports of their findings but allow the legal decision makers to decide the critical legal question of whether the plaintiff should be compensated.

Not all civil cases involve civil wrongs or torts. Litigants often approach courts with claims for employment benefits, health benefits, insurance, or veterans' benefits that they believe have been unjustly denied. To discuss these civil wrongs would take us far afield from the main topics in this section of the chapter. Another important topic, however, is the psychological evaluations of civil capacities, to which we now turn our attention.

CIVIL CAPACITIES

Many psychologists, including neuropsychologists, perform civil capacity evaluations (sometimes referred to as civil competency evaluations) as part of their clinical work. For example, in one survey of practicing neuropsychologists, they reported that capacity issues arose in 75% of their cases (Demakis & Mart, 2017). The professional literature often uses the term *competency* to refer to a court's legal decision, and the term *capacity* to refer to a psychologist's assessment of a person's decision-making ability (Lichtenberg, Qualls, & Smyer, 2015). Nevertheless, in much of the research as well as in practice, the terms are used interchangeably. Capacity (or competency) evaluations are not limited to older individuals, of course, but with the aging of the U.S. population, the frequency of these evaluations will certainly rise (Demakis, 2012; Mossman & Farrell, 2015; Quickel & Demakis, 2013). MHPs will be asked to evaluate whether an individual was or is capable of making a critical decision in his or her best interest. Persons who have reached adulthood are presumed to be capable of making these decisions. Likewise, they are expected to take responsibility for decisions that resulted in disastrous consequences. This decisional autonomy extends to such areas as consenting to medical treatment, joining a cult, engaging in a business contract, enlisting in the military, drafting a will, refusing medication or life-prolonging treatment, or consenting to participate in psychological or medical research.

The presumption that one is capable of making decisions can be nullified if it can be demonstrated to the satisfaction of a court that the person was not mentally or physically competent at the time the decision was made (or is being considered). In most jurisdictions, the party claiming that a person is not competent bears the burden of proving that by a preponderance of the evidence, but some jurisdictions require clear and convincing evidence, which is a higher standard. Put another way, if you want to challenge Uncle David's testamentary capacity, you have to prove that at the time he drafted his will, he was not able to make the decision to give all of his money to the person he met just 6 months ago. When a court determines that an individual is or was not competent, it invalidates a decision that was made (e.g., the terms of a will or a decision to forego medical treatment). If the person is still alive, the court will usually appoint a guardian to decide what is in the person's best interest. We focus more on testamentary capacity below.

Testamentary Capacity

One decision that is frequently challenged—though not often successfully—is the ability to make a will, called **testamentary capacity**. In most states, this would come under the purview of a probate court. As Slovenko (1999) has noted, making a will actually requires only minimal competency and is an easy task, and Melton et al. (2007) comment that it does not demand high cognitive skills. Others (e.g., Shulman, Cohen, & Hull, 2005) suggest that it is an advanced activity mediated by higher cognitive functions.

Today, people are encouraged to make wills at relatively young ages, particularly if they have children, and to update them periodically as assets or their life situations change. Testamentary capacity usually comes into question when the testator (will-maker) is an older person, whether or not this is a first will or one that has been revised. Few would disagree that when it comes to testamentary competence, the older-adult population is an unusually high-risk group and presents a number of unique challenges for the evaluator (Regan & Gordon, 1997). Some members of the older-adult population (age 65 or older) have a collection of potential incapacities, such as mental illness, dementia, poor judgment, and variety of concurrent medical illnesses and limitations. Fortunately, the law is not concerned with whether people are functioning at their highest level of mental or psychological functioning at the time the will is completed. The law requires only that one be "of sound mind" when making a will. Specific requirements are that individuals (1) know they are making a will, (2) know the nature and extent of their property, (3) know the objects of their bounty, and (4) know how their property is being divided (Melton et al., 2007). As Melton et al. point out, it is possible for someone to be forgetful, addicted to narcotics or alcohol, mentally disordered, or have a low threshold of cognitive functioning, yet still be capable of making a will.

It is presumed, then, that people—including older adults—are competent or capable when making a will. As Mossman and Farrell (2015, p. 541) point out, suspicions about capacity are most likely to arise in four situations: (1) when the person's will is strikingly different from his or her previously-expressed wishes; (2) when the person had a mental or neurologic disorder that could impair thinking and judgment; (3) when the person was dependent on others and particularly vulnerable; or (4) when the person changed his or her will several times, apparently to control the actions of persons who were critical to his or her well-being.

The evaluation of testamentary capacity is usually retrospective, such that it requires the evaluator to interview those who knew the individual, review any available records, and draw inferences about the individual's mental state at the time the will was formulated. In many respects, it is similar to the psychological autopsy (discussed in Chapter 3), although far less detailed (Drogin & Barrett, 2013). As usual, the forensic psychologist would be expected to review, with counsel's guidance and support, the relevant statutes, regulations, and case law pertinent to the jurisdiction where the testamentary capacity assessment is conducted (Drogin & Barrett, 2013). In some situations, lawyers advise their clients to be evaluated for testamentary capacity at the time they execute their wills. Psychological assessment would especially be warranted if the individual exhibits signs of dementia, has a mental disorder that includes periods of cognitive incapacity, or has some intellectual disability. One instrument, the Legal Capacity Questionnaire (LCQ: Walsh, Brown, Kaye, & Grigsby, 1994) assesses a person's competence to make a will. It is an easily scored instrument intended for use by lawyers, not by psychologists. However, a variety of general mental capacity psychological measures may be used by forensic psychologists who engage in this enterprise, including measures of mental disorders, dementias, and neurological problems. In addition to choosing a test or measure to use, however, the examiner reviews records, interviews collateral sources (e.g., family members), and of course the individual him or herself, if they are still alive. Sample questions that might be asked include the following: "Would you describe your financial assets for me and tell me about their value?" "How do you get along with your relatives?" "Who are the important people in your life now?" "Tell me about how you decided to choose the people who will inherit from you?" (Mossman & Farrell, 2015, p. 546). If the testator is deceased and the will is being challenged after the death, something more akin to a psychological autopsy is needed.

In 2014, the American Psychological Association published the "Guidelines for Psychological Practice With Older Adults." The Guidelines were necessary because psychological science and clinical practice in the area of psychology and aging have expanded rapidly. "Clinicians and researchers have made impressive strides toward identifying the unique aspects of knowledge that facilitate the accurate psychological assessment and effective treatment of older adults as the psychological literature in this area has burgeoned" (APA, 2014d, pp. 34–35). The need for psychological services for older adults will be increasingly substantial over the next two decades as the baby boomers get older. The prominent demand will largely be in the forensic assessments of cognitive deficits and dysfunction as they pertain to testamentary capacities and other categories of decision making.

An appreciable minority of older persons exhibit significantly impaired cognition, such as dementia, that significantly affects functional abilities. "The prevalence of dementia increases dramatically with age, with approximately 5% of the population between ages 71 and 79 years and 37% of the population above age 90 suffering with this condition" (APA, 2014d, p. 43). During the early stages of dementia or periodic bouts of severe mental illness, the psychologist or other MHP may be asked to evaluate the person, not only for his or her capacity to execute a will, but also for the need for guardianship.

Legal Guardianship Determinations

A guardianship is a legal right given to an individual to be responsible for the care and needs of a person deemed fully or partially incapable of providing for his or her own care and needs. Minor children and adults with cognitive impairment or mental disorder are those most often in need of guardianships. Our focus in this section will be on aging adults who, under certain conditions, demonstrate declining cognitive and decision-making abilities that may hinder their capacity to carry out certain tasks for daily living. Frequently, cognitive impairment leads to an increase in susceptibility to financial fraud and scams, an apparent inability to make reasonable decisions, and signs of considerable dependence on others, which may also lead to exploitation.

On the other hand, many persons of advanced age are perfectly capable of making decisions that affect their health and their financial status, even though these decisions may not be favored or recommended by those around them. Health care and financial decisions are the two categories that are most likely to be challenged in courts and most likely to require the assessment of mental health professionals. A decision that one lacks the capacity to make such a decision is what leads to a guardian being appointed.

Some people have a durable power of attorney and advance directives for handling the possible loss of cognitive ability later in life. In a *power of attorney* document, the individual appoints an agent or agents (usually a family member) to manage financial affairs, make health care decisions, and conduct other business when he or she shows significant declines in cognitive, planning, and decision-making abilities. Advance directives are discussed later in the chapter.

When an aging parent or other relative begins to show signs of mental deterioration, and in the absence of a signed power of attorney document, a family may ask for legal guardianship. In order to act as someone's legal guardian, the first step is to go to court to have the person declared incompetent based on a psychological expert's opinion. "In most jurisdictions, any interested person can petition to have someone declared incompetent and subject to guardianship" (Melton et al., 2007, p. 371). A guardian can only be appointed if the court hears sufficient evidence that the person lacks mental capacity in some or all areas of his or her life. The burden of proof is typically on the person seeking guardianship. In other words, he or she must demonstrate, usually by clear and convincing evidence, that the mental capacity is lacking. If the court is satisfied with the evidence, it may grant either a "limited" or "full" guardianship. Limited guardianships allow some self-determination in specified aspects of the person's daily life but place restrictions on other areas deemed too risky for the person to make his or her own decisions. If the court feels a full guardianship is in order, it would transfer the responsibility for managing finances, living arrangements, and medical decisions to the guardian. A guardianship assignment may take effect immediately or sometime in the future. In many cases, the guardian will need to report to the court annually to affirm he or she is meeting the assigned responsibilities outlined by the court. As might be expected, however, there is considerable variation in the application of guardianship statutes from jurisdiction to jurisdiction. Some states require substantial evidence of incompetency before entering an order for guardianship, while others do not (Melton et al., 2007). Some states do not even require psychological evaluations prior to a guardianship proceeding. If they did, the demand for competent psychological evaluations would be overwhelming in many jurisdictions (Melton et al., 2007).

In states that require or expect psychological evaluations for guardianship proceedings, the court will typically ask for one that is designed to identify the extent of the declining mental conditions and to suggest options for how to proceed. The psychologist who conducts these evaluations or presents testimony to the court will be expected to indicate current competencies and predict future declining mental conditions. The clinical assessment should focus on the range of *functions* that the person can perform, not the nature of any mental disorder or diagnosis. "Thus, despite the difficulty of doing so, clinicians should pinpoint as precisely as possible the tasks the allegedly incompetent person can and cannot do" (Melton et al., 2007, p. 373).

There is a wide spectrum of functional and psychological tests used in guardianship and other civil capacity evaluations (Quickel & Demakis, 2013). Melton et al. (2007) note that there are at least five instruments designed to assess independent activities of daily living skills. They are (1) the Adult Functional Adaptive Behavior Scale, (2) the Multidimensional Functional Assessment Questionnaire, (3) the Philadelphia Geriatric Center Multilevel Assessment Inventory, (4) the Direct Assessment of Functional Status, and (5) the Everyday Problems Test. Another useful measure that should be added to the list is the Independent Living Scales. As Mossman and Farrell (2015) emphasize in a discussion of capacity assessment instruments, many of the tools presented have not been subjected to extensive research or been broadly accepted for specific use in guardianship proceedings.

In addition, the psychologist should identify in what ways the person may be helped in performing certain tasks on his or her own. These guardianship determinations are important, and they present "a delicate balance between preserving individual freedom and autonomy and protecting individuals from harm and exploitation" (Quickel & Demakis, 2013, p. 155). "It is easy to forget that the very nature of guardianship can deprive an individual of fundamental rights of choice, movement, and association, and even life and death decisions, authorized and enabled through state power" (Reinert, 2006, p. 40). In the guardianship legal context, Drogin and Barrett (2013) assert that from the forensic psychologist's perspective, "the stakes may be no less dire than those encountered in the course of criminal law matters" (p. 301). They suggest that psychologists evaluating guardianships might find the APA's (1998) "Guidelines for the Evaluation of Dementia and Age-Related Cognitive Decline" helpful. In addition, the forensic psychologist who conducts guardianship evaluations should stay closely attuned to the newest strategies for performing them, as there surely will be many updates in the future (Melton et al., 2007).

In summary, forensic psychologists can make significant contributions to the welfare and quality of life for individuals who need competently done evaluations regarding guardianships. Another challenging undertaking in competence evaluations is the assessing of competency or capacity to consent to treatment.

Competence to Consent to Treatment

Perhaps even more frequent than evaluations of testamentary capacity and guardianships are evaluations of a person's ability to make decisions regarding medical and psychological treatment. These decisions require informed consent, which generally means that the individuals must be told of the possible consequences of treatment (disclosure); must be mentally capable of understanding what they are consenting to; and must be doing so of their own free will, without coercion. Each of these three elements is scrutinized separately by courts when questions of informed consent come before them. Interestingly, research suggests that disclosure is particularly problematic. "The most general thing that can be said about disclosure in health and mental health settings is that there is rarely adherence to the spirit of informed consent" (Melton et al., 1997, p. 352). Melton et al. note that consent forms are lengthy and beyond comprehension, patients often lack information about alternative treatments, and negative information (e.g., about side effects) is often omitted. A variety of explanations are offered for this failure to adhere to the spirit of disclosure requirements. For example, treatment providers may wish to protect their patients from excessive worry, or they may fear that they themselves will appear professionally weak by not knowing precisely how the patient will react to the treatment. Obviously, the quality of disclosure is an important component in a subsequent evaluation of consent to treatment. That is, if the individual did not receive sufficient information about treatment alternatives or about the risks associated with the treatment, the consent was not informed.

Measures of Competence to Consent to Treatment

The competence of mentally disturbed individuals to consent to treatment has been studied extensively by researchers associated with the MacArthur Foundation (e.g., Appelbaum & Grisso, 1995; Grisso, Appelbaum, Mulvey, & Fletcher, 1995). Their research has, in turn, been the subject of considerable scholarly comment (see, generally, Winick, 1996). The MacArthur Competence Study (Appelbaum & Grisso, 1995) assessed and compared decision-making competence in three groups: persons hospitalized with serious mental illness, persons hospitalized with medical illness, and community volunteers who were not patients. Despite some decision-making deficits, those hospitalized with mental illness were still capable of making decisions, as reflected on measures of decision-making ability. The exceptions were patients with schizophrenia who had severe psychiatric symptoms; nevertheless, the majority of patients with schizophrenia still performed adequately. Hospitalized patients with depression demonstrated intermediate levels of decision making. The MacArthur researchers developed a tool—the **MacArthur Competence Assessment Tool–Treatment (MacCAT-T)**, which is distinct from the MacCAT-CA described in Chapter 5—for use by clinicians who evaluate treatment competence. The interview format allows clinicians to test decision-making competence in four areas: (1) ability to state a choice, (2) ability to understand relevant information, (3) ability to appreciate the nature of one's own situation, and (4) ability to reason with the information provided.

Although the MacCAT-T has received favorable reviews and commentary (e.g., Lichtenberg, Qualls, & Smyer, 2015; Mossman & Farrell, 2015; Winick, 1996), some researchers and scholars have issued cautionary notes. Kirk and Bersoff (1996) suggest that the instrument sets too low a standard for decision-making competence, focusing as it does on competencies rather than disabilities. In other words, using the instrument, too many individuals would be found to make competent decisions in their best interest, and their decisional disabilities would be overlooked. Kapp and Mossman (1996) believe there are inherent problems in any attempt to construct a universal test of decisional capacity to make medical choices. Although the MacArthur group clearly warned that their measures were still in the experimental stage, Kapp and Mossman express concern that clinicians will rush too quickly to adopt the competency assessment tool and that courts will accept it too readily. They note also that numerous other instruments are currently available to assess competency, many of which are accompanied by research testing their validity (e.g., the Mini-Mental State Examination [MMSE], the Geriatric Depression Scale, the Alzheimer's Disease Assessment Scale). Kapp and Mossman believe it is far more useful to develop a *process* than a universal test for evaluating competency to consent to treatment: "What is needed . . . is a credible process for collecting, critically examining, and drawing up usable guidelines from our extensive research and practice experience" (p. 95). Nevertheless, the MacCat-T has earned mostly positive reviews, but no one suggests that it or any other single measure be used to the exclusion of others.

Lichtenberg, Qualls, and Smyer (2015) note that none of the instruments that are designed to assess capacity in older adults investigate the values they hold. "It is important to understand the older adult's long-held and cherished values that might affect the health decision the older adult is making, through review of any legal documents created to guide health decisions, direct discussion with the older adult, and communication with informants" (p. 561). The same could be said of cherished values that might affect financial decisions.

An important factor in evaluating older adults is to recognize their needs for autonomy. Although protecting them is often paramount to decision makers, this should not be the sole consideration.

Incapacitation: Special Condition

Another decisional competency area that has been controversial involves persons who are comatose or cognitively incapacitated and in a permanent vegetative state. Obviously, they cannot make decisions in their best interest. However, if their wishes are known, they will generally (although not invariably) be honored.

A number of tragic cases have brought this issue to public attention. For example, in the 1970s, Karen Ann Quinlan was comatose and on life support systems with physicians giving no hope to her parents that she would ever be revived. The parents went to court to secure permission to remove their daughter from life support. The state supreme court in that case (*In re Quinlan*, 1976) ruled that the wishes of a comatose person should be honored if she had made it perfectly clear what she would want in the event that she became incompetent; the parents then had to persuade the courts that this was what she would have wanted. They were allowed to remove her from a respirator in 1976, and she died of pneumonia in 1985.

Nancy Cruzan was a young woman severely injured in an automobile accident in 1983 that left her in a permanent vegetative state. In that case, the U.S. Supreme Court supported Missouri's law requiring clear and convincing evidence that Cruzan would want life-sustaining procedures to be terminated (*Cruzan v. Director, Missouri Department of Health*, 1990). Her parents were able to provide this evidence, she was removed from life support, and she died shortly thereafter.

The case of Terri Schiavo also attracted nationwide attention. She was a young woman in Florida who apparently suffered cardiac arrest with resulting brain damage, in 1990. After 2 months, she was said to be in a persistent vegetative state, but her husband and her physicians attempted a number of medical options to revive her, without success. After 8 years, her husband petitioned the court to remove feeding tubes that were keeping her alive, but her parents and the state of Florida objected. Schiavo had no living will, so the case revolved around what people believed her wishes would be—the husband had one point of view, while the parents had another. This very complex case went through numerous court proceedings, even to the point of being denied review four times by the U.S. Supreme Court. The feeding tube was alternately removed and replaced. Schiavo's husband ultimately was successful in his pleas; the tubes were removed; and Schiavo died in March 2005, 15 years after her tragic collapse.

These cases—and similar situations in other states—prompted many people to prepare **advance directives** in case they should become physically incapacitated. In some cases, family members or other interested parties have challenged these advance directives, maintaining that the incapacitated person was not mentally competent at the time he or she formulated them. In these situations, the forensic clinician is asked to make an assessment similar to that involved in testamentary capacity.

Although the U.S. Supreme Court has made it clear that competent individuals have a constitutional right to refuse life-prolonging treatment, it has not thus far supported the idea of aggressively hastening one's death. To date, it has been left to states to craft their own legal rules in this matter. At this writing, five states (Oregon, Vermont, Washington, California, and Colorado) along with the District of Columbia allow terminally ill, competent individuals to request, and physicians to administer, medication that will help them die. In Montana, it was ruled that physicians could not be prosecuted for prescribing lethal drugs. Similar bills have been introduced in many other states. (See Focus 6.4 for more information.) Medical assistance in dying is permitted in Canada but restricted to Canadian citizens, as well as in other Western nations (e.g., Switzerland, Belgium). The Netherlands has an extremely liberal policy, requiring no proof of a terminal illness.

Aid in dying laws and favorable court rulings have spurred the need for a new form of psychological assessment: the evaluation of competency to make decisions that will hasten one's death. **Hastened death evaluations** began to be discussed in the forensic psychology literature around the turn of the 21st century, along with proposed guidelines for conducting them (e.g., Allen & Shuster, 2002; Werth, Benjamin, & Farrenkopf, 2000). Thus far, however, there is little evidence that they are a common undertaking by forensic psychologists. This is perhaps because medical professionals who are willing to provide assistance in dying (and many are not) do not question the competence of the patients who request it. Although opponents of these laws say they undermine the value of life, supporters say they recognize the dignity and privacy of the individual who does not wish to prolong the inevitable death he or she faces in the near future.

INVOLUNTARY CIVIL COMMITMENT

Closely related to competency to consent to treatment is the issue of hospitalizing individuals for psychological or psychiatric treatment against their will. Every state allows such commitment, both on emergency and extended bases. The typical statute allows an emergency commitment of 3 to 10 days and an extended commitment for a 3- to 6-month period subject to recommitment proceedings. When people are recommitted, their status must be reviewed at specified intervals. In recent years, though, the number of beds available for involuntary commitment has decreased, and many mental health advocates bemoan accompanying problems,

FOCUS 6.4. COMPASSION AND CHOICE: IS THERE A RIGHT TO AID IN DYING?

Brittany Maynard, a 29-year-old woman with terminal brain cancer, moved to Oregon with her husband in order to have access to medical assistance in dying. She died in November 2014, after ingesting a lethal drug that had been legally prescribed. Brittany Maynard was one of a very small number of individuals who have chosen this option, but it was her right to do so.

Oregon was the first state to pass a "Death with Dignity" act, in 1997. Since then, aid in dying has been allowed in California, Colorado, Vermont, Washington, Montana, and Washington, D.C. In Montana, an effort to establish this as a right under the state constitution failed, but that state's supreme court ruled that a physician who prescribed lethal drugs at the request of a competent, terminally ill patient could not be prosecuted. Bills have been introduced to pass similar laws in many other states, including Maryland, Hawaii, and New York. As a group, aid in dying laws in the United States require that the person be emotionally competent and terminally ill with a prognosis of six months or less. Typically two but sometimes three physicians must accede to the request (one prescriber and one or two consulting physicians). If there is suspicion that the person is not mentally competent or psychologically stable enough to make the decision, a mental health professional must be consulted. The laws also allow physicians to opt out—that is, they can refuse to prescribe the medication. Finally, the laws state that the individuals themselves must ingest the drugs.

Also typically, the patient must be fully informed of the progress of the illness, and there must be safeguards in place to prevent a rash decision and improve the quality of end-of-life care. Typically, the patient must make that request on more than one occasion.

Virtually all research on this issue indicates that in the states where this is allowed, a very small number of people (1% of people with terminal diagnoses) have been prescribed drugs for the purpose of ending their lives, and only about one third of those who receive them actually use them. Moreover, many physicians are opposed to prescribing life-ending medication, so patients must find a physician willing to cooperate. Recently, the pharmaceutical company that produced the drug most commonly prescribed—Seconal—raised its prices to an exorbitant level. It is now estimated that, in those states where such assistance is legal, the cost of ending one's life can be $3,000 to $4,000.

As discussed in the text, although end-of-life evaluations for competence have received some attention in the literature, this is not an active area for forensic psychologists. Nevertheless, as medical aid in dying gains more adherents, mental health practitioners as a group may see more involvement.

Questions for Discussion

1. Review the arguments that might be offered by someone who is opposed to aid in dying legislation.
2. The American Medical Association (AMA) has expressed its opposition to medical assistance in dying legislation, but it commissioned a study to continue to examine the issue. A report of this study was due sometime in 2017. If the report has been released, summarize and discuss its findings.
3. Assuming one is in favor of aid in dying legislation, should it be extended to persons who have incurable diseases but are believed to have more than 6 months to live? For example, should a person with ALS or a diagnosis of early Alzheimer's disease be able to obtain drugs to hasten his or her death?
4. Explain how an evaluation of one's competence to make an end-of-life decision might end up in a court proceeding.

such as waiting lists for beds in psychiatric facilities or patients with severe mental illness being treated in emergency rooms of public hospitals. (See Perspective 10.1 in Chapter 10, in which Dr. Lavita Nadkarni refers to this crisis.)

Although standards vary somewhat depending on the state, the party seeking the commitment always has to prove by at least clear and convincing evidence that the individual is mentally ill and in need of treatment (*Addington v. Texas*, 1979). Interestingly, in the case of intellectual disability, however, commitment to a care facility can be achieved by a less rigid standard, preponderance of the evidence (*Heller v. Doe*, 1993). Whether mentally disordered or intellectually disabled, the individual must be deemed a danger to self or others *or* so gravely disabled that this person is unable to meet his or her basic needs. It should be noted that, although individuals have a right to legal representation at commitment hearings, there is evidence that lawyers often function paternalistically or maternalistically instead of advocating for the legal rights of their clients (Perlin & Dorfman, 1996). This is not unlike the situation of lawyers representing juveniles in delinquency proceedings, when they believe it is in the juvenile's interest to obtain treatment rather than aggressively forcing the state to prove the juvenile's guilt beyond a reasonable doubt.

An extremely controversial area in involuntary commitment is the civil commitment of sexual predators. Less controversial, but still of concern, are the civil commitments of persons found incompetent to stand trial but not restorable to competence, or persons not guilty by reason of insanity. The latter is less controversial because the length of commitment is decreasing in many jurisdictions, with increases in conditional release. Sexual predators are far less likely to be considered eligible for conditional release. These topics were addressed in Chapter 5, and they will not be revisited here.

The U.S. Supreme Court has ruled that persons who are seriously mentally disordered are unable to consent "voluntarily" to being institutionalized (*Zinermon v. Burch*, 1990). Burch, a mentally disordered individual who was found wandering along a highway in a highly disoriented condition, had signed forms voluntarily admitting himself into a mental institution, where he remained for about five months. He later sued the state, maintaining that he was not competent to sign his admission forms. The Supreme Court agreed, declaring his original admission invalid because, in his severely mentally disordered state, he could not have validly consented. Accordingly, persons who are unable to make competent decisions must be admitted to mental institutions via the involuntary commitment route described above (Slovenko, 1999). Despite this decision, however, it is doubtful that psychiatric facilities scrutinize voluntary admissions to determine whether the person seeking admission has the capacity to make that decision (Melton et al., 2007).

Outpatient Civil Commitment

Civil commitment also can be achieved on an outpatient basis—in fact, statutes often require this least restrictive alternative if it can reasonably be provided. Courts are empowered to issue **outpatient treatment (OT) orders**, also called community treatment orders (CTOs), and occasionally orders of non-hospitalization (ONH). These orders typically require that the individual live in his or her own home or alternative group or foster home and comply with a medication regimen. The resulting effect on the individual is referred to as **assisted outpatient treatment (AOT)**. If the person does not comply with the treatment order, he or she is subject to psychiatric hospitalization.

Outpatient civil commitment has been a hot topic in the research literature, probably surpassing interest in institutional confinement (Lareau, 2013; Winick & Kress, 2003b). The creation of laws enabling such commitment is often spurred by a tragic event, such as the death of journalist Kendra Webdale in 1999, which produced New York's "Kendra's Law." Webdale was pushed into the path of a subway train by a man who had been diagnosed with schizophrenia, had a history of violence, but was not taking medication. Kendra's Law allows judges to order individuals to receive psychiatric treatment in the community for up to 6 months; in 2013, this time period was expanded to 1 year. At the end of the specified time period, they may or may not be reevaluated. Until recently, most states required that an outpatient order be based on showing that the individual was both mentally disordered and dangerous to the self or others. However, some states are now beginning to allow outpatient orders without the dangerousness component. Called **preventive outpatient treatment (or commitment)**, this approach allows the state to intervene before the individual's condition becomes worse (Lareau, 2013). "The new broadened criteria still require mental illness, but instead of the dangerousness standard, they require a need for treatment to prevent further deterioration that would predictably lead to dangerousness based on the individual's illness history" (Hiday, 2003, p. 11). Hiday adds that the person must be judged unable to seek or comply with treatment voluntarily. In addition, like the outpatient orders based on a dangerousness standard, it must be determined that the individual can survive safely in the community with available supervision. Supervision or monitoring is a crucial component in outpatient commitment. Although some research questions its effectiveness (Pfeffer, 2008), other studies emphasize positive results when appropriate monitoring occurs (Swanson et al., 2013).

Schopp (2003) and Lareau (2013) provide additional descriptions of outpatient civil commitment that help clarify the situations under which it occurs. In sum, outpatient commitment can take three forms. First, persons who were institutionalized under civil commitment statutes requiring mental disorder and the dangerousness standard are *conditionally released* to the community; if they fail to meet the conditions of their release, they are subject to being returned to the institution. Second, persons who are eligible for institutional confinement under the civil commitment statutes are given an alternative mandatory treatment status in the community, rather than being institutionalized. This is considered the *least restrictive alternative*. Third, persons who would not qualify under the dangerousness standard but who are considered to need treatment to prevent further deterioration are assigned to *preventive commitment*. The last—an option available in about 10 states—is the most controversial among those concerned about civil liberties, because the commitment standards are less stringent than customary civil commitment standards (Lareau, 2013).

Researchers are continuing to explore the effectiveness of involuntary outpatient treatment, which is increasingly being used in all three forms described above. The main questions revolve around whether individuals can be "coerced" to get better; in other words, does treatment "work" if a person is forced to get it?

In reviewing this literature, Hiday (2003) notes that early studies almost invariably found positive outcomes on a number of factors. For example, patients ordered to outpatient treatment had lower rehospitalization rates; better compliance with medication and other treatment; and generally better adjustment in the community than comparison groups of patients, such as those who were discharged without outpatient orders. Hiday also reports on a second generation of research, conducted in North Carolina (Swartz, Swanson, & Hiday, 2001) and New York City (Steadman, Gounis, & Dennis, 2001), that is more empirically based, including random assignment to outpatient commitment and non-outpatient commitment groups. Both groups received mental health and social services in the community. The North Carolina study again found that patients under outpatient orders had significantly more positive outcomes than those not under these orders. The New York study, though, found no significant differences, a finding that Hiday attributes to technical problems in the research. She notes that, despite the study's conclusions, New York State's Department of Mental Health remains supportive of outpatient commitment and reports positive outcomes for patients under those orders—including declines in harmful behavior and homelessness and an increase in medication compliance.

As noted above, the most recent research suggests outpatient commitment is cost effective and produces positive results, but monitoring is an essential component (Swanson et al., 2013; Swartz, Swanson, Steadman, Robbins, & Monahan, 2009). This can be challenging to do, though, particularly when the patient moves to another community or another state and does not contact a mental health provider. Nevertheless, when monitoring occurs, outpatient treatment is not only cost effective, but people who are treated in the community also recover faster, have fewer relapses, deteriorate less from dependency fostered by hospitalization, and maintain employment better than similar patients who are treated in hospital settings (Swartz et al., 2009).

Not everyone is supportive of outpatient commitment, however, particularly when it is not based on dangerousness criteria. Such preventive commitment raises many legal questions without ensuring that effective treatment will be provided (Pfeffer, 2008; Winick, 2003).

Persons who would otherwise not qualify for civil commitment are forced to take medications and comply with other treatment regimens against their will, and it appears that they often feel pressured to do so. A recent study (Pridham et al., 2016) analyzed 23 articles and 14 empirical studies on this matter and found that coercion was widely perceived. Civil libertarians see this as a dangerous expansion of the already overwhelming power of the state. The New York study (Steadman, Gounis, et al., 2001), which reported no differences between those subjected to mandatory treatment and those who were not, provides additional support for this perspective—if forced treatment is no better than voluntary treatment, why force treatment? Such debates among reasonable people have a long history in the literature on civil commitment and will not likely be resolved in the near future.

It is also important to note that the research supportive of any form of outpatient commitment generally indicates that such treatment is effective only if it continues for a period of at least 6 months and is accompanied by the provision of intensive services (Winick & Kress, 2003a). Some maintain that the treatment should span years rather than months (Durham & La Fond, 1990). Thus, psychologists who are providing treatment to patients under such orders should be aware of the need to sustain these services. And, as suggested above, if patients intend to move away, referrals should be made to mental health services at their destination.

Role of Forensic Psychologists

Regardless of the nature of the involuntary commitment (inpatient or outpatient and its variations), the assessment skills of forensic psychologists are required to help determine whether the individual meets the standards for commitment. If a showing of dangerousness is required, the psychologist again engages in the risk-assessment enterprise we have discussed above and in earlier chapters. Melton et al. (1997, 2007) warn that this is an area where clinicians must exercise extreme caution, considering the inadequate legal representation provided to so many individuals and the potential loss of freedom they are encountering. Demonstrating the presence of mental illness and determining treatment needs of the individual are probably the easier of the clinician's tasks. The accompanying assessment of dangerousness (or risk) is more formidable. All of the cautions about risk assessment referred to in earlier chapters should be recalled here as well.

The individual's potential for dangerousness to self involves an assessment of suicide risk. Clinicians should be informed about general research on demographics of suicide (e.g., males at higher risk, married persons at lower risk) as well as the individual's own clinical history. Interviews with the individual also may uncover *suicide ideation*, or fantasies of killing oneself. Both the frequency and intensity of such ideations should be considered. However, as Melton et al. (1997, 2007) note, the track record of MHPs at predicting suicide is very poor. They urge clinicians to refer to the person's risk compared with others in the population rather than simply state that he or she is a danger to himself or herself.

We now shift our attention to the increasingly important topic of sexual and gender harassment. More recently, gender harassment has especially drawn attention from the civil court system.

SEXUAL AND GENDER HARASSMENT

Sexual harassment may be broadly defined as unwelcome sexual advances, requests for sexual favors, and other unwanted verbal or physical conduct of a sexual nature (Hellkamp & Lewis, 1995; Till, 1980). Civil claims of sexual harassment arise most frequently in employment and educational contexts, where harassment qualifies as discrimination in violation of Title VII of the Civil Rights Acts of 1964, amended in 1971. This is an important point to emphasize: harassment is a form of discrimination, and federal law prohibits discrimination in the workplace, in hiring, in education, and in public accommodations, among many contexts. Courts have differed over whether Title VII's prohibition against employment discrimination in the workplace applies to LGBT individuals. Most recently, in April 2017, the 7th Circuit Court of Appeals ruled 8–3 that LGBT individuals are indeed protected against discrimination in the workplace. Shortly after that ruling, however, in July of 2017, the Department of Justice under Attorney General Jeff Sessions filed a brief in a New York discrimination case, arguing that LGBT individuals were *not* covered by the law. It remains to be seen how that case will be determined. The U.S. Supreme Court has never ruled on the matter.

In recent years, more courts and commentators have indicated that **gender harassment** should also be included under a broad definition of sexual harassment (Kabat-Farr & Cortina, 2014; Leskinen, Cortina, & Kabat, 2011). This is behavior directed at individuals who appear to violate their so-called gender roles, such as women who work in a previously all-male environment; women who are assertive, competent, and persistent; or men who are perceived as weak or emotional. Gender harassment does not necessitate unwelcome advances or a request for sexual favors; it too, though, conveys a degrading attitude toward the individual at whom it is directed. Gender harassment examples include female- or male-bashing jokes, comments that women do not belong in management or that men have no place in childcare, and crude gender-related terms of address (e.g., denigrating a coworker as a "hussy" or "male whore") (Kabat-Farr & Cortina, 2014, p. 60). Thus, a pattern of making derisive comments about the ability of women to do a job or comments like, "Shouldn't you be at home making dinner for your husband?" further illustrate gender harassment. In essence, gender harassment parallels the legal concept of hostile environment harassment (Kabat-Farr & Cortina, 2014).

Many people work in environments where "dirty jokes," innuendoes, sexual banter, or comments on a coworker's clothes are a regular occurrence. Such behavior is unacceptable and inappropriate but some apparently do not mind it. Many others do mind but try to ignore it, or they put the offending individual in his or her place. This is easier done if the offending person is on the same level—when the person is a supervisor or boss, the problem becomes magnified. Numerous illustrations of this came to public attention in recent years, as sexual harassment suits were filed, and often settled out of court, against public figures, including entertainers, business people, cable executives and personalities, studio executives, and public officials.

When harassing behaviors reach extremes, and/or when individuals are denied promotions because they do not cooperate with a harasser, this is when the legal system is most likely to be brought into the picture, but as noted above, numerous claims are settled out of court, typically with the respondent not admitting guilt. Although public figures accused of sexual harassment often claim they will countersue (e.g., for defamation), this rarely occurs. Instead, the matter is settled quietly with plaintiffs receiving some financial compensation and often signing nondisclosure agreements, indicating they will no longer pursue the case and will not reveal further information.

To qualify as illegal in the workplace, the behavior must be more than irritating or mildly offensive. It must be severe and pervasive, so much so that it alters conditions of the victim's employment. In many sexual harassment cases, an employer or supervisor has offered a promotion in exchange for sex or, alternately, has threatened a demotion if denied. The conduct also must be objectively offensive—or offensive to a reasonable person—not just subjectively offensive to the plaintiff (*Harris v. Forklift Systems, Inc.*, 1993). Examples of such conduct from actual court cases include the following: a fellow worker posting pictures of erect penises on women's lockers; a supervisor ordering a clerk to reach into his (the supervisor's) pocket for change; constant repetition of extremely vulgar jokes, even after a request that these cease; consistent, noticeable ogling of a person's body, particularly focusing on women's breasts or the genital area; and sending images of violent pornography and degradation of women via office computers. If we add gender harassment, examples might include some of the above, as well as persistent comments that criticize a male teacher for coaching girls' basketball teams, telling women they cannot do a job as well as men can, and excluding the sole woman—or the sole man—from significant group work assignments.

It is important to emphasize that sexual harassment is "sex neutral," in that both women and men can be victims (*Oncale v. Sundowner Offshore Services*, 1998). Reviewing research in this area, Stockdale, Sliter, and Ashburn-Nardo (2015) note that women are more likely than men to experience it, but "incidence rates for men are not trivial" (p. 522). Finally, although plaintiffs typically seek compensation for mental anguish and pain and suffering (e.g., anger, anxiety, loss of self-esteem, fear, or feelings of humiliation), extensive psychological harm need not be demonstrated for a plaintiff to prevail (*Harris v. Forklift Systems, Inc.*, 1993). In other words, the Supreme Court has recognized that some victims of sexual harassment may experience its negative effects without also experiencing debilitating psychological deterioration.

Psychologists have a variety of tasks to perform relating to sexual harassment. They may consult with employers in setting up educational programs on the topic. They can provide guidance to employers and training to employees so that harassment will be prevented (Stockdale, Sliter, & Ashburn-Nardo, 2015). Such consultation would include both education in the laws relating to discrimination and the psychological theory that helps explain it, such as research on stereotyping.

They may also offer counseling services to victims of harassment. In the present chapter, we discuss their role in civil suits. Either side—plaintiff or defendant—might hire a psychologist to evaluate the claims of emotional distress made by the plaintiff. The psychologist is also asked to address the question of whether the particular behavior of the defendant, if it did occur, could reasonably lead to the mental injury experienced by the plaintiff. In these examinations, the evaluator is asked not only to document the disorder, but also to eliminate other possible causes that are unrelated to the alleged harassment. Both clinical and research psychologists also might be called as expert witnesses to testify on gender stereotyping or on the general psychological effects of sexual or gender harassment.

So far, psychology and the law have largely neglected gender harassment in comparison to traditionally defined sexual harassment, but it is likely to become more of a key issue in civil suits in the future (Kabat-Farr & Cortina, 2014). Gender harassment is especially relevant when considering the experiences of women in mostly male settings and workplaces. Gender harassment "alienates and isolates women, reducing their access to information and opportunities . . . and involves interpersonal derogation, scorn, and rejection" (Kabat-Farr & Cortina, 2014, p. 60).

In sexual harassment suits, the alleged victim may be compelled to undergo a psychological or psychiatric evaluation at the request of the respondent. Compelled examinations occur when the plaintiff claims any more than ordinary distress as a result of the harassment. For example, she may claim that the actions of the respondent not only were irritating or embarrassing, but also caused a mental disorder, such as a major depressive disorder (Kovera & Cass, 2002) or PTSD. In compelled evaluations, the respondent asks the court to order an evaluation by a clinician contacted by his or her attorney and must show good cause for why the plaintiff should undergo it. Kovera and Cass note that courts tend to deny motions for a compelled examination if the disorder occurred in the past rather than being current. Furthermore, "simply claiming emotional damages does not put one's mental health into controversy and thus does not warrant a compelled mental health examination" (p. 99). Rather, motions are more likely to be granted if the plaintiff meets a number of criteria, such as claiming *severe* disorder and signifying intent to put forth her or his own expert to substantiate any claims. A compelled evaluation is likely to open the way for a psychologist to gain information about sexual history, including sexual abuse, and this information is then made available to the opposing party. As in all evaluations, then, it is critical that the examining clinician inform the person being evaluated of the potential use of the report.

Psychological Measures of Sexual Harassment

The dominant instrument for assessing sexual harassment from the perspective of the alleged victim is the **Sexual Experiences Questionnaire (SEQ)** (Fitzgerald & Shullman, 1985), which has developed with updated versions (e.g., Fitzgerald, Magley, Drasgow, & Waldo, 1999). The SEQ has been referred to as "the most theoretically and psychometrically sophisticated instrument available for assessing incidence and prevalence of sexual harassment" (Cortina, 2001, p. 165). Despite this comment, it is important to emphasize that, for legal purposes, the mental health practitioner does not decide whether sexual harassment occurred in a particular case. Furthermore, some researchers are more guarded in their appraisal of the SEQ as it pertains to the *legal* questions at stake: "As a measure of the psychological definition of sexual harassment, the SEQ has been shown to be a reliable and valid assessment of unwanted social-sexual workplace treatment, which generally (but not legally) conforms to the construct of sexual harassment" (Stockdale, Logan, & Weston, 2009).

The SEQ lists 29 specific behaviors and asks respondents whether they have ever experienced them on a scale of *never* to *often*. Five types of harassment are measured: gender harassment, seductive behavior, sexual bribery, sexual coercion, and sexual imposition.

As with many instruments described in this text, the SEQ was developed from research focusing almost exclusively on white participants. Although acknowledging the usefulness of the SEQ, several researchers have noted that research on sexual harassment does not sufficiently take into consideration differences in ethnic and cultural norms that might affect nonwhite victims. J. H. Adams (1997) argues persuasively that sexual harassment of blacks is reflective of both sex and race discrimination and that it perpetuates both gender and racial stereotypes. Cortina (2001) notes that Latinas might be more likely than non-Latinas to take offense at unwanted sex-related behavior in the workplace because of cultural norms emphasizing respect, dignity, and harmony in in-group relations. On the other hand, those Latinas who emigrated from countries where sexual harassment is more normative might interpret fewer of the behaviors on the SEQ as harassing behaviors. After conducting focus group interviews with Latina workers, Cortina added new items to the SEQ (SEQ-L) to assess behaviors that were particularly relevant to Latina experiences. For example, focus group interviews suggested that the Latinas were offended by being addressed informally in Spanish when a more formal mode of address was expected and by being called Spanish pet names. They were also offended when someone stood too close or expected them to behave in certain ways *because of their ethnicity* (e.g., as a Latina, she was expected to wear sexy clothes). None of these behaviors was included in the original SEQ.

We have only touched the surface of the rapidly developing research on ethnic and race differences in attitudes and responses to sexual harassment. Clearly, though, it is incumbent on forensic psychologists working with culturally diverse groups to be aware of these findings and to be sensitive to between-group differences.

SUMMARY AND CONCLUSIONS

As we have stated throughout these early chapters, there is no shortage of tasks for forensic psychologists to perform in a given context. Consultation with the civil courts is no exception. In this chapter, we have attempted to provide a representative sampling, but several areas were left untouched or only lightly addressed. For example, forensic psychologists participate in a wide variety of personal injury litigation and disability evaluations other than the employment compensation claims that were highlighted here. Fortunately, the perspective written by Dr. Piechowski covers this territory. Likewise,

forensic psychologists participate in discrimination suits other than sexual harassment, such as race, age, disability, and gender discrimination in both employment and non-employment situations. They perform child welfare evaluations, such as assessments of families and of children at risk in child protection proceedings. They evaluate children who have been sexually abused and whose parents wish to file civil charges against the alleged perpetrators. These and numerous other areas have contributed to making forensic psychology the exciting and growing field that it is.

Family law has changed dramatically over the past quarter century, particularly in light of changes in the definition of family and the many contemporary issues that have developed. The types of decisions to be made have remained essentially the same, regardless of the makeup of the family: Family court judges decide which parent or which caretaker gets custody of a child or children, they decide on visitation arrangements, and they decide whether to allow a custodial parent or guardian to relocate the children to a different geographical area. It is important to stress, however, that in the vast majority of divorces, parents arrive at a mutually acceptable agreement in these matters without having to litigate them in the courts.

When court intervention is needed, psychologists, sometimes called family forensic psychologists, help by conducting custody evaluations, alternatively called parenting evaluations. Many psychologists consider these among the most difficult and controversial assessments to make. They are emotionally laden, have engendered ethics complaints, and raise numerous questions as to what is the proper standard to apply. The dominant best interest of the child standard, though logical and commendable, is also vague and subjective. A major concern in custody disputes is the instruments that are sometimes used to assess parental abilities, as few have been submitted to empirical validation. Furthermore, because there is no one clearly identified preferred custody arrangement, psychologists must be cautious about research that suggests one form of custody is superior to another.

We covered a variety of contexts in which psychologists are involved in other civil matters, such as the assessment of civil capacities in various contexts. These include assessment of testamentary capacity and of competency to make medical decisions, such as decisions to consent to treatment, refuse treatment, or even hasten one's own death. With the aging of the population, the capacity of individuals to make decisions in their own best interest is likely to be assessed even more.

The chapter also included discussion of involuntary civil commitment, most particularly commitment to outpatient treatment. This form of commitment is increasing in virtually every state, but it raises important questions about the civil liberties of individuals who would otherwise not be eligible for institutional confinement. Many forensic psychologists are supportive of this form of commitment, primarily because it allows individuals to receive needed treatment in a community setting. Thus far, research on outpatient treatment effectiveness has demonstrated positive results, particularly if the treatment continues beyond a 6-month period and is accompanied by intensive services. In many cases, however, it is difficult to maintain continuity and adequate monitoring.

We ended the chapter with discussion of research and issues relating to sexual and gender harassment. Evaluations of persons who bring sexual harassment claims—particularly compelled evaluations—should be done with extreme caution. Although a number of inventories, including the SEQ, are available, they are just beginning to address the perceptions and experiences of different cultural groups.

KEY CONCEPTS

Advance directives 223
Approximation rule 201
Assisted outpatient treatment (AOT) 225
Best interest of the child (BIC) standard 201
Case-blind consultant 210
Child custody evaluations (CCEs) 199
Compensatory damages 211
Employment compensation claims 212
Family courts 196
Forensic neuropsychology 214
Friendly-parent rule 201

Gender harassment 228
Hastened death evaluations 223
Injunction 211
Least detrimental alternative standard 201
Legal parental authority 208
MacArthur Competence Assessment Tool–Treatment (MacCAT-T) 221
Outpatient treatment (OT) orders 225
Parental relocation 205
Parenting evaluation 199
Physical parental authority 208
Plaintiff 210

Preventive outpatient treatment (or commitment) 225
Probate courts 196
Projective instruments 205
Punitive damages 211
Respondent 210
Sexual Experiences Questionnaire (SEQ) 229
Sexual harassment 227
Tender years doctrine 201
Termination of parental rights 200
Testamentary capacity 218
Tort 210
Visitation risk assessments 205

QUESTIONS FOR REVIEW

1. Provide three findings from the research literature on custody evaluations and the effects of custody arrangements on children.

2. Define the following: BIC standard, tender years doctrine, least detrimental alternative standard, and friendly-parent rule.

3. Summarize the reasons why custody or parenting evaluations are considered among the most difficult forensic evaluations.

4. List any five civil capacities that may be assessed by forensic psychologists.

5. Give illustrations of when a forensic psychologist might be asked to assess competence to consent to treatment or to refuse treatment.

6. What is a hastened death evaluation?

7. What is AOT? What has research demonstrated about its effectiveness?

8. Both sexual harassment and gender harassment are forms of discrimination. Although gender harassment can be considered a form of sexual harassment, what is the distinction?

 SAGE edge™

Want a better grade? Go to **edge.sagepub.com/bartol5e** for the tools you need to sharpen your study skills. Access practice quizzes, eFlashcards, an action plan, and SAGE journal articles for enhanced learning.

CRIMINAL PSYCHOLOGY

CHAPTER SEVEN

THE DEVELOPMENT OF DELINQUENT AND CRIMINAL BEHAVIOR

"You can't go to jail for what you're thinking."

"It may be an ethics violation, but it's no crime."

"Well, there was probably bad judgment involved, but she didn't commit a crime!"

"He's just a kid, he can't be held responsible for something he didn't really mean to do. The kids are only 9 years old; they didn't know the gun was loaded, and they were both fooling around with it. It's tragic that one lost his leg, but it was an accident."

The quotes above represent actions or thoughts that do not qualify as crime. It's true that you can't go to jail for what you're thinking, even if you are thinking of poisoning your boss, and violations of ethics rules are not crimes. It is not a crime to exercise poor judgment unless that judgment leads one to conduct that is criminal. (Contrast the poor judgment of spending your entire paycheck on one lottery ticket versus thinking you can fool the IRS and not file an income tax return, for example.) And in the case of the 9-year-old boy, he did not commit a crime if he truly thought the gun was not loaded and did not intend to harm his friend. (His parents could, though, be sued in a civil court for negligence, depending upon the circumstances surrounding the case.)

A crime is "an intentional act in violation of the criminal law committed without defense or excuse, and penalized by the state as a felony or misdemeanor" (Tappan, 1947, p. 100). In other words, criminal behavior is intentional behavior that violates a criminal code—it did not occur accidentally, and the person's action cannot be justified (as in self-defense) or excused (as in the person was insane). To convict someone of a criminal offense, the prosecution (the government) generally must prove that the defendant committed a *voluntary act (actus reus)* intentionally, or with a *guilty* state of mind (*mens rea*). The statute defining the offense will specify what actions and what mental states (together called "elements") constitute a particular crime (La Fond, 2002). If a case goes to trial, the judge or jury can convict the defendant only if the prosecutor proves all elements beyond a reasonable doubt. However, if a defendant pleads guilty or does not contest the charges, the prosecutor is spared the burden of proving guilt, but a conviction is still entered on the record.

The spectrum of criminal behavior is extremely wide, ranging from minor offenses like criminal trespass to murder. In recent years, the public has become much more aware of corporate and political

Chapter Objectives

- Define criminal behavior and juvenile delinquency.
- Define antisocial behavior, conduct disorder, and antisocial personality disorder.
- Review the offenses for which juveniles are most frequently charged.
- Review the developmental approach to criminal behavior.
- Summarize theories of Terrie Moffett and Laurence Steinberg.
- Identify developmental factors most relevant to criminal behavior.
- Specify the relationship between ADHD and delinquency.
- Identify those firesetting behaviors that are precursors to offending.
- Review research on adult psychopathy and juveniles with psychopathic characteristics.

crimes, categories of offenses that have long captured the interest of criminologists who believe that extensive harm can be perpetrated by those holding extreme wealth or political power. Presidential administrations are sometimes at the forefront—one president, Richard M. Nixon, resigned in disgrace after members of his reelection campaign first burglarized, then colluded in covering up the burglary. As this book is going to press, investigations of possible illegal activity by people associated with the president are ongoing. Major corporations, such as Enron (a dominant energy leader), WorldCom (a telecommunications giant), Global Crossing (worldwide computer networking services), and others were involved in serious accounting improprieties that misled and betrayed investors. In the case of Enron, the wrongdoing affected the retirement, security, and jobs of its employees. Fraud in the banking industry, insider trading, violations of human rights, and corruption among public officials are examples of other criminal offenses that began to receive more public attention at the turn of the 21st century. Environmental disasters—such as the BP oil spill in the Gulf of Mexico—have demonstrated still more criminal activity that resulted in great harm. Readers are undoubtedly aware of numerous other instances, on national, international, state, and local levels.

Also in recent years, we have seen more interest in the decriminalization of some offenses, particularly the possession of marijuana in small amounts. Although "hard drugs" such as heroin and cocaine are recognized as having harmful effects, marijuana has long been regarded as parallel to or less damaging than alcohol, a legal substance. Cannabis, the marijuana plant, is extremely complex, containing over 400 chemical entities and 60 cannabinoid compounds, many of which have medicinal properties (Atakan, 2012). Whereas medical marijuana has increasingly been made available by prescription in many states, recreational marijuana is now gaining greater acceptance as well. In Colorado and Washington, it is no longer a criminal offense to possess marijuana in small amounts, and these states now allow its sale in regulated "pot shops" for recreational use. Washington, D.C., in early 2014, changed the possession of an ounce of marijuana to an infraction incurring a civil fine ($25) from a criminal offense incurring possible jail time. Smoking pot in public in Washington, D.C., though, remains a criminal offense. Approximately 15 other states have taken steps toward decriminalizing marijuana by lifting restrictions on the possession of small amounts. Twenty-nine states and the District of Colombia currently have laws broadly legalizing marijuana in some form (ProCon.org, 2017). Furthermore, many states are authorizing the dispensing of marijuana for medicinal purposes.

Our intention in this chapter, as well as in this text, is to focus on serious offenses that presumably produce the greatest harm to society. Although many people from all socioeconomic groups break criminal laws, only a small percentage of them become persistent offenders who commit numerous serious crimes, including crimes of a violent nature. An even smaller number of people commit the unusual, high-profile crimes that gain media attention, such as the individual who randomly opens fire on shoppers in a mall or students and teachers in a school. Because psychologists have been particularly interested in studying these two groups, and forensic psychologists most likely to come into contact with them, we focus on them in this text. As a result, other crimes that also produce great harm to society (e.g., many political and environmental crimes) are given less attention.

In the present chapter, we discuss people who demonstrate a habitual, persistent offending history of committing serious crimes. We will especially concentrate on those offenders who have had a *lifelong* criminal career of engaging in a wide variety of criminal offenses. Good examples of repetitive, chronic offenders are the life course–persistent offender discussed in the section on juvenile delinquency and the psychopath. Although the chapter focuses on juvenile offenders, we are primarily interested in the processes and factors involved in development of serious, lifelong offending. Consequently, although we do give more attention to juveniles in the development of criminal behavior, both adult offending and juvenile offending will be part of the discussion throughout the chapter. In Chapters 8 and 9, we will narrow our focus to crimes involving sexual assault; intimidation; and violence, such as murder, stalking, hate crime, and arson—again, crimes that lend themselves particularly well to psychological research and theory. They are also important topics for forensic psychologists, who frequently perform risk assessments of people charged with these offenses.

The overall purpose of the present chapter is to provide an overview of the developmental factors that are involved in the formation of serious or repetitive criminal behavior. Empirical research indicates that persistent antisocial behavior does not *usually* begin in adulthood but rather quite early in life, with signs sometimes appearing even during the preschool years (Moffitt, 1993a, 1993b). Consequently, the best place to start is by examining the developmental trajectory of the emerging juvenile offender.

It is important to avoid the temptation to seize on one cause or single explanation of crime, though. "The crime problem" *as a whole* can be attributed to any number of broad societal factors—the availability of handguns and assault weapons, racism, poverty, media glorification of violence, sexism, and an emphasis on obtaining power and material goods are examples. The cause of a *given individual's* criminal behavior is unlikely to be one-dimensional as well. What may at first appear to be relatively straightforward and simple is typically complex when studied by researchers or assessed and treated by clinicians. The causes of crime and delinquency are multiple and probably result mostly from a complicated interaction of many different influences.

THE JUVENILE OFFENDER

Definition of Juvenile Delinquency

Juvenile delinquency is an imprecise, social, clinical, and legal label for a broad spectrum of law- and norm-violating behavior. At first glance, a simple legal definition appears to be adequate: *Delinquency is behavior against the criminal code committed by an individual who has not reached adulthood.* But the term *delinquency* has numerous definitions and meanings beyond this one-sentence definition. In some states, the legal definition also includes status offending, which is not behavior against the "adult" criminal code but is behavior prohibited *only* for juveniles. For example, running away, violating curfew laws, and truancy all qualify as juvenile **status offenses**.

In addition, social, legal, and psychological definitions of delinquency overlap considerably. Social definitions of delinquency encompass a broad gamut of youthful behaviors considered inappropriate, but not all are technically crimes. These youthful behaviors include aggressive actions, truancy, petty theft, vandalism, drug abuse, sexual promiscuity, and even incorrigibility. The behavior may or may not have come to the attention of the police and, in fact, often does not. If the behavior is known to the police, it is not unusual for "social delinquents" to be referred to community social service agencies or to juvenile courts, but these youth do not fit the legal definition of delinquent unless they are found at a court hearing to have committed the crime for which they are charged, if their behavior did indeed constitute a crime. Therefore, *legally speaking*, a **juvenile delinquent** is one who commits an act against the criminal code *and who is adjudicated delinquent by an appropriate court.* The legal definition is usually restricted to persons younger than age 18, but in some states persons up to age 21 can be designated youthful offenders, meaning that they are likely to get leniency at sentencing. In addition, all states allow juveniles—in some cases as young as age 10—to be tried as adults in criminal courts under certain conditions and for certain offenses.

Psychological or *psychiatric* definitions of delinquency include the symptom-based labels of "conduct disorder" or "antisocial behavior." **Conduct disorder** (often abbreviated **CD**) is a diagnostic designation used to represent a group of behaviors characterized by *habitual* misbehavior, such as stealing, setting fires, running away from home, skipping school, destroying property, fighting, or being cruel to animals. Under this definition—like the social definition discussed above—the "delinquent" may or may not have been arrested for these behaviors, and some are not even against the criminal law. CD is described more fully in the most recent *Diagnostic and Statistical Manual of Mental Disorders (DSM-5)* of the American Psychiatric Association (2013). The *DSM* has traditionally been regarded as a decision-making tool for clinicians and as a guidepost for researchers (Moffitt et al., 2008). However, its classification of disorders and the criteria it suggests for identifying them are not universally accepted by clinicians. The latest revision, the *DSM-5*, received considerable criticism as it was being revised over more than a decade (Francis, 2012), and it remains to be seen whether this dissatisfaction will continue as mental health clinicians have more experience with this revision. Nevertheless, the *DSM-5* is likely to remain an important guide to forensic psychologists, psychiatrists, and other mental health professionals.

The more psychological term **antisocial behavior** is usually reserved for serious habitual misbehavior, which involves actions that are directly harmful to the well-being of others. Both antisocial behavior and conduct disorder should be distinguished, however, from **antisocial personality disorder** (**ASP**, also referred to as **APD**), which is a psychiatric diagnostic label reserved primarily for *adults* at least 18 years of age who displayed conduct disorder as children or adolescents and who continue serious offending well into adulthood. The *DSM-5* recognizes four categories of ASP which may occur alone or in combination: (1) aggression to people and animals, (2) destruction of property, (3) deceitfulness, and (4) serious violations of rules.

Although psychologists use the terms conduct disorder and antisocial behavior, a growing number of them describe and try to understand crime and delinquency through developmental, cognitive, and even biopsychological processes. For example, Terrie Moffitt's (1993a) developmental theory explains crime from a developmental perspective, and Robert Hare's (1996) concept of criminal psychopathy offers an intriguing delineation of the emotional, cognitive, and biopsychological factors involved in repetitive, serious offending over a lifetime. As we discuss later in the chapter, Hare and his followers believe that there are fundamental differences in brain functioning between the true psychopath and the "normal" population. More recently, Laurence Steinberg and his colleagues (Steinberg, 2007, 2014a; Steinberg, Cauffman, Woolard, Graham, & Banich, 2009; Steinberg & Monahan, 2007) have gathered revealing scientific evidence on adolescent cognitive and psychosocial development and how these relate to decision making, peer influence, and impulsivity. The research by Steinberg and his colleagues is often included in amicus curiae briefs submitted to courts by the APA and cited in subsequent court opinions (e.g., juvenile sentencing cases). We will review each of these perspectives shortly.

THE NATURE AND EXTENT OF JUVENILE OFFENDING

The amount of delinquent behavior—both what is reported and what is unreported to law enforcement agencies—is essentially an unknown area. We simply do not have complete data on the incidence of juvenile delinquency, broadly defined. However, although incomplete, we do have some statistics collected by law enforcement agencies, the courts, and juvenile correctional facilities.

Unlawful acts committed by juveniles can be divided into five major categories:

1. Unlawful acts against persons
2. Unlawful acts against property
3. Drug offenses
4. Offenses against the public order
5. Status offenses

The first four categories listed above are comparable in definition to crimes committed by adults. Juvenile status offenses, on the other hand, are acts that are not illegal if committed by an adult and that can be dealt with only by a juvenile court. However, these courts are increasingly shying away from dealing with status offenses, and the government keeps only limited statistics. Typical status offenses range from misbehavior, such as violations of curfew, underage drinking, running away from home, and truancy, to offenses that are interpreted very subjectively, such as unruliness and ungovernability (beyond the control of parents or guardians). Interestingly, a major source of crime data in the United States, the Uniform Crime Reports (UCR), stopped collecting data on runaways in 2010. We discuss the UCR below. In the early 2000s, when status offenses were still reported by law enforcement agencies, the most common were underage drinking (92%), running away from home (40%), ungovernability (11%), and truancy (10%) (Sickmund, 2003).

The juvenile justice system historically supported differential treatment of male and female status offenders. Adolescent girls, for example, were often detained for incorrigibility or running away from home, while the same behavior in adolescent boys was ignored or tolerated. In recent years, as a result of suits brought on behalf of juveniles, many courts put authorities on notice that this discriminatory approach was unwarranted. In the first decade of the 21st century, the arrest rate for status offenses of runaways was about equal for girls and boys (Puzzanchera, 2009; Snyder, 2008). Changes in juvenile justice policies have led to new approaches to juveniles, however. As noted above, there is less emphasis on keeping official statistics on running away from home and other status offenses, although a few jurisdictions still do. A small but growing trend across the nation is now to initiate girls' courts, mentioned in Chapter 4. These are usually offshoots of juvenile or family courts and are intended to meet specific needs of adolescent girls, particularly those who are engaged in juvenile prostitution (P. L. Brown, 2014).

Youth crime data are collected from a mixture of sources: (1) official records of police arrests, such as the FBI's Uniform Crime Reports (UCR); (2) reports from victims, such as the National Crime Victimization Survey (NCVS); (3) self-reports of delinquent involvement, in which national samples of youth are asked to complete questionnaires about their own behavior, such as in the National Youth Survey (Elliott, Ageton, & Huizinga, 1980) and Monitoring the Future (MTF); (4) juvenile court processing, as reported by the National Center for Juvenile Justice (NCJJ); (5) juvenile corrections, as reported in the monograph *Children in Custody* (*CIC*); and (6) probation and parole statistics, as reported in various governmental publications.

The last three sources of information have the major disadvantage of greatly underestimating the number of actual offenses because so many cases are either undetected or dismissed before reaching the courts. Some of the positive reasons for this include parental involvement, negotiations, and community programs, as a result of which many youthful offenders are diverted before they go to juvenile court. The most complete official nationwide compilation of juvenile offending is the FBI's UCR, which keeps records of crimes reported to police as well as arrests. Consequently, we will touch briefly on the juvenile offending data presented in this document, even though these data have many shortcomings. However, knowledge about the UCR will be useful in discussing adult crime as well.

The Uniform Crime Reports (Crime in the United States)

The FBI's **Uniform Crime Reports (UCR)**, first compiled in 1930, is the most frequently cited source of U.S. crime statistics. The UCR is an annual document containing accounts of crime *known to law enforcement* agencies across the country, as well as *arrests*. The UCR does not include conviction data; it is strictly law enforcement information and does not tell us anything about whether individuals arrested were found guilty. The UCR and the annual Crime in the United States Report are available on the FBI website at www.fbi.gov.

The UCR tabulates information on crime in several ways, including by age, gender, and race of persons arrested, as well as city and region of the country where crimes are reported and arrests occur. The two major divisions of serious crimes are classified as violent crimes and property crimes. The four offenses that qualify as violent are (1) murder and nonnegligent manslaughter, (2) forcible rape (distinguished from statutory rape), (3) robbery, and (4) aggravated assault. The four offenses that qualify as property are (1) burglary, (2) larceny-theft, (3) motor vehicle theft, and (4) arson. Table 7.1 illustrates the distribution of juvenile arrests for these offenses for the year 2015.

The UCR is not the sole method of recording police data on reported crimes and arrests. Since 1989, the FBI has collected data through the National Incident-Based Reporting System (NIBRS). The NIBRS collects data on crime incidents and arrests within 22 categories. For each offense known to law enforcement within these categories, incident, victim, property, offender, and arrestee information are gathered when available. The goal of the NIBRS is to modernize crime information and address many of the shortcomings that had been identified in the UCR.

Nationally, juveniles made up about 7.6% of the persons arrested for violent and property crime in the United States during 2015 (FBI, 2016a). It should be noted that they are arrested in greater numbers than their proportions in the population, but this is partly due to the fact that they often commit their crimes in groups, including crews and gangs. Juveniles were arrested for 10% of the violent crime and 14% of the property crime in 2015. It should also be emphasized that crime and arrest rates move in cycles, often due to the social, economic, and political climates within a society at any given time. Therefore, although rates have decreased in recent years, they may—for a variety of reasons—also suddenly increase in future years. Furthermore, distinctions must be made between specific crimes. For example, in the first half of 2015, violent crime reported to law enforcement decreased overall, but rapes increased (FBI, 2016a).

It is also important to note that a small percentage of offenders are responsible for a large proportion of the total crimes committed (Chaiken, 2000; Coid, 2003). This is true whether we are referring to juveniles or adults. In any given population, the most persistent 5% or 6% of offenders are responsible for at least 50% to 60% of known crimes (Farrington, Ohlin, & Wilson, 1986; Lynam, 1997). On the other hand, many reported serious offenses never result in police contact. Self-report surveys—those in which people report their own offending—suggest that serious, repetitive juvenile offenders escape detection about 86% of the time (D. S. Elliott, Dunford, & Huizinga, 1987). These figures clearly indicate that measures of juvenile offending substantially underestimate the overall juvenile crime rate. The adult crime rate is underestimated as well, because many crimes committed by adults are not reported to police, and unlike juveniles, adults are not often asked to report their own offending. Finally, frequent offenders usually do not specialize in any one particular kind of crime,

Table 7.1 Juvenile Arrests for Violent and Property Crimes, 2015			
Offense Charged	**Total Arrests, All Ages**	**Under Age 18**	**Under Age 15**
Total (violent and property crimes)	1,415,913	185,660	51,800
Violent crimes	**361,241**	**35,886**	**10,053**
Murder	7,519	521	47
Rape	15,934	2,515	991
Robbery	66,138	12,347	2,348
Aggravated assault	271,650	20,503	6,667
Property crimes	**1,054,672**	**149,774**	**41,747**
Burglary	156,419	25,527	7,543
Larceny-theft	838,874	113,114	31,006
Motor vehicle theft	53,315	8,236	2,055
Arson	6,064	1,897	1,143

Source: Federal Bureau of Investigation (2016a).

such as theft, larceny, or drug trafficking. Instead, they tend to be involved in a wide variety of offenses, ranging from minor property crimes to highly violent acts.

THE DEVELOPMENTAL PERSPECTIVE

Over the past three decades, the contemporary study of crime and delinquency has adopted a developmental perspective. If we follow groups of individuals from birth to adulthood, we learn a great deal about how antisocial behavior develops (Hartup, 2005). There is solid research evidence, for example, that serious, persistent delinquency patterns and adult criminality begin in early childhood, and some signs even can be seen during the preschool years. Researchers have discovered discernible differences between young children who ultimately became serious delinquents and those who did not. For example, there are differences in childhood experiences, biological and genetic predispositions, social skills, and expressions of feelings for others. The emerging developmental approach emphasizes the neurological, biological, mental, emotional, and social influences on children and how these in turn may affect the emergence of delinquency and adult criminal behavior.

Perhaps the most fruitful approach is to conceptualize development as following a path or trajectory. Research has strongly supported the hypothesis that people follow different developmental pathways in their offending or non-offending histories. Some youth, for example, engage in defiant and disobedient behavior at very young ages, and this sometimes progresses into more severe forms of violence and criminal behavior during adolescence and young adulthood (Dahlberg & Potter, 2001; Frick, Ray, Thornton, & Kahn, 2014). Other youth display early signs of cruelty to animals, bullying, firesetting, and substance abuse, and these behavioral patterns continue well into adulthood. Many young people display very few signs of antisocial behavior during their childhood but participate in some vandalism, theft, alcohol consumption, and drug experimentation during adolescence. Developmental theory has clearly been the most instrumental in identifying and documenting the various developmental pathways and trajectories related to antisocial behavior.

The Moffitt Developmental Theory

Seminal research conducted by Terrie Moffitt (1993a, 1993b) indicated that delinquency could be best understood if we viewed it as progressing along at least two developmental paths. Because the Moffitt theory is one of the dominant theories in the psychology of crime and delinquency today, it is important that we cover it in some detail. We must emphasize at the outset that, although most of Moffitt's research identifies the *two* paths that will be covered below, more recent research by Moffitt and many other scholars strongly suggests that a two-path theory, though still viable, is not totally sufficient. However, it is a good place to begin.

On one path, we see a child developing a lifelong trajectory of delinquency and crime beginning at a very early age, probably around 3 or even younger. Moffitt (1993a) reports that

> across the life course, these individuals exhibit changing manifestations of antisocial behavior: biting and hitting at age four, shoplifting and truancy at age ten, selling drugs and stealing cars at age sixteen, robbery and rape at age 22, and fraud and child abuse at age 30. (p. 679)

These individuals, whom Moffitt calls **life course–persistent offenders (LCPs)**, continue their antisocial ways across all kinds of conditions and situations. The occasional hitting by a 4-year-old is not cause for concern; if it persists, though, it may be. Moffitt (1993a, 1993b) finds that many LCPs exhibit neurological problems during their childhoods, such as difficult temperaments as infants, attention deficit disorders or hyperactivity in elementary school, and additional learning problems during their later school years. Some of these neurological problems are present before or soon after birth. These same children may develop judgment and problem-solving deficiencies that become apparent when they reach adulthood.

LCPs generally commit a wide assortment of aggressive and violent crimes over their lifetimes. Moreover, LCPs as children miss opportunities to acquire and practice prosocial and interpersonal skills at each stage of development. This is partly because they are rejected and avoided by their childhood peers and partly because their parents and other caretakers become frustrated and may give up on them (Coie, Belding, & Underwood, 1988; Coie, Dodge, & Kupersmith, 1990; Moffitt, 1993a). Furthermore, disadvantaged living conditions, inadequate schools, and violent neighborhoods are factors that are very likely to exacerbate the ongoing and developing antisocial behavioral pattern, although research also indicates that these socioeconomic factors can be mediated by supportive parenting (Odgers et al., 2012). Based on available data, the number of LCPs in the male juvenile offender population is estimated to be somewhere between 5% and 10% (Moffitt, Caspi, Dickson, Silva, & Stanton, 1996). "Less than 10% of males should show extreme antisocial behavior that begins during early childhood and is thereafter sustained at a high level across time and across circumstances, throughout childhood and adolescence" (Moffitt, 1993a, p. 694). Less than 2% of females can be classified as early starters in a persistent career of crime (Coid, 2003).

The great majority of "delinquents" are those individuals who take a second path: They *begin* offending during their adolescent years and *stop* offending somewhere around their 18th birthday. In essence, these adolescent delinquent behaviors arise from peer, brain developmental, and social environmental factors, and the offending tends to be temporary. Moffitt labels these individuals **adolescent-limited offenders (ALs)**. Moffitt (1993a) estimates that a majority of adolescents are involved in some form of antisocial behavior during their teens, but then it stops as their brain matures neurologically and they approach the responsibilities of young adulthood.

The developmental histories of the ALs do not demonstrate the early and persistent antisocial problems that members of the LCP group manifest. Interestingly, the frequency—and, in some cases, the violence level—of the offending *during the teen years* may be as high as that of the LCP youth, however. In effect, the teenage offending patterns of ALs and LCPs may be highly similar during the teenage years (Moffitt et al., 1996):

> The two types cannot be discriminated on most indicators of antisocial and problem behavior in adolescence; boys on the LCP and AL paths are similar on parent-, self-, and official records of offending, peer delinquency, substance abuse, unsafe sex, and dangerous driving. (p. 400)

That is, a professional could not easily identify the group classification (AL or LCP) simply by examining juvenile arrest records, self-reports, or the information provided by parents *during the teen years.*

According to Moffitt, the AL delinquent is most likely to be involved in offenses that symbolize adult privilege and demonstrate autonomy from parental control, such as vandalism (usually school property), theft, drug and alcohol offenses, and other status offenses like running away or truancy. In addition, AL delinquents may engage in crimes that are profitable or rewarding, but they also have the ability to abandon these actions when more socially approved behavioral patterns become more rewarding and acceptable to significant others. For example, the onset of young adulthood brings new opportunities, such as leaving high school for college, obtaining a full-time job, and entering a relationship with a prosocial person. AL delinquents are quick to learn that they have something to lose if they continue offending into adulthood. During childhood, in contrast to LCP children, AL youngsters have learned to get along with others. Research has consistently shown that social rejection by peers in the elementary school grades is a potent risk factor for the development of antisocial behavior problems in adolescence and adulthood (Dodge & Pettit, 2003; Laird, Jordan, Dodge, Pettit, & Bates, 2001). Therefore, by adolescence, AL youth normally have a satisfactory repertoire of academic, social, and interpersonal skills that enable them to "get ahead" and develop lasting relationships. Their developmental histories and personal dispositions allow them the option of exploring new life pathways, an opportunity not usually afforded the LCP youth.

A growing body of research is finding, though, that a simple dual developmental path may not adequately capture all the variations in criminal careers (Donnellan, Ge, & Wenk, 2000). Moreover, researchers are exploring differences in the antisocial trajectories of males and females over the life course (e.g., Odgers et al., 2008). Using data from three studies of crime and delinquency conducted in London; Philadelphia; and Racine, Wisconsin, some researchers (D'Unger, Land, McCall, & Nagin, 1998; Nagin, Farrington, & Moffitt, 1995; Nagin & Land, 1993) have identified four developmental paths that perhaps more comprehensively reflect the reality of offending patterns. The four paths are (1) the adolescent-limited offenders, (2) the life course–persistent offenders (also called "high-level chronic offenders"), (3) the low-level chronic offenders (LLCs), and (4) those with a non-offending pattern (NCs). The ALs followed Moffitt's (1993a, 1993b) hypothesized offending pattern, beginning in their early teens, peaking at around age 16, and then showing a steady decline during their late teens and early adulthood (Nagin et al., 1995). The LLCs, on the other hand, exhibited a rise in offending through early adolescence, reached a plateau by mid-teens, and remained at the same offending level well past age 18. The LCPs demonstrated their usual pattern of beginning antisocial behavior early and remaining at a high level throughout their lifetimes. Interestingly, research by H. R. White, Bates, and Buyske (2001) suggests that it might be meaningful to introduce a fifth category, characterized by youth who engage in relatively little delinquency in early adolescence but for whom delinquency increases from late adolescence into adulthood. (See Focus 7.1 for a case study relating to developmental pathways.)

Other researchers are interested in exploring gender differences in pathways, which is referred to as the **gendered pathways approach**. Moffitt (Moffitt & Caspi, 2001) found evidence that her theory fit both males and females, and Odgers et al. (2008) found evidence of LCP and AL pathways in both genders as well. Odgers et al. also found that LCP males and females were similar on risk factors during childhood, such as those related to social, family, and individual neurodevelopmental variables (e.g., high family conflict, hyperactivity, low family SES, reading difficulties). Studied at age 32, both LCP males and females were engaging in serious violence and experiencing significant problems in emotional and physical health. Interestingly, both women and men on the AL pathway still had problems, but to a lesser extent. They demonstrated little continuity in their antisocial behavior into adulthood. However, AL women still demonstrated significant deficits in economic status at age 32. The researchers concluded that the overall prognosis for LCP offenders was poor, but for AL female offenders, "interventions should focus on factors that may ensnare antisocial adolescent girls into a pathway to poor economic outcomes as women" (Odgers et al., 2008, p. 707). With respect to gender, other researchers (e.g., Fontaine, Carbonneau, Vitaro, Barker, & Tremblay, 2009) have found significantly lower percentages of girls falling squarely into the theory, particularly on the LCP path. In addition, scholars focusing on gendered pathways refer to differences in risk factors between girls and boys that can lead to a later onset of antisocial behavior in girls. In sum, the topic of gendered pathways represents one that should be of continuing interest to scholars.

Adolescent Brain Development

Laurence Steinberg and his associates have formulated a theoretical model that offers an intriguing *neurological* explanation for Moffitt's adolescence-limited offenders. The model is based on an increasingly large collection of empirical studies from developmental psychology and neuroscience. Steinberg (2008, 2010b) hypothesizes that reward seeking and impulsivity

FOCUS 7.1. LENNY'S STORY*

"Lenny"—a Native American boy—was 12 years old when his parents died in an incident that took the lives of over 30 people at a party they were attending. The tragedy left over a dozen children suddenly needing care. Lenny was placed in a foster home some 50 miles away from the town he had known. His younger sister was placed in a different home, in a different community. Lenny's foster parents, though well intentioned, were unfamiliar with his cultural heritage. It should be noted that this occurred several years before the passage of a federal law that may have made it less likely for this type of placement to be made. Lenny had great difficulty adjusting to his new school as well as to his new home and neighborhood environment. He had never been an outstanding student, but his grades now plummeted. He was quiet and sullen in the foster home—where several other foster children were also housed—but not otherwise a behavior problem. He had no friends at school, however, refused to do school-work, and was often called to the principal's office because of disruptive—though never violent—behavior. The small rural school had no social worker, psychologist, or other counselor on staff. The community was homogeneous in race, cultural identity, socioeconomic class, and even religion. On all counts, Lenny felt isolated. He lost all contact with his previous friends and saw his sister only bimonthly when a social worker brought her to visit. Other than the fact that they had all lost or were separated from their parents, he had little in common with the other foster children in the home.

He saw his social worker on a weekly basis, but Lenny—though polite and compliant—was noncommunicative and never expressed his feelings. Social workers left and were replaced by others. The foster parents, the social workers, and the school principal were concerned about his future, but these adults were frustrated as to how to help him.

Lenny had difficulty with one teacher in particular—she was a woman with young children and a husband who held a management position in a nearby factory. Though not wealthy, the family had a nice home, and they were regarded as a model family in the community. The teacher's academic standards were rigid, and she had little sympathy for Lenny's plight.

Lenny was almost 14—he had been in the foster home for about 2 years—when he burglarized the teacher's home, taking inexpensive jewelry and almost $200 in cash. Although foster parents were willing to give Lenny another chance, the teacher advocated that he be punished. Shortly thereafter, he appeared before a judge, was removed from his foster home, and was sent to a juvenile rehabilitation center, where he remained until his 18th birthday. A few years after his release, he committed an armed robbery of a service station in another state, which resulted in a 5-year prison term. After his release, he moved back to his home state and held a series of laborer jobs.

The above occurred many years ago, before many resources for juveniles—including legal assistance—were available. (For many juveniles today, they are still not available.) Lenny is now in his 50s. In the very recent past, Lenny was arrested and charged with disorderly conduct and aggravated assault—he had spent a day drinking in a bar and had returned home and battered the woman with whom he was living.

Based on a true case, with some identifying details changed.

Questions for Discussion

1. What further information is needed to decide whether Lenny qualifies as a LCP offender? What other developmental pathways are a possibility?
2. If one considers only the above information, what could have made a significant positive difference in Lenny's life (other than his parents not dying)?
3. If the above scenario occurred today, at what point or points would a forensic psychologist be most likely to be called in, and in what capacity?

develop along different timetables and have different neurological influences during adolescent and young adult development. "The inconvenient truth in adolescence brain science is that different structures, regions, circuits, systems, and processes mature along different timetables" (Steinberg, 2016, p. 345). Moreover, the differences in the timetables help account for the well-known high levels of risk taking during adolescence. Steinberg's model is known as the **developmental dual systems model**.

Steinberg (2016) and his colleagues have recently completed a study of approximately 5,500 young persons (ages 10 to 30) from 11 different countries characterized by considerable cultural diversity. The results underscore the validity of the dual system model in explaining risk taking and offending behavior across cultures. The study found compelling evidence that sensation-seeking peaked at late adolescence, whereas self-regulation increases in a steady linear pattern through adolescence and young adulthood.

As a general rule, and as most parents and caretakers have learned, adolescent behavior is characterized by impulsiveness, sensation seeking, a lack of future orientation, and strong susceptibility to peer pressure and influence. Risk taking during this period includes reckless driving, binge drinking, smoking cigarettes, and engaging in spontaneous unprotected sex. (See Photo 7.1.) Teenagers "know" they should not drag race at 95 miles an hour, they "know" the harm in smoking tobacco, they "know" the dangers of sexually transmitted diseases, but nevertheless many, both adolescent males and adolescent females, still engage in risky behaviors. But the adolescent risk-taking behavior plays a primary role in greater mortality as a result of such behaviors as substance abuse, violent and nonviolent criminal behavior, and unprotected sex (Luna & Wright, 2016).

Impulsivity and rapid mood swings, so characteristic of many teens, are likely associated with immature self-control mechanisms, which take time to develop during the adolescent and young adult years. Sensation seeking "refers to the tendency to seek out novel, varied, and highly stimulating experiences, and the willingness to take risks in order to attain them" (Steinberg et al., 2008, p. 1765). Developmental psychologists have long observed that teens as a group lack a "future orientation." Compared with adults, they are more likely to focus on the here and now and less likely to think about the long-term consequences of their decisions or actions. When they do think about the long-term consequences, they are inclined to give less weight to future effects than to immediate risks and benefits (Scott & Steinberg, 2008). Moreover, as highlighted by Moffitt's theory, risk taking during the teen years may also involve committing a variety of criminal acts. Self-report studies have revealed that nearly 90% of adolescent boys admit to committing offenses for which they could be incarcerated (Scott & Steinberg, 2008).

Considerable research evidence supports the conventional wisdom that adolescents are more oriented toward peers and more responsive to peer influence than to the influence of adults (Scott & Steinberg, 2008). The increased importance of peers leads teens to modify their behavior in order to fit in and receive peer approval. Furthermore, numerous studies have consistently shown that susceptibility to peer influence plays a significant role in instigating adolescents to engage in antisocial behavior (K. Erickson, Crosnoe, & Dornbusch, 2000; Scott, Reppucci, & Woolard, 1995). Risky behaviors and most crimes committed by adolescents are usually committed in groups and are seldom premeditated (K. C. Monahan, Steinberg, & Cauffman, 2009; Warr, 2002; Zimring, 1998). In fact, both Moffitt (1993a) and Steinberg (2014a) contend that adolescents' desire to impress peers is the core reason for most delinquency. The greater prevalence of group risk-taking behaviors and criminal offending is probably due to the fact that adolescents spend more time with their peer groups than adults do (Steinberg, 2008).

▶ **Photo 7.1** Teenagers at a house party.
Source: © iStockphoto.com/sturti.

It should be noted that very similar models have been developed by Beatriz Luna and Catherine Wright (2016), known as the driven dual system model, and by B. J. Casey and associates (Casey & Caudle, 2013; Casey, Getz, & Galvan, 2008), called the maturational imbalance model. Both models are dual models that view the interaction between the socio-emotional system and the cognitive control system as being slightly different. Similar to Steinberg's model, the development of these two models was greatly helped by neuroimaging technologies.

Magnetic Resonance Imaging (MRI)

The very way the human brain develops may explain much of the behavior of adolescent youth. Especially since the 1990s, researchers have had a strong and sustained interest in patterns of brain development during adolescence and young adulthood (Steinberg, 2008).

In recent years, high-resolution imaging technologies, such as magnetic resonance imaging (MRI), functional MRI (fMRI), and diffusion tensor imaging (DTI), have allowed neuroscientists and neuropsychologists to map significant differences in brain maturation in children, adolescents, and adults (Luna & Wright, 2016). MRI evidence also is being used increasingly in a variety of court cases (Miller & Lindbergh, 2017). These technologies require no injections or medications, are noninvasive, painless, and safe, and are well suited for the study of brain development and changes across all age groups.

Neuroimaging studies provide cogent evidence that the adolescent brain undergoes substantial structural, neurochemical, and functional changes during adolescence (Luna & Wright, 2016). These changes affect risk taking and delinquent behavior. The well-cited observation that criminal offending increases "dramatically from age ten until eighteen, when they reach their peak, and then they decline precipitously between ages eighteen and twenty-five . . ." (Steinberg, 2014a, p. 88) underscores the importance of understanding these adolescent brain changes as valuable explanations for their behavior.

The Social Brain and Peer Influence

The growing number of neuroimaging studies are also discovering that brain development and function significantly affect how adolescents view and interpret their social world. This field of study is called **social cognition**, which refers to how individuals process, store, and apply information about other people and their social interactions. Social cognition allows us to make inferences about another person's intentions, feelings, and thoughts (Adolphs, 2009). In addition, social cognitions, which are developed by the social brain, appear to be strongly influenced by one's culture and ethnic background. For example, adolescents pay close attention to facial expression in others, such as the direction of gaze and emotional expressions. During adolescence, face processing of the social-cognition system becomes more specialized in line with the norms of the culture with which the person is most familiar. For instance, the "eye-roll" is likely to communicate different things within various cultures.

The social brain rapidly develops throughout adolescence, before stabilizing in early to mid-20s (Kilford, Garrett, & Blakemore, 2016). As Luna and Wright (2016) emphasize, "Adolescence is a time of increased socialization when bonding with peers and potential romantic partners takes priority over established family relationships" (p. 106). Due to ongoing changes in social brain development, adolescence is a period of heightened sensitivity to sociocultural signals in the social environment (Blakemore & Mills, 2014). Several neuroimaging studies have revealed significant changes in adolescent social brain networks associated with social cognitions of face processing, peer evaluation, and peer influence (Blakemore & Mills, 2014). One thing is clear: Peer evaluations of adolescents affect their feelings of social or personal worth, especially for adolescents between the ages of 13 and 17 years. In their desire to be accepted by their peers and avoid rejection, adolescents are often driven to engage in risky, dangerous, and even criminal behavior. "Studies of peer rejection in adolescence . . . repeatedly find that peer rejection is associated with worsened mood, increased distress and increased anxiety compared to child and adult groups . . ." (Kilford et al., 2016, p. 113).

Although peer influences are largely associated with negative outcomes, they also can have a positive influence on behavior (Kilford et al., 2016). Peers can help one another get through rough times and encourage others to do the right thing. Parents or guardians also provide a protective effect on risk taking in adolescence, especially if they keep appropriate tabs on their behavior and with whom they associate. Gang affiliations and association with peers who encourage and engage in risky, criminal behaviors are examples where parents and other adults can play protective roles.

Neuroscience and Sex Differences in Adolescence

Diffusion tensor imaging (DTI) has been increasingly applied to uncover sex differences in the brain maturation level of adolescents (Gur & Gur, 2016). Preliminary results indicate that adolescent males tend to outperform adolescent females on motor and spatial cognitive tasks. Adolescent females do better on emotion identification and nonverbal reasoning. Neuroimaging studies have also found that adolescent males tend to rely on cognitive processing within a single hemisphere of the brain while completing various tasks, whereas female adolescents rely on using both hemispheres of the brain. Although these neuroimaging studies of sex differences are new, they are apt to shed some light on why sex differences are so prominent in some neurodevelopmental disorders, such as attention-deficit/hyperactivity disorders and conduct disorders.

As Luna and Wright (2016) point out, developmental neuroscience and neuroimaging findings have played crucial roles in informing the juvenile justice system, especially as it relates to sentencing involving the death penalty and life without parole. Neuroscience findings are also increasingly making their way to the U.S. Supreme Court, typically presented to the Justices in amicus curiae briefs. For example, in *Graham v. Florida* (2010), the Court cited Steinberg's research in ruling that a sentence of life without parole was cruel and unusual punishment for individuals who committed their crimes during adolescence, at least when the crime was not murder. Later, in cases that did involve murder (*Miller v. Alabama* and *Jackson v. Hobbs*, 2012), the Court again cited Steinberg's research and ruled that a mandatory life without parole sentence violated the due process rights of the juvenile, because it did not allow the sentencing judge to take into consideration the possibility that the juvenile had rehabilitative potential. The Court had already determined that the death penalty is cruel and unusual punishment for anyone who was 17 or under when they had committed their crime (*Roper v. Simmons*, 2005). In all of these juvenile cases, research on cognitive abilities of adolescents helped inform the decisions of the majority of the Supreme Court Justices.

Interestingly, extremely lengthy sentences may have the same effect as life without parole sentences. In a case decided after *Miller v. Alabama*, the California Supreme Court ruled that a 110-year sentence given to a juvenile who was 16 years old at the time of his crimes (three attempted murders) was a constitutional violation (*People v. Caballero*, 2012). Under that sentence, the prisoner would not have been eligible for parole for 100 years.

In sum, "Within the past decade . . . juvenile law has increasingly looked to scientific findings regarding the differences between adolescents' and adults' brains to make informed, scientifically based legal decisions in cases involving delinquents" (Luna & Wright, 2016, p. 92). Forensic psychologists must be extensively familiar with this research and be ready to inform the court and its participants about the developmental neuroscientific findings concerning the different maturational trajectories of the adolescent brain. Furthermore, as pointed out by researchers (e.g., S. L. Anderson, 2016; Luna & Wright, 2016) adolescence is also the most vulnerable period for the emergence of a variety of psychological disorders, such as anxiety disorders, mood disorders, eating disorders, personality disorders, drug abuse, and psychosis. In fact, the average age of onset for serious psychological disorders is age 10 (Steinberg, 2014a).

Steinberg (2008) asks two fundamental questions about the high risk-taking propensity of teens: Why does risk-taking behavior increase between childhood and adolescence? And, why does risk taking decline between adolescence and adulthood? He theorizes that risk taking increases between childhood and adolescence because of developmental changes in the regions of the brain he calls the *socio-emotional system*. The specific regions of the brain believed to be involved include a complex neurological network consisting of the amygdala, nucleus accumbens, orbitofrontal cortex, medial prefrontal cortex, and superior temporal sulcus. These neurological changes lead to significant increases in reward-seeking and stimulation-seeking activity during adolescence.

On the other hand, risk-taking behavior *declines* between adolescence and adulthood because of developmental changes in the regions of the brain he labels the *cognitive control system*, which is primarily located in the front areas of the brain, called the frontal lobe. These growth changes, Steinberg contends, improve the person's capacity for self-regulation and regulate the socio-emotional system. Cognitive control refers to "the ability to persist in goal-directed behavior in the face of competing cognitive and behavioral demands and is a crucial component of self-regulation" (Zeier, Baskin-Sommers, Racer, & Newman, 2012, p. 284). The increase in reward-seeking needs occurs early and is relatively abrupt, whereas the increase in self-regulatory competence occurs gradually and is not usually complete until an individual has reached his or her mid-20s (see Figure 7.1). These two systems constitute the basic components for Steinberg's dual systems model. Steinberg argues that risk taking and criminal behavior during adolescence can be best understood and explained by the interaction between the socio-emotional and cognitive control systems.

From Steinberg's (2008) perspective, the observed high and abrupt risk-taking behavioral patterns of adolescence are primarily due to increases in sensation seeking that are linked to increases in neurotransmitter activity within the socio-emotional system areas of the brain. The neurotransmitter dopamine and an increase in dopamine receptors are largely responsible for these changes. On the other hand, the emergence of the cognitive control system lags behind the socio-emotional system. The gradual development of cognitive control or self-regulation systems during adolescence and early adulthood is linked to neurological and network maturation in the frontal lobe, especially the prefrontal regions. Research confirms the hypothesis that adolescents tend to recruit the cognitive control network less selectively and efficiently than do adults (Steinberg, 2008, 2016).

Steinberg believes resistance to peer influence is achieved by cognitive control of the impulsive reward-seeking behavior (the socio-emotional system). Steinberg and Monahan (2007) found that gains in self-reported resistance to peer influence continue to age 18 and

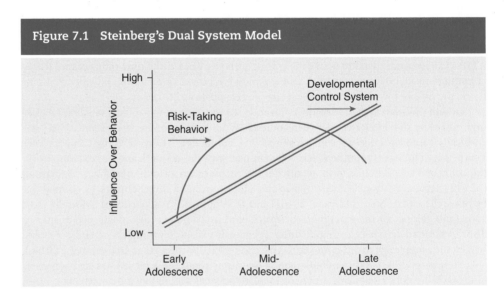

Figure 7.1 Steinberg's Dual System Model

beyond. However, the impact of peers on risky behavior continues to be very evident even among college undergraduates averaging 20 years of age (M. Gardner & Steinberg, 2005). (During political campaigns, it is sometimes remarked that—with the exception of a serious violent offense—no candidate for office should be judged on anything that occurred when he or she was in high school or college.) As the cognitive control system matures, however, conditions of heightened arousal in the socio-emotional system that in earlier years led to risk taking are increasingly controlled. As mentioned previously, this maturity is largely completed by the mid-20s in most individuals. "Some things just take time to develop, and mature judgment is probably one of them" (Steinberg, 2008, p. 100).

Steinberg emphasizes that not all teens exhibit dangerous, harmful, or reckless behaviors. As we have noted earlier in the chapter, individuals follow different developmental trajectories and reach different levels of maturity at different ages (Steinberg, Graham, et al., 2009). In addition, a wide assortment of factors influence sensation-seeking and risky behavior, including opportunities to engage in antisocial risk taking, parental and adult supervision levels, individual temperamental differences, and availability of alcohol and drugs. These same factors also play an important role in the early formation of persistent or life-course antisocial behavior.

Interestingly, there is growing scientific evidence that intellectual maturity is reached several years before psychosocial maturity (Steinberg, Cauffman, et al., 2009). Adolescents age 16 or older have basically the same logical reasoning abilities and verbal skills as adults. In addition, "adolescents are no worse than adults at perceiving risk or estimating their vulnerability to it" (Steinberg, 2008, p. 80). In other words, as mentioned above, they "know" that drag racing at high speeds on a country road is dangerous. However, even though teens can articulate the risks involved in some of their behavior, the socio-emotional system takes over in certain situations, especially in the presence of peers. These situations are most likely to occur when adolescents are emotionally aroused, absent adult supervision, and facing choices with apparent immediate rewards and few obvious or immediate costs—the very conditions that are likely to undermine adolescents' decision-making competence (Steinberg, 2007). "The adolescent brain is bad at some things (impulse control) but very good at others (learning) . . ." (Steinberg, 2016, p. 345).

In sum, Steinberg's dual systems theory provides an excellent conceptual platform for understanding the adolescent-limited offenders and why teenagers often engage in risky, dangerous behavior, even when they know better. Fortunately, risky behavior in most cases fades as the individual gets older. For the serious, persistent offender, however, violent antisocial behavior persists well into adulthood. Studies consistently underscore the fact that specific early behavior problems frequently precede the development of serious antisocial behavior. In the next sections, specific developmental factors that are believed to be most closely linked to these antisocial patterns well into adulthood will be presented.

DEVELOPMENTAL FACTORS IN THE FORMATION OF PERSISTENT CRIMINAL BEHAVIOR

Disruptive behavior is a term that has been applied to a variety of actions that create problems for some children and their caretakers. "[D]isruptive behavior problems in childhood typically include hyperactivity, impulsivity, inattention, oppositional behaviors, defiance, aggression, and disregarding the rights of others" (Waschbusch, 2002, p. 118). According to Waschbusch, these disruptive behavior problems affect 5% to 10% of children and adolescents and account for more than 50% of referrals to mental health clinics. When left untreated, disruptive children are likely to experience peer rejection, have problems in school, demonstrate difficulties getting along with others, and exhibit persistent delinquent behaviors. In many instances, the persistent delinquency behaviors develop into long-term chronic, adult, violent, and antisocial behavioral patterns.

Disruptive behaviors are included in at least two of the four prominent features of Moffitt's LCPs or serious, persistent offenders that are continually reported in the research literature. The four are (1) hyperactive-impulsive attention problems, (2) conduct problems, (3) deficient cognitive ability, and (4) poor interpersonal or social skills (often resulting in peer rejection). In order to understand more fully the formation of life-course antisocial behavior, we cover each in some detail.

Attention-Deficit/Hyperactivity Disorder (ADHD) and Delinquency

The term *attention-deficit/hyperactivity disorder* (**ADHD**) encompasses a wide variety of terms frequently used in medical and educational contexts, such as minimal brain dysfunction (MBD), attention deficit disorder (ADD), and hyperactive-impulsive attention (ADHD-HI) problems or simply "hyperactivity." We will use the term most commonly used today, ADHD. All the terms, however, refer basically to three central behaviors: (1) excessive motor activity (cannot sit still, fidgets, runs about, is talkative and noisy), (2) impulsivity (acts before thinking, shifts quickly from one activity to another, interrupts others, does not consider consequences of behavior), and (3) inattention (does not seem to listen, is easily distracted, loses things necessary for tasks or activities). Together, the three behaviors result in the child's inability to regulate and organize his or her behavior in different situations. ADHD is considered a neurodevelopmental disorder which begins early in life and is associated with "significant impairment across multiple areas of functioning, including academic, psychological, social, and occupational functioning" (Weyandt, Oster, Gudmundsdottir, DuPaul, & Anastopoulos, 2017, p. 160).

Another symptom cluster that should not be confused with ADHD is **oppositional defiant disorder (ODD)**, which has often been linked to crime. ODD symptoms include arguing with adults, refusing adults' requests, deliberately trying to annoy others, blaming others for mistakes, and being spiteful or vindictive (Kosson, Cyterski, Steuerwald, Neumann, & Walker-Matthews, 2002). Many mental health practitioners are skeptical that ODD is a legitimate disorder; nevertheless, its prevalence is still considered low, at an estimated 3% in boys and 1.4% in girls (von Polier, Vloet, & Herpertz-Dahlmann, 2012). It should be mentioned that some children diagnosed with ADHD also show behavioral patterns of ODD (Biederman, 2005).

Although ADHD is the leading psychological diagnosis for children living in the United States (Flory, Milich, Lynam, Leukefeld, & Clayton, 2003; Nigg, John, et al., 2002), estimates of the incidence of ADHD in school-age children in most cultures is about 5% (American Psychiatric Association [APA], 2013). It is estimated to range between 5% and 10% in children and adolescents in all parts of the world (Ramsay, 2017; Taylor & Sonuga-Barke, 2008; von Polier et al., 2012). ADHD is also estimated to range from 3% to 9% in the adult population (Ramsay, 2017; Sevecke, Kosson, & Krischer, 2009). To date, however, no systematic nationwide research has been conducted to identify the extent, seriousness, or nature of ADHD. However, the research has consistently revealed that boys outnumber girls, with ratios ranging from 2:1 to 9:1 (R. W. Root & Resnick, 2003). According to R. W. Root and Resnick, black children appear to receive the diagnosis more often than other racial or ethnic minority children, although the reasons for this finding are unclear. In addition, ADHD symptoms manifest themselves early in development, usually during the preschool years (Deault, 2010). It is important to realize that all children (and adults) have certain levels of inattention, overactivity, and impulsivity in certain situations, but for the diagnostic label of ADHD to be assigned, the symptoms must be unusually persistent and pronounced (R. W. Root & Resnick, 2003). In his description of ADHD, Ramsay (2017) writes the "syndrome represents a subgroup of individuals whose self-regulation deficits fall at the extreme end of a range of functioning" (p. 63). Although most studies have been carried out in the United States and Europe, research has also supported the validity of ADHD in developing countries (Rohde et al., 2001) and across different cultures (Barkley, 1998; Polanczyk, Lima, Horta, Biederman, & Rohde, 2007).

A significant percentage of children with diagnosed ADHD show the same persistent symptoms into adulthood (Lara et al., 2009; Nigg, Butler, Huang-Pollock, & Henderson, 2002; Weyandt et al., 2017). In a comprehensive study of 10 countries, Lara et al. report that roughly 50% of childhood cases of ADHD continue to meet the full criteria for the disorder as adults. Other studies find that an estimated 30% to 65% of children with ADHD continue to exhibit clinically significant symptoms as adults (Cahill et al., 2012). In other words, many people do not "outgrow" ADHD. The observation that ADHD is prevalent among adults is a recent conclusion, however. In the past, ADHD was largely considered a childhood disorder.

Educators find that ADHD children have difficulty staying on task, remaining cognitively organized, sustaining academic achievement in the school setting, and maintaining control over their behavior. Associated features may include low frustration tolerance, irritability, and rapid mood changes (American Psychiatric Association, 2013). ADHD is puzzling, and its causes are largely unknown. Some scientists contend that ADHD children are born with a biological predisposition toward inattention and excessive movement; others maintain that some children are exposed to environmental factors that damage the nervous system. Loeber (1990) reveals how exposure to toxic substances during the preschool years can interfere with a child's neurological development, often resulting in symptoms of ADHD. For example, children exposed to even low levels of lead toxicity (e.g., from paint, airborne contaminants, or drinking water) are more hyperactive and impulsive and are easily distracted and frustrated. They also show notable problems in following simple instructions. Some researchers (e.g., Nigg & Huang-Pollock, 2003; Séguin & Zelazo, 2005) observe that ADHD children do not possess effective strategies and cognitive organization with which to deal with the daily demands of the traditional school setting. These children often have particular difficulty in understanding and using abstract concepts. ADHD children also seem to lack cognitive organizational skills for dealing with new knowledge and information. Nonetheless, it is believed that numerous gifted, brilliant individuals were or could have been diagnosed with ADHD when they were children, so it is a mistake to focus on the problematic aspects of this diagnosis. In addition, it is believed that numerous children are misdiagnosed. This, accompanied by concerns about drugs prescribed for children with ADHD, has led to spirited and sometimes vituperative arguments in the professional literature. Most forensic psychologists confronting this issue in the process of conducting various assessments are well aware of these concerns.

Some research suggests that one of the primary causal factors of ADHD appears to be inhibitory problems due to neuropsychological deficits (Barkley, 1997, 1998; Nigg, Butler, et al., 2002). The inhibitory problems may be primarily due to motor (behavioral) control (Nigg, 2000). Overall, however, the extant research underscores the possibility that the causes of ADHD are probably multiple and extremely difficult to tease out of the many ongoing interactions occurring between the nervous system and the environment.

Although many behaviors have been identified as accompanying ADHD, the major theme is that ADHD children are perceived as annoying and aversive to those around them, and therein may lie the problematic aspects. ADHD children often continually seek and prolong interpersonal contacts and eventually irritate and frustrate those people with whom they interact. Because of these annoying and socially inappropriate behaviors, they are often rejected by peers, especially if they are perceived as aggressive (Henker & Whalen, 1989). This pattern of peer rejection appears to continue throughout the developmental years (Dodge & Pettit, 2003; J. B. Reid, 1993). In many ways, then, ADHD appears to be more a disorder of interpersonal relationships than simply a disorder of hyperactivity. Some researchers find that ADHD children generally lack friendship and intimacy (Henker & Whalen, 1989). Moffitt (1990) reports that children between the ages of 5 and 7 who demonstrate the characteristics of both ADHD and antisocial behavior not only have special difficulty with social relationships, but also have a high probability of demonstrating these problems into adolescence and beyond.

Experts argue that the most common problem associated with ADHD is delinquency and substance abuse (Beauchaine, Katkin, Strassberg, & Snarr, 2001). The data strongly suggest that youth with symptoms of both ADHD and delinquent behavior are at very high risk for developing lengthy and serious criminal careers (Mannuzza, Klein, Bessler, Malloy, & LaPadula, 1998; Moffitt, 1990; Odgers et al., 2008; Pfiffner et al., 1999). One study of antisocial youth in a secure facility found that nearly half of the adolescents demonstrated symptoms of ADHD (S. Young et al., 2010). Other studies indicate that prevalence estimates for adjudicated adolescents range from 14% to 19% and from 20% to 72% for incarcerated adolescents (Vermeiren, 2003). David Farrington (1991), in his well-regarded research, also found that violent offenders often have a history of hyperactivity, impulsivity, and attention deficit problems. A study by Cahill and associates (2012) revealed that the prevalence rate of ADHD in adult prison inmates is substantially higher than reported in the general population. Surprisingly, the study found that ADHD may be higher in female inmates than in male inmates.

The relationship between ADHD and delinquency and adult crime is an area demanding much more research by forensic psychologists interested in studying crime and delinquency. It must be stressed, however, that the child with ADHD should not be labeled as the delinquent or the criminal of tomorrow. Many children and adolescents with ADHD do not become serious delinquents or adult offenders. However, they often do have much greater genetic, neurocognitive, and psychosocial burdens than do non-ADHD children and adolescents (von Polier et al., 2012). As noted above, they tend to have more learning difficulties and problems in school (especially reading problems), more problems interacting with peers, and more neurological problems.

The most common method of treatment for ADHD is medication (especially methylphenidate, more commonly known as Ritalin, and the central nervous system stimulant Adderall and its derivatives). However, although medication apparently helps many children, many others exhibit numerous side effects, some of them severe. Counseling and psychotherapy are frequently used, especially cognitive-behavior therapy, often in conjunction with medication, but with limited success with this puzzling phenomenon, particularly over the long term. As many practitioners realize, ADHD children generally demonstrate multiple problems that can be best managed through treatment strategies that take into account all the factors impinging on the child at any given time. (See R. W. Root & Resnick, 2003, for an excellent review.) These treatment approaches are called "multisystemic" and will be dealt with more fully in Chapter 13.

Conduct Disorder (CD)

ADHD frequently co-occurs with a diagnostic category called "conduct disorder" (Coid, 2003; Connor, Steeber, & McBurnett, 2010; Offord, Boyle, & Racine, 1991; J. B. Reid, 1993). Waschbusch (2002) reports, for instance, that about 50% of disruptive children exhibit the basic symptoms of both ADHD and a conduct disorder (CD). If disruptive children have the symptoms of one, about half of them also have symptoms of the other. Not only does the presence of CD increase the symptoms of ADHD, but the combination of the two is an especially powerful predictor of a lifelong course of violence, persistent criminal behavior, and drug abuse (Erskine et al., 2016; Flory et al., 2003; Molina, Bukstein, & Lynch, 2002; Pfiffner et al., 1999). According to Erskine et al. (2016), CD was associated with increased signs of depression, anxiety, substance abuse problems, and decreased educational achievement. As mentioned previously, conduct disorder consists of a cluster of maladaptive behaviors characterized by a variety of antisocial behaviors. Examples of this misbehavior include stealing, firesetting, running away from home, skipping school, destroying property, fighting, telling lies on a frequent basis, and being cruel to animals and people. CD is generally considered to be a serious childhood and adolescent disorder because it appears to be a precursor to chronic criminal behavior during adulthood (Lahey et al., 1995). In fact, "the relationship between conduct disorder and violence is well documented" (Baskin-Sommers et al., 2016, p. 352). According to the *DSM-5* (American Psychiatric Association, 2013), the central feature of conduct disorder is the *repetitive* and *persistent* pattern of behavior that violates the basic rights of others.

The *DSM-5* recognizes two subtypes of conduct disorder: childhood onset and adolescent onset. Childhood-onset CD occurs when the pattern begins before the age of 10. This pattern often worsens as the child gets older and is more likely to lead to serious and persistent criminal behavior into adulthood (Frick et al., 2003). According to Frick and colleagues, "In addition, children in the childhood-onset group are characterized by more aggression, more cognitive and neuropsychological disturbances, greater impulsivity, greater social alienation, and more dysfunctional backgrounds than are children in the adolescent-onset group" (p. 246).

On the other hand, adolescent-onset CD is characterized by the absence of any maladaptive behavior before the age of 10. After age 10, those with adolescent-onset CDs tend to exhibit fewer problems in interpersonal and social skills but do reject traditional rules and formal procedures. They often associate with deviant peers in forbidden activities to show their independence and self-perceived maturity (Frick et al., 2003). In many respects, the two types of CD follow the developmental paths of Moffitt's (1993a, 1993b) LCPs (childhood onset) and ALs (adolescent onset).

Behavioral indicators of childhood-onset CDs can be observed in children's interactions with parents or caretakers well before school entry (J. B. Reid, 1993). For example, children who are aggressive, difficult to manage, and noncompliant in the home at age 3 often continue to have similar problems when entering school. Furthermore, as we noted, these behaviors show remarkable continuity through adolescence and into adulthood. CD children frequently have significant problems with school assignments, a behavioral pattern that often results in their being mislabeled with a "learning disability." It is important to note that students with genuine learning disabilities are not necessarily conduct disordered. In other words, the two designations may overlap, but each is also a distinct categorization. Similar to ADHD children, aggressive CDs are at high risk for strong rejection by their peers. This rejection generally lasts throughout the school years and is very difficult to change (J. B. Reid, 1993). As described above, children who are consistently socially rejected by peers miss critical opportunities to develop normal interpersonal and social skills. Lacking effective interpersonal skills, these youth *may* meet their needs through more aggressive means, including threats and intimidation.

Prevalence estimates of CD ranges from 2% to more than 10%, with a median of 4% (American Psychiatric Association, 2013). Overall, the sex ratio for CD appears to be 2.5 males to each female (Moffitt et al., 2008). According to the *DSM-5*, boys with CD tend to display fighting, stealing, vandalism, and school discipline problems, whereas girls are more likely to participate in lying, truancy, running away, substance abuse, and prostitution. Some feel that the current diagnostic category in the *DSM-5* fails to accurately detect CD among girls. (See Moffitt et al., 2008 for a comprehensive review.) In addition, severe conduct-problem children often show deficits in verbal abilities and problems in executive control of behavior (Frick & Viding, 2009). Although the *DSM-5* stipulates that a youth with CD exhibits a lack of remorse or guilt and shows no empathy toward others, a majority of studies have discovered that children with severe CD do not show problems in empathy and guilt (Frick et al., 2014). "In fact, they often show high rates of anxiety, and they appear to be highly distressed by the effects of their behavior on others" (Frick et al., 2014, p. 27).

An interesting study by Bardone, Moffitt, and Caspi (1996) found that CD patterns in girls are a strong predictor of a lifetime of problems, including poor interpersonal relations with partners/spouses and peers, criminal activity, early pregnancy without supportive partners, and frequent job loss and firings. Similar to CD boys, CD girls—without intervention—often lead a life full of interpersonal conflict. One observation that continually emerges in studies of CD is that these youths are frequently raised in families that are hostile to them, and their parents engage in inconsistent parenting practices (Frick et al., 2014).

We must remind ourselves that there are multiple factors associated with delinquency, including delinquency characterized by serious and chronic offending. This part of the chapter has focused on various deficiencies within the individual—hyperactivity, conduct disorder, and impulsivity, to name a few. Children live within a social system, however. The behavior and reactions of adults such as parents, caretakers, and teachers significantly affect the child's behavior. In some cases, the "deficiencies" described here are due to abuse, maltreatment, neglect, or simply ignorance about effective child-rearing techniques. In these, as well as other cases, intervention by competent and caring adults can avert a lifetime of continual offending. Moreover, researchers also bring attention to crucial macro-level variables, such as the neighborhood or community in which one is raised or the health care one has received (Chauhan, 2015).

Cognitive Ability and Crime

In addition to the emphasis on developmental pathways, ADHD, and conduct disorder, recent research on crime and delinquency has identified the importance of cognition and mental processes in the development of antisocial behavior and violence. These include language acquisition, self-regulation, and executive functions. (We also covered self-regulation to some extent in the sections on Steinberg's dual systems model and neurodevelopment.) Developmental research also has been instrumental in identifying the enormous influence of multiple contexts (e.g., school, peers, and families) in the learning and continuation of delinquency and criminal behavior. This emphasis has highlighted the importance of considering the many complex interactions among neurodevelopment and the environment, family members, peers and friends, and cultural and ethnic background in all discussions of antisocial behavior.

Intelligence

A number of developmental theories posit a role for intelligence in the development of delinquency. For example, Moffitt (1993a) hypothesizes that the more serious, persistent offenders should demonstrate lower intelligence or cognitive ability than non-offenders. She writes, "The verbal deficits of antisocial children are pervasive, affecting receptive listening and reading, problem solving, expressive speech and writing, and memory" (p. 680). It is clear that a person's intellectual performance will vary on different occasions, in different domains—as judged by different criteria—and across the life span. In the past few decades, there has been a concentrated effort to develop the idea of multiple intelligences, rather than just one single type of intelligence, and to have an appreciation of abilities that previously either were ignored or were considered not very important in understanding human behavior. Every student reading this book knows that some people are "book smart but not street smart." Some people find it difficult to express themselves orally or in writing but are able to create works of art or build a sturdy house. Who would argue that the street-smart person or the creator of art or builder of houses is not intelligent?

Although intelligence is a controversial topic—particularly due to skepticism about the validity of "IQ" testing—it has become apparent today that intelligence exists in multiple forms and relates to a wide assortment of abilities. Howard Gardner (2000), for example, describes nine different types of intelligences or cognitive styles (see Table 7.2). There are probably more types, such as wisdom, spirituality, synthesizing ability, intuition, metaphoric capacities, humor, and good judgment (H. Gardner, 1983, 1998, 2000), many of which have been used to describe resilient persons. Gardner considered the last two of the primary nine—insight into oneself and the understanding of others—features of emotional intelligence. **Emotional intelligence** is the ability to know how people and oneself are feeling and the capacity to use that information to guide thoughts and actions, such as we find in the social brain. A deficiency in this form of intelligence may play a prominent role in human violence.

Standard intelligence tests (IQ tests) measure only the first three forms of the Gardner multiple intelligences model: linguistic, visual-spatial, and logical-mathematical. Even if we presume that standard tests are valid (and caution is urged here), the delinquent individuals who scored low on the standard tests may well be higher in other types of intelligence. Likewise,

Table 7.2 Gardner's Different Intelligences Model

Intelligence Type	Definition
(1) Linguistic	Possessing a good vocabulary and reading comprehension skills
(2) Visual-spatial	Ability to visualize objects, find one's orientation in space, and navigate from one location to another
(3) Logical-mathematical	Ability to think logically, reason deductively, detect patterns, and carry out mathematical operations
(4) Interpersonal	Ability to understand and interact with others effectively
(5) Intrapersonal	Ability to understand and know oneself
(6) Existential	Tendency to ponder the meaning of life, death, and the nature of reality
(7) Kinesthetic	Ability to dance well, handle objects skillfully, and be a competent athlete
(8) Musical	Ability to hear, recognize, and manipulate patterns in music
(9) Naturalistic	Ability to see patterns in nature and discriminate among living things (plants and animals)

Source: Adapted from Gardner (1983, 1998, 2000).

people who score high on standard tests may be quite deficient at understanding and interacting with others.

Individuals who chronically engage in violence—regardless of how they score on traditional IQ tests— also may lack significant insight into their own behavior and possess little sensitivity toward others. They tend to misread emotional cues from others and become confused and angry in ambiguous social situations. For example, highly aggressive children often have a **hostile attribution bias**. That is, they are more likely than less aggressive children to interpret ambiguous actions of others as hostile and threatening. Research consistently indicates that highly aggressive and violent adolescents "typically define social problems in hostile ways, adopt hostile goals, seek few additional facts, generate few alternative solutions, anticipate few consequences for aggression, and give higher priority to their aggressive solutions" (Eron & Slaby, 1994, p. 10). These hostile cognitive styles, combined with deficient interpersonal skills, are more likely to result in aggression and violence in certain social situations.

Highly aggressive and antisocial children appear to be less equipped cognitively for dealing with ambiguous or conflict-laden situations. Research strongly supports the idea that highly aggressive individuals possess biases and cognitive deficits for dealing with and solving problematic social encounters with others. Children and adolescents who engage in severe peer aggression show more distorted thought patterns that support aggressive behavior. According to Pornari and Wood (2010), "They make more justifications and rationalizations in order to make a harmful act seem less harmful and to eliminate self-censure" (pp. 88–89). Research also indicates that serious delinquent offenders are deficient in being able to cognitively put themselves in the place of others or to empathize (Pepler, Byrd, & King, 1991). As a result, these youth are less concerned about the negative consequences of violence, such as the suffering of the victim or the social rejection they receive from their peers.

Ironically, although the early research on IQ and delinquency can be criticized for its lack of attention to social factors, it is likely that intelligence, in a broader sense, *does* play a role. Most particularly, Gardner's (1983) concept of emotional intelligence may be a key factor in the development of habitual and long-term offending. Put another way, the chronic offender may or may not be "intelligent" in the traditional sense; however, he or she is unlikely to be high in emotional intelligence. However, early school failure seems to play a more critical role in the development of delinquency and crime than the traditional measures of intelligence predict (Dodge & Pettit, 2003). In addition, research indicates that retention in kindergarten and in the early grades—being "held back"—has significant detrimental effects on healthy development (Dodge & Pettit, 2003).

Related to verbal intelligence and thinking is language development. A number of studies indicate that low language proficiency is associated with antisocial behavior, as will be discussed in the next section.

Language Development

Verbal deficits and impaired language development are closely associated with behavior problems and serious delinquency (Leech, Day, Richardson, & Goldschmidt, 2003; Muñoz, Frick, Kimonis, & Aucoin, 2008; Petersen et al., 2013; Vermeiren, De Clippele, Schwab-Stone, Ruchkin, & Deboutte, 2002). Antisocial behavior and aggression have been linked to low language proficiency as early as the second year of life and throughout the life span (Dionne, 2005). According to Keenan and Shaw (2003), language is the "primary means by which children learn to solve problems nonaggressively and effectively decrease negative emotions such as anger, fear, and sadness" (p. 163). By the end of the preschool period, the average child has internalized—primarily through the use of language—rules that are associated with the ability to inhibit behavior, follow rules, and manage negative emotions (Keenan & Shaw, 2003; Kochanska, Murray, & Coy, 1997). In addition, according to Keenan and Shaw, the child demonstrates more empathy and prosocial behavior toward others as a result of language development. As noted by Dionne, "language becomes for most children a social tool for increased prosocial interactions" (p. 335).

Delayed language development appears to increase stress and frustration for many children and impede normal socialization (Keenan & Shaw, 2003). Toddlers, especially boys, who do not meet language development milestones at ages 6 months, 18 months, and 24 months, often display later delinquency and antisocial behavior, even when other influences are accounted for (Nigg & Huang-Pollock, 2003; Stattin & Klackenberg-Larsson, 1993). A higher incidence of language delay also has been observed among male children who display disruptive behaviors during the preschool years and antisocial behaviors during the school years (Dionne, Tremblay, Boivin, Laplante, & Pérusse, 2003; Stowe, Arnold, & Ortiz, 2000). However, the evidence for a similar pattern for girls remains sparse and inconclusive.

How might the above relationships be explained? Early language delay and limited communication skills may predispose a child to use more physically aggressive tactics for dealing with others, especially peers. Frustrated about not getting his needs met through normal communication and social strategies, the child is drawn to more physically aggressive behaviors to get his way. This aggressive behavioral pattern, however, is likely to produce a circular effect, since aggressive and disruptive behaviors interfere with creating a positive social environment for language development and normal peer interactions. Therefore, aggressive or antisocial behaviors may, in turn, curtail language development. In contrast to children with language deficits, verbally advantaged children may benefit from their verbal skills by developing prosocial behaviors and may thus steer away from the antisocial trajectories (Dionne, 2005; Dionne et al., 2003).

N. J. Cohen (2001) asserts that language provides an important cognitive tool for controlling one's own behavior, impulses, and emotions. According to Dionne (2005), "Emotion regulation and self-regulation are generally viewed as requiring complex linguistic tools such as the ability to analyze social situations, organize thoughts about one's own emotions, and plan behavior according to social roles" (p. 346).

Self-Regulation Skills

As emphasized by Steinberg and his associates, whose research was discussed above, self-regulation is one of the most important skills in the prevention of antisocial behavior. **Self-regulation** is defined as the capacity to control and alter one's behavior *and* emotions. It also includes the ability to shift focus and attention and to activate and change behavior (Eisenberg et al., 2004). The reader will recognize that self-regulation includes *both* behavioral and emotional regulation. Being able to control and shift emotions, especially anger, is a pivotal skill important for maintaining prosocial behavior and avoiding aggressive or violent behavior. Research documents that not only is poor behavioral and emotional self-regulation related to aggression and violent delinquency, but it is also related to the early onset of substance use and the escalation of use during adolescence (Wills & Stoolmiller, 2002; Wills, Walker, Mendoza, & Ainette, 2006).

In their relationships with adults, children begin to acquire strategies that enable them to control their behavior and emotions in numerous ways. Although self-regulation skills may reflect some temperamental qualities whose origins may have some genetic component, it is clear that such skills are malleable and can be taught or improved upon by parents, caregivers, or others in the social environment (Buckner, Mezzacappa, & Beardslee, 2003). Sensitive and consistent caregiving and warm but firm parenting styles have been associated with the development of self-control and compliance with social rules. As we learned from Steinberg's dual systems research, self-regulation abilities take time to mature fully. Still, young children can learn to control many of their basic impulses and behaviors at a fairly early age.

Features of self-control begin to emerge in the second year, as does the concern for others. During the third year of life, children are expected to become reasonably compliant with parental requests and to internalize the family standards and values for behavior. By 17 months of age, however, approximately 80% of children show some form of physically aggressive behavior (Tremblay et al., 1996). Moreover, this physical aggression is not usually learned but appears to be a "natural" development of childhood. In addition, while most demonstrate physical aggression at 17 months, not all do so at the same frequency and with the same vigor (Tremblay & Nagin, 2005). As self-regulation develops, physically aggressive behavior usually decreases substantially from the third year onward. During mid-adolescence, however, many exhibit another peak in physical aggression but show a decrease during early adulthood (Dionne, 2005). However, there is a significant increase in verbal and indirect aggressions with age (Vaillancourt, 2005), suggesting that aggression may still exist but that children learn how to be aggressive in different ways (Tremblay & Nagin, 2005). A large factor in this learning or socialization is the development of self-regulation and enhanced executive functions.

Executive Functions

Closely related to self-regulation is the concept of **executive functions**, which refers to deliberate problem solving and the regulation of one's thoughts, actions, and emotions (Tremblay, 2003; Zelazo, Carter, Reznick, & Frye, 1997). Executive function is important in understanding aggression and antisocial behavior because "people with executive function deficits are less able to override maladaptive response inclinations in order to maintain more appropriate and personally beneficial behavior" (Zeier et al., 2012, p. 284). Executive functioning can deteriorate with age or be damaged, such as following a traumatic brain injury or stroke. As indicated in Chapter 6, people with dementia have often experienced significant loss in this function, leading to comments that "they have no filters." Not only do executive functions recognize and inhibit inappropriate behavior, but they also prioritize the steps necessary for solving problems effectively. In sum, executive functions are involved in the planning, regulation, and control of purposive behavior. As further described by Banich (2009), "[executive function] involves an *individual* guiding his or her behavior, especially in novel, unstructured, and nonroutine situations that require some degree of judgment" (p. 89).

Current research and theory supposes that executive functioning resides predominantly in the prefrontal lobe of the cortex (or front part of the brain). As noted earlier in this chapter, the prefrontal lobe or cortex develops a rich network of neurological pathways that enable it to communicate and perhaps control many regions of the brain. As we also learned earlier, the development of these pathways peaks during adolescence and levels off during young adulthood. Not surprisingly, studies have also repeatedly reported strong links between those individuals with symptoms of ADHD and poor executive functioning (Brocki, Eninger, Thorell, & Bohlin, 2010; M. Miller & Hinshaw, 2010).

Several studies of children and adolescents have documented a relationship between different aspects of executive function and antisocial behavior (A. B. Morgan & Lilienfeld, 2000; Nigg, Quamma, Greenberg, & Kusche, 1999; Séguin & Zelazo, 2005; Tremblay, 2003). In fact, poor executive functioning is one of the hallmarks of antisocial personality disorder (Zeier et al., 2012). By contrast, children and adults with good executive functions are well-organized, diligent, focused on completing tasks, and skillful in their approach to solving problems (Buckner et al., 2003). They are adept at focusing attention, able to concentrate well, and flexible in their thinking. All these features are the opposite characteristics of those persons who manifest persistent and violent offending histories.

Deficient Interpersonal Skills and Peer Rejection

As described earlier, research examining social influences has discovered that peer rejection is one of the strongest predictors of later involvement in persistent, serious offending, especially violence (Cowan & Cowan, 2004; Dodge, 2003). This rejection starts early. Even around age 5, aggressive, belligerent children are unpopular and are excluded from peer groups (Dodge & Pettit, 2003; Patterson, 1982).

Children may be rejected by peers for a variety of reasons, but aggressive behavior appears to be a prominent one. Kids reject those peers who rely on various forms of physical and verbal aggression as a method for getting what they want. These peer-rejected children are not only aggressive, but they also tend to be argumentative, inattentive, and disruptive. Furthermore, boys who are both peer rejected and aggressive have a variety of behavioral, social, and cognitive deficits and display low levels of prosocial behavior in general (Coie & Miller-Johnson, 2001). This cluster of deficits frequently results in poor school and academic performance (Buh & Ladd, 2001; Dodge & Pettit, 2003). Peer acceptance is crucial during early development, and those who receive it turn out far differently from their rejected peers. Children who are liked and accepted by their peer group in the early school years are much less likely to become antisocial in their later years (Laird et al., 2001; Rubin, Bukowski, & Parker, 1998). It should be emphasized, however, that almost all the research on the effects of peer rejection, aggression, and delinquent behavior has focused on boys, although neuroimaging studies have begun to focus on girls, especially teenage girls.

As pointed out previously, recent research on the development of delinquent and criminal behavior has identified ADHD features, which appear to have strong neurodevelopmental components. There are many other potential biological and neurological development factors that may contribute to the development of antisocial behavior, including genetics and temperament.

ADDITIONAL SOCIAL DEVELOPMENTAL INFLUENCES

Many other developmental factors have been identified as contributing to a child's trajectory toward a life of committing serious crime and violence. For example, the experience of physical abuse in early life significantly increases the risk of future antisocial conduct (Dodge & Pettit, 2003; Mayfield & Widom, 1996). On the other hand, emotional warmth and appropriate behavioral management by parents have been found to have very positive outcomes on the developmental trajectories of their children (Dishion & Bullock, 2002; Dodge & Pettit, 2003). The amount of exposure that the child has to aggressive peers in day care or preschool also appears to have significant effects on the child's later aggressive behavior. In addition, children who spend large amounts of time in unsupervised after-school self-care in the early elementary grades are also at high risk of participating in antisocial behavior (Sinclair, Pettit, Harrist, & Bates, 1994).

Poverty is also a powerful risk factor. Although the vast majority of children growing up poor do not engage in serious antisocial behavior or delinquency, poverty does create multiple barriers to healthy development. Communities under financial strain are often plagued by inadequate educational and health systems and often have a large number of families experiencing disruption brought about by limited occupational resources and family breakdown. In these areas, schools tend to be inadequate and day care services limited. Moreover, unsafe levels of lead and other toxic materials have been found in significantly higher amounts in economically deprived areas than in middle- or upper income communities (Narag, Pizarro, & Gibbs, 2009). Although it is crucial to emphasize that economic circumstances do not have a causal effect on delinquency—and that most children raised in poverty do not become persistent or even occasional offenders—poverty must be recognized as a risk factor that should be addressed.

JUVENILE FIRESETTING: AN ILLUSTRATION OF THE DEVELOPMENTAL PERSPECTIVE

Up to this point in the chapter, we have discussed various theoretical approaches and studies that are relevant to the development of criminal behavior that often comes to the attention of forensic psychologists. As noted, the pathways to crime include numerous variables, ranging from early childhood experiences to neighborhood influences, individual factors, and educational experiences, to name just a few. In this section, we illustrate the developmental perspective by highlighting one juvenile offense, firesetting, that receives substantial attention in the psychological literature.

Arson, or firesetting, is a criminal offense that is often perpetrated by juveniles, although children also are often the victims of these crimes. Although firesetting behavior is not unusual in young children, if continued it can be a symptom of serious psychological disorder and also can be a precursor to many years of chronic offending.

The term *firesetting* refers to "intentional acts planned to produce a disturbance or to bring about damage or harm" (Chen, Arria, & Anthony, 2003, p. 45). "Intentional" is a key word, since many fires are accidentally caused by young children playing with matches. Our primary focus in this section will be on children and adolescents who *deliberately* light fires to cause damage, but for a variety of reasons.

In a comprehensive study of 1,016 juveniles and adults arrested for arson and fire-related crimes, Icove and Estepp (1987) discovered that vandalism—prompted by a wish to get back at authority—was the most frequently identified motive, accounting for 49% of the arsons in the sample. Similar results had been found by other researchers using smaller samples (e.g., E. Robbins & Robbins, 1964), which revealed that most fires set by juveniles are motivated by the wish to get back at authority or gain status or are prompted by a dare or a need for excitement. Feelings of anger, being ignored, or depression are commonly reported before acts of firesetting (Chen et al., 2003).

Many arson fires set by youth go undetected, unreported, or unsolved (Zipper & Wilcox, 2005). It is estimated, for example, that less than 10% of the fires set by juveniles are reported (Adler, Nunn, Northam, Lebnan, & Ross, 1994). Zipper and Wilcox report that, of the 1,241 Massachusetts juveniles referred for counseling services because of firesetting, only 11% of the blazes these youths started were reported to law enforcement. No one reported these incidents because witnesses or caretakers did not consider the behavior dangerous; no loss of life or significant destruction of property occurred. Furthermore, many people worry that charging juveniles with arson will give them a criminal record that will hamper their future careers. In essence, though firesetting is a serious antisocial behavior, it is believed to be vastly underreported in official statistics.

Developmental Stages of Firesetting

Child firesetters have attracted considerable interest among developmental psychologists. The general consensus is that childhood firesetting goes through discernible stages. For example, Gaynor (1996) identifies three developmental phases: (1) fire interest, (2) fireplay, and (3) firesetting. Fascination and experimentation with fire appear to be common features of normal child development. Kafrey (1980) discovered that fascination with fire appears to be nearly universal in children between 5 and 7 years old. This fascination begins early, with 1 in 5 children setting fires before the age of 3. As the child gets older, fireplay (experimentation) usually takes place between the ages of 5 and 9. In this stage, the child experiments with how a fire starts and how it burns. Unfortunately, children during this phase are especially vulnerable to the hazards of fire because of their lack of experience with it and ways to extinguish it if it flares out of control (Lambie, McCardle, & Coleman, 2002). By age 10, most children have learned the dangers of fire. However, if they continue to set fires at this point—especially damaging ones—they probably have graduated into the firesetting stage. These youths most often intend to use fires to destroy, as a form of excitement, or as a communicative device to draw attention to themselves and their perceived problems.

Experts find that children who *continue* to set fires after age 10 frequently demonstrate poor social skills, inadequate social competence, and poor impulse control compared to their peers (Kolko, 2002; Kolko & Kazdin, 1989). Some experts have found that persistent firesetters, compared to non-firesetters, are more likely to have ADHD (Forehand, Wierson, Frame, Kempton, & Armistead, 1991), and many are rejected by their peers. Some studies report that approximately 74% of youth firesetters have been diagnosed with CD (Chen et al., 2003). In addition, a majority of children who set fires beyond the normal fascination and experimental stages tend to have poor relationships with their parents and also appear to be victims of physical abuse (H. F. Jackson, Glass, & Hope, 1987). One investigation found that maltreated and abused children, compared to their non-maltreated peers, set significantly more fires, demonstrated more versatility in their ignition sources, had more variety in the items or targets they burned, and were more likely to set fires out of anger due to family stressors (C. Root, MacKay, Henderson, Del Bove, & Warling, 2008).

Lambie, McCardle, and Coleman (2002) report that firesetting is often only one segment of a cluster of antisocial behaviors that occur for a variety of reasons but typically include impulse control problems and misdirected anger and boredom. Following their comprehensive review of the research literature, Lambie and Randell (2011) conclude that "firesetting is unlikely to exist in isolation and is best understood within the framework of antisocial behavior" (p. 326). Other researchers have commented on the wide range of criminal offending engaged in by firesetters, beyond firesetting (Gannon & Pina, 2010). For instance, there is some evidence that children who are consistently cruel to animals and other children also tend to engage in consistent firesetting behavior (Slavkin, 2001). Furthermore, a very large majority of firesetters known to the juvenile justice system have committed many other serious juvenile acts besides arson (Ritvo, Shanok, & Lewis, 1983; Stickle & Blechman, 2002). Interestingly, Stickle and Blechman found that "firesetting juvenile offenders exhibit a pattern of developmentally advanced, serious antisocial behavior consistent with an early starter or life-course–persistent trajectory" (p. 190). Most firesetters are young males. Male firesetters outnumber females by a magnitude of two to three times (Lambie, Ioane, Randell, & Seymour, 2013).

Firesetters often come from dysfunctional families and unstable homes, where faulty or maladaptive parenting is present (Lambie et al., 2013). This is even more frequent in the background of female firesetters, where abuse and neglect are common (Hickle & Roe-Sepowitz, 2010). Negative peer relationships, serious school problems, and high rates of truancy are also typical for female firesetters. Mental disorders and substance abuse tend to be common for both male and female firesetters (MacKay, Paglia-Boak, Henderson, Marton, & Adlaf, 2009; Tyler & Gannon, 2012).

Firesetting Typologies

Based on clinical assessments of known firesetters, Kolko (2002) developed a typology that identifies four types of firesetters: (1) curious, (2) pathological, (3) expressive, and (4) delinquent. The typology is built on the assumption of differences in motivation, although it does take into consideration individual and environmental influences. In brief, the curious firesetter uses fire for fascination purposes, the pathological is driven by psychological or emotional problems, the expressive sets fires as a cry for help, and the delinquent uses fire as a means to antisocial or destructive ends (Putnam & Kirkpatrick, 2005). The types are not mutually exclusive, in that a juvenile could use fire as a cry for help for his or her psychological distress.

In the following section, we discuss another topic that lends itself well to a developmental perspective on criminal behavior. Psychopathy, as will be demonstrated below, has been the subject of intense research and theoretical interest by mental health professionals at least since the groundbreaking work of Hervey Cleckley (1941), followed by Robert Hare (e.g., 1965, 1970, 1991). Psychopathy remains one of the most important constructs to be considered by forensic psychologists, particularly but not exclusively as they interact with the criminal justice system.

THE CRIMINAL PSYCHOPATH

Probably no topic has caught the attention of forensic psychologists interested in the development of habitual criminal behavior more in recent years than that of psychopathy. Nicholls and Petrila (2005) assert, "One of the most important concepts to ever emerge in forensic psychology and law is psychopathy" (p. 729). The term **psychopath** is currently used to describe a person who demonstrates a discernible cluster of psychological, interpersonal, and neuropsychological features that distinguish him or her from the general population.

Although psychopathy is usually associated with repetitive criminal or other antisocial behavior, not all researchers and theorists agree that this association is necessary. Some argue (e.g., Lilienfeld, Patrick, et al., 2012) that although the psychopath may be a charming but unscrupulous con artist, he or she does not have to engage in criminal behavior to qualify for psychopathy. (See Perspective 7.1 later in the chapter, in which Dr. Lilienfeld discusses psychopathy and other research interests.) Others (e.g., Neumann, Schmitt, Carter, Embley, & Hare, 2012) contend that antisocial behavior is a central factor in the definition of psychopathy. The debate is a crucial one and will be discussed in more detail below. It is important at this point, however, to distinguish the psychopath from a **sociopath**, the common term for someone who commits *repeated* crime. Although they engage in repetitive crime, sociopaths—unlike psychopaths—have a sense of morality, show genuine empathy for others, and generally possess a well-developed conscience even though their criminal activity may suggest otherwise (Pemment, 2013). To illustrate, the sociopath may be sympathetic to the plight of the homeless and may feel guilty about the crimes he commits. Psychopaths, on the other hand, demonstrate very little empathy, compassion, and conscience compared to the general population, and they also have additional emotional deficits in certain areas. Basically, the psychopath seems to have a reduced capacity for emotional experience (Brook & Kosson, 2013). We will cover the distinguishing behavioral, emotional, interpersonal, and neurological characteristics of the psychopath in more detail in the sections to follow.

Many psychopaths have no history of serious antisocial behavior, and many persistent, serious offenders are not psychopaths. For our purposes here, the term *criminal psychopath* will be reserved for those psychopaths who demonstrate a wide range of persistent antisocial behavior.

As a group, they tend to be "dominant, manipulative individuals characterized by an impulsive, risk-taking and antisocial lifestyle, who obtain their greatest thrill from diverse sexual gratification and target diverse victims over time" (S. Porter et al., 2000, p. 220). S. Porter and associates go on to say, "Given its relation to crime and violence, psychopathy is arguably one of the most important psychological constructs in the criminal justice system" (p. 227). Nevertheless, many scholars believe the emphasis on psychopathy is unjustified, particularly as it relates to juveniles, as we will discuss shortly.

General Behavioral Characteristics of Psychopaths

Hervey Cleckley (1941) was one of the first to outline the behavioral characteristics of psychopaths. He was a professor of psychiatry and neurology at the Medical College of Georgia during the 1930s and remained there until the 1950s. Cleckley is credited with completing one of the most comprehensive works on the psychopath, titled *The Mask of Sanity*. The book went through five editions, and his clear writing style, in combination with the subject area, captivated public and scholarly interests for many years.

Cleckley (1941) identified what he thought were 10 cardinal behavioral features characteristic of the true psychopath: (1) selfishness (also called egocentricity), (2) an inability to love or give genuine affection to others, (3) frequent deceitfulness or lying, (4) lack of guilt or remorsefulness (no matter how cruel the behavior), (5) callousness or a lack of empathy, (6) low anxiety proneness, (7) poor judgment and failure to learn from experience, (8) superficial charm, (9) failure to follow any life plan, and (10) cycles of unreliability. By no means do all researchers in the field of psychopathy agree with this list, but the behavioral features outlined serve as a starting point for further discussion in this section. Cleckley also believed that the typical psychopath exhibited superior intelligence, but that observation has not been supported by the research literature. For example, various measures of psychopathy have shown little—if any—correlations with IQ measures (Hare, 2003). Some recent research has suggested that many psychopaths may possess good amounts of emotional intelligence, however (Copestake, Gray, & Snowden, 2013) and that they use this ability to manipulate, deceive, and control others. In this context, emotional intelligence refers to "the capacity to perceive and understand emotions and the ability to use this information as part of decision-making and the management of behavior" (Copestake et al., 2013, p. 691).

In this respect, the psychopath differs from more traditional chronic offenders, who—as discussed above—are typically not high in emotional intelligence.

An important feature underlying all behavioral descriptions is the psychopath's profound and pathological stimulation seeking (Quay, 1965). According to Quay, the actions of the psychopath are motivated by an excessive *neuropsychological* need for thrills and excitement. It is not unusual to see psychopaths drawn to such interests as race car driving, skydiving, and motorcycle stunts.

Antisocial Personality Disorder and Psychopathy

Psychiatrists, clinical psychologists, and mental health workers often use the term mentioned earlier, *antisocial personality disorder* (ASP/APD), to summarize many of the same features found in the criminal psychopath. As defined in the *DSM-5*, antisocial personality disorder refers specifically to an individual who exhibits "a pervasive pattern of disregard for and violation of the rights of others, occurring since age 15 years" (American Psychiatric Association, 2013, p. 659). This definition is followed by seven criteria, any three or more of which must be met (e.g., failure to conform to social norms, deceitfulness). The person diagnosed with APD must be at least 18 years of age, but, as we discussed earlier, there is evidence of CD disorder with onset before age 15. In other words, the antisocial personality disorder appears closely aligned with the persistent offender, such as the LCP offender.

It should be emphasized that, although there are many behavioral similarities, the terms *antisocial personality disorder* and *psychopathy* are not synonymous. Nevertheless, the *DSM-5* states that "This pattern has also been referred to as *psychopathy*, *sociopathy*, or *dissocial personality disorder*" (p. 659). Most research psychologists want to preserve a distinction. Antisocial personality disorder refers to broad behavioral patterns based on clinical observations, whereas psychopathy refers not only to specific behavioral patterns, but also to measurable cognitive, emotional, and neuropsychological differences. Overall, psychopathy and ASP do not reflect the same underlying psychopathology (Riser & Kosson, 2013). In addition, ASP is so broad in its scope that between 50% and 80% of male inmates qualify as meeting its criteria (Correctional Services of Canada, 1990; Hare, 1998; Hare, Forth, & Strachan, 1992). In contrast, only 11% to 25% of male inmates meet the criteria for psychopathy (Hare, 1996).

Prevalence of Criminal Psychopathy

Overall, Hare (1998) estimates that the prevalence of psychopaths in the general population is about 1%, whereas in the adult prison population, estimates range from 15% to 25%. Some researchers (e.g., Simourd & Hoge, 2000) wonder, however, whether these estimates are not somewhat inflated. Simourd and Hoge report that only 11% of the inmate population they studied could be identified as criminal psychopaths. The inmates used in their study were not simply inmates in a medium-security correctional facility. All 321 were serving a current sentence for violent offending, more than half of them had been convicted of a previous violent offense, and almost all of them had extensive criminal careers. Even so, they did not qualify as psychopaths according to the criteria for achieving that designation; they were antisocial personalities. Simourd and Hoge's research underscores the need to not assume high percentages of criminal psychopathy within any given population, even a population of incarcerated offenders.

Offending Patterns of Criminal Psychopaths

Although some psychopaths have little contact with the criminal justice system, many have continual contact with the system because of persistent, serious offending. For example, Gretton, McBride, Hare, O'Shaughnessy, and Kumka (2001) point out that criminal psychopaths generally

> lack a normal sense of ethics and morality, live by their own rules, are prone to use cold-blooded, instrumental intimidation and violence to satisfy their wants and needs, and generally are contemptuous of social norms and the rights of others. (p. 428)

Criminal psychopaths manifest violent and aggressive behaviors—including verbal abuse, threats, and intimidation—at a much higher rate than is found in other populations (Hare, Hart, & Harpur, 1991). In some cases, this persistent offending is extremely violent in nature.

Criminal psychopaths are "responsible for a markedly disproportionate amount of the serious crime, violence, and social distress in every society" (Hare, 1996, p. 26). Hare posits, "The ease with which psychopaths engage in . . . dispassionate violence has very real significance for society in general and for law enforcement personnel in particular" (p. 38). Hare refers to a 1992 report by the FBI that found that nearly half of the law enforcement officers who died in the line of duty were killed by individuals who closely matched the behavioral and personality profile of the psychopath. In addition, the crimes of psychopathic sex offenders are likely to be more violent, brutal, unemotional, and sadistic than those of other sex offenders (Hare, Clark, Grann, & Thornton, 2000). Some serial murders described as unusually sadistic and brutal also tend to have many psychopathic features (Hare et al., 2000; M. H. Stone, 1998). It should be emphasized, though, that very few psychopaths—even criminal psychopaths—are serial killers.

The relationship between psychopathy and sexual offending appears to be a complex one. For example, the prevalence of psychopaths among child sex offenders is estimated to be from 10% to 15%; among rapists, it is between 40% and 50% (Gretton et al., 2001; S. Porter et al., 2000). Research also indicates that rapists who have psychopathic characteristics are more likely to have "nonsexual" motivations for their crimes compared to rapists who are not psychopaths, such as anger, vindictiveness, sadism, and opportunism (Hart & Dempster, 1997). Rape, however, is always a violent crime and should not be attributed predominately to sexual motivations.

With regard to other violent offenses, many murders and serious assaults committed by non-psychopaths occurred during domestic disputes or extreme emotional arousal. However, this pattern of violence is rarely observed for criminal psychopaths (Hare et al., 1991; Williamson, Hare, & Wong, 1987). Criminal psychopaths frequently engage in violence as a form of revenge or retribution or during a bout of drinking. Many of the attacks of non-psychopaths are against women they know well, whereas many of the attacks of criminal psychopaths are directed toward women who are strangers. Hare et al. (1991) observe that the violence committed by criminal psychopaths was callous and cold-blooded, "without the affective coloring that accompanied the violence of nonpsychopaths" (p. 395).

According to S. Porter et al. (2000), research suggests that psychopaths reoffend faster, violate parole sooner, and perhaps commit more institutional violence (i.e., in jails, prisons, or psychiatric facilities) than non-psychopaths. In one study (Serin, Peters, & Barbaree, 1990), the number of failures—or violations of the conditions of their release—of male offenders released on an unescorted temporary absence program was examined. The failure rate for psychopaths was 37.5%, whereas none of the non-psychopaths failed. The failure rate during parole was also examined. Although 7% of non-psychopaths violated parole requirements, 33% of the psychopaths violated their requirements. In another study (Serin & Amos, 1995), 299 male offenders were followed for up to 8 years after their release from a federal prison. Sixty-five percent of the psychopaths were convicted of another crime within 3 years, compared to a reconviction rate of 25% for non-psychopaths. Quinsey, Rice, and Harris (1995) found that within 6 years of release from prison, more than 80% of the psychopaths convicted as sex offenders had violently recidivated, compared to a 20% recidivism rate for non-psychopathic sex offenders.

High recidivism rates are also characteristic of adolescent offenders with psychopathic characteristics. According to Gretton et al. (2001), these offenders are more likely than other adolescent offenders to escape from custody, violate the conditions of probation, and commit nonviolent and violent offenses over a 5-year follow-up period. The high recidivism rates among adult and juvenile psychopathic offenders have prompted some researchers to conclude that there is "nothing the behavioral sciences can offer for treating those with psychopathy" (Gacono, Nieberding, Owen, Rubel, & Bodholdt, 2001, p. 119). Other researchers take a decidedly different perspective and believe that untreatability statements concerning the psychopath are unwarranted (Salekin, 2002; Skeem, Monahan, & Mulvey, 2002; Skeem, Poythress, Edens, Lilienfeld, & Cale, 2003; Wong, 2000). There is *some* evidence that psychopaths who receive larger "doses" of treatment are less likely to demonstrate subsequent violent behavior than those who receive less treatment (Skeem et al., 2003).

Psychological Measures of Psychopathy

Currently, the most popular instrument for measuring criminal psychopathy is the 20-item **Psychopathy Checklist-Revised (PCL-R)** (Hare, 1991). It is an instrument familiar to most forensic psychologists who interact with the criminal justice system in various ways. More recently, the PCL-R has been published in a second edition, which includes new information on its applicability in forensic and research settings. It has been expanded for use with offenders in other countries and includes updated normative and validation data on male and female offenders.

A 12-item short-form version has also been developed, called the **Psychopathy Checklist: Screening Version (PCL:SV)** (Hart, Cox, & Hare, 1995; Hart, Hare, & Forth, 1993), as well as the **Psychopathy Checklist: Youth Version (PCL:YV)** and the **P-Scan: Research Version.** The P-Scan is a screening instrument that serves as a *rough* screen for psychopathic features and as a source of working hypotheses to deal with managing suspects, offenders, or clients. It is designed for use in law enforcement, probation, corrections, civil and forensic facilities, and other areas in which it would be useful to have some information about the possible presence of psychopathic features in a particular person.

The above instruments are largely based on Cleckley's (1941) conception of psychopathy but are specifically designed to identify psychopaths in male prison, forensic, or psychiatric populations. Because the PCL-R is currently the most frequently used as both a research and clinical instrument, it will be the center of attention for the remainder of this section. The PCL:YV is beginning to be researched more extensively and will be covered in more detail in the section on juveniles with psychopathic features.

Several other inventories or tests to measure psychopathic traits have been developed besides the PCL-R, the PCL:YV, and their derivatives. For example, one of the more recent measures is the **Triarchic Psychopathy Measure (TriPM)** developed by Patrick and colleagues (Drislane, Patrick, & Arsal, 2014; Patrick, Drislane, & Strickland, 2012; Patrick, Fowles, & Krueger, 2009). The TriPM consists of three scales: Boldness, Meanness, and Disinhibition. The Boldness scale measures dominance, emotional stability, and venturesomeness. The Meanness scale measures such traits as manipulativeness, lack of empathetic concern, and cruelty. Some experts view meanness as the core component of psychopathy (Herpers, Rommelse, Bons, Buitelaar, & Scheepers, 2012). Disinhibition entails such traits as impulsivity, irresponsibility, and hostility (Drislane et al., 2014). Other measures of psychopathy include the Youth Psychopathic Traits Inventory (YPI; Andershed, Kerr, Stattin, & Levander, 2002), the Child Psychopathic Scale (CPS; Lynam, 1997), the Psychopathic Personality Inventory (PPI; Lilienfeld & Andrews, 1996), and the Psychopathic Personality Inventory-Revised (PPI-R; Lilienfeld & Widows, 2005). Coverage of all these measures of psychopathy are beyond the scope of this chapter. Despite the proliferation of psychopathic measures, the PCL-R clearly remains the "gold standard" for researchers and practicing clinicians.

The PCL-R assesses the affective (emotional), interpersonal, behavioral, and social deviance facets of criminal psychopathy from various sources, including self-reports; behavioral observations; and collateral sources, such as parents, family members, friends, and arrest and court records, which can help to establish the credibility of self-reports (Hare, 1996; Hare et al., 1991). In addition, item ratings from the PCL-R, for instance, require some integration of information across multiple domains, including behavior at work or school; behavior toward family, friends, and sexual partners; and criminal behavior (Kosson et al., 2002). Typically, highly trained examiners use all this information to score each item on a point scale of 0 to 2, which measures the extent to which an individual has the disposition described by each item on the checklist (0 = *consistently absent*, 1 = *inconsistent*, 2 = *consistently present*). Scoring is, however, quite complex and requires substantial time, extensive training, and access to a considerable amount of background information on the individual. A score of 30 or above usually qualifies a person as a primary psychopath (Hare, 1996). In some research and clinical settings, cutoff scores ranging from 25 to 33 are often used (Simourd & Hoge, 2000). Hare (1991) recommends that persons with scores between 21 and 29 be classified as "middle" subjects who show many of the features of psychopathy but do not fit all the criteria. Scores below 21 are considered "non-psychopaths."

So far, the research has strongly supported the reliability and validity of the PCL-R for distinguishing criminal psychopaths from criminal non-psychopaths and for helping correctional psychologists in risk assessments of inmates (Hare, 1996; Hare et al., 1992). In addition, the instrument provides researchers and mental health professionals with a universal measurement for the assessment of psychopathy that facilitates international and cross-cultural communication concerning theory, research, and eventual clinical practice (Hare et al., 2000). Currently, the PCL-R is increasingly being used as a clinical instrument for the diagnosis of psychopathy across the globe, although it appears to be most powerful in identifying psychopathy among

North American white males (Hare et al., 2000). However, it is also an instrument that many forensic psychologists prefer to use to assess an offender's risk of violence and "to inform decisions about whether to incarcerate, treat, indefinitely detain, or even execute him or her" (Camp, Skeem, Barchard, Lilienfeld, & Poythress, 2013, p. 468). This extensive use of the PCL-R is highly controversial, as we see below.

The PCL-R as a Risk Assessment Tool

In U.S. courts, the PCL-R is increasingly being used as an important—and sometimes required—risk assessment tool. "The mental health field clearly has embraced the applied use of the PCL-R, as evidenced by its popularity in various surveys of instruments used in civil and criminal cases" (DeMatteo et al., 2014b, p. 96). Not only has the PCL-R become a popular tool for forensic psychologists to use in risk assessment measures for U.S. courts, but it has also actually become a required assessment for some types of cases in some states. These cases involve sexually violent predator hearings, parole hearings, capital sentencing, civil commitment, and transfer to adult court hearings (DeMatteo & Edens, 2006; DeMatteo et al., 2014b; Walsh & Walsh, 2006). In cases involving sexually violent predators, "many of these laws have in one form or another focused on the concept of 'psychopathy' as relevant to the classification of being a dangerous sexual offender, with some laws specifically referring to these offenders as 'sexual psychopaths'" (DeMatteo et al., 2014a). In addition, it appears that evidence of psychopathy is highly influential to judicial decision making in a sizeable portion of court cases (Viljoen, MacDougall, Gagnon, & Douglas, 2010). More important, the evidence of psychopathy often plays an instrumental role in decisions concerning whether the defendant can be successfully rehabilitated.

DeMatteo et al. (2014b) comment, "The PCL-R remains a popular and widely used measure among forensic practitioners, and the results of this case law survey suggest that the number of U.S. court cases reporting the use of the PCL-R continues to accelerate" (p. 105). There is also every indication the number of cases involving the PCL-R will continue to increase well into the future.

Moreover, results of the PCL-R submitted by forensic psychologists are rarely challenged in court, a fact that troubles researchers who are concerned with possible overuse of this instrument (DeMatteo et al., 2014a). Considering the amount of stigmatizing effects that the label "psychopath" carries, the low challenge rate is surprising. As things stand now, a defendant labeled a psychopath is in danger of receiving the maximum sentence allowed because he or she is *perceived* as highly dangerous with little chance of being rehabilitated or successfully treated. For example, J. Cox, Clark, Edens, Smith, and Magyar (2013) found that mock jurors are more likely to support execution in capital cases when the defendant was diagnosed as a "psychopath." In fact, the researchers made a call for a moratorium on the use of the PCL-R in court cases involving capital offenses. Not surprisingly, scores on the PCL-R are used primarily by the prosecution (DeMatteo & Edens, 2006; Edens & Cox, 2012; Edens, Davis, Fernandez Smith, & Guy, 2013) to buttress its argument for longer sentences. What may be surprising, though, is that some judges may respond in an unexpected manner if provided with evidence that psychopathy is biologically based. In a recent study in which sitting judges were given scenarios based on an actual case, the judges who were given such biological information were more lenient in their sentencing than those who were not provided it (Aspinwall, Brown, & Tabery, 2012; G. Miller, 2012).

Core Factors of Psychopathy

One finding that has clearly emerged from the research on the PCL-R is that psychopathy is multidimensional in nature. **Factor analysis** is one statistical procedure designed to find different dimensions or factors in test data. When expert ratings of psychopathy on the PCL-R were submitted to a factor analysis, at least two behavioral dimensions or factors came to light (Hare, 1991; Harpur, Hakstian, & Hare, 1988; Hart et al., 1993). Factor 1 reflects the interpersonal and emotional components of the disorder and consists of items that measure a tendency to be deceitful, unemotional, remorseless, socially dominant, and manipulative. The typical psychopath feels no compunction about using others strictly to meet his or her own needs. Some studies have found that Factor 1 is related "to levels of anxiety and fear, decreased physiological reactivity to threatening cues, and resilience against mood disorders" (Sadeh, Javdani, & Verona, 2013, p. 167). This factor is commonly referred to as the interpersonal-affective factor.

Factor 2 is most closely associated with a socially deviant lifestyle and antisocial attitudes, as characterized by a tendency to be irresponsible, impulsive, and aggressive. The factor is also associated with a strong tendency to engage in an antisocial lifestyle combined with unrealistic goals and ambitions. In contrast to Factor 1, Factor 2 is related to high levels of anxiety and distress and various forms of psychopathology (Sadeh et al., 2013). This factor is often referred to as the impulsive factor. In criminal psychopaths, some researchers have found that Factor 1 appears to be associated with planned predatory violence, whereas Factor 2 appears to be related to spontaneous and disinhibited violence (Hart & Dempster, 1997). Factor 1 is also linked to resistance to and inability to profit from psychotherapy and treatment programs (Olver & Wong, 2009). Factor 2 appears related to socioeconomic status, educational attainment, and cultural/ethnic background, whereas Factor 1 may be more connected with biopsychological influences (Cooke & Michie, 1997). Research also suggests that Factor 1 may be a more powerful predictor of psychopathic violence than Factor 2 (Cooke, Michie, Hart, & Hare, 1999; Olver, Lewis, & Wong, 2013).

Although the first two core factors have received the bulk of the research attention to date, some studies with both adolescents and adults reveal that there may be at least *three* behavioral dimensions at the core of psychopathy rather than just the original two (Cooke & Michie, 2001; Frick, Bodin, & Barry, 2000; Kosson et al., 2002). Cooke and Michie (1997), for example, found from their factor analysis of PCL-R data that psychopathy probably consists of three core factors: (1) arrogant and deceitful interpersonal style, (2) impulsive and irresponsible behavioral style (highly similar to the original Factor 2), and (3) deficient affective experience. Factors 1 and 3 are actually subdivisions of the original Factor 1 reported in earlier studies. The term *deficient affective experience* refers to the lack of sincere positive emotions toward others and the demonstration of callousness and lack of empathy. The terms *arrogant* and *deceitful interpersonal style*, on the other hand, refer to the glibness, superficial charm, and grandiose sense of self-worth that are so characteristic of the psychopath. The three factors are now termed interpersonal (Factor 1), deviant lifestyle (Factor 2), and deficient affective (Factor 3).

An increasing amount of evidence indicates that a fourth core factor of psychopathy should be included in the discussion (Hare, 2003; Hare & Neumann, 2008; Neumann et al., 2012; Salekin, Brannen, Zalot, Leistico, & Neumann, 2006; Vitacco, Neumann, & Jackson, 2005; Walters & Heilbrun, 2010). According to the **four-factor perspective**, the factors are as follows: (1) interpersonal, such as pathological lying and conning; (2) impulsive lifestyle, such as irresponsible behavior, sensation seeking, and impulsiveness; (3) affective, meaning shallow affect or emotional reactions, lack of remorsefulness for their actions; and (4) antisocial tendencies, such as poor self-regulation and a wide array of antisocial behavior (see Table 7.3 for a summary).

The argument for a fourth factor is based on the finding that individuals manifesting psychopathic traits often exhibit violence and a large collection of other antisocial behaviors that go beyond the poor planning and impulsivity associated with Factor 2. As noted by Neumann et al., 2012, "Both clinical tradition and empirical evidence clearly show that psychopathic propensities are fundamentally linked with antisociality" (p. 559). Lynam and Miller (2012) write that any description of psychopathy is incomplete without including antisocial behavior. Therefore, researchers backing inclusion of this factor in defining psychopathy contend that we are missing a critical ingredient in the understanding of the psychopath if measures of antisocial behavior

Table 7.3	Summary Table of Four Core Factors of Psychopathy	
Factor	**Behavior Description**	**Factor Label**
Factor 1	Arrogant, deceitful, takes advantage of others, manipulative	Interpersonal
Factor 2	Impulsive, irresponsible, unreliable	Impulsive
Factor 3	Unemotional, remorseless, callous, shows lack of empathy	Affective
Factor 4	Wide array of antisocial behavior, poor self-regulation	Antisocial

are left out of the equation. Salekin et al. (2006) maintain that much of the predictive power of psychopathy measures is enhanced if we include past antisocial behavior in defining psychopathy. In fact, research has found that Factor 4 appears to be the most important factor for predicting psychopathic recidivism (Hawes, Boccaccini, & Murrie, 2013; Walters & Heilbrun, 2010). Recent research has also discovered that Factor 4 emerges as a key component in defining psychopathy for both male and female adult psychopaths as well as for male and female juvenile psychopaths (Kosson et al., 2013). The fourth factor has become known as the antisocial factor.

Other researchers disagree with the requirement that antisocial behavior should be considered a core factor of psychopathy. Lilienfeld et al. (2012), for example, maintain that the inclusion of antisocial behavior as a core definition of psychopathy leaves little room for the psychopath who is slick, smooth, likeable, socially poised, and charming but does not engage in a life of antisocial or criminal behavior. They propose a "boldness" factor, which will be discussed below.

The Boldness Factor

In recent years, scholars have debated whether the personality trait of boldness should be included as a core factor for describing psychopathy. The **boldness factor** (also called fearless dominance) refers to an "interpersonal style that is characterized by fearlessness, being relatively immune to stress or anxiety, and being successful at negotiating social interactions to achieve desired goals" (Douglas, Nikolova, Kelley, & Edens, 2015, p. 265). Several researchers (e.g., Patrick, Fowles, & Krueger [2009] and Skeem, Polaschek, Patrick, & Lilienfeld [2011]) describe psychopathic boldness as the ability to remain calm and focused in stressful or life-threatening situations, and to exhibit high self-assurance and social efficacy in a wide variety of social situations. The trait boldness also reflects the capacity to recover rapidly from disastrous events.

Scott Lilienfeld and his colleagues (Lilienfeld, Watts, & Smith, 2015; Lilienfeld, Smith, Savigné, et al., 2016; B. Murphy, Lilienfeld, Skeem, & Edens, 2016) believe that boldness (fearless dominance) may represent the key trait that separates successful psychopaths from unsuccessful psychopaths. "Recent studies suggest that fearless dominance may be a marker of the successful features of psychopathy and may bear important implications for leadership" (Lilienfeld et al., 2015, p. 301).

Fearless dominance also appears to be associated with occupational choice. For example, Lilienfeld and his colleagues discovered that the trait was significantly linked to leadership positions in many organizations and high-risk occupations (Lilienfeld et al., 2015). Examples of high-risk occupations include firefighters, law enforcement, and dangerous sports. At this point, there is a growing interest in the search for the elusive successful psychopath (Smith, Watts, & Lilienfeld, 2014).

Boldness also emerges as a key component in the triarchic model of psychopathy (Patrick, Fowles, & Krueger, 2009). The triarchic model was discussed earlier in the chapter under the section psychological measures of psychopathy, where we briefly covered the Triarchic Psychopathy Measure (TriPM). The model consists of three traits that some scholars believe are best representative of psychopathy: (1) boldness, (2) meanness, and (3) disinhibition. Meanness refers to "deficient empathy, disdain for and lack of close attachments with others, rebelliousness, excitement seeking, exploitiveness, and empowerment through cruelty" (Patrick et al.,

2009, p. 927). It can be expressed through extreme arrogance, defiance of authority, destructive excitement seeking, and physical cruelty toward people and animals (Skeem et al., 2011). Patrick et al. believe that meanness may be a central feature of psychopathic crime and delinquency that is actively directed at hurting others.

FROM MY PERSPECTIVE 7.1

Love Science, Find Your Muse, and Check Your Ego at the Door

Scott O. Lilienfeld, PhD

Courtesy of Scott O. Lilienfeld.

Serendipity often plays a pivotal role in scientific discovery (Bosenman, 1988). Chance also often plays a key role in people's life choices, including their career paths. Such was the case for me. I would love to say that my interests in psychopathic personality (psychopathy), now my primary focus of research, followed a coherent, straight-line path from college to graduate school to academia. But that would be untrue, as my research interests arose almost entirely by happenstance.

As a psychology major at Cornell University in the late 1970s and early 1980s, I initially knew next to nothing about psychopathy. Then, as a junior, I enrolled in a course taught by Robert Dworkin on advanced issues in psychopathology research. Bob divided his course into three modules: schizophrenia, mood disorders, and psychopathy. During the psychopathy module, he introduced us to laboratory work of David Lykken (1957), who had more or less single-handedly launched the experimental study of this puzzling condition. In a clever set of studies conducted for his doctoral dissertation, Lykken demonstrated that psychopaths display striking deficits in the capacity to experience fear. For example, on a "mental maze" task that required participants to learn a complex sequence of lever presses, some of which result in electric shock, psychopaths failed to learn from punishment—even though they mastered the maze sequence just as rapidly as did non-psychopaths. I recall being impressed with the sheer ingenuity with which Lykken put his theoretical conjectures to rigorous tests.

Soon after, I applied to graduate programs in clinical psychology, and was fortunate to be admitted to my first-choice school, the University of Minnesota. I was aware of the interests of the faculty members in the program, and had initially planned to focus my research

in graduate school on schizophrenia, which was a particular strength of the program. A few months before starting graduate school, however, I happened to be watching a television documentary featuring research on identical twins then being conducted at the University of Minnesota. Suddenly, an imposing man with a beard appeared on screen, and his name was David Lykken; David spoke eloquently of the power of twin designs to elucidate the human condition. I immediately recognized that this was the same researcher whose work I had admired as an undergraduate (because David had moved from the University of Minnesota's Department of Psychology to the Department of Psychiatry, he had not been listed as a member of the clinical psychology program, so I had not realized that he was there). Soon after arriving at Minnesota in 1982, I introduced myself to David to discuss the possibility of working in his laboratory. To my surprise, he immediately agreed to supervise me on research on psychopathy. The more I learned about this condition, the more intrigued I became—and I have never looked back.

Finding a research area to pursue can be a challenge, but students should not despair. Although I am in my mid-50s, I at times still feel as though I am trying to figure out what I want to do when I grow up. That does not concern me, as I have continually managed to reinvent myself. For example, I am no longer certain that I fully understand what psychopathy is despite having studied it for three decades. I began my academic career convinced that psychopathy is a single entity. Now I am exceedingly doubtful. I have since come to believe that psychopathy is instead a configuration of largely distinct traits drawn from the realm of general personality. Hence, I suspect that large bodies of research devoted to discovering "the" cause of psychopathy, including some to which I contributed, are based on an erroneous premise (Lilienfeld, Smith, & Watts, 2016). This belated recognition has led me into a novel body of research,

(Continued)

(Continued)

namely, the question of how basic personality traits combine to create "interpersonal syndromes"—constellations of traits that yield noxious social outcomes.

I am frequently asked what advice I can give to aspiring scholars in forensic psychology and allied fields. I may not be the best person to ask, as I have always been something of a contrarian, and readers of this book should know that my advice may differ in significant ways from that of many other scholars. But for what it's worth, here are three suggestions.

First, find a muse and follow it. Discover a burning scientific question that fascinates you and pursue it doggedly. Incidentally, if you don't have a deep passion for science, don't go into academia. At the risk of being slightly facetious, one needs to be a bit "crazy" to want to be a professor. By that, I do not mean that one needs to be mentally disturbed, but rather that one must be sufficiently passionate about a question to want to devote a sizeable chunk of one's life to exploring it.

Second, stay broad in your knowledge and interests. Difficult as it may be, try to resist the incessant pressure toward hyperspecialization that has consumed much of academic life, especially in research-intensive universities. Despite my avid interest in psychopathy, I am an extreme generalist by nature. For example, I have also conducted work on anxiety disorders, dissociative disorders, psychiatric classification, evidence-based assessment and therapeutic practices, psychological

misconceptions, and scientific thinking in psychology. I would not recommend that young scholars be quite as catholic in their interests as I am. Still, to be an outstanding scholar, one needs to draw upon and synthesize insights from seemingly unrelated fields. As an academic friend of mine likes to say, it's precisely at the intersection of diverse disciplines that the "magic" in science typically arises.

Third, don't take yourself too seriously. Take your research seriously, to be sure, but don't get too big of an ego. Precious few of us will be remembered, let alone be famous, a century from now (Roediger, 2016). So don't aspire for fame. Aim to make a modest discovery in your domain of interest, and be sure to have fun along the way.

I consider it an enormous privilege to be a professor. Yes, one has to work long hours and deal with the inevitable frustrations of academic bureaucracy. But I have to continually remind myself—and at times pinch myself—that I am being paid to do what I dearly love, and that is more than ample reward for me.

Dr. Lilienfeld is Samuel Candler Dobbs Professor of Psychology at Emory University in Atlanta, Georgia, and Editor of the journal, Clinical Psychological Science. His primary areas of research interest are the causes and assessment of personality disorders, especially psychopathy; psychiatric classification and diagnosis; and the application of scientific thinking to psychology.

Disinhibition is characterized by a "lack of planfulness and foresight, impaired regulation of affect and urges, insistence on immediate gratification, and deficient behavioral restraint" (Patrick et al., 2009, p. 925). In proposing the triarchic model, Patrick et al. believe that these three distinct dispositions provide a cogent summary which reconciles and accommodates the extensive research and alternative descriptions of psychopathy over the past three decades.

Juvenile Psychopathy

One of the serious shortcomings of the extensive research conducted on psychopathy is that it originally focused almost exclusively on adult males (Frick, Barry, & Bodin, 2000). Consequently, research on juvenile (primarily adolescent) psychopathy as well as psychopathy in females has been limited. It is now growing rapidly. However, attempts to apply the label *psychopathy* to juvenile populations are strongly resisted, and they "raise several conceptual, methodological, and practical concerns related to clinical/forensic practice and juvenile/criminal justice policy" (Edens, Skeem, Cruise, & Cauffman, 2001, p. 54).

Over the past decade, scholars have engaged in spirited debates on this issue (Edens & Vincent, 2008; Salekin, Rosenbaum, & Lee, 2008; Viljoen, MacDougall, et al., 2010). Some debate has focused on whether psychopathy can or should be applied to juveniles at all. Can features of adult psychopathy be found in adolescents in the first place? Second, even if psychopathy can be identified in adolescents, the label may have too many negative connotations. More specifically, the label implies that the prognosis for treatment is poor, a high rate of offending and recidivism can be expected, and the intrinsic and biological basis of the disorder means little can be done outside of biological interventions. A third debate contends that psychopathy assessments of youth must achieve a high level of confidence before they can be employed in the criminal justice system (Seagrave & Grisso, 2002).

Several instruments for measuring pre-adult psychopathy have been developed in recent years, including the Psychopathy Screening Device (PSD; Frick, O'Brien, Wootton, & McBurnett, 1994), the Childhood Psychopathy Scale (CPS; Lynam, 1997), and the PCL:YV (Forth, Kosson, & Hare, 1997). All three instruments began primarily as research measures rather than as clinical-diagnostic measures but are now likely to be seen in clinical practice. This is particularly true of the PCL:YV.

The PCL:YV, designed for assessing psychopathy in adolescents age 13 or older, is a modified version of the PCL-R. Basically, the instrument attempts to assess psychopathy across the youth's life span, with an emphasis on school adjustment and peer and family relations. Similar to the adult PCL-R, the PCL:YV requires a lengthy standardized, semi-structured clinical interview and a review of documents by a well-trained psychologist. Scores of 0 (*consistently absent*), 1 (*inconsistent*), or 2 (*consistently present*) for each of the 20 behavioral dimensions of psychopathy represent the scoring system. The instrument—like the PCL-R—generates a total score and two factor scores. Factor 1 reflects an interpersonal/affective dimension and includes items that measure glibness/superficial charm, grandiosity, manipulativeness, dishonesty, and callousness. Factor 2 reflects behavioral or lifestyles features such as impulsiveness, irresponsibility, early behavioral problems, and lack of goals.

The PSD is a behavior rating scale in which some of the items on the PCL-R were rewritten for use with youth (Frick, Barry, et al., 2000). Currently, the PSD comes in three versions: (1) a teacher version, (2) a parent version, and (3) a self-report version. Using the teacher and parent versions of the PSD, Frick et al. (1994) found (through a factor analysis) that juvenile psychopathy may be made up of two major dimensions. One dimension was labeled callous-unemotional and the other impulsivity-conduct problems. The callous-unemotional dimension, however, appeared to be especially useful for predicting more severe aggression, conduct problems, and delinquency (Marsee, Silverthorn, & Frick, 2005). Later, Frick, Bodin, et al. (2000) found evidence (again through a factor analysis) to support a *three*-dimensional core for juvenile psychopathy. Two of the factors (callous-unemotional and impulsivity) were similar to the core dimensions found for adults in Frick, Bodin, et al.'s earlier study. However, the construct of impulsivity seems to be much more complex in youth than in adults, and the researchers discovered that the construct may be subdivided into impulsivity and narcissism (grandiose sense of self-worth).

Callous-Unemotional (CU) Traits

The validity and value of the **callous-unemotional (CU) traits** has been supported by considerable research in recent years (Frick et al., 2014). Many experts view CU traits as defining signs and symptoms of juvenile and adult psychopathy, but these traits can be displayed in young children as well. CU trait theory was first proposed by Paul Frick and his colleagues (C. T. Barry et al., 2000; Frick, Barry, et al., 2000). The research team conducted a series of research projects designed to detect developmental precursors to adult psychopathy. They were able to identify a group of children who had been diagnosed with conduct disorders but who exhibited particularly severe and chronic patterns of antisocial behavior beyond what is normally seen in other children with conduct disorders. They also discovered a group of children and adolescents who displayed a significant lack of empathetic concern for others, limited capacity for guilt, and deficits in emotional expression. They noticed that these characteristics were highly similar to those behavioral patterns found in adult psychopaths. The researchers referred to this cluster of traits as callous-unemotional. Further study revealed that high levels of impulsivity and egocentricity were apparent in these youths, and that they were not only diagnosed with severe conduct disorders but were also highly aggressive and often violent (Frick et al., 2014). Moreover, the youths displayed significant cognitive difficulties, such as the inability to take the perspective of others, self-serving cognitive distortions such as blaming others for their mistakes, and underestimating the likelihood they will be punished for misbehavior.

Additional research revealed that children with CU traits are not afraid of being punished for their aggressive actions and are convinced that aggression is an effective means for dominating and controlling others (Pardini & Byrd, 2012). The CU children in the study spoke in a way that minimized the extent to which their aggression caused victim suffering, and they openly acknowledged caring very little about the distress and suffering of others. Not surprisingly, other studies found that CU traits in childhood and adolescence strongly predicted psychopathy patterns in adulthood (Kahn, Frick, Youngstrom, Findling, & Youngstrom, 2012).

It should be noted that CU traits were included as a "specifier" under the general category of conduct disorder in the *DSM-5*. A specifier, in this context, provides an opportunity to distinguish this group of conduct disorders as different from the other subgroups of CDs. The intent was to notify practitioners that this group is more likely to engage in aggression that is planned for instrumental gain (American Psychiatric Association, 2013).

One of the major problems of identifying juvenile psychopaths is that psychopathy may be very difficult to measure reliably because of the transient and constantly changing developmental patterns across the life span, especially during the early years. For example, psychopathic symptoms in childhood may look very different from those exhibited in adulthood (Hart, Watt, & Vincent, 2002). That is, some of the behavioral patterns of children and adolescents may be similar to psychopaths for a variety of reasons but may not really be signs of psychopathy. Moreover, children and adolescents who display serious antisocial and conduct problems show great variability in the types of problem behaviors they have, making it difficult for researchers and clinicians to easily classify them into neat categories (Frick et al., 2014).

Children in abusive homes often demonstrate an abnormally restricted range of emotions that are similar to the emotional characteristics of psychopathy. Actually, they may be the child's way of coping in a very stressful home environment (Seagrave & Grisso, 2002). Furthermore, Seagrave and Grisso assert, "Some adolescent behavior may . . . appear psychopathic by way of poor anger control, lack of goals, and poor judgment, but is actually influenced by parallel developmental tasks encountered by most adolescents" (p. 229). Going against the rules is part of many adolescents' attempts to gain autonomy from adult dominance, such as what is found in adolescent-limited offending. In addition, adult criminal psychopaths often have been psychologically scarred by years of drug and alcohol abuse, physical fighting, lost opportunities, and multiple incarcerations (Lynam, 1997). Consequently, adult psychopaths may present a very different population pool compared to the juvenile psychopath.

Appropriateness of PCL-R and PCL:YV for Testing Adolescents

Edens, Skeem, et al. (2001) also point out that some of the items on the various psychological measures of psychopathy (especially the PCL-R and PCL:YV) are inappropriate for use with adolescents, or for use with certain populations, such as female adolescents (Edens, Campbell, & Weir, 2007) or various ethnic groups (Leistico, Salekin, DeCoster, & Rogers, 2008). Some items focus on such things as lack of goals and irresponsibility. If these features are not present in the adolescent, then he or she might receive scores in the psychopathy direction. However, adolescents generally have not crystallized their life goals or had to take on many responsibilities, and consequently such items "seem less applicable as definitive markers of psychopathy for adolescence than for adults" (Edens et al., 2007, p. 58). We must be careful, then, not to generalize what we know about the adult psychopath to a juvenile who has been given the same label.

Nevertheless, many researchers are persisting in their attempts to identify juvenile psychopaths and measure psychopathic tendencies. In a study examining the prevalence rate of psychopathy among children, Skilling, Quinsey, and Craig (2001) found in a sample of more than 1,000 boys in Grades 4 to 8 that 4.3% of the sample could be classified as psychopathic on every measure employed in the study.

Lynam (1997) designed a research project that compared juvenile and adult psychopaths. Using the CPS, Lynam reported results that suggested psychopathy begins in childhood and can be measured reliably in young adolescents (ages 12 and 13). Lynam found that, like their adult counterparts, they were the most aggressive, severe, frequent, and impulsive offenders, a characteristic that was stable across time. Moreover, he discovered that the CPS was a better predictor of serious delinquency than was socioeconomic status, previous delinquency, IQ, or impulsivity.

Research so far does indicate that there is some validity in measures of juvenile psychopathy (Kosson et al., 2002; Murrie & Cornell, 2002). Recent research also indicates that juvenile psychopathy may have a genetic basis and may run in families (Forsman, Lichtenstein, Andershed, & Larsson, 2010; Viding & Larsson, 2010). In addition, preliminary functional magnetic resonance imaging studies show areas of the brain are active in juveniles who were labeled as psychopaths when performing certain tasks (Salekin, Lee, Schrum Dillard, & Kubak, 2010). Other studies suggest that psychopathic youth may have specific physical brain abnormalities (J. P. Newman, Curtin, Bertsch, & Baskin-Sommers, 2010; Shirtcliff, Vitacco, Gostisha, Merz, & Zahn-Waxler, 2009). However, many scholars remain concerned about the implications of bringing evidence of psychopathy or psychopathic features to the attention of the courts, particularly when it comes to young offenders.

In an important study involving courts, Viljoen, MacDougall, et al. (2010) reviewed 111 American and Canadian cases of adolescent offenders and found that psychopathy evidence is becoming increasingly common and appears to be influential in the decision making of judges, although it was not necessarily a key factor. Evidence of psychopathy or psychopathic features was found in about half the cases. Juveniles whose cases did not indicate psychopathy or psychopathic features received more lenient sentences than those whose cases did. In addition, "psychopathy evidence appeared very influential in some cases, including those in which decisions were made to transfer a youth to adult court or place the youth in an adult jail" (p. 271). According to Viljoen, MacDougall, et al., "psychopathy evidence was commonly used to infer that a youth would be very difficult or impossible to treat" (p. 271).

The Female Psychopath

The study of criminal behavior has traditionally concentrated on men, "as males are overrepresented in the criminal justice system and are significantly more likely to engage in antisocial behavior" (Javdani, Sadeh, & Verona, 2011, p. 1325). Similarly, there are few statistics on the ratio of male to female psychopaths, but it has been generally assumed that males far outnumber their female counterparts. Based on PCL-R data, Salekin, Rogers, and Sewell (1997) reported that the prevalence rate of psychopathy for female offenders in a jail setting was 15.5%, compared to a 25% to 30% prevalence rate estimated for men.

Little research has been conducted on the extent to which psychopathy exists in females. For example, female psychopathic traits in large, culturally diverse, general populations have yet to be fully examined (Neumann et al., 2012). Because the known psychopathic population is dominated by men, little research has been directed at women, but the studies that have been conducted are frequently cited. Salekin, Rogers, Ustad, and Sewell (1998) found, using a PCL-R cutoff score of 29, that 12.9% of their sample of 78 female inmates qualified as psychopaths. In another investigation involving 528 adult women incarcerated in Wisconsin, Vitale, Smith, Brinkley, and Newman (2002) reported that 9% of their participants could be classified as psychopaths, using the recommended cutoff score of 30 on the PCL-R. Some preliminary studies using the PCL-R suggest that female criminal psychopaths may demonstrate different behavioral patterns from those of male criminal psychopaths (Hare, 1991; Vitale et al., 2002).

Female Psychopaths Compared to Male Psychopaths

Based on the limited research that has been done, there appear to be many similarities between male and female psychopaths, but there also may be some differences (Neumann et al., 2012; Verona, Bresin, & Patrick, 2013; Walters, 2014). Early studies reported that female psychopaths might be less aggressive and violent than male psychopaths (Mulder, Wells, Joyce, & Bushnell, 1994). Earlier research also indicated that female psychopaths seemed to recidivate less often than male psychopaths. In fact, the evidence suggested that psychopathic female inmates recidivated at rates that were no different from those reported for non-psychopathic female inmates (Salekin et al., 1998).

However, more recent research reports that—compared to male psychopaths—female psychopaths tend to be more subtle and skillful in their aggression, exploitative relationships, and manipulation of others, which results in their harmful acts going largely unnoticed by the authorities (Kreis & Cooke, 2011). Furthermore, female psychopaths are more likely than male psychopaths to target family, friends, or acquaintances rather than strangers (Nicholls & Petrila, 2005). In contrast, male psychopaths rely on greater use of physical aggression, dominance, and status seeking, which makes their harmful actions more noticeable and more likely to be officially recorded. Kreis and Cooke assert that the incidence of female psychopathy is probably underestimated because of behavioral differences. They write, "Measures (e.g., the PCL-R) that rely strongly on officially recorded criminality and antisocial behavior, and of more male typical presentations of it, are clearly going to miss a great proportion of psychopathic women" (p. 645).

Preliminary evidence further suggests that female psychopaths suffer greater levels of environmental deprivation, victimization, and mental health problems compared to their male counterparts (Hicks et al., 2012; Javdani et al., 2011). These findings may mean that environmental and cultural influences play a greater role in the development of psychopathy in women. The Hicks et al. research also underscores the importance of a complex interaction between genes and the environment in the development of psychopathy. It is clear that research focusing on the potential influences of different cultures and social backgrounds on psychopathic traits would certainly add a deeper understanding of the development of female and male psychopathic behavior.

Racial/Ethnic Differences

Kosson, Smith, and Newman (1990) noticed that most measures of psychopathy have been developed using white inmates as subjects. In their research, they found that psychopathy, as measured by Hare's PCL, exists in black male inmates in a pattern that resembles that of white male inmates. However, Kosson et al. found one important difference: black criminal psychopaths tended to be less impulsive than white criminal psychopaths.

On one hand, this finding raises some questions as to whether the PCL is entirely appropriate to use with African American inmates. On the other hand, Vitale et al. (2002) found no significant racial differences in the scores and distributions of female psychopaths. More specifically, Vitale et al. reported that 10% of the 248 incarcerated white women who participated in their study reached the cutoff scores of 30 or higher on the PCL-R compared to 9% of the 280 incarcerated black women who had similar scores. A meta-analysis by Skeem, Edens, and

Colwell (2003) supports the conclusion that the differences between blacks and whites are minimal. Questions remain, however, as to the potential differences among other racial or ethnic groups.

Some researchers have raised the intriguing and serious issue of whether the stigmatizing diagnosis of psychopathy is likely to be used in a biased manner among minority or disadvantaged groups (Edens, Petrila, & Buffington-Vollum, 2001; Skeem, Edens, & Colwell, 2003; Skeem, Edens, Sanford, & Colwell, 2003). In essence, the consequence of being diagnosed a psychopath is becoming more serious (Skeem, Edens, Sanford, et al., 2003). As pointed out by Skeem, Edens, and Colwell, Canada and the United Kingdom use the diagnosis of psychopathy to support indeterminate detention for certain classes of offenders, and that furthermore,

> There is evidence that psychopathy increasingly is being used as an aggravating factor in the sentencing phase of U.S. death penalty cases, where it has been argued that the presence of these personality traits renders a defendant a "continuing threat to society." (p. 17)

In addition, as we learned earlier, there is concern that a diagnosis of psychopathy may be used to justify decisions to transfer juvenile offenders to the adult criminal justice system, typically based on the assumption that psychopathy is untreatable. Therefore, any differences in psychopathy scores related to race, ethnicity, or age would raise significant criminal justice and public policy issues (Skeem, Edens, & Colwell, 2003). Edens, Petrila, et al. (2001) suggest that perhaps the PCL-R should be excluded from capital sentencing until more solid research on its ability to assess violence risk in minority and disadvantaged individuals is established. It would be wise, therefore, for forensic psychologists to refrain from using diagnostic indicators of psychopathy at the sentencing phase until considerably more research is undertaken.

Treatment and Rehabilitation of Psychopaths

For nearly a century, the treatment and rehabilitation of criminal psychopaths have been shrouded with pessimism and discouragement. The leading researcher on psychopathy, Robert Hare (1996), lamented that, "There is no known treatment for psychopathy" (p. 41). To add to the discouragement, a long list of research projects continually discovered that nothing seemed to work to reduce their violence, criminal recidivism, and antisocial attitudes (Hare et al., 2000). Gacono et al. (2001) concluded from their comprehensive review of the treatment literature that "simply stated, at this time there is no empirical evidence to suggest that psychopathy is treatable" (p. 111). Other studies reported that psychopaths are either completely unresponsive to treatment or play the treatment game well, pretending to cooperate but skillfully "conning" the treatment provider (Bartol & Bartol, 2014). In fact, some researchers (e.g., Rice, Harris, & Cormier, 1992) concluded that inappropriate treatment programs may make psychopathic offenders worse. Others suggested that psychopaths are difficult clients primarily because of their interpersonal and emotional style (Olver & Wong, 2009).

Farrington (2005) probably made the most comprehensive statement when he wrote, it seems to be generally believed that psychopaths are difficult to treat because (a) they are an extreme, qualitatively distinct category; (b) psychopathy is extremely persistent throughout life; (c) psychopathy has biological causes which cannot be changed by psychosocial interventions; and (d) the lying, conning, and manipulativeness of psychopaths make them treatment resistant (pp. 494–495).

Frick, Ray, Thornton, and Kahn (2014) paint an equally bleak picture of the intervention success with children and adolescents with both CD and CU traits. In their review of the research literature, they conclude, several studies of adolescents in the juvenile justice system demonstrated that adolescents with elevated psychopathic or CU traits were less likely to participate in treatment, showed lower rated quality of participation in treatment, showed poorer institutional adjustment, and were more likely to reoffend after treatment than those low on these traits. (p. 42)

Although children and adolescents with a combined CU and CD trait cluster present a true treatment challenge, Frick et al. also contend that if interventions "are tailored to the unique emotional, cognitive, and motivational styles of children and adolescents with CU traits, treatments can reduce their behavior problems" (p. 44).

Other research is beginning to suggest there is hope, and there are some indications that certain psychotherapies could be effective if applied competently and appropriately (Salekin, 2002; Skeem, Monahan, & Mulvey, 2002; Skeem et al., 2003; Wong & Hare, 2005). We discuss this further in Chapter 12. In his review of 42 studies on psychopaths, Salekin found several treatment approaches that appeared effective in reducing the severity of psychopathic attitudes and behavioral patterns. Olver and Wong (2009) report some success with incarcerated psychopathic sex offenders when appropriate treatment programs were applied. Success was measured by sexual and violent recidivism rates, 10 years after the treatment. Olver and Wong concluded, "The results do not support the notion that psychopaths are untreatable or that treatment makes psychopaths worse or more likely to recidivate" (p. 334). It is clear there is encouraging news about the treatment of psychopaths as well as children and adolescents with psychopathic characteristics.

SUMMARY AND CONCLUSIONS

Criminal behavior involves an extremely wide range of human conduct and is committed by individuals of all ages and across all economic circumstances. In this chapter, we have been concerned with that subset of criminal behavior that includes persistent, serious offending over time. Consequently, we have examined early origins of such offending by focusing on developmental factors associated with the antisocial acts of chronic juvenile offenders. To illustrate this developmental perspective, juvenile firesetting behavior was highlighted. In addition, we have examined offending patterns over the life span by focusing on the criminal psychopath.

As a group, juvenile offenders tend to grow out of crime—which is to say, they do not grow up to become chronic adult offenders. From the statistics on juvenile arrests, it is impossible to tell how many different juveniles are involved (as some are arrested more than once) as well as which of these particular juveniles will become long-term offenders. We know from the research that a small percentage (5%–6%) of offenders is responsible for a large proportion of juvenile crime. We know also that chronic offenders do not specialize but rather are involved in a wide variety of offenses. Forensic psychologists attempt to identify those juveniles who are at risk for serious, chronic offending. Psychologists working in juvenile corrections are also involved in providing treatment for these juveniles, a topic we will return to in Chapter 13.

In their attempts to identify juveniles at risk, many psychologists today have adopted developmental or cognitive approaches. Developmental studies—such as those conducted by Terrie Moffitt and her colleagues—suggest that differences in impulsivity, aggressiveness, social skills, and empathy for others can distinguish persistent from nonpersistent offenders. Moffitt's (1993a) dual-pathway hypothesis (LCP vs. AL offenders) has contributed significantly to theory development in this area. Most recently, though, Moffitt as well as other researchers have suggested that more than two developmental pathways are needed.

Research by Steinberg on the adolescent brain has documented that adolescents develop intellectually at a faster pace than emotionally. To a great extent, this explains the typical adolescent's tendency to take risks and make spur-of-the-moment decisions. Although there are individual differences among adolescents, as a general principle this age group is believed by developmental psychologists to be responsible for their behavior, but less responsible than adults. For this reason, Steinberg's research is frequently cited in court decisions that relate to the future of juveniles who have committed criminal acts.

The most recent developmental studies have identified such factors as early exposure to aggressive peers and rejection by peers as contributing to later antisocial conduct. Developmental theory also suggests that conduct disorders, differences in cognitive abilities, and ADHD all play a significant role in facilitating chronic antisocial behavior in children and adolescents. However, they certainly do not "cause" it. Although each of these correlates with delinquency, a cautionary note is necessary. "Deficiencies" in children may well be due to abuse, neglect, or lack of resources or understanding on the part of the adults in their lives. Larger, macro-level variables also must be considered, including neighborhood factors and health challenges, such as those due to environmental toxins. It is unwarranted to focus on behavioral problems in children without attending to their broader social systems.

We discussed in some detail the criminal psychopath, a designation that has been given to a significant minority of adults. Although it is estimated that only 1% of the total adult population would qualify as psychopathic, estimates of the number of imprisoned psychopaths have reached over 15% (although some believe these estimates are inflated). Psychopaths are problematic, not only because of their offending patterns, but also because of their apparent resistance to change. For this reason, a diagnosis of psychopathy may be the "kiss of death" at capital sentencing in those states where future dangerousness is an important consideration as well as at civil commitment proceedings for sexually violent predators. A variety of instruments are offered to measure psychopathy, the most widely known being Robert Hare's (1991) PCL-R. We noted that gender, race, and ethnicity differences in psychopathy are beginning to attract research attention.

Although there is debate over whether the concept of psychopathy can be applied to juveniles, efforts to develop instruments for measuring this construct are robust and ongoing, and the instruments are increasingly being used in clinical practice. However, the concept of juvenile psychopathy—*if such a construct exists*—may have important implications for the prevention of serious delinquency if clinicians can intervene and provide effective treatment. Nevertheless, as in the adult population, psychopathy is likely to be limited to a very small subset of juvenile offenders. Even so, the concerns expressed by many researchers should be very carefully considered. A psychopathic label placed on a juvenile may virtually guarantee his or her transfer to a criminal court.

KEY CONCEPTS

Adolescent-limited offenders (ALs)   242

Antisocial behavior   238

Antisocial personality disorder (APD or ASP)   238

Attention-deficit/hyperactivity disorder (ADHD)   250

Boldness factor   268

Callous-unemotional (CU) traits   271

Conduct disorder (CD)   238

Developmental dual systems model   244

Emotional intelligence   254

Executive functions   257

Factor analysis   266

Firesetting   259

Four-factor perspective   267

Gendered pathways approach   243

Hostile attribution bias   255

Juvenile delinquency   237

Juvenile delinquent   237

Life course–persistent offenders (LCPs)   241

Oppositional defiant disorder (ODD)   250

P-Scan: Research Version   265

Psychopath   261

Psychopathy Checklist: Screening Version (PCL:SV)   264

Psychopathy Checklist: Youth Version (PCL:YV)   265

Psychopathy Checklist-Revised (PCL-R)   264

Self-regulation   257

Social cognition   246

Sociopath   261

Status offenses   237

Triarchic Psychopathy Measure (TriPM)   265

Uniform Crime Reports (UCR)   239

QUESTIONS FOR REVIEW

1. Discuss the differences among legal, social, and psychological definitions of delinquency.

2. What are the main sources of youth crime data?

3. Explain how Moffitt's original dichotomy of juvenile offending has been modified in recent years.

4. What are at least three explanations of ADHD?

5. What are three alternative explanations for the IQ–delinquency connection?

6. What is intelligence? How has Howard Gardner contributed to psychology's understanding of this concept?

7. List Cleckley's behavioral features of the psychopath.

8. State the controversy over labeling juveniles as psychopaths.

 SAGE edge™

Want a better grade? Go to **edge.sagepub.com/bartol5e** for the tools you need to sharpen your study skills. Access practice quizzes, eFlashcards, an action plan, and SAGE journal articles for enhanced learning.

CHAPTER EIGHT

PSYCHOLOGY OF VIOLENCE AND INTIMIDATION

In May 2017, 22 people were killed and scores of others were wounded when a bomb strapped to a 23-year-old man exploded during a concert in Manchester, England. Shortly after that, in June, a van plowed down people on London Bridge and people were stabbed in a nearby bar, leaving seven dead and multiple others wounded.

In August, in Barcelona, Spain, a truck zig-zagged through a plaza milling with people enjoying a sunny day. At least 13 people were killed and at least 80 were injured. In Charlottesville, Virginia, also in August, a car driven by a white supremacist careened through a crowd of people protesting racism—one woman was killed and many were wounded. In New York City, a rental truck sped down a bicycle path on Halloween, killing 8 and injuring many bikers and pedestrians. The assailant allegedly planned his attack for a year.

A mass shooting at an outdoor concert venue in Las Vegas, Nevada, on October 1, 2017, left 58 people dead and more than 500 injured. The gunman opened fire from a hotel suite high above the concert.

Ninety-eight percent of video games rated for teens have violent content, and 64% of those rated for everyone have violent content (Calvert et al., 2017).

Violence terrifies us, angers us, fascinates us, and entertains us. Although we are concerned about perceived increases in violent crime rates and fearful of becoming victims of violence, we also support images and depictions of violent activity in the entertainment media and often demand such details in the news media. Real incidents of violent crime like those described above are reported and replayed extensively by the news media, but they should be, because they are in the public interest. We need to be told when there is violence, just as we need to be told when public figures behave badly. Interestingly, violence is somewhat difficult to define, precisely because it has so many meanings and conjures up such a broad spectrum of images (G. Newman, 1979). Moreover, it occurs in many situations and under a wide variety of conditions, and there are numerous explanations for why it occurs.

Violence is commonly defined as *physical* force exerted for the purpose of inflicting injury, pain, discomfort, or abuse on a person or persons or for the purpose of damaging or destroying property. Such physical force, however, may be condoned by society. We allow police

Chapter Objectives

- Introduce the reader to the statistical and research data on violent crime.

- Assess the psychological effects of violent media and electronic video games on aggressive behavior.

- Describe threat assessment and school violence.

- Examine the research and clinical data on criminal homicide, including multiple murder and serial killers.

- Review the psychological factors involved in workplace violence.

- Review the demographic and psychological aspects involved in hate and bias crimes.

- Review the psychological trauma and potential violence of being stalked, bullied, or cyberbullied.

- Cover the key aspects of traditional bullying and modern cyberbullying.

to use reasonable force against an individual resisting arrest, a football player to tackle his opponent, a soldier to kill his or her enemy, and crime victims to protect themselves from serious bodily harm. It is the violence committed without justification that we are concerned with in this chapter, specifically criminal violence.

It should be noted that *violence* and *aggression* are not interchangeable terms. Whereas violence involves physical force, aggression may or may not involve such force. ***Aggression*** can be defined as behavior perpetrated or attempted with the intention of harming another individual (or group of individuals) physically or psychologically. A protester who blocks someone's entry into a business that allegedly discriminates against a racial or ethnic group is performing an aggressive act, not a violent act. Even though we may agree with the protester's action as a matter of principle, it is still aggressive. Likewise, refusing to speak to someone who has insulted you in the past is an aggressive act, not a violent act. It would qualify as what psychologists call "passive aggression." Thus, all violent behavior is aggressive, but not all aggressive behavior is violent. Although the concept of aggression has been studied extensively by psychologists, we are concerned primarily in this chapter with the subset that is violent behavior. Nevertheless, nonviolent aggression will also have its place, particularly when we discuss crimes of intimidation.

Two increasingly interconnected streams of research on violence have emerged in recent years. One research stream has examined the many characteristics and demographics of the individual violent offender; the other has examined the immediate contexts and environments in which violence most often occurs (Hawkins, 2003). Studies focusing on the former have examined the social, psychological, and biological factors in interpersonal offending. Studies in the latter tradition have examined family, peer, local community, and neighborhood effects on varying levels of violence. Each area of research has recognized the importance of the other. That is, researchers acknowledge that both individual factors and environmental influences must be taken into account in their efforts to understand violence. Research has shown, for example, that the relationships among racial/ethnic composition; feelings of anger, resentment, and frustration; and homicide rates are contingent—at least in part—on the level of economic deprivation, joblessness, drug use, and number of gangs within a given community (C. C. Johnson & Chanhatasilpa, 2003).

Forensic psychologists frequently encounter violence—as well as aggression in general—sometimes even on a daily basis. Their clients may threaten to harm others. They may be asked to assess the risk of violence in a given individual. They may themselves be placed at risk of violence. In a court setting, they may be asked to testify about the effects of violence on a victim of a crime or a plaintiff in a civil suit. Therefore, an understanding of the prevalence, causes, and effects of violence is critical for forensic psychologists.

We will begin this chapter with data on violent crime, including information on gender and race/ethnic differences. This will be followed by a discussion of theoretical perspectives on violence offered by research psychologists. Efforts to prevent violence from occurring are covered in a section on threat assessment, which is different from the risk assessment enterprise discussed in previous chapters. Closely related to threat assessment is the topic of school violence, of intense interest to mental health practitioners as well as the public in general. We will

▶ **Photo 8.1** Former congresswoman Gabrielle Giffords, who was shot in the head in 2011 while meeting with her constituents, speaks at a "Not One More" Event in 2015 along with her husband, Captain Mark Kelly.
Source: Monica Schipper/ Getty Images.

then focus on the specific violent crimes of homicide and workplace violence. The chapter ends with a discussion of crimes of intimidation, which represent a form of aggression that may or may not result in violence but produce fear in the victims.

UCR DATA ON VIOLENT CRIME

In the Uniform Crime Reporting System (UCR), as discussed in the previous chapter, the four violent crimes are murder and nonnegligent manslaughter, rape, robbery, and aggravated assault. Together, reports of these crimes comprise the violent crime rate provided annually to the public (see Figure 8.1 for trends in violent crime). In addition, arrest data on the above crimes as well as simple assault are also provided. According to the UCR (FBI, 2016a), aggravated assault accounted for the largest share of violent crimes known to police (approximately 74%) in 2015 in the United States, and murder accounted for the smallest share (approximately 1.3%) (see Figure 8.2). Personal weapons, such as hands, fists, and feet, were used in 4.6% of the homicides committed in 2015; firearms in 71.4%; and knives or cutting instruments in 11.4% of the incidents. Other dangerous weapons were used in the remaining 12.6% of the offenses.

Gun deaths in the United States are a disturbing reality that remains unaddressed by meaningful legislation on gun safety and control. Every year, approximately 31,000 deaths occur, and there are 78,000 nonfatal injuries attributed to guns (Centers for Disease Control and Prevention [CDC], 2013). Although not all of the deaths are the result of criminal offenses—some are accidental deaths or shootings, suicides or attempted suicides, or instances of self-defense—the vast majority represent criminal activity. We should note that firearms-related homicides declined 39% between 1993 and 2011, and nonfatal firearm crimes declined 69% during the same period (Planty & Truman, 2013). However, the majority of these declines occurred between 1993 and 2002. The number of firearm homicides increased between 1999

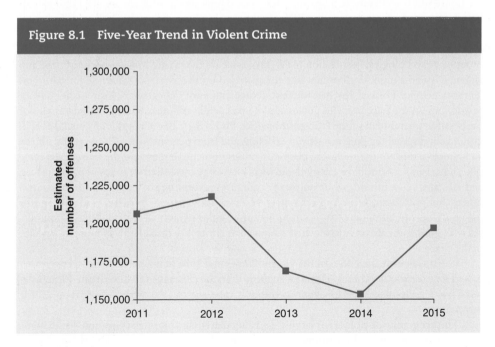

Figure 8.1 Five-Year Trend in Violent Crime

Source: FBI (2016a).

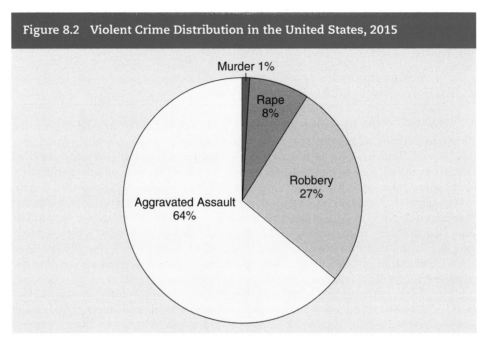

Figure 8.2   Violent Crime Distribution in the United States, 2015

Murder 1%

Rape 8%

Robbery 27%

Aggravated Assault 64%

Source: FBI (2016a).

and 2006. According to a recent government report, although the number of firearms crimes has declined over time, the percentage of *all* violence involving a firearm has not changed substantively. In 1993, an estimated 9% of all violence was committed with a firearm; in 2011, the figure was 8% (Planty & Truman, 2013). Handguns account for the greatest majority of both fatal and nonfatal incidents—70% of all homicides and just under 10% of all nonfatal violent crime.

Clearly, firearms-related crime remains a huge problem in the United States. In 2014, an American Psychological Association (APA) task force on the prediction and prevention of gun violence issued a number of policy statements based on the available scientific literature on gun violence (see Focus 8.1). Over the past decade, numerous efforts have been made to place restrictions on the purchase and possession of guns, while still maintaining the guarantees of the Second Amendment of the Constitution. (See Photo 8.1.) These restrictions include background checks, keeping guns away from ex-felons and from persons with serious mental illness, and gun-free safe zones in schools, hospitals, entertainment venues, and the like. At the same time, however, 12 states allow licensed gun owners to carry concealed weapons in public places, and 10 states allow this on public university campuses (excepting stadiums and administrative offices, but not classrooms). Approximately 40 states allow people to carry handguns and/or long guns openly, although some restrictions apply. Although not all violent crime is committed with guns, guns are often associated with violent crime. We discuss this in more detail later in the chapter.

In 2015, an estimated 46% of the violent crimes and 19% of property crimes were cleared by arrest or some other means. During that same year, the clearance (or solved) rate for murder was 62%. The clearance rates for aggravated assault, rape, and robbery were 54%, 38%, and 29%, respectively.

The geography of violence is largely distributed across two primary locations—the home and the street. Additional locations—for example, schools, bars, places of work—comprise smaller percentages of violence. Until recently, much of the emphasis on stopping violent crimes has been directed at the more visible street crimes and less at violence within the home.

Street crimes are far more likely to come to the attention of police and thus more likely to be represented in official statistics. However, women and children are more likely to be harmed by violence in their homes and by people they know than by strangers on the street. Thus, both researchers and law enforcement officials have given increasing attention to studying, preventing, and responding to this category of violent crime. Workplace and school violence also are drawing more attention, as we discuss later in this chapter.

GENDER, RACE, AND ETHNIC DIFFERENCES IN CRIMINAL VIOLENCE

UCR data consistently indicate that males account for 80% to 90% of total arrests for violent crimes in any given year. Males account for about 89% of the annual arrests for murder (FBI, 2016a). This 9:1 ratio is characteristic of other countries as well. Arrest rates for aggravated

FOCUS 8.1. EXPERT REPORT ON GUN VIOLENCE

In December 2013, the APA released a policy report on gun violence, prepared by a panel of experts including clinicians; professors of psychology, public health, pediatrics, and public policy; and representatives from private and public foundations. The complete report is available at http://www.apa.org/pubs/info/reports/gun-violence-prevention.aspx.

Following are some high points and recommendations of the report, adapted from its summary:

- No single profile can reliably predict who will use a gun in a violent act.
- Prevention is most effective at the community level, when the community is engaged in collective problem solving.
- Males in particular face gendered expectations that emphasize self-sufficiency, toughness, and violence. Knowledge of developmental psychologists must be used to change these expectations.
- Training police in crisis intervention and training community members in mental health first aid has shown success; more such community programs should be considered.
- Public health messaging campaigns on safe gun storage are needed.
- Depressed individuals or those with severe mental illness are more likely to commit suicide with a gun than to commit homicide with a gun.
- Most mentally ill individuals are not dangerous, but for those at risk for violence, mental health treatment can often prevent gun violence; at

present, access to mental health services in the United States is woefully inadequate.
- Firearms prohibitions for high-risk groups have been shown to reduce violence. High-risk groups include domestic violence offenders, persons convicted of violent misdemeanor crimes, and those with mental illness who have been adjudicated as being a threat to themselves or others.
- Threat assessment teams in schools, the workplace, and government agencies are a crucial component in preventing violence and intervening to assist a person posing a threat of violence or self-harm.
- Additional policies to reduce gun violence include licensing of handgun purchases, background-check requirements for all gun sales, and close oversight of retail gun sellers.

Questions for Discussion

1. What would you add to the above list? Is any important context or policy missing?
2. Comment on the above points from the perspective of (a) a mental health professional, (b) a law enforcement officer, (c) a person who says he owns guns primarily for sport, and (d) a person who says she owns a gun primarily for protection.
3. In the past few years, terrorists—including domestic terrorists—have used vehicles as weapons to kill or injure large numbers of people. Assuming you agree that some restrictions on guns are reasonable, should there be similar restrictions on vehicle ownership?

assault are slightly different, with 77% male and 23% female. Although women's violent crime rate increased faster than the men's rate for a brief period in the mid-1990s, women continue to be far underrepresented in the violent crime statistics. The two dominant explanations for the gender discrepancies in violent offending are (1) socialization factors (the fact that women are less likely than men to be encouraged to be violent) and (2) biological factors (with some researchers linking the male hormone testosterone to aggression).

Women also are said to have less opportunity to commit the violent street crimes that come to the attention of police. Thus, some theorists have suggested that violence perpetrated by women may go undetected and unreported because it is more likely to occur in the privacy of the home. Even if this were so, it would be unlikely to narrow the gender gap in violent offending because much male violence in the home also goes undetected and unreported. As noted in the APA panel report highlighted above, males are often encouraged to adhere to stereotypical masculinity, which includes risk taking, use of aggression, and toughness.

Although gender differences in violent offending have garnered some interest, it is racial and ethnic differences that have produced the most commentary. Race differences in crime and violence remain emotionally and politically charged, divisive topics in the United States and in many other societies around the world (Hawkins, 2003). National surveys conducted in the United States, for example, suggest that a majority of white respondents believe blacks and Latinos are more prone (innately and culturally) to violence than whites or Asians (Bobo & Kluegel, 1997; Unnever & Cullen, 2012). These beliefs demonstrate the continual existence of stereotypes as misguided explanations of criminal violence in the United States.

Official crime data can be partly blamed for perpetrating these stereotypes. According to these data, African Americans in the United States are involved in criminal homicide and other forms of violence at a rate that far exceeds their numbers in the general population. For example, although African Americans make up about 13.5% of the U.S. population, they accounted for more than 50% of all arrests for murder in 2015 (FBI, 2016a). These statistics hold for both adult and juvenile black Americans. These figures reflect social inequalities such as lack of employment and educational opportunities, racial oppression in its many forms, discriminatory treatment at the hands of the criminal justice system, and law enforcement practices in geographical areas where many African Americans reside. It is extremely important to emphasize that race or ethnic differences in violent crime are *not* due to genetic or biological factors, such as racial differences in innate aggressive traits. As we shall see shortly, researchers have explored and sometimes uncovered links between biology and aggression, but these links are not racially or ethnically connected.

Latinos are now the largest ethnic minority group in the United States. The Latino population in the United States more than doubled between 1980 and 2000 but in recent years has shown a decrease in growth rate. The U.S. Latino population reached 57 million in 2015 (U.S. Census Bureau, 2016) but a drop-off in immigration and a declining birth rate among Hispanic women has lowered the overall growth rate of Hispanics in the United States (Krogstad, 2016). As of 2015, California had the largest Hispanic population of any state (15.2 million).

Shihadeh and Barranco (2010) assert that it is a mistake to characterize Latino communities as one undifferentiated group. They point out that some Latino communities have changed in recent years in ways that encourage more crime, including violent crime. For example, years ago Latino migrants were more likely to settle in large Latino communities where they were protected by a shell of common culture and language. Today, Latino migrants are more likely to venture into new, less established communities that are more isolated from their culture and language. This recent shift in migration patterns may lead to higher rates of crime and violence among some sectors of the Latino population. Still, much more research needs to be undertaken before meaningful conclusions about the relationship between violence and Latino ethnicity can be advanced.

Interestingly, research findings from industrialized nations across the globe do not lend themselves to simple explanations for the different rates of violence among groups, cultures, or subcultures. "Group differences in rates of crime and violence observed in those areas of the world do not appear to be easily explained by traditional notions of minority versus majority, white versus nonwhite, and possibly economically disadvantaged versus advantaged" (Hawkins, 2003, p. xxiii).

Furthermore, we must be careful not to focus exclusively on any one racial or ethnic group, to the exclusion of others. Although great attention has been paid to the street crimes of black males, the research microscope has ignored other groups. Researchers do not generally focus on whites as a separate group, despite the fact that violence among whites occurs regularly. Researchers do filter out other racial and ethnic groups, however. There is an indication, for example, that intimate partner and family violence may be far more prevalent among Asian Americans than among other ethnic groups. In the National Violence Against Women Survey, 25% of Asian women indicated they had been physically or sexually assaulted by family members or intimates (M. Lee, 2002). Overall, many puzzles remain in any attempts to explain the ethnic and racial distribution of violence and its changes over time (Hawkins, 2003). In addressing that distribution, participation of whites should not be ignored. Furthermore, as society increasingly becomes multiracial and multiethnic, it will difficult to justify placing people in racial or ethnic categories.

In addition, more research needs to be conducted across a variety of settings and environments. Using simple categories such as black, Latino/Hispanic, Asian, Native American, Middle Eastern, and white does not truly capture the multiethnic mixture characteristics of communities across the nation. Cultures and subcultures are complex and psychologically rich, and meaningful research investigations on ethnic/minority differences in violence require a deep appreciation of this complexity.

Practicing forensic psychologists must become highly knowledgeable about the beliefs, attitudes, values, traditions, and expected behaviors of each ethnic or racial group or subculture with which they interact if they are to be effective and helpful to offenders and their victims. **Ethnocentrism**, or viewing others strictly through one's own cultural perspectives, often encourages people—including mental health professionals—to form stereotypes and biases that limit their ability to assess and treat those from diverse backgrounds (Feindler, Rathus, & Silver, 2003).

THEORETICAL PERSPECTIVES ON VIOLENCE

Criminal violence can be classified along several continuums. For example, one continuum can represent the amount of planning involved in the act. At one pole, the act is highly calculated and planned (cold-blooded), but at the other pole, the act can be characterized as highly impulsive and emotionally driven behavior with virtually no planning (e.g., crimes of passion). In psychological literature, violence may represent different forms of aggression, ranging from instrumental to reactive, with equal elements of both occurring at the middle sections of the continuum. **Instrumental violence** "occurs when the injury of an individual is secondary to the acquisition of some other external goal" (Woodworth & Porter, 2002, p. 437). The external goal may be money, status, security, or material goods. **Reactive violence**—also called **expressive violence**—refers to physical violence precipitated by a hostile and angry reaction to a perceived threat or dangerous situation. Reactive violence, therefore, "is often the impulsive and unthoughtful response to a provocation, real or imagined" (American Psychological Association [APA], 1996, p. 8). An angry person who "flies off the handle" and shoots a friend over a petty argument represents an obvious example. More often than not, the aggressor—once the emotions calm down—cannot believe what he or she did or understand how he or she could lose control to that level. In many cases, though, it is difficult to clearly differentiate whether the violence is instrumental or reactive—it often appears to include some mixture of both instrumental and reactive factors. Consequently, violent actions often fall in the middle ranges of the instrumental–reactive continuum, similar to what is found in the normal curve.

An interesting question emerges when we examine these two polar opposites on the violence continuum in reference to the criminal psychopaths discussed in Chapter 7: Are they more likely to commit instrumental or reactive forms of violence? Recall that psychopaths demonstrate a lack of empathy or remorse and have shallow emotions in general. However, they are also impulsive and highly reactive to provocative situations. Woodworth and Porter (2002) have initiated some research into this area by studying both psychopathic and non-psychopathic offenders who committed homicide. According to these researchers, psychopaths tend to engage in the more instrumental, goal-driven (e.g., to obtain money or drugs) homicides, whereas non-psychopathic offenders engage in predominately reactive, spontaneous violence (e.g., in the context of a heated argument). Psychopaths who murdered were primarily motivated to advance their own cause and exhibited little empathy or concern for their victims. Woodworth and Porter were surprised, though, at the overall level of instrumental violence characterizing *all* homicides, whether committed by psychopaths or non-psychopaths. The majority of the offenders did not simply "snap" and kill their victims in an uncontrollable emotional rage. The researchers suggest that future study should examine whether the results might generalize to other types of criminal violence and offenders.

The Causes of Violence

The causes of violence are multiple and complex. The psychological literature usually divides these causes into four highly overlapping categories: (1) neurobiological, (2) socialization, (3) cognitive, and (4) situational factors. It is important to stress that they are overlapping, because contemporary research on criminal behavior increasingly takes a developmental perspective, as indicated in Chapter 7. Moreover, scholars from different perspectives, even from different disciplines, collaborate to study violence and other social problems.

Neurobiological Factors

The neurobiological factors refer to a wide array of neurological and neurochemical influences on the brain during the life course that may result in high levels of aggressive and violent behavior. Recent advances in the neurosciences have revealed links between violence and brain damage or dysfunction resulting from a variety of environmental risk factors (Hubbs-Tait, Nation, Krebs, & Bellinger, 2005; Raine, 2013). Among the more prominent environmental risk factors are the neurotoxins. "Neurotoxins are trace elements, pesticides, chemicals, and biological elements that have toxic effects on the human nervous system" (Hubbs-Tait et al., 2005, p. 58). Examples of neurotoxins are lead, cadmium, and manganese, all of which are trace elements found in the environment. Neurotoxins have the potential of producing neurocognitive dysfunction which predisposes individuals to engage in antisocial behavior and violence (Raine, 2013).

Malnutrition may also significantly affect the neurodevelopment of the brain. It is estimated that malnutrition affects the neurodevelopment of 167.2 million preschool children worldwide (Waber et al., 2014). Several studies have indicated that prenatal and early childhood malnutrition "is associated with adverse outcomes in school-aged children and adolescents, including an increased prevalence of conduct problems and aggressive behaviors" (Galler et al., 2012, p. 239). Galler and her associates found that the conduct problems and aggressive behavior were significantly elevated in adolescence, despite improvements in diet during infancy.

Alcohol, drug ingestion, and tobacco use by the mother adversely affects critical fetal development. Traumatic head injury as a result of child abuse or accident may also be a contributing factor, especially if the injury occurs in the frontal cortex region.

The best approach, of course, is to prevent these from occurring in the first place. Once the deficits do occur, attempts to remove or remedy the neurobiological problems may include neurological intervention in the form of medication. However, and equally important, a supportive and competent social environment has been found to neutralize or mitigate the effects of these neurobiological factors on any propensity toward violence. As Adrian Raine (2013), one of the leading researchers on the relationship between brain damage and violence writes, "I want to stress that social factors are critical both in interacting with biological forces in causing crime, and in directly producing the biological changes that predispose a person to violence" (p. 9).

Socialization Factors

Socialization factors refer to those processes through which a person learns patterns of thinking, behavior, and feeling from his or her early life experiences (APA, 1996). More specifically, according to the American Psychological Association, "Scientists use the term socialization to describe the process by which a child learns the 'scripts' for specific social behavior, along with the rules, attitudes, values, and norms that guide interactions with others" (p. 3). Furthermore, children can learn as much from observing significant or admired others in their environment as from their own experiences. Considerable research indicates that aggressive, antisocial, and violent behaviors are often learned from significant others (including TV, movie, on-line, or fictional characters) and are held in reserve for response to specific social situations. This is a good argument for limiting young children's exposure to violent media images, a topic that will be addressed shortly.

Cognitive Factors

Cognitive factors refer to the ideas, beliefs, and patterns of thinking that emerge as a result of interactions with the world during a person's lifetime. Research has revealed that violent individuals have different ways of processing and interpreting that information. "They tend to perceive hostility in others when there is no hostility" (APA, 1996, p. 5). As you may recall from Chapter 7, this notable tendency is referred to as *hostile attribution bias*. Violent people are also less efficient at thinking of nonviolent ways to solve social conflicts and disagreements. They also tend to be more accepting of violence in general. Some young males—especially members of violent peer groups or gangs—have adopted the belief that it is acceptable to react to every perceived or imagined sign of disrespect with aggression. Simply put, aggressive children and adolescents have more antisocial, violent beliefs than their nonaggressive peers (Shahinfar, Kupersmidt, & Matza, 2001).

Situational Factors

Situational factors refer to the characteristics of the environment, such as stress or aggression in others, that encourage or engender violent behavior. As pointed out by many researchers, "Often we seek the causes of violence in the person and ignore the contributing effects of the situation" (APA, 1996, p. 6). Almost any aversive situation—such as excessive heat, continuous loud noise, or crowded living conditions—can provoke aggression and violence in those persons submitted to such conditions. Neighborhoods, schools, family, and peers can all be conducive to the development of violent behavior. The presence of weapons increases the chances that the conflict will occur in the first place and that it will have lethal consequences once it does (see Focus 8.2 dealing with gun-related legislation).

It is also clear that children who grow up in deprived environments where poverty, frustration, and hopelessness are prevalent are at much greater risk for later involvement in violence than other children, although most children growing up under these conditions do not

FOCUS 8.2. STAND YOUR GROUND, OPEN CARRY, AND CONCEALED CARRY LAWS: DO THEY ENCOURAGE OR DISCOURAGE VIOLENCE?

In the early 21st century, several high-profile incidents in the news focused public attention on laws allowing people to use force, including deadly force, in the face of a perceived threat of bodily harm. Known collectively as "stand your ground" laws, they differ from traditional self-defense laws—some call them expanded self-defense.

At about the same time, attention was given to laws—some long standing, some newly passed—that allowed people to carry guns, including handguns, openly on public streets. The laws varied considerably across states and communities. For example, many laws banned *open* carry, but allowed people to carry *concealed* weapons on their persons if they have a license to do so. At this writing, the carrying of concealed weapons on one's person by someone other than law enforcement is permitted in approximately 12 states, and some of these have extended this to public colleges and universities, as noted in the text.

Self-defense is a recognized justification for killing another person, but stand your ground laws go beyond the traditional law of self-defense. Self-defense laws allow (a) a reasonable person, (b) being somewhere he or she has a right to be, (c) perceiving himself or herself in immediate danger of grave bodily harm, (d) to use force against an aggressor. However, self-defense laws often say the force used may not be disproportionate to the threat. They also generally expect that one will flee if one can do so. The exception in many states is the so-called "castle doctrine," which states there is no obligation to retreat if one is in one's own home, office, or similar location. The state of Florida passed the nation's first stand your ground law in 2005. Approximately 15 other states now have similar laws. As the name implies, what they have in common is that they carry no responsibility to flee. They also allow disproportionate force to be used.

Critics of stand your ground laws, open carry legislation, and concealed carry licenses argue, among other things, that they encourage violence and lead to the death of innocent people. In addition, they promote an armed society by encouraging people to purchase and carry weapons, and gun violence in our society is already too high. Supporters of the laws say, again among other things, that they discourage additional violence because potential aggressors never know when someone else is carrying a weapon and is ready to use it. Some also say the traditional law of self-defense does not go far enough, because fleeing the scene is unrealistic. However, it is important to stress that the traditional law of self-defense requires a duty to flee only if one is able to do so.

Advocates of gun control legislation are persistent in their efforts to promote gun safety and place reasonable restrictions on ownership. Legal restrictions on the purchase of weapons, background checks, gun buy-back programs, education, and alternatives to violence programs have all been tried, with varying degrees of success. Powerful lobbying groups such as the NRA strongly resist many of these measures, although ironically gun owners as a group are said to support background checks and safety education. Since the *Heller* decision (2008) which reified the Second Amendment's guarantee of the right to bear arms as a personal guarantee, the Supreme Court has been reluctant to expand the right (such as by extending it outside one's home). In June 2017, the Court announced that it would not hear a case, *Peruta v. California*, that would address the question of whether the individual constitutional right to bear arms announced in *Heller* applies equally on public streets.

Questions for Discussion

1. If the law already recognizes self-defense and defense of others as a justification for harming another individual, why is a stand your ground law needed?
2. Under traditional self-defense law, one is not expected to try to flee if in one's own home. In some states, this includes one's office or place of business. Where should the line be drawn? What about in the home of a friend? At school? In one's car?
3. Should college and university students be allowed to carry concealed weapons on campus if they have the necessary permits? If so, should this be prohibited in certain areas? Administrative buildings? Classrooms? The football stadium? Dining halls? Residence halls?
4. Review the laws on gun purchases and ownership in your state or local community. Who is allowed to buy guns, carry guns, and where are guns allowed? Are there restrictions on where guns are allowed?

follow a destructive path. Childhood aggression can predict adult violence in some individuals, though. Research has discovered that approximately 10% of highly aggressive children grow up to account for 50% to 60% of the majority of violent crimes (Bartol & Bartol, 2011). During their childhood, these individuals exhibit aggression, disobedience, and disruptions at home and in school; are disliked and avoided by peers; are neglected by parents and teachers; and are likely to fail in school, eventually dropping out. Unsupervised and susceptible to the pernicious influence of other delinquent youth, they grow up to be antisocial, aggressive, and sometimes violent young adults. They are likely to become involved in abusive spousal relationships, and they often abuse their own children.

Despite the complexity and multitude of causes, human violence is ultimately a learned behavior. Because it is learned, it can be unlearned or altered, or conditions can be changed so that it is not learned in the first place. Furthermore, violence is a behavior that is acquired early in life—in many cases, *very* early. Consequently, prevention of violence should likewise begin very early in life.

THE EFFECTS OF VIOLENT MEDIA

Over the past 40 years, a significant amount of research literature has strongly supported the observation that media violence viewing is one factor contributing to the development of aggression and violence (Bushman & Huesmann, 2012; Huesmann, Moise-Titus, Podolski, & Eron, 2003). The majority of the research has focused on the effects of watching dramatic violence on TV, video, and film. A wide variety of research projects have continually arrived at the same fundamental conclusion: Exposure to dramatic violence on TV, other media, and in the movies is related to violent behavior. In addition to the hundreds of research findings, three major national studies have concluded that *heavy* exposure to media violence is one of the most significant causes of violence in society (APA, 2003c). They include the Surgeon General's Commission Report (Surgeon General's Scientific Advisory Committee on Television and Social Behavior, 1972), the National Institutes of Mental Health's (1982) 10-year follow-up study on "Television and Behavior," and the American Psychological Association's Task Force on Television in Society (1992). According to the APA (2003c), these reports indicate that viewing a steady diet of violence on the screen has the following negative effects:

- It increases the viewer's fear of becoming a victim, with a corresponding increase in self-protective behaviors and increased distrust of others.

- It desensitizes the viewer to violence. That is, viewers often become less sensitive to the pain and suffering of others.

- It encourages some individuals to become more involved in violent actions.

- It demonstrates how desired goods and services can be obtained through the use of aggression and violence.

- Sexual violence in X- and R-rated films has been shown to increase sexual aggression in some males.

It is important to distinguish between short-term and long-term effects of media on aggressive behavior and violence. Long-term effects occur as a result of learning and storing violent and aggressive material in the cognitive system that eventually "crystallizes" and is difficult to change as the child gets older. Young children are especially open to new learning, and these experiences often have a greater impact during the early developmental years than learning events that occur during adulthood. Moreover,

In recent theorizing, long-term relations have been ascribed mainly to acquisition through observational learning of three social-cognitive structures: schemas about a hostile world, scripts for social problem solving that focus on aggression, and normative beliefs that aggression is acceptable. (Huesmann et al., 2003, p. 201)

Observational learning refers to the very strong tendency of human beings to imitate any significant or admired person or model they observe. Children are especially prone to doing this. Consequently, observation of specific aggressive behaviors around them increases children's likelihood of behaving exactly that way. Over time and with frequent exposure to aggressive behavior, children develop beliefs (schemas) that the world is basically a hostile place, that aggression is an acceptable social behavior, and that the best way to solve conflicts and to get things is to be aggressive.

Huesmann and his colleagues (2003) found strong long-term effects of media violence observed in early childhood that carried over into adulthood:

Overall, these results suggest that both males and females from all social strata and all levels of initial aggressiveness are placed at increased risk for the development of adult aggressive and violent behavior when they view a high and steady diet of violent TV shows in early childhood. (p. 218)

Media violence encourages, stimulates, and reinforces aggressive behavior. Furthermore, aggressive children tend to enjoy aggressive media. Huesmann et al. (2003) suggest that "aggressive children feel happier and more justified if they believe they are not alone in their aggression, and view media violence to make them feel happier because it convinces them that they are not alone" (p. 202). The authors also posit that media violence appears to have *short-term* effects on adults, but the real *long-term* effects seem to occur only with children. The effects are not only found in children who are already violence prone, but also in almost all children.

In addition, the Huesmann et al. (2003) study found that violent films, TV programs, and other media that have the most deleterious effects on children are not always the ones that adults and critics perceive as most violent. What type of scene is the most deleterious to children? "It is one in which the child identifies with the perpetrator of the violence, the child perceives the scene as telling about life like it is, and the perpetrator is rewarded for the violence"(p. 218). In other words, violent media that portray an admired perpetrator as successful through the use of violence appear to have a greater impact on the child's observational learning of aggression and violence over the long haul. The researchers suggest that the easiest way to reduce the effects of media violence on children is to restrict children's exposure to such violence. The persons in the best position to do this, particularly with young children, are parents or caretakers.

Violent Video and Electronic Games

Young people today are growing up in a media-saturated environment. In fact, some scholars refer to this generation as "born digital" (Palfrey & Gasser, 2008). The earliest investigations of video game play in the United States indicated that 97% of adolescents (ages 12–17) played computer, Web, tablet, cell phone, or console video games (Lenhart et al., 2008; Willoughby, Adachi, & Good, 2012). Ninety-nine percent of boys and 94% of girls played the games (Lenhart et al., 2008). Furthermore, as cited at the beginning of the chapter, 98% of the games rated for teens have violent content, and 64% of those rated for everyone had such content. Early surveys also revealed that approximately half of the adolescents played video games on a mobile device, such as a cell phone, i-Pad, or other handheld system, which is not entirely surprising considering that the year 2007 marked the "explosion" of mobile technological devices (Friedman, 2016). Prior to the digital explosion of 2007, surveys estimated that the average youth observed more than 100,000 violent episodes and some 20,000 murders on television before reaching adolescence.

Virtually everyone reading this textbook has likely played video games, some perhaps for hours at a time. Many of you have played *violent* video games. Has that made you more violent? Has it desensitized you to the effects of violence? Has it caused you serious psychological harm? Some predicted that the U.S. Supreme Court would address this last question, when it announced its decision in *Brown v. Entertainment Merchants Association* (2011). The case involved a California law passed in 2005 banning the sale of violent video games to children under 18 and imposing a $1,000 fine on any retailer caught doing so. The games in question were those that depicted killing, maiming, dismembering, or sexually assaulting the image of a human. However, the California Supreme Court struck down the law in 2009, stating there was no conclusive evidence that these games seriously harmed children. The U.S. Supreme Court agreed, noting that research on the effects of exposure to such violence was equivocal. The Court supported the First Amendment right of the Entertainment Merchants Association to distribute their products and refused to allow a fine on retailers who sold them.

The effect of violent video games on violence became a serious topic for study after a series of school shootings that occurred during the late 1990s. The shooters in these cases were often students who habitually played violent video games. For example, Eric Harris and Dylan Klebold, the Columbine (Colorado) High School students who murdered 13 persons and wounded 23 before killing themselves, were fascinated with the bloody video game *Doom*, one of the earliest and most successful of all violent video games. "Harris created a customized version of Doom with two shooters, extra weapons, unlimited ammunition, and victims could not fight back—features that are eerily similar to aspects of the actual shootings" (C. A. Anderson & Bushman, 2001, p. 353).

A comprehensive report by a task force assigned by the American Psychological Association to assess the impact of violent video games (Calvert et al., 2017) is revealing. The 10-member task force reviewed all relevant and methodologically sound studies on the topic through 2013. Its conclusions are sobering. Exposure to violent video games was associated with increased aggressive behavior, cognitions, affect, desensitization, and decreased empathy. Even controlling for other risk factors (e.g., poor academic achievement, parental conflict, exposure to deviant peers), exposure to violent video games was considered a robust risk factor for aggressive outcomes. Nevertheless, the task force could not conclude that there was a direct link between violent video games and either delinquency or adult crime because there was insufficient research addressing this specific question. Also needed is research specifically focusing on gender, ethnic, and socioeconomic groups, as well as research examining features of the games (e.g., plots), the player's perspective, and the player's motivations for playing the games. This important task force report (Calvert et al., 2017) merits careful study by anyone interested in this topic.

The overwhelming majority of people who play video games today, including violent games, do not commit acts of violence. Nevertheless, the Calvert et al. report suggests that the games have an overall negative effect on many users. Some research still indicates they may have a particularly negative effect on individuals who are already violence prone (e.g., as a result of witnessing violence in their homes or having exhibited violent behavior in the past). This leads us to topics that are of great interest to forensic psychologists today, specifically, threat assessment and school and workplace violence.

THREAT ASSESSMENT

"A threat is an expression of intent to do harm or act out violently against someone or something. A threat can be spoken, written, or symbolic—for example, motioning with one's hands as though shooting at another person" (O'Toole, 2000, p. 6). **Threat assessment** is concerned with predicting future violence or other undesirable actions targeted at specific individuals or institutions after an expressed threat has been communicated (Bartol & Bartol, 2013). Forensic psychologists engaged in threat assessment work, however, often add that their focus is more on preventing violence than on predicting it. According to Dewey Cornell (cited in A. Miller, 2014,

p. 40), "We don't intervene because we predict someone is dangerous, we want to intervene because they're troubled or there's conflict or people are worried about them." Put another way, threat assessment aims to interrupt people on a pathway to commit violence (Meloy, cited in A. Miller, 2014). Recall also that the APA (2013a) panel on gun violence highlighted the fact that threat assessments in schools, the workplace, and government agencies were crucial to preventing violence in those environments.

Not everyone who poses a threat actually makes a threat. In other words, some shooters have not made direct threats, but reviewing their history after a tragedy, investigators could see many red flags (A. Miller, 2014). Caution is needed, however, because what are identified as red flags (e.g., overreacting to minor disturbances and owning and using guns for recreational purposes, such as hunting or target practice)—can be seen in the backgrounds of many individuals who never display violent behavior. Many gun owners would be outraged at the suggestion that they pose a threat because they own and use a gun. Rather, a combination of factors taken together lead the threat assessor to conclude that the individual poses a threat. However, we cannot assume that those who truly pose a threat are also likely to perpetrate violence. Nevertheless, researchers and clinicians who specialize in threat assessment recommend that attention be given to those who pose a threat whenever possible (A. Miller, 2014). The strategies for intervention are discussed below.

Threat assessment is a process to determine the credibility and seriousness of a threat and the likelihood that it will be carried out. It involves three basic functions: identify, assess, and manage (see Table 8.1). Similar to the risk assessment instruments discussed in earlier chapters, forensic psychologists have devised instruments that can be used for assessing the likelihood that a threat will be carried out. Little research is available on the extent to which these instruments are used, however. There is also a professional group, the Association of Threat Assessment Professionals, and a number of publications (e.g., J. R. Meloy & Hoffmann, 2013) that provide guidance to forensic psychologists and other mental health professionals conducting threat assessments. In addition, a new APA journal, the *Journal of Threat Assessment and Management*, was launched in 2014.

Because an enormous amount of research in recent years has concentrated on school shootings, we will discuss in the next section what is known about threat assessment as it pertains to that context. Workplace violence is also a prominent issue demanding threat assessment procedures, and that will be covered later in the chapter.

Table 8.1	Some Tasks Associated With Threat Assessment
Identify	Be aware of "markers" of possible impending violence (e.g., expressed threat, uncharacteristic and violent behavior, hostility toward others).
	Report concerns to authorities (threat assessment teams, law enforcement, school officials, workplace supervisors).
Assess	Obtain and gather information from various sources.
	Talk with individual and his or her peers.
	Appraise person's current situation (e.g., problems at home, health issues, access to weapons) with or without using threat assessment instruments.
	Determine underlying problem (e.g., depression, bullying).
Manage	Provide counseling/treatment for underlying problem.
	Make use of family conferences when appropriate.
	Warn or protect potential victims.
	Monitor the individual or obtain a restraining order if necessary.

School Shootings

The term *school shooting* most often refers to those violent incidents occurring within the school building or on the school grounds. Some believe (Daniels & Bradley, 2011) that the definition should include one or more fatalities that happen "in school, on school property, at school sponsored activities, or to a member of the school community on his or her commute to or from school" (p. 3). Recent data on violent deaths in schools (e.g., the School-Associated Violent Deaths Surveillance Study [SAVD]) also include these broader contexts. Thus, administrators, teachers, and other staff members are included along with students, and suicides as well as homicides are tabulated. The SAVD is a study developed by the Centers for Disease Control and Prevention, and has been collecting data since 1992. All data from 1999 to the present are considered "preliminary" (Planty & Truman, 2013), so statistics should be cited with caution. It is believed, on the basis of the data that are available, that homicides of youth at school comprise just over 1% of the total homicides in the United States in any given year (Planty & Truman, 2013). However, in these statistics, "at school" includes not only on school property and while attending school, but also on the way to or from school and while attending or traveling to or from a school-sponsored event. Student homicides while at school are rare.

"Aggressive behavior such as fighting and bullying are common problems in school, yet lethal attacks or more serious violence such as rape or aggravated assault are rare" (Nekvasil & Cornell, 2015, p. 99). Student threats of violence, on the other hand, are relatively common at schools, but they are often expressions of anger and frustration rather than serious plans of an imminent shooting (Nekvasil & Cornell, 2015). Fighting, bullying, and threats of violence are more common in the middle school (Grades 6 through 8) than in any other grade level.

For our purposes, we will restrict our discussion to those lethal attacks that take place within the school building or immediately outside the building—and it is unknown precisely how many of these have occurred. The great majority of these shootings have been carried out by one or more students against others. The horrific massacre of 20 first graders and 6 school staff members at Sandy Hook Elementary School in Newtown, Connecticut, in 2012 is an exception, because it was carried out by a 20-year-old who lived in the community. Other exceptions are shootings of a staff member by another adult who gained entrance into the school. For our purposes, the latter examples better qualify as workplace violence, a topic to be discussed later in the chapter.

In recent years, some writers (e.g., Langman, 2013; Madfis & Levin, 2013) have preferred the term *school rampage shootings*, defined as involving "attacks on multiple parties, selected almost at random" (K. Newman, Fox, Harding, Mehta, & Roth, 2004, pp. 14–15). However, as noted by Böckler, Seeger, Sitzer, and Heitmeyer (2013), the term *rampage* suggests an impulsive, *random* act. School shootings are usually carefully planned by the perpetrator, sometimes over a period of months or even years. In addition, the shooter often develops a "hit list" or a plan to kill a specific group of students, such as athletes (Daniels et al., 2007; Daniels & Page, 2013).

Another problem with the terms *school shooting* or *rampage shooting* is the word *shooting*. Although a vast majority of school violence in the United States involves a gun, not all does. Böckler et al. (2013) also observe that outside the United States, there are many cases where, because of the extensive restrictions on firearms, perpetrators resort to other weapons such as explosives, swords, knives, or axes: The United States is not immune to such attacks, however. In April 2014, a 16-year-old Pennsylvania student stabbed 20 students and a security guard before being restrained. "Even if such incidents are not 'shootings' in the literal sense, they exhibit clear similarities in perpetrator profile, contextual factors, developments in the lead-up to the attack, and modus operandi" (p. 6). Consequently, we agree with Böckler et al. that these non-firearm incidents should be included under the rubric **school shootings**. Therefore, in this section, we will continue to use the term *school shootings* to describe serious violence involving a lethal weapon, but not necessarily a gun, within the school and immediate school grounds.

Research has discovered that school shootings are a rapidly growing phenomenon in modern Western societies over the past two decades. In addition, more school shootings have occurred in the United States during that time frame than in all other countries combined (Böckler, Seeger, Sitzer, & Heitmeyer, 2013). Statistically, though, school shootings are rare, accounting for a very small percentage of youth deaths (Daniels & Page, 2013). However, the psychological impact of a school shooting is widespread and long lasting within the local community and, to some extent, across the nation as a whole (Ardis, 2004; Daniels & Bradley, 2011; Larkin, 2007; M. L. Sullivan & Guerette, 2003). The school shootings at Columbine High School in 1999 and Sandy Hook Elementary School in 2012 had an impact far beyond the communities in which they occurred. As posited by O'Toole (2013), "While these lethal school shootings are rare, when they occur they are devastating, life-changing events, and always leave people shaking their heads" (p. 173).

Types of School Threats

According to the FBI (O'Toole, 2000), school threats may be divided into four types: (1) direct, (2) indirect, (3) veiled, and (4) conditional. A *direct* threat specifies a target and is delivered in a straightforward, clear, and explicit manner. For example, a caller—sometimes a student, sometimes someone from outside—might say, "I placed a bomb in the school cafeteria, and it will go off at noon today." An *indirect* threat is more vague and ambiguous. The specific motivation, the intention, and the target are unclear and open to speculation: "If I wanted to, I could kill many at the school at any time." This is the type of threat that has most frequently been made.

A *veiled* threat strongly implies but does not explicitly threaten violence. For example, a student might receive an anonymous note in his locker that reads, "We would be better off without you around anymore." The message clearly hints at a potential violent act but leaves the seriousness and meaning of the note for the threatened victim to interpret. A *conditional* threat is most often seen in extortion cases. It often warns that a violent act will occur unless certain demands or terms are met, such as what occurred during the Washington, D.C., sniper killings in the fall of 2002. The message was this: "If you don't pay us 10 million dollars, none of your children will be safe."

When school children themselves become aware of a threat, they do not necessarily report it to school authorities. This occurs even when they themselves are personally threatened. A recent study indicated that only about one fourth of high school students who received a personal threat told anyone in authority (Nekvasil & Cornell, 2012). A major task of threat assessment teams is to encourage everyone in the school to report any suspicious behavior or threats.

The Safe School Initiative (SSI) Report

In June 1999, following the attack at Columbine High School, the U.S. Secret Service in collaboration with the Department of Education began conducting a study of school shootings and other school-based attacks between the years 1974 and 2000 (Borum, Fein, Vossekuil, & Berglund, 1999; Vossekuil, Fein, Reddy, Borum, & Mozeleski, 2002). The study, called the **Safe School Initiative (SSI)**, examined 37 school shooting incidents involving 41 student shooters. The study involved extensive review of police records, school records, court documents, and other source material, including interviews with 10 school shooters. The goal of the project was to examine thoroughly the thinking, planning, communications, and behaviors engaged in by students who carried out school attacks. In addition, the perceived rash of school violence has thrust mental health professionals and school psychologists into the role of assisting school districts and the local communities in the development of prevention and treatment programs directed at juvenile violence (G. D. Evans & Rey, 2001). It also has initiated considerable applied research by forensic psychologists and other mental health professionals across the country.

In the Safe School Initiative report, researchers concluded that those involved in school shootings did not "just snap"; they planned their attacks ahead of time (Vossekuil et al., 2002). According to the report, the findings of which are summarized in Focus 8.3, for more than half of the school shooters, the motive was revenge. In many cases, long-standing bullying or harassment played a key role in the decision to attack. However, there are many other motives or reasons for school violence and for making the threats that may precede them.

> Threats are made for a variety of reasons. A threat may be a warning signal, a reaction to fear of punishment or some other anxiety, or a demand for attention. It may be intended to taunt; to intimidate; to assert power or control; to punish; to manipulate or coerce; to frighten; to terrorize; to compel someone to do something; to strike back for an injury, injustice or slight; to disrupt someone's or some institution's life; to test authority, to protect oneself. The emotions that underlie a threat can be love; hate, fear; rage; or desire for attention, revenge, excitement, or recognition. (O'Toole, 2000, p. 6)

Most school shooters in the United States had easy access to guns. In nearly two thirds of the incidents, school shooters obtained guns from their own home or the home of a relative. The shooter responsible for the Newtown school tragedy had access to many weapons, including one recently purchased for him by his mother, whom he killed in their home before setting out for Sandy Hook Elementary School. Guns may be easy to obtain for many youth, but when other "red flags" are in evidence—threats, changes in behavior, or increasing despondency—making them inaccessible should be a priority. With respect to school shooters, the SSI report suggests that additional efforts to acquire, prepare, or use a weapon may signal an attacker's progression from thought to action.

After the attack at Columbine High School in 1999, some mental health professionals were intent on developing a psychological profile of the typical school shooter (Borum, Cornell, Modzeleski, & Jimerson, 2010; J. McGee & DeBernardo, 1999). However, according to the SSI report, there is no accurate or useful profile of "the school shooter" or threatener. Furthermore, researchers who prepared the report found that the personalities and social characteristics of the shooters varied considerably. They came from a variety of social backgrounds and varied in age from 11 to 21 years. Family situations ranged from intact families to foster homes. Academic performance ranged from excellent to failing. Although mental illness is often believed to be at the root of school shootings (and mass murders in general), most school shooters were not diagnosed with any mental disorder, and a majority had no history of drug or alcohol abuse. However, more than three fourths of school shooters did threaten to kill themselves, made suicidal gestures, or tried to kill themselves before their attacks.

Statistics do show that school shootings are committed predominately by male adolescents at secondary schools (Böckler et al., 2013). Studies also suggest that most school shooters are average or above average academically (Vossekuil et al., 2002). Ultimately, it must be emphasized that school shootings are the result of numerous interacting risk factors; there appears to be no one single cause (Böckler et al., 2013). According to Böckler et al., risk factors include the following:

1. Factors that influence the socialization of children and adolescents, such as the family and the culture. For example, lack of parental supervision and dysfunctional family relationships, or a family atmosphere that resorts to violence to solve problems, represent risk factors that may result in violence at school.

2. The school atmosphere, policies, and culture. For instance, a school environment that allows bullying and rejection by peers, or tolerates or ignores disrespectful behavior—these represent common risk factors in school shootings. Vossekuil et al. (2002) discovered that 75% of school shooters felt persecuted by peers at school.

3. Individual factors, such as personality traits, genetic makeup, and mental health. For example, depression or uncontrollable rage may be contributing factors.

Prevention of School Shootings and Other Violence

Of the three categories of risk factors, addressing the school-related factors may represent the best preventive efforts. Effective anti-bullying programs, crisis planning, training for crises, and school–community collaboration are all measures that are likely to mitigate school shootings (Daniels & Page, 2013). Rules and expectations should be clearly articulated, and consequences for disrespectful behavior and other misbehavior should be consistently and fairly meted out (Daniels & Page, 2013). Recall that only about 25% of students who report being threatened by others report these threats to someone in authority. Attempting to break the student code of silence by educating students about the difference between snitching and helping to save lives of others appears to be a helpful strategy.

In an important study, Daniels and Bradley (2011) examined the culture of schools where shootings occurred compared to the culture of schools where a planned shooting was successfully averted because authorities were attuned to signs of danger or alerted by students. Four common themes emerged. In those schools where a shooting occurred, there was considerable evidence of (1) an inflexible culture, (2) inequitable discipline, (3) tolerance for disrespectful behavior, and (4) a code of silence. The *inflexible culture* created, among certain students, a sense of not belonging. *Inequitable discipline* occurs when staff members and teachers apply school rules differently to different groups. Concerning *tolerance for disrespectful behavior*, Daniels and Page (2013) write,

FOCUS 8.3. SUMMARY OF SECRET SERVICE SAFE SCHOOL INITIATIVE (SSI) REPORT

What we know about school shooters:

- Attackers talk about their plans to others, usually through e-mail, Facebook, Twitter, or face-to-face conversations. Prior to most incidents, the attacker told someone about his idea or plan. In more than three fourths of incidents, the attacker told a friend, schoolmate, or sibling about his idea for a possible attack before taking action. This communication about violent intentions is often referred to by threat investigators as leakage.
- Attackers make plans. Incidents of targeted violence at school are rarely impulsive. In almost all incidents, the attacker developed the idea to harm the target before the attack.
- There is no stereotype or profile. There is no accurate or useful profile of the "school shooter." The personality and social characteristics of the shooters vary substantially.
- Attackers had easy access to guns. Most attackers had used guns previously and had access to guns. In nearly two thirds of incidents, the attackers obtained guns used in the attack from their own home or that of a relative.

- School staff are often first responders. Most shooting incidents were not resolved by law enforcement intervention. More than half of the attacks ended before law enforcement responded to the scene. In these cases, faculty or fellow students stopped the attacker. (This finding has led to calls for more school resource officers [SROs], typically police officers assigned to every school.)
- Attackers are encouraged by others. In many cases, other students were involved in some capacity. In almost half of the cases, friends or fellow students influenced or encouraged the attacker to act.
- Bullying can be a factor. In a number of cases, bullying played a key role in the decision to attack. A number of attackers had experienced bullying and harassment that were long-standing and severe.
- Warning signs are common. Almost every attacker engaged in some behavior prior to the incident that seriously concerned at least one adult, and in many cases, several adults.

Source: Adapted from U.S. Secret Service (2002).

If a school permits, or is perceived to permit, disrespectful behavior, such as bullying, racism, and overt rudeness, the students bearing the brunt of such actions may feel they have no one to turn to, especially if they are aware that the school's policies are very lenient. (p. 413)

The code of silence develops when students are resistant to reporting threats because of fear of repercussions or lack of an adequate or clearly defined reporting system.

Daniels and Bradley conclude that developing and maintaining a school culture of dignity and respect will go a long way toward eliminating the code of silence. Although this is important information, we should not assume that the school culture is at fault whenever a school shooting occurs. Preventive efforts are crucial, but they may be no match for one or more students who are intent upon harming others.

Guidelines

Guidelines for preventing threats of violence from becoming serious may be found in the Virginia Student Threat Guidelines, a project spearheaded by Dewey Cornell (Cornell & Allen, 2011; Cornell, Gregory, & Fan, 2011). The guidelines were developed for K–12 schools in response to the FBI and Secret Service recommendation that schools utilize a threat assessment approach to reduce school violence. The guidelines use a decision tree to evaluate threats of violence (Cornell & Sheras, 2006; see Figure 8.3), which outlines a process whereby school personnel determine at the outset whether a threat is transient or substantive. Substantive threats are indications that the individual or individuals intend to carry out the threat. If the threat appears serious, various steps are taken to insure that the threat is not carried out. At this point, law enforcement and mental health assessments are likely involved. The final step proceeds with a written safety plan based on the findings of the assessment and investigations. A manual for the guidelines can be found at Cornell and Sheras (2006).

We now turn to discussing violence in another context, the work environment. Workplace violence (which includes school violence as the school pertains to the education professionals, paraprofessionals, and staff) has increased in recent years, possibly for reasons discussed below.

WORKPLACE VIOLENCE

Workplace violence is a complex phenomenon, encompassing a wide assortment of threatening and injurious behaviors that occur within one's place of employment. Workplace violence is somewhat of a misnomer because it refers not only to the more physically violent incidents, but also to the subtle behavior that *threatens* violence, such as coercion, intimidation, outright threats, and harassment. In the public mind, workplace violence usually means a worker killing his or her coworkers or supervisors. However, the data reveal that the assailants of most serious workplace violence come from outside the workplace (Piquero, Piquero, Craig, & Clipper, 2013).

From 2000 to 2012, over half of the workplace homicides occurred within three occupations: sales and related occupations (especially fast-food restaurants and beverage stores), protective service occupations (especially law enforcement officers), and transportation occupations (especially ground-passenger transportation services) (Bureau of Labor Statistics, 2013). Shootings account for 80% of all workplace homicides (Bureau of Labor Statistics, 2010). Coworkers or former coworkers were the assailants in 12% of all shootings. Robbers were assailants in 40% of the shootings. Figure 8.4 depicts gun-related workplace homicides by industry in 2010.

Figure 8.3   Decision Tree for Student Threat Assessment

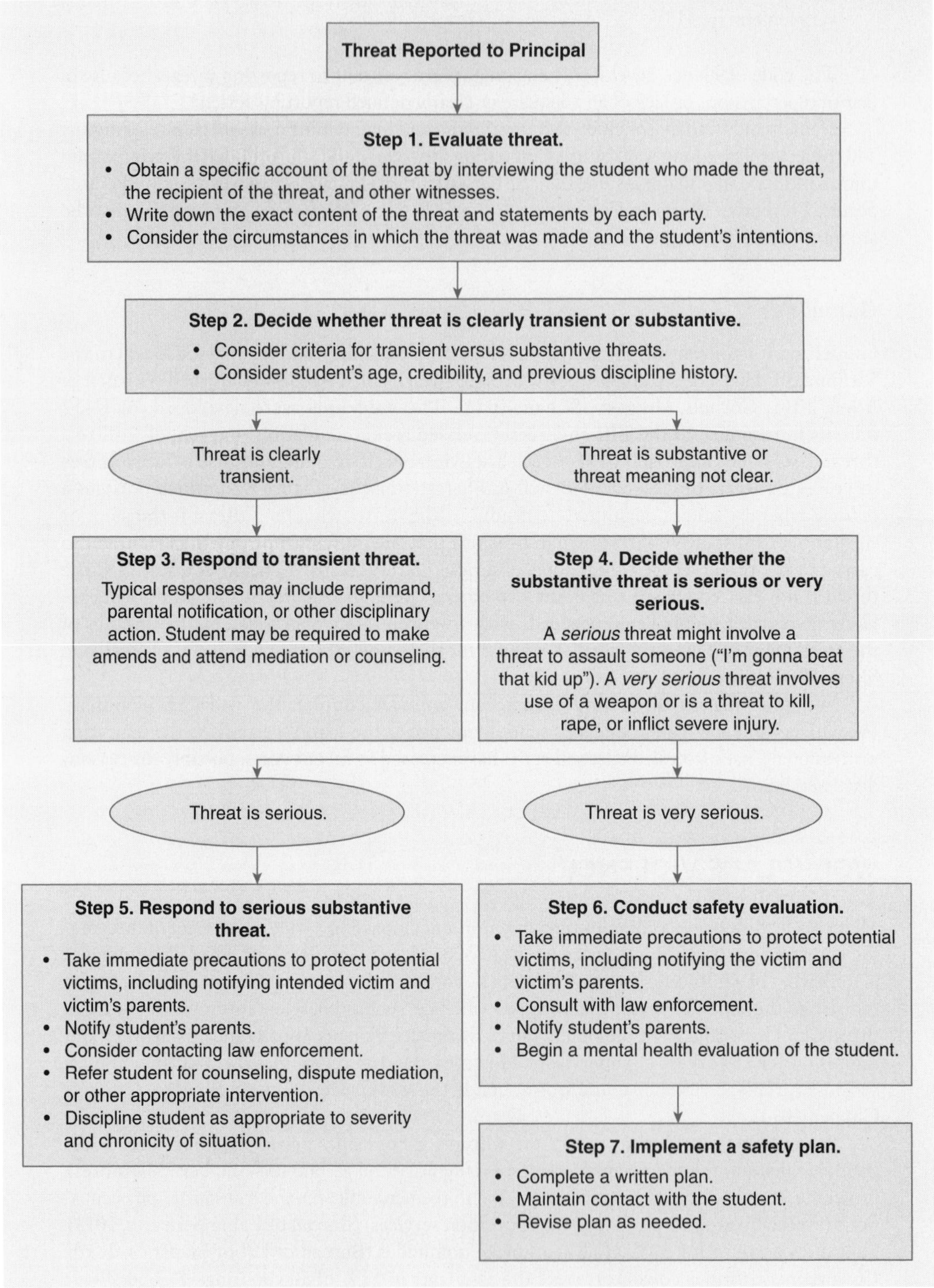

Threat Reported to Principal

Step 1. Evaluate threat.
- Obtain a specific account of the threat by interviewing the student who made the threat, the recipient of the threat, and other witnesses.
- Write down the exact content of the threat and statements by each party.
- Consider the circumstances in which the threat was made and the student's intentions.

Step 2. Decide whether threat is clearly transient or substantive.
- Consider criteria for transient versus substantive threats.
- Consider student's age, credibility, and previous discipline history.

Threat is clearly transient.

Threat is substantive or threat meaning not clear.

Step 3. Respond to transient threat.

Typical responses may include reprimand, parental notification, or other disciplinary action. Student may be required to make amends and attend mediation or counseling.

Step 4. Decide whether the substantive threat is serious or very serious.

A *serious* threat might involve a threat to assault someone ("I'm gonna beat that kid up"). A *very serious* threat involves use of a weapon or is a threat to kill, rape, or inflict severe injury.

Threat is serious.

Threat is very serious.

Step 5. Respond to serious substantive threat.
- Take immediate precautions to protect potential victims, including notifying intended victim and victim's parents.
- Notify student's parents.
- Consider contacting law enforcement.
- Refer student for counseling, dispute mediation, or other appropriate intervention.
- Discipline student as appropriate to severity and chronicity of situation.

Step 6. Conduct safety evaluation.
- Take immediate precautions to protect potential victims, including notifying the victim and victim's parents.
- Consult with law enforcement.
- Notify student's parents.
- Begin a mental health evaluation of the student.

Step 7. Implement a safety plan.
- Complete a written plan.
- Maintain contact with the student.
- Revise plan as needed.

Source: Cornell, D. G., & Sheras, P. L. (2006). *Guidelines for responding to student threats of violence.* Dallas, TX: Sopris West Educational Services. Reprinted with permission.

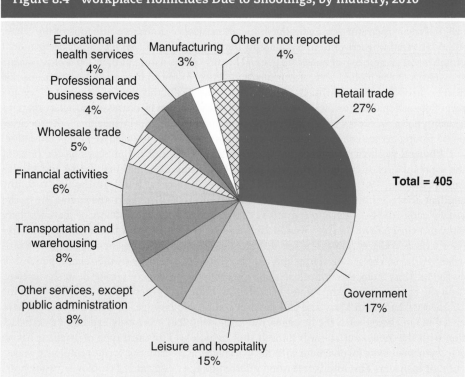

Figure 8.4 Workplace Homicides Due to Shootings, by Industry, 2010

Educational and health services 4%
Manufacturing 3%
Other or not reported 4%
Professional and business services 4%
Retail trade 27%
Wholesale trade 5%
Total = 405
Financial activities 6%
Transportation and warehousing 8%
Government 17%
Other services, except public administration 8%
Leisure and hospitality 15%

Source: U.S. Department of Labor Statistics (2013).

Homicide is the leading cause of death for women in the workplace, and it appears to be increasing (Tiesman, Gurka, Konda, Coben, & Amandus, 2012). Although 39% of women killed in the workplace were killed during criminal events such as robbery, theft, or other criminal activity, those killed by intimate partners were a close second at 33%. Women in protective service occupations usually have the highest overall homicide victimization rates, but women in health care (especially nursing), production (e.g., food services, factory work), and office/administration have the highest proportion of homicide victimization associated with intimate partner violence. Over half of the homicides committed by intimate partners occurred in parking lots and public buildings associated with the workplace.

As noted above, schools are the workplace for many adults, and neither schools nor colleges and universities are immune from workplace violence. In April 2017, a special education teacher was shot to death in her classroom, along with one of her students, by her estranged husband. Another child in the classroom was also shot but survived. The husband committed suicide at the scene. In February 2010, a 42-year-old college professor at the University of Alabama in Huntsville opened fire on her colleagues during a biology department meeting, killing three and wounding three.

Other examples of workplace violence in academe have included graduate students who shot professors on their dissertation committees and teachers killed by former boyfriends in the parking lot of the school. In 2009, a laboratory technician at Yale University was charged with the on-campus murder of a graduate student shortly before her scheduled wedding day. Note that we are making a distinction between these work-related incidents and the school violence directed specifically at students, which was discussed previously.

Obviously, most workplace violence does not end in death. Robbery, aggravated assaults, and sexual assaults are the most common violent crimes that occur in the workplace (Harrell, 2011). One third of victims of workplace violence between 1993 and 1999 reported that they believed the perpetrator was under the influence of alcohol or drugs at the time of the crime. Although retail workers tend to be the most frequent victims of *homicide*, other occupational groups are at greater risk of *violence* in general because of the nature of their job. Police officers are victims of the highest rate of workplace violence, followed by correctional officers, taxi drivers, private security guards, and bartenders. In the 1980s, the phrase "*going postal*" became part of the national lexicon after a series of workplace shootings by distressed postal workers. In actuality, postal workers were no more likely to commit workplace violence than other occupational groups, but the convergence of several crimes among this group led to the misconception.

Physical workplace violence has been classified into four major types on the basis of the assailant's relationship to the workplace (California Occupational Safety and Health Administration, 1995; Gregorie, 2000; LeBlanc & Kelloway, 2002). In the first type, the assailant does not have a legitimate relationship to the workplace or to the victim. He or she usually enters the workplace to commit a criminal action, such as a robbery or theft. Robbery is the principal motive for most workplace homicide, accounting for 85% of workplace deaths (Gregorie & Wallace, 2000). The second type of assailant is the recipient of some service provided by the workplace or victim and may be either a current or former client, patient, or customer. Most often, this individual is unhappy with the product or service he or she received from the agency or company. In August 2010, an individual entered the headquarters of the Discovery Channel in Maryland and took several people hostage. Although this could have ended in violence toward the hostages, the man—who had previously expressed dissatisfaction with the media outlet—was himself shot by police. The third type of assailant has an employment-related involvement with the workplace, as a current or former employee, supervisor, or manager. This assailant is often referred to as a "disgruntled employee" who enters the workplace to punish or get back at some individual or the agency or company in general. According to Gregorie and Wallace, disgruntled employees account for approximately 10% of workplace homicides. The fourth type has an indirect involvement with the workplace because of a relationship with an employee, such as a current or former spouse or partner.

One thing is clear concerning the survivors of workplace violence. Workplace violence "can lead to many adverse outcomes including [those related to] personal safety concerns, job insecurity, fear, lowered job performance, job satisfaction, affective commitment, intent to turnover, psychological distress, emotional exhaustion, depression, physical well-being, interpersonal deviance, and organizational deviance" (Piquero et al., 2013, p. 390). Forensic psychologists sometimes are asked to assess victims of workplace violence in civil suits against present or former employers, in which the victims allege that the employers were negligent in protecting them from harm. Psychologists and other mental health professionals also can play an instrumental role in helping employees recover from these stressful incidents. This is especially important when it comes to employees who witness a coworker or supervisor being killed or brutalized. Mental health professionals also play critical roles in the prevention of workplace violence when it comes to violence between employees and supervisors. The threat assessments discussed earlier in the chapter become crucial when there is concern that a particular employee may pose a danger to the workplace. The National Standards Institute endorsed threat assessment teams in workplaces in 2011 (A. Miller, 2014). Stress management interventions have been shown to be highly effective in addressing coworker dissatisfactions and other stress-related issues (Limm et al., 2011).

Few systematic studies have examined the predictors or causes of workplace violence. Most of the work to date has focused on either (a) describing the assailant or (b) identifying the job characteristics that increase the risk for violence (LeBlanc & Kelloway, 2002). Considerably more research is needed to identify the causes and implement preventive measures in the workplace. Nevertheless, many places of employment have been sensitized to this issue and have increased their levels of security in response to fear and uneasiness among employees.

This may be due, at least partly, to the dramatic increase in workplace violence litigation (Kaufer & Mattman, 2002). According to Kaufer and Mattman, the legal action and civil lawsuits at this point in time concentrate on four major areas: (1) negligent hiring (failure to screen employees properly), (2) negligent retention (failure to terminate unsuitable and threatening employees), (3) negligent supervision (failure to monitor performance), and (4) inadequate security.

Consequently, legal and regulatory obligations for employers to provide safe and secure work environments are bound to increase, and mandatory prevention and training programs are likely to be commonplace across all private and public organizations in the near future, at least at state and local levels. As should be apparent, forensic psychologists increasingly are called on to conduct threat assessments or to assess the risk of violence in an individual about whom fellow workers or supervisors are concerned. Perhaps more important, however, psychologists working within employment settings should be attuned to the culture of the workplace and play a critical role in facilitating an environment that promotes cooperation and mutual respect among and between employees and supervisory personnel.

We have thus far discussed only violence and threats of violence in the workplace, but we must emphasize that other workplace issues also merit careful attention. Discrimination—be it on the basis of race, gender, ethnicity, age, sexual orientation, or religion—remains an area of major concern. One particular form of discrimination is sexual harassment, which we covered in Chapter 6. In fiscal year 2016, the U.S. Equal Employment Opportunity Commission (EEOC) received 12,880 charges of sexual harassment (U.S. Equal Employment Opportunity Commission [EEOC], 2017). Seventeen percent of those charges were filed by men. Moreover, even though there has been a leveling off of filings with the EEOC over the past 10 years, the data underscore the fact that sexual harassment is still quite common in the workplace. One study (Fineran & Gruber, 2009) found that more than half of teenage girls experience some form of sexual harassment at their place of work. It is a distressing behavior that explicitly or implicitly affects an individual's employment; unreasonably interferes with an individual's work performance; and creates an intimidating, hostile, or offensive work environment. In addition, a number of investigations have substantiated a link between PTSD and depression, and sexual harassment (Fineran & Gruber, 2009). More pertinent to our discussion here, harassing behavior may lead to stalking, which may in turn lead to violence.

Likewise, racial, religious, and ethnic discrimination in the workplace also may lead to violence. In addition, discrimination in all of its contexts has similarities to bias crimes and to crimes of intimidation, which will be discussed later in the chapter.

In the next section, we direct our attention to the most serious violent act, the taking of human life. Although homicide was illustrated in much of the previous material, we will now discuss its overall prevalence as well as its specific forms.

CRIMINAL HOMICIDE

Homicide is the killing of one person by another. **Criminal homicide** is the causing of the death of another person without legal justification or excuse. Under certain conditions, the killing of another person can be justified (such as in self-defense) or excused (such as if the perpetrator was legally insane).

The criminal law recognizes two major levels of criminal homicide: murder and manslaughter. **Murder** is the term reserved for the "unlawful killing of one human by another with malice aforethought, either expressed or implied" (H. C. Black, 1990, p. 1019). Many states recognize "degrees" of murder, labeling those unlawful killings that are committed with planning and premeditation as murder in the first degree. First-degree murder is usually considered a capital offense, punishable by death or life in prison. Second-degree murder suggests less planning and premeditation, but still malice. The man who drove his car through a crowd of people protesting racism in Charlottesville, Virginia, in August 2017, killing one woman, was charged with murder in the second degree. Some states have done away with the distinction in degrees, the argument being that "planning" can occur in an instant, and the essential feature of murder is malice and intent.

Manslaughter usually refers to an *unintended* killing that results from *unjustifiable* conduct that places others at risk (Morawetz, 2002). The individual who aimlessly fires a loaded weapon and ends up killing someone, even if he or she did not "intend" to, is still responsible for that person's death. However, manslaughter also may include an *intended* killing "for which there is mitigation, acts that are provoked by the victim, or that result[s] from temporary and understandable circumstances that compromise the actor's normal responsibility" (Morawetz, 2002, p. 398). For example, a father who comes upon a car accident, discovers that his daughter has been killed, and chokes to death the inebriated driver of the car that hit her would likely be charged with nonnegligent manslaughter, not murder.

The UCR includes both murder and nonnegligent manslaughter under the term *criminal homicide* for reporting purposes. According to the UCR, approximately 15,696 persons were victims of murder or nonnegligent manslaughter in 2015 (FBI, 2016a). The murder rate in the United States during that year was 4.9 murders for every 100,000 inhabitants. The murder rate as reported in the UCR is based solely on police investigations as opposed to the determination of a court, medical examiner, coroner, jury, or other judicial body. In other words, the UCR provides data on the criminal homicides known to police and—if solved—on the persons arrested. Recall also that the UCR does not tell us, for instance, whether the 11,092 persons arrested and charged for murder and nonnegligent manslaughter in 2015 were convicted. Also not included in the UCR murder statistics are deaths police believe were caused by negligence, suicide, accidents, or justifiable homicide.

During 2015, UCR-contributing agencies submitted supplemental information concerning 13,455 homicides. The Supplementary Homicide Report (SHR) collects data on the age, sex, and race of both the victim and the offender; the type of weapon used; the relationship of the victim to the offender; and circumstances surrounding the incident. The circumstances are listed in Table 11.1 in Chapter 11. The relationship of the victim to the offender will also be reported in Chapter 11, which deals with violent victimology.

Criminal homicide, like sexual assault, is a heterogeneous phenomenon associated with different contexts, motivations, and types of offenders (Woodworth & Porter, 2002). Consequently, any attempt to make broad generalizations about people who commit criminal homicide—particularly murder—is risky. Nevertheless, researchers have drawn tentative conclusions about the types of individuals who commit this ultimate violent act. For example, most murders are single-incident offenses involving only one victim—and murderers generally do not commit another murder, even after release from prison. The "typical murder" is committed either during the course of committing another offense—most often a robbery—or is perpetrated against an intimate partner or an acquaintance. The typical murder also is committed between the ages of 18 and 34 (see Table 8.2).

An unknown number of murderers kill themselves after they have committed their crimes—typically very shortly thereafter and in the same location. The clinical characteristics of homicide-suicide are similar across the globe. Perpetrators of homicide-suicide are mostly men (95% in the United States), and the homicide victims are usually women (85% in the United States) (Hillbrand, 2001). In a majority of cases, the offender and victim(s) are relatives. Most cases involve one killer and one victim (90%) (Hillbrand, 2001). Despair, hopelessness, and depression are common among perpetrators of murder-suicides. In fact, the clinical or psychological characteristics are more typical of suicide than homicide. For example, there is not a lifelong pattern of impulsivity or violence.

A distinct form of homicide-suicide involves politically motivated terrorists who commit acts such as suicide bombings. In such incidents, a single terrorist may strap himself or herself with explosives that are later detonated at targeted locations. As in the September 11, 2001, attacks on the World Trade Center and the Pentagon, and the attack that was thwarted by passengers who sacrificed themselves by flying a plane into the ground in Shanksville, Pennsylvania, these may be perpetrated by individuals acting in small groups. Individuals who commit homicide-suicide, whether politically motivated or not, seldom utter threats or give warnings of the impending killings.

Forensic psychologists are most likely to be called on to consult regarding the atypical murder. A psychologist may be asked for a "profile" of a serial killer or to assess the risk that he will strike again within a given locality. These activities are engaged in by police and public safety psychologists, whose work was discussed in Chapters 2 and 3. The field of investigative psychology includes consulting with police to help in solving crimes. Forensic

Table 8.2 Age Distribution of Murder Offenders, 2015			
Age	**Total**	**Male**	**Female**
Total (all ages)	8,533	7,549	934
Under 10	0	0	0
Under 15	52	46	6
Under 18	605	566	39
18–24	3,198	2,896	302
25–34	2,527	2,192	335
35–44	1,136	985	151
45–54	657	543	114
55 and over	410	362	48

Source: FBI (2016a).

psychologists also may be called to testify in a murder trial, and most particularly at the sentencing phase when the court is deciding on the length and nature of a sentence. Finally, even mass murderers may be eligible for parole, and clinicians may be asked to assess their risk of future violence if released. The mass murderer Anders Breivik, who killed 77 people in a bombing and gun rampage in Norway in 2011, was sentenced to the maximum term of 21 years in the Norwegian prison system. However, his term could be extended if he is considered a continuing danger to society, a determination that would presumably require input from mental health professionals. Because forensic psychologists do encounter those who murder many victims in various capacities, we devote more coverage to these atypical crimes. The topic of single or typical murders is revisited in Chapters 10 and 11, where we discuss the effects of violent crime on victims.

Multiple Murder

Multiple murder (also called multicide) is usually divided into three somewhat overlapping major-offender patterns based on the timing of the act. **Serial murder** usually refers to incidents in which an individual (or individuals) separately kills a number of people (usually a minimum of three) over time. The time interval—sometimes referred to as the "cooling-off period"—may be days or weeks but more likely months or even years. **Spree murder** normally refers to the killing of three or more individuals without a cooling-off period, usually at two or three different locations. The designation spree murder is problematic, however, because some of these killings share characteristics of mass murders, while other seem more like serial murders. Neither law enforcement nor psychological researchers have found this to be a helpful designation, either for crime control or for research purposes. Compared with serial and mass murderers, spree murderers have received very little research attention and will not be discussed in detail below.

Mass murder involves the killing of three or more persons at a single location with *no* cooling-off period between the killings. The FBI identifies two types: classic and family. The school shootings discussed above; the Las Vegas mass shooting in October 2017; the Navy Yard shooting in 2013; the Virginia Tech tragedy of 2007; the Aurora, Colorado, movie theater shootings in 2012; and the 2014 stabbings and shootings in Isla Vista, California (to be described more below), are all examples of classic mass murder. In a family mass murder—which is by far the more common of the two—at least three family members are killed by another immediate family member or relative. Very often, the perpetrator kills himself or herself. Both classic and family mass murders, but particularly the latter, are also often examples of homicide-suicides. In the classic mass murder, it is more likely that the perpetrator—if not alive—has been shot by police at the scene.

What the public knows about multiple murder is largely based on misinformation and myth. The more sensational aspects of serial murder, for example, associate it with sexual sadists who prey on strangers to satisfy sexual fantasies. Movies or shows with multiple-murder themes, especially serial killings, almost invariably portray these killers with sexual, cruel, and often bizarre characteristics.

Researchers and scholars do not seem immune to the alluring features of multiple murder either. Fox and Levin (1998) have observed that the scholarly accounts are too often based on media sources or unstructured interviews with convicted offenders: "Indeed, the ratio of scholarly books to research articles is unusually high, reflecting an abundance of speculation and a paucity of hard data" (pp. 409–410). It is with this caveat in mind that we review the following information.

What little empirical research on multiple murder has been conducted has occurred within the past 20 years, largely in response to high-profile multiple-homicide incidents, such as those perpetrated by serial offenders David Berkowitz ("Son of Sam"), Theodore Bundy, Robert Yates, John Wayne Gacy, Donald Harvey, Jeffrey Dahmer, and Gary Ridgway. Ridgway, known as the "Green River Killer," pleaded guilty in November 2003 to the murders of 48 women, more than any other serial killer in U.S. history to date. In the past, researchers and criminologists assumed that multiple murderers were basically similar to single-victim offenders and therefore did not require special study. Later research, however, revealed that multiple murder does involve motivations, victims, demographics, and psychological features that differentiate much of it from the more ordinary single-victim homicide.

The considerable variation in the behavioral, emotional, and cognitive features of multiple murderers has prompted some researchers (R. M. Holmes & DeBurger, 1988; R. M. Holmes & Holmes, 1998; Ressler, Burgess, & Douglas, 1988) to develop typologies, or classification systems, that allow some appreciation of the complexity of the crime. We will cover one of these typologies later in the chapter.

Although multiple murders receive considerable media attention because of their drama and sensational qualities, they are statistically rare occurrences. The frequent onslaught of violence and multiple murder in the entertainment media eventually develops the impression that these incidents are much more frequent than they actually are. When multiple murders do occur, news media depict repetitive, graphic, and dramatic accounts of the violence. The normal cognitive reaction of people watching is to store the vivid details and then have these details ready at the "top of their mind" for future reference. The result of this process is the public's tendency to conclude that violence and multiple murders are dramatically increasing when they really are not. Mass and serial murders *seem* to be on the increase in the United States because accounts in the media are readily available. However, a careful review of the data simply does not lend support to this perspective. Even if statistics sometimes indicate that serial murders have increased, this apparent increase may be due to better communication and computer systems between state and federal law enforcement agencies over the past 20 years. For example, the **Violent Criminal Apprehension Program (ViCAP)** (see Focus 8.4) is designed to communicate with and help the nation's law enforcement agencies to investigate, identify, track, apprehend, and prosecute violent serial offenders. (See Perspective 8.1 later in the chapter, in which Dr. Angela Eke discusses her research and her work with a similar violent crime analysis program in Canada.)

FOCUS 8.4. VICAP: SHARING DATA TO SOLVE VIOLENT CRIME

ViCAP—the Violent Criminal Apprehension Program—is an FBI-sponsored data information center for the analysis of serial violent and sexual crimes. Law enforcement officials across the United States are able to enter information on solved cases into the database, as well as request the FBI's assistance in solving particularly difficult cases. The cases examined by ViCAP include the following:

- Solved or unsolved homicides or attempts, especially those that (1) involve an abduction; (2) are apparently random, motiveless, or sexually oriented; or (3) are known or suspected to be part of a series;
- Missing persons, in which the circumstances indicate a strong possibility of foul play and the victim is still missing; and

Source: FBI (2010).

- Unidentified dead bodies, in which the manner of death is known or is suspected to be homicide.

As cases are entered into the database, they are compared continually against all other cases to detect signature aspects of homicide—such as a note left at the scene—and similar patterns (e.g., victim's age, season of the year). If ViCAP analysts detect similar patterns, as they would in the case of serial murder, the law enforcement agencies involved are notified. ViCAP can then assist agencies in coordinating an investigation, such as obtaining search warrants and conducting laboratory tests.

Serial Killers

Despite the extensive commentary and media interest, there has been surprisingly little empirical research on serial murder. Most of the scientific research is limited to archival research or case studies. *Archival research* is seeking out and analyzing evidence from past records, such as police records, newspaper stories, diaries, historical notes in private collections, or other documents pertaining to serial murders. A *case study* is an extensive examination of the background, behavior, and crimes of one particular serial killer. "The literature on serial murder is largely the product of broad-based descriptive study of large numbers of cases of serial killers or the result of individual case studies" (Skrapec, 2001, p. 46). Consequently, most of the following information will be descriptive in nature, and the identification of motives will be largely based on self-reports provided by the killers themselves. Self-reports, although informative, are not the most objective measures available. They only provide information pertaining to what offenders want to reveal.

What does a serial killer look like? Physically, serial killers can be placed on a continuum, with Theodore Bundy, the handsome, charming, intelligent law student who brutally killed dozens of women in the Pacific Northwest, at one pole, and Arthur Shawcross, the dour, rumpled, aging serial killer of primarily prostitutes in the Rochester, New York, area at the other pole. Some television buffs may want to add the fictional Dexter Morgan of *Dexter* fame. An innocuous-looking, mild-mannered blood-spatter analyst, Morgan carried out revenge killings of people who had escaped the justice system. Many of his victims were themselves serial killers. It is not difficult to find additional images and depictions from the entertainment media and crime novels.

There is no single identifiable serial killer type based on physical appearance, social class, or personality attributes. Research suggests that most serial killers are males, but there are exceptions, such as Aileen Wuornos, convicted of killing six men, who was executed by lethal injection in 2002. Research on female serial killers has been limited and has focused on small samples, but it is now believed that approximately 16% of all serial killers are female, suggesting that additional studies on this group are warranted (Harrison, Murphy, Ho, Bowers, & Flaherty, 2015). Unless otherwise noted, the material below relates to male offenders, but it cannot be assumed that female offenders are different.

Serial killers have many of the same personality traits or behavioral features as the general public. However, the one trait that appears to separate them from the norm is their exceptional interpersonal skill in their presentation of self (Fox & Levin, 2003). Their ability to charm and "fool" others often elevates them beyond suspicion and makes them difficult to apprehend. This may explain why victims allow serial killers into their homes or go willingly with them on dates or other engagements. In reference to this issue, Joseph Fisher (1997) describes a serial killer who held two communities in constant fear for several months. He writes,

> Perhaps most unsettling for the community was the behavior of the victims; some of whom were reported to have gone willingly with their killer even though they may have known what lay ahead. This blind trust and the killer's exploitation of that trust seemed to have an eerie, supernatural quality. (pp. xiii–xiv)

It is a mistake to assume that serial murderers are seriously mentally disordered in the clinical sense of that term. Some are, but most are not. Although their thought patterns may be considered extremely aberrant when it comes to sensitivity and concern for other human beings, a vast majority of serial killers fail to qualify as psychotic or "crazy" in the traditional diagnostic categories of mental disorders. Serial killers have developed versions of the world characterized by values, beliefs, perceptions, and general cognitive processes that facilitate repetitive murder, often in a brutal, demeaning, and cold-blooded manner. They are prone to committing murders that draw interest and send spine-chilling fear into the community, and their motives appear incomprehensible to the general public. The motives of many serial killers seem to be based on psychological rewards of control, domination, media attention, and excitement rather than material gain. But the labels "sick," "crazy," or "psychotic" explain little and offer little hope in the quest for understanding the processes in the development of this behavior.

Although some serial killers have extensive police records, the records mainly reflect a series of petty thefts, embezzlements, and forgeries rather than a history of violence (Jenkins, 1988). Single-victim homicides often involve family, intimates, or acquaintances, whereas serial murder most often involves strangers, especially if the offender is male. Female serial murderers present a different story, however, because they most often murder those with whom they share a relationship such as husbands, intimates, and acquaintances, including individuals who are in their care (Harrison et al., 2015). For example, female serial murderers have included women in the nursing and home health care professions or who operated boarding homes. The crimes were undetected for long periods because it was assumed that the victims had suffered natural deaths (Hickey, 2010).

An examination of the victim selection of known male serial murderers will reveal that they prefer victims offering easy access and transience. Often the victim's disappearance is not reported to police. For example, victims are often prostitutes, runaways, young male drifters, and itinerant farm workers whose family and friends may not immediately realize that they are missing. With experience, improving skills, and a need for greater challenge, serial killers often move to more difficult victims, such as university or college students, children, the elderly, or the solitary poor. Very rarely do serial murderers break in and terrorize, torture, and kill strangers in their homes.

The geographic location preferred by serial killers most often tends to be a specific one. For some unknown reason, serial murderers seldom kill victims in the communities where they (the murderers) were born. They do, however, often select victims near their *current* residence or place of work. Hickey (1997) estimates, for example, that 14% of serial killers use their homes or workplaces as the preferred location, whereas another 52% commit their murder in the same general location or area, such as the same neighborhood or city. This tendency suggests that geographical profiling may be an invaluable aid in the identification of serial murderers. However, this still leaves more than 30% of offenders who apparently commit crime across a much wider geographical area.

As noted above, serial killers are primarily males, and they often have a preference for one gender over the other. Jeffrey Dahmer, for instance, murdered at least 17 young males in Wisconsin and Ohio during the early 1990s. Dahmer drugged, strangled, dismembered, and—in some cases—consumed the flesh of his victims. John Wayne Gacy sexually assaulted and killed at least 33 boys in Illinois during the 1970s. He buried most of his victims in the dirt basement of his house. Robert Yates, on the other hand, murdered at least 17 prostitutes and homeless women in the state of Washington during the 1990s. Gary Ridgway targeted women in the Seattle area during the 1980s and 1990s, mainly runaways and prostitutes.

A serial murderer may choose his victims because they hold profound meaning for him in terms of his life experiences (Skrapec, 2001). Interviews and descriptions of serial killers suggest that one of the dominant motives for their behavior is the power and control over another person's life that the crime offers them. "For these killers, murder is a form of expressive, rather than instrumental, violence" (Fox & Levin, 1998, p. 415). In keeping with the control theme, serial killers, unlike typical murderers, usually do not use a firearm to murder their victims. Although they may use a firearm to intimidate and control their victims, serial killers prefer a method of killing that provides the maximum amount of control and dominance. Choking, stabbing, and other methods of delayed death are ways the killer can maintain the life-or-death mastery over the helpless victims.

Serial killers also tend to be inspired by detailed and elaborate fantasies rich with themes of dominance (Fox & Levin, 2003; Skrapec, 1996). Prentky et al. (1989), for instance, found that 86% of the 25 serial killers they studied had violent fantasies on a regular basis, compared with only 23% of the 17 single-victim murderers. However, it should be mentioned that a majority (58%) of the serial killers in their sample had above-average intelligence compared to only 29% of the single-victim murderers. Therefore, the two groups were not completely matched in all important factors. In reference to this difference, Prentky et al. state, "While intelligence seems to have little bearing on the quality or content of the fantasy, it does influence how well fantasy is translated into behavior (i.e., how organized the crime is) and how successfully the offender eludes apprehension" (p. 888). The researchers further state that "fantasy, as it is defined in this study, is an elaborated set of cognitions (or thoughts) characterized by preoccupation (or rehearsal), anchored in emotion, and originating in daydreams" (p. 889). Furthermore, the more the fantasy is rehearsed in the mind of the potential killer, the stronger the association between the fantasy content and the actual behavior becomes, eventually lowering the restraints that normally would inhibit acting out the fantasy itself. Eventually, the individual will actually act on the fantasy. At this point, Prentky et al. suggest, the serial killer engages in a series of progressively more accurate "trial runs" in an attempt to enact the fantasy as it is imagined. In other words, the killer will continue to try to improve on his cognitive script through trial and error. Because the trial runs can never quite match the fantasy entirely, the need to restage the fantasy with a new victim is always there. As Fox and Levin (1998) note, "The killer's crime can increase in severity as he constantly updates his fantasy in a never-ending spiral of image and action" (p. 417).

Many serial killers augment their fantasies with hard-core pornography, which often contains themes of violence, dominance, and bondage (Fox & Levin, 1998, 2003). In the past, police investigators often uncovered extensive libraries of films and tapes that portrayed acts of rape and murder. Today, they would likely also uncover pornographic sites on the person's computer and other electronic equipment. It is not clear, however, whether the violent pornography engenders thoughts of violence or whether violence-prone individuals prefer violent pornography. The answer may lie in some combination of both.

Many serial killers also collect memorabilia of their victims, such as items of clothing, audiotapes or photographs of the murder, and—in rare cases—body parts. Called *trophies*, these "souvenirs" vividly remind the killer of the incident, enhancing his fantasies even further.

Serial Killer Typologies

In contemporary psychology, the term *typology* refers to a particular system for classifying personality or behavior patterns. Usually, the typology is used to classify a wide assortment of behaviors into a more manageable set of brief descriptions. There are many problems with typologies, however, including considerable overlap between categories. Rarely is one classification independent and separate from the others. In addition, some individuals can qualify for two or more classifications at once. For example, if the typology is based primarily on motive, the offender may demonstrate a combination of motives for the crime. Moreover, placing individuals into various categories is based on the questionable assumption that behavior is consistent across both time and place. Still, typologies are useful in highlighting the complexity of human behavior and the variety of motives and scripts.

Several typologies of serial killers have been proposed (L. Miller, 2014), but we will concentrate only on the R. M. Holmes and DeBurger (1985, 1988) and R. M. Holmes and Holmes (1998) scheme for illustrative purposes. It is widely cited, but researchers question its validity, as we note shortly. Holmes and DeBurger classify serial killers into a typology based on motive. The typology outlines four types: (1) visionary, (2) mission oriented, (3) hedonistic, and (4) power/control. The **visionary type** is driven by delusions or hallucinations that compel him to kill a particular group of individuals. According to R. M. Holmes and DeBurger (1988), this type of serial killer is psychotic—which is atypical because serial killers are not usually mentally disordered—and suffers from a severe break with reality. He or she is probably the most difficult to understand for investigators and the public alike. The crime scene is chaotic and has an abundance of physical evidence, often including fingerprints and even the murder weapon (R. M. Holmes & Holmes, 1998).

When the visionary type does kill, it will usually be well within his comfort zone (near his residence, place of recreation, or workplace). Therefore, geographical profiling would seem to be a very useful tool in the detection of this offender. Unlike most serial killers, however, the visionary murderer has no *ideal victim type (IVT)*. That is, there are rarely any common physical (hair color, sex, age, or race), occupational, or personality traits that connect the victims. In addition, the murder is usually spontaneous and characterized by very little planning, and the victim is simply in the wrong place at the wrong time.

The **mission-oriented type** believes that there is a particular group of people who are considered undesirable and who must be destroyed or eliminated. The undesirables may be prostitutes; gays, lesbians, and transgender individuals; "street people"; or members of a particular religious, racial, or ethnic minority group. Unlike the visionary type, this serial killer is not psychotic or otherwise mentally ill.

The **hedonistic type** strives for pleasure and thrills, and, in the killer's mind, people are simply objects to use for one's own enjoyment. According to R. M. Holmes and Holmes (1998), hedonistic killers may be divided into three subtypes based on the primary motive for the murder: lust, thrill, and comfort. The *lust* serial killer's primary motive is sex, even if the victim is already dead (an activity called necrophilia): "He kills for sex; it is a propelling element in the motivation to kill and in the enjoyment he receives from his activities" (p. 93). Furthermore, "The killer kills in ways that reflect both the fantasy and the manner in which the fantasy is to be satisfied" (p. 93). The lust killer, according to Holmes and Holmes, is always seeking the IVT that is sexually appealing to him. Ted Bundy, for example, reported that the way a woman walked and talked was an important factor in his victim selection.

The *thrill killer* is primarily motivated to induce pain or a terrified reaction from the victim. The pain and terror engendered, in combination with the process of the murder itself, are highly stimulating and exciting for the killer. Usually, the killer has no relationship with his victim, although he may have followed her for some time. Similar to the lust killer, the thrill murderer selects victims based on certain physical characteristics that feed into his fantasies.

The motive for the *creature comfort killer* is to acquire activities (business interests) or objects (money) that provide a comfortable and luxurious lifestyle. The killer's victims presumably stand in the way of achieving this. "The comfort killer's main objective is to enjoy life and to be sufficiently in control of immediate circumstances so that 'the good life' can be attained" (R. M. Holmes & Holmes, 1998, p. 119). Moreover, "overt, blatant displays of fatal aggression are not characteristics of this type; most comfort-oriented murderers tend to kill quietly if the situation permits" (p. 119). For the comfort killer, the act of murder is incidental to the pursuit of material gain and a comfortable lifestyle. Presumably, comfort killers dispose of their victims when they have identified a potential *new* "mark." In many ways, comfort killers resemble the behavioral characteristics of a criminal psychopath. Some writers (e.g., S. T. Holmes, Hickey, & Holmes, 1991) have pointed out that female serial killers often fall into this category.

The **power-control killer** obtains satisfaction from the absolute life-or-death control he has over the victim. Sexual components may or may not be present, but the primary motive is the extreme power and dominance over the helpless victim. These killers also tend to seek specific victims who appear especially vulnerable and easy to victimize.

Canter and Youngs (2009) contend that the Holmes typology is largely based on the motivation of the offender, which they believe is fraught with problems that often result in marginally useful or unsuccessful profiles of the offender. Canter (Canter & Wentink, 2004) believes the best approach for the development of helpful profiles is to examine the offending style and dominant theme that is reflected in the way that the offender interacts with the victim and the role the offender assigns to the victim. More research is needed before we can determine which approach is most useful to investigators.

Mass Murder

Compared to serial murder, relatively little research has been done on mass murders. Perhaps this is because mass murder, although horrible and troubling, is not as intriguing, mysterious, or frightening as serial murder. It is, of course, devastating to all who experience it, either directly or indirectly. We have only to mention such recent events as the mass killings in Newtown, Las Vegas, and Aurora, the Navy Shipyard incident, the killings at Fort Hood on two separate occasions, stabbings and gun deaths near the University of California Santa Barbara campus, and Virginia Tech to recall the horror of those occurrences.

It should be noted, as well, that the specific form of mass murder associated with terrorism is not usually included in the mass murder literature. Although instances of multiple deaths caused by terrorists, including domestic terrorists, have occurred for many years, these incidents are studied from a different perspective because they are either committed by groups of individuals for political purposes or by individuals affiliated with specific hate groups. The terrorist incidents referred to at the opening of this chapter are examples.

Mass murder usually happens suddenly and unpredictably—rarely is there any sequel. A long-term search for the perpetrator is not necessary. It is often clear who the offender is, although the motives are sometimes unclear. The offender often dies at the scene, either by his own hand or at the hands of police. It has been suggested that mass murderers often commit "suicide by cop," placing themselves directly and deliberately in the line of fire, rather than allowing themselves to be captured. In fact, it is commonly assumed that suicide is a primary motive of many mass murderers. However, Grant Duwe (2000), on the basis of his examination of 495 mass killings over a 21-year time period, concluded that only 21% of mass murderers committed suicide, another 2% attempted suicide, and 3% were fatally shot by the police. It appears that family mass murders are the type most likely to result in the perpetrator taking his or her own life.

The motives of mass murderers are highly variable. "The motivations for mass murder can range from revenge to hatred, from loyalty to greed; and the victims can be selected individually, as members of a particular category or group, or on a random basis" (Fox & Levin, 1998, p. 430). However, according to Fox and Levin, a majority of mass murderers are driven by revenge, and their victims are apparently chosen because of what they have done or what they represent. When targeting of victims belonging to specific groups occurs, the crimes may also qualify as hate crimes, which will be discussed below.

Mass murderers are frequently described as frustrated, angry people who feel helpless about their lives. They are usually between the ages of 25 and 45 (average age at time of murder is approximately 30), and they are generally convinced there is little chance that things will get better for them. They have often suffered some tragic or serious loss, such as losing a job or being abandoned by a spouse or partner. Their personal lives have been failures by their standards, but they often blame others for this. In May 2014, a 22-year-old stabbed to death his two roommates and a third young man who was visiting. He then drove his BMW through Isla Vista, California, a town heavily populated with college students, shooting at random while pursued by police. He ultimately killed three more people and wounded 13 others before shooting himself in the head. The killer had apparently posted frequent online messages expressing his hatred of women. He also posted a chilling "manifesto" on YouTube, detailing his frustrations and railing against women who did not pay attention to him. He vowed to punish them and the fraternity men they chose over him.

Mass murderers are often socially isolated and withdrawn people who lack a strong social network of friends or supporters. Compared with serial murderers, they are more likely to be mentally disordered in the clinical sense. The Newtown shooter; the shooter of patrons in a theater in Aurora, Colorado; and the above-mentioned 22-year-old in California all had had contact with mental health professionals, as did the Virginia Tech shooter discussed below. Their isolation was probably due to some combination of their emotional problems, an active dislike of people, and their own inadequate social and interpersonal skills. Attacking several or many others at one time provides these lonely, angry people a chance to get even, to dominate others, to take control, and to gain recognition.

The Virginia Tech massacre in April 2007, where 32 people were killed and 25 others wounded on the campus of Virginia Polytechnic University in Blacksburg, is a good illustration of a classic mass murder. The perpetrator, a 23-year-old senior, was described by those who knew him as a lonely, troubled, isolated, bullied, and peer-rejected individual who was extremely angry about the way he was treated by the world outside his immediate family. Some of his professors found his creative writing papers unusually violent and frightening. On the Virginia Tech campus, he was seen by students as quiet, strange, and basically noncommunicative. He had come into contact with law enforcement on several occasions for stalking female students. Two of the incidents resulted in verbal warnings from campus police.

Mass murderers often take a very active interest in guns. Unlike serial murder, about two thirds of the mass killings (both classic and family) involved the use of guns, usually semiautomatic firearms with high magazine capacities (Duwe, 2000). In other words, they prefer weapons that make it easier to kill many people quickly. It is not unusual for an arsenal of weapons to be found in the homes, vehicles, or hotel rooms of mass murderers.

In the following chapter, we will discuss research and theory related to other crimes of violence, specifically sexual offenses, and in Chapter 10 we will focus on family violence. For the present, we review information about crimes that may not involve direct violence—although they often do—but are serious by nature of the fear they engender.

HATE OR BIAS CRIMES

Hate crimes—also called **bias crimes**—are criminal offenses motivated by an offender's bias against a group to which the victim either belongs or is believed to belong. Neither hatred nor prejudice alone is sufficient to constitute a hate crime. There must be an underlying criminal offense—for example, an assault, vandalism, arson, or murder—that is *motivated* by the hatred or prejudice. It is not a crime to hate; however, demonstrated hatred against the victim of a crime based on prejudice can enhance the sentence given the perpetrator if convicted. One of the most notorious hate crime incidents in recent years was the killing of nine people at a Mother Emanuel Church prayer meeting by Dylann Roof in 2015. Roof expressed no regret about his actions and said he committed his actions to preserve the Aryan race.

The groupings—or protected categories—most commonly identified in bias crime laws are race, religion, gender, disability, sexual orientation, and ethnicity. (See Focus 8.5 for illustrations of incidents that qualify as hate crimes. See also Photo 8.2.) It is important to note that these are inclusive categories; that is, bias crime statutes protect all members of all races (not just blacks or whites) and persons of all sexual orientations (not just gays and lesbians). In addition, statutes in some states also provide penalties for bias crimes against certain age groups (e.g., the elderly) or members of the military.

The **Hate Crime Statistics Act** of 1990 requires the FBI to collect data and provide information on the nature and prevalence of violent attacks, intimidation, arson, or property damage directed at persons or groups because of bias against their race, religion, sexual orientation, or ethnicity. In September 1994, the Violent Crime Control and Law Enforcement Act amended the Hate Crime Statistics Act to include physical and mental disabilities in the data collection. Gender—commonly covered in hate crime statutes in many states—is not one of the specified categories. However, gender is now covered as a result of the **Violence Against Women Act** (VAWA), first passed in 1994 and reauthorized in 2000 and 2013.

Also in 1994, Congress passed the Hate Crime Sentencing Enhancement Act, which provides for longer sentences for such crimes. In 1996, due to dramatic increases in the burning of places of worship (especially African American churches located in the southeastern sections of the United States), the Church Arson Prevention Act was signed into law. The Hate Crime Prevention Act of 1999 prohibits persons from interfering with an individual's civil or constitutional rights, such as voting or employment, by violence or threat of violence due to his or her race, color, religion, or national origin. In October 2009, Congress passed the Matthew Shepard and James Byrd, Jr. Hate Crimes Prevention

▸ **Photo 8.2** Anti-Muslim graffiti on a mosque at the Islamic Center of America in Dearborn, Michigan.

Source: Bill Pugliano/Getty Images.

Act in response to the brutal murders of both men because of their sexual orientation and race, respectively. This new federal law not only encouraged prosecution of hate crimes and allowed enhanced sentences, but also expanded the protected categories to include gender and sexual orientation along with those aforementioned. Despite these laws, crimes against gay, lesbian, bisexual, and transgender individuals remain frequent and tend to be the most violent of all hate crimes (Cramer et al., 2013). The Human Rights Campaign reported that at least 22 transgender people (mostly women of color) were killed in the United States in the year 2016 alone.

FOCUS 8.5. HATRED ON DISPLAY

The following are illustrations of recent bias-related incidents reported in the media. Although criminal activity is indicated in most—but not all—of them, the perpetrators were not necessarily charged with committing bias crimes—and in some cases the perpetrators were not caught.

- Shortly after the presidential election of 2016, a youth baseball dugout was spray painted with racist and anti-Semitic slogans. A photograph of the dugout was displayed on the front page of USA Today.
- Similarly, both during the presidential campaign and after the election, numerous mosques across the United States were defaced or otherwise vandalized.
- In 2017, nooses and swastikas began to appear in greater numbers in graffiti, on campuses, and even in the nation's capital. In Charlottesville, Virginia, hate groups including white supremacists and neo-Nazis marched with torches, many shouting racist slogans and raising their fists in a Nazi salute.
- In 2017, a black family living in a rural community in New York was awakened shortly before midnight to find their garage on fire and the house itself at risk of burning. The father, mother, and five children left the house, physically unharmed but emotionally distraught. A swastika and racist graffiti had been spray-painted on the house. A teenage boy was later charged.

- In June 2016, 49 people were killed and 53 wounded at a nightclub in Orlando, Florida, that was a popular gathering spot for LGBT individuals.
- Seven teens were implicated in the stabbing death of an Ecuadorean immigrant as he was walking near a train station. The person who did the stabbing received a 25-year sentence for manslaughter as a hate crime. Prosecutors said the group of teens went to the area "in search of Hispanics."
- An intellectually disabled youth was beaten by four young people in Chicago; images of the beating were posted on Facebook. Advocates for the disabled said that such incidents against the disabled were common and seldom came to public attention.

Questions for Discussion

1. Which of the above incidents does not, as described, suggest criminal activity?
2. For purposes of the criminal law, we could rank the incidents in order of severity, with the murders being the most serious. Should they also be ranked according to a moral perspective? According to psychological damage to the victims? Should they be ranked according to any other perspective?
3. When nooses and swastikas are put on display, who are the victims?

In 2017 a 29-year-old man became the first person sentenced for killing a transgender woman under the federal hate crime statute. He was sentenced to 49 years.

Based on national statistics, hate crimes appear to account for a relatively small percentage of all criminal violence, usually about 4%. In 2015, a total of 5,850 hate crime incidents were reported (FBI, 2016b), and this number includes both violent and nonviolent offenses. Documenting hate or bias crimes is difficult because the intentions of the offender are not always obvious or clear cut. In addition, it is an enormous challenge to estimate accurately the prevalence of hate crimes because of varying statutes and methods of data collection across jurisdictions. Consequently, law enforcement agencies record hate crimes only when the investigation reveals facts sufficient to conclude that the offender's actions were bias motivated. Evidence most often used to support the existence of bias includes oral comments, written statements, or gestures made by the offender at the time of the incident, or drawings or graffiti left at the crime scene (Strom, 2001). In addition, there is tremendous state-to-state variation in the degree to which law enforcement officers are trained and encouraged to recognize and record hate crimes. For this reason, the most egregious examples are often turned over to federal investigators for possible prosecution under federal civil rights laws.

Available data indicate that a majority of hate crimes are motivated by race/ethnicity/ancestry bias (56.9%), followed by religious bias (21.4%), sexual orientation bias (18.1%), gender identity bias (2%), and disability bias (1.3%) (FBI, 2016b). It is estimated that 60% of the total hate crime victimizations are not reported to the police (M. M. Wilson, 2014). Sexual orientation hate crimes are the least likely to be reported by the victim. Although substantially unreported, LGBT hate crimes are usually more violent and involve greater victim injury (Briones-Robinson, Powers, & Socia, 2016). Religious-bias crimes usually target Jews (Cheng, Ickes, & Kenworthy, 2013). Anti-Muslim hate crimes escalated rapidly after the attacks of September 11, 2001, but then leveled off for a few years (Cheng et al., 2013). However, according to data released by the FBI in November 2016, the number of assaults, attacks on mosques, and other hate crimes against Muslims in 2015 reached the highest total since the immediate aftermath of September 11, 2001 (Clay, 2017). In 2015, there were 257 anti-Islamic (Muslim) incidents involving 301 victims, a 67% increase from the previous year 2014. Currently, Muslim women in the United States wearing the hijab are often targets of harassment and racial microaggressions (casual degradations) (Nadal et al., 2015). An example of a microaggression is asking someone, "What country are you from?" implying that she is not American. Muslim men draw perceptions of terrorism, violence, and criminal behavior (Clay, 2017).

Examples of a disability bias include biases against a person with AIDS, a mental disorder, or intellectual disability. Hate crimes on college campuses demonstrate a broad spectrum of criminal conduct, ranging from threats to sexual assaults to bombings. They occur at virtually every type of college or university and in every part of the country and are a significant problem on many campuses (Stotzer, 2010; Wessler & Moss, 2001).

Approximately two thirds of hate crimes are directed at individuals, whereas the remaining targets are businesses, religious institutions, or other institutions and organizations. About 4 out of 5 violent hate crimes reported in the FBI's hate crime statistics involve the victimization of a single individual within a single incidence (FBI, 2016b). The greatest proportion of persons suspected of committing hate crimes are white males (48%). FBI data indicate that 85% of those arrested for hate crimes are age 18 or older. Younger persons (younger than age 18) are more likely to be arrested for property-related offenses, such as vandalism, whereas older persons are more likely to be arrested for violent hate crime, such as aggravated assault.

Hate crime violence appears to have its roots in an individual's learned prejudice against particular social groups. This, combined with fear and association with like-minded individuals, can escalate into violence when members of the prejudicial group believe their lifestyle is under attack. The chilling images of primarily young white men marching with their fists raised, and chanting racist and anti-Semitic slogans in Charlottesville in August 2017 were a sad and stark wake-up call that society has done too little to eradicate prejudicial views.

Forensic psychologists can play major roles in understanding and preventing hate crimes and treating those who commit them. For example, they can research and apply knowledge of how bias against certain groups influences juries, lawyers, judges, and law enforcement. They can study how hate crimes differ from other forms of violent crime. They can work with and train mental health professionals who work with hate crime victims. Forensic psychologist also can participate in advancing legislation aimed at addressing bias crimes at the state and federal levels.

STALKING: THE CRIME OF INTIMIDATION

Stalking is defined as "a course of conduct directed at a specific person that involves repeated physical or visual proximity, nonconsensual communication, or verbal, written, or implied threats sufficient to cause fear in a reasonable person" (Tjaden, 1997, p. 2). The term refers to

> repeated and often escalating unwanted intrusions and communications, including loitering nearby, following or surveying a person's home, making multiple telephone calls or other forms of unwanted direct and indirect communications, spreading

gossip, destroying personal property, harassing acquaintances or family members, sending threatening or sexually suggestive "gifts" or letters, and aggressive and violent acts. (K. M. Abrams & Robinson, 2002, p. 468)

Stalking is as old as the history of human relationships, and yet it has only been within the past three decades that the behavior has been recognized as unlawful (Beatty, Hickey, & Sigmon, 2002). The release of films such as *Fatal Attraction* (Paramount Pictures, released 1987), *Sleeping With the Enemy* (20th Century Fox, released 1991), and *Cape Fear* (Universal Studios, released 1991) contributed to increasing salience about this problem in the minds of the public. Increased coverage by the news media of the stalking of celebrities (e.g., David Letterman, Rebecca Schaeffer) also led to stalking becoming a household term at the end of the 20th century. Today, attention has been directed to cyberstalking and a related phenomenon, cyberbullying.

Whether in person, over cell phones, or online, stalking is an extremely frightening, emotionally distressful, and depressing crime of intimidation. Since the 1990s and to the present, it has been the subject of extensive psychological research. Not surprisingly, clinicians have discovered that the longer the duration of the stalking—regardless of whether the behaviors are intrusive, violent, or some combination of both—the greater the potential damage to the victim (McEwan, Mullen, & Purcell, 2007). Anti-stalking laws exist in all 50 states, the District of Columbia, and Canada. Although most states define stalking in their statutes as the willful, malicious, and repeated following and harassing of another person, some include such activities as lying-in-wait, surveillance, nonconsensual communication, telephone harassment, and vandalism (Tjaden & Thoennes, 1998a). Some states require that at least two stalking incidents occur before the conduct is considered criminal. With the rapid development of technology, the laws in some states have now added cyberstalking to their list of prohibited behaviors.

One of the most comprehensive studies on stalking was conducted by the Center for Policy Research and published in a monograph titled *Stalking in America: Findings From the National Violence Against Women Survey* (Tjaden & Thoennes, 1998b). The project, cosponsored by the National Institute of Justice and Centers for Disease Control and Prevention, was a nationally representative phone survey of 8,000 women and 8,000 men, 18 years or older. The survey was conducted between November 1995 and May 1996 and provides empirical data on the prevalence, characteristics, and consequences of stalking during that time period.

The survey found that 8% of women and 2% of men reported that they had been stalked at some point in their lives (Tjaden, 1997). In most instances, the stalking lasted less than 1 year, but some individuals were stalked for more than 5 years. According to the research reported by Mullen, Pathé, and Purcell (2001), however, repeated unwanted communications and imposed contacts that go on for more than 2 weeks are highly likely to last for months or even years. In one recent, extensive survey (National Crime Victimization Survey), 11% of the victims of stalking said they had been stalked by the same person for 5 years or more (Baum, Catalano, Rand, & Rose, 2009).

Researchers believe that the motives of most stalkers are to control, intimidate, or frighten their victims. The fears and emotional distress generated by stalking behavior are many and varied. About 1 in 5 victims feared bodily harm to themselves and 1 in 6 feared for the safety of a child or other family member (Baum et al., 2009). About 1 in 20 feared being killed by the stalker.

In the study referenced above (Baum et al., 2009), the stalker was male 87% of the time, and the victim was female 80% of the time. Eighty percent of the stalkers are believed to be white, at least 50% are between the ages of 18 and 35, and many earn above-average incomes. In most stalking incidents, the victims (particularly women) knew their stalker. Approximately half of the female victims were stalked by current or former marital or cohabiting partners, and a majority of these women (80%) had been physically assaulted by that partner either during the relationship, during the stalking episode, or both. In about a third of the cases, the stalkers vandalized the victim's property, and about 10% of the time, the stalker killed or threatened to kill the victim's pet. Only 7% of the victims thought their stalkers were mentally disordered, psychotic, crazy, or abusers of alcohol or drugs.

Another comprehensive study of stalking was cosponsored by the National Institute of Justice and the Bureau of Justice Statistics (B. S. Fisher, Cullen, & Turner, 2000). The project involved a phone survey of 4,446 female students at 223 colleges and universities, conducted from February to May 1997. The primary screening question used to measure stalking was the following: "Since school began in fall 1996, has anyone—from a stranger to an ex-boyfriend—repeatedly followed you, watched you, phoned, written, e-mailed, or communicated with you in other ways that seemed obsessive and made you afraid or concerned for your safety?"

The key findings of the study were the following:

- Thirteen percent of the college women had been stalked since the school year began.

- Of the victims, 80.3% knew or had seen their stalker before.

- Stalking incidents lasted on average about 2 months.

- Thirty percent of the women reported being injured emotionally and psychologically from being stalked.

- In 10.3% of incidents, the victim reported that the stalker forced or attempted sexual contact.

- Overall, 83.1% of stalking incidents were not reported to police or campus law enforcement.

It should also be noted that some mental health professionals who deal regularly with persons having mental or emotional difficulties have become the victims of stalking by their clients (Gentile, Asamen, Harmell, & Weathers, 2002). According to Gentile, Asamen, Harmell, and Weathers, the stalkers of mental health professionals may be either single or divorced at the time of the stalking. The majority of these clients (62%) were diagnosed as having a mood disorder. In another survey, about 2 out of 3 university counselors had experienced some type of harassing behavior or stalking behavior from a current or former client (Romans, Hays, & White, 1996).

In an effort to better understand stalkers, some researchers have proposed typologies, or classification systems. One of the first systematic studies on stalkers was done by Zona, Sharma, and Lane (1993) in their work with the Los Angeles Police Department's Threat Management Unit. These researchers developed a classification system that focused on individuals who stalked entertainment celebrities and divided stalkers into three behavioral clusters: (1) eroto-manic, (2) love obsessional, and (3) simple obsessional (categories that will be defined shortly). A few years later, researchers shifted their focus from "star stalkers" to men who stalked their ex-partners (Emerson, Ferris, & Gardner, 1998; Kurt, 1995). Star stalkers were assumed to be predominately mentally disordered persons who were driven by delusions in their pursuit of their favorite celebrity, whereas ex-partner stalkers were seen as asserting their power over women through violence and intimidation (Mullen et al., 2001).

Mohandie, Meloy, Green-McGowan, and Williams (2006) studied a large sample of 1,005 male and female stalkers. They concluded that they could be grouped into four categories based on their relationship to the victim: (1) the Intimate stalker, who pursues a current or former sexual intimate; (2) the Acquaintance stalker, who pursues someone he or she knows but with whom he or she has not ever been sexually intimate; (3) the Public Figure stalker, who pursues a public figure with whom he or she has never had a relationship; and (4) the Private Stranger stalker, who pursues someone he or she has never met but is aware of because the victim is in the stalker's environment (such as a neighbor or fellow college student). Mohandie et al. found that these groups had different violence rates, with the Intimate stalker being the most likely (74%) to use violence against his or her victim and the Public Figure stalker being the least likely (2%). Using the same data set, M. Meloy, Mohandie, and Green McGowan (2008) and M. Meloy and Mohandie (2008) have published studies focusing only on female stalkers.

Another often-cited stalking typology, one that focuses more on the motives for stalking than on the relationship between the stalker and his or her victim, was outlined by Beatty, Hickey, and Sigmon (2002). It consists of four broad categories, the first three of which are similar to those proposed by Zona et al. (1993): (1) simple obsession stalking, (2) love obsession stalking, (3) erotomania stalking, and (4) vengeance stalking. The term *obsession* refers to recurrent ideas, thoughts, impulses, or images that a person tries to control or satisfy through various actions. It should be emphasized that this typology has not been validated by empirical research but should serve as a springboard for future research and hypothesis development. The following descriptions of the four stalker categories follow Beatty et al.'s definitions.

Simple obsession stalkers are the most common, accounting for 60% of the stalkers. They represent behavior that is a continuation of a previous pattern of domestic violence and psychological abuse in an intimate relationship. Consequently, the targeted victim is often a former spouse, and the majority of offenders are males. These stalkers appear to be more intelligent and better educated than most other stalkers (J. R. Meloy & Gothard, 1995). The stalking is hypothesized to be prompted by the offender's feelings of low self-esteem and helplessness. Apparently, the offender increases his own self-esteem by demeaning and demoralizing his former spouse or partner and may take drastic steps if he perceives the victim is trying to remove herself from the controlling situation. Simple obsession is the category of stalking that is most likely to result in murder. It is very similar to the Intimate stalker described by Mohandie et al. (2006).

Love obsession stalkers and their victims tend to be casual acquaintances, such as neighbors or coworkers, but such stalking may also involve complete strangers, such as a celebrity. The primary motivation of these stalkers is to establish a personal relationship with the targeted victim. Like simple obsession stalkers, these individuals may have very low self-esteem and may be haunted by feelings of helplessness and depression. Presumably, these stalkers believe that by associating with persons who display exceptional qualities and high status, they can correspondingly raise their own levels of self-esteem and worthiness. Often, the love obsession stalker is so desperate to develop a relationship with the victim that he or she is willing to accept a negative or destructive relationship, sometimes resorting to violence in an effort to win the attention of the unwilling victim. A classic example of this type of stalker is John Hinckley, who was convinced he could win the love of actress Jodi Foster by shooting President Ronald Reagan.

Erotomania stalkers are considered highly delusional, and the offender is often plagued by serious mental disorders, most often schizophrenia. Erotomania stalkers believe that the relationship with their victim already exists, in contrast to the simple and love obsession stalkers. Erotomania stalkers are usually less dangerous to the victims, but their irrationality is troubling and unpredictable to the victims. The woman who stalked talk show host David Letterman for nearly 10 years illustrates this type of stalker. She apparently believed throughout that time that she was Letterman's wife and the mother of his child. She was discovered on his New Canaan, Connecticut, property on many occasions; was arrested driving his car; and sent him flowers and candy. Eventually, the troubled woman committed suicide by kneeling in front of a speeding train in Colorado.

Vengeance stalkers are quite different from the other three types because they do not seek a personal relationship with their targeted victims. Instead, these stalkers try to elicit a particular response—such as fear, or change of behavior such as moving to another area—from their victims. Vengeance is their prime motivation. An illustration of this kind of stalker is when an employee who is fired from his job begins to stalk and harass the supervisor who he believes is responsible for the firing, in hopes of ruining the supervisor's life.

When Does Stalking Usually Stop?

What terminates stalking? Some stalkers stop pursuing their current victim when they find a new "love" interest. About 18% of the victims in the Center for Policy Research Survey (Tjaden & Thoennes, 1998b) indicated that the stalking stopped when stalkers entered into a relationship with a new person. Law enforcement interventions also seem to help. Fifteen percent of victims said the stalking ceased when their stalkers received a warning from the police. Interestingly, more formal interventions such as arrest, conviction, or restraining orders do not appear to be very effective—perhaps serving to antagonize the stalker. Angela Eke and her colleagues (Eke, Hilton, Meloy, Mohandie, & Williams, 2011), in a nine-year follow-up study of stalkers with police contacts, found that 77% committed new offenses over that time period, over half being charged with stalking offenses. About one third were charged with violent offenses. Eke et al. also found that stalkers with previous diagnoses of mental illness had significantly more contact with police, but their recidivism was more likely to be nonviolent. (See Perspective 8.1, in which Dr. Eke discusses her research interest in stalking and violent crime.) When it comes to persistent, frightening stalking that creates risks to personal safety, the Tjaden and Thoennes survey (1998b) suggests that the most effective method to stop it may be for the victim to relocate as far away from the offender as possible, providing no information of the person's whereabouts to the stalker or to individuals who might communicate that information. Victims of stalking should not be expected to bear the burden of such an impractical approach, however.

Predictions of Violence in Stalking Cases

Many stalking victims want to know the likelihood that they will become the victim of a violent act (Rosenfeld & Harmon, 2002). According to Rosenfeld and Harmon, "Determining which stalkers represent a significant risk of violence, and differentiating those individuals from the remaining offenders who may pose less risk of physical harm, has clear and significant implications for victims, clinicians, and the legal system" (p. 685). Recall that Mohandie et al. (2006) found that intimate stalkers had the highest rate of violence in their four groups, and Eke et al. (2011) found that stalkers with mental illness were less violent than those without.

In an effort to identify features that may differentiate violent stalkers from nonviolent stalkers, Rosenfeld and Harmon (2002) analyzed 204 stalking and harassment cases referred for court-ordered mental health evaluations in New York City. Results supported the findings of previous researchers (e.g., Palarea, Zona, Lane, & Langhinrichsen-Rohling, 1999) who found that former spouses or intimates of stalkers were most at risk.

> Specifically, intimate stalkers threatened persons and property (including physical violence toward the victim), were more likely to "make good" on their threats by following them with some form of violent behavior, and used more physical approach behaviors in contacting their victims than non-intimate stalkers. These results illustrate the importance of accounting for the presence of an intimate relationship when assessing for violence risk in stalking cases. (Palarea et al., 1999, p. 278)

Violent *threats* and drug abuse also appear to be significant predictors of stalking violence. Rosenfeld and Harmon (2002) also found that variables such as the stalker's prior criminal history and previous violent *behavior* did *not* emerge as good predictors of violence. This was surprising because Palarea et al. reported that a history of violence was the strongest predictor in their data. McEwan, Mullen, MacKenzie, and Ogloff (2009) also found that stalkers who are rejected ex-intimates, who have a history of violent behavior, and who have made threats present the greatest risk of violence. The differences between the studies, however, may be due to the fact that Rosenfeld and Harmon (2002) had access to much more information—official records of arrest and convictions as well as stalker self-reports and victim reports—than the

Applying Research to Practice

Angela Wyatt Eke, PhD

Courtesy of Angela Wyatt Eke.

I've always had an interest in psychology and an interest in law. When I was in high school, the counsellors engaged students in a career assessment. The goal was to suggest potential matches between expressed skills and interests and various career paths. My results highlighted law, medicine, psychology, and policing. It was perhaps no surprise then when I went on to attend the University of Toronto (U of T) for my bachelor of science degree; I focused on psychology with additional courses in criminology. I completed my master's and PhD in psychology at York University. While at U of T, two specific experiences stand out as both relevant and fortunate regarding my later career path.

First, I attended a volunteer fair and signed up to do some work in corrections. It was a great experience; I learned about the practical side of psychology and participated in one-on-one as well as group work with individuals. I volunteered many hours during my undergraduate days and continued during my graduate work, later completing a graduate research practicum in corrections. Throughout this time, my interest in applied research really began to develop—it was exciting to incorporate research into practice while also gaining ideas of where we should go with research, based on real-life settings. This has led to my focus on operational research such as risk assessment and case management in cases of stalking, intimate partner violence, as well as child sexual exploitation.

Second, as an undergraduate, I took a course on the psychology of aggression taught by Professor Lester Krames, who supervised my undergraduate research work. One year, Dr. Krames invited a guest lecturer to one of his classes—an Ontario Provincial Police (OPP) officer named Kate Lines. She was one of the first police criminal profilers in Canada and also a leader in developing a behavioural sciences section within the OPP. The short of this story is Kate later hired me as an Analytical Assistant and Research Assistant within the Provincial Violent Crime Linkage and Analysis Section (ViCLAS). I've worked with the OPP ever since.

Although I work within a police environment, on a daily basis, I'm in contact with colleagues from hospital settings, academia, and other government environments. A lot of this contact relates to collaborations on various research projects that generally involve the familiar process of project development, grant writing, proposal writing, research ethics, and so forth. I have the good fortune of working with great colleagues. When you bring together individuals from multiple environments you can build projects that have direct relevance across areas; in addition, you're working with a range of expertise and experience, which adds so much to the quality of the work.

With technology today, there are so many opportunities for disseminating research findings and discussing applied practice. Along with traditional conferences and training sessions, we can sign up for webinars or join listserves, which allow for immediate access and conversation with others. We can all follow our favorite researchers, practitioners, and experts via Twitter, ResearchGate, and myriad other applications. Technology also makes it easier to engage and work with colleagues from around the world. For one of our larger projects examining cases of child pornography, we now have a project page where we can share developments with other researchers and practitioners (https://www.researchgate.net/project/Child-Pornography-Offender-Risk-Tool-CPORT).

Like many others, though, I do wonder if all of our connectivity and the ease of checking in on work can blur our personal and family time. While important to follow your interests and passion, it is also important to be mindful of overall wellness and keep work and personal life in balance.

On a related note, while the information we're working with can be unique, it can also involve material and case facts that may evoke strong emotional reactions (child abuse, intimate partner violence, sexual offending). It is important to protect the overall wellness of those engaged in this work (e.g., police, clinicians, social workers, researchers). For example, Dr. Michael Seto and I have collaborated for years on research examining child sexual exploitation. To protect the wellness of research members we established a "safeguard" program that is psychologically based and involves clinicians and therapists external to the OPP and external to the project. Project staff meet with them on an individual basis at least once a year, or more often if they prefer or as needed; we've had good feedback about the program. I also see various wellness programs evolving and becoming more standard across a variety of positions. I believe there will be much more growth in this area over time—from organizational considerations relating to how we can support and assist colleagues, to how we recognize psychological and emotional trauma in our clients and our cases.

Part of my work involves providing training to police and other audiences as well as involvement in case consults. These are generally collaborative round table discussion with threat analysts, criminal profilers and forensic psychiatrists or psychologists.

I maintain some direct ties to academia, teaching an undergraduate course in forensic psychology and supervising student research practicum and theses.

Many of these students are researchers and practitioners well on their way in their own careers and I've had the pleasure of learning from them, attending their conference presentations or working with them on projects.

I've enjoyed my career. When I was in school, psychology related positions within policing were few. It has been exciting to see new research and applied psychology roles developing in police settings, as well as a general growth in work intersecting policing, clinical practice, and research. I believe students will find many more career opportunities developing over time. I look forward to meeting the students of today as future professionals.

Dr. Eke is the Research Coordinator for the Criminal Behaviour Analysis Unit, Behavioural Sciences and Analysis Section of the Ontario Provincial Police. She is an adjunct faculty member at Laurentian University. She was recently appointed a Member of the Order of Merit of the Police Forces. She balances her work with time spent with family and friends, travel, and renovation projects with her husband.

Palarea group did. Palarea et al. used data obtained from 223 police files maintained by the LAPD. Consequently, the difference between the two studies might be a function of the quality and quantity of the data collected.

Some research suggests that juvenile stalkers may be more dangerous and violent than adults. In an investigation of 299 juvenile stalkers, Purcell, Moller, Flower, and Mullen (2009) found that juveniles participated in higher levels of threats and violence than typically found in adult stalking. Over half of the victims (54%) of juvenile stalkers were physically attacked, some sustaining significant injuries, and another 2% were sexually assaulted resulting in serious injury. On the other hand, a recent study by Sheridan, North, and Scott (2015) found little difference in the violence displayed among three age groups of stalkers—16 and under, 17 to 59, and 60 and over. However, there were significant differences in ages of the *victims*. Older victims were the most likely to be injured and also the less likely to be taken seriously by law enforcement.

Cyberstalking

Cyberstalking is analogous to traditional forms of stalking in that it incorporates persistent behaviors that engender apprehension and fear. However, with the advent of new technologies, traditional stalking has taken on entirely new forms through media like e-mail, text messaging, tweets, and other avenues of social networking. It is possible that such incidents may be more common than traditional forms of stalking. This is because the basic apparatus of the Internet facilitates not only anonymity but also contact with an immense field of potential victims. Cell phones and the Internet have provided far-reaching and unregulated opportunities for cyberstalkers to harass unsuspecting victims. In addition, there is a considerable amount of personal information available through the Internet, and cyberstalkers can easily and quickly locate private information about a target.

Unsolicited e-mail is one of the most common forms of harassment, including hate, obscene, or threatening mail. Text messaging, Instagram, Twitter, and other social media outlets are becoming increasingly popular. Other forms of harassment include sending the victim computer viruses or high volumes of electronic junk mail (spamming). Electronic stalking can result from an attempt to initiate a relationship, repair a relationship, or threaten and traumatize a person. It is often accompanied by traditional stalking such as threatening phone calls, vandalism of property, threatening mail, and physical attacks (Gregorie, 2000).

It is extremely difficult to hold someone accountable for cyberstalking, however, as a recent U.S. Supreme Court decision illustrates. In *Elonis v. U.S.* (2015), a man was convicted under a federal law making it a crime to transmit via interstate communication (e.g., cyberspace) a threat to injure someone. Elonis had periodically posted violent images and rap lyrics on his Facebook account, along with disclaimers that these did not refer to real persons. In addition, he posted rantings against his estranged wife, his employer, and various government officials. His boss and estranged wife both perceived these as threats—the former fired him and the latter obtained an order of protection from abuse. However, the U.S. Supreme Court, in a unanimous decision (8–0), said prosecutors had not demonstrated that he intended to threaten these particular individuals. Although it was argued that Elonis had at least been negligent in his postings and should have known better, the Court said negligence was not sufficient to convict him of that crime.

Cyberbullying is becoming more prominent and, although similar to cyberstalking, it largely involves adolescents bullying adolescents on line. Age is a major determining factor in distinguishing the two terms, but this is not to say that adults do not get cyberbullied, in both workplace and non-workplace settings. Most studies focus on adolescents, however. At this point, we will cover the psychological aspect of bullying and then extend the coverage to include cyberbullying, which is increasing while traditional physical, face-to-face bullying is decreasing.

Peer Non-Cyberbullying

During the past two decades, "peer victimization, and especially bullying, has become recognized as a pervasive and often neglected problem in school around the world" (Cornell, Gregory, Huang, & Fan, 2013, p. 138). In one national survey, 28% of adolescents in the United States reported being victims of bullying at school during the past year (Robers, Zhang, Truman, & Snyder, 2012). Other studies have found very similar results (Faris & Felmlee, 2011b). In addition, bullying is pervasive in elementary schools, middle school, high school, and the workplace. Bullying, then, is not limited to children and adolescents.

Bullying is a form of peer aggression in which one or more individuals physically, verbally, or psychologically harass a victim who is perceived to be weaker. Examples of physical bullying include hitting, spitting, kicking, punching, pushing, or taking or destroying personal items. Verbal bullying includes name calling, taunting, malicious teasing, and verbal threats. Psychological bullying is spreading destructive or mean rumors and engaging in social exclusion, extortion, or intimidation. Very often, those who bully have been victims of bullying themselves.

Bullying can adversely affect all students in a particular school, even if they are not direct victims (Cornell et al., 2013; Vanderbilt & Augustyn, 2010). More specifically, "Bystanders may have various roles that range from assisting and reinforcing the bully to being frightened and experiencing vicarious victimization" (Cornell et al., 2013, p. 139). Bullying affects the entire climate of the school. Researchers have found that widespread bullying creates a school environment of fear and insecurity, reduces school attendance, and results in poor academic performance and dedication to schoolwork (Glew, Fan, Katon, & Rivara, 2008; Swearer, Espelage, Vaillancourt, & Hymel, 2010). As a result of chronic bullying, victims often suffer psychological problems, including depression, PTSD, and suicidal thoughts (T. Shaw, Dooley, Cross, Zubrick, & Waters, 2013). Many of these problems may continue into adulthood.

Rather than focusing on the personality traits of those who bully or are bullied, Faris and Felmlee (2011b), in a very important study, investigated the social networks in which bullying takes place. The authors argue that the role of personal deficiencies in bullying is overstated. Rather, it is the role of peer status that often leads to bullying and peer-directed aggression. The results of their study revealed that, "for the vast majority of adolescents, increases in status are, over time, accompanied by increases in aggression toward their peers" (p. 67). Their findings indicate that bullying does not emerge from isolated adolescents who are on the fringes of the school hierarchy, but rather occurs most often among relatively popular young people seeking additional status—in other words, students at the mid levels of status. A very similar finding is reported by Reijntjes and his associates (2013). High amounts of bullying were significantly related to high social status as measured by perceived popularity. Apparently, in some peer circles, aggression and bullying are a way of gaining status among that specific group of adolescents. Interestingly, Faris and Felmlee found that once bullies gained the top status level, their aggression and bullying generally stopped or were greatly reduced.

Adolescents who engage in bullying are unlikely to target strangers but often select those peers with whom they previously had close relationships. Both girls and boys engaged in bullying, but in slightly different ways. Girls were less likely to use direct forms (verbal harassment or physical violence) but somewhat more likely to spread rumors and ostracize (Faris & Felmlee, 2011b). Girls, however, were also more likely to be victimized.

Studies also show that bullying behaviors are partly maintained by the responses of those peers who witness the bullying (Salmivalli, Voeten, & Poskiparta, 2011). "Bystanders are present for 80% of bully incidents, and therefore can influence the bullying situation by promoting or reducing bullying" (Banks, Blake, & Joslin, 2013, p. 10). Studies continually show that bystanders that defend victims have the greatest likelihood of decreasing bullying. Consequently, research that focuses on the prevention of and intervention in bullying has shifted toward recognizing bullying as a group process (Howard, Landau, & Pryor, 2014). That is, the bully is often reinforced by the peer-group dynamics that occur during the episode. For example, peers spend a majority of the time watching the bullying incident and try not to get involved (O'Connell, Pepler, & Craig, 1999). Experts believe that passively watching the behavior sends a message to the bully that the bystanders approve of his or her actions. Only about 17% of peers try to defend the victim (Howard et al., 2014). More important, "When peers do intervene, either by actively defending the victim or aggressing against the bully, a majority of these efforts have proven effective" (Howard et al., 2014, p. 266).

Psychologists, particularly school psychologists and other school personnel, can help greatly in reducing peer bullying by educating students that peers are central to occurrence, maintenance, and escalation of that bullying. Howard, Landau, and Pryor (2014) warn, however, that bullying-prevention programs cannot be applied without careful consideration of the individual differences among students. Failure to appreciate and address the important differences in how children and adolescents respond to bullying will lead to only partial success in bullying reduction. As noted by Banks, Blake, and Joslin (2013),

> Many students may choose not to defend for fear of stigmatization or rejection by peers, whereas others may defend intermittently because the bully is their friend or simply because they assume someone else will speak up first on behalf of the victim. (p. 10)

In addition, most parents discuss how their children should respond to bullying, which also influences whether and how bystanders intervene. Studies reveal that children whose parents tell them not to become involved in the bullying incident are more likely to just watch or even join in the bullying (Banks et al., 2013; T. N. Sullivan et al., 2012; Traube et al., 2007).

The above findings suggest that parents should also be involved in bully-intervention programs. A study conducted by Ttofi and Farrington (2011) confirmed this approach. The researchers discovered that anti-bullying interventions that included the training of parents on how to handle bullying reduced both school bullying and victimization.

Cyberbullying

"The time has come for developmental and clinical psychologists to pay attention to the hidden world of adolescent peer culture revealed by examining adolescents' digital communication" (Underwood & Ehrenreich, 2017, p. 145). Best estimates indicate that 88% of adolescents in the United States own or have access to mobile phones, and about 25% report going online almost constantly (George & Odgers, 2015). On average, adolescents send and receive 67 text messages daily on their phones (Lenhart, 2015), and 80% of adolescent mobile phone owners report sleeping with (or presumably very near) their phones (Lenhart, Ling, Campbell, & Purcell, 2010). Most adolescents consider their phones indispensable to their social lives (Barlett, Gentile, & Chew, 2016). Adolescents turn to social media as a way of understanding how they fit in with their peers and keep tabs on what their friends are doing and whom they are with. Many, if not most, adolescents prefer to communicate with friends and peers through text messages rather than any other form of communication, including face-to-face interactions (Lenhart et al., 2010; Underwood & Ehrenreich, 2017).

The heavy use of electronic communications renders adolescents highly susceptible to become victims of cyberbullying, defined as the intentional use of electronic communication to intimidate, threaten, or embarrass another person. In one major survey of 28,104 adolescents (Grades 9–12) attending 58 Maryland high schools (Waasdorp & Bradshaw, 2015), 12.5% reported being cyberbullied in the past 3 months. Middle school students (Grades 6–8) appear to be especially susceptible to cyberbullying. A survey by Hinduja and Patchen (2009) found that 9% of middle school students reported being cyberbullied within the last 30 days, and 17% during their lifetime. Eight percent of the middle school students admitted cyberbullying someone. In another survey of 3,767 middle school students, Kowalski and Limber (2007) discovered that 18% had been cyberbullied at least once within the previous 2 months. Eleven percent said they had cyberbullied others during the past 2 months. Girls appear most likely to be both victims and perpetrators during the middle school years, while boys tend to be both victims and perpetrators in high school. A recent study by the Cyberbullying Research Center (Hinduja & Patchin, 2016a) revealed that 33.8% of students between ages 12 and 17 were victims of cyberbullying in their lifetime. In addition, the same study found that 11.5% of students between those ages had engaged in cyberbullying in their lifetime.

Cyberbullying has become a worldwide problem. In the United Kingdom, 1 in 4 youths between 11 and 19 said they had been cyberbullied (Li, 2006). Similar data were reported by Canadian youth (Li, 2006, 2010). Spain and Italy also appear to have significant problems with youth cyberbullying (Ortega et al., 2012). (See Kowalski, Giumetti, Schroeder, & Lattanner, 2014, for a complete listing of the many countries facing cyberbullying problems.)

Effects of Cyberbullying

The psychological impact of even a single episode of cyberbullying can be quite devastating to the victim (Underwood & Ehrenreich, 2017). This is especially the case if the perpetrator was believed by the victim to be a friend or known peer. "Adolescents may be deeply wounded by even a single experience of cyber victimization, which will most often happen at the hands of a friend" (Underwood & Ehrenreich, 2017, p. 155). In 2017, news media reported on the case of an 11-year-old boy who killed himself after seeing a video of his 14-year-old girlfriend who was supposedly dead. The girl herself, along with a friend, had apparently sent him the video. Many other incidents have been reported of teens either harming themselves, killing themselves, or experiencing serious psychological problems after embarrassing photos have been posted online. In the Waasdorp and Bradshaw study described previously, nearly one third of the victims said they thought it was a friend who cyberbullied them. Unfortunately, perpetrators who feel they are anonymous can be even more daring, vicious, and threatening than those who bully face to face.

Not only does the cyberattack cause havoc to the victim's self-esteem and self-image, but the message also can be immediately viewed by friends and followers (Underwood & Ehrenreich, 2017). Moreover, it potentially remains in digital space forever. Studies find that the effects on youth include anxiety disorders, sleep problems, loneliness, depression, substance use, low academic achievement, low life satisfaction, and in extreme cases, suicide attempts

(Mehari, Farrell, & Le, 2014; Underwood & Ehrenreich, 2017). Because of its established links to physical and mental health problems in youth, cyberbullying has become an emerging public health concern (Selkie, Fales, & Moreno, 2016).

Studies have generally reported that girls are more likely to be victims and perpetrators of cyberbullying than boys. However, as noted earlier, a recent study suggests that girls report more cyberbullying in early adolescence (e.g., middle school), whereas boys report more in late adolescence (Barlett & Coyne, 2014). Very little research has focused on the extent that youths of various races, ethnicities, and religions are subjected to cyberbullying.

To date, all states have a bullying law, but only 23 have laws specially pertaining to cyberbullying (Hinduja & Patchin, 2016b). There is no cyberbullying law in the United States at the federal level. In Canada, several provinces and territories have laws specifically dealing with online and offline bullying. At the federal level, Canada's parliament passed Bill C-13 which criminalizes nonconsensual distribution of intimate images online but do not include other types or content of cyberbullying.

The difficulty enacting laws directed at cyberbullying in the United States is illustrated by the fate of the Megan Meier Cyberbullying Prevention Act of 2009, a proposed federal law that would have forbade interstate or foreign digital or electronic communication with the intent to coerce, intimidate, harass or cause substantial emotional distress to a person. The proposed penalty for violating the law was a fine of $10,000 or imprisonment not more than 2 years, or both. The bill was introduced twice in the House of Representatives but failed to gain support for passage because of concerns about infringement on the First Amendment (free speech) and the overbroad aspects of the law that might provide prosecutors with too much latitude. Megan Meier was a 14-year-old girl who committed suicide after receiving a hostile, demeaning message from "Josh Evan," a "boy" she met on Myspace. Eventually, it was learned that "Josh" was really another girl, an acquaintance of Megan who lived down the street.

So far, punishment for cyberbullying has been limited to suspensions from school, provided the actions significantly disrupted the school environment. Adolescents are often reluctant to share hurtful online experiences with their parents, however (Underwood & Ehrenreich, 2017). Waasdorp and Bradshaw (2015) found that only one third of adolescents told their parents about being cyberbullied. Parental monitoring and support are helpful but, as Underwood and Ehrenreich point out, adolescents are continually embracing new digital platforms which become overwhelming to understand. Even for parents who try to monitor the digital lives of adolescents, this is a major challenge—70% of teens admit they are skillful at avoiding parental monitoring.

SUMMARY AND CONCLUSIONS

Violence, the definition of which indicates that it requires some display of physical force, is essentially atypical human behavior when we compare it with the vast amount of human behavior that is nonviolent. Nonetheless, it remains a fascinating area of study as well as a pervasive aspect of popular culture. In fact, as we saw in this chapter, the increasingly violent images in the media have prompted research studies that in turn have led to calls for limiting the exposure of children—particularly young children—to these images. We saw that aggression, a construct frequently studied by psychologists, does not necessarily result in the physical force that we defined as violence. In addition, society actually condones some forms of violence, which further complicates any attempts to prevent it, predict it, or treat those who display violence or who are its victims.

The chapter focused primarily on criminal violence as it is defined in the law and in crime statistics. The four Part I violent crimes—murder and nonnegligent manslaughter, rape, aggravated assault, and robbery—together comprise about one third of the total Part 1 crimes committed. Persons arrested for these crimes are predominantly male (87%–90%), although the violent crime rate for females began to increase faster than the male rate in the 1990s. Women continue to appear in arrest statistics far less often than men, however, a phenomenon for which a variety of explanations has been proposed. The most common explanations relate to either socialization or biological differences.

Race and ethnic differences in violent crime have received greater attention, and these differences are among the most troubling to researchers and policy makers alike. African Americans, particularly males, continue to make up a disproportionate part of official statistics on violent crime. The chapter emphasized that numerous social factors can explain these differentials and warned against attributing any biological factors to the differences.

We also cautioned against focusing on one racial or ethnic group to the exclusion of others, noting that researchers are beginning to explore differences among these groups. Psychologists and criminologists as a group often discuss violence as being instrumental, or reactive-expressive, or some combination of both. Studies suggest that the great majority of criminal violence—including homicide—is instrumental. Offenders commit the crime to achieve a particular goal, be it material goods, recognition, or political change. Psychologists and criminologists also have explored biological, social, cognitive, and situational factors as explanations for violent behavior. At present, it appears that a combination of all four categories of factors is the best way to approach the study of violence. However, we emphasize that, although some researchers have found biological links to aggression, any biological predisposition can be attenuated (or lessened) with careful attention to social, cognitive, and situational factors. To use one example, the social environment of a child who is highly aggressive as the result of some brain damage can be modified to make it less likely that that child will display violent behavior.

The chapter covered criminal homicide, the violent crime that is the least frequent but has received considerable research attention. The typical homicide is the single killing committed either in the course of another felony—most often a robbery—or committed against a relative or acquaintance. Young adult males are the most likely perpetrators of these single murders. Atypical murders—particularly those that qualify as multiple murders (serial, spree, and mass murders)—have most fascinated and frightened the public. We discussed in detail both serial and mass murderers because they have received the most research attention.

Serial murderers—so called because of the time interval between their killings—generally begin their murderous behavior at a later age than single murderers. Most are male, but their victims may be male or female—they generally show a preference for one or the other. Although there is no "serial murderer personality" or profile, serial murderers as a group appear to be persuasive and to delude their victims into thinking that they pose no danger to them. Serial murderers *as a group* are not mentally disordered in the traditional sense; that is, they do not fit traditional diagnostic categories of mental illness, although some qualify as criminal psychopaths. In some typologies of serial murderers, however, one type does display psychotic behavior.

Mass murderers—who kill three or more individuals during one incident—are generally divided into classic and family types, but a terrorist mass murder type should also be added. Although there are highly publicized illustrations of mass murders in public places, most mass murders seem to be family murders. When the perpetrator is a member of the family, he or she is also likely to commit suicide in conjunction with the incident. Compared with serial murderers, mass murderers are more likely to be isolated, disenchanted, and ineffective individuals whose crime is precipitated by what they perceive as a tragic loss, such as abandonment by a significant other or loss of employment.

Violence in schools and in the workplace has attracted intense media attention. Although school shootings are statistically rare in light of the vast number of schools in the United States, they continue to occur with regularity. Even when only one life is lost, the tragedy touches the entire community. No one profile of a school shooter exists, but researchers have identified some common features as well as "red flags" that *may* alert school officials. When an individual student is believed to pose a threat, mental health practitioners may be asked to conduct a threat assessment. Workplace violence includes homicides, but the vast majority of workplace violence incidents do not end in death. In fact, most of these incidents are not actually violence but rather *threats* of violence. Forensic psychologists have critical roles, not only in alerting employers to potentially violent individuals in the workplace, but also in facilitating a working environment that fosters acceptance and cooperation among all employees. However, a substantial portion of workplace violence is committed by outsiders or by former workers or supervisors.

The chapter ended with a discussion of bias crimes, stalking, and bullying, and the cyber versions of each of these. Of these, bias crimes qualify more directly as criminal violence, if the underlying offense is a violent crime, such as assault. Vandalism, such as spray-painting racist slogans, defacing mosques, or upending cemetery markers, is a continuing problem and one in which the perpetrator is often not identified. Although incidents of bias or hate crimes have increased in recent years, the number reported nationwide does not seem overwhelming, but we cautioned that many bias crimes go unreported to police. In addition, police agencies vary greatly in the extent to which they enforce bias crime statutes or record bias crimes.

Stalking was sometimes referred to as the crime of the 1990s. Its traditional form—following, sending mail, or telephoning victims—is now supplemented by cyberstalking, which is stalking via electronic communication. Researchers have proposed typologies of stalkers that are similar to the typologies proposed for serial killers and mass murderers. One very recent typology is that proposed by Beatty et al. (2002), who describe simple, love obsession, erotomania, and vengeance stalking. Although not violent in itself, stalking (whether in traditional or online form) engenders fear—sometimes debilitating fear—in its victims. An undetermined percentage of stalkers do ultimately exhibit violent behavior. For the forensic psychologist, this is another illustration of the risk assessment enterprise discussed in Chapters 4 and 5 that is such an essential component of many clinical practices. We discussed recent efforts to distinguish between those stalkers who are likely to be violent and those who will cease their stalking behavior without harming their victims. At present, it appears that victims who are former intimate partners of the stalker are most at risk of being physically harmed. Past violent behavior does not appear to be a strong predictor of violence associated with stalking, but the research is somewhat inconsistent on this point and needs further attention.

Psychologists, particularly those consulting with schools, have been concerned with bullying, including cyberbullying, in recent years, in light of evidence that this is an increasing problem, particularly among children and adolescents. Although we focused on bullying among children and adolescents, because this is where the research takes us, it is important to recognize that bullying also occurs among adults. Research suggests a complex interaction between bullying and being bullied. Adolescents who bully others were often bullied themselves in their childhoods, so early detection and prevention are crucial aspects to be considered. Bullying also may be used as a means of gaining status among some peers; when the status is achieved, the bullying behavior no longer continues. Recent research on bullying indicates that both peer intervention (encouraging peers to speak out against it) and adequate parental education about bullying represent the most effective means to address this problem.

KEY CONCEPTS

QUESTIONS FOR REVIEW

1. What are the four categories of the causes of violence discussed in the psychological literature?

2. Provide illustrations of gender, race, and ethnic differences in violence.

3. Summarize the negative effects of constant viewing of violence in the media.

4. Distinguish among single murder, serial murder, mass murder, and spree murder.

5. List and define the typologies of serial killers.

6. What are the two major types of mass murder?

7. Why is the term *workplace violence* somewhat of a misnomer?

8. Describe the four major categories of workplace violence.

9. Define hate or bias crime and tell how the criminal justice system has responded to these crimes.

10. List any five findings from the research on (a) stalking and (b) bullying.

 SAGE edge™

Want a better grade? Go to **edge.sagepub.com/bartol5e** for the tools you need to sharpen your study skills. Access practice quizzes, eFlashcards, an action plan, and SAGE journal articles for enhanced learning.

CHAPTER NINE

A man in Chicago held captive three women in the basement of his home before they ultimately managed to escape, along with a child born during the period of captivity.

A study reported that nearly one-fourth of juveniles held in detention facilities nationwide reported being sexually assaulted by staff or other juveniles.

Both political figures and academic researchers have brought attention to the problem of sexual assault on college campuses and in the military.

A presidential candidate bragged about the unwanted groping of women by the genitals, but his comments were brushed off by many as "locker-room talk."

Sexual assault is a pervasive global crime. Human rights organizations have reported widespread examples of assaults, particularly but certainly not exclusively against women and girls, in many countries including the United States. Those who commit these crimes attack for a wide variety of reasons.

After three decades of research, it is clear that sexual assault is a multidetermined behavior committed by a heterogeneous group of offenders. Although desire for power, control, and dominance is usually the primary reason, sexual gratification may be the primary reason as well. Even when gratification is a primary motive, however, the exertion of power and control are almost as important—if not equally so. Addressing the heterogeneity of sexual offenders and their motives is critical if we are to identify effective strategies for offender management and treatment (S. L. Brown & Forth, 1997).

Forensic psychologists encounter sex offenders primarily as individuals they are evaluating in a number of contexts. An alleged sex offender may be assessed before a judge decides to grant bail; a convicted offender may be assessed before a judge determines a sentence. Psychologists often conduct risk assessments of juvenile sex offenders and evaluate them with respect to their amenability for rehabilitation. Correctional psychologists also offer treatment to sex offenders both in community and prison settings. A sex offender being released from prison may be assessed as to whether he is dangerous and should be involuntarily civilly committed. Forensic psychologists also may help police investigating

Chapter Objectives

- Define sexual assault and rape and identify the incidence of each.

- Examine the characteristics of men who rape and sexually assault.

- Acquaint the reader with the Massachusetts Treatment Center and Groth typologies for rapists and child molesters.

- Define and review the research and clinical data on pedophilia.

- Review research on juvenile sex offenders, both male and female.

- Discuss sexual exploitation of children through the Internet.

- Describe the procedures for the psychological assessment of sex offenders.

sex crimes, such as by identifying categories of sex offenders, or testify in court as experts on the treatment of sexual offenders. We cover research relating to each of these contexts in the chapter.

In this chapter, we also provide a comprehensive summary of the incidence and complexity of sexual assault, the known characteristics and developmental histories of various sex offenders, and the methods commonly used to assess and evaluate them. The effect of sexual assault on victims will be covered in Chapter 11, and the treatment of convicted sex offenders will be described in Chapter 12. It will be emphasized there, as it is in the present chapter, that sex offenders are a diverse group. The etiology or causes of such offending varies widely, and there are surprisingly few common demographic factors in their backgrounds. Furthermore, professionals who work in this area in many contexts (e.g., police officers investigating crimes, clinicians evaluating offenders or offering treatment, mental health practitioners providing services to victims, and even researchers gathering data) are susceptible to emotional burnout (Recall Perspective 8.1 in the previous chapter in which Dr. Angela Eke discusses this. Also see Perspective 9.1 in which Dr. Leigh Harkins refers to her work in sex offender treatment settings.)

This chapter will also cover typologies of sexual offenders that are often used by both law enforcement officials and mental health professionals. As explained in the previous chapter, typologies, which place people into categories or groupings, are an important first step in the understanding and management of crimes and perpetrators, including sexual assault. A typology is useful in classifying a wide assortment of behaviors, attitudes, motives, and beliefs into a manageable set of meaningful descriptions. It helps put order into an otherwise chaotic mass of observations, a process that enables research, assessment, prevention, treatment, and policy planning to take place. Offender typologies also highlight the enormous complexity of sexual offending and emphasize that there is no single type of sex offender. Nevertheless, as previously mentioned, typologies are not perfect tools and must continually be revised and validated.

FROM MY PERSPECTIVE 9.1

No Single Path, But Persistence and Guidance Can Get You There

Leigh Harkins, PhD

Courtesy of Leigh Harkins.

When I was working on my undergraduate degree, if someone had told me I could be a professor one day, I'd have laughed and told them they 100% had the wrong person. It wasn't that I didn't think I was smart or willing to work hard, but to me that kind of achievement seemed so unattainable. I had only begun to start thinking about the possibility of graduate school in my 4th year through the support of my undergraduate

thesis supervisor (and because everyone else in my Honours Thesis class was!).

Around the same time, I had also begun a placement (or internship) at the Centre for Addiction and Mental Health in Toronto, which really set me on the path to where I am today. As part of this placement, I was given the opportunity to sit in on treatment groups for men who had committed sexual offenses. I was initially shocked hearing details about the offenses they had committed, but as I got to know them, it became increasingly easier to see past the offenses to the person. For example, I started to care about how their job interviews had gone. The realization that these men were so much more than their offenses solidified for me the importance of treatment, not just for preventing future crimes and sparing more victims, but also for ensuring a future for the men who had committed the offenses.

As a result of being involved in this treatment group, I was offered a volunteer research assistant position (which eventually evolved into a paid position). I read and coded hundreds of treatment files of men who had committed sexual offenses. The tremendous range of experiences and factors that contributed to their offenses was fascinating to me. That opportunity really ignited in me a passion for research that ultimately resulted in pursuing a MA in counselling psychology from the Ontario Institute for Studies in Education at the University of Toronto (which also included another opportunity for a practicum working in treatment groups with the Correctional Service of Canada), and PhD in forensic psychology from the University of Birmingham in the United Kingdom, examining important factors in the effectiveness of treatment for men who had committed sexual offenses. For example, I found that denying one's offense was related to lower levels of reoffending instead of higher as is commonly assumed.

However, I don't want to suggest that this path was straight and easy, or clear cut. When I discovered how much I enjoyed treatment, I thought the next logical step was to apply to clinical psychology programs. I did loads of research into clinical psychology programs and potential supervisors throughout Canada and the United States; I worked tirelessly on my statements of intent; I studied and wrote my GREs; and I submitted my applications. Unfortunately, after all that, I didn't get in to any of them! Looking back, I know now that this was not surprising because clinical programs have limited openings and are notoriously difficult to get into. Although I had pretty much decided my career was over before it had even started, I sought guidance and support from my supervisors and mentors. They helped me see how many other options there were out there, including counselling psychology and pursuing research degrees on clinical psychology related topics. Their guidance, along with their continuous support and encouragement, helped me persevere until I found programs that were the right fit for my interests.

So, seek and accept support and guidance where it is offered. It can help you see your way through doors you hadn't noticed before. Also, try to take advantage of opportunities that come your way. Throughout my PhD, I tried my best to take every opportunity that my supervisor offered, even if it wasn't directly related to my PhD. These opportunities took me off in a variety of different directions, including travelling around to prisons all across the United Kingdom with a theatre group called Geese Theatre Company that uses interactive theatre and facilitates drama-based group work in criminal justice settings, to evaluate some of Geese's programs. I also did an evaluation for the Ministry of Justice in the United Kingdom that eventually led to me being invited to give training and presentations in Finland and Sweden on the Good Lives Model of Offender Rehabilitation (i.e., a strengths-based rehabilitation framework). As much as you have to be pro-active about carving your path, also remain open to opportunities. You never know what unexpected and wonderful directions they may take you and how or where new passions and ideas might be sparked.

Dr. Harkins is an Associate Professor in forensic psychology at University of Ontario Institute of Technology. She enjoys biking, playing volleyball, music festivals, vegan cooking, and being bossed around by a small ginger wiener dog.

DEFINITIONS OF SEXUAL ASSAULT AND RAPE

Legal definitions of what constitutes a sexual offense vary widely from state to state. In a majority of states, the broad term **sexual assault** has replaced the term rape in the criminal statutes. **Rape** is a narrower term, referring to forced penetration of vaginal, anal, or oral regions of the body. Sexual assault recognizes that victims also may be violated in ways that do not involve penetration, such as groping or fondling. In addition, in an effort to include males as victims, the statutes are becoming increasingly gender neutral.

The definitions used in federal criminal law parallel the changes in definitions in many states. To begin with, the Federal Criminal Code (Title 18, Chapter 109A, Sections 2241–2243) definition of sexual assault does not use the term *rape* and does not require the victim to label the act as rape to meet the criteria (legally called the elements) for the crime (Kilpatrick, Whalley, & Edmunds, 2002). Second, the federal code distinguishes between two types of sexual assault on the basis of the degree of force or threat of force used: (1) aggravated sexual assault and (2) sexual assault.

Aggravated sexual abuse by force or threat of force, according to the federal code, is when a person

> knowingly causes another person to engage in a sexual act or . . . attempts to do so by using force against the person, or by threatening or placing that person in fear that the person will be subjected to death, serious bodily injury, or kidnapping. (n.p.)

The federal code also tries to take into consideration recent increases in the use of "date rape drugs" or "acquaintance rape drugs" by defining aggravated sexual abuse by other means. This occurs when a person knowingly renders another person unconscious and thereby engages in a sexual act with that person. Aggravated sexual abuse by other means also occurs when a person administers to another person by force or threat of force, or without the knowledge or permission of that person, a drug, intoxicant, or similar substance and thereby (1) substantially impairs the ability of that person to appraise or control conduct and (2) engages in a sexual act with that person.

The Federal Criminal Code defines sexual abuse—as opposed to aggravated sexual abuse—in two ways, in terms of whether it involves

1. Causing another person to engage in a sexual activity by threatening or placing that person in fear; or

2. Engaging in a sexual act with someone when that person is incapable of declining participation in or communicating unwillingness to engage in that sexual act.

Definitions for Gathering Statistics

As we discussed in Chapter 7, the U.S. government has three major crime measures, each published in a separate document: the *Uniform Crime Reports* (UCR), the *National Incident-Based Reporting System* (NIBRS), and the *National Crime Victimization Survey* (NCVS). All three measures define sexual assault slightly differently.

The Uniform Crime Reports (UCR)

The UCR divides sexual offenses into two categories: (1) **forcible rape** and (2) [other] sexual offenses. Beginning in 2013, the FBI began collecting rape data under a revised definition. Before that time, "forcible rape" was defined as "the carnal knowledge of a female forcibly and against her will." As of December 2013, the term *forcible* was removed from the definition. The revised definition of rape is "penetration, no matter how slight, of the vagina or anus with any body part or object, or oral penetration of a sex organ of another person, without the consent of the victim." Attempts or assaults to commit rape are also included in UCR rape data, but statutory rape and incest are not. In UCR data, the old definition is referred to as the legacy definition, and the new description is called the revised definition. In the 2015 rape statistics, the UCR continues to present the data under the legacy definition.

The UCR counts one offense as rape, regardless of whether it was rape, attempted rape, or assault with intent to rape, and regardless of the victim's age or sex. Note the change from the legacy definition, which included only rapes in which the victim was a female. Sexual relations without the victim's consent which involves a family member is classified as a rape and not an act of incest.

All other crimes of a sexual nature are classified as Part II offenses. They include such behaviors as fondling or groping sexual parts of another's body and lewd and lascivious actions, such as exposing one's sexual organs to unsuspecting others.

Statutory rapes, in which no force is used but the female victim is under the age of consent, are part of a list of offenses for which only arrest data are collected in the UCR. This is not to say that the offenses are not serious; many qualify as felonies. It is estimated, however, that approximately 25% of the sex crimes committed against minors and reported to the police involve statutory rape (Troup-Leasure & Snyder, 2005). However, even if a statutory rape is reported to police, it will appear in the UCR only if someone is arrested. The UCR program counts each offense in which a female of any age is forcibly raped or on whom an assault to rape or attempt to rape is made. Of the total rapes reported for 2012, about 93% were classified as rapes, and the remainder were categorized as attempts (Federal Bureau of Investigation [FBI], 2013a).

Note that until 2013, the UCR program did not recognize rape when males were the victims. Although this has now changed, the gathering of statistics is still in transition and will likely take a few years to accomplish. Thus, to this point, the statistics reported in the UCR and in this chapter will be based on the legacy definition, where only females are victims. Until recently, reported sexual attacks on males were considered aggravated assaults or other sex offenses, depending on circumstances and the extent of injuries; they were not considered rapes.

The UCR also does not tabulate cases in which the offender uses threats of *nonphysical* force to obtain sex, such as threatening a person with the loss of a job or other punishment if this person does not comply. However, some state legislatures have broadened the definition of force and have criminalized sex obtained by certain nonphysical forms of coercion (Kinports, 2002).

The National Incident-Based Reporting System (NIBRS)

The NIBRS, to be discussed again in Chapter 11, has the potential to yield fairly detailed descriptions of sexual assaults reported by participating law enforcement agencies. The NIBRS divides crimes into two major categories: Group A and Group B. Group A contains the 46 most serious crimes, including sexual offenses, and Group B contains 11 of the less serious offenses, such as passing bad checks. The sex offenses in Group A are divided into two subcategories, forcible and non-forcible. The forcible offenses include forcible rape (distinguished from statutory), forcible sodomy, sexual assault with an object, and forcible fondling. For these offenses, the NIBRS provides, among other things, data that include the following:

- Demographic information on all victims;

- Levels of victim injury;

- Victim's perceptions of offender's age, gender, race, and ethnicity;

- Victim–offender relationship.

The NIBRS also collects information on the weapons used, location of the incident, and the demographics of the offender (if arrested). Like the UCR, the NIBRS is based on law enforcement data and does not include information on convictions.

The National Crime Victimization Survey (NCVS)

The **National Crime Victimization Survey (NCVS)** is a government-sponsored survey of victims of crime. In the NCVS, rape is defined as forced sexual intercourse in which the victim may be either male or female. Sexual assault—on the other hand—includes a wide range of victimizations involving attacks in which unwanted sexual contact occurs between the victim and the offender(s). Threats and attempts to commit such offenses are included in the victimization data reported by the NCVS.

Many existing laws require that both force and lack of consent be proved before an individual can be convicted of rape or sexual assault. Traditionally, for example, a lack of resistance by the victim was interpreted as evidence of consent. Ironically, at the same time, victims were often advised not to resist because that would only anger the rapist even more. Although no jurisdiction still adheres to the requirement that the victim must have resisted "to the utmost," some state courts continue to require some reasonable resistance unless the force exercised by the offender prevented the victim from resisting (Kinports, 2002). The issue of consent is a critical component in most court cases involving rape or sexual assault because persons accused of these crimes who choose to go to trial often use consent as their defense when their alleged victim was an adult.

Statutory Rape Statistics

As noted above, **statutory rape** is the unlawful sexual intercourse with a female younger than the age of consent, which may be anywhere between 12 and 18, depending on the jurisdiction and state statute. Most states, however, use a cutoff point of age 16 or 18. The age of consent is an arbitrary legal cutoff considered to be the age at which the person has the cognitive and emotional maturity to give meaningful consent and understand the consequences. If the female was below the age of consent, the state is not required to prove that the intercourse was without her consent, as she is presumed incapable of consenting because of her young age. Moreover, a mistake made by the offender as to the victim's age is usually not a valid defense. Kinports (2002) writes that though making statutory rape a crime was "traditionally justified as a means of preserving an unmarried girl's economic value to her father, today it is seen as a way of protecting vulnerable children" (p. 737). Increasingly, many contemporary state statutes are becoming gender neutral, encompassing both boys and girls. Therefore, the female teacher who has "consensual" sex with her 15-year-old male student can be charged with statutory rape. Furthermore, most states exempt peer relationships from statutory rape laws by requiring a minimum age for the offender or an age differential (typically 2 years) for the youths.

Rape by Fraud

Rape by fraud refers to the act of having sexual relations with a consenting adult under fraudulent conditions. A frequently cited example is when a professional psychotherapist has sexual intercourse with a patient under the guise of "effective treatment."

Despite these broad and much-needed shifts in definition, the terms *rape* and *sexual assault* are still used interchangeably in both law and research to describe crimes that involve unwanted and illegal sexual acts. This is especially true with official government documents, such as those published by the U.S. Department of Justice. Even there, use of the term *rape* is increasingly reserved for sexual acts that involve actual or threatened sexual penetration, whereas sexual assault refers to a wide range of sexual attacks, including rape. Put another way, rape is always sexual assault, but sexual assault is not always rape.

Mindful of the distinctions and changes in definitions and requirements, we will continue to use the term *rape* when it is clear that penetration is an issue. Otherwise, sexual assault will be used. In addition, our discussion of research studies and typologies will employ the terminology favored by the researchers who conducted and developed them.

Prevalence and Incidence of Rape and Other Sexual Assaults

National victimization surveys indicate that the vast majority of sexual assaults are never reported to law enforcement (Kilpatrick et al., 2002; Langton, Berzofsky, Krebs, & Smiley-McDonald, 2012). Both the NCVS and data from nongovernmental sources support this observation. According to the NCVS, only about one third of sexual assaults were reported to authorities over the 5-year period 2005–2010. (Langton et al., 2012). Most of the victims in the NCVS said they did not report rape because they were afraid of reprisal or getting the offender in trouble (see Table 9.1).

National studies also indicate that victims are reluctant to label the experience as a sexual assault if the attacker is a spouse, boyfriend, or acquaintance (Acierno, Resnick, & Kilpatrick, 1997). Victims with disabilities are even less likely to report sexual assaults because of their social isolation and fear (Kilpatrick et al., 2002). Many of the assailants are family members or caretakers, and the victims do not want to get them in trouble, and fear loss of support or services if they report. In recent years, the public has been made more aware of sexual assaults in correctional facilities, college campuses, and within the military, where the rates of reporting are believed to be even lower. (See Focus 9.1 for a discussion of sexual assault in the military.)

Table 9.1 Rape and Sexual Assault Victimizations Against Women and Girls Reported and Not Reported to Police, 2005–2010	
Total	**100%**
Reported	**36%**
Primary Reason Reported	
To stop incident or prevent recurrence or escalation	25%
To get help or recover lost possessions	3%
To protect respondent and household from further crimes by offender	28%
To catch/punish/prevent offender from reoffending	17%
To improve police surveillance/duty to tell police	21%
Other/unknown/not one most important reason	6%
Not Reported	**64%**
Primary Reason Not Reported	
Reported to different official (e.g., school personnel)	8%
Personal matter	13%
Not important enough to respond	8%
Police could not do anything to help	2%
Police would not do anything to help	13%
Did not want to get offender in trouble with law	7%
Advised not to report	1%
Fear of reprisal	20%
Other/unknown/not one most important reason	30%

Source: Adapted from Planty, Langton, Krebs, Berzofsky, & Smiley-McDonald (2013).

Military sexual assaults reported to the Department of Justice have increased in recent years. According to a Pentagon report released in early 2014, covering the period July 1, 2012, through June 30, 2013, the Defense Department had received 3,553 such reports, which represented an increase of 43% from the year before. Sexual assaults include rapes and attempted rapes and forcible touchings but do not include sexual harassment, which is reported under a different system. Although both women and men may be victims of sexual assault, data on women are more available. Some statistics suggest that between 20% and 48% of servicewomen are sexually assaulted, that every day more than 70 incidents of unwanted sexual conduct occur, that more military women live with PTSD as a result of rape than PTSD from combat experiences, and that female soldiers are 15 times more likely to be raped by a comrade than killed by the enemy.

The sexual assaults include civilians against service members and service members against civilians in addition to service members against service members. The increase in numbers in recent years reflects some willingness of those assaulted to come forward, suggesting that steps are being taken to address the problem.

Psychologists—typically though not exclusively military psychologists—are likely to be involved in this issue in several ways. They may evaluate survivors who bring civil suits against their aggressors, consult with attorneys on the psychological consequences of sexual abuse, provide treatment for victims of sexual assault, participate in educational and prevention programs for all military personnel, and testify before Congress on related legislation, or testify in court about the effects of sexual trauma. These are just a few tasks awaiting the attention of psychologists.

Questions for Discussion

1. Of the tasks mentioned above, which are the most likely to be undertaken by *forensic* psychologists if that term is narrowly defined?
2. How can psychologists be most effective in addressing the problems of sexual assault in the military?
3. What are the challenges of obtaining accurate information about sexual assault (a) in the military, (b) on college campuses, and (c) in correctional facilities?

According to the UCR, 83,376 rapes of females (both women and girls are counted) were recorded during 2015 (FBI, 2016a). The total number of both females and male victims, under the revised definition, was 124,047. Based on that volume, 28.1 of every 100,000 females (legacy definition) and 38.8 per 100,000 of the general population were victims of rape during 2015. The rate of forcible rapes during the past 10 to 15 years has shown a discernible downward trend, but as always we should be cautious in interpreting these statistics. About 8 out of 10 rapes and sexual assaults go unreported to the police and an estimated 73% to 93% of sexual assaults that *are* reported are never prosecuted (Campbell et al., 2014; Lonsway & Archambault, 2012; Shaw, Campbell, Cain, & Feeney, 2016).

For UCR purposes, an offense is "cleared" when at least one person is arrested and charged or when circumstances beyond the control of law enforcement preclude an arrest for a crime that police believe has been solved. The latter would occur when a victim decides not to cooperate with police after initially doing so, or a suspect dies before an arrest can be made. Nationally, 38.2% of rapes (legacy definition) and 37.8% (revised definition) were cleared during 2015 (FBI, 2016a). However, it is important to remind ourselves that—for a variety of reasons—a majority of rapes are not reported to police. Moreover, as noted above, only a small percentage are prosecuted.

Numerous studies have been conducted by both independent and government-sponsored researchers to shed light on the prevalence of sexual assault in general and among specific groups (e.g., college students, ethnic populations, emotionally and intellectually disabled people). The National Intimate Partner and Sexual Violence Survey (NIPSV) reports that about 1 in 5 women (18.3%) and 1 in 71 men in the United States have been raped sometime during their lives, whether it was completed forced penetration, attempted forced penetration, or alcohol- or drug-facilitated completed penetration (M. C. Black et al., 2011). More than half (51.1%) of female victims said they had been raped by an intimate partner, and another 40.8% had been raped by an acquaintance, such as a boyfriend or date. About one half (52.4%) of the male victims reported they were raped by an acquaintance and 15.1% by a stranger. Half of the female victims stated they experienced their first completed rape before age 18.

Survey research in the United States and Canada suggests that more than 50% of college women have been victims of some form of sexual assault (Morry & Winkler, 2001). The National Women's Survey (Kilpatrick, Edmunds, & Seymour, 1992) found that about 13% of adult women had been victims of completed rape, and about 14% had been victims of other types of sexual assault. The National Survey of Adolescents (Kilpatrick & Saunders, 1997) determined that an estimated 13% of female adolescents and 3.4% of male adolescents had been victims of sexual assault at some point.

A substantial percentage of American youth date and have romantic relationships at an early age (Garthe, Sullivan, & McDaniel, 2017). For example, about half of all adolescents have been on at least one date by age 12 (Garthe et al., 2017; Steinberg, 2014b). Unfortunately, a large number of adolescent youths who date are victimized by violence and sexual assault.

DATE OR ACQUAINTANCE RAPE

Date rape (also known as **acquaintance rape**) refers to a sexual assault that occurs within the context of a dating relationship. Date and acquaintance rape is far more common than generally realized, representing about 80% of all rapes (Planty, Langton, Krebs, Berzofsky, & Smiley-McDonald, 2013). These data imply that only one fifth of the sexual violence in the United States is committed by strangers. Although the terms *date rape* and *acquaintance rape* are often used interchangeably, date rape technically refers to sexual assault that occurs within the context of a dating relationship, while acquaintance rape refers to a sexual assault by a person whom the victim knows out of the context of a dating relationship—e.g., a friend, neighbor, classmate, or relative. Approximately one third of these assaults are committed by an intimate partner (former or current spouse, girlfriend or boyfriend) and 38% are committed by a friend or acquaintance (Planty et al., 2013). Women ages 18 to 24 have the highest incidence of rape and sexual assault victimization compared with females (women and girls) in other age groups (Sinozich & Langton, 2014).

Thus far, research in this area has focused primarily on college students (Post, Biroscak, & Barboza, 2011). In a national study of nearly 4,500 college women, Bonnie Fisher et al. (2000) found that 10% reported having been raped in their lifetimes, and another 11% reported having experienced an attempted rape involving threatened or actual physical force. Another 35% said they had experienced some form of nonconsensual sexual contact. A very large portion of the rapes occurred during a college dating situation. The Fisher et al. study estimates that 9 out of 10 of the college women knew the man who raped them. In another survey, over one fourth of the college women had experienced unwanted sexual contact ranging from kissing and petting to oral, anal, or vaginal intercourse since enrolling in college (Gross, Winslett, Roberts, & Gohm, 2006). The survey discovered that 41% of the offenders were boyfriends, followed by friends (29%), and acquaintances (21%). (See Photo 9.1.)

The connection between alcohol use and date or acquaintance rape is strong. In more than half of sexual assaults involving dating partners, alcohol had been consumed by either one or both partners (Gross, Bennett, Sloan, Marx, & Jurgens, 2001; Ullman, Karabatsos, & Koss,

▶ **Photo 9.1** Students on a university campus listen to a speaker on sexual assault shortly after misogynistic and hateful posts appeared on a Facebook page allegedly operated by students. The posts included comments supporting the drugging and raping of women. *Source:* © iStockphoto.com/shaunl.

1999). Women who consume alcohol may be perceived by many young males as sexually available (Abbey, Zawacki, & McAuslan, 2000), and thus are more likely to be the targets of sexual predators (Abbey, Zawacki, Buck, Clinton, & McAuslan, 2004). However, as Sarah Ullman (2007b) warns, "women's drinking in and of itself should not be assumed to increase their risk of sexual victimization" (p. 419). She notes that research has found that rapes where only offenders were drinking were related to greater rape completion and victim injury, "suggesting a greater role of offender, not victim, drinking in assault outcomes" (p. 419). Clearly, the role of drinking with respect to injury received is a complicated one.

In many date rapes, the male believes he is entitled to "payback" because he probably initiated the date; paid most of the expenses; and drove his vehicle or provided transportation, if transportation was needed. Over a decade ago, M. S. Hill and Fischer (2001) found in their study of male college students that "feelings of entitlement" appear to be a central feature in date rape behaviors and attitudes. Changing concepts of "dating," such as the couple agreeing to share the cost or the woman initiating the date, will likely begin to diminish this payback attitude.

One of the more consistent findings in the research literature on date rape is that men, compared to women, tend to assign more blame to victims and less blame to perpetrators (Basow & Minieri, 2010; Munsch & Willer, 2012). However, not all of the research supports these gender differences. K. A. Black and McCloskey (2013) suggest that belief in traditional gender roles held by both men and women may still play a very significant role in date rape situations as well as reacting to them, such as attributing blame or giving opinions about punishment. They point out that some men who believe in traditional male–female roles "may feel compelled to behave in ways that establish authority and maintain control in intimate relationships" (p. 951). Some women who hold traditional attitudes, on the other hand, may see other women as objectifying themselves to attract men's attention, or place greater priority on maintaining the relationship. K. A. Black and McCloskey argue that these beliefs in traditional gender roles not only get incorporated into a person's attitudes about sexual relations, but also strongly influence judgments about what happens in dating situations. In their important date rape study, the researchers discovered the following:

> Participants with traditional gender role attitudes attributed greater responsibility to the victim and less responsibility to the perpetrator, were less likely to agree that the woman should report the incident and that the perpetrator should be arrested and found guilty of rape, and recommended a more lenient sentence for the perpetrator than did participants with liberal attitudes. (p. 962)

Belief in traditional gender roles may influence the behavior of those who interact with rape victims as well, such as police, medical personnel, and acquaintances. Judgmental behavior on the part of these individuals may be a reflection of traditional gender role attitudes and the existence of rape myths that society has yet to eradicate. For example, sexual assault nurse examiners (SANEs), who are called into emergency rooms when a rape victim comes in, indicate that triage nurses and other medical personnel unfortunately too often display little empathy for these victims. Rape myths will be discussed again below.

DEMOGRAPHICS OF MEN WHO RAPE

One of the most consistent demographic findings about rapists is that, as a group, they tend to be young. According to data reported in the UCR, for instance, 41% of those arrested for rape are younger than age 25, and more than 15% of those arrested are younger than age 18 (FBI, 2016a). Another consistent finding is that *many* men convicted of rape manifest a wide spectrum of antisocial behavior across their early life span. In other words, many of these sex offenders engage in both sexual and nonsexual crimes. One extensive study (Mercado, Jeglic, Markus, Hanson, & Levenson, 2011) found that about 70% of the sexual offenders had been charged with a prior *nonsexual* offense. Warren, Hazelwood, and Reboussin (1991) report that in their sample of serial rapists, 71% were involved with shoplifting, 55% were assaultive to adults, 24% set fires, and 19% were violently cruel to animals during childhood and adolescence. Hanson and Morton-Bourgon (2005) found that most sexual offenders are not caught for another sexual crime. On average, they were more likely to be arrested for a nonsexual offense rather than a sexual offense. The overall recidivism rate for all sex offenders in the study was 36%, which included both sexual and most often nonsexual offenses. The point to remember is that most sex offenders, but especially rapists, do not specialize in any one type of crime, but engage in a wide spectrum of criminal behavior.

Sexual Homicide

Approximately 40% of rape victims reported that they had also been physically beaten during the incident (Tjaden & Thoennes, 2006). Eleven percent indicated the attacker used a weapon to gain submission from their victim. When murder involves rape and other sex offenses, it is referred to as a *sexual assault murder*. Although they draw a great deal of attention from the entertainment media, sexual assault murders account for less than 1% of all homicides with known circumstances in the United States (Chan, Heide, & Myers, 2013; Chan, Myers, & Heide, 2010). It should be noted that the UCR and most law enforcement agencies in North America and the United Kingdom treat sexual homicide as an "ordinary" homicide for purposes of official reporting (Chan et al., 2010). Part of the problem in obtaining statistical data on the offense is that there is considerable debate about what defines sexual homicide, and furthermore, such a distinction is not always apparent at the crime scene. Surprisingly, though, according to Greenfeld (1997) and A. Hill, Haberman, Klussman, Berner, and Briken (2008), offenders younger than age 18 had accounted for 10% to 11% of the sexual assault murders that took place during a 30-year period.

In a large sample of nearly 4,000 offenders arrested for sexually related homicides, Chan, Myers, and Heide (2010) found that a majority (72%) of the reported victims were white. In addition, 64% of the victims were adults, 13% were elderly, 12% were adolescents, and 11% were children. Forty-one percent of the offenders arrested were black. In addition, sexual assault murders are more likely to involve strangers than rape alone or nonlethal sexual assault, but the overall differences (stranger vs. known victim) were relatively small (Chan et al., 2013). In another study by Chan and Frie (2013), focusing on 204 female sexual homicide offenders (27 juveniles and 177 adults), it was discovered that the majority of their victims were adult males with whom they shared a relationship.

As a group, sex offenders appear to be deficient in social skills and intimacy and are often described as lonely. Furthermore, child molesters, on average, appear to be more deficient in intimacy and are lonelier than rapists, who, in turn, appear to be lonelier and more lacking in intimacy than non–sex offenders (W. B. Marshall, 1996). Despite these generalizations, researchers know that sex offenders are not a homogeneous group. Several attempts have been made to capture their heterogeneity into categories or types. In the following sections, we will discuss the best known of these attempts to classify offenders.

TYPOLOGIES OF MEN WHO RAPE

As mentioned earlier, classification systems, based on either personality traits or behavioral patterns of individuals, are called typologies, and they have been moderately successful in their ability to add to our understanding of criminal behavior. Chief among the criminal typologies are those pertinent to men who rape. It is important to realize, however, that individuals do not always fit neatly into a particular type; they only approximate it.

Another problem with typologies is that very few of them have been subjected to empirical verification or validation studies, and they sometimes encourage stereotypes of offenders (B. K. Schwartz, 1995). That is, typologies can promote a tendency for the public and professionals to jam people into their favorite categories without empirical support or thoughtful consideration of individual differences among offenders.

However, typologies can be very useful in organizing a vast array of behavioral patterns that would otherwise be a confusing muddle. They are also useful in correctional facilities for risk management, such as deciding where to place an inmate, or in treatment programming, such as deciding what particular treatment technique or strategy might be most beneficial for an inmate or offender. To some researchers, the "acid test" of the usefulness of a typology is its ability to estimate the risk of particular offenders to reoffend (Quinsey, 1986).

Many rape typologies have been suggested, including the one originally used by the FBI (Hazelwood & Burgess, 1987), the Selkin typology (Selkin, 1975), the Nagayama-Hall typology (Nagayama-Hall, 1992), and the Nicholas Groth typology (Groth, 1979). However, the most extensively studied sex offender typologies are the ones developed by researchers and clinicians associated with the Massachusetts Treatment Center (MTC) (Knight & Prentky, 1987; Prentky & Knight, 1986). One typology was developed for rapists and the other for child molesters. The MTC typologies are among the most rigorously tested classification systems in sex offender research to date (Goodwill, Alison, & Beech, 2009).

The MTC typologies have undergone several revisions over the course of the development and are currently in their fourth revision (R. A. Knight, 2010; R. A. Knight & King, 2012). In this chapter, we will concentrate on the third revision of both the rapist and child molester typologies (Figures 9.1 and 9.2, presented later in the chapter), as they have drawn the most research interest to date.

The Massachusetts Treatment Center Rapist Typology

A group of researchers at the Massachusetts Treatment Center (MTC) (M. Cohen, Garafalo, Boucher, & Seghorn, 1971; M. Cohen, Seghorn, & Calmas, 1969; R. A. Knight & Prentky, 1987; Prentky & R. A. Knight, 1986) has developed an empirically based and useful typology that focuses on the behavioral patterns of convicted rapists, including the appearance of aggressive and sexual patterns in the sexual assaults. It also provides an excellent framework for describing the psychological characteristics of rapists in general.

The MTC researchers believe that rape is a multidetermined behavior that can best be explained by models incorporating a multitude of dimensions. An empirically based typology that takes into account all possible categories of rape behavior is such a model. Originally, the researchers identified four categories of rapists: displaced aggressive, compensatory, sexual aggressive, and impulsive. These have been replaced with a new typology. The MTC classification system now identifies four major types, based on the rapist's primary motivation (opportunistic, pervasively angry, sexual, vindictive), and nine subtypes (R. A. Knight, Warren, Reboussin, & Soley, 1998; see Figure 9.1). The new system is called the **MTC:R3** and has been subjected to extensive research by the MTC group as well as other researchers (Barbaree & Serin, 1993; Barbaree, Seto, Serin, Amos, & Preston, 1994; Goodwill et al., 2009; G. T. Harris, Rice, & Quinsey, 1994). R3 signifies the third revision.

The nine discrete rape subtypes are differentiated on the basis of six variables that have been consistently found by clinicians and researchers to play an important role in the behavioral, emotional, and thought patterns of a wide array of rapists (and child molesters). Before covering the typologies themselves, we will discuss the six variables, which are as follows:

- Aggression
- Impulsivity
- Social competence

- Sexual fantasies
- Sadism
- Naïve cognitions or beliefs

In a sense, these six variables form the "building blocks" for the development and ongoing revision of the MTC rape typology, and each should be described separately to get a deeper understanding of typology subtypes. It should be understood at the outset that certain variables appear to be more prominent in some rapists than in others.

Aggression

For our purposes here, aggression may be divided into two broad categories: (1) instrumental or strategic violence, and (2) expressive aggression or nonstrategic violence (Prentky & R. A. Knight, 1991). The former represents the type of aggression used by rapists to gain victim compliance. There is usually no anger present in instrumental aggression, except in reaction to a victim's lack of cooperation or compliance. Expressive aggression, on the other hand, is used by rapists to hurt, humiliate, abuse, or degrade the victim in some way. This form of aggression goes way beyond simply obtaining victim compliance and is often extremely violent. This instrumental–aggressive dichotomy model does have its limitations, however, as some rapists demonstrate a mixture of both. As Prentky and Knight (1991) point out, "Those rapists who intend only to force victim compliance are likely to vary widely in the amount of aggression evident in their offenses" (p. 647). It may depend on the extent of victim resistance, the level of alcohol or drugs ingested by the offender, the presence of other aggressors or victims, and the context in which the attack occurs. Furthermore, sometimes the expressive aggression is "sexualized," and sometimes it is not. However, the instrumental–expressive dichotomy does serve as a useful springboard for discussing most of the MTC subtypes.

Impulsivity

There is considerable research and clinical evidence that impulsivity is a significant factor in many sexual assaults and criminal behavior in general. Lifestyle impulsivity has been found to be a powerful predictor of recidivism and frequency of offending (Prentky & Knight, 1986, 1991). Some impulsive people seem to have an overpowering deficiency in self-control and continually revert to old behavioral patterns, regardless of the costs. Research has consistently found that lifestyle impulsivity emerges as one of the strongest and most meaningful ways to differentiate repetitive rapists from other repeat sex offenders such as child molesters. It is also the major focus of many treatment programs designed to change the antisocial behavior of sex offenders. As noted by Prentky and Knight (1991), "Clinicians have long recognized the importance of impulsivity for relapse and have introduced self-control and impulsivity management modules into treatment" (p. 656).

Social Competence

Sexual offenders have often been described as having poor social and interpersonal skills, especially when dealing with the opposite sex (Prentky & Knight, 1991). The Massachusetts Treatment Center researchers refer to this characteristic as *social competence*, a concept that plays an important role in developing the various subtypes of the MTC typology. This feature is especially prominent in the behavioral patterns of child molesters. There are also consistent research findings that rapists as a group are not assertive in their everyday relationships with others. It should be realized that social competence represents a wide range of different abilities, such as social assertiveness, communication skills, social problem solving, social comfort, and political savvy, and consequently should be understood as a complex skill that is developed within a variety of contexts.

Sexual Fantasies

Sexual fantasy refers to any mental imagery that is sexually arousing or erotic to the individual (Leitenberg & Henning, 1995). Many clinicians believe that sexual fantasy is a necessary precursor to deviant sexual behavior. As stated by Leitenberg and Henning, "There seems to be little question that many men who commit sexual offenses frequently have sexually arousing fantasies about these acts and masturbate to these fantasies regularly and presumably more often than nonoffenders" (p. 487). In one clinical study of men who had been convicted of sexual homicide, approximately 80% had sexual fantasies related to sexually assaultive behavior (Burgess, Hartman, & Ressler, 1986), and the percentage appears to be even higher for those convicted of serial sexual murders (Prentky et al., 1989). In fact, most treatment programs for sex offenders include a component designed to directly change sexual fantasies (Leitenberg & Henning, 1995; W. L. Marshall, Boer, & Marshall, 2014). Some research has discovered that the content, frequency, and intensity of deviant sexual fantasies often differentiate between single and serial sexual murderers (Prentky & Knight, 1991).

It should be noted that it is not unusual for people to have sexual fantasies that would be inappropriate, or even criminal, for them to act on. Briere and Runtz (1989) found that 21% of male college students in an anonymous survey admitted that children sometimes attracted them sexually, and 9% of the sample said they have sexual fantasies about children (Leitenberg & Henning, 1995). In a survey conducted by Malamuth (1981), 35% of male college students felt there was some likelihood that they would sexually assault if they could be sure of getting away with it. In another study, 60% of a group of 352 male undergraduates indicated that they might rape or force a female to perform sexual acts against her will if given the opportunity (Briere, Malamuth, & Ceniti, 1981). Nevertheless, research (e.g., Dean & Malamuth, 1997) suggests that although aggressive or violent sexual fantasies are common in some college males, the degree to which these fantasies translate into an actual sexual assault depends on the individual's empathy for others. More specifically, those men who are highly self-centered are more likely to be sexually aggressive and act out their sexual fantasies. "There is no evidence that sexual fantasies, by themselves, are either a sufficient or a necessary condition for committing a sexual offense" (Leitenberg & Henning, 1995, p. 488).

Sadism

"Typically, central to the definition of sadism is a pattern of extreme violence in the offense that has often focused on erogenous areas of the body and that may be considered bizarre or appear ritualized" (Prentky & Knight, 1991, p. 652). Sadism is illustrated by cruel and malicious acts that are enjoyed by and often sexually arousing to the offender. Sadistic rapists, compared to other types of rapists, tend to offend more frequently against victims who are close friends, intimates, or family (Prentky, Burgess, & Carter, 1986).

Naïve Cognitions or Beliefs

Research indicates that offense-justifying attitudes are prevalent among males prone to rape and, to some extent, among the general male population as well. Similar to sexual fantasies, irrational attitudes and cognitive distortions usually are a major focus of most treatment programs for sex offenders.

Sexual socialization and social learning play very critical roles in the development of those who choose to sexually assault. Sexual behavior and attitudes toward women are acquired through the day-to-day contacts with family members, peers, images of entertainment figures, and the media in general. Koss and Dinero (1988) found that sexually aggressive men expressed greater hostility toward women, frequently used alcohol, frequently viewed violent and degrading pornography, and were closely connected to peer groups that reinforced highly sexualized and dominating views toward women. These same men were more likely to believe that force and coercion are legitimate ways to gain compliance in sexual relationships. Koss and Dinero conclude, "In short, the results provided support for the developmental sequence for sexual aggression in which early experiences and psychological characteristics establish conditions for sexual violence" (p. 144).

Research reveals that a majority of sexually aggressive men subscribe to attitudes and ideology that encourage men to be dominant, controlling, and powerful, whereas women are expected to be submissive, permissive, and compliant. Such an orientation seems to have a particularly strong disinhibitory effect on sexually aggressive men, encouraging them to interpret ambiguous behaviors of women as come-ons, to believe that women are not really offended by coercive sexual behaviors, and to perceive rape victims as desiring and deriving gratification from being sexually assaulted (Lipton, McDonel, & McFall, 1987).

Rape Myths

Rape myths and misogynistic attitudes appear to play a major role in sexual assault. Rape myths are "attitudes and beliefs that are generally false but widely and persistently held, and that serve to deny and justify male sexual aggression against women" (Lonsway & Fitzgerald, 1994, p. 134). Not all rapists tend to have these attitudes, but men who do subscribe to them hold more rape-supportive points of view (Chapleau & Oswald, 2010; Good, Heppner, Hillenbrand-Gunn, & Wang, 1995; Johnson & Beech, 2017) and date rape–supportive points of view (M. S. Hill & Fischer, 2001; D. M. Truman, Tokar, & Fischer, 1996). Recent research on rape in prisons—a topic that is gaining more attention from the research community— suggests that inmates who sexually assault others and prison officials who ignore or deny the seriousness of this behavior tend to subscribe to rape myths (Neal & Clements, 2010).

According to findings reported by Chapleau and Oswald (2010), the stronger the cognitive association between power and sex, the more likely it is that men endorse rape myths and report a higher likelihood that they would rape. Furthermore, the more strongly men accept rape myths, the higher the tendency that they will misperceive women's attire and behavior as "asking for it" or misperceive their own sexual interest as "uncontrollable." Similarly, an important European study by Bohner, Jarvis, Eyssel, and Siebler (2005) provides further evidence that rape myths serve to justify sexual aggression, "not only after it has occurred but also by increasing the likelihood of future violence" (p. 827).

Researchers have also explored the "macho personality constellation," which is characterized by having callous sexual attitudes, believing that violence is manly, and getting excitement from taking high risks (M. S. Hill & Fischer, 2001; Mosher & Anderson, 1986). Some sexually aggressive men also believe that women must be kept in their place—even if it means humiliating them—and the best way to achieve this world order is to assault them physically and sexually. The underlying cognitive framework that most sexually aggressive men seem to have is hostility toward women (Lonsway & Fitzgerald, 1995).

In his ongoing research on sexual aggression, Neil Malamuth and his colleagues (Malamuth, Linz, Heavey, Barnes, & Acker, 1995) identified several characteristics that distinguish sexually aggressive males from their nonaggressive counterparts. The more important characteristics include (1) an insecure, defensive, hypersensitive, and hostile-distrustful orientation toward women; (2) gratification from being able to control and dominate women; and (3) a strong tendency to misread cues from women.

Malamuth and his associates (Malamuth, Heavey, & Linz, 1993; Malamuth, Sockloskie, Koss, & Tanaka, 1991) argue that sexually aggressive men have beliefs (or schema) that predispose them to regard women as untrustworthy. These men do not believe what women say or do, especially when it pertains to romantic or sexual interests. In short, these men are highly suspicious of women and perceive communication from women as having the opposite meaning of what was intended. Malamuth, Sockloskie, Koss, & Tanaka (1991) note that societies and subcultures that regard power, toughness, dominance, aggressiveness, and competitive selfishness as masculine qualities tend to produce men who are hostile to women and to the qualities associated with femininity, such as gentleness, empathy, and sensitivity. "The display of these traditionally feminine characteristics may signify to some men a loss of appropriate identity, whereas engaging in dominance and aggression, including in the sexual arena, may reinforce the idea that they are 'real men'" (Malamuth et al., 1995, p. 354). For such men, sexual aggression may be a way to reaffirm their sense of masculinity, as advocated by that particular society or subculture.

Malamuth also found that sexually aggressive men have information-processing deficits in their ability to separate seductive from friendly behavior or hostile from assertive behavior (Malamuth & Brown, 1994; W. D. Murphy, Coleman, & Haynes, 1986). For example, rapists are less accurate than non-rapists in reading women's cues in first-date interactions (Lipton et al., 1987). This deficit is especially apparent when the woman's communication is direct, clear, and strong. If she protests too much, it indicates—to the sexually aggressive male—that she really means the opposite. To the sexually aggressive male, she is game-playing and attempting to be seductive by using assertiveness or aggression.

The misinterpretation of communication (both verbal and nonverbal) is not limited to the sexual assault context. It is often a key element found in highly aggressive and violent persons, including children. Kenneth Dodge (2003; Dodge & Pettit, 2003), for example, discovered that highly aggressive children often have what he calls a *hostile attribution bias*, as described in Chapter 7. That is, children prone to high levels of aggression are more likely to interpret ambiguous actions of others as hostile and threatening than their less aggressive peers (Dodge, 2003). They are apt to perceive aggression where none was intended. Research has consistently shown that violent youth "typically define social problems in hostile ways, adopt hostile goals, and seek few additional facts, generate few alternative solutions, anticipate few consequences for aggression, and give higher priority to their aggressive solutions" (Eron & Slaby, 1994, p. 10). This information-processing deficiency may be the result of the lack of opportunity during early childhood to develop social and interpersonal skills for detecting correct cues from others.

On the other hand, there is some empirical evidence that women who have severe victimization histories are less adept at identifying the cues that signal risky situations. Yeater, Treat, Viken, and McFall (2010) conducted a study using 194 undergraduate women between the ages of 18 and 24 who were from diverse ethnic and cultural backgrounds. As part of the study, the students read vignettes describing social situations that varied on dimensions of sexual victimization risk and potential impact on women's popularity. Near the end of the study, the participants were administered the Sexual Experiences Survey (SES) and the Rape Myths Acceptance Scale. The SES responses were used to quantify the severity of victimization experiences. The researchers found that those women who had severe victimization histories had difficulty identifying those situations that suggested high risks of being sexually assaulted. In addition, the researchers found that fear of losing the relationship with a man or losing popularity in general obscured their ability to identify high-risk situations. Lastly, those participants who demonstrated a higher acceptance of rape myths were less skillful at identifying high-risk situations. According to Yeater and her colleagues, "endorsement of rape-supportive attitudes appears to interfere with both women's and men's use of information that may help guide effective decision making in heterosexual interactions" (p. 383).

We should be careful not to imply that these women would be at fault if they were raped, simply because they misread high-risk situations. The tendency to blame victims for their victimization is one that often occurs in society, particularly but not exclusively in cases of sexual assault: "If you had locked your door, you wouldn't have been burglarized." "How could you fall for that scam? If it sounds too good to be true, it isn't." "If you hadn't gone to that bar, you wouldn't have been raped." However, women as well as men can benefit from information that disproves rape myths and from learning effective strategies to help avoid victimization (Ullman, 2007a).

Rape myths reside not only in many rapists. Research has found that they exist in members of the clergy, college students, high school students, and military personnel (Shaw, Campbell, Cain, & Feeney, 2016), and they are not exclusive to men. They have been found among law enforcement officers (Shaw et al., 2016; Smith, Wilkes, & Bouffard, 2016), and in jury members (Dinos, Burrowes, Hammond, & Cunliffe, 2015; Shaw et al., 2016). In a study of police officers' rape beliefs, Shaw et al. found that explicit rape myths have been reduced to some extent in recent years but continue to operate implicitly during rape investigations. Shaw et al. write, "Such beliefs now operate at a more implicit level, undetectable on rape myth surveys yet still influential in decision-making and action" (p. 9). These beliefs come across in police attitudes during the interview, investigation, and report writing. (See Focus 9.2 for more discussion of this study.)

FOCUS 9.2. THE PERSISTENCE OF RAPE MYTHS

Despite decades of sensitization and education by rape survivors and their supporters, many myths associated with this crime have persisted. Within the past few years, a candidate for public office made the statement that when a woman was raped, her body has a way of "shutting down" biologically so that she would not become pregnant. Although his statement was roundly condemned, other rape myths persist. As noted in the text, these myths are held by many in the general population, including some law enforcement officers. Although most police officers do not believe that rape victims are promiscuous or secretly desire to be raped, many apparently still believe that victims often put themselves in dangerous situations and are partly to blame for the assault. In other words, the victim should have known better.

Shaw et al. (2016) examined police records of actual sexual assault investigations to determine the extent to which police endorsed rape myths. They found statements implying acceptance of rape myths in over half of

the case records. The statements were categorized into three victim-blaming groups:

- Circumstantial—these statements minimized the rape on the basis of the circumstances of the assault (e.g., the victim was not injured or was not "emotional" enough about the attack);
- Characterological—these statements focused on the character of the victim (e.g., she was a regular drug user or she should not have been out alone that late);
- Investigatory—these statements made excuses for a less-than-thorough investigation because the victim was unwilling to assist, without considering what may have led to a victim's noncooperation during the early stages of the investigation.

The last group, the investigatory statements, suggested to the researchers a lack of understanding of the reality facing rape victims. Research has consistently reported that nearly half of rape victims who report the

(Continued)

assault to police are treated in a manner they described as upsetting or humiliating (D. Patterson, 2011). Under that situation, it is not surprising that a victim would be reluctant to cooperate. Police psychologists and other mental health professionals would be wise to train police officers to be aware of their implicit myths and blaming attitudes toward rape victims.

Questions for Discussion

1. More than half of the investigation reports contained statements implying acceptance of rape myths. Does this mean that, for those cases, a perpetrator was not found and prosecuted? In your opinion, what is the significance of that finding?

2. What methods should police psychologists use to help law enforcement personnel recognize their implicit myths?

3. The text cites very recent research indicating that rape myths persist not only among rapists, but also in the general population. Do they persist on your campus, in your workplace, or in community settings where you interact with a cross-section of people? If yes, why might this be so? If no, why might it not be so?

The MTC:R3

As described previously, the MTC:R3 rape typology consists of nine discrete rapist types who are differentiated on the basis of the six variables already discussed. This section describes these nine types in more detail, and the typology is illustrated in Figure 9.1. Thus far, the research has focused almost exclusively on male rapists. Although a small percentage of reported rapes involve women as offenders, these women are almost invariably operating in partnership with a male offender. In recent years, though, some researchers have suggested that the prevalence of independent female sexual offending has been underestimated, chiefly due to society's reluctance to accept that women sexually offend or that their offending is harmful to their victims (Becker, Hall, & Stinson, 2001). Based on official records, however, the proportion of independent female sex offenders among all sex offenders across the globe is 4.6% (Cortoni, Hanson, & Coache, 2010). Moreover, in victimization studies for Australia, Canada, New Zealand, the United Kingdom, and the United States, the proportion of sex offenders who were females ranged from 3.1% for New Zealand to 7.0% for Australia, an average of 4.8%. Our discussion of the MTC:R3 typology focuses on the male as perpetrator. Later in the chapter, we discuss typologies for female offenders.

The Opportunistic Rapist (Types 1 and 2)

The impulsive or **opportunistic rapist** engages in sexual assault simply because the opportunity to rape presents itself. Thus, this offender type is motivated more by contextual factors and opportunity than by any internally driven sexual fantasy (Prentky & Knight, 1991). The rape may occur within the context of some other antisocial act, such as a robbery or burglary. Alternatively, the rape may be perpetrated on a woman encountered at a bar or party. The most prominent characteristic of these offenders is their impulsivity and lack of self-control, resembling those qualities of an immature child. More important, this poor impulse control leads to a pervasive and enduring lifestyle of impulsive and irresponsible behavior, frequently leading to an extensive criminal career. Thus, rape becomes only one of many antisocial behaviors in this person's repertoire.

The opportunistic rapist is not perceived to be "person oriented" and sees the victim only as a sexual object. He seems to have little concern for the victim's fear or discomfort. Opportunistic offenders consistently engage in troublesome acting-out behavior throughout their childhood, adolescence, and into adulthood. To be classified as an opportunistic rapist according to the MTC:R3, the offender must show the following:

- Callous indifference to the welfare and comfort of the victim

- Presence of no more force than is necessary to get the compliance of the victim (instrumental aggression). Any excessive force or aggression—beyond what is needed to carry out the offense—rules out this type.

- Evidence of adult impulsive behavior, such as frequent fighting, vandalism, and other impulse-driven antisocial behaviors

The Massachusetts Treatment Center researchers have discovered that opportunistic rapists can be subdivided on the basis of their social competence and the developmental stage at which their high impulsivity is first noticed. The opportunistic offender who is high in social competence—a Type 1 rapist—manifests impulsivity in adulthood. The Type 2 rapist, on the other hand, is low in social competence and demonstrates impulsivity during adolescence.

The Pervasively Angry Rapist (Type 3)

The **pervasively angry rapist** demonstrates a predominance of global and undifferentiated anger that pervades all areas of the offender's life. These rapists are angry at the world in general, and their anger is directed at both men and women. The acts reflect capricious and random violence directed at whoever gets in the way at the wrong time and wrong place (Prentky & Knight, 1991). When these men attack women, their violent and aggressive behaviors exhibit a minimum or total absence of sexual arousal. Their attacks are characterized by high levels of aggression, and they inflict considerable injury on their victims. S. L. Brown and Forth (1997) report that psychopaths who sexually assault fall most often into the opportunistic or the pervasively angry categories.

The occupational history of the pervasively angry rapist is usually stable and often reveals some level of success. He perceives himself as athletic, strong, and masculine. More often than not, his occupation is a "masculine" one, such as truck driver, carpenter, mechanic, electrician, or plumber. His friends typically describe him as having a quick, violent temper (S. T. Holmes & Holmes, 2002). These offenders experienced chaotic and unstable childhoods and family life. Many of them were adopted or foster children who were often neglected or abused.

According to R. A. Knight and Prentky (1987), an offender must demonstrate the following characteristics to be classified as the pervasively angry type:

- Presence of a high degree of nonsexualized aggression or rage expressed through verbal or physical assault that clearly exceeds what is necessary to gain compliance of the victim (expressive aggression)

- Evidence of adolescent *and* adult sexual and nonsexual antisocial behavior

- Carries out attacks that are usually unplanned and unpremeditated

So far, no particular subtypes have been identified for the pervasively angry rapist. Therefore, this type of rapist is referred to simply as Type 3.

Sexually Motivated, Sadistic Rapists (Types 4 and 5)

The motivation for the next four types is "sexual" in that their attacks are characterized by the presence of protracted sexual or sadistic fantasies that strongly influence the assaults. A discernible pattern of sexual preoccupation and fantasy is what all four have in common. The **sexually motivated rapist** category is subdivided into sadistic and non-sadistic, and each is further subdivided (see Figure 9.1). Sadistic sexual offenders are either "overt" (Type 4) or "muted" (Type 5), depending on whether their sexually aggressive acts are directly expressed in violent

Figure 9.1 Breakdown of Four Categorizations of Rapist Types Into Nine Rapist Subtypes (MTC:R3)

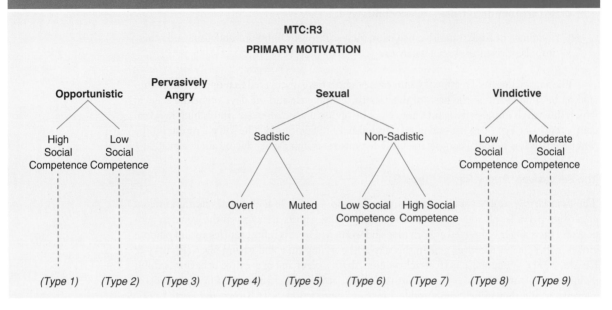

Source: Knight, Warren, Reboussin, & Soley, B. J. (1998). *Criminal Justice and Behavior*, Vol. 25, p. 57, Fig. 2. Copyright © SAGE, 1998. Reprinted with permission of SAGE Publications, Inc.

attacks (overt) or are only fantasized (muted). The *muted* offender's motive is the victim's fear or some violent fantasy that aids in his sexual arousal. That is, the victim's fear excites him, or he relies on some rehearsed sexual fantasy during the act to excite him. It should be noted, however, that Type 5 (muted sadistic rapist) has been deleted in the new revision 4, which is still under development. The research data did not support the subtype. All other MTC:R3 subtypes have been retained. The *overt* sadistic rapist demonstrates *both* sexual and aggressive elements in his assault. In essence, the victim's actual (not fantasized) pain and discomfort are prerequisites for his sexual excitement. He believes his victims fundamentally "enjoy" being abused, forcefully raped, aggressively dominated, and controlled. Therefore, this type of rapist interprets the victim's resistance and struggle as a game, and the more the victim resists, the more excited and aggressive he becomes. At first, the attack may begin as attempts at seduction, but with increasing resistance from the victim, aggressive behaviors become increasingly prominent. On the other hand, rage or high levels of violence are precipitated in the offender when the victim, out of abject fear or helplessness, becomes passive and submissive, so it seems to be a no-win situation for the victim. In this context, in the offender's eyes, the victim is no longer playing the "game" properly.

Overt sadistic rapists are frequently married, but they show little commitment to the marriage. Their backgrounds often are replete with sexual and nonsexual offending, beginning during adolescence or before and ranging from truancy to rape-murder. They have often had severe behavior problems in school, and throughout their lifetimes they have displayed poor behavior control and a low frustration tolerance. They manifest more paraphilias than the other types of rapists. The term *paraphilia* "denotes an intense and persistent sexual interest other than sexual interest in genital stimulation or preparatory fondling with phenotypically normal, physically mature, consenting human partners" (American Psychiatric Association, 2013, p. 685). A paraphilia becomes a disorder when it causes distress or impairment to the individual or entails personal harm or risk of harm to others. (See Table 9.2 for examples of paraphilias.)

Table 9.2 Various Paraphilias and Their Definitions

Frotteurism	Sexual arousal from touching or rubbing against a nonconsenting person, usually in a crowded public place
Voyeurism	Sexual arousal from observing an unsuspecting person who is undressing, naked, or engaged in sexual activity
Sexual masochism	Sexual arousal in response to being humiliated, beaten, whipped, bound, or otherwise made to suffer
Sexual sadism	Sexual arousal gained from inflicting real or simulated physical pain or psychological suffering on another person
Fetishism	Achieving sexual arousal by using, fondling, or smelling inanimate objects, such as shoes, undergarments, leather, stockings, or purses
Partialism	Achieving sexual arousal by touching or fondling body parts not normally associated with sexual activity, such as feet, hair, ears, and so on

On occasion, the Type 4 rapist engages in sexual sadism that is so extreme that the victim may be murdered. To qualify as an overt, sadistic rapist, the offender must demonstrate the following:

- A level of aggression or violence that clearly exceeds what is necessary to force compliance of the victim

- Explicit, unambiguous evidence that aggression is sexually exciting and arousing to him. This can be illustrated either by descriptions indicating that the offender derives sexual pleasure from injurious acts to the victim, or by the fact that the injurious acts are focused on parts of the body that have sexual significance.

To qualify as a sadistic, muted rapist (a type that has been excluded from the latest version of the MTC, the MTC-R4) on the other hand, the offender must demonstrate the following:

- Instrumental aggression or enough force to gain compliance

- Evidence that sexual fantasies of violence or the victim's fear excite him

Sexually Motivated, Non-Sadistic Rapists (Types 6 and 7)

The **non-sadistic rapist** engages in a sexual attack because of an intense sexual arousal prompted by specific stimuli identified in the intended victim. Although rape is, by definition, clearly a violent act, aggression is not the significant feature in the attack of the sexually motivated, non-sadistic rapist. Rather, the fundamental motivation is the desire to prove sexual prowess and adequacy to the victim. This type is also known as the "power reassurance rapist" (S. T. Holmes & Holmes, 2002). These men live in a world of fantasy, oriented around themes of how victims will yield eagerly under attack, submit to pleasurable intercourse, and even request further contact with the rapist. These rapists fantasize that they will at last be able to prove their masculinity and sexual competence to themselves and the victims. In their sexual assaults, these rapists are described as being highly sexually aroused and showing obvious disturbances involving lack of control and cognitive-perceptual distortions of reality.

The victim of such a rapist is most often a stranger, but the rapist has probably watched and followed the victim for some time. Certain stimuli have drawn his attention and excited him.

For instance, he may be attracted to college women or women who are tall or wear uniforms. S. T. Holmes and Holmes (2002) report that non-sadistic, sexually motivated rapists prefer women who are approximately their own age and race, especially those residing in the same neighborhood or close to their place of employment. The attacks are often done at night, with a time interval between attacks of 7 to 15 days. If the victim physically resists his attack, the non-sadistic rapist is likely to flee from the scene. During the entire incident, there will be very low levels of aggressive behavior on his part. Sometimes, if he is successful, he may contact the victim at a later time to inquire about her well-being or even to ask for a date. Generally, this type of rapist confines his illegal activity to sexual assault and is not involved in other forms of antisocial behavior.

Assignment to the non-sadistic categories requires the following behavioral indicators:

- Presence of verbalizations aimed at self-reassurance and self-affirmation

- Behaviors that reflect, albeit in a distorted fashion, an attempt at establishing an amorous relationship with the victim

- Concerns for the victim's welfare, comfort, and enjoyment of the sexual experience

Research (e.g., R. A. Knight & Prentky, 1987; R. A. Knight et al., 1998) has shown that there may be at least two subtypes of non-sadistic, sexually motivated rapists, similar to the two subdivisions of the opportunistic rapist. One group may be described as quiet, shy, submissive, and socially inadequate. Although they are dependable workers, their poor social skills and resulting low self-esteem prevent them from succeeding at occupational advancement. This type of person is usually classified as low socially competent, or Type 6. The second subtype may be more socially adaptable and competent and achieve more occupational advancement and professional development. This rapist is classified as highly socially competent (Type 7) (see Figure 9.1).

Vindictive Rapists (Types 8 and 9)

In an effort to express anger toward women, the **vindictive rapist** uses the act of rape to harm, humiliate, and degrade them. A violent sexual assault is, in this rapist's eyes, the most humiliating and dominating act possible. The victims are brutally assaulted and subjected to sadistic acts such as biting, cutting, or tearing of parts of the body. In most instances, the victims are complete strangers, although the victim may possess certain characteristics that attract the assailant's attention. Often, in addition to using physical abuse, this attacker will use a great deal of profanity and emotional abuse through threats. Resisting this particular rapist may engender more violence from him. Nevertheless, as we will note below, women threatened by rape cannot be expected to distinguish among rapist types and should never be discouraged from using resistance strategies whenever possible (Ullman, 2007b).

Although many vindictive rapists are married, their relationships with women are characterized by periodic irritation and violence, and they probably engage in domestic violence and partner abuse. These men generally perceive women as demanding, hostile, and unfaithful individuals who need to be dominated and controlled. They sometimes select their victim because they perceive something in her behavior or appearance that communicates assertiveness, independence, and professional activity. The assault usually follows some precipitating events involving a wife, girlfriend, or mother that he generalizes to all women. Upon arrest, the offender often attributes his offense to an "uncontrollable impulse." Like the opportunistic and non-sadistic rapists, vindictive rapists can be subdivided by their degree of social competence, although here they are divided into low and moderate rather than low and high.

To qualify as a vindictive rapist, the following behaviors must be evident:

- Clear evidence, in verbalization or behavior, of the intent to demean, degrade, or humiliate the victim

- No evidence that the aggressive behavior is eroticized or that sexual pleasure is derived from the injurious acts

- The injurious acts are not focused on parts of the body that have sexual significance

Raymond Knight (2010), in response to studies that have identified several problems with the MTC:R3, has started to revise some aspects of the typological model. In the newly developed MTC:R4 version, Knight deleted subtype 5, the muted sadistic rapist, as mentioned earlier in this section, but all other MTC:R3 subtypes remain.

Summary

Although human beings rarely fit neatly into typologies, the MTC rape typology is useful in understanding rape and helps in treatment and in the prediction of recidivism. Even so, psychologists are more likely to use various risk assessment measures for this latter purpose, as we note later in the chapter. The MTC typology is of value because it takes into consideration behavioral patterns, rather than simply personality traits, as well as the context within which the behavior patterns occur. However, the typology needs refinement and reconstruction, a process the group has been pursuing for a number of years. R. A. Knight and Prentky (1990) conclude that

> the MTC:R3 is a typological system that was developed to increase understanding of the etiology of sexual offending and to help predict recidivism. It might be that an alternative typology or a variant of MTC:R3 can be developed to maximize detection. (p. 78)

The MTC:R3 has received favorable reports from many research studies (Goodwill et al., 2009).

However, rape typologies in general may be of little use to the *victim* of sexual assault, and may even be a liability. Some typologies, for example, suggest that resisting certain rapist types will only make them angrier and will also make it more likely that the victim will be severely physically harmed or even killed. Ullman (2007a) remarks that the woman in the process of being assaulted is unlikely to make a determination about which category the rapist falls into. More important, however, contemporary research indicates that women who scream loudly or fight back—if they are able to do so—are more likely to avoid a completed rape; on the other hand, begging, pleading, and trying to reason with the rapist are less likely to be effective (Ullman, 2007a).

The Groth Rapist Typology

Nicholas Groth (1979; Groth, Burgess, & Holmstrom, 1977) has proposed typologies for both rapists and child molesters that are somewhat similar to the MTC systems. We will cover the **Groth rape typology** in this section and the **Groth child molester typology** in the next section. Whereas the MTC:R3 was largely built on research and statistical analyses, the Groth typology has been predominately clinically developed and has not been adequately tested for reliability and validity. Many mental health workers, though, like the Groth classification system because it is simple and straightforward to use. In addition, many police investigators continue to use the system in crime scene profiling. For example, the behaviors associated with the types listed below—power, anger, and sadistic—are seen as helpful in identifying an unknown rapist.

The Groth system is based on the *presumed* motivations and aims that underlie almost all rapes. According to Groth (1979), rape is a "pseudosexual act" in which sex serves merely as a vehicle for the primary motivations of power and aggression. He asserts that "rape is never the result simply of sexual arousal that has no other opportunity for gratification. . . . Rape is always a symptom of some psychological dysfunction, either temporary and transient or chronic and repetitive" (p. 5). Rape, he says, "is always and foremost an aggressive act" (p. 12). On this basis, Groth divides rape behavior into three major categories: (1) anger rape, (2) power rape, and (3) sadistic rape.

In **anger rape**, the offender uses more physical force than necessary to gain compliance and engages in a variety of sexual acts that are degrading or humiliating to the woman. He also expresses his contempt for the victim through abusive and profane language. Rape, for the anger rapist, is a violent act of conscious anger and rage toward women. According to Groth (1979), sex is actually "dirty," offensive, and disgusting to the anger rapist, and this is the reason why he uses the sexual act to defile and degrade the victim. To illustrate, Groth quotes one rapist: "I wanted to knock the woman off her pedestal, and I felt rape was the worst thing I could do to her" (p. 14). Very often, his attacks are prompted by a previous conflict with or humiliation by some significant woman in his life, such as a wife, supervisor, or mother. However, some anger rapists are also reacting to a recent upset that does not necessarily involve a woman, such as being rejected from military service, being fired, being burdened by financial debts, or being harassed by others. Considerable physical injury to the victim is common in such rapes.

The offender in **power rape** seeks to establish power and control over his victim. Consequently, the amount of physical force and threat used will depend on the degree of submission shown by the victim. In the words of one rapist, "I told her to undress and when she refused I struck her across the face to show her I meant business" (Groth, 1979, p. 26). The goal of the power rapist is sexual conquest, and he will try everything in his power to overcome any resistance. Sexual intercourse is his way of establishing his masculine identity, authority, potency, mastery, and domination as well as achieving sexual gratification. According to Groth, the victim is sometimes kidnapped or held captive in some fashion, and she may be subjected to repeated sexual assaults over an extended period of time. However, the offender is often disappointed that the assault did not live up to his expectations and fantasies.

The third pattern of rape proposed by Groth is the **sadistic rape**, which includes both sexual aspects and extreme nonsexual aggression. The sadistic rapist experiences sexual arousal and excitement at the victim's maltreatment, helplessness, and suffering. The assault may involve bondage and torture, and he often administers physical abuse to various parts of the victim's body. Prostitutes, women he considers promiscuous, or women representing symbols of something he wants to punish or destroy often incur the wrath of the sadistic rapist. The victim may be stalked, abducted, abused, and sometimes murdered.

Groth (1979) estimated that more than half of the offenders evaluated or treated by his agency were power rapists, 40% were anger rapists, and only 5% were sadistic rapists. Interestingly, Groth asked convicted sex offenders to rate the sexual pleasure they had received from the rape on a scale from 1 (*little or none*) to 10 (*extremely satisfying*). Most of the offenders gave ratings of 3 or less, indicating low sexual pleasure from the act. In fact, Groth found that many men failed to have orgasms during the rape. Most reactions from the sex offenders in the sample to the sexual aspects of the attack ranged from disappointment to disgust. Moreover, none of the offenders thought rape was more rewarding or gratifying sexually than consensual sex. Similar results have been reported by Warren, Reboussin, Hazelwood, and Wright (1989).

One of the major contributions of the Groth typology is that it questions the notion that rapists are motivated largely by sexual desire or that rapists are all the same. Since he first introduced this concept, however, other researchers—like those at the MTC—have developed it in a more sophisticated fashion. Although the descriptions of Groth's offenders are intuitively appealing, empirical evidence in support of the reliability and validity of the typology is lacking. Very few research studies have examined the typology in recent years. Of the two major typologies, the MTC version is by far the more heavily researched and validated.

CHILD SEX OFFENDERS

If you are reading this text, you probably consider sexual crimes against children among the most heinous in our society. If the statistics are accurate, it is also likely that you or someone you know has been victimized by such crimes. As we discuss below, the incidence of childhood sexual victimization both nationally and globally is highly disturbing; moreover, like other crimes against children, it is often not reported to police or social service agencies.

Definitions of Pedophilia

Pedophilia is *commonly* known as "child molestation" or child sexual abuse, but pedophilia—as defined in the *DSM-5*—is not necessarily a crime. It is a psychological condition, defined as one in which, "over a period of at least 6 months, recurrent, intense sexually arousing fantasies, sexual urges, *or behaviors* involving sexual activity with a prepubescent child or children (generally age 13 years or younger)" occur (American Psychiatric Association, 2013, p. 697, emphasis added). We added the italics to emphasize that the fantasies or urges themselves are not criminal; they become so only if and when the individual acts upon them. It is also important to note that not all child molesters have the fantasies and urges that have traditionally been associated with pedophilia (W. L. Marshall, Boer, & Marshall, 2014). W. L. Marshall (1998) reported that an examination of his own extensive clinical files found that there was no clear evidence of recurrent fantasies or urges in about 60% of nonfamilial child molesters or over 75% of incest offenders. The phrase "or behaviors" in the *DSM-5* recognizes that child molestation is not only a crime but also should be clinically treated. Virtually all clinicians believe treatment should be available for anyone who commits sex crimes, even though persons who commit these crimes may not have a serious mental disorder.

The *DSM-5* further specifies that some pedophiles are sexually attracted only to children (the exclusive type), whereas others are attracted sexually to both children and adults (nonexclusive type). The psychologist, then, wants to prevent the urges—if they are recurrent—from translating into criminal activity or, if the activity has already occurred, treat the person so that it does not happen again. Child molesters who do not have recurrent urges and fantasies should be treated using evidence-based-treatment approaches (W. L. Marshall et al., 2014). As noted in Chapter 5, some forensic psychologists today often conduct sexually violent predator evaluations, which are intended to assess the likelihood that persons convicted of a sexual crime against either children or adults will reoffend in a similar manner.

For the purposes of this text, we are focusing on the pedophile who has taken the step into criminal activity and is considered a child sex offender. He may or may not have the fantasies and urges discussed in the clinical literature, but he has at least evinced the behavior. In this section, we use the term *child sex offender* in line with current research literature. A child sex offense may be rape, as defined earlier in the chapter, or another form of sexual assault. Although some researchers have specifically studied the topic of child rape, the great majority make reference to child sexual assault, which may or may not include that offense.

If the child victim is the offender's relative—sometimes referred to as *intrafamilial* child molestation—the criminal behavior is called **incest**. By far the largest group in this category is fathers who molest their sexually immature daughters or stepdaughters (Rice & Harris, 2002). *Extrafamilial* child molestation, on the other hand, refers to sexual abuse from a person *outside* the family. However, the two categories probably overlap, perhaps to a large extent. Rice and Harris, for example, report that a significant number of intrafamilial molesters have also offended outside the family.

Some Demographics of Child Sex Offenders

Best estimates of the prevalence of child sex offenders (CSOs) among men in the general population is less than 1% (Ahlers et al., 2011; A. F. Schmidt, Mokros, & Banse, 2013). In a recent online survey of both men and women, it was discovered that 6% of men and 2% of women indicated some likelihood of having sex with a child if they were guaranteed they would not get caught or punished (Wurtele, Simons, & Moreno, 2014). In another anonymous survey, approximately 4% of college-age men admitted having had sexual contact with a prepubescent girl (Ahlers et al., 2011). It should be noted, however, that some research has discovered that a large segment of child-attracted men either do not commit sexual offenses (Bailey, Bernard, & Hsu, 2016) or they go undetected. For example, Bailey, Bernard, and Hsu found only 1 of 122 child-attracted men in their survey reported an arrest or conviction for a sexual offense against children, and that was for possession of child pornography.

Prentky, Knight, and Lee (1997) assert that the more an offender's sexual preference is limited to children, the less socially competent he is likely to be. In this context, social competence refers to the offender's strength and range of social and sexual relationships with adults. Although some child sex offenders may demonstrate some interpersonal inadequacies, a large number appear to be quite interpersonally skillful in their strategies to gain access to children while hiding their true motivations and actions (Owens, Eakin, Hoffer, Muirhead, & Shelton, 2016). "Some offenders appear to be charming, sincere, compassionate, morally sound, and socially responsible" (Owens et al., 2016, p. 11). Often, they attempt to work in occupations that put them in frequent contact with children, such as coaches, counselors, clergy, school crossing guards, school bus drivers, and even law enforcement.

Although we urge caution in discussing victim characteristics, it must be stated that some researchers have found that victims of CSOs tend to have similar traits. In her summary of the research literature, A. C. Butler (2013) finds that CSOs tend to select children who do not have many friends and "who appear to lack confidence, to have low self-esteem, and to be unhappy and emotionally needy" (p. 643). All of these characteristics are likely to be a reflection of a child's living environment—such as living with a CSO in a family under stress and conflict. Furthermore, disabilities of any kind tend to increase the vulnerability of children to sexual predators. For example, children with learning difficulties, language impairments, health problems, and intellectual disabilities are vulnerable targets for CSOs. Children from families in which parents do not show the child sufficient attention or affection are also especially vulnerable.

Perhaps because of the extremely negative attitudes the public has toward child sexual abuse, CSOs rarely take full responsibility for their actions. Many claim that they went blank, were too intoxicated to know what they were doing, could not help themselves, or did not know what came over them. Overall, they demonstrate a strong preference for attributing their behavior to external forces or motivating factors largely outside their personal control. The tendency of sex offenders of children to deny, distort, or minimize the psychological damage they do is a relatively consistent finding in the research literature (Nunes & Jung, 2012). Many therapies for CSOs are designed to address and hopefully change these cognitions.

Few crimes are considered as despicable as the sexual abuse of children, and yet so little is understood about its causes, incidence, and reoffense risk (Prentky et al., 1997). In the United States, data on CSOs are difficult to obtain because there are no central or national objective recording systems for tabulating sexual offenses against children. Across the world, human rights groups report numerous instances of children being abused, kidnapped, sold, and killed by individuals, tyrannical governments, and militant groups. In many parts of the world, children are not cherished and protected.

The available evidence suggests that, in the United States, child sexual abuse is grossly underreported, both to police and in official statistics. This is due partly to children's fears of retaliation from the perpetrator. However, in some cases it is also because another adult is aware of the offending but persuades the child not to reveal it. The child sexual offender also may be protected by his own family—let's keep this a private matter, relatives have been known to say. With regard to official statistics, offenders may be arrested and prosecuted under a variety of statutes and for a variety of offenses, including child rape, aggravated assault, sodomy, incest, indecent exposure, and lewd and lascivious behavior. Although the UCR program lists arrests for sex offenses, it does not differentiate child sexual abuse from the mixture of other possible sexual offenses. In addition, arrests are reported for crimes against children, but not all crimes against children are sex offenses. Self-report surveys are somewhat more instructive. The best data available indicate that 1 in 4 girls and 1 in 20 boys in the United States have been sexually abused or assaulted by the time they reach their 17th birthday (Finkelhor, Shattuck, Turner, & Hamby, 2014). Perhaps more surprising is the discovery that many of these abuses and assaults were committed by their peers. Over half of the total sexual offenses against children and adolescents were committed by juveniles; many of them were acquaintance peers. Overall, self-report victimization survey data reveal high rates of lifetime experience of sex abuse and assault at the hands of both adults and peers.

The classification, diagnosis, and assessment of CSOs—like those of rapists—are complicated by a high degree of variability among individuals in relation to personal characteristics, life experiences, criminal histories, and motives for offending. "There is no single 'profile' that accurately describes or accounts for all child molesters" (Prentky et al., 1997, p. v). Perhaps the best way to provide a solid framework for any presentation on the complex nature of pedophilia and the offenders involved is through a discussion of two well-known typologies. Again, they are the research-based typology of the Massachusetts Research Center (MTC:CM3) and the more clinically based Groth typology. Like the rapist typologies discussed earlier, these typologies have been formulated primarily with reference to male offenders, but this situation has changed in recent years, as we will discuss shortly.

The MTC:CM3

Similar to their development of the MTC:R3 for rape typing, the Massachusetts Treatment Center researchers (M. L. Cohen et al., 1969; R. A. Knight, 1989; R. A. Knight & Prentky, 1990; R. A. Knight, Rosenberg, & Schneider, 1985) have also developed one of the most useful typologies or empirically based classification systems for CSOs yet constructed. Called the **MTC:CM3** (Child Molesters, Revision 3), the system underscores the importance of viewing child sex offending as characterized by multiple behavioral patterns and intentions. The MTC:CM3 classifies child molesters according to variables on two basic dimensions, or axes (see Figure 9.2). The first dimension focuses on the degree of fixation the offender has on children and the level of social competence demonstrated by the offender. The second dimension focuses on the amount of contact with children, the level of injury to the victim, and the amount of sadism manifested in the attack.

The First Dimension

The MTC researchers have distinguished four types of child molesters based on this dimension:

- High fixation, low social competence (Type 0)

- High fixation, high social competence (Type 1)

- Low fixation, low social competence (Type 2)

- Low fixation, high social competence (Type 3)

The term *fixation* refers to the intensity of pedophilic interest or the degree to which the offender is focused on children as sexual objects. High fixation means that the offender

Figure 9.2 A Flow Chart of the Decision Process for Classifying Child Molesters (MTC:CM3)

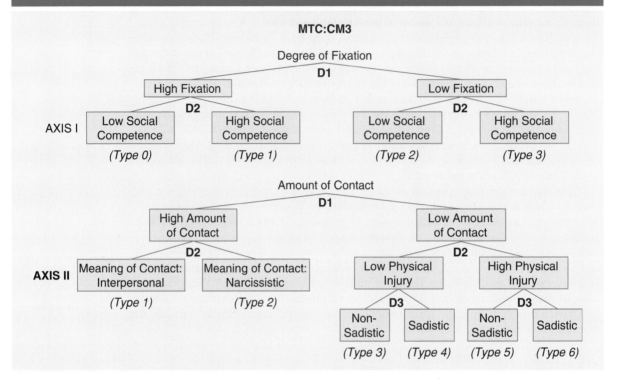

Source: R. A. Knight, Carter, & Prentky (1989). A system for the classification of child molesters: Reliability and application. *Journal of Interpersonal Violence*, Vol. 4, p. 8, Fig. 1. Copyright © 1989 by SAGE Publications, Inc. Reprinted by permission of SAGE Publications, Inc.

demonstrates an exclusive and long-standing preference for children as sexual objects, whereas a low fixation connotes that both children and adults can serve or have served as sexual objects for the offender. Social competence refers to the level of social and interpersonal skills, assertiveness, and self-esteem possessed by the offender. Low social competence signifies that the offender has inadequate social skills, is unassertive in dealing with adults, and demonstrates poor self-esteem. High social competence means the opposite.

The Type 0 child molester displays a long-standing preference for children as both sexual and social companions. He has never been able to form a mature relationship with adult peers, male or female, and he is described by people who know him as socially immature, passive, timid, and dependent. He feels most comfortable with children. The Type 0 CSO is rarely married or in a long-lasting relationship and has a history of steady employment, although the type of work is often below his ability and intellectual capacity. Sexual contact with the child occurs after the two become fully acquainted through a number of social encounters. He rarely is aggressive or uses physical force and rarely engages in genital intercourse. The behavior is generally restricted to touching, fondling, or caressing the child. However, this pedophile is the most difficult to treat and is most likely to recidivate because he is not disturbed or troubled about his exclusive preference for children.

Type 1 is similar to Type 0 in his child molestation strategies. However, he tends to be more socially competent in dealing with the world, has higher self-esteem, and usually has a good work history in line with his competence.

Type 2 child molesters have low fixation. They have had a fairly normal adolescence and good peer relationships and sexual experiences, but they later developed feelings of sexual inadequacy and self-doubt. These feelings of inadequacy were further exacerbated by failures in their occupational, social, or sexual lives. The Type 2 offender's background almost always includes alcohol abuse, divorce, and a poor employment history. Each pedophilial act is usually precipitated by a significant disappointment related to the offender's sexual and social adequacy in interaction with either female or male peers. Unlike Types 0 and 1, the low fixated/low socially competent offender prefers victims who are strangers and who live outside his neighborhood or area. The victims are nearly always female, and he seeks genital sex with the victim. Unlike Type 0 and 1 child molesters, this offender often feels remorseful for his actions and is willing to change.

The Second Dimension

MTC researchers have also discovered that CSOs can be distinguished on the basis of how much daily contact they seek with children (see Figure 9.2).

The "amount of contact" dimension identifies six types of CSOs:

- High contact, interpersonal interests (Type 1)

- High contact, sexual interests (Type 2)

- Low contact, low physical injury, exploitative (Type 3)

- Low contact, low physical injury, psychologically sadistic (Type 4)

- Low contact, high physical injury, aggressive (Type 5)

- Low contact, high physical injury, victim pain (Type 6)

A high-contact offender has regular contact with children within both sexual and nonsexual contexts (R. A. Knight et al., 1989). These high-contact offenders often engage in occupations or recreational activities that bring them into frequent contact with children. Many occupations and much volunteer work can fall under this categorization (e.g., teachers, coaches, camp counselors, bus drivers, clergy, child care workers, scout leaders, social workers, karate teachers, clowns at children's parties, tutors, to name but a few), and we must be careful not to make assumptions about the individuals associated with them. The MTC research team identified two kinds of offenders who intentionally seek more extensive contact with children: (1) the interpersonal offender (Type 1), who seeks the frequent company of children for both social and sexual needs; and (2) the narcissistic offender (Type 2), who seeks the company of children primarily for sexual needs. Narcissistic offenders molest children they do not know, and their sexual acts with children are typically genitally oriented (R. A. Knight, 1989).

Another group of CSOs includes low-contact seekers. In general, low-contact child molesters come into contact with children only when they decide to sexually assault a child. Low-contact child molesters are subdivided into those who administer very little physical injury to their victims and those who administer high physical injury. Low physical injury is indicated by the absence of physical harm to the victim and the presence of such acts as pushing, shoving, slapping, holding, verbal threats, or other intimidation tactics. Low physical injury offenders are further classified into two types: (1) exploitative, non-sadistic offenders (called Type 3); and (2) muted or symbolic, sadistic offenders (Type 4). The Type 3 offender uses no more aggression or violence than is necessary to obtain victim compliance. Type 4, on the other hand, engages in a variety of frightening, painful, or threatening acts, none of which causes significant physical injury to the child.

Finally, the MTC:CM3 classifies two types of child molesters who administer a high amount of physical injury to their victims: (1) the aggressive offender (Type 5) and (2) the sadistic offender (Type 6). High injury is characterized by hitting; punching; choking; sodomizing; or forcing the child to ingest disgusting things, such as urine or feces. The Type 5 offender is drawn to children for both aggressive and sexual reasons, but sadism is not the primary need. He is extremely angry about all things in his life and is generally violent toward people, including children. The sadistic or Type 6 offender obtains sexual pleasure from the pain, fear, and physical harm he inflicts on the child. He exploits the child's vulnerability any way he can and attempts various strategies and ploys to get the child to comply. This offender does not care about the emotional or physical well-being of the victim and sees the child strictly as a sexual object. He usually has a long history of criminal and antisocial behavior. His relationships with peers are unpredictable, difficult, and stormy. He is unpleasant to be around, uncomfortable to work with, and generally moody and irritable. His very poor and abrasive interpersonal skills may be the principal reason he selects children as victims (R. A. Knight et al., 1985).

The aggressive-sadistic or Type 6 child molester is apt to have a long history of antisocial behavior and poor adjustment to his environments. Type 6 CSOs most often prefer male children. Because the primary motive is to obtain sexual gratification without consideration for the victim, these offenders often assault the child viciously and sadistically. The more harm and pain inflicted, the more this individual becomes excited. Type 6 CSOs are most often responsible for child abductions and murders by strangers. They are very difficult to treat, but, fortunately, they are also very rare. A well-known example of this offender would be John Wayne Gacy Jr., who raped and sadistically murdered 33 teenage boys and young men and buried their bodies in the cellar of his suburban Chicago home.

The Groth Typology

Another often-cited typology that classifies child molesters is the one proposed by Nicholas Groth (1979; Groth & Burgess, 1977). Groth classifies child molesters on the basis of the longevity of the behavioral patterns and the offender's psychological aims. If the sexual preference for children has existed persistently since adolescence, he is classified as an **immature or fixated child molester**. Like the MTC system's high-fixation type, the fixated child molester has been sexually attracted to children throughout his life. Groth (1979) argues that this fixation is due to poor psychological development. On the other hand, if the child molester has managed to develop some normal aspects to his relationships with adults but turns to children for sexual comfort when stressed or when he experiences a blow to his self-esteem, he is called a **regressed child molester**.

As mentioned above, Groth further subdivides child molesters on the basis of their intentions or psychological goals. He identifies two basic types: (1) sex-pressure offenders and (2) sex-force offenders. The *sex-pressure offender* tries to entice the child into sexual acts through persuasion or cajolement or to entrap the child by placing him or her in a situation in which he or she feels indebted or obligated. Attractive gifts or "thoughtful" favors are the most common strategies. The *sex-force offender*, on the other hand, uses threat of harm or brute physical force. The offender either intimidates the child by exploiting the child's helplessness, naïveté, or trust, or simply physically overpowers the child.

Groth and his colleagues (Groth & Burgess, 1977; Groth, Burgess, & Holmstrom, 1977) believe the sex-force type can be subdivided into the *exploitative* type, who use the threat of force to overcome victim resistance, and the *sadistic* type, who derive great pleasure in harming the child. The exploitative offender employs verbal threats, restraint, manipulation, intimidation, and physical strength to overcome the child's resistance. His intent is not to physically harm the child but to obtain the child's compliance. According to these researchers, the sadistic type eroticizes the pain he administers to the child. He uses more force than necessary to gain compliance and may even commit what some police investigators call a "lust murder." The physical and psychological abuse is necessary for him to experience sexual excitement and gratification. Often, the child is beaten, choked, tortured, and violently sexually abused. Fortunately, like the sadistic offender of the MTC:CM3 typology, this type of offender is very rare.

The Groth system has traditionally been the one most often used by law enforcement investigators, largely because it is intuitively appealing. Like Groth's rapist typologies, his system has behavioral indicators that can be used to identify an offender based upon the crime scene or evidence provided by the victim. In many ways, the Groth typology is similar to the MTC child molester classification system, although it has not been developed much beyond Groth's original formulation. Furthermore, and as pointed out by Heilbrun, Marczyk, and DeMatteo (2002), the Groth child molester typology remains speculative and continues to have very little empirical research to support it.

FEMALE SEX OFFENDER TYPOLOGIES

Traditionally, female sex offenders have received very little research attention, and consequently, have been poorly understood, but this research neglect has been changing in recent years. For example, and as noted earlier, Cortoni, Hanson, and Coache (2010) estimate that females constitute 5% of all sex offenders in industrialized countries across the world. Vandiver and Kercher (2004) developed a clinically useful and research-derived typology of female sex offenders. They based their typology on 471 registered adult female sex offenders in Texas and were able to identify six types. They are the following:

1. Heterosexual nurturers
2. Noncriminal homosexual offenders
3. Female sexual predators
4. Young adult child exploiters
5. Homosexual criminals
6. Aggressive homosexual offenders

Heterosexual nurturers represented the largest group. The women in this group victimized only males with an average age of 12. The offenders were generally in mentorship, caretaking, or teacher roles, such as the teacher–lover category in which a teacher engages in a "romantic" relationship with one of her students or a counselor with one of her clients. A large segment of the women in this group did not believe the relationship was abusive or psychologically damaging to their child victim. These offenders appeared to be motivated by a desire for intimacy to compensate for unmet emotional and social needs and did not recognize the inappropriateness of the relationship. Vandiver and Kercher (2004) found that this group had a low recidivism rate.

Noncriminal homosexual (same sex) offenders made up the second-largest group. This group preferred early-adolescent females as victims with an average age of 13. These female offenders appeared to have similar characteristics as heterosexual nurturers except that their victim preferences were females. Similar to heterosexual nurturers, these offenders were unlikely to have a criminal record or to recidivate.

Female predators sexually abused both male (60%) and female children (40%) who averaged 11 years of age. Members of this group were largely repeat offenders who engaged in a wide variety of crimes.

Females who fell into the young adult child exploiters group were those who sexually assaulted young victims (average age of 7) of both genders. These offenders themselves were the youngest of the six offender groups, with an average age of 28. About half of the victims were related to the offender and were sometimes the offender's own child. Their sexual offenses appeared to be associated with domestically violent relationships with other women.

In a study of 390 female sex offenders in New York State, Sandler and Freeman (2007) also were able to identify six categories. In addition, their sample was highly similar to Vandiver and Kercher's (2004) on demographic variables, such as offender age and race. However, Sandler and Freeman's research did not completely support some of the offender characteristics reported by Vandiver and Kercher. This is to be expected, as the development of female sex offender typologies is in its earliest stages.

Sandler and Freeman (2007) did find support for the heterosexual nurturer and young adult child exploiter categories identified by Vandiver and Kercher (2004), but some descriptors of the four other categories were different. One major difference was the gender of the victims. Sandler and Freeman discovered that many of the female offenders did not *consistently* victimize one gender more than the other.

Overall, the samples between the two studies were different. For one thing, the two states, Texas and New York, had different codes or registry requirements for sex offenders, so that an offender registered at a certain level in one may not have been registered at the same level in the other state. Furthermore, Vandiver and Kercher's (2004) sample included females who may or may not have served time in prison, although their offenses were considered serious enough to warrant arrest and prosecution (Gannon & Rose, 2008).

Although the two studies advance our knowledge concerning female offenders, neither project was able to obtain additional data relating to co-offenders (Gannon & Rose, 2008). That is, did the females offend alone or with a co-offender, such as a male partner? In one study conducted in the Netherlands between 1994 and 2005, Wijkman, Bijleveld, and Hendricks (2010) found approximately 8 of 10 female child sex offenders had abused their own children, often with a male co-offender. In about 75% of those cases, the co-offender was the woman's husband or intimate partner (Nicholls, Cruise, Greig, & Hinz, 2015). The study also revealed that female sex offenders were often raised in highly dysfunctional homes characterized by sexual abuse and conflict.

ONLINE CHILD SEXUAL PREDATORS

The explosive growth of Internet use among youth has both positive and negative effects on the health and development of children and adolescents (Ybarra & Mitchell, 2007). Because of the Internet's anonymity, one negative impact is the opportunity for sex offenders to exploit children and adolescents, both for online behavior, such as promoting sexual performances, and for in-person meetings. According to the Growing Up With Media Survey involving 1,588 youth, 15% of the participants reported an unwanted sexual solicitation online in 2006 (Ybarra & Mitchell, 2007). Other surveys support these data (Mitchell, Wolak, & Finkelhor, 2005). Surveys also indicate that most of the sexual solicitations occurred via instant messaging or public chat rooms.

According to Janis Wolak and her colleagues (Wolak, Finkelhor, Mitchell, & Ybarra, 2008), most Internet-initiated sex crimes involve adult men who use the Internet to meet and entice underage youth into sexual encounters. They also tend to be white males, often older than 25 years (Owens et al., 2016). They utilize various online communications in these endeavors, including instant messages, social networking avenues (blogs, Facebook), e-mail, gaming sites, and chat rooms. One study (Malesky, 2007) found that three quarters of online offenders said they monitor chat room dialogues in an attempt to identify potential victims. As a result of these and other activities, many states now have passed "luring" statutes, making it a crime to deceive children or adolescents through the electronic media for purposes of engaging them in sexual activity.

Current research indicates that the typical Internet child sex offender does not use trickery to assault children (Wolak, Finkelhor, & Mitchell, 2004). In a great majority of cases, the victims are fully aware they are communicating with adults; only 5% of the offenders pretended to be adolescents. In addition, those offenders who ultimately want a meeting (they would be in the contact-driven group) rarely deceive victims about their sexual interests. "Sex is usually broached online, and most victims who meet offenders face to face go to such meetings expecting to engage in sexual activity" (Wolak et al., 2008, p. 113) in exchange for money or drugs. Moreover, the sexual intention of a majority of the offenders are made clear and introduced early in the Internet conversation with the target (Winters, Kaylor, & Jeglic, 2017). Perhaps surprisingly, the National Juvenile Online Victimization (N-JOV) study reports that three quarters of victims who had face-to-face sexual encounters with offenders did so more than once (Wolak, Mitchell, & Finkelhor, 2003). Ninety-nine percent of the victims of Internet-initiated sex crimes were 13 to 17 years old, and none was younger than 12. Available data suggest that online molesters do not usually seek unsuspecting victims as much as they seek those youths who may be susceptible to seduction because they are offered gifts, are curious, or are lonely for companionship (Wolak et al., 2008).

Viewing a victim as "susceptible to seduction," or focusing on the victim's motives for meeting, though, distracts us from the behavior of the offender. Furthermore, online offenders also may engage in **grooming** unsuspecting victims, or preparing them for sexual abuse. Kloess, Beech, & Harkins (2014) provided a helpful review of research on grooming in both the physical and online world. In the physical world, the practice is well recognized—it can involve the environment, significant others, as well as the potential victim. For example, the offender may align himself with community organizations in which children are involved, may get to know the victim's caretakers well, and ultimately ingratiate himself with the child, making the child feel special or offering gifts. Researchers also note that, in the physical world, the offenders may isolate the child and may introduce sexual activities gradually, such as by showing pictures, minor touching, before moving on to blatant acts (Kloess et al., 2014, and resources therein).

Grooming online occurs in different ways. Integrating and expanding on other research in this area (e.g., Briggs, Simon, & Simonsen, 2011) Kloess et al. note that offenders often but not invariably begin by posing as adolescents themselves. (And increasing numbers of online offenders *are* in fact adolescents.) They exchange pictures and gradually form on-line friendships via a number of stages, ultimately ending with a request for pornographic images, incitement to sexual acts, or arrangement of in-person meetings. Kloess et al. add that "In the absence of a meeting occurring between an offender and a victim, sexually exploitative interactions, via computer-mediated communication, may only ever come to the attention of police authorities when a victim comes forward or discloses the abuse, or as a result of proactive undercover police investigations" (p. 132).

Wolak and her colleagues (2008) assert that many youths are vulnerable to online child sex offenders because they lack the mature judgment and emotional self-regulation necessary for healthy relationships that involve sexual intimacy (recall the Steinberg research discussed in Chapter 7). Engaging in early sexual behavior, especially with an unknown adult, presupposes risk taking, a common behavioral pattern of adolescence. Adolescents who have histories of sexual or physical abuse appear to be especially vulnerable (Mitchell, Finkelhor, & Wolak, 2007).

In their study of convicted online CSOs, Owens, Eakin, Hoffer, Muirhead, and Shelton (2016) reported that, although the CSOs were predominantly white males, they varied widely in most other demographic variables, such as age, education, income, occupation, marital status, and community standing. In another study of online CSOs (Shelton, Eakin, Hoffer, Muirhead, & Owens, 2016), the researchers concluded, "The characteristics of the offenders in this sample were somewhat diverse, perhaps more than other criminal populations, suggesting that there does not appear to be a set demographic profile for Internet offenders" (p. 20). It should be mentioned that both studies (Shelton et al., 2016 and Owens et al., 2016) used offenders who had gone through investigations for an online child sexual exploitation offense through the FBIs Innocent Images National Initiative (IINI) and were convicted in either state or federal court. All cases involved the use of the Internet in some capacity to facilitate the sexual exploitation of a child. In total, the studies used 251 resolved FBI online child sexual exploitation cases which involved possessing, distributing, or producing child pornography, traveling to have sex with a child, and/or sexual contact offending against a child.

Online child offenders are usually not violent or sadistic, nor do they lack interpersonal skills to gain the confidence and acquiescence of victims. That said, the word "usually" should be emphasized. About 5% of the offenders in the N-JOV survey used threats or violence or attempted sexual assault. Abduction, however, is rare. For example, none of victims in the N-JOV study (Wolak et al., 2004) were forced to accompany offenders. Still, about one quarter of the cases began with missing persons reports, because the victim either ran away to be with the offender or lied to parents about his or her whereabouts.

Seto, Hanson, and Babchishin (2011) emphasize that although many online offenders are strongly aroused by child pornography, these pedophilic interests do not necessarily result in sexual contact with children. Their research finds that only half of those online offenders have acted on these sexual interests. Moreover, those who have acted on their pedophilic interests "are likely to have personality traits and life circumstances that facilitate antisocial behavior and criminality" (p. 140).

It is important to emphasize that Internet-initiated sexual offenses do not always result in physical encounters—in fact, they typically do not. In a study of convicted offenders, Briggs, Simon, and Simonsen (2011) identified two subtypes, based on their motivations: fantasy driven and contact driven. Fantasy-driven offenders were interested in pursuing a cyber relationship for purposes of self-gratification or engaging in cybersex. The contact-driven offenders wished to build a relationship and arrange a meeting for the purpose of sexual activity. The fantasy-driven offenders were older, married, or divorced. Contact-driven offenders tended to be younger, less well educated, and unemployed.

Similarly, Babchishin, Hanson, and Hermann (2011) note that research and clinical literature have identified several typologies of online sexual offenders.

> For example, online offenders have been categorized as those who (a) access child pornography out of curiosity or impulse, without specific sexual interest in children; (b) access child pornography to satisfy sexual fantasies, but do not commit contact sex offenses; (c) create and distribute child pornography solely for financial gain; and, lastly, (d) use the Internet to facilitate contact sex offenses. (p. 93)

Note that each of the above categories still represents exploitation of children, even if only the last refers to contact.

Although we have emphasized in this section those offenders who use the Internet to facilitate contact sex offenses, we will pay more attention to the first three offenders in the next chapter on victimology.

JUVENILE SEX OFFENDERS

According to the most recent FBI statistics (FBI, 2016a), about 16% of those arrested for rape and 17% of those arrested for all other sex offenses (except prostitution) are younger than age 18. The extent of the offending may be underestimated because, for a variety of reasons, many (perhaps a majority) of juvenile sex offenders are unknown to the criminal justice system. Several studies do suggest, however, that juvenile sex offenders may account for about 20% of all sexual assaults and perhaps as much as 50% of child sexual abuse (Barbaree & Marshall, 2006; Keelan & Fremouw, 2013). Most of the research on juvenile sex offenders has concentrated on adolescent males while neglecting preadolescent males and females and adolescent female sex offenders. Nevertheless, there are exceptions, as we will see shortly.

Juvenile male sex offenders represent a heterogeneous population and defy any unitary profile or simple description. They come from all ethnic, racial, and socioeconomic groups. "However, what is known is that about 70% of adolescent sexual offenders come from two-parent homes, most attend school and achieve average grades, and less than 4% suffer from major mental illness" (Becker & Johnson, 2001, p. 274). Further research indicates that the median age of juvenile male sex offenders is between 14 and 15, more than 90% knew their victims, and more than one third of the offenses involved the use of force (National Council of Juvenile and Family Court Judges [NCJFCJ], 1993). The victims are often substantially younger than the juvenile offender, are most often female (75%), and are usually relatives or acquaintances (Righthand & Welch, 2001). The median age of victims is 7 years old (NCJFCJ, 1993). Babysitting or some form of child care frequently provides the opportunity to offend, especially for female sex offenders.

Juvenile sex offenders frequently engage in a wide range of nonsexual criminal and anti-social behavior (Carpentier, Leclerc, & Proulx, 2011). They tend to shoplift, steal, set fires, bully, assault others (including adults), and are often cruel to animals. Although most juvenile sex offenders attend school and achieve average grades, a significant number are truant, demonstrate behavioral problems, and have learning disabilities. Moreover, although juvenile sex offenders are described as ranging from social outcasts to popular athletes and from academically gifted students to tough delinquents (Cellini, 1995), research continually reveals that most juveniles with sexual behavior problems have significant deficits in social competence and getting along with others (Becker, 1990; R. A. Knight & Prentky, 1993). As we found in Chapter 7 for life course–persistent (LCP) delinquents in general, inadequate interpersonal skills, poor peer relationships, and social isolation are among the social difficulties identified in these juveniles (Righthand & Welch, 2001).

The types of sexual offenses committed by juveniles vary widely, ranging from noncontact offenses (such as exhibitionism and voyeurism) to sexual penetration. About half of the contact offenses involve oral–genital contact or attempted or actual vaginal or anal penetration (Righthand & Welch, 2001). Juvenile sex offenders usually use more force when assaulting peers or adults than they do with younger children.

Many adult sex offenders began their sexually abusive behavior in their youth. Studies report that 47% to 58% of adult sex offenders committed their first offense during adolescence or younger (Cellini, 1995; Cellini, Schwartz, & Readio, 1993). Many experts and mental health professionals have made the point that a juvenile's own sexual victimization in childhood is a primary cause of later sex offending. Yet, such abusive experiences have not consistently been found to differ significantly from those of other juvenile offenders (R. A. Knight & Prentky, 1993; Spaccarelli, Bowden, Coatsworth, & Kim, 1997). However, Dennison and Leclerc (2011) find that, although sexual victimization in childhood is not a necessary condition for later sexual offending, it does appear to influence developmental pathways into sexual offending for some individuals. In one British study, the researchers found that only 12% of the 224 boys who had been sexually abused as children later became sexually abusive themselves (Salter et al., 2003). Although the figure seems low and may reflect only the abuse that came to official attention, it does underscore the point that most children who are sexually abused do not become victimizers themselves. Some scholars (e.g., Hunter & Figueredo, 2000) maintain that the timing and frequency of sexual abuse is likely to affect the person's psychosocial and psychosexual development. They report data suggesting that early and frequent sexual victimizations are associated with adolescent sexual offending.

The role of child maltreatment in the etiology of sex offending appears unclear and much more complicated than previously supposed (R. A. Prentky, Harris, Frizzell, & Righthand, 2000).

There is some evidence, though, that abused children as a group exhibit less empathy toward others than their non-abused peers, have trouble recognizing appropriate emotions in others, and have difficulty taking another person's perspective (R. A. Knight & Prentky, 1993). Abuse in this context refers not only to sexual abuse but also to physical and emotional abuse and neglect.

Female Juvenile Sex Offenders

According to the latest FBI statistics, juvenile females accounted for only 2% of all juveniles (under 18) arrested for sex offenses (excluding rape and prostitution) (FBI, 2016a). For our purposes, we will not treat prostitution as a sex offense, because engaging in prostitution does not involve the victimization of others. Although juvenile prostitution (both female and male) is a social problem, if there is a victim, it is the person who is committing the offense. For example, many juvenile as well as adult prostitutes are victims of human trafficking, a topic to be covered in the next chapter.

Research on girls who have committed sex offenses has been relatively rare, and existing studies have been limited by small sample sizes and other methodological restrictions and problems (Becker et al., 2001; Righthand & Welch, 2001). Most of the available research on sex differences in sexual offending has focused on adult females (Bumby & Bumby, 1997), and—as discussed above—that research itself is very limited. As Becker, Hall, and Stinson observe, "Society in the past has been disbelieving in regards to the presence or potential threat of female sexual perpetrators" (p. 30). They add that the mental health professionals in routine clinical interviews rarely or never ask females about possible sexual aggression or paraphilias.

Fehrenbach and Monasterky (1988) report that most adolescent girls who sexually victimized young children did so while taking care of children or babysitting. The victims of the 28 female sex offenders they studied were 12 years old or younger, and they were mostly acquaintances (57%), followed by siblings (29%) and other relatives (14%). Mathews, Hunter, and Vuz (1997) provided data on 67 female adolescent offenders who ranged in age from 11 to 18. More than 90% of their victims were acquaintances or relatives. Both of the above studies also found that a high percentage of the abusers (50% and 77.65%, respectively) themselves had a history of being sexually abused. Some studies report that adolescent female sex offenders are younger than male sexual offenders at the time of arrest, and also are more likely to sexually abuse both male and female victims (Nicholls et al., 2015). Bumby and Bumby (1997) found that adolescent female sex offenders tended to be depressed, have a poor self-concept, have a suicide ideation, and have been victims of sexual abuse during childhood.

Future Directions

Becker and Johnson (2001) recommend that future clinical research on juvenile sex offending concentrate on the following four areas: (1) theory development that addresses the etiology of the behavior, (2) the development of classification systems or typologies that encompass all juvenile ages and both genders, (3) further development of treatment interventions for different classifications of juvenile sexual offenders, and (4) treatment outcomes studies with long-term follow-ups.

RECIDIVISM RATES OF SEX OFFENDERS

Recidivism refers to the repetition of criminal behavior. Usually, it is measured in four ways: (1) rearrest, (2) reconviction, (3) resentence to prison, and (4) return to prison with or without a new sentence (Langan & Levin, 2002). The observed rate of new sexual offenses among known sexual offenders is 10% to 15% after 4 or 6 years (Hanson, 2001; Hanson & Bussière, 1998; Hanson & Morton-Bourgon, 2004, 2005). However, not all offenders reoffend at the same rate. Hanson, Bourgon, Helmus, and Hodgson (2009), in their meta-analytic study of nearly 7,000 sex offenders, found the sexual recidivism rate for treated offenders was 10.9% compared to a sexual recidivism rate of 19.2% for untreated offenders. Female sex offenders appear to have an extremely low recidivism rate (less than 3%) compared to males (Cortoni et al., 2010). As a group, child sex offenders commit a new but similar sexual offense at a higher rate than rapists. On the other hand, as mentioned earlier in the chapter, research finds that rapists generally do not confine their repeat crimes to sexual offenses but engage in a wide variety of violent crimes, including violent sexual ones (Carpentier et al., 2011; Quinsey, Harris, Rice, & Cormier, 1998). Among male sexual offenders, for example, studies have revealed that recidivism rates are 13.5% for new sexual offenses, 25.5% for violent (including sexual) offenses, and 36% for any type of recidivism (Cortoni et al., 2010; Hanson & Morton-Bourgon, 2004).

Age Factors

A study by R. Karl Hanson (2001) confirms prior research that, on average, the rate of recidivism for rapists decreases with age. Hanson analyzed data from 10 follow-up studies of sex offenders released from prisons. He found important differences in recidivism risk according to both age and offense type. The highest risk age period for adult rapists was between 18 and 25 years, with a gradual decline in recidivism risk as the offender got older. Extrafamilial child molesters were far more likely to recidivate than either intrafamilial child molesters or rapists. The highest risk period for extrafamilial child molesters was between the ages of 25 and 35; moreover, there were only modest declines in their recidivism risk until after the age of 50. Intrafamilial child molesters, on the other hand, were at highest risk between the ages of 18 and 25, and they were the least likely of the three groups to recidivate, particularly after age 25.

Hanson (2001) notes that the age differential in recidivism between rapists and child molesters as a group might be attributable to a greater delay in the detection and prosecution of offenses against children than for offenses against adults. Another factor that may enter into the reported differences in age is that child molesters may be more skillful at avoiding detection.

Recidivism of Juvenile Sex Offenders

In general, research has found that the juvenile offender recidivism rate for sex offenses ranges between 2% and 14% (Reitzel, 2003; Rubinstein, Yeager, Goodstein, & Lewis, 1993; Sipe, Jensen, & Everett, 1998). M. A. Alexander (1999) reports an overall sexual recidivism rate (based on rearrest) of 7%, with juvenile rapists having the highest sexual reoffending rate of all juvenile sex offenders. More important, however, is the finding by some researchers (Alexander, 1999; Hunter & Becker, 1999) that juvenile sex offenders are less likely to reoffend than adult offenders.

ASSESSMENT OF SEX OFFENDERS

Assessment of sex offenders is an extremely challenging undertaking because of the heterogeneous and multidimensional nature of the persons who commit such crimes. Comprehensive assessment strategies include evaluations of the offender's needs (psychological, social, cognitive, and medical), family relationships, risk factors, past criminal history, and risk management considerations (Righthand & Welch, 2001). Forensic psychologists assess sex offenders not only to decide on a treatment plan, but also to gauge their likelihood of further offending. These **psychosexual evaluations** often are conducted at the request of judges, lawyers, parole officers, or other agents of the criminal justice system. In recent years, as discussed in Chapter 5, some forensic psychologists have engaged in conducting risk assessments of sex offenders who have completed their criminal sentences but are subject to involuntary civil commitment under sexually violent predator (SVP) laws. Recall that these laws are controversial, and some mental health practitioners refuse to participate in these assessments. Although treatment may be provided after commitment, the quality of treatment varies, and convicted offenders are rarely released once they are civilly committed in this manner.

Assessment of Adult Sex Offenders

Unstructured clinical interviews have traditionally been the most commonly used assessment procedure for evaluating adult sex offenders (Dougher, 1995). An unstructured interview is one that imposes minimal structure on the interviewee by asking open-ended questions rather than preset questions that are designed to control the discussion. The interviewee is allowed to answer the questions with wide freedom and minimal direction. The assessment interview with sex offenders is usually problematic, though, because the sex offender has a strong tendency to deny or conceal his "true" thoughts, feelings, or deviant behaviors (Abel, Lawry, Karlstrom, Osborn, & Gillespie, 1994). Consequently, the information gathered is often unreliable and distorted and must be viewed with skepticism. It is important, therefore, that the clinician obtain as much collateral or outside information as possible during the assessment process to corroborate or supplement the interview material. Collateral information includes psychological and medical reports, previous statements made by the offender, police reports, arrest reports, and other information from those persons who know the offender (Dougher, 1995). Even when all these informational sources are taken into account, forensic psychologists and other practitioners who rely on unstructured assessment methods and clinical judgment are often inaccurate in their predictions of sexual offending. "It is widely accepted that evaluations based on unstructured professional judgment are less accurate than structured risk assessments" (Hanson & Morton-Bourgon, 2009, p. 1). As mentioned in Chapter 3, this observation was also made over 50 years ago by Paul Meehl (1954). In recent years, however, even researchers strongly devoted to actuarial risk assessment have been receptive to including *structured* clinical or professional judgment in these methods. This method recommends specific questions and allows clinicians to add their unique observations to data gathered from the actuarial instruments.

The use of various psychological tests for the assessment of male sex offenders also has a long history. These tests are primarily focused on identifying personality characteristics or developing a psychological profile of the already-known offender. Usually, the tests are of the paper-and-pencil variety, where respondents answer "true" or "false" to items that ask about their thoughts, attitudes, and behaviors. Assessments based on psychological tests and inventories have largely focused on risk assessment measures, specifically the likelihood of recidivism or reoffense. The most prominent actuarial instruments are the SORAG (Quinsey et al., 2006), the Static-99 (Hanson & Thornton, 2000), the J-SORRAT-II (Epperson, Ralston, Fowers, DeWitt, & Gore, 2006), and the MnSOST-R (Epperson et al., 2004). Several structured professional judgment (SPJ) risk assessment measures specifically designed to assess risk in sexual offenders also are available. These include the SVR-20 (Boer, Hart, Kropp, & Webster, 1997), ERASOR (Worling & Curwen, 2001), and RSVP (Hart, Boer, Otto, & Douglas, 2010). Some of these measures are discussed below, and most are also periodically revised to compensate for shortcomings in the original measure that are identified by subsequent research. (See also Table 4.2 in Chapter 4 listing violence risk assessment instruments.)

Although these instruments are used to assess the risk of future offending and as aids in treatment planning, they are also used in various jurisdictions to place sex offenders in risk tiers. The tiers are relevant to community sexual offender notification regulations and civil commitment statutes (Heilbrun et al., 2002). For example, sex offender registration and notification (SORN) statutes typically require that low-risk offenders only register with police. In the case of high-risk offenders, it is expected both that they register and that police notify the community where they take up residence. As mentioned in Chapter 5, researchers often question the effectiveness of these laws in reducing recidivism (e.g., Sandler, Letourneau, Vandiver, Shields, & Chaffin, 2017).

The success of psychological inventories in identifying those male sex offenders who will reoffend is, at best, very marginal. However, the development of actuarial risk assessment measures over the past 15 years has been a major improvement in prediction of sexual offending. Actuarial prediction is based on quantified experience and data rather than on the more subjective information, such as clinical judgment alone, but once again, structured professional judgment should not be undermined. Although no single risk tool has been identified as clearly superior in predictive accuracy, the Static-99 is currently the most widely used sex offender risk assessment tool in the world (Hanson, Babchishin, Helmus, & Thornton, 2012). It is primarily used for predicting crime and violence and sexual reoffending. Furthermore, its use has expanded to treatment planning, community supervision, and civil commitment evaluations.

The Static-99

It is important to emphasize that neither the Static-99 nor any of the other risk assessment instruments are without critics. Research is ongoing on virtually every dominant measure used. It is often observed that the most positive results in support of an instrument are found in research by the instrument's developers in comparison to studies by independent researchers (W. L. Marshall et al., 2014).

The Static-99 is a 10-item actuarial instrument created by R. Karl Hanson and David Thornton (2000). The items cover static, historical factors, such as the number of prior offenses, victim characteristics, and the offender's age. The items were selected strictly on the basis of empirical relationships with recidivism and ease of administration (Hanson & Morton-Bourgon, 2009). The popularity of Static-99 is probably due to its cost-effectiveness and its applicability to a wide range of sexual offenders (Hanson, Helmus, & Thornton, 2010). Nevertheless, because it was developed on the basis of research with rapists and child molesters, there are questions as to its relevance to other sex offenders. Its accuracy in predicting sexual and violent recidivism also could be improved. In an effort to improve predictive accuracy, Hanson and Thornton (2003) developed the Static-2002. Preliminary study has, indeed, indicated that the Static-2002 is more accurate for the prediction of sexual, violent, and general recidivism, but more research is needed on the power of subscales to identify psychologically meaningful attributes (Hanson et al., 2010).

The Sexual Violence Risk-20 (SVR-20)

According to a survey of forensic psychologists conducted by Archer, Buffington-Vollum, Stredny, and Handel (2006), the second most commonly used risk assessment instrument for adult sex offenders is the Sexual Violence Risk-20 (SVR-20), developed by Boer, Hart, Kropp, and Webster (1997). The SVR-20—an SPJ rather than an actuarial instrument—covers aspects of the offender's criminal history and psychological characteristics. The items are designed to evaluate the risk for sexual recidivism and to help in case management.

It should be emphasized that fully effective risk assessment for sex offender recidivism will require more than a single risk assessment instrument. The forensic psychologist should be prepared to examine a wide range of complex factors in the assessment process. The best methods of combining risk factors into an overall evaluation remain an active topic of scientific debate in forensic psychology. For example, Hanson and Morton-Bourgon (2009) argue that the ideal risk assessment procedure should not only provide accurate prediction of criminal sexual behavior, but it should also provide information useful for case management. Others have made similar observations, emphasizing that, ideally, all sex offenders should be treated (W. L. Marshall et al., 2014). This approach involves the utilization of dynamic risk factors, which are those characteristics of a person that can be changed. Case management that focuses on changeable risk factors should also be able to reduce recidivism. Hanson and Morton-Bourgon (2005) were able to identify several dynamic factors characteristic of persistent sexual offenders that have the potential of being useful case management and treatment targets, including sexual preoccupation, deviant attitudes, intimacy deficits, and self-regulation problems.

Assessment of Juvenile Sex Offenders

The instruments described above are largely intended for adult sex offenders. There have also been several risk assessment methods devised for evaluating juvenile sex offenders. Both actuarial and SPJ instruments are available. Examples include the Juvenile Sex Offender Assessment Protocol–II (J-Soap-II; Prentky, Harris, Frizzell, & Righthand, 2000; Prentky & Righthand, 2003); the Estimate of Risk of Adolescent Sexual Offender Recidivism (ERASOR; Worling & Curwen, 2001); the Juvenile Sexual Offense Recidivism Risk Assessment Tool–II (JSORRAT-II; Epperson et al., 2006); the Multiplex Empirically Guided Inventory of Ecological Aggregates for Assessing Sexually Abusive Adolescents and Children (MEGA; Miccio-Fonseca, 2006); and the Structured Assessment of Violence Risk Among Youth (SAVRY; Borum, Bartel, & Forth, 2006). Some of these instruments are based on static risk factors (those that are historical or unchangeable), while others utilize dynamic factors (Griffin, Beech, Print, Bradshaw, & Quayle, 2008).

Importantly, juvenile risk assessment procedures pay attention not only to dynamic risk factors, but also to strength and resilience factors (also called protective factors) in the life of the youthful offender and his or her family. Examples of protective factors are the consistent presence of a stable adult in the youth's life—such as a grandparent or respected teacher—and having someone in whom the youth can confide. One relatively new and promising assessment instrument, the AIM2 (Griffin et al., 2008), incorporates static and dynamic strengths along with concerns (risk factors). The instrument is intended for young men between 12 and 18 years of age who are known to have sexually abused or assaulted others. The AIM2 consists of 75 items, designed to measure static concerns, dynamic concerns, static strengths, and dynamic strengths. Although there is much research needed, the assessment approach represented by the AIM2 seems warranted for both juvenile and adult sex offenders.

The above risk assessment procedures have been largely developed on male offenders. They are not entirely appropriate for female offenders because their offending and recidivism patterns are different (Cortoni et al., 2010). Forensic psychologists are encouraged to follow the research on risk factors and recidivism among female offenders and to use caution in the choice of assessment instruments.

SUMMARY AND CONCLUSIONS

Sex offending is of grave concern in contemporary society. Statistics indicate that sexual victimization is a reality for many individuals, and it is well acknowledged that most such victimization does not come to official attention. Forensic psychologists are highly likely to come into contact with both offenders and victims. In this chapter, we covered the assessment tasks of psychologists in relation to sexual offending; sex offender treatment and work with victims will be covered in later chapters.

The terms rape and sexual assault are often used interchangeably, but we have made some distinction between them. Sexual assault is a broader term that

covers a wide range of offenses, including rape. Rape is typically used to refer to sexual crimes in which vaginal, anal, and sometimes oral penetration of the victim occurred. Increasingly, more state statutes are forgoing the term rape, however, and instead define the forms and degrees of sexual assault (e.g., aggravated; sexual assault of a child; sodomy). Much research literature continues to report studies using the term rape, and offenders are routinely called rapists as opposed to sexual assaulters.

Statistics reporting on the incidence and prevalence of sexual offending often are not comparable, partly because of the differences in terminology. Nevertheless, it is possible to discern a variety of patterns. It appears, for example, that probably no more than one third of all sexual assaults are reported to authorities. Victims themselves may not label the attacks as rapes or as sexual assaults; when they do, they are often fearful of the consequences of revealing their victimization. Although the official rate of rape has shown a downward trend, statistics and surveys about date rape, child sexual abuse, sexual assaults on campus and in the military, and juvenile sex offending indicate continuing cause for concern. Also of increasing interest is the topic of sexual offending by both adult and adolescent females. Although some studies in this area are available, they are often limited by their small sample sizes. By far, the greatest amount of research has focused on male offenders.

Research has indicated that men who rape often manifest a wide range of antisocial behavior in addition to their sexual offenses. Sex offenders as a group appear to be deficient in social skills and in their ability to maintain positive intimate relationships with others. A number of variables have also been found to play a key role in the behaviors, emotions, and thoughts of sex offenders. These include aggression, impulsivity, social competence, sexual fantasies, sadism, and naïve beliefs such as those demonstrated in a rapist's acceptance of society's "rape myths."

Nevertheless, sex offenders are not a homogeneous group. That very clear conclusion, based on numerous research studies, has led to the development of typologies or methods of classifying sex offenders for the purpose of both predicting deviant sexual behavior and providing treatment to offenders. We reviewed two prominent typologies for both rapists and child molesters: the research-based typologies developed by the Massachusetts Treatment Center and the more clinically based typologies offered by Nicholas Groth. Mental health professionals as well as law enforcement and correctional officials are probably more familiar with the Groth typologies, but they are the least validated. The MTC rapist typology divides rapists according to one of four primary motivations: opportunistic, pervasively angry, sexual, and vindictive. Three of the four are further subdivided, resulting in nine rapist subtypes. The Groth typology identifies three forms of rape: anger, power, and sadistic rape.

Much of the chapter focused on the sexual victimization of children by child sex offenders. Although "pedophiles" is a commonly used term for CSOs, an important point must be made. Pedophilia is the clinical term for a condition in which the individual repeatedly experiences sexually arousing fantasies, urges, or behaviors involving sexual activity with children. Unless the behavior occurs, pedophilia is a psychological condition, not a crime. It is a challenge to obtain data on the prevalence of sexual abuse of children, and available evidence suggests that these behaviors are widely underreported and often difficult to treat.

Both the MTC researchers and Groth have developed classification systems for child molesters, as they have for rapists. The MTC system classifies child molesters on two separate axes, one focusing on the offender's degree of fixation, and the other on the amount of contact, level of injury, and extent of sadism demonstrated in the attack. Several radically different types of child molesters are especially difficult to treat. The first is the Type 0 offender, who has a long-standing and highly fixated preference for children as both sexual and social companions. Types 5 and 6, aggressive and sadistic offenders, inflict pain and physical harm on their victims, including harm that may result in death. Because of the nature of their crimes, they are unlikely to be included in treatment programs. Forensic psychologists who treat child molesters often do work with Type 0 offenders, however.

Groth's typology classifies offenders first on the basis of the longevity of their behavior patterns: They are either immature (or fixated) or regressed. Groth also considers their psychological aims: They pressure or they force. Finally, offenders who force are subdivided into exploitative and sadistic types.

Although most research has been carried out with male sex offenders, female offenders are receiving increasingly more attention. For example, recent research has found that women constitute approximately 17% to 23% of all adult offenders, but they constitute only about 10% of all violent offenders and 5% of all sexual offenders (Blanchette & Brown, 2006; Cortoni et al., 2009, 2010). It is highly unlikely that female offenders can be conceptualized or treated in the same way as male offenders. In the chapter, we reviewed proposed typologies as well as some of the characteristics that distinguish them from male offenders. Although some female sex offenders engage in highly predatory behavior with strangers, the great majority appear to offend against those who are in their care.

In recent years, researchers have been paying increasing attention to the problem of juvenile sex offenders. Statistics suggest that between 25% and 50% of sexual assaults may be perpetrated by adolescents. Although we must be guarded in accepting these figures, it is clear that juvenile sexual offending is of concern. As with adult offending, most of the research to date has been directed at males as perpetrators. Juvenile sex offenders are a heterogeneous group, and they frequently engage in a wide variety of nonsexual offending and exhibit behavioral problems. The typical juvenile sex offender has significant deficits in social competence, but again there are exceptions. It is important to point out that children who are sexually victimized do not usually become sex offenders. However, it is likely that significant numbers of juvenile sex offenders—both male and female—were themselves victimized. Even so, the relationship between prior sexual victimization and juvenile sex offending is not clear and merits additional research before firm conclusions can be offered. The recommendations made by Becker and Johnson (2001) bear repeating: Theory development, typologies, additional treatment interventions for different classifications of juveniles, and evaluation research are all sorely needed.

Also receiving more attention is the online sexual exploitation of children. The Internet has afforded more opportunity for producers of child pornography to distribute their images and videos, and for users to access them and to initiate contact with victims. Researchers have begun to distinguish between those who produce and those who access child pornography, and among those users who do not have a specific interest in children, those who do, and those who use the Internet to make actual physical contact with victims. All are forms of child sexual exploitation, but different characteristics of the perpetrator are implied.

Sex offender recidivism rates reflect the importance of preventing and treating the behaviors discussed in this chapter. Adult offenders as a group show higher recidivism rates than juveniles, although the sex offending of adults decreases with advancing age. These rates vary among offender types, though. Furthermore, not all reoffend at the same rate. Child molesters, for example, commit new offenses more often than rapists. Rapists, however, have been found to engage in other violent crimes in addition to rape.

The psychological assessment of sex offenders is a crucial task for forensic psychologists. Offenders are assessed not only for their amenability to treatment, but also for their level of risk—or dangerousness—to society. Dominant instruments for assessing risk in sex offenders (e.g., the Static-99, Static-2002, and SVR-20) were discussed, but it should be emphasized that all risk assessment measures have critics and all require continued validation across ranges of offenders.

KEY CONCEPTS

QUESTIONS FOR REVIEW

1. Define rape, and explain how and why the term is being replaced by sexual assault in many criminal statutes.

2. What are the demographic features of men who rape?

3. Briefly summarize the MTC:R3 classification system, along with what it is based on.

4. What six variables have consistently been found to play an important role in the behavior, emotional, and thought patterns of rapists?

5. Contrast the MTC and the Groth rapist typologies on both their (a) classification system and (b) research support.

6. What are the two basic dimensions on which child molesters are classified according to the MTC:CM?

7. Contrast the MTC and Groth child molester typologies on both their (a) classification system and (b) research support.

8. Discuss juvenile sex offenders according to their antisocial conduct, the victims they choose, and their own history of victimization.

9. Are female juvenile sex offenders different from male juvenile sex offenders? Explain your answer.

10. List and define briefly any five psychological measures designed to assess recidivism among adult or juvenile sex offenders.

 SAGE edge™

Want a better grade? Go to **edge.sagepub.com/bartol5e** for the tools you need to sharpen your study skills. Access practice quizzes, eFlashcards, an action plan, and SAGE journal articles for enhanced learning.

VICTIMOLOGY AND VICTIM SERVICES

CHAPTER TEN

FORENSIC PSYCHOLOGY AND THE VICTIMS OF CRIME

A couple filed their income tax, expecting a refund, only to be told they had already filed it and a refund had been sent to them. They subsequently learned that someone had stolen their identity, filed a return in their name, and received the refund.

An 8-year-old girl riding in a boat with her family was killed when another boat crashed into them. The second boat was piloted by a 24-year-old intoxicated man who was subsequently convicted of manslaughter.

One person was killed and 19 others were injured when a car careened through Times Square in the middle of a sunny day in May 2017.

We are all victims of crime. Whether or not we have been robbed, had our personal identity confiscated, been assaulted, been deprived of our life savings or pension funds, or been burglarized, we have all experienced the social and financial costs of crime. Even so-called **victimless crimes**—illegal drug use, prostitution, and illegal gambling—can be said to be harmful to society and leave victims in their wake. Many of us have experienced the fear of crime as well. It is not unusual to hear of women applying for permits to carry guns or signing up for self-defense classes following a string of sexual assaults in a small town or city, for example. In addition, many people are victimized by crime without being aware of it. Medical insurance fraud is a good example of this. How many beneficiaries of Medicare or Medicaid are able to review and monitor the statements submitted by medical practitioners on their behalf? It is estimated that health insurance fraud costs taxpayers millions of dollars annually.

When we speak of crime victims, however, we are most likely referring to individuals who have been physically or emotionally harmed by known crimes against themselves or their property. In these cases, "criminal victimization's impact is multidimensional, including physical (injury, pain, disability), financial (loss of income, possessions, housing, medical bills), and emotional (fear, anxiety, depression, self-blame, insecurity, posttraumatic stress disorder) consequences" (Neff, Patterson, & Johnson, 2012, p. 609).

Chapter Objectives

- Describe the psychological effects of being victimized, and introduce the reader to the role played by mental health professionals in working with victims.

- Emphasize the multicultural and multiethnic aspects of working with victims.

- Describe the legal rights of victims.

- Recap official victimization data.

- Review homicide victimization research.

- Review rape and sexual assault victimization research.

- Review sex online solicitation.

- Address human trafficking and sexual exploitation trafficking.

- Review the psychological effects of commercial sexual exploitation of minors.

The U.S. government, which has been collecting victimization data for over 40 years, focuses its efforts on the types of crime that are highlighted in the media—assaults, burglaries, robberies, larcenies—and rarely on white-collar offenses or political crimes. Likewise, forensic psychologists and other mental health providers are far more likely to assess and treat victims of rape, child abuse, attempted murder, or robbery than victims of insider trading or illegal government surveillance. Moreover, when members of the public are asked about their fear of crime, they are more worried about child abduction than they are about credit card fraud, despite the relative rarity of the former and frequency of the latter. Child abduction is, of course, a serious, emotionally wrenching crime compared with fraud, yet the person who is the victim of credit card fraud suffers both financial and emotional harm. The point made here is that victimization comes in many forms and touches people in numerous ways. Although we may focus in this chapter on the forms of victimization most likely to be encountered by forensic psychologists and other mental health professionals, the backdrop is victimization in its broadest sense.

Psychologists will be increasingly employed as consultants, instructors, expert witnesses, evaluators, therapists, and service providers to victim service organizations in the coming years. Forensic psychologists have a major role to play in several areas such as the following: consulting with attorneys, assessing crime victims, providing expert testimony on the psychological effects of violent victimization, assessing psychological harm of plaintiffs in civil suits, and providing psychological information for victim impact statements. Although the criminal justice system does deal with victims to some extent, its primary responsibility is to apprehend and prosecute offenders (Neff et al., 2012). Today, with the passage of victims' rights legislation at both the state and federal level, victims have gained more attention in ways we will discuss shortly. However, the tasks of providing forensic and other mental health services fall to psychologists, social workers, psychiatrists, and other mental health professionals. Crime victims, including victims of intimate partner violence, sexual assaults and abuse, sexual exploitation, child abuse, elderly abuse, violent crime, and hate/bias crimes, need help in many areas. One skill area that will be especially in demand is the assessment of a victim's crime-related experiences and responses. For example, such assessments are desirable when someone sues for damages or seeks disability or other compensation relating to a crime (Carlson & Dutton, 2003). Another important forensic task is the assessment of a child to determine if a crime occurred or, if it did, the extent to which it had negative psychological effects on the child.

Psychological evaluation and assessment of victims of child sexual exploitation will be especially in demand in the near future. Psychological therapy and counseling for a wide spectrum of victims of crime, ranging from children to the elderly, will be a critical need in the coming years. The National Survey of Children's Exposure to Violence (NatSCEV), for instance, has discovered that 6 out of every 10 children were exposed to violence within 1 year, either directly or indirectly such as from being a witness to a violent act; by learning of a violent act against a family member, neighbor, or close friend; or from a threat against their home or school (Finkelhor, Turner, Ormrod, Hamby, & Kracke, 2009). Nearly 40% of children surveyed experienced more than one type of direct victimization in the previous year (Finkelhor, Turner, Hamby, & Ormrod, 2011). Children exposed to violence often display a variety of psychological problems that will require psychological services, including assessment and therapy from professionals who are familiar with the research and clinical literature on victimization. These professionals should also be very familiar with the cultural backdrop from which these children come. Results of these assessments often find their way into courts, including trials of persons accused of crimes against children, and the custody disputes and civil suits brought by victims against offenders that were referred to in Chapter 6. (See Perspective 10.1, in which Dr. Lavita Nadkarni discusses her extensive work in many of these areas.)

The chapter begins with an overview of the issues that forensic psychologists must deal with concerning victimization of people of diverse cultures and backgrounds, sexual orientation, disability, and religious preferences. We will then discuss victims' rights and their ramifications; cover statistical information on victimization; and give special attention to victims of homicide, sexual violence, and sexual trafficking.

Although we are focusing on criminal victimization, it is important to emphasize that much victimization occurs in the civil context; that is, people are victims of civil wrongs, such as discrimination, sexual harassment (which is a form of discrimination), unsafe working conditions, and negligence on the part of others in numerous other settings. Sometimes, the wrongs

FROM MY PERSPECTIVE 10.1

Bridges and Gaps: Building Connections and Training the Next Generation to Meet the Mental Health Needs of Diverse Populations

Lavita Nadkarni, PhD

Courtesy of Lavita Nadkarni.

The intersection of personal and professional identities has been very true of my journey within the field of forensic psychology. *Quincy M.E.* was a television show broadcast from 1977 to 1984—right around the time was an undergraduate student at Queen's University, majoring in psychology and volunteering in prisons—not that unusual when you consider the university was surrounded by five prisons. I initiated an inmate visitation program in one of the minimum security prisons and learned from some of the Elders (my professors at Queen's University) in the field. I then entered a MA program in forensic psychology at John Jay College of Criminal Justice in 1983. *Quincy* was still on television—quite popular—and many people didn't understand what it meant to be a forensic psychologist; people would ask how I was going to "counsel" dead people. I later obtained my PhD from Adelphi University. Fast forward nearly 30 years later, and the ironic thing is that I am the Director of Forensic Studies at the University of Denver's Graduate School of Professional Psychology, in which one of our current field placements and a career for some of our graduates is as a death investigator for the M.E.'s office!

The above captures some of my professional identity. My personal narrative is that I am a South Asian immigrant whose parents valued education, community service, and relationships near and far. As such, I am aware of the impact of my work, both direct and indirect, on the welfare of others. I strive to lead by example and teach my students to recognize both the value and humility of what we do. Psychology is not a career choice for many South Asian families—law or psychiatry would have been a more traditional choice. I come from a family of lawyers and judges; my mother was the first female person of color to be a citizenship judge and magistrate in Canada; my great-grandfather was the Chief Justice of the High Court in Mumbai. Their choice of work had an enormous impact on the communities in which they lived and on my own career choice. I have spent my career finding creative entry points to meet the mental health needs of our communities—this has been my passion and my inspiration for continuing to do this work.

A sense of belonging has not always been a "given" for me, so I understand the challenges that face many immigrants in our society today. I have lived as an immigrant in three countries, residing in very diverse communities, amongst and working with underserved populations. I was born in the United Kingdom, began school in India, and spent my childhood in Canada, before moving to the United States as an adult for graduate school. My parents never forgot

(Continued)

the generosity of the Canadian community, spending countless volunteer hours serving the public, promoting social justice, and taking a stand against injustice. This immigration journey and model of service has affected my choice of work and my involvement in social justice. I know the feeling of being unheard, invalidated, discriminated against, and being disenfranchised—experiences many of our clients have had with the behavioral, mental health, and criminal justice systems, which are not quite meeting their needs.

For nearly 30 years, I have worked in various mental health capacities, providing forensic psychological evaluations relating to matters of trauma, immigration and asylum, competency, social security disability, parental custody and access, child abuse and neglect, and domestic violence. Today, I supervise doctoral level students on court-ordered psychological evaluations through our in-house clinics, and I teach forensic courses to masters- and doctoral-level students.

I stress to them that the mental health care system across this nation is in crisis. Individuals with severe mental health difficulties are being seen in emergency rooms, jails, and shelters, but many in need of mental health treatment never get any because of the lack of resources and stigma attached to mental illness. We need to train a workforce who understands the diverse needs of this (often) legally involved mentally ill (or disordered) population. We have an obligation to help alleviate the pain and suffering in our communities.

Dr. Nadkarni is a clinical psychologist, licensed in Colorado and New York State. She is the Associate Dean and Director of Forensic Studies at the University of Denver's Graduate School of Professional Psychology and has a clinical forensic private practice. She is the coauthor of Principles of Forensic Report Writing and has coauthored and coedited many publications related to diversity issues. She is currently the President of the National Council of Schools and Programs of Professional Psychology. Her family includes her husband, Michael, daughter Maya, and pets Tilly and Opal.

done by others result in physical losses, such as brain damage or the loss of a limb; at other times, wrongs can result in severe psychological symptoms, such as depression or posttraumatic stress disorder (PTSD). Thus, while the greater part of the chapter will focus on what is known about victims of *crime*, it is important to keep in mind that the psychological impact of being victimized and the various roles played by forensic psychologists in victim services are similar in civil contexts.

MULTICULTURALISM AND VICTIMIZATION

"Multiculturalism, in its broadest terms, not only is defined by race and ethnicity but also involves topics of gender, sexual orientation, and disability" (Bingham, Porché-Burke, James, Sue, & Vasquez, 2002, p. 75, emphasis added). Recognizing and respecting individual differences in culture, religious preference, sexual orientation, disabilities, and gender are important to sensitive and effective work with victims. Each person has his or her unique way of viewing the world through the lens of cultural and linguistic experiences. Recent data indicate that the racial/ethnic composition of the United States is approximately 63% white; 14% black; 5% Asian; 0.7% American Indian and Alaska natives, and 16% Hispanic, Latino, or Spanish origin (U.S. Census Bureau, 2011a). One in 50 Americans now identifies as "multiracial." Currently, there are 57 possible race combinations involving five major race/ethnicity categories, according to the U.S. Census Bureau. Consequently, it is becoming increasingly difficult to place many Americans into a specific racial classification. By the year 2050, it is estimated that 54% of the population will be members of what are now regarded as minority groups. Native Americans are now recognized by the Census Bureau as represented by more than 500 separate nations and tribes with 187 different languages (Ogawa & Belle, 2002).

In addition, there are an estimated 3.7 million Arab Americans (U.S. Census Bureau, 2011a), who have represented one of the most misunderstood ethnic groups in this country (C. D. Erickson & Al-Timini, 2001). Two thirds are concentrated in 10 states, mostly in

California, New York, and Michigan. They are also one of the most diverse ethnic groups in terms of their cultural and linguistic backgrounds, political and religious beliefs, family structures and values, and acculturation to Western society. Arab Americans represent 22 countries as varied as Egypt, Lebanon, Morocco, Tunisia, Syria, Palestine, and Yemen. The majority of the Arab world is Muslim, but Arab Americans may be affiliated with other religions or no religion at all. However, Arab American Muslims are currently the fastest growing population in the Arab American community. Accurate numbers of Arab Americans and American Muslims are unknown because they are often reluctant to identify themselves for fear of possible negative social reactions, particularly in the wake of the terrorist attacks of September 11, 2001, and renewed attacks on them beginning in 2016 after that year's divisive presidential campaign. The Federal Bureau of Investigation (FBI) reported a 1,600% increase in hate crimes against this population in the year after the events of September 11 (Padela & Heisler, 2010). A survey conducted by Padela and Heisler, 2 years after September 11, found evidence that many Arab Americans continued to experience negative emotional states that led to a variety of mental health problems, such as depression and stress disorders. The 9-11 backlash against Muslim Americans and Arab Americans continues more than a decade later (U.S. Department of Justice, Civil Rights Division, 2011) but soared to their highest level since 9-11 during the 2016 election (Lichtblau, 2016).

It is important to emphasize that most members of minority groups in the United States are citizens, either born in the United States or naturalized. Others are on various temporary visas (e.g., student or work visas), and a minority are undocumented. Included in the undocumented are the "dreamers," the children of undocumented immigrants who were brought into the United States by their parents or others. It is fair to say, with the exception of the Native America population, we are all immigrants. Nevertheless, when we discuss serving immigrant populations, we refer primarily to people who have immigrated in recent years and have not been assimilated totally into the dominant culture. As noted above, by the year 2050, it is projected that over 50% of the U.S. population will consist of persons now considered ethnic minorities (Bernal & Sharrón-Del-Río, 2001; C. I. Hall, 1997). The shift in racial/ethnic composition is projected to be more dramatic in some states, such as California and Texas, and will present enormous challenges and opportunities to victim services providers, as well as to providers of other social services. Members of immigrant families are often afraid to ask for help due to language barriers, fear of deportation, and poor understanding of their rights in the community (Ogawa & Belle, 2002). If they are here temporarily or are undocumented, the challenges are multiplied, because there may be abrupt interruptions of services and difficulties in long-range planning.

> Once in the United States, [the undocumented] become easy prey for employment exploitation, consumer fraud, housing discrimination, and criminal victimization because assistance from government authorities is attached to the fear of deportation. There is an epidemic of sexual assaults, for example, committed upon undocumented Latinas. (Ogawa & Belle, 2002, p. 6)

As we commented in Chapter 1, these concerns have intensified in recent years, with irrational fears of "other" groups, current immigration policies, and the unsettled state of the economy contributing to the mix. Meaningful, sensible, and compassionate legislation under the umbrella term "immigration reform" has yet to be successfully passed in Congress. Despite the fact that non-citizens do not have identical legal rights to citizens, immigration status should not dictate whether individuals get an education, get protection from a society, or receive victim services. Nearly two decades ago, it was observed that "almost 20 million international refugees throughout the world have been forced by extreme abuse of human rights to flee their home countries" (Gorman, 2001, p. 443), many fleeing to the United States. At that time, the then-named U.S. Immigration and Naturalization Service (INS, now Immigration and Customs

Enforcement [ICE]) had authorized about 200,000 asylum cases, and another 90,000 undocumented immigrants received amnesty permitting them to stay in the country (Gorman, 2001). Many of them had been abused and tortured in their home countries, and they were vulnerable to becoming victims of crime here. For example in 2016, U.S. Customs and Border Protection intercepted nearly 46,900 unaccompanied children and more than 70,400 families from Central America arriving at the U.S.–Mexican border (Lesser & Batalova, 2017).

In working with refugees, promoting a sense of safety is an important task that requires a high degree of cross-cultural sensitivity. Today, refugees from many Middle Eastern nations ravaged by wars have sought to build new lives in the United States and other Western nations. In addition, an unknown number of immigrants—chiefly women and both male and female adolescents—are lured to this country for work purposes, only to be victimized by those who engage in sex trafficking.

Well-trained forensic psychologists and other clinicians must recognize that the traditional psychological concepts and theories used in assessment and treatment approaches were developed from predominately Euro-American contexts and may be limited in their application to racial and culturally diverse populations (Sue, Bingham, Porché-Burke, & Vasquez, 1999). Christine Iijima Hall (1997) has admonished that Euro-American psychology may become culturally obsolete if it is not adapted to reflect a multicultural perspective. According to Hall, this will require psychology to make "substantive revisions in its curriculum, training, research, and practice" (p. 642). Heeding these words as well as those from many other scholars, professional associations such as the American Psychological Association (APA) have published guidelines for working with diverse populations, as mentioned in Chapter 1. For example, the APA has published the *APA Handbook of Intercultural Communication*, edited by David Matsumoto (2010), which should be of great help to practicing psychologists.

Forensic psychologists should be especially attuned to the potential injustices and oppression that may result from monocultural psychology. C. I. Hall (1997) writes that "people of color and women have been misdiagnosed or mistreated by psychology for many decades" (p. 643). Even psychologists of color or those who are gay/lesbian/bisexual/transgender or from diverse backgrounds are not always knowledgeable about the psychological issues of other cultural groups or of their own groups. As Hall notes, "Color, gender, and sexual orientation do not make people diversity experts" (p. 644). Although these challenges are crucial to all forensic settings, they may be particularly important for those who provide victim services. Without appreciation of their cultural backgrounds, some individuals become not only victims of crime, but also victims of the criminal justice system and victims of the mental health professions that do not truly recognize their needs. (See Focus 10.1 for additional discussion on this topic.)

Victims With Disabilities

A neglected area in victimization research and practice is consideration of persons with disabilities. Victims in this instance extend not only to criminal victimization, but also to discrimination and harassment in the workplace, as well as emotional abuse and neglect in the home that fall short of criminal offending. Laws banning discrimination against persons with disabilities in work settings and public services open up new areas of opportunity for forensic psychologists. It should be noted that individuals with drug addictions are often covered by these laws.

> Psychologists may find opportunities to consult in the determination of reasonable workplace accommodation for persons with psychiatric, learning, and intellectual disabilities and to provide expert testimony in employment discrimination cases. Psychologists also have an essential role in evaluating neurological, learning, and psychological impairment and function as part of the process of determining reasonable accommodation for both students and employees with disabilities. (C. J. Gill, Kewman, & Brannon, 2003, p. 308)

FOCUS 10.1. SERVING IMMIGRANT POPULATIONS

In the United States, immigrants—persons born in other countries (of non-American parents)—are crucial to who we are as a nation. The same may be said of other nations who have welcomed immigrants more enthusiastically than the United States in recent years (e.g., Canada and some European nations). The great majority of immigrants are here legally, having migrated voluntarily for a variety of reasons (e.g., better economic opportunities, education). A subset of immigrants are refugees who left their countries of origin to escape persecution or violence or repressive regimes. Increasingly, "environmental refugees" migrate to the United States to escape environmental disasters or degradation (Bemak & Chi-Ying Chung, 2014). As noted in Chapter 1, immigrants in the United States tend to represent both ends of the education and skills continuum—the professions at one end, and the agriculture, service, and construction sectors at the other (American Psychological Association [APA], 2012).

A minority of immigrants are undocumented because their visas have expired or because they entered illegally. These undocumented immigrants have received negative political and media attention in recent years and, as noted in Chapter 5, deportation proceedings have accelerated. Misconceptions abound about their numbers and their intentions, and there is great lack of recognition of the contributions they make to society (e.g., they pay taxes but cannot receive benefits).

Forensic psychologists are called on increasingly to offer service to immigrants in numerous contexts, including the competency to participate in immigration proceedings, which we discussed in Chapter 5.

As this book is going to press, however, the current political climate is such that many legal protections for undocumented immigrants are fragile. The political climate in the United States has changed so rapidly that it is impossible to tell at this time how policy changes and legal challenges to immigration laws will affect immigration groups. Legal immigrants and the children of the undocumented are affected as well, as families are torn apart or are kept in abeyance about the status of their loved ones.

What is not likely to change, however, is the need for psychologists to offer their assessment and treatment services (Bemak & Chi-Ying Chung, 2014; Butcher, Hass, Greene, & Nelson, 2015; Vaisman-Tzachor, 2012). In these capacities, they may face language and cultural barriers because some immigrants, particularly refugees, may have difficulty communicating or may distrust an examiner who resembles an authority figure. A common task is assessing the trauma that has been experienced by the individual in the past, as well as the individual's reasonable fear of what may happen in the future. Posttraumatic stress disorder (PTSD) is often found in immigrants and refugees who have experienced such events as torture, rape, sex trafficking, or famine (APA, 2012). Experts are quick to point out, however, that the effects of traumatic events may be displayed differently in different cultural groups and according to education or social class (Butcher et al., 2015, and references therein).

Psychological instruments used by forensic examiners must be carefully chosen because many have not been normed on immigrant populations and are not culturally appropriate (Butcher et al., 2015). In addition, the testing process itself may be disturbing to many immigrants who may be even more likely than nonimmigrants to see it as intrusive (Pope, 2012). Scholars recommend that carefully selected instruments as well as structured professional interviews be conducted, together with review of case records.

Questions for Discussion

1. Given the current political climate and concerns about immigration, discuss additional challenges that might be faced by forensic psychologists working with immigrant populations.
2. As noted in the text, undocumented immigrants are often victims of crime. What challenges face the psychologist who is involved in the psychological *treatment* of victims who are undocumented immigrants?

Americans with Disabilities Act (ADA)

Much of the activity in working with the disabled has been prompted by the Americans with Disabilities Act (ADA), implemented July 26, 1992, and discussed briefly in Chapter 2. The act applies to public employers and private employers with 15 or more employees. It prohibits discrimination (a) in the hiring process; (b) regarding terms, conditions, and benefits of employment; and (c) in access to work-related amenities, facilities, and functions

(Goodman-Delahunty, 2000). The Crime Victims with Disabilities Awareness Act (Public Law 105-301) of 1998 was designed to increase public awareness of the extent and nature of crime against victims with developmental disabilities. After its initial passage, the ADA was the subject of numerous lawsuits as well as decisions by the U.S. Supreme Court that interpreted some of its provisions quite narrowly. Commenting on these decisions, some researchers pointed out that the ADA went from protecting 43 million Americans when it was first passed, to protecting a mere 13.5 million (Rozalski et al., 2010). Legal scholars in general believed the law had been severely limited (Foote, 2013). Partly in response to decisions by the Court and other federal courts, Congress passed the Americans with Disabilities Act Amendments Act of 2008 (ADAAA), which was intended to once again broaden protections afforded to disabled Americans. It is too soon to tell whether the relatively new law has significantly affected this population in a positive way.

Employees with disabilities who become victims of crime may suffer substantial, long-term psychological problems that may interfere with or hamper their employment opportunities, advancement, and quality of life. The interested reader is encouraged to consult an article by Jane Goodman-Delahunty (2000), who identifies some common legal pitfalls for practitioners and forensic psychologists and provides suggestions for how to avoid these pitfalls when providing services to employers or to employees with psychological impairments.

Approximately 14% to 20% of the U.S. population has some type of disability (C. J. Gill et al., 2003; Harrell, 2012a; Olkin & Pledger, 2003), broadly defined as a physical or mental condition that substantially limits one or more of the individual's major life activities. It should be noted that disability is listed along with race, gender, age, sexual orientation, and other dimensions of human diversity in the "Ethical Principles of Psychologists and Code of Conduct" (APA, 2002). Psychologists working in forensic settings, therefore, may require specialized training and experience to be competent professionals in working with the disabled.

Well-executed research on the victimization of people with disabilities and the impact it has on their lives is desperately needed. Some data are beginning to emerge on the extent of disability victimization. Criminal victimization data indicate that victimization rates for children and adults with disabilities far exceed those of individuals who do not have disabilities (Harrell 2012a; Office for Victims of Crime, 2009). For example, youth (ages 12 to 19) with a disability experience violence at twice the rate as youth without a disability (Rand & Harrell, 2009). For disabled youth ages 16 to 19, the rates are even higher—they experience violence more than three times as those without a disability (Harrell, 2012a). Persons with cognitive disabilities had the highest rate of violent victimization from 2009 to 2011 (Harrell, 2012a). (See Table 10.1.)

In addition to violent victimization, persons with disabilities are often victims of harassment, discrimination, and emotional abuse. Many people with disabling conditions are especially vulnerable to victimization because of their real or perceived inability to fight or flee or to notify others. About 68% to 83% of women with developmental disabilities (which includes both serious mental and physical impairments) will be sexually assaulted in their lifetime, which represents a 50% higher rate than in the rest of the population (Tyiska, 1998). In addition, people with these disabilities are more likely to be victimized again by the same person, and more than half of those victimized never seek assistance from legal or treatment services (Pease & Frantz, 1994).

Table 10.1 Violent Victimization Against Persons With Disabilities, by Disability Type, 2009–2011

Disability Type	2009	2010	2011
Hearing	16.7	10.6	17.3
Vision	28.6	24.9	23.5
Ambulatory	20.5	19.7	22.7
Cognitive	46.0	43.5	51.0
Self-care	18.3	17.8	27.8
Independent living	24.4	26.4	25.7

Source: Harrell (2012a).

Note: The above percentages represent the proportion of individuals with a disability who are violently victimized. For example, in 2009, an estimated 16.7% of persons with hearing disability were violently victimized. In 2011, 51% of persons with cognitive disability were violently victimized. Persons in self-care or independent living categories have one or more of the listed disabilities.

Although it can be said that victims of crime—particularly violent crime—will always be affected by what happened to them, society has taken some steps to try to "make up for" their victimization. Crime victims' bills of rights have been enacted in all states, half of which provide for mandatory restitution unless compelling reasons to the contrary are stated on the record. In addition, at least 31 states have passed victims' rights constitutional amendments, and at least 10 of these provide for mandatory restitution (M. Murray & O'Ran, 2002). At the present time, every state has some form of victims' rights legislation. In addition, Congress in 2004 passed the Crime Victims' Rights Act. (See Focus 10.2 for a list of rights guaranteed under this law.)

Restitution or **compensation** is a remedy for the recovery of some measure of economic and psychological wholeness. It is an attempt to restore a victim's original financial, physical, or psychological position that existed prior to the loss or injury. Undoubtedly, this is a laudable if somewhat high-sounding goal. However, crime victims have consistently reported their frustrations in obtaining adequate and timely restitution both from offenders and from public funds allocated for this purpose (Karmen, 2013).

Victims of crime can use two legal venues for obtaining justice: criminal courts and civil courts. Criminal courts deal with the aspect of the justice system that determines guilt or innocence with reference to crime and metes out criminal sanctions. Criminal courts allow victims to speak out at sentencing or have their statements read to the court. In some states,

FOCUS 10.2. CRIME VICTIMS' RIGHTS ACT OF 2004*

Congress in 2004 passed legislation providing the following rights to victims of crime. Every state has similar legislation or recognizes victims' rights in its constitution or court decisions. State laws differ, however. For example, some states limit the rights to victims of serious crimes.

Victims' rights under the federal law are as follows:

- The right to be reasonably protected from the accused;
- The right to reasonable, accurate, and timely notice of any public court proceeding, or any parole proceeding, involving the crime or of any release or escape of the accused;
- The right not to be excluded from any such public court proceeding, unless the court, after receiving clear and convincing evidence, determines that testimony by the victim would be materially altered if the victim heard other testimony at that proceeding;
- The right to be reasonably heard at any public proceeding in the district court involving release, plea, sentencing, or any parole proceeding;
- The reasonable right to confer with the attorney for the government in the case;
- The right to full and timely restitution as provided in law;
- The right to proceedings free from unreasonable delay;
- The right to be treated with fairness and with respect for the victim's dignity and privacy.

Questions for Discussion

1. Discuss any problems you might infer with respect to enforcement of this law. In other words, are any of the above rights more or less difficult to guarantee to victims?
2. Is the above list comprehensive or should victims be afforded other specific rights under the law?
3. In the case of federal crimes, does the release of 911 calls to the public violate the rights of crime victims?
4. Locate the victims' rights law in your state. Compare it with the federal law.

Source: 18 U.S.C. Section 3771.

Amended slightly in 2013, but above listed guarantees remain.

victims are also notified prior to all court appearances, and—if the defendant is eventually convicted and imprisoned—they are notified of parole hearings. They also may be given the opportunity to speak out at these hearings. In recent years, with the passage of victims' rights legislation, some victims have been able to seek financial compensation through the criminal justice process.

The civil courts also allow crime victims to seek civil remedies for the physical, financial, and psychological injuries they have suffered as a result of criminal acts, permitting vindication of their rights and recovery of financial reparations from the offenders (Gaboury & Edmunds, 2002). As illustrated in the high-profile O. J. Simpson case of the early 1990s, a defendant may be acquitted in criminal court but found responsible for a death or an assault in a civil court, but these instances are rare. Simpson was found not guilty of killing Nicole Brown Simpson and Ronald Goldman in criminal court; later, however, a civil jury held him responsible and awarded the families $3.5 million.

Civil litigation can be a complex, difficult, and expensive process. Lawyers may ask forensic psychologists, such as those specializing in neuropsychology, to help determine the extent of injuries. For example, as noted in the previous chapters, psychologists may assess a victim of crime or a civil wrong for the presence of PTSD or other psychological aftereffects of victimization. This is done to determine a value that can be placed on the victim's injuries, which in turn helps a jury award damages. Compensation for the cost of psychotherapy can be included in the damages awarded.

Cases involving personal injuries or civil wrongs that are not crime related include sexual harassment, wrongful termination due to gender discrimination, unnecessary medical procedures, and injuries suffered from using faulty products, to name but a few. Sexual harassment suits are a particularly controversial area, especially when the victim of harassment has possible symptoms of PTSD. Although both the civil and the criminal process can be stressful for the victim, the criminal justice process is especially intimidating and frustrating. From the moment some victims call police, they may find themselves faced with a spiral of events that is seemingly out of their control. They may perceive that police do not respond quickly enough, for example, and when police do arrive, victims may believe that police are not sensitive enough to the experience they suffered. Victims often find it difficult to understand why their property cannot be recovered or, if recovered, why it cannot be immediately returned. Victims of violent crime are fearful that their aggressor will be released on bail; if convicted and imprisoned, they are fearful that he or she will be released on parole.

It is a reality in law that the U.S. Constitution protects the rights of suspects and defendants but not the rights of victims. As we discussed in Chapter 3, criminal suspects do not have to speak with police, and if they choose to do so, they are guaranteed the right to an attorney during police questioning if they want one. Defendants have the right to an attorney during every critical stage of the court proceedings, including arraignments, pretrial hearings, trials, and sentencing. In contrast, victims are not represented by lawyers unless they choose to hire a lawyer during a civil proceeding. Although it can be argued that the prosecutor is essentially the lawyer for the victim, the prosecutor is technically the lawyer for the government and may pay very little attention to the physical, financial, or emotional needs of victims. Victims often have to take time off from work or other obligations to appear in court, and when cases go to trial, they are subjected to the scrutiny of the media and grueling cross-examination in a courtroom in which they must be confronted by the defendant. As a result, victims have often complained that they are the forgotten component of the criminal justice process or are twice victimized— once when the crime first occurs and again when they encounter the criminal justice process.

Although the above reality strikes many people as unfair, it occurs because suspects and defendants have so much to lose from the criminal justice process, in which the awesome power of the state is brought to bear against the individual. A person accused of crime stands to lose his or her freedom, sometimes for life. Under the law, if we are ready to take away a person's freedom—in some cases even his or her life—we must "do it right" by providing the protections in accordance with the Constitution. The law does not plan to take away the freedom of the victim, and hence the victim's rights are not guaranteed in the Constitution.

This logic often does not convince victims or their advocates, however. In the 1970s, the nation saw a major trend in the direction of ensuring that victims, too, would have certain rights under the law. Thus, beginning in 1980, when Wisconsin passed the first "victims' bill of rights," states began to pass laws providing victims with certain statutory, if not constitutional, guarantees and protections. As noted above, Congress passed a Crime Victims' Rights Act in 2004. Its provisions mirror many of the rights afforded victims under the laws of their respective states.

Most states have laws requiring **notification** of victims at various stages during the criminal justice process. For example, if a person charged with a violent crime against the victim is about to be released on bail, the victim is notified; if a convicted offender is about to be released from jail or prison, the victim is notified. Even if an offender will be out of prison for a limited time period, as in a work release program, the victim may be notified. Some states also require notification when a plea negotiation has been reached. Not surprisingly, all states require that victims be notified if an offender has escaped from prison.

There are several decision-making points at which a victim's input may be accepted. The right of **allocution** is the right to speak out during these proceedings. Chief among them are the bail hearing, the sentencing hearing, and the parole board hearing. At bail setting, victims are sometimes allowed to argue for a higher bail or, more commonly, to ask that the defendant be forbidden from contacting them. All states allow victims to speak out at sentencing hearings, either in person or in prepared written statements.

Presentence reports—which are documents prepared by probation officers or other professionals to help judges reach sentencing decisions—typically include a *victim impact statement*. The person preparing the report interviews the victim and obtains information about the extent of his or her suffering. A victim of an aggravated assault, for example, might describe being unable to sleep peacefully, recurring nightmares, expensive meetings with a psychiatrist, and his continuing fear of walking alone. When there is no presentence report, victims are allowed to present statements to the presiding judge or to appear in court and testify directly about what they have experienced. In death penalty cases, survivors of the victim are allowed to have the sentencing jury hear details about the suffering they themselves have experienced (*Payne v. Tennessee*, 1991). Some states also allow victims to appear at parole board hearings to protest an offender's release.

Although the physical and psychological impact of crime may be considered the most obvious aspect, the financial impact can also be devastating. "The financial losses incurred as a result of crime (unforeseen medical expenses, psychological counseling costs, and the need to replace stolen property) can be as debilitating as any other type of injury suffered by crime victims" (Gaboury & Edmunds, 2002, p. 2).

All 50 states, plus the District of Columbia, Puerto Rico, and the Virgin Islands, have compensation programs that can pay for medical and counseling expenses, lost wages and support, funeral bills, and a variety of other costs (Eddy & Edmunds, 2002). In some cases, the money is derived from state taxes or grant sources; in others, it comes from offenders themselves. It is also common for states to deny convicted offenders the right to profit from books they may write about their crimes. Called "Son of Sam" laws, after the infamous serial murderer David Berkowitz, who claimed he was controlled by the devil through a dog called "Sam," these laws sometimes redirect the income to the victim or to a victim's fund.

Despite the enactment of the above laws, they do not seem to be working to the advantage of the great majority of victims. Research has indicated that only a small percentage of victims are even aware of their existence (Karmen, 2013; National Center for Victims of Crime [NCVC], 1999). As noted earlier, victims also report that compensation takes time and is rarely provided in total.

Notification, which places an added burden on agents of the criminal justice system, seems particularly problematic. It is often unclear who has the responsibility to keep the victim informed, and consequently, no one takes on this task. In communities with well-funded victims' advocates or victims' assistance programs, notification is more likely to occur, but victims' assistance programs may be the first to go when budgets are tight. Likewise, most victims do not exercise their right of allocution at bail, sentencing, or parole hearings. When they do, the research is mixed with respect to their effectiveness, although results are slightly weighed in favor of their having influenced parole decision makers. For example, several studies document that victims appearing before parole boards have been successful at delaying the offender's release (Karmen, 2009).

Victims are not typically successful at having sentences *increased*, however. After reviewing studies on the effect of victims' rights legislation, Karmen (2001) notes, "Even with all the new options, does institutionalized indifference toward the victims' plight still pervade the justice system? The answer seems to be a qualified 'yes,' according to some preliminary findings gathered from evaluation studies" (p. 317).

Restorative Justice

One philosophical approach that directly provides services to victims is **restorative justice**. Restorative justice—sometimes called reparative justice—is not easy to define because it encompasses a vast array of practices in different areas of the criminal justice system (Daley, 2002). According to Daley, "Restorative justice is used not only in adult and juvenile criminal matters, but also in a range of civil matters, including family welfare and child protection, and disputes in schools and workplace settings" (p. 57). Programs that focus on restorative justice are often initiated in religious organizations, and some send representatives into prisons where organized prison ministries operate. (See Perspective 13.1 in Chapter 13, in which Dr. Eve Brank refers to one such program.) Rather than focusing exclusively on punishing the individual offender, the primary goal of restorative justice is to involve a larger segment of the community in deciding what should be done about criminal offending and the harm perpetrated on its victims. Basically, the mission of restorative justice is to "make whole" the victims and the community that have suffered from the offender's crime, while also reintegrating the offender into the community when appropriate (Karmen, 2001). "It is guided by values that emphasize healing and social well-being of those affected by crime" (Presser & Van Voorhis, 2002, p. 162). Typically, a community reparative board functions as mediators to help resolve conflict and restore or repair both the victim and the offender. The victim plays a major role in the process and may receive some form of restitution.

Restorative justice approaches are often used in school or neighborhood settings where no crime has been committed, but where a problem has erupted, such as bullying behavior. The goal is to settle the dispute in an informal manner and achieve a satisfactory outcome for all involved. In schools, groups of students meet in circles discussing common problems and giving each other support (National Council on Crime and Delinquency [NCCD], 2013). Adults facilitating the programs may be teachers, social workers, trained community volunteers, or mental health practitioners. Restorative justice programs have been praised by the National Council on Crime and Delinquency (NCCD), which sees them as an alternative to traditional juvenile and criminal justice programs.

Restorative or reparative justice is closely associated with a "mediation" philosophy, or an approach that attempts to solve problems by compromising and finding common ground rather than by using conflict tactics. Schoolchildren today are often exposed to mediation strategies to avoid playground fights or resolve a variety of peer conflicts, and mediation may be used in workplaces to resolve disputes between frontline workers and supervisors or administrators. Likewise, attempts at peaceful resolution may be recommended in divorce situations, including custody disputes.

Mediation approaches are used in the criminal context as well, primarily as part of a diversion program to avert formal processing for those charged or at risk of being charged for minor crimes. These programs do not focus only on mediation; they try to hold offenders accountable for their actions and make them responsible for repairing harm to victims and the community (Lemley, 2001). This is done through the process of negotiation, mediation, victim empowerment, and reparation (Rodriguez, 2007).

Restorative justice has a place in both criminal and civil contexts. In criminal cases, the balance of power between a victim and the perpetrator must be taken into account, however. Mediation is not the best alternative when the perpetrator is an adult and the victim is a child, for example, or in many domestic conflict situations. Restorative justice appears to be an especially valuable approach in school and perhaps workplace settings. In recent years, schools have begun to shy away from "zero tolerance" policies, whereby students are suspended for unacceptable behavior. Critics of these policies argue that suspending a misbehaving student only increases the chances of his being unsupervised in the community and isolated from pro-social peers. Restorative justice "circles" within a school setting may be better ways of dealing with antisocial behavior (NCCD, 2013). Nevertheless, restorative justice programs—which vary across the country in how they are developed and how they operate—need continuing evaluation research to measure their degree of success.

CRIME VICTIMIZATION DATA

Information about victimization in our society is best obtained from victims themselves. Persons who have been assaulted or burglarized can tell us when and where the crime occurred, whether they reported it to police, and the degree of physical and emotional harm they experienced, among many other things. These victimization statistics also help us understand the distribution of crime, including its geographical and temporal characteristics. Are certain regions of the country more "crime-prone" than others, for example, or are certain months of the year more likely to see a reduction in crime? When victims know something about the person or persons who victimized them, victimization data also can provide information about those who commit crime.

Measurements of Victimization

The National Crime Victimization Survey (NCVS)

The preeminent victimization survey in the United States is the National Crime Victimization Survey (NCVS), sponsored by the Bureau of Justice Statistics (BJS) and conducted by the Census Bureau. The most recent NCVS—which was mentioned briefly in the previous chapter—reports the results of contacts with a large national sample of households (95,760) representing 163,880 persons older than age 12 (Truman & Morgan, 2016). On an annual basis, a member of the household is first asked whether anyone over 12 experienced crime during the previous 6 months. If the answer is yes, the victim is interviewed more extensively on the frequency, characteristics, and consequences of the criminal victimization. The same households are recontacted every 6 months for a period of 3 years. The NCVS is currently designed to measure the extent to which households and individuals are victims of rape and other types of sexual assault, robbery, assault, burglary, motor vehicle theft, and larceny. The survey includes both crimes reported and those not reported to the police. Consequently, there are differences between NCVS data and the FBI's Uniform Crime Report data.

The NCVS was introduced in 1973 and was then known as the National Crime Survey (NCS). Until that time, the government's main measure of crime in the United States was the FBI's UCR, which reflected crimes that were known to police along with arrest data. Many people—for a variety of reasons—do not report their victimizations to police, however. The NCS was developed to try to tap the "dark figure" of crime, or the crime that did not come to the attention of police. A victimization rate, expressed by the number of victimizations per 1,000 potential victims, is reported to the public. Developers of the NCS reasoned that some crime victims might be more willing to report their victimization to interviewers than to police. Furthermore, interviewers could probe and learn more about the effects of victimization. Over the years, these predictions have been borne out because victimization data continually indicate that, overall, at least half of all crimes are not reported to police. Not surprisingly, this figure varies according to specific crimes; reporting rates of auto theft, for example, are dramatically higher than reporting rates of sexual assault.

The NCS was revised in the 1980s and substantially redesigned in 1992, when its name was changed to the National Crime Victimization Survey. Among the changes were the addition of questions asking victims how law enforcement officials responded when they reported their victimizations. Victims also were asked more details about the crime, including whether the perpetrator appeared to be under the influence of alcohol or illegal substances and what they were doing at the time of the crime (e.g., going to work, shopping). The redesign also included a more sensitive and comprehensive approach to asking victims about sexual assault (Karmen, 2001). In addition to reports of household victimization, the BJS also sponsors supplementary reports, such as surveys of school and workplace victimization and victimization of commercial establishments.

The National Survey of Children's Exposure to Violence (NatSCEV)

In June 1999, the Office of Juvenile Justice and Delinquency Prevention (OJJDP) created the Safe Start Initiative to prevent and reduce the impact of children's exposure to violence (Finkelhor, Turner, & Hamby, 2011). Through this initiative, with the support of the Centers for Disease Control and Prevention (CDC), OJJDP introduced the **National Survey of Children's Exposure to Violence (NatSCEV)**. The survey's goal was to provide a comprehensive presentation of the nature and extent of child and adolescent victimization in the United States. The project estimates children's exposure to violence, crime, and abuse, including child maltreatment, bullying, community violence, domestic violence, and sexual victimization. The survey was conducted between January and May 2008. It measured that past year as well as lifetime exposure to violence for children age 17 and younger across a number of victimization categories: conventional crime, child maltreatment, victimization by peers and siblings, sexual victimization, witnessing and indirect victimization, school violence and threats, and Internet victimization.

Together, the above two important surveys, as well as other studies, provide information about victimization data. We cover these data below.

Violent Victimization Committed by Strangers

The most recent NCVS indicates that violent victimizations committed by strangers accounted for approximately 40% of all nonfatal violence during 2015 in the United States (Truman & Morgan, 2016). The rate of stranger violence reported to the police was 2.8 per 1,000 persons age 12 or older. The rate of serious stranger violence reported was 1.4 per 1,000 persons age 12 or older. Both rates represented declines from previous years.

Ethnic/Minority Differences in Criminal Victimization

NCVS data, tabulated by the BJS (Rand, 2009), provide information on the criminal victimization of five ethnic/minority or racial groups: white, black, American Indian, Hispanic, and Asian. The American Indian classification is based on those NCVS respondents who identified themselves as persons of Indian, Eskimo, or Aleut descent. Asians were defined in this context as Japanese, Chinese, Korean, Asian Indian, Vietnamese, and Pacific Islander. Pacific Islander includes those persons who identified themselves as Filipino, Hawaiian, Guamian, Samoan, and other Asian. Respondents who identified themselves as Mexican American, Chicano, Mexican, Puerto Rican, Cuban, Central or South American, or other Spanish origins were classified as Hispanic. All the groups are extremely diverse, but the rapidly growing Hispanic/Latino group reflects perhaps the greatest diversity. Because of this diversity, the BJS considered the "Hispanic" category as consisting of persons of any race in this tabulation. In other words, some Hispanics also report that they consider themselves white, black, American Indian, or Asian, a point that needs to be considered when examining the statistical data on crime and victimization rates.

The 2010 NCVS data (Truman & Planty, 2012) show that individuals of more than one race experience violent crime at rates that are 2 to 3 times higher than persons belonging to one race or ethnic group. In addition, people of American Indian/Alaska Native origin experience higher rates of violence than all persons who claim only one race or ethnicity. Blacks as a group were second in victimizations of violent crime (see Table 10.2). For decades, blacks—especially young black males—have consistently been disproportionately represented among homicide victims. Blacks are usually 6 times more likely than whites and 8 times more likely than persons of other races to be murdered (Rennison, 2001; E. L. Smith & Cooper, 2013). Firearms, especially handguns, were by far the most frequently used weapon. Firearms were reportedly used in 73% of all murders of males and in 49% of all murders of females (E. L. Smith & Cooper, 2013).

Table 10.2	Rate of Violent Victimization by Race of the Victim per 1,000 Persons Age 12 or Older		
Race	**2002**	**2010**	**2015**
White	32.6	18.3	17.4
Black	36.1	25.9	22.6
Hispanic	29.9	16.8	16.8
American Indian/ Alaska Native	62.9	77.6	Not reported
Asian/Native Hawaiian/Other Pacific Islander	11.7	10.3	25.7*
Persons of two or more races	Not reported	52.6	Not reported

Source: Truman & Planty (2012, p. 5), Truman & Morgan (2016, p. 9).

*American Indian/Alaska Native combined with Asian/Native Hawaiian/other Pacific Islander.

Criminal Victimization as a Function of Age

From 1994 to 2010, the overall rate of serious violent crime against youth (ages 12 to 17) decreased by 77% (N. White & Lauritsen, 2012). Although this decline has been documented by the NCVS, we must keep in mind that the majority of violent crime against youth is not reported to police (White & Lauritsen, 2012). During the 2002 to 2010 period, approximately 56% of serious violent crime and 72% of less serious violent crime (simple assault) were not reported. The reasons given by youth for not reporting violent crime to law enforcement were multiple and included the following: The incident was already reported to another official (such as school personnel); the victim did not think it was important enough to be reported; or he or she considered the incident to be a private or personal manner or feared reprisal. A few thought that the police really wouldn't do much about the incident anyway. These are some of the same reasons adults give for not reporting their victimizations.

Studies have shown that approximately 40% of urban youth have been exposed to a shooting, and many report witnessing serious forms of community violence (Gardner & Brooks-Gunn, 2009; Stein, Jaycox, Kataoka, Rhodes, & Vestal, 2003). In some communities, many youth have reported being victims of violent acts, including being threatened, chased, hit, beaten up, sexually assaulted, or attacked with a knife or gun, and 85% report having witnessed violent acts (Kliewer, Lepore, Oskin, & Johnson, 1998). Approximately 25% of the victims of violent crime are injured, many of them severely (T. Simon, Mercy, & Perkins, 2001). A significant number of children (11%) reported five or more direct exposures to different types of violence, and 1.4% reported 10 or more direct victimizations (Finkelhor, Turner, Hamby, & Ormrod, 2011). Repeated exposure to direct victimization, either of one crime or different crimes, is referred to as **polyvictimization**. Many children and youth (from ages 6 to 18) who are continually exposed to violence develop difficulty concentrating and learning, as well as anxiety, fear, depression, and posttraumatic stress disorder.

Various kinds of violence have different types of impact on those individuals who experience and witness it. In other words, all violence is not the same. Further, several studies have shown that the psychological impact of being a victim of violence differs from that of being a witness to violence (Shahinfar, Kupersmidt, & Matza, 2001). Research also has found that adolescents who had been physically abused are at a higher risk to commit violent behavior themselves than those who had simply witnessed abuse (Shahinfar et al., 2001).Violence between parents (interparental violence) may be more damaging to the psychological health of a young child than being beaten and chased at school. Furthermore, interparental violence in which weapons are used, such as guns or knives, may be more upsetting to children than those incidents not involving weapons (Jouriles et al., 1998). Moreover, individual reactions to being exposed or subjected to violence exist on a continuum, with some youth showing unusual amounts of resilience and ability to cope at one pole, and others being more vulnerable at the other pole. Most are somewhere in the middle.

PSYCHOLOGICAL EFFECTS OF CRIMINAL VICTIMIZATION

Psychological Impact of Violence

The impact of criminal violence extends even beyond the direct victims and their families and friends. For several decades, it has been widely recognized that people have a substantial fear of becoming victims of crime, and that this fear is especially strong among women and the elderly (Dansie & Fargo, 2009; Schafer, Huebner, & Bynum, 2006). Daily reports of crime victimization in the media exacerbate the fear, but other things do too. Perceptions of neighborhood safety, the ability to defend oneself, and other factors also contribute. In the United States, since the events of September 11, 2001, fears of terrorism create additional stress. Incidents such as the Boston Marathon bombing of 2013, the San Bernardino incident in December 2015, and the Charlottesville incident in 2017— which many consider an example of domestic terrorism— intensify those fears. Terrorist activity is no stranger in other parts of the world, as illustrated by recent incidents in Madrid and Barcelona, Spain and Manchester, England.

The psychological impact of criminal violence on its direct victims is substantial and far-reaching. In fact, in many cases, the psychological trauma experienced by victims of crime may be more troubling to the victim than the physical injury or the loss of property. Psychological reactions to criminal victimization can range from mild to severe. The picture becomes even more serious when children become *polyvictims*. The National Survey of Children's Exposure to Violence finds that 1 in 10 children in the United States are polyvictims (Finkelhor et al., 2011). Mild reactions to stress are characterized by a variety of symptoms, including minor sleep disturbances, irritability, worry, interpersonal strain, attention lapses, and the exacerbation of prior health problems (Markesteyn, 1992). Severe reactions, on the other hand, may include serious depression, anxiety disorders, alcohol and drug abuse problems, and thoughts about or attempts at suicide (S. D. Walker & Kilpatrick, 2002). One of the most devastating and common reactions to criminal victimization is posttraumatic stress disorder. PTSD is so important to the understanding and treatment of criminal victimization that it will be worthwhile to discuss the symptoms and what is known about it in some detail.

Recall that PTSD was mentioned in earlier chapters. It is sometimes used as a defense to criminal conduct, for example, and it may be highly relevant in civil cases in which psychologists testify about the effects of a civil harm (e.g., personal injury resulting from a respondent's negligence, or sexual harassment).

Posttraumatic Stress Disorder (PTSD)

Posttraumatic stress disorder (PTSD) is a common psychological reaction to a highly disturbing, traumatic event, and it is usually characterized by recurrent, intrusive memories of the event. The memories tend to be vividly sensory, are experienced as relatively uncontrollable, and evoke extreme distress (Halligan, Michael, Clark, & Ehlers, 2003). As we will note below, it is now documented that many veterans of wars in Vietnam, the Persian Gulf, Iraq, and Afghanistan have suffered or still suffer from PTSD, and it is likely that veterans of earlier wars did as well, although the condition was not recognized. According to the *DSM-5* (American Psychiatric Association, 2013), PTSD may occur when a person has exposure to actual or threatened death, serious injury, or sexual violence. It may develop when the person has directly experienced a traumatic event, witnessed the event, or learned that the traumatic event happened to a close family member or close friend.

PTSD is diagnosed by a mental health professional when the biological, psychological, and social effects of trauma are severe enough to have impaired a person's social and occupational functioning. PTSD may be either acute (when duration of symptoms is less than 3 months) or chronic (when symptoms last longer than 3 months), or the victim may show a delayed onset—now called delayed expression—when months or even years have passed between the traumatic event and the onset of symptoms. The usual course is for symptoms to be strongest soon after the event and then diminish over time. Symptoms may be more severe and longer lasting if the trauma is perceived by the victim as intentionally human made rather than an accident or a natural catastrophe. In other words, victims of violence such as rape, war, or a terrorist attack would be more likely to have long-lasting and more severe symptoms than those persons who experience a hurricane, earthquake, tornado, or an accidental plane crash.

PTSD symptoms include intense fear, helplessness, or horror. It should be noted, though, that the *DSM-5* no longer requires that these particular emotional reactions be in evidence. Some individuals, according to the *DSM-5*, may display different mood states, negative cognition, or dissociative symptoms. In addition, the victims continually reexperience the traumatic event in their thoughts and reactions, consistently avoid things that remind them of the incident, and have persistent symptoms of high levels of anxiety and stress that were not present before the trauma. The symptoms usually wax and wane, coming back and then going into remission for a time. Some research on memory, however, suggests that people tend to remember more trauma than they actually experienced, and when they do, they have more symptoms of PTSD (Strange & Takarangi, 2012). This is not to say that trauma was not experienced, it is merely to suggest that replaying the event in one's mind may have the effect of intensifying the experience, thus causing more distress in the individual. (In Perspective 4.1 in Chapter 4, Dr. Strange alludes to this research.)

Surveys estimate that lifetime prevalence of PTSD (meaning PTSD is experienced sometime in their lifetime) among American adults ranges between 7% and 12% (Breslau, 2002; Kessler et al. 2005; Ozer, Best, Lipsey, & Weiss, 2003), a percentage that increased slightly after the events of September 11. Prior to that time, research indicated that of the 50% to 60% of the U.S. population who were exposed to traumatic stress, only 5% to 10% developed PTSD (Ozer et al., 2003). These data suggest that people's reactions to stress are unique and different for each individual. Nevertheless, for many years, PTSD was under-recognized in routine clinical practice when PTSD symptoms were not the presenting complaint (Franklin, Sheeran, & Zimmerman, 2002), but with more knowledge about its existence, this could be changing. Nevertheless, critics of *DSM-5* changes in criteria for PTSD say the changes will lead to more misdiagnosis of the disorder (Francis, 2013).

The lifetime prevalence of PTSD for women is twice that for men (10.4% vs. 5.0%), according to a nationally representative sample of 5,877 people ages 15 to 45 years (Kessler, Sonnega, Bromet, Hughes, & Nelson, 1995), a discrepancy likely explained at least partially by exposure to sexual assault. Rape is considered one of the most severe of all traumas, causing multiple, long-term negative outcomes (R. Campbell, 2008). Consequently, rape victims—who often prefer to refer to themselves as survivors—have extensive post-assault needs and require help from multiple health and psychological systems. These needs sometimes require months or years before some progress is made toward adaptation or adjustment in the victim's life. However, the data suggest that surprisingly few survivors (less than 35%) seek mental health services, especially adolescents (Ullman, 2007a). Instead, most (about two thirds) seek help from friends and family members. However, many victims simply lack access to professional care for psychological problems. In concluding her comprehensive review of the research literature, Ullman writes, "Multiple interacting dimensions of gender, race, and social class, to name a few, need specific attention to understand help-seeking from all survivors' viewpoints, so that innovative mental health services can be developed and made available to sexual assault survivors" (p. 77).

In a national survey of male and female Vietnam War veterans (D. S. Weiss et al., 1992), it was estimated that 30.9% of men and 26.0% of women met the diagnostic criteria for PTSD at some point since their service in Vietnam (Ozer et al., 2003). Fifty percent of the veterans of the wars in Iraq and Afghanistan seeking treatment screen positive for PTSD, although much fewer receive an "official" diagnosis of the disorder (Ramchand et al., 2010). Among those previously deployed military personnel not seeking treatment, the prevalence estimates range from 5% to 20%. Additional research on men and women deployed in the Iraq and Afghanistan wars suggest that the amount of PTSD symptoms resulting from military sexual trauma (sexual harassment and sexual assault) and exposure to multiple war-related stressors may be even higher than those reported previously (Katz, Cojucar, Beheshti, Nakamura, & Murray, 2012).

The psychological aftermath of exposure to traumatic life experiences is highly variable, with some persons adjusting well and others showing significant adverse emotional and psychological consequences of considerable duration (G. N. Marshall & Schell, 2002). Again, it is possible that memory distortion in some individuals may intensify the symptoms of PTSD. Some crime victims express anger in addition to their PTSD symptoms (Orth, Cahill, Foa, & Maercker, 2008). In addition, the more severe the PTSD symptoms, the stronger the anger expressed. Many researchers continue to search for an array of personal, social, and environmental factors that may contribute to PTSD. However, it is unclear from the research who is most susceptible to PTSD. It is apparent, though, that social support is both a prevention factor before the person experiences trauma and a factor that helps the person recover faster after the trauma has occurred (Ozer et al., 2003).

The research literature suggests that psychological harm is not qualitatively dissimilar for victims of different criminal offenses but rather is a matter of degree. That is, although the psychological reactions displayed by victims of sexual assault, robbery, burglary, and kidnapping vary in intensity, the nature of their distress is similar (Markesteyn, 1992). Therefore, Markesteyn proposes that, in general, a victim's reactions and recovery may be mediated by three classes of variables: (1) victims' pre-victimization characteristics, (2) victims' post-victimization abilities to cope, and (3) factors related to the criminal event. Pre-victimization variables refer to such things as ethnic/minority background, religious or spiritual beliefs, socioeconomic status, gender, and age. As noted above, one of the most important pre-victimization variables is the quality and availability of supportive relationships. Factors related to the criminal event include the degree of violence involved and the location of the crime (e.g., at home or outside the home). Victims who are attacked in an environment they perceive as being "safe" have been shown to experience more negative reactions than those attacked in "unsafe" locations (Markesteyn, 1992). Post-victimization factors include the various coping mechanisms available to crime victims, such as ability to place the blame appropriately, perceived control over their lives, and social and professional support. Fear of being revictimized is especially powerful as a post-victimization reaction. For example, victims of street robbery report an increased sense of vulnerability and an extreme awareness of themselves as potential targets of another crime. They may refrain from going out at night, change their place of employment, move to a new house, or acquire weapons for self-defense (Cohn, 1974). On the basis of an extensive research literature review, Markesteyn concluded that, "almost without exception, the research has demonstrated a correlation between the positive support people receive and their ability to adapt to and successfully overcome stressful life events" (p. 25). Victim services intervention appears to be especially critical.

Short-term psychological reactions to nondomestic assaults (robbery, aggravated and simple assaults) experienced by 40% of victims include anger, difficulty sleeping, uneasiness, confusion, bewilderment, denial, and fear (Markesteyn, 1992). The most serious reactions of depression, helplessness, loss of appetite, nausea, and malaise are reported by 20% to 40% of the victims. About 5% of victims report having lifelong reactions. Victims who do not receive support from others, especially professional intervention and treatment, are particularly at risk for developing subsequent psychological problems.

HOMICIDE VICTIMIZATION

In 2015, approximately 13,455 people were murdered (or were victims of non-negligent manslaughter) in the United States (FBI, 2016a). Although the number of homicides reported to law enforcement has shown a steady decline over the past two decades, the year 2015 showed a 11% increase from 2014 estimates. Homicide victims represent the smallest proportion (1.3%) of violent crime victims, but the psychological devastation experienced by those who survive them is enormous. The nation's youth are especially vulnerable, with nearly 3 of every 10,000 young males likely to be victims of criminal homicide prior to their 18th birthday (APA, 1996). Murder rates of young minority males living in impoverished areas of large cities are much higher, with 1 in every 333 becoming a victim of a homicide before reaching the age of 25. The homicide rate of juveniles in the United States is very high compared to other developed, industrialized nations.

Homicides of young children are committed primarily by family members (71%), usually by "personal weapons" (such as hands and feet) used to batter, strangle, or suffocate victims (Finkelhor & Ormrod, 2001b). According to Finkelhor and Ormrod, although victims include approximately equal numbers of boys and girls, offenders include a disproportionate number of women. Children at the highest risk for homicide are those younger than age 1. Usually, children in this age group are killed by relatives who do not want the child or believe they are ill-equipped to provide for the child. When young children (younger than 5 years of age) are killed by parents, it is usually as a result of the constant attention they require. Two of the most common triggers of young-child homicide are crying that will not stop and toileting accidents (U.S. Advisory Board on Child Abuse and Neglect, 1995). These fatalities appear to be more common in conditions of poverty and in families marked by divorce or absence of the father. The aggressor, however, may be another male figure in the household.

Middle childhood (ages 6–11) is a time when homicide risk is relatively low, whereas the risk of homicide for teenagers (ages 12–17) is high, remaining constant at 10% higher than the average homicide rate for all persons (Fox & Zawitz, 2001). Unlike homicides of children younger than age 12, relatively few homicides of teenagers (9%) are committed by family members.

As pointed out by Finkelhor and Ormrod (2001b), the actual homicide rate for young children may be higher than the statistics suggest. Homicides of young children are difficult to document because they can resemble deaths resulting from accidents and other causes. A child who dies from sudden infant death syndrome (SIDS) may be difficult to distinguish from one who has been smothered, or a child who has been thrown down may have injuries similar to those who died from an accidental fall (Finkelhor & Ormrod, 2001b).

Relationship of the Victim to the Offender

Table 10.3 shows the relationship of the victim to the offender, based on 2015 data reported by the FBI. As illustrated, about 13% of the homicides were a result of one family member killing another family member. Table 10.4 shows the number of victims killed within the family compared to other known relationships.

Table 10.3 Family Relationship of Victim to Offender		
Total Family Murder Victims	1,711	100%
Husband	113	6.5%
Wife	509	29.6%
Mother	125	7.3%
Father	131	7.6%
Son	255	14.8%
Daughter	162	9.4%
Brother	108	6.3%
Sister	22	1.2%
Other Family	286	16.6%

Source: FBI (2016a).

Table 10.4 Murder by Known and Unknown Relationships, 2015		
Total Murder Victims	13,455 Victims	100%
Family	1,711 victims	12.7%
Other Known (e.g., acquaintances, boyfriends, girlfriends, neighbors)	3,909 victims	29.1%
Strangers	1,375 victims	10.2%
Unknown	6,450 victims	47.9%

Source: FBI (2016a).

Death Notification

Notification of family members of a death that resulted from violent crime is among the most challenging tasks for professionals whose responsibility it is to deliver the message (Ellis & Lord, 2002). The best available data indicate that nearly 2% of the adults in the U.S. population have lost an immediate family member due to criminal homicide (Amick-McMullan, Kilpatrick, & Resnick, 1991; S. D. Walker & Kilpatrick, 2002). It is also very often the most traumatic event in the lives of family members and loved ones. Not only is **death notification** highly stressful and intense, but the survivors have also had no time to prepare psychologically.

An inappropriate or poorly done notification can prolong survivors' grieving process and delay their recovery from the trauma for years. In the victimology literature, survivors are often referred to as *co-victims,* a term that will be defined and discussed below. During notification and thereafter, the co-victim's needs may include (1) an opportunity for venting of emotion; (2) calm, reassuring authority; (3) restoration of control; and (4) preparation for what the co-victim needs to do next (Ellis & Lord, 2002).

Forensic psychologists would most likely be involved in death notification by training and providing supportive counseling to police officers, mental health professionals, and death notification teams who are expected to provide the services to families and co-victims of violent crime on a regular basis. There are several models for training death notifiers, but the best-known and probably the most heavily relied on model was developed by Mothers Against Drunk Driving (MADD) (Ellis & Lord, 2002). Even with the availability of the training protocol offered by MADD, however, many death notifiers lack formal training (Stewart, Lord, & Mercer, 2001). Several other handbooks or manuals with training suggestions for death notification are also available. The U.S. Office for Victims of Crime (OVC), in cooperation with the National Sheriffs' Association, has prepared a handbook titled *First Response to Victims of Crime 2001* (Gillis, 2001), and the National Organization for Victim Assistance (1998) has published the second edition of the *Community Crisis Response Team Training Manual.* Chapter 6 of the manual is directly related to procedures and suggestions for death notification. Janice Lord (1997, 2001) has also been a leading expert in developing practices for death notification and has written several manuals or brochures for the OVC. In 1995, the OVC supported the MADD protocol in revising their death notification curriculum and tested it in seven sites (Ellis & Lord, 2002). Experienced death notifiers reported that their greatest unmet educational needs were the following:

- Specific details on how to deliver a notification

- How to manage immediate reactions of the family

- How to manage their own reactions

- General aspects of death notification

According to Ellis and Lord (2002), death notifiers should be sensitive, mature, positive, and calm persons who sincerely wish to become notifiers. Stressed, anxious individuals who lack confidence in delivering the message properly should not be selected as notifiers. Because death notification is a stressful event for all participants, burnout is a prominent danger for those professionals who are intimately involved on a regular basis. An important role for the psychologists in these situations is to provide support and counseling to the victim service providers and be watchful for burnout symptoms.

Reactions of Homicide Co-Victims

My brother was killed by another kid 16 years ago, when he was 15. My family's never been the same. People who talk about "closure" or "moving on" just don't get it. There's never "closure."

My father's in prison because he killed my mother. He can rot there forever. I don't care.

These statements, made some years ago by students in our classes, highlight the terrible suffering and grief faced by what are called **co-victims** of violent crime. Both direct victims and those who are close to them are likely to feel the effects of what occurred for many years to come. This is particularly so with violent crimes.

The term *co-victim* is often used to emphasize the depth of the homicide's emotional impact. In the aftermath of the murder, it is the co-victim who deals with the medical examiner, the criminal and juvenile justice system, and the media. The term co-victim may be expanded to any group or community that is touched by the murder: a classroom, a dormitory, a school, an office, or a neighborhood. Most of the individuals who make up these communities are wounded emotionally, spiritually, and psychologically by a murder, some more deeply than others (Ellis & Lord, 2002, p. 2). The tragedy at Sandy Hook Elementary School in 2012 produced numerous co-victims, both children and adults, although they surely prefer to call themselves survivors. Other examples are the co-victims in the Colorado theater shooting case of 2012, the Boston Marathon bombing, and the Mother Emanuel church killings, among many other crimes. Some co-victims have responded to these tragedies by becoming activists seeking to bring about changes in gun laws, while others have sought privacy and shied away from public appearances. Some have turned to victim service mental health providers or other community resources, while others have preferred to obtain support from one another. Co-victims or survivors of individual tragedies, such as the killing of a single youth, have responded in similar variable fashion.

To be effective, victim service providers must be knowledgeable and carefully trained to deal with the wide range of reactions and needs of victims and co-victims as well as the investigative and judicial processes involved in homicide cases. Such service providers recognize cultural diversity, understand the role that culture and ethnicity play with regard to individuals and groups, and understand the socioeconomic and political factors that affect these groups (C. I. Hall, 1997). Co-victims may respond to the notification of the death of their loved one in a way that is compatible with their cultural/ethnic ways of dealing with death, in combination with their psychological, emotional, and spiritual strengths and weaknesses.

Family members exhibit a wide range of emotions when a loved one is murdered. The available research suggests that the reactions of survivors of homicidal death differ significantly from those of people who grieve the loss of a loved one who died nonviolently (Sprang, McNeil,

& Wright, 1989). The process of mourning, for families of murder victims, lasts longer, is more intense, and is more complex (Markesteyn, 1992). The grief reactions of homicide survivors appear to be deeper, display rage and vengefulness more often, and result in longer lasting anxiety and phobic reactions (Amick-McMullen, Kilpatrick, Veronen, & Smith, 1989; Markesteyn, 1992). As pointed out by L. Miller (2008), "the cruel and purposeful nature of murder compounds the rage, grief, and despair of the survivors" (p. 368). The greater the perceived intentionality and malevolence of the murder, the higher is the co-victims' distress. Co-victims often suffer from intrusive and repetitive images of the violence; nightmares; and episodic, turbulent emotions of anger and grief. Excessive yearning or searching for the deceased, feelings of loneliness or emptiness, a sense of purposelessness or futility, and emotional numbness or detachment are also frequent symptoms of grief brought on by the violent death of a loved one (Carlson & Dutton, 2003). In addition to these symptoms, homicidal death bereavement responses include rage, desire for revenge directed toward the killer, and frustrations with the criminal justice system (S. A. Murphy et al., 1999).

Co-victim reactions may be especially intense if the deceased was subjected to torture, sexual assault, or other intrusive or heinous acts (Ellis & Lord, 2002). Co-victims often need to be reassured that the death was quick and painless and that suffering was minimal. "If the death was one of torture or of long duration, they may become emotionally fixated on what the victim must have felt and the terror experienced" (Ellis & Lord, 2002, Chap. 12, p. 8). If the offender was of another racial/ethnic or other minority group, the co-victim may develop a biased view of that particular group, which may have to be dealt with during counseling.

Complicated Bereavement

A particular challenge for counselors and psychologists is when the survivors cannot find any kind of meaning in the death, a situation that is quite common for parents who lose a child through a violent death, such as murder or suicide (L. Miller, 2008). In his review of the grief literature, Neimeyer (2000) writes,

> Taken together, these studies document that the "search for meaning" plays a compelling role in the grief of the great majority (70–85%) of persons experiencing sudden, potentially traumatizing bereavement, although a significant minority apparently copes straightforwardly with their loss, without engaging in deep-going reflection about its significance. (p. 549)

According to Neimeyer, the quest for meaning in a violent death is an individual odyssey but appears to center around finding benefit in the experience—although *benefit* is a difficult word to use in this context. Grief counselors find it is helpful to survivors to shift from an early emphasis on finding an answer to the question of "why" the death occurred, to a later focus on the positive benefits of the loss. For example, an individual may find new meaning in his or her life and set forth on a path to a new, positive life direction. More specifically, a person may decide to live more fully in the present and develop a more compassionate and expressive approach to others.

Some experts indicate that survivors who cannot "find meaning" are far more likely to experience a syndrome called **complicated bereavement** (Neimeyer, Prigerson, & Davies, 2002). Complicated bereavement as discussed by Neimeyer, Prigerson, and Davies involves symptoms that are not considered psychologically healthy. They can include prolonged and obsessive searching for the loved one, preoccupation with thoughts of the death, excessive irritability and bitterness, disbelief, and lack of acceptance of the death. There often are serious suicidal thoughts, in a desire to rejoin the loved one. While some of these symptoms are characteristic of the grieving process, it is their length and intensity that distinguish complicated bereavement from "normal" bereavement.

The grief literature indicates that most survivors of loved ones who died *nonviolently* eventually make a reasonable recovery and move on as best they can. By contrast, survivors of those who die violent deaths take longer to recover. S. A. Murphy et al. (1999) reported that one third of the parents of children who died violent deaths continued to show their trauma responses and psychological distress at least 2 years after the child's death. In a later study (S. A. Murphy, Johnson, & Lohan, 2002), two thirds of the parents (both mothers and fathers) met the diagnostic criteria for mental distress (depression, anxiety, cognitive disorganization, detachment from their world) 5 years after the violent death of their child. Clinicians and researchers interested in bereavement believe that the grief process that follows the violent death of a loved one represents a distinctive type of grief response that requires special training and skills to treat effectively (Carlson & Dutton, 2003).

SEXUAL ASSAULT VICTIMIZATION

This section provides an overview of sexual violence victimization, including characteristics of the victim and the effects of the sexual violence on the victim's life and mental health. The assailant could be an intimate partner, a relative, a friend, a date, a known person, or a stranger. A large portion of the sexual violence (approximately one third) is perpetrated by an intimate partner, which could be a current or former spouse, girlfriend, or boyfriend. The next chapter will describe intimate partner and family violence with an emphasis on physical violence and psychological abuse.

Characteristics of the Victims

Age

Rape and sexual assault are primarily crimes against youth, at least according to available statistics. These statistics must be viewed guardedly, however, in light of the low reporting rates of sexual assault in general. Older women, married women, and men, for example, may be less likely to report this type of victimization. The National Women's Study (Tjaden & Thoennes, 1998a) reported the following data concerning the age of victims:

- 32% of sexual assaults occurred when the victim was between the ages of 11 and 17;

- 29% of all rapes occurred when the victim was younger than age 11;

- 22% occurred between the ages of 18 and 24;

- 7% occurred between ages 25 and 29;

- 6% occurred when the victim was older than 29.

Again, these data must be viewed cautiously, because sexual assault of older individuals—including the elderly—within their residences are likely to go unreported, as are incidents of marital and acquaintance rape. For example, Rennison (2002b) estimates on the basis of self-report surveys that 63% of completed rapes, 65% of attempted rapes, and 74% of completed and attempted sexual assaults are not reported in the United States.

Additional data collected from the National Incident-Based Reporting System (NIBRS) add a more comprehensive picture, but the age distribution differs. NIBRS indicates that more than two thirds of all victims of sexual assault reported to law enforcement agencies were juveniles (younger than age 18) (Snyder, 2000). More than half of all juvenile victims were younger than age 12. More specifically, 33% of all victims of sexual assault reported to law enforcement

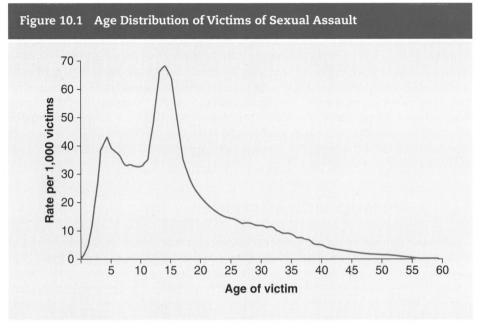

Figure 10.1 Age Distribution of Victims of Sexual Assault

Source: Snyder (2000).

were ages 12 through 17, and 34% were younger than age 12. Fourteen percent of victims were younger than age 5 (see Figure 10.1).

NIBRS data indicate that juveniles were the largest majority of the victims of fondling (84%), sodomy (79%), and sexual assault with an object (75%), but they were the victims in less than half (46%) of rapes (Snyder, 2000).

Although babysitters are responsible for a relatively small portion of the crimes against young children (4.2%), the children at risk of physical assaults by babysitters are younger (ages 1–3) than those at risk of sex crimes (ages 3–5) (Finkelhor & Ormrod, 2001a). Males constitute the majority of sex-offending babysitters reported to the police (77%), whereas females make up the majority of physical assaulters (64%).

Gender

Overall, according to official statistics, an estimated 90% of the victims of rape and sexual assault are female (FBI, 2016a; Greenfeld, 1997). Research data indicate that between 18% and 26% of women in the United States have been sexually assaulted at some point in their lives (Finkelhor, Shattuck, Turner, & Hamby, 2014; Kilpatrick, Resnick, Ruggerio, Conoscent, & McCauley, 2007; Post, Biroscak, & Barboza, 2011). Although data on the number of male victims who have been sexually assaulted over their lifetimes are difficult to find, the best estimates have ranged between 5% and 14% (Finkelhor et al., 2014; Rosin, 2014). However, two recent surveys conducted independently by the Centers for Disease Control and Prevention and the Bureau of Justice Statistics discovered widespread sexual victimization among men in the United States (Stemple & Meyer, 2014). In fact, some forms of male victimization are "roughly equal to those experienced by women" (Stemple & Meyer, 2014, p. e19). Recent data are beginning to reveal "an alarmingly high prevalence of both male and female victimization" (p. e19). (See Focus 10.3 for more information on this topic.) Children and college students, persons with disabilities, and incarcerated individuals are most vulnerable to be raped or otherwise sexually assaulted.

The child sex offender is almost always male, but the victim may be of either gender. As mentioned in Chapter 9, however, researchers are beginning to question the assumption that females rarely commit sexual assaults against children (Becker & Johnson, 2001; Sandler & Freeman, 2007). Heterosexual sexual assault—male adult with female child—appears to be the more common type, with available data suggesting that three quarters of male sex offenders choose female victims exclusively (Langevin, 1983; Lanyon, 1986). Homosexual child sex offending—adult male with male child—appears to be substantially less frequent, occurring in about 20% to 23% of the reported cases. A small minority of child sex offenders choose children of either gender.

Extent of Injury to Victims

Data on physical injury from sexual assault reveal that 58% of female victims of sexual violence suffered physical injury during the attack, such as cuts, bruises, internal injuries, broken bones, gunshot wounds, or rape injuries (Planty, Langton, Krebs, Berzofsky, & Smiley-McDonald, 2013).

FOCUS 10.3. SEXUAL VICTIMIZATION OF MALES

Over the past 20 years, a number of high-profile media stories highlighted the fact that sexual assault cannot be defined only as male against female. Chief among these media accounts were the priest-abuse scandals, wherein men in the United States as well as across the world revealed that, as young boys, they had been abused by priests. (Although girls also were abused by priests, boys were more vulnerable because they often came into contact with priests as altar boys. Furthermore, despite their vows of celibacy, priests were not unknown to have consensual sexual relationships with adult women or men.) Another media story was the case of Jerry Sandusky, the Penn State assistant football coach who was imprisoned after being charged and convicted of some 45 counts of child sexual abuse occurring between 1994 and 2009. Receiving less public attention were studies of sexual assault in juvenile facilities, and prison rape, indicating that both male and female inmates were extremely vulnerable to sexual assault by both prison and jail staff and other inmates.

In an incisive article, Stemple and Meyer (2014) have argued that a new approach to studying sexual assault is needed. They note that both official statistics and research paradigms focus on sexual assault primarily as a male against female crime and view females as powerless and helpless victims. Some assumptions (e.g., that male victims experience less harm or that all sex is welcome to men) discourage further inquiry into male victimization. Furthermore, while it is well acknowledged that female rape victims often do not report their experience to police, male rape victims are just as likely to not report, and sometimes for different reasons.

Stemple and Meyer say that, because of the dominant methods of gathering sexual assault data and the dominant paradigms for studying it, we ignore the harm suffered by males raped by females, same-sex assaults of males, and highly vulnerable males with disabilities or in institutional settings.

Questions for Discussion

1. Sexual assault is often not reported to authorities for many different reasons. Are these reasons the same regardless of one's gender? If not, what reasons would be the same and which ones would be different?
2. Should sexual assault of adult females be considered more harmful than sexual assault of adult males?
3. Unequal power relationships are often at the root of the sexual assault of women and girls (e.g., the jailer against the inmate, the uncle against the niece, the trio of college fraternity brothers against the first-year student attending their party). Are power relationships at work when males are assaulted as well?

Sexual violence refers to the completed, attempted, or threatened rape or sexual assault. About 35% of the females who received physical injury during the attack said they sought treatment for their injuries, usually at a hospital, doctor's office, or emergency room.

These data suggest that the majority of victims will not exhibit overt physical evidence that most people believe is characteristic of violent sexual attacks. One reason offenses against adult males are not taken seriously is that they do not evidence the same amount of force. NCVS data indicate that women do require medical care for rape reported injuries more than men, but both did have significant injuries (12.6% of women, 8.5% of men) (Stemple & Meyer, 2014). Unfortunately, many people who see no clear evidence of physical injury will conclude that the victim must have consented. In addition, even though some attacks do not result in physical injury or death, sexual assaults inflict enormous psychological harm on victims, especially children. Similar to women, "men who experience sexual abuse report problems such as depression, suicidal ideation, anxiety, sexual dysfunction, loss of self-esteem, and long-term relationship difficulties" (Stemple & Meyer, 2014, p. e20).

Relationship of the Victim to the Offender

Intimate Partner and Dating Violence

The legal scope of rape has traditionally been confined to imposed sexual contact or assault of adolescent and adult females who are not related to the offender. In view of the fact that rape most often occurs between acquaintances, relatives, and spouses, this traditional definition is drastically outdated. Kilpatrick, Whalley, and Edmunds (2002), for example, report compelling evidence that most rapes are of intimate partners and not strangers. Their data indicate that

- 24.4% of rapists were strangers;
- 21.9% were husbands or ex-husbands;
- 19.5% were boyfriends or ex-boyfriends;
- 9.8% were relatives; and
- 14.6% were other nonrelatives, such as friends or neighbors.

More recent data from the NCVS covering the years 2005 to 2010 show similar results (Planty et al., 2013). The survey indicates that 8 out of 10 victims of sexual violence knew the offender. About one third of victims who knew the assailant said the victimization was committed by an intimate partner. Another 6% revealed the offender was a relative or family member, and 38% said the offender was a friend or acquaintance. Strangers committed 22% of the attacks, a percentage that has remained basically unchanged from 1994 to 2010.

Still, many people (including the victims themselves) do not define sexual attacks as rape unless the assailant is a stranger. Thus, if the victim is sexually assaulted by a husband, boyfriend, or a "date," she is unlikely to report the incident. Depending on the study, 15% to 20% of female college students report experiencing date rape or other dating violence (Eshelman & Levendosky, 2012). In fact, sexual assault on college campuses has received very recent public attention, much like the sexual assault in the military discussed earlier. Many young women have reported being sexually assaulted during or after fraternity or other parties, for example, but others have been assaulted walking to their residence halls from an evening class.

Dating and intimate-partner rape victims may suffer three types of abuse: sexual, physical, and psychological (Eshelman & Levendosky, 2012). Sexual abuse includes refusing to use a condom or other contraception or demanding or physically forcing sexual actions. Physical abuse includes a continuum of actions "from slapping or hitting to more severe acts such as stabbing, burning, and choking" (Eshelman & Levendosky, 2012, p. 216). Psychological abuse includes behavior such as intimidation, social isolation, humiliation, and other behavioral patterns designed to control the victim. Victims of dating violence often receive repeated trauma from their "dates" or boyfriends, and the psychological effects of repetitive abuse tend to be more severe than the effects of single-event abuse. Moreover, "the experience of multiple abuse types is more likely to lead to mental health problems than exposure to only one type of abuse" (Eshelman & Levendosky, 2012, p. 224). Depression and PTSD are two of the more common psychological problems associated with intimate partner or dating sexual violence (Taft, Resick, Watkins, & Panuzio, 2009).

Criminal justice officials and the general public frequently feel that marital or date rape is unimportant because they believe that it is less psychologically traumatic to the victim and more difficult to prove. Some prosecutors, for example, admit they are reluctant to prosecute marital or date rape cases because of concerns that it is difficult to convince juries that husbands or boyfriends could be sexual assailants. However, as mentioned earlier, available data suggest that more than a third of the total rapes and sexual assaults are committed by an intimate partner, often a spouse (Planty et al., 2013).

Additional Victimization Data

Approximately 90% of the time, the sexual assault victimization involves a single offender, a percentage that has been consistent over the past two decades (Planty et al., 2013). During the years 2005 to 2010, victims reported that the assailant possessed or used a weapon 11% of the time. According to the victims, the offender had a firearm 6% of the time and a knife in 4% of the attacks. The most common reason given by adult victims of rape or sexual assault for reporting the crime to the police was to prevent further crimes by the offender against them. The most common reason given by the victim for *not* reporting the crime to the police was that it was considered a personal matter. Nationally, per capita rates of rape are found to be highest among residents ages 16 to 19, low-income residents, and urban residents (Greenfeld, 1997). There are no significant differences in the rate of rape or sexual assault among racial groups.

Juvenile victims were more likely to be victimized in a residence than adult victims (Snyder, 2000). The most common nonresident locations for sexual assaults of juveniles are roadways, fields/woods, schools, and hotels/motels. The weapons most commonly used in sexually assaulting juveniles were hands and fists.

Child Sexual Abuse

Child sexual abuse is the exploitation of a child or adolescent for another person's sexual and control gratification (Whitcomb, Hook, & Alexander, 2002). The global prevalence of child sexual victimization is estimated to be about 27% among girls and approximately 14% among boys (Garcia-Moreno, Guedes, & Knerr, 2012). In the United States, the prevalence of child sexual victimization is approximately 25% to 27% in girls and an estimated 16% in boys (Pérez-Fuentes et al., 2013). A survey study by Wurtele, Simons, and Moreno (2014) revealed that 6% of the men and 2% of the women indicated some likelihood of having sex with a child (age 12 or younger) if they were guaranteed they would not get caught or punished. In addition, 9% of the men and 3% of the women revealed some likelihood of viewing child pornography on the Internet.

In most cases of child sexual abuse, the offender and the victim know one another, often very well, and the crime frequently involves relatives (incest). Many victims are simply looking for affection, wanting only to be hugged or cuddled or to have human contact. Some offenders justify their own behavior by saying the child acted "seductively." Very often, the child may participate in the molestation primarily because he or she is too frightened to protest. Although this is difficult for many to understand, research indicates that child sex offenders, on average, tend to have positive feelings toward their victims, generally perceiving them as willing participants, and that they frequently victimize children living in their immediate households (Miner, Day, & Nafpaktitis, 1989). These "positive feelings" are presumably restricted to crimes that do not involve sexual penetration, however. In many cases, the sexual behavior between the offender and the same child has gone on for a sustained period of time.

Psychological Effects

Research indicates strongly that any form of sexual abuse in childhood results in long-term, interpersonal, social, and psychological problems in many children, adolescents, and adults (Cantón-Cortés, Cortés, & Cantón, 2015; Domhardt, Münzer, Fegert, & Godbeck, 2015; Hillberg, Hamilton-Giachrisis, & Dixon, 2011). Some of the psychological and behavioral problems are even found in preschool victims (Hébert, Langevin, & Bernier, 2013; Langevin, Hébert, & Cossette, 2015). Reports of depression, shame, suicidality, sleep disorders, substance abuse, feelings of isolation, fears and intense anxiety are not uncommon in both male and female victims. Depression and PTSD are the symptoms most commonly found among adolescents and adults who were sexually assaulted as children (Gospodarevskaya, 2013; Wherry, Baldwin, Junco, & Floyd, 2013). Some studies report that 30% to 40% of individuals who experienced sexual abuse in childhood report a lifetime history of depression, compared with 10% to 20% of individuals without a childhood history of sexual abuse (Musliner & Singer, 2014). Both male and female victims report these psychological and interpersonal problems.

The overwhelming evidence from both clinical and empirical studies is that most victims of sexual abuse are negatively affected by their experience (Pérez-Fuentes et al., 2013). However, the long-term effects of child sexual abuse appear to differ significantly from individual to individual. Although some victims apparently suffer no negative long-term consequences, studies with adults confirm the long-term effects of sexual abuse mentioned in the clinical literature for a majority of the victims (Browne & Finkelhor, 1986).

Studies also suggest that sexual abuse by fathers or stepfathers may have a more negative impact than abuse by perpetrators outside the home. Furthermore, and not surprisingly, the use of force or physical coercion in the assault usually results in more trauma for the child (Browne & Finkelhor, 1986). Experiences involving intercourse or attempted intercourse and genital contact by mouth are more troubling than acts involving touching of unclothed breasts or genitals.

Child Sexual Abuse Accommodation Syndrome (CSAAS)

The child sexual abuse syndrome (CSAS), or **child sexual abuse accommodation syndrome (CSAAS)**, originally proposed by Summit (1983), is reserved for a cluster of behaviors that occur in children who have been victims of sexual abuse by a family member or by a trusted adult. According to Summit, children do not necessarily have an innate sense that sexual activity with an adult is wrong. However, if the sexual activity continues, the adult usually must pressure or threaten the child to prevent others from knowing about the activity. Often, the abuser presents these threats and pressures in such a way that the child is led to believe something terrible will happen (perhaps to a family member) if this "private" knowledge becomes known. Hence, the child is placed in the position of being responsible for the welfare of the family. The child also feels helpless to stop the activity. Thus, the child must "accommodate" these secrets and incorporate them into his or her daily living pattern.

According to this view, children who have been sexually abused feel ashamed, fail to report the abuse, and deny that it occurred when questioned. Summit believed that mental health professionals could verify that sexual abuse had occurred if they found behavioral indicators of the CSAAS, such as comments by a child indicating precocious sexual knowledge. In addition, those who support the existence of CSAAS believe it is acceptable for the interviewer to be more suggestive in questioning these children, asking specific and sometimes leading questions.

However, there is question about the validity of the CSAAS, specifically because it may prompt the child to hide or deny the abuse, and leading questions are needed to draw out the correct information. Reviewing the literature on this topic, Bruck and Ceci (2009) noted that children who are abused may not initially report it for the reasons noted above. However, when questioned directly, but not suggestively, they do not deny it. "These findings lend no support to the notion that children who deny having been abused must be pursued with relentless suggestive questioning because otherwise they will not disclose the details of their abuse" (p. 156). Bruck and Ceci also note that, while highly suggestive interviews prompted children to report abuse, children also gave false reports, or reported events that did not occur.

Almost three decades ago, J. E. B. Myers (1991) observed, "At this point, professionals have not reached consensus on whether a syndrome exists that can detect child sexual abuse" (p. 82). Haugaard and Reppucci (1988) wrote, "The principal flaw with the notion of a specific syndrome is that no evidence indicates that it can discriminate between sexually abused children and those who have experienced other trauma" (pp. 177–178). Many of the behaviors listed by Summit (1983) may occur in any child who has experienced other types of trauma besides sexual abuse, although the behaviors usually do not demonstrate precocious sexual awareness. "As a result, one cannot reliably say that a child exhibiting a certain combination of behaviors has been sexually abused rather than, for instance, physically abused, neglected, or brought up by psychotic or antisocial parents" (Haugaard & Reppucci, 1988, p. 178).

In sum, CSAAS has questionable validity as a meaningful diagnostic tool or indicator of sexual abuse. Even precocious sexual awareness may not be reflective of abuse. Moreover, it is particularly problematic if it results in highly suggestive questioning of children, leading to false reports. On the other hand, some have observed that children are highly vulnerable to PTSD, a more useful concept in describing the psychological impact of child sexual abuse (Whitcomb et al., 2002).

In child sexual abuse cases, the forensic psychologist may be asked to evaluate the child to determine if the allegations have foundation and, if they do, what level of trauma has been experienced. It is crucial, then, for the psychologist to be aware of current research on the reliability of children's reports of victimization (Bruck & Ceci, 2009). This is relevant information in both criminal cases, when someone is charged with the abuse, and civil cases, such as when child custody is at issue, as we discussed in Chapter 6. The forensic psychologist may also be asked to assess the competency of the child to testify in the case and may help in preparing the child to testify. Finally, the psychologist may act as an expert witness in the case, such as testifying about the validity of children's memory or level of understanding.

Psychological Impact

Sexual assault produces a broad spectrum of psychological reactions in its victim. In much of the literature on sexual assaults, "victims" are now often referred to as a "survivors," "a label that emphasizes their strength and avoids the connotation of passivity associated with the label of 'victim'" (Felson, 2002, p. 136). However, we continue to use the more recognized term *victim* in this context because we are talking about *victimization* of all kinds in this chapter and discussing the many *victim* services available. Nevertheless, it is understandable that people who have experienced such attacks prefer to refer to themselves as survivors, because that term connotes emotional strength and emphasizes that they are in control of their lives.

Sexual victimization usually provokes some type of reaction and physical, social, psychological, and often economic or—in the case of students—academic loss. After a sexual assault, some student victims have difficulty concentrating, begin to miss classes, and fall behind in their school assignments. Some withdraw completely from high school or college. Furthermore, service providers and psychologists should be aware that many victims of sexual assault are often concerned about people finding out about it, including family members (Kilpatrick et al., 2002). As one student commented, "I never wanted to tell my mother; it would have broken her heart."

Among the more common psychological reactions to sexual assault are PTSD, shame, helplessness, anger, or depression. The quality of life usually suffers as victims experience sleeplessness, nightmares, social isolation, flashbacks, and intense feelings of insecurity. Studies find that rates of PTSD in victims are significantly higher after a rape than after nonsexual assault (Elklit & Christiansen, 2013; Faravelli, Giugni, Salvatori, & Ricca, 2004). Some evidence also suggests that women who are sexually attacked by strangers are more likely to develop PTSD than women who know their assailants (Elklit & Christiansen, 2013; Ullman, Filipas, Townsend, & Starzynski, 2006). Although this research focused on women as victims, it is important to stress that similar findings might be found with respect to men as victims. Some research has found that 94% of rape victims met symptomatic criteria for PTSD shortly after the assault, and 47% continued to show symptoms of PTSD 3 months after the assault (Foa, Rothbaum, Riggs, & Murdock, 1991). In another study, 16.5% of rape victims showed PTSD symptoms 17 years after the assault (Kilpatrick, Saunders, Veronen, Best, & Von, 1987). Some of the mental health problems become life threatening in nature. Rape victims are 4 times more likely than non–crime victims to have contemplated suicide. Moreover, "rape victims were also 13 times more likely than non–crime victims to have actually made a suicide attempt (13% vs. 1%)" (Kilpatrick et al., 2002, Chap. 10, p. 15).

Forensic psychologists and other psychologists working in forensic settings are often asked to do an assessment, provide treatment, or become an expert witness in sexual assault cases. The assessment may be done to evaluate the victim's suffering, responses, and reactions, especially if they appear to be life threatening. The psychologist should be knowledgeable about the victim's cultural and ethnic background and how that culture perceives victims of sexual assault. A number of rating scales and psychological inventories are available to document the victim's level of trauma.

Expert testimony might occur in a criminal or a civil case. A civil case may involve a victim suing an alleged attacker to recover damages or suing a third party for failing to provide adequate protection. A psychologist might testify in support of the victim's claim of severe emotional injuries, such as PTSD, which has led to the devastation of the victim's social, occupational, and/or financial life.

INTERNET VICTIMIZATION

Online Sexual Solicitation

In recent years, the news media have raised alarms about the dangers of the Internet. The major theme centers around the contention that child and adolescent online profiles and other social media channels frequently attract aggressive sexual predators. Based on their extensive research on the issue, Wolak, Finkelhor, Mitchell, and Ybarra (2008) conclude, "The research about Internet-initiated sex crimes makes it clear that the stereotype of the Internet child molester who uses trickery and violence to assault children is largely inaccurate" (p. 112). They find that most Internet-initiated sex crimes consist of adult men who use the Internet to meet and entice underage teenagers into sexual meetings. Very frequently, as we noted in Chapter 9, the teenagers realize they are communicating with an adult. The behavior of the perpetrator is still criminal, however, because even if a "consensual" sexual encounter occurs, he is committing statutory rape. In addition, he may be charged under "luring" statutes.

Many online sexual solicitors are not dangerous, as few (less than 5%) online solicitors are arrested for violent contact sexual offenses (Seto, Hanson, & Babchishin, 2011). However, the use of the Internet specifically for the commercial sexual exploitation of children and youth is another matter. This includes such behaviors as circulating pornographic images of children or of children being assaulted. It also includes luring children for purposes of sex trafficking and offering children to others for sexual purposes—a topic to be discussed below. An estimated

570 arrests for Internet-facilitated commercial sexual exploitation of children were made in the United States in 2006 (Mitchell, Jones, Finkelhor, & Wolak, 2011). Increasingly, offenders and traffickers are using the Internet to facilitate the sexual trafficking and exploitation of children. As noted by Mitchell, Jones, Finkelhor, and Wolak, "The domain of technology-facilitated crimes against children has been characterized by two features: rapid growth and changing dynamics" (p. 46). The Internet is an effective and efficient medium for reaching large and diverse audiences interested in the sexual exploitation of minors.

Much of the current information about the extent of Internet sexual exploitation of minors has been drawn from the National Juvenile Online Victimization (N-JOV) Study. The study was designed to investigate the characteristics and extent of Internet-related sex crimes against minors (Mitchell et al., 2011). The study provides some estimation on how new technologies, including the Internet and other digital media, are being used to produce, advertise, distribute, and sell materials and contact information pertaining to the use of minors for sexual purposes.

HUMAN TRAFFICKING

Human trafficking is the third leading criminal enterprise in the world and is one of the fastest growing and possibly represents the most lucrative criminal enterprise globally (Cecchet & Thoburn, 2014; Rafferty, 2013). **Human trafficking** is the economic exploitation of an individual through force, fraud, or coercion (APA, 2014c). (See Photo 10.1; see also Focus 10.4 regarding APA recommendations on trafficking.) The U.S. Department of State (2010) broadly defines it as when "one person obtains or holds another in compelled service" (p. 7). "Trafficking occurs within domestic services, agriculture and food processing, construction, hospitality and service industries, textile and garment work, health care, and the commercial sex trades, among other areas" (Hume & Sidun, 2017, p. 9).

Although the term *trafficking* implies travel or movement from one location to another, victims do not have to be literally transported to be labelled victims of trafficking (Miller-Perrin & Wurtele, 2017). Trafficking is defined by exploitation rather than movement.

The number of trafficked victims is extremely difficult to estimate. Currently, there is no uniform system for collecting data on the victims (Miller-Perrin & Wurtele, 2017). Second, the covert nature of human trafficking often prevents identifying who is a victim and who is not, especially involving sexual exploitation victims. Third, victims are fearful of retribution from their traffickers. Victims also tend to be highly distrustful of authority figures such as law enforcement because they may be

▶ **Photo 10.1** Then UNICEF ambassador Angie Harmon and a human rights worker comfort a teenager who is a survivor of sexual exploitation.
Source: © Kike Calvo/U.S. FUND FOR UNICEF via AP Images.

runaways or undocumented immigrants. Despite these drawbacks, the best estimates report that approximately 20.9 million people across the globe are victims, and many of them are children (Muraya & Fry, 2016; United Nations Office on Drugs and Crime [UNODC], 2012). In the *UNODC's Global Report on Trafficking in Persons 2012*, sexual exploitation was by far the most common form of human trafficking (79%), followed by forced labor (18%). The UNODC noted that other forms of exploitation—forced or bonded labor, domestic servitude and forced marriage, organ removal, and the exploitation of children in begging, the sex trade, and as soldiers—are underreported. Although victims (survivors) of human trafficking often suffer a life of slavery under psychologically and physically damaging living conditions, our focus in this section of the chapter will be on sexual exploitation, especially pertaining to children and adolescents.

Child and Adolescent Sex Trafficking

The most lucrative of all human trafficking is sexual exploitation, especially involving women and girls. Girls between the ages of 12 and 16 are at the greatest risk for exploitation (APA, 2014c). However, it has been reported that the age of trafficked children has been getting younger, as young as 7 to 10 years of age (B. Wilson & Butler, 2014).

Child sex trafficking "is the act of recruitment, transportation, transfer, harboring, or receipt of a child for the purpose of exploitation, regardless of the use of illicit means, either within or outside a country" (Rafferty, 2013, p. 559). Usually, the definition includes children and adolescents under the age of 18. It is estimated that 300,000 children and adolescents become victims of commercial sexual exploitation in the United States each year (W. Adams, Owens, & Small, 2010; Hopper, 2017). Some are brought in from other regions of the world, including Africa, Asia, Central and South America, and eastern Europe. Many are also from Mexico and Canada.

Although women and girls represent a majority of the victims of commercial sexual exploitation, a significant proportion of victims are men and boys (Raney, 2017). The vulnerability appears prevalent for runaway, homeless boys who self-identify as gay, bisexual, and transgender/transsexual (J. A. Reid, 2012). Many of these boys feel misunderstood and rejected by family, friends, and peers due to their sexual identity, and they seek other avenues outside the home for acceptance and companionship. They are often easy prey for traffickers. Of the estimated 1.7 million runaway/throwaway children in the United States, about 23% are considered at risk to become sexually exploited (Hammer, Finkelhor, & Sedlak, 2002).

The commercial sexual exploitation of children (CSEC) comes primarily in two forms: child prostitution and the production and distribution of child pornography. Traffickers usually select children who appear to be the most vulnerable, largely because they are easier to control. Traffickers are not only strangers; they may be mothers, fathers, siblings, relatives, friends, and adult acquaintances. In a notorious case whose facts were recounted in a 2014 Supreme Court decision (*Paroline v. United States*), an 8-year-old girl was raped by her uncle, who videotaped the assault and circulated it on the Internet. Law enforcement officials ultimately uncovered more than 35,000 images of the rape on home computers in the United States alone. The uncle was convicted, imprisoned, and ordered to pay restitution. The Paroline case centered on a man who had downloaded the images on his computer and had served some time in prison for this offense. The Supreme Court case focused on how much compensation he should pay the victim under the Crime Victims' Rights Act of 2004 (see Focus 10.1) as a result. In similar cases of individuals downloading images of the girl's rape, courts across the United States had attached various amounts, from $100 to $3,000. A federal appeals court had determined that Paroline was responsible for the total suffering the girl had experienced, which was estimated at $3.4 million. The Supreme Court disagreed, and indicated that Congress should come up with some sort of formula for deciding how to assess compensation in similar instances. The reader may wonder, as did the dissenter, Justice Kagan, how such a formula could be devised. Justice Kagan would have had Paroline be responsible for the total amount.

Psychological Effects on CSEC Victims

CSEC victims (which include adolescents as well as children) often show symptoms of depression, anxiety, shame, low self-esteem, hopelessness, sleep disorders, and PTSD. In addition, they also may have physical injuries, sexually transmitted diseases, and a variety of other health concerns.

Clinical psychologists and other mental health professionals have discovered that trauma resulting from an accumulation of traumatic events such as experienced by CSEC victims often results in a more pervasive and complicated form of PTSD, called Complex PTSD (Muraya & Fry, 2016). Complex PTSD pertains to significant psychopathology encompassing several psychological functions including relationships, emotions, behavioral and cognitive domains (Herman, 1992; Muraya & Fry, 2016). CSEC victims during their captivity "may be gagged, stripped, kept naked, drugged, given alcohol, starved, burned, or even undergo genital mutilation" (B. Wilson & Butler, 2014, p. 497). These conditions may exist over an extended period of time, compounded by repeated sexual exploitation. Complex PTSD usually emerges after prolonged and repeated trauma.

CSEC victims often come from homes where they were maltreated. Some studies suggest that 85% of sexually exploited and trafficked children and adolescents may have been abused or neglected by parents or caretakers (Gragg, Petta, Bernstein, Eisen, & Quinn, 2007). In addition, the childhood households of trafficked children and adolescents are frequently characterized by parental substance abuse, domestic violence, poverty, and constant crises. In many cases, children and adolescents run away and live on the streets, a lifestyle that renders them vulnerable to trafficking and prostitution. Often runaway youth turn to "survival sex" for their daily needs, where sexual acts are exchanged for shelter, food, and in some cases drugs (Institute of Medicine & National Research Council, 2013). In addition, "gay and transgendered youth are frequently cut off from family and peers, experience considerable stigma and isolation, and are at greater risk for being homeless, which, in turn, increases the likelihood of selling sex" (Miller-Perrin & Wurtele, 2017, p. 132).

Dire poverty is perhaps one of the dominant factors that lands children, adolescents, and adults into commercial sex trafficking. In many areas of the world, parents are forced to sell one or more of their children to traffickers so that the family can survive. It should be mentioned that women and girls in many parts of the world experience gender inequality and gender-based discrimination, and are overall devalued as persons (Miller-Perrin & Wurtele, 2017). Traffickers therefore take advantage of the devaluation of women and girls in disadvantaged communities and are willing to pay for them at low prices in their recruitment strategies.

Psychological Services

Unfortunately, research on the extent and manner in which psychological services are being delivered to victims of sexual exploitation is extremely sparse. Moreover, there is a paucity of research concerning the best practices to effectively address the lifetime trauma experienced by victims of commercial sexual exploitation (Rafferty, 2017; B. Wilson & Butler, 2014). One thing is clear: Intervention starts with a comprehensive assessment of each child or adolescent victim. As asserted by McIntyre (2014), "Child survivors of commercial sexual exploitation and trafficking are in need of comprehensive assessment as a critical first step in providing assistance post-exploitation" (p. 39). Children who have been sexually exploited in this way may be unwilling, reluctant, or unable to tell who they are, where they came from, and what happened to them in the early stages of post-exploitation experiences (McIntyre, 2014). The comprehensive assessment process should capture two domains of the victim's life: (1) the trafficking experience and (2) the cultural, social, and family environment from which she or he came.

According to McIntyre (2014), the assessment of the trafficking experience should develop into four stages that determine the following: (1) the victim's vulnerabilities before recruitment; (2) the methods and strategies used in the victim's recruitment; (3) the trafficking process, including the travel, transportation, and transfer of the child or adolescent to the intended location of exploitation (brothel, club, pub, hotel, private home); and (4) the intended category of exploitation. The social and personal environment evaluation should include a narrative of the victim's views and perceptions of self (including strengths and weaknesses), and a social history about the family, culture, and community of origin. McIntyre believes that the child's discovery of, and ability to increase, personal strengths and resources will help the victim thrive in recovery and safeguard against future threats.

As has been mentioned earlier in the book, psychologists and other mental health professionals should be able to provide culturally relevant services (Rafferty, 2017). This is crucial in the assessment of CSEC survivors, who often come from developing countries. Psychologists must be culturally knowledgeable and sensitive to the beliefs and values that exist in the communities from which these survivors came. Rafferty emphasizes that Western-based assessment procedures and therapeutic approaches are not always compatible or effective for dealing with the needs of victims from developing countries. For example, some cultures disapprove of receiving assistance for emotional problems and shame those who do. Spirituality is another strong component for resolving problems in many cultures and communities. When working with CSEC victims, Rafferty suggests nonverbal activities, such as art therapy, music, dance movement therapy, yoga, and drama participation.

The APA Task Force (APA, 2014c), Rafferty (2017), and M. Crawford (2017) have outlined or identified a number of ways mental health practitioners can help commercially sex trafficked victims. (See Focus 10.4 for a list of examples.) A number of other researchers have

FOCUS 10.4. PREVENTING HUMAN TRAFFICKING, HELPING SURVIVORS

Many researchers, advocates, and mental health professionals are concerned about the extent of commercial sex trafficking in the United States, as well as globally. As noted in the text, an APA task force has issued recommendations to combat this problem and help survivors. APA members have also testified before Congress when it considered legislation such as the Runaway and Homeless Youth and Trafficking Prevention Act. In that testimony, psychologists emphasized that human trafficking is extremely difficult to measure because of the lack of a centralized database, the diversity of situations, and difficulty obtaining information from the victims. They also emphasized the severe physical and mental health consequences experienced by the victims but emphasized as well that they can and do heal.

Here are some of the recommendations directed specifically to psychologists. They are encouraged to do the following:

- Develop and validate psychological measures for the assessment of the mental health and psychological needs of the victims.
- Provide career counseling and psychotherapy in line with the cultures and abilities of the survivors.
- Contribute toward the prevention of human trafficking through community involvement, teaching, and informing the general public.
- Design, conduct, analyze, and publish investigations related to human trafficking.

- Work within law enforcement agencies on investigations of human trafficking as well as help in the prosecution of traffickers. (This recommendation is especially directed at forensic psychologists who consult with law enforcement, serve as trial consultants, or testify in court.)
- Provide culturally sensitive assessments of sexually exploited trafficked survivors.
- Provide services to juvenile justice agencies in identifying juveniles who have been victims of sexually exploited trafficking and refer the victims to the proper social and psychological services.

Questions for Discussion

1. Survivors can and do heal. Discuss how such healing is most likely to occur.
2. Do you agree that all arrested juveniles should be screened for evidence of sexual exploitation? What about all homeless or runaway children?
3. The Runaway and Homeless Youth and Trafficking Prevention Act referred to above modified an earlier law by, among other things, extending shelter services to 30 days and allowing shelters to provide trauma-informed and gender-responsive services for youth. What other services should be offered to runaway, homeless, and/or sexually exploited children and adolescents?

been active in uncovering the needs of survivors of CSEC (e.g., Salisbury, Dabney, & Russell, 2015). Furthermore, because CSEC is not easily detected, there are calls for uncovering this form of victimization in children and adolescents who are reticent about revealing what has happened to them. Adolescents in particular are often arrested for minor offenses, such as theft, burglary, or drug possession. According to Andretta, Woodland, Watkins, and Barnes (2016), "The availability of a brief, objective, and nonintrusive screener for the purpose of generating likelihood of CSEC victimization is sorely needed in cities where thousands of youth are arrested per year" (p. 266).

SUMMARY AND CONCLUSIONS

Forensic psychologists and other mental health practitioners will be increasingly employed as consultants, instructors, expert witnesses, evaluators, therapists, and service providers to victim service organizations in the coming years. In this chapter, we explored some of the many areas in which their services will be most needed in the very near future and emphasized the need for a deep appreciation for multiculturalism and diverse cultural norms and values. The knowledgeable forensic psychologist will also be capable of working with many victims with disabilities, a group that represents a very large, diverse, but underserved population in American society.

We reviewed some highlights of victims' rights, with an emphasis on victims who must deal with the criminal justice system. In addition to a federal law guaranteeing rights to crime victims, all states make some provisions for addressing the rights of victims. Nevertheless, programs and providers often are not funded sufficiently, and court interpretations of the statutes vary.

Crime victimization data were covered briefly, focusing on some of the racial and ethnic-minority differences reported in the available victimization statistics. The psychological effects of criminal victimization, particularly violent victimization, were described in some detail. PTSD appears to be the most common psychological reaction to crime of all kinds, although the reactions are usually most intense and long lasting after a violent incident. The *co-victims* of homicide incidents, especially when the dead victim is a family member, are particularly devastated and in many cases may never fully recover. Sexual assault also represents a highly traumatic event that is often followed by a wide range of psychological reactions and disorders, especially PTSD. Child sexual abuse is not only common, but also has long-lasting

psychological damage for many of its victims. However, the chapter also emphasized that victims respond to trauma and disaster differently, with some coping extremely well while others struggle. Consequently, the existence of "textbook syndromes" as a direct result of victimization should be viewed cautiously and with the expectation that many—perhaps most—victims do not exhibit a set pattern of symptoms.

Many children today are victims of sexual crimes, including the production and distribution of child pornography, luring on the Internet, and child sex trafficking. The psychological effects of these victimizations cannot be overestimated, but effects are individual. Psychologists often must assess the impact and submit reports in both criminal and civil cases. The child sexual abuse accommodation syndrome, proposed in the 1980s, has not been sufficiently documented and has questionable validity. Some mental health examiners have found evidence of PTSD in exploited children, but this is not necessarily universal. Negative psychological consequences are invariably documented, however, just as they are in other forms of sexual crimes against children.

The chapter focused on serious, predominantly violent crime, but it is important to know that property crimes such as burglary and identity theft take a toll on their victims. Because there is scant research in this area, we have alluded to it only briefly here. Research on the effects of white-collar crime victimization is needed as well. All crimes engender psychological effects and leave emotional scars on their victims. Therefore, an area worth exploring for those forensic psychologists interested in doing research would be the psychological effects of these understudied but very common offenses.

KEY CONCEPTS

Allocution   383
Child sexual abuse accommodation
   syndrome (CSAAS)   400
Child sex trafficking   404
Complicated bereavement   394
Co-victims   393
Death notification   392

Human trafficking   403
Multiculturalism   376
National Survey of Children's
   Exposure to Violence
   (NatSCEV)   386
Notification   383
Polyvictimization   387

Posttraumatic stress disorder
   (PTSD)   388
Restitution/compensation   381
Restorative justice   384
Victimless crimes   373

QUESTIONS FOR REVIEW

1. What is monocultural psychology, and what challenges does it present to forensic psychologists?

2. Are persons with disabilities more likely to be victims of crime? Explain your answer.

3. What are the two venues in which victims of crime may seek recourse?

4. List and describe any five rights granted to victims as a result of the Crime Victims' Rights Act of 2004.

5. What type of information about victimization is available from the NCVS?

6. List some of the common psychological effects of crime on its victims.

7. What role do forensic psychologists play in dealing with the co-victims of criminal homicide?

8. What role do forensic psychologists play in dealing with adult victims of sexual assault?

9. What role do forensic psychologists play in dealing with victims of child sexual abuse?

10. Describe Summit's child sexual abuse accommodation syndrome and state the controversy associated with it.

Want a better grade? Go to **edge.sagepub.com/bartol5e** for the tools you need to sharpen your study skills. Access practice quizzes, eFlashcards, an action plan, and SAGE journal articles for enhanced learning.

CHAPTER ELEVEN

FAMILY VIOLENCE AND CHILD VICTIMIZATION

The wall between the two apartments was thin, and Brenda often heard shouting and cursing coming from next door. The day after she heard banging noises, she knocked on her neighbor's door, saw her bruises, and urged her to contact a woman's shelter, which had a mental health consultant on its staff.

School officials were concerned when Eric, always a sullen child, arrived at school one morning with scrapes on his face. In the nurse's office, it was learned that he also had a sprained wrist. An on-site school psychologist spoke with Eric, determined he was being abused at home, and called Child Protective Services.

Forensic psychologists and other clinicians working within forensic settings frequently encounter both perpetrators and victims of violence in families and between intimate acquaintances. The tasks they perform include doing assessments, consulting with legal authorities and social service providers, and testifying in courts. Psychologists conducting child custody evaluations—discussed in Chapter 6—are advised to consider whether there is violence in the home as well as the effects of that violence on parents and dependent children. Forensic psychologists working in law enforcement and corrections may conduct workshops on preventing and responding to family violence, and some provide psychotherapy for victims as well as offenders. As will be seen throughout this chapter, family violence in all of its manifestations is found at all socioeconomic levels and spares no age, race, religion, or ethnic group.

The chapter begins with a discussion of the violence directed at spouses or other intimate partners, then moves to child abuse and the more serious or unusual physical forms of abuse, including infanticide, Munchausen syndrome by proxy, and shaken baby syndrome. Repressed and recovered memory is covered in some detail because this topic has received considerable attention in research and clinical literature, and also because it sometimes plays a significant role in the courtroom concerning various kinds of child abuse and other traumatic experiences. It continues to be one of the most controversial topics in clinical and forensic psychology today. Child and adolescent abduction–though rare–is presented as a special area that has not received the professional attention it deserves. The chapter ends with another neglected topic, elder abuse. There is a rapidly growing demand for forensic geropsychologists throughout the country, and we will provide some of the career opportunities in that expanding discipline.

Chapter Objectives

- Review the various issues around family violence and its psychological consequences.

- Describe intimate partner violence.

- Describe forensic assessment of violence in the family and between intimate partners, including assessment instruments used.

- Review research on child abuse and its psychological consequences.

- Emphasize the strengths and limitations of human memory in reporting victimization and crime.

- Examine child abduction and its psychological effects.

- Introduce elder abuse and neglect, and review its devastating effects.

The broad term family violence (also known as domestic or intrafamilial violence) refers to any assault, including sexual assault, or other crime that results in the personal injury or death of one or more family or household member(s) by another who is or was residing in the same dwelling. It often occurs in intimate relationships, such as between current or former spouses, partners, or significant others. As such, it is more likely to be called intimate partner violence (IPV), a term that also encompasses violence in a relationship where the two individuals may not be living together (or have lived together but are now living apart). Approximately 13% of all homicides involve one family member killing another family member (FBI, 2013a). Nearly one third of the victims of family homicides were wives slain by a husband or ex-husband, usually during an argument (see Table 11.1) (FBI, 2016a). Table 11.1 also shows other circumstances that have led to spousal-victim homicides. Approximately 1 in 4 American, British, and Australian women report experiencing a physical assault by an intimate partner at some point in their lives (Bedi & Goddard, 2007; Perez, Johnson, & Wright, 2012). Forty percent of these women reported being injured enough to require medical attention (although they did not necessarily seek it) during their most recent assault (Perez et al., 2012).

Whether referred to as domestic, family, intrafamilial, or intimate partner violence, it is found across all ethnic and racial groups and all socioeconomic classes. It occurs against people of all ages, cultures, and living conditions. However, research indicates that violence directed at women is more likely to occur in homes characterized by poverty, communities with few resources, socially isolated families, and subcultures where there is greater acceptance of gender inequities (L. E. Walker, 1999). In recent years, however, it has become apparent that women's improving economic contributions are increasingly important resources for a family's financial well-being and are likely to result in a decline in family violence (Powers & Kaukinen, 2012). Some data have supported this hypothesis for brief periods, but latest reports show an increase in homicides (FBI, 2016a). Despite ebbs and flows, violence in the home and between intimate partners continues to occur at all socioeconomic levels and is a major social problem.

It should be emphasized that both men and women perpetrate violence, and some studies suggest that there is little difference in aggression between the sexes in this regard (e.g., Archer, 2002; Straus & Gelles, 1990). As pointed out by Menard, Anderson, and Godboldt (2009), however, these studies often are based on large community samples that self-report aggression using such measures as the Conflict Tactics Scales (CTS), to be discussed below. Self-reported aggression in this context includes situations in which a couple may have a physical altercation that does not necessarily result in calling police and that does not represent a pattern of continuing or escalating violence (M. P. Johnson, 2006). By contrast, official data such as the National Crime Victimization Survey (NCVS), records from shelters, and studies by other researchers indicate that IPV *that is persistent and escalating* is perpetrated chiefly by men against women.

Table 11.1 Murder Circumstances, by Victim Relationship to Offender, 2015*			
Circumstances	Family Murder Victims	Husband as Victim	Wife as Victim
Total (family killing family)	1,721	113	509
Romantic triangle	20	3	14
Argument over money/property	35	2	5
Other arguments	637	64	242
Brawl under influence of alcohol	21	0	2
Brawl under influence of narcotics	14	0	2
Arson	5	0	2

Source: FBI (2016a).

*Note: When neither spouse is listed as a victim, other family members, such as children, siblings, or other relatives, were the victims.

Although *domestic violence (DV)* has been the term used in the past to define a pattern of behaviors used by one partner to establish and maintain power and control over the other, *intimate partner violence*, or *IPV*, is the term that is increasingly used in its place (Daire, Carlson, Barden, & Jacobson, 2014). IPV has emerged as a term to describe various types of relationship violence. Daire, Carlson, Barden, and Jacobson write, "IPV encompasses the traditional power and control violence described by the term DV but also includes relationship violence that does not stem from one partner's attempt to control his or her partner" (p. 170). Although IPV and DV are used interchangeably in the literature, Daire et al. view IPV to be a more inclusive term and one that reflects current trends in the research literature. Where appropriate, we will use the term IPV in place of DV.

Despite changes in relationship trends in recent years, there appear to be different *motivations* for the violence used by men and women (Menard, Anderson, & Godboldt, 2009, citing the research in this area). The motivations for IPV—as they are for all forms of human violence—are highly variable, but the overriding motive of male offenders who abuse women is believed to be to establish or maintain power and control over them. Even so, we cannot assume that this is characteristic of all male-perpetrated violence within the home (J. B. Kelly & Johnson, 2008). When women use violence against their partners in domestic situations, it is most often for self-defense, in anticipation of violence, or in retaliation for violence perpetrated against them (Meuer, Seymour, & Wallace, 2002). Many male abusers are serial abusers. That is, if they leave or are left by one partner they have been abusing, they quickly become involved with another partner whom they soon abuse. Furthermore, this cycle or pattern of abuse is not easily broken, as we shall see.

It is important to stress, however, that recent research suggests that in many relationships, the desire on the part of one partner to control the other is *not* always a significant factor in explaining the violence (J. B. Kelly & Johnson, 2008). Some research even suggests that a relationship in which a violent individual seeks control over his partner is the least common domestic violence situation (Jaffe, Johnston, Crooks, & Bala, 2008). For example, in conflict-instigated violence, the violence is perpetrated by both partners who demonstrate limited skills at resolving conflict. According to Jaffe et al., these cases "involve bilateral assertions of power by the man and woman, without a regular primary instigator, and are identified more often in community samples" (p. 501). However, serious violence is most likely to occur in those relationships where one partner (usually the man) shows an ongoing pattern of using force, threat, emotional abuse, or other coercive means.

The Typical Development of an IPV Relationship Based on Power and Control

Over a decade ago, Meuer et al. (2002) outlined the typical sequence that characterizes the pattern of such violence, which they refer to broadly as domestic violence. Again, in light of recent findings, it is important to stress that the typical sequence outlined below specifically describes the type of relationship in which one partner seeks excessive control and power over the other.

Meuer et al. (2002) identify nine stages of domestic violence or IPV. It should be noted that we use opposite-sex pronouns (he and she) in the illustrations below because heterosexual relationships are the most common in society. We also refer to the abuser as male because that is the most typical for these abusive relationships. However, IPV also occurs in same-sex relationships, a topic we will return to in the pages ahead.

The *first stage* of such relationships identified by Meuer et al. (2002) seems wonderful and intense, with the husband or partner taking an active interest in everything his spouse or partner does and everywhere she goes. He wants to be with her all the time, flatters her, confides in her, and proclaims he wants to spend the rest of his life with her. Meuer et al. observe that many victims mistake these obsessive and controlling behaviors as devotion, rather than recognizing them as red flags that may lead to an abusive relationship. *Stage 2* emerges when he begins to insist on knowing her whereabouts at all times, begins making decisions for her, and demands her loyalty to the relationship. He indicates he is in charge, will make the rules, and expects her to follow them and attend to his needs. During this stage, he also may begin to blame a former spouse or partner for the problems in a previous relationship, saying— for example—that that person had him arrested without cause or unjustifiably obtained a restraining order against him. During *Stage 3*, the woman becomes adjusted to the attention, jealousies, and control he displays. She makes a commitment to him—usually under his pressure—and convinces herself that she is happy to be with someone who cares so much for her. *Stage 4* is characterized by the beginning of excessive control through psychological and emotional abuse. He begins to demand control over things dealing with all phases of her life, including clothing, hairstyles, and how she should act. He becomes angry if she deviates from his requests. His actions communicate that she is unattractive or that her appearance is somehow faulty.

Stage 5 is characterized by the first incident of physical abuse. The victim will probably view the response as an aberration that is unlikely to occur again. The abuser says he is sorry and that it will never happen again. She accepts his apology and explanation and may wonder what she did to prompt his behavior. In *Stage 6*, the psychological and physical abuse occurs again. The victim will ask the abuser why he is repeating such behavior, and he will, in turn, blame the victim for prompting his abusive behavior by not meeting his expectations. He makes it clear that she is responsible for setting him off and that it will not happen again if she changes her ways. The victim at this stage begins to internalize the blame more completely. *Stage 7* occurs roughly simultaneously with Stage 6. Meuer et al. (2002) refer to this stage as the beginning of the isolation process. The abuser wants to know who she spends time with and either asks her to not see them again or forbids her to do so. He further makes it difficult for her to see anyone and gets excessively suspicious if she has a good time with anyone but him. Eventually, she stops seeing people of whom he disapproves, and she becomes increasingly isolated.

As the relationship continues, she experiences considerable emotional conflict and confusion. This phase represents *Stage 8*. The abuser blames the victim, and the victim is confused about what is wrong. In *Stage 9*, the abuser increases his use of psychological threats and physical force to gain and maintain control and dominance. If she confronts him or threatens to leave him, he escalates his use of threats and force. The victim may eventually conclude that it is safer to stay in the relationship than to leave. She may feel she cannot make it on her own for a variety of reasons.

During the later stages, the abusive behavior is usually followed by promises that he will never do it again. As noted by Meuer and her colleagues (2002), most IPV victims repeatedly attempt to leave the relationship but return when they believe they cannot overcome the obstacles of getting away from the abuser.

According to these researchers, leaving the relationship is not always the best approach and may increase the potential danger to the victim. Unfortunately, there has been evidence that victims who attempt to leave are often stalked, harassed, and threatened on an ongoing basis. The stalking may occur even when a divorce is filed or granted. It was originally believed that if a battered woman could be persuaded to leave the abusive relationship, the violence would stop, but "many batterers continue to harass, stalk, and harm the woman long after she has left him, sometimes resulting in someone's death" (L. E. Walker, 1999, p. 25). In many cases, most of the reported injuries from domestic violence occur *after* the separation of the couple. Some evidence also suggests that women who leave their batterers are at a 75% greater risk of being killed by their batterers than those who stay (Wilson & Daly, 1993).

The above perspective—that leaving may not be the best thing—is strongly resisted by advocates of victims of IPV, who maintain that getting out of the relationship is still precisely what victims must do. For the person being abused, it seems to be a no-win situation: "If I stay, this will get worse; if I leave, he will come after me." In addition, society itself places obstacles in the victim's path. For example, economic options are limited, and deeply entrenched cultural norms hold the victim responsible for dealing with the violence against herself (Dobash & Dobash, 2000). Also, community support is too often unavailable. If shelters, support groups, and a supportive law enforcement response were *consistently* present, the chances for successfully escaping an abusive situation would increase. In general, advocates maintain, the risk of staying is much greater than the risk of leaving. This is a complex issue and one not

▸ **Photo 11.1** A mother and her two sons who have suffered domestic violence leave their home for a women's shelter, carrying their belongings.
Source: Viviane Moos/CORBIS/Corbis via Getty Images.

clearly resolved by the empirical data. However, it is probably fair to say that most practicing psychologists working with victims of abuse would be supportive of their efforts to leave but would also help them to identify the resources necessary to enable them to do that. (See Photo 11.1.)

It is also a reality that—for a multitude of economic and psychological reasons—some women who are abused often return to their abusers, sometimes over and over (M. E. Bell, Goodman, & Dutton, 2007; Eckstein, 2011; Silke, 2012). Explanations for this phenomenon have been numerous and varied: lack of financial resources, blaming oneself for the violence, believing the children need a father, masochistic tendencies, pressure from family members, inadequacy of temporary shelters, and a strong emotional attachment to the abuser.

Psychological Characteristics of Batterers

Battering is a term often reserved for *physical violence* experienced in intimate relationships, such as in a dating relationship, marriage or partnership, or separation and divorce. Some researchers use the term *battering* to represent the more serious and frequent abuse, including the more severe psychological abuse. Men who batter often deny or minimize their use of violence, or they blame it on others. In fact, the shoving, kicking, striking, choking, hitting, or punching inflicted on the victim is often not seen by the batterer as abuse (Meuer et al., 2002). Rather, he justifies his behavior as being provoked by, triggered by, or in response to something done by the victim. In other words, he perceives his behavior as a natural and understandable reaction to frustration. Again, however, we must emphasize that this refers to the relationship in which the violence is perpetrated to exert power and control over the victim. It may not be characteristic of all relationships in which IPV occurs.

A strong predictor of whether a man will abuse his spouse or significant other appears to be whether he has experienced or witnessed violence in his own family while growing up (Meuer et al., 2002). Violence is learned behavior that is passed down from one generation to the next (Eron, Gentry, & Schlegel, 1994; L. E. Walker, 1999). Not all men from abusive or violent homes become abusers themselves, of course. Those who do, compared to those who do not, are less capable of attachment to others; are more impulsive; are more lacking in social skills; and possess different attitudes toward women, the masculine role in the family, and violence. Some research has also indicated that many batterers have serious mental disorders in addition to their problems with power and control over women that encourage their use of violence (D. Dutton & Golant, 1995; L. E. Walker, 1999). It appears, therefore, that treatment programs that focus on both the batterer's emotional problems and his misguided beliefs and values may help in the amelioration of IPV for those abusers who show signs of psychopathology.

Similar to other offenders discussed in earlier chapters (e.g., rapists, stalkers), batterers also have been studied for purposes of developing typologies or batterer types. A well-validated typology of batterers would allow a systematic examination of how and why different men use violence against their wives and partners, as well as help design effective prevention and treatment strategies for dealing with them. After a thorough review of the research literature on batterers in domestic situations, Holtzworth-Munroe and Stuart (1994) were able to identify three types of male batterers that emerge with consistency in a variety of studies: (1) family only, (2) dysphoric/borderline, and (3) generally violent/antisocial. The typology is based on the severity and frequency of the marital violence, the generality of the violence (only within the family or outside the family), and the amount of emotional or mental dysfunction exhibited by the batterer.

Family-only batterers are typically not violent outside the family and engage in the least amount of severity and frequency of violence. Their violence tends to be periodic, primarily when stress and frustration reach a peak, and they do not demonstrate discernible indications of severe mental disorders or psychopathology. In addition, they are least likely to have previous arrest records and alcohol problems and are most likely to apologize after the violence. Their major problems are being inappropriately assertive in their relationships and their tendency to misinterpret social cues. Consequently, they have resorted to violence rather than appropriate nonviolent means to resolve conflicts with their partners. This group is estimated to constitute about 50% of the known batterers (Holtzworth-Munroe & Stuart, 1994).

Dysphoric/borderline batterers exhibit mental disorders and are psychologically disturbed and emotionally volatile. These individuals often engage in moderate to severe spousal abuse, including psychological and sexual abuse. Although this group's violence is mainly confined to the family, they may also exhibit some extrafamilial violence. Their anger is generalized and explosive in nature and is apt to be displayed anytime they become frustrated. The disturbed batterer also tends to have serious alcohol and drug abuse problems. It is estimated that this group comprises about 25% of the known batterers.

Generally violent/antisocial batterers are more likely to use weapons and more prone to inflict severe injury on wives, partners, and other family members, in addition to engaging in extrafamilial violence. They also are more likely to have an extensive history of contacts with police, including arrests and convictions. Generally violent batterers tend to be highly impulsive and explosive. Moreover, they exhibit serious problems with alcohol and drug abuse, and many show characteristics of psychopathy. Overall, they probably make up about 25% of the batterer group (Holtzworth-Munroe & Stuart, 1994).

Mental health professionals have made some progress in the treatment of batterers, both with programs in the community and in prison settings. However, researchers have not yet concluded that any specific approach to treating batterers is significantly more effective than others, assuming equivalent training of the providers and a comprehensive treatment strategy (American Psychological Association [APA], 2003b). Most treatment programs include some form of cognitive-behavioral psychotherapy, although the specifics vary with the types of abuse for which the offender is being treated. Waltz, Babcock, Jacobson, and Gottman (2000) suggest that generally violent batterers and disturbed batterers are unlikely to benefit from short-term treatments focusing on anger management. According to Waltz et al., these approaches often assume—incorrectly—that the acquisition of anger control and attitude change are sufficient. However, a variety of broader, more complex issues may interfere with short-term treatment approaches. Long-term treatment strategies that concentrate on cognitive-behavioral and psychopathological issues are more likely to be effective. How effective these strategies are for psychopaths who are batterers remains an unfinished story, however. We simply do not have enough empirical data to know what works with this troubling group.

For family-only batterers, treatments that focus on violence, abusive behavior, and relationship problems are likely to be successful because they appear to be more sensitive and empathic to the needs of others. One thing is clear, however. The form of treatment used by mental health professionals must address the offender's use of dominance and control, as well as the attitudes and cognitions that underlie his acts of violence.

Dropping out of treatment programs is a common problem that many clinicians face with their clients. Research has found that batterers who complete their treatment programs are less likely to recidivate (Cattaneo & Goodman, 2005). Interestingly, the source of referral to treatment as well as supervision appear to have some effect on the completion of treatment; that is, batterers who are referred by courts—rather than enrolling in a program voluntarily—and who are supervised while attending the programs are more likely to complete their treatment (S. J. Barber & Wright, 2010). It seems clear, then, that efforts should be made on three fronts: mandate treatment, encourage retention in treatment, and supervise offenders to make it less likely that they will drop out of the program.

Battered Woman Syndrome

Battered woman syndrome (BWS) is a term first used by psychologist L. E. (Lenore) Walker (1979), who identified the syndrome based on a volunteer sample of abused middle-class women. In her clinical practice, Walker observed a cluster of behavioral, cognitive, and emotional features that she believes are frequently found in women who have been battered and psychologically abused *over a period of time* by their partners. She later documented BWS more fully on the basis of extended interviews with 435 battered women of various socioeconomic groups (L. E. Walker, 1984). The core features she identified include feelings of learned helplessness (Seligman, 1975), the development of survival rather than escape skills (e.g., appeasing the batterer rather than planning to leave), low self-esteem, and feelings of depression. Later, Walker (2009) began to view BWS as a form of posttraumatic stress disorder. In recent years, she has developed and modified the Battered Woman Syndrome Questionnaire (BWSQ).

In her earliest and still often-cited work, Lenore Walker (1984) contended that battering relationships generally follow a three-stage cycle of violence: (1) the tension-building phase, (2) the acute battering incident phase, and (3) the honeymoon or contrition phase. The cycle has similarities to the nine-stage sequence later proposed by Meuer et al. (2002) and discussed above. During the tension-building phase, there may be minor physical, emotional, or verbal abuse, and the victim often tries to placate her abuser but with only limited success. This initial phase is followed by a second one that is characterized by an escalation of serious physical violence and the inability of the woman to placate the batterer at all, no matter what she does. This acute battering phase is followed by the "honeymoon stage" (also referred to as the "loving and contrition stage"), in which the batterer expresses his regret for the assaultive behavior and vows to change his ways. He may send her flowers, give her gifts, and pay a great deal of attention to her. At some point, however, he communicates to her that the violent incident was her fault. Soon, the violence cycle is repeated.

According to L. E. Walker (1979), a woman qualifies for BWS when she has experienced the complete cycle at least *twice*. Walker (1989) further suggested that the third stage of the cycle often disappears as the relationship continues to deteriorate over time and the violence increases. She argued that, over time, the tension-building phase becomes more common, whereas the contrition phase eventually drops out of the cycle completely. Unless some effective intervention takes place, when Stage 3 disappears, many battered women are in grave danger of becoming homicide victims.

Although Lenore Walker admitted that not all battered women report many of the features she described, other researchers challenged her general propositions on BWS (Levesque, 2001) and its scientific validity (see McMahon, 1999). Some observed that syndrome evidence in general—including battered women syndrome—is ripe for challenge in the courtroom because its scientific underpinning is questionable (Petrila, 2009). Levesque (2001) argued that one of the real dangers of indiscriminately applying the BWS label to all battered women is that it may mistakenly lead the public, lawmakers, and the courts to perceive women's positions in violent relationships to be essentially identical. As Levesque points out, cross-cultural analysis indicates that the abusive relationship dynamics found in U.S. studies on mainstream culture may not apply to other societies, cultures, or even subcultures within the United States: "Thus, different groups may experience maltreatment events differently, which may exacerbate the difficulties others face in situations that happen to garner the same label" (p. 51).

The term BWS also portrays a stereotypical image of battered women as helpless, passive, or psychologically impaired, and the battering relationship is seen as matching a single, stereotypical pattern of all domestic violence cases (M. A. Dutton, 1996). In contrast to the expected stereotypical pattern of depression, helplessness, and passivity, many battered women demonstrate a wide range of behavioral patterns and emotions that often reflect survival skills and effective adaptations to a serious, life-threatening situation. Unfortunately, the BWS label undermines the enormous coping skills and psychological strength of many—if not most—battered women across a broad spectrum of cultural and social circumstances.

Evan Stark (2002) strongly recommends that psychologists and other mental health practitioners, when preparing forensic assessments and legal testimony for the courts, emphasize the *process* of unique coercive control used by some batterers, rather than focusing strictly on the generalized psychological trauma assumed to be experienced by all battered women. Stark argues that stressing the systematic use of the abuse, coercion, and control in a *particular* relationship and the harms associated with this complete domination is a more meaningful approach than simply trying to identify the psychological damage done to the victim. Many victims, he notes, do not exhibit clearly discernible clusters of psychological maladjustment, depression, and helplessness outlined in much of the literature, even though they may have been subjected to incredible amounts of coercion, domination, and abuse during a lengthy relationship. Furthermore, Stark concludes from the extant research that most battered women experience neither the cycle of violence nor learned helplessness. Some experience a range of psychological and behavior problems that fall outside the purview of BWS, whereas others demonstrate virtually no mental health problems at all. Stark also cautions about a common misconception that the severity of domestic violence can be measured by those physical injuries and emotional disturbances that come to the attention of the police and medical personnel. These groups do not learn about the tyrannical control and low-level violence that, when administered chronically and over an extended period of time, severely affect the victim's quality of life. Nevertheless, the behaviors may not follow an identifiable syndrome.

Same-Sex IPV

Researchers in recent years have given considerable attention to the issue of IPV between members of the same sex. As a general proposition, virtually all of the literature reviewed above applies in this context as well. For example, Potoczniak, Mourot, Crosbie-Burnett, and Potoczniak (2003) find some striking similarities in the research literature in the violence cycle and stages of abuse between same-sex IPV (SS-IPV) and opposite-sex IPV (OS-IPV). Similar to OS-IPV perpetrators, SS-IPV perpetrators blame their partners, are extremely controlling, and are highly self-focused. SS-IPV victims also often follow many of the same characteristics described for OS-IPV victims (Hellemans, Loeys, Buysse, Dewaele, & DeSmet, 2015; Messinger, 2011). The major difference between OS-IPV and SS-IPV incidents appears to be how the community, police, medical personnel, and available social service programs (e.g., women's shelters) respond to the victims.

Turrell (2000) investigated same-sex domestic violence among lesbians, gay women, and gay men (female participants were allowed to choose between the labels *lesbian* and *gay woman*). Turrell discovered a sexual abuse prevalence rate of 13% for gay men, 11% for gay women, and 14% for lesbians in a past or present relationship. Of those who reported sexual abuse, other physical abuse was also common. Specifically, 44% of the gay men, 58% of the gay women, and 55% of the lesbians reported being physically abused in a past or present same-sex relationship.

Potocizniak et al. (2003) point out, based on a study by J. Hill (2000), that gay, lesbian, and bisexual (GLB) persons involved in IPV are perceived by jurors as having a lower moral character than their heterosexual counterparts. In line with this type of reasoning, jurors feel also that rape committed against a GLB person by another GLB person is not as serious as a heterosexual rape and consequently should receive a less severe penalty in a judicial setting (J. Hill, 2000).

Research also suggests that female victims of same-sex IPV find help at different places from those of the female victims of opposite-sex IPV. For example, OS-IPV victims find domestic violence shelters more helpful than many other resources, whereas female victims of same-sex IPV reported these same shelters to be the *least* helpful (Potocizniak, Mourot, Crosbie-Burnett, & Potocizniak, 2003; Renzetti, 1992). Furthermore, SS-IPV female victims most often find friends to be the most helpful resources, followed by counselors and relatives. It is no surprise that SS-IPV female victims report that the police, attorneys, and medical professionals are generally *not* helpful. Interestingly, one of the very few studies that examined the help-seeking behaviors of gay male victims of SS-IPV (Merrill & Wolfe, 2000) found that many male victims not only sought help from friends and counselors, but also found gay domestic violence programs very helpful (Potocizniak et al., 2003).

Mental Health Needs of Children Exposed to IPV

Research on the effects of IPV on children began in the early 1980s and has experienced a rapid growth since that time (Goddard & Bedi, 2010). Exposure to intimate partner violence occurs when children "see, hear, are directly involved in, or experience the aftermath of violence between their caretakers" (Olaya, Ezpeleta, de la Osa, Granero, & Doménech, 2010, p. 1004). According to this definition, approximately 15.5 million children living in the United States are exposed to IPV incidents every year (McDonald, Jouriles, Ramisetty-Mikler, Caetano, & Green, 2006). Some believe this estimate is too low (Knutson, Lawrence, Taber, Bank, & DeGarmo, 2009).

A large number of studies report that children exposed to IPV have different mental health needs than those children not exposed (Goddard & Bedi, 2010; Olaya et al., 2010). More specifically, these children are more likely to have symptoms of PTSD, mood problems, loneliness, lowered self-esteem, and a greater tendency toward self-harm. Other studies (Cummings, El-Sheikh, Kouros, & Buckhalt, 2009; Gelles & Cavanaugh, 2005; Goddard & Bedi, 2010) report that IPV exposure affects the child's ability to regulate his or her emotions and appears to be linked to a greater tendency to violence during adolescence and into adulthood. Witnessing domestic violence has also been associated with psychopathic traits in adult male offenders (Dargis & Koenigs, 2017).

McGee (2000) (cited in Bedi & Goddard, 2007) describes some of the self-reports provided by IPV-exposed children and teens.

One [nightmare] was that when I was asleep he got a knife and stabbed me. (Boy, age 5; p. 71)

I'd think about my mom being hit and then I just would walk out of school and come home. . . . I didn't like the thought of her being on her own with him, so I stayed home all the time. (Girl, age 15; p. 81)

The relationship between child abuse and IPV exposure has been the subject of much controversy. Some researchers and practitioners argue that the two are different and therefore should remain distinct categories. On the other hand, evidence that IPV results in negative outcomes for the child has led some countries, such as Australia and the United States, to consider IPV as a form of psychological child abuse, a topic to be discussed in the next section (Bedi & Goddard, 2007; Goddard & Bedi, 2010).

The first step for clinicians working with troubled children is to identify the IPV home environment; that is, does IPV occur and if so, what is its severity and frequency? Most IPV-exposed children are reluctant to report or discuss the situation, and they may feel shame, guilt, or fear (Olaya et al., 2010). In addition, it is important for the psychologist to realize that there may be more than violence between adult partners happening. Research has demonstrated that co-occurring or different forms of child abuse are common in families identified for domestic violence (Margolin et al., 2009). The more frequent and severe the IPV, the more likely that various kinds of child abuse are also occurring.

Roles of the Forensic Psychologist in IPV Cases

Forensic psychologists are often asked to do risk assessments of batterers at all stages of the criminal justice process, from pretrial assessment to sentencing to correctional release. Early on, a victim of partner abuse may request a restraining order or order of protection from the court. This is a judicial command that the abuser refrain from contacting the victim for a specified time period. The psychologist may be asked to be an expert witness during a civil or criminal trial. If the batterer is a defendant in a criminal case, the psychologist may be asked to assess his level of danger if released on bail before the next court appearance. In a criminal trial in which a defendant assaulted or killed an abusive partner, the defense may request the forensic psychologist to identify whether the defendant qualified for BWS or PTSD. During the jury-selection process in criminal cases, the forensic psychologist may also be asked to evaluate the extent of myths about family violence within the jury pool or community; once a jury has been chosen, a jury consultant might be asked to assess how these individuals are likely to respond to the testimony presented by both sides of the case. In civil matters, the psychologist may be asked to evaluate the family dynamics or parental suitability to help in custody decisions involving the children. Finally, in many instances, psychologists and other mental health professionals will provide crisis intervention or treatment consultation or provide the services themselves.

Risk Assessment: Is the Victim Safe?

One of the most frequent tasks performed by forensic psychologists in this context is risk assessment—that is, predicting the likelihood of recidivism. The one thing that all practitioners who work with family violence can agree on is that the ongoing safety of the victim must be considered first and foremost (Petretic-Jackson, Witte, & Jackson, 2002). Failure to put this factor into the equation may result in the death or serious injury of one or more family members. As discussed in previous chapters, many risk assessment instruments, both actuarial and based on structured professional judgment (SPJ), are available for assessing the risk of violence. In the case of IPV, forensic psychologists may use the **Ontario Domestic Assault Risk Assessment (ODARA)** (Hilton et al., 2004), which is a brief actuarial measure that can be scored by police officers, because it contains items referring to information that is readily available to them (e.g., prior domestic violence, number of children, substance abuse, threats of violence). Results of the ODARA have been used to assist in making bail decisions early in the criminal justice process. Continuing research suggests that the ODARA holds predictive power for general risk of recidivism among IPV offenders. This research indicates that these offenders often have criminal careers that include stalking, sexual assault, and some nonviolent property offenses (Eke, Hilton, Meloy, Mohandie, & Williams, 2011; Hilton & Eke, 2016). (Recall Dr. Eke's Perspective 8.1 in Chapter 8.)

Hilton and her colleagues (e.g., Hilton, Harris, & Rice, 2010a, 2010b) have also studied a more extensive use of the ODARA in combination with other risk assessment instruments. Recognizing that forensic psychologists have more case material available to them, they posited that such information as an offender's antisocial behavior, the presence of a mental disorder, childhood abuse, and a juvenile record might be combined with the data available from the ODARA to render the risk assessment even more reliable when applied to domestic violence. Interestingly, they discovered that some of the above variables added little to the information already included in the ODARA. However, clinical information about an offender's history of antisocial behavior was critical. Antisocial behavior is tapped well by the Psychopathy Checklist-Revised (PCL-R). Thus, Hilton et al. developed a new measure, the **Domestic Violence Risk Appraisal Guide (DVRAG)** (Hilton, Harris, Rice, Houghton, & Eke, 2008), which combines risk factors identified in both the ODARA and the PCL-R for a presumably more effective instrument to measure domestic violence recidivism by male assailants. It is not intended to be a replacement for the ODARA, but rather as a measure accompanying it. Because the DVRAG is still quite new, it awaits further research on its effectiveness. Thus far, both the ODARA and the DVRAG have received positive reviews in the IPV literature. Nonetheless, they are subject to the same criticisms that have been leveled at other actuarial instruments, as we discussed in Chapter 4 (K. S. Douglas, Hart, Groscup, & Litwack, 2014).

Another instrument that may be useful for predicting violence risk in family situations is the **Spousal Assault Risk Assessment (SARA)**, developed by Kropp, Hart, Webster, and Eaves (1998). The SARA is a 20-item checklist designed to screen for risk factors in individuals suspected of or being treated for spousal or family-related assault. It is used when a clinician wishes to determine the degree to which an individual poses a threat to his or her spouse, children, or other family members. The SARA is an example of an SPJ instrument. Recall that SPJ instruments offer guidance to clinicians and encourage them to weigh the risk factors that are present in reference to that particular case (that is, using their professional judgment). They are also intended to help in the management of risk, based on the result of the assessment.

Another non-actuarial risk assessment measure specifically intended to predict domestic violence recidivism is Danger Assessment (DA), developed by Jacquelyn Campbell (1995). The first part of the DA is designed to determine the severity and frequency of battering by presenting the victim with a calendar of the past year. She or he is then asked to mark the approximate dates when physically abusive events occurred and to rank the severity of the incident on a 1 to 5 scale (ranging from 1 *low* to 5 *use of weapon*). The second part of the DA is a 15-item questionnaire requiring a yes or no response to each item. The items are intended to provide an overview of the range of tactics used by the batterer.

Again, researchers and clinicians continue to debate the validity of actuarial instruments versus those based on structured professional judgment. Hilton, Harris, and Rice (2010b) report that they as well as other researchers found that the DA and SARA had only a modest ability to distinguish recidivists from non-recidivists. Others, however, have reported better results (Belfrage et al., 2012; Helmus & Bourgon, 2011). Clinicians now have a wealth of meta-analyses and individual studies on risk assessment measures to guide their decisions as to which to use.

Forensic Assessment in IPV—Other Factors

In addition to predicting recidivism, psychologists are often engaged in the treatment of both victims of domestic violence and the offenders themselves. In the case of the victim, the mental health practitioner must be keenly aware of the impact of cultural and lifestyle variables on the battered person's response to the abuse and her recovery (M. A. Dutton, 1992; T. L. Jackson, Petretic-Jackson, & Witte, 2002). For example, many cultural and social barriers impede help-seeking behavior for a wide spectrum of cultural groups. In some cultures, violence may even be condoned within the secrecy of the family, although there have been worldwide attempts to change this tolerance (Kozu, 1999; McWhirter, 1999). For some minority women or immigrants, a language barrier makes it doubly hard to find help and support.

A multimodal approach is most often recommended for the assessment and treatment of battered victims as well as battering offenders. The term *multimodal* refers to the use of a combination of psychological instruments and information-gathering strategies, including open-ended interviews, structured interviews, questionnaires, and standard psychological measures. As mentioned above, however, when recidivism is the primary focus, one or two dominant instruments have received good research results. Most clinicians are quick to point out, though, that instruments—though helpful—are insufficient for a more generalized assessment of the problem and should not be used in isolation.

An open-ended interview allows people to respond "in their own words" or tell their "own story" with a minimum of redirection from the clinician. It allows considerable flexibility for the clinician to modify the goals, the questions, and the general flow of information from the person being interviewed. The structured interview involves a more standardized set of procedures and questions that lessen the clinician's freedom to redirect the information-gathering process. It normally asks specific, predetermined questions that restrict the evaluator's inquiries during the administration of the interview. However, the predetermined questions of the structured interview procedure tend to be more accurate in predictions of behavior, while the open-ended interview questions can be most helpful in obtaining the full story.

Conflict Tactics Scale (CTS)

One of the most commonly used assessment instruments for determining the *extent* of intimate partner violence (rather than or in addition to the likelihood of recidivism) is the **Conflict Tactics Scale (CTS)**, developed by Murray Straus (1979). The CTS measures the frequency and severity of behaviors that partners engage in during an argument (Levensky & Fruzzetti, 2004).

During the early stages of its development, CTS-generated data were surprising and controversial, indicating that 1 in 6 marriages had included an incident of physical violence, and that IPV appeared to be as high among women as it was among men (Langhinrichsen-Rohling, 2005). According to Langhinrichsen-Rohling, the CTS data gave us a look behind closed doors of intimate partner violence early on. Although the CTS is still widely used, researchers and practitioners have identified many limitations (see Levensky and Fruzzetti, 2004, for a comprehensive review of its limitations). As we observed above, some studies using the CTS led to the misleading conclusion that men and women were equally likely to engage in interpersonal violence, without taking into consideration the forms and motivation for the behavior. In an attempt to address the criticisms, a Revised Conflict Tactics Scale and child–parent CTS were later developed.

Assessment of Victim Reactions

Although the BWS, discussed earlier in the chapter, is facing considerable opposition in the research community, there is support for the presence of PTSD symptoms in the victims of IPV, with rates ranging from 45% to 84% (T. L. Jackson et al., 2002; Jones, Hughes, & Unterstaller, 2001; Perez et al., 2012). For example, battered women residing in domestic violence shelters usually display higher rates and severity of IPV-related PTSD symptoms compared to battered women not in shelters (Perez et al., 2012). This is partly attributed to the higher rates of violence they have experienced during the pre-shelter period, along with the fear of retribution from their abuser because they have fled the home. Assuring long-term safety for the survivor, therefore, is a priority. Lack of this assurance is a reason battered women return to their homes after seeking shelter, particularly when the abuser promises to reform or threatens further harm to children or even pets if the victim does not return.

Several measures commonly used to assess the level of PTSD symptomatology are the PTSD Symptom Scale (Foa, Riggs, Dancu, & Rothbaum, 1993), the Posttraumatic Diagnostic Stress Scale (Foa, Cashman, Jaycox, & Perry, 1997), the Crime-Related Post-Traumatic Stress Disorder Scale (Saunders, Arata, & Kilpatrick, 1990), the Distressing Event Questionnaire (Kubany, Leisen, Kaplan, & Kelly, 2000), and the Traumatic Life Events Questionnaire (Kubany, Haynes, et al., 2000).

Assessing PTSD in victims is important if the assault case is prosecuted as well as for treatment purposes. Documentation of PTSD is crucial in many respects. For example, it may prompt prosecutors to pursue the case more aggressively and it may be a factor to consider in plea negotiation or at sentencing. Documentation of PTSD also may be relevant to an eventual civil case against the abuser. In the very rare cases where a battered woman kills her abuser, a defense based on PTSD is more effective than one based on BWS. Documentation of PTSD is also relevant to the treatment of victims of violence and sexual assault and the treatment of women offenders.

The forensic psychologist is likely to administer formal psychological tests and inventories or other appropriate psychological measures to determine whether any discernible changes in attitude, cognitive functioning, behavior, and emotions are a result of the abuse. In any forensic setting, documentation is critical at all phases of the assessment process. Documentation may include court records; police reports; mental health and medical records; investigative reports of friends, family, or neighbors or other witnesses; and related legal proceedings such as depositions, trial transcripts, and protection orders. The evaluator should be aware that "unconventional sources" might provide invaluable documentation as well. These include "date books, logbooks, telephone messages, diaries, letters (including threatening letters from partners), tapes, photographs, and other records" (Stark, 2002, p. 232).

The family makeup and situation is also relevant. This considers the ages of family members, social class, occupational status, level of acculturation, prior exposure to violence, normative approval of violence, family structure, and cultural coping strategies (T. L. Jackson et al., 2002; West, 1998). It is important for the clinician to realize that the victim may have the distorted belief that she is the cause of the abuse and is at a loss regarding what to do about it. Unfortunately, very little empirical research on the effectiveness of therapeutic interventions with battered women has been conducted (Petretic-Jackson et al., 2002).

PTSD is especially common in intimate partner violence when the abusive partner engages in stalking, various forms of harassment, and threats of violence after the relationship has ended (Eshelman & Levendosky, 2012). As described earlier, "Stalking is defined as a course of conduct directed at a specific person that would cause a reasonable person to feel fear" (Catalano, 2012, p. 1). The threats of violence are especially destructive to the psychological well-being of the victim. Risk assessment procedures are important, particularly when the court is contemplating issuing a permanent order of protection. Although temporary restraining orders (TROs) are not as difficult to obtain in most jurisdictions, permanent orders need a stronger showing that the person against whom the order is sought poses a threat to the person seeking the protection.

Cattaneo and Chapman (2011) point out, however, that although research on risk assessment has been very helpful in prediction, it has not been particularly helpful in the management of risk. That is, the goal of clinicians and practitioners who work with cases of IPV is to prevent future abuse, not just predict it. This is one reason why some researchers favor SPJ instruments over actuarial instruments; SPJ instruments facilitate risk management by encouraging clinicians to create scenarios of possible violence and develop management plans in light of these scenarios (K. S. Douglas et al., 2014).

As noted by Kropp (2004), the term *risk assessment* is not synonymous with victim safety planning. He writes, "In practice . . . decisions about risk likely involve consideration of the imminence, nature (e.g., emotional, physical, sexual), frequency, and seriousness of the violence in addition to the likelihood that it will occur" (p. 678). In addition, Kropp emphasizes that there is no such thing as "no risk" in the context of spousal or intimate partner violence. All spousal or intimate partner assaulters are dangerous to some degree, and risk assessment instruments do not allow us to rule out the danger completely. Risk assessment can, however, inform us "regarding the nature, form, and degree of the danger" (p. 677). Several forensic risk assessment instruments are good at predicting future violence—including IPV—but *prevention* of future violence demands more research attention.

Necessary Training for IPV Assessment

Forensic psychologists and other mental health workers who deal with IPV and its victims should have special training that emphasizes that assault by an intimate partner is a unique form of violence that differs in important ways from other forms. It is also important that forensic psychologists are thoroughly trained in empirically based, best-practice guidelines. Whereas violence from strangers is often an isolated, one-time event, the type of violence found in IPV is an ongoing occurrence characterized by repetitive abuse from a once-trusted person over a long period of time. In short, IPV is a process that has incalculable cumulative effects over time. Moreover, the victim may feel trapped in the home or situation in which it occurs, often with no *perceived* hope for escape. "Because of marital commitments, financial ties, and child care, victims of intimate partner violence cannot as easily remove themselves from the situations as can victims of abuse by a nonintimate" (Petretic-Jackson et al., 2002, pp. 300–301). This perceived hopelessness may lead to depression and inhibiting feelings of helplessness for some victims, but—as noted above—many other victims handle the situation quite differently. Consequently, forensic psychologists and other clinicians must be prepared for the wide range of psychological symptoms and coping mechanisms that victims will display.

IPV, as well as domestic violence in general, is also apt to engender a variety of reactions from psychologists, especially if they or someone close to them have personally experienced such violence. Working with victims of domestic abuse (in both adults and children) is especially stressful, and when clinicians are exposed to trauma victims, it leads to a high incidence of professional burnout. The term **vicarious traumatization** has sometimes been used to describe the psychological distress that clinicians themselves experience as a result of working with traumatized victims (D. A. Harris, 2013; S. F. Lambert & Lawson, 2013; Petretic-Jackson et al., 2002).

CHILD ABUSE

"Children are the most victimized segment of the population" (Finkelhor, 2011, p. 14). In 2011, state and local child protective services in the United States received an estimated 3.4 million referrals of children being abused or neglected (U.S. Department of Health and Human Services [DHHS], 2017). An estimated 683,000 children were victims of a combination of maltreatments, such as neglect and physical abuse. Nearly 40% of the children reported as abused or neglected were under the age of 6. Approximately 50% of the maltreated children were found to have been maltreated two, three, or more times. Overall, studies estimate that 1 in 7 children in the United States experience some form of child maltreatment in their lifetimes (Finkelhor et al., 2009). Most police departments today have assigned special investigators designated to conduct investigations of child abuse.

About 1,750 children died of maltreatment in 2011 in the United States, a rate of 2.10 per 1,000 children. Of the child maltreatment fatalities, approximately 82% occurred among children younger than age 4. Children younger than 1 year have the highest rate of victimization (21.2 per 1,000 children). About 50% of the children who died of maltreatment in the United States had already been referred to a child protection agency (National Resource Center on

Child Sexual Abuse, 1996). Parents and other caretakers account for about one fifth of all *violent* crimes committed against children, and more than half of these crimes are against children 2 or younger (D. E. Abrams, 2013).

Types of Maltreatment

There are four major types of child maltreatment: (1) neglect, (2) physical abuse, (3) sexual abuse, and (4) emotional abuse. *Neglect* refers to failure to provide for a child's basic needs, such as lack of appropriate supervision or failure to provide necessary food, shelter, or medical care, and represents the largest category of maltreatment. Neglect may also include failure to educate a child or attend to special education or emotional needs. *Physical abuse* refers to anything that may cause physical injury such as punching, beating, kicking, biting, shaking, throwing, stabbing, choking, burning, or hitting. This category of maltreatment is the second most frequent (see Photo 11.2). *Sexual abuse* includes activities by a parent or caretaker such as sexual fondling, rape, sodomy, indecent exposure, and commercial exploitation through prostitution or the production of pornographic materials. *Emotional abuse* refers to behavior that impairs a child's emotional development or sense of self-esteem or worth and may include such things as constant criticism or rejection.

▸ **Photo 11.2** A child cowers in fear before an adult male's wrath.
Source: © iStock/princessdlaf.

According to the U.S. Department of Health and Human Services (2010), over two thirds (70%) of maltreatment victims experience neglect. About 15% are physically abused, and 9% are sexually abused. Only 7% reportedly are emotionally abused, a figure that probably is greatly underestimated. Boys and girls are about equally neglected or physically abused, but girls are 4 times more likely to experience sexual abuse. About one quarter of the victims experience more than one type of maltreatment. An estimated 60% of children seen by a physician for a physical abuse injury will return with further inflicted injuries. Approximately 10% will eventually die from the continual abuse. About 10% of all children seen in emergency rooms have some form of non-accidental injury. Although abusive injuries are seen at all socioeconomic levels, fatal cases of abuse are most common in the poorer segments of the population. Children of all races and ethnicities experience child abuse.

It should be mentioned that rates of child sexual abuse have declined 62% since the 1990s (Finkelhor & Jones, 2012). This conclusion is based on three independent sources of agency data and four separate large victim surveys (Finkelhor & Jones, 2012). However, this decline has not been conclusively reported for other forms of child abuse, such as physical abuse in particular. The reasons for the decline are multiple and complex, and they include such factors as better awareness and prevention programs.

Pet Abuse

Research has discovered that pet abuse often accompanies child abuse (Arkow, 1998; Levitt, Hoffer, & Loper, 2016). That is, adults who abuse their children also tend to abuse the family pet, which is usually a treasured companion of abused children. Abusers often threaten to harm or kill a pet to frighten a child into secrecy about the abuse, particularly about sexual abuse. A strong relationship also exists between pet cruelty and spousal abuse. In one study, more than half of the victims at a women's shelter reported that their pets had been harmed or killed by their partner and that they delayed coming to the shelter for fear of harm to their pets left at home (Ascione, 1997). A growing body of research also suggests that violent people often commit considerable cruelty against animals in general, particularly against pets and stray animals (Merz-Perez, Heide, & Silverman, 2001). In their study, Levitt, Hoffer, and Loper (2016) discovered that of 150 adult male offenders who were charged with animal cruelty, 144 had other documented criminal offenses prior to and/or following the animal cruelty offenses. The Levitt et al. study examined 400 incident reports of animal cruelty and neglect by adult males from police and sheriff departments, animal control agencies, and district attorney's offices across the United States. Males under age 18 were excluded from the study because juvenile records are usually sealed, and women were excluded because of the rarity of cases.

Levitt et al. also divided the animal cruelty offenses into three types: active, passive, and sexual animal abuse. The first two types are likely familiar to most readers, while the third may be surprising. Active abuse included strangling, kicking, beating, stabbing, burning, and mutilation. Passive abuse included failure to provide adequate food, water, shelter, or veterinary care. Sexual animal abuse includes a wide range of behaviors, such as vaginal, anal, or oral penetration, fondling, penetration using an object, and killing or injuring an animal for sexual gratification (Vermont Humane Federation, 2017).

In the Levitt et al. study (2016), over 50% of those who were arrested for active cruelty had an arrest for interpersonal violence, including domestic violence. In addition, one third of those arrested for animal sexual abuse had been arrested for sexually assaulting a person, with many of the victims being under age 18. Specific relationships between passive abuse and criminal behavior were unclear in this study.

Up to this point, research concerning animal sexual abuse has been rare. However, beginning in 2016, the National Incident-Based Reporting System (NIBRS) began to collect more data on animal cruelty reports, ranging from dog fighting to animal sex abuse. According to DeGloria (2015), this expanded collection occurred because FBI investigators were finding high rates of animal sexual abuse among serial sexual homicide predators. Given the apparent connection between various forms of animal cruelty and violence toward humans, continuing research on this topic is needed.

Dynamics of Family Violence

Abusive families tend to be socially isolated and lack an extended network of family and friends for social, financial, and emotional support. The family situation is usually unstable, punctuated by stormy relationships between adults, one or more children who are resented or unwanted, financial constraints, heavy alcohol or drug abuse, or feelings of being trapped with little way out. As discussed earlier in the chapter, male abusers tend to be impulsive, immature, frustrated persons who believe it is their right as the "man of the household" to dominate the female. Not all family violence is based on this need to control, however. Data and concepts relating to adult violence were covered earlier in the chapter. In this section, we focus on the violence committed against children.

The psychological factors associated with the abuse may differ according to gender, but also from person to person. Some men become especially abusive if they are forced into providing primary care while the woman works because they interpret this situation as a loss of self-esteem and their traditional masculine role. Women who abuse tend to be overstressed, depressed, and frustrated. For both male and female abusers, the precipitating event for the abuse tends to be the infant's or child's crying or lack of toileting.

In a long-ago case, a young divorced mother with three children under age 3 (including 18-month-old twins), living in a small stark apartment far away from her parents and siblings, was receiving public assistance. Her check failed to arrive on time, and she was unable to heat her apartment or buy sufficient groceries; her telephone and electricity were shut off, and the landlord threatened to evict her. When one of her twins cried constantly, she "lost it" and beat him, leaving severe bruises and nearly breaking his arm. Cases such as this are often reported in the news media, and they abound in the files and in the minds of human service workers.

There are uncertainties concerning the relative contribution of child abuse to later psychopathology in the victim (Knapp & VandeCreek, 2000). According to Knapp and VandeCreek,

> Little is known about the impact of mitigating factors, such as having otherwise positive parental figures, receiving an early treatment after the abuse, or having a robust personality or a strong social network. Similarly, more needs to be known about the impact of exacerbating factors, such as having otherwise destructive parental figures, receiving blame or no treatment after the abuse, having a fragile personality, or lacking a strong social network. (p. 370)

Infanticide, Neonaticide, and Filicide

When parents kill or try to kill their children, we react with horror. Although these are rare occurrences, they inevitably attract extensive media attention. In shocking incidents that occurred many years ago but are still familiar to many, Andrea Yates drowned her five children in a bathtub. As we noted in Chapter 5, she was found not guilty by reason of insanity and remains hospitalized in a psychiatric facility. In another tragic case, the then-lawyer Joel Steinberg physically beat Lisa, the 6-year-old girl whom he and his partner, Hedda Nussbaum, had illegally adopted to the point where she was hospitalized and died from her injuries shortly thereafter. An infant boy, also illegally in their care, was found tethered in his crib and was returned to his biological mother. Nussbaum, who had lived with Steinberg for some 12 years, had been severely beaten and fit the classic profile of a battered woman. Although first charged, she testified against him and was not prosecuted. Both adults were apparently heavy drug users, and the children were physically and emotionally neglected. A photograph of Lisa at school taken before her death depicted a very sad-looking little girl with dark circles under her eyes. Steinberg, subsequently disbarred, was convicted of manslaughter. He spent 17 years in prison and was released on parole in 2004. Nussbaum changed her name shortly afterward and moved to a different state.

An estimated 1,200 to 1,500 young children are killed each year by a parent or other person, representing about 12% to 15% of the total homicides in the United States (Child Welfare Information Gateway, 2012; Emery & Laumann-Billings, 1998). In 2015, it was estimated that nationally 1,670 children age 12 and under died of abuse and neglect at a rate of 2.25 per 100,000 children in the U.S. population (DHHS, 2017). Three quarters (74.8%) of all child fatalities due to abuse and neglect in 2015 were younger than 3 years, many of them younger than 1 year old. Boys had a slightly higher child fatality rate than girls (2.42 per 100,000 boys compared to 2.09 per 100,000 girls in the population). Forty-two percent of child fatalities were white, 31% were African American, and 15% were Hispanic. The African American fatality rate is about 2.5 times greater than the rate of white children, and 3.0 times greater than the rate of Hispanic children. Parents are responsible for a majority of homicides of children under age 5. Thirty-three percent were killed by their fathers, and 30% were killed by their mothers. Children under 5 who were not killed by a parent were murdered by a male offender in a majority of cases (80%) (Cooper & Smith, 2011, pp. 6–7).

Infanticide, although the term literally means the killing of an infant, has become the umbrella term for homicide of children up to 2 years of age. Because there are significant differences between parents who commit infanticide within the first 24 hours after birth and those who kill a slightly older child, two additional terms are often used in the research and clinical literature. Specifically, **neonaticide** refers to the killing of the newborn within the first 24 hours, whereas **filicide** refers to the killing of a child older than 24 hours. It should be noted that neonaticide is rarely used in legal settings; infanticide is usually the preferred legal term for lawmakers and legal scholars (Nesca & Dalby, 2011). Again, infanticide in the legal system refers to the killing of children up to the age of 2. We will continue to use the term *neonaticide* in this section, since researchers have consistently used it to distinguish different psychological motivations of the offender. In addition, almost all of the research focuses on women who kill their children rather than men who do so.

Mothers who commit neonaticide tend to be young, unmarried women who deny or conceal their pregnancy, fearing the disapproval or rejection from their family and society (Dobson & Sales, 2000). Mothers who commit filicide (children older than 1 day and up to 2 years) tend to be older and married and often demonstrate symptoms of depression. Mothers of the second group are most often in situations they perceive as hopeless and dire. They believe that killing the child is the only way to prevent the child's suffering or potential suffering living under adverse conditions. When mothers kill or try to kill more than one child, however, these age distinctions may not apply.

Traditionally, women who kill their children—regardless of the age of the children—have been viewed by the legal system (and the public) as very likely suffering from serious mental problems. When the children are infants, the clinical diagnosis is often "postpartum depression," a depressive episode believed to be brought on by childbirth. However, it is important to realize that three categories of mental reactions may be apparent after childbirth: postpartum blues, postpartum depression, and postpartum psychosis (Dobson & Sales, 2000). The most common is *postpartum blues*, characterized by crying, irritability, anxiety, confusion, and rapid mood changes. Approximately 50% to 80% of women show some minor features of postpartum blues between 1 and 5 days after delivery (Durand & Barlow, 2000). The symptoms may last for a few hours to a few days and are clearly linked to childbirth. Although researchers indicate that the symptoms do not generally last more than 12 days, the sheer exhaustion that accompanies many if not most births can extend "blues" to a longer time span. The connection between postpartum blues and infanticide has not been supported by the research literature. As noted by Dobson and Sales,

> This mental disturbance is unlikely to play a major causative role in either neonaticide or filicide, because it occurs too late to affect mental status in women who commit neonaticide, and because its duration of less than 10 days is too short to play a major role in filicide, which can occur at any time during the 1st postpartum year. (p. 1105)

Note that Dobson and Sales place 1 year, not 2 years, as the cutoff for filicide.

Postpartum depression occurs during the weeks and months following childbirth. The symptoms—some of which also occur with postpartum blues—include depression, loss of appetite, sleep disturbances, fatigue, suicidal thoughts, disinterest in the newborn child, and a general loss of interest in life's activities. The woman with postpartum depression often feels guilty for being depressed when she should be happy about a new baby. The incidence rate among childbearing women ranges from 7% to 17% in North America (Dobson & Sales, 2000). However, in contrast to postpartum blues, postpartum depression does not appear to be directly connected to childbirth but is more a clinical form of depression that is present before childbirth and may or may not be a recurring disorder across the life cycle of the woman. Although women with postpartum depression may commit infanticide or filicide, research finds that this not common after childbirth, and the child's death is not directly caused by it.

The third category of mental problems associated with the postpartum period is *postpartum psychosis*, a severe mental disorder that is rare, occurring in 1 out of every 1,000 women following delivery. Usually, the psychotic features are highly similar to the symptoms of serious bipolar depression and appear to be directly connected to childbirth. Many years ago, a young mother took a rifle and shot to death her infant, who was approximately 3 months old. In the weeks preceding the tragedy, she had remained in her home with shades drawn and had refused the entreaties of her husband to seek mental health services. Prosecutors did not charge her in the death, because they could not find any mental health expert to testify that she was not suffering from postpartum psychosis. Although some believed this was an abuse of prosecutor discretion and that the woman received favorable treatment, the prosecutor obviously believed the defense would easily be able to find a mental health expert who would testify to the presence of postpartum psychosis.

As noted by Dobson and Sales (2000), "A number of epidemiological studies have provided clear scientific evidence supporting the link between childbirth and postpartum psychosis" (p. 1106). Sometimes the psychosis is severe enough to lead to the mother's attempted suicide, together with an attempt to kill her baby (Kendall & Hammen, 1995). There is some documentation that many women (estimates range from 20% to 40%) who commit filicide are suffering from postpartum psychosis (Dobson & Sales, 2000).

Nesca and Dalby (2011) contend that many infanticides (both neonaticides and filicides) may also be a result of PTSD. They point out that studies have reported a PTSD prevalence rate of 24% to 33% following an uncomplicated childbirth. They further argue that forensic research using comprehensive evaluations revealed that PTSD—in combination with depression—was the major clinical finding of these studies. Although these results are intriguing as another explanation of infanticide, considerably more research needs to be undertaken before any tentative conclusions can be drawn.

Overall, few infanticides are committed by mothers who suffer depression, despair, PTSD, or psychosis. In the case of neonaticide, it "is generally committed by women who often conceal the pregnancy, give birth away from a hospital and then suffocate, strangle, or drown the unwanted newborn before hiding the corpse" (T. Porter & Gavin, 2010, p. 99). However, the reality is that another adult—such as the baby's father or the father of the mother—may also be responsible for the infant's death. In some cases, the baby's father is the father of the mother.

An incapacitating mental illness of the mother is rarely an explanation. However, infant homicides can result from acts of omission, such as neglecting to watch the child in a hazardous environment, or acts of commission, such as delivering a swift blow to silence a crying infant. In these cases, a manslaughter (nonnegligent) charge or verdict is more likely to be rendered. The adult may not have intended to cause death, but he or she is still responsible.

Munchausen Syndrome by Proxy (Medical Child Abuse)

Munchausen syndrome by proxy (MSBP) is a rare form of child abuse in which a parent (almost always the mother) *consistently* and *chronically* subjects a child to medical attention without any "true" medical condition or symptoms being present. "Munchausen is characterized by an adult's chronic and relentless pursuit of medical treatment, involving some combination of consciously self-inflicted injury and falsely reported symptomatology" (Robins & Sesan, 1991, p. 285). The term *Munchausen syndrome* was apparently coined by the London physician Richard Asher (1951) to describe patients who consistently produced false stories about themselves to receive needless medical examinations, operations, and treatments. Asher named the syndrome after Baron von Munchausen, a distinguished German soldier and politician who was born in 1720 (Dowdell & Foster, 2000). Asher named the behavior after von Munchausen because of the many fabricated stories of incredible travels and brave military exploits he would tell to friends and acquaintances, including his physicians (Raspe, 1944). Today the term commonly used by researchers to replace the cumbersome term MSBP is *medical child abuse* (Yates & Bass, 2017).

In Munchausen syndrome by proxy, the child's presenting symptoms are either falsified or directly induced *by the parent*. In fact, the term *by proxy* refers to the parent's dominating influence in the presentation of symptoms to the medical staff. The most common cluster of symptoms reported by the parent concerning the child's condition involves seizures, failure to thrive, vomiting, diarrhea, asthma/allergies, and infections (see M. S. Sheridan, 2003, pp. 441–443 for a complete list of symptoms). Symptom inducement by the parent may include adding fat to stools in order to produce a laboratory abnormality, initiating starvation in the child, placing blood into the child's urine sample before lab testing, or injecting contaminating or toxic material intravenously into the child's bloodstream (J. B. Murray, 1997; Pearl, 1995).

MSBP cases are found in homes of all socioeconomic levels, and the victims are most often young children ranging in age from 6 months to 8 years. Both sexes appear to be equally susceptible to being victimized. The term *serial MSBP* is reserved for those cases involving more than one child in the same family (R. A. Alexander, Smith, & Stevenson, 1990).

The case histories of MSBP commonly illustrate an "overinvolved" mother and an "emotionally distant" or physically absent father. MSBP mothers are often described as "emotionally empty" and lonely and frequently have experienced significant emotional, physical, and sexual abuse during their own childhood and young adulthood (Robins & Sesan, 1991). The mother often appears to others as the ideal parent and comes across as very concerned, devoted, attentive, and loving. However, she is also seen as overprotective and obsessed with the child's illness (M. L. Brown, 1997; Voltz, 1995).

The offending mother is often sophisticated about medical conditions, has some fascination with medical procedures and diagnoses, and may even be a health professional herself. Suspicions that MSBP may be present should be entertained when the parent is unusually attentive to the child and is very reluctant to leave the child's side during a medical examination or treatment. This, though, can be said of many if not most parents. A better sign is when a child has a series of recurring medical conditions that do not respond to treatment or follow an unanticipated course that is persistent, puzzling, and unexplained. Another indicator is when laboratory findings or symptomatology are highly abnormal and discrepant with existing medical knowledge. The extreme forms of this child abuse may lead to serious injury or death. Verification of MSBP can also be achieved when the symptoms disappear after the suspected perpetrator and victim are separated (M. S. Sheridan, 2003).

Although there have been many cases of MSBP reported in the literature, the prevalence or incidence of the problem is difficult to determine, largely due to the challenge of identifying actual illnesses as opposed to fabricated ones and the general lack of knowledge about this unusual form of child abuse. The best estimates range from 2 to 2.8 per 100,000 in children under 1 year of age and 0.4 per 100,000 in children younger than 16 years of age (Ferrara et al., 2013; Schreier, 2004; Sharif, 2004). Ferrara et al. report some research evidence that the prevalence of the disorder may be even higher in some populations. Furthermore, the mortality rate for children who are victims of MSBP appears to range from 6% to 10%, when suffocation and poisoning are involved (Ferrara et al., 2013). Poisoning may occur when the parent or caretaker either injects or forces intake of substances that are poisonous in nature in order to make the child sick. Suffocation may occur with the forced ingestion of drugs, medications, or substances that cause breathing problems.

It has been reported in some cases that the "proxy" is a family pet (Tucker, 2002). In a survey sent to 1,000 veterinary surgeons asking them about non-accidental injuries in animals, a small number of the respondents believed that they had encountered MSBP perpetrated by some pet owners. In other words, some pet owners may deliberately hurt their pets to get sympathy and medical attention.

In most cases, child protective services are brought into play if MSBP is suspected. Rarely are criminal charges filed unless the behavior has resulted in serious injury or the child has died. The forensic psychologist may become involved at both the child protection and the prosecution stages of the case. If the parent is unwilling or unable to stop the behavior, the child may need to be removed from the home until effective intervention or some appropriate arrangement with the parent is accomplished. If the case is serious enough to warrant criminal charges, the forensic psychologist may become a *court-appointed* evaluator, which means he or she is being asked directly by the court to provide pertinent information (Sanders & Bursch, 2002). Recall that, as mentioned in Chapter 1, many states now require special training and certification for those who provide these and similar services for courts (Heilbrun & Brooks, 2010).

In the case of MSBP, the psychologist must review all available medical records on both the child and the suspected parent and do a psychological assessment of both parent and child. According to Sanders and Bursch (2002), a significant number of women who engage in falsifying illness in their children also complain of many unsubstantiated illnesses within themselves. Siblings should also be evaluated, as they too may have been subjected to MSBP. In most cases, the court will be interested in whether there is evidence that child abuse occurred, as well as how the child has been harmed as a result of the alleged abuse. The court may also be interested in treatment options for the perpetrator and what management or treatment programs are recommended. In keeping with forensic guidelines, though, psychologists should avoid serving as both the evaluator and the treatment provider.

Abusive Head Trauma

Another form of child abuse is **abusive head trauma (AHT)**, previously known as **shaken baby syndrome**. This is when a parent or caretaker shakes a baby so hard that serious brain damage occurs. The brain damage can result in intellectual disability, speech and learning disabilities, blindness, paralysis, seizures, hearing loss, or death. A baby's brain and blood vessels are very fragile and can be easily damaged by whiplash motions, such as shaking, jerking, and jolting. The neck muscles are not strong enough to control head movements, and rapid movement of the head can result in the brain being damaged from banging against the skull wall.

SBS is difficult to diagnose, unless a witness accurately describes the incident. Medical personnel report that many babies who are symptomatic of AHT are brought in for medical attention for a fall, difficulty breathing, seizures, vomiting, altered consciousness, or choking. Sometimes the adults in these cases admit that they shook the baby, but that it was done only in an effort to resuscitate the infant. To diagnose AHT, physicians look for bleeding in the retina or retinal detachment, blood in the brain, and increased head size indicating excessive accumulation of fluid in the tissues of the brain. Fixed pupils, inactivity, and breathing problems may also be evident. In addition, spinal cord damage and broken ribs may be present, depending on how the baby was held during the shaking.

Although there are incomplete statistics on the frequency of AHT, there is consensus that brain trauma is the leading cause of death and disability in infants and young children (Dubowitz, Christian, Hymel, & Kellogg, 2014) and that shaking is involved in many of these cases (Duhaime, Christian, Rorke, & Zimmerman, 1998; Showers, 1999; Smithey, 1998). Russell (2010) writes that, of those children diagnosed with SBS, about 30% die as a result of their injuries, and only 15% survive with no lasting effects. Ellis and Lord (2002) estimate that 10% to 12% of all infant deaths related to abuse and neglect can be attributed to AHT. Furthermore, studies indicate that 70% to 80% of the perpetrators of AHT are male, and most often they are the parent of the child (Child Abuse Prevention Center, 1998; Ellis & Lord, 2002). The offender is usually in his early twenties (Showers, 1997). Both male and female babies are equally victimized, and AHT cuts across all socioeconomic levels. Frustration from a baby's incessant crying or from eating and toileting problems is usually reported as the precipitating event leading to the severe shaking. Ignorance of the dangers of shaking a baby is typical, and the overwhelming majority of offenders have poor child-rearing skills. In many hospitals today, parents are asked to watch educational videos on AHT and on infant care in general before leaving the hospital with their newborns.

REPRESSED AND RECOVERED MEMORIES

In the late 20th century, one of the most controversial topics in forensic psychology was the question of whether a "lost" memory of abuse or other crime can be recovered at a later time. The topic remains of great interest to some researchers today, although there is increasing skepticism that significant memories are buried and suddenly recovered (e.g., Alison, Kebbell, & Lewis, 2006). The topic is often referred to as **repressed memory**; recovered memory; or, less frequently, false memory (to imply questionable validity of the reported memory itself). The raging debate (also known as the "memory wars") was especially prominent during the 1990s, when there was a dramatic increase in reports of repressed memories of child sexual abuse and satanic ritual abuse (Patihis, Ho, Tingern, Lilienfeld, & Loftus, 2014). On one side are those who believe that memories of personal traumatic events can be repressed and remain inaccessible for years. Moreover, this side is convinced that with skillful therapy, these repressed memories can be fully and accurately recovered when the person feels it is psychologically safe to do so. On the other side of the debate are those who believe that the existence of repressed memories is highly unlikely and—at the very least—questionable. This side argues that recovered memories of abuse are largely false memories that sometimes can be inadvertently developed by therapists.

The notion of repressed memories has been around at least since the time of Sigmund Freud (1915/1957), who was certainly the most influential in bringing the concept into the limelight. Freud wrote that "the essence of repression lies simply in the function of rejecting and keeping something out of consciousness" (p. 105). To minimize anxiety and fear, we supposedly push out of our awareness painful or extremely troubling memories, and it is assumed we do this unconsciously. Current clinical thinking broadens the term *repression* to include a wide range of cognitive processes.

> Repression refers to the psychological process of keeping something out of awareness because of unpleasant affect connected with it. The "something" may be a memory (or part of a memory), a fantasy, a thought, an idea, a feeling, a wish, an impulse, a connection, and so forth. (Karon & Widener, 1999, p. 625)

Repression may include loss of memory of the trauma (amnesia) in some individuals and partial, fragmentary memory in others.

According to Freud (1915/1957)—and some contemporary clinicians—a repressed or submerged memory continues to linger in the unconscious until it is retrieved during psychotherapy or under certain other conditions, such as dream analysis, hypnosis, or some other "method of recovery." For many individuals, these repressed memories are never satisfactorily retrieved and may continue to raise havoc by causing psychological problems across their life spans—at least, this is the position held by some clinicians. These clinicians are convinced that they encounter many forms of repression—particularly memories of early childhood abuse—during their routine practice. On the other side of the ledger are cognitive scientists who question the frequency of "true" repression and the clinical assumptions of how or why it occurs.

The courts have had to face the issue of repressed memories in numerous cases. Adults who were allegedly the victims of abuse, especially sexual abuse, claim in civil or criminal trials that they had initially forgotten these traumatic experiences but eventually remembered them, usually with the help or guidance of therapists and often under hypnosis or some other "discovery" process. The courts refer to repressed-then-recovered memory as "delayed discovery." The alleged abuser, often the father or another family member, having been named, disclaims abuse, countering that the victim's memories are false and that they have been implanted by the psychotherapist, investigator, or evaluator (Partlett & Nurcombe, 1998). The accuracy of these recollections has been the center of the contentious debate of experts spanning nearly 30 years, as well as among the experts providing testimony in the courtroom. As noted by Patihis, Ho, Tingern, Lilienfeld, and Loftus (2014), "In the courtroom, beliefs about memory often determine whether repressed-memory testimony is admitted into evidence" (p. 519).

It should be mentioned that criminal prosecutions cannot be brought against someone after the statute of limitations for that crime has expired (*Stogner v. California*, 2003). The *statute of limitations* is the legal time limit placed on the filing of criminal charges or a civil complaint. In criminal cases, it is typically 1 to 3 years after the event, except for murder, for which the time period does not expire. In civil cases, the time for filing a complaint varies, but is typically under a few years. However, many states have begun to extend statutes of limitations, particularly in civil cases, when sexual abuse was at issue. This is in recognition that it may take years for victims of sexual abuse to come forward—even when repressed memories are not at issue. Those who support these extensions believe they are needed to procure justice for survivors of sexual abuse, while those who do not support the extensions believe they are unfair to people accused of crime or civil wrongs.

In both civil and criminal cases, the defense tries to call an expert witness to challenge the testimony offered by the prosecution's or the plaintiff's witness. The focus is usually on questioning the circumstances under which the original report was elicited and the interviewing methods of investigators or other involved professionals (Berliner, 1998). Some victims, under the repeated urging of their psychotherapists and often combined with discovery methods such as hypnosis, come to remember (often suddenly) that they were sexually abused by parents, siblings, relatives, or strangers. Convinced that these abuses are the core ingredient of their maladjustment or current difficulties or that their abusers should be punished, a significant number of these victims seek redress through the courts, primarily civil courts. Although these recovered memories may have foundation in some (perhaps many) cases, these claims must be evaluated very carefully by the forensic psychologist before proceeding to the legal arena. Lilienfeld and Loftus (1998) write, "The question of whether traumatic memories can be repressed for long periods of time (i.e., years or decades) and then suddenly recovered in intact form is perhaps the most controversial issue in clinical psychology today" (p. 471). (See Focus 11.1 for a discussion of two repressed-memory cases.)

There is little information on how frequently repressed memory occurs in clinical practice. In one of the few studies conducted so far, Polusny and Follette (1996) reported that 72% of the psychologists whom they surveyed had *not* encountered a case of "repressed" memory in the past year, and 15% had seen only one repressed memory case during that time. However, it is not unusual for clinicians to report anecdotally that they have seen many in their practices, as did one of the experts referred to in Focus 11.1.

Special-Expert Panels on Repressed Memory

According to McNally, Perlman, Ristuccia, and Clancy (2008), the controversy surrounding repressed and recovered memories of child sexual abuse has been among the most bitter in the history of psychology. In an effort to clear up some of the controversy and debate on repressed or recovered memories, the APA appointed a "working group" of researchers and clinicians to study the issue and arrive at some consensus on what is known and how to proceed. Called the American Psychological Association (APA) Working Group on Investigation of Memories of Childhood Abuse ("Final Conclusions," 1998), the panel of clinicians and researchers was able to come to the following five conclusions:

1. Controversies regarding adult recollections should not be allowed to obscure the fact that child sexual abuse is a complex and pervasive problem in America that has historically gone unacknowledged.

2. Most people who were sexually abused as children remember all or part of what happened to them.

3. It is possible for memories of abuse that have been forgotten for a long time to be remembered.

4. It is also possible to construct convincing pseudo-memories for events that never occurred.

5. There are gaps in our knowledge about the processes that lead to accurate and inaccurate recollections of childhood abuse.

FOCUS 11.1. RECOVERED MEMORY IN COURT: TWO CASES

The controversy over whether traumatic memories can be buried and recovered after many years is settled in some quarters but still rages in others. Many psychologists, primarily those involved in memory research, say that while the *details* of a traumatic event may be forgotten and possibly recovered, the *fact* that a traumatic event occurred after one has reached a certain age (usually 5 or above) is not forgotten. For example, if you were sexually assaulted as an 8-year-old, you would not forget it. Others, though, represented primarily by some clinicians, believe traumatic events can be repressed and later recovered, both spontaneously and through therapeutic methods.

Joan Borawick was 38 years old when she sued an aunt and uncle, alleging that they had sexually abused her many years ago when she visited them in Connecticut from her home in Washington State. At the time of the alleged abuse, 1961 and 1964, she was 8 and 12 years old. Borawick claimed that she did not remember the abuse for many years. About 20 years after the alleged incidents, she began to experience panic attacks. She sought and received psychiatric treatment as well as medical treatment for chronic physical illness. In addition, she underwent 12 to 14 sessions with a hypnotist who used regression therapy. During pretrial depositions, the hypnotist testified that Borawick revealed sexual abuse during these sessions, but he did not tell her this, because they would probably surface in time. As he predicted, several months after her last session, non-hypnotic memories of sexual abuse began to surface. She claimed to have memories of bizarre rituals and abuse by her father, other family members, and her father's friends, as well as her aunt and uncle.

In *Borawick v. Shay* (1995), an appeals court agreed with a lower court that Borawick's memories were refreshed by hypnosis, and that the technique did not achieve scientific credibility to be admitted into a court proceeding. The court noted that hypnotically recalled memory was apt to be a mosaic of actual events, irrelevant events, fantasy, and fantasized details. It is important to note that the court did not completely ban evidence obtained as a result of hypnosis; rather, it adopted a list of requirements or safeguards for its admission, most of which were not met in this case. Consequently, Borawick was not allowed to testify about her memories of being abused. She later appealed this decision to the U.S. Supreme Court, but the Court denied certiorari.

John Doe 76C v. Archdiocese of Saint Paul and Minneapolis (2012) was a priest abuse case. "John Doe" filed a civil suit alleging that he had been sexually abused in 1980 and 1981 on four separate occasions when he was a teenager by a priest in his parish. It was undisputed that the priest had a history of sexually abusing children and that the Diocese did not make this known to the public until the mid-1980s. Back then, the revelation was followed by extensive media publicity, and many victims came forward. Doe was not one of them, he said, because he had no recollection of the incidents. In 2002, however, he began to get flashbacks to the incidents, and he began therapy to deal with the rage and anger he felt

Under Minnesota law, the statute of limitations had expired, but Doe sought to introduce expert testimony on repressed and recovered memory to support his claim that he should be allowed to sue, despite the fact that so much time had elapsed. In other words, he said he could not have filed suit earlier because he had repressed the traumatic events. To decide whether to allow expert testimony on repressed memory, the district court in his case first held a hearing in which psychologists and psychiatrists on both sides of this issue testified. One expert in support of Doe indicated that he had seen dozens if not hundreds of patients who had repressed and recovered memories. Nevertheless, after hearing all the testimony, the court concluded that the theory of repressed and recovered memory was fundamentally unreliable for the purposes of being admitted into court; therefore, Doe was not allowed to present an expert on his behalf and the case was summarily dismissed.

An intermediate appeals court reversed this decision, ruling that the expert testimony might be admissible, but the Minnesota Supreme Court ruled against Doe. Acknowledging that other courts have been more accepting of repressed memory evidence, this court agreed with the lower court that the theory that memory could be repressed and recovered was unreliable and did not meet the standards for admitting scientific evidence into the courtroom.

But there were important issues on which the APA Working Group could not agree, mostly concerning the nature of early memory of abuse and its recovery. Although the group clearly strove to find consensus, the debate between some clinicians and researchers apparently became heated and polarized, resulting in a special issue in the December 1998 edition of *Psychology, Public Policy, and Law* that presents both sides. In this section, we will focus on the dominant view generally accepted by the cognitive and developmental scientists, but we will also give some attention to other perspectives where appropriate.

Before we proceed, however, we should mention that a similar panel of experts on repressed or recovered memory met in the United Kingdom shortly before the APA group convened. The group, called the British Psychological Society's (BPS) Working Party on Recovered Memories, was convened for the purpose of publishing a position statement on the phenomenon for members of the BPS, the media, and the interested citizen. The resulting document, which took more than 10 months to be finalized, is commonly referred to as the BPS Report (see British Psychological Society, 1995). The conclusions of the BPS Report generally coincide closely with the conclusions of the APA Final Report described above. For example,

> Like the BPS Report, the APA Final Report concluded that it was possible for memories of abuse that had been forgotten for a long time to be remembered, but that it was possible to construct convincing pseudomemories for events that never occurred. (Davies, Morton, Mollon, & Robertson, 1998, p. 1080)

However, Davies et al. also concluded that the APA Working Group neglected some important research findings that should have been addressed. They thought, for instance, that the APA panel neglected to establish an agreed-on scientific framework on which to base their discussions. More specifically,

> there appears to be little consensus over the relevant evidence and methods of proof. In the absence of such fundamentals, the temptation is to revert to a political framework, which is unproductive from the standpoint of advancing theory and practice. (Davies et al., 1998, p. 1080)

But even more relevant to our discussion here is the observation that

> the Final [APA] Report contains little serious discussion as to how memory mechanisms might mediate such diverse effects: The cognitivists merely accuse the therapists of clinging to a scientifically unsupported view of repression, and the therapists

look in turn to the recent work of Van der Kolk (e.g., Van der Kolk & Fisler, 1995) as providing a rationale for a special and different form of memory associated with trauma. (Davies et al., 1998, p. 1080)

Where does the repressed memory debate stand today? In one recent study, Magnussen and Melinder (2012) asked licensed psychologists in Norway whether they believed in the existence of recovered memories of traumatic events. Sixty-three percent of the psychologists said "yes." In the United States, Patihis et al. (2014) found high levels of belief in repressed memories among college undergraduates (78%). A majority of these students (65%) also thought that repressed memories could accurately be recovered through therapy. Similar results were found among the general public in the United States, with 84% accepting the existence of repressed memories and 78% believing in their accurate recovery. On the other hand, the Patihis et al. study discovered that experimental and research clinical psychologists were, by far, the most skeptical about repressed memories and their recovery. However, other mental health professionals, including *practicing* clinical psychologists, were more accepting of repressed-memory possibilities.

Because the topic of repressed or false memory is so important in forensic psychological practice and because it sets the stage for understanding memory processes in witness and expert testimony in the courtroom, we will pay special attention to the issue in this section. We begin by briefly outlining some of what research has revealed about human memory in general.

Research Sketches of Human Memory and Its Limitations

In its simplest terms, memory involves acquisition, storage, and retrieval. Acquisition, also called the encoding or input stage, is the initial step in the memory process and overlaps considerably with the sensory perceptual process. Sensory perception is the process of organizing and making sense of the information received from the senses, such as sight, hearing, smell, taste, somatosensory receptors, and vestibular and kinesthetic senses. Memory storage, also called retention, is when information becomes "resident in memory" (Loftus, 1979). In the retrieval stage, the brain searches for the pertinent information and retrieves it, a process somewhat like searching for a document in a filing cabinet or laptop.

In any discussion of forensic matters and memory, it will be helpful to begin with four important points about memory made by three of the leading scientists in the area: Peter Ornstein, Stephen Ceci, and Elizabeth Loftus (1998a).

- Not everything gets into memory.

- What gets into memory may vary in strength.

- The status of information in memory changes across time.

- Retrieval is not perfect (i.e., not all that is stored gets retrieved).

In reference to the first point, some experiences may not be recalled because they were not entered into memory in the first place. The human cognitive system is limited in its information-processing capacity and cannot simultaneously attend to everything going on in the environment. We have to be selective in what is noticed. Consequently, considerable information is never processed. Furthermore, information processing is influenced by prior knowledge and experience. In other words, to understand and interpret what is being experienced, the brain compares "new" material to "old," stored material. By analogy, the new material is fitted onto a "cognitive template" to see how it compares. How one "sees" the world is dictated to a large extent by "cognitive templates" that are already in place from previous experiences and knowledge.

Concerning the second point raised by Ornstein et al. (1998a), several factors may influence the strength and organization of the resulting memory "trace." In addition, strong memory traces may be readily retrieved, whereas weak traces may be more difficult to recover. The strength of the trace depends on such factors as the length of exposure to an event, the number of exposures, the age of the individual, and how significant or prominent the event is to the person. With increasing age (at least through young adulthood), there are corresponding changes in information-processing skills and the cognitive templates that have been developed from previous experiences.

The third point refers to what may happen once the information is stored and perhaps is one of the most important points concerning forensic issues. That is,

> the memory trace can be altered during the course of the interval between the actual experience and a report of it. The passage of time, as well as a variety of intervening experiences, can influence strongly the strength and organization of stored information. (Ornstein et al., 1998a, p. 1028)

A considerable amount of research indicates that humans continually alter and reconstruct their memory of past experiences rather than simply store past events permanently and unchangingly (Loftus, 2005; Strange & Takarangi, 2015; Sutton, 2011). Memory is not like a video camera that accurately stores events to be played back when necessary. (Recall Dr. Strange's Perspective 4.1 in Chapter 4.) Moreover, this alteration or "reconstructive process" is often done without the person's complete awareness. The individual is aware of the content of memory but is not usually aware of the transformations that have occurred during encoding, retention, and retrieval. The perspective that memory is continually vulnerable to revision is known as the **reconstructive theory of memory**. Overall, though, this reconstructive process probably does not *substantially* alter the *major* theme of the original memory for most people, but it does introduce a number of errors in *specific* descriptions of the event. For example, witnesses to a car accident may all report that two cars collided (as opposed to one car and one truck), but the specific details of the incident may vary considerably.

> Moreover, without reinstating events or experiences (e.g., through rehearsal, prompts, or visualizations), the strength of a memory trace decreases over time, and this trace decay combines with interferences in the delay interval to make access to stored information and successful retrieval more difficult. (Ornstein et al., 1998a, p. 1028)

In young children, memory traces are often not as strong because children generally lack the requisite knowledge and experience to fully appreciate the event. Thus, they may undergo more rapid decay than the memory traces of older children. A growing body of research also indicates that young children (such as preschoolers) are usually more susceptible to the influences of misleading information received after the event than are older children and adults (Bruck & Ceci, 2009; Ceci, Ross, & Toglia, 1987; Ornstein et al., 1998a).

The fourth point refers to the common observation that not everything in memory can be retrieved all the time. Social pressures, stress, anxiety, information overload, and the low strength of the information itself are some of the many factors that may interfere with quick and immediate retrieval under certain conditions. People's names are especially difficult to retrieve for many people.

Many clinicians believe that memory of traumatic events may be encoded differently from memory for unremarkable events (Alpert, Brown, & Courtois, 1998). More specifically, some suggest that the enormous differences between normal resting states and high levels of arousal might result in changing the entire process of how memories are stored and retrieved. In the APA Working Group Report, as mentioned previously, the clinical group placed considerable reliance on the work of Van der Kolk and Fisler (1994, 1995) as evidence for memory repression.

As pointed out by Davies and his colleagues (1998), Van der Kolk and Fisler emphasized the difference between memories of traumatic events and memories of events that are merely stressful. More specifically, Van der Kolk and Fisler (1994) stated that traumatic memories may somehow be "frozen" in their original form and unmodified by further experience. Consequently, reliving these traumatic experiences can be retraumatizing because retrieving them is actually like reexperiencing them. But note that this phenomenon refers to actively *avoiding* reliving the trauma, not *repressing* the event. If anything, Davies et al. note, Van der Kolk and Fisler are referring to state-dependent memory rather than repressed memory. **State-dependent memory** refers to the research findings that the things we experience in one emotional or physiological state—such as happiness, fear, or even intoxication—are sometimes easier to recall when we are again in that same state. Recent research has indicated, for example, that witnesses who were moderately intoxicated should be interviewed immediately if possible rather than waiting until they have "sobered up" (Compo et al., 2017). (See Focus 11.2 for more on this interesting phenomenon.) Although a person who does not like to revisit that same state of pain and trauma may avoid doing so as much as possible, it does not mean that person is *repressing* the memory, at least according to the typical clinical definition of repression.

In addition, the scientific evidence clearly indicates that memories from early infancy are highly unreliable, incomplete, and full of error. The phenomenon of infantile or childhood "amnesia" has long been noted by developmental psychologists (Dudycha & Dudycha, 1941). (See Focus 11.3.) Infantile amnesia refers to the common observation that adults are usually unable to recall events that occurred before the age of around 3 years. According to the BPS Report (BPS, 1995), for instance, "nothing can be recalled accurately from before the first birthday and little from before the second. Poor memory from before the fourth birthday is normal" (p. 29). Most of us have little trouble remembering certain things that occurred when we were

FOCUS 11.2. STATE-DEPENDENT MEMORY

State dependent refers to the observation that a memory acquired in one state of consciousness cannot be recalled until the person returns to the same state of consciousness. The person will have great difficulty remembering the events if in a different psychological state. For example, if a person learns new material while under the influence of alcohol, he tends to recall it better if he is again under the influence of alcohol.

State-dependent learning was first described in 1784 but was not subjected to much scientific study until the 1960s (Schramke & Bauer, 1997). Early research concentrated on differences induced by drugs and alcohol, and then interest shifted to the effects of mood or emotion states on memory and learning. For example, research has discovered that the negative events are recalled better when people are in a negative mood (Lewinsohn & Rosenbaum, 1987), and positive events are recalled better while in a positive mood (Ehrlichman & Halpern, 1988). Research later found that state-dependent learning may be influenced by drugs, moods, level of activation (e.g., anxiety levels), arousal (i.e., sleep

and wakefulness), or environmental settings (i.e., where the original memory was acquired) (Slot & Colpaert, 1999; Weingartner, Putnam, George, & Ragan, 1995). Pertaining to environmental settings, if you misplace your keys, trying to remember where you left them is often not as effective as physically retracing your steps in the actual environment. If a person hides money while intoxicated and forgets where the money was hidden, recall is likely to be enhanced by being similarly intoxicated and placed in the same environment.

Questions for Discussion

1. What are some ways in which police investigating a crime might make use of the research on state-dependent learning?
2. What might be an explanation for the research findings that positive events are remembered better when one is in a positive mood and negative events remembered better when one is in a negative mood?

FOCUS 11.3. INFANTILE AMNESIA

It is widely believed by psychologists that a vast majority of humans cannot recall events that occurred prior to age 3, a phenomenon called infantile amnesia. For some unknown reason, adolescent and adult memory of early childhood events appears to begin sometime after the third or fourth birthday. Consequently, all those hours spent with baby—rocking to sleep, playing, changing diapers, feeding, laughing, and cuddling—may be lost forever in the baby's mind. Childhood memories are fragile, but the common assumption is that infant memories are virtually nonexistent.

However, some research (Bauer, 1996) suggests that a baby may store those events in a different kind of "preverbal memory." It appears that even infants in the first year of life are able to retain bits of information about unique episodes over time (Mandler, 1988, 1990), but because they do not possess language skills, they cannot put these experiences into words at a later time. Very young children often rely on forms of memory (e.g., kinesthetic memory) that do not depend on verbal processing to be cognitively stored.

Other factors probably also contribute to the difficulty in recalling early childhood memories. Howe and Courage (1997) propose that childhood memories emerge as the cognitive self develops: The cognitive self is "a knowledge structure whose features serve to organize memories of experiences that happened to 'me'" (p. 499). If the cognitive self is immature, the ability to recall remains disorganized and partly inaccessible. As children get older, the ability to maintain and organize

information seems to increase. Other developmental aspects that probably affect childhood memory are the dramatic neurological and perceptual changes that occur during early childhood.

Although there is some question of whether memories of childhood events prior to age 3 can be recovered, some recent research suggests that emotionally laden events that occurred when some preschool children were 4 years of age were remembered into late childhood and adulthood (C. Peterson, Morris, Baker-Ward, & Flynn, 2014). In addition, preschool children who had an elaborate discussion with their parents concerning a recent experience were more likely to remember the event later in life (C. Peterson et al., 2014). Furthermore, young children who are encouraged to tell coherent narratives about what happens to them also appear to increase later memory of early childhood events.

Questions for Discussion

1. What is your earliest childhood memory? Approximately how old were you when the event you remember occurred? Was it an emotionally laden event?
2. In light of the research cited in the last paragraph above, consider the pros and cons of discussing with a preschool child emotionally laden events that (a) happened to him and (b) happened on a national scale.

7 years of age, such as a birthday party or a special occasion, but prior to that, things often become quite hazy. Even some things about our seventh birthday or other ordinary memories of early childhood may be nothing more than reconstructions based on stories told to us by parents or relatives (Knapp & VandeCreek, 2000, p. 367). However, scientists are not in complete agreement as to when this period of infantile amnesia ends for most children (Bruck & Ceci, 2012; Ornstein, Ceci, & Loftus, 1998b) or exactly why it occurs (Harley & Reese, 1999; see Focus 11.3).

Claims and assertions of abuse during childhood are complicated by the fact that the very definition of abuse is culturally determined, and behaviors that would be taken by adults to be clear instances of abuse might not be viewed in a comparable fashion by children and vice versa (Ornstein et al., 1998b). For example, as Ornstein et al. point out, insertions of anal suppositories, urinary catheterization, and other invasive medical procedures during the first few years of life may be perceived by the young child as "abusive."

Many practitioners believe that traumatized children are more likely to reenact traumatic events than to describe them verbally (Alpert et al., 1998). Although many children are unable to give verbal descriptions of events that had taken place in their early years, they showed evidence of their memory in their behavior and play, where they reenacted the abuse events (Alpert et al., 1998). It is clear that children interpret and respond to trauma according to their developmental level and maturity, but description of the behavioral pattern in children has been limited. Terr (1991, 1994) developed a model (derived from clinical observations of hundreds of traumatized children) of two types of childhood trauma, each with corresponding memory encoding and retrieval. By her description, Type I trauma consists of sudden, external, single events that result in stereotyped symptoms of childhood PTSD along with detailed memories, but also with misperceptions and mistimings regarding characteristics of the events. Type II traumas are those that involve "long-standing or repeated exposure to extreme external events." According to Terr, memory loss is most common in this kind of trauma. However, as pointed out by Ornstein et al. (1998b), scientists who study memory have found that repetition enhances memory rather than diminishing it: "Research on memory with children and adults suggests that people are more likely to forget an isolated event than a series of repeated events, even though the repeated events may become blended into a typical script" (p. 1000).

Perhaps more troubling for the courts and to the psychological profession is that under certain circumstances, *false* memories of abuse can be created, often by psychotherapists or evaluators themselves. Note that this is a different issue from children's reports of *contemporary* abuse, a topic discussed in the previous chapter. As reported by Roediger and Bergman (1998), "A substantial body of experimental evidence (buttressed by a long collection of anecdotal cases) shows that events that never happened can be vividly remembered, or that events can be remembered in ways quite different from the way they occurred" (p. 1102). Repeated suggestions, confrontations, or the use of highly suggestive "memory recovery" techniques may cause the creation of memories that are not true (Knapp & VandeCreek, 2000). (Recall that highly suggestive interviewing is also problematic in obtaining reports of contemporary abuse.)

A growing literature further suggests that it is relatively easy to create pseudo-memories in some individuals, but it may be more difficult in others. "The available evidence makes clear that individuals who have been exposed to repeated suggestive techniques over long periods of time sometimes provide highly detailed and coherent narratives that happen to be false"(Ornstein et al., 1998a, p. 1045). Hypnosis as a memory-recovery technique especially runs the risk of creating, distorting, or magnifying memories (see, again, the case discussed in Focus 11.1). At the very least, hypnosis as a discovery technique is considered by many forensic experts to be a very dangerous method of persuasion, if not indoctrination. On the other hand, some hypnotic techniques, used by well-trained hypnotists, are effective in encouraging the person being hypnotized (e.g., a victim or a witness) to relax and remember the facts of a case that he or she otherwise would not recall (Scheflin, 2014). Thus, as mentioned in Chapter 3, hypnotism may be used early in police investigations.

The tendency of clinicians to unintentionally engender symptoms or recollections in their patients is called the iatrogenic effect (*iatros* is the Greek word for physician, and *genic* refers to cause). In other words, clinicians who firmly believe in and are perceptually sensitive to certain symptoms as indicative of a specific disorder may, in effect, prompt the patient to think similarly. In this sense, certain therapists who are convinced that childhood sexual abuse is the basic cause of many symptoms of maladjustment may have a strong propensity to look for and interpret a variety of behaviors as symptoms of sexual abuse. In effect, the clinician may encourage the reconstruction of memory in the patient to include accounts of sexual abuse that may have never occurred. In addition, the scientific research indicates that young children may be disproportionately vulnerable to suggestive influences, either during psychotherapy or more generally through daily living (Ceci & Bruck, 1993). However, Bruck and Ceci (2004) have also noted that susceptibility to suggestion is highly common in middle childhood as well.

In summary, repressed memory of childhood abuse and its recovery by psychotherapists or through suggestions via self-help books or workshops should raise some red flags for further inquiry and reasonable evaluation and assessment by the forensic psychologist. We do not mean to imply that it could not happen—only that the overwhelming bulk of the research evidence suggests that if it does, it is very likely subject to error and will need further corroboration from independent sources and careful assessment.

As asserted by two well-respected scientists, Roediger and Bergman (1998),

> Far more mysterious is how painful events, banished to an unconscious state for years through some mechanism of dissociation or repression, could be brought back to consciousness and recollected with great fidelity . . . no evidence from the voluminous literature on human memory makes us think this is possible. (p. 1095)

This is especially the case for adults who suddenly recollect from their "unconscious" traumatic events that happened 20 to 40 years previously. Furthermore, and as noted by McNally and Geraerts (2009), some of the "recovered" memories are extremely implausible, including memories of satanic ritual abuse, space alien abduction, and living in past lives. Secondly, people typically remember these episodes after undergoing procedures specifically designed to unleash repressed memories (e.g., guided imagery, hypnosis). Thirdly, a large number of people who reported having recovered memories of terrible abuse have later retracted their reports. Finally, a few studies also demonstrate that false memories can be created in some individuals (about 30% in college students) (S. Porter, Yuille, & Lehman, 1999). Overall, McNally and Geraerts find very little convincing scientific evidence to support the repressed memory–recovery paradigm.

The research clearly indicates that memories of emotional events are reasonably good and accurate, and very, very rarely are they repressed or forgotten (Alison et al., 2006; Roediger & Bergman, 1998). Many people have reported their memories for high-impact events with considerable accuracy, a phenomenon referred to as **flashbulb memory** (R. Brown & Kulick, 1977). People in their 60s and older remember vividly what they were doing when they heard that President Kennedy was assassinated, and those older than 35 or 40 remember where they were when the space shuttle *Challenger* that contained teacher-astronaut Christa McAuliffe exploded in 1986. All but the youngest among us remember what we were doing when two hijacked airliners crashed into the World Trade Center on September 11, 2001. You also likely recall some high-impact event that occurred during your childhood. People often feel that they remember with high accuracy even minor details of emotional events, such as earthquakes, tornadoes, and other natural disasters (Roediger & Bergman, 1998). Nevertheless, these are not all personal traumatic events, such as a sexual assault.

It is interesting to note that today a majority of people in the U.S. general public have beliefs that run counter to the extensive research findings on memory. For example, two thirds of the U.S. public still believe memory acts like a video camera, nearly half believe memory is permanent and unchanging, and over half think that memory can be enhanced through hypnosis (Simons & Chabris, 2011, 2012).

Roles of the Forensic Psychologist in Child Abuse Cases

In the past, clinicians rarely became involved in addressing forensic issues in child abuse before the cases were adjudicated (Melton, Petrila, Poythress, & Slobogin, 1997). This has changed in recent years, however. Forensic psychologists are becoming involved much earlier in the process. Today, the forensic psychologist may assume a crucial role in the early stages of a case and then be asked to return to the role of a "neutral" expert in the adjudication and disposition. For example, the clinician may be asked by a court to determine whether child abuse or neglect likely occurred and, if so, what should be done about it. The answer to the second question— what should be done?—may require immediate (emergency), short-term, or long-term predictions and decisions and is essentially a risk assessment determination.

According to Melton, Petrila, Poythress, and Slobogin (1997), the second question focuses on the extent to which the child is in imminent danger. Early in the case, this might involve removing the child from the home for his or her protection. This usually only happens when there is some credible evidence that the child is being abused or neglected. What constitutes credible evidence of child abuse or neglect varies from state to state. If credible evidence is established, subsequent measures are taken to ensure the safety of the child. About four fifths of all complaints reported to child protective services are not substantiated. This may be because no credible evidence is available, or it may be because there is no abuse. Unfortunately, when high-profile child abuse cases are publicized in the media, there is often anecdotal evidence that complaints were filed but were not investigated properly.

In most states, the credible evidence standard does not require the psychologist or mental health professional (usually a caseworker) to consider conflicting evidence or to complete a comprehensive report in the case, but "merely requires the fact finder to present minimal evidence to support the allegations against the alleged perpetrator" (Owhe, 2013, p. 316). In most areas of the country, anyone can make a report of suspected child abuse or neglect, and this is often done anonymously. Perhaps more important, the finding that abuse or neglect probably exists (regardless of the standard of proof) can affect children and families significantly (Owhe, 2013).

It should be emphasized that many jurisdictions are beginning to establish multidisciplinary teams for investigation, assessment, and intervention in child abuse or neglect cases. Consequently, the forensic psychologist rarely acts alone or without the expertise of other mental health professionals. Still, as pointed out by Melton et al. (1997, 2007), the forensic psychologist may be regarded as the team's sole expert in a variety of assessments and predictions.

The adjudication and disposition of the case refers primarily to the criminal proceedings against the alleged abuser. However, they may also occur in civil proceedings, such as custody hearings or hearings to decide whether visitation should be allowed. During adjudication, four issues that may involve the forensic psychologist are

1. What is the most appropriate procedure for taking a child's testimony?

2. Under what conditions is a child's out-of-court statement (hearsay) admissible?

3. Is the child competent enough to provide accurate testimony in abuse cases?

4. Did abuse or neglect occur, and if so, who is responsible?

The first issue—which first emerged in sexual abuse cases—concerns identifying what special procedures would allow a child to testify without placing him or her under enormous duress in the presence of the defendant. In many cases, the child's disclosures are the strongest, if not the only, piece of evidence and are vital to identification and prosecution (McWilliams, 2016). Moreover, "the child is notoriously vulnerable while giving evidence against abusers, especially parents, when proof of the charge will result in separation. Many children are highly suggestible and subject to recantation when faced with the reality of parental separation" (Partlett & Nurcombe, 1998, p. 1260). These problems of recantation and suggestibility are especially troubling when accusations of abuse made during custody proceedings give one parent an advantage over the other.

In criminal cases, recent legal rules in many states limit the defendant's confrontation with the child by allowing, under special circumstances, the child's testimony to be taken through closed-circuit TV, courtroom closure during the child's testimony, or in some other way. Thus, the jury can observe and hear the testimony and the cross-examination while the child's distress and the defendant's intimidation are presumably minimized. If such a limitation on the defendant's right to confront witnesses against him is to occur, it first requires an assessment of the emotional consequences of the child's "interaction with a particular adult in a specific context" (Melton et al., 1997, p. 458). In 1987, the U.S. Supreme Court (e.g., *Maryland v. Craig*, 1987) "opened the door to testimony by mental health professionals in hearings to determine whether there is a necessity for special procedures to protect particular child witnesses" (Melton et al., 1997, p. 458).

Clinicians who evaluate abused children are required to be skillful and sensitive to a wide range of factors. For example, open-ended questions are widely recognized as revealing the most quality information when interviewing young children (McWilliams, 2016). Close-ended questions (yes/no or forced choice questions) result in significantly less information, especially when interviewing children. Suggestive questioning, on the other hand, is likely to contaminate the child's (or adult's) memory and reliable information. Suggestive questioning implies or leads to a certain answer which may result in misinformation from the child.

In addition, the reports must be "fair, unbiased, and measure up to standard of proof equal to the gravity and seriousness of the allegations and impending consequences" (Owhe, 2013, p. 325). K. S. Budd, Felix, Poindexter, Naik-Polan, and Sloss (2002) report that

> clinicians may be asked to assess the child's developmental or emotional functioning and needs, the effects of maltreatment on the child, the risk of harm should the child be united with his or her parents, the impact of separation from the biological family on the child's functioning, or the advantages and disadvantages of potential visitation or placement options. (p. 3)

"Guidelines for Psychological Evaluations in Child Protection Matters" were first passed in 1999 and were recently revised (APA, 2013b). The Guidelines list six questions psychologists are frequently asked to address: (1) What, if any, maltreatment occurred? (2) How seriously has the child's psychological well-being been affected? (3) What therapeutic intervention is recommended? (4) Can the parent(s) be successfully treated to prevent harm to the child in the future; if so, how, and if not, why not? (5) What would be the psychological effect upon the child if returned to the parent(s)? (6) What would be the psychological effect upon the child if separated from the parent(s) or if parental rights were terminated?

The Guidelines, along with multiple other guides in the professional literature, caution psychologists against allowing their personal biases and values to influence their assessments, and they recommend the use of multiple methods during the assessment process (tests, interviews), not unlike assessments in child custody evaluations. The psychologist also should be highly sensitive to and knowledgeable about the cultural, socioeconomic, and diversity issues relevant to the child's situation and aware of any cultural norms that may be relevant (e.g., involvement of extended family members, variations in disciplinary approaches). With regard to the ultimate issue question discussed in other chapters (e.g., should this child be removed from the custody of his parents?), the choice of providing the answer is again left to the individual psychologist. However, if he or she chooses to offer such an opinion, the recommendations "should be based on articulated assumptions, data, interpretations, and inferences based upon established professional and scientific standards" (Guideline 13).

Assessment in child protection matters is very common, as are suggestions for how these assessments should be conducted (Condie, 2014). Very few surveys describe in detail current practice—for example, how they are actually being done—or which procedures are most useful. In their survey of one urban juvenile court system, K. S. Budd et al. (2002) found that psychologists conducted 90% of the evaluations of children. Unfortunately, many of the evaluations were not based on multisource, multisession information but were based on much more limited data. However, many of the evaluations did emphasize the strengths of the child.

In some cases, anatomically detailed dolls are used to help young children suspected of being sexually abused express themselves verbally on sexual topics. The practice of using them, however, has been questioned. Some experts (e.g., Bruck, Ceci, & Francoeur, 2000; Ceci & Bruck, 1993) contend that these dolls heighten the child's suggestibility and promote false stories. Others (e.g., Koocher et al., 1995) believe that, in the hands of well-trained professionals, they may be a useful communication tool, as long as they are used cautiously.

In recent years, training of forensic psychologists in interviewing skills has advanced considerably (Lamb, 2016). Proper training is not accomplished overnight. According to Lamb,

"There is now clear evidence that improvements in interviewing practice occur reliably only when training courses involve multiple modules, distributed over time, with repeated opportunities for interviewers to consolidate learning and to obtain feedback on the quality of the interviews they do conduct" (p. 710).

CHILD ABDUCTION

A person is guilty of **child abduction** (kidnapping) if he or she unlawfully leads, takes, entices, or detains a child under a specified age with intent to keep or conceal the child from his or her parent, guardian, or other person having lawful custody. Child abduction is relatively rare among violent crimes against children and adolescents. It makes up less than 2% of all violent crimes against juveniles reported to law enforcement (Finkelhor & Ormrod, 2000). Child abductions are most often divided into three classifications based on the identity of the perpetrator: (1) family abductions (representing 49% of reported abductions cases), (2) acquaintance abductions (27%), and (3) stranger abductions (24%). Many of the following statistics are drawn from the U.S. Department of Justice report, *Kidnapping of Juveniles*, prepared by Finkelhor and Ormrod.

Family Abduction

Family abduction is committed mostly by parents (80%), a phenomenon so common in child abduction cases that it is labeled *parental abduction*. "Parental abduction encompasses a broad array of illegal behaviors that involve one parent taking, detaining, concealing, or enticing away his or her child from the parent having custodial access" (J. J. Wilson, 2001, p. 1). The U.S. Department of Justice (2010) estimates that there are 200,000 parental abductions annually in the United States. Noncustodial parental abduction usually involves a child younger than age 6—most often around age 2. Both genders are equally victimized. The perpetrators are also evenly distributed (50% each) between men and women. The abduction generally originates in the home. Those children who become victims of family abduction are often thrust into a life of uncertainty and isolation, because the abductor is always fearful that he or she will be discovered and the child returned to the custodial parent.

Juveniles are more likely to be kidnapped by family members or acquaintances than by complete strangers. Acquaintances are people they know but who are not family members. Acquaintance kidnapping most often involves a teenage female victim (72%). The perpetrator is often a juvenile himself (30%) and is frequently a boyfriend or former boyfriend (18%). The most common motives are to seek revenge for being spurned, to force a reconciliation, to commit a sexual assault, or to evade parents who want to break up the relationship. In some instances, gang members kidnap other teenagers (whom they know) for intimidation, retaliation, or recruitment. A third type of acquaintance abduction involves family friends or employees (e.g., babysitters) who remove children from their home for the purpose of sexual assault or retaliation against the family. Acquaintance abduction victims suffer a higher rate of injury compared to victims of the other forms of abduction, possibly because the victim is usually older and therefore more likely to resist the abduction. Another reason may be that intimidation, which often is associated with more physical force, is the primary motive in many of these abductions.

Parents and caretakers are not particularly satisfied with how law enforcement officials handle family abductions. In one extensive survey, only 45% were satisfied with how police handled their family abduction situation, compared to 75% satisfaction with how police responded to reports of abduction by strangers (Hammer, Finkelhor, Ormrod, Sedlak, & Bruce, 2008).

Acquaintance and Stranger Child Abductions

Acquaintances are people the child or adolescent knows or has seen but are not immediate family members or other relatives. The child may recognize them from the neighborhood, doing repair work at school, spending time in the playground, or working at a local ice cream store. Stranger abductors are those the child does not recognize, although usually the offender has some level of familiarity with the child (e.g., by watching the child from a distance).

According to A.-J. Douglas (2011), although parents usually admonish their children to stay away from strangers, most neglect to tell them not to allow anyone, even someone they know or recognize, to take them somewhere without parent consent. Many parents have established "code words" with their children and warn them not to go with an acquaintance other than a police officer unless he or she uses the code word. Tragically, some abductors have dressed as police officers.

Victims are typically abducted from either a public outdoor location or their own residence. Outdoor locations, such as streets, highways, parks, playgrounds, beaches, lakes, and amusement parks, are especially favorite locations of stranger abductors (Finkelhor & Ormrod, 2000). Based on NIBRS data, the school is usually not the location for child abductions, including family abductions.

Two recent and important studies on acquaintance and stranger child abductions were conducted by Janet Warren and associates (2016) and Shelton, Hilts, and MacKizer (2016). The Warren study investigated 463 incidents of single-victim child abduction identified by federal law enforcement agencies as serious. The Shelton study examined 32 incidents in which the child was abducted from inside his or her residence. The Shelton data were gathered from the FBI Behavioral Analysis Unit as well as local and state law enforcement.

Both studies found that most acquaintance and stranger abductions were motivated by the offender's sexual interest in the child, with the majority of the child victims being Caucasian females between the ages of 6 and 17 (average age of 11). Surprisingly, very few of the abductors were on a state or federal sex offender registry. Warren et al. found that 55% of the abducted female and 49% of the male victims were killed or never found. Asphyxiation was the primary cause of death in most cases.

Other studies report that when the child is murdered, it is usually within the first 24 hours after the abduction (W. D. Lord, Boudreaux, & Lanning, 2001). Some experts on child abduction investigations believe the first three hours are the most critical, as 74% of the abducted children who are murdered are killed within that time period (Bartol & Bartol, 2013). About one third of the child survivors of these extreme abductions are injured enough to require medical attention.

As mentioned above, the Shelton et al. (2016) study focused on residential abductions by an acquaintance or stranger. About 60% of residential abductors were known by the victim or the victim's family. In most cases, the offender entered through the front door, which was typically unlocked. Entry usually occurred between midnight and 8 a.m. while the family was sleeping. Upon exiting the residence, the child old enough to walk went with the offender without resistance, suggesting that the offender was nonthreatening in his approach. Interestingly, siblings were sometimes sleeping in the same room as the victim during the abduction and often witnessed the event. According to Shelton et al., far too often the siblings did not mention seeing the abduction, probably due to fear of reprisal from the offender. Shelton et al. recommended that trained forensic interviewers be involved in the investigation to uncover what the sibling knew about the incident.

Research on stranger and acquaintance abductions also indicates that many of the offenders have criminal records, but most of their previous crimes were not sexual in nature (Beasley et al., 2009). The most common previous offense is burglary.

On average, approximately 115 "stranger" abductions ended in the death of the child each year (Bartol & Bartol, 2013). Because of the seriousness of stranger or near-stranger child abductions, federal law enforcement is usually involved, putting into action its Child Abduction Rapid Deployment (CARD) teams. Although 115 is a relatively small number compared to the number of family or close-acquaintance abductions, the nature of the crimes has far-reaching, traumatizing effects on both the family and the entire community. In addition, these abductions receive considerable media publicity and have been highly influential in molding public opinion about the risk and frequency of stranger abduction sexual homicides.

NISMART

The National Incidence Study of Missing, Abducted, Runaway and Throwaway Children (NISMART) (Finkelhor, Hotaling, & Sedlack, 1990; Johnston & Girdner, 2001) is a report describing the results of a nationwide telephone survey conducted in 1988. The study determined estimates of the number of family abductions to both domestic and international destinations nationwide. It is the most up-to-date, comprehensive study currently available. More important to our discussion here, the NISMART survey reported some of the common behavioral and psychological characteristics of parental abductors. The following characteristics were outlined by Johnston and Girdner:

- Abducting parents are likely to deny and dismiss the other parent's value to the child. They believe that they, more than anyone else, know what is best for their child. In some cases, the motivation to abduct may also be an attempt to protect the child from a parent who is perceived to be likely to molest, abuse, or neglect the child, which in some instances may be a legitimate concern.

- Abducting parents usually take very young children (the mean age is 2 to 3). Such children are easier to transport and conceal, are unlikely to protest verbally, and may be unable to tell others their name or provide other identifying information.

- Most abducting parents are likely to have a supportive social network of family, friends, or social communities that provide assistance and emotional and moral support. This pattern is especially prevalent when the abductor has no financial or emotional ties to the geographical area from which the child was taken.

- Most custody violators do not consider their actions illegal or morally wrong, even after the involvement of the district attorney's office.

- Mothers and fathers are equally likely to abduct their children, although at different times. Fathers tend to abduct before there is a child custody order in place, whereas mothers tend to abduct after the court has issued a formal custody decree (p. 5).

Parental kidnappers who appear to be the most dangerous to the other parent or the child manifest paranoid, irrational beliefs and delusions that do not dovetail with reality (Johnston & Girdner, 2001). This risk is especially high in those abductors who have a history of domestic violence, hospitalization for mental disorders, or serious substance abuse. They may feel overwhelmed by their divorce and may be convinced that their former partners have betrayed and exploited them. Revenge may emerge as a dominant motive for the abduction. Fortunately, this type of parental abductor is relatively rare. Interestingly, one study found that approximately 75% of male abductors and 25% of female abductors had exhibited violent behavior in the past (Greif & Hegar, 1993).

Psychological Impact of Family Abduction

The experience of family abduction can be emotionally traumatic to both the child and the left-behind parent (Chiancone, 2001). The incident can be particularly damaging in cases in which force is used to carry out the abduction, the child is concealed, or the child is held for a long period of time. According to the NISMART survey, abductors use force in 14% of parental abductions and coercive threats in 17% (Chiancone, 2001; Finkelhor et al., 1990). The length of time separated from the left-behind parent is one of the major determinants of the emotional impact the incident has on the abducted child (Agopian, 1984). According to Chiancone, children held for short periods (less than a few weeks) usually do not give up hope of being reunited with the other parent and do not suffer the emotional reactions found in long-term abductions.

However, the story is different for those children who experience long-term abductions. In reference to the Agopian study, Chiancone writes,

They [the children] were often deceived by the abducting parent and frequently moved to avoid being located. This nomadic, unstable lifestyle made it difficult for children to make friends and settle into school, if they attended at all. Over time, younger children could not easily remember the left-behind parent, which had serious repercussions when they were reunited. Older children felt angry and confused by the behavior of both parents—the abductor for keeping them away from the other parent and the left-behind parent for failing to rescue them. (p. 5)

Chiancone (2001) also indicates that left-behind parents commonly experienced feelings of loss, rage, and impaired sleep, and more than half reported loneliness, fear, and/or severe depression. Social support and professional intervention are often important in helping them adjust to this traumatic experience. The psychological damage done to both the child and the left-behind parents prompted all 50 states and the District of Columbia to enact laws that treat family abductions as a felony under certain circumstances (U.S. Department of Justice, 2010).

ELDER ABUSE AND NEGLECT

Approximately 1 to 2 million older Americans are victims of various kinds of abuse each year (National Center on Elder Abuse [NCEA], 2013). In addition, approximately 5% of all homicide victims between 1980 and 2008 were elderly (Cooper & Smith, 2011). *Elder abuse* is defined as the physical, financial, emotional, or psychological harm of an older adult, usually defined as age 65 or above (C. E. Marshall, Benton, & Brazier, 2000). Some researchers (Acierno et al., 2010) use 60 as a minimum age of the victim for studying elder abuse.

Abandonment is usually included in the definition of neglect and is characterized by such things as desertion of an elder at a hospital, a nursing facility, or other similar institution or public place such as a bus station. Financial abuse is also prevalent in cases of elder abuse. This refers to the illegal or improper use of an elder's funds, property, or assets. Sexual abuse, on the other hand, is relatively uncommon and refers to nonconsensual sexual contact of any kind with an elderly person. The laws that protect elders and definitions of elder abuse vary from state to state, although all states have some form of legislation that addresses the problem (Berson, 2010). Many states have passed laws that require the police and the courts to formally respond to accusations of elder abuse (E. Morgan, Johnson, & Sigler, 2006; Payne, 2008). Furthermore, 16 states mandate that certain professionals who suspect elder abuse must report it (Payne, 2008).

According to the National Elder Mistreatment Study (Acierno et al., 2010)—a study based on self-reports of the victims over a 1-year period—the prevalence of elder abuse in the United States was 4.6% for emotional abuse, 1.6% for physical abuse, 0.6% for sexual abuse, 5.1% for neglect, and 5.2% for financial abuse by a family member. Overall, approximately 1 in 10 cognitively intact, elderly respondents reported experiencing some form of abuse during 2008. Relatively little of this mistreatment was reported to authorities. (See Photo 11.3.)

▶ **Photo 11.3** An older woman whose black eyes and facial expression are signs of abuse.
Source: © iStock/triffitt.

Adult children are the most frequent abusers of their elderly parents (NCEA, 1999). Other family members and spouses ranked as the next most likely abusers of older people. Men tend to be the most likely perpetrators of elder mistreatment, although women are more likely to be involved in elder neglect (Administration on Aging, 1998). Most cases of elder abuse and neglect take place at home because most older Americans live at home rather than in nursing homes or institutions.

The emotional or psychological abuse can range from name-calling or giving the "silent treatment" to intimidating and threatening the individual. It may also involve treating the older person like a child and isolating the person from family, friends, or regular activities. Because elder maltreatment is often subtle and provides few clear or recognizable signs of the mistreatment, it is extremely difficult to say exactly how many cases there are in the United States each year. The best estimates indicate that only 1 out of 14 domestic elder abuse incidents comes to the attention of authorities, even after the enactment of mandatory reporting laws in many states (Acierno et al., 2010; Pillemer & Finkelhor, 1988; Payne, 2008). Payne writes, "Those providing care to older persons, criminal justice officials, human service professionals, researchers, and policy makers must come to agreement that failing to intervene in elder abuse cases is, in and of itself, a form of mistreatment" (p. 711). Meeting the many needs of older adults is an important role for psychologists today, some of whom specialize in this area as geropsychologists.

Roles of the Forensic Psychologist in Elder Abuse Cases

Melton and his colleagues (1997) posit that, for the forensic psychologist, the issues of elder abuse and neglect are closely related to child abuse cases in many respects: "Evaluators should address many of the same domains in dispositional evaluation, and they should be alert to many of the same potential problems and role confusion" (p. 479). *Dispositional evaluation* refers to an assessment of the attitudes, desires, and motivations of an individual. There are, however, two major differences between forensic evaluations for child abuse and those for elder abuse.

> First, clinicians conducting dispositional evaluations in cases involving elders or other dependent adults need to be aware of the service alternatives for adults with disabilities, and they need to have a realistic view of the care needs that the victim presents. In that sense, the scope of an evaluation in an elder maltreatment case may have much in common with an evaluation for limited guardianship. (Melton et al., 1997, p. 479)

Guardianship refers to the appointment of authority over an individual's person or estate to another person when that individual is considered incapable of administering his or her own affairs. Guardianship—touched on briefly in Chapter 6—can come in many forms, but the two that are most pertinent here are general and specific or special guardianship. As the name implies, a *general guardian* is one who has the responsibility for general care and control of the person and the estate, whereas the *specific guardian* is one who has special or limited powers and duties with respect to the person. For example, the specific guardian may have the legal authority to make only certain treatment decisions, whereas in other areas, the affected person is free to make other decisions.

The second major difference between child abuse and elder abuse evaluations is that the victim, unlike in child abuse or protection cases, is presumed to be competent until there is a legal determination otherwise. In addition, about one fourth of the complainants in the elder abuse cases are the victims themselves (Melton et al., 1997). Furthermore, there may be significant financial conflicts of interest, especially if the assigned caregivers are financially (and perhaps emotionally) dependent on the victim. Consequently, the clinician needs to be aware of and sensitive to the complicated relationships that may exist between the guardians and the victim.

The APA (2014d) published "Guidelines for Psychological Practice With Older Adults," intended to assist psychologists in evaluating their readiness for working with older adults.

The Guidelines represent an update of the guidelines published in 2003. In the updated Guidelines, the APA emphasizes that,

> Unquestionably, the demand for psychologists with a substantial understanding of later-life wellness, cultural, and clinical issues will expand in future years as the older population grows and becomes more diverse and as cohorts of middle-aged and younger individuals who are receptive to psychological services move into old age. (p. 35)

The Guidelines list 21 recommendations that psychologists who work or plan to work with older adults should consider in their practice.

SUMMARY AND CONCLUSIONS

Forensic psychologists are all too familiar with the results of violent victimization. When the perpetrator of the violence is a family member or an intimate partner, the effects are particularly devastating. Psychologists evaluate victims of violent crime to assess the extent of their psychological injury. Results of those evaluations may then be used in civil or criminal proceedings. Psychologists also may evaluate or offer treatment to violent offenders, a topic that will be covered more fully in the remaining chapters. In this chapter, we focused on the services provided to victims of family violence, as well as the information that has been gathered on the characteristics and extent of the crime itself.

Family violence is a very broad term that includes spouse or intimate partner violence (IPV), child abuse, and sibling on sibling violence, among other permutations. In this chapter, we focused on IPV, child abuse, and elder abuse. We also discussed child abduction by noncustodial parents and strangers. An area of growing concern and research interest is the abuse of animals, which has been associated with violence against children and partners.

Many researchers today refer to IPV rather than spousal assault or domestic violence between adult partners. This is because intimate partners often are not married or do not reside in the same domicile. Yet, the characteristics of the violence and the relationships are similar. Researchers have made considerable progress in their study of IPV. Whereas earlier studies focused primarily on female victims, often describing them as passive, depressed, and helpless, later research focused on descriptions of the abuse relationship and features of the male batterer. Likewise, researchers have explored IPV between same-sex couples and between couples in which the woman is the abuser. In the great majority of intimate partner abuse situations, however, the male is the abuser. We explored some of the issues faced by forensic psychologists who treat abusers

and victims, as well as the challenges they face when giving expert testimony. Recently, researchers have focused more attention on the effect of IPV on the children who witness it. Many believe that exposing children to violence between adults is a form of emotional abuse.

Child abuse—also referred to as maltreatment—can take one or more of four forms: neglect, physical abuse, sexual abuse, and emotional abuse. In any form, it is a continuing and disturbing problem. After reviewing statistics associated with this crime, we focused on the most severe forms, including infanticide, sexual abuse, the little-researched Munchausen syndrome by proxy—or medical child abuse—and abusive head trauma. Evaluations of children who have allegedly been abused, including sexually abused, are among the most challenging for psychologists in forensic practice. These evaluations often occur in the context of divorce proceedings, which were covered in Chapter 6. A related area, alleged instances of child abuse in the distant past, has been extremely controversial for many psychologists. These cases often—but not inevitably—revolve around the issue of repressed or recovered memory. We presented the research associated with this topic as well as conclusions from both American and British working groups. Although the repressed memory issue is far from resolved—and it often pits research psychologists against clinicians—it is important to note that the empirical research to this point does not strongly support widespread forgotten memories. It is possible, though, that some victims of sexual assault do forget and later recall their victimization many years after the abuse.

The chapter ended with coverage of services to older age groups and elder abuse. Until recently, this topic has been under-researched by psychology, but not ignored by the law or by victim advocates. Data indicate that the elderly often do not report to officials the abuse or neglect they experience from family members. When such abuse is reported, it may result in guardianship proceedings, in which the care and custody of an older person may be removed from family members and transferred to other individuals or to the state. Psychologists in forensic practice are likely to encounter these issues primarily when they are involved in such guardianship proceedings or when they assess the civil capacities discussed in Chapter 6, such as testamentary capacity or capacities to consent or refuse treatment. With a growing population of older individuals, these and other services are likely to be needed well into the future.

KEY CONCEPTS

Abusive Head Trauma (AHT)   429
Battered woman syndrome (BWS)   415
Battering   413
Child abduction   442
Conflict Tactics Scale (CTS)   420
Domestic Violence Risk Appraisal Guide (DVRAG)   419
Dysphoric/borderline batterers   414
Elder abuse   445
Family violence   410

Family-only batterers   414
Filicide   425
Flashbulb memory   439
Generally violent/antisocial batterers   414
Iatrogenic effect   438
Infanticide   425
Infantile amnesia   436
Intimate partner violence (IPV)   410
Munchausen syndrome by proxy (MSBP)   427

Neonaticide   425
Ontario Domestic Assault Risk Assessment (ODARA)   418
Reconstructive theory of memory   435
Repressed memory   429
Repression   430
Shaken baby syndrome (SBS)   429
Spousal Assault Risk Assessment (SARA)   419
State-dependent memory   436
Vicarious traumatization   422

QUESTIONS FOR REVIEW

1. Summarize Meuer, Seymour, and Wallace's stage theory of domestic violence.

2. What obstacles are placed in the path of victims of intimate partner violence who want to leave the relationship?

3. Why is the term *battered woman syndrome* controversial?

4. What progress has been achieved in the treatment of batterers?

5. What are the major differences between same-sex intimate partner violence (SS-IPV) and opposite-sex intimate partner violence (OS-IPV)?

6. List five measures used to assess symptoms of PTSD.

7. List and describe briefly the four major types of child maltreatment.

8. What are the key psychological features of Munchausen syndrome by proxy, now referred to as medical child abuse?

9. What conclusions were reached by the APA Working Group on Investigation of Memories of Childhood Abuse?

10. What is the role of the forensic psychologist in child abuse? In parental abduction? In elder abuse?

 SAGE edge™

CORRECTIONAL PSYCHOLOGY

CHAPTER TWELVE

CORRECTIONAL PSYCHOLOGY IN ADULT SETTINGS

The correctional officer who was serving as the "tour guide" for the college students visiting the maximum-security facility seemed to be enjoying the break from his usual routine. Early on, he rolled up his pants leg and showed students the scars he sported from fights with inmates; then he showed them the collection of makeshift weapons that had been confiscated from their cells. During a walk through one of the cell blocks, he stopped and positioned two students in front of a prisoner's cell and joked while the man leered at the young women. In a nearby cell, another inmate was looking downward, probably wishing he could disappear. The tour guide briefly took the students past a few observation cells, where mentally ill prisoners were in stripped down surroundings, one sobbing quietly. As the group was leaving the facility, a student muttered, "Just get me out of here."

During a different prison visit, graduate students were allowed to observe a disciplinary hearing, in which a prisoner was facing a 30-day stay in segregation following an altercation in the prison yard. If found responsible for the fight, the man would also lose "good-time credits," delaying his potential release date from prison. The prisoner was given the opportunity to speak on his own behalf, but he said nothing. The hearing lasted less than 5 minutes, and the prisoner was moved to a segregated cell.

Corrections today is a high-profile, complex operation that consumes very large portions of the operating budgets of the federal government and virtually all states. Nevertheless, beginning in 2008, the population of people under correctional supervision in the United States began to decline (Kaeble & Glaze, 2016). At year-end 2015, about 6,741,400 persons were under such supervision, a decrease of about 115,600 from the year before (Kaeble & Glaze, 2016). At year-end 2015, 2.7% of adults were under some form of correctional supervision, representing the lowest rate since 1994. Persons under correctional supervision include those in prisons and jails as well as in the community, on probation or on parole. (See Table 12.1 for a comparison of two recent years.)

The decline is due primarily to lower numbers of incarcerated prisoners in federal and state prisons; declining numbers in jails are less dramatic. However, many factors can account for the overall fewer number

Chapter Objectives

- Describe the tasks of psychologists and other mental health professionals in adult corrections.

- Sketch the correctional system and how it operates.

- Summarize the legal rights of inmates, including the right to treatment.

- Review the research on the psychological effects of imprisonment.

- Describe treatment approaches to dealing with specific groups of offenders.

Table 12.1 Estimated Number of Persons Supervised by Adult Correctional Systems (Both Federal and State), by Correctional Status, 2011 and 2015

Correctional Populations	2011		2015	
	Population	Percentage	Population	Percentage
Total	6,994,500	100%	6,741,400	100%
Probation	3,973,800	56.8	3,789,800	56.2
Parole	855,500	12.2	870,500	9.6
Prison	1,599,000	22.9	526,800	.08
Local jail	735,600	10.5	728,200	10.8

Source: Kaeble & Glaze, 2016, p. 2.

Note: Chart excludes territorial prisons, military facilities, and jails in Indian country, but includes persons held in private prisons and special facilities such as prison hospitals.

of individuals under correctional supervision, including the falling crime rates and the diversion of low-level offenders to special courts, both discussed in earlier chapters. Furthermore, court decisions requiring solutions to overcrowded prisons in the 1990s prompted states to decriminalize some offenses or shorten sentences. California, for example, lost a long battle in the courts when the U.S. Supreme Court in *Brown v. Plata* (2011) upheld lower court decisions requiring the state to reduce its prison population. California's system had been designed for 80,000 inmates, but its population had doubled that by the time the initial suits were brought. Significantly for mental health professionals, a key component of the decision was the finding that the state of mental health care for inmates had deteriorated because of overcrowding conditions.

Mental health care is a major issue, not only in the nation's prisons, but also in its jails. Jails serve primarily as both (a) temporary detention facilities for those awaiting trial or a resolution of their cases and (b) facilities for convicted offenders serving short sentences, typically under a year. Although some offenders are in jail for other purposes (e.g., awaiting transfer to a prison or awaiting extradition to another state), the majority are there as detainees or short-term inmates convicted of misdemeanor crimes. Jail conditions are often unstable, overcrowded, and understaffed. In early 2014, a homeless veteran, charged with trespassing, died while in custody in New York's Rikers Island, one of the nation's largest jails, where the average daily population is 12,000. His cell had heated to 100 degrees because of a faulty heating system. The incident resulted in the demotion of the superintendent and the appointment of a new one, but the new one resigned in 2017 after only 3 years on the job. Although some positive changes had occurred during his tenure, an administrative scandal involving the use of official cars for private business and deteriorating conditions and violence contributed to his departure.

In another incident, in a different jail, a detainee was not provided with needed medication for her heart condition and died as a result. Such anecdotes, not always widely reported, are not unusual within the nation's jails. We will visit the issue of jail violence and mental health later in the chapter.

In March 2014, the Federal Bureau of Prisons (BOP) was responsible for the custody and care of over 215,566 prisoners; by the end of 2015, this number had decreased to 195,700 (Kaible & Glaze, 2016). Most of the federal inmates are serving time for crimes involving weapons, illegal drugs, or bank robbery (Tyner, 2013). A smaller number serve sentences for "white collar" crimes such as embezzlement, bank and credit card fraud, and securities violations.

The majority of all offenders (approximately two thirds) in both federal and state systems are under community supervision, which includes probation, parole, and their many variants. House arrest, electronic monitoring, halfway houses for newly released offenders, day reporting, and intensive supervision are examples of sanctions included under the term **community corrections**. Probationers traditionally represent the majority of offenders under community supervision (Kaeble & Glaze, 2016; Glaze & Herberman, 2013), because they are predominantly nonviolent offenders. Community supervision consists primarily of probation and parole, with or without intermediate measures such as intensive supervision programs and halfway houses. **Probation** is a court-ordered period of correctional supervision in the community, usually as an alternative to incarceration, but it could also occur after a short stay in jail. **Parole** is a period of conditional supervised release in the community following a prison term, and it represents approximately 18% of offenders under community supervision.

A separate group of individuals are persons detained under immigration laws. In 2015, the Department of Homeland Security (which includes the U.S. Border Patrol and Immigration and Customs Enforcement [ICE]) apprehended 460,000 individuals, the fewest since 420,000 were apprehended in 1971 (Baker & Williams, 2017). Moreover, the apprehension rate declined more than 30% from 2014 to 2015, primarily driven by the continuing decline in the apprehension of Mexican nationals on the southwest border. This decline further represents a continuing trend since the peak in apprehension reported in 2011. Despite these drops in illegal immigration, ICE maintains the largest immigration detention system in the world, operating centers throughout the United States that house immigrants who are apprehended and placed in removal proceedings. On average, 32,000 immigrants are detained on any given day (Baker & Williams, 2017). Approximately 95% are Mexican nationals and immigrants from the North Triangle (Honduras, Guatemala, and El Salvador). (Recall that services to immigrants in removal proceedings was discussed in Chapter 5.)

Of special note, as this book is going to press, is the possible rise of private prisons. Although the prison population has declined in recent years, there is also fear of a law-and-order punitive mentality that does not bode well for continuing decreases. We cannot predict what data will emerge from future population studies, but one thing is clear: the federal government and many states are showing interest in turning to the private sector to manage inmates. These for-profit facilities developed rapidly in the 1980s and 1990s, then began to lose favor as researchers questioned their effectiveness. Today, there appears to be interest in giving private prisons a second look. (See Focus 12.1 for more discussion on private prisons.)

In this chapter, we will focus on the services offered by forensic psychologists to the wide variety of individuals under correctional supervision, particularly in prisons and jails. As we noted in Chapter 1, correctional psychologists sometimes prefer to use that title rather than calling themselves "forensic psychologists." Some have also expressed concern that the broad field of forensic psychology has not given sufficient attention to the type of graduate training that is of benefit to those who want to pursue careers in corrections (Magaletta et al., 2013). Recognizing the great need for services of qualified mental health professionals in the correctional system, correctional psychologists advocate practicums and internships early in a graduate student's career (Magaletta, Patry, Cermak, & McLearen, 2017).

In the United States, correctional psychology is a vibrant and growing field. In Canada, a long and rich tradition of correctional psychology has had an enormous impact on the field, particularly in the United States and Europe (see Wormith & Luong, 2007, for a comprehensive review). Correctional treatment research by Canadian correctional psychologists (e.g., Andrews & Bonta, 1994; Hanson, Bourgon, Helmus, & Hodgson, 2009; Hanson & Harris, 2000) has been instrumental in the development of correctional psychology as a viable profession.

The chapter begins by providing an overview of key concepts and the legal rights of inmates that are pertinent to psychological concepts. We then examine the assessment and treatment roles of correctional psychologists as well as aspects of the prison and jail environments that present obstacles to effective treatment. By far the greatest research attention is paid to the work of psychologists who consult with or work in institutional settings, yet correctional and forensic psychologists as a group are more likely to come into contact with persons under community supervision than inmates within correctional facilities. During the latter part of the chapter, therefore, we will focus on community corrections and the contributions of forensic psychologists in that realm.

INSTITUTIONAL CORRECTIONS

The United States has the highest incarceration rate of any industrialized country, with the numbers of inmates behind bars having increased steadily over the past quarter century and only beginning to decrease in recent years. Incarceration rate refers to the number of individuals who are incarcerated, per 100,000 population. About 1 in every 108 adults in the United States was incarcerated in prison or jail in 2012 (Glaze & Herberman, 2013). By the end of the 20th century, every state was facing overcrowding in at least one, and typically more, of its correctional facilities. In recent years, however, this overcrowding has eased somewhat as more states have taken steps to move offenders out of institutional settings or divert them to community programs, as noted at the beginning of the chapter.

The crimes for which offenders are incarcerated are not only those considered the most heinous. As of 2011, in state prisons, 53.5% of all offenders were serving time for violent offenses, 16.6% for drug offenses, 10.6% for public order offenses, and 18.6% for property offenses such as burglary or larceny (Carson & Golinelli, 2013). As might be expected, robbery, murder, rape/sexual assault, and aggravated assault accounted for the great majority of violent crimes sentenced offenders in state prisons had committed. Interestingly, the violent crimes were fairly evenly distributed, ranging from 10.3% (assault) to 13.7% (robbery). Although robbery is a serious crime and its effect on the victim should not be discounted, it does not necessarily include the *use* of force. The taking of property through *threat* of force—such as a weapon shown to the victim—is sufficient to classify a crime as a robbery.

Women are less likely than men to be incarcerated for violent offenses. Yet, between 1991 and 2011, the number of women committed to state prisons for violent crimes increased 83% (compared with an increase of 30% for men) (Carson & Golinelli, 2013), though to our knowledge, no one is predicting that women will ever "catch up" to men. At year-end 2014, there were 201,200 women incarcerated in state and federal facilities and 1,978,700 men (Kaeble & Glaze, 2016).

Despite the high incarceration numbers, imprisonment does not seem to deter or rehabilitate a substantial number of offenders. Research on recidivism—typically measured by new arrests, new convictions, or sometimes by self-report data—is not encouraging. An oft-cited, but somewhat dated, government survey of persons released from prison in 15 states found that, over a 3-year period, a very high number were rearrested, particularly those who had been imprisoned for property offenses (Langan & Levin, 2002). Of the 272,000 persons released from prison, 68% were rearrested for a felony or serious misdemeanor, 47% were reconvicted, and 25% were resentenced to prison for a new crime. Although these data suggest that neither the imprisonment itself nor programs offered to inmates had a positive effect on those who reoffended, recidivism data must be interpreted very cautiously.

An arrest does not necessarily mean that an individual has indeed committed another offense. Even if he or she has, however, it does not mean that the offender has not benefited in other ways from the rehabilitation and mental health programs offered in a correctional setting. As will be noted later in the chapter, various programs and psychological treatment within the correctional system should not be judged solely on whether or not the individual reoffends (Rosenfeld, Howe, Pierson, & Foellmi, 2015).

FOCUS 12.1. CORPORATIZING PUNISHMENT

Shortly before leaving office, in August 2016, President Barack Obama urged the Federal Bureau of Prisons to begin phasing out its use of private prisons for federal offenders. In February 2017, Attorney General Jeff Sessions announced an opposite stance: Under the new administration, private prisons would be encouraged. This, he argued, would give the Bureau of Prisons the flexibility to manage federal inmates. The announcement was encouraging news to states that sought more development of for-profit prisons as well. Stocks in the two largest private prison corporations—CoreCivic (formerly the Corrections Corporation of America) and Geo Group rose 100% after the presidential election of 2016.

Private, for-profit incarceration facilities have a long history in corrections, but they were used primarily for juveniles, and presumably with an emphasis on rehabilitation. In the modern era, they began to re-emerge in the 1980s and developed rapidly between 1990 and 2009. Between 1990 and 2009, the number of prisoners in private prisons increased by over 1600%. (Shapiro, 2011). Private prisons now hold approximately 6% of state prisoners and 16% of federal prisoners. In 2016, ICE reported that private prisons held nearly three quarters of federal immigration detainees. In addition, many juvenile facilities remain privately operated. However, with the renewed focus on law and order and emphasis on incarceration, a prison boom in the near future would not be unanticipated.

The yearly cost of maintaining one inmate in a government-operated prison is often greater than one year's college tuition. Proponents of private prisons indicate they are cost effective, reduce recidivism, and produce jobs. However, a significant amount of research indicates that cost savings are minimal, that private prisons do not reduce recidivism any more than public prisons, and that they have an overall negative impact on all services (Bales, Bedard, Quinn, Ensley, & Holley, 2005; Mason, 2012; Shapiro, 2011). Anecdotal accounts of conditions in many private prisons indicate additional problems, such as poor staff training, poor quality medical care, and high levels of violence. A 2012 U.S. Supreme Court decision (*Minneci v. Pollard*) also limited the options for inmates held in private prisons to sue these entities for constitutional violations.

Prisoner advocacy groups now fear that privatization of prisons and juvenile facilities will lead to continuing cuts in services, including mental health services, because these institutions are seeking profit. In addition, because there will be beds to fill, there will be great incentive for imprisoning more individuals rather than reduce the overall prison population.

Questions for Discussion

1. Obtain more information about CoreCivic or the GEO Group and discuss what you have learned.
2. Does the government (federal or state) have an obligation to "manage" offenders directly, or is it acceptable to contract out this management to the private sector?
3. What might be advantages and disadvantages for the correctional psychologist working in public versus private facilities?

Nevertheless, recidivism statistics such as those reported above lead some observers to question whether incarceration is the best route to take in dealing with the problem of crime, and others to question whether rehabilitation is a realistic goal. Furthermore, many legal scholars and researchers in the social sciences are concerned about the disproportionate confinement of the poor and racial or ethnic minorities. The conditions within many prisons, including overcrowding and violence within the facility, give further cause for concern. In recent years, for example, the disturbing topic of prison rape has received increasingly more research attention (Neal & Clements, 2010; Stemple & Meyer, 2014). Although few scholars advocate the total abolition of jails and prisons, many are calling for alternatives to incarceration, especially for nonviolent offenders.

Forensic psychologists working within or in consultation with institutional corrections, then, must find ways to do their work within a system that is placed in the position of justifying its operations, and many perform this work admirably (Gendreau & Goggin, 2014; R. D. Morgan, Kroner, Mills, & Batastini, 2014). (See Perspective 12.1, in which Dr. Kroner discusses

From Prison Psychologist to Academe and Back—and Back Again

Daryl G. Kroner, PhD

I began my correctional psychology career in 1986. I had completed my MA in clinical psychology at North Carolina State University and accepted a psychologist position at Grande Cache Correctional Centre at the base of the Rocky Mountains. This place was stunningly beautiful, which fed into my backpacking, fishing, and photography hobbies.

I was excited about applying the clinical skills that I had learned and looked forward to gaining new knowledge through doing research. The first time entering the main gates, who I met, and how the first morning went is all something I remember with much detail. The prison was recently built and the furniture inside was new. Within a few months, I was amazed at the cultural diversity and the range of mental health symptoms that were present with the offenders. In addition to trying to understand this population's clinical needs, I began collecting self-report, staff ratings, and institutional outcome data.

This research endeavor met with practical realities. Yes, there was the need to get system approvals, there were those who chose not to participate, there were incomplete forms, and I had to convince some that it was a good idea to do research.

But I learned a valuable lesson as the result of an incident involving an offender in disciplinary segregation. When I first saw him, he was psychologically incapacitated, curled up in a fetal position. Retrospectively, after more familiarity with DSM, I realized that this offender was experiencing a brief reactive psychosis. At the time, though, I strongly recommended that he be removed from disciplinary segregation because of his very low level of mental health functioning. He was placed in an alternate housing unit at the institution, one that was more open and where there was more interaction with others. Within days he began exhibiting the very aggressive behavior that initially had him placed in segregation. This offender was subsequently sent to another institution. Removing this offender from disciplinary segregation was the right decision, but the staff had perceived that I had inappropriately let him out of segregation. Because of this, the research project received almost no cooperation and was placed on hold for a number of months. Eventually this project was completed, but with a much longer timeframe. The strength of interconnectedness in institutional life was a lesson that has stuck with me.

Another practical lesson has to do with the nature of offender data. During the 1980s, it was common to use psychological measures that were not developed on offender samples. The conducting of basic psychometric research with offenders found different scale means, factor structures (often simpler), poorer construct and predictive validities. Repeatedly being humbled by offender data led to a more cautious clinical interpretation of testing results. So, instead of relying on non-offender norms, a goal became to gather offender norms with previously standardized scales.

During the late 1990s, I completed my PhD at Carleton University. It was great to be there with the likes of Don Andrews, Adelle Forth, Bob Hoge, and Jim Bonta. After 22 years as a prison psychologist, I accepted an academic position at Southern Illinois University. One benefit of working in an academic setting is being able to finish projects that had their seeds in clinical practice. Whether looking at risk assessment or treatment change, it is satisfying to be able to bring projects to a close. This is something we can't always do in prison settings because of the daily clinical demands. A second benefit is the interaction with students. Students bring a different perspective on issues with considerable energy. For example, the importance of sub-threshold diagnoses would not have been highlighted if not for an inquisitive student.

My daily routine involves getting into the office just after 6:00 a.m., keeping my door shut until 10:00 a.m. (reading and research time), walking to the gym over the lunch hour, and then leaving the office around 5:00 p.m. Now, instead of seeing offenders, my days involve meetings with students, teaching classes, and doing research. Maybe students "catch" some of the gratifying experiences that I have had working with offenders.

Dr. Kroner is a professor in the Department of Criminology and Criminal Justice at Southern Illinois University. Prior to this position, he was employed as a correctional psychologist for over 20 years. During this time, he worked at maximum, medium, and minimum facilities delivering intervention services to offenders. His current research interests include risk assessment, measurement of intervention outcomes, interventions among offenders with mental illness, and criminal desistance.

his career as a correctional psychologist in prison settings and academe.) The public wants its prisons but is resentful of the fiscal costs. Moreover, although public opinion surveys suggest continuing support for rehabilitation, individuals working in corrections have learned that rehabilitation-oriented programs are among the first to go when budgets need to be cut, especially in state-run prisons. Even with scaled-down programming, it is not unusual for the corrections budget to consume a greater share of state coffers than the education budget.

The psychologist in a correctional setting also must work in an environment that often diminishes the likelihood of therapeutic success. Inmates get transferred to other prisons, correctional officers may not support the psychologist's role, administrators may cut their budgets, there is little time to conduct research, and the limitations on confidentiality suggest to prisoners that psychologists are representatives of the prison administration rather than advocates for their own interests. We will cover these and other issues later in the chapter.

For the time being, it is important to note that many professional groups have established a variety of guidelines and standards for providing services in correctional facilities. These include the "Standards for Health Services in Prisons," published by the National Commission on Correctional Health Care (NCCHC, 2008), as well as the recently updated standards developed by the International Association for Correctional and Forensic Psychology (IACFP) (Althouse, 2010). The IACFP has published 66 standards intended to offer direction and support to practitioners. Focus 12.2 contains a list of topics covered in the standards. In addition, psychologists working in corrections are expected to conform to the ethical code of the American Psychological Association. The "Specialty Guidelines for Forensic Psychology" (American Psychological Association [APA], 2013c) also are relevant to the work of psychologists working within the correctional field. Finally, psychologists must be aware of all state and federal laws and regulations that pertain to the care and custody of jail and prison inmates.

OVERVIEW OF CORRECTIONAL FACILITIES

Persons detained, accused, or convicted, when not allowed to remain in their own homes, are housed in several types of facilities: detention centers, jails, prisons, and community-based facilities. The term *detention center* is applicable primarily to the federal facilities that hold people on a temporary basis while their status is being reviewed (e.g., immigration status), but jails—which are operated by local governments, are also used to detain. As noted earlier in the chapter, **jails** are distinct from prisons, because they primarily hold persons for short time periods. People in jail are temporarily detained, held for lack of bail while awaiting trial or other court proceedings, or sentenced to confinement after having been convicted of a misdemeanor. (See Photo 12.1.) **Prisons** are facilities operated by the federal government and all states for persons convicted of felonies, and typically sentenced to terms of more than 1 year. **Community-based facilities** are less secure institutions, such as halfway houses or transition homes, typically intended as **intermediate sanctions** for offenders deemed to need less security than would be provided in jails or prisons but more than would be available in their own homes. Community-based facilities will be discussed later in the chapter.

On any given day, approximately half of the individuals held in jails are innocent; they are detainees, not convicted of the crime of which they are accused. Ultimately, some may be found guilty, but until then, they are considered innocent. Approximately another half are serving short-term sentences for misdemeanor offenses. The proportion of detainees and sentenced misdemeanants varies widely by jurisdiction, however. In some facilities, up to 70% of the population comprises **pretrial detainees** who were unable to afford bail or who were denied bail because they were considered dangerous. Jails also may house a vast array of individuals awaiting transfer to prison, to a mental institution, to another state, to a juvenile facility, or to a military detention facility, though such individuals awaiting transfer usually make up a small portion (rarely more than 5%) of the jail population. In effect, though, jails hold a collection of persons at various stages of criminal, civil, or military justice processing. In some communities,

FOCUS 12.2. IACFP STANDARDS

The International Association for Correctional and Forensic Psychology (IACFP), formerly the American Association for Correctional Psychology, has developed a set of standards that provide the minimum acceptable levels for psychological services offered to offenders held in local, state, or federal facilities, as well as in the community (Althouse, 2010; Standards Committee, 2000). Below are examples of topics and subtopics covered in the standards. Interested readers are advised to read the standards (see Althouse, 2010), which include a discussion section explaining the rationale behind each one.

- Roles and services: Appropriate roles include but are not limited to consultation to correctional administration for mental health program design; psychological screening of security staff employed in specialized mental health units; classification for mental health program assignments; training of staff; assessment, diagnosis, and treatment of mental illness; crisis intervention; and advocacy for and evaluation of mental health programs and services.
- Staffing requirements: At least one person responsible for psychological services in the facility has a doctoral degree that is primarily psychological in nature, is licensed/certified, and has training/experience in correctional psychology.
- Documentation: All services and mental health information will be documented or maintained in a file specific to the offender in compliance with current professional and legal standards and guidelines.
- Limits of confidentiality: Inmates will be informed both verbally and in writing of the limits of confidentiality as well as legally and administratively mandated duties to warn.

- Informed consent: All screenings, assessments, treatments, and procedures shall be preceded by an informed-consent procedure.
- Employer and ethical/practice standards conflicts: There is a documented policy for the resolution of conflicts between the facility and the psychological services staff.
- Screening/evaluation: All screening is performed only by psychological staff or facility staff trained by them. At no time are psychological data made available to inmate workers (this includes filing).
- Inmate treatment: Diagnostic and treatment services are provided to inmates of the facility; those needing emergency evaluation and/or treatment are housed in a specially designated area with close supervision by staff or trained volunteers and with sufficient security.
- In-service training: Written procedures provide for the training of facility and community staff (e.g., in recognizing psychological emergency situations and in procedures for making referrals to psychological services).
- Research: Psychological services staff are encouraged to conduct applied and/or basic research to improve the delivery of psychological services.

Questions for Discussion

1. The above represent standards, but with some exceptions they are not legal requirements. After reviewing the section on legal rights of inmates later in the chapter, discuss which of the above are likely required under law.
2. Choose any one standard and discuss how it might be implemented in a maximum-security facility.

jails also serve as temporary overnight shelters for individuals whom police arrest on minor charges, believing they need a safe haven.

As noted above, in the federal system, pretrial detainees are held in detention centers. When space in federal detention centers is not available, persons accused of federal crimes or awaiting sentencing are detained in state or local jails. Federal detention centers have been heavily publicized since the terrorist attacks of September 11, 2001, because the government held individuals for questioning about possible terrorist involvement. "Makeshift" detention centers were opened, and numerous individuals were turned over to Immigration and Naturalization Services (INS)—now Immigration and Customs Enforcement (ICE)—and deported after secret deportation proceedings before immigration judges. In 2016, ICE reported that nearly three quarters of federal immigration detainees were held in private facilities.

Prisons, operated by states or by the federal government, hold only persons convicted of felonies. They are classified by the level of security maintained over the inmates: minimum, medium, and maximum, with gradients sometimes in between these three main alternatives. Different custody levels are also found within as well as among prisons. Thus, an inmate may be kept in close custody in a medium-security prison for disciplinary reasons, and an inmate in a maximum-security prison may have attained "trustee" status, requiring minimal custody.

In the 1990s, **supermax prisons** were introduced in the federal government and approximately 41 states. These are extremely high-security facilities (or units within a maximum-security prison) supposedly intended to hold the most troublesome, violent inmates. As we will see later in the chapter, however, numerous concerns have been raised about these facilities and about solitary confinement in general. Prison systems also may include specialized facilities, such as work camps, hospitals, classification centers, and units for inmates with mental disorders. Boot camps, prison farms, forestry centers, and ranches for young offenders who have committed primarily nonviolent crimes are other examples of specialized facilities.

In some states, jails are under the control of the state rather than local government, and jail/prison functions are combined. Thus, detainees and sentenced offenders—both misdemeanants and felons—may be kept within the same facility, though they may be placed in separate housing units. A typical approach in these "mixed systems" is to have one or two facilities designated as maximum security, with the balance being medium- or minimum-security facilities capable of housing persons accused of crime as well as those who have been convicted and sentenced.

▸ **Photo 12.1** A woman under arrest, awaiting cell assignment in a local jail.
Source: © Stockbyte/Thinkstock.

The federal prison system is highly organized and centralized under the **Federal Bureau of Prisons (BOP)**. It consists of a network of facilities that are called penitentiaries, correctional institutions, prison camps, and halfway houses, as well as the detention centers referred to above. They are located on a continuum of five security levels: minimum, low, medium, high, and administrative. The nation's one federal supermax facility, located in Florence, Colorado, is classified at the administrative level. The facility houses approximately 900 male inmates. (See Focus 12.3 on career opportunities for psychologists in the BOP.) In addition to the features summarized above, jails and prisons can be contrasted on an important point that affects the work of psychologists. Prisons are far more likely than jails to offer programs, including recreation, work programs, substance abuse treatment, and a variety of rehabilitative programs. This can be attributed to several factors. First, because a jail stay is relatively short, inmates are less likely to benefit from meaningful programming. Second, most jails are operated by local governments and do not have funds available for much beyond their custodial function. Third, most jails are operated by law enforcement professionals, such as county sheriffs, rather than corrections professionals. The law enforcement community is not trained to provide services to offenders or alleged offenders; it is trained to enforce the law, protect the public, and provide service to the community. Programming for detainees and inmates is not considered a priority. Nevertheless, there are exceptions, and programming can be found in many jails nationwide. Short-term programs, such as those addressing substance abuse, domestic violence, and prevention of disease, are examples. Furthermore, a professional organization—the American Jail Association—publishes standards for operating jails that include training staff and offering a variety of services to detainees and inmates.

Although psychologists are less likely to be involved in treatment programs in jails than in prisons, their *assessment* and *crisis intervention* services are often in demand in these short-term

FOCUS 12.3. CAREER OPPORTUNITIES IN THE FEDERAL BUREAU OF PRISONS

Employment opportunities in the U.S. Federal Bureau of Prisons (BOP) are expected to increase, and there is a constant need for mental health professionals. BOP states that they have a continuing need for doctoral-level clinical psychologists in facilities around the country (Magaletta et al., 2013). Similar career opportunities exist in the Canadian correctional system, which offers multiple opportunities for practicum sites (Olver, Preston, Camilleri, Helmus & Starzomski, 2011). About 60% of the doctoral psychologists in the BOP have completed internships in federal prisons. Some are also board certified in forensic psychology.

The roles of these psychologists vary depending on the overall mission of the facility (McKenzie, 2013). The Bureau is a national leader in offering quality pre-doctoral internship training for students interested in becoming a professional or correctional psychologist. The internships are fully accredited by the American Psychological Association, which is an important stamp of approval for the extensive and meaningful training provided. Interns receive a stipend of approximately $49,000, annual (vacation) leave and sick leave, and liability coverage for professional activities performed. Interns receive graduated exposure to the clinical role, practicing with greater independence as their skills and confidence improve (Tyner, 2013). A number of clinical and educational seminars are continually available to increase the intern's general fund of clinical knowledge.

Staff psychologists in the BOP are autonomous. They are the main providers of mental health services and—in contrast to psychologists in some state prison systems and mental hospitals—are not under the supervision of psychiatrists. Broadly, psychologists provide crisis intervention to acutely suicidal and psychotic individuals, as well as long-term psychotherapy to those individuals seeking to resolve emotional and behavioral problems. They also provide assessments on a regular basis. Staff psychologists have the opportunity to be involved in the following:

- Forensic evaluations for the federal courts
- Psychological evaluations of candidates for the witness protection program
- Assessments of sex offenders for possible civil commitment proceedings
- Hostage negotiation training
- Drug abuse treatment programs
- Suicide prevention programs
- Crisis intervention response teams for trauma victims
- Predoctoral internship training programs
- Employee assistance programs
- Inpatient mental health programs
- Staff training
- Research

Source: U.S. Bureau of Prisons (http://www.bop.gov).

settings. Some pretrial detainees, for example, need to be assessed for their competency to stand trial and the variety of other competencies that were discussed in Chapter 5. Whether or not competencies are in question, pretrial detainees are often confused; frightened; and worried about their social, legal, and financial status. In a confusing, noisy, often crowded environment, detainees may experience "entry shock." This is particularly—but not exclusively—a problem for persons being held in jail for the first time. Suicide is the leading cause of death in jails (Clear & Cole, 2000). Research also documents that suicide rates are higher in jail than in prison; some estimates indicate they are at least 5 times higher (F. Cohen, 2008; Steadman, McCarty, & Morrissey, 1989). Although screening for suicide risk is typically done by non-psychological staff upon a detainee's or inmate's entry into the facility, mental health professionals are needed to do a more comprehensive assessment and to offer treatment to individuals who are at risk of taking their own lives. Despite this, jails are much less likely than prisons to have well-developed mental health services available to inmates (Steadman & Veysey, 1997). It is for this reason that many communities have now begun to experiment with the mental health courts that were discussed in Chapter 4.

Correctional facilities—both jails and prisons—can be violent, noisy, disorganized, demeaning places that promote isolation, helplessness, and subservience through the use of overwhelming power, often by instilling fear. Although this is particularly true of large, urban jails and maximum-security prisons, there are clearly exceptions. In comparison to state-run correctional institutions, facilities run by the BOP tend to be less violent, noisy, chaotic, and disorganized. Overall, though, many correctional professionals maintain that both jails and prisons can be operated in a humane fashion and can achieve society's dual hope of protecting the public from crime and rehabilitating offenders.

LEGAL RIGHTS OF INMATES

It is a well-established principle in law that prisoners do not lose their constitutional rights at the prison gate. In a great number of U.S. Supreme Court decisions, especially during the 1960s and 1970s, the Court specified minimum rights that were guaranteed to inmates under the Constitution. The cases decided by the Court involved procedures, practices, and conditions of confinement in jails and prisons. In addition to federal constitutional protections, inmates also may have rights that are guaranteed under their state constitutions or under both federal and state statutes, or state courts (e.g., rights pertaining to visitations or educational benefits). In this section, we will summarize the key doctrines that are most relevant to psychologists consulting with correctional systems or offering direct services to inmates. This will, of necessity, omit legal protections that are important to inmates but are at most peripheral to the professional concerns of psychologists. For example, inmates have a constitutional right to receive mail (although it may be censored) and to observe religious practices (including dietary practices), unless those practices interfere with institutional security or create excessive economic burdens. Readers are referred to the excellent treatises by Fred Cohen (1998, 2000, 2003, 2008) and J. W. Palmer and Palmer (1999) for comprehensive coverage of correctional law that encompasses many areas not to be discussed here. (Table 12.2 lists key U.S. Supreme Court cases dealing with prisoner rights cited in this chapter.)

The principles to be discussed below clearly apply to cases involving prisoners, but they also apply to those serving jail sentences. For this reason, we will use the term *inmate* throughout this section as a more generic term to cover both groups. The rights of pretrial *detainees*, however, are somewhat different because these individuals have not been convicted of a crime. Nevertheless, in the name of institutional security, detainees can be subjected to many of the same conditions as sentenced misdemeanants, as will be noted shortly. A question still unanswered, though, is the extent to which all of these rights apply to inmates being held in private prisons. In two Supreme Court cases involving federal prisoners held in private prisons (*Correctional Services Corporation v. Malesko*, 2001; *Minneci v. Pollard*, 2012), the Court denied the inmate the right to sue officials of the private prisons for violation of constitutional rights, maintaining that there were adequate state tort remedies. The most recent case, Minneci, involved an inmate's claim that he was denied adequate medical treatment in violation of the Eighth Amendment prohibition against cruel and unusual punishment. (As is noted below, the right to treatment is a basic constitutional guarantee.) Dissenting in the case, Justice Ruth Bader Ginsburg noted that, if Pollard has been held in a federal or state public prison, he would not have been denied the opportunity to sue prison officials.

Right to Treatment

A right closely aligned with the interests of psychologists is the constitutional right of the inmate to receive adequate medical treatment. The case that established this right is *Estelle v. Gamble* (1976), in which an inmate argued that his Eighth Amendment protection against cruel and unusual punishment had been violated by the failure of prison officials to attend to his medical needs.

Table 12.2	Representative U.S. Supreme Court Cases Relevant to Inmates Cited in Chapter
Case	**Significance**
Estelle v. Gamble (1976)	Right to treatment, including mental health
Bell v. Wolfish (1979)	Limits on rights of pretrial detainees
Vitek v. Jones (1980)	Right to hearing before transfer to mental health facility
Hudson v. Palmer (1984)	Limits on privacy within one's cell
Ford v. Wainwright (1986)	Disallows execution of the severely mentally ill
Panetti v. Quarterman (2007)	Mentally ill inmates must appreciate why they are being put to death. Awareness is not enough.
Washington v. Harper (1990)	Psychoactive medication may be administered against will; administrative hearing sufficient
McKune v. Lile (2002)	Loss of privileges for refusal to participate in treatment program
Brown v. Plata (2011)	California ordered to reduce crowded prison population
Atkins v. Virginia (2002)	Disallows execution of intellectually disabled
Hall v. Florida (2014)	States may set their own criteria for intellectual disability
Moore v. Texas (2017)	State criteria for intellectual disability subject to review
Correctional Services Corp. v. Malesko (2001)	Limits on rights to sue private prisons
Minneci v. Pollard (2013)	Right to sue private prisons again restricted

Gamble, a Texas inmate, was on a prison work assignment when a bale of cotton that he was loading on a truck fell on him. There followed 3 months of repetitive visits to prison medical staff, during which he was provided with muscle relaxants and other medications. By the end of this time period, he had received numerous different medications, blood tests, and blood pressure measurements, along with cell passes permitting him to stay in his cell. At one point, a prescription was not filled for 4 days because the staff had lost it. Eventually, he refused to work, saying that his pain was not dissipating, and he was brought before a prison disciplinary committee and then placed in solitary confinement as punishment. While in solitary, he asked to see a doctor for chest pains; a medical assistant saw him 12 hours later and hospitalized him.

Although *Estelle v. Gamble* (1976) involved treatment for a variety of physical ailments, it has widely been interpreted to include psychological or psychiatric assistance for serious mental disorders (F. Cohen, 2008). To deprive the inmate of adequate medical care violates the Eighth Amendment ban on cruel and unusual punishment. The question naturally arises, "What is 'adequate' medical treatment?" Inmates clearly do not have a right to "state-of-the art" treatment or therapy. In fact, in the *Gamble* case, even failure to obtain an X-ray of an inmate's lower back was not considered inadequate treatment. Although the Supreme Court in that case made it clear that inmates had a **right to treatment**, it did not second-guess the judgment of medical professionals who chose not to order the X-ray.

Estelle v. Gamble (1976) is an important case because it not only clearly stated that inmates have a constitutional right to medical treatment, but also set the standard for deciding whether the Constitution had been violated. Inmates alleging such a violation would have to prove that prison officials were "deliberately indifferent" to their serious medical needs. Simple "negligence" would not be enough to amount to a constitutional violation (although negligence would be sufficient under some *state* laws). In a later case, *Farmer v. Brennan* (1994), the Court said that a prison official would not be liable unless that official both knew of and disregarded an excessive risk to an inmate's health and safety. The Court added that if an official *should have known* of a substantial risk but did not, the official's failure to alleviate the risk did *not* constitute cruel and unusual punishment.

Applied in the context of psychological treatment, it is clear that inmates should be offered treatment at least for their serious mental disorders, including psychoses, clinical depression, and schizophrenia. The IACFP (Althouse, 2010) Standards do not distinguish between serious and milder disorders, suggesting that mental health treatment should be available for *all* mental disturbances. Moreover, the Standards indicate that it is generally inappropriate for inmates needing acute, chronic, or convalescent mental health care to be treated in jails and prisons. Rather, they should be transferred to facilities that are set up specifically for these purposes. This is the ideal, however, and rarely occurs in reality.

The Extent of Inmates With Mental Disorders

In reality, both jails and prisons hold substantial numbers of individuals with severe mental disorders. In fact, despite some reductions in the correctional population in recent years, there is little indication that the percentage of inmates with serious mental disorders is declining. The lack of adequate mental health care in jails and prisons across the United States is widely acknowledged by commentators and courts alike (F. Cohen, 2008; Heilbrun & Griffin, 1999; R. D. Morgan, Gendreau et al., 2016). Recall that in the recent U.S. Supreme Court case, *Brown v. Plata* (2011), the Court agreed with lower courts that the state of mental health care in California prisons had deteriorated to the point that Eighth Amendment rights of prisoners were violated.

A great number of individuals with mental disorders continue to languish in jails and prisons without adequate psychological intervention (see Photo 12.2). It has been estimated that at least 10% to 15% of men in jails and state prisons have severe mental disorders and are in need of treatment (Ax et al., 2007; H. R. Lamb, Weinberger, & Gross, 2004; Steadman, Osher, Robbins, Case, & Samuels, 2009). Preliminary data from the Mental Health Prevalence Project (MHPP; Magaletta, Dietz, & Diamond, 2005) suggest that the rates of psychiatric disorder among *federal inmates* may not be that different:

> [O]ur overall estimates suggest that the populations may actually be more similar than previously thought. Although the two jurisdictions (i.e., federal and state) do house correctional populations that are dissimilar along certain demographic and criminological dimensions, mental health might not be one of them. (Magaletta, Diamond, Faust, Daggett, & Camp, 2009, p. 241)

Studies also indicate that the need among female inmates is even greater than among males (Magaletta et al., 2009), an estimate that is somewhat confounded by the fact that women, compared with men, may be more likely to self-disclose their need for mental health services. Some studies reveal that two thirds of women inmates in a state correctional institution report symptoms of psychological and mental disorders (Faust & Magaletta, 2010; Reichert, Adams, & Bostwick, 2010). In a survey of women inmates, James and Glaze (2006) reported that 77% of women in the federal correctional system and 70% in the state

▶ **Photo 12.2** A mentally ill man is silhouetted as he peers out from the small opening of his cell door.
Source: © AP Photo/Troy Maben.

correctional systems used mental health services while incarcerated. In addition, 60% of male inmates reported receiving these services while incarcerated. Faust and Magaletta (2010) found that female inmates who had a history of mental health treatment (inpatient and outpatient), suicide attempts, and drug abuse before incarceration used psychological services at a greater level than those who did not show these pre-incarceration characteristics. Faust and Magaletta concluded that these results suggest "those familiar with accessing mental health services in the community are more comfortable with and able to request them once incarcerated" (p. 6).

The segregation of inmates with mental disorders raises many legal questions. Courts have allowed severely disturbed inmates to be placed in stripped-down observation cells—sometimes referred to as "safe cells"—for their own protection. They may be kept under extremely stark conditions while awaiting transfer to a treatment facility or until they can be stabilized with appropriate medication, but there are legal limitations on this type of confinement. A suit against the New York Department of Corrections (*Perri v. Coughlin*, 1999) is illustrative. Perri was an extremely disruptive, severely disordered inmate in the New York State prison system. He was held in an observation cell on three separate occasions, for a total of 108 days. The cell contained only a sink and toilet, and a brightly glaring light was on 24 hours a day. He had no clothes or blankets and had to sleep naked on the floor. The observation unit provided no opportunity for exercise, recreation, or group therapy. The lengthy confinement, coupled with failure to provide treatment, led to the court's decision to hold the New York State Department of Corrections liable for damages (F. Cohen, 2000). The adequacy of medical services, including both physical and mental health, is a frequent point of litigation in class action suits brought by incarcerated individuals. (A *class action suit* is one brought on behalf of a group of people who have all allegedly been harmed by the actions of a defendant.)

Right to Refuse Treatment

Although inmates have a right to treatment, they cannot be forced to participate in treatment programs. This applies to both physical and psychological treatment. However, if the state has a very strong interest in seeing the inmate's behavior changed, some leeway exists. In the Supreme Court case, *McKune v. Lile* (2002), the Court allowed prison officials to effectively punish an inmate for refusing to participate in a program, although the state argued—and the Court agreed—that it was not acting punitively.

Lile was a convicted rapist within 2 years of completing his sentence and being released. The state of Kansas had a strong interest in enrolling him in a sex offender treatment program that required him to disclose his history of offending, but it did not guarantee that the information would be confidential. This requirement that offenders take responsibility for their actions is common in treatment programs and is not limited to sex offenders. Lile—apparently concerned that disclosing information could lead to future prosecution for crimes he had not previously been accused of—refused to participate. Prison officials told him that his refusal could lead to his being transferred to a more secure and restrictive level, where he would lose such privileges as canteen access and more appealing work assignments. Lile then argued that he was essentially being forced to incriminate himself, a violation of the Fifth Amendment, and a federal court of appeals had agreed. However, in a close decision (5–4), a majority of Justices on the U.S. Supreme Court did not agree. Thus, although inmates still may not be forced to participate in a treatment program, they can be persuaded to do so with threatened loss of privileges, provided that the state's interest in rehabilitation is high, as it was in this case.

In a similar fashion, inmates have a right to refuse medication, but this right can be overridden. Obviously, inmates cannot refuse treatment for a communicable disease, such as tuberculosis, that poses a risk to the prison population. Perhaps less obviously, the preservation of life may be given more weight than the inmate's own wishes. In a 1995 case, for example, an inmate with diabetes was forced to submit to monitoring of his blood sugar and to take insulin or other medications if ordered to by physicians (*North Dakota ex rel. Schuetzle v. Vogel*, 1995). On the other hand, a quadriplegic inmate who wished to die a dignified death was allowed by courts in California to reject force-feeding and other painful medical intervention (*Thor v. Superior Court*, 1993). One could argue that, had the diabetic inmate been allowed to have his way, the prison system would have been faced with significant medical costs resulting from complications associated with his disease. The quadriplegic inmate presented no such economic threats. The cases were not decided on the economic issue, however, but rather on the right of competent individuals to self-determination of their medical needs balanced against the state's interest in preserving life.

The U.S. Supreme Court has issued one decision on the right of inmates to refuse treatment in the form of psychoactive drugs (*Washington v. Harper*, 1990). In Washington State, felons with severe mental disorders were housed in a special unit within the prison system. Antipsychotic drugs were frequently used to control disruptive behavior. If an inmate refused to be treated with these medications, he or she was allowed to challenge the treatment in an administrative hearing before a three-person panel comprising a psychologist, a psychiatrist, and a member of the prison administration. Harper and other inmates wanted a judicial review, before an independent court, rather than an administrative review. They also wished to be afforded a right to counsel, rather than the lay adviser allowed in the administrative hearing. The Supreme Court, in a 6–3 ruling, however, found no fault with the procedure in use. Essentially, prison officials can give an inmate psychoactive drugs against his or her will, but it must be determined in an administrative hearing that such medication is necessary to control the inmate's disruptive behavior. It is important to note, though, that state statutes may be even more restrictive than this, prohibiting medication that might be more for the convenience of the staff than truly medically necessary.

Courts have also begun to address the issue of forcing an inmate to take medication to render him or her competent to be executed. In 1986, in *Ford v. Wainwright*, the U.S. Supreme Court ruled that executing a death row inmate who was "insane"—or too mentally disordered to appreciate what was happening to him—violated the Constitution. (See also *Panetti v. Quarterman* [2007], in which a slim majority [5–4] of the court said that the fact of the mentally disordered offender being *aware* that the state was putting him to death was not enough; the inmate must *appreciate the purpose* of this being done.) Since the *Wainwright* ruling, many forensic psychologists and psychiatrists have been troubled. Some psychologists resist participating in evaluations of an inmate's **competency to be executed**, knowing that their recommendation could facilitate the inmate's death. Some psychiatrists—who have the authority to prescribe medication—have not wanted to prescribe psychoactive medication that would stabilize the inmate enough to allow him or her to be put to death. Furthermore, lawyers representing these death row inmates have argued that they should have a right to refuse the medication. In February 2003, a federal appeals court became the first federal court to rule that death row inmates do *not* have such a right.

Right to Rehabilitation

People are often surprised to learn that, although there is a right to *treatment* for physical and mental disorders, an inmate has no constitutional right to *rehabilitation* in correctional settings. In this context, **rehabilitation** refers to a variety of programs that presumably should increase the likelihood that the inmate will not reoffend upon release from prison. In a wide range of cases, inmates have asked the courts to grant them constitutional rights to participate in substance abuse programs, job training programs, educational programs, and programs for violent offenders, among many others. They have consistently been rejected. This is not to say that such programs should not exist. In fact, "It is clear . . . that a penal system cannot be operated in such a manner that it impedes the ability of inmates to attempt their own rehabilitation, or simply to avoid physical, mental, or social deterioration" (J. W. Palmer & Palmer, 1999, p. 221). Thus, lack of *any* meaningful rehabilitative opportunities, particularly within a prison system, would be regarded with suspicion by the courts. The key principle is that individual prisoners do not have a constitutional right to participate in any particular program. Corrections officials are given the discretion to decide who will be assigned to these programs.

Prison Transfers

Inmates have no constitutional right to be held in a specific facility, including one in their home state or close to their family. In many prison systems, it is not unusual for prisoners to be moved from one facility to another, often with little or no notice. One prominent correctional scholar was fond of commenting wryly that, on any given day, half his state's prison population was on a bus.

The type of **prison transfer** that has constitutional implications is the transfer to a civil mental institution. Inmates with mental disorders who are facing a transfer to a mental health facility outside of the prison system are entitled to a hearing before this occurs (*Vitek v. Jones*, 1980). In reality, transfers to mental institutions are rarely challenged (F. Cohen, 2000, 2008). Furthermore, inmates with mental disorders, when transferred, are usually sent to a mental health unit or facility within the prison system. Because it is not clear whether such transfers require hearings such as those outlined in the *Vitek* case, prison systems sometimes provide them as a matter of policy if the inmate protests the transfer. In addition, the IACFP (Althouse, 2010) Standards assume that hearings are required: "This requirement is not obviated by the receiving institution being in the same jurisdiction or the special management unit being within the same correctional facility" (Standard D-36, Discussion).

Privacy and Confidentiality

Inmates have very little right to privacy in prison or jail settings. Despite the fact that inmates often call their cells their "houses" or "homes," the law does not treat them this way. In the leading case on this issue, *Hudson v. Palmer* (1984), the Court gave corrections officials wide leeway in conducting unannounced cell searches without the presence of inmates. Prisoners had asked to be allowed to be present when the cell searches were conducted, arguing that their property—including objects having sentimental value—was sometimes destroyed or was missing after these searches. Although not condoning malicious destruction of property, the Court majority nevertheless left these searches to the discretion of prison officials, in the name of maintaining institutional security.

Confidentiality of psychological records is a topic of direct concern to the forensic psychologist. Psychologists have an ethical obligation to preserve inmate confidentiality to the maximum extent possible. The IACFP Standards (Althouse, 2010) indicate that non-psychological staff should have access to confidential information only on a "need to know" basis and that psychological staff should supervise such releases and interpret information.

In the event that third parties within or outside the facility are provided with psychological information, "release of confidential information" forms should be completed by inmates and kept in the files. The Standards also make it clear that inmates should be informed verbally and in writing of limits of confidentiality. For example, they should be informed that if a psychologist is made aware of an escape plan or of a plan to harm another inmate, he or she is obliged to notify prison officials. In addition, psychologists should obtain completed informed consent forms from inmates before conducting an assessment or initiating treatment.

Interestingly, even more basic than confidentiality is the actual *adequacy* of the records. Despite the fact that lower courts have made it clear that adequate records are prerequisite to continuity of care (F. Cohen, 2008), there is widespread concern about poor record keeping in many correctional facilities. According to Fred Cohen, a lawyer and a scholar of correctional law,

> In my own work encompassing a large number of prisons, I would say that broadly deficient mental health records is the most consistently encountered problem I uncover. . . . What may be surprising is that even in relatively sophisticated systems, the mental health records are sometimes so deficient that there often is no treatment plan or only an old one that has not been changed or updated; what is there is illegible; there is no medical history or a clinically inadequate one; treatment recommendations are sparse or nonexistent; and there are no follow-up or progress notes. (pp. 10–12)

Cohen adds that "decent treatment" may in fact be occurring in some cases, but this would not be evident from the files. He includes in his 2008 book a helpful guide for ensuring a properly prepared mental health file.

The limits on confidentiality and requirements for informed consent are problematic for many psychologists who are considering work in correctional settings. According to the IACFP (Althouse, 2010),

> The correctional mental health services provider works *with* their clients, but *for* the department, facility, or agency, and must be able to differentiate and balance the ethical/legal obligations owed to the correctional organization or agency, community safety, and the offender, inmate, or resident client. (Standard C-6, Discussion)

This can be difficult for the psychologist who is accustomed to working both for and with the same client. Furthermore, some psychologists are concerned that a number of inmates who "consent" to assessment and treatment do so because they believe they have no choice.

Segregation

Segregation, also referred to as solitary confinement or isolation, refers to the separation of an inmate from the general jail or prison population. This may be done for a variety of reasons. We referred above to the isolation of those with mental disorders in observation cells. In addition, inmates may be placed in **disciplinary segregation**, as punishment for violation of rules, or in **protective custody**, to keep them away from other inmates who may prey on them. Supermax or ultramax facilities hold large numbers of allegedly violent and recalcitrant inmates in **administrative segregation** for years at a time, and this term is also sometimes used for the temporary isolation of inmates while an alleged violation is being investigated. And, of course, in death penalty states, prisoners in death row are usually held in solitary in single cells for years at a time.

Whatever terminology is used, and for whatever purpose, it is clear that isolating prisoners is a common practice in North America, in both the United States and Canada (Morgan, Gendreau et al., 2016). Although only about 5% of the prisoner population is in isolation at any one time, it is also estimated that close to one fifth of all prisoners in the United States have served some time in segregation (Beck, 2015). It is important to emphasize that confinement conditions vary widely. Prisoners almost invariably spend 23 hours in their cells, with meals delivered there, and 1 hour allowed for exercise in small yards. They are typically allowed a shower three times a week. Some prisons allow limited visitations, and reading materials or even television may be allowed. (In the critically acclaimed and highly recommended Sundance drama *Rectify*, death row inmate Daniel Holden communicates verbally with a fellow death row inmate through the vents between their cells, and he is able to hear and touch music on a tape recorder a chaplain brings—but he cannot keep the recorder in his cell.)

Courts have allowed corrections officials to segregate inmates but have placed some restrictions on the duration and the conditions of the confinement, particularly in the case of disciplinary segregation. Inmates also have a right to a hearing before being placed in disciplinary segregation, but this right is rarely exercised, and even if exercised, hearings are run in a perfunctory fashion, as illustrated by the anecdote at the beginning of this chapter. Challenges to being placed in segregation are rarely successful.

Conditions of segregation have been monitored more carefully than *duration* by the courts, though they are often considered in relation to the duration. Thus, placement in a stark cell with no opportunity to shower for 48 hours is not legally problematic; placement in the same cell and under the same conditions for 2 weeks probably would be. Hygiene, nutrition, the physical condition of the cell, and the physical condition of the inmate are all taken into consideration. "It is clear that there is not yet a minimum standard set on the number of days or other conditions that will constitute cruel and unusual punishment in punitive isolation in every situation" (J. W. Palmer & Palmer, 1999, p. 80). Thus, although psychologists may be concerned about the effects of isolation on the mental state of the inmate, and although inmates have argued unsuccessfully that isolation is per se cruel and unusual, the courts have placed limits on only the most egregious of situations.

Few limitations have been placed on the duration of protective custody or administration segregation, but again, conditions may be scrutinized. The Supreme Court has yet to hear a case involving conditions of confinement in supermax facilities, but lower courts have weighed in on this issue. As noted above, conditions vary in these facilities, depending upon the state. The extraordinarily high level of security needed to house inmates in supermax facilities results in extreme isolation and unprecedented restrictions on personal freedoms (DeMatteo, 2005b). Essentially, these institutions often function "very close to the edge of what the Constitution allows" (Collins, 2004, p. 2).

A lower federal court (*Madrid v. Gomez*, 1995) has made it clear that the above conditions are particularly harmful to inmates who are at psychological risk or are presently mentally disordered. Reviewing conditions in the secure housing unit (SHU) at Pelican Bay State Prison in California, the court found that the following violated the Constitution's prohibition against cruel and unusual punishment: a pattern of excessive force by correctional officers within the facility, the lack of adequate provision of medical and mental health care, and the holding of inmates with mental illness in the SHU.

Nevertheless, the court did not find a constitutional violation in the SHU for *stable* inmates:

> Conditions in the SHU may well hover on the edge of what is humanly tolerable for those with normal resilience, particularly when endured for extended periods of time. They do not, however, violate exacting Eighth Amendment standards, except for the specific population subgroups [the mentally ill] identified in this opinion. (*Madrid v. Gomez*, 1995)

The vast majority of the psychological literature has condemned the use of solitary confinement for extended periods, and most particularly for prisoners with fragile mental states (e.g., Grassian, 1983; Haney, 2008; Immarigeon, 2011; Toch, 2008). Civil liberties groups across the nation have sought to limit the use of extreme isolation in the nation's jails and prisons (e.g., S. Kim, Pendergrass, & Zelon, 2012). While the consensus is that isolation may be necessary as a punitive measure for violent inmates for short periods of time, it is also believed to be used unnecessarily and for extended time periods. Depending upon the jurisdiction and the prison, isolation can range from separation in a sparse but clean cell to placement in a cell the size of a parking space with another inmate. Kim et al. (2012) reported that interviews with inmates, family members, and corrections officers—as well as reviews of prison documents—documented highly negative effects of solitary confinement on both inmates and corrections officers.

Not everyone is in agreement that isolation is inevitably problematic, however. Interestingly, a 1-year study of the effects of solitary confinement in Colorado (Metzner & O'Keefe, 2011; O'Keefe, Klebe, Stucker, Sturm, & Leggett, 2010) showed that only a small percentage of offenders (7%) were adversely affected, the majority were stable, and 20% actually showed improvement in their level of functioning. The study has been widely criticized because its findings were so different from other literature on negative effects of isolation. However, it also has been praised for its methodological rigor (Gendreau & Goggin, 2014). Gendreau and Goggin note that it is imperative that the Colorado study be replicated in other jurisdictions.

Most recently, Morgan, Gendreau et al. (2016), reported on two meta-analytic reviews of the effects of administrative segregation on inmates' well-being. Interestingly, the reviews were conducted simultaneously but by two groups of researchers unaware of each other's involvement in a meta-analytic review. The two groups—one at the University of Cincinnati (14 studies) and the other at Texas Tech University (19 studies) reached essentially the same conclusions—that the negative effects of segregation had been quite exaggerated. Ten studies overlapped—that is, they appeared in both meta-analyses.

The researchers found that, despite the fact that there were negative effects, they were not significantly different from the negative effects experienced by incarceration in general or the negative effects experienced by non-segregated prison populations. Even when isolation occurred for more than 60 days—a time period considered extremely harmful—the researchers found no reason for greater concern. They studied such effects as anger, depression, psychosis, cognitive functioning, and physical health. However, two exceptions were highlighted: Some inmates displayed mood disturbance and self-injurious behavior, but they were not of the magnitude that would be expected based on previous commentary and research. The researchers also found a small increase in recidivism after release from prison, but a decrease in institutional misconduct.

The weight of opinion among mental health professionals is to employ solitary confinement in very limited ways and to avoid its use altogether for offenders with mental disorders. Morgan, Gendreau, et al. (2016) emphasize that, although their research results must be considered carefully, they are not advocating a greater use of segregation or placing inmates in isolation for long periods of time. They also point out that, for those inmates who are placed in these restrictive environments, mental health services should be available. "Currently, services typically consist of psychotropic medications, brief check-ins at the inmate's cell front, or infrequent meetings in private with a clinician" (p. 458). This, they suggest, is not sufficient and not consistent with a best practices approach.

Rights of Pretrial Detainees

Under the law, persons accused of crime and held in jails or detention centers may not be punished. As noted earlier, they are innocent unless and until they are proven guilty. Thus, a detainee cannot be placed in disciplinary segregation and lose good time credits because he or she is not serving time. However, courts allow detainees to be placed in highly restrictive conditions and to suffer significant invasions of privacy in the name of institutional security. In addition, a detainee can be placed in isolation for violating the rules of the facility. In the landmark U.S. Supreme Court case on this issue, *Bell v. Wolfish* (1979), detainees in a federal facility challenged a number of actions taken by administrators in the name of institutional security. For example, detainees were placed in groups of three and more in what were intended to be two-person cells, and they were sometimes put in makeshift accommodations due to overcrowding. They were not allowed to stand and watch if their cells were searched. They were not allowed to receive packages containing food items or personal items from outside the institution. Finally, they were submitted to visual body cavity searches after contact visits (visits from the outside). In a 6–3 decision, the U.S. Supreme Court ruled that these were not punitive conditions and were justified in the name of institutional security.

In addition to the constitutional protections discussed above, inmates may have certain rights under their state constitutions or laws passed by state legislatures. Confidentiality of records, rights to participate in rehabilitation programs, and visitation rights (e.g., the right to see one's biological children) are all areas that vary widely from state to state. The psychologist working in a correctional setting, then, must be aware not only of the rights guaranteed under the U.S. Constitution, but also of the laws specific to the state where the facility is located.

ROLES OF THE CORRECTIONAL PSYCHOLOGIST

Correctional psychologists are sometimes distinguished from psychologists working in correctional facilities. The correctional psychologist typically has "specific academic and/or program training in correctional philosophy, systems, offender management, forensic report writing, treatment aimed at reducing recidivism, and outcome research" (Althouse, 2000, p. 436). Many—if not most—psychologists working in corrections do not have this specific background. Furthermore, not all psychologists hold doctorates, whether PhDs or PsyDs. Although it is estimated that more than 90% of psychologists working in the Federal Bureau of Prisons hold doctorates, it appears that those working in state prisons and local jails are more likely to have master's degrees or certificates of advanced study. The future, however, holds far greater opportunity for doctoral psychologists to be employed in both federal and state correctional facilities.

Psychologists at all levels clearly offer valuable services to corrections. For our purposes, therefore, we use the terms *correctional psychologist* and *psychologist working in corrections* interchangeably. This is consistent with the IACFP (Althouse, 2010) Standards, which note that the same level of professional practice is needed irrespective of the training level or educational background of the service provider. The Standards also recognize that these service providers often include other professional groups as well as psychologists. Finally, as mentioned in Chapter 1 and earlier in this chapter, correctional psychologists often do not consider themselves *forensic psychologists*, though in the broad sense of this term, we do so in the text. For some psychologists, a limitation of working in correctional settings is the amount of time they are able to allocate for research. (Dr. Kroner alludes to this in his Perspective essay earlier in the chapter.) In one study (Boothby & Clements, 2000), psychologists reported that research endeavors occupied approximately 2% of their time. The IACFP (Althouse, 2010) Standards recognize the difficulty of setting aside time for research due to the increasing demand for psychological services. Nevertheless, Standard F-1 encourages applied or basic research, and its discussion section recommends that qualified mental health staff be "afforded the opportunity for engaging in at least one evaluation or research project having practical relevance for correctional or forensic psychology" (Standard F-1, Discussion). Mental health staff also are encouraged to facilitate research projects from outside parties when possible.

Some research suggests that psychologists working in correctional settings were only "moderately satisfied" with their jobs, particularly due to lack of opportunities for advancement and professional atmosphere (Boothby & Clements, 2002). Other research projects reveal that correctional psychologists report a high degree of job satisfaction when they are employed at facilities with a higher security level as compared to minimum-security facilities (Garland, McCarty, & Zhao, 2009; Magaletta, Patry, & Norcross, 2012). Although it may be tempting to think that perceived safety issues were a reason, a similar study (MacKain, Myers, Ostapiej, & Newman, 2010) found that safety was not a major concern among the psychologists they studied, nor was it a factor in the earlier Boothby and Clements (2002) study.

A number of other studies have examined job satisfaction or burnout among staff in correctional facilities, although these studies are often not limited to psychology staff (e.g., Garland et al., 2009). Two exceptions are the work of MacKain, Myers, Ostapiej, and Newman (2010) and Senter, Morgan, Serna-McDonald, and Bewley (2010). MacKain et al., (2010) using scales similar to those used by Boothby and Clements (2002), studied specific facets of satisfaction among prison psychologists in North Carolina and found that economic factors (health benefits, job security), work relationships, and perceived administrative support were related to job satisfaction. Interestingly, correctional psychologists appear to be more satisfied with their personal lives than psychologists working in such settings as public psychiatric hospitals. These results suggest that psychologists employed in correctional facilities should be educated about the potential stressors of their work. Furthermore, students planning to become correctional psychologists should receive course work about the inherent stressors of correctional settings as well as its benefits. In addition, the stressors may not be as apparent as one would think, as MacKain et al. (2010) found. In sum, as Magaletta et al. (2013) observed, the field of forensic psychology in general needs to do a better job of preparing students for these careers.

PSYCHOLOGICAL ASSESSMENT IN CORRECTIONS

Psychological assessment refers to all of the techniques used to measure and evaluate an individual's past, present, or future psychological status. Assessment usually includes, but is not limited to, the use of psychological tests, or personality inventories, questionnaires, or other measuring instruments. The last two decades of the 20th century saw a large increase in the number of commercially available measures and tests specifically intended for use in forensic and other clinical settings. This includes a variety of psychological measures that are presently in use in prisons and jails across the United States. As an example, all inmates entering the Federal Bureau of Prisons are administered the Psychology Services Inmate Questionnaire (PSIQ), a fill-in-the-blank self-report form that assesses past mental health services and evidence of current psychological problems (Magaletta et al., 2009). In addition to questionnaires and other psychological instruments, assessment involves interviews with the individuals being assessed, interviews with others, direct observations, and reviews of case records.

In corrections, assessment is warranted *at a minimum* at several points in an inmate's career: (1) at the entry level, when he or she enters the correctional system; (2) when decisions are to be made concerning the offender's reentry into the community; and (3) at times of psychological crisis. Beyond these very minimal requirements, however, reassessments should be done on an ongoing basis. "Behavioral changes in inmates, which occur as time is served, demand constant reassessment and reassignment" (J. W. Palmer & Palmer, 1999, p. 307).

More specialized types of assessment are also performed, depending upon the jurisdiction. For example, in death penalty states, psychologists may be involved in assessing inmates for intellectual disability (in light of the *Atkins, Hall, and Moore* cases: *Atkins v. Virginia*, 2002; *Hall v. Florida*, 2014; *Moore v. Texas*, 2017) or extent of mental disorder (*Ford v. Wainwright*, 1986) with reference to their competency to be executed. (See Focus 12.4 for additional information on *Moore v. Texas*.) In the federal government and those states that have sexually violent predator (SVP) laws, psychologists may administer measures to assess inmates about to be released for the likelihood of future sexual offending. As noted earlier in the text, risk of future sexual offending may lead to involuntary civil commitment as a sexually dangerous person.

For the correctional system intent on pursuing both security needs and rehabilitative goals, assessment also is a key component to providing treatment. James Bonta (1996) has identified three historical generations of assessment for the purpose of offering treatment. During the first generation, assessment was performed chiefly by individual clinicians who relied on their own professional experience and judgment. In the second generation, standardized assessment instruments were adopted, although these included primarily static risk factors

FOCUS 12.4. *MOORE V. TEXAS:*
INTELLECTUAL DISABILITY AND DEATH, REVISITED

In 1980, Bobby James Moore was convicted of murder after the attempted robbery of a food market, during which he shot and killed a 70-year-old grocery clerk. He was 20 years old at the time of the crime, and he was subsequently sentenced to death. In 1995, he was granted a new sentencing hearing because his lawyers in the first trial had failed to present mitigating evidence, including the fact of impaired mental development. He was resentenced to death in 2001. In 2017, the U.S. Supreme Court vacated that death sentence.

As a child, Moore twice failed first grade, but was promoted to second grade because the school believed he should be with children his age. In fifth grade, he was hit by other children with a chain and brick. Neuropsychologists examining him said he had likely suffered a traumatic brain injury (TBI) as a result. Through his early years, he was beaten by a father who called him stupid, and he was socially promoted from grade to grade. He eventually dropped out of school in the ninth grade. At the age of 13, he could not tell time, did not know days of the week, months of the year, or seasons. He was thrown out of his home, lived on the streets, played pool, and mowed lawns for money. Once imprisoned, he obeyed rules and was able to learn some skills.

Between 1971 and 1989, Moore was administered IQ tests seven times, attaining an average score of 70.66, which indicated mild intellectual disability. In addition, mental health practitioners reviewed his adaptive performance at cognitive, social, and practical skills and found significant deficits.

Although a lower court found that these deficits should reduce his sentence to life in prison or even merit a new trial, the highest appellate court for criminal appeals in Texas (CCA) did not agree. First, that court focused on scores of 78 and 74 that Moore had attained, but did not consider the scores below 70. The Court did not consult current medical standards to determine intellectual disability, a point made by the judge who dissented in the CCA's decision. Instead, the court used outdated criteria for assessing intellectual disability, and the focus was on Moore's adaptive strengths, rather than his deficits. The CCA then ruled that his death sentence should stand.

Moore appealed to the U.S. Supreme Court, arguing that current psychological and psychiatric standards for determining intellectual disability—not the outdated standards—should be applied in this case. Amicus curiae briefs on his behalf were submitted by national and international groups, including the APA. By current professional standards, these briefs argued, Moore was an intellectually disabled individual and therefore—in keeping with *Atkins v. Virginia* and *Hall v. Florida*, ineligible for the death penalty. In a 5–3 decision, the U.S. Supreme Court agreed that contemporary professional standards should apply, and sent Moore's case back to the Texas court for resentencing consistent with the decision.

Questions for Discussion

1. It is clear that an IQ score alone is not sufficient to find a person eligible or ineligible for the death penalty. In its previous cases, the U.S. Supreme Court gave leeway to states to decide on their own standard for assessing intellectual disability. Does this case represent a retreat of that position? Assuming that the death penalty will remain an option in some states, should there be a national standard for determining intellectual disability?

2. In the three Supreme Court cases referred to above, the majority gave considerable deference to the psychiatric/psychological professions, essentially ruling that current professional standards should inform but not dictate the legal decision. Dissenters, however, believed that this deference to experts was not warranted. What is your opinion on this?

3. Moore obviously had some strengths and was able to manage living in his community. Why is it important to focus on adaptive deficits rather than adaptive strengths in assessing whether to put someone to death?

(such as prior record or number of violent incidents within a facility) focused mostly on making decisions about an offender's custody level. The third and present generation of assessment includes both risk and needs factors. Thus, a standardized risk/needs assessment instrument takes into consideration both prior violent incidents (a risk factor) and an offender's attitude toward authority (a needs factor). We will discuss risk/needs assessments as well as its associated RNR (risk/needs/responsivity) treatment approach in more detail shortly.

Initial Inmate Screening and Classification

As a matter of institutional or systemwide policy, correctional facilities require entry-level assessments so that inmates can be "psychologically processed" and assigned to a particular facility or unit. Ideally, no individual should be placed in the general correctional population without having been screened for evidence of problem behaviors or mental states. Thus, screening should be done as soon as possible after entry into the facility.

In jails, especially for pretrial detainees, this screening process may be very cursory. It will focus on whether the person is a suicide risk, indications of substance abuse, history of hospitalizations and medications, and indicators of violence. Because few facilities have psychological staff available round the clock, initial screening may be done by corrections staff, such as caseworkers or corrections officers. The IACFP Standards (Althouse, 2010) condone this practice as long as these individuals have been trained by psychological staff and this staff reviews all written reports. If there is evidence of mental disorder, suicide ideation, or depression or anxiety greater than would be normally expected, the individual should be referred for a more extensive evaluation. It appears that initial psychiatric evaluations of inmates occur in virtually all jails (Steadman et al., 1989).

In prisons, screening and classification become more complex. In many states, an offender is first sent to a classification or reception center, which may or may not be within the facility to which the offender is eventually sent. States with large prison systems (e.g., Texas, New York, California, and Florida) have centralized processing centers. The new prisoner may spend several days or even many weeks in this assessment center, separated from those already in the system, until assigned to an institution based on security needs as well as to specific programs. The classification committee may recommend, for example, that a prisoner be assigned to an aggression management program or an educational program to improve his reading level. The committee might recommend that another prisoner be offered substance abuse treatment and that contacts with her children be facilitated.

The reception unit in many prisons includes psychologists, psychiatrists, social workers, or other professionals who administer tests, interview the offender, review records, and offer programming and treatment recommendations. The IACFP Standards recommend that all newly received inmates be briefly screened for mental disorders and suicide risk "prior to being placed in a general population room or cell" and that those in need of a more comprehensive mental health evaluation be referred immediately to a qualified mental health provider (Standard D-17a). Detailed recommendations for the contents of these screenings are provided in Standards D-17b through D-17g. "Initial assessment of the mental health status of the inmate at this crucial point can also prevent additional complications, including assault, suicide attempts, or rapid cognitive and emotional deterioration" (Standard D-17, Discussion).

Principles of Risk, Needs, and Responsivity (RNR)

In corrections, it is important to assess both needs and risks, particularly if a treatment regimen is to follow. In previous chapters, we have given some attention to risk factors, those that make it more likely that an individual will engage in antisocial behavior (e.g., early onset of offending), as well as protective factors, those that cushion or protect the individual (e.g., a caring adult). Principles of **risk/needs/responsivity (RNR)** (Andrews & Bonta, 1994) are now firmly established in the criminology literature and have been demonstrated to be effective in achieving rehabilitative goals (Gendreau & Goggin, 2014).

Andrews and Bonta (1994) identified two main categories of needs: criminogenic and non-criminogenic. **Criminogenic needs** are dynamic factors (Gendreau, Cullen, & Bonta, 1994) subject to change. An offender's attitude toward employment or his or her degree of alcohol use are examples. "The importance of criminogenic needs is that they serve as treatment goals: when programs successfully diminish these needs we can reasonably expect reduction in recidivism" (Gendreau et al., 1994, p. 75). **Noncriminogenic needs** are those that may be subject to change but have been found to have little influence on an offender's criminal behavior. Psychological states such as depression, anxiety, or low self-esteem are examples. Although these states may lead to adjustment problems for the individual, they are not strongly correlated with criminal behavior in the great majority of offenders. However, these needs should still be addressed in treatment. The depressed or highly anxious offender still needs help.

One of the foremost risk/needs scales available in corrections is the **Level of Service Inventory–Revised (LSI-R)** (Andrews & Bonta, 1995), which was developed in Canadian correctional facilities and has since been introduced in American corrections. A similar instrument, the **Level of Service/Case Management Inventory (LS/CMI)** (Andrews, Bonta, & Wormith, 2004b) helps identify risks and needs as well as interventions that might be used to change an offender's patterns. The LSI-R—which is scored on the basis of records reviews and interviews with offenders—assesses offenders' criminogenic needs along 10 domains, including personality characteristics, pro-criminal attitudes, family/marital history, and substance abuse. The LSI-R has been the focus of considerable research (e.g., Gendreau, Little, & Goggin, 1996; Simourd & Malcolm, 1998). Many studies have supported its use with male offenders (Hollin, Palmer, & Clark, 2003); female offenders (Folsom & Atkinson, 2007; E. J. Palmer & Hollin, 2007); and youthful offenders, both male and female (Catchpole & Gretton, 2003). Not all research supports its use with female offenders, however; as we will note below, a considerable amount of research suggests that the needs of female offenders are different and are not tapped by many of the actuarial instruments in use (Van Voorhis, Wright, Salisbury, & Bauman, 2010). Although earlier surveys suggested that psychologists in the United States were less inclined to use actuarial instruments (Boothby & Clements, 2000; Gallagher, Somwaru, & Ben-Porath, 1999), this has changed, at least among clinicians engaged in the practice of forensic psychology (Heilbrun & Brooks, 2010). Part of this is due to the fact that, as Otto and Heilbrun (2002) predicted, instruments with good predictive ability are increasingly being sought as courts demand more scientific accountability. Recall from our discussion of structured professional judgment instruments in previous chapters that many clinicians continue to prefer instruments that leave room for their professional judgment.

As prisoners approach the end of their sentence, or as they approach a parole date, the psychologist may be called on to assess their risk of reoffending, including, as noted above, sexual assault recidivism. Similar assessments also may be conducted when prison officials are considering a change in the offender's status, such as shifting him or her from a medium- to a minimum-security level. Because this is pertinent to the classification issues discussed above, it is important to keep in mind that the various assessment instruments may be used for classification as well as release decision making.

Assessments for **release decisions** are usually prepared at the request of state parole boards (Brodsky, 1980), particularly in the case of inmates who have a history of mental disturbance or predatory behavior. The psychologist typically meets with the inmate, reviews his or her prison files, and administers psychological tests. As we have seen in previous chapters, psychology has made substantial progress in developing risk assessment instruments over the past 20 years (e.g., J. Monahan, Steadman et al., 2001; Steadman et al., 1989). Boothby and Clements (2000) found that risk assessment *instruments* are not widely used. Nevertheless, instruments recommended for this purpose include the revised Psychopathy Checklist (PCL-R); the Violence Risk Appraisal Guide (VRAG); and the Historical, Clinical, and Risk Management Scale (HCR-20), all of which were referred to in earlier chapters, as well as instruments developed specifically to assess sex offender risk.

Crisis Intervention

Inmates in both jails and prisons are susceptible to a wide variety of psychological crises that may require a forensic psychologist's assessment and treatment skills. Psychologist Hans Toch (e.g., Toch, 1992; Toch & Adams, 2002) has written extensively about the "mosaic of despair" that can overwhelm some inmates and even lead them to injure themselves or take their own lives. Crises of self-doubt, hopelessness, fear, or abandonment are not unusual in an incarcerated population, and most particularly among inmates whose mental health is fragile (Toch, 2008). In addition, any inmate may be confronted with a situation that warrants a psychological consultation. Victimization by other prisoners, news of the death of a loved one, and denial of parole are all examples of situations that can precipitate a psychological crisis in an otherwise stable inmate. When such a crisis occurs, prison officials are interested in obtaining from the psychologist both an immediate resolution of the crisis and long-range solutions that will help avoid a similar problem in the future.

As noted above, prisoners who have been placed in segregation also have specific mental health needs, including those that might be a direct result of the isolation. Although some may appreciate the respite from the general population as well as the protection it provides them from possible violence, extended periods in isolation are problematic. Recall that Morgan, Gendreau et al. (2016) urged psychologists to uncover and adopt best practices for serving this population of prisoners.

Competency to Be Executed

One very specialized area demanding the assessment skills of correctional psychologists revolves around the death penalty. The U.S. Constitution prohibits the execution of an offender who is so mentally disordered that he or she is unaware of the punishment that is about to be imposed and why he or she has to suffer it (*Ford v. Wainwright*, 1986). The question of competency can be raised for any person who has been sentenced to death and who appears to have become severely mentally disordered while awaiting execution (Zapf, 2015).

Severe intellectual disability also can save an offender from being put to death. In *Atkins v. Virginia*, 2002, the Court ruled that some intellectually disabled persons (then referred to as mentally retarded) could not be executed. Intellectual disability is a chronic condition that should ideally be taken into consideration at the sentencing phase in a capital case. Because the Supreme Court ruled on this only in 2002, persons who challenge their execution in this manner are often already on death row. However, the Court in the *Atkins* case did not specify how mental disability should be decided. In a later decision on this matter (*Hall v. Florida*, 2014), the Court still did not do so, but it did indicate that the decision could not be made on the basis of an IQ score alone. In its latest decision on this matter (*Moore v. Texas*, 2017), discussed above and in Focus 12.4, the Court made it clear that assessment should be in keeping with current professional mental health standards.

In sum, then, if an offender on death row challenges the execution on the basis of his or her mental disorder or intellectual disability, the forensic psychologist may be called in to perform an assessment of the offender's competency for execution. It should be noted though, that in the case of mentally disordered offenders, they cannot refuse psychoactive medication intended to make them competent for execution. This interpretation has raised ethical concerns among mental health practitioners who resist restoring a prisoner's mental state or prescribing drugs against his wishes, only to make the prisoner eligible to be put to death (Weinstock, Leong, & Silva, 2010).

Together, these Supreme Court decisions reignited a long-standing philosophical debate on the critical role of mental health professionals with respect to offenders sentenced to die (e.g., Bonnie, 1990; Brodsky, 1980; Mossman, 1987; Weinstock et al., 2010). (See Focus 12.5 for a discussion of additional issues relating to the death penalty.) Competency for execution

FOCUS 12.5. DEATH IS DIFFERENT

The United States is the only North American or Western European nation in which capital punishment is employed. Public support for this approach has declined steadily over the past 30 years, with now roughly one-third of the adult population supporting its use. Approximately 31 states as well as the federal government continue to have capital punishment on the books, but the number of individuals who have actually been executed remains small. In four or five states, governors have placed a moratorium on putting prisoners to death. As of June 2017, there were approximately 2,800 prisoners on "death row," with their time since sentencing ranging from just over a year (e.g., the Boston Marathon Bomber) to over 20 years. Ironically, the Boston Marathon Bomber was sentenced to death under federal law, but in a state that does not have the death penalty on its books.

Throughout this text, we have referred to the death penalty in a variety of contexts—assessment of competency to be executed, who is eligible for the death penalty, research on death qualified jurors, jury instructions, the constitutionality of certain drug protocols used in lethal injections, and the role of sentencing juries, among other topics.

Arguments against the death penalty may be morally based, pragmatic, research-based or all three. They include but are not limited to the following:

- It is morally wrong for government to take a life in this manner.
- The death penalty is extremely costly to carry out; it costs more to execute someone than to keep him or her in prison for life.
- Jurors who are death qualified differ demographically, educationally, and politically from those who are not.

- The death penalty is given disproportionately to members of minority groups, particularly African Americans.
- The race of the victim affects who will get the death penalty; it is given more when victims are white and the perpetrator is black than for any other racial or ethnic victim–offender relationship.
- People have been wrongfully convicted, including some who were on death row.
- The drugs used to give lethal injection are difficult to obtain and/or are ineffective, causing unnecessary suffering during the killing process.
- It is a greater punishment to keep someone in prison for life than to put them to death.
- Even someone convicted of killing can atone for the crime and can make positive contributions within a prison setting.
- It is not fair for someone to be put to death in one state for committing the same crime as a person in another state that does not have the death penalty.

Questions for Discussion

1. Why do you think public support for the death penalty has declined in recent years?
2. What are the arguments *in favor of* the death penalty? Do they outweigh those against? Are there more arguments against the death penalty that are not listed above? Where do you stand on this issue?
3. Which of the arguments against or for the death penalty are relevant to psychological research and the practice of forensic psychology?

---

assessments have been fraught with much controversy and debate as to "whether, and to what extent, psychologists (or psychiatrists and other mental health professionals) should become involved in this type of evaluation" (Zapf, 2015, p. 229).

The great majority of psychologists working in correctional settings will never be asked to conduct an evaluation of a death row inmate's competency to be executed, for two main reasons. First, in states with the death penalty, the death row population is usually kept at one maximum-security facility, at least as these prisoners approach their execution date. Only a small minority of psychologists work in or contract with these facilities. Second, prisoners under sentence of death are far more likely to appeal their death sentence on other grounds (e.g., inadequate assistance of counsel) than to raise the issue of incompetency. However, the Court's recent rulings in

Hall v. Florida (2014) and *Moore v. Texas* (2017) may increase significantly the number of offenders who challenge their execution on the basis of intellectual disability.

A number of forensic psychologists have offered suggestions to their colleagues who may be conducting evaluations of competency to be executed (e.g., Heilbrun, 1987; Heilbrun, Marczyk, & DeMatteo, 2002; Small & Otto, 1991), particularly on the basis of mental disorder. In a model report published by Heilbrun, Marczyk, and DeMatteo, psychologist Mark Cunningham used the following techniques in his competency assessment:

- Clinical and forensic interview of the prisoner;

- Psychological testing, including the MMPI-2 and the Personality Assessment Inventory (PAI);

- Interview of a corrections officer on the death row unit;

- Cell observation;

- A second interview with the prisoner;

- Telephone interviews with friends, relatives, the prisoner's ex-wife, and his spiritual adviser, which ranged in length from 12 minutes to 70 minutes; and

- Reviews of numerous legal, health, military, and prison records, as well as journal entries and letters in support of clemency (p. 96).

Small and Otto (1991) note that it is important to inform the prisoner of the purpose of the evaluation, describe its procedure, and explain who will get the results as well as the implications of the findings. In addition, they recommend videotaping the assessment to document that the above steps have been taken, under the assumption that a court may scrutinize the evaluation process itself. Central to the evaluation, they say, is the clinical interview, in which the clinician should try to determine whether the prisoner understands that he or she was convicted and is about to be executed. In a more recent Supreme Court decision (*Panetti v. Quarterman*, 2007), the Court suggested more was needed. It was not enough for the person to "know" he had committed a crime and was being executed, but must also have an appreciation that he was being executed because of his own actions. The prisoner in that case was delusional, and his delusions were believed to interfere with appreciating the connection between his crime and his planned execution (Weinstock et al., 2010). The Court's struggles in attempting to give guidance to mental health professionals on this critical issue are enough to discourage many from participating in the process.

TREATMENT AND REHABILITATION IN CORRECTIONAL FACILITIES

A dominant task of the psychologist in the correctional system is to provide *psychological treatment*, a term that encompasses a wide spectrum of strategies, techniques, and goals. Boothby and Clements (2000) reported that direct treatment took up approximately 26% of psychologists' time in correctional settings, second only to administrative tasks. In addition to providing services to those inmates who are mentally disordered, psychologists also offer services directly targeting substance abusers, sexual offenders, psychopaths, arsonists, and those prone to violence such as domestic abusers. In addition, virtually any inmate, regardless of his or her offense, may require treatment of symptoms such as depression, anxiety, and stress (including posttraumatic stress) that might not necessarily qualify as a full-fledged mental disorder.

R. D. Morgan, Kroner, Mills, and Batastini (2014) observe that the goals of treatment can be characterized broadly as either mental health stabilization or rehabilitation. In the first goal, prisoners are helped to adjust to their environment and to develop effective coping skills. The prisoner who is depressed upon hearing that his wife is seeking a divorce or is fearful of being assaulted in prison may be in need of mental health stabilization. High levels of violence in a prison and overuse of isolation can contribute to an increase in mental health problems among prisoners. The second goal relates to providing treatment that will prompt the individual to desist from future offending. Substance abuse treatment, anger management, and sex offender treatment all fall into this second category. Several recent meta-analyses have indicated that treatment is effective when it is offered (R. D. Morgan et al., 2014).

The most common treatments used within correctional institutions are person-centered therapy, cognitive therapy, behavior therapy, group and milieu therapy, transactional analysis, reality therapy, and responsibility therapy (Kratcoski, 1994; Lester, Braswell, & Van Voorhis, 1992). In recent years, more attention has been given to the benefits of motivational interviewing, the primary objective of which is "increasing an offender's problem acceptance and recognition, highlighting the benefits of change, and helping him or her reach a decision to change while continuing to support self-efficacy" (Rosenfeld et al., 2015). Dialectical behavior therapy, particularly as it targets anger, aggression, and impulsivity, also has received attention (Rosenfeld et al., 2015).

Today, as mentioned above, psychological treatment often follows the risk/needs/responsivity principles of Andrews and Bonta, most specifically by reducing an offender's criminogenic needs (Andrews & Bonta, 2010; Gendreau & Goggin, 2014). Additional research has found that treatment that adheres to principles of RNR is both effective in reducing recidivism and cost-effective compared to no treatment or treatment that does not adhere to RNR principles (Romani, Morgan, Gross, & McDonald, 2012).

It should be noted that psychologists are just one of several professional groups providing this therapy. Psychiatrists, social workers, and mental health counselors are also involved in most correctional facilities. This is an important point because the method of treatment used depends largely on the professional training and orientation of the clinician. Psychiatrists, for example, are more likely to favor psychoactive drugs as part of a treatment regimen, although recent studies suggest that this approach is increasingly being supplemented with individual therapy (Heilbrun & Griffin, 1999). Social workers are more likely to use group treatment approaches, in which inmates talk about their concerns, experiences, and anxieties while the social worker generally directs and controls the topic flow. As indicated by the Boothby and Clements (2000) study, group therapy does not seem to be the norm among psychologists in correctional facilities, but it is still widely used by other clinical professionals. Sixty percent of the treatment provided by the psychologists in that study was in an individual format. The researchers found this problematic, given the high need for mental health services in the nation's jails and prisons.

A different survey of 162 professionals representing a range of professional groups (R. D. Morgan, Winterowd, & Ferrell, 1999) indicated a far greater use of group therapy. In that study, 72% of the respondents offered group therapy to inmates, and their time was about equally divided between group and individual treatment. These practitioners also estimated that 20% of all inmates in their facilities received some group therapy. When delivered effectively, group therapy has several advantages over individual therapy in correctional settings. It is, of course, more practical, given the limited number of treatment staff and high prison population. In addition, group therapy provides prisoners with opportunities for socializing, group decision making, developing altruism, and developing functional peer relationships that individual treatment typically does not provide (R. D. Morgan et al., 1999).

On a more negative note, few professionals in the above study (only 16%) reported that their departments were conducting research on the effectiveness of group or other therapy.

Perhaps more sobering, 20% indicated that no supervision was offered to therapists who facilitated group therapy sessions.

Common Psychological Treatment in Corrections

A wide variety of treatment options are available to forensic psychologists offering therapy in correctional settings (Kratcoski, 1994). The treatment model—or treatment approach—adopted by a given professional may be influenced by a host of factors, including the psychologist's training; perceptions of "what works"; and, of course, the available resources within the facility. In the Boothby and Clements (2000) study, a large majority of respondents (88%) reported using a cognitive model, whereas 69% used a **behavioral model** and 40% a rational-emotive approach. As is obvious from these percentages, psychologists used various models, depending on the situation.

Behavioral Models

In the 1960s, psychologists consulting with correctional facilities made extensive use of behavior modification as a means of encouraging inmates to change (Bartol, 1980). Behavior modification included rewarding inmates for "good behavior" within the facility and removing privileges when behavior was unacceptable. For example, an inmate who had no disciplinary violations for a month might be given an increase in visits to the commissary, or prison store, while disruptive behavior might result in a loss of visiting privileges. By themselves, approaches that are based on such reinforcement strategies have shown little effectiveness. The main objection to such approaches is that change generated within the facility did not generalize to the real world, once inmates were released. Furthermore, in some facilities, legal advocates argued that the punishments imposed were sometimes arbitrary and in violation of inmate rights. Behavior modification as the sole approach to treatment eventually lost favor.

Cognitive-Behavioral Models

Cognitive models seek to change the very beliefs and assumptions that are at the core of an individual's behavior. Some researchers have argued (e.g., Mandracchia, Morgan, Gross, & Garland, 2007; Walters, 1996, 2006) that offenders as a group possess thinking styles or make thinking errors that encourage them to persist in antisocial behavior. Cognitive models, which are strongly based on social learning theory, encourage prisoners to examine their beliefs and assumptions, recognize problems in judgment that have led them to criminal activity, develop self-awareness, and accept responsibility for their actions. Once this has been accomplished, offenders are taught decision-making strategies and social skills, as needed, for replacing behaviors that got them into trouble with pro-social behaviors. Because cognitive programs often have components that resemble aspects of behavioral programs, the term *cognitive-behavioral* is used. For example, many cognitive-behavioral programs make use of contracts and token economy systems, whereby individuals gain points when they demonstrate pro-social behaviors.

The **cognitive-behavioral approach** appears to have the most promise in a variety of treatment contexts (Rosenfeld et al., 2015; Wormith et al., 2007). Pearson, Lipton, Cleland, and Yee (2002) performed a meta-analysis on the 69 primary research studies of the effectiveness of behavioral and cognitive-behavioral treatment and found the latter significantly associated with lower recidivism rates. The effect was mainly due to the cognitive components rather than the behavior-modification interventions, however. That is, such aspects as problem solving, interpersonal skills training, role-playing, and negotiation skills training—all associated with a cognitive approach—were linked with effectiveness. Token economies, contingency management, and behavioral contracts—all associated with behavior modification—had little effect.

At its best, cognitive-behavioral therapy also involves the reduction of criminogenic needs, in accordance with the theory of Andrews and Bonta (2010) and the principles of risk, needs, and responsivity.

Wormith et al. (2007) also discuss a revived interest in positive psychology, which is closely related to principles of cognitive psychology. *Positive psychology* "promotes ideas and principles that facilitate optimal mental and physical health and militate against mental illness and dysfunctional thoughts, feelings, and behaviors" (p. 886). Clinicians who use this approach in correctional settings try to help inmates work toward desirable goals such as achieving meaning and happiness in their lives. Wormith et al. note that, while this does not seem consistent with a punitive-retributive model of criminal justice, it is worthwhile to consider as an alternative to traditional forms of treatment.

TREATMENT OF SPECIAL POPULATIONS

Like the general population, offenders vary widely in their background experiences and their needs. Although treatment should be individualized as much as possible to recognize these differences, programs are often established to address common needs of groups of offenders. For example, prisons—and to a lesser extent jails—may offer programs for inmates who are elderly or very young, female inmates who killed their abusers, sex offenders, psychopaths, inmates who are parents, substance abusers, inmates with intellectual disabilities, and inmates under sentence of death. Although we will not cover all of these categories below, readers are advised that an extensive literature in correctional psychology is available covering each of these areas (e.g., Becker & Johnson, 2001; Kratcoski, 1994; R. D. Morgan et al., 2014, and references therein).

Substance-Abusing Offenders

Substance abuse often co-occurs with mental disorders. Nevertheless, many individuals with substance abuse problems are not mentally disordered. With or without accompanying mental disorder, though, their numbers within correctional facilities are increasing. Statistics in recent years suggest that about one fifth of state prisoners and slightly over half of all federal prisoners are serving time for drug offenses. Even more revealing, however, is the fact that 53% of state and 45% of federal inmates in 2004 met the *DSM-IV* criteria for drug dependence or abuse (Welsh, 2007). Even with recent moves to reduce sentencing for persons convicted of drug offenses, the problem of substance misuse among persons convicted of non–drug-related offenses will remain.

Although correctional facilities recognize the need for treatment of offenders with substance abuse problems, the availability of professional treatment is limited (Belenko & Peugh, 2005). Welsh (2007) reports that, although nearly half of drug-dependent inmates are in some type of substance abuse program, fewer than 15% receive treatment from a trained professional. Peer counseling or self-help groups (such as Alcoholics Anonymous or Narcotics Anonymous) or drug education is more likely to be available. It is significant that current literature reviews on treatment of prisoners often do not mention substance abuse treatment (e.g., R. D. Morgan et al., 2014) but focus instead on treatment of special populations such as the seriously mentally disordered, the intellectually disabled, violent offenders, and sex offenders. In addition to the need for more professional programs, there is great need for more research on identifying the specific needs of offenders and their performance in treatment programs (see, generally, Simpson & Knight, 2007).

One approach to the treatment of substance abusers that has received favorable research results is the therapeutic community (TC), discussed again later in this chapter. In this model, trained counselors interact with a small group of offenders, establishing therapeutic relationships and engaging them in a process of taking responsibility for and changing their substance-abusing behavior (De Leon, Hawke, Jainchill, & Melnick, 2000). Prisons with TCs in place often contract out this program to private providers in the community, and it is typically offered to inmates who are preparing to leave the prison setting. At its best, a prison-based TC can be highly effective for offenders with substance problems. In general, research has documented the effectiveness of TCs when they are intensive, behavior based, and focused on targeting an offender's drug use (MacKenzie, 2000). However, TCs also encounter obstacles to their smooth operation, including untrained staff, staff turnover, budget cuts, and changes in treatment providers (Farabee, 2002; Saum et al., 2007). On the whole, however, "prison-based TCs coupled with aftercare treatment in the community can reduce both recidivism and relapse into drug use" (Wormith et al., 2007, p. 883).

Violent Offenders

Violent behavior has been defined as the intentional and malevolent physical injuring of another without adequate social justification (Blackburn, 1993). Psychological services to inmates who have committed violent crimes or who otherwise demonstrate propensities toward violent behavior are common in many correctional facilities. Corrections officials place a high priority on both controlling such behavior within prison and jail settings and reducing its likelihood once an inmate has been released. Therefore, programs that address this problem in the inmate population are appreciated, if not always well funded. As a group, however, violent offenders are extremely challenging. "When compared to other offenders, they tend to be less motivated for treatment, more resistant or noncompliant while in treatment, have higher attrition rates, demonstrate fewer positive behavioral changes while in treatment, and demonstrate higher recidivism rates posttreatment" (Serin & Preston, 2001, p. 254).

Serin and Preston (2001) also note that a major impediment to treating violent offenders has been confusion over the definition of the population along with failure to recognize that violent individuals are not all alike. This lack of homogeneity, the authors emphasize, requires differential treatment, but it is rarely offered. For example, programs for violent offenders too often do not distinguish between offenders displaying instrumental aggression and offenders who have anger-control problems. Instrumental aggression is coolly committed for the purposes of achieving a particular goal. Thus, it makes little sense to place an offender who commits his crimes using instrumental aggression into a program teaching him to control his anger. On the other hand, anger control is an important skill to develop in individuals who are impulsive; have substance abuse problems or mental disorders; or lack social, relationship, or parenting skills. Although differential treatment is an important goal, it is very difficult to achieve, particularly within an institutional setting. As Serin and Preston acknowledge, few settings have the resources—both financial and human—to provide multiple programs for different types of violent offenders. Even when more than one program is offered, the identification and matching of offenders with specific programs are challenging tasks. In addition, the population of violent offenders who qualify as psychopaths requires different strategies, as we will see shortly.

R. D. Morgan et al. (2014) are far more optimistic about treatment programs for violent individuals, providing they last a minimum of 6 months and are based on RNR principles. Their goal is to help offenders learn nonviolent alternatives by providing them with skills to identify negative lifestyles and "heighten their awareness of violence, responsibility, and control" (p. 809). Essential components of these programs include encouraging offenders to address their own cognitive distortions and develop effective conflict-resolution skills.

Programs for violent offenders differ widely in their approach, but many have two common features: (1) teaching techniques for self-regulating aggression and (2) addressing cognitive deficits. In the first category, motivated offenders are taught relaxation skills or "stress inoculation" approaches to reduce the arousal that results in inappropriate aggression. In the second category, motivated offenders are challenged to confront the irrational beliefs or biases that lead to violence. Defining problems in hostile ways or failing to anticipate the consequences of aggressive behavior are examples. Programs that address cognitive deficits, therefore, strive to change the thinking patterns of offenders by persuading them that the approaches they have used to this point have not resulted in successful outcomes in their relationships with society or with others in their environment. A prerequisite to a successful program outcome, however, is the motivation of the offender.

Although a variety of violent offender programs have produced some positive treatment effects, "few provide the rigor (i.e., control groups) to conclude that intervention for violent adults reduces violent recidivism" (Serin & Preston, 2001, p. 260). Advocates of violent offender programs maintain that such programs at the least *reduce the risk* of future violence and should ideally be followed up with community supervision and treatment once inmates are released. Furthermore, even when studies do not demonstrate positive posttreatment effects, the design of the study itself—not the treatment offered—may be the problem. As always, more methodologically sound research is needed to continue the progress toward effective programming.

Interestingly, some research indicates that it is far more difficult to provide intensive treatment for high-risk offenders in the community than in a controlled prison environment. Despite the numerous challenges within an institutional setting that were discussed above, the clinician has more control within a residential program. In addition, *milieu* treatment—such as can be found in therapeutic communities within the facility—is a possibility. A major disadvantage of institutional treatment is the difficulty in generalizing it to noninstitutional settings (Quinsey, Harris, Rice, & Cormier, 1998).

It should be mentioned that pharmacological approaches are also used in the management of violent offenders, particularly those for whom violence can be attributed partially to biological factors. These would include some individuals with brain injuries, schizophrenia, dementia, and clinical depression, among other disorders. Anti-psychotic medications are often used in prison settings to control acute violent behavior in a crisis situation, such as a psychotic episode. Nevertheless, the vast majority of violent offenders neither require nor would benefit from pharmacological treatment (Serin & Preston, 2001), and correctional psychologists as a group are unlikely to advocate it. When such treatment is indicated, it should also be accompanied by psychological interventions such as those mentioned above.

Criminal Psychopaths

Individuals who qualify as criminal psychopaths present special challenges to society as well as to prison administrators. It has been a long-standing conclusion that psychopaths are essentially untreatable and continually demonstrate low motivation in treatment or rehabilitation programs. Hare (1996) asserts,

> There is no known treatment for psychopathy…. This does not necessarily mean that the egocentric and callous attitudes and behaviors of psychopaths are immutable, only that there are no methodologically sound treatments or "resocialization" programs that have been shown to work with psychopaths. Unfortunately, both the criminal justice system and the public routinely are fooled into believing otherwise. (p. 41)

In fact, Hare suggests that group therapy and insight-oriented treatment programs may actually help the psychopath develop better ways of manipulating and deceiving others.

Psychopaths often volunteer for various prison treatment programs, show "remarkable improvement," and present themselves as model prisoners. They are skillful at convincing therapists, counselors, and parole boards that they have changed for the better. Upon release, however, there is a high probability that they will reoffend, and their recidivism rate is not usually reduced following treatment. "Treatment participated in by many psychopaths may be superficial, intended mainly for impression management" (S. Porter et al., 2000, p. 219). Other research has concluded that psychopaths are less motivated to seek treatment, more likely to drop out, and more likely to reoffend following treatment than those who did not receive treatment (Polaschek & Daly, 2013).

Rice, Harris, and Cormier (1992) investigated the effectiveness of an intensive therapeutic community program offered in a maximum-security psychiatric facility. The study was retrospective, in that the researchers examined records and files 10 years after the program was completed. Results showed that psychopaths who participated in the therapeutic community exhibited higher rates of violent recidivism than psychopaths who did not. For non-psychopaths, the results were the reverse: Non-psychopaths were less likely to reoffend if they had participated in the program. Rice et al. note that the psychopaths in their study were an especially serious group of offenders, with 85% having a history of violent crimes. It is possible that a group of less serious offenders would show better results. Nevertheless, the researchers concluded, "The combined results suggest that a therapeutic community is not the treatment of choice for psychopaths, particularly those with extensive criminal histories" (p. 408).

It should be mentioned that the treatment program reported on in the Rice et al. (1992) article had controversial features, including emotion-laden encounter groups among inmates in the facility. Although often cited as evidence of the difficulty in effectively treating psychopaths, the study cannot be generalized to psychopaths in other institutional settings. As Skeem, Polaschek, and Manchak (2009) have observed, these high-risk offenders were subjected to intensive, radical, and involuntary treatment.

Rosenfeld, Howe, Pierson, and Foellmi (2015) note that the pessimistic research on the treatment of psychopaths has primarily relied on the PCL-R scale and also has used recidivism as an outcome. That dominantly used scale does not sufficiently capture short-term reductions in psychopathic traits, which might be achieved by some of the modern treatment approaches. For example, some studies do suggest that *under certain conditions*, some psychopaths do benefit from treatment (Skeem, Monahan, & Mulvey, 2002; Skeem, Polaschek, & Manchak, 2009). Specifically, both the level of violence and the frequency of offending can be reduced, if psychopaths are provided *intensive* treatment in a *conventional* violence reduction program. Skeem et al. (2002) found that psychopathic psychiatric patients who received seven or more treatment sessions during a 10-week period were approximately 3 times less likely to be violent than psychopathic patients who received six or fewer sessions. These results support earlier findings reported by Salekin (2002), who also discovered that a range of treatment interventions appeared to be moderately successful for psychopaths, especially if the treatment was lengthy and intensive.

Likewise, Bonta (2002) has suggested that psychopathy should be considered a dynamic factor, not a static variable: "Antisocial personality . . . does not need to be viewed as such a stable, intractable aspect of the person" (p. 369). Note that Bonta is not differentiating psychopathy from antisocial personality disorder (APD), which may be the dominant way of viewing it in the future. That is, both psychopaths and those with APD may receive similar treatment. Bonta argues that certain features of the antisocial personality—impulsiveness, risk taking, callous disregard for others, shallow affect, pathological lying—can be linked with realistic treatment goals. All of these are features of the psychopath as well.

Sex Offenders

As noted in Chapter 9, sex offenders are an extremely heterogeneous group. Most of the research has focused on two predominant groups: rapists and child molesters or child sex offenders (CSOs), the two sex offender groups that are the most likely to be imprisoned and the most difficult to treat, although within each group, some types of offenders are more amenable to treatment. Recall that we gave considerable attention to the typologies developed in an attempt to understand these offenders. However, extreme care should be used in applying these typologies, very few of which have been submitted to empirical validation (Heilbrun et al., 2002). The classification system developed and revised by the Massachusetts Treatment Center research group—again, discussed in Chapter 9—is the most respected system available, but it is also relatively complex. An especially negative label (e.g., sadistic rapist) may have unfair consequences for the individual. In prison, it may hinder his adjustment to incarceration, may affect his security level, or may limit his chances for an early release. In addition, although many psychologists believe the risk assessment instruments specifically devised for sex offenders are useful, these instruments also have many limitations (T. W. Campbell, 2003).

The number of sex offenders under state correctional supervision at year-end 2011 numbered 166,383, or 12.4% of the total state prisoner population (Carson & Golinelli, 2013). As of July 2012, the Federal Bureau of Prisons held 21,717 current or prior sex offenders, representing roughly 10% of the BOP inmate population (Cameron, 2013). Federal sex crimes occur in three major categories: (1) child pornography/child abuse image distribution or production across state lines, (2) transportation of illegal sex activity (sex trafficking), and (3) sex abuse crimes that occur on federal lands or in areas under federal jurisdiction.

Psychologists and other clinicians continue to search for effective strategies to prevent future crime by sex offenders who, *as a group*, are highly resistant to changing their deviant behavior patterns (Bartol, 2002). The BOP reports that half of the sex offenders held under its jurisdiction are rated recidivism risk, according to their scores on the Static-99 (Cameron, 2013). Psychological treatment for these sex offenders—which is voluntary—concentrates on improving basic cognitive skills, such as reducing criminal thinking or criminal lifestyles, and improving emotional self-management and interpersonal skills. Success rates were not indicated in the Cameron report.

After an extensive review of the research and clinical literature on sex offender treatment, Furby, Weinroth, and Blackshaw (1989) concluded, "There is as yet no evidence that clinical treatment reduces rates of sex reoffenses in general and no appropriate data for assessing whether it may be differentially effective for different types of offenders" (p. 27). The Furby et al. review included all variants of therapeutic approaches.

Despite this pessimistic appraisal, other reviews have been more favorable. For example, meta-analyses of the sex offender treatment literature have indicated that, on the whole, sex offenders are better if they are treated than if they are untreated (e.g., Gallagher et al., 1999). A meta-analysis examining 69 studies (Schmucker & Losel, 2008) indicated that cognitive-behavioral programs had positive effects. The cognitive-behavioral approach has also received positive reviews from Laws (1995) and Hanson, Bourgon, Helmus, and Hodgson (2009), who conducted a meta-analysis of 23 treatment programs offered in institutions and the community. Surveys indicate that the majority of sex offender treatment programs in the United States and Canada are cognitive-behavioral and social learning in orientation (Oliver, Nicholaichuk, Gu, & Wong, 2012).

This treatment contends that maladaptive sexual behaviors are learned according to the same principles as normal sexual behaviors and are largely the result of attitudes and beliefs. Cognitive-behavioral therapy, compared to traditional verbal, insight-oriented therapy, has demonstrated short-term effectiveness in eliminating exhibitionism and fetishism (Kilmann, Sabalis, Gearing, Bukstel, & Scovern, 1982), some forms of pedophilia (W. L. Marshall & Barbaree, 1990), and sexual violence and aggression (N. G. C. Hall, 1995; Polizzi, MacKenzie, & Hickman, 1999). Cognitive-behavioral treatment currently offers the most effective method for the temporary cessation of deviant sexual behavior in motivated individuals. (See Focus 12.6 for common features of cognitive-behavioral treatment programs.)

The key words relative to the success of cognitive-behavioral treatment are *temporary cessation* and *motivated individual*. There is now widespread agreement among researchers and clinicians that sex offenders cannot be "cured." The challenge of cognitive-behavioral therapy—and all therapies for that matter—is not in getting the motivated offender to stop

FOCUS 12.6. THE COGNITIVE-BEHAVIORAL APPROACH: KEY ELEMENTS

Of the many therapeutic interventions that have been tried in corrections, the cognitive-behavioral approach seems to hold the most promise. It consists of counseling (group and individual) and training whereby offenders develop cognitive skills that will presumably help them to adopt alternative, pro-social behaviors rather than the antisocial behaviors that resulted in their criminal convictions. There is no universally implemented cognitive-behavioral treatment program; rather, treatment providers decide on an approach consistent with their own training and the needs of the offenders under their care. Any or all of the following elements might be found in a cognitive-behavioral treatment program:

- Social skills development training (e.g., learning to communicate, to be assertive rather than aggressive, and to resolve conflicts appropriately)
- Decision making (e.g., learning to weigh alternatives, learning to delay gratification)
- Identifying and avoiding "thinking errors"—misguided assumptions that facilitated criminal offending (e.g., "Women want to be shown who's boss.")
- Training at solving problems (e.g., interpersonal problems with one's intimate partner)

- Self-control training and anger management (e.g., avoiding hostile attribution)
- Building self-esteem (e.g., recognizing good qualities and providing self-reinforcement)
- Cognitive skills training (e.g., learning to reason)
- Relapse prevention (learning to avoid situations that might lead to further offending)
- Practical skills training (e.g., applying for work)

As noted in the text, the cognitive-behavioral approach has shown success when programs are properly implemented and carried out and offenders are motivated to change. It is not perfect. However, although other therapeutic approaches (e.g., behavior modification) have not had promising results (with some exceptions), cognitive-behavioral therapy gives reason to hope.

Questions for Discussion

1. Assuming that the elements listed above are important, what other services and programs should be available to prisoners?
2. Is cognitive-behavioral therapy likely to be more or less effective for certain groups of offenders?

---

the deviant sexual patterns but in preventing relapse across time and situations. Thus, a treatment approach demonstrating much promise in the treatment of sex offenders is called **relapse prevention (RP)**. "RP is a self-control program designed to teach individuals who are trying to change their behavior how to anticipate and cope with the problem of relapse" (W. H. George & Marlatt, 1989, p. 2). The program emphasizes self-management; clients are considered responsible for the solution of the problem.

In accordance with the principles outlined by Andrews and Bonta (2010), however, clinicians also need to work on reducing criminogenic needs in high-risk sexual offenders and in matching their treatment to the learning style of the client (Hanson et al., 2009). Negative peer associations, aimless use of time, an antisocial lifestyle, deviant sexual interests, and attitudes tolerant of sexual crime are examples of criminogenic needs. Interestingly, Bourke and Hernandez (2009) found that federal inmates convicted of offenses relating to Internet child pornography had a high incidence of self-reporting prior instances of hands-on child sex offenses. The study was criticized on methodological grounds and for premature conclusions, although the authors did note that it was preliminary and merited replication studies.

Sex offender treatment programs exist in virtually every state and in the federal prison system, and they represent a major endeavor engaged in by correctional psychologists, as well as community psychologists who have sex offenders among their patients. Group therapy is a common approach to working with sex offenders, just as it is with violent offenders or substance abusers. The vast majority of programs require the offender to take responsibility for his or her crime as a first step. In fact, denying responsibility for the crime is considered a significant risk factor for future offending. Recall the case *McKune v. Lile* (2002) in which the Supreme Court essentially allowed punishment of an inmate who refused to participate in a treatment program, partly because it required him to reveal offenses for which he had not been charged, and there was no guarantee that by revealing these offenses he would not be prosecuted—a classic "Catch-22" situation. Interestingly, however, some recent research is suggesting that this assumption should be reconsidered. In one study, sex offenders were found to participate effectively in treatment even when they denied their offense (Watson, Harkins, & Palmer, 2016). In another study, denial of responsibility was not significantly associated with recidivism for certain offender types (Harkins, Howard, Barnett, Wakeling, & Miles, 2015). (See Perspective 9.1 in Chapter 9, in which Dr. Harkins mentions this research.)

Sex offender treatment programs vary widely in approach, in the extent to which they are evaluated, and in the degree of success when evaluation research is conducted. Recent meta-analyses (Hanson et al., 2009) are making progress in identifying the common features of those programs that are most likely to reduce recidivism. Treatment programs are less likely to be available to jail inmates because of the short-term nature of jail confinement. However, inmates who are subsequently released to the community may be referred to community treatment programs.

Women Prisoners

In recent years, women's rates of incarceration have increased faster than men's rates, although, as noted earlier, very few scholars predict that they will ever "catch up." In 1970, there were only 5,600 women in prison; by 1980, there were 12,500; and by 1998 there were over 75,000 (Reichert et al., 2010). As indicated at the beginning of the chapter, by 2012, a total of 101,289 women were serving prison sentences of more than 1 year, compared to 1,225,933 men (Carson & Golinelli, 2013). Most women are in prison because of drug (7%) or property offending (20%). Typical female offenders are mothers who are poor, under-educated, unskilled, and victims of physical and sexual abuse (Reichert et al., 2010).

Although increasing research attention is now being given to incarcerated women, they still remain forgotten offenders compared with incarcerated men. Recent studies have focused on assessing needs and validating actuarial risk assessment instruments with female offenders (e.g., Folsom & Atkinson, 2007; E. J. Palmer & Hollin, 2007; Van Voorhis et al., 2010), but research on effective treatment approaches is not widely available. Yet mental health concerns are becoming increasing apparent. For example, in one study (Reichert et al., 2010), 60% of the incarcerated women in a state prison showed symptoms of PTSD or other mental disorders. Other studies have identified similar statistics (Owen, 2000). Since most female prisoners are likely to have prior abuse histories (between 60% and 85%), they are generally in need of trauma-based treatment (Messina, Grella, Burdon, & Prendergast, 2007). A vast majority of women offenders are also in need of substance abuse services.

As mentioned in the previous paragraph, many women serving time have had a history of victimization—often violent victimization and often at the hands of fathers, spouses, or intimate partners. As Owen (2000) observes, "Closely related to mental health problems is the need to recognize the impact of the physical, sexual, and emotional abuse experienced by women offenders" (p. 196). Treatment approaches that increase their self-confidence, recognize their victimization but enable them to take charge of their lives, and teach them life skills offer the best hope for women who are incarcerated.

Scholars agree that problems faced by female prisoners are similar to but also distinct from the problems faced by male prisoners. For example, due to the small numbers of women in prison, there are far fewer correctional facilities available, thus severely restricting opportunities for female inmates to be near their families or to have occupational, educational, or social activities while incarcerated. More important, their relationships with their children are often severely hampered, resulting in a more severe deprivation than is typically found for the male parent (MacKenzie, Robinson, & Campbell, 1989). This parent–child deprivation is especially severe for long-term inmates, who may lose their major source of identity when they lose their parental role (Weisheit & Mahan, 1988). In essence, the available literature suggests that different treatment priorities may be warranted for women who are incarcerated (Van Voorhis et al., 2010).

Treatment in Jail Settings

Psychological treatment of inmates in jail settings is considerably different from treatment in prisons. The short-term nature of the jail stay suggests that **crisis intervention** and limited treatment goals are typical. Moreover, treatment in jail settings is far more likely to consist of stabilizing medication rather than therapy. Nevertheless, the treatment models discussed above can still be implemented, even in short-term jail settings.

Providing treatment services to the non-sentenced jail population—the detainees—is especially challenging. First, it is impossible to predict how long the individual will remain in detention because pretrial release is a continuing possibility for the majority of detainees. Some detainees may have charges dismissed, or they may plead guilty to their offenses, meaning that they will be placed on probation or transferred to prison. Second, even while in custody, numerous disruptions will occur in the individual's schedule. For example, court appearances, visits, meetings with attorneys, population head counts, and even recreational opportunities are unpredictable. Third, treatment services must be generic and not tied to criminal activity because the detainee is only charged with, not convicted of, crime. Thus, sex offender treatment or a program for domestic abusers is inappropriate when applied to detainees who are presumed innocent until proven guilty.

Even sentenced inmates serving time in jail provide challenges to the forensic psychologist, largely due to the short-term nature of their sentence. The therapist therefore must forego long-term goals, even if he or she believes such goals are in the greater interest of the client. "Mental health professionals who are willing to work toward less traditional treatment goals can function within the jail with minimal goal conflict" (Steadman et al., 1989, p. 103). They are advised to develop release-planning goals that will link the individual to community-based mental health agencies. In addition, they are urged to keep in mind that the jail environment itself is crowded, noisy, and lacking in privacy, and that inmates have very little control over their lives. Such conditions can exacerbate mental disorder. Not surprisingly, therefore, "the primary treatment goals for jail inmates will usually be crisis stabilization and maintenance at an appropriate level of functioning while in custody" (J. F. Cox, Landsberg, & Paravati, 1989, p. 223).

As discussed at the beginning of this chapter, jails—sometimes even more than prisons—have a number of features that can impede efforts to offer treatment. Today, limited budgets and overcrowding are major concerns (Luskin, 2013). For these reasons, the processing of mentally disordered offenders in specialized mental health courts is a good option, particularly if they have been charged with less serious offenses. As numerous researchers have noted, the cost of providing mental health services to severely disordered inmates in both jails and prisons is enormous (Heilbrun et al., 2012). In the case of newly arrested individuals with severe mental disorders, well-functioning mental health courts assist in diverting them to effective community resources.

OBSTACLES TO THE TREATMENT OF INMATES

The correctional environment itself creates numerous challenges for the clinician offering services to inmates. In this section, we discuss some of the main obstacles.

Confidentiality

As noted in earlier chapters, forensic psychologists often find that they cannot guarantee total confidentiality to the persons whom they assess or treat. This is clearly true of psychologists working in correctional settings, particularly prisons and jails. For example, when the security of the institution is at stake, the inmate presents a threat of suicide, or a third party is in danger, confidentiality cannot be guaranteed. Limitations on confidentiality include "knowledge of escape plans, intentions to commit a crime in prison, introduction of illegal items (e.g., contraband) into prison, in addition to suicidal or homicidal ideation and intention, court subpoenas, and reports of child or elder abuse or neglect" (R. D. Morgan et al., 1999, p. 602). Psychologists and other treatment providers are advised to inform inmates of these limitations on confidentiality prior to the provision of assessment and treatment services (IACFP Standards). As a result of these limits, the inmate may perceive the treatment provider as a representative of the administration. When this happens, the work of psychologists in correctional facilities becomes especially challenging (Milan, Chin, & Nguyen, 1999).

Coercion

Another obstacle to successful treatment is its coercive aspect. Institutional treatment often—although not invariably—operates on the principle that psychological change can be coerced. Conversely, traditional forms of psychological treatment have been successful only when subjects were willing and motivated to participate. This basic principle applies regardless of whether the person is living in the community or within the walls of an institution that has overwhelming power over the lives of its inmates. Thus, although inmates have a right to refuse treatment, their refusal can create far more problems than their grudging acceptance. For example, refusal may mean transfer to another facility, delay in being released, or a restriction on privileges (*McKune v. Lile*, 2002).

In recent years, however, some researchers have begun to question the conventional wisdom that coercion and treatment cannot coexist (see, generally, Farabee, 2002). The critical variable appears to be not the fact that the individual is incarcerated, but rather the individual's willingness to participate or his or her perceived need for treatment. In addition, some studies indicate that even a recalcitrant inmate can eventually benefit from treatment programs (e.g., Burdon & Gallagher, 2002; Gendreau & Goggin, 2014; Harkins et al., 2015; Prendergast, Farabee, Cartier, & Henkin, 2002).

Reviewing studies on inmate participation in treatment, R. D. Morgan et al. (2014) note that inmate reluctance to *seek* treatment can be a major barrier. In this case, the inmate is not refusing help, but rather is deciding not to ask for it. In addition to concerns about confidentiality mentioned above, inmates also may perceive the need to seek psychological help as a weakness and may fear being stigmatized by other inmates. In addition, in some cases they worry that seeking treatment will result in being placed in isolation or losing good-time credits toward early release. R. D. Morgan et al. recommend that mental health professionals try to overcome this barrier by providing information about available resources and how to access them during inmate orientation programs, as well as providing outreach services to inmates in their living units.

Environment

Another obstacle to effective treatment in prisons and jails is the unusual nature of the prison environment itself. The list of negative features ranges from overcrowding, violence, and victimization by other prisoners and staff, to isolation from families and feelings of a lack of control over one's life.

In the late 1950s and 1960s, a number of psychologists working in correctional settings helped establish therapeutic communities for inmates facing adjustment problems in prisons (Toch, 1980). As mentioned earlier in the chapter, these TCs were special living quarters where inmates would be housed separately from the rest of the prison population and would be involved in decision making, group therapy, and operating their own living quarters within the broad prison setting. Although these inmates did not have significantly better recidivism rates than other inmates (Gendreau & Ross, 1984), prison life was made more tolerable for them, and job satisfaction for the staff improved. Today, few prison programs offer therapeutic community settings, primarily because of budgetary constraints and space limitations. When available, they are more likely to be offered to inmates with substance abuse problems. In general, research has documented the effectiveness of therapeutic communities when they are intensive, behavior based, and focused on targeting an offender's drug use (MacKenzie, 2000). Continuing research has shown positive results with the therapeutic community approach with respect to drug offenders (Saum et al., 2007).

Many observers note that prison environments are worse today than they were in the 1960s, when therapeutic communities were first proposed. Overcrowding, violence, and deteriorating physical conditions characterize a substantial number of the nation's prisons and jails. By the end of the 20th century, for example, state prisons as a group were operating between full capacity and 15% above capacity, and federal prisons were operating at 31% above capacity (Bureau of Justice Statistics [BJS], 2001a). The overcrowding problem in jails was even more severe. Overcrowding was the contributing factor spurring court orders to reduce prison populations, such as mentioned at the beginning of the chapter (*Brown v. Plata*, 2011). Although prison populations have gone down in recent years, there is no guarantee that they will remain stable. Furthermore, if the U.S. Justice Department persists in its advocacy of private prisons, incarceration rates could once again rise. Ironically, private prisons are even less likely than public facilities to offer effective psychological services (Bales et al., 2005; Shapiro, 2011).

Violence is also endemic in many prisons. It has been estimated that about 25,000 nonsexual assaults and close to 300,000 sexual assaults occur each year in the nation's jails and prisons (Clear & Cole, 2000), and this is believed to be a conservative estimate. It is impossible to know the true number because many assaults may not be reported. In 2003, in an attempt to address this issue, Congress passed the **Prison Rape Elimination Act (PREA)**, which, among other things, mandates prisons and jails to report incidences of rape of which they are aware. Mental health professionals have written about the need to research the problem of prison rape and design programs for both prevention and treatment (Stemple & Meyer, 2014; Neal & Clements, 2010).

Living conditions for inmates who are kept in isolation for disciplinary reasons or presumably for their own protection (e.g., those with mental disorders) are particularly problematic from a psychological perspective, especially if the stays in isolation extend for months or even years at a time. As mentioned above, however, not everyone agrees that isolation is damaging, particularly because offenders are kept under varying conditions. Although it would be unfair to suggest that the typical jail or prison faces these seemingly intractable problems, correctional psychologists encounter them all too often, and they contribute significantly to the stress experienced by both inmates and staff.

Treatment is also made difficult by other aspects of even the most humane jail or prison environment. The drop-out factor, wherein inmates do not complete a planned treatment program, is a major obstacle to providing effective treatment (R. D. Morgan et al., 2014). Jail sentences are typically short, so continuous treatment is highly unlikely to occur. In both jails and prisons, inmates "miss" appointments with clinicians for a wide variety of reasons. Even when inmates themselves want to attend, they may be prevented from doing so for security or disciplinary reasons. A cellblock may be locked down for a day, for example, while officials conduct cell searches, investigate a disturbance, or conduct medical tests. An inmate involved in an altercation may be placed in disciplinary segregation, making it unlikely that regular visits to a therapist will be allowed. As noted in the section on isolation, therapy for inmates in segregation typically consists of medication, visits at an inmate's cell door, or an occasional one-on-one session (R. D. Morgan et al., 2016). For security reasons, prison inmates are transferred to other facilities with little warning. Finally, budgetary constraints in many facilities result in cutbacks to all but the most essential services. Interestingly, recent efforts to bring telepsychology to prisoners (as well as parolees) have been lauded as a possible solution (Batastini & Morgan, 2016; Farabee, Calhoun, & Veliz, 2016). Telepsychology involves patients working with therapists at a distance, such as when an inmate is seated in a therapy room in prison and the mental health professional is in his or her office. Telepsychology may be a way of not only reducing costs, but also be an efficient method to maximize the number of treatment sessions.

Despite these difficulties, studies show that when psychological treatment is provided, it is effective. Citing their earlier meta-analysis (R. D. Morgan et al., 2012), R. D. Morgan et al. (2014) write, "a comprehensive meta-analytic review of interventions for incarcerated offenders found significant improvements for general mental health outcomes, improved coping skills, and improved institutional adjustment with fewer behavior problems . . . all goals of basic mental health services in jails and prisons" (p. 806). M. S. Martin, Dorken, Wamboldt, and Wootten (2012) found similar positive results for persons with major mental illnesses. Recent publications by other correctional psychologists (e.g., Gendreau & Goggin, 2014; W. L. Marshall, Boer, & Marshall, 2014; Rosenfeld et al., 2015) also support the effectiveness of psychological treatment within jails and prisons.

COMMUNITY-BASED CORRECTIONS

As we noted at the beginning of the chapter, the great majority of adults under correctional supervision remain within the community, either in their own homes or in transitional or group homes, camps, ranches, or similar facilities. Community-based placements other than one's own home generally hold individuals for less than 24 hours a day, allowing them opportunity to work, attend school, participate in job training, or attend counseling or treatment sessions. Community-based facilities are operated by state or federal governments or by private organizations under government contract. In the criminal justice literature, such placements are referred to as "intermediate sanctions," representing points on a continuum between probation and jail or prison, as well as between prison and parole. They may also be referred to as "probation plus" or "parole plus." The offender who lives in a halfway house upon release from prison, for example, is on parole with the added restrictions imposed by the rules and supervision of the halfway house administration.

Intermediate sanctions are also used with offenders who remain in their own homes, such as offenders assigned to house arrest or electronic monitoring. The forensic psychologist offering services to offenders under community correctional supervision, therefore, soon learns that they have a variety of living arrangements as well as conditions of release.

A common condition of release is the requirement that an offender attend counseling or therapy. Thus, many community psychologists have on their caseload individuals who have been ordered to seek treatment, not unlike the orders of outpatient treatment discussed in Chapter 6. We will not revisit here the issue discussed earlier in the present chapter, revolving around whether change can be coerced. Although it is not irrelevant in this context, the coercion here is not as clear-cut as coercion within the institutional environment of the jail or prison, particularly the latter. Nevertheless, the forensic psychologist should be alert to the fact that his or her clients might only be seeking help because of the fear that they could be incarcerated if they do not meet the conditions of release.

Like the psychologist working with detainees and inmates, the psychologist working in community settings performs both assessment and treatment tasks. Evaluations of an individual's competency to stand trial or competency to participate in a variety of judicial proceedings are often performed in the community. In addition, the community psychologist may assess an offender's appropriateness for a particular treatment program, such as a program for sex offenders. Risk assessments are increasingly being performed within the community, as well. For example, before downgrading a probationer from an intensive supervision program (defined further below) to "regular" probation, the court or the probation authority may ask the psychologist to assess the risk to the community if the probationer is no longer supervised as diligently. The principles associated with risk assessment, as well as with risk/needs assessment discussed earlier in this chapter and in Chapters 4 and 5, will not be repeated here.

The role of the psychologist in treating offenders in the community deserves our careful attention. In most ways, the principles applied and the standard of practice are no different from what the psychologist would adopt in the treatment of any other client. Nevertheless, a number of factors render the correctional client distinctive. The common thread among all of these factors is the importance of communication between the psychologist and the representatives of the criminal justice system. First, as noted above, the coercive nature of the treatment may create problems, although it is far less coercive than treatment in jails and prisons. Second, the psychologist may be placed in the untenable position of being an "enforcer," similar to the probation officer. Thus, if the client misses an appointment, the psychologist must decide whether to report this lapse to the probation officer, who may or may not see this as a serious problem. Third, in a somewhat related vein, the psychologist may be called on to make decisions involving privileges that he or she would rather not have to make. A parolee receiving treatment may wish to attend the out-of-state wedding of a sibling, for example, a decision that would typically be left to the supervising officer. Community psychologists are often called on to render opinions on such matters, which many believe are out of their purview. Fourth, the limits of confidentiality must be recognized and communicated to the individual. Typically, the client in these situations is not the offender but the supervising agency, which may be a court or a probation/parole department. In some jurisdictions, the court imposing the conditions of release may require periodic progress notes from the treating clinician. In addition, in the event that probation or parole is revoked, summary notes from the psychologist's records may be subjected to court scrutiny. Fifth and finally, the criminogenic needs of the offender require continual assessment and addressing.

The last decade of the 20th century saw some promising work describing and evaluating the work of psychologists vis-à-vis conditionally released offenders in community settings. Heilbrun and Griffin (1999), describing a number of well-regarded programs in the United States, Canada, and the Netherlands, concluded that there was no single "ideal" program; rather, it was important to use

> the full range of treatment modalities that have been developed during the past decade. . . . By employing treatments such as recently developed psychotropic medications, psychosocial rehabilitation, skill-based psychoeducational interventions designed to improve relevant areas of deficits, and relapse prevention, it is likely that treatment response in a forensic program will be enhanced. (p. 270)

Despite the fact that there is no single "ideal" program, however, it is likely that programs based on the now well-established RNR principles of Andrews and his colleagues (e.g., Andrews & Bonta, 2010; Andrews, Zinger, et al., 1990), described earlier in the chapter, have the greatest chance of success at reducing reoffending.

Heilbrun and Griffin (1999) provide illustrations of community-based programs in eight states as well as Canada. Most of the programs described provided services to a hybrid population of individuals with mental disorders, including individuals found not guilty by reason of insanity, as well as probationers and parolees assigned to treatment programs as a condition of their release or referred by probation/parole officers. Thus, most contacts were on an involuntary basis. Included were both outpatient and residential rehabilitation programs, with outpatient clinics offering both assessment and treatment. Some clinics offering substance abuse treatment also accepted voluntary clients.

In summarizing the programs they describe, Heilbrun and Griffin (1999) note that all emphasized the treatment of psychopathology and the management of aggressive behavior. "In order to meet both goals, programs may refuse to accept high-risk patients, who are generally regarded as more antisocial individuals" (p. 264). Interestingly, it is precisely high-risk offenders who been found to benefit the most from intensive treatment programs.

This is a finding that has consistently emerged from research focusing on the variant of intermediate sanctions known as intensive supervision. **Intensive supervision programs (ISPs)** were intended for high-risk probationers and parolees who were nevertheless deemed not to require incarceration if a less costly alternative were available. (In reality, low-risk offenders were placed in these programs as well [Tonry, 1990].) Probation or parole officers supervising offenders on ISPs have smaller caseloads, provide round-the-clock team supervision, make frequent contacts, and presumably are less tolerant of any failure on the part of the offender to meet the conditions of release. Alcohol and illegal drug use are monitored closely and without notice. Despite these punitive conditions, evaluations of community ISPs have not been promising, and they have not proved cost effective (Gendreau, Paparozzi, Little, & Goddard, 1993; Tonry, 1990).

Gendreau, Cullen, and Bonta (1994) later proposed **intensive rehabilitation supervision (IRS)** as a "second generation" approach to community supervision. "Based on the existing empirical evidence, a persuasive case can be made for abandoning intensive supervision programs that seek only to control and punish offenders in favor of programs that give equal primacy to changing offenders" (p. 74).

Because of their potential for frequent contact with high-risk offenders, IRS programs are likely to be able to match the risk level of offenders with their criminogenic and noncriminogenic needs. As noted earlier, criminogenic needs are dynamic risk factors, or factors that can change over time, such as an individual's attitude toward authority or employment. "The importance of criminogenic needs is that they serve as treatment goals: when programs successfully diminish these needs, we can reasonably expect reduction in recidivism" (Gendreau et al., 1994, p. 75). Targeting noncriminogenic needs (e.g., anxiety, depression, and self-esteem) is less likely to produce significant reductions in recidivism (Andrews & Bonta, 2010).

Thus, Gendreau and his colleagues (1994) have faith in community corrections treatment, particularly if it is targeted specifically at high-risk offenders and uses the intensive treatment approach. "The empirical evidence regarding ISPs is decisive: without a rehabilitation component, reductions in recidivism are as elusive as a desert mirage" (p. 77).

This is not to suggest that *non-intensive* treatment is ineffective for low-risk offenders, however. As studies reviewed by Heilbrun and Griffin (1999) have demonstrated, substance abuse treatment and assistance in working toward independent living can be beneficial for motivated low-risk offenders. Programs with strong community ties; written contracts; group meetings; vocational resources; and assistance at tasks of daily living, such as managing money, have garnered positive research results.

SUMMARY AND CONCLUSIONS

This chapter has provided a description of the role of forensic psychologists working primarily with adult offenders (and sometimes with detainees) in both institutional and community settings. We began with an overview of jails and prisons, focusing on distinctions between the two that are most relevant to the psychologist. Because of their short-term nature, for example, jails offer fewer programs and are less likely to enable the psychologist to have long-range treatment goals. Jails also engender more crisis situations, such as suicide attempts by detainees. The chapter also included a review of those legal rights of inmates that are most likely to affect the work of psychologists. The right to treatment, the right to refuse treatment, and the right not to suffer cruel and unusual punishment are examples.

The work of psychologists in adult corrections can be divided into the two broad but overlapping areas of assessment and treatment. We reviewed the many situations under which psychologists are asked to assess various abilities of detainees and inmates, as well as their mental states. In recent years, psychology has seen the development of many assessment instruments for use in these forensic settings; studies indicate, however, that psychologists are not making extensive use of these instruments, preferring more traditional measures such as the clinical interview and the MMPI. At a minimum, assessment is needed when inmates enter the facility, before they are released, and when they are in crisis situations. Ideally, though, assessment should be a continuing enterprise and should occur as indicated throughout the inmate's stay.

The assessment of a death row inmate's competency to be executed is unlikely to involve the typical correctional psychologist. Nevertheless, this is an area of immense importance and one that has engendered considerable debate. Some psychologists, such as those who are philosophically opposed to the death penalty, believe they should not be involved in such assessments. Others believe it is their professional duty to offer the services as they are required. Furthermore, because a federal court has now given authorities the go-ahead to force medication on a death row inmate to render him or her stable enough to be executed, this issue will undoubtedly trouble some clinicians even more. In states where psychologists have or will have prescription privileges, the matter will be especially salient. We did not cover this debate in detail within the chapter, but we discussed suggestions given to those forensic psychologists who conduct "competency for execution" assessments. With the Supreme Court's recent decisions in *Atkins v. Virginia* (2002), *Hall v. Florida* (2014), and *Moore v. Texas* (2017), assessments of cognitive ability may become more frequent as well.

Psychologists are only one of several professional groups offering treatment services to inmates, both individually and in groups. The treatment model—or treatment approach—that tends to be the most favored is the cognitive-behavioral approach, although others are also in evidence. Cognitive-behavioral approaches—which have received the most positive evaluation results—are based on social learning theory. They assume that criminal behavior is learned much like other behavior and that the motivated inmates can "unlearn" the behavior. Consequently, these approaches encourage inmates to identify their thinking patterns, their assumptions, and their expectations, and to recognize the consequences of their behavior both for themselves and their victims. Research indicates that motivated inmates can benefit from these approaches, which are often used with a wide range of offenders, including violent offenders, sex offenders, and substance abusers. Among the least motivated inmates for such treatment are persistent violent offenders and psychopaths, although we hesitate to draw generalizations, particularly about the first group.

Features of the prison and jail settings can present numerous obstacles to effective treatment, so much so that some psychologists prefer not to approach this challenge. Limitations on confidentiality, budgetary restraints, violence and overcrowding within the facility, inmate schedules and inmate transfers, and sometimes lack of support from administrators and correctional officers are not unusual. Yet many psychologists find immense satisfaction performing this work. Professional organizations offer guidelines and provide support, and increasingly more research is published identifying effective strategies and approaches in a wide variety of situations.

The chapter ended with a review of community treatment programs with offenders who are on probation; on parole; or under intermediate sanctions, such as intensive supervision. In recent years, we have begun to see more descriptions and evaluations of community programs within the psychological literature. Although community programs provide their own special challenges (e.g., offenders not appearing for their treatment session), they also have the advantage of being in a more realistic environment that does not present the numerous obstacles of institutional settings.

KEY CONCEPTS

Administrative segregation   467

Behavioral model   479

Cognitive-behavioral approach   479

Community corrections   453

Community-based facilities   457

Competency to be executed   465

QUESTIONS FOR REVIEW

1. Explain the difference between institutional and community corrections.

2. List any five topics covered in the IACFP Standards.

3. List the main differences between prisons and jails.

4. Does the constitutional right to treatment include a right to psychiatric/psychological treatment? Explain your answer.

5. Which two categories of adult offenders have been determined incompetent to be executed, according to the U.S. Supreme Court? Discuss the implication of these Court rulings for forensic psychologists.

6. Identify the tasks that might be assumed by psychologists in relation to both screening and classification of inmates.

7. Provide an illustration of a treatment program for each of the following special populations: violent offenders, criminal psychopaths, women offenders, sex offenders, and inmates in jail.

8. Discuss the advantages of supervising low-level offenders in the community as opposed to incarcerating them in jails and prisons.

 SAGE edge™

Want a better grade? Go to **edge.sagepub.com/bartol5e** for the tools you need to sharpen your study skills. Access practice quizzes, eFlashcards, an action plan, and SAGE journal articles for enhanced learning.

CHAPTER THIRTEEN

JUVENILE JUSTICE AND CORRECTIONS

L. R. was thrown out of her home at age 13, following several years of "incorrigibility" both at home and at school. She joined a group of street kids, who offered her protection, but also introduced her to drugs and prostitution. Police took her into custody for drug possession at age 15. The juvenile court wanted to know how best to help her.

O. T., a 15-year-old who had been belligerent toward both classmates and teachers, arrived at school one morning with an Army knife he had obtained from his father. He tried to stab a teacher and assaulted a fellow student before he was stopped. The prosecutor declined to have him tried in criminal court. "In this state, we help kids, we don't punish them," he said.

B. A. joined a violent gang at age 14. As part of the gang initiation, he robbed an elderly couple in their home and physically assaulted the 8-year-old brother of a rival gang member. The juvenile court wanted to know if he would be violent in the future.

The juvenile justice system provides numerous opportunities for the forensic psychologist. For over a century, juveniles who are accused of crime, particularly minor offenses, have been treated differently from adults. Although still held responsible, they are not considered as responsible as adults due to their immaturity. Even when their crimes are serious ones, juveniles as a group are considered more likely to be rehabilitated. Juvenile courts, then, were established to recognize these differences and to attempt to arrive at suitable dispositions that would reduce the likelihood that young offenders would continue on a path of offending.

Various data indicate that juveniles today are more likely to come into contact with police, courts, and correctional facilities than at any other time in history, although fluctuations in arrest rates suggest that the situation is not dire. For example, arrest data for 2011 reveal that police took into custody some 1.47 million juveniles that year, indicating that arrests were down 11% from 2010 and down 31% since 2002 (Puzzanchera,

Chapter Objectives

- Introduce the juvenile justice system and its history.

- Review landmark U.S. Supreme Court cases pertaining to the rights and protections of juveniles.

- Introduce the methods and procedures used in psychological assessments of juveniles.

- Discuss juvenile comprehension of constitutional rights.

- Review social science research on false confessions of juveniles.

- Describe rehabilitative options available for juveniles.

- Review representative approaches to the rehabilitation of juveniles.

- Describe and assess multisystemic therapy.

- Review model approaches to the treatment of violent offenders and juvenile sex offenders.

2013). In 2015, police arrested 649,970 persons under age 18, representing an 8.4% decline from the previous year (FBI, 2016a). These decreases may reflect numerous factors, ranging from police ignoring petty offenses or referring youth to community resources to an actual decline in the number of crimes committed by youth. There were increases, however, in murder, rape, and motor vehicle theft.

Another source of data is the number of cases that are processed in juvenile courts. In 2010, juvenile courts in the United States handled approximately 1.4 million delinquency cases, or cases in which juveniles ages 10 or over were charged with violations of the criminal law (Puzzanchera & Robson, 2014). The number decreased slightly in 2014, at 975,000 cases (Hockenberry & Puzzanchera, 2017). While most juveniles reach juvenile court as a result of an arrest, about 15% to 19% are referred by parents, school personnel, social agencies, or probation departments (C. Knoll & Sickmund, 2010; Puzzanchera, Adams, & Sickmund, 2010; Sickmund, 2004). (See Focus 13.1 for additional juvenile court data. See also Focus 13.4 for more information about youth in confinement.)

All states have established an upper age of jurisdiction—that is, the maximum age at which juveniles can appear in juvenile courts—(age 16 or 17, depending on the state). However, all states also have various laws that allow juveniles younger than that maximum age to be tried as adults (Puzzanchera & Addie, 2014). For example, 10-year-olds can be tried as adults in a small number of states, although that rarely happens. It is not unusual, though, to find cases of 14-year-olds in criminal courts. Juveniles are generally not processed in the federal system, even when federal laws are involved. For example, in 2008 only 152 juveniles were handled by the federal courts, and one half of those were tribal youths (Motivans & Snyder, 2011).

In a typical year, juvenile court judges waive jurisdiction over an estimated 1% of all formally handled delinquency cases (Puzzanchera & Addie, 2014; Puzzanchera & Robson, 2014).

FOCUS 13.1. JUVENILE COURTS, JUVENILE FACILITIES, AND DELINQUENCY

Juvenile courts in the United States handled almost one million delinquency cases in 2014, but this represent a 42% decrease in cases since 2005 (Hockenberry & Puzzanchera, 2017). In addition, approximately 31 million youths are under some form of juvenile court jurisdiction in any given year, with the great majority being between the ages of 10 and 15 (Puzzanchera et al., 2010). In 2013, approximately 60,227 juveniles were in residential placement in publicly or privately operated juvenile facilities (Hockenberry, 2016). Eighty-six percent of juvenile offenders held in residential placement were male, and black male youth were disproportionately represented. These data do not include juveniles whose cases were heard in criminal courts rather than juvenile courts, and who were sentenced to incarceration in adult jails or prisons.

Recent data indicate that 27% of the cases handled by juvenile courts concerned offenses against persons (violent offenses), 34% of the cases were property offenses, 13% dealt with drug law violations, and 26% were public order offenses (Hockenberry & Puzzanchera, 2017). Public order offenses include obstruction of justice, disorderly conduct, weapons offenses, liquor law offenses, and nonviolent sex offenses such as lewd behavior.

Questions for Discussion

1. Status offenses, traditionally included in juvenile arrest and court data, are no longer reported in the latest statistics. What might be possible explanations for this?
2. Obtain any one of the above cited government reports and discuss additional findings.

The vast majority (90%) of waived cases involve males, age 16 or older. An unknown number of juveniles, chiefly between the ages of 14 and 18 (but sometimes younger), are tried in criminal rather than juvenile courts because prosecutors had the discretion to bring their cases there rather than to juvenile courts (Redding, 2010).

Despite the large numbers reported above, the juvenile crime rate—which began to rise quite dramatically in the 1980s—has been declining, suggesting that juveniles today are less likely than in the past to commit crimes, particularly serious crimes. And, as mentioned above, the number of juveniles arrested and the number of juvenile cases processed in juvenile courts has declined. However, public officials, clinicians, and legal and social service professionals alike are concerned about the still-disturbing patterns of juvenile crime, particularly substance abuse, violence, and sex offending.

JUVENILE COURTS

Juvenile courts may exist as separate entities or may be part of the broader "family court" or "domestic court" system that was covered in Chapter 6. In general, they operate more informally than criminal courts and employ a different lexicon or terminology. (See Focus 13.2 for a list of terms used in many juvenile courts.) Regardless of how these courts are structured, judges, lawyers, and social service representatives consult with psychologists and other clinicians for a wide variety of reasons. In addition, many juveniles are now having their cases heard in criminal courts, as we note below. As some researchers have observed (e.g., Viljoen, McLachlan, Wingrove, & Penner, 2010), the juvenile justice system as a whole has become more adult-like, with juvenile court judges giving tougher sentences and more juveniles being processed in criminal courts.

Thus, whether in juvenile or criminal court, a defense lawyer may require an assessment of her client's overall intellectual functioning. When juveniles waive their constitutional rights, such as the right to remain silent or the right to a lawyer during police interrogation, judges (and defense lawyers) often want to know whether the juveniles possessed the necessary cognitive skills to make such a waiver. Psychological assessments may be sought to assess a youth's risk of violence or determine if he or she is amenable to rehabilitation. In addition to this, juvenile court judges, and some criminal court judges, as well as lawyers often want to know whether treatment is available to meet the needs of a given young offender, along with the cost of such treatment and the probability that it will be effective.

In addition to the above assessment tasks, psychologists are called on to offer treatment to juveniles, both within juvenile facilities and in community settings. In this chapter, we will discuss the involvement of psychologists at each of these stages, from the early contact with the justice system to the treatment of juveniles in correctional facilities or in the community. To begin though, we provide a brief history of the juvenile courts and review legal rights of juveniles that are relevant to the practice of forensic psychology.

A BRIEF HISTORY OF THE JUVENILE COURT

The first juvenile court was established in the United States in 1899, in the state of Illinois. A broad group of social activists had influenced the Illinois legislature to establish a judicial system for children that was to be separate from that faced by adults. Children were presumed to be in need of protection, less accountable for their offenses than adults, and more amenable to rehabilitation once they had strayed. It was also believed that many children were neglected by their caretakers and required the intervention of the state for their own best interest. Thus, the first juvenile court was intended to serve the needs of *all* children who needed supervision (at-risk children), not only those who were charged with violating

FOCUS 13.2. COMMON TERMS USED IN JUVENILE COURTS

Intake

The intake is the juvenile's first contact with the juvenile justice system following police custody. Here, a decision is made whether to dismiss the case, handle it informally, or refer it formally to juvenile court. About half of all cases are handled informally. This may include referral to a social service agency, informal probation, or even the payment of some fines or voluntary restitution.

Intake workers also decide whether a juvenile should be detained, though a judge must review the detention, typically within 48 hours. Intake officers may be probation officers, social workers, or representatives from the prosecutor's office.

Diversion

This is the process of steering youth away from court and referring them to a structured program. The decision to refer a youth to diversion is usually made by intake workers or by prosecutors. Diversion programs vary widely, usually requiring youth to admit their actions, sign contracts, and agree to certain conditions (e.g., perform community service).

Delinquency Petition

A delinquency petition is the formal document prepared by the prosecutor or an intake worker that states the allegations against the juvenile and asks the juvenile court to adjudicate the case. Petitions are sometimes dismissed before a delinquency hearing occurs.

Preventive Detention

Juveniles have no guarantee of bail under the Constitution. They may be detained securely (i.e., through preventive detention) to prevent them from committing additional offenses. Although an intake worker may make the initial detention decision, a judge or magistrate must review the need for continued detention. Juvenile courts often use detention as an opportunity to order psychological evaluations and other tests.

Waiver Petition

A waiver petition is the prosecutor's request that the juvenile's case be transferred to criminal court. Waivers or transfers also can be made by judges or in accordance with a statute passed by the legislature of the state.

Delinquency Hearing (or Adjudicatory Hearing)

A delinquency hearing is the equivalent of a trial in criminal court. Like adults, the juvenile has a right to have a lawyer, to confront and cross-examine witnesses, and to remain silent. The prosecutor must prove all elements of the offense beyond a reasonable doubt. However, in juvenile court the juvenile does not have a constitutional right to an open hearing or a trial by jury.

Disposition

A disposition is the equivalent of a sentencing in criminal court. If the juvenile has been adjudicated a delinquent, the juvenile court judge decides on the appropriate sanction (e.g., probation, out-of-home placement).

Blended Sentencing

In approximately half the states, both juvenile and criminal courts are allowed to use blended sentencing, or to impose juvenile or adult sanctions on certain juveniles (usually dependent on ages of juveniles and crime charged). However, a juvenile cannot be tried in both juvenile and criminal court for the same offense. This would be an example of double jeopardy.

Aftercare

Aftercare is the equivalent of adult parole. This involves supervision of the juvenile after release from some form of residential treatment.

the law. Today, every state has juvenile courts, either standing on their own or as part of a larger family court system.

The first juvenile courts were strongly based on a *parens patriae* rationale. The doctrine of **parens patriae** (literally, "parent of the country") gives the state the power to intervene in a child's life, even over the objections of the parents, because such intervention is presumed

Don't Be Afraid to Change What You Know

Eve Brank, JD, PhD

Courtesy of Eve Brank.

At 14, I knew I wanted to be a prison psychologist. Over the course of the next 14 years, my pursuit of that career shifted three times to lead me to where I am today.

My interest in crime and prisons started because I was too busy to buy a book or visit a library before a family vacation in 1988. I was heading into the ninth grade the following year, and my time was consumed with cheer practices, trips to the beach, and hanging out with my friends. As I was packing for a two-week RV trip with my parents, I realized I had not taken the time to get a book to take with me—there were no e-readers in 1988. Thankfully, we had a bookcase full of books at home that I had not read. I chose two: *The Scarlet Letter* by Nathanial Hawthorne and *Life Sentence* by Chuck Colson. I do not remember why I chose either; perhaps the thought of being in an RV for two weeks with my parents felt like a life sentence to my 14-year-old self, and maybe it was the drawing of Hester Prynne on the cover of Hawthorne's book that intrigued me.

You are probably familiar with *The Scarlet Letter* and the strict legal code that ruled Hester and her daughter, Pearl. That unforgiving historical society was juxtaposed with the words of Colson that focused on notions of rehabilitation and restorative justice for those in prison and released from prison. Colson, a top aide to then-President Nixon, pled guilty to obstruction of justice in a case related to the Watergate scandal. His pre-prison religious conversion combined with his experiences with fellow inmates led Colson to start Prison Fellowship when he was released. Prison Fellowship focuses from a religious perspective on the restoration of prisoners and their families.

I read these books as my mom, dad, and I rolled across the country in our old RV. Swirling around together with these two books were the different parts of the country I was seeing—from the back roads of Tennessee to the strip of Las Vegas. There were so many different people and paths they chose or had thrust upon them. The sights, people, and these books, drew me to the idea of working within the adult criminal justice system.

In college, I majored in sociology and psychology thinking I wanted to be a clinical psychologist. During this time, two somewhat trivial things happened that changed my course. First, I was working on my honors thesis and I wanted to do a study with inmates and their relationships with prison staff. My faculty advisor had a contact in the juvenile detention facility and suggested I do my study there instead of in a prison. Preparing for that project and working in the detention facility turned my attention to juveniles and their needs within the juvenile justice system, and my interest in adult prisons lessened.

As I was preparing to submit my applications to graduate school in clinical psychology, I had the opportunity to do an internship at an early delinquency intervention program. My internship supervisor allowed me to lead group and individual sessions. This is where the second hiccup came that changed my path. I really did not enjoy talking to these juveniles. I remember my mind wandering to research questions while they talked and thinking, "When do I get to talk?" I stubbornly thought I still needed to apply to clinical psychology because that was what I had planned to do. Thankfully, I also applied and was admitted to the University of Nebraska's Law-Psychology program. As a graduate and law student, I was able to focus on social psychology and law. I was also able to work on issues relevant to the juvenile justice and child welfare systems.

Throughout my graduate school training, I vowed I did not want to be a professor and worked to establish myself to be most suitable for work in a research or policy advocacy center. Here is where my third shift came. I had a one-year-old daughter when I finished graduate school, and my husband was entering medical school. I ended up getting a job as a lecturer at the same university where my husband was in school because there weren't any research or policy advocacy centers in the city where we were. I enjoyed teaching classes and getting to do some research; working with graduate students made me realize I wanted to be a professor. I absolutely loved the mentoring, the exchange of knowledge, and the apprenticeship model. I was very fortunate to become a professor at the University of

(Continued)

Florida and later at the University of Nebraska, where my research focuses on the way the law intervenes, and sometimes interferes, in family and personal decision making.

As you can see, I did not set out to be a college professor, but I absolutely love my career. In a somewhat ironic twist, I recently became the director of a research center that was only an option for me because of my background as a professor. Because I allowed myself to shift my focus and not be too inflexible in my pursuit of what I thought I wanted to do, I ended up in a fulfilling career with wonderful students and colleagues.

I was fortunate to meet Chuck Colson relatively early in my career. I told him that one of his books indirectly influenced me to pursue my career as a professor. After our meeting, he followed up with a personal letter that I have framed and sitting in my home office. I reread that letter whenever I need a reminder to be flexible with my goals and take chances. My advice to you is the same: Know what you want to do but don't be afraid to change what you know.

Dr. Brank is the Director of the Center on Children, Families, and the Law and an Associate Professor of Psychology and Courtesy Professor of Law at the University of Nebraska, Lincoln. She enjoys knitting while other people talk, running with friends, and doing home improvement projects. Dr. Brank lives in Lincoln with her husband, Adam, daughter, and two chubby cats.

to be in the best interest of the child (BIC). The doctrine has survived and remains a strong component of much juvenile law today, including custody-related law discussed in Chapter 6. With regard to juvenile delinquency, the law is also very oriented toward recognizing the legal rights of juveniles, at least in principle. (See Perspective 13.1, in which Dr. Eve Brank refers to her interests in corrections, juveniles, and policy issues relating to families and the law.)

Prior to the establishment of the juvenile courts, children who allegedly broke the law were handled through the social service system or were taken before criminal courts. In the mid-19th century, the nation's largest cities had **Houses of Refuge**, which were institutional settings presumably intended to protect, nurture, and educate neglected or wayward children. Children who were sent to Houses of Refuge were poor or homeless, were considered incorrigible, or had committed usually minor law violations—or some combination of the above. Houses of Refuge in the 19th century—with some exceptions—very rapidly earned the reputation of being emotionally cold facilities that often exploited their young charges by contracting their domestic and manual labor to households in the community (Bernard, 1992).

Young offenders who were processed in criminal courts were allowed to remain in the community if they stayed out of trouble. This is similar to the probation of today, but there were few probation officers available to monitor behavior and offer support and guidance as needed. The early probation officers were volunteers or police officers assigned to this special duty (Cromwell, Killinger, Kerper, & Walker, 1985). It was not until the end of the 19th century that states began to authorize probation and provide funds for probation officers on a systematic basis. Before that time, probationary status was available only in areas where there were volunteers or police willing to take on these supervisory tasks. Many young offenders thus were sentenced by criminal courts to serve time in prisons or reformatories. The latter were intended primarily for first-time offenders. Their purpose was to give these offenders a second chance, offering them education and discipline in preparation for a law-abiding life. Like the Houses of Refuge, many of those reformatories were criticized for abusing young offenders, ruling by fear, and not delivering on their promise to provide education and rehabilitation (Bernard, 1992; R. Johnson, 1996).

The juvenile courts clearly were trying to change children and their families, but it is highly questionable whether they were effective. Until the 1960s, they operated very informally, and judges and other court officers had very broad discretion over the lives of juveniles. The courts were supposedly intended to help juveniles, preferably within the community and within their own homes. Sometimes, parents themselves took their children to these courts if they considered them "incorrigible." Proceedings were informal and closed to the public, and all aspects of the juvenile's life were subjected to inquiry by the court. Psychiatrists and psychologists working in child guidance clinics provided judges with cognitive and personality test results and offered recommendations based on their interviews with the child and family members (Rothman, 1980).

Gradually, despite the allegedly good intentions of the founders of the juvenile court movement, the courts gained the reputation of being authoritarian, imposing unreasonable expectations on juveniles and their families, particularly the economically disadvantaged. When these expectations were not met, juvenile judges were not averse to sending juveniles to secure training schools, where they encountered punitive treatment rather than effective rehabilitation. These decisions to institutionalize were routinely made with little attention to due process of the law; juveniles in most courts did not have the assistance of lawyers, nor did they have reasonable opportunity to confront the witnesses against them or to challenge the actions of court officials. Juvenile courts also routinely urged—and in some cases required—juveniles to confess their offenses. When juvenile court judges believed that the juveniles were not appropriate for juvenile court, they would transfer them to criminal court, where they would presumably be treated the same as adults.

Supreme Court Decisions

Two U.S. Supreme Court cases in the 1960s signaled a need to change procedures in juvenile court. One—*Kent v. United States* (1966)—required that a judge hold a hearing before transferring a juvenile to adult court. Morris Kent Jr. was no angel. The 16-year-old was charged with housebreaking, robbery, and rape while on probation. When arrested, he admitted committing the crimes and was confined in a receiving home for children. The juvenile court, however, quickly transferred his case to adult criminal court over the very strong objections of his attorney, who argued that Kent could be rehabilitated if maintained in a juvenile setting.

In criminal court, Kent was found not guilty by reason of insanity regarding the rape charge but was found guilty of housebreaking and robbery. He was sentenced to 30 to 90 years and transferred to a mental institution in accordance with the insanity finding. Kent's lawyer appealed the original decision of the juvenile court to transfer his case to criminal court.

The U.S. Supreme Court ruled unanimously that the juvenile had a constitutional right to have the assistance of an attorney and to challenge the transfer. The Court also suggested factors that judges could consider in deciding whether a transfer was appropriate. These included (1) the juvenile's sophistication, maturity, and general living environment; (2) the seriousness of the alleged crime; (3) the manner in which it was committed (e.g., level of violence); (4) whether the alleged crime was against persons or property; (5) the juvenile's prior record with the criminal or juvenile system; (6) the prospect of rehabilitation if kept in the juvenile system as well as prospects of adequate protection of the public; (7) the prosecutorial merit of the case; and (8) if two or more defendants were charged, the benefit of having them tried in the same court. These eight factors were later adapted and adopted for use by juvenile courts in many states. The Supreme Court opinion in *Kent* also presents a scathing indictment of the juvenile court system as it operated at that time, serving as a precursor of the landmark case that would follow, *In re Gault* (1967).

A year after *Kent v. United States* (1966), in *In re Gault*, the Supreme Court dramatically altered procedures associated with delinquency hearings. Gerald Gault had been taken into custody by police, taken to the police station, and subjected to two hearings before a judge who ultimately adjudicated him delinquent and sent him to a juvenile training school, where he could have been kept until his 21st birthday. Gerald was 15 years old at the time of his offense. His crime? He had placed an obscene phone call to his next-door neighbor. Although his parents were present at the delinquency hearing, Gerald was not represented by counsel, and his alleged victim did not appear in court to testify against him.

In a lengthy opinion that traced the history of the juvenile court in the United States, the Supreme Court noted that Gerald Gault, like Morris Kent before him, had been subjected to proceedings that could only be characterized as "a kangaroo court"—a term sometimes used for court proceedings that disregard the law or do not uphold its spirit. The Court therefore ruled that juveniles facing delinquency proceedings and possible institutionalization had, at a minimum, the following constitutional rights:

- The right to confront and cross-examine witnesses against them;

- The right against self-incrimination (often referred to as a privilege, but actually a right);

- The right to written notice of the charges against them;

- The right to the assistance of a lawyer in their defense.

The Court did want to preserve the privacy of juveniles, however, noting that closed proceedings could still be the norm in juvenile courts. In a later decision (*McKeiver v. Pennsylvania*, 1971) it refused to extend the constitutional right to a jury trial to juveniles. States do have the option of allowing delinquency proceedings to be open, as well as to allow juries in juvenile courts, but very few do.

Although *In re Gault* (1967) was a decision widely hailed by children's rights advocates, it should not be assumed that it cured all of the ills of juvenile courts. Just over 20 years after the *Gault* case, Barry Feld (1988) reported research that fewer than half of all juveniles were represented by lawyers in delinquency proceedings. Other research across 15 states suggested higher rates of representation, 65% to 97% depending on the jurisdiction. As recently as a decade ago, fewer than half of all juveniles were represented by lawyers in delinquency hearings (Kehoe & Tandy, 2006). In some jurisdictions, as many as 80% of youth waive their right to counsel (Kehoe & Tandy, 2006). It is also well recognized that the *quality* of legal representation varies widely across the nation and is often poor (Melton, Petrila, Poythress, & Slobogin, 2007).

When juveniles are *not* represented by lawyers, it is likely that they waived that right. In some cases, this was done on the advice of parents or other authority figures. Juveniles also have a constitutional right to a lawyer during custodial interrogation, but most juveniles speak to police without a lawyer present (Grisso, 1998; Melton et al., 2007; Viljoen, Zapf, & Roesch, 2007). Thus, the validity of waivers—that is, whether the juveniles understood the consequences of giving up their rights—is another topic of great interest to researchers to the present day (Eastwood, Snook, Luther, & Freedman, 2016; Rogers et al., 2010).

Shortly after these Court rulings in the *Kent* and *Gault* cases were announced, Congress also began to scrutinize the juvenile justice system. In 1974, Congress passed the **Juvenile Justice and Delinquency Prevention Act (JJDPA)**, a law that encouraged states to do better by the juveniles in their care. The act strongly advocated the diversion of juveniles from formal court processing whenever this could be accomplished. This prompted the establishment of numerous community programs across the country aimed at keeping juveniles out of the justice system and providing them with a second chance.

In addition, Congress was particularly concerned about two groups of juveniles. These were (a) the juveniles who were being detained in adult jails, sometimes within sight and hearing distance of adults who were also detained or had been convicted and were serving sentences, and (b) the status offenders who had committed no "crimes" but were nevertheless being held in secure institutions, often with more serious delinquents. Recall that status offenders are juveniles whose offenses might include running away from home, "incorrigibility," or truancy (skipping school)—in other words, behaviors that only they can commit by virtue of their status as children or adolescents. The JJDPA mandated that states receiving funds for juvenile justice programs must remove all juveniles from adult jails and must also remove status offenders from secure institutions. The latter mandate is referred to as the **deinstitutionalization of status offenders (DSO)** requirement.

Throughout the 1980s and 1990s, Congress passed numerous amendments to the JJDPA, some of which extended deadlines for states to meet the mandates of the law (I. M. Schwartz, 1989). Nevertheless, the JJDPA remains a strong piece of legislation supporting the rights of children in the juvenile justice system. A national office, the **Office of Juvenile Justice and Delinquency Prevention (OJJDP)**, oversees the legislation, provides grants for research on juvenile issues, and helps set national juvenile justice policy to this day.

By the end of the 20th century, then, both court decisions and legislation were in place to recognize the rights of juveniles while also providing them with protection and treatment. Despite this, numerous observers commented that the juvenile justice system was in disarray (e.g., Amnesty International, 1998; Feld, 1999). Of particular concern was increasing evidence that racial and ethnic minorities were disproportionately detained and incarcerated (Leiber, 2002; Snyder & Sickmund, 1995). This problem became known as **disproportionate minority confinement (DMC)**. It should be pointed out that the latest available government statistics show some decline in the overall use of detention and out-of-home placement for black versus white youth, but the rates are still disproportionate, as noted above in Focus 13.1.

The treatment of girls and ethnic minorities also gained more attention as the 20th century came to a close. Researchers and scholars noted that, although girls had benefited from the movement to deinstitutionalize status offenders, the needs of girls in detention and treatment were not being met by the juvenile justice system (Chesney-Lind & Shelden, 1998; Federle & Chesney-Lind, 1992). Still others pointed to the need for culturally sensitive programs within the juvenile justice system to recognize the needs of Native American, black, Latino, and Asian American youth (Eron, Gentry, & Schlegel, 1994). Those who support such ethnocentric programming do not say that it alone will make a difference if other principles for facilitating positive change are not applied. As W. R. King, Holmes, Henderson, and Latessa (2001) observed, these programs are syringes rather than cures: "Syringes do not heal people by themselves; however, syringes are indispensable tools for delivering medicine" (p. 501).

The overall conditions in juvenile detention and treatment facilities also received considerable attention nationwide (Amnesty International, 1998; Parent et al., 1994; Puritz & Scali, 1998). Change, however, has been slow to occur. By statute and case law, juveniles held in institutions have a variety of legal rights, but they need advocates to see that these rights are acknowledged, and advocacy is lacking for many. They have a right to be in a sanitary environment and to be protected from other violent juveniles and abusive staff, but researchers have identified problems—including problems of sexual victimization—in a number of states (Beck, Cantor, Hartge, & Smith, 2013; Beck, Guerino, & Harrison, 2010). Juveniles also may not be held in excessive isolation or under unreasonable restraints, but most institutions permit the use of isolation and restraints when needed (Snyder & Sickmund, 1995). Juveniles must receive adequate medical care, mental health care, and education, and they must have access to legal counsel, family communication, recreation, exercise, and programming (del Carmen, Parker, & Reddington, 1998; Puritz & Scali, 1998). Despite these rights, reviews of conditions of confinement in detention centers, training schools, camps, ranches, farms, and other facilities for juveniles nationwide have indicated substantial and widespread problems in living space, health care, security, solitary confinement, and control of suicidal behavior (American Civil Liberties Union, 2014; Parent et al., 1994).

Against this backdrop, we now turn to the specific tasks that are performed by forensic psychologists in consultation with the juvenile justice system.

JUVENILE ASSESSMENT: AN OVERVIEW

As we have noted throughout the book, assessment is an essential component of the daily professional life of the forensic psychologist. Also called psychological evaluation, assessment refers to all the techniques used to measure and evaluate an individual's past, present, or future psychological status. It may be considered "the act of determining the nature and causes of a client's problem" (Lewis, Dana, & Blevins, 1994, p. 71). Thus, interviews, observations, and reviews of records and other documents are all part of the assessment process. Typically, when assessing a juvenile, the psychologist also administers a variety of tests to measure the juvenile's cognitive abilities and personality attributes, and in many cases measures to assess risk of violence or sexual offending.

The assessment usually includes phone or in-person interviews with relevant adults, including family members, and peers. Some forensic psychologists recommend observing the juvenile in a natural setting (e.g., in school, with parents and siblings at home) if possible. Although some forensic psychologists urge very wide-ranging assessment, others believe assessments should be limited in scope and should address only the referral question (e.g., did this juvenile possess the necessary cognitive ability to waive his or her right to a lawyer? Is it likely that this juvenile is competent to stand trial?). Until recently, in most jurisdictions there were no clinical requirements and few legal restrictions associated with these assessments; the specific approach taken was left to the individual clinician. Now, more states are endorsing specific guidelines or certification procedures for clinicians who will be submitting evaluation results to the courts (Heilbrun & Brooks, 2010). In addition, there is a wealth of information in the form of handbooks, guidelines, and research studies that offer suggestions to clinicians (e.g., American Psychological Association [APA], 2013b, 2013c; Grisso, 1998; Kruh & Grisso, 2009; Melton et al., 2007; Weiner & Otto, 2014).

The clinical literature advises forensic psychologists to be extremely cautious in assessing juveniles if their practice has been limited primarily to adults. "It is possible to conduct a seemingly competent evaluation but fail to obtain the data necessary to construct a complete picture of the developmental and familial context for the youth's clinical presentation and delinquent behavior" (Heilbrun, Marczyk, & DeMatteo, 2002, p. 187). Heilbrun et al. add that normal adolescent defensiveness and mistrust may make youths appear cold and remorseless. For instance, children of ethnic and racial groups that have experienced discrimination in society may be distrustful of authority figures, including the mental health professionals evaluating them. Adolescents as a group also may be reluctant to disclose embarrassing information that may actually help in their defense. For example, a juvenile may be charged with assaulting an individual who sexually abused him in the past, and the juvenile may be reluctant to disclose that abuse. Examiners also must be alert to the possibility of serious psychopathology, which can be overlooked in adolescents by clinicians accustomed to the symptomatology and clinical presentations of adults (Heilbrun et al., 2002).

Although assessment is an essential component of treatment, treatment does not necessarily accompany assessment. In fact, as we mentioned in earlier chapters, psychologists are warned to avoid—or at least be cautious of—dual roles of evaluator and treatment provider. The mental health practitioner evaluating the juvenile's competency should not be the person who has treated the juvenile in the past, nor should she be the person asked to restore the juvenile to competency if found not competent. Nevertheless, clinicians are often advised to include recommendations for treatment in assessment reports, if such treatment is known to be available (Grisso, 1998).

Risk Assessment

As mentioned in earlier chapters throughout the book, assessing risk is a common task of the forensic psychologist in numerous settings. With respect to juveniles, courts and juvenile facilities in particular are interested in knowing the likelihood that a juvenile will commit violence or other serious offending in the future. Judges take this into consideration in deciding whether to transfer juveniles to criminal courts (or vice versa) or deciding whether to impose community or institutional sanctions. Juvenile corrections decision makers often want to match a juvenile's placement setting or program with his or her risk level. A number of risk assessment instruments have been designed especially for juveniles, the two most prominent being the Structured Assessment of Violence Risk in Youth (SAVRY; Borum, Bartel, & Forth, 2006) and the Youth Level of Service/Case Management Inventory (YLS/CMI; Hoge & Andrews, 2002). (See Table 4.3 in Chapter 4 for other risk assessment measures.)

Risk assessment instruments are widely used by forensic psychologists assessing both juveniles and adults, and there is a rich literature evaluating their validity and effectiveness. Both commentators and professional standards warn mental health practitioners to choose the instruments they use very carefully and assure that they reflect best practices. The SAVRY and the YLS/CMI have both received favorable reviews and have demonstrated good predictive validity (e.g., Olver, Stockdale, & Wormith, 2014). In a recent article, however, Viljoen, Shaffer, Gray, & Douglas (2017) emphasized that risk assessment of juveniles should take into consideration the enormous changes in adolescent development and the likelihood that risk level fluctuates as a result. In their study of adolescent probationers, Viljoen et al. found that both the SAVRY and YLS/CMI could use improvement in their ability to measure short-term changes, though each instrument still holds promise for continued use with adolescents.

Assessment of Competence to Waive Miranda Rights

There is good evidence that many juveniles, like many adults, cannot understand their constitutional rights (Grisso & Schwartz, 2000; Rogers et al., 2010). Psychologists who evaluate them must be knowledgeable not only about the law, but also about adolescent development and decision making (Grisso, 1998; Heilbrun et al., 2002). Like adults, juveniles have a constitutional right not to incriminate themselves during their dealings with the criminal justice system. Juveniles do not have to answer questions posed by police while in custody (*Fare v. Michael C.*, 1979; *Miranda v. Arizona*, 1966). In addition, they do not have to take the stand during a delinquency proceeding, and they have the right to confront witnesses against them (*In re Gault*, 1967). The above cases also established that juveniles have a right to have an attorney present during custodial interrogation and have a right to the assistance of counsel in delinquency proceedings. (See Table 13.1 for a summary of Supreme Court cases relevant to juveniles.)

In reality, many if not most juveniles waive these constitutional rights, as do many adults. The police questioning of juveniles who have been taken into custody is far more likely to occur solely in the presence of a parent or non-lawyer guardian than in the presence of an attorney. Research suggests strongly that these adults often encourage the juveniles to cooperate with police, answer their questions, and confess to their offenses. "At the time of their children's arrests, many parents themselves are anxious, fearful, or confused during the police encounter. Others are angry at the youth and contribute to the coercive pressure of the interrogation" (Grisso, 1998, p. 44).

Under the law, a waiver is a valid one if it is made willingly, knowingly, and intelligently. At what age can the average juvenile meet this standard? Moreover, even if the average juvenile can meet the standard, what about *this* juvenile who is being confronted by police under stressful conditions? In *Fare v. Michael C.* (1979), the Supreme Court noted that a juvenile's waiver of the right to a lawyer before being questioned by police while in their custody (custodial interrogation) should be given very careful scrutiny if it comes to the court's attention (see Focus 13.3 for this and a more recent case on this issue). Thus, when defense attorneys challenge these waivers or when judges themselves decide there is reason to question their validity, forensic psychologists may be called in to evaluate the juveniles' cognitive development and the extent to which they understood what they were doing. A psychologist also may be asked to testify as an expert witness regarding research on adolescent development.

Psychologist Thomas Grisso has been one of the leading experts in adolescent development, the legal rights of juveniles, and a variety of forensic assessments. Early research by Grisso (1981) found that most juveniles age 14 and younger did not understand the meaning of the *Miranda* warning, nor the implications if they chose to waive their rights. Juveniles who were

Table 13.1 Representative U.S. Supreme Court Cases Relevant to Juveniles

Case Name and Year	Key Ruling
Kent v. United States (1966)	Juveniles have a right to a hearing before judges can transfer their cases to criminal court.
In re Gault (1967)	Juveniles have constitutional rights similar (but not identical) to those of adults in delinquency proceedings.
Breed v. Jones (1975)	Juveniles are protected from double jeopardy; cannot be charged in criminal court for same offense after being adjudicated delinquent in juvenile court.
McKeiver v. Pennsylvania (1978)	Juveniles have no constitutional right to jury trial in delinquency proceedings.
Fare v. Michael C. (1979) and *J.D.B. v. North Carolina* (2011)	Juveniles have right against self-incrimination at interrogation stage; age of juvenile waiving rights is crucial factor to consider.
Roper v. Simmons (2005)	Prohibits death penalty for juveniles.
Graham v. Florida (2010)	Prohibits mandatory life without parole for juveniles convicted of crimes other than murder.
Miller v. Alabama (2012) *Jackson v. Hobbs* (2012)	Prohibits mandatory life without parole for juveniles convicted of murder.
Montgomery v. Louisiana (2016)	Persons sentenced to life without parole prior to *Miller* should have their sentences reconsidered in light of that case.

slightly older—15 and 16—had similar difficulty if they were of below-average intelligence. As noted earlier, most recent research (e.g., Eastwood et al., 2016; N. E. S. Goldstein et al., 2013; Redlich, Silverman, & Steiner, 2003) has continued to document that age and suggestibility are strong predictors of comprehension of one's legal rights.

Grisso (1998) recommends that mental health professionals use three categories of instruments to assess whether a juvenile had sufficient competency to waive his or her rights. First, an instrument specifically designed for that purpose, such as the Comprehension of Miranda Rights (CMR) and its offshoots (e.g., the Comprehension of Miranda Rights–Recognition [CMR-R], the Comprehension of Miranda Vocabulary [CMV], and the Function of Rights in Interrogation [FRI]). Second, the examiner can use any standardized test of cognitive ability. Third, he or she may use a standard personality inventory. Grisso also recommends a review of school, mental health, and juvenile court records, when available, as well as interviews with parents or caretakers along with the youth himself or herself. In other words, Grisso recommends conducting a very extensive assessment in an effort to determine whether the youth provided a valid waiver of the right to an attorney during custodial interrogation.

Psychologist Richard Rogers and his colleagues (e.g., Rogers, Hazelwood et al., 2009; Rogers, Rogstad et al., 2010) also have conducted extensive research on comprehension of *Miranda* rights, including by juvenile suspects. They have developed and validated a Miranda Vocabulary Scale (MVS) to assess an individual's understanding of very basic terms used by police. Rogers (2011) notes that juveniles present formidable challenges to *Miranda* comprehension because of their young age, lack of maturity, and limited education. Based on available data, Rogers provided a conservative estimate that—out of 1.5 million juvenile arrests—311,000 juvenile suspects had impaired *Miranda* abilities (Rogers, 2011).

FOCUS 13.3. FROM *MICHAEL C.* TO *J. D. B.*: QUESTIONS OF INTERROGATION AND CUSTODY

The U.S. Supreme Court case *Fare v. Michael C.* (1979) involved a juvenile's waiver of his right to an attorney during police interrogation. Michael C. was a 16-year-old charged with murder. After arrest and at the police station, he was told he had a right to see an attorney, but he apparently interpreted this *Miranda* warning as a police trick. Described as immature, distraught, and poorly educated, Michael C. repeatedly asked to see his probation officer instead of a lawyer. He was told his probation officer would be contacted after he answered some police questions. Asked again if he wished to see an attorney, he said he did not.

The U.S. Supreme Court ruled against Michael C., in a 5–4 decision, though the Court did express concern as to whether juveniles have the capacity to fully understand the warning given to them, and warned judges to consider the social circumstances of the interrogation, including the age, education, intelligence, and background of the youth. Nevertheless, Michael C.'s request to see the probation officer was not considered the equivalent of a request to see a lawyer, and the Court said police did not err in refusing to grant the request.

About 30 years later, J.D.B., a 13-year-old seventh grader, was taken out of his classroom by a uniformed police officer, led to a conference room, and questioned about his involvement in a burglary and theft of a digital camera (*J.D.B. v. North Carolina*, 2011). Two police officers (one a school resource officer) and two representatives of the school administration were in the room, and the door was shut. J.D.B.'s grandmother, who was his legal guardian, was not contacted. The adults engaged him in small talk over a 45-minute period and at one point encouraged him to do the right thing and tell police what he knew. After he admitted to the burglary, he was told he didn't have to keep talking and could leave the room if he wanted to. Attorneys later representing J.D.B. argued that he was in custody, was not given adequate *Miranda* warnings, and that his confession was not a valid one.

Lower courts had determined that the youth was not in custody when questioned, and therefore that the *Miranda* warning was not even required. The Supreme Court cited psychological research on adolescent development, and noted that J.D.B.'s age should have been taken into consideration in deciding whether he perceived himself free to leave. Because age had not been sufficiently taken into consideration at the trial court level, the Supreme Court sent the case back to the state courts for a further review of the circumstances surrounding the questioning.

Questions for Discussion

1. The crime these two juveniles were accused of were very different. Does that matter?
2. Why might Michael C. have asked to see his probation officer rather than a lawyer? Should he have been allowed to do so?
3. What factors would you consider in deciding whether J.D.B. perceived himself to be free to leave the conference room?

False Confessions

In addition to evidence that juveniles have trouble understanding their legal rights, there is evidence that they sometimes confess to crimes they did not commit. As we discussed in Chapter 3, a false confession may occur for a wide range of reasons, some of which relate to psychological tactics used by police (e.g., Kassin, 1997; Kassin et al., 2010). For example, police may deceive a suspect into thinking they have evidence that they do not actually have, or they may befriend the suspect and convince the person that they are his or her only link to freedom. A juvenile eager to go home, or a juvenile who wants to protect a family member or friend, may decide to tell police what they want to hear. The highly publicized Central Park jogger case is only one illustration of many similar cases that have been documented. An evaluating clinician clearly should be alert to the possibility of a false confession.

Although false confessions are of concern regardless of the age of the suspect, it should come as no surprise that juveniles may be particularly susceptible to making them. Redlich and Goodman (2003) examined the suggestibility of three different age groups (12- and 13-year-olds, 15- and 16-year-olds, and 18- to 26-year-olds) in an experimental situation similar to many used in the false confession research (e.g., Kassin, 1997). Participants were given a computer task and told to not press a particular key. They were then told that they had pressed it when they really had not. In some experimental situations, the experimenter provides participants with "false evidence," in this case that they pressed the key. Researchers then tabulate the number of "false confessions" and try to determine what, in addition to age, distinguishes participants who "admit" to something they did not actually do from those who do not.

Redlich and Goodman (2003) examined whether (a) scores on the Gudjonsson Suggestibility Scale (GSS) and (b) the presentation of false evidence would predict and facilitate a false confession. The GSS is an instrument designed to measure the extent to which individuals are susceptible to being influenced by others. Results indicated that 69% of all participants falsely confessed or complied, 39% internalized (believed they had pressed the forbidden key), and 4% confabulated (made up details about their behavior during the study). However, significant age differences emerged. For the mid-level age group (15- and 16-year-olds), false confessions occurred particularly when false evidence was presented. The youngest age group falsely confessed both when false evidence was presented and when it was not. In general, the two youngest age groups were more likely to say they had done something wrong than were the young adults. With respect to individual differences, scores on the GSS predicted compliance (admitting to the "offense") but not internalization or confabulation.

Evaluating Adjudicative Competence

Juveniles whose cases are heard in criminal courts must, like adults, be competent to stand trial. Otherwise, the trial of an incompetent defendant violates due process of the law (*Drope v. Missouri*, 1975; *Dusky v. United States*, 1960). When a juvenile's case is heard in criminal court, competency to stand trial—if it is raised—is measured in accordance with the *Dusky* standard: sufficient present ability to consult with one's lawyer and a rational and factual understanding of the proceedings. Although most courts have not set a separate standard for juveniles, the *Dusky* standard is altered in some jurisdictions to inquire more carefully into the juvenile's decision-making abilities (Oberlander, Goldstein, & Ho, 2001).

Requiring courts to inquire more carefully into a juvenile's competence is a good move because many developmental psychologists and legal advocates for children believe that adjudicative competence in juveniles and adults is not identical. Even if a juvenile is knowledgeable about the role of the attorney and able to understand the charges, he or she may not be an *effective* participant in these proceedings. According to Richard Bonnie (1992), effective participation requires an ability to make decisions, weigh alternatives, and understand consequences—abilities he referred to as "decisional competency."

Juveniles may be particularly at a disadvantage when it comes to **decisional competency**. Although adults also may have deficits related to effective participation, juveniles—given their stage of development—are more likely to have these deficits and are thus at greater jeopardy. In addition, those juveniles who come before the juvenile courts are even more likely than other juveniles to be intellectually disabled, mentally disordered, or emotionally or socially immature. The problem does not disappear if the juveniles are transferred to criminal court. In fact, it might be even greater, because criminal court judges are not attuned to the needs of juveniles, having dealt with the legal question of competency primarily with adult defendants.

Competency to stand trial—or adjudicative competence—in the *juvenile* court with respect to delinquency proceedings has emerged as an issue only since the early 1990s (K. Larson & Grisso, 2012). Since then, there has been an explosion of research in this area (Fogel, Schiffman, Mumley, Tillbrook & Grisso, 2013). At this point, statutes or case law in about half the states *require* an inquiry into adjudicative competency in juvenile courts. In the remaining states, the competency inquiry is raised on a case-by-case basis. Precipitating the interest in juvenile competence has been research conducted by the MacArthur Research Network, discussed below, as well as the extensive research on adolescent cognitive development and decision making by Steinberg and his colleagues, cited in earlier chapters (e.g., Steinberg, 2010a; Steinberg & Cauffman, 1996).

MacArthur Juvenile Competence Study

In an effort to shed some light on the juvenile competency question, the MacArthur Research Network began gathering data in 1999 for a multisite study of adjudicative competence in juveniles. Major questions addressed by the research were the following (see the **MacArthur Juvenile Competence Study** home page at www.mac-adoldev-juvjustice.org):

- Compared to adults in the criminal justice system, do youth in the juvenile justice system more often manifest deficits in abilities related to adjudicative competence?

- If so, in what abilities are these differences most apparent, and how are those abilities related to development?

- What types of youth are at greatest risk of adjudicative incompetence due to developmental immaturity? Might developmental immaturity interact with mental disorders to create increased risks of deficits in abilities related to adjudicative incompetence? Is there an age below which incompetence to stand trial should be presumed?

- What methods could clinicians and courts use to identify youth who are seriously deficient in abilities related to adjudicative competence?

In the first phase of the above study, Grisso et al. (2003) compared abilities of 927 adolescents in juvenile detention facilities and community settings and 466 young adults (ages 18–24) in jails and community settings in Philadelphia, Los Angeles, northern and eastern Virginia, and northern Florida. In addition to a standard battery of tests and record reviews, the groups were asked to respond to vignettes and were administered the MacArthur Competence Assessment Tool–Criminal Adjudication (MacCAT-CA) and a newly developed MacArthur Judgment Evaluation. The two youngest adolescent groups (ages 11–13 and 14–15) were found to be 3 times and 2 times (respectively) as likely as the young adults to be seriously impaired in competence-relevant abilities. The 16- and 17-year-old juveniles did not differ from the young adults.

In addition to age, intelligence was also a predictor of poor performance. Gender, ethnicity, socioeconomic background, prior experience with the legal system, and symptoms of mental health problems were not predictors (although few individuals with serious mental health problems were included in the sample). The adolescents also tended to make choices that reflected compliance with authority and psychosocial immaturity. Grisso and his colleagues (2003) recommend that legal standards recognize immaturity as a possible indicator of incompetence to stand trial. In other words, children who are immature are unlikely to meet the standard for competency in criminal court. They recommend also that states rethink transferring juveniles age 13 and younger to criminal courts, given the high proportion of youth in that age group who were considered significantly impaired (about 30% total, but more than half of those with below-average intelligence).

JUVENILE AMENABILITY TO REHABILITATION

The decision as to whether a juvenile is likely to benefit from rehabilitative services and what types of services are most promising may be made at several points during juvenile justice processing. In addition, **amenability to rehabilitation** commonly takes into consideration a juvenile's present treatment needs. Two contexts in which courts request these evaluations are the judicial waiver decision and the disposition decision.

Waiver Decisions

Judges in both criminal and juvenile courts are often faced with the decision of whether to transfer jurisdiction of juveniles, or "waive" a juvenile to the other court. Most **judicial waivers** are made at the request of prosecutors who want to prosecute juveniles in adult criminal courts. In making the transfer decision, judges consider factors such as those recommended by the U.S. Supreme Court in *Kent v. United States* (1966), discussed earlier in the chapter.

The transfer by judges is only one of several possible forms of waiver. A great number of juveniles are tried in criminal courts as a result of **legislative waiver**, also called **statutory exclusion** or **waiver by statute**. These are waivers whereby the legislative branch has ordained that juveniles of specified ages will have their cases heard in criminal courts when charged with specific crimes. For example, in the vast majority of states, a 15-year-old charged with murder will automatically be tried in criminal court. (A criminal court judge may transfer his or her case to juvenile court, but this rarely occurs.) Still another form of waiver, **prosecutorial waiver**, gives prosecutors the authority to decide whether the case will be taken to juvenile court or criminal court. Most state statutes allow some combination of these waivers, depending on the age of the juvenile and the seriousness of the offense.

Important policy debates have occurred with respect to juvenile waivers. Should juvenile cases be heard in criminal or juvenile courts? Those who want to keep them in juvenile courts (such as the prosecutor referred to in the anecdote at the beginning of this chapter) argue that too many adolescents are consigned to the adult system, where the emphasis is on punishment more than on rehabilitation (Bishop, 2000). In addition, research indicates that transferring juveniles to adult criminal courts increases their recidivism and promotes life-course criminality. Furthermore, the potential of having their cases heard in criminal court apparently does not deter juveniles from committing crime (Redding, 2010).

Even when juveniles have been transferred to criminal courts, however, an amenability for rehabilitation evaluation may be requested. A defense attorney, for example, may desire such an assessment for help during the plea negotiation process or during the sentencing phase, if his or her client is convicted. Those who believe that some juvenile cases should be heard in criminal courts believe that a more punitive orientation is required, particularly for older adolescents. They argue that when the crime is a serious one, such as sexual assault or murder, it is not fair to the victim or survivors if the offender receives punishment of a few years in a juvenile facility and is then allowed to go free.

There is considerable debate about even trying juveniles in criminal courts, a phenomenon that has increased steadily in recent years. All but one state (Nebraska), along with the District of Columbia, enacted or expanded transfer provisions between 1992 and 1999 (Sickmund, 2003). In 2010, juvenile court judges waived jurisdiction over an estimated 6,000 juveniles, primarily males age 16 or 17 (Puzzanchera & Addie, 2014; Puzzanchera & Robson, 2014). By 2014, juvenile courts waived approximately 5,200 juveniles, a decrease of 42% from the highest number of waivers in 2006. These data suggest "a nationwide trend away from overreliance on out-of-home placements for juveniles toward community-based alternatives (Cruise, Morin, & Affleck, 2016, p. 611). Part of this trend reflects the increasing effectiveness of evidence-based treatment for juveniles within the juvenile justice system and outside institutional settings. Recall the material in Chapter 7, in which we discussed Steinberg's research on adolescent brain development. Opponents of trying juveniles in criminal courts argue that their emotional immaturity is such that they do not understand the consequences of their actions and must be treated differently from "full blown adults."

Juveniles being considered for transfer to criminal court have a good deal to lose. Prosecution in criminal court involves public proceedings, a criminal record if found guilty, and possible incarceration in an adult prison. A juvenile who is considered an unlikely candidate for rehabilitation in the juvenile system is not likely to get rehabilitative services once transferred to adult settings. Research has also documented that juveniles charged with serious crimes in criminal courts and juveniles facing property offenses in juvenile courts both get harsh dispositions (Podkopacz & Feld, 1996). However, juveniles sentenced in criminal courts typically get longer sentences than those in juvenile court for similar crimes (Redding, 2010).

Life Without Parole

A recent juvenile justice decision delivered by the U.S. Supreme Court, *Graham v. Florida* (2010), highlights the importance of amenability for rehabilitation. Graham, who was on probation, took part in a home invasion during which an elderly couple was harmed. He was tried in criminal court and was given a sentence of life without parole (LWOP), without the opportunity to argue that society should not give up on him and that he had potential to be rehabilitated. (See Focus 13.4 for more information about this and other LWOP cases.)

At the beginning of the 21st century, some 2,500 prisoners who were juveniles at the time of their crimes were serving LWOP sentences. In Graham's case, the U.S. Supreme Court established that a LWOP sentence is cruel and unusual punishment for juveniles, at least for those not convicted of murder. In two later companion cases, the Supreme Court ruled that *mandatory* life without parole in a murder case was also unconstitutional (*Jackson v. Hobbs*, 2012 and *Miller v. Alabama*, 2012). Although state laws required judges to sentence juveniles convicted of murder to life-without-parole sentences, the Court ruled that judges should have the discretion to give less severe sentences upon consideration of the juvenile's age, the nature of the crime, and possible mitigating factors. The Supreme Court has since ruled that prisoners who had been given LWOP sentences before the Jackson and Miller cases were announced, could have their sentences reconsidered (*Montgomery v. Louisiana*, 2016).

For some sentencing judges, though, a life without parole option was not needed: They imposed lengthy regular sentences that would effectively keep young offenders incarcerated for their whole lives. For example, a judge in California gave a 110-year-sentence to a 16-year-old, which would have made him eligible for parole—but not for 100 years. The California Supreme Court vacated that sentence (*People v. Caballero*, 2012).

Disposition

Disposition is the equivalent of sentencing in the adult context. Once a juvenile has been adjudicated a delinquent in a delinquency hearing, the judge chooses from a variety of disposition alternatives, ranging from community-based services to confinement in a secure facility. In most jurisdictions, however, juvenile judges themselves do not choose among a variety of community alternatives. The judges place juveniles in the custody of juvenile justice officials (e.g., a juvenile correctional agency or a department of human services) who determine the best program approach for each juvenile. That said, placement in a secure facility must be made by a juvenile court. In either case—community setting or institution—psychological assessment may occur later in the process rather than in consultation with the juvenile court. Juvenile correctional officials may want help deciding on a programmatic approach for a particular juvenile. A juvenile probation officer, for example, may wonder whether a boy on her caseload is a good candidate for a substance abuse program in the community.

The extent to which psychologists actually do consult with the juvenile courts for amenability to rehabilitation evaluations varies by jurisdiction. It appears that they are used more prior to judicial waivers than prior to disposition, though after *Graham v. Florida* and *Miller v. Alabama* we may see them occurring more in criminal courts. Podkopacz and Feld (1996) found that court psychologists had examined and filed reports on 46% of juveniles facing transfer proceedings in their Minnesota sample, with percentages increasing in later years (63% in 1991 and 57% in 1992). By comparison, Hecker and Steinberg (2002) found that only 2% to 3% of juvenile cases in the jurisdiction they studied were referred for psychological assessment *prior to disposition*. A slightly higher

FOCUS 13.4. JUVENILE LIFE WITHOUT PAROLE

Terrance Jamar Graham's family background is littered with unfortunate circumstances, including parents addicted to crack cocaine and a diagnosis of ADHD (attention-deficit/hyperactivity disorder). He was 16 years old when he was arrested and charged with armed burglary and attempted robbery of a restaurant. Graham's case was heard in criminal court, and he was convicted and placed on probation. While on probation, he was allegedly involved in a home invasion, although he denied this charge. He did admit to associating with the young adults who perpetrated the offense and fleeing from the scene. Because he violated the conditions of his probation, he was returned to court and then sentenced to life without parole (LWOP) for a combination of offenses including the original armed burglary, attempted robbery, and probation violations. Graham did not kill anyone.

The U.S. Supreme Court ruled in *Graham v. Florida* (2010)—along with a similar companion case—that a sentence of life without the possibility of parole for juvenile offenders who did not commit murder was cruel and unusual punishment in violation of the Eighth Amendment of the Constitution. Observers wondered whether the Court would rule the same way if a juvenile had been convicted of murder. Two years later, the Court answered that question.

In both *Miller v. Alabama* and *Jackson v. Hobbs* (2012), a 14-year-old had been convicted of murder and given a mandatory sentence of life without the possibility of parole, essentially insuring that the two offenders would spend the rest of their lives in prison. In both cases, the sentencing judge had no discretion to give a lighter sentence. The Supreme Court ruled that a *mandatory* sentence of this nature was unconstitutional. However, judges could still impose such a sentence if individual circumstances of a case warranted. As noted in the text, the recent case of *Montgomery v. Louisiana* applies the Miller and Jackson rule retroactively to prisoners who

as juveniles were previously sentenced to life without parole.

Along with other professional organizations (the American Psychiatric Association, the National Association of Social Workers, and Mental Health America), the American Psychological Association had filed an amicus curiae brief arguing against the life sentences in each of the above cases.

Citing extensive research in developmental psychology and neuroscience, the briefs stated, among other things, the following:

- Compared with adults, juveniles have a lesser capacity for mature judgment.
- Juveniles are more vulnerable to negative external influences than are adults.
- Their unformed identity makes it less likely that their offenses evince a fixed bad character and more likely that they will reform.
- Their psychosocial immaturity is consistent with emerging research on brain development.
- It is disproportionate punishment to sentence them to die in prison with no opportunity to demonstrate reform.

Questions for Discussion

1. The Supreme Court decision in the *Miller* and *Jackson* cases indicates that *mandatory* LWOP sentences are unconstitutional, even for juveniles convicted of murder. However, it left open the possibility that a judge could give such a sentence if circumstances warranted it. Should the Court have set a complete ban on LWOP sentences for all persons who commit their offenses while juveniles?
2. What are the advantages of having professional groups such as the APA submit amicus briefs to appellate courts?

---

percentage (10%–15%) was referred for screening, as opposed to full assessment. (It is possible, though, that the records of juveniles not referred contained psychological reports of evaluations that had been conducted earlier in the juvenile process.) It should be noted that in both of the above studies, the recommendations of the clinicians carried heavy weight with judges.

Conducting the Evaluation

A number of manuals and suggestions are available for psychologists conducting psychological evaluations relating to transfer and disposition decisions (e.g., Grisso, 1998; Melton et al.,

1997, 2007). As Hecker and Steinberg (2002) observed, though, "an empirically validated 'gold standard' for the predisposition evaluation of juvenile offenders remains elusive" (p. 300). Psychologists are typically advised to review the juvenile's files, including school, social service, and juvenile court records. In addition, they are advised to obtain information about family history and substance use and abuse, as well as to assess intellectual, academic, personality, and vocational functioning, using a range of possible measures. Furthermore, although most juvenile offenders are not *seriously* emotionally disturbed, mental health needs are common, and—according to recent research—very prevalent (e.g., Grisso, 2008). Juveniles in correctional facilities, for example, are believed to have mental health issues ranging from conduct disorders to severe depression and suicidal tendencies (LeCroy, Stevenson, & MacNeil, 2001). Developmental disabilities and cognitive impairment also plague both institutionalized juveniles and those under community supervision (K. Day & Berney, 2001). Many juvenile offenders also are substance abusers, often with significant chemical dependency problems, and many others are sex offenders. Developing and validating instruments for the evaluation of juvenile sex and violent offenders (e.g., J-SOAP, ERASOR, Static-99, Static-2002) have become robust activities in recent years. The psychologist assessing juveniles, therefore, should be aware of both assessment techniques and the range of treatment and rehabilitation services available, in the community as well as within institutional settings.

Many psychologists are concerned about the possible negative effects of labeling juveniles. Of particular concern are those labels that suggest the prospects for change are not good. In recent years, for example, juvenile psychopathy has received considerable research attention. It has prompted the development of a special version of Hare's Psychopathy Checklist, the Psychopathy Checklist: Youth Version (PCL:YV) (Forth, Kosson, & Hare, 1997). Recall from Chapter 7 that some researchers have argued that it is premature to place this pessimistic label on juveniles who may possess psychopathic characteristics that they may well outgrow (Edens, Skeem, Cruise, & Cauffman, 2001; Edens & Vincent, 2008; Seagrave & Grisso, 2002). Edens, Skeem, Cruise, and Cauffman (2001) also suggest that labeling adolescents this way may violate the two ethical principles of social responsibility and do no harm. In addition, there is concern that labeling a juvenile as a psychopath will be harmful in various legal proceedings (Viljoen, MacDougall, Gagnon, & Douglas, 2010). In an evaluation of a juvenile's amenability for rehabilitation, for example, labeling the juvenile a psychopath would almost assuredly guarantee that he or she will be transferred to criminal court. Somewhat in response to the above controversy, many researchers now prefer to refer to "juveniles with psychopathic characteristics" (e.g., callousness) rather than "juvenile psychopaths." In addition, research on both identification and treatment of such juveniles is expanding rapidly (Salekin, Leistico, Trobst, Schrum, & Lochman, 2005) as is research on protective factors that might reduce the likelihood that psychopathy would develop (Salekin & Lochman, 2008).

Another pessimistic label that might be problematic is *life course–persistent offender* (LCP), in accordance with Moffitt's (1993a) adolescent limited AL–LCP dichotomy, also covered in Chapter 7. Some diagnostic categories in the *DSM-5* (e.g., ADHD, conduct disorder) are problematic if the individuals working with the juvenile after the assessment do not understand the limitations of these diagnoses as well as their significance. Labels that make their way into files of juveniles in correctional facilities or community programs may be as damaging as the labels that make their way into school files of non-delinquent children.

Hecker and Steinberg (2002) appraised the quality of psychological evaluations submitted to juvenile courts prior to disposition as well as the effect of the reports on judges' decision making. They reviewed 172 predisposition reports submitted to juvenile courts in Philadelphia between 1992 and 1996 by four independent practitioners who were licensed psychologists in Pennsylvania.

Findings included the following:

- A vast majority of the assessments included a standardized measure of intellectual functioning, but few included a standardized personality measure; instead, projective tests were typically administered for measuring personality.

- There were no statistically significant individual differences in either judges' acceptance or rejection of recommendations or among clinicians in whether their recommendations were accepted or rejected.

- A high percentage of recommendations were accepted; in fact, recommendations were fully rejected in only 8 of the 172 cases.

- Many reports lacked information about the juvenile's mental health, criminal, or substance abuse history, all of which the researchers considered crucial information because of their links to recidivism.

- Judges were most likely to accept recommendations if the reports included information about mental health, regardless of the quality of this information. This was troubling to the researchers, who believed that reports did not include sufficient detail in this area, as noted above.

Hecker and Steinberg (2002) emphasized that their study may not be representative of other jurisdictions, considering the small number of judges and clinicians as well as the small number of cases in their sample. Nevertheless, they described a useful coding scheme by which researchers might evaluate predisposition reports, along with their impact on judicial decisions in other jurisdictions.

In sum, research on amenability to rehabilitation evaluations suggests that they vary widely in quality, despite the fact that there is some consensus on what should be included in the evaluation reports. Most sources recommend comprehensive evaluations that will assess the juvenile's family background; determine developmental, cognitive, and emotional functioning; and identify promising treatment options. Evaluators are advised to avoid labels that might be pessimistic and suggest that there is little hope for the juvenile. As Grisso (1998) has noted, a pessimistic report may become a self-fulfilling prophecy if the rehabilitation staff becomes discouraged. "Reservations about the prospect for change . . . should always be coupled with suggestions to staff that might increase the prospects" (p. 192).

OUT-OF-HOME PLACEMENTS

As noted earlier in the chapter, cases handled by juvenile courts have decreased in numbers in recent years, and this has been accompanied by a decrease in out-of-home placements. Nonetheless, although probation remains the modal disposition for juveniles in juvenile court, some 1,852 juveniles were held in confinement out of their homes in 2015. These placements included training schools, treatment centers, wilderness camps, and group homes, both public and private (see Table 13.2 for total numbers of residential placements).

Facilities that hold juvenile offenders vary widely in size, organizational complexity, and layout (Sedlak & McPherson, 2010a). They range from the simple, one- or two-building structures to complex facilities that consist of multiple buildings. Some are small, handling as few as 10 youths, while the largest may hold into the hundreds.

It may be surprising that about 12% of youth in residential placement live in facilities that house both offenders and non-offenders (Sedlak & McPherson, 2010a). This is because some youth facilities house youth who are in custody because the juvenile court wants to protect them (Sedlak & McPherson, 2010a). For example, they may have been abused or neglected, or they do not have a parent or guardian. In some instances, families may have voluntarily placed them in a private facility for mental health or substance abuse treatment. Although such facilities are not of high security, they are still considered highly restrictive placements.

Juveniles, like adults, also may be provided with intermediate sanctions, which are less restrictive than residential placement but more restrictive than the standard probation under

Table 13.2 Number and Types of Facilities Holding Youth in Residential Placement Nationwide, Including Both Detained and Committed Youth

	Total	Detention Center	Shelter	Reception/ Diagnostic Center	Group Home	Ranch/ Wilderness Camp	Training School	Residential Treatment Center
Number of facilities	1,852	664	143	61	360	37	176	726
All facilities	100%	100%	100%	100%	100%	100%	100%	100%
Public	54	92	38	72	19	76	91	33
State	21	21	3	56	7	22	68	19
Local	33	71	35	16	12	54	24	14
Private	46	8	62	28	81	24	9	67

Source: Adapted from Hockenberry et al., 2016.

which the juvenile remains in his or her own home with conditions attached. Examples of intermediate sanctions are day reporting centers and intensive supervision programs. In intensive supervision programs, probation officers ideally have a small caseload, conduct frequent monitoring, and provide intensive counseling and other services to juveniles.

A major difference between juvenile and adult corrections is the number of private facilities available, although as was noted in the previous chapter, the private prison industry for adults is now growing. Although they do not hold as many juveniles (only 31% of the total youth offenders), there are more privately operated than publicly operated facilities for juveniles (Bayer & Pozen, 2003; Hockenberry, 2013; Snyder & Sickmund, 2006). Private facilities are operated by private nonprofit or for-profit corporations or organizations. Those who work in such facilities are employees of the private corporation or organization. Private facilities have the advantage of restricting their populations to those juveniles they believe they are best able to help, but they are not necessarily the best option for youth and may suffer from lack of oversight. Nevertheless, some innovative treatment programs have been tried and tested in private facilities.

Juvenile Detention

As Table 13.2 indicates, also included under the rubric of juvenile corrections is **juvenile detention**, which is defined as a *temporary* secure or nonsecure placement pending adjudication or during adjudication proceedings, up to a final disposition. In other words, some youth are held in detention following arrest; through their delinquency hearing; and up until the time the judge decides whether to place them on probation, order them to residential treatment, or neither one. Although the term *detention* is widely used to pertain to placement at any point in time, it should technically be used in the above limited sense.

Like adults, juveniles are presumed innocent until proven guilty. Adults, though, have a greater presumption of being released prior to their next court appearance. Adults may be denied bail and held in preventive detention if they are charged with a capital crime or demonstrated to be dangerous (*United States v. Salerno*, 1987). Juveniles, however, may be held in preventive detention for their own protection or if there is a serious risk that they will commit *any* crime before their next court appearance (*Schall v. Martin*, 1984). This gives juvenile judges a wide leeway to detain juveniles, although most juveniles are *not* detained. The number of delinquency cases involving detention increased 48% from 1985 to 2007 (Puzzanchera et al., 2010) but decreased 17% between 2007 and 2010 (Hockenberry, 2013).

▶ Photo 13.1 Juveniles in a classroom in a youth correctional facility. *Source:* Mikael Karlsson / Alamy Stock Photo.

Far more male juvenile offenders are held in *residential placements* than female juvenile offenders (86% compared to 14%) (Hockenberry, 2016). In addition, racial minorities are disproportionately represented among *detained* youth populations, even though they have lower violence risks on average than white youths (Desari, Falzer, Chapman, & Borum, 2012). The most recent statistics had black youths detained at 6 times the rate of white youths (Hockenberry, 2016).

Juveniles in detention—technically defined—have not been adjudicated and thus cannot be placed in a rehabilitation program. For example, a youth accused of sexual assault should not be placed in a treatment program for juvenile sex offenders because he has not been found guilty of that offense. Many public juvenile facilities have detention and treatment wings, with treatment reserved for those juveniles who have been adjudicated delinquent. On the other hand, juveniles in detention *can* be provided with substance abuse treatment, sex education, remedial education, and other such services during the time they are held, similar to youth in residential placement (see Photo 13.1).

Detention centers have come under scrutiny for their overcrowded conditions and disproportionate confinement of minority youth. The most recent survey of youths in residential placement, including both detained and committed youth, indicated that minority youth accounted for 68% of the population, with black males forming the largest share (Hockenberry, 2016). As noted above, the detention rate for black youth was nearly 6 times the rate for white youth, and their commitment rate was more than 4 times the rate for white youth. Put another way, black youth are significantly more likely than youth of any other race to be detained and committed to an out-of-home placement facility. Generally, numerous problems are detected for youth in confinement, whether they be in "detention" or "rehabilitation" (see Focus 13.5). However, because of important differences, we will preserve the "pure" meaning of *detention*. Whenever the word is used, the reader should realize that it refers to *temporary* placement and that the youth under these conditions have not yet been adjudicated delinquent, with the exception of those who have been so adjudicated and are awaiting the judge's disposition (sentencing) decision.

PSYCHOLOGICAL TREATMENT IN JUVENILE FACILITIES

Numerous studies have documented mental health needs of juveniles in the care of the juvenile justice system, particularly those in institutional settings. Some research indicates that nearly two thirds of males and three quarters of females in juvenile detention centers and correctional facilities meet the criteria for one or more mental disorders (Abram et al., 2013; Grisso, 2008). It is also known that the symptoms of mental disorders in adolescence often lead to impulsive, aggressive, and violent behaviors, particularly when the adolescent has two or more mental disorders. In an anonymous survey of youth in residential placements across the United States, 60% reported that they were easily upset, quick to lose their temper, and often angry (Sedlak & McPherson, 2010b). These characteristics do not necessarily indicate mental disorder, however. More significantly, according to Grisso (2008), various forms of clinical depression are found in about 10% to 25% of youth in juvenile justice settings.

FOCUS 13.5. YOUTH IN CONFINEMENT

In 2010 and again in 2013, the U.S. Department of Justice released reports (Beck et al., 2010; Beck et al., 2013) that gained considerable attention in the media. Surveys of youth in juvenile confinement facilities, both state owned and operated and private, indicated that about 12% in the first survey and 9.5% in the second had experienced one or more incidents of sexual victimization over the past year (or since their admission if they had not been confined that long). The facilities included both state and large private residential centers. Incidents involving staff victimization were more prevalent than those involving other youth, but the decline in overall victimization was attributed to a decline in staff victimization (from about 11.2% of youth reporting victimization in the 2010 report to 8.7% in the second). In both surveys, about 2.5% of the youth reported an incident involving another youth. The majority of the incidents involving other youth occurred with force or threats of force, while about one fourth involved offers of favors or protection. In the remainder, the victims were given drugs or alcohol to engage in sexual conduct.

In a separate news item, a state director of an office of family and children's services stepped down from her position after it was learned that juvenile males in a state-run facility were rewarded for their good behavior by being allowed to have a party to which they could invite female friends and prostitutes from the outside. Drug use and sexual activity allegedly occurred at these parties.

In still other news flashes, juvenile detention or treatment centers have been closed after evidence of physical abuse and neglect of the mental health needs of the residents was obtained. Stories like these come as no surprise to advocates for juveniles, many of whom argue forcefully that juveniles should be placed in secure confinement only as a last resort.

Nevertheless, like adult prison populations, the numbers of youth in residential placement have gone down in recent years, now being at its lowest since 1997 (Hockenberry, 2016). Additionally, nationwide data indicate that the great majority of facilities do provide services to youth in their care. In a recent report (Hockenberry, Wachter, & Stadky, 2016, p. 1), it is noted that "Almost all facilities (87%) reported that a portion of all residents attended some type of school. Most responding facilities routinely evaluated all residents for substance abuse (74%), mental health needs (58%), and suicide risk (90%)."

Questions for Discussion

1. Given the assumption that at least *some* youths should be confined in secure institutions or given out-of-home placement, discuss the "ideal" way of accomplishing this.

2. Comment on the above quoted statistics related to the services provided to youth in residential facilities.

3. Are any of the following groups more or less appropriate for secure (locked-down) confinement: girls, mentally disordered juveniles, juveniles with suicidal tendencies, substance abusers, juvenile sex offenders, gang members? To what extent should these characteristics be taken into consideration in deciding whether a youth should be confined?

The national survey by Sedlack and McPherson (2010b) also found that about half of the youth offenders indicated they were depressed. Fazel, Doll, and Långström (2008) found similar results, although they also discovered that girls in detention or correctional facilities were 3 times more likely to be diagnosed with severe depression than boys. Available data (e.g., Sedlak & McPherson, 2010b) indicate that girls in custody have more mental health and substance use problems, and experience a more extensive history of abuse, than boys in custody (Blum, Ireland, & Blum, 2003; Hubbard & Pratt, 2002; Teplin, Abram, McLelland, Dulcan, & Mericle, 2002).

Grisso (2008) observes that depressed adolescents, male or female, are commonly very irritable, sullen, and hostile, unlike depressed adults who tend to be sad and withdrawn. The irritable moodiness of these youth increases the likelihood that they will provoke angry responses from their social environments, including peers. In far too many instances, these angry responses escalate to physical aggression and potential violence. This connection between anger and aggression may, in some cases, lead to self-injurious behavior like cutting or head banging.

In addition, Fazel and associates (2008) found that adolescents in detention and correctional facilities are about 10 times more likely to have psychosis (serious mental disorder) than the general adolescent population. These figures held for both boys and girls. Research also links psychiatric disorder in juveniles with suicidal behavior (Wasserman, McReynolds, Schwalbe, Keating, & Jones, 2010).

Related to the above discussion are the observations by Sedlak and McPherson (2010a) concerning the mental health services provided in delinquent youth facilities. In their extensive survey, they discovered that mental health services in the form of evaluation, ongoing therapy, or counseling are nearly universal in the facilities studied. Recall, though, that in the most recent census of residential facilities (Hockenberry et al., 2016), just under 60% evaluated all residents for mental health needs. Moreover, Sedlak and McPherson found that many mental health personnel were untrained or marginally capable of meeting the needs of the youth held in many of the facilities, a fact that suggests that the quality of the programs—seen as an essential factor by Lipsey (2009)—is lacking. For instance, only half of the youth surveyed were in facilities that provide mental health evaluations or appraisals. Moreover, despite the relatively high suicide risk in the juvenile population in residential placement, screening for suicide risk was not common. Again in the latest survey (Hockenberry et al., 2016), though, 90% routinely screened for suicide risk. Given concerns expressed by Sedlak and McPherson, however, adequate staff training must be assured. They conclude,

> Overall, current mental health services for youth in custody still fall short of key recommendations for practice, which suggest that all youth offenders receive suicide risk and other mental health screens and that all mental health screens and assessments be administered by properly trained staff. (Sedlak & McPherson, 2010b, p. 3)

Treatment for mental disorders are not the only needs of youth in institutional settings, of course. In addition to educational needs, they may benefit from substance abuse treatment, self-efficacy, alternatives to violence, nutritional and other health information, and improvement of social skills, among others. Yet research continually shows that good-quality interventions that would be of benefit are not available to many juvenile offenders, both institutionalized and on probation (Haqanee, Peterson-Badali, & Skilling, 2015; Peterson-Badali, Skilling, & Haqanee, 2015).

Developmental disabilities and cognitive impairments also plague both institutionalized juveniles and those under community supervision (K. Day & Berney, 2001). Many juvenile offenders also are substance abusers, often with significant chemical dependency problems. For instance, Loeber, Burke, and Lahey (2002) discovered that 40% to 50% of delinquent youth were found to have substance abuse disorders compared to only 15% of non-delinquent youth. Youth offenders with multiple limitations abound. It is not unusual, for example, for a juvenile rehabilitation facility to receive a depressed sex offender who abuses alcohol and has attempted suicide.

Grisso (2008) observes that some adolescents have a mental disorder for a significant period of time, while others show symptoms of a mental disorder for only a short time. On the other hand, some juvenile offenders do not have mental disorders, developmental disabilities, or substance abuse problems at all. Nevertheless, these adolescents would benefit from treatment programs addressing their violent behaviors or their chronic property offending. Furthermore, a substantial number of juvenile offenders have been victims of violence, including sexual assault, and many have witnessed intimate partner violence (IPV) in their homes. Others have experienced the effects of intense conflict between parents or a bitter separation or divorce. Over two thirds of the youth responding to the Sedlak and McPherson (2010b) survey reported experiencing some form of trauma, including physical or sexual abuse. Consequently, programs that focus on treatment of juvenile offenders often address the effects of victimization. For example, they offer strategies for developing social skills and improving a self-concept that may have been shattered by years of abuse. A significant number of programs for juveniles incorporate family treatment along with individual and group treatment.

At the end of the 20th century, numerous questions were raised about the efficacy of treatment provided to juveniles, particularly in institutional settings. A noteworthy meta-analytic review of juvenile treatment programs (Whitehead & Lab, 1989) produced discouraging results. The authors analyzed evaluations of juvenile correctional treatment that had appeared in professional journals from 1975 to 1984 and found little positive impact on recidivism. In fact, many of the programs appeared to exacerbate recidivism. The authors also found no support for the superiority of behavioral interventions over other forms. Diversionary approaches, those intended to steer juveniles away from formal court processing, did show some favorable results, however. Numerous researchers since have advocated keeping youth in community settings as much as possible (e.g., Grisso, 2008; Lambie & Randell, 2013)

Not all reviewers were as pessimistic as the Whitehead and Lab (1989) meta-analysis would suggest. As we noted in the chapter on adult corrections, many scholars and researchers have not given up on rehabilitation and are intent on documenting the effectiveness of some programs for some individuals. Psychologists have uncovered a number of principles associated with effective treatment, even in institutional settings. For example, cognitive-behavioral approaches and "multimodal approaches" that integrate group, individual, and family treatment to the extent possible have received good reviews. In a recent meta-analytic overview, Lipsey (2009) found three factors that were associated with program effectiveness: (1) a therapeutic intervention philosophy; (2) serving of high-risk offenders; and (3) quality of the program, meaning that the treatment providers were carefully trained and supervised and lapses in quality were quickly corrected. Interestingly, the Lipsey meta-analysis also found that the level of juvenile justice supervision (e.g., intensive supervision, probation, secure custody) did not show a relationship to the success of the intervention, suggesting that "effective treatment is not highly context dependent" (p. 143).

APPROACHES TO REHABILITATION

At one point, there was a widely held belief that nothing works in the treatment of juvenile offenders, but in recent years, there has been a discernible shift toward identifying and enabling better treatment (Heilbrun et al., 2016). "This shift . . . parallels and incorporates advancements in the understanding of adolescents' cognitive, emotional, behavioral, and neurological development" (Heilbrun et al., 2016, p. 14). The research evaluating treatment effectiveness studies is also better. Effective treatment and rehabilitation are best described as that which reduces illegal, antisocial behavior and meets the juvenile's individual needs. There is reason for optimism, as many treatment programs for juvenile offenders are beginning to demonstrate such effectiveness (Baldwin, Christian, Berkeljion, & Shadish, 2012; Cruise et al., 2016; van der Stouwe, Asscher, Stams, Dekovic', & van der Laan, 2014). These optimistic trends are especially apparent in community placement approaches, many but not all of which are out of home. In this section, we review some of the more common forms of treatment available in out-of-home placements.

Group Home Models

For a wide variety of reasons, many juveniles cannot remain in their own homes, yet they do not need to be placed in a *secure* treatment facility. Group homes are a common alternative, allowing juveniles to remain in their community, attend school, and be provided with services in the community on an outpatient basis (e.g., counseling, therapy, substance abuse prevention program). It is an important principle of juvenile justice that the least restrictive placement should be used, a principle that critics charge is too often not honored in practice.

One of the most common models for the treatment of adolescents in a group home setting is the **teaching-family model,** initiated in 1967 with the opening of the Achievement

Place home in Kansas. By the turn of the 21st century, there were approximately 134 such group homes in the United States for delinquents, abused and neglected children, and autistic and developmentally challenged children and young adults (Bernfeld, 2001). In the typical teaching-family home, the teaching parents are a couple with specialized training and usually with master's degrees in human services. They live in a family-like situation with up to seven youths and have assistants available on a daily basis. Consultants serve in a supervisory capacity and integrate treatment, training, and specialized services as needed. "Almost without exception, consultants started out as practitioners and then obtained the extra training to become consultants" (Fixsen, Blasé, Timbers, & Wolf, 2001, p. 163).

Fixsen, Blasé, Timbers, and Wolf (2001) have candidly reviewed the growing pains of the teaching-family model, noting how earlier attempts to replicate the apparent success of Achievement Place produced discouraging results. In 1978, the first meetings of the Teaching-Family Association were held, and the association continues to identify goals, produce ethical standards, and provide training and other services to individuals involved in this model (Teaching-Family Association, 1993, 1994). In addition, the model has attracted positive reviews in the literature (American Psychological Association (2003a); Fixsen, Blasé, Timbers, & Wolf, 2007).

Teaching-family homes originally operated primarily on a token-economy model—a behavior-modification approach that was quite popular in psychology in the 1960s and 1970s for institutional settings. Residents would receive tokens or points for good behavior and could then exchange these points for privileges, such as longer recreation time or a more desirable work assignment. However, "bad" behavior resulted in loss of tokens and, consequently, the removal of privileges. Transferring the token economy to a natural setting, such as a group home, is more of a challenge (Reppucci & Saunders, 1974; Wolf, Kirigin, Fixsen, Blasé, & Braukmann, 1995). As a result, although reinforcement for good behavior and a system of points and privileges remain important aspects of the teaching-family home, additional treatment services are provided. The concept is usually not recommended, however, for adolescents with serious mental health problems or for those who have been charged with or found to have committed serious offenses.

The teaching-family home has many positive features that should be helpful to *nonserious* delinquents who are unable to remain in their own homes, at least temporarily. Warm and compassionate teaching parents, the maintenance of ties with natural family and with the community, and the opportunity to learn prosocial behaviors are among these features. Nevertheless, studies indicate that behavioral gains—including reductions in substance use and increases in prosocial behaviors—while adolescents are in the teaching-family home are typically not maintained when they have left (Mulvey, Arthur, & Reppucci, 1993).

In recent years, many have argued that group homes—like juvenile justice programs in general—should give more attention to cultural diversity and specific cultural needs of individual juveniles (e.g., Eron et al., 1994). Black, Latino, and Asian American youth, for example, can benefit from a group home placement that encourages them to acknowledge, learn about, and celebrate their cultural heritage. Evaluations of culturally sensitive programs indicate that they lower recidivism and increase self-efficacy (Eron et al., 1994; W. R. King et al., 2001). One such program, the House of Umoja in Philadelphia, provides education, cultural treatment, counseling, and substance abuse treatment to black male at-risk youth ages 15 to 18. Similar programs funded by the Office of Juvenile Justice and Delinquency Prevention (OJJDP) operate across the nation, primarily in urban areas.

Likewise, gender-specific programming is critical. Girls, including delinquent girls, often have needs that are very different from those of boys. Delinquent girls are more likely than boys to have been victims of child sexual abuse and intimate partner violence; in addition, they are more likely to be lacking in self-esteem (Budnick & Shields-Fletcher, 1998; Sedlak & McPherson, 2010b; Sorensen & Bowie, 1994). They are also less likely than boys to be charged with a violent offense (Snyder & Sickmund, 1999). Adolescent girls also are more likely than adolescent boys to suffer from mental disorders, particularly depression (Sedlack & McPherson, 2010b; Teplin et al., 2002). However, girls also may be more likely than boys to self-report symptoms of depression. Although group home options may appear to be warranted for girls, they often come to these homes with family backgrounds that may be even more complex than those of delinquent boys.

Family Preservation Models

Many advocates for children maintain that they should be kept in their own homes, with their own parents or close relatives, if at all possible (e.g., D. A. Gordon, 2002; Henggeler, 1996). They believe that providing a wide range of support services, even to highly dysfunctional families, is in the best interest of the children and adolescents who are part of these families. It must be acknowledged, however, that family preservation is not in the best interest of all children and adolescents. Despite the optimistic appraisals and documented success of family preservation that will be covered below, some juveniles may not be well served by intense efforts to make their family situation work for them. This is particularly true of children and adolescents who have been victimized in their own homes, by parents or caretakers or by siblings. As Chesney-Lind and Shelden (1998) indicate,

> Family counseling that is grounded in the notion that maintenance of the family unit is uppermost needs to be critically reviewed in light of the extreme physical and sexual violence that some girls in the juvenile justice system report. In some instances, the victimized girl or boy must be allowed to live away from the parents. (p. 219)

With this caveat, we turn now to a discussion of the positive aspects of family preservation.

Homebuilders

One highly regarded family preservation approach is the **Homebuilders model**, an exemplary program for families in which one or more children are at risk of being removed from the home because of their antisocial behavior (Haapala & Kinney, 1988; Whittaker, Kinney, Tracy, & Booth, 1990). It is probably the oldest intensive family preservation services program in the United States. In the Homebuilders model, one or two caseworkers—typically social workers with master's degrees—work intensively with a family for a short period of time; they are available to the family around the clock and are highly proactive in obtaining needed services. The goal is to prevent the out-of-home placement of children through intensive, on-site intervention, and to teach families new problem-solving skills. These services might be wide ranging. For example, they might include helping find a job for one of the family members, transportation, tutoring, family therapy, after-school programming, or a mentor for a young adolescent. An evaluation of the homebuilders program by Haapala and Kinney produced highly favorable results, with 87% of the children avoiding out-of-home placement within a year. The forensic psychologist is most likely to come into contact with Homebuilders as a consultant offering evaluation or treatment services in the community. The youth involved in the program are not those with serious delinquency problems, however.

Multisystemic Therapy

Another program that has received extensive research attention is the family preservation approach advocated by social psychologist Scott Henggeler, **multisystemic therapy (MST)**. MST was specifically developed for application with serious juvenile offenders, including those responsible for violent crimes. MST is heavily based on the systems theory pioneered by psychologist Urie Bronfenbrenner (1979). According to this view, behavior is multidetermined and influenced heavily by interactions with one's social environment. Children and adolescents are embedded in various social systems (their families, their peer groups, their schools, and their neighborhoods). Effective intervention requires that the child or adolescent and all of his or her social systems be considered. Thus, MST attempts to promote behavior change within the youth's natural environment and uses the strengths within each of the various social systems to bring this about.

Despite efforts to place limits on the numbers of juveniles sent to secure facilities, the United States leads the world and any other developed country in the incarceration of juveniles (Henggeler, 2016). Therefore Henggeler (1996, 2016; Henggeler & Borduin, 1990) has long argued that secure institutions should be avoided if at all possible because antisocial behaviors are only reinforced when serious offenders live among other serious offenders. Thus, in addition to keeping juveniles in their own homes, another goal of MST is to help juveniles break bonds with antisocial peers and develop bonds with prosocial peers. Henggeler has acknowledged that this is one of the most difficult goals to achieve.

Like Homebuilders, MST makes a small team of treatment providers—in this case, therapists—available to families around the clock and helps facilitate a wide range of services. Most treatment providers are master's-level mental health professionals specially trained in the multisystemic approach. Clinical or forensic psychologists supervise the therapists and provide intensive treatment if needed. Therapists meet with youth in natural settings (e.g., the home or school or even in a local park). They identify both risk and resilience factors in a juvenile's life, across all of his or her social systems. For example, a risk factor at school may be an older boy who has goaded the juvenile into committing offenses in the past. A resilience factor at school may be an art class or a history class that the juvenile likes. Likewise, genuine affection among siblings is a resilience factor in the family; the impending loss of a father's employment is a risk factor. The treatment providers then provide strategies for addressing the risk factors and capitalizing on the resilience factors.

MST may involve intensive individual counseling, a factor that distinguishes it from Homebuilders and other **family preservation models** that target youth whose behavioral problems are usually less serious. MST therapists are generalists. "Because of the varying demands of each family, [they] must be capable of applying a range of empirically based therapeutic approaches. . . . and tailoring interventions to the unique needs and strengths of each family" (T. L. Brown, Borduin, & Henggeler, 2001, p. 458). MST youth are often on probation after having been adjudicated delinquent, with offenses ranging from substance abuse to aggravated assault. However, MST also has been used for non-offending child and adolescent populations and with youth from a variety of cultural and ethnic backgrounds (T. L. Brown et al., 2001; Edwards, Schoenwald, Henggeler, & Strother, 2001). Thus far, it has drawn favorable research reviews (e.g., Burns, Schoenwald, Burchard, Faw, & Santos, 2000; Henggeler, 2001; Tate & Redding, 2005).

To illustrate, Borduin, Schaeffer, and Heiblum (2009) conducted an evaluation of MST as compared to the usual community services (UCS) mandated by the juvenile court. All the youths and their families who participated in the study were referred by juvenile court personnel. The arrest histories of the youths attest to their serious criminal involvement. The youths, whose mean age was 14, averaged 4.33 previous arrests for sexual and nonsexual felonies. Ninety-five percent of the youths were boys, and most (73%) were white.

Families and youths received MST for 31 weeks on average, whereas the UCS group received cognitive-behavioral therapy for about the same length of time. The researchers measured the effectiveness of the treatment 9 years after initial contact. They selected a follow-up time period that was long enough to allow for adult arrest data on every youth.

Overall, MST had favorable results on family relations (increased cohesion and adaptability), peer relations (increased emotional bonding, social maturity, and decreased aggression), and improved academic performance. In addition, MST created both short- and long-term changes in the youths' criminal behavior and incarceration. "Youths treated with MST reported decreases in person and property crimes at posttest and were less likely to be rearrested for sexual and nonsexual crimes within the 8.9-year follow-up period than were youths who received UCS" (Borduin et al., 2009, p. 35).

Similar positive results for MST have been reported by Curtis, Ronan, Heiblum, and Crellin (2009) in New Zealand, and by Glisson et al. (2010) in the Appalachian region of eastern Tennessee. Schwalbe, Gearing, MacKenzie, Brewer, and Ibrahim (2012) noted that programs that included the intensive family-based therapies such as those provided by MST had positive results for juveniles who were treated in community settings.

It is important to highlight the fact that MST programs do not generally deal with youths who have serious mental disorders, nor are the programs available for youth who are incarcerated. MST is essentially a program delivered in community settings.

Functional Family Therapy

A program similar to MST is **functional family therapy (FFT)**, which was developed in the 1970s for behaviorally disturbed adolescents whose parents were unable to control their acting-out behaviors. According to Sexton and Turner (2010), "FFT has an established record of outcome studies that demonstrate its efficacy with a wide variety of adolescent-related problems, including youth violence, drug abuse, and other delinquency-related behavior" (p. 339). Furthermore, the positive outcomes of the therapy remain even after a 5-year follow-up, and it also appears to have a positive influence on the siblings of the targeted adolescent. It seems to be especially effective in reducing substance abuse (Alexander, Waldron, Robbins, & Neeb, 2013; Waldron & Turner, 2008).

FFT combines social learning, cognitive-behavioral, interpersonal, and family systems theories (D. A. Gordon, 2002). Cognitive-behavioral approaches focus on a person's expectations and appraisals. The person is encouraged to examine how attitudes and beliefs may have contributed to his or her present situation. The individual works with the therapist to identify strategies for behavioral change. In functional family therapy, therapists work with the family as a unit and attempt to identify features of family dynamics that result in problematic interactions among members. Attention is focused away from the adolescent as the problem; rather, the family is viewed as a system, with members affecting one another's behaviors. Communication and problem-solving skills are taught, and participants are typically given homework assignments between sessions. Like MST, FFT is used in a wide variety of contexts, not just with youth who have come into conflict with the law.

Although FFT has been used successfully with delinquents, including those referred by juvenile courts (D. A. Gordon, 2002), it seems less suited for serious delinquents remaining in the community than MST. The latter was specifically formulated to deal with serious delinquency, and it places considerable emphasis on intensive individual treatment as well as strengthening social systems both within and outside the family group. On the other hand, FFT may be better than MST at providing all members of the family group with skills and strategies to function effectively as a self-supporting group. Nonetheless, according to T. L. Brown, Borduin, and Henggeler (2001), behavioral parent training approaches have not been demonstrably effective with serious juvenile offenders, primarily because of the multiple risk factors (e.g., marital distress, socioeconomic disadvantage, parental depression) that are relatively common in their families. Although FFT is not exclusively focused on parent training, it closely resembles such a model. However, Schwalbe et al. (2012) did find that parent training had positive effects on reducing recidivism, so the efficacy of parent training programs should not be completely discounted.

Another promising program that is modeled after MST and FFT is **Multidimensional Treatment Foster Care (MTFC),** which is designed to work with chronic juvenile offenders in the child welfare system (Chamberlain, 2003; Chamberlain, Leve, & DeGarmo, 2007). Although it follows MST principles, MTFC's major goal is to minimize youth associations with deviant peers, and to surround the youth with competent adults (specially trained foster parents) who are positive and encouraging.

MST, FFT, and MTFC—to ensure program integrity—require extensive training on the part of those who will deliver the services, but neither one requires that treatment providers hold terminal degrees in the field. Those with master's degrees—and sometimes less—are able to offer treatment when they are well trained and supervised by clinical psychologists. Sexton and Turner (2010) also point out that FFT must be delivered in a clinically specific and precise manner to produce positive results. That is, the therapists must be well trained and supervised before the full desired effects can be achieved. Edwards, Schoenwald, Henggeler, and Strother (2001) and D. A. Gordon (2002) have summarized the challenges faced in implementing each of these approaches in communities that have expressed interest in them. Supporters of both approaches have emphasized the need for continual communication between developers of these programs and the service providers, as well as the extensive training and initial supervision required to ensure that treatment will be delivered effectively.

Numerous studies on MST, FFT, and MTFC have extremely encouraging results. In his literature review of the three programs, Henggeler (2016) states, "Although significant treatment effects were not observed in all studies, the vast majority demonstrated meaningful decreases in recidivism and confinement, which were sometimes sustained for many years posttreatment" (p. 588). In addition, the studies showed significant improvements in youth functioning, decreased behavioral problems, less association with delinquent peers, and improved school performance.

Cognitive-Behavioral Treatment

Virtually every juvenile rehabilitation center today incorporates some form of cognitive-behavioral treatment (CBT), which—as noted in Chapter 12—is the psychological treatment approach with demonstrated efficacy for adult offenders as well. CBT is typically used in conjunction with other forms of treatment, such as substance abuse programs or sex offender treatment programs. CBT can be used with any of the treatment approaches discussed above. Focus 13.6 provides an illustration of a cognitive-behavioral approach for serious juvenile offenders used in one juvenile correctional system.

▶ Photo 13.2 An adolescent girl settling into her room in a substance abuse treatment center.
Source: Anne Cusack/Los Angeles Times via Getty Images.

Substance Abuse Models

Like adult offenders, juvenile offenders very often have substance abuse problems that accompanied past offenses and are predictive of future delinquent activity (Puzzanchera, 2013; Snyder & Sickmund, 1999; Weekes, Moser, & Langevin, 1999). In the case of juvenile offenders, however, the treatment must take into account their rapid physiological, psychological, and sociocultural development (McNeece, Springer, & Arnold, 2001). In other words, treatment providers must factor in the emotional turmoil and search for identity and acceptance that are often characteristic of adolescence. Like the other treatment programs discussed, programs that provide individual, group, and family therapy—a multimodal approach—seem to be the most effective for substance abusers.

We should note that many of the approaches discussed thus far in this chapter might include a substance abuse component. For example, both group home and family preservation models frequently implement substance abuse treatment. (See Photo 13.2.) As stated above, for example, FFT seems to be particularly well suited for treating adolescent substance abuse

FOCUS 13.6. A COGNITIVE INTERVENTION PROGRAM FOR JUVENILES

Cognitive-behavioral therapy (CBT) is regarded by many mental health practitioners as the most effective form of psychological treatment for both juvenile and adult offenders, and it is delivered in many different forms across institutional and community programs. Various forms of CBT have stressed victim impact, thinking errors or cognitive distortion, behavior modification, and positive thinking, among many factors. In addition, CBT may be used individually or in group settings. We describe below one example.

The Juvenile Cognitive Intervention Program (JCIP) is provided to incarcerated juvenile delinquents in Wisconsin in three secure juvenile correctional facilities, two for boys and one for girls. Researchers describe the premise of the program thusly: "If we can change how someone thinks, we can change their behavior" (McGlynn, Hahn, & Hagan, 2012, p. 1111). Treatment providers—who are typically trained social workers—help juveniles recognize their cognitive distortions, change their thinking patterns, and practice using these skills in dealing with problems they may encounter both within the facility and when they are released. Examples of distortions include

- blaming problems on others;
- perceiving that others are out to harm them, which we refer to in the text as hostile attribution bias;
- minimizing the seriousness of their own antisocial behavior;
- thinking that one's own views and needs are more important than those of others.

The Wisconsin program uses a questionnaire (the HIT [How I Think] Questionnaire; Barriga & Gibbs, 1996) to measure the extent of cognitive distortions in juveniles before and after treatment. The questionnaire is self-administered, and the higher the score, the greater the extent of distorted thinking. McGlynn, Hahn, and Hagan (2012) evaluated the effectiveness of the JCIP with 431 males and 103 females between the ages of 12 and 18. All were adjudicated delinquents, and most had been in several treatment programs and had numerous acts of violent delinquency in their records.

Overall, the program reduced the HIT scores of the participants, indicating that the treatment changed cognitive thinking in a positive direction. Males had higher scores before treatment than females, but scores of both males and females were reduced as a result of the treatment. Interestingly, age was a significant factor in the research. Younger juvenile offenders demonstrated higher scores. The researchers noted that—because efforts are usually made to keep young offenders out of institutional settings—those who are incarcerated are likely to be the ones with the most serious behavioral problems.

The McGlynn et al. (2012) study had limitations, as the authors acknowledge. Nevertheless, they find the study supportive of the use of the JCIP for juvenile offenders.

Questions for Discussion

1. On the basis of the above admittedly sketchy description of the program, what questions are left if one is to assess its efficacy? Put another way, what would you want to know before deciding whether this is a valuable program to use with serious delinquents?
2. Given that CBT approaches have been demonstrated to be effective and should be used, what more can and should be done for serious, incarcerated delinquents?
3. Is it possible to change how another person thinks? Explain your answer.

problems. Such treatment also is a component of virtually every publicly supported juvenile rehabilitation center. Private facilities, in which parents enroll their adolescents for inpatient substance abuse treatment, are also common. Interestingly, Ira Schwartz (1989), a one-time head of the OJJDP, has argued forcefully that these private placements are overused and unwarranted for many youth, calling private treatment centers the new jail for middle-class kids. Moreover, there is very little evidence to support inpatient treatment over outpatient approaches for the vast majority of juvenile substance abusers (McNeece et al., 2001).

McNeece. Springer, and Arnold (2001) reviewed the variety of programs available for both adult and juvenile substance abusers. These include individual, group, and family therapy;

self-help programs; psychoeducational approaches; pharmacotherapy (e.g., Antabuse, methadone, and naltrexone); acupuncture; case management; and both inpatient and outpatient programs. They note that several states are developing specific assessment and receiving centers for juveniles with substance abuse problems. These centers may be attached to the juvenile court or a local drug court, or they may operate independently. Although such assessment and treatment centers may be a step in the right direction, follow-up services are desperately needed, particularly in light of today's nationwide opioid crisis. In a study of six such assessment centers, McNeece and his colleagues (1997) learned that they provided short-term stabilization, but recommendations for extended treatment often were not followed due to lack of resources and shortage of staff. The crucial importance of follow-up services has been demonstrated in evaluation studies of many other juvenile programs as well.

The professional literature contains numerous descriptions and evaluations of other treatment programs for both adult and juvenile offenders. For our purposes, we will discuss two illustrations, one representing inpatient and one representing outpatient treatment.

Violence-Prevention Programs

Violence is commonly defined as physical force exerted for the purpose of inflicting injury, pain, discomfort, or abuse on a person or persons. Some definitions include damage to or destruction of property. Thus, vandalism—an offense often seen in juvenile crime statistics—would be included. Programs for juveniles that are aimed at preventing and controlling violence focus primarily on physical harm done to other persons. They are good candidates for cognitive-behavioral intervention because juveniles who commit violent crimes may minimize their actions, and they often display a hostile attribution bias. Like juvenile sex offenders, they may blame others for their actions. Sexual assault is a violent crime; however, it is typically approached in a separate (or additional) treatment program, as we will discuss shortly.

Violence may begin very early in a child's life and often occurs as a result of modeling significant individuals in the child's social network—particularly parents, caretakers, peers, or media heroes. In recent years, as discussed in Chapter 8, increasing attention has been given to violent video games that are thought by many to desensitize children to brutality and encourage them to adopt violent strategies in their own lives. Also gaining attention is the **biological/ neurological perspective**, with some researchers suggesting that biological, genetic, or neuropsychological factors make a significant contribution to aggression (e.g., Fishbein, 2000; Moffit, 1993a; Raine, 1993). Although these researchers do not suggest that these factors "cause" violent crime or delinquency, they do indicate that some individuals may be predisposed to committing violent acts. Consequently, they urge early identification and intervention into the lives of individuals who may be at risk.

Violent behavior may suddenly appear in adolescence—for example, the 14-year-old who takes a gun to school and kills the principal or the 15-year-old who stabs his father to death. However, this one-time violence is highly atypical. Far more typical is the progression from early, aggressive behavior to more serious aggression as a child develops. Psychologist Arnold M. Goldstein (2002a) says, "Catch it low to prevent it high," indicating that low-level aggression could, if not nipped, turn into more serious behavior later on. He goes on to say,

> My central belief—a belief increasingly finding at least initial empirical support—is that we, as a society, have far too often ignored the very manifestations of low-level aggression which, when rewarded, grow (often rapidly) into those several forms of often intractable high-level aggression which are currently receiving a great deal of society's attention. (p. 169)

The author also believes that cursing, threats, insults, incivilities, vandalism, bullying, and harassment are all precursors to serious aggression. Thus, the 6- or 7-year-old who consistently bullies, bites, or hits his playmates will likely, if reinforced, move on to more serious assaultive behavior as an adolescent. Reinforcement may be in the form of internal or external rewards. Gaining status on the playground or having other children be afraid of him may be sufficient reinforcement, even if adult authority figures "punish" him for his misbehavior.

Most children who reach the juvenile courts on delinquency petitions are older than 10—most are between the ages of 12 and 17. Even so, approximately 9% of juvenile arrests involve children age 14 and younger. In addition, recent juvenile court statistics indicate that 24% of delinquency cases involving *crimes against persons* (e.g., assault, rape, robbery, violent sexual offenses) were committed by youths younger than age 14 (C. Knoll & Sickmund, 2010). By the teen years, the individual has already "learned" that his or her violent behavior brings some rewards. Therefore, the treatment of violent behavior usually involves "unlearning" strategies that have seemingly worked up to that point.

Most violence-prevention programs geared at juveniles adopt a cognitive-behavioral or social learning perspective. "Cognitive interventions assume that an angry, aggressive state is mediated through a person's expectations and appraisals and that the likelihood of violence is increased or decreased as a result of this process" (Tate, Reppucci, & Mulvey, 1995, p. 778). Violent youth often see hostility where none is intended. Therefore, they are encouraged to reassess their assumptions that others are a threat to them. In some programs, these cognitive distortions are referred to as "thinking errors," a concept proposed by Yochelson and Samenow (1976). Youth—particularly those in residential treatment programs—may be asked to write down their thoughts and emotions as they occur. In group therapy sessions, they reveal what they have written, and the group and the treatment provider identify the thinking errors and suggest strategies for thinking differently.

A victim empathy component may be part of the treatment. For example, the juveniles are encouraged to put themselves in the place of the victim to appreciate what the victim suffered, sometimes through role-playing exercises. Restorative justice, which we discussed in Chapter 10, focuses on making the victim whole after experiencing victimization. This approach has shown good results when the offender is a juvenile (Bergseth & Bouffard, 2012; Schwalbe, Gearing, MacKenzie, Brewer, & Ibrahim, 2012). In other words, many juvenile offenders across age, gender, racial groups, offending history, and crimes committed demonstrate empathy for their victims and appreciate the consequences of their criminal activity.

Violence-prevention programs also typically provide juveniles with alternatives to violent behavior, teaching them decision-making skills to put to use when a potentially violent situation erupts. They are encouraged also to avoid placing themselves in volatile situations. Alcoholic substances, for example, are known to facilitate violent behavior, so substance abuse prevention is an important component of many violence-prevention programs.

A. P. Goldstein and Glick (1987, 2001) describe **aggression replacement training (ART)**, an approach taken with children and adolescents in a variety of settings, including community and residential treatment programs for delinquents. They note that adolescents who display highly aggressive behaviors are often also deficient or inadequate in socially desirable behaviors, such as identifying their own feelings or responding appropriately to slights or anger. The ART curriculum consists of (1) skillstreaming (teaching a broad range of prosocial behaviors), (2) anger control training, and (3) moral reasoning. In small groups, chronically aggressive adolescents are taught such skills as asking permission, having a conversation, giving a compliment, and dealing with embarrassment. They are also taught to identify triggers to their aggression and provided with techniques for reducing the level of their anger (e.g., counting backward, imagining a peaceful scene). The juveniles are also presented with moral dilemmas and encouraged to find a solution that is fair and just. The ART curriculum has been implemented in numerous residential and community facilities, as well as in a variety of school systems and gang-prevention programs (see A. P. Goldstein & Glick, 2001, for a review). Although ART has produced cognitive-behavioral changes in violent adolescents, it has not yet been demonstrated to reduce violent behavior in juveniles after release from correctional facilities (Tate et al., 1995). A. P. Goldstein and Glick acknowledge that maintaining anger control beyond facility walls can be problematic. Nevertheless, they maintain that positive effects of the program persist, although not as strongly as in a controlled environment.

Guerra, Tolan, and Hammond (1994) observe that a common element related to treatment effectiveness for adolescent violence is the development of social interaction skills: "Improved social skills not only help individuals resolve conflict-producing situations with their peers, but enable them to get along in multiple social contexts" (p. 397).

In the juvenile justice system, programs for serious violent offenders generally operate within institutional settings, primarily in secure settings for youth. From a therapeutic perspective, institutionalization has the obvious advantages of intervening in a controlled setting, away from criminogenic influences in the youth's natural environment. It also allows intensive treatment, using both group and individual models. Unfortunately, evaluations of institutional treatment have produced mixed results, which is not surprising because the youth themselves are the most challenging to work with. Critics of institutionalization also point out, however, that a major disadvantage of secure treatment is the tendency of adolescents to align with one another and reinforce their own deviant behaviors (Henggeler, 1996), so criminogenic influences remain. Interestingly, M. S. Jackson and Springer (1997) recommend taking advantage of this tendency to align; they suggest that those working with juveniles in incarcerated settings encourage the forming of "therapeutic gangs," which incorporate positive aspects of the juvenile gangs to which many incarcerated youth belonged. The therapeutic gang members work together to identify negative attitudes and values and look for positive alternatives.

Juvenile Sex Offender Treatment Programs

It is believed that a high percentage of all juvenile sex offenders were themselves sexually abused. Gray, Pithers, Busconi, and Houchens (1997) found that 86% of the children in their sample of serious juvenile offenders had been sexually abused themselves. Children who are sexually abused typically do not become abusers. Rather, the devastating effects of sexual abuse are more likely to be internalized and displayed in adjustment problems such as depression, self-destructive behavior, anxiety, and poor self-esteem in both children and adults (Browne & Finkelhor, 1986). Those victims who do become abusers suffer many of these adjustment problems as well. If we consider the well-documented effects of childhood sexual abuse, it is clear that juvenile sex offenders need a treatment program that not only works to prevent future offending, but also recognizes and addresses the emotional trauma they are likely to have experienced.

Adolescent sex offenders, left untreated, are highly likely to continue to offend into adulthood. It has been estimated that 47% to 58% of adult sex offenders committed their first offense during adolescence (Cellini, Schwartz, & Readio, 1993). Becker and Johnson (2001) note that researchers and clinicians are becoming increasingly aware also that prepubescent children commit sexual offenses and that many of these offenses continue into adolescence. Recent juvenile court data show a noteworthy decrease in the percentage of sex offenses committed by juveniles, however (Puzzanchera, 2013). For example, over the 10-year period from 2002 to 2011, sexual offenses committed by juveniles declined quite dramatically (36% for forcible rape; 35% for other sexual offenses). Despite this significant decrease, juvenile sex offender treatment, much like substance abuse treatment, remains an essential component of many clinical practices. It is available in most public and many private juvenile rehabilitation facilities.

The assessment that precedes treatment for juvenile sex offenders often occurs before they have been adjudicated, however. Youth suspected of or charged with sexual offenses may be referred for evaluation, both by juvenile courts and by social service agencies. In these situations, "it is the job of the assessor to determine the probability that a deviant sexual act occurred, the reason for its occurrence, and whether or not there is need for intervention" (Becker & Johnson, 2001, p. 274).

Whether it occurs before or after a juvenile has been adjudicated delinquent, assessment of sex offenders is controversial. Because of the nature of sexual offending, courts and other juvenile justice officials are particularly interested in knowing not only whether the juvenile is likely to respond to treatment, but also whether the juvenile is likely to reoffend. Considerable progress has been made in developing assessment instruments for juvenile sex offending since the following pessimistic appraisal: There simply is no way to make clinical assumptions about the risk of re-offense or progression of adolescents' deviant sexual patterns" (Cellini, 1995, p. 6-4 [Chap. 6, p. 4]). As noted earlier, two instruments—the SAVRY and the YLS/CMI both have received favorable reviews. Nevertheless, researchers continue to urge caution in these assessments, such as by noting that instruments used may not always be able to measure short-term changes in adolescent development (Viljoen et al., 2017).

Practicing forensic psychologists and researchers recommend the gathering of extensive background and clinical information in any evaluations of juvenile sex offenders. According to Becker and Johnson (2001), the psychologist conducting the assessment should obtain the following:

- Family social, medical, and mental histories;

- Developmental history of the juvenile, including information about temperament as infant and toddler;

- School information;

- History of violent behavior;

- Alcohol and other substance abuse history;

- A detailed sexual history;

- Information about mental status.

Becker and Johnson made the additional comment, "One should assess the youth's general fund of knowledge and intelligence as well as insight and judgment" (2001, p. 276).

A very wide range of treatment modalities is available for juvenile sex offenders, including individual and group treatment, family counseling, and psychoeducational classes. Worling and Langton (2012) have summarized treatment goals that are common to many sexual offender treatment programs. They include enhancing accountability and awareness of the impact of the offense on the victim(s), promoting healthy sexual interests and prosocial sexual attitudes, establishing plans to prevent future offending, and if possible involving parents and caregivers in treatment planning. Like many other researchers, however, Worling and Langton note that the confined setting of incarceration is a barrier to effective treatment.

According to Cellini (1995), "Peer groups are the preferred method of treatment for 98% of the juvenile and adult programs currently being offered for sex offenders" (p. 6-6). The typical peer group program takes a cognitive-behavioral approach, with sex offenders discussing their offenses and the effects on their victims, under the direction of a clinical moderator. Sex education is an important component; juvenile sex offenders are given factual information about human sexuality, and nondeviant sexual interests are promoted. They are encouraged to identify thinking errors—mistaken assumptions regarding their crimes or their victims—and to develop strategies to avoid future offending. Social skills and assertiveness training is an important component of many sex offender treatment programs as well. Although peer group treatment may be dominant, the literature also strongly advocates individual and family therapy when possible (Becker & Johnson, 2001). As is the case with programs for violent offenders, a multimodal approach, emphasizing group, individual, and family treatment, is most likely to be effective.

It is widely believed that sex offenders are never completely "cured" but are always susceptible to reoffending (Cellini, 1995; Pithers et al., 1995). Thus, an important component of sex offender treatment programs is relapse prevention, whereby offenders are taught strategies for recognizing situations and avoiding stimuli that have led to their offenses in the past (e.g., visiting with a particular acquaintance, going to a certain playground, viewing violent pornography).

It is often noted that the literature on sex offender treatment is long on description and short on careful evaluation (Becker & Johnson, 2001; Worling & Langton, 2012). Although many articles are published outlining the treatment methods used, there are very few controlled studies of effectiveness. In addition, the literature discusses primarily the sex offending of adolescent males, with very little written regarding female sex offenders or prepubescent children. This, too, is changing, though, as more researchers become aware that the sexual offending of women and girls is a topic worthy of attention (Becker, Hall, & Stinson, 2001).

Summary of Institutional Treatment

Although we have discussed just a few approaches to the treatment of juveniles in institutional settings, it is apparent that psychologists are faced with a formidable task. Many of the obstacles to treatment that were described in the previous chapter relative to adult offenders exist in juvenile institutions as well. In addition, institutional programs are unable to place much emphasis on working with the family, the environment to which the adolescent frequently returns. Supporters of multisystemic therapy make a good case for its use with violent youth who are allowed to remain in the community and within their own family environment. In addition, there is evidence that a longer stay in an institution does not reduce recidivism (Mulvey, 2011). As Mulvey and others (e.g., Henggeler, 2016) note, community-based supervision and treatment are more effective at reducing recidivism for youth who have committed serious offenses. However, for a few dangerously violent juvenile offenders, incarceration is a necessary alternative for society's protection. In these cases, intensive treatment should be provided.

Like many earlier researchers, Lambie and Randell (2013) list and document the numerous negative effects of incarceration of juveniles in juvenile facilities as well as in adult prisons, where juveniles are typically but not always separated from adults. It is not unusual to see 16- and 17-year-old youth incarcerated with the adult population. The negative effects—whether incarcerated with adults or other juveniles—include victimization by other inmates as well as staff, lack of mental health care, suicidal behaviors, lack of adult guidance and prosocial relationships with peers, damages to physical health, educational deficiencies, and difficulty reentering into the community upon release. Lambie and Randell also make the point that, even when evidence-based treatment is provided within the facility, its positive effects are outweighed by lack of improvement in other factors, such as family cohesion or relationships with peers. In other words, when youth are released, they must still return to an often problematical family situation and find themselves in communication with antisocial peers.

SUMMARY AND CONCLUSIONS

In 1999, the U.S. juvenile justice system celebrated its 100th anniversary, if one marks its beginning with the establishment of the first juvenile court in 1899. As would be expected, the juvenile justice process of today hardly resembles the process of the first half of the 20th century. Or does it? Early juvenile courts were informal, paternalistic, often very judgmental, and children were rarely represented by lawyers. Clinicians—primarily psychiatrists and psychologists—consulted regularly with these courts, providing wide-ranging evaluations of a juvenile's emotional, cognitive, and mental status, as well

as background information on the youth's social history. Although the courts were supposedly intended to "save" children from a life of poverty, they too often placed them in institutions that failed to provide the education, nurturing, and overall physical and emotional care that children need. In the 1960s, a rights-oriented Supreme Court recognized these deficiencies in the juvenile justice system and attempted to correct them by providing juveniles with legal representation and other due process rights. In the 1970s, Congress passed the Juvenile Justice and Delinquency Prevention Act, landmark legislation that, among many other things, began to address conditions in juvenile facilities.

It is important for forensic psychologists working with the juvenile justice system to be aware of its history. Many concerned advocates for juveniles today fear that problems similar to those of old have reoccurred or, in some cases, never really disappeared. In this chapter, our discussion ranged from issues relating to juvenile comprehension of their rights early in the criminal process to their detention and incarceration as adjudicated delinquents.

Much recent research attention has focused on evaluating juveniles' competence to waive their *Miranda* rights and their adjudicative competence. Questions also are raised about the extent to which they are susceptible to making false confessions and even whether they trust their lawyers. Consequently, in evaluating juveniles who are faced with various juvenile court proceedings, forensic psychologists should pay special attention to these factors. Assessments of juvenile's mental health needs are also warranted. Research indicates that many juveniles in detention and treatment facilities have mental disorders that may co-occur with substance misuse.

Conditions of confinement in many secure facilities are appalling. There is documented overrepresentation of minority youth, particularly in secure confinement. On the whole—there are always exceptions—the needs of juvenile girls have been overlooked, and the needs of juveniles from ethnic, racial, or sexual orientation minorities have been ignored. The results of surveys of conditions and needs of institutionalized juveniles lead many observers to advocate for greater use of community-based approaches, such as intensive services provided to families or group homes. Similar to what has been found with adult treatment programs, some common features of successful programs can be identified. Those based on cognitive-behavioral models, for example, have received very favorable reviews. Multimodal programs—those that attempt to incorporate group, individual, and family treatment—also produce good results. Programs that target offenders with high risks and high needs, work intensively with those offenders, and include a follow-up component are also well rated. The follow-up component is particularly important for juveniles because they so frequently return to an environment that facilitates their antisocial behavior. This may be why multisystemic therapy—the community-based approach that attempts to address strengths and weaknesses in the juvenile's various social systems (e.g., individual, family, school, community, employment setting)—is highly promising.

KEY CONCEPTS

Aftercare 498

Aggression replacement training (ART) 527

Amenability to rehabilitation 509

Biological/neurological perspective 526

Blended sentencing 498

Decisional competency 508

Deinstitutionalization of status offenders (DSO) 502

Delinquency petition 498

Delinquency hearing (or adjudicatory hearing) 498

Disposition 498

Disproportionate minority confinement (DMC) 503

Diversion 498

Family preservation models 522

Functional family therapy (FFT) 523

Homebuilders model 521

Houses of Refuge 500

Intake 498

Judicial waivers 510

Juvenile detention 515

Juvenile Justice and Delinquency Prevention Act (JJDPA) 502

Legislative waiver, statutory exclusion, or waiver by statute 510

MacArthur Juvenile Competence Study 509

Multidimensional Treatment Foster Care (MTFC) 523

Multisystemic therapy (MST) 521

Office of Juvenile Justice and Delinquency Prevention (OJJDP) 503

Parens patriae 498

Preventive detention 498

Prosecutorial waiver 510

Teaching-family model 519

Waiver petition 498

QUESTIONS FOR REVIEW

1. Why is it important to distinguish between detention and treatment/rehabilitation?

2. List and describe briefly assessment roles of forensic psychologists in juvenile justice settings.

3. Discuss the significance of the Supreme Court cases *Kent v. United States* and *In re Gault* to juveniles charged with criminal offenses.

4. Discuss reasons why juveniles as a group may be especially susceptible to waiving their constitutional rights and to making false confessions.

5. What are the strengths and weaknesses of the teaching-family approach?

6. Compare and contrast Homebuilders, FFT, MST, and MTFC on such factors as population served, treatment approaches, and evaluation research.

7. What is ART? Briefly summarize its curriculum.

8. What is CBT? Illustrate how it might be used with a juvenile offender found to have committed a sexual assault.

 SAGE edge™

Want a better grade? Go to **edge.sagepub.com/bartol5e** for the tools you need to sharpen your study skills. Access practice quizzes, eFlashcards, an action plan, and SAGE journal articles for enhanced learning.

GLOSSARY

Abusive head trauma (AHT) Severe damage to a child's brain as a result of head injury sustained by the actions of another, typically a parent or caretaker (e.g., shaking, throwing against a wall). Formerly called shaken baby syndrome.

Accusatorial approach In police interrogation, an aggressive questioning procedure that assumes the suspect is responsible for a criminal offense and has the goal of obtaining a confession. Compare with information-gathering approach.

Actuarial predictions These are predictions that employ statistics to identify certain facts about a person's background and known behavior that can be related to the behavior being predicted, based on how groups of individuals with similar characteristics have acted in the past.

Acute dynamic factors Psychological characteristics that change rapidly (within days, hours, or even minutes) and include such things as mood swings, emotional arousal, and alcohol or other drug-induced effects.

Adjudicative competence The ability to participate in a variety of legal proceedings, including plea bargaining and participating in a criminal trial.

Administrative segregation A form of custody exercised by prison administrators to isolate an inmate physically from the rest of the prison population for a variety of reasons, including but not limited to protection of the inmate.

Adolescent-limited offenders (ALs) Individuals who usually demonstrate delinquent or antisocial behavior only during their teen years and then stop offending during their young adult years.

Advance directives Documents that allow persons to make advance decisions about life-sustaining procedures in the event of a terminal condition or persistent vegetative state, or any other later health care decision.

Aftercare In the juvenile justice system, this term is the equivalent of parole.

Aggravating factors Circumstances surrounding a crime that heighten its seriousness for purposes of sentencing. An example would be an excessively heinous or cruel method of carrying out a crime, such as a torture murder.

Aggression Behavior that is intended to cause harm or damage to another person.

Aggression replacement training (ART) Treatment program for aggressive children and adolescents consisting of *skillstreaming* (teaching a broad range of pro-social behaviors), anger control training, and moral reasoning.

Allocution The right to speak out during court proceedings, such as at the bail hearing, the sentencing hearing, or the parole board hearing. In all states, for example, victims are allowed to speak out at sentencing hearings.

Amenability to rehabilitation Refers to the extent to which an offender, particularly a juvenile, is likely to benefit from programs or services available within an institutional or community setting.

American Psychological Association (APA) The largest professional association for psychologists in the world, with 134,000 members as of 2012.

Americans with Disabilities Act (ADA) A federal law that guarantees equal opportunity for individuals with disabilities in state and local government services, public accommodations, employment, transportation, and telecommunications.

Amicus curiae briefs Documents submitted to appellate courts by outside parties to call attention to some matter that might otherwise escape the courts' attention.

Anger rape A rape situation, identified by Groth, in which an offender uses more force than necessary for compliance and engages in a variety of sexual acts that are particularly degrading or humiliating to the victim.

Antisocial behavior Any behavior that is considered a violation of social norms in society; antisocial behaviors may or may not be defined as crimes.

Antisocial personality disorder (APD or ASP) A disorder characterized by a history of continuous behavior in which the rights of others are violated.

Appellate jurisdiction A court's authority to hear appeals from decisions of lower courts.

Approximation rule Court looks at the amount of caretaking done by each parent before making a decision on child custody.

Arraignment Court proceeding during which criminal defendants are formally charged with an offense, informed of their rights, and asked to enter a plea.

Assisted outpatient treatment (AOT) Court-ordered mental health treatment in the community, on the condition that a person will be hospitalized or rehospitalized if not cooperative with treatment providers.

Association for Psychological Science (APS) An organization of psychologists dedicated to the advancement of science in psychology. After the APA, it is the next-largest psychological association in the United States.

Attention-deficit/hyperactivity disorder (ADHD) Traditionally considered a chronic neurological condition characterized by developmentally poor attention, impulsivity, and hyperactivity. More contemporary perspectives also see the behavioral pattern as a deficiency in interpersonal skills.

Availability heuristic The cognitive shortcuts that people use to make inferences about their world. It is the information that is most readily available to use mentally, and is usually based extensively on the most recent material we gain from the news or entertainment media.

Battered woman syndrome (BWS) A cluster of behavioral and psychological characteristics believed common to women who have been abused in relationships.

Battering A term often reserved for *physical violence* experienced in intimate relationships, such as in a dating relationship, marriage or partnership, or separation and divorce.

Behavioral model Treatment approach based on the assumption that rewarding people (e.g., inmates or incarcerated juveniles) for "good behavior" and removing privileges when behavior is unacceptable will produce positive changes in behavior.

Bench trial/court trial A civil or criminal trial in which the judge, rather than a jury, is the finder of fact, responsible for reviewing the evidence and rendering a verdict.

Best interest of the child (BIC) standard The legal doctrine that the parents' legal rights should be secondary to what is best for the child.

Beyond a reasonable doubt The burden of proof that must be met by the government in all criminal cases.

Bias crimes Also called hate crimes, these are criminal offenses motivated by an offender's bias against a group to which the victim either belongs or is believed to belong.

Biological/neurological perspective The research perspective that biological, genetic, or neuropsychological factors make a significant contribution to aggression. Although this perspective does not suggest that these factors "cause" violent crime or delinquency, it does indicate that some individuals may be biologically or neurologically predisposed to committing violent acts.

Blended sentencing In the juvenile justice system, this refers to giving juveniles a mix of juvenile and adult sanctions, such as a juvenile treatment program followed by adult parole supervision once the juvenile has reached adulthood.

Boldness factor Interpersonal style characterized by fearlessness, calmness, and low stress level when confronted with crises or stress inducing situations. Believed by some scholars to be a core factor in psychopathy.

Bullying A form of peer aggression in which one or more individuals physically, verbally, or psychologically harass a victim who is perceived to be weaker. Although primarily directed at children and adolescents, bullying also may be directed at adult peers.

California Psychological Inventory (CPI) A personality measure often used in the screening of law enforcement officers. It focuses on normal or adaptive personality traits, rather than on abnormal traits. Approximately 25% of police agencies are believed to use the CPI for candidate screening.

Callous-unemotional (CU) traits Group of personality characteristics believed to be associated with psychopathy, such as self-centeredness and lack of empathy. See also, four-factor perspective.

Case-blind consultant Professional who consults with lawyers or judges on issues relating to a case without direct contact with the litigants; may review work of other consultants or provide legal professionals with relevant research data.

Challenge for cause Exercised by an attorney or judge whenever it can be demonstrated that a would-be juror does not satisfy the statutory or other requirements for jury duty.

Child abduction Unlawfully leading, taking, enticing, or detaining a child under a specified age with intent to keep or conceal the child from the parent, guardian, or other person having lawful custody.

Child custody evaluations (CCEs) Also called parenting evaluations or assessments, these are assessments prepared for courts by mental health professionals to help judges make decisions in disputed custody situations.

Child sexual abuse accommodation syndrome (CSAAS) A term reserved for a cluster of behaviors that occur in children who have been victims of sexual abuse by a family member or an adult with whom the child has a trusting relationship. The syndrome is controversial and has little empirical support.

Child sex trafficking Associated with child abduction of some children, this refers to their exploitation for sexual purposes, such as the production of child pornography or prostitution.

Clear and convincing evidence Legal standard achieved when the truth of the facts asserted is highly probable but does not reach the standard of beyond a reasonable doubt.

Clinical predictions Predictions of behavior (e.g., violence) that are based primarily on clinical knowledge rather than on statistical or actuarial data. Compare with actuarial predictions and structured professional judgment (SPJ).

Coerced-compliant false confessions Admissions of guilt most likely to occur after prolonged and intense interrogation experiences, such as when sleep deprivation is a feature. The suspect, in desperation to avoid further discomfort, admits to the crime even knowing that he or she is innocent.

Coerced-internalized false confessions These occur when innocent persons—who are tired, confused, and highly psychologically vulnerable—come to believe that they actually committed the crime.

Cognitive factors The internal processes that enable humans to imagine, to gain knowledge, to reason, and to evaluate. Each person has his or her own cognitive version of the world.

Cognitive-behavioral approach An approach to therapy that focuses on changing beliefs, fantasies, attitudes, and rationalizations that justify and perpetuate antisocial or other problematic behavior. Believed to be the most effective treatment approach for both adult and juvenile offenders.

Cognitive-behavioral viewpoint Related to hypnosis, this is the perspective that hypnotic participants are not in an altered state of consciousness but rather are playing a role suggested by the hypnotist.

Cognitive interview Method of interviewing that uses memory retrieval and various communication techniques aimed at increasing the amount of accurate information from witnesses and victims. Its goal is to make the interviewee aware of all events that happened in a situation.

Cognitive lie detection Method of interviewing and interrogation that asks questions the suspect does not anticipate.

Cognitive load During police interviewing and interrogation, this refers to the cognitive demands placed on the interviewee, with the premise that this will make it more difficult for the interviewee to be deceptive. An example would be asking the person to recount events of the past day in reverse order of when they occurred.

Commitment bias The phenomenon that once a witness commits to a certain viewpoint, such as identification of a face, the witness is less likely to change his or her mind.

Community corrections The broad term for a wide variety of options that allow persons convicted of crime to be supervised in the community, such as being placed on probation. Term also applies to parole, the supervision of former prisoners in the community.

Community-based facilities Correctional facilities that are not institutions and allow supervision of juveniles or adults within their own homes or in special community facilities, such as halfway houses.

Compensatory damages Money awards given in civil suits to make up for the harm that the plaintiff has suffered.

Competency restoration The treatment given to someone found incompetent to stand trial for the specific purpose of rendering the person competent to be tried.

Competency Screening Test (CST) Sentence-completion examination intended to provide a quick assessment of a defendant's competency to stand trial. The test taps the defendant's knowledge about the role of the lawyer and the rudiments of the court process.

Competency to be executed The legal requirement that a person convicted of a capital crime and sentenced to death must, at the time of execution, be emotionally stable or intellectually capable enough to understand the meaning of being put to death.

Competency to stand trial The legal standard that requires that criminal defendants be able to understand and appreciate criminal charges and help their attorneys in preparing a defense.

Complicated bereavement A course of bereavement following the death of a loved one that is more psychologically disturbing than the typical bereavement process and that may be responsive to mental health treatment.

Composition bias Characteristic of a police lineup that unfairly encourages a witness to identify the suspect in custody (e.g., no lineup members approximate the suspect's age).

Concurrent validity In psychological testing, validity measured by comparing one test with another, already established one.

Conditional release Judicial or administrative release from an institutional setting (jail, prison, psychiatric hospital) on the condition that one demonstrates good behavior in the community or participates in mental health treatment.

Conduct disorder (CD) A diagnostic label used to identify children who demonstrate habitual misbehavior.

Confirmation bias The tendency to look for evidence that confirms one's preexisting expectations or beliefs.

Conflict Tactics Scale (CTS) A measure used by researchers and clinicians to gauge the level of disruption and violence in interpersonal relationships.

Control question technique (CQT) The most preferred procedure by professional polygraphers in cases requiring the investigation of specific incidents, such as criminal acts. Compare with Guilty Knowledge Test.

Correctional psychology The branch of forensic psychology that interacts with prisons, jails, and other correctional facilities and programs, both in institutional and community settings. Correctional psychologists often prefer that term rather than forensic psychologist.

Co-victims People close to the victim of a serious crime, such as a murder, who must deal with the medical examiner, the criminal or juvenile justice system, and the media in the aftermath of the crime. Term is often used to emphasize the depth of homicide's emotional impact on the victim's survivors.

Crime scene profiling The development of a rough behavioral or psychological sketch of an offender based on clues identified at the crime scene.

Criminal homicide The unlawful and intentional killing of a human being. The term encompasses both murder and nonnegligent homicide.

Criminal investigative analysis A broad term for the investigation of crime. May or may not include crime scene profiling.

Criminal responsibility evaluations Assessment designed to determine whether a defense of insanity can be supported. Also called "mental state at time of offense" evaluation or "insanity" evaluation.

Criminogenic needs Those dynamic risk factors that have been empirically found to be related to criminal behavior, such as substance abuse or misogynistic attitudes.

Crisis intervention The intervention of mental health practitioners into emergency or crisis situations, such as suicide attempts, emotional agitation, or psychotic behavior displayed during confinement.

Critical incidents Emergencies and disasters that are nonroutine and unanticipated.

Cyberstalking Threats or unwanted advances directed at another using the Internet or other forms of online communication.

Date or acquaintance rape A sexual assault that occurs within the context of a dating or social relationship.

***Daubert* standard** Guide to help determine whether expert scientific testimony meets criteria established by the U.S. Supreme Court for reliability and relevance.

Death notification Procedure or process used for informing family members of a death resulting from violent crime, accident, or some other incident.

Death penalty mitigation In capital cases, attempts by the defense team to reduce or avoid the sentence of death for their client based on factors that lessen the offender's culpability. Examples of mitigating factors are the offender's age and a history of child abuse.

Decisional competency Ability to make decisions in one's own best interest. Research indicates that juveniles—given their stage of development—are unlikely to have the emotional sophistication and maturity to make such decisions when confronted with the criminal justice process.

Deinstitutionalization of status offenders (DSO) Mandate from the JJDPA that states receiving funds for juvenile justice programs must remove all juveniles from adult jails and must also remove status offenders from secure institutions.

Delinquency hearing (or adjudicatory hearing) The equivalent of a criminal trial in adult courts. Juveniles have constitutional rights similar to adult offenders, including rights to an attorney, to confront and cross-examine their accusers, and to not testify against themselves. They do *not* have a constitutional right to a jury or to an open proceeding, though some states grant these rights.

Delinquency petition In juvenile courts, the prosecutor's document charging a juvenile with an offense that, if proven, would qualify the juvenile as a delinquent.

Deposition Proceedings during which potential witnesses are questioned by attorneys for the opposing side, under oath and in the presence of a court recorder, although typically away from the courtroom.

Detention centers Facilities where pretrial detainees are held. Jails serve as detention centers as well as incarceration for persons sentenced to short terms, typically under 1 year.

Developmental dual systems model Proposed by Laurence Steinberg, it refers to the difference in cognitive and emotional brain development in adolescents, making them more prone to sensation-seeking and risk-taking behaviors.

Differential experience hypothesis States that individuals will have greater familiarity or experience with members of their own race and will thus—in identification procedures—be better able to discern differences among members of their own race.

Digital investigative analysis Forensic electronic data recovery, usually for legal purposes.

Diplomate Professional designation signifying that a person has been certified as having advanced knowledge, skills, and competence in a particular specialty.

Disciplinary segregation In prisons and jails, punishment (physical isolation) for violation of rules. Also may be called solitary confinement.

Discovery process The pretrial procedure by which one party in a civil or criminal case discloses to the other party information vital for his or her defense.

Disposition The resolution of a legal matter. In criminal law, an example would be the sentence a defendant receives. In civil law, the disposition of a case may be a judgment in favor of the plaintiff. In juvenile law, a disposition is the equivalent of a criminal sentence.

Disproportionate minority confinement (DMC) The observation that racial and ethnic minorities are disproportionately detained and incarcerated.

Diversion Any one of a number of programs used to steer someone away from formal or traditional court processing, such as diversion of juveniles to a substance abuse program or diversion of some defendants to mental health courts.

Domestic Violence Risk Appraisal Guide (DVRAG) One of the measures used to assess the extent of violence in a relationship and predict the likelihood of future occurrence.

Double-blind lineup A lineup procedure in which neither the person making an identification nor the person administering the lineup knows the identity of the suspect.

Dual-purpose evaluations Assessment of both a defendant's competency to stand trial and criminal responsibility during the same evaluation. Dual-purpose evaluations are highly discouraged in legal and psychological literature but still occur with some frequency in many jurisdictions.

Dual-court system Refers to the fact that federal and state courts in the United States exist side by side, independent of one another, sometimes in the same geographical location.

Dusky standard Relates to juvenile and adult competency to stand trial and decision-making abilities. The rule holds that defendants must be able to understand and appreciate the criminal proceedings against them and be able to assist their attorneys in their defense.

Duty to warn or protect Requirement from the *Tarasoff* case that clinicians must take steps to warn or to protect possible victims of serious bodily harm as a result of threats made by the clinicians' clients.

Dynamic risk factors Aspects of a person's developmental history that change over time, such as attitudes, opinions, and knowledge.

Dysphoric/borderline batterers Batterers who exhibit mental disorders and are psychologically disturbed and emotionally volatile. These individuals often engage in moderate to severe spousal abuse, including psychological and sexual abuse.

Early intervention system (EIS) Also called an early warning system, this is a program that helps identify psychological and performance problems in law enforcement officers early and provide them with support services.

Early warning systems See early intervention system.

Elder abuse Defined as the physical, financial, emotional, or psychological harm of an older adult, usually defined as age 65 or older.

Emotional intelligence Ability to know how one's own self and others are feeling and the capacity to be able to use that information to guide thoughts and actions.

Employment compensation claims Claims involving physical injuries, psychological damage, or emotional distress sustained as a result of one's employment. Employers are required to insure their workers against injury while on the job.

Equivocal death analysis (EDA) Reconstruction of the personality profile and cognitive features (especially intentions) of deceased persons when the cause of death is not clear. Also called psychological autopsy.

Erotomania stalkers This type of stalker usually has serious mental disorder and is often considered delusional. Public figures are typically the targets of this type of stalking.

Ethical Principles of Psychologists and Code of Conduct (EPPCC) Provides ethical standards and guidelines for what is appropriate behavior in clinical and research practice for psychologists.

Ethnocentrism Refers to the tendency to interpret events in accordance with one's own cultural heritage.

Excessive force Refers to situations in law enforcement where the level of force exceeds the level considered justifiable under the circumstances.

Executive functions Higher order mental abilities involved in goal-directed behavior. They include organizing behavior, memory, inhibition processes, and planning strategies.

External stress Stress that is outside of one's daily tasks. In the law enforcement context, they include frustrations with the courts, the prosecutor's office, the criminal process, the correctional system, the media, and public attitudes toward policing.

Face (or content) validity Refers not to what a psychological test actually measures, but to what it superficially *appears* to measure.

Facial composites Computerized or artist drawings of faces from information supplied by witnesses.

Factor analysis A statistical procedure by which underlying patterns and personality characteristics are identified.

False confessions Admissions of guilt that are not valid and are often but not necessarily induced by coercive interrogation procedures.

Family courts Specialized courts dealing with issues relating to families, such as divorce and child custody, orders of protection, delinquency proceedings, and guardianship proceedings.

Family forensic psychology A specialty whose practitioners have extensive knowledge about human development, family dynamics, and the court system.

Family preservation models Approaches that try to prevent youth with minor behavioral problems and their family from becoming more dysfunctional. The major intention is to keep the family unit together, presuming that this is in the best interest of the family as a whole.

Family violence Refers to any assault, including sexual assault, or other crime that results in the personal injury or death of one or more family or household member(s) by another who is or was residing in the same dwelling.

Family-only batterers These are violent offenders who usually do not engage in violence outside the family. Their violence tends to be periodic, primarily when stress and frustration reach a peak.

Federal Bureau of Prisons (BOP) The major federal agency that coordinates all services provided in federal facilities, such as detention centers, prisons, and hospitals. The BOP also supports research on many aspects of corrections and provides internships for doctoral students interested in careers in corrections.

Filicide Killing of one's child who is older than 1 year.

Firesetting An abnormal fascination with fire accompanied by successful or unsuccessful attempts to start harmful fires. Term used in child psychopathology literature.

Fitness-for-duty evaluations (FFDEs) Assessments conducted to determine the psychological ability of law enforcement officers to perform their essential job functions, particularly after experiencing a major stressful event.

Flashbulb memory Refers to memory—usually considerably accurate—of high-impact events, such as an automobile accident or a mass shooting.

Forcible rape Terminology used by the FBI to refer to rape without consent. Distinguished from statutory rape, which involves an underage victim who was not forced, but who is believed to be unable to consent because of age.

Forensic entomology Study of insects (and their arthropod relatives) as it relates to legal issues.

Forensic mental health assessments (FMHAs) Conducted by psychologists and psychiatrists consulting with criminal courts. Competency to stand trial assessments and criminal responsibility evaluations are prominent examples.

Forensic neuropsychology The application of knowledge from the neuropsychological profession to legal matters. Neuropsychology is the study of the psychological effects of brain and neurological damage and dysfunction on human behavior.

Forensic psychiatrists Medical doctors trained to provide assessment services to courts in relation to persons who may evidence emotional, cognitive, or behavioral problems.

Forensic psychology The production of psychological knowledge and its application to the civil and criminal justice systems.

Forensic school psychology Branch of psychology dealing with legal matters within an educational context.

Forensic social workers Social workers, typically with a master's degree, who provide services relative to legal matters, such as custody evaluations or assessments in guardianship cases.

Four-factor perspective A model that sees psychopathy as consisting of four core factors: interpersonal, impulsive, affective, and antisocial. There is continuing debate in the literature as to whether the fourth should be considered a separate factor.

Friendly parent rule In child custody determinations, the rule that preference will be given to the parent who is most likely to nurture the child's relationship with the other parent, provided the other parent is not abusive.

Functional family therapy (FFT) Developed in the 1970s for behaviorally disturbed adolescents whose parents were unable to control their acting-out behaviors. It combines social learning, cognitive-behavioral, interpersonal, and family systems theories.

Gender harassment A form of discrimination, and sometimes recognized in sexual harassment law, it refers to persistent, unwanted comments or behavior directed at an individual because of his or her gender. Distinguished from sexual harassment in that it implies the harasser has no interest in sexual contact with the target of the harassment.

Gendered pathways approach Research that indicates that girls and boys or women and men develop criminal behavior in different ways.

General acceptance rule Standard for admitting scientific evidence into court proceedings that allows it if it is generally accepted as valid in the scientific community. This was the essence of the *Frye* standard that dominated in courts until the late 20th century.

General jurisdiction Refers to courts with broad authority over a vast array of both simple and complex cases, both civil and criminal.

Generally violent/antisocial batterers Batterers who are likely to use weapons and who are more prone to inflict severe injury on wives, partners, and other family members, in addition to engaging in extrafamilial violence.

Geographical jurisdiction Court authority over a specified geographical area of the country or state.

Geographical mapping Concerned with analyzing the spatial patterns of crimes committed by numerous offenders over a period of time.

Geographical profiling Focuses on the location of the crime and how it relates to the residence or base of operations of the offender. Assumes that serial offenders prefer to commit their crimes near their own residences.

Grand jury A body of citizens (usually 23 in number) that is directed by the prosecutor to weigh evidence and decide whether there is enough to charge a person with a criminal offense.

Grooming Pertains to a strategy of sex offenders who use various methods to ingratiate themselves to their targeted victim, usually a child or adolescent.

Groth child molester typology Clinically developed system to classify pedophiles.

Groth rape typology Clinically developed system to classify rapists.

Guilty but mentally ill (GBMI) A verdict alternative in some states that allows defendants to be found guilty while seemingly affording them treatment for mental disorders.

Guilty Knowledge Test (GKT) A polygraph test that assesses the extent to which the polygraph examinee is aware of facts about a crime. See also control question technique (CQT). The GKT is preferred by researchers, but is used less often by practicing polygraphers than the CQT.

Hastened death evaluations In states allowing individuals to hasten their death with the help of physician-prescribed medication, these assessments may be conducted if there are questions about the patient's capacity to make such a decision.

Hate crimes Also called bias crimes, these are criminal offenses motivated by an offender's bias against a group to which the victim either belongs or is believed to belong.

Hate Crime Statistics Act Federal law that requires law enforcement officials to collect extensive data on reported crimes allegedly motivated by hatred or bias against someone belonging or believed to belong to a specific group.

Hedonistic type Serial killer who strives for pleasure and thrill-seeking. To this killer, people are simply objects to use for one's own enjoyment. The hedonistic type is divided into lust, thrill, and creature comfort killers.

Homebuilders model Family preservation approach that tries to keep antisocial children in their homes and offers highly intensive services to the family for a short period of time.

Hostile attribution bias The tendency of some individuals to perceive hostile intent in others even when it is lacking.

Houses of Refuge Institutional settings presumably intended to protect, nurture, and educate neglected or wayward children during the mid-19th century.

Human trafficking The luring or kidnapping and exploitation of people, including children, for monetary gain. Usually but not necessarily involves sexual exploitation.

HUMINT (HUManINTelligence) interrogation Effective method of interrogation designed to acquire knowledge for intelligence and national security purposes.

Hypnotic hypermnesia The enhancement or revival of memory through hypnosis.

Hypnotic trance theory The perspective that hypnosis represents a special state of consciousness that promotes a high level of responsiveness to suggestion and changes in bodily feelings.

Iatrogenic effect A process whereby mental or physical disorders are unintentionally induced or developed in patients by physicians, clinicians, or psychotherapists.

Idiographic approach Searching for general principles which can be applied to large groups by intense study of one individual. The detailed case study of one person illustrates an idiographic approach. Compare with nomothetic approach.

Immature or fixated child molester Type of child molester who never developed satisfactory sexual relationships with other adults.

Incarceration rate Number of persons incarcerated in prisons and jails per specified number in the population—on national level, reported per 100,000 U.S. population.

Incest Sexual abuse of adolescents or children by immediate family or relatives.

Infanticide Although this term literally means the killing of an infant, it is also used for the killing of a child by a parent, and is then divided into neonaticide and filicide.

Infantile amnesia Normal lack of memory of events that happened very early in one's life, typically but not necessarily before age 4.

Information-gathering approach A method of police interviewing and interrogation that does not presume guilt on the part of the person being questioned, but rather seeks to obtain information about events surrounding a crime. Compare with accusatorial approach.

Initial appearance A court appearance if an arrested individual is being held in jail rather than released or cited to appear in court at a later date. Its purpose is to review the need for continuing detention. However, it also may apply to the first proceeding before a judge, whether or not the individual was detained.

Injunction A court order to stop or refrain from doing something or to stay away from a person or place, usually based on a request from a party who is allegedly harmed by the activity.

Insanity In the legal context, this term describes a judicial determination that an individual's mental disorder relieves him or her of criminal responsibility for illegal actions.

Insanity Defense Reform Act (IDRA) The federal law passed in 1984 that changed the standard for determining insanity in federal courts and made it more difficult for defendants to use this defense.

Institutional corrections Broad term for facilities that confine inmates; applies also to their rules, policies, and practices.

Instrumental violence Occurs when the injury of an individual is secondary to the acquisition of some other external goal of the offender.

Intake In juvenile law, this is the youth's first official contact with the juvenile court system; the intake officer often has discretion to warn the youth, refer the youth for prosecution, or divert the youth to community services.

Intensive rehabilitation supervision (IRS) Community supervision programs that match the risk level of offenders with their criminogenic and noncriminogenic needs.

Intensive supervision programs (ISPs) Correctional supervision of offenders who are on probation or parole but are assigned to heightened supervision or offered additional services.

Interdisciplinary Fitness Interview–Revised (IFI-R) One of the available measures for assessing competency (fitness) to stand trial.

Intermediate sanctions Supervision that is less restrictive than residential placement but more restrictive than the standard probation under which the juvenile or adult offender remains in his or her own home with conditions attached. Sometimes referred to as probation-plus or parole-plus. Examples may include intensive supervision, day-reporting requirements, or electronic monitoring.

Intimate partner violence (IPV) Violent crimes committed against persons by their current or former spouses, boyfriends, or girlfriends.

Investigative psychology Umbrella term that refers to a scientific approach designed to improve our understanding of criminal behavior and the investigative process.

Inwald Personality Inventory (IPI) Developed for use with corrections officers, this personality inventory is used by some clinicians to measure personality in law enforcement officers as well.

Jails Facilities operated by local governments to hold persons temporarily detained, awaiting trial, or sentenced to short-term (typically under 1 year) confinement after having been convicted of a misdemeanor.

Job analysis Identification and analysis of the skills, abilities, knowledge, and psychological characteristics that are needed to do a job.

Judicial waivers The process by which a judge transfers a juvenile's case to criminal court.

Juvenile delinquency Broad term for variety of antisocial acts committed by youth; some but not all are criminal offenses.

Juvenile delinquent Young person who commits an act against the criminal code and who is adjudicated delinquent by an appropriate court.

Juvenile detention Temporary secure or nonsecure placement pending adjudication or during adjudication proceedings, up to a final disposition.

Juvenile Justice and Delinquency Prevention Act (JJDPA) Landmark federal legislation passed in 1974 that attempted to address the needs of juveniles in the juvenile justice system as well as those considered at risk for delinquency.

Leakage Term used for behaviors that presumably indicate deception on the part of someone being interviewed.

Least detrimental alternative standard In custody decisions, the standard that chooses the arrangement that would cause the child the least amount of harm.

Legal parental authority Having the authority to make legal decisions for the child, such as medical needs and choice of educational system.

Legal psychology Umbrella term for the scientific study of a wide assortment of topics reflecting the close relationship between psychology and the courts.

Legislative waiver, statutory exclusion, or waiver by statute Terms used for the automatic processing of juveniles in criminal courts, typically for serious crimes. Many states, for example, require by statute that juveniles 14 and above who are charged with murder be tried in criminal courts. In some jurisdictions, criminal court judges have the authority to transfer the juvenile to juvenile court.

Level of Service Inventory–Revised (LSI-R) Assesses dynamic and static risk factors to determine offender needs for services as well as risk of reconviction, including for violent offenses.

Level of Service/Case Management Inventory (LS/CMI) A modification of the LSI that focuses on determining the clinical and social services the individual should ideally receive.

Life course–persistent offenders (LCPs) Offenders who demonstrate a lifelong pattern of antisocial behavior and who are often resistant to treatment or rehabilitation.

Limited jurisdiction Refers to authority of lower courts that can only settle small disputes or deal with preliminary issues in a major case.

Linkage analysis An investigative method that looks at similarities between crimes and attempts to connect them to the same offender.

Love obsession stalkers Stalkers who seek a love relationship with a stranger or casual acquaintance with whom they are obsessed.

MacArthur Competence Assessment Tool–Treatment (MacCAT-T) Used by clinicians to evaluate ability to benefit from treatment.

MacArthur Competency Assessment Tool–Criminal Adjudication (MacCAT-CA) Used by clinicians to evaluate competence to stand trial.

MacArthur Juvenile Competence Study Multisite study of adjudicative competence in juveniles.

Malingering Response style in which the individual consciously fabricates or grossly exaggerates his or her symptoms.

Manslaughter The unjustified killing of a human being without premeditation. May be negligent or non-negligent, and does not require intent to kill.

Mass murder Involves the killing of three or more persons at a single location with no cooling-off period between the killings.

Mens rea In criminal law, the guilty mind. It refers to the intent that is needed in order to be found guilty of a crime.

Mental State at the Time of the Offense Screening Evaluation (MSE) One of several tools used by clinicians to assess criminal responsibility, typically to determine whether an insanity defense could be supported.

Minnesota Multiphasic Personality Inventory–Revised (MMPI-2) Self-administered personality inventory used in numerous contexts, including law enforcement screening.

Minnesota Multiphasic Personality Inventory-Revised-Restructured Form (MMPI-R-RF) Self-report personality inventory used in clinical practice, especially in the selection of law enforcement and public safety personnel. Although the inventory uses many questions from the MMPI-2, researchers have developed its own norms and clinical scales.

Mission-oriented type Serial killer who believes that there is a particular group of people who are considered undesirable and who must be destroyed or eliminated.

Modus operandi (MO) Actions and procedures an offender uses to commit a crime successfully.

MTC:CM3 Empirically based classification system for pedophiles that underscores the importance of viewing pedophilia as characterized by multiple behavioral patterns and intentions.

MTC:R3 Rape typology consisting of nine discrete rapist types that are differentiated on the basis of six variables.

Multiculturalism Refers to differences in race, ethnicity, gender, sexual orientation, and disability.

Multidimensional Treatment Foster Care (MTFC) Treatment model developed specifically with chronic offenders in the child welfare system.

Multisystemic therapy (MST) A community treatment approach for serious juvenile offenders that focuses on the family while being responsive to the many other contexts surrounding the family, such as the peer group, the neighborhood, and the school.

Munchausen syndrome by proxy (MSBP) An unusual form of child abuse in which the parent (usually the mother) or parents consistently bring a child for medical attention with symptoms falsified or directly induced by the parent or parents. Term is gradually being replaced by the term *child medical abuse*.

Murder The intentional and premeditated killing of one human being by another without justification or excuse.

National Crime Victimization Survey (NCVS) A government survey that attempts to measure the extent to which households, individuals, and commercial establishments are victims of serious crime.

National Survey of Children's Exposure to Violence (NatSCEV) A government-sponsored survey designed to measure the violent victimization of children.

NEO Personality Inventory–Revised (NEO PI-R) Personality inventory based on the five-factor model of personality traits.

Neonaticide The killing of a newborn, usually under 48 hours old, sometimes defined as under 24 hours old.

Nomothetic approach Refers to the search for general principles, relationships, and patterns by examining and combining data from many individuals. Compare with idiographic approach.

Noncriminogenic needs Needs that are subject to change but have been found to have little influence on an offender's criminal behavior. Psychological states such as depression, anxiety, or low self-esteem are examples used by some researchers.

Non-hypnotic hypermnesia Enhancement or recovery of memory through non-hypnotic methods, such as free association, fantasy, and recall techniques.

Non-sadistic rapists Those who engage in a sexual attack because of an intense sexual arousal prompted by specific stimuli identified in the intended victim. Although rape is always a violent act, the perpetrator's aggression is not considered the significant feature in the attack.

Notification In victims' rights legislation, refers to the requirement that victims be told about the status of an offender at various stages of the criminal justice process.

Observational learning The process by which individuals learn patterns of behavior by observing another person performing the action.

Office of Juvenile Justice and Delinquency Prevention (OJJDP) The federal agency charged with overseeing juvenile justice on the national level, providing grants for juvenile research and programs, and taking a leadership role in setting policies nationwide relative to juveniles.

Ontario Domestic Assault Risk Assessment (ODARA) Instrument recommended for use by law enforcement officers and others to determine the likelihood that an individual will commit future violence within the family.

Opportunistic rapist One who engages in sexual assault simply because the opportunity to rape presents itself.

Oppositional defiant disorder (ODD) In children, this is a disorder whose symptoms include arguing with adults, refusing adults' requests, deliberately trying to annoy others, blaming others for mistakes, and being spiteful or vindictive.

Organizational stress Refers to the emotional and stressful effects that the policies and practices of the police department have on the individual officer.

Outpatient treatment (OT) orders Court orders that allow an individual to live in his or her own home or alternative group or foster home on condition that the individual receive mental health treatment and usually comply with a medication regimen. Also sometimes called community treatment orders or assisted outpatient treatment (AOT).

Own-race bias (ORB) The tendency of people to be able to discriminate between faces of their own race better than those of other races.

Paraphilia The clinical term for various psychological conditions that are exhibited in fantasies, urges, or behaviors involving nonhuman objects, suffering or humiliation of oneself or one's partner, or children or other nonconsenting persons. The paraphilias are not considered mental disorders unless they involve behaviors that are harmful to the individual or others.

Parens patriae The doctrine in law that establishes the right of the state to substitute its presumably benevolent decision making for that of individuals who are thought to be unable or unwilling to make their own decisions. Applied particularly in cases involving children, juveniles, mentally disordered individuals, and intellectually disabled people.

Parental relocation An increasingly frequent topic for family courts, in which they are asked to make a decision as to whether the custodial parent should be allowed to relocate the child to a geographical area away from the non-custodial parent.

Parenting evaluation A term preferred to custody evaluations in some jurisdictions. Assessment of parenting plans is also frequently used.

Parole The conditional release of an offender after completing a portion of his or her sentence.

Pedophilia Clinical term for sexual attraction to children. However, it may or may not result in actual child molestation or other sexual abuse.

Peremptory challenge A rule that allows a lawyer to request the removal of a prospective juror without giving a reason.

Personal stress Stress related to marital relationships, health problems, addictions, peer group pressures, feelings of helplessness and depression, and lack of achievement.

Personality Assessment Inventory (PAI) A self-administered, objective inventory of adult personality that provides information on critical clinical variables.

Pervasively angry rapist This rapist demonstrates a predominance of global and undifferentiated anger that pervades all areas of his life.

Physical parental authority In custody decision making, the right to make day-to-day decisions affecting the child, such as curfew hours or whether the child can go out with friends. Compare with legal parental authority.

Plaintiff Person or party who initially brings a civil suit.

Police and public safety psychology Branch of psychology focusing on services provided to law enforcement personnel, including assessment, clinical treatment, and consulting on administrative matters.

Police culture A set of behaviors and attitudes that are presumed to be characteristic of individuals involved in law enforcement work, such as suspicion, toughness, and protectiveness of other law enforcement officers.

Polyvictimization Victim's repeated exposure to direct victimization, either involving one type of crime or a variety of crimes.

Post-shooting traumatic reaction (PSTR) Represents a collection of emotions and psychological response patterns that may occur after a law enforcement officer shoots a person in the line of duty.

Posttraumatic stress disorder (PTSD) A cluster of behavioral patterns that result from a psychologically distressing event that is outside the usual range of human experience.

Power-control killer Type of serial murderer who obtains satisfaction from the absolute life-or-death control he has over the victim.

Power rape A rape situation described by Groth in which the assailant seeks to establish power and control over his victim. The amount of force used depends on the degree of submission shown by the victim.

Predictive validity The extent to which a test predicts a person's subsequent performance on the dimensions and tasks the test is designed to measure.

Preemployment psychological screening The psychological evaluation that is conducted prior to a conditional offer of employment.

Preponderance of the evidence Proof that one side in a legal dispute has more evidence in its favor than the other. It is the standard required in most civil suits and may be relevant to criminal proceedings as well, but not to establish guilt, which requires proof beyond a reasonable doubt.

Presentence investigation (PSI) Social history, typically prepared by probation officers, that includes information about the offender's family background, employment history, level of education, substance abuse, criminal history, medical needs, and mental health history. Used by courts for sentencing purposes.

Pretrial detainees Those persons held in jail before trial because either they are unable to afford bail, or they were denied bail because they were considered dangerous.

Preventive detention The term used when defendants are jailed before trial specifically because they might flee or are considered too dangerous for pretrial release. Preventive detention for juveniles can be used if they are at risk of committing more crime, not necessarily violent crime.

Preventive outpatient treatment (or commitment) Court-ordered community treatment to prevent a person from becoming dangerous. A controversial option because it does not require the high standard of dangerousness needed for other involuntary civil commitment, either to an institution or to community treatment.

Prison Rape Elimination Act (PREA) Federal law requiring prisons and jails to address the problem of sexual assault within such facilities.

Prison transfer Process whereby prisoners are moved from one facility to another, sometimes without notice.

Prisons Correctional facilities operated by state and federal governments to hold persons convicted of felonies and sentenced generally to terms of more than 1 year.

Probate courts Courts that have jurisdiction over a range of civil matters, such as wills and estates, property transfers, and—in some states—divorce and child custody matters.

Probation A sentence to serve time in the community, subject to supervision and conditions imposed by courts or probation officers.

Projective instruments Psychological tests that require the individual to interpret ambiguous stimuli (e.g., photos or inkblots).

Prosecutorial waiver Provision that gives prosecutors the authority to decide whether the case will be taken to juvenile court or criminal court.

Protective custody A form of isolation in which the inmate is separated from others for his or her own safety.

P-Scan: Research Version Measure of psychopathy intended primarily for research purposes but now used by some mental health practitioners in their clinical practice.

Psychological assessment Refers to all the techniques used to measure and evaluate an individual's past, present, or future psychological status. Usually includes interviews, observations, and various measuring procedures that may or may not include psychological tests.

Psychological autopsy Primarily undertaken in an effort to make a reasonable determination of what may have been in the mind of the deceased person leading up to and at the time of death—particularly if the death appears to be a suicide.

Psychological profiling The gathering of information on a known individual, generally one who poses a threat or is believed to be dangerous. Psychological profiles also may be prepared on public persona, such as presidents or historical figures.

Psychology of crime and delinquency The science of the behavioral and mental processes of the adult and juvenile offender.

Psychopath An individual who demonstrates a distinct behavioral pattern that differs from the general population in its lack of sensitivity, empathy, compassion, and guilt. Often involved in antisocial—including criminal—activity. Distinguished from the sociopath in that psychopathy is believed to have a biological origin associated with an inordinate need for stimulation.

Psychopathy Checklist: Screening Version (PCL:SV) A relatively quick measure of psychopathy.

Psychopathy Checklist: Youth Version (PCL:YV) An instrument used for the measurement of psychopathic characteristics in young people.

Psychopathy Checklist–Revised (PCL-R) Developed by Robert Hare, it is the best known and most heavily researched instrument for the measurement of criminal psychopathy.

Psychosexual evaluations Assessment of sex offenders not only to decide on a treatment plan, but also to gauge their likelihood of further offending.

Punitive damages Awards in civil cases that are assessed to punish the defendant or respondent for the harm caused to the plaintiff. Compare with compensatory damages.

Questioned document examination or analysis Examination of the validity of documents, such as wills or suicide notes.

Racial profiling Illegal singling out of someone (e.g., by law enforcement) solely on the basis of his or her race or ethnicity.

Rape A form of sexual assault characterized by force or threat of force that involves penetration. See also, statutory rape and sexual assault.

Rape by fraud The act of having sexual relations with a supposedly consenting adult female under fraudulent conditions, such as when a physician or psychotherapist has sexual intercourse with a patient under the guise of effective treatment.

Rape myths A variety of mistaken beliefs about the crime of rape and its victims held by many men and women.

Reactive or expressive violence Refers to physical violence precipitated by a hostile and angry reaction to a perceived threat or dangerous situation.

Recidivism A return to criminal activity (usually measured by arrest) after being convicted of a criminal offense.

Reconstructive psychological evaluation (RPE) Reconstruction of the personality profile and cognitive features (especially intentions) after a person is deceased. Also called psychological autopsy.

Reconstructive theory of memory Perspective that memory is continually vulnerable to revision.

Regressed child molester The child molester who is attracted to and victimizes children after experiencing sexual relationships with adults. Compare with fixated child molester.

Rehabilitation Any attempt intended to bring about changes in behavioral or thought patterns.

Reid method The predominant method used by law enforcement in the United States to interview and interrogate criminal suspects. See also, accusatorial method.

Relapse prevention (RP) A method of treatment primarily designed to prevent a relapse of an undesired behavioral pattern. Often used in sexual offender treatment.

Release decisions Judges' decisions concerning whether to confine an individual or place him or her on probation or release prior to trial.

Repressed memory State of being unaware that a traumatic event occurred.

Repression Refers to the psychological process of keeping something out of awareness because of the traumatic effect connected with it.

Respondent Another term for defendant in a civil suit.

Restitution/compensation Refers to the victim's right to receive restitution or compensation from the offender for the harm suffered.

Restorative justice Sometimes called reparative justice. An approach to attempt to heal victims, the community, and sometimes the offender (particularly a juvenile offender) after a crime has been committed. It may involve victim–offender mediation or reconciliation, and is intended primarily as a means of making the victim "whole" after a criminal event.

Right to treatment Statutory right that stipulates that incarcerated and institutionalized persons have a right to receive care and treatment suited to their needs.

Risk assessment The enterprise in which clinicians offer probabilities that a given individual will engage in violent or otherwise antisocial behavior based on known factors relating to the individual.

Risk/needs/responsivity (RNR) Principles identified by Andrews and Bonta, widely believed and documented to be associated with effective psychological treatment.

Rogers Criminal Responsibility Assessment Scales (R-CRAS) Measures designed to assess criminal responsibility and detect malingering in cases where the defendant is considering raising or has raised an insanity defense.

Sadistic rape A rape situation, identified by Groth, in which the offender experiences sexual arousal and excitement as a result of the victim's torment, distress, helplessness, and suffering. The assault usually involves bondage and torture.

Safe School Initiative (SSI) A variety of federal programs designed to increase safety in schools; includes violence prevention as well as ways to deal with problems related to bullying and harassment.

School shootings General term for school violence, including events involving guns and other weapons.

Scientific jury selection Procedures used by social scientists consulting with lawyers in efforts to help lawyers select jurors who are most sympathetic to their side. May involve community attitude surveys or other methods to "predict" the ultimate decision of members of the jury pool.

Screening-in procedures Intended to identify those attributes (almost invariably personality) that distinguish one candidate over another as being potentially a more effective police officer.

Screening-out procedures Designed to eliminate those law enforcement applicants who demonstrate significant signs of psychopathology or emotional instability or who lack the basic ability or mental acuity to perform the job in a safe and responsible manner.

Self-regulation The ability to control one's behavior in accordance with internal cognitive standards.

Sequential lineup A live or photo lineup in which a witness views individuals in a series, requiring the witness to decide on whether to identify one individual before moving on to another. Compare with simultaneous lineup.

Serial murder Incidents in which an individual (or individuals) kill a number of people (usually a minimum of three) over time.

Sexual assault The broad term to cover a range of sexual offenses, not limited to rape; a term now preferred in many statutes and in research literature.

Sexual Experiences Questionnaire (SEQ) Instrument available for assessing incidence and prevalence of sexual harassment.

Sexual harassment A form of discrimination evidenced by unwelcome sexual comments or behavior directed toward a person based on sex; creates a hostile working environment. See also, gender harassment.

Sexual masochism Refers to sexual arousal in response to being humiliated, beaten, whipped, bound, or otherwise made to suffer.

Sexual sadism Sexual arousal gained from inflicting real or simulated physical pain or psychological suffering on another person.

Sexually motivated rapist Characterized by the presence of protracted sexual or sadistic fantasies that strongly influence the assaults.

Sexually violent predator (SVP) Term used for the sex offender who is believed to be a continuing danger to society. Under SVP statutes, such offenders are civilly committed after the end of their prison sentences.

Shadow juries Used by some trial consultants, these are individuals who match demographically and possibly in attitudes the members of an actual jury. Consultants note how the shadow jury is responding to the trial as it proceeds in order to suggest strategies to the lawyer who hired the consultant.

Shaken baby syndrome (SBS) See Abusive head trauma.

Show-up Identification procedure in which police present a single suspect to the eyewitness(es) to see if the person or persons will identify that individual as the perpetrator.

Simple obsession stalkers Stalkers who seek power and control after a failed relationship with the victim; often associated with past domestic violence.

Simultaneous lineup A live or photo lineup in which a witness views individuals all at once, such as standing in a row or in a photo array. Compare with sequential lineup.

Situational factors Characteristics of the psychosocial environment, such as stress or aggression in others, that encourage or engender violent behavior.

Sixteen Personality Factor Questionnaire (16-PF) A psychological instrument with good validity and reliability used to measure normal or core personality traits in adults. Does not necessarily predict success in law enforcement.

Social cognition Refers to how people process, store, and apply social and interpersonal information about other people.

Socialization factors Those processes through which a person learns patterns of thinking, behavior, and feeling from his or her early life experiences.

Sociopath The individual with a history of serious and typically violent criminal activity. Should be distinguished from psychopath, who does not necessarily commit crimes, but who is distinguished by having an inordinate biological need for stimulation.

Specialized courts Courts that deal only with particular matters. Family courts, drug courts, mental health courts, girls' courts, and domestic violence courts are all examples.

Specialty Guidelines for Forensic Psychology APA and AP-LS Guidelines offered in a number of subject areas associated with research and clinical practice in forensic psychology. Most recent guidelines were published in 2013.

Spousal Assault Risk Assessment (SARA) Evaluates an individual's risk of committing violence against a spouse or intimate partner.

Spree murder Refers to the killing of three or more individuals *without* a cooling-off period, usually at two or three different locations.

Stable dynamic factors Although they are changeable, these factors usually change slowly and may take months or even years to change.

Stalking Defined as "a course of conduct directed at a specific person that involves repeated physical or visual proximity, nonconsensual communication, or verbal, written, or implied threats sufficient to cause fear in a reasonable person" (Tjaden, 1997, p. 2).

State-dependent memory Refers to the research finding that the things we experience in one emotional or physiological state—such as happiness, fear, or even intoxication—are sometimes easier to recall when we are again in that same state.

Static risk factors Aspects of a person's developmental history that place the person at risk for antisocial activity but that cannot be changed. Examples are parents with a history of criminal activity or the person's own early-onset of criminal offending. Also called historical factors.

Status offenses A class of illegal behavior that only persons with certain characteristics or status can commit. Used almost exclusively to refer to the behavior of juveniles. Examples include running away from home, violating curfew, buying alcohol, or skipping school.

Statutory rape Rape for which the age of the victim is the crucial distinction, with the premise that a victim below a certain age (usually 16) cannot validly consent to sexual intercourse with an adult.

Structured professional judgment (SPJ) Relevant to risk assessment, it refers to a mental health practitioner assessing the likelihood of violence by using clinical judgment aided by guidelines. Some risk assessment instruments are developed based on the premise that SPJ has more validity than—or at least as much validity as—actuarial risk assessment.

Subject matter jurisdiction The authority of courts over specific issues or legal matters. For example, a family court may have authority over divorce, custody, adoption, and delinquency matters.

Supermax prisons High-security facilities (or units within a maximum-security prison) supposedly intended to hold the most troublesome, violent inmates, either in complete isolation or in two-person quarters.

Suspect-based profiling The process of collecting data on behavioral, personality, cognitive, and demographic data on previous offenders in an attempt to identify other offenders. Used to detect drug trafficking and terrorism-related criminal activity.

Tarasoff requirement Generic term used for the statutory stipulation or court decision that a therapist has the duty to warn or a duty to protect individuals threatened by the therapist's client. The duty to warn implies a need to inform the individual directly; the duty to protect may involve notifying authorities or taking steps to have the patient hospitalized.

Task-related stress Stress related to the nature of the work itself. In a law enforcement context, for example, this includes the possibility of being killed in the line of duty.

Teaching-family model A model used particularly in group homes for delinquents or for children at risk. It includes adults playing the role of "parent," encouraging youth to be socialized in a healthy family context.

Tender years doctrine A legal assumption, derived from the traditional belief that the mother is the parent ideally and inherently best suited to care for children of a "tender age." The doctrine is no longer officially used in virtually all states, though in many the mother is presumptively given custody of the child.

Termination of parental rights The rare judicial determination that a parent or parents is/are not fit to care for children. Legal authority for the children is removed. Abandonment and severe child abuse may be reasons.

Testamentary capacity The mental ability to make a will.

Threat assessment Set of investigative and operational activities designed to identify, assess, and manage individuals who may pose a threat of violence to identifiable targets, such as the school environment.

Tort Legal term for a civil wrong in which a plaintiff alleges some negligence on the part of the defendant or respondent.

Trans-situational consistency Tendency of people to exhibit the same behavior and tendencies across different situations.

Trans-temporal consistency Tendency of people to exhibit the same behavior and tendencies across time.

Trial consultants Also called litigation consultants. Professionals, often but not necessarily psychologists, who assist lawyers in such tasks as selecting jurors, preparing witnesses to testify, and identifying effective strategies for the cross-examination (e.g., of children).

Triarchic Psychopathology Measure (TriPM) Represents the major three traits that some scholars argue best describe psychopathic individuals: (1) boldness; (2) meanness; (3) impulsiveness.

Ultimate issue Final question that must be decided by the court. For example, should the expert provide an opinion about whether the defendant was indeed insane (and therefore not responsible) at the time of his crime?

Unconscious transference Occurs when a person seen in one situation is confused with a person seen in another situation.

Uniform Crime Reports (UCR) A program operated by the FBI, it is the government's main method of collecting national data on crimes reported to police and arrests. See also NIBRS and NCVS.

Vengeance stalkers Stalkers who do not seek a relationship with their victims, but rather are trying to elicit a response, such as fear, or change of behavior, such as moving to a new geographical area.

Vicarious traumatization Occurs when clinicians are exposed to a series of trauma victims, which often leads to a high incidence of professional burnout.

Victimless crimes Crimes that are said to have no victim with the exception of the person who himself or herself is committing them. Examples are gambling, drug offenses, and prostitution.

Victimology The psychological and criminological study of crime victimization, including but not limited to characteristics of victims, victims' rights, and victim assistance programs.

Vindictive rapist Offender who uses the act of rape to harm, humiliate, and degrade his victims.

Violence Use of physical force or destruction.

Violence Against Women Act Federal law containing multiple provisions for preventing and responding to crimes perpetrated against women and girls, particularly in areas of domestic violence and sexual assault.

Violent Criminal Apprehension Program (ViCAP) Program designed to communicate with and help the nation's law enforcement agencies to investigate, identify, track, apprehend, and prosecute violent serial offenders by sharing information across jurisdictional boundaries.

Visionary type Serial killer driven by delusions or hallucinations that compel the person to kill a particular group of individuals.

Visitation risk assessments Evaluations provided to family courts for help in deciding whether and how often children should be allowed to visit non-custodial parents or others.

Voir dire A process through which the judge and attorneys question the prospective jurors and possibly disqualify them from jury duty. In some jurisdictions, the questioning can be done only by lawyers.

Voluntary false confessions Confessions to crimes one did not commit, offered without coercion by others such as police or family members.

Voyeurism The tendency to gain sexual excitement and gratification from observing unsuspecting others who are naked, undressing, or engaging in sexual activity.

Waiver petition An official request to the court that a juvenile's case be transferred to criminal court, or transferred from criminal court to juvenile court.

Workplace violence The aggressive actions, including deaths, that occur at the workplace, not necessarily caused by those who work within the organization.

CASES CITED

Addington v. Texas, 99 S.Ct. 1804 (1979).

Ake v. Oklahoma, 470 U.S. 68 (1985).

Argersinger v. Hamlin, 407 U.S. 25 (1972).

Atkins v. Virginia, 536 U.S. 304 (2002).

Barefoot v. Estelle, 463 U.S. 880 (1983).

Batson v. Kentucky 476 U.S. 79 (1986).

Bell v. Wolfish, 441 U.S. 520 (1979).

Borawick v. Shay, 68 F.3d 597 (2d Cir. 1995), cert. denied, 517 U.S. 1229.

Brady v. Maryland, 373 U.S. 83 (1963).

Breed v. Jones, 421 U.S. 519 (1975).

Brown v. Board of Education, 347 U.S. 483 (1954).

Brown v. Entertainment Merchants Association, 564 U.S. _____ (2011).

Brown v. Plata, 131 S.Ct. 1910 (2011).

Clark v. Arizona, 126 S.Ct. 2709 (2006).

Coker v. Georgia, 433 U.S. 584 (1977).

Cone v. Bell, 129 S.Ct. 1769 (2009).

Cooper v. Oklahoma, 116 S. Ct. 1373 (1996).

Correctional Services Corporation v. Malesko (00-860) 534 U.S. 61 (2001)

Cruzan v. Director, Missouri Department of Health, 497 U.S. 261 (1990).

Daubert v. Merrill Dow Pharmaceuticals, Inc., 509 U.S. 579 (1993).

Delling v. Idaho, cert. denied 133 S.Ct 504 (2012).

District of Columbia v. Heller, 554 U.S. 570 (2008).

Drope v. Missouri, 420 U.S. 162 (1975).

Durham v. United States, 214 F.2d 862 (D. C. Cir. 1954).

Dusky v. United States, 362 U.S. 402 (1960).

Elonis v. U.S. 575 U.S. ___ (2015).

Estelle v. Gamble, 429 U.S. 97 (1976).

Ewing v. Goldstein, 5 Cal.Rptr.3d 864 (2004), 120 Cal.App.4th 807 (2004).

Fare v. Michael C., 442 U.S. 707 (1979).

Faretta v. California, 422 U.S. 806 (1975).

Farmer v. Brennan, 511 U.S. 725 (1994).

Finger v. State, 27 P.3d 66 (Nev. 2001).

Ford v. Wainwright, 477 U.S. 399 (1986).

Foster v. Chatman, 578 U.S. _____ (2016).

Foucha v. Louisiana, 504 U.S. 71 (1992).

Franco-Gonzalez v. Holder, No. CV 10-02211 DMG (DTBx), 2013 WL 3674492 (C. D. Cal. Apr. 23, 2013).

Frye v. United States, 54 app. D.C., 46, 47; 293 F 1013, 1014 (1923).

Furman v. Georgia, 408 U.S. 238 (1972).

General Electric Co. v. Joiner 522 U.S. 136 (1997).

Gideon v. Wainwright, 372 U.S. 335 (1963).

Glossip v. Gross, 576 U.S. _____ (2015).

Godinez v. Moran, 113 S.Ct. 2680 (1993).

Graham v. Florida, 130 S. Ct. 2011 (2010).

Gruber v. Gruber, 583 A.2d 434 (Pa. Super. 1990).

Hall v. Florida, 572 U.S. _____ (2014).

Harris v. Forklift Systems, Inc., 510 U.S. 17 (1993).

Heller v. Doe, 509 U.S. 312 (1993).

Hollingsworth v. Perry, 570 U.S. _____ (2013).

Hudson v. Palmer 468 U.S. 517 (1984).

In re Gault, 387 U.S. 1 (1967).

In re M-A-M, 251. & N. Dec. 474 (2011).

In re Quinlan, 70 N.J. 10, 355 A.2d. 647, cert. denied sub nom. (1976).

Indiana v. Edwards, 554 U.S. 164 (2008)

Jackson v. Indiana, 406 U.S. 715 (1972)

Jaffe v. Redmond, 116 S. Ct. 1923 (1996).

J.D.B. v. North Carolina, 564 U.S. 261 (2011).

Jenkins v. United States 307 F.2d 637 (1962).

John Doe 76C, v. Archdiocese of Saint Paul and Minneapolis, No. A10–1951 (July 25, 2012).

Kansas v. Crane, 534 U.S. 407 (2002).

Kansas v. Hendricks, 521 U.S., 117 S.Ct. 2072 (1997).

Kennedy v. Louisiana, 554 U.S., 128 S.Ct. 2072 (2008).

Kent v. United States, 383 U.S. 541 (1966).

Kumho Tire Co. v. Carmichael 526 U.S. 137 (1999).

Lockett v. Ohio, 438 U.S. 586 (1978).

Madrid v. Gomez, 889 F. Supp. 1149 (N.D. Cal. 1995).

Maryland v. Craig, 497 U.S. 836 (1987).

McKeiver v. Pennsylvania, 403 U.S. 528 (1971).

McKune v. Lile, 536 U.S. 24 (2002).

McWilliams v. Dunn, __ U.S. ___ (2017).

Miller v. Alabama and Jackson v. Hobbs, 132 S.Ct. 2455 (2012).

Minneci v. Pollard 607 F. 3d 583 and 629 F. 3d 843, reversed (2012).

Miranda v. Arizona, 384 U.S. 436 (1966).

Montgomery v. Louisiana, 577 U.S. ___ (2016).

Moore v. Texas, 581 U.S. _____ (2017).

North Dakota ex rel. Schuetzle v. Vogel 557 N.W.2d 358 (N.D. 1995).

Obergefell v. Hodges, 576 U.S. _____ (2015).

Oncale v. Sundowner Offshore Services, 523 U.S. 75 (1998).

Packingham v. North Carolina 582 US ___ (2017).

Panetti v. Quarterman, 127 S. Ct. 852 (06-6407) (2007).

Paroline v. United States, 572 U.S. _____ (2014).

Payne v. Commonwealth of Virginia, Court of Appeals of Virginia, Record No. 151524, Decided December 29, 2016.

Payne v. Tennessee 501 U.S. 808 (1991).

Pena-Rodriguez v. Colorado, 580 U.S. _____ (2017).

People v. Caballero, 55 Cal 4th 262 (2012).

People v. Hickey, 86 Ill. App. 20 (1889).

Perri v. Coughlin, WL 395374 (N.D.N.Y. 1999).

Perry v. New Hampshire, 132 S.Ct. 716 (2012).

Peruta v. California, Petition for certiorari denied on June 26, 2017

Regina v. M'Naughten, 8 Eng. Rep. 718 (1843).

Riggins v. Nevada, 504 U.S. 127 (1992).

Riley v. California, 573 U.S. 783 (2014).

Ring v. Arizona, 536 U.S. 584 (2002).

Roper v. Simmons, 543 U.S. 551 (2005).

Schall v. Martin, 467 U.S. 253 (1984).

Sell v. United States 539 U.S. 166 (2003).

Shannon v. U.S. 512 U.S. 573 (1994).

Stogner v. California 539 U.S. 607 93 Cal. App. 4th 1229, 114 Cal. Rptr. 2d 37, reversed (2003).

Stovall v. Denno, 388 U.S. 293 (1967).

Tarasoff v. Regents of the University of California, 17 Cal. 3d 425, 551 P.2d 334, 131 Cal. Rptr. 14 (Cal. 1976).

Thompson v. Oklahoma, 487 U.S. 815 (1988).

Thor v. Superior Court, 855 P.2d 375 (Cal. 1993).

Troxel v. Granville, 530 U.S. 57 (2000).

United States v. Alexander, 526 F. 2d 161. 168 (1975 [8th Cir.]).

United States v. Brawner 471 F.2d 969,153 U.S. App. D.C. 1; 1972 U.S. App. (1972).

United States v. Comstock, 560 U.S. 130 S.Ct. 1949 (2010).

United States v. Salerno, 481 U.S. 739 (1987).

United States v. Windsor, 570 U.S._____ (2013).

U.S. v. Jones, 132 S.Ct. 945 (2012).

Vitek v. Jones, 445 U.S. 480 (1980).

Volk v. DeMeerleer, 2016 386 P.3d 254 (2016).

Washington v. Harper 494 U.S. 210 (1990).

Zinermon v. Burch, 110 S.Ct. 975 (1990).

REFERENCES

Aamodt, M. G. (2008). Reducing misconceptions and false beliefs in police and criminal psychology. *Criminal Justice and Behavior, 35*, 1231–1240.

Aamodt, M. G., & Stalnaker, H. (2001). Police officer suicide: Frequency and officer profiles. In D. C. Sheehan & J. I. Warren (Eds.), *Suicide and law enforcement* (pp. 383–398). Washington, DC: FBI Academy.

Aamodt, M. G., Stalnaker, H., & Smith, M. (2015, October). *Law enforcement suicide: Updated profiles and the quest for accurate suicide rate*. Paper presented at the Annual Meeting of the Society for Police and Criminal Psychology, Atlanta, GA.

Abbey, A., Zawacki, T., Buck, P. O., Clinton, A. M., & McAuslan, P. (2004). Sexual assault and alcohol consumption: What do we know about their relationship and what types of research are still needed? *Aggression and Violent Behavior, 9*, 271–305.

Abbey, A., Zawacki, T., & McAuslan, P. (2000). Alcohol's effects on sexual perception. *Journal of Studies on Alcohol, 61*, 688–697.

Abel, G. G., Lawry, S. S., Karlstrom, E., Osborn, C. A., & Gillespie, C. E. (1994). Screening tests for pedophilia. *Criminal Justice and Behavior, 21*, 115–131.

Abram, K. M., Teplin, L. A., King, D. C., Longworth, S. L., Emanuel, K. M., Romero, E. G., . . . & Olson, N. D. (2013, June). *PTSD, trauma, and comorbid psychiatric disorders in detained youth*. Washington, DC: U.S. Department of Justice, Office of Juvenile Justice and Delinquency Prevention.

Abrams, D. E. (2013). A primer on criminal child abuse and neglect law. *Juvenile and Family Court, 64*, 1–27.

Abrams, K. M., & Robinson, G. E. (2002). Occupational effects of stalking. *Canadian Journal of Psychiatry, 47*, 468–472.

Acierno, R. H., Hernandez, M. A., Arnstadter, A. B., Resnick, H. S., Steve, K., Muzzy, W., & Kilpatrick, D. G. (2010). Prevalence and correlates of emotional, physical, sexual, and financial abuse and potential neglect in the United States: The National Elder Mistreatment Study. *American Journal of Public Health, 100*, 292–297.

Acierno, R. H., Resnick, H., & Kilpatrick, D. G. (1997, Summer). Health impact of interpersonal violence 1: Prevalence rates, case identification, and risk factors for sexual assault, physical assault, and domestic violence in men and women. *Behavioral Medicine, 23*, 53–67.

Ackerman, M. J., & Ackerman, M. C. (1997). Custody evaluation practices: A survey of experienced professionals (revisited). *Professional Psychology: Research and Practice, 28*, 137–145.

Ackerman, M. J., & Gould, J. W. (2015). Child custody and access. In B. L. Cutler & P. A. Zapf (Eds.), *APA handbook of forensic psychology, Vol. 1. Individual and situational influences in criminal and civil courts* (pp. 425–469). Washington, DC: American Psychological Association.

Ackerman, M. J., & Pritzl, T. B. (2011). Child custody evaluation practices: A 20-year follow up. *Family Court Review, 49*, 618–628.

Adam, K. S., & Brady, S. N. (2013). Fifty years of judging family law: The Cleavers have left the building. *Family Court Review, 51*, 28–33.

Adams, G. A., & Buck, J. (2010). Social stressors and strain among police officers: It's not just the bad guys. *Criminal Justice and Behavior, 37*, 1030–1040.

Adams, J. H. (1997). Sexual harassment and Black women: A historical perspective. In W. O'Donahue (Ed.), *Sexual harassment: Theory, research, and treatment* (pp. 213–224). Boston, MA: Allyn & Bacon.

Adams, K., Alpert, G. P., Dunham, R. G., Garner, J. H., Greenfield, L. A., Henriquez, M. A., . . . & Smith, S. K. (1999, October). *Use of force by police: Overview of national and local data series: Research report*. Washington, DC: National Institute of Justice and Bureau of Justice Statistics.

Adams, W., Owens, C., & Small, K. (2010). *Effects of federal legislation on the commercial sexual exploitation of children*. Washington, DC: U.S. Department of Justice, Office of Juvenile Justice and Delinquency Prevention.

Adler, R., Nunn, R., Northam, E., Lebnan, V., & Ross, R. (1994). Secondary prevention of childhood firesetting. *Journal of the American Academy of Child and Adolescent Psychiatry, 33*, 1194–1202.

Administration on Aging. (1998, September). *The National Elder Abuse Incidence Study: Final report*. Washington, DC: U.S. Department of Health and Human Services, Administration on Aging.

Adolphs, R. (2009). The social brain: Neural basis of social knowledge. *Annual Review of Psychology, 60*, 693–716.

Agopian, M. W. (1984). The impact on children of abduction by parents. *Child Welfare, 63*, 511–519.

Ahlers, C. J., Schaefer, G. S., Mundt, I. A., Roll, S., Englert, H., Willich, S. N., & Beier, K. M. (2011). How unusual are the contents of paraphilias? Paraphilia-associated sexual arousal patterns in a community-based sample of men. *Journal of Sexual Medicine, 8*, 1362–1370.

Alexander, J. F., Waldron, H. B., Robbins, M. S., & Neeb, A. A. (2013). *Functional family therapy for adolescent behavior problems.* Washington, DC: American Psychological Association.

Alexander, M. A. (1999). Sexual offender treatment efficacy revisited. *Sexual Abuse: A Journal of Research and Treatment, 11,* 101–116.

Alexander, R. A., Smith, W., & Stevenson, R. (1990). Serial Munchausen syndrome by proxy. *Pediatrics, 8,* 581–585.

Alison, L. J., Bennell, C., Ormerod, D., & Mokros, A. (2002). The personality paradox in offender profiling: A theoretical review of the processes involved in deriving background characteristics from crime scene actions. *Psychology, Public Policy, and Law, 8,* 115–135.

Alison, L. J., & Canter, D. V. (1999). Professional, legal and ethical issues in offender profiling. In D. V. Canter & L. J. Alison (Eds.), *Profiling in policy and practice* (pp. 21–54). Aldershot, England: Ashgate.

Alison, L. J., Kebbell, M., & Lewis, P. (2006). Considerations for experts in assessing the credibility of recovered memories of child sexual abuse: The importance of maintaining a case-specific focus. *Psychology, Public Policy, and Law, 4,* 419–441.

Alison, L. J., Smith, M. D., Eastman, O., & Rainbow, L. (2003). Toulmin's philosophy of argument and its relevance to offender profiling. *Psychology, Crime & Law, 9,* 173–183.

Alison, L. J., Smith, M. D., & Morgan, K. (2003). Interpreting the accuracy of offender profiles. *Psychology, Crime & Law, 9,* 185–195.

Allen, R. S., & Shuster, J. L. (2002). The role of proxies in treatment decisions: Evaluating functional capacity to consent to end-of-life treatments within a family context. *Behavioral Sciences & the Law, 20,* 235–252.

Alpert, J., Brown, L. S., & Courtois, C. A. (1998). Symptomatic clients and memories of childhood abuse: What the trauma and sexual abuse literature tells us. *Psychology, Public Policy, and Law, 4,* 941–945.

Althouse, R. (2010). Standards for psychology services in jails, prisons, correctional facilities, and agencies. *Criminal Justice and Behavior, 37,* 749–808.

Amato, P. R. (2000). The consequences of divorce for adults and children. *Journal of Marriage and the Family, 62,* 1269–1287.

Amato, P. R. (2001). Children of divorce in the 1990s: An update of the Amato and Keith (1991) meta-analysis. *Journal of Family Psychology, 15,* 355–370.

Amato, P. R. (2010). Research on divorce: Continuing trends and new developments. *Journal of Marriage and the Family, 72,* 650–666.

American Bar Association (2009). Due process for people with mental disabilities in immigration removal proceedings. *Mental and Physical Disability Law Reporter, 33,* 882–900.

American Civil Liberties Union. (2014). *Alone and afraid: Children held in solitary confinement and isolation in juvenile detention and correctional facilities.* New York, NY: Author.

American Psychiatric Association. (2013). *Diagnostic and statistical manual of mental disorders* (5th ed.). Washington, DC: Author.

American Psychological Association. (1992). Ethical principles of psychologists and code of conduct. *American Psychologist, 47,* 1597–1611.

American Psychological Association. (1996). *Reducing violence: A research agenda.* Washington, DC: Author.

American Psychological Association. (1998). Guidelines for the evaluation of dementia and age-related cognitive decline. *American Psychologist, 53,* 1298–1303.

American Psychological Association. (2002). Ethical principles of psychologists and code of conduct. *American Psychologist, 57,* 1060–1073.

American Psychological Association. (2003a). *Family-like environment better for troubled children and teens.* Retrieved from http://www.apa .org/research/action/family.aspx

American Psychological Association. (2003b). Guidelines on multicultural education, training, research, practice, and organizational change for psychologists. *American Psychologist, 58,* 377–402.

American Psychological Association. (2003c). Is youth violence just another fact of life? In *APA Online: Public Interest Initiatives.* Washington, DC: Author. Retrieved from http://www.APA.org

American Psychological Association. (2010a). Amendments to the 2002 "Ethical Principles of Psychologists and Code of Conduct." *American Psychologist, 65,* 493.

American Psychological Association. (2010b). Guidelines for child custody evaluations in family law proceedings. *American Psychologist, 65,* 863–867.

American Psychological Association. (2012). Guidelines for psychological practice with lesbian, gay, and bisexual clients. *American Psychologist, 67,* 10–42.

American Psychological Association. (2013a). *Gun violence: Prediction, prevention, and policy.* APA Panel of Experts Report. Washington, DC: Author. Retrieved from http://www.apa.org/pubs/info/reports/ gun-violence-prevention.aspx

American Psychological Association. (2013b). Guidelines for psychological evaluations in child protection matters. *American Psychologist, 68,* 20–31.

American Psychological Association. (2013c). Specialty guidelines for forensic psychology. *American Psychologist, 68,* 7–19.

American Psychological Association. (2014a). *Pursuing a career in forensic and public service psychology.* Washington, DC: Author. Retrieved from www.apa.org/action/science/forensic/education-training.aspx

American Psychological Association. (2014b). *2012 APA state licensing board list (unpublished special analysis).* Washington, DC: Author.

American Psychological Association. (2014c). *Report of the Task Force on Trafficking of Women and Girls.* Washington, DC: Author.

American Psychological Association. (2014d). Guidelines for psychological practice with older adults. *American Psychologist, 69*, 34–65.

American Psychological Association. (2016a). *APA practice central.org*. Retrieved from www.apapracticecenter.org/advocacy/prescriptive authority/retrieved 1/18/17

American Psychological Association. (2016b). *APA membership statistics*. Washington, DC: Author.

American Psychological Association Center for Workforce Studies. (2015). Retrieved from http://www.apa.org/workforce/about/index.aspx

American Psychological Association's Task Force on Television in Society. (1992). *Big world, small screen: The role of television in American society*. Lincoln: University of Nebraska Press.

Amick-McMullan, A., Kilpatrick, D. G., & Resnick, H. S. (1991). Homicide as a risk factor for PTSD among surviving family members. *Behavioral Modification, 15*, 545–559.

Amick-McMullen, A., Kilpatrick, D. G., Veronen, L. J., & Smith, S. (1989). Family survivors of homicide victims: Theoretical perspectives and an exploratory study. *Journal of Traumatic Stress, 2*, 21–35.

Amnesty International. (1998). *Betraying the young* (Special report). New York, NY: Author.

Andershed, H., Kerr, M., Stattin, H., & Levander, S. (2002). Psychopathic traits in non-referred youths: Initial test of a new assessment tool. In E. Blaauw, J. M. Philippa, K. C. M. P. Ferenschild, & B. van Lodesteijn (Eds.), *Psychopaths: Current international perspectives* (pp. 131–158). The Hague, Netherlands: Elsevier.

Anderson, C. A., & Bushman, B. J. (2001). Effects of violent video games on aggressive behavior, aggressive cognition, aggressive affect, physiological arousal, and prosocial behavior: A meta-analytic review of the scientific literature. *Psychological Science, 12*, 353–359.

Anderson, N. B. (2010). Connecting with our members. *APA Monitor, 41*, 9.

Anderson, S. D., & Hewitt, J. (2002). The effect of competency restoration training on defendants with mental retardation found not competent to proceed. *Law and Human Behavior, 26*, 343–351.

Anderson, S. L. (2016). Commentary on the special issue on the adolescent brain: Adolescence, trajectories, and the importance of prevention. *Neuroscience and Biobehavioral Review, 70*, 329–333.

Andretta, J. R., Woodland, M. H., Watkins, K. M., & Barnes, M. E., (2016). Towards the discreet identification of commercial sexual exploitation of children (CSEC) victims and individualized interventions: Science to practice. *Psychology, Public Policy, and Law, 22*, 260–270.

Andrews, D. A., & Bonta, J. (1994). *The psychology of criminal conduct*. Cincinnati, OH: Anderson.

Andrews, D. A., & Bonta, J. (1995). *The Level of Service Inventory–Revised*. Toronto, Canada: Multi-Health Systems.

Andrews, D. A., & Bonta, J. (1998). *The psychology of criminal conduct* (2nd ed.). Cincinnati, OH: Anderson.

Andrews, D. A., & Bonta, J. (2010). *The psychology of criminal conduct* (4th ed.). New Providence, NJ: Matthew Bender.

Andrews, D. A., Bonta, J., & Hoge, P. D. (1990). Classification for effective rehabilitation: Rediscovering psychology. *Criminal Justice and Behavior, 17*, 19–52.

Andrews, D. A., Bonta, J., & Wormith, J. S. (2004a). *The Level of Service/Case Management Inventory (LS/CMI)*. Toronto, Canada: Multi-Health Systems.

Andrews, D. A., Bonta, J., & Wormith, J. S. (2004b). *Manual for the Level of Service/Case Management Inventory (LS/CMI)*. Toronto, Canada: Multi-Health Systems.

Andrews, D. A., Zinger, I., Hoge, R. D., Bonta, J., Gendreau, P., & Cullen, F. T. (1990). Does correctional treatment work? A psychologically informed meta-analysis. *Criminology, 28*, 369–404.

Appelbaum, P. S., & Grisso, T. (1995). The MacArthur Treatment Competence Study I: Mental illness and competence to consent to treatment. *Law and Human Behavior, 19*, 105–126.

Archer, J. (2002). Sex differences in physically aggressive acts between heterosexual partners: A meta-analytic review. *Aggression and Violence, 7*, 313–351.

Archer, R. P., Buffington-Vollum, J. K., Stredny, R. V., & Handel, R. W. (2006). A survey of psychological tests used among forensic psychologists. *Journal of Personality Assessment, 87*, 84–94.

Ardis, C. (2004). School violence from the classroom teacher's perspective. In W. L. Turk (Ed.), *School crime and policing* (pp. 131–150). Upper Saddle River, NJ: Prentice Hall.

Arkow, P. (1998). The correlations between cruelty to animals and child abuse and the implications for veterinary medicine. In R. Lockwood & F. R. Ascione (Eds.), *Cruelty to animals and interpersonal violence: Readings in research and application* (pp. 409–414). West Lafayette, IN: Purdue University Press.

Ascione, F. R. (1997). *Animal welfare and domestic violence*. Logan: Utah State University.

Asher, R. (1951). Munchausen's syndrome. *The Lancet, 1*, 339–341.

Aspinwall, L. G., Brown, T. R., & Tabery, J. (2012, August 17). The double-edged sword: Does biomechanism increase or decrease judges' sentencing. *Science, 337*, 846–849.

Atakan, Z. (2012). Cannabis, a complex plant: Different compounds and different effects on individuals. *Therapeutic Advances in Psychopharmacology, 2*, 241–254.

Atkinson, J. (2010). The law of relocation of children. *Behavioral Sciences & the Law, 28*, 563–579.

Ault, R., & Reese, J. T. (1980, March). A psychological assessment of crime profiling. *FBI Law Enforcement Bulletin, 49*, 22–25.

Aumiller, G. S., & Corey, D. (2007). Defining the field of police psychology: Core domains and proficiencies. *Journal of Police and Criminal Psychology*, *22*, 65–76.

Austin, W. G. (2008a). Relocation, research, and forensic evaluation. Part I: Effects of residential mobility on children of divorce. *Family Court Review*, *46*, 136–149.

Austin, W. G. (2008b). Relocation, research, and forensic evaluation. Part II: Research support for the relocation risk assessment model. *Family Court Review*, *46*, 347–365.

Aviv, R. (2013, January 14). The science of sex abuse: Is it right to imprison people for heinous crimes they have not yet committed? *The New Yorker*, 36–45.

Ax, R. K., Fagan, T. J., Magaletta, P. R., Morgan, R. D., Nussbaum, D., & White, T. W. (2007). Innovations in correctional assessment and treatment. *Criminal Justice and Behavior*, *34*, 893–905.

Babchishin, K. M., Hanson, R. K., & Hermann, C. A. (2011). The characteristics of online sex offenders: A meta-analysis. *Sexual Abuse: A Journal of Research and Treatment*, *23*, 92–123.

Bailey, J. M., Bernard, P. A., & Hsu, K. J. (2016). An Internet study of men sexually attracted to children: Correlates of sexual offending against children. *Journal of Abnormal Psychology*, *125*, 989–1000.

Baird, K. A. (2007). A survey of clinical psychologists in Illinois regarding prescription privileges. *Professional Psychology, Research and Practice*, *38*, 196–202.

Baker, B., & Williams, C. (2017, July). *Immigration enforcement actions, 2015*. Washington, DC: Department of Homeland Security, Office of Immigration Statistics.

Bakker, A. B., & Heuven, E. (2006). Emotional dissonance, burnout, and in-role performance among nurses and police officers. *International Journal of Stress Management*, *13*, 423–440.

Baldwin, S. A., Christian, S., Berkeljion, A., & Shadish, W. R. (2012). The effects of family therapies for adolescent delinquency and substance abuse: A meta-analysis. *Journal of Marital and Family Therapy*, *38*, 281–304.

Bales, W. D., Bedard, L. E., Quinn, S. T., Ensley, D. T., & Holley, G. P. (2005). Recidivism of public and private state prison inmates in Florida. *Criminology and Public Policy*, *4*, 57–82.

Balkin, J. (1988). Why policemen don't like policewomen. *Journal of Police Science and Administration*, *16*, 29–37.

Ballie, R. (2001, December). Where are the new psychologists going? *Monitor on Psychology*, *32*, 24–25.

Banich, M. T. (2009). Executive function: The search for an integrated account. *Current Directions in Psychological Science*, *18*, 89–94.

Banks, C. S., Blake, J. J., & Joslin, A. K. (2013, Fall). Stand up or stay out of it: How do parents teach their children to respond to bullying situations? *The School Psychologist*, 10–15.

Barbaree, H. E., & Marshall, W. L. (Eds.). (2006). *The juvenile sex offender* (2nd ed.). New York, NY: Guilford Press.

Barbaree, H. E., & Serin, R. C. (1993). Role of male sexual arousal during rape in various rapist subtypes. In G. C. Nagayama, G. C. N. Hall, R. Hirchman, J. R. Graham, & M. S. Zaragoza (Eds.), *Sexual aggression: Issues in etiology, assessment, and treatment* (pp. 99–106). Washington, DC: Taylor & Francis.

Barbaree, H. E., Seto, M. C., Serin, R. C., Amos, N. L., & Preston, D. L. (1994). Comparisons between sexual and nonsexual rapist subtypes: Sexual arousals to rape, offense precursors, and offense characteristics. *Criminal Justice and Behavior*, *21*, 95–114.

Barber, S. J., & Wright, E. M. (2010). Predictors of completion in a batterer treatment program. *Criminal Justice and Behavior*, *37*, 847–858.

Barber, T. X., Spanos, N. R., & Chaves, J. F. (1974). *Hypnosis, imagination, and human potentialities*. New York, NY: Pergamon.

Bardone, A. M., Moffitt, T. E., & Caspi, A. (1996). Adult mental health and social outcomes of adolescent girls with depression and conduct disorder. *Development and Psychopathology*, *8*, 811–829.

Barkley, R. (1997). Behavioral inhibition, sustained attention, and executive functions: Constructing a unifying theory of ADHD. *Psychological Bulletin*, *121*, 65–94.

Barkley, R. (1998). *Attention-deficit hyperactivity disorder* (2nd ed.). New York, NY: Guilford Press.

Barlett, C., & Coyne, S. M. (2014). A meta-analysis of sex differences in cyber-bullying behavior: The moderating role of age. *Aggressive Behavior*, *40*, 474–488.

Barlett, C. P., Gentile, D. A., & Chew, C. (2016). Predicting cyberbullying from anonymity. *Psychology of Popular Media Culture*, *5*, 171–180.

Barnard, G. W., Thompson, J. W., Freeman, W. C., Robbins, L., Gies, D.,, & Hankins, G. (1991). Competency to stand trial: Description and initial evaluation of a new computer-assisted assessment tool (CAD-COMP). *Bulletin of the American Academy of Psychiatry and the Law*, *19*, 367–381.

Baron, R. A., & Byrne, D. (2000). *Social psychology* (9th ed.). Boston, MA: Allyn & Bacon.

Barrick, M. R., & Mount, M. K. (1991). The Big Five personality dimensions and job performance: A meta-analysis. *Personnel Psychology*, *44*, 1–26.

Barrick, M. R., & Mount, M. K. (2005). Yes, personality matters: Moving on to more important matters. *Human Performance*, *18*, 359–372.

Barriga, A. Q., & Gibbs, J. C. (1996). Measuring cognitive distortion in antisocial youth: Development and preliminary evaluation of the How I Think questionnaire. *Aggressive Behavior*, *22*, 333–343.

Barry, C. T., Frick, P. J., DeShazo, T. M., McCoy, M. G., Ellis, M., & Loney, B. R. (2000). The importance of callous-unemotional traits for extending the concept of psychopathy to children. *Journal of Abnormal Psychology, 109*, 335–340.

Bartol, C. R. (1980). *Criminal behavior: A psychosocial approach.* Englewood Cliffs, NJ: Prentice Hall.

Bartol, C. R. (1996). Police psychology: Then, now, and beyond. *Criminal Justice and Behavior, 23*, 70–89.

Bartol, C. R. (2002). *Criminal behavior: A psychosocial approach* (6th ed.). Upper Saddle River, NJ: Prentice Hall.

Bartol, C. R., & Bartol, A. M. (1987). History of forensic psychology. In I. B. Weiner & A. K. Hess (Eds.), *Handbook of forensic psychology* (pp. 3–21). New York, NY: Wiley.

Bartol, C. R., & Bartol, A. M. (2004). *Psychology and law: Theory, research, and application* (3rd ed.). Belmont, CA: Wadsworth/Thomson.

Bartol, C. R., & Bartol, A. M. (2011). *Criminal behavior: A psychological approach* (9th ed.). Upper Saddle River, NJ: Prentice Hall.

Bartol, C. R., & Bartol, A. M. (2013). *Criminal and behavioral profiling.* Thousand Oaks, CA: Sage.

Bartol, C. R., & Bartol, A. M. (2014). *Criminal behavior: A psychological approach* (10th ed.). Columbus, OH: Pearson.

Bartol, C. R., & Bartol, A. M. (2015). *Psychology and law: Research and practice.* Thousand Oaks, CA: Sage.

Baskin-Sommers, A. R., Baskin, D. R., Sommers, I., Casados, A. T., Crossman, M. K., & Javdani, S. (2016). The impact of psychopathology, race, and environmental context on violent offending in a male adolescent sample. *Personality Disorders: Theory, Research, and Treatment, 7*, 354–362.

Basow, S. A., & Minieri, A. (2010). "You owe me": Effects of date cost, who pays, participant gender, and rape myth beliefs on perceptions of rape. *Journal of Interpersonal Violence, 26*, 479–497.

Batastini, A. B., & Morgan, R. D. (2016). Connecting the disconnected: Preliminary results and lessons learned from a telepsychology initiative with special management inmates. *Psychological Services, 13*, 283–291.

Bauer, P. J. (1996). What do infants recall of their lives? Memories for specific events by one- to two-year-olds. *American Psychologist, 51*, 29–41.

Baum, K., Catalano, S., Rand, M., & Rose, K. (2009, January). *Stalking victimization in the United States.* Washington, DC: U.S. Department of Justice, Bureau of Justice Statistics.

Bauserman, R. (2002). Child adjustment in joint-custody versus sole-custody arrangements: A meta-analytic review. *Journal of Family Psychology, 16*, 38–53.

Bauserman, R. (2012). A meta-analysis of parental satisfaction, adjustment, and conflict in joint custody and sole custody following divorce. *Journal of Divorce & Remarriage, 53*, 464–488.

Bayer, P., & Pozen, D. E. (2003). *The effectiveness of juvenile correctional facilities: Public versus private management.* New Haven, CT: Economic Growth Center, Yale University.

Beasley, J. D., Hayne, A. S., Beyer, K., Cramer, G. L., Benson, S. B., Muirhead, Y., & Warren, J. L. (2009). Patterns of prior offending by child abductors: A comparison of fatal and nonfatal outcomes. *International Journal of Law and Psychiatry, 32*, 273–280.

Beatty, D., Hickey, E., & Sigmon, J. (2002). Stalking. In A. Seymour, M. Murray, J. Sigmon, M. Hook, C. Edwards, M. Gaboury, & G. Coleman (Eds.), *2002 National Victim Assistance Academy textbook.* Washington, DC: U.S. Department of Justice, Office of Victims of Crime.

Beauchaine, T. P., Katkin, E. S., Strassberg, Z., & Snarr, J. (2001). Disinhibitory psychopathology in male adolescents: Discriminating conduct disorder from attention-deficit/hyperactivity disorder through concurrent assessment of multiple autonomic states. *Journal of Abnormal Psychology, 110*, 610–624.

Beck, A. J. (2015). *Use of restrictive housing in U.S. prisons and jails, 2011–2012.* Washington, DC: U.S. Department of Justice.

Beck, A. J., Cantor, D., Hartge, J., & Smith, T. (2013). *Sexual victimization in juvenile facilities reported by youth, 2012.* Washington, DC: U.S. Department of Justice, Bureau of Justice Statistics.

Beck, A. J., Guerino, P., & Harrison, P. M. (2010). *Sexual victimization in juvenile facilities reported by youth, 2008–2009.* Washington, DC: U.S. Department of Justice, Bureau of Justice Statistics.

Becker, J. V. (1990). Treating adolescent sexual offenders. *Professional Psychology: Research and Practice, 21*, 362–365.

Becker, J. V., Hall, S. R., & Stinson, J. D. (2001). Female sexual offenders: Clinical, legal and policy issues. *Journal of Forensic Psychology Practice, 1*, 29–50.

Becker, J. V., & Johnson, B. R. (2001). Treating juvenile sex offenders. In J. B. Ashford, B. D. Sales, & W. H. Reid (Eds.), *Treating adult and juvenile offenders with special needs* (pp. 273–289). Washington, DC: American Psychological Association.

Becker, K. (2014). *Importance of factors associated with competence for immigration proceedings: A survey of immigration attorneys.* Retrieved from ProQuest Dissertations and Theses Global (Order No. 3581895).

Bedi, G., & Goddard, C. (2007). Intimate partner violence: What are the impacts on children? *Australian Psychologist, 42*, 66–77.

Beech, A. R., & Craig, L. A. (2012). The current status of static and dynamic factors in sexual offender risk assessment. *Journal of Aggression, Conflict and Peace Research, 4*, 169–185.

Belenko, S., & Peugh, J. (2005). Estimating drug treatment needs among prison inmates. *Drug and Alcohol Dependence, 77*, 269–281.

Belfrage, H., Strand, S., Storey, J. E., Gibas, A. L., Kropp, P. R., & Hart, S. D. (2012). Assessment and management of risk for intimate partner violence by police officers using the Spousal Assault Risk Assessment Guide. *Law and Human Behavior, 36*, 60–67.

Bell, M. E., Goodman, L. A., & Dutton, M. A. (2007). The dynamics of staying and leaving: Implications for battered women's emotional well-being and experiences of violence at the end of a year. *Journal of Family Violence, 22*, 413–428.

Bemak, F., & Chi-Ying Chung, R. (2014). Immigrants and refugees. In F. T. L. Leong (Ed.), *APA handbook of multicultural psychology: Vol. 1. Theory and Research* (pp. 503–517). Washington, DC: American Psychological Association.

Ben-Porath, Y. S., Corey, D. M., & Tarescavage, A. M. (2017). Using the MMPI-2-RF in preemployment evaluations of police officer candidates. In C. L. Mitchell & E. H. Dorian (Eds.), *Police psychology and its growing impact on modern law enforcement* (pp. 51–78). Hershey, PA: IGI Global.

Ben-Porath, Y. S., Fico, J. M., Hibler, N. S., Inwald, R., Kruml, J., & Roberts, M. R. (2011, August). Assessing the psychological suitability of candidates for law enforcement positions. *The Police Chief, 78*, 64–70.

Ben-Porath, Y. S., & Tellegen, A. (2008). Minnesota Multiphasic Personality Inventory-2-Restructured Form: Manual for Administration, Scoring, and Interpretation. Minneapolis: University of Minnesota Press.

Ben-Shakhar, G. (2002). A critical review of the Control Question Test (CQT). In M. Kleiner (Ed.), *Handbook of polygraph testing* (pp. 103–126). San Diego, CA: Academic Press.

Ben-Shakhar, G. (2008). The case against the use of polygraph examinations to monitor post-conviction sex offenders. *Legal and Criminological Psychology, 13*, 191–207.

Benson, E. (2002, November). The perils of going solo. *Monitor on Psychology, 33*, 25.

Bergman, M. E., Walker, J. M., & Jean, V. A. (2016). A simple solution to policing problems: Women! *Industrial and Organizational Psychology, 9*, 590–597.

Bergseth, K. J., & Bouffard, J. A. (2012). Examining the effectiveness of a restorative justice program for various types of juvenile offenders. *International Journal of Offender Therapy and Comparative Criminology, 57*, 1054–1075.

Berliner, L. (1998). The use of expert testimony in child sexual abuse cases. In S. J. Ceci & H. Hembrooke (Eds.), *Expert witnesses in child abuse cases* (pp. 11–27). Washington, DC: American Psychological Association.

Bernal, G., & Sharrón-Del-Río, M. R. (2001). Are empirically supported treatments valid for ethnic minorities? Toward an alternative approach for treatment research. *Cultural Diversity and Ethnic Minority Psychology, 7*, 328–342.

Bernard, T. (1992). *The cycle of juvenile justice.* New York, NY: Oxford University Press.

Bernfeld, G. A. (2001). The struggle for treatment integrity in a "dis-integrated" service delivery system. In G. A. Bernfeld, D. P. Farrington, & A. W. Leschied (Eds.), *Offender rehabilitation in practice* (pp. 167–188). Chichester, England: Wiley.

Berson, S. B. (2010, June). Prosecuting elder abuse cases. *NIJ Journal, 265*, 8–9.

Beune, K., Giebels, E., & Taylor, P. J. (2010). Patterns of interaction in police interviews: The role of cultural dependency. *Criminal Justice and Behavior, 37*, 904–925.

Biederman, J. (2005). Attention-deficit/hyperactivity disorder: A selective overview. *Biological Psychiatry, 57*, 1215–1220.

Bingham, R. P., Porché-Burke, L., James, S., Sue, D. W., & Vasquez, M. J. T. (2002). Introduction: A report on the National Multicultural Conference and Summit II. *Cultural Diversity and Ethnic Minority Psychology, 8*, 75–87.

Bishop, D. M. (2000). Juvenile offenders in the adult criminal justice system. *Crime and Justice: A Review of Research, 27*, 81–167.

Black, H. C. (1990). *Black's law dictionary* (6th ed.). St. Paul, MN: West.

Black, J. (2000). Personality testing and police selection: Utility of the "Big Five." *New Zealand Journal of Psychology, 29*, 2–9.

Black, K. A., & McCloskey, K. A. (2013). Predicting date rape perceptions: The effects of gender, gender role attitudes, and victim resistance. *Violence Against Women, 19*, 949–967.

Black, M. C., Basile, K. C., Breiding, M. J., Smith, S. G., Walters, M. L., Merrick, M. T., . . . & Stevens, M. R. (2011). *The National Intimate Partner and Sexual Violence Survey (NISVS): 2010 summary report.* Atlanta, GA: National Center for Injury Prevention and Control, Centers for Disease Control and Prevention.

Blackburn, R. (1993). *The psychology of criminal conduct.* Chichester, England: Wiley.

Blair, J. P. (2005). What do we know about interrogation in the United States? *Journal of Police and Criminal Psychology, 20*, 44–57.

Blakemore, S. I., & Mills, K. L. (2014). Is adolescence a sensitive period for sociocultural processing? *Annual Review of Psychology, 65*, 187–207.

Blanchette, K., & Brown, S. L. (2006). *The assessment and treatment of women offenders: An integrated perspective.* Chichester, England: Wiley.

Blau, T. (1994). *Psychological services for law enforcement.* New York, NY: Wiley.

Blum, J., Ireland, M., & Blum, R. W. (2003). Gender differences in juvenile violence: A report from Add Health. *Journal of Adolescent Health, 32*, 234–240.

Blumberg, M. (1997). Controlling police use of deadly force: Assessing two decades of progress. In R. G. Dunham & G. P. Alpert (Eds.), *Critical issues in policing: Contemporary readings* (3rd ed., pp. 442–464). Prospect Heights, IL: Waveland.

Bobo, L. D., & Kluegel, J. (1997). The color line, the dilemma, and the dream: Racial attitudes and relations in American at the close of the twentieth century. In J. Higham (Ed.), *Civil rights and social wrongs: Black–White relations since World War II* (pp. 31–35). University Park: Pennsylvania State University Press.

Boccaccini, M. T. (2002). What do we really know about witness preparation? *Behavioral Sciences & the Law, 20,* 161–189.

Boccaccini, M. T., & Brodsky, S. L. (2002). Believability of expert and lay witnesses: Implications for trial consultation. *Professional Psychology: Research and Practice, 33,* 384–388.

Böckler, N., Seeger, T., Sitzer, P., & Heitmeyer, W. (2013). School shootings: Conceptual framework and international empirical trends. In N. Böckler, T. Seeger, P. Sitzer, & W. Heitmeyer (Eds.), *School shootings: International research, case studies, and concepts for prevention* (pp. 1–26). New York, NY: Springer.

Boer, D., Hart, S., Kropp, P., & Webster, C. (1997). *Manual for the Sexual Violence Risk–20 (SVR-20).* Vancouver, Canada: Family Violence Institute.

Boes, J. O., Chandler, C. J., & Timm, H. W. (2001, December). *Police integrity: Use of personality measures to identify corruption-prone officers.* Monterey, CA: Defense Personnel Security Research Center.

Bohm, R. M. (1999). *Deathquest: An introduction to the theory and practice of capital punishment in the United States.* Cincinnati, OH: Anderson.

Bohner, G., Jarvis, C. I., Eyssel, F., & Siebler, F. (2005). The causal impact of rape myth acceptance on men's rape proclivity: Comparing sexually coercive and noncoercive men. *European Journal of Social Psychology, 35,* 819–828.

Boney-McCoy, S., & Finkelhor, D. (1995). Psychosocial sequelae of violent victimization in a national youth sample. *Journal of Consulting and Clinical Psychology, 63,* 726–736.

Bonnie, R. J. (1990). Dilemmas in administering the death penalty: Conscientious abstentions, professional ethics, and the needs of the legal system. *Law and Human Behavior, 14,* 67–90.

Bonnie, R. J. (1992). The competence of criminal defendants: A theoretical reformulation. *Behavioral Sciences & the Law, 10,* 291–316.

Bonnie, R. J., & Grisso, T. (2000). Adjudicative competence and youthful offenders. In T. Grisso & R. Schwartz (Eds.), *Youth on trial: A developmental perspective on juvenile justice* (pp. 73–103). Chicago, IL: University of Chicago Press.

Bonta, J. (1996). Risk-needs assessment and treatment. In A. T. Harland (Ed.), *Choosing correctional options that work: Defining the demand and evaluating the supply* (pp. 18–32). Thousand Oaks, CA: Sage.

Bonta, J. (2002). Offender risk assessment: Guidelines for selection and use. *Criminal Justice and Behavior, 29,* 355–379.

Boothby, J. L., & Clements, C. B. (2000). A national survey of correctional psychologists. *Criminal Justice and Behavior, 27,* 716–732.

Boothby, J. L., & Clements, C. B. (2002). Job satisfaction of correctional psychologists: Implications for recruitment and retention. *Professional Psychology: Research and Practice, 33,* 310–315.

Borduin, C. M., Schaeffer, C. M., & Heiblum, N. (2009). A randomized clinical trial of multisystemic therapy with juvenile sexual offenders: Effects on youth social ecology and criminal activity. *Journal of Consulting and Clinical Psychology, 77,* 26–37.

Borum, R., Bartel, P., & Forth, A. (2006). *Manual for the Structured Assessment of Violence Risk in Youth (SAVRY).* Odessa, FL: Psychological Assessment Resources.

Borum, R., Cornell, D. G., Modzeleski, W., & Jimerson, S. R. (2010). What can be done about school shootings? A review of the evidence. *Educational Researcher, 39,* 27–37.

Borum, R., Fein, R., Vossekuil, B., & Berglund, J. (1999). Threat assessment: Defining an approach for evaluating risk of targeted violence. *Behavioral Sciences & the Law, 17,* 323–337.

Borum, R., & Fulero, S. M. (1999). Empirical research on the insanity defense and attempted reforms: Evidence toward informed policy. *Law and Human Behavior, 23,* 375–394.

Borum, R., & Grisso, T. (1995). Psychological tests used in criminal forensic evaluations. *Professional Psychology: Research and Practice, 26,* 465–473.

Borum, R., & Philpot, C. (1993). Therapy with law enforcement couples: Clinical management of the "high-risk lifestyle." *American Journal of Family Therapy, 21,* 122–135.

Borum, R., & Strentz, T. (1993, April). The borderline personality: Negotiation strategies. *FBI Law Enforcement Bulletin, 61,* 6–10.

Bosco, D., Zappalà, A., & Santtila, P. (2010). The admissibility of offender profiling in the courtroom: A review of legal issues and court opinions. *International Journal of Law and Psychiatry, 33,* 184–191.

Bosenman, M. F. (1988). Serendipity and scientific discovery. *The Journal of Creative Behavior, 22,* 132–138.

Bourke, M., & Hernandez, A. E. (2009). The "Butner Study" redux: A report of the incidence of hands-on child victimization by child pornography offenders. *Journal of Family Violence, 24,* 182–191.

Bow, J. N., Gottlieb, M. C., & Gould-Saltman, D. (2011). Attorney's beliefs and opinions about child custody evaluations. *Family Court Review, 49,* 301–312.

Bow, J. N., & Quinnell, F. A. (2001). Psychologists' current practices and procedures in child custody evaluations: Five years post American Psychological Association guidelines. *Professional Psychology: Research and Practice, 32,* 261–268.

Bradshaw, J. (2008, July/August). Behavioral detectives patrol airports. *The National Psychologist,* p. 10.

Braffman, W., & Kirsch, I. (1999). Imaginative suggestibility and hypnotizability: An empirical analysis. *Journal of Personality and Social Psychology, 77,* 578–587.

Brakel, S. J. (2003). Competency to stand trial: Rationalism, "contextualism" and other modest theories. *Behavioral Sciences & the Law, 21,* 285–295.

Brandon, S. E. (2014). Towards a science of interrogation. *Applied Cognitive Psychology, 28,* 945–946.

Brent, D. A. (1989). The psychological autopsy: Methodological issues for the study of adolescent suicide. *Suicide and Life-Threatening Behavior, 19,* 43–57.

Breslau, N. (2002). Epidemiologic studies of trauma, posttraumatic stress disorder, and other psychiatric disorders. *Canadian Journal of Psychiatry, 47,* 923–929.

Bresler, S. A. (2010, Summer). The fitness for duty assessment: An evaluation well-suited for the forensic psychologist. *American Psychology-Law Society News, 30*(2), 1, 4.

Brewster, J., Stoloff, M. L., Corey, D. M., Greene, L. W., Gupton, H. M., & Roland, J. E. (2016). Education and training guidelines for the specialty of Police and Public Safety Psychology. *Training and Education in Professional Psychology, 10,* 171–178.

Bricklin, B., & Elliot, G. (1995). Postdivorce issues and relevant research. In B. Bricklin (Ed.), *The child custody evaluation handbook: Research-based solutions and applications* (pp. 27–62). New York, NY: Bruner/Mazel.

Bridge, B. J. (2006). Solving the family court puzzle: Integrating research, police, and practice. *Family Court Review, 44,* 190–199.

Briere, J., Malamuth, N., & Ceniti, J. (1981). *Self-assessed rape proclivity: Attitudinal and sexual correlates.* Paper presented at the American Psychological Association meeting, Los Angeles, CA.

Briere, J., & Runtz, M. (1989). University males' sexual interest in children: Predicting potential indices of "pedophilia" in a non-forensic sample. *Child Abuse & Neglect, 13,* 65–75.

Briggs, P., Simon, W. T., & Simonsen, S. (2011). An exploratory study of Internet-initiated sexual offenses and the chat room sex offender. Has the Internet enabled a new typology of sex offender? *Sexual Abuse: A Journal of Research and Treatment, 23,* 72–91.

Brigham, J. C. (1999). What is forensic psychology, anyway? *Law and Human Behavior, 23,* 273–298.

Briones-Robinson, R., Powers, R., & Socia, K. M. (2016). Sexual orientation bias crimes: Examination of reporting, perception of police bias, and differential police response. *Criminal Justice and Behavior, 43,* 1688–1709.

British Psychological Society. (1995). Recovered memories: The report of the Working Party of the British Psychological Society. Leicester, England: Author.

Brocki, K. C., Eninger, L., Thorell, L. B., & Bohlin, G. (2010). Inter-relations between executive function and symptoms of hyperactivity/impulsivity and inattention in preschoolers: A two-year longitudinal study. *Journal of Abnormal Child Psychology, 38,* 163–171.

Brodsky, S. L. (1980). Ethical issues for psychologists in corrections. In J. Monahan (Ed.), *Who is the client? The ethics of psychological intervention in the criminal justice system* (pp. 63–92). Washington, DC: American Psychological Association.

Brodsky, S. L. (1999). *The expert expert witness: More maxims and guidelines for testifying in court.* Washington, DC: American Psychological Association.

Brodsky, S. L. (2004). *Coping with cross-examination and other pathways to effective testimony.* Washington, DC: American Psychological Association.

Brodsky, S. L. (2012). On the witness stand [Perspective essay]. In C. R. Bartol & A. M. Bartol, *Introduction to Forensic Psychology* (3rd ed., pp. 138–140). Thousand Oaks, CA: Sage.

Bronfenbrenner, U. (1979). *The ecology of human development: Experiment by nature and design.* Cambridge, MA: Harvard University Press.

Brook, M., & Kosson, D. S. (2013). Impaired cognitive empathy in criminal psychopathy: Evidence from a laboratory measure of empathic accuracy. *Journal of Abnormal Psychology, 122,* 156–166.

Brown, M. L. (1997). Dilemmas facing nurses who care for Munchausen syndrome by proxy. *Pediatric Nursing, 23,* 416–418.

Brown, P. L. (2014, January 28). A court's all-hands approach aids girls most at risk. *New York Times,* p. A11.

Brown, R., & Kulik, J. (1977). Flashbulb memories. *Cognition, 5,* 73–99.

Brown, S. L., & Forth, A. E. (1997). Psychopathy and sexual assault: Static risk factors, emotional precursors, and rapists subtypes. *Journal of Consulting and Clinical Psychology, 65,* 848–857.

Brown, T. L., Borduin, C. M., & Henggeler, S. W. (2001). Treating juvenile offenders in community settings. In J. B. Ashford, B. D. Sales, & W. H. Reid (Eds.), *Treating adult and juvenile offenders with special needs* (pp. 445–464). Washington, DC: American Psychological Association.

Browne, A., & Finkelhor, D. (1986). Impact of child sexual abuse: A review of the research. *Psychological Bulletin, 99,* 66–77.

Brucia, E., Cordova, M. J., & Ruzek, J. I. (2017). Critical incident interventions: Crisis response and debriefing. In C. L. Mitchell & E. H. Dorian (Eds.), *Police psychology and its growing impact on modern law enforcement* (pp. 119–142). Hershey, PA: IGI Global.

Bruck, M., & Ceci, S. J. (2004). Forensic developmental psychology: Unveiling four common misconceptions. *Current Directions in Psychological Science, 13,* 229–232.

Bruck, M., & Ceci, S. J. (2009). Reliability of child witnesses' reports. In J. L. Skeem, K. S. Douglas, & S. O. Lilienfeld (Eds.), *Psychological science in the courtroom: Consensus and controversy* (pp. 149–174). New York, NY: Guilford Press.

Bruck, M., & Ceci, S. J. (2012). Forensic developmental psychology in the courtroom. In D. Faust (Ed.), *Coping with psychiatric and psychological testimony* (pp. 723–737). New York, NY: Oxford University Press.

Bruck, M., Ceci, S. J., & Francoeur, E. (2000). Children's use of anatomically detailed dolls to report genital touching in a medical examination. *Journal of Experimental Psychology: Applied, 6,* 74–83.

Buckner, J. C., Mezzacappa, E., & Beardslee, W. R. (2003). Characteristics of resilient youths living in poverty: The role of self-regulatory processes. *Development and Psychopathology, 15,* 139–162.

Budd, K. S., Felix, E. D., Poindexter, L. M., Naik-Polan, A. T., & Sloss, C. F. (2002). Clinical assessment of children in child protection cases: An empirical analysis. *Professional Psychology: Research and Practice, 33,* 3–12.

Budnick, K. J., & Shields-Fletcher, E. (1998). *What about girls?* Washington, DC: U.S. Department of Justice, Office of Juvenile Justice and Delinquency Prevention.

Buh, E. S., & Ladd, G. W. (2001). Peer rejection as an antecedent of young children's school adjustment: An examination of mediating processes. *Developmental Psychology, 37,* 550–560.

Bull, R., & Milne, R. (2004). Attempts to improve the police interviewing of suspects. In D. Lassiter (Ed.), *Interrogations, confessions, and entrapment* (pp. 182–196). New York, NY: Kluwer Academic.

Bull, R., & Soukara, S. (2010). Four studies of what really happens in police interviews. In G. D. Lassiter & C. A. Meissner (Eds.), *Police interrogations and false confessions: Current research, practice, and policy recommendations* (pp. 81–95). Washington, DC: American Psychological Association.

Bumby, K. M. (1993). Reviewing the guilty but mentally ill alternative: A case of the blind "pleading" the blind. *Journal of Psychiatry and Law, 21,* 191–220.

Bumby, K. M., & Bumby, N. H. (1997). Adolescent female sexual offenders. In H. R. Cellini & B. Schwartz (Eds.), *The sex offender: New insights, treatment innovations and legal developments* (Vol. 2, pp. 10.1–10.16). Kingston, NJ: Civil Research Institute.

Burcham, A. M. (2016, June). *Sheriffs' officer personnel, 1993–2013.* Washington, DC: U.S. Department of Justice, Bureau of Justice Statistics.

Burdon, W. M., & Gallagher, C. A. (2002). Coercion and sex offenders: Controlling sex-offending behavior through incapacitation and treatment. *Criminal Justice and Behavior, 29,* 87–109.

Bureau of Justice Assistance. (2001, June). *Recruiting & retaining women: A self-assessment guide for law enforcement.* Washington, DC: U.S. Department of Justice.

Bureau of Justice Statistics. (2001a). *Prisoners in 2000.* Washington, DC: U.S. Department of Justice.

Bureau of Justice Statistics. (2015, May). *Local police departments, 2013: Personnel, policies, and practices.* Washington, DC: U.S. Department of Justice.

Bureau of Justice Statistics. (2016, November). *Publicly funded forensic crime laboratories: Quality assurance practices, 2014.* Washington, DC: U.S. Department of Justice.

Bureau of Labor Statistics. (2010, July). *Workplace shootings.* Washington, DC: U.S. Department of Labor.

Bureau of Labor Statistics. (2013, August). *National census of fatal occupational injuries in 2012.* Washington, DC: U.S. Department of Labor.

Burgess, A. W., Hartman, C. R., & Ressler, R. K. (1986). Sexual homicide: A motivational model. *Journal of Interpersonal Violence, 1,* 251–272.

Burgoon, J. K., Blair, J. P., & Strom, R. E. (2008). Cognitive biases and nonverbal cues availability in detecting deception. *Human Communication Research, 34,* 572–599.

Burl, J., Shah, S., Filone, S., Foster, E., & DeMatteo, D. (2012). A survey of graduate training programs and coursework in forensic psychology. *Teaching of Psychology, 39,* 48–53.

Burns, B. J., Schoenwald, S. K., Burchard, J. D., Faw, L., & Santos, A. B. (2000). Comprehensive community-based interventions for youth with severe emotional disorders: Multisystemic therapy and the wraparound process. *Journal of Child and Family Studies, 9,* 283–314.

Bush, S. S. (2017). Introduction. In S. S. Bush (Ed.), *APA handbook of forensic neuropsychology* (pp. xvii–xxii). Washington, DC: American Psychological Association.

Bushman, B. J., & Huesmann, L. R. (2012). Effects of violent media on aggression. In D. Singer & J. L. Singer (Eds.), *Handbook of children and the media* (2nd ed., pp. 231–248). Thousand Oaks, CA: Sage.

Butcher, J. N., Bubany, S., & Mason, S. N. (2013). Assessment of personality and psychopathology with self-report inventories. In K. F. Geisinger (Ed.), *APA handbook of testing and assessment in psychology: Vol. 2. Testing and assessment in clinical and counseling psychology* (pp. 171–192). Washington, DC: American Psychological Association.

Butcher, J. N., Hass, G. A., Greene, R. L., & Nelson, L. D. (2015). *Using the MMPI-2 in forensic assessment.* Washington, DC: American Psychological Association.

Butcher, J. N., & Miller, K. B. (1999). Personality assessment in personal injury litigation. In A. K. Hess & I. B. Weiner (Eds.), *The handbook of forensic psychology* (2nd ed., pp. 104–126). New York, NY: Wiley.

Butler, A. C. (2013). Child sexual assault: Risk factors for girls. *Child Abuse & Neglect, 37,* 643–652.

Butler, W. M., Leitenberg, H., & Fuselier, G. D. (1993). The use of mental health professional consultants to police hostage negotiation teams. *Behavioral Sciences & the Law, 11,* 213–221.

Cahill, B. S., Coolidge, F. L., Segal, D. L., Klebe, K. J., Marle, P. D., & Overmann, K. A. (2012). Prevalence of ADHD in subtypes in male and female adult prison inmates. *Behavioral Sciences & the Law, 30,* 154–166.

Caillouet, B. A., Boccaccini, M., Varela, J. G., Davis, R. D., & Rostow, C. D. (2010). Predictive validity of the MMPI-2 Psy 5 scales and facets for law enforcement employment outcomes. *Criminal Justice and Behavior, 37*, 217–238.

California Occupational Safety and Health Administration. (1995). *Guidelines for workplace security*. Sacramento, CA: Author.

Call, J. A. (2008). Psychological consultation in hostage/barricade crisis negotiation. In H. V. Hall (Ed.), *Forensic psychology and neuropsychology for criminal and civil cases* (pp. 263–288). Boca Raton, FL: CRC Press.

Callahan, L. A., & Silver, E. (1998). Factors associated with the conditional release of persons acquitted by reason of insanity: A decision tree approach. *Law and Human Behavior, 22*, 147–163.

Callahan, L. A., Steadman, H. J., McGreevy, M. A., & Robbins, P. C. (1991). The volume and characteristics of insanity defense pleas: An eight-state study. *Bulletin of Psychiatry and the Law, 19*, 331–338.

Calvert, S. L., Appelbaum, M., Dodge, K. A., Graham, S., Hall, G. C. N., Hamby, S., . . . & Hedges, L. V. (2017). The American Psychological Association task force assessment of violent video games: Science in the service of public interest. *American Psychologist, 72*, 126–158.

Cameron, B. W. (2013, March). *The Federal Bureau of Prison's sexual offender treatment and management programs*. Dallas, TX: U.S. Department of Justice, Federal Bureau of Prisons.

Camp, J. P., Skeem, J. L., Barchard, K., Lilienfeld, S. O., & Poythress, N. G. (2013). Psychopathic predators? Getting specific about the relation between psychopathy and violence. *Journal of Consulting and Clinical Psychology, 81*, 467–480.

Campbell, J. C. (1995). Prediction of homicide of and by battered women. In J. C. Campbell (Ed.), *Assessing dangerousness: Violence by sexual offenders, batterers, and child abusers* (pp. 96–113). Thousand Oaks, CA: Sage.

Campbell, R. (2008). The psychological impact of rape victims' experiences with the legal, medical, and mental health systems. *American Psychologist, 63*, 702–717.

Campbell, R., Bybee, D., Townsend, S. M., Shaw, J., Karin, N., & Makowitz, J. (2014). The impact of Sexual Assault Nurse Examiners (SANE) programs in criminal justice outcomes: A multisite replication study. *Violence Against Women, 20*, 607–625.

Campbell, T. W. (2003). Sex offenders and actuarial risk assessments: Ethical considerations. *Behavioral Sciences & the Law, 21*, 269–279.

Canter, D. V. (1999). Equivocal death. In D. Canter & L. J. Alison (Eds.), *Profiling in policy and practice* (pp. 123–156). Burlington, VT: Ashgate.

Canter, D. V., & Alison, L. (2000). Profiling property crimes. In D. V. Canter & L. J. Alison (Eds.), *Profiling property crimes* (pp. 1–30). Burlington, VT: Ashgate.

Canter, D. V. & Wentink, N. (2004). An empirical test of Holmes and Holmes' serial murder typology. *Criminal Justice and Behavior, 31*, 489–515.

Canter, D. V., & Youngs, D. (2009). *Investigative psychology: Offender profiling and the analysis of criminal action*. West Sussex, England: Wiley.

Cantón-Cortés, D., Cortés, M. R., & Cantón, I. (2015). Child sexual abuse, attachment style, and depression: The role of the characteristics of abuse. *Journal of Interpersonal Violence, 30*, 420–436.

Carlson, E. H., & Dutton, M. A. (2003). Assessing experiences and responses of crime victims. *Journal of Traumatic Stress, 16*, 133–148.

Carone, D. A., & Bush, S. S. (Eds.). (2013). *Mild traumatic brain injury: Symptom validity assessment and malingering*. New York, NY: Springer.

Carpentier, J., Leclerc, B., & Proulx, J. (2011). Juvenile sexual offenders: Correlates of onset, variety, and desistance of criminal behavior. *Criminal Justice and Behavior, 38*, 854–873.

Carrión, R. E., Keenan, J. P., & Sebanz, N. (2010). A truth that's told with bad intent: An ERP study of deception. *Cognition, 114*, 105–110.

Carroll, O. (2017). Challenges in modern digital investigative analysis. *U.S. Attorneys' Bulletin, 65*, 25–28.

Carson, E. A., & Golinelli, D. (2013, December). *Prisoners in 2012: Trends in admissions and releases, 1991–2012*. Washington, DC: U.S. Department of Justice, Bureau of Justice Statistics.

Casey, B. J., & Caudle, K. (2013). The teenage brain: Self-control. *Current Directions in Psychological Science, 22*, 82–87.

Casey, B. J., Getz, S., & Galvan, A. (2008). The adolescent brain. *Developmental Review, 28*, 62–77.

Catalano, S. (2012, September). *Stalking victims in the United States—revised*. Washington, DC: U.S. Department of Justice, Bureau of Justice Statistics.

Catchpole, R. E. H., & Gretton, H. M. (2003). The predictive validity of risk assessment with violent young offenders: A 1-year examination of criminal outcome. *Criminal Justice and Behavior, 30*, 688–708.

Cattaneo, L. B., & Chapman, A. R. (2011). Risk assessment with victims of intimate partner violence: Investigating the gap between research and practice. *Violence Against Women, 17*, 1286–1298.

Cattaneo, L. B., & Goodman, L. A. (2005). Risk factors for reabuse in intimate partner violence: A cross-disciplinary critical review. *Trauma, Violence, and Abuse, 6*, 141–175.

Cecchet, S. J., & Thoburn, J. (2014). The psychological experience of child and adolescent sex trafficking in the United States: Trauma and resilience in survivors. *Psychological Trauma: Theory, Research Practice, and Policy, 6*, 482–491.

Ceci, S. J., & Bruck, M. (1993). The suggestibility of the child witness: A historical review and synthesis. *Psychological Bulletin, 113*, 403–439.

Ceci, S. J., Ross, D. F., & Toglia, M. P. (1987). Suggestibility of children's memory: Psycholegal implications. *Journal of Experimental Psychology: General, 116*, 38–49.

Cellini, H. R. (1995). Assessment and treatment of the adolescent sexual offender. In B. Schwartz & H. R. Cellini (Eds.), *The sex offender: Corrections, treatment and legal practice* (Vol. 1). Kingston, NJ: Civil Research Institute.

Cellini, H. R., Schwartz, B., & Readio, S. (1993, December). *Child sexual abuse: An administrator's nightmare.* Washington, DC: National School Safety Center.

Centers for Disease Control and Prevention. (2013, August 23). *Injury prevention and control: Data and statistics (WISQARS™).* Retrieved from http://www.cdc.gov/injury/wisqars/index.html

Chaiken, M. R. (2000, March). *Violent neighborhoods, violent kids. Juvenile Justice Bulletin, 6–18.* Washington, DC: U.S. Department of Justice.

Chamberlain, P. (2003). *Treating chronic juvenile offenders: Advances made through the Oregon multidimensional treatment foster care model.* Washington, DC: American Psychological Association.

Chamberlain, P., Leve, L. D., & DeGarmo, D. S. (2007). Multidimensional treatment foster care for girls in the juvenile justice system: 2-year follow-up of a randomized clinical trial. *Journal of Consulting and Clinical Psychology, 66*, 624–633.

Chan, H. C., & Frie, A. (2013). Female sexual homicide offenders: An examination of an underresearched offender population. *Homicide Studies, 17*, 96–118.

Chan, H. C., Heide, K. M., & Myers, W. C. (2013). Juvenile and adult offenders arrested for sexual homicide: An analysis of victim–offender relationship and weapon used by race. *Journal of Forensic Sciences, 58*, 85–89.

Chan, H. C., Myers, W. C., & Heide, K. M. (2010). An empirical analysis of 30 years of U.S. juvenile and adult sexual homicide offender data: Race and age differences in the victim–offender relationship. *Journal of Forensic Sciences, 55*, 1282–1290.

Chapleau, K. M., & Oswald, D. L. (2010). Power, sex, and rape myth acceptance: Testing two models of rape proclivity. *Journal of Sex Research, 47*, 66–78.

Chappelle, W., & Rosengren, K. (2001). Maintaining composure and credibility as an expert witness during cross-examination. *Journal of Forensic Psychology Practice, 1*, 51–67.

Chauhan, P. (2015). There's more to it than the individual. In C. R. Bartol & A. M. Bartol, *Introduction to forensic psychology: Research and application* (4th ed., pp. 225–227). Thousand Oaks, CA: Sage.

Chen, Y.-H., Arria, A., & Anthony, J. C. (2003). Firesetting in adolescents and being aggressive, shy, and rejected by peers: New epidemiologic evidence from a national sample survey. *Journal of the American Academy of Psychiatry and Law, 31*, 44–52.

Cheng, W., Ickes, W., & Kenworthy, J. B. (2013). The phenomenon of hate crimes in the United States. *Journal of Applied Social Psychology, 43*, 761–794.

Chesney-Lind, M., & Shelden, R. G. (1998). *Girls, delinquency, and juvenile justice* (2nd ed.). Belmont, CA: West/Wadsworth.

Chiancone, J. (2001, December). Parental abduction: Review of the literature. *Juvenile Justice Bulletin* (pp. 14–18). Washington, DC: U.S. Department of Justice, Office of Juvenile Justice and Delinquency Prevention.

Child Abuse Prevention Center. (1998). *Shaken baby syndrome fatalities in the United States.* Ogden, UT: Author.

Child Welfare Information Gateway. (2012, May). *Child abuse and neglect fatalities 2010: Statistics and interventions.* Washington, DC: Children's Bureau.

Chiroro, P., & Valentine, T. (1995). An investigation of the contact hypothesis of the own-race bias in face recognition. *Quarterly Journal of Experimental Psychology, 48A*, 979–894.

Choe, I. (2005). The debate over psychological debriefing for PTSD. *The New School Psychology Bulletin, 3*, 71–82.

Churcher, F. P., Mills, J. F., & Forth, A. E. (2016). The predictive validity of the Two-Tiered Violence Risk Estimates Scale (TTV) in a long-term follow-up of violent offenders. *Psychological Services, 13*(3), 232–245.

Cirincione, C., Steadman, H., & McGreevy, M. (1995). Rates of insanity acquittals and the factors associated with successful insanity pleas. *Bulletin of the American Academy of Psychiatry and Law, 23*, 399–409.

Clark, D. W., & White, E. K. (2017). Law officer suicide. In C. L. Mitchell & E. H. Dorian (Eds.), *Police psychology and its growing impact on modern law enforcement* (pp. 176–197). Hershey, PA: IGI Global.

Clark, D. W., White, E. K., & Violanti, J. M. (2012, May). Law enforcement suicide: Current knowledge and future directions. *The Police Chief, 79*, 48–51.

Clark, S. E. (2012). Costs and benefits of eyewitness identification reform: Psychological science and public policy. *Perspectives on Psychological Science, 7*, 238–259.

Clay, R. A. (2017, April). Islamophobia. *APA Monitor, 48*, 34.

Clear, T. R., & Cole, G. F. (2000). *American corrections* (5th ed.). Belmont, CA: West/Wadsworth.

Cleary, H. M. D. (2017). Applying the lessons of developmental psychology to the study of juvenile interrogations: New directions for research, policy, and practice. *Psychology, Public Policy, and Law, 23*, 118–130.

Cleary, H. M. D., & Warner, T. C. (2016). Police training in interviewing and interrogation methods: A comparison of techniques used with adult and juvenile suspects. *Law and Human Behavior, 40*, 270–284.

Cleckley, H. (1941). *The mask of sanity.* St. Louis, MO: C.V. Mosby.

Cochrane, R. E., Grisso, T., & Frederick, R. I. (2001). The relationship between criminal charges, diagnoses, and psycholegal opinions among federal defendants. *Behavioral Sciences & the Law, 19,* 565–582.

Cochrane, R. E., Herbel, B. L., Reardon, M. L., & Lloyd, K. P. (2013). The Sell effect: Involuntary medication treatment is a "clear and convincing" success. *Law and Human Behavior, 37.* doi 10.1037/lhb0000003.

Cochrane, R. E., Tett, R. P., & Vandecreek, L. (2003). Psychological testing and the selection of police officers: A national survey. *Criminal Justice and Behavior, 30,* 511–527.

Cohen, F. (1998). *The mentally disordered inmate and the law.* Kingston, NJ: Civic Research Institute.

Cohen, F. (2000). *The mentally disordered inmate and the law, 2000–2001 supplement.* Kingston, NJ: Civic Research Institute.

Cohen, F. (2003). *The mentally disordered inmate and the law, 2003 cumulative supplement.* Kingston, NJ: Civic Research Institute.

Cohen, F. (2008). *The mentally disordered inmate and the law* (2nd ed.). Kingston, NJ: Civic Research Institute.

Cohen, M. E., & Carr, W. J. (1975). Facial recognition and the von Restorff effect. *Bulletin of the Psychonomic Society, 6,* 383–384.

Cohen, M. L., Garafalo, R., Boucher, R., & Seghorn, T. (1971). The psychology of rapists. *Seminars in Psychiatry, 3,* 307–327.

Cohen, M. L., Seghorn, T., & Calmas, W. (1969). Sociometric study of the sex offender. *Journal of Abnormal Psychology, 74,* 249–255.

Cohen, N. J. (2001). *Language development and psychopathology in infants, children, and adolescents.* Thousand Oaks, CA: Sage.

Cohn, Y. (1974). Crisis intervention and the victim of robbery. In I. Drapkin & E. Viano (Eds.), *Victimology: A new focus* (pp. 17–28). Lexington, MA: Lexington Books.

Coid, J. W. (2003). Formulating strategies for the primary prevention of adult antisocial behaviour: "High risk" or "population" strategies. In D. F. Farrington & J. W. Coid (Eds.), *Early prevention of adult antisocial behaviour* (pp. 32–78). Cambridge, England: Cambridge University Press.

Coie, J. D., Belding, M., & Underwood, M. (1988). Aggression and peer rejection in childhood. In B. Lahey & A. Kazdin (Eds.), *Advances in clinical child psychology* (Vol. 2, pp. 125–158). New York, NY: Plenum.

Coie, J. D., Dodge, K., & Kupersmith, J. (1990). Peer group behavior and social status. In S. R. Asher & J. D. Coie (Eds.), *Peer rejection in childhood* (pp. 17–57). Cambridge, England: Cambridge University Press.

Coie, J. D., & Miller-Johnson, S. (2001). Peer factors and interventions. In R. Loeber & D. P. Farrington (Eds.), *Child delinquents: Development, intervention, and service needs* (pp. 191–209). Thousand Oaks, CA: Sage.

Cole, G. F., & Smith, C. E. (2001). *The American system of criminal justice* (9th ed.). Belmont, CA: Wadsworth/Thompson.

Collins, W. C. (2004). *Supermax prisons and the Constitution: Liability concerns in the extended control unit.* Washington, DC: U.S. Department of Justice, National Institute of Corrections.

Colwell, L. H., & Gianesini, J. (2011). Demographic, criminogenic, and psychiatry factors that predict competency restoration. *Journal of the American Academy of Psychiatry and Law, 39,* 297–306.

Compo, N. S., Carol, R. N., Evans, J. R., Pimentel, P., Holness, H., Nichols-Lopez, K., . . . & Furton, K. G. (2017). Witness memory and alcohol: The effects of state-dependent recall. *Law and Human Behavior, 41,* 202–215.

Condie, L. O. (2014). Conducting child abuse and neglect evaluations. In I. B. Weiner & R. K. Otto (Eds.), *The handbook of forensic psychology* (4th ed., pp. 237–278). Hoboken, NJ: Wiley.

Conley, J. M. (2000). Epilogue: A legal and cultural commentary on the psychology of jury instructions. *Psychology, Public Policy, and Law, 6,* 822–831.

Conn, S. M., & Butterfield, L. D. (2013). Coping with secondary traumatic stress by general duty police officers: Practical implications. *Canadian Journal of Counselling and Psychotherapy, 47,* 272–298.

Connell, M. (2010). Parenting plan evaluation standards and guidelines for psychologists: Setting the frame. *Behavioral Sciences & the Law, 28,* 492–510.

Connor, D. F., Steeber, J., & McBurnett, K. (2010). A review of attention-deficit/hyperactivity disorder complicated by symptoms of oppositional defiant disorder or conduct disorder. *Journal of Developmental & Behavioral Pediatrics, 31,* 427–440.

Cooke, D. J., & Michie, C. (1997). An item response theory analysis of the Hare Psychopathy Checklist–Revised. *Psychological Assessment, 9,* 3–14.

Cooke, D. J., & Michie, C. (2001). Refining the construct of psychopathy: Toward a hierarchical model. *Psychological Assessment, 13,* 171–188.

Cooke, D. J., Michie, C., Hart, S. D., & Hare, R. D. (1999). Evaluation of the screening version of the Hare Psychopathy Checklist–Revised (PCL–SV): An item response theory analysis. *Psychological Assessment, 11,* 3–13.

Cooley, C. M. (2012). Criminal profiling on trial: The admissibility of criminal profiling evidence. In B. E. Turvey (Ed.), *Criminal profiling: An introduction to behavioral evidence analysis* (4th ed., pp. 627–654). Amsterdam, Netherlands: Elsevier/Academic Press.

Cooper, A., & Smith, E. L. (2011, November). *Homicide trends in the United States, 1980–2008.* Washington, DC: U.S. Department of Justice, Bureau of Justice Statistics.

Copestake, S., Gray, N. S., & Snowden, R. J. (2013). Emotional intelligence and psychopathy: A comparison of trait and ability measures. *Emotion, 13,* 691–702.

Copson, G. (1995). *Coals to Newcastle? Part I: A study of offender profiling*. London, England: Home Office, Police Research Group.

Corey, D. M. (2013, September 27). An update on specialty milestones. *Police Psychological Services Section Newsletter, 10*, 4.

Corey, D. M. (2017). Police and public safety psychologists. In R. J. Sternberg (Ed.), *Career paths in psychology* (3rd ed., pp. 409–420). Washington, DC: American Psychological Association.

Corey, D. M., & Borum, R. (2013). Forensic assessment for high-risk occupations. In I. B. Weiner & R. K. Otto (Eds.), *Handbook of psychology. Vol. 11. Forensic psychology* (2nd ed., pp. 246–270). Hoboken, NJ: Wiley.

Corey, D. M., Cuttler, M. J., Cox, D. R., & Brower, J. (2011, August). Board certification in police psychology: What it means for public safety. *Police Chief, 78*, 100–104.

Cornell, D. G., & Allen, K. (2011). Development, evaluation, and future direction in the Virginia Student Threat Assessment Guidelines. *Journal of School Violence, 10*, 88–106.

Cornell, D. G., Gregory, A., & Fan, X. (2011). Reductions in long-term suspensions following adoption of the Virginia Student Threat Assessment Guidelines. *NASSP Bulletin, 95*, 175–194.

Cornell, D. G., Gregory, A., Huang, F., & Fan, X. (2013). Perceived prevalence of teasing and bullying predicts high school dropout rates. *Journal of Educational Psychology, 105*, 138–149.

Cornell, D. G., & Sheras, P. L. (2006). *Guidelines for responding to student threats of violence*. Dallas, TX: Sopris West Educational Services.

Correctional Services of Canada. (1990). *Forum on corrections research. 2*(1) [Entire issue]. Ottawa, Canada: Author.

Correll, J., Park, B., Judd, C. M., Wittenbrink, B., Sadler, M. S., & Keesee, T. (2007). Across the thin blue line: Police officers and racial bias in the decision to shoot. *Journal of Personality and Social Psychology, 92*, 1006–1023.

Cortina, L. M. (2001). Assessing sexual harassment among Latinas: Development of an instrument. *Cultural Diversity and Ethnic Minority Psychology, 7*, 164–181.

Cortoni, F., Hanson, R. K., & Coache, M.-É. (2009). Les délinquantes sexuelles: Prévalence et récidive [Female sexual offenders: Prevalence and recidivism]. *Revue international de criminologie et de police technique et scientifique, LXII*, 319–336.

Cortoni, F., Hanson, R. K., & Coache, M.-É. (2010). The recidivism rates of female sexual offenders are low: A meta-analysis. *Sexual Abuse: A Journal of Research and Treatment, 22*, 387–401.

Costa, P. T., & McCrae, R. R. (1992). *NEO PI-R: The Revised NEO Personality Inventory*. Odessa, FL: Psychological Assessment Resources.

Cowan, P. A., & Cowan, C. P. (2004). From family relationships to peer rejection to antisocial behavior in middle childhood. In J. B. Kupersmidt & K. A. Dodge (Eds.), *Children's peer relations: From development to intervention* (pp. 159–178). Washington, DC: American Psychological Association.

Cox, J., Clark, J. C., Edens, J. F., Smith, S. T., & Magyar, M. S. (2013). Jury panel member perceptions of interpersonal-affective traits in psychopathy predict support for execution in a capital murder trial simulation. *Behavioral Sciences & the Law, 31*, 411–428.

Cox, J. F., Landsberg, G., & Paravati, M. P. (1989). A practical guide for mental health providers in local jails. In H. J. Steadman, D. W. McCarty, & J. P. Morrissey (Eds.), *The mentally ill in jail: Planning for essential services*. New York, NY: Guilford Press.

Cox, W. T. L., Devine, P. G., Plant, E. A., & Schwartz, L. L. (2014). Toward a comprehensive understanding of officers' shooting decisions: No simple answers to this complex problem. *Basic and Applied Social Psychology, 36*, 356–364.

Cramer, R. J., Kehn, A., Pennington, C. R., Wechsler, H. J., Clark, J. W., & Nagle, J. (2013). An examination of sexual orientation- and transgender-based hate crimes in the post-Matthew Shepard era. *Psychology, Public Policy, and Law, 3*, 355–368.

Crawford, M. (2017). International sex trafficking. *Women & Therapy, 40*, 101–122.

Crawford, N. (2002, November). Science-based program curbs violence in kids. *Monitor on Psychology, 33*, 38–39.

Crespi, T. D. (1990). School psychologists in forensic psychology: Converging and diverging issues. *Professional Psychology: Research and Practice, 21*, 83–87.

Cromwell, P. F., Killinger, G. C., Kerper, H. B., & Walker, C. (1985). *Probation and parole in the criminal justice system* (2nd ed.). St. Paul, MN: West.

Cromwell, P. F., Olson, J. F., & Avary, D. W. (1991). *Breaking and entering: An ethnographic analysis of burglary*. Newbury Park, CA: Sage.

Crozier, W. E., Strange, D., & Loftus, E. F. (2017). Memory errors in alibi generation: How an alibi can turn against us. *Behavioral Sciences & the Law, 35*, 6–17.

Cruise, K. R., Morin, S. L., & Affleck, K. (2016). Residential interventions with justice-involved youths. In K. Heilbrun (Ed.), *APA handbook of psychology and juvenile justice* (pp. 611–639). Washington, DC: American Psychological Association.

Cruise, K., & Rogers, R. (1998). An analysis of competency to stand trial: An integration of case law and clinical knowledge. *Behavioral Sciences & the Law, 16*, 35–50.

Cummings, E. M., El-Sheikh, M., Kouros, C. D., & Buckhalt, J. A. (2009). Children and violence: The role of children's regulation in the marital aggression–child adjustment link. *Clinical Child and Family Psychological Review, 12*, 3–15.

Cunningham, M. D., & Reidy, T. J. (1998). Integrating base rate data in violence risk assessments at capital sentencing. *Behavioral Sciences & the Law, 16*, 71–96.

Cunningham, M. D., & Reidy, T. J. (1999). Don't confuse me with the facts: Common errors in violence risk assessment at capital sentencing. *Criminal Justice and Behavior, 26*, 20–43.

Cunningham, M. D., Sorensen, J. R., Vigen, M. P., & Woods, S. O. (2011). Correlates and actuarial models of assaultive prison misconduct among violence-predicted capital offenders. *Criminal Justice and Behavior, 38*, 5–25.

Curtis, N. M., Ronan, K. R., Heiblum, N., & Crellin, K. (2009). Dissemination and effectiveness of multisystemic treatment in New Zealand: A benchmarking study. *Journal of Family Psychology, 23*, 119–129.

Cutler, B. (2015). Reality is more exciting than fiction [Perspective essay]. In C. R. Bartol & A. M. Bartol, *Introduction to forensic psychology: Research and application* (4th ed., pp. 127–128). Thousand Oaks, CA: Sage.

Cutler, B. L., & Penrod, S. D. (1995). *Mistaken identification: The eyewitness, psychology, and law*. New York, NY: Cambridge University Press.

Cutler, B. L., Penrod, S. D., & Dexter, H. R. (1989). The eyewitness, the expert psychologist, and the jury. *Law and Human Behavior, 13*, 311–322.

Cutler, B. L., Penrod, S. D., & Martens, T. K. (1987). Improving the reliability of eyewitness identification: Putting content with context. *Journal of Applied Psychology, 72*, 629–637.

D'Unger, A. V., Land, K. C., McCall, P. L., & Nagin, D. S. (1998). How many latent classes of delinquent/criminal careers? Results from mixed Poisson regression analysis. *American Journal of Sociology, 103*, 1593–1630.

Dahlberg, L. L., & Potter, L. B. (2001). Youth violence: Developmental pathways and prevention challenges. *American Journal of Preventive Medicine, 20*(1s), 3–14.

Daire, A. P., Carlson, R. G., Barden, S. M., & Jacobson, L. (2014). An intimate partner violence (IPV) protocol readiness model. *The Family Journal: Counseling and Therapy for Families, 22*, 170–178.

Daley, K. (2002). Restorative justice: The real story. *Punishment & Society, 4*, 55–79.

Daniels, J. A., & Bradley, M. C. (2011). *Preventing lethal school violence*. New York, NY: Springer.

Daniels, J. A., Buck, I., Croxall, S., Gruber, J., Kime, P., & Govert, H. (2007). A content analysis of news reports of averted school rampages. *Journal of School Violence, 6*, 83–99.

Daniels, J. A., & Page, J. W. (2013). Averted school shootings. In N. Böckler, T. Seeger, & P. Sitzer (Eds.), *School shootings: International research, case studies, and concepts for prevention* (pp. 421–440). New York, NY: Springer.

Daniels, J. A., Royster, T. E., Vecchi, G. M., & Pshenishny, E. E. (2010). Barricaded captive events in schools: Mitigation and response. *Journal of Family Violence, 25*, 587–594.

Dansie, E. J., & Fargo, J. D. (2009). Individual and community predictors of fear of criminal victimization: Results from a national sample of urban US citizens. *Crime Prevention and Community Safety, 11*, 124–140.

Dargis, M., & Koenigs, M. (2017). Witnessing domestic violence during childhood is associated with psychopathic traits in adult male criminal offenders. *Law and Human Behavior, 41*, 173–179.

Davies, G., Morton, J., Mollon, P., & Robertson, N. (1998). Recovered memories in theory and practice. *Psychology, Public Policy, and Law, 4*, 1079–1090.

Davis, R. D., & Rostow, C. D. (2008, December). M-PULSE: Matrix-psychological uniform law enforcement selection evaluation. *Forensic Examiner*, 19–24.

Day, A., & Casey, S. (2009). Values in forensic and correctional psychology. *Aggression and Violent Behavior, 14*, 232–238.

Day, K., & Berney, T. (2001). Treatment and care for offenders with mental retardation. In J. B. Ashford, B. D. Sales, & W. H. Reid (Eds.), *Treating adult and juvenile offenders with special needs* (pp. 199–220). Washington, DC: American Psychological Association.

De Leon, G., Hawke, J., Jainchill, N., & Melnick, G. (2000). Therapeutic communities: Enhancing retention in treatment using "senior professor" staff. *Journal of Substance Abuse Treatment, 19*, 375–382.

Dean, K. E., & Malamuth, N. M. (1997). Characteristics of men who aggress sexually and of men who imagine aggressing: Risk and moderating variables. *Journal of Personality and Social Psychology, 72*, 449–455.

Deault, L. C. (2010). A systematic review of parenting in relation to the development of comorbidities and functional impairments in children with attention-deficit/hyperactivity disorder (ADHD). *Child Psychiatry and Human Development, 41*, 168–192.

DeClue, G., & Rogers, C. (2012). Interrogations 2013: Safeguarding against false confessions. *The Police Chief, 79*, 42–46.

DeGloria, P. (2015, March 5). Recognizing sexual abuse in animals. *VINS News Service*.

del Carmen, R. V., Parker, M., & Reddington, F. P. (1998). *Briefs of leading cases in juvenile justice*. Cincinnati, OH: Anderson.

Delprino, R. P., & Bahn, C. (1988). National survey of the extent and nature of psychological services in police departments. *Professional Psychology: Research and Practice, 19*, 421–425.

Demakis, G. J. (2012). Introduction to basic issues in civil capacity. In G. J. Demakis (Ed.), *Civil capacities in clinical neuropsychology: Research findings and practical applications* (pp. 1–16). New York, NY: Oxford University Press.

Demakis, G. J., & Mart, E. G. (2017). Civil capacities. In S. S. Bush (Ed.). *APA handbook of forensic neuropsychology* (pp. 309–339). Washington, DC: American Psychological Association.

DeMatteo, D. (2005a, Winter). Legal update: An expansion of *Tarasoff*'s duty to protect. *American Psychology–Law News, 25*, 2–3, 20.

DeMatteo, D. (2005b, Fall). Legal update: "Supermax" prison: Constitutional challenges and mental health concerns. *American Psychology-Law News, 25*, 8–9.

DeMatteo, D., Burl, J., Filone, S., & Heilbrun, K. (2016). *Training in forensic assessment and intervention: Implications for principle-based models. Learning forensic assessment: Research and practice* (2nd ed., pp. 3–31). New York, NY: Routledge.

DeMatteo, D., & Edens, J. F. (2006). The role and relevance of the Psychopathy Checklist–Revised in courts: A case law survey of U.S. courts (1991–2004). *Psychology, Public Policy, and Law, 12*, 214–241.

DeMatteo, D., Edens, J. F., Galloway, M., Cox, J., Smith, S. T., & Formon, D. (2014a). The role and reliability of the Psychopathy Checklist–Revised in U.S. sexually violent predator evaluations: A case law survey. *Law and Human Behavior, 38*, 248–255.

DeMatteo, D., Edens, J. F., Galloway, M., Cox, J., Smith, S. T., Koller, J. P., & Bersoff, B. (2014b). Investigating the role of the psychopathy checklist–revised in United States case law. *Psychology, Public Policy, and Law, 20*, 96–107.

DeMatteo, D., Marczyk, G., Krauss, D. A., & Burl, J. (2009). Educational and training models in forensic psychology. *Training and Education in Professional Psychology, 3*, 184–191.

Dennison, S., & Leclerc, B. (2011). Developmental factors in adolescent child sexual offenders: A comparison of nonrepeat and repeat sexual offenders. *Criminal Justice and Behavior, 38*, 1089–1102.

Dern, H., Dern, C., Horn, A., & Horn, U. (2009). The fire behind the smoke: A reply to Snook and colleagues. *Criminal Justice and Behavior, 36*, 1085–1090.

Desari, R. A., Falzer, P. R., Chapman, J., & Borum, R. (2012). Mental illness, violence risk, and race in juvenile detention: Implications for disproportionate minority contact. *American Journal of Orthopsychiatry, 82*, 32–40.

Detrick, P., & Chibnall, J. T. (2006). NEO PI-R personality characteristics of high-performance entry-level police officers. *Psychological Services, 3*, 274–285.

Detrick, P., & Chibnall, J. T. (2013). Revised NEO personality inventory normative data for police officer selection. *Psychological Services, 10*, 372–377.

Detrick, P., & Chibnall, J. T. (2017). A five-factor model inventory for use in screening police officer applicants: The Revised NEO Personality Inventory (NEO PIO-R). In C. L. Mitchell & E. H. Dorian (Eds.), *Police psychology and its growing impact on modern law enforcement* (pp. 79–92). Hershey, PA: IGI-Global.

Detrick, P., Chibnall, J. T., & Luebbert, M. C. (2004). The NEO PI–R as predictor of police academy performance. *Criminal Justice and Behavior, 31*, 676–694.

Detrick, P., Chibnall, J. T., & Rosso, M. (2001). Minnesota Multiphasic Personality Inventory–2 in police officer selection: Normative data and relation to the Inwald Personality Inventory. *Professional Psychology: Research and Practice, 32*, 481–490.

Dietz, A. S. (2000). Toward the development of a roles framework for police psychology. *Journal of Police and Criminal Psychology, 15*, 1–4.

Dinos, S., Burrowes, N., Hammond, K., & Cunliffe, C. (2015). A systematic review of juries' assessment of rape victims: Do rape myths impact juror decision-making? *International Journal of Law, Crime, and Justice, 43*, 36–49.

Dionne, G. (2005). Language development and aggressive behavior. In R. E. Tremblay, W. W. Hartup, & J. Archer (Eds.), *Developmental origins of aggression* (pp. 330–352). New York, NY: Guilford Press.

Dionne, G., Tremblay, R., Boivin, M., Laplante, D., & Pérusse, D. (2003). Physical aggression and expressive vocabulary in 19-month-old twins. *Developmental Psychology, 39*, 261–273.

Dirks-Linhorst, P. A., & Kondrat, D. (2012). Tough on crime or beating the system: An evaluation of Missouri Department of Mental Health's not guilty by reason of insanity murder acquittees. *Homicide Studies, 16*, 129–150.

Dishion, T. J., & Bullock, B. M. (2002). Parenting and adolescent problem behavior: An ecological analysis of the nurturance hypothesis. In J. G. Borkowski, S. L. Ramey, & M. Bristol-Power (Eds.), *Parenting and the child's world: Influences on academic, intellectual, and social-emotional development* (pp. 231–249). Mahwah, NJ: Erlbaum.

Dixon, L., & Gill, B. (2002). Changes in the standards for admitting expert evidence in federal civil cases since the *Daubert* decision. *Psychology, Public Policy, and Law, 8*, 251–308.

Dobash, R. P., & Dobash, R. E. (2000). Feminist perspectives on victimization. In N. H. Rafter (Ed.), *Encyclopedia of women and crime* (pp. 179–205). Phoenix, AZ: Oryx.

Dobolyi, D. G., & Dodson, C. S. (2013). Eyewitness confidence in simultaneous and sequential lineups: A criterion shift account for sequential mistaken identification overconfidence. *Journal of Experimental Psychology: Applied, 19*, 345–357.

Dobson, V., & Sales, B. (2000). The science of infanticide and mental illness. *Psychology, Public Policy, and Law, 4*, 1098–1112.

Dodge, K. A. (2003). Do social information-processing patterns mediate aggressive behavior? In B. B. Lahey, T. E. Moffitt, & A. Caspi (Eds.), *Causes of conduct disorder and juvenile delinquency* (pp. 254–274). New York, NY: Guilford Press.

Dodge, K. A., & Pettit, G. S. (2003). A biopsychological model of the development of chronic conduct problems in adolescence. *Developmental Psychology, 39*, 349–371.

Domhardt, M., Münzer, A., Fegert, J. M., & Goldbeck, L. (2015). Resilience in survivors of child sexual abuse: A systematic review of literature. *Trauma, Violence, & Abuse, 16*, 476–493.

Donn, J. E., Routh, D. K., & Lunt, I. (2000). From Leipzig to Luxembourg (via Boulder and Vail): A history of clinical training in Europe and the United States. *Professional Psychology: Research and Practice, 31,* 423–428.

Donnellan, M. B., Ge, X., & Wenk, E. (2000). Cognitive abilities in adolescent-limited and life-course–persistent criminal offenders. *Journal of Abnormal Psychology, 109,* 396–402.

Dougher, M. J. (1995). Clinical assessment of sex offenders. In B. K. Schwartz & H. R. Cellini (Eds.), *The sex offender: Corrections, treatment and legal practice* (pp. 182–224). Kingston, NJ: Civic Research Institute.

Douglas, A.-J. (2011, August). Child abductions: Known relationships are the greater danger. *FBI Law Enforcement Bulletin, 80,* 8–9.

Douglas, K. S., Hart, S. D., Groscup, J. L., & Litwack, T. R. (2014). Assessing violence risk. In I. B. Weiner & R. K. Otto (Eds.), *The handbook of forensic psychology* (4th ed., pp. 385–441). Hoboken, NJ: Wiley.

Douglas, K. S., Nikolova, N. L., Kelley, S. E., & Edens, J. E. (2015). Psychopathy. In B. L. Cutler & P. A. Zapf (Eds.), *APA handbook in forensic psychology: Vol. 1. Individual and situational influences in criminal and civil contexts* (pp. 257–323). Washington, DC: American Psychological Association.

Douglas, K. S., & Ogloff, J. R. P. (2003). The impact of confidence on the accuracy of structured professional and actuarial violence risk judgments in a sample of forensic psychiatric patients. *Law and Human Behavior, 27,* 573–587.

Dowdell, E. B., & Foster, K. L. (2000). Munchausen syndrome by proxy: Recognizing a form of child abuse. *Nursing Spectrum.* Retrieved from http://nsweb.nursingspectrum.com/ce/ce209.hum

Dowling, F. G., Moynihan, G., Genet, B., & Lewis, J. (2006). A peer-based assistance program for officers with the New York City Police Department: Report of the effects of September 11, 2001. *American Journal of Psychiatry, 163,* 151–153.

Drislane, L. E., Patrick, C. J., & Arsal, G. (2014, June). Clarifying the content coverage of differing psychopathy inventories through reference to the triarchic psychopathy measure. *Psychological Assessment, 26,* 350–362.

Drizin, S. A., & Leo, R. A. (2004). The problem of false confessions in the post-DNA world. *North Carolina Law Review, 82,* 891–1007.

Drogin, E. Y., & Barrett, C. L. (2013). Civil competencies. In R. K. Otto & I. B. Weiner (Eds.), *Handbook of psychology, Vol. 11. Forensic psychology* (2nd ed., pp. 648–663). Hoboken, NJ: Wiley.

Drogin, E. Y., Hagan, L. D., Guilmette, T. J., & Piechowski, L. D. (2015). Personal injury and other tort matters. In B. L. Cutler & P. A. Zapf (Eds.), *APA handbook of forensic psychology: Vol. 1. Individual and situational influences in criminal and civil contexts* (pp. 471–509). Washington, DC: American Psychological Association.

Dubowitz, H., Christian, C. W., Hymel, K., & Kellogg, N. D. (2014). Forensic medical evaluations of child maltreatment: A proposed research agenda. *Child Abuse & Neglect, 38,* 1734–1746.

Dudycha, G. J., & Dudycha, M. M. (1941). Childhood memories: A review of the literature. *Psychological Bulletin, 38,* 668–682.

Duhaime, A., Christian, C. W., Rorke, L. B., & Zimmerman, R. A. (1998). Nonaccidental head injury in infants: The "shaken-baby syndrome." *New England Journal of Medicine, 338,* 1822–1829.

Durand, V. M., & Barlow, D. H. (2000). *Abnormal psychology: An introduction.* Belmont, CA: Wadsworth.

Durham, M. L., & La Fond, J. Q. (1990). A search for the missing premise of involuntary therapeutic commitment: Effective treatment of the mentally ill. In D. B. Wexler (Ed.), *Therapeutic jurisprudence* (pp. 133–163). Durham, NC: Carolina Academic Press.

Dutton, D., & Golant, S. K. (1995). *The batterer: A psychological profile.* New York, NY: Basic Books.

Dutton, M. A. (1992). *Empowering and healing the battered woman.* New York, NY: Springer.

Dutton, M. A. (1996, May). *Validity and use of evidence concerning battering and its effects in criminal trials: NIJ Report to Congress.* Washington, DC: U.S. Department of Justice, National Institute of Justice and U.S. Department of Health and Human Services, National Institute of Mental Health.

Duwe, G. (2000). Body-count journalism: The presentation of mass murder in the news media. *Homicide Studies, 4,* 364–399.

Eastwood, J., & Snook, B. (2010). Comprehending Canadian police cautions: Are the rights to silence and legal counsel understandable? *Behavioral Sciences & the Law, 28,* 366–377.

Eastwood, J., & Snook, B. (2012). The effect of listenability factors on the comprehension of police cautions. *Law and Human Behavior, 36,* 177–183.

Eastwood, J., Snook, B., & Au, D. (2016). Safety in numbers: A policy capturing study of the alibi assessment process. *Applied Cognitive Psychology, 30,* 260–269.

Eastwood, J., Snook, B., & Luther, K. (in preparation). Measuring the effectiveness of the sketch procedure in investigative interviews.

Eastwood, J., Snook, B., Luther, K., & Freedman, S. (2016). Engineering comprehensible youth interrogation rights. *New Criminal Law Review, 91,* 42–62.

Ebert, B. W. (1987). Guide to conducting a psychological autopsy. *Professional Psychology: Research and Practice, 18,* 52–56.

Eckstein, J. J. (2011). Reasons for staying in intimately violent relationships: Comparisons of men and women and messages communicated to self and others. *Journal of Family Violence, 26,* 21–30.

Eddy, D., & Edmunds, C. (2002). Compensation. In A. Seymour, M. Murray, J. Sigmon, M. Hook, C. Edmunds, M. Gaboury, & G. Coleman (Eds.), *National Victim Assistance Academy textbook.* Washington, DC: U.S. Department of Justice, Office of Victims of Crime.

Edens, J. F., Campbell, J., & Weir, J. (2007). Youth psychopathy and criminal recidivism: A meta-analysis of the psychopathy checklist measures. *Law and Human Behavior, 31*, 53–75.

Edens, J. F., & Cox, J. (2012). Examining the prevalence, role and impact of evidence regarding antisocial personality, sociopathy and psychopathy in capital cases: A survey of defense team members. *Behavioral Sciences & the Law, 30*, 239–255.

Edens, J. F., Davis, K. M., Fernandez Smith, K., & Guy, L. S. (2013). No sympathy for the devil: Attributing psychopathic traits to capital murderers also predicts support for executing them. *Personality Disorders: Theory, Research and Treatment, 4*, 175–181.

Edens, J. F., Petrila, J., & Buffington-Vollum, J. K. (2001). Psychopathy and the death penalty: Can the psychopathy checklist–revised identify offenders who represent "a continuing threat to society?" *Journal of Psychiatry and Law, 29*, 433–481.

Edens, J. F., Skeem, J. L., Cruise, K. R., & Cauffman, E. (2001). Assessment of "juvenile psychopathy" and its association with violence: A critical review. *Behavioral Sciences & the Law, 19*, 53–80.

Edens, J. F., & Vincent, G. M. (2008). Juvenile psychopathy: A clinical construct in need of restraint. *Journal of Forensic Psychology Practice, 8*, 186–197.

Edwards, D. L., Schoenwald, S. K., Henggeler, S. W., & Strother, K. B. (2001). A multi-level perspective on the implementation of multisystemic therapy (MST): Attempting dissemination with fidelity. In G. A. Bernfeld, D. P. Farrington, & A. W. Leschied (Eds.), *Offender rehabilitation in practice* (pp. 97–120). Chichester, England: Wiley.

Ehrlichman, H., & Halpern, J. N. (1988). Affect and memory: Effects of pleasant and unpleasant odors on retrieval of happy and unhappy memories. *Journal of Personality and Social Psychology, 55*, 769–779.

Einhorn, J. (1986). Child custody in historical perspective: A study of changing social perceptions of divorce and child custody in Anglo-American law. *Behavioral Sciences & the Law, 4*, 119–135.

Eisenberg, N., Spinrad, T. L., Fabes, R. A., Reiser, M., Cumberland, A., Shepard, S. A., . . . & Murphy, B. (2004). The relations of effortful control and impulsivity to children's resiliency and adjustment. *Child Development, 75*, 25–46.

Eke, A. W., Hilton, N. Z., Meloy, J. R., Mohandie, K., & Williams, J. (2011). Predictors of recidivism by stalkers: A nine-year follow-up of police contacts. *Behavioral Sciences & the Law, 29*, 271–283.

Ekman, P. (2009). *Telling lies: Clues to deceit in the marketplace, politics, and marriage.* New York, NY: Norton.

Elklit, A., & Christiansen, D. M. (2013). Risk factors for posttraumatic stress disorder in female help-seeking victims of sexual assault. *Violence and Victims, 28*, 552–568.

Elliott, D. S., Ageton, S. S., & Huizinga, D. (1980). *The National Youth Survey.* Boulder, CO: Behavioral Research Institute.

Elliott, D. S., Dunford, T. W., & Huizinga, D. (1987). The identification and prediction of career offenders utilizing self-reported and official data. In J. D. Burchard & S. N. Burchard (Eds.), *Prevention of delinquent behavior.* Newbury Park, CA: Sage.

Ellis, C. A., & Lord, J. (2002). Homicide. In A. Seymour, M. Murray, J. Sigmon, M. Hook, C. Edmunds, M. Gaboury, & G. Coleman (Eds.), *National Victim Assistance Academy textbook.* Washington, DC: U.S. Department of Justice, Office of Victims of Crime.

Ellsworth, P. C., & Reifman, A. (2000). Juror comprehension and public policy: Perceived problems and proposed solutions. *Psychology, Public Policy, and Law, 6*, 788–821.

Emerson, R. M., Ferris, K. O., & Gardner, C. B. (1998). On being stalked. *Social Problems, 45*, 289–314.

Emery, R. E., & Laumann-Billings, L. (1998). An overview of the nature, causes, and consequences of abusive family relationships. *American Psychologist, 53*, 121–135.

Epperson, D. L., Kaul, J. D., Goldman, R., Huot, S., Hesselton, D., & Alexander, W. (2004). *Minnesota sex offender screening tool–revised (MnSOST-R).* St. Paul: Minnesota Department of Corrections.

Epperson, D., Ralston, C., Fowers, D., DeWitt, J., & Gore, K. (2006). Juvenile Sexual Offense Recidivism Rate Assessment Tool–II (JSOR-RAT-II). In D. Prescott (Ed.), *Risk assessment of youth who have sexually abused.* Oklahoma City, OK: Wood N' Barnes.

Erickson, C. D., & Al-Timini, N. R. (2001). Providing mental health services to Arab Americans: Recommendations and considerations. *Cultural Diversity and Ethnic Minority Psychology, 7*, 308–327.

Erickson, K., Crosnoe, R., & Dornbusch, S. M. (2000). A social process model of adolescent deviance: Combining social control and differential association perspectives. *Journal of Youth and Adolescence, 29*, 395–425.

Erickson, S. K., Lilienfeld, S. O., & Vitacco, M. J. (2007). A critical examination of the suitability and limitations of psychological testing in family court. *Family Court Review, 45*, 157–174.

Eron, L., Gentry, J. H., & Schlegel, P. (Eds.). (1994). *Reason to hope: A psychosocial perspective on violence and youth.* Washington, DC: American Psychological Association.

Eron, L., & Slaby, R. G. (1994). Introduction. In L. D. Eron, J. H. Gentry, & P. Schlegel (Eds.), *Reason to hope: A psychosocial perspective on violence and youth* (pp. 1–22). Washington, DC: American Psychological Association.

Erskine, H. E., Norman, R. E., Ferrar, A. J., Chan, G. C. K., Copeland, W. E. N., Whiteford, H. A., . . . & Scott, J. G. (2016). Long-term outcomes of attention-deficit/hyperactivity disorder and conduct disorder: A systematic review and data analysis. *Journal of the American Academy of Child & Adolescent Psychiatry, 55*, 602–609.

Eshelman, L., & Levendosky, A. A. (2012). Dating violence: Mental health consequences based on type of abuse. *Violence and Victims, 27*, 215–228.

Evans, G. D., & Rey, J. (2001). In the echoes of gunfire: Practicing psychologists' responses to school violence. *Professional Psychology: Research and Practice, 32*, 157–164.

Evans, J. R., Houston, K. A., Meissner, C. A., Ross, A. M., Labianca, J. R., Woestehoff, S. A., & Kleinman, S. M. (2014). An empirical evaluation of intelligence-gathering interrogation techniques from the United States Army Field Manual. *Applied Cognitive Psychology, 28*, 867–875.

Evans, J. R., Meissner, C. A., Brandon, S. E., Russano, M. B., & Kleinman, S. M. (2010). Criminal versus HUMINT interrogations: The importance of psychological science to improving interrogation practice. *Journal of Psychiatry & Law, 38*, 215–249.

Evans, J. R., Meissner, C. A., Ross, A. B., Houston, K. A., Russano, M. B., & Hogan, A. J. (2013). Obtaining guilty knowledge in human intelligence interrogations: Comparing accusatorial and informational gathering approaches with a novel experimental paradigm. *Journal of Applied Research in Memory and Cognition, 2*, 83–88.

Eve, P. M., Byrne, M. K., & Gagliardi, C. R. (2014). What is good parenting? The perspectives of different professionals. *Family Court Review, 52*, 114–127.

Everly, G., Flannery, R., Eyler, V., & Mitchell, J. (2001). Sufficiency analysis of an integrated multicomponent approach to crisis intervention. *Advances in Mind–Body Medicine, 17*, 174.

Farabee, D. (Ed.). (2002). Making people change [Special issue]. *Criminal Justice and Behavior, 29*(1).

Farabee, D., Calhoun, S., & Veliz, R. (2016). An experimental comparison of telepsychiatry and conventional psychiatry for parolees. *Psychiatric Services, 67*, 562–565.

Faravelli, C., Giugni, A., Salvatori, S., & Ricca, V. (2004). Psychopathology after rape. *American Journal of Psychiatry, 161*, 1483–1485.

Faris, R., & Felmlee, D. (2011b). Status struggles: Network centrality and gender segregation in same- and cross-gender aggression. *American Sociological Review, 76*, 48–73.

Farrington, D. P. (1991). Childhood aggression and adult violence: Early precursors and later life outcomes. In D. J. Pepler & K. H. Rubin (Eds.), *The development and treatment of childhood aggression* (pp. 5–29). Hillsdale, NJ: Erlbaum.

Farrington, D. P. (2005). The importance of child and adolescent psychopathy. *Journal of Abnormal Child Psychology, 33*, 489–497.

Farrington, D. P., Ohlin, L. E., & Wilson, J. Q. (1986). *Understanding and controlling crime*. New York, NY: Springer.

Faust, E., & Magaletta, P. R. (2010). Factors predicting levels of female inmates' use of psychological services. *Psychological Services, 7*, 1–10.

Fay, J. (2015). Police officer to police and public safety psychologist: A valuable journey. In C. R. Bartol & A. M. Bartol, *Introduction to Forensic Psychology* (4th ed., pp. 37–38). Thousand Oaks, CA: Sage.

Fazel, S., Doll, H., & Långström, N. (2008). Mental disorders among adolescents in juvenile detention and correctional facilities: A systematic review and metaregression analysis of 25 surveys. *Journal of American Academy of Child and Adolescent Psychiatry, 47*, 1010–1019.

Federal Bureau of Investigation. (2008). *Expanded homicide data—Crime in the United States, 2007*. Washington, DC: U.S. Department of Justice.

Federal Bureau of Investigation. (2010). *Crime in the United States—2009*. Washington, DC: U.S. Department of Justice.

Federal Bureau of Investigation. (2013a). *Crime in the United States—2013*. Washington, DC: U.S. Department of Justice.

Federal Bureau of Investigation. (2013b). *Hate crime statistics, 2012*. Washington, DC: U.S. Department of Justice.

Federal Bureau of Investigation. (2016a). *Crime in the United States—2015*. Washington, DC: U.S. Department of Justice.

Federal Bureau of Investigation. (2016b). *Hate crime statistics, 2015*. Washington, DC: U.S. Department of Justice.

Federal Bureau of Investigation. (2016c, October 18). *FBI releases 2015 on law enforcement officers killed and assaulted*. Washington, DC: FBI National Press Office.

Federle, K. H., & Chesney-Lind, M. (1992). Special issues in juvenile justice: Gender, race and ethnicity. In I. M. Schwartz (Ed.), *Juvenile justice and public policy: Toward a national agenda* (pp. 165–195). New York, NY: Maxwell-Macmillan.

Fehrenbach, P. A., & Monasterky, C. (1988). Characteristics of female sexual offenders. *American Journal of Orthopsychiatry, 58*, 148–151.

Feindler, E. L., Rathus, J. H., & Silver, L. B. (2003). *Assessment of family violence: A handbook for researchers and practitioners*. Washington, DC: American Psychological Association.

Feld, B. C. (1988). In re Gault revisited: A cross-state comparison of the right to counsel in juvenile court. *Crime & Delinquency, 34*, 393–424.

Feld, B. C. (Ed.). (1999). *Readings in juvenile justice administration*. New York, NY: Oxford University Press.

Feld, B. C. (2013). *Kids, cops, and confessions: Inside the interrogation room*. New York, NY: New York University Press.

Felson, R. B. (2002). *Violence and gender reexamined*. Washington, DC: American Psychological Association.

Ferrara, P., Vitelli, O., Bottaro, G., Gatto, A., Liberatore, P., Binetti, P., . . . & Stabile, A. (2013). Factitious disorders and Münchausen syndrome: The tip of the iceberg. *Journal of Child Health Care, 17*, 366–374.

Filone, S., & King, C. M. (2015). The emerging standard of competence in immigration removal proceedings: A review for forensic mental health professionals. *Psychology, Public Policy, and Law, 21*, 60–71.

Final conclusions of the American Psychological Association Working Group on Investigation of Memories of Childhood Abuse. (1998). *Psychology, Public Policy, and Law, 4*, 931–940.

Fineran, S., & Gruber, J. E. (2009). Youth at work: Adolescent employment and sexual harassment. *Child Abuse & Neglect, 33,* 550–559.

Finkelhor, D. (2011). Prevalence of child victimization, abuse, crime, and violence exposure. In J. W. White, M. P. Koss, & A. E. Kazdin (Eds.), *Violence against women and children, Vol. 1. Mapping the terrain* (pp. 9–29). Washington, DC: American Psychological Association.

Finkelhor, D., Hotaling, G., & Sedlak, A. (1990). *Missing, abducted, runaway, and thrownaway children in America: First report.* Washington, DC: Juvenile Justice Clearinghouse.

Finkelhor, D., & Jones, L. (2012, November). *Have sexual abuse and physical abuse declined since the 1990s?* Durham: University of New Hampshire, Crimes Against Children Research Center.

Finkelhor, D., & Ormrod, R. (2000, June). *Kidnapping of juveniles: Patterns from NIBRS.* Washington, DC: U.S. Department of Justice, Office of Juvenile Justice and Delinquency Prevention.

Finkelhor, D., & Ormrod, R. (2001a, September). *Crimes against children by babysitters.* Washington, DC: U.S. Department of Justice, Office of Juvenile Justice and Delinquency Prevention.

Finkelhor, D., & Ormrod, R. (2001b, October). *Homicides of children and youth.* Washington, DC: U.S. Department of Justice, Office of Juvenile Justice and Delinquency Prevention.

Finkelhor, D., Shattuck, A., Turner, H. A., & Hamby, S. L. (2014). The lifetime prevalence of child sexual abuse and sexual assault in late adolescence. *Journal of Adolescent Health, 55,* 329–333.

Finkelhor, D., Turner, H., & Hamby, S. (2011). *National Survey of Children's Exposure to Violence: Questions and answers about the National Survey of Children's Exposure to Violence.* Washington, DC: U.S. Department of Justice, Office of Justice Programs.

Finkelhor, D., Turner, H., Hamby, S., & Ormrod, R. (2011, October). *Polyvictimization: Children's exposure to multiple types of violence, crime, and abuse.* Washington, DC: U.S. Department of Justice, Office of Juvenile Justice and Delinquency Prevention.

Finkelhor, D., Turner, H., Ormrod, R., Hamby, S., & Kracke, K. (2009, October). *Children's exposure to violence: A comprehensive survey.* Washington, DC: U.S. Department of Justice, Office of Juvenile Justice and Delinquency Prevention.

Finkelman, J. M. (2010). Litigation consulting: Expanding beyond jury selection to trial strategy and tactics. *Consulting Psychology Journal: Practice and Research, 62,* 12–20.

Finn, P., & Tomz, J. E. (1997, March). *Developing a law enforcement stress program for officers and their families.* Washington, DC: U.S. Department of Justice.

Fishbein, D. (2000). Neuropsychological function, drug abuse, and violence: A conceptual framework. *Criminal Justice and Behavior, 27,* 139–159.

Fisher, B. S., Cullen, F. T., & Turner, M. G. (2000). *Sexual victimization of college women.* Washington, DC: U.S. Department of Justice, National Institute of Justice.

Fisher, J. C. (1997). *Killer among us: Public reactions to serial murder.* Westport, CT: Praeger.

Fisher, R. P., & Geiselman, R. E. (1992). *Memory-Enhancing techniques for investigative interviewing: The cognitive interview* (NCJ 140158). Washington, DC: U.S. Department of Justice, National Criminal Justice Reference Service.

Fisher, R. P., & Geiselman, R. E. (2010). The cognitive interview method of conducting police interviews: Eliciting extensive information and promoting therapeutic jurisprudence. *International Journal of Law and Psychiatry, 33,* 321–328.

Fitzgerald, L. F., Magley, V. J., Drasgow, F., & Waldo, C. R. (1999). Measuring sexual harassment in the military: The sexual experiences questionnaire (SEQ-DoD). *Military Psychology, 11,* 243–263.

Fitzgerald, L. F., & Shullman, S. L. (1985). *Sexual experiences questionnaire.* Kent, OH: Kent State University.

Fixsen, D. L., Blasé, K. A., Timbers, G. D., & Wolf, M. M. (2001). In search of program implementation: 792 replications of the teaching-family model. In G. A. Bernfeld, D. P. Farrington, & A. W. Leschied (Eds.), *Offender rehabilitation in practice* (pp. 149–166). Chichester, England: Wiley.

Fixsen, D. L., Blasé, K. A., Timbers, G. D., & Wolf, M. M. (2007). In search of program implementation: 792 replications of the teaching-family model. *The Behavior Analyst Today, 8,* 96–110.

Flory, K., Milich, R., Lynam, D. R., Leukefeld, C., & Clayton, R. (2003). Relation between childhood disruptive behavior disorders and substance use and dependence symptoms in young adulthood: Individuals with symptoms of attention-deficit/hyperactivity disorder and conduct disorder are uniquely at risk. *Psychology of Addictive Behaviors, 17,* 151–158.

Foa, E. B., Cashman, L., Jaycox, L., & Perry, K. (1997). The validation of a self-report measure of posttraumatic stress disorder: The Posttraumatic Diagnostic Scale. *Psychological Assessment, 9,* 445–451.

Foa, E. B., Riggs, D. S., Dancu, C. V., & Rothbaum, B. O. (1993). Reliability and validity of a brief instrument for assessing posttraumatic stress disorder. *Journal of Traumatic Stress, 6,* 459–474.

Foa, E. B., Rothbaum, B. O., Riggs, D. S., & Murdock, T. B. (1991). Treatment of posttraumatic stress disorder in rape victims: A comparison between cognitive-behavioral procedures and counseling. *Journal of Consulting and Clinical Psychology, 59,* 715–723.

Fogel, M. H., Schiffman, W., Mumley, D., Tillbrook, C., & Grisso, T. (2013). Ten year research update (2001–2010): Evaluations for competence to stand trial (Adjudicative competence). *Behavioral Sciences & the Law, 31,* 165–191.

Folsom, J., & Atkinson, J. L. (2007). The generalizability of the LSI-R and the CAT to the prediction of recidivism in women offenders. *Criminal Justice and Behavior, 34,* 1044–1056.

Fontaine, N., Carbonneau, R., Vitaro, F., Barker, E. D., & Tremblay, R. E. (2009). Research review: A critical review of studies on the developmental trajectories of antisocial behavior in females. *Journal of Child Psychology and Psychiatry, 50,* 363–385.

Foote, W. E. (2013). Forensic evaluations in Americans with Disabilities Act cases. In R. K. Otto & I. B. Weiner (Eds.), *Handbook of psychology: Vol. 11. Forensic psychology* (2nd ed., pp. 271–294). Hoboken, NJ: Wiley.

Foote, W. E. (2016). Evaluations of individuals for disability in insurance and social security contexts. In R. Jackson & R. Roesch (Eds.), *Learning forensic assessment: Research and practice* (2nd ed., pp. 413–433). New York, NY: Routledge.

Foote, W. E., & Lareau, C. R. (2013). Psychological evaluation of emotional damages in tort cases. In R. K. Otto & I. B. Weiner (Eds.), *Handbook of psychology: Vol. 11. Forensic psychology* (2nd ed., pp. 172–200). Hoboken, NJ: Wiley.

Forehand, R., Wierson, M., Frame, C. L., Kempton, T., & Armistead, L. (1991). Juvenile firesetting: A unique syndrome or an advanced level of antisocial behavior? *Behavioral Research and Therapy, 29,* 125–128.

Forsman, M., Lichtenstein, P., Andershed, H., & Larsson, H. (2010). A longitudinal twin study of the direction of effects between psychopathic personality and antisocial behavior. *Journal of Child Psychology and Psychiatry, 51,* 39–47.

Forth, A. E., Kosson, D. S., & Hare, R. D. (1997). *Hare Psychopathy Checklist: Youth Version.* Toronto, Canada: Multi-Health Systems.

Fournier, L. R. (2016). The *Daubert* guidelines: Usefulness, utilization, and suggestions for improving quality control. *Journal of Applied Research in Memory and Cognition, 5,* 308–313.

Fox, J. A., & Levin, J. (1998). Multiple homicide: Patterns of serial and mass murder. In M. Tonry (Ed.), *Crime and justice: A review of research* (Vol. 23, pp. 407–455). Chicago, IL: University of Chicago Press.

Fox, J. A., & Levin, J. (2003). Mass murder: An analysis of extreme violence. *Journal of Applied Psychoanalytic Studies, 5,* 47–64.

Fox, J. A., & Zawitz, M. A. (2001). *Homicide trends in the United States.* Washington, DC: U.S. Department of Justice, Bureau of Justice Statistics.

Francis, A. (2012, December 8). *In distress: The DSM's impact on mental health practice and research.* Retrieved from http://www.psychologytoday.com.blog/dsm5-in-distress/201212/misleading-medical-illness-mental disorder

Francis, A. (2013). *DSM-5 is guide not bible–ignore its ten worst changes.* Retrieved from http://www.psychologytoday.com/blog/dsm5-in-distress/201212

Franklin, C. L., Sheeran, T., & Zimmerman, M. (2002). Screening for trauma histories, posttraumatic stress disorder (PTSD), and subthreshold PTSD in psychiatric outpatients. *Psychological Assessment, 14,* 467–471.

Freedman, S., Eastwood, J., Snook, B., & Luther, K. (2014). Safeguarding youth interrogation rights: The effect of grade level and reading complexity of youth waiver forms on the comprehension of legal rights. *Applied Cognitive Psychology, 28,* 427–431.

Freeman, N., & Sandler, J. (2009). Female sex offender recidivism: A large-scale empirical analysis. *Sexual Abuse: Journal of Research and Treatment, 21,* 455–473.

Frenda, S. J., Nichols, R. M., & Loftus, E. F. (2011). Current issues and advances in misinformation research. *Current Directions in Psychological Science, 20,* 20–23.

Freud, S. (1957). Repression. In J. Strachey (Ed. & Trans.), *The standard edition of the complete psychological works of Sigmund Freud* (Vol. 14, pp. 147–156). London, England: Hogarth. (Original work published 1915)

Frick, P. J., Barry, C. T., & Bodin, S. D. (2000). Applying the concept of psychopathy in children: Implications for the assessment of antisocial youth. In C. B. Gacono (Ed.), *The clinical and forensic assessment of psychopathy* (pp. 3–24). Mahwah, NJ: Erlbaum.

Frick, P. J., Bodin, S. D., & Barry, C. T. (2000). Psychopathic traits and conduct problems in community and clinic-referred samples of children: Further development of the psychopathy screening device. *Psychological Assessment, 12,* 382–393.

Frick, P. J., Cornell, A. H., Bodin, S. D., Dane, H. E., Barry, C. T., & Loney, B. R. (2003). Callous-unemotional traits and developmental pathways to severe conduct problems. *Developmental Psychology, 39,* 246–260.

Frick, P. J., O'Brien, B. S., Wootton, J., & McBurnett, K. (1994). Psychopathy and conduct problems in children. *Journal of Abnormal Psychology, 103,* 700–707.

Frick, P. J., Ray, J. V., Thornton, L. C., & Kahn, R. E. (2014). Can callous-unemotional traits enhance the understanding, diagnosis, and treatment of serious conduct problems in children and adolescents? A comprehensive review. *Psychological Bulletin, 140,* 1–57.

Frick, P. J., & Viding, E. M. (2009). Antisocial behavior from a developmental psychopathology perspective. *Development and Psychopathology, 21,* 1111–1131.

Friedman, T. L. (2016). *Thank you for being late: An optimist's guide to thriving in the age of accelerations.* New York, NY: Farrar, Straus, and Giroux.

Furby, L., Weinroth, M. R., & Blackshaw, L. (1989). Sex offender recidivism: A review. *Psychological Bulletin, 105,* 3–30.

Fuselier, G. D. (1988). Hostage negotiation consultant: Emerging role for the clinical psychologist. *Professional Psychology: Research and Practice, 19,* 175–179.

Fuselier, G. D., & Noesner, G. W. (1990, July). Confronting the terrorist hostage taker. *FBI Law Enforcement Bulletin,* pp. 9–12.

Fyfe, J. J. (1988). Police use of deadly force: Research and reform. *Justice Quarterly, 5,* 165–205.

Gaboury, M., & Edmunds, C. (2002). Civil remedies. In A. Seymour, M. Murray, J. Sigmon, M. Hook, C. Edwards, M. Gaboury, & G. Coleman.

(Eds.), *National Victim Assistance Academy textbook*. Washington, DC: U.S. Department of Justice, Office of Victims of Crime.

Gacono, C. B., Nieberding, R. J., Owen, A., Rubel, J., & Bodholdt, R. (2001). Treating conduct disorder, antisocial, and psychopathic personalities. In J. B. Ashford, B. D. Sales, & W. H. Reid (Eds.), *Treating adult and juvenile offenders with special needs* (pp. 99–129). Washington, DC: American Psychological Association.

Gallagher, R. W., Somwaru, D. P., & Ben-Porath, Y. S. (1999). Current usage of psychological tests in state correctional settings. *Corrections Compendium, 24*, 1–3, 20.

Galler, J. R., Bryce, C. P., Aber, D. P., Hock, R. S., Harrison, R., Eaglesfield, G. D., & Fitzmaurice, G. (2012). Infant malnutrition predicts conduct problems in adolescents. *Nutritional Neuroscience, 15*, 186–192.

Gallo, F. J., & Halgin, R. P. (2011). A guide for establishing a practice in police preemployment postoffer psychological evaluations. *Professional Practice: Research and Practice, 42*, 269–275.

Gannon, T. A., & Pina, A. (2010). Firesetting: Psychopathology, theory and treatment. *Aggression and Violent Behavior, 15*, 224–238.

Gannon, T. A., & Rose, M. R. (2008). Female child sexual offenders: Toward integrating theory and practice. *Aggression and Violent Behavior, 13*, 442–461.

Garcia-Moreno, C., Guedes, A., & Knerr, W. (2012). *Sexual violence*. Geneva, Switzerland: World Health Organization.

Gardner, B. O., Boccaccini, M. T., Bitting, B. S., & Edens, J. F. (2015). Personality Assessment Inventory scores as predictors of misconduct, recidivism, and violence: A meta-analytic review. *Psychological Assessment, 27*, 534–544.

Gardner, H. (1983). *Frames of mind: The theory of multiple intelligences*. New York, NY: Basic Books.

Gardner, H. (1998). Are there additional intelligences? The case for naturalist, spiritual, and existential intelligence. In K. Kane (Ed.), *Education, information, and transformation* (pp. 111–131). Englewood Cliffs, NJ: Prentice Hall.

Gardner, H. (2000). *Intelligence reframed: Multiple intelligences for the 21st century*. New York, NY: Basic Books.

Gardner, M., & Brooks-Gunn, J. (2009). Adolescents' exposure to community violence: Are neighborhood youth organizations protective? *Journal of Community Psychology, 37*, 505–525.

Gardner, M., & Steinberg, L. (2005). Peer influence on risk taking, risk preference, and risky decision making in adolescence and adulthood: An experimental study. *Developmental Psychology, 41*, 625–635.

Garland, B. E., McCarty, W. P., & Zhao, R. (2009). Job satisfaction and organizational commitment in prisons: An examination of psychological staff, teachers, and unit management staff. *Criminal Justice and Behavior, 36*, 163–183.

Garrett, B. L. (2011). *Convicting the innocent: Where criminal prosecutors go wrong*. Cambridge, MA: Harvard University Press.

Garthe, R. C., Sullivan, T. N., & McDaniel, M. A. (2017). A meta-analytic review of peer risk factors and adolescent dating violence. *Psychology of Violence, 7*, 45–57.

Gates, M. A., Holowka, D. W., Vasterling, J. J., Keane, T. M., Marx, B. P., & Rosen, R. C. (2012). Posttraumatic stress disorder in veterans and military personnel: Epidemiology, screening, and case recognition. *Psychological Services, 9*, 361–382.

Gay, J. G., Vitacco, M. J., & Ragatz, L. (2017, March 1). Mental health symptoms predict competency to stand trial and competency restoration success. *Legal and Criminological Psychology*. Advance online publication. doi:10.1111/lcrp.12100

Gaynor, J. (1996). Firesetting. In M. Lewis (Ed.), *Child and adolescent psychiatry: A comprehensive textbook* (pp. 591–603). Baltimore, MD: Williams & Wilkins.

Gelles, M. G., & Palarea, R. (2011). Ethics in crisis negotiation: A law enforcement and public safety perspective. In C. H. Kennedy & T. J. Williams (Eds.), *Ethical practice in operational psychology: Military and national intelligence operations* (pp. 107–123). Washington, DC: American Psychological Association.

Gelles, R. J., & Cavanaugh, M. M. (2005). Violence, abuse, and neglect in families and intimate relationships. In P. C. McHenry & S. J. Price (Eds.), *Families & change: Coping with stressful events and transitions* (3rd ed., pp. 129–154). Thousand Oaks, CA: Sage.

Gendreau, P., Cullen, F. T., & Bonta, J. (1994). Intensive rehabilitation supervision: The next generation in community corrections? *Federal Probation, 58*, 72–78.

Gendreau, P., & Goggin, C. (2014). Practicing psychology in correctional settings. In I. B. Weiner & R. K. Otto (Eds.), *Handbook of forensic psychology* (4th ed., pp. 759–793). Hoboken, NJ: Wiley.

Gendreau, P., Little, T., & Goggin, C. (1996). A meta-analysis of the predictors of adult recidivism: What works! *Criminology, 34*, 401–433.

Gendreau, P., Paparozzi, M., Little, T., & Goddard, M. (1993). Punishing smarter: The effectiveness of the new generation of alternative sanctions. *Forum on Correctional Research, 5*, 31–34.

Gendreau, P., & Ross, R. R. (1984). Correctional treatment: Some recommendations for effective intervention. *Juvenile and Family Court Journal, 34*, 31–39.

Gentile, S. R., Asamen, J. K., Harmell, P. H., & Weathers, R. (2002). The stalking of psychologists by their clients. *Professional Psychology: Research and Practice, 33*, 490–494.

George, J. A. (2008). Offender profiling and expert testimony: Scientifically valid or glorified results? *Vanderbilt Law Review, 61*, 221–260.

George, M. J., & Odgers, C. L. (2015). Seven fears and the science of how mobile technologies may be influencing adolescents in the digital age. *Perspectives in Psychological Science, 10*, 821–851.

George, W. H., & Marlatt, G. A. (1989). Introduction. In D. R. Laws (Ed.), *Relapse prevention with sex offenders* (pp. 1–31). New York, NY: Guilford Press.

Gershon, R. R. M., Lin, S., & Li, X. (2002). Work stress in aging police officers. *Journal of Occupational and Environmental Medicine, 44,* 160–167.

Giebels, E., & Noelanders, S. (2004). *Crisis negotiations: A multiparty perspective.* Veenendall, Netherlands: Universal Press.

Giebels, E., & Taylor, P. J. (2009). Interaction patterns in crisis negotiations: Persuasive arguments and cultural differences. *Journal of Applied Psychology, 94,* 5–19.

Gill, C. J., Kewman, D. G., & Brannon, R. W. (2003). Transforming psychological practice and society: Policies that reflect the new paradigm. *American Psychologist, 58,* 305–312.

Gillis, J. W. (2001). *First response to victims of crime 2001.* Washington, DC: U.S. Department of Justice, Office for Victims of Crime.

Glaze, L. E., & Herberman, E. J. (2013, December). *Correctional populations in the United States, 2012.* Washington, DC: U.S. Department of Justice, Bureau of Justice Statistics.

Glew, G. M., Fan, M.-Y., Katon, W., & Rivara, F. P. (2008). Bullying and school safety. *Journal of Pediatrics, 152,* 123–128.

Glisson, C., Schoenwald, S. K., Hemmelgarn, A., Green, P., Dukes, D., Armstrong, K. S., . . . & Chapman, J. E. (2010). Randomized trial of MST and ARC in a two-level evidence-based treatment implementation strategy. *Journal of Consulting and Clinical Psychology, 78,* 537–550.

Goddard, C., & Bedi, G. (2010). Intimate partner violence and child abuse: A child-centered perspective. *Child Abuse Review, 19,* 5–20.

Goff, P. A., Jackson, M. C., DiLeone, B. A., Culotta, M. C., & DiTomasso, N. D. (2014). The essence of innocence: Consequences of dehumanizing black children. *Journal of Personality and Social Psychology, 106,* 526–545.

Goff, P. A., & Kahn, K. B. (2012). Racial bias in policing: Why we know less than we should. *Social Issues and Policy Review, 6,* 177–210.

Golding, S. L. (1993). *Interdisciplinary Fitness Interview–Revised: A training manual.* Salt Lake City: University of Utah, Department of Psychology.

Golding, S. L. (2016). Learning forensic examinations of adjudicative competency. In R. Jackson & R. Roesch (Eds.), *Learning forensic assessment: Research and practice* (2nd ed., pp. 65–96). New York, NY: Routledge.

Golding, S. L., & Roesch, R. (1987). The assessment of criminal responsibility: A historical approach to a current controversy. In I. B. Weiner & A. K. Hess (Eds.), *Handbook of forensic psychology* (pp. 395–436). New York, NY: Wiley.

Golding, S. L., Skeem, J. L., Roesch, R., & Zapf, P. A. (1999). The assessment of criminal responsibility: Current controversies. In A. K.

Hess & I. B. Weiner (Eds.), *The handbook of forensic psychology* (2nd ed., pp. 379–408). New York, NY: Wiley.

Goldkamp, J. S., & Irons-Guynn, C. (2000). *Emerging judicial strategies for the mentally ill in the criminal caseload: Mental health courts in Fort Lauderdale, Seattle, San Bernardino, and Anchorage.* Washington, DC: U.S. Department of Justice, Bureau of Justice Statistics.

Goldstein, A. M. (2002a). Low-level aggression: Definition, escalation, intervention. In J. McGuire (Ed.), *Offender rehabilitation and treatment* (pp. 169–192). Chichester, England: Wiley.

Goldstein, A. M., Morse, S. J., & Packer, I. K. (2013). Evaluation of criminal responsibility. In I. B. Weiner (Ed.), *Handbook of psychology* (2nd ed., pp. 440–472). Hoboken, NJ: Wiley.

Goldstein, A. P., & Glick, B. (1987). *Aggression replacement training.* Champaign, IL: Research Press.

Goldstein, A. P., & Glick, B. (2001). Aggression replacement training: Application and evaluation management. In G. A. Bernfeld, D. P. Farrington, & A. W. Leschied (Eds.), *Offender rehabilitation in practice* (pp. 121–148). Chichester, England: Wiley.

Goldstein, N. E. S., Goldstein, A. M., Zelle, H., & Condie, L. O. (2013). Capacity to waive Miranda rights and the assessment of susceptibility to police coercion. In R. K. Otto & I. B. Weiner (Eds.), *Handbook of psychology: Forensic psychology, Vol. 11,* (2nd ed., pp. 381–411). Hoboken, NJ: Wiley.

Gongola, J., Scurich, N., & Quas, J. A. (2017). Detecting deception in children: A meta-analysis. *Law and Human Behavior, 41,* 44–54.

Good, G. E., Heppner, M. J., Hillenbrand-Gunn, T. L., & Wang, L. F. (1995). Sexual and psychological violence: An exploratory study of predictors in college men. *The Journal of Men's Studies, 4*(1), 59–71.

Goodman-Delahunty, J. (2000). Psychological impairment under the Americans with Disabilities Act: Legal guidelines. *Professional Psychology: Research and Practice, 31,* 197–205.

Goodwill, A. M., Alison, L. J., & Beech, A. R. (2009). What works in offender profiling? A comparison of typological, thematic, and multivariate models. *Behavioral Sciences & the Law, 27,* 507–529.

Goodwill, A. M., Lehmann, R. J. B., Beauregard, E., & Andrei, A. (2016). An action phase approach to offender profiling. *Legal and Criminological Psychology, 21,* 229–250.

Gordon, D. A. (2002). Intervening with families of troubled youth: Functional family therapy and parenting wisely. In J. McGuire (Ed.), *Offender rehabilitation and treatment* (pp. 193–220). Chichester, England: Wiley.

Gorman, W. (2001). Refugee survivors of torture: Trauma and treatment. *Professional Psychology: Research and Practice, 32,* 443–451.

Gospodarevskaya, E. (2013). Post-traumatic stress disorder and quality of life in sexually abused Australian children. *Journal of Child Sexual Abuse, 22,* 277–296.

Gothard, S., Rogers, R., & Sewell, K. W. (1995). Feigning incompetency to stand trial: An investigation of the Georgia Court Competency Test. *Law and Human Behavior, 19*, 363–373.

Gough, H. G. (1987). *California Psychological Inventory administrator's guide*. Palo Alto, CA: Consulting Psychologists Press.

Gould, J. W., & Martindale, D. A. (2013). Child custody evaluations: Current literature and practical applications. In R. K. Otto & I. B. Weiner (Eds.), *Handbook of Psychology, Vol. 11. Forensic psychology* (2nd ed., pp. 101–138). Hoboken, NJ: Wiley.

Gowensmith, W. N., Frost, L. E., Speelman, D. W., & Therson, D. E. (2016). Lookin' for beds in all the wrong places: Outpatient competency restoration as a promising approach to modern challenges. *Psychology, Public Policy, and Law, 22*, 293–305.

Gowensmith, W. N., Murrie, D. C., & Boccaccini, M. T. (2012). Field reliability of competence to stand trial opinions: How often do evaluators agree, and what do judges decide when evaluators disagree? *Law and Human Behavior, 36*, 130–139.

Gowensmith, W. N., Murrie, D. C., & Boccaccini, M. T. (2013). How reliable are forensic evaluations of legal sanity? *Law and Human Behavior, 37*, 98–106.

Gragg, F., Petta, I., Bernstein, H., Eisen, K., & Quinn, L. (2007). *New York prevalence study of commercially exploited children*. Renssaelaer: New York State Office of Children and Family Services.

Grandey, A. A. (2000). Emotion regulation in the workplace: A new way to conceptualize emotional labor. *Journal of Occupational Health Psychology, 5*, 95–110.

Granhag, P. A., & Strömwall, L. A. (2002). Repeated interrogations: Verbal and nonverbal cues to deception. *Applied Cognitive Psychology, 16*, 243–257.

Granhag, P. A., Vrij, A., & Meissner, C. A. (2014). Information gathering in law enforcement and intelligence settings: Advancing theory and practice. *Applied Cognitive Psychology, 28*, 815–816.

Grassian, S., (1983). Psychopathological effects of solitary confinement. *American Journal of Psychiatry, 140*, 1450–1454.

Gray, A. S., Pithers, W., Busconi, A. J., & Houchens, P. (1997). Children with sexual behavior problems: An empirically derived taxonomy. *Association for the Treatment of Sexual Abusers, 3*, 10–11.

Greenberg, S. A., Otto, R. K., & Long, A. C. (2003). The utility of psychological testing in assessing emotional damages in personal injury litigation. *Assessment, 10*, 411–419.

Greenburg, M. M. (2011). *The mad bomber of New York: The extraordinary true story of the manhunt that paralyzed a city*. New York, NY: Union Square Press.

Greenfeld, L. A. (1997). *Sex offenses and offenders: An analysis of data on rape and sexual assault*. Washington, DC: U.S. Department of Justice, Bureau of Justice Statistics.

Gregorie, T. (2000). *Cyberstalking: Dangers on the information highway*. Arlington, VA: National Center for Victims of Crime.

Gregorie, T., & Wallace, H. (2000). Workplace violence. In A. Seymour, M. Murray, J. Sigmon, M. Hook, C. Edmonds, M. Gaboury, & G. Coleman. (Eds.), *National Victim Assistance Academy textbook*. Washington, DC: U.S. Department of Justice, Office for Victims of Crime.

Gregory, N. (2005). Offender profiling: A review of the literature. *British Journal of Forensic Practice, 7*, 29–34.

Greif, G. L., & Hegar, R. L. (1993). *When parents kidnap: The families behind the headlines*. New York, NY: Free Press.

Gretton, H. M., McBride, M., Hare, R. D., O'Shaughnessy, R., & Kumka, G. (2001). Psychopathy and recidivism in adolescent sex offenders. *Criminal Justice and Behavior, 28*, 427–449.

Griffin, H. L., Beech, A., Print, B., Bradshaw, H., & Quayle, J. (2008). The development and initial testing of the AIM2 framework to assess risk and strengths in young people who sexually offend. *Journal of Sexual Aggression, 14*, 211–225.

Griffin, P. (2011, Winter). Presidential column. *AP-LS News, 31*, 2.

Griffith, J. D., Hart, C. L., Kessler, J., & Goodling, M. M. (2007). Trial consultants: Perceptions of eligible jurors. *Consulting Psychology Journal: Practice and Research, 59*, 148–153.

Grisso, T. (1981). *Juveniles' waiver of rights: Legal and psychological competence*. New York, NY: Plenum.

Grisso, T. (1986). *Evaluating competencies: Forensic assessments and instruments*. New York, NY: Plenum.

Grisso, T. (1988). *Competency to stand trial evaluations: A manual for practice*. Sarasota, FL: Professional Resource Exchange.

Grisso, T. (1998). *Forensic evaluation of juveniles*. Sarasota, FL: Professional Resource Press.

Grisso, T. (2003). *Evaluating competencies: Forensic assessments and instruments* (2nd ed.). New York, NY: Kluwer/Plenum.

Grisso, T. (2008). Adolescent offenders with mental disorders. *The Future of Children, 18*, 143–164.

Grisso, T., Appelbaum, P., Mulvey, E., & Fletcher, K. (1995). The MacArthur treatment competence study: II. Measures of abilities related to competence to consent to treatment. *Law and Human Behavior, 19*, 127–148.

Grisso, T., & Schwartz, R. G. (Eds.). (2000). *Youth on trial: A developmental perspective on juvenile justice*. Chicago, IL: University of Chicago Press.

Grisso, T., Steinberg, L., Woolard, J., Cauffman, E., Scott, E., Graham, S., . . . & Schwarz, R. (2003). Juveniles' competence to stand trial: A comparison of adolescents' and adults' capacities as trial defendants. *Law and Human Behavior, 27*, 333–364.

Gross, A. M., Bennett, T., Sloan, L., Marx, B. P., & Jurgens, J. (2001). The impact of alcohol and alcohol expectancies on male perceptions of female sexual arousal in a date rape analog. *Experimental and Clinical Psychopharmacology, 9,* 380–388.

Gross, A. M., Winslett, A., Roberts, M., & Gohm, C. L. (2006). An examination of sexual violence against women. *Violence Against Women, 12,* 288–300.

Grossman, N. S., & Okun, B. F. (2003). Family psychology and family law: Introduction to the special issue. *Journal of Family Psychology, 17,* 163–168.

Groth, A. N. (1979). *Men who rape: The psychology of the offender.* New York, NY: Plenum.

Groth, A. N., & Burgess, A. W. (1977). Motivational intent in the sexual assault of children. *Criminal Justice and Behavior, 4,* 253–271.

Groth, A. N., Burgess, A. W., & Holmstrom, L. (1977). Rape: Power, anger, and sexuality. *American Journal of Psychiatry, 134,* 1239–1243.

Grubb, A. (2010). Modern day hostage (crisis) negotiation: The evolution of an art form within the policing arena. *Aggression and Violent Behavior, 15,* 341–348.

Grubin, D. (2002). The potential use of polygraph in forensic psychiatry. *Criminal Behaviour and Mental Health, 12,* 45–55.

Grubin, D. (2008). The case for polygraph testing of sex offenders. *Legal and Criminological Psychology, 13,* 177–189.

Gudjonsson, G. H. (1992). *The psychology of interrogations, confessions and testimony.* London, England: Wiley.

Gudjonsson, G. H. (2003). *The science of interrogations and confessions: A handbook.* Chichester, England: Wiley.

Guerette, R. T. (2002). Geographical profiling. In D. Levinson (Ed.), *Encyclopedia of crime and punishment* (Vol. 2, pp. 780–784). Thousand Oaks, CA: Sage.

Guerra, N. G., Tolan, P. H., & Hammond, W. R. (1994). Prevention and treatment of adolescent violence. In L. D. Eron, J. H. Gentry, & P. Schlegel (Eds.), *Reason to hope: A psychosocial perspective on violence and youth* (pp. 383–403). Washington, DC: American Psychological Association.

Guilmette, T. J. (2013). The role of clinical judgement in symptom validity assessment. In D. A. Carone & S. S. Bush (Eds.), *Mild traumatic brain injury: Symptom validity assessment and malingering* (pp. 31–43). New York, NY: Springer.

Gunnoe, M. L., & Braver, S. L. (2001). The effects of joint legal custody on mothers, fathers, and children: Controlling for factors that predispose a sole maternal versus joint legal award. *Law and Human Behavior, 25,* 25–43.

Gur, R. E., & Gur, R. C. (2016). Sex differences in brain and behavior in adolescence: Findings from the Philadelphia neurodevelopmental cohort. *Neuroscience and Biobehavioral Reviews, 70,* 159–170.

Haapala, D. A., & Kinney, J. M. (1988). Avoiding out-of-home placement of high-risk status offenders through the use of intensive home-based family preservation services. *Criminal Justice and Behavior, 15,* 334–348.

Haber, R. N., & Haber, L. (2000). Experiencing, remembering, and reporting events. *Psychology, Public Policy, and Law, 6,* 1057–1097.

Hall, C. I. (1997). Cultural malpractice: The growing obsolescence of psychology with the changing U.S. population. *American Psychologist, 52,* 642–651.

Hall, N. G. C. (1995). Sexual offender recidivism revisited: A meta-analysis of recent treatment studies. *Journal of Consulting and Clinical Psychology, 63,* 802–809.

Halligan, S. L., Michael, T., Clark, D. M., & Ehlers, A. (2003). Post-traumatic stress disorder following assault: The role of cognitive processing, trauma memory, and appraisals. *Journal of Consulting and Clinical Psychology, 71,* 410–431.

Hammer, H., Finkelhor, D., Ormrod, R., Sedlak, A. J., & Bruce, C. (2008, August). Caretaker satisfaction with law enforcement response to missing children. (NCJ217090). *National Incidence Studies of Missing, Abducted, Runaway, and Thrownaway Children.* Washington, DC: U.S. Department of Justice, Office of Juvenile Justice and Delinquency Prevention.

Hammer, H., Finkelhor, D., & Sedlak, A. J. (2002, October). Runaway/throwaway children: National estimates and characteristics. In *National Incidence Studies of Missing, Abducted, Runaway, and Throwaway Children (NISMART)* (pp. 1–12). Washington, DC: U.S. Department of Justice, Office of Juvenile Justice and Delinquency Prevention.

Hancock, K. J., & Rhodes, G. (2008). Contact, configural coding, and the other-race effect in face recognition. *British Journal of Psychology, 99,* 45–56.

Haney, C. (2008). A culture of harm: Taming the dynamics of cruelty in supermax prisons. *Criminal Justice and Behavior, 35,* 956–984.

Hanson, R. K. (2001). *Age and sexual recidivism: A comparison of rapists and child molesters.* Ottawa, Canada: Department of Solicitor General Canada.

Hanson, R. K. (2005). Twenty years of progress in violence risk assessment. *Journal of Interpersonal Violence, 20,* 212–217.

Hanson, R. K. (2009). The psychological assessment of risk for crime and violence. *Canadian Psychology, 50,* 172–182.

Hanson, R. K., Babchishin, K. M., Helmus, L., & Thornton, D. (2012). Quantifying the relative risk of sex offenders: Risk ratios for Static-99R. *Sexual Abuse: A Journal of Research and Treatment, 25,* 482–515.

Hanson, R. K., Bourgon, G., Helmus, L., & Hodgson, S. (2009). *A meta-analysis of the effectiveness of treatment for sexual offenders: Risk, need, and responsivity.* (User Report 2009–01). Ottawa, Canada: Public Safety Canada.

Hanson, R. K., & Bussière, M. T. (1998). Predicting relapse: A meta-analysis of sexual offender recidivism studies. *Journal of Consulting and Clinical Psychology, 66,* 348–362.

Hanson, R. K., & Harris, A. J. R. (2000). Where should we intervene? Dynamic predictors of sexual offense recidivism. *Criminal Justice and Behavior, 27,* 6–35.

Hanson, R. K., Helmus, L., & Thornton, D. (2010). Predicting recidivism amongst sexual offenders: A multi-site study of Static-2002. *Law and Human Behavior, 34,* 198–211.

Hanson, R. K., & Morton-Bourgon, K. E. (2004). *Predictors of sexual recidivism: An updated meta-analysis* (User Report 2004-02). Ottawa, Canada: Public Safety and Emergency Preparedness Canada.

Hanson, R. K., & Morton-Bourgon, K. E. (2005). The characteristics of persistent sexual offenders: A meta-analysis of recidivism studies. *Journal of Consulting and Clinical Psychology, 73,* 1154–1163.

Hanson, R. K., & Morton-Bourgon, K. E. (2009). The accuracy of recidivism risk assessment for sexual offenders: A meta-analysis of 118 prediction studies. *Psychological Assessment, 21,* 1–21.

Hanson, R. K., & Thornton, D. (1999). *Static-99: Improving actuarial risk assessments for sex offenders.* User Report 99–02. Ottawa, Canada: Department of the Solicitor General.

Hanson, R. K., & Thornton, D. (2000). Improving risk assessment for sex offenders: A comparison of three actuarial scales. *Law and Human Behavior, 24,* 119–136.

Hanson, R. K., & Thornton, D. (2003). *Notes on the development of Static-2002.* (Corrections Research User Report No. 2003–01). Ottawa, Canada: Department of the Solicitor General of Canada.

Haqanee, Z., Peterson-Badali, M., & Skilling, T. (2015). Making "what works" work: Examining probation officers' experiences addressing the criminogenic needs of juvenile offenders. *Journal of Offender Rehabilitation, 54*(1), 37–59.

Hare, R. D. (1965). A conflict and learning theory analysis of psychopathic behavior. *Journal of Research in Crime and Delinquency, 2,* 12–19.

Hare, R. D. (1970). *Psychopathy: Theory and research.* New York, NY: Wiley.

Hare, R. D. (1991). *The Hare Psychopathy Checklist–Revised.* Toronto, Canada: Multi-Health Systems.

Hare, R. D. (1996). Psychopathy: A clinical construct whose time has come. *Criminal Justice and Behavior, 23,* 25–54.

Hare, R. D. (1998). Psychopathy, affect, and behavior. In D. Cooke, A. Forth, & R. Hare (Eds.), *Psychopathy: Theory, research, and implications for society* (pp. 105–137). Dordrecht, Netherlands: Kluwer.

Hare, R. D. (2003). *The Hare Psychopathy Checklist–Revised (PCL-R).* Toronto, Canada: Multi-Health Systems.

Hare, R. D., Clark, D., Grann, M., & Thornton, D. (2000). Psychopathy and the predictive validity of the PCL-R: An international perspective. *Behavioral Sciences & the Law, 18,* 623–645.

Hare, R. D., Forth, A. E., & Strachan, K. E. (1992). Psychopathy and crime across the life span. In R. D. Peters, R. J. McMahon, &

V. L. Quinsey (Eds.), *Aggression and violence throughout the life span* (pp. 285–300). Newbury Park, CA: Sage.

Hare, R. D., Hart, S. D., & Harpur, T. J. (1991). Psychopathy and the DSM-IV criteria for antisocial personality disorder. *Journal of Abnormal Psychology, 100,* 391–398.

Hare, R. D., & Neumann, C. S. (2008). Psychopathy as a clinical and empirical construct. *Annual Review of Clinical Psychology, 4,* 217–246.

Harkins, L., Howard, P., Barnett, G., Wakeling, H., & Miles, C. (2015, January). Relationships between denial, risk, and recidivism in sexual offenders. *Archives of Sexual Behavior, 44,* 157–166.

Harley, K., & Reese, E. (1999). Origins of autobiographical memory. *Developmental Psychology, 35,* 1338–1348.

Harpur, T. J., Hakstian, A., & Hare, R. D. (1988). Factor structure of the Psychopathy Checklist. *Journal of Consulting and Clinical Psychology, 56,* 741–747.

Harrell, E. (2011, March). *Workplace violence, 1993–2009.* Washington, DC: U.S. Department of Justice, Bureau of Justice Statistics.

Harrell, E. (2012a, December). *Crime against persons with disabilities, 2009–2011—statistical tables.* Washington, DC: U.S. Department of Justice, Bureau of Justice Statistics.

Harris, A. J., Fisher, W., Veysey, B. M., Ragusa, L. M., & Lurigio, A. J. (2010). Sex offending and serious mental illness: Directions for policy and research. *Criminal Justice and Behavior, 37,* 596–612.

Harris, A. J., Lobanov-Rostovsky, C., & Levenson, J. S. (2010). Widening the net: The effects of transitioning to the Adam Walsh Act's federally mandated sex offender classification system. *Criminal Justice and Behavior, 37,* 503–519.

Harris, A. J., & Lurigio, A. J. (2010). Special Issue: Sex offenses and offenders: Toward evidence–based public policy. *Criminal Justice and Behavior, 37,* 477–481.

Harris, D. A. (2013). Review of clinical work with traumatized young children. *Infant Mental Health Journal, 34,* 173–174.

Harris, G. T., Rice, M. E., & Quinsey, V. L. (1993). Violent recidivism of mentally disordered offenders: The development of a statistical prediction instrument. *Criminal Justice and Behavior, 20,* 315–325.

Harris, G. T., Rice, M. E., & Quinsey, V. L. (1994). Psychopathy as a taxon: Evidence that psychopaths are a discrete class. *Journal of Consulting and Clinical Psychology, 62,* 387–397.

Harrison, M. A., Murphy, E. A., Ho, L. Y., Bowers, T. G., & Flaherty, C. V. (2015). Female serial killers in the United States: Means, motives, and makings. *The Journal of Forensic Psychiatry & Psychology, 26,* 383–406).

Hart, S. D., Boer, D. P., Otto, R. K., & Douglas, K. S. (2010). Structured professional judgement guidelines for sexual violence risk assessment: The Sexual Violence Risk–20 (SVR–20) and Risk For Sexual Violence Protocol (RSVP). In R. K. Otto & K. S. Douglas

(Eds.), *Handbook of violence risk assessment: International perspectives on forensic mental health* (pp. 269–294). New York, NY: Routledge/Taylor & Francis.

Hart, S. D., Cox, D. N., & Hare, R. D. (1995). *The Hare Psychopathy Checklist: Screening Version.* Toronto, Canada: Multi-Health Systems.

Hart, S. D., & Dempster, R. J. (1997). Impulsivity and psychopathy. In C. D. Webster & M. A. Jackson (Eds.), *Impulsivity: Theory, assessment, and treatment.* New York, NY: Guilford Press.

Hart, S. D., Hare, R. D., & Forth, A. E. (1993). Psychopathy as a risk marker for violence: Development and validation of a screening version of the Revised Psychopathy Checklist. In J. Monahan & H. Steadman (Eds.), *Violence and mental disorder: Developments in risk assessment* (pp. 81–98). Chicago, IL: University of Chicago Press.

Hart, S. D., Watt, K. A., & Vincent, G. M. (2002). Commentary on Seagrave and Grisso: Impressions of the state of the art. *Law and Human Behavior, 26,* 241–245.

Hartup, W. W. (2005). The development of aggression: Where do you stand? In R. E. Tremblay, W. W. Hartup, & J. Archer (Eds.), *Developmental origins of aggression* (pp. 3–24). New York, NY: Guilford Press.

Hasselbrack, A. M. (2001). Opting in to mental health courts. *Corrections Compendium,* Sample Issue, 4–5.

Hatcher, C., Mohandie, K., Turner, J., & Gelles, M. G. (1998). The role of the psychologist in crisis/hostage negotiations. *Behavioral Sciences & the Law, 16,* 455–472.

Haugaard, J. J., & Reppucci, N. D. (1988). *The sexual abuse of children.* San Francisco, CA: Jossey-Bass.

Haugen, P. T., Evces, M., & Weiss, D. S. (2012). Treating posttraumatic stress disorder in first responders: A systematic review. *Clinical Psychology Review, 32,* 370–380.

Hawes, S. W., Boccaccini, M. T., & Murrie, D. C. (2013). Psychopathy and the combination of psychopathy and sexual deviance as predictors of sexual recidivism: Meta-analytic findings using the Psychopathy Checklist–Revised. *Psychological Assessment, 25,* 233–243.

Hawkins, D. F. (2003). Editor's introduction. In D. F. Hawkins (Ed.), *Violent crime: Assessing race and ethnic differences* (pp. xiii–xxv). Cambridge, England: Cambridge University Press.

Hazelwood, R., & Burgess, A. (1987). *Practical aspects of rape investigation: A multidisciplinary approach.* New York, NY: Elsevier.

Hébert, M., Langevin, R., & Bernier, M. J. (2013). Self-reported symptoms and parents' evaluation of behavior problems in preschoolers disclosing sexual abuse. *International Journal of Child, Youth, and Family Studies, 4,* 467–483.

Hecker, T., & Steinberg, L. (2002). Psychological evaluation at juvenile court disposition. *Professional Psychology: Research and Practice, 33,* 300–306.

Heilbronner, R. L., Sweet, J. J., Morgan, J. E., Larrabee, G. J., & Millis, S. (2009). American Academy of Clinical Neuropsychology consensus conference statement on the neuropsychological assessment of effort, response bias, and malingering. *Clinical Neuropsychologist, 23,* 1093–1129.

Heilbrun, K. (1987). The assessment of competency for execution: An overview. *Behavioral Sciences & the Law, 5,* 383–396.

Heilbrun, K. (2001). *Principles of forensic mental health assessment.* New York, NY: Kluwer Academic/Plenum.

Heilbrun, K., & Brooks, S. (2010). Forensic psychology and forensic sciences: A proposed agenda for the next decade. *Psychology, Public Policy, and Law, 16,* 219–253.

Heilbrun, K., DeMatteo, D., & Goldstein, N. E. S. (Eds.). (2016). *APA handbook of juvenile justice.* Washington, DC: American Psychological Association.

Heilbrun, K., DeMatteo, D., Goldstein, N. E. S., Locklair, B., Murphy, M., & Giallella, C. (2016). Psychology and juvenile justice: Human development, law, science, and practice. In K. Heilbrun (Ed.), *APA handbook of psychology and juvenile justice* (pp. 3–20). Washington, DC: American Psychology Association.

Heilbrun, K., DeMatteo, D., Yashuhara, K., Brooks-Holliday, S., Shah, S., King, C., . . . & Laduke, C. (2012). Community-based alternatives for justice-involved individuals with severe mental illness: Review of the relevant research. *Criminal Justice and Behavior, 39,* 351–419.

Heilbrun, K., & Griffin, P. (1999). Forensic treatment: A review of programs and research. In R. Roesch, S. D. Hart, & J. R. P. Ogloff (Eds.), *Psychology and law: The state of the discipline* (pp. 241–274). New York, NY: Kluwer Academic/Plenum.

Heilbrun, K., Grisso, T., & Goldstein, A. M. (2009). *Foundations of forensic mental health assessment.* New York, NY: Oxford University Press.

Heilbrun, K., Marczyk, G. R., & DeMatteo, D. (2002). *Forensic mental health assessment: A casebook.* New York, NY: Oxford University Press.

Hellemans, S., Loeys, T., Buysse, A., Dewaele, A., & DeSmet, O. (2015). Intimate partner violence victimization among non-heterosexuals: Prevalence and associations with mental and sexual well-being. *Journal of Family Violence, 30,* 71–88.

Hellkamp, D. T., & Lewis, J. E. (1995). The consulting psychologist as an expert witness in sexual harassment and retaliation cases. *Consulting Psychology Journal: Practice and Research, 47,* 150–159.

Helmus, L., Babchishin, K. M., Camilleri, I. A., & Olver, M. E. (2011). Forensic psychology opportunities in Canadian graduate programs: An update of Simourd and Wormith's (1995) survey. *Canadian Psychology, 52,* 122–127.

Helmus, L., & Bourgon, G. (2011). Taking stock of 15 years of research on Spousal Assault Risk Assessment Guide: A critical review. *International Journal of Forensic Mental Health, 10,* 64–75.

Henderson, N. D. (1979). Criterion-related validity of personality and aptitude scales. In C. D. Spielberger (Ed.), *Police selection and evaluation: Issues and techniques* (pp. 36–44). Washington, DC: Hemisphere.

Henggeler, S. W. (1996). Treatment of violent juvenile offenders—we have the knowledge. *Journal of Family Psychology, 10*, 137–141.

Henggeler, S. W. (2001). Multisystemic therapy. *Residential Treatment for Children and Youth, 18*, 75–85.

Henggeler, S. W. (2016). Community-based intervention for juvenile offenders. In K. Heilbrun (Ed.), *APA handbook of psychology and juvenile justice* (pp. 575–595). Washington, DC: American Psychology Association.

Henggeler, S. W., & Borduin, C. M. (1990). *Family therapy and beyond: A multisystemic approach to treating the behavior problems of children and adolescents.* Pacific Grove, CA: Brooks/Cole.

Henker, B., & Whalen, C. K. (1989). Hyperactivity and attention deficits. *American Psychologist, 44*, 216–244.

Henry, M., & Greenfield, B. J. (2009). Therapeutic effects of psychological autopsies: The impact of investigating suicides on interviewees. *Crisis, 30*, 20–24.

Herman, J. L. (1992). Complex PTSD: A syndrome in survivors of prolonged and repeated trauma. *Journal of Traumatic Stress, 5*, 377–391.

Herndon, J. S. (2001). Law enforcement suicide: Psychological autopsies and psychometric traces. In D. C. Sheehan & J. I. Warren (Eds.), *Suicide and law enforcement* (pp. 223–234). Washington, DC: FBI Academy.

Herpers, P. C. M., Rommelse, N. N. J., Bons, D. M. A., Buitelaar, J. K., & Scheepers, F. E. (2012). Callous-unemotional traits as a cross-disorders construct. *Social Psychiatry and Psychiatric Epidemiology, 47*, 2045–2064.

Hess, A. K. (2006). Serving as an expert witness. In I. B. Weiner & A. K. Hess (Eds.), *The handbook of forensic psychology* (3rd ed., pp. 652–700). Hoboken, NJ: Wiley.

Hess, K. D. (2006). Understanding child domestic law issues: Custody, adoption, and abuse. In I. B. Weinter & A. K. Hess (Eds.), *The handbook of forensic psychology* (3rd ed., pp. 98–123). Hoboken, NJ: Wiley.

Heuven, E., & Bakker, A. B. (2003). Emotional dissonance and burnout among cabin attendants. *European Journal of Work and Organizational Psychology, 12*, 81–100.

Hickey, E. W. (1997). *Serial murderers and their victims.* Belmont, CA: Wadsworth.

Hickey, E. W. (2010). *Serial murderers and their victims* (5th ed.). Belmont, CA: Thomson/Wadsworth.

Hickle, K. E., & Roe-Sepowitz, D. E. (2010). Female juvenile arsonists: An exploratory look at characteristics and solo and group arson offences. *Legal and Criminological Psychology, 15*, 385–399.

Hickman, M. J. (2006, June). *Citizen complaints about police use of force.* Washington, DC: U.S. Department of Justice, Office of Justice Programs.

Hicks, B. M., Carlson, M. D., Blonigen, D. M., Patrick, C. J., Iacono, W. G., & MGue, M. (2012). Psychopathic personality traits and environmental contexts: Differential correlates, gender differences, and genetic mediation. *Personality Disorders: Theory, Research, and Treatment, 3*, 209–227.

Hiday, V. A. (2003). Outpatient commitment: The state of empirical research on its outcomes. *Psychology, Public Policy, and Law, 9*, 8–32.

Hilgard, E. R. (1986). *Divided consciousness: Multiple controls in human thought and action* (Expanded ed.). New York, NY: Wiley.

Hill, A., Haberman, N., Klussman, D., Berner, W., & Briken, P. (2008). Criminal recidivism in sexual homicide perpetrators. *International Journal of Offender Therapy and Comparative Criminology, 52*, 5–20.

Hill, J. (2000). The effects of sexual orientation in the courtroom: A double standard. *Journal of Homosexuality, 39*, 93–111.

Hill, M. S., & Fischer, A. R. (2001). Does entitlement mediate the link between masculinity and rape-related variables? *Journal of Counseling Psychology, 48*, 39–50.

Hillberg, T., Hamilton-Giachrisis, C., & Dixon, L. (2011). Review of meta-analysis on the association between child sexual abuse and adult mental health difficulties: A systematic approach. *Trauma, Violence, & Abuse, 12*, 38–49.

Hillbrand, M. (2001). Homicide-suicide and other forms of co-occurring aggression against self and against others. *Professional Psychology: Research and Practice, 32*, 626–635.

Hiller, M., Belenko, S., Taxman, F., Young, D., Perdoni, M., & Saum, C. (2010). Measuring drug court structure and operations: Key components and beyond. *Criminal Justice and Behavior, 37*, 933–950.

Hilton, N. Z., & Eke, A. W. (2016). Non-specialization of criminal careers among intimate partner violence offenders. *Criminal Justice and Behavior, 43*, 1347–1363.

Hilton, N. Z., Harris, G. T., & Rice, M. E. (2010a). Assessing the risk of future violent behavior. In N. Z. Hilton, G. T. Harris, & M. E. Rice (Eds.). *Risk assessment for domestically violent men: Tools for criminal justice, offender intervention, and victim services* (pp. 25–45). Washington, DC: American Psychological Association.

Hilton, N. Z., Harris, G. T., & Rice, M. E. (2010b). In-depth risk assessment and theoretical explanation. In N. Z. Hilton, G. T. Harris, & M. E. Rice (Eds.), *Risk assessment for domestically violent men: Tools for criminal justice, offender intervention, and victim services* (pp. 67–88). Washington, DC: American Psychological Association.

Hilton, N. Z., Harris, G. T., Rice, M. E., Houghton, R. E., & Eke, A. W. (2008). An in-depth actuarial assessment for wife assault recidivism: The Domestic Violence Risk Appraisal Guide. *Law and Human Behavior, 32*, 150–163.

Hilton, N. Z., Harris, G. T., Rice, M. E., Lang, C., Cormier, C. A., & Lines, K. J. (2004). A brief actuarial assessment for the prediction of wife assault recidivism: The Ontario Domestic Assault Risk Assessment. *Psychological Assessment, 16*, 267–275.

Hinduja, S., & Patchin, J. W. (2009). *Bullying beyond the schoolyard: Preventing and responding to cyberbullying*. Thousand Oaks, CA: Corwin Press.

Hinduja, S., & Patchin, J. W. (2016a). *2016 Cyberbullying Data*. Retrieved from https://cyberbullying.org/2016-cyberbullying-data

Hinduja, S., & Patchin, J. W. (2016b, January). *State cyberbullying laws*. Cyberbullying Research Center.

Hockenberry, S. (2013, June). *Juveniles in residential placement, 2010*. Washington, DC: U.S. Department of Justice, Office of Juvenile Justice and Delinquency Prevention.

Hockenberry, S. (2016). *Juveniles in residential placement, 2013*. Washington, DC: U.S. Department of Justice, Office of Juvenile Justice and Delinquency Prevention.

Hockenberry, S., & Puzzanchera, C. (2017). *Juvenile court statistics 2014*. Pittsburgh, PA: National Center for Juvenile Justice.

Hockenberry, S., Wachter, A., & Stadky, A. (2016). *Juvenile residential facility census, 2014: Selected findings*. Washington, DC: U.S. Department of Justice, Office of Juvenile Justice and Delinquency Prevention.

Hoge, R. D., & Andrews, D. A. (2002). *The Youth Level of Service/Case Management Inventory manual and scoring key*. Toronto, Canada: Multi-Health Systems.

Hoge, S. (2010). Commentary: Resistance to Jackson v. Indiana—Civil commitment of defendants who cannot be restored to competence. *Journal of the American Academy of Psychiatry and the Law, 38*, 359–364.

Hoge, S. K., Bonnie, R. G., Poythress, N., & Monahan, J. (1992). Attorney–client decision-making in criminal cases: Client competence and participation as perceived by their attorneys. *Behavioral Sciences & the Law, 10*, 385–394.

Hoge, S. K., Bonnie, R. G., Poythress, N., Monahan, J., Eisenberg, M., & Feucht-Haviar, T. (1997). The MacArthur Adjudicative Competence Study: Development and validation of a research instrument. *Law and Human Behavior, 21*, 141–179.

Hollin, C. R., Palmer, E. J., & Clark, D. (2003). Level of Service Inventory–Revised profile of English prisoners: A needs analysis. *Criminal Justice and Behavior, 30*, 422–440.

Holmes, R. M., & DeBurger, J. (1985). Profiles in terror: The serial murderer. *Federal Probation, 39*, 29–34.

Holmes, R. M., & DeBurger, J. (1988). *Serial murder*. Newbury Park, CA: Sage.

Holmes, R. M., & Holmes, S. T. (1998). *Serial murder* (2nd ed.). Thousand Oaks, CA: Sage.

Holmes, S. T., Hickey, E., & Holmes, R. M. (1991). Female serial murderesses: Constructing differentiating typologies. *Contemporary Journal of Criminal Justice, 7*, 245–256.

Holmes, S. T., & Holmes, R. M. (2002). *Sex crimes: Patterns and behavior* (2nd ed.). Thousand Oaks, CA: Sage.

Holtzworth-Munroe, A., & Stuart, G. L. (1994). Typologies of male batterers: Three subtypes and the differences among them. *Psychological Bulletin, 116*, 476–497.

Homant, R. J., & Kennedy, D. B. (1998). Psychological aspects of crime scene profiling: Validity research. *Criminal Justice and Behavior, 25*, 319–343.

Hopper, E. K. (2017). Trauma-informed psychological assessment of human trafficking survivors. *Women & Therapy, 40*, 12–30.

Horry, R., Memon, A., Wright, D. B., & Milne, R. (2012). Predictors of eyewitness identification decisions from video lineups in England: A field study. *Law and Human Behavior, 36*, 257–265.

Horvath, L. S., Logan, T. K., & Walker, R. (2002). Child custody cases: A content analysis of evaluations in practice. *Professional Psychology: Research and Practice, 33*, 557–565.

Howard, A. M., Landau, S., & Pryor, J. B. (2014). Peer bystanders to bullying: Who wants to play with the victim? *Journal of Abnormal Child Psychology, 42*, 265–276.

Howe, M. L., & Courage, M. L. (1997). The emergence and early development of autobiographical memory. *Psychological Review, 104*, 499–523.

Hubbard, D. J., & Pratt, T. C. (2002). A meta-analysis of the predictors of delinquency among girls. *Journal of Offender Rehabilitation, 34*, 1–13.

Hubbs-Tait, L., Nation, J. R., & Krebs, N. F., & Bellinger, D. C. (2005). Neurotoxins, micronutrients, and social environments. *Psychological Science in the Public Interest, 6*, 57–121.

Huesmann, L. R., Moise-Titus, J., Podolski, C. L., & Eron, L. D. (2003). Longitudinal relations between children's exposure to TV violence and their aggressive and violent behavior in young adulthood: 1977–1992. *Developmental Psychology, 39*, 201–221.

Hugenberg, K., Young, S. G., Bernstein, M. J., & Sacco, D. F. (2010). The categorization-individuation model: An integrative account of the other-race recognition deficit. *Psychological Review, 117*, 1168–1187.

Hume, D. L., & Sidun, N. M. (2017). Human trafficking of women and girls: Characteristics, commonalities, and complexities. *Women & Therapy, 40*, 7–11.

Hunt, J. W. (2010). *Admissibility of expert testimony in state courts*. Minneapolis, MN: Aircraft Builders Council.

Hunter, J. A., & Becker, J. V. (1999). Motivators of adolescent sex offenders and treatment perspectives. In J. Shaw (Ed.), *Sexual aggression* (pp. 211–234). Washington, DC: American Psychiatric Press.

Hunter, J. A., & Figueredo, A. J. (2000). The influence of personality and history of sexual victimization in the prediction of juvenile perpetrated child molestation. *Behavior Modification, 24*, 241–263.

Hyland, S., Langton, L., & Davis, E. (2015, November). *Police use of nonfatal force, 2002–11*. Washington, DC: U.S. Department of Justice, Bureau of Justice Statistics.

Iacono, W. G. (2008). Effective policing: Understanding how polygraph tests work and are used. *Criminal Justice and Behavior, 35*, 1295–1308.

Iacono, W. G. (2009). Psychophysiological detection of deception and guilty knowledge. In J. L. Skeem, K. S. Douglas, & S. O. Lilienfeld (Eds.), *Psychological science in the courtroom: Consensus and controversy* (pp. 224–241). New York, NY: Guilford Press.

Iacono, W. G., & Patrick, C. J. (1999). Polygraph ("lie detector") testing: The state of the art. In A. K. Hess & I. B. Weiner (Eds.), *The handbook of forensic psychology* (2nd ed., pp. 440–473). New York, NY: Wiley.

Iacono, W. G., & Patrick, C. J. (2014). Employing polygraph assessment. In I. B Weiner & R. K. Otto (Eds.), *Handbook of forensic psychology* (4th ed., pp. 613–658). New York, NY: Wiley.

IACP Police Psychological Services Section. (2010, February 5). FFDE guidelines adopted by IACP Board in January, 2010. *Police Psychological Services Section Newsletter, 9*, 1.

Icove, D. J., & Estepp, M. H. (1987, April). Motive-based offender profiles of arson and fire–related crime. *FBI Law Enforcement Bulletin*, 17–23.

Immarigeon, R. (Ed.). (2011). *Women and girls in the criminal justice system Policy issues and practice strategies*. Kingston, NJ: Civic Research Institute.

In re M-A-M-, 25 I. & N. Dec. 474 (2011).

Inbau, F. E., Reid, J. E., Buckley, J. P., & Jayne, B. C. (2004). *Criminal interrogation and confessions* (4th ed.). Boston, MA: Jones & Bartlett.

Inbau, F. E., Reid, J. E., Buckley, J. P., & Jayne, B. C. (2013). *Criminal interrogation and confessions* (5th ed.). Burlington, MA: Jones & Bartlett Learning.

Innocence Project. (2010, December 14). *Fact sheet: Eyewitness identification reform*. Retrieved from www.innocenceproject.org

Innocence Project. (2014, January 8). *Home page*. Retrieved from http://www.innocenceproject.org

Institute of Medicine & National Research Council. (2013). *Confronting commercial sexual exploitation and sex trafficking of minors in the United States*. Washington, DC: National Academic Press.

International Association of Chiefs of Police (IACP). (2002). *Fitness for duty evaluation guidelines*. Alexandria, VA: Author.

Inwald, R. E. (1992). *Inwald Personality Inventory technical manual* (Rev. ed.). Kew Gardens, NY: Hilson Research.

Inwald, R. E., & Brobst, K. E. (1988). *Hilson Personnel Profile/Success Quotient manual*. Kew Gardens, NY: Hilson Research.

Jackson, H. F., Glass, C., & Hope, S. (1987). A functional analysis of recidivistic arson. *British Journal of Clinical Psychology, 26*, 175–185.

Jackson, J. L., van Koppen, P. J., & Herbrink, J. C. M. (1993). Does the service meet the needs? An evaluation of consumer satisfaction profile analysis and investigative advice offered by the Scientific Research Advisory Unit of the National Criminal Intelligence Division (CRI)—The Netherlands (NISCALE Report NSCR, 93-05). Leiden, Netherlands: Netherlands Institute for the Study of Criminality and Law Enforcement.

Jackson, M. S., & Springer, D. W. (1997). Social work practice with African-American juvenile gangs: Professional challenge. In C. A. McNeece & A. R. Roberts (Eds.), *Policy and practice in the justice system* (pp. 231–248). Chicago, IL: Nelson-Hall.

Jackson, T. L., Petretic-Jackson, P. A., & Witte, T. H. (2002). Mental health assessment tools and techniques for working with battered women. In A. R. Roberts (Ed.), *Handbook of domestic violence intervention strategies* (pp. 278–297). New York, NY: Oxford University Press.

Jaffe, P. G., Johnston, J. R., Crooks, C. V., & Bala, N. (2008). Custody disputes involving allegations of domestic violence: The need for differentiated approaches to parenting plans. *Family Court Review, 46*, 500–522.

James, D. J., & Glaze, L. E. (2006). *Mental health problems in prison and jail inmates*. Washington, DC: U.S. Department of Justice.

Janus, E. S. (2000). Sexual predator commitment laws: Lessons for law and the behavioral sciences. *Behavioral Sciences & the Law, 18*, 5–21.

Janus, E. S., & Meehl, P. E. (1997). Assessing the legal standard for predictions of dangerousness in sex offender commitment proceedings. *Psychology, Public Policy, and Law, 3*, 33–64.

Janus, E. S., & Walbek, N. H. (2000). Sex offender commitments in Minnesota: A descriptive study of second-generation commitments. *Behavioral Sciences & the Law, 18*, 343–374.

Javdani, S., Sadeh, N., & Verona, E. (2011). Expanding our lens: Female pathways to antisocial behavior in adolescence and adulthood. *Clinical Psychology Review, 31*, 1324–1348.

Jenkins, P. (1988). Serial murder in England, 1940–1985. *Journal of Criminal Justice, 16*, 1–15.

Jenkins, P. (1993). Chance or choice: The selection of serial murder victims. In A. V. Wilson (Ed.), *Homicide: The victim/offender connection* (pp. 461–477). Cincinnati, OH: Anderson.

Johnson, C. C., & Chanhatasilpa, C. (2003). The race/ethnicity and poverty nexus of violent crime: Reconciling differences in Chicago's community area homicide rates. In D. F. Hawkins (Ed.), *Violent crime: Assessing race and ethnic differences*. Cambridge, England: Cambridge University Press.

Johnson, L. B., Todd, M., & Subramanian, G. (2005). Violence in police families: Work–family spillover. *Journal of Family Violence, 20*, 3–12.

Johnson, L. G., & Beech, A. (2017, May). Rape myth acceptance in convicted rapists: A systematic review of the literature. *Aggression and Violent Behavior, 34*, 20–34.

Johnson, M. P. (2006). Conflict and control: Gender symmetry and asymmetry in domestic violence. *Violence Against Women, 12,* 1003–1018.

Johnson, R. (1996). *Hard time: Understanding and reforming the prison* (2nd ed.). Belmont, CA: Wadsworth.

Johnston, J. R. (1995). Research update: Children's adjustment in sole custody compared to joint custody families and principles for custody decision making. *Family and Conciliation Courts Review, 33,* 415–425.

Johnston, J. R., & Girdner, L. K. (2001, January). Family abductors: Descriptive profiles and prevention interventions. *Juvenile Justice Bulletin.* Washington, DC: U.S. Department of Justice, Office of Juvenile Justice and Delinquency.

Jones, L., Hughes, M., & Unterstaller, U. (2001). Post-traumatic stress disorder (PTSD) in victims of domestic violence: A review of the research. *Trauma, Violence, & Abuse, 2,* 99–119.

Jouriles, E. N., McDonald, R., Norwood, W. D., Ware, H. S., Spiller, L. C., & Swank, P. R. (1998). Knives, guns, and interparent violence: Relations with child behavior problems. *Journal of Family Psychology, 12,* 178–194.

Kabat-Farr, D., & Cortina, L. M. (2014). Sex-based harassment in employment: New insights into gender and context. *Law and Human Behavior, 38,* 58–72.

Kaeble, D., & Glaze, L. (2016). *Correctional populations in the United States,* 2015. Washington, DC: U.S. Department of Justice, Bureau of Justice Statistics.

Kafrey, D. (1980). Playing with matches: Children and fire. In D. Canter (Ed.), *Fires and human behaviour* (pp. 47–62). Chichester, England: Wiley.

Kahn, K. B., & McMahon, J. M. (2015). Shooting deaths of unarmed racial minorities: Understanding the role of racial stereotypes on decisions to shoot. *Translational Issues in Psychological Science, 1,* 310–320.

Kahn, K. B., Steele, J. S., McMahon, J. M., & Stewart, G. (2017). How suspect race affects police use of force in an interaction over time. *Law and Human Behavior, 41,* 117–126.

Kahn, R. E., Frick, P. J., Youngstrom, E., Findling, R. L., & Youngstrom, J. K. (2012). The effects of including a callous-unemotional specifier for the diagnosis of conduct disorder. *Journal of Child Psychology and Psychiatry, 53,* 271–282.

Kamena, M. D., Gentz, D., Hays, V., Bohl-Penrod, N., & Greene, L. W. (2011). Peer support teams fill an emotional void in law enforcement agencies. *Police Chief, 78,* 80–84.

Kapp, M. B., & Mossman, D. (1996). Measuring decisional capacity: Cautions on the construction of a "Capacimeter." *Psychology, Public Policy, and Law, 2,* 45–95.

Karmen, A. (2001). *Crime victims: An introduction to victimology* (4th ed.). Belmont, CA: Wadsworth.

Karmen, A. (2009). *Crime victims: An introduction to victimology* (7th ed.). Florence, KY: Cengage Learning.

Karmen, A. (2013). *Crime victims: An introduction to victimology* (8th ed.). Belmont, CA: Wadsworth/Cengage Learning.

Karon, B. P., & Widener, A. J. (1999). Repressed memories: Just the facts. *Professional Psychology: Research and Practice, 30,* 625–626.

Kassin, S. M. (1997). The psychology of confession evidence. *American Psychologist, 52,* 221–233.

Kassin, S. M. (2008). Confession evidence: Commonsense myths and misconceptions. *Criminal Justice and Behavior, 35,* 1309–1322.

Kassin, S. M., Drizin, S., Grisso, T., Gudjonsson, G. H., Leo, R. A., & Redlich, A. D. (2010). Police-induced confessions: Risk factors and recommendations. *Law and Human Behavior, 34,* 3–38.

Kassin, S. M., Goldstein, C. G., & Savitsky, K. (2003). Behavior confirmation in the interrogation room: On the dangers of presuming guilt. *Law and Human Behavior, 27,* 187–203.

Kassin, S. M., & Gudjonsson, G. H. (2004). The psychology of confessions: A review of the literature and issues. *Psychological Science in the Public Interest, 5,* 33–67.

Kassin, S. M., & Kiechel, K. L. (1996). The social psychology of false confessions: Compliance, internalization, and confabulation. *Psychological Science, 7,* 125–128.

Kassin, S. M., Leo, R. A., Meissner, C. A., Richman, K. D., Colwell, L. H., Leach, A.-M., . . . & Fon, D. L. (2007). Police interviewing and interrogation: A self-report survey of police practices and beliefs. *Law and Human Behavior, 31,* 381–400.

Kassin, S. M., Perillo, J. T., Appleby, S. C., & Kukucka, J. (2015). Confessions. In B. L. Cutler & P. A. Zapf (Eds.), *APA handbook of forensic psychology: Vol. 2. Criminal investigation, adjudication, and sentencing outcomes* (pp. 245–270). Washington, DC: American Psychological Association.

Kassin, S. M., & Wrightsman, L. S. (1985). Confession evidence. In S. M. Kassin & L. S. Wrightsman (Eds.), *The psychology of evidence and trial procedure* (pp. 67–94). Beverly Hills, CA: Sage.

Katz, L. S., Cojucar, G., Beheshti, S., Nakamura, E., & Murray, M. (2012). Military sexual trauma during deployment to Iraq and Afghanistan: Prevalence, readjustment, and gender differences. *Violence and Victims, 27,* 487–499.

Kaufer, S., & Mattman, J. W. (2002). *Workplace violence: An employer's guide.* Palm Springs, CA: Workplace Violence Research Institute.

Kaufman, R. L. (2011). Forensic mental health consulting in family law: Where have we come from? Where are we going? *Journal of Child Custody, 8,* 5–31.

Kebbell, M. R., & Wagstaff, G. G. (1998). Hypnotic interviewing: The best way to interview eyewitnesses. *Behavioral Sciences & the Law, 16,* 115–129.

Keelan, C. M., & Fremouw, W. J. (2013). Child versus peer/adult offenders: A critical review of the juvenile sex offender literature. *Aggression and Violent Behavior, 18*, 732–744.

Keenan, K., & Shaw, D. (2003). Starting at the beginning: Exploring the etiology of antisocial behavior in the first years of life. In B. B. Lahey, T. E. Moffitt, & A. Caspi (Eds.), *Causes of conduct disorder and juvenile delinquency* (pp. 153–181). New York, NY: Guilford Press.

Kehoe, E. G., & Tandy, K. B. (2006, April). *An assessment of access to counsel and quality of representation in delinquency proceedings.* Washington, DC: National Juvenile Defender Center.

Keilin, W. G., & Bloom, L. J. (1986). Child custody evaluation practices: A survey of experienced professionals. *Professional Psychology: Research and Practice, 17*, 338–346.

Keita, G. P. (2014, September 9). *Testimony on militarization of police forces* [Transcript]. Presented at the U.S. Senate Committee on Homeland Security and Governmental Affairs, Washington, DC. Retrieved from http://www.apa.org/about/gr/pi/news/2014/militarization-testimony.aspx

Kelly, C. E., Miller, J. C., Redlich, A. D., & Kleinman, S. M. (2013). A taxonomy of interrogation methods. *Psychology, Public Policy, and Law, 19*, 165–178.

Kelly, J. B., & Johnson, M. P. (2008). Differentiation among types of intimate partner violence: Research update and implications for interventions. *Family Court Review, 46*, 476–499.

Kelly, J. B., & Lamb, M. E. (2003). Developmental issues in relocation cases involving young children: When, whether, and how? *Journal of Family Psychology, 17*, 193–205.

Kelman, H. (1958). Compliance, identification, and internalization. *Journal of Conflict Resolution, 2*, 51–60.

Kendall, P. C., & Hammen, C. (1995). *Abnormal psychology.* Boston, MA: Houghton Mifflin.

Kessler, R. C., Berglund, P., Demler, O., Jin, R., Merikangas, K. R., & Walter, E. E. (2005). Lifetime prevalence and age-of-onset distributions of DSM-IV disorders in the National Comorbidity Survey Replication. *Archives of General Psychiatry, 62*, 593–602.

Kessler, R. C., Sonnega, A., Bromet, E., Hughes, M., & Nelson, C. B. (1995). Posttraumatic stress disorder in the National Comorbidity Survey. *Archives of General Psychiatry, 52*, 1048–1060.

Kihlstrom, J. F. (2001). Martin T. Orne (1927–2000). *American Psychologist, 56*, 754–755.

Kilford, E. J., Garrett, E., & Blakemore, S. J. (2016). The development of social cognition in adolescence: An integrated perspective. *Neuroscience and Biobehavioral Reviews, 70*, 106–120.

Kilmann, P. R., Sabalis, R. F., Gearing, M. L., Bukstel, L. H., & Scovern, A. W. (1982). The treatment of sexual paraphilias: A review of the outcome research. *Journal of Sex Research, 18*, 193–252.

Kilpatrick, D. G., Edmunds, C., & Seymour, A. (1992). *Rape in America: A report to the nation.* Arlington, VA: National Center for Victims of Crime.

Kilpatrick, D. G., Resnick, H. S., Ruggerio, K., Conoscent, L. M., & McCauley, J. (2007, February). *Drug-facilitated, incapacitated, and forcible rape: A national study.* Charlestown: Medical University of South Carolina.

Kilpatrick, D. G., & Saunders, B. E. (1997, November). *Prevalence and consequences of child victimization: Results from the National Survey of Adolescents: Final report.* Washington, DC: U.S. Department of Justice, National Institute of Justice.

Kilpatrick, D. G., Saunders, B. E., Veronen, L. J., Best, C. L., & Von, J. M. (1987). Criminal victimization: Lifetime prevalence, reporting to police, and psychological impact. *Crime and Delinquency, 33*, 479–489.

Kilpatrick, D. G., Whalley, A., & Edmunds, C. (2002). Sexual assault. In A. Seymour, M. Murray, J. Sigmon, M. Hook, C. Edwards, M. Gaboury, & G. Coleman. (Eds.), *National Victim Assistance Academy textbook.* Washington, DC: U.S. Department of Justice, Office for Victims of Crime.

Kim, H. S. (2011). Consequences of parental divorce for child development. *American Sociological Review, 76*, 487–511.

Kim, S., Pendergrass, T., & Zelon, H. (2012). *Boxed in: The true cost of extreme isolation in New York's prisons.* New York: New York Civil Liberties Union.

King, L., & Snook, B. (2009). Peering inside a Canadian interrogation room: An examination of the Reid model of interrogation, influence tactics, and coercive strategies. *Criminal Justice and Behavior, 36*, 674–694.

King, R., & Norgard, K. (1999). What about families? Using the impact on death row defendants' family members as a mitigating factor in death penalty sentencing hearing. *Florida State University Law Review, 26*, 1119–1176.

King, W. R., Holmes, S. T., Henderson, M. L., & Latessa, E. J. (2001). The community corrections partnership: Examining the long-term effects of youth participation in an Afrocentric diversion program. *Crime & Delinquency, 47*, 558–572.

Kinports, K. (2002). Sex offenses. In K. L. Hall (Ed.), *The Oxford companion to American law* (pp. 736–738). New York, NY: Oxford University Press.

Kirby, R., Shakespeare-Finch, J., & Palk, G. (2011). Adaptive and maladaptive coping strategies predict post-trauma outcomes in ambulance personnel. *Traumatology, 17*, 25–34.

Kircher, J. C., & Raskin, D. C. (2002). Computer methods for the psychophysiological detection of deception. In M. Kleiner (Ed.), *Handbook of polygraph testing* (pp. 287–326). San Diego, CA: Academic Press.

Kirk, T., & Bersoff, D. N. (1996). How many procedural safeguards does it take to get a psychiatrist to leave the light bulb unchanged? A due process analysis of the MacArthur Treatment Competence Study. *Psychology, Public Policy, and Law, 2*, 45–72.

Kirkland, K., & Kirkland, K. (2001). Frequency of child custody evaluation complaints and related disciplinary action: A survey of the association of state and provincial psychology boards. *Professional Psychology: Research and Practice, 32*, 171–174.

Kirschman, E. (2007). *I love a cop: What police families need to know* (Rev. ed.). New York, NY: Guilford Press.

Kitaeff, J. (2011). *Handbook of police psychology*. New York, NY: Routledge/Taylor & Francis.

Kleim, B., & Westphal, M. (2011). Mental health in first responders: A review and recommendation for prevention and intervention strategies. *Traumatology, 17*, 17–24.

Kliewer, W., Lepore, S. J., Oskin, D., & Johnson, P. D. (1998). The role of social and cognitive processes in children's adjustment to community violence. *Journal of Consulting and Clinical Psychology, 66*, 199–209.

Kloess, J. A., Beech, A. R., & Harkins, L. (2014). Online child sexual exploitation: Prevalence, Process, Offender Characteristics. *Trauma, Violence & Abuse, 15*, 126–139.

Knapp, S., & VandeCreek, L. (2000). Recovered memories of child abuse: Is there an underlying professional consensus? *Professional Psychology: Research and Practice, 31*, 365–371.

Knight, K., & Simpson, D. D. (2007, September). Special issue: Offender needs and functioning assessments from a national cooperative research program. *Criminal Justice and Behavior, 34*, 1105–1112.

Knight, R. A. (1989). An assessment of the concurrent validity of a child molester typology. *Journal of Interpersonal Violence, 4*, 131–150.

Knight, R. A. (2010). Typologies for rapists—the generation of a new standard model. In A. Schlank (Ed.), *The sexual predator: Legal issues of assessment treatment: Vol. IV* (pp. 17.2–17.24). Kingston, NJ: Civic Research Center.

Knight, R. A., Carter, D. L., & Prentky, R. A. (1989). A system for the classification of child molesters: Reliability and application. *Journal of Interpersonal Violence, 4*(1), 3–23.

Knight, R. A., & King, M. W. (2012). Typologies for child molesters: The generation of a new structured model. In B. K. Schwartz (Ed.), *The sexual offender: Vol. 7* (pp. 5.2–5.7). Kingston, NJ: Civil Research Institute.

Knight, R. A., & Prentky, R. A. (1987). The developmental antecedents and adult adaptations of rapist subtypes. *Criminal Justice and Behavior, 14*, 403–426.

Knight, R. A., & Prentky, R. A. (1990). Classifying sexual offenders: The development and corroboration of taxonomic models. In W. L. Marshall, D. R. Laws, & H. E. Barbaree (Eds.), *The handbook of sexual assault: Issues, theories, and treatment of the offender* (pp. 23–52). New York, NY: Plenum.

Knight, R. A., & Prentky, R. A. (1993). Exploring characteristics for classifying juvenile offenders. In H. E. Barbaree, W. L. Marshall, & S. M. Hudson (Eds.), *The juvenile sex offender* (pp. 45–78). New York, NY: Guilford Press.

Knight, R. A., Rosenberg, R., & Schneider, B. A. (1985). Classification of sexual offenders: Perspectives, methods, and validation. In A. W. Burgess (Ed.), *Rape and sexual assault* (pp. 222–293). New York, NY: Garland.

Knight, R. A., Warren, J. I., Reboussin, R., & Soley, B. J. (1998). Predicting rapist type from crime-scene variables. *Criminal Justice and Behavior, 25*, 46–80.

Knoll, C., & Sickmund, M. (2010, June). *Cases in juvenile court, 2007*. Washington, DC: U.S. Department of Justice, Office of Juvenile Justice and Delinquency Prevention.

Knoll, C., & Sickmund, M. (2012, October). *Cases in juvenile court, 2009*. Washington, DC: U.S. Department of Justice, Office of Juvenile Justice and Delinquency Prevention.

Knoll, J. L. (2008). The psychological autopsy, Part I: Applications and methods. *Journal of Psychiatric Practice, 14*, 393–397.

Knutson, J. F., Lawrence, E., Taber, S. M., Bank, L., & DeGarmo, D. S. (2009). Assessing children's exposure to intimate partner violence. *Clinical Child and Family Psychology Review, 12*, 157–173.

Kochanska, G., Murray, K., & Coy, K. (1997). Inhibitory control as a contributor to conscience in childhood: From toddler to early school age. *Child Development, 68*, 263–277.

Kocsis, R. N. (2009). Criminal profiling: Facts, fictions, and courtroom admissibility. In J. L. Skeem, K. S. Douglas, & S. O. Lilienfeld (Eds.), *Psychological science in the courtroom: Consensus and controversy* (pp. 245–262). New York, NY: Guilford Press.

Kohout, J., & Wicherski, M. (2010). *2011 graduate study in psychology snapshot: Applications, acceptances, enrollments, and degrees awarded to master's- and doctoral-level students in U.S. and Canadian graduate departments of psychology: 2009–1010*. Washington, DC: Center for Workforce Studies, American Psychological Association.

Kois, L., Wellbeloved-Stone, Chauhan, P., & Warren, J. I. (2017). Combined evaluations of competency to stand trial and mental state at the time of the offense: An overlooked methodological consideration? *Law and Human Behavior, 41*, 217–229.

Kolko, D. (Ed.). (2002). *Handbook on firesetting in children and youth*. Boston, MA: Academic Press.

Kolko, D. J., & Kazdin, A. E. (1989). The children's firesetting interview with psychiatrically referred and nonreferred children. *Journal of Abnormal Child Psychology, 17*, 609–624.

Koocher, G. P., Goodman, G. S., White, C. S., Friedrich, W. N., Sivan, A. B., & Reynolds, C. R. (1995). Psychological science and the use of anatomically detailed dolls in child-sexual assessments. *Psychological Bulletin, 118*, 199–222.

Koss, M. P., & Dinero, T. E. (1988). Predictors of sexual aggression among a national sample of male college students. In R. A. Prentky & V. L. Quinsey (Eds.), *Human sexual aggression: Current perspectives* (pp. 133–147). New York, NY: New York Academy of Sciences.

Kosson, D. S., Cyterski, T. D. Steuerwald, B. L., Neumann, C. S., & Walker-Matthews, S. (2002). The reliability and validity of the Psychopathy Checklist: Youth Version in non–incarcerated adolescent males. *Psychological Assessment, 14*, 97–109.

Kosson, D. S., Neumann, C. S., Forth, A. E., Salekin, R. T., Hare, R. D., Krischer, M. K., . . . & Sevecke, K. (2013). Factor structure of the Hare Psychopathy Checklist: Youth Version (PCL: YV) in adolescent females. *Psychological Assessment, 25*, 71–83.

Kosson, D. S., Smith, S. S., & Newman, J. P. (1990). Evaluating the construct validity of psychopathy in Black and White male inmates: Three preliminary studies. *Journal of Abnormal Psychology, 99*, 250–259.

Kostelnik, J. O., & Reppucci, N. D. (2009). Reid training and sensitivity to developmental maturity in interrogation: Results from a national survey of police. *Behavioral Sciences and the Law, 27*, 361–379.

Kourlis, R. L. (2012). It is just good business: The case for supporting reform in the divorce court. *Family Court Review, 50*, 549–557.

Kovera, M. B., & Cass, S. A. (2002). Compelled mental health examinations, liability decisions, and damage awards in sexual harassment cases: Issues for jury research. *Psychology, Public Policy, and Law, 8*, 96–114.

Kovera, M. B., Russano, M. B., & McAuliff, B. D. (2002). Assessment of the commonsense psychology underlying *Daubert:* Legal decision makers' abilities to evaluate expert evidence in hostile work environment cases. *Psychology, Public Policy, and Law, 8*, 180–200.

Kowalski, R. W., Giumetti, G. W., Schroeder, A. N., & Lattanner, M. R. (2014). Bullying in the digital age: A critical review and meta-analysis of cyberbullying research among youth. *Psychological Bulletin, 140*, 1073–1137.

Kowalski, R. W., & Limber, S. P. (2007). Electronic bullying among middle school students. *Journal of Adolescent Health, 41*, s22–s30.

Kozu, J. (1999). Domestic violence in Japan. *American Psychologist, 54*, 50–54.

Krapohl, D. J. (2002). The polygraph in personnel selection. In M. Kleiner (Ed.), *Handbook of polygraph testing* (pp. 217–236). San Diego, CA: Academic Press.

Kratcoski, P. C. (1994). *Correctional counseling and treatment* (3rd ed.). Prospect Heights, IL: Waveland.

Krauss, D. A., & Sales, B. D. (2000). Legal standards, expertise, and experts in the resolution of contested child custody cases. *Psychology, Public Policy, and Law, 6*, 843–879.

Krauss, D. A., & Sales, B. D. (2001). The effects of clinical and scientific expert testimony on juror decision making in capital sentencing. *Psychology, Public Police, and Law, 7*, 267–310.

Krauss, D. A., & Sales, B. D. (2014). Training in forensic psychology. In I. B. Weiner & R. K. Otto (Eds.), *The handbook of forensic psychology* (4th ed., pp. 111–134). New York, NY: Wiley.

Kreeger, J. L. (2003). Family psychology and family law—a family court judge's perspective: Comment on the special issue. *Journal of Family Psychology, 17*, 260–262.

Kreis, M. K. F., & Cooke, D. J. (2011). Capturing the psychopathic female: A prototypicality analysis of the assessment of psychopathic personality (CAPP) across gender. *Behavioral Sciences & the Law, 29*, 634–648.

Krogstad, J. M. (2016, September 8). *Key facts about how the U.S. Hispanic population is changing.* Pew Research Center. Retrieved from www.pewresearch.org

Kropp, P. R. (2004). Some questions regarding spousal assault risk assessment. *Violence Against Women, 10*, 676–697.

Kropp, P. R., Hart, S. D., Webster, C. E., & Eaves, D. (1998). *Spousal Assault Risk Assessment: User's guide.* Toronto, Canada: Multi-Health Systems.

Kruh, I., & Grisso, T. (2009). *Evaluation of juveniles' competence to stand trial.* New York, NY: Oxford University Press.

Kubany, E. S., Haynes, S. N., Leisen, M. B., Ownes, J. A., Kaplan, A. S., Watson, S. B., . . . & Burns, K. (2000). Development and preliminary validation of a brief broad-spectrum measure of trauma exposure: the Traumatic Life Events Questionnaire. *Psychological Assessment, 12*, 200–224.

Kubany, E. S., Leisen, M. B., Kaplan, A. S., & Kelly, M. P. (2000). Validation of a brief measure of posttraumatic stress disorder: The Distressing Event Questionnaire (DEQ). *Psychological Assessment, 12*, 197–209.

Kurke, M. I., & Scrivner, E. M. (Eds.). (1995). *Police psychology into the 21st century.* Hillsdale, NJ: Erlbaum.

Kurt, J. L. (1995). Stalking as a variant of domestic violence. *Bulletin of the American Academy of Psychiatry and Law, 23*, 219–230.

Kuther, T. L., & Morgan, R. D. (2013). *Careers in psychology: Opportunities in a changing world* (4th ed.). Belmont, CA: Wadsworth/Cengage Learning.

La Fon, D. S. (2008). The psychological autopsy. In B. E. Turvey (Ed.), *Criminal profiling: An introduction to behavioral evidence analysis* (pp. 419–430). London, England: Academic Press.

La Fond, J. Q. (2000). The future of involuntary civil commitment in the U.S.A. after *Kansas v. Hendricks. Behavioral Sciences & the Law, 18*, 153–167.

La Fond, J. Q. (2002). Criminal law principles. In K. L. Hall (Ed.), *The Oxford companion to American law.* New York, NY: Oxford University Press.

La Fond, J. Q. (2003). Outpatient commitment's next frontier: Sexual predators. *Psychology, Public Policy, and Law, 9*, 159–182.

LaFortune, K. A., & Carpenter, B. N. (1998). Custody evaluations: A survey of mental health professionals. *Behavioral Sciences & the Law, 16*, 207–224.

Lahey, B. B., Loeber, R., Hart, E. L., Frick, P. J., Applegate, B., Zhang, Q., . . . & Russo M. F. (1995). Four-year longitudinal study of conduct disorder in boys: Patterns and predictors of persistence. *Journal of Abnormal Psychology, 104,* 83–93.

Laird, R. D., Jordan, K., Dodge, K. A., Pettit, G. S., & Bates, J. E. (2001). Peer rejection in childhood, involvement with antisocial peers in early adolescence, and the development of externalizing problems. *Development and Psychopathology, 13,* 337–354.

Lamb, H. R., Weinberger, I. E., & Gross, B. H. (2004). Mentally ill persons in the criminal justice system: Some perspectives. *Psychiatric Quarterly, 75,* 107–126.

Lamb, M. E. (2016). Difficulties translating research on forensic interview practices and practitioners: Finding water, leading horses, but can we get them to drink? *American Psychologist, 71,* 710–718.

Lamb, M. E., & Malloy, L. C. (2013). Child development and the law. In R. M. Lerner, M. A. Easterbrook, J. Mistry, & I. B. Weiner (Eds.), *Handbook of psychology: Vol. 6. Developmental psychology* (2nd ed., pp. 571–593). Hoboken, NJ: Wiley.

Lambert, S. F., & Lawson, G. (2013). Resilience of professional counselors following Hurricanes Katrina and Rita. *Journal of Counseling and Development, 91,* 261–268.

Lambie, I., Ioane, J., Randell, I., & Seymour, F. (2013). Offending behaviours of child and adolescent firesetters over a 10-year follow-up. *Journal of Child Psychology and Psychiatry, 54,* 1295–1307.

Lambie, I., McCardle, S., & Coleman, R. (2002). Where there's smoke there's fire: Firesetting behaviour in children and adolescents. *New Zealand Journal of Psychology, 31,* 73–79.

Lambie, I., & Randell, I. (2011). Creating a firestorm: A review of children who deliberately light fires. *Clinical Psychology Review, 31,* 307–327.

Lambie, I., & Randell, I. (2013). The impact of incarceration on juvenile offenders. *Clinical Psychology Review, 33,* 448–459.

Lancaster, G. L. J., Vrij, A., Hope, L., & Waller, B. (2013). Sorting the liars from the truth tellers: The benefits of asking unanticipated questions on lie detection. *Applied Cognitive Psychology, 27,* 107–114.

Langan, P. A., & Levin, D. J. (2002, June). *Recidivism of prisoners released in 1994.* Washington, DC: U.S. Department of Justice, Bureau of Justice Statistics.

Langevin, R. (1983). *Sexual strands.* Hillsdale, NJ: Erlbaum.

Langevin, R., Hébert, M., & Cossette, L. (2015). Emotion regulation as a mediator of the relation between sexual abuse and behavior problems in children. *Child Abuse and Neglect, 46,* 16–26.

Langhinrichsen-Rohling, J. (2005). Top 10 greatest "hits": Important findings and future directions for intimate violence research. *Journal of Interpersonal Violence, 20,* 108–118.

Langman, P. (2013). Thirty-five rampage school shooters: Trends, patterns, and typology. In N. Böckler, T. Seeger, & P. Sitzer (Eds.), *School shootings: International research, case studies, and concepts for prevention* (pp. 131–158). New York, NY: Springer.

Langton, L. (2010, June). *Women in law enforcement, 1987–2008.* Washington, DC: U.S. Department of Justice, Bureau of Justice Statistics.

Langton, L., Berzofsky, M., Krebs, C., & Smiley-McDonald, H. (2012, August). *Victimizations not reported to the police, 2006–2010.* Washington, DC: U.S. Department of Justice, Bureau of Justice Statistics.

Lanyon, R. I. (1986). Theory and treatment in child molestation. *Journal of Consulting and Clinical Psychology, 54,* 176–182.

Lara, C., Fayyad, J., de Graaf, R., Kessler, R. C., Aguilar-Gaxiola, S., Angermeyer, M., . . . & Sampson, N. (2009). Childhood predictors of adult attention-deficit/hyperactivity disorder: Results from the World Health Organization World Mental Health Survey initiative. *Biological Psychiatry, 65,* 46–54.

Lareau, C. R. (2013). Civil commitment and involuntary hospitalization of the mentally ill. In R. K. Otto & I. B. Weiner (Eds.), *Handbook of psychology: Vol. 11. Forensic psychology* (2nd ed., pp. 308–331). Hoboken, NJ: Wiley.

Larkin, R. W. (2007). *Comprehending Columbine.* Philadelphia, PA: Temple University Press.

Larson, K., & Grisso, T. (2012, Summer). Juvenile competence to stand trial: Issues in research, policy, and practice. *American Psychology-Law Society Newsletter,* 18–20.

Lassiter, G. D., & Meissner, C. A. (Eds.). (2010). *Police interrogation and false confessions: Current research, practice, and policy recommendations.* Washington, DC: American Psychological Association.

Lavigne, J. E., McCarthy, M., Chapman, R., Petrilla, A., & Knox, K. L. (2012). Exposure to prescription drugs labeled for risk of adverse effects of suicidal behavior or ideation among 100 Air Force personnel who died by suicide, 2006–2009. *Suicide and Life-Threatening Behavior, 42,* 561–566.

Laws, D. R. (1995). Central elements in relapse prevention procedures with sex offenders. *Psychology, Crime, and Law, 2,* 41–53.

LeBlanc, M. M., & Kelloway, K. E. (2002). Predictors and outcomes of workplace violence and aggression. *Journal of Applied Psychology, 87,* 444–453.

LeCroy, C. W., Stevenson, P., & MacNeil, G. (2001). Systems considerations in treating juvenile offenders with mental disorders. In J. B. Ashford, B. D. Sales, & W. H. Reid (Eds.), *Treating adult and juvenile offenders with special needs* (pp. 403–418). Washington, DC: American Psychological Association.

Lee, H., & Vaughn, M. S. (2010). Organizational factors that contribute to police deadly force liability. *Journal of Criminal Justice, 38,* 193–206.

Lee, M. (2002). Asian battered women: Assessment and treatment. In A. R. Roberts (Ed.), *Handbook of domestic violence: Intervention strategies* (pp. 472–482). New York, NY: Oxford University Press.

Lee, S. M., & Nachlis, L. S. (2011). Consulting with attorneys: An alternative hybrid model. *Journal of Child Custody, 8*, 84–102.

Leech, S. L., Day, N. L., Richardson, G. A., & Goldschmidt, L. (2003). Predictors of self-reported delinquent behavior in a sample of young adolescents. *Journal of Early Adolescence, 23*, 78–106.

Lehrmann, D. H. (2010). Advancing children's rights to be heard and protected: The model representation of Children in Abuse, Neglect, and Custody Proceedings Act. *Behavioral Sciences & the Law, 28*, 463–479.

Leiber, M. J. (2002). Disproportionate minority confinement (DMC) of youth: An analysis of state and federal efforts to address the issue. *Crime & Delinquency, 48*, 3–45.

Leistico, A., Salekin, R., DeCoster, J., & Rogers, R. (2008). A large-scale meta-analysis relating the Hare measures of psychopathy to antisocial conduct. *Law and Human Behavior, 32*, 28–45.

Leitenberg, H., & Henning, K. (1995). Sexual fantasy. *Psychological Bulletin, 117*, 469–496.

Lemley, E. C. (2001). Designing restorative justice policy: An analytical perspective. *Criminal Justice Policy Review, 12*, 43–65.

Lenhart, A. (2015). *Teens, social media and technology overview, 2015*. Washington, DC: The Pew Center Internet & American Life Project.

Lenhart, A., Kahne, J., Middaugh, E., Macquill, A. R., Evans, C., & Vitak, J. (2008). *Teens, video games and civics* (Report No. 202–415–4500). Washington, DC: Pew Internet and American Life Project.

Lenhart, A., Ling, R., Campbell, S., & Purcell, K. (2010). *Teens and mobile phones*. Washington, DC: University of Michigan Department of Communication Studies; The Pew Center Internet & American Life Project.

Lenton, A. P. (2007). Matters of life and death: Justice in judgments of wrongful death. *Journal of Applied Social Psychology, 37*, 1191–1218.

Leo, R. A. (1996). *Miranda's* revenge: Police interrogation as a confidence game. *Law & Society Review, 30*, 259–288.

Leo, R. A., & Ofshe, R. J. (1998). The consequences of false confessions: Deprivations of liberty and miscarriages of justice in the age of psychological interrogation. *Journal of Criminal Law & Criminology, 88*, 429–440.

Leonard, E. L. (2015). Forensic neuropsychology and expert witness testimony: An overview of forensic practice. *International Journal of Law and Psychiatry, 42–43*, 177–182.

Leskinen, E. A., Cortina, L. M., & Kabat, D. B. (2011). Gender harassment: Broadening our understanding of sex-based harassment at work. *Law and Human Behavior, 35*, 25–39.

Lesser, G. E., & Batalova, J. (2017, April 5). Central American immigrants in the United States. *Migration Policy Institute*. Retrieved from www.migrationpolicy.org

Lester, D., Braswell, M., & Van Voorhis, P. (1992). *Correctional counseling* (2nd ed.). Cincinnati, OH: Anderson.

Levensky, E. R., & Fruzzetti, A. E. (2004). Partner violence: Assessment, prediction, and intervention. In W. T. O'Donohue & E. R. Levensky (Eds.), *Handbook of forensic psychology: Resource for mental health and legal professionals* (pp. 714–743). Amsterdam, Netherlands: Elsevier.

Levesque, R. J. R. (2001). *Culture and family violence: Fostering change through human rights law*. Washington, DC: American Psychological Association.

Levitt, L., Hoffer, T. A., & Loper, A. E. (2016). Criminal histories of a subsample of animal cruelty offenders. *Aggression and Violent Behavior, 30*, 48–59.

Lewinsohn, P. M., & Rosenbaum, M. (1987). Recall of parental behavior by acute depressives, remitted depressives, and nondepressives. *Journal of Personality and Social Psychology, 52*, 611–619.

Lewis, J. A., Dana, R. Q., & Blevins, G. A. (1994). *Substance abuse counseling: An individualized approach* (2nd ed.). Pacific Grove, CA: Brooks/Cole.

Li, Q. (2006). Cyberbullying in schools: A research on gender differences. *School Psychology International, 27*, 157–170.

Li, Q. (2010). Cyberbullying in high schools: A study of students' behaviors and beliefs about the new phenomenon. *Journal of Aggression, Maltreatment & Trauma, 19*, 372–292.

Lichtblau, E. (2016, September 7). Hate crimes against American Muslims most since post-9/11 era. Retrieved from https://www.nytimes.com/2016/09/18/us/politics/hate-crimes-american-muslims-rise.html

Lichtenberg, P. A., Qualls, S. H., & Smyer, M. A. (2015). Competency and decision-making capacity: Negotiating health and financial decision making. In P. A. Lichtenberg & P. T. Mast (Eds.), *APA handbook of clinical geropsychology: Vol. 2. Assessment, treatment, and issues of later life* (pp. 553–578). Washington, DC: American Psychological Association.

Lieberman, J. D. (2011). The utility of scientific jury selection. Still murky after 30 years. *Current Directions in Psychological Science, 20*, 48–52.

Lilienfeld, S. O., & Andrews, B. P. (1996). Development and preliminary validation of a self-report measure of psychopathic personality traits in noncriminal population. *Journal of Personality Assessment, 66*, 488–524.

Lilienfeld, S. O., & Loftus, E. F. (1998). Repressed memories and World War II: Some cautionary notes. *Professional Psychology: Research and Practice, 29*, 471–475.

Lilienfeld, S. O., Patrick, C. J., Benning, S. D., Berg, J., Sellbom, M., & Edens, J. F. (2012). The role of fearless dominance in psychopathy: Confusions, controversies, and clarifications. *Personality Disorders: Theory, Research, and Treatment, 3*, 327–340.

Lilienfeld, S. O., Smith, S. F., Savigné, K. C., Patrick, C. J., Drislane, L. E., Latzman, R. D., . . . & Krueger, R. F. (2016). Is boldness relevant to psychopathic personality? Meta-analytic relations with non-psychopathy checklist-based measures of psychopathy. *Psychological Assessment, 28*, 1172–1185.

Lilienfeld, S. O., Smith, S. F., & Watts, A. L. (2016). The perils of unitary models of the etiology of mental disorders: The response modulation hypothesis of psychopathy as a case example. Rejoinder to Newman and Baskin-Sommers (2016). *Psychological Bulletin, 142*, 1394–1403.

Lilienfeld, S. O., Watts, A. L., & Smith, S. F. (2015). Successful psychopathy: A scientific status report. *Current Directions in Psychological Science, 24*, 298–303.

Lilienfeld, S. O., & Widows, M. R. (2005). *Psychopathic Personality Inventory–Revised: Professional manual.* Lutz, FL: Psychological Assessment Resources.

Limm, H., Gündel, H., Heinmüller, M., Martin-Mittage, B., Nater, U., Siegrist, J., . . . & Angerer, P. (2011). Stress management interventions in the workplace to improve stress reactivity: A randomized controlled trial. *Occupational and Environmental Medicine, 68*, 126–133.

Lipsey, M. W. (2009). The primary factors that characterize interventions with juvenile offenders: A meta-analytic overview. *Victims and Offenders, 4*, 124–147.

Lipsitt, P. D., Lelos, D., & McGarry, A. L. (1971). Competency for trial: A screening instrument. *The American Journal of Psychiatry, 128*, 105–109.

Lipton, D. N., McDonel, E. C., & McFall, R. M. (1987). Heterosexual perceptions in rapists. *Journal of Consulting and Clinical Psychology, 55*, 17–21.

Loeber, R. (1990). Development and risk factors of juvenile antisocial behavior and delinquency. *Clinical Psychological Review, 10*, 1–41.

Loeber, R., Burke, J., & Lahey, B. (2002). What are adolescent antecedents to an antisocial personality disorder? *Criminal Behaviour and Mental Health, 12*, 24–36.

Loftus, E. F. (1979). *Eyewitness testimony.* Cambridge, MA: Harvard University Press.

Loftus, E. F. (2004). The devil in confessions. *Psychological Science in the Public Interest, 5*, i–ii.

Loftus, E. F. (2005). Planting misinformation in the human mind: A 30-year investigation of the malleability of memory. *Learning and Memory, 12*, 361–366.

Loftus, E. F. (2013). 25 years of eyewitness science . . . finally pays off. *Perspectives on Psychological Science, 8*, 556–557.

Logue, M., Book, A. S., Frosina, P., Huizinga, T., & Amos, S. (2015). Using reality monitoring to improve deception detection in the context of the cognitive interview for suspects. *Law and Human Behavior, 39*, 360–367.

Loh, W. D. (1981). Perspectives on psychology and law. *Journal of Applied Social Psychology, 11*, 314–355.

Lonsway, K. A., & Archambault, J. (2012). The "justice gap" for sexual assault cases: Future directions for research and reform. *Violence Against Women, 18*, 145–168.

Lonsway, K. A., & Fitzgerald, L. F. (1994). Rape myths: In review. *Psychology of Women Quarterly, 18*, 133–164.

Lonsway, K. A., & Fitzgerald, L. F. (1995). Attitudinal antecedents of rape myth acceptance: A theoretical and empirical reexamination. *Journal of Personality and Social Psychology, 68*, 704–711.

Lord, J. (1997). *Death notification: Breaking the bad news with concern for the professional and compassion for the survivor.* Washington, DC: U.S. Department of Justice, Office for Victims of Crime.

Lord, J. (2001). Death notification training of trainers seminars. *OVC Bulletin.* Washington, DC: U.S. Department of Justice, Office for Victims of Crime.

Lord, W. D., Boudreaux, M. C., & Lanning, K. (2001, April). Investigating potential child abduction cases: A developmental perspective. *FBI Law Enforcement Bulletin*, 1–10.

Luke, T., Crozier, W. E., & Strange, D. (2017, March 23). Memory errors in police interviews: The bait question as a source of misinformation. *Journal of Applied Research in Memory and Cognition.* Advance online publication. doi:10.1016/j.jarmac.2017.01.011

Luna, B., & Wright, C. (2016). Adolescent brain development: Implications for the juvenile criminal justice system. In K. Heilbrun (Ed.), *APA handbook of psychology and juvenile justice* (pp. 91–114). Washington, DC: American Psychological Association.

Luskin, M. L. (2013). More of the same? Treatment in mental health courts. *Law and Human Behavior, 37*, 255–266.

Lykken, D. T. (1957). A study of anxiety in the sociopathic personality. *Journal of Abnormal and Social Psychology, 55*, 6–10.

Lykken, D. T. (1959). The GSR in the detection of guilt. *Journal of Applied Psychology, 43*, 385–388.

Lynam, D. R. (1997). Pursuing the psychopath: Capturing the fledgling psychopath in a nomological net. *Journal of Abnormal Psychology, 106*, 425–438.

Lynam, D. R., & Miller, J. D. (2012). Fearless dominance and psychopathy: A response to Lilienfeld et al. *Personality Disorders: Theory, Research, and Treatment, 3*, 341–353.

Lynn, S. J., Boycheva, E., Deming, A., Lilienfeld, S. O., & Hallquist, M. N. (2009). Forensic hypnosis: The state of the science. In J. L. Skeem, K. S. Douglas, & S. O. Lilienfeld (Eds.), *Psychological science in the courtroom: Consensus and controversy* (pp. 80–99). New York, NY: Guilford Press.

Maccoby, E., Buchanan, C., Mnookin, R., & Dornsbusch, S. (1993). Postdivorce roles of mother and father in the lives of their children. *Journal of Family Psychology, 1*, 24–38.

MacKain, S. J., Myers, B., Ostapiej, L., & Newman, R. A. (2010). Job satisfaction among psychologists working in state prisons: The relative impact of facets assessing economics, management, relationships, and perceived organizational support. *Criminal Justice and Behavior, 37*, 306–318.

MacKain, S. J., Tedeschi, R. G., Durham, T. W., & Goldman, V. J. (2002). So what are master's level psychology practitioners doing? Surveys of employers and recent graduates in North Carolina. *Professional Psychology: Research and Practice, 33*, 408–412.

MacKay, S., Paglia-Boak, A., Henderson, J., Marton, P., & Adlaf, E. (2009). Epidemiology of firesetting in adolescents: Mental health and substance abuse correlates. *Journal of Child Psychology and Psychiatry, 50*, 1282–1290.

MacKenzie, D. L. (2000). Evidence-based corrections: Identifying what works. *Crime & Delinquency, 46*, 457–471.

MacKenzie, D. L., Robinson, J. W., & Campbell, C. S. (1989). Long-term incarceration of female offenders: Prison adjustment and coping. *Criminal Justice and Behavior, 16*, 223–238.

MacLin, O. H., MacLin, M. K., & Malpass, R. S. (2001). Race, arousal, attention, exposure, and delay: An examination of factors moderating face recognition. *Psychology, Public Policy, and Law, 7*, 134–152.

MacLin, O. H., & Malpass, R. S. (2001). Racial categorization of faces: The ambiguous race face effect. *Psychology, Public Policy, and Law, 7*, 98–118.

Madfis, E., & Levin, J. (2013). School rampage in international perspective: The salience of cumulative strain theory. In N. Böckler, T. Seeger, & P. Sitzer (Eds.), *School shootings: International research, case studies, and concepts for prevention* (pp. 79–104). New York, NY: Springer.

Magaletta, P. R., Diamond, P. M., Faust, E., Daggett, D., & Camp, S. D. (2009). Estimating the mental illness component of service need in corrections: Results from the Mental Health Prevalence Project. *Criminal Justice and Behavior, 36*, 229–244.

Magaletta, P. R., Dietz, E. F., & Diamond, P. M. (2005). *The prevalence of behavioral and psychological disorders among an admissions cohort of federal inmates* (Bureau of Prisons, Research Review Board 01–038). Washington, DC: U.S. Department of Justice.

Magaletta, P. R., Patry, M. W., Cermak, J., & McLearen, A. M. (2017). Inside the world of corrections practica: Findings from a national survey. *Training and Education in Professional Psychology, 11*, 10–17.

Magaletta, P. R., Patry, M. W., & Norcross, J. C. (2012). Who is training behind the wall? Twenty-five years of psychology interns in corrections. *Criminal Justice and Behavior, 39*, 1405–1420.

Magaletta, P. R., Patry, M. W., Patterson, K. L., Gross, N. R., Morgan, R. D., & Norcross, J. C. (2013). Training opportunities for corrections practice: A national survey of doctoral psychology programs. *Training and Education in Professional Psychology, 7*, 291–299.

Magnussen, S., & Melinder, A. (2012). What psychologists know and believe about memory: A survey of practitioners. *Applied Cognitive Psychology, 26*, 54–60.

Malamuth, N. M. (1981). Rape proclivity among males. *Journal of Social Issues, 37*, 138–157.

Malamuth, N. M., & Brown, L. M. (1994). Sexually aggressive men's perceptions of women's communications: Testing three explanations. *Journal of Personality and Social Psychology, 67*, 699–712.

Malamuth, N. M., Heavey, C. L., & Linz, D. (1993). Predicting men's antisocial behavior against women: The "interaction model" of sexual aggression. In N. G. Hall & R. Hirschman (Eds.), *Sexual aggression: Issues in etiology and assessment treatment and policy*. New York, NY: Hemisphere.

Malamuth, N. M., Linz, D., Heavey, C. L., Barnes, G., & Acker, M. (1995). Using the confluence model of sexual aggression to predict men's conflict with women: A 10-year follow-up study. *Journal of Personality and Social Psychology, 69*, 353–369.

Malamuth, N. M., Sockloskie, R., Koss, M., & Tanaka, J. (1991). The characteristics of aggressors against women: Testing a model using a national sample of college students. *Journal of Consulting and Clinical Psychology, 59*, 670–681.

Maldonado, S. (2017). Bias in the family: Race, ethnicity, and culture in custody disputes. *Family Court Review, 55*, 213–242.

Malesky, L. A., Jr. (2007). Predatory online behavior: Modus operandi of convicted sex offenders in identifying potential victims and contacting minors over the Internet. *Journal of Child Sexual Abuse: Research, Treatment & Program Innovations for Victims, Survivors, & Offenders, 16*, 23–32.

Malloy, L. C., Shulman, E. P., & Cauffman, E. (2014). Interrogations, confessions, and guilty pleas among serious adolescent offenders. *Law and Human Behavior, 38*, 181–193.

Mandler, J. M. (1988) How to build a baby: On the development of an accessible representational system. *Cognitive Development, 3*, 113–136.

Mandler, J. M. (1990). Recall of events by preverbal children. In A. Diamond (Ed.), *The development and neural bases of higher cognitive functions* (pp. 485–516) . New York, NY: New York Academy of Science.

Mandracchia, J. T., Morgan, R. D., Gross, S., & Garland, J. T. (2007). Inmate thinking patterns: An empirical investigation. *Criminal Justice and Behavior, 34*, 1029–1043.

Manguno-Mire, G. M., Thompson, J. W., Shore, J. H., Croy, C. D., Artecona, J. F., & Pickering, J. W. (2007). The use of telemedicine to evaluate competence to stand trial: A preliminary randomized controlled study. *Journal of the American Academy of Psychiatry and the Law, 35*, 481–489.

Mann, S., Ewens, S., Shaw, D., Vrij, A., Leal, S., & Hillman, J. (2013). Lying eyes: Why liars seek deliberate eye contact. *Psychiatry, Psychology and Law, 20*, 452–461.

Manning, P. K. (1995). The police occupational culture in Anglo-American societies. In W. Bailey (Ed.), *The encyclopedia of police science*. New York, NY: Garland Publishing.

Mannuzza, S., Klein, R. G., Bessler, A., Malloy, P., & LaPadula, M. (1998). Adult psychiatric status of hyperactive boys grown up. *American Journal of Psychiatry, 155*, 493–498.

Margolin, G., Vickerman, K. A., Ramos, M. C., Serrano, S. D., Gordis, E. B., Iturralde, M. C., . . . & Spies, L. A. (2009). Youth exposed to violence: Stability, co-occurrence, and context. *Clinical Child and Family Psychology Review, 12*, 39–54.

Markel, H. (2014, September 29). *How the Tylenol murders of 1982 changed the way we consume medication*. Retrieved from http://www.pbs.org/newshour/updates/tylenol-murders-1982

Markesteyn, T. (1992). *The psychological impact of nonsexual criminal offenses on victims*. Ottawa, Canada: Ministry of the Solicitor General of Canada, Corrections Branch.

Marsee, M. A., Silverthorn, P., & Frick, P. J. (2005). The association of psychopathic traits with aggression and delinquency in non-referred boys and girls. *Behavioral Sciences & the Law, 23*, 803–817.

Marshall, C. E., Benton, D., & Brazier, J. M. (2000). Elder abuse: Using clinical tools to identify clues of mistreatment. *Geriatrics, 55*, 42–53.

Marshall, G. N., & Schell, T. L. (2002). Reappraising the link between peritraumatic dissociation and PTSD symptom severity: Evidence from a longitudinal study of community violence survivors. *Journal of Abnormal Psychology, 111*, 626–636.

Marshall, W. B. (1996). Assessment, treatment, and theorizing about sex offenders. *Criminal Justice and Behavior, 23*, 162–199.

Marshall, W. L. (1998). Diagnosing and treating sexual offenders. In A. K. Hess & I. B. Weiner (Eds.), *The handbook of forensic psychology* (2nd ed., pp. 640–670). New York, NY: Wiley.

Marshall, W. L., & Barbaree, H. (1990). Outcome of comprehensive cognitive-behavioral treatment programs. In W. L. Marshall & H. E. Barbaree (Eds.), *Handbook of sexual assault: Issues, theories, and treatment of offenders* (pp. 363–385). New York, NY: Plenum.

Marshall, W. L., Boer, D., & Marshall, L. E. (2014). Assessing and treating sex offenders. In I. B. Weiner & R. K. Otto (Eds.), *The handbook of forensic psychology* (4th ed., pp. 839–866). Hoboken, NJ: Wiley.

Martin, M. S., Dorken, S. K., Wamboldt, A. D., & Wootten, S. E. (2012). Stopping the revolving door: A meta-analysis on the effectiveness of interventions for criminally involved individuals with major mental disorders. *Law and Human Behavior, 36*, 1–12.

Martin, S. E. (1989). Women on the move? A report on the status of women in policing. *Women and Criminal Justice, 1*, 21–40.

Martin, S. E. (1992). The effectiveness of affirmative action: The case of women in policing. *Justice Quarterly, 8*, 489–504.

Mason, C. (2012). *Too good to be true: Private prisons in America*. (NCJ 240782). Washington, DC: Sentencing Project.

Mason, M. A., & Quirk, A. (1997). Are mothers losing custody? Read my lips: Trends in judicial decision-making in custody disputes—1920, 1960, 1990, and 1995. *Family Law Quarterly, 31*, 215–236.

Mathews, J. K., Hunter, J. A., & Vuz, J. (1997). Juvenile female sexual offenders: Clinical characteristics and treatment issues. *Sexual Abuse: A Journal of Research and Treatment, 9*, 187–199.

Matsumoto, D. (Ed.). (2010). *APA Handbook of interpersonal communication*. Washington, DC: American Psychological Association.

Mayer, M. J., & Corey, D. M. (2015). Current issues in psychological fitness-for-duty evaluations of law enforcement officers: Legal and practice implications. In C. L. Mitchell & E. H. Dorian, *Police psychology and its growing impact on modern law enforcement* (pp. 93–118). Hershey, PA: IGI Global.

Mayfield, M. G., & Widom, C. S. (1996). The cycle of violence. *Archives of Pediatric and Adolescent Medicine, 150*, 390–395.

McAuliff. B. D., & Groscup, J. L. (2009). *Daubert* and psychological science in court: Judging validity from the bench, bar, and jury box. In J. L. Skeem, K. S. Douglas, & S. O. Lilienfeld (Eds.), *Psychological science in the courtroom: Consensus and controversy* (pp. 26–52). New York, NY: Guilford Press.

McCann, J. T. (1998). A conceptual framework for identifying various types of confessions. *Behavioral Sciences & the Law, 16*, 441–453.

McCormick, E. J. (1979). *Job analysis: Methods and applications*. New York, NY: Amacom.

McDonald, R., Jouriles, E. N., Ramisetty-Mikler, S., Caetano, R., & Green, C. E. (2006). Estimating the number of American children living in partner-violence families. *Journal of Family Psychology, 20*, 137–142.

McElvain, J. P., & Kposowa, A. J. (2008). Police officer characteristics and the likelihood of using deadly force. *Criminal Justice and Behavior, 35*, 505–521.

McEwan, T. E., Mullen, P. E., MacKenzie, R. D., & Ogloff, J. R. P. (2009). Violence in stalking situations. *Psychological Medicine, 39*, 1469–1478.

McEwan, T. E., Mullen, P. E., & Purcell, R. (2007). Identifying risk factors in stalking: A review of current research. *International Journal of Law and Psychiatry, 30*, 1–9.

McEwan, T. E., Pathé, M., & Ogloff, J. R. P. (2011). Advances in stalking risk assessment. *Behavioral Sciences & the Law, 29*, 180–201.

McGee, C. (2000). *Childhood experiences of domestic violence*. London, England: Jessica Kingsley.

McGee, J., & DeBernardo, C. (1999). The classroom avenger: A behavioral profile of school-based shootings. *Forensic Examiner, 8*, 16–18.

McGlynn, A. H., Hahn, P., & Hagan, M. P. (2012). The effect of a cognitive treatment program for male and female juvenile offenders. *International Journal of Offender Therapy and Comparative Criminology, 57*, 1107–1119.

McGowan, M. R., Horn, R. A., & Mellott, R. N. (2011). The predictive validity of the Structured Assessment of Violence Risk in youth in secondary educational settings. *Psychological Assessment, 23*, 478–486.

McGrath, A., & Thompson, A. P. (2012). The relative predictive validity of the static and dynamic domain scores in risk-need assessment of juvenile offenders. *Criminal Justice and Behavior, 39*, 250–263.

McGrath, R. J., Cumming, G. F., & Burchard, B. L. (2003). *Current practices and trends in sexual abuser management: The Safer Society 2002 Nationwide Survey.* Brandon, VT: Safe Society Press.

McIntyre, B. L. (2014). More than just rescue: Thinking beyond exploitation to creating assessment strategies for child survivors of commercial sexual exploitation. *International Social Work, 57,* 39–63.

McKenzie, J. (2013, May). *Postdoctoral psychology internship 2014–2015.* Rochester, MN: U.S. Bureau of Prisons, Federal Medical Center.

McLawsen, J. E., Scalora, M. J., & Darrow, C. (2012). Civilly committed sex offenders: A description and interstate comparison of populations. *Psychology, Public Policy, and Law, 18,* 453–476.

McMahon, M. (1999). Battered women and bad science: The limited validity and utility of battered women syndrome. *Psychiatry, Psychology, and Law, 6,* 23–49.

McMains, M. J., & Mullins, W. C. (2013). *Crisis negotiations: Managing critical incidents and hostage situations in law enforcement and corrections* (5th ed.). Waltham, MA: Anderson.

McNally, R. J., Bryant, R. A., & Ehlers, A. (2003). Does early psychological intervention promote recovery from posttraumatic stress? *American Psychological Society, 4,* 45–70.

McNally, R. J., & Geraerts, E. (2009). A new solution to the recovered memory debate. *Perspectives on Psychological Science, 4,* 126–134.

McNally, R. J., Perlman, C. A., Ristuccia, C. S., & Clancy, S. A. (2008). Clinical characteristics of adults reporting repressed, recovered, or continuous memories of childhood sexual abuse. *Journal of Consulting and Clinical Psychology, 74,* 237–242.

McNeece, C. A., Springer, D. W., & Arnold, E. M. (2001). Treating substance abuse disorders. In J. B. Ashford, B. D. Sales, & W. H. Reid (Eds.), *Treating adult and juvenile offenders with special needs* (pp. 131–170). Washington, DC: American Psychological Association.

McNeece, C. A., Springer, D. W., Shader, M. A., Malone, R., Smith, M. A., Touchton-Cashwell, S., et al. (1997). *An evaluation of juvenile assessment centers in Florida.* Tallahassee: Florida State University, Institute for Health and Human Services Research.

McWhirter, P. T. (1999). La violencia privada: Domestic violence in Chile. *American Psychologist, 54,* 37–40.

McWilliams, K. (2016, Spring). Best practice guidelines for child forensic interviewing: What we know and where we are going. *Section on Child Maltreatment Insider, 21,* 2–3.

Meehl, P. E. (1954). *Clinical versus statistical prediction: A theoretical analysis and a review of the evidence.* Minneapolis: University of Minnesota Press.

Meesig, R., & Horvath, F. (1995). A national survey of practices, policies and evaluative comments on the use of pre-employment polygraph screening in police agencies in the United States. *Polygraph, 24,* 57–136.

Mehari, K. R., Farrell, A. D., & Le, A.-T. (2014). Cyberbullying among adolescents: Measures in search of a construct. *Psychology of Violence, 4,* 399–415.

Meissner, C. A., & Brigham, J. C. (2001). Thirty years of investigating the own-race bias in memory for faces: A meta-analytic review. *Psychology, Public Policy, and Law, 7,* 3–35.

Meissner, C. A., Hartwig, M., & Russano, M. B. (2010). The need for a positive psychological approach and collaborative effort for improving practice in the interrogation room. *Law & Human Behavior, 34,* 43–45.

Meissner, C. A., & Lassiter, G. D. (2010). Conclusion: What have we learned? Implications for practice, policy, and future research. In G. D. Lassiter & C. A. Meissner (Eds.), *Police interrogations and false confessions: Current research, practice, and policy recommendations* (pp. 225–230). Washington, DC: American Psychological Association.

Meissner, C. A., Redlich, A. D., Bhatt, S., & Brandon, S. E. (2012). Interview and interrogation methods and their effects on true and false confessions. *Campbell Systematic Reviews, 13,* 1–53.

Meissner, C. A., Russano, M. B., & Narchet, F. M. (2010). The importance of a laboratory science for improving the diagnostic value of confession evidence. In G. D. Lassiter & C. A. Meissner (Eds.), *Police interrogations and false confessions: Current research, practice, and policy recommendations* (pp. 111–126). Washington, DC: American Psychological Association.

Meloy, J. R., & Gothard, S. (1995). Demographic and clinical comparison of obsessional followers and offenders with mental disorders. *American Journal of Psychiatry, 152,* 258–263.

Meloy, J. R., & Hoffmann, J. (Eds.). (2013). *The international handbook of threat assessment.* New York, NY: Oxford University Press.

Meloy, M., & Mohandie, K. (2008). Two case studies of corporate-celebrity male victims: The stalking of Steven Spielberg and Stephen Wynn. In J. R. Meloy, L. Sheridan, & J. Hoffman (Eds.), *Stalking, threatening, and attacking public figures: A psychological and behavioral analysis* (pp. 245–270). New York, NY: Oxford University Press.

Meloy, M., Mohandie, K., & Green McGowan, M. (2008). A forensic investigation of those who stalk celebrities. In J. R. Meloy, L. Sheridan, & J. Hoffman (Eds.), *Stalking, threatening, and attacking public figures: A psychological and behavioral analysis* (pp. 37–54). New York, NY: Oxford University Press.

Melton, G. B., Petrila, J., Poythress, N. G., & Slobogin, C. (1997). *Psychological evaluations for the courts: A handbook for mental health professionals and lawyers* (2nd ed.). New York, NY: Guilford Press.

Melton, G. B., Petrila, J., Poythress, N. G., & Slobogin, C. (Eds.). (2007). *Psychological evaluations for the courts: A handbook for mental health professionals and lawyers* (3rd ed.). New York, NY: Guilford Press.

Memon, A., Meissner, C. A., & Fraser, J. (2010). The cognitive interview: A meta-analytic review and study space analysis of the past 25 years. *Psychology, Public Policy, and Law, 16,* 340–372.

Menard, K. S., Anderson, A. L., & Godboldt, S. M. (2009). Gender differences in intimate partner recidivism: A 5-year follow-up. *Criminal Justice and Behavior, 36*, 61–76.

Mental Health Court Showing Gains. (March/April 2017). *The National Psychologist, 26*, 10.

Mercado, C. C., Jeglic, E., Markus, K., Hanson, R. K., & Levenson, J. (2011, January). *Sex offender management, treatment, and civil commitment: An evidence base analysis aimed at reducing sexual violence.* Washington, DC: U.S. Department of Justice, National Institute of Justice.

Merrill, G. S., & Wolfe, V. A. (2000). Battered gay men: An exploration of abuse, help-seeking, and why they stay. *Journal of Homosexuality, 39*, 1–30.

Merry, S., & Harsent, L. (2000). Intruders, pilferers, raiders, and invaders: The interpersonal dimension of burglary. In D. Canter & L. Alison (Eds.), *Profiling property crimes.* Dartmouth, England: Ashgate.

Merz-Perez, L., Heide, K. M., & Silverman, I. J. (2001). Childhood cruelty to animals and subsequent violence against humans. *International Journal of Offender Therapy and Comparative Criminology, 45*, 556–573.

Messina, N., Grella, C., Burdon, W., & Prendergast, M. (2007). Childhood adverse events and current traumatic distress: A comparison of men and women drug-dependent prisoners. *Criminal Justice and Behavior, 34*, 1385–1401.

Messinger, A. M. (2011). Invisible victims: Same-sex IPV in the National Violence Against Women Survey. *Journal of Interpersonal Violence, 26*, 2228–2243.

Metzner, J. L., & O'Keefe, M. L. (2011). Psychological effects of administrative segregation: The Colorado Study. *Corrections Mental Health Report, 13*, 1–2, 13–14.

Meuer, T., Seymour, A., & Wallace, H. (2002, June). Domestic violence. In A. Seymour, M. Murray, J. Sigmon, M. Hook, C. Edwards, M. Gaboury, & G. Coleman (Eds.), *National Victim Assistance Academy textbook.* Washington, DC: U.S. Department of Justice, Office for Victims of Crime.

Meyer, J. R., & Reppucci, N. D. (2007). Police practices and perceptions regarding juvenile interrogation and interrogative suggestibility. *Behavioral Sciences & the Law, 25*, 757–780.

Mez, J., Daneshvar, D. H., Kierman, P. T., Abdolmohammadi, B., Alarez, V. E., Huber, B. R., . . . & McKee, A. C. (2017). Clinicopathological evaluation of traumatic encephalopathy in players of American football. *JAMA, 318*, 360–370.

Miccio-Fonseca, L. C. (2006). *Multiplex Empirically Guarded Inventory of Ecological Aggregates for assessing sexually abusive youth (ages 19 and under) (MEGA).* San Diego, CA: Author.

Michalski, D., Kohout, J., Wicherski, M., & Hart, B. (2011). *2009 Doctorate Employment Survey.* Washington, DC: American Psychological Association, Center for Workplace Studies.

Mickes, L., Flowe, H. D., & Wixted, J. T. (2012). Receiver operating characteristics analysis of eyewitness memory: Comparing the diagnostic accuracy of simultaneous vs. sequential lineups. *Journal of Experimental Psychology: Applied, 18*, 361–376.

Milan, M. A., Chin, C. E., & Nguyen, Q. X. (1999). Practicing psychology in correctional settings: Assessment, treatment, and substance abuse programs. In A. K. Hess & I. B. Weiner (Eds.), *Handbook of forensic psychology* (2nd ed., pp. 580–602). New York, NY: Wiley.

Miller, A. (2014). Threat assessment in action. *Monitor on Psychology, 45*(2), 37–38, 40.

Miller, G. (2012, August 17). In mock cases, biological evidence reduces sentences. *Science, 337*, 788.

Miller, L. (1995). Tough guys: Psychotherapeutic strategies with law enforcement and emergency services personnel. *Psychotherapy, 32*, 592–600.

Miller, L. (2008). Death notification for families of homicide victims: Healing dimensions of a complex process. *Omega: Journal of Death and Dying, 57*, 367–380.

Miller, L. (2014). Serial killers: I. Subtypes, patterns, and motives. *Aggression and Violent Behavior, 19*, 1–11.

Miller, L. (2015). Why cops kill: The psychology of police deadly force encounters. *Aggression and Violent Behavior, 22*, 97–111.

Miller, L. S., & Lindbergh, C. A. (2017). Neuroimaging techniques in the courtroom. In S. S. Bush (Ed.), *APA handbook of forensic neuropsychology* (pp. 111–144). Washington, DC: American Psychological Association.

Miller, M., & Hinshaw, S. F. (2010). Does childhood executive function predict adolescent functional outcomes in girls with ADHD? *Journal of Abnormal Child Psychology, 38*, 315–326.

Miller, R. D. (2003). Hospitalization of criminal defendants for evaluation of competence to stand trial or for restoration of competence: Clinical and legal issues. *Behavioral Sciences & the Law, 21*, 369–391.

Miller-Perrin, C., & Wurtele, S. K. (2017). Sex trafficking and the commercial sexual exploitation of children. *Women & Therapy, 40*, 123–151.

Millon, T. (1994). *MCMI-III: Manual.* Minneapolis, MN: National Computer Systems.

Miner, M. H., Day, D. M., & Nafpaktitis, M. K. (1989). Assessment of coping skills: Development of situational competency test. In D. R. Laws (Eds.), *Relapse prevention with sex offenders* (pp. 127–136). New York, NY: Guilford Press.

Mischel, W. (1968). *Personality and assessment.* New York, NY: Wiley.

Mischel, W., & Peake, P. K. (1982). Beyond déjà vu in the search for cross-situational consistency. *Psychological Review, 89*, 730–755.

Mitchell, C. L. (2017). Preemployment psychological screening of police officer applicants: Basic considerations and recent advances. In

C. L. Mitchell & E. H. Dorian (Eds.), *Police psychology and its growing impact on modern law enforcement* (pp. 28–50). Hershey, PA: IGI Global.

Mitchell, K., Finkelhor, D., & Wolak, J. (2007). Youth Internet users at risk for the most serious online sexual solicitations. *American Journal of Preventive Medicine, 32,* 532–537.

Mitchell, K., Jones, L. M., Finkelhor, D., & Wolak, J. (2011). Internet-facilitated commercial sexual exploitation of children: Findings from a nationally representative sample of law enforcement agencies in the United States. *Sexual Abuse: A Journal of Research and Treatment, 23,* 43–71.

Mitchell, K., Wolak, J., & Finkelhor, D. (2005). Police posing as juveniles online to catch sex offenders: Is it working? *Sexual Abuse: A Journal of Research and Treatment, 17,* 241–267.

Moffitt, T. E. (1990). The neuropsychology of delinquency: A critical review of theory and research. In M. Tonry & N. Morris (Eds.), *Crime and Justice* (vol. 12, p. 99–169). Chicago, IL: University of Chicago Press.

Moffitt, T. E. (1993a). Adolescent-limited and the life-course persistent antisocial behavior: A developmental taxonomy. *Psychological Review, 100,* 674–701.

Moffitt, T. E. (1993b). The neuropsychology of conduct disorder. *Development and Psychopathology, 5,* 135–151.

Moffitt, T. E., Arseneault, L., Jaffee, S. R., Kim-Cohen, J., Koenen, K. C., Odgers, C. L., . . . & Viding, E. (2008). Research review: DSM-V conduct disorder: Research needs for an evidence base. *Journal of Child Psychology and Psychiatry, 49,* 3–33.

Moffitt, T. E., & Caspi, A. (2001). Childhood predictors differentiate life-course persistent and adolescence limited antisocial pathways among males and females. *Development and Psychopathology, 13,* 355–375.

Moffitt, T. E., Caspi, A., Dickson, N., Silva, P., & Stanton, W. (1996). Childhood-onset versus adolescent-onset antisocial conduct problems in males: Natural history from ages 3 to 18. *Development and Psychopathology, 8,* 399–324.

Mohandie, K., Meloy, J. R., Green McGowan, M., & Williams, J. (2006). The RECON typology of stalking: Reliability and validity based upon a large sample of North American stalkers. *Journal of Forensic Sciences, 51,* 147–155.

Molina, B. S. G., Bukstein, O. G., & Lynch, K. G. (2002). Attention-deficit/hyperactivity disorder and conduct disorder symptomatology in adolescents with alcohol use disorder. *Psychology of Addictive Behaviors, 16,* 161–164.

Monahan, J. (1996). Violence prediction: The past twenty years and the next twenty years. *Criminal Justice and Behavior, 23,* 107–120.

Monahan, J., Steadman, H., Appelbaum, P., Grisso, T., Mulvey, E., Roth, L., . . . & Silver, E. (2005). *The classification of violence risk.* Lutz, FL: Psychological Assessment Resources.

Monahan, J., Steadman, H. J., Silver, E., Appelbaum, P. S., Robbins, P. C., Mulvey, E. P., . . . & Banks, S. M. (2001). *Rethinking risk assessment: The MacArthur Study of Mental Disorder and Violence.* New York, NY: Oxford University Press.

Monahan, K. C., Steinberg, L., & Cauffman, E. (2009). Affiliation with antisocial peers, susceptibility to peer influence, and antisocial behavior during the transition to adulthood. *Developmental Psychology, 45,* 1520–1530.

Morawetz, T. H. (2002). Homicide. In K. L. Hall (Ed.), *The Oxford companion to American law.* (pp. 398–400). New York, NY: Oxford University Press.

Moreland, M. B., & Clark, S. E. (2016). Eyewitness identification: Research, reform, and reversal. *Journal of Applied Research in Memory and Cognition, 5,* 277–283.

Morey, L. C. (1991). *The Personality Assessment Inventory: Professional manual.* Odessa, FL: Psychological Assessment Resources.

Morey, L. C. (2007). *The Personality Assessment Inventory professional manual.* Lutz, FL: Psychological Assessment Resources.

Morgan, A. B., & Lilienfeld, S. O. (2000). A meta-analytic review of the relation between antisocial behavior and neuropsychological measures of executive functions. *Clinical Psychology Review, 20,* 113–136.

Morgan, E., Johnson, I., & Sigler, R. (2006). Public definitions and endorsement of the criminalization of elder abuse. *Journal of Criminal Justice, 34,* 275–283.

Morgan, R. D., Flora, D. B., Kroner, D. C., Mills, J. F., Varghese, F., & Steffan, J. S. (2012). Treating offenders with mental illness: A research synthesis. *Law and Human Behavior, 36,* 37–50.

Morgan, R. D., Gendreau, P., Smith, P., Gray, A. L., Labrecque, R. M., MacLean, N., . . . & Mills, J. F. (2016). Quantitative syntheses of the effects of administrative segregation on inmates' well-being. *Psychology, Public Policy, and Law, 22,* 439–461.

Morgan, R. D., Kroner, D. G., Mills, J. F., & Batastini, A. B. (2014). Treating criminal offenders. In I. B. Weiner & R. K. Otto (Eds.), *The handbook of forensic psychology* (4th ed., pp. 795–837). Hoboken, NJ: Wiley.

Morgan, R. D., Kuther, T. L., & Habben, C. (2005). *Life after graduate school: Insider's advice from new psychologists.* New York, NY: Psychology Press.

Morgan, R. D., Mitchell, S. M., Thoen, M. A., Campion, K., Bolanos, A. D., Sustaita, A. D., & Henderson, S. (2016). Specialty courts: Who's in and are they working? *Psychological Services, 13,* 246–253.

Morgan, R. D., Winterowd, C. L., & Ferrell, S. W. (1999). A national survey of group psychotherapy services in correctional facilities. *Professional Psychology: Research and Practice, 30,* 600–606.

Morris, A. (1996). Gender and ethnic differences in social constraints among a sample of New York City police officers. *Journal of Occupational Health Psychology, 1,* 224–235.

Morris, R. (2000). *Forensic handwriting identification: Fundamental concepts and principles*. San Diego, CA: Academic Press.

Morry, M. M., & Winkler, E. (2001). Student acceptance and expectation of sexual assault. *Canadian Journal of Behavioural Science, 33*, 188–192.

Morse, S. J. (2003). Involuntary competence. *Behavioral Sciences & the Law, 21*, 311–328.

Mosher, D. L., & Anderson, R. D. (1986). Macho personality, sexual aggression, and reactions to guided imagery of realistic rape. *Journal of Research in Personality, 20*, 77–94.

Mossman, D. (1987). Assessing and restoring competency to be executed: Should psychologists participate? *Behavioral Sciences & the Law, 5*, 397–409.

Mossman, D. (2003). *Daubert*, cognitive malingering, and test accuracy. *Law and Human Behavior, 27*, 229–249.

Mossman, D. (2007). Predicting restorability of incompetent criminal defendants. *Journal of the American Academy of Psychiatry and the Law, 35*, 34–43.

Mossman, D., & Farrell, H. M. (2015). Civil competencies. In B. L. Cutler & P. A. Zapf (Eds.), *APA handbook of forensic psychology: Vol. 1. Individual and situational influences in criminal and civil contexts* (pp. 533–558). Washington, DC: American Psychological Association.

Motivans, M., & Snyder, H. (2011). *Summary: Tribal youth in the federal justice system*. Washington, DC: U.S. Department of Justice, Bureau of Justice Statistics.

Mulder, R., T., Wells, J. E., Joyce, P. R., & Bushnell, J. A. (1994). Antisocial women. *Journal of Personality Disorders, 8*, 279–287.

Mullen, P. E., Pathé, M., & Purcell, R. (2001). Stalking: New constructions of human behaviour. *Australian and New Zealand Journal of Psychiatry, 35*, 9–16.

Mulvey, E. P. (2011). *Highlights from pathways to desistance: A longitudinal study of serious adolescent offenders*. Washington, DC: U.S. Department of Justice, Office of Juvenile Justice and Delinquency Prevention.

Mulvey, E. P., Arthur, M. W., & Reppucci, N. D. (1993). The prevention and treatment of juvenile delinquency: A review of the research. *Clinical Psychology Review, 13*, 133–167.

Mumcuoglu, K. Y., Gallili, N., Reshef, A., Brauner, P., & Grant, H. (2004). Use of human lice in forensic entomology. *Journal of Medical Entomology, 41*, 803–806.

Mumley, D. L., Tillbrook, C. E., & Grisso, T. (2003). Five-year research update (1996–2000): Evaluations for competence to stand trial (adjudicative competence). *Behavioral Sciences & the Law, 21*, 329–350.

Muñoz, L. C., Frick, P. J., Kimonis, E. R., & Aucoin, K. J. (2008). Verbal ability and delinquency: Testing the moderating role of psychopathic traits. *Journal of Child Psychology and Psychiatry, 49*, 414–421.

Munsch, C. L., & Willer, R. (2012). The role of gender identity threat in perceptions of date rape and sexual coercion. *Violence Against Women, 18*, 1125–1146.

Muraya, D. N., & Fry, D. (2016). Aftercare services for child victims of sex trafficking: A systematic review of policy and practice. *Trauma, Violence, & Abuse, 17*, 204–220.

Murphy, S. A., Braun, T., Tillery, L., Cain, K. C., Johnson, L. C., & Beaton, R. D. (1999). PTSD among bereaved parents following the violent deaths of their 12- to 28-year-old children: A longitudinal prospective analysis. *Journal of Traumatic Stress, 12*, 273–291.

Murphy, B., Lilienfeld, S., Skeem, J., & Edens, J. F. (2016). Are fearless dominance traits superfluous in operationalizing psychopathy? Incremental validity and sex differences. *Psychological Assessment, 28*, 1597–1607.

Murphy, K. R., & Davidshofer, C. O. (1998). *Psychological testing: Principles and applications* (4th ed.). Upper Saddle River, NJ: Prentice Hall.

Murphy, S. A., Johnson, L. C., & Lohan, J. (2002). The aftermath of the violent death of a child: An integration of the assessments of parents' mental distress and PTSD during first 5 years of bereavement. *Journal of Loss and Trauma, 7*, 202–222.

Murphy, W. D., Coleman, E. M., & Haynes, M. R. (1986). Factors related to coercive sexual behavior in a nonclinical sample of males. *Violence and Victims, 1*, 255–278.

Murray, J. B. (1997). Munchausen syndrome/Munchausen syndrome by proxy. *Journal of Psychology, 131*, 343–350.

Murray, M., & O'Ran, S. (2002). Restitution. In A. Seymour, M. Murray, J. Sigmon, M. Hook, C. Edwards, M. Gaboury, & G. Coleman (Eds.), *National Victim Assistance Academy textbook*. Washington, DC: U.S. Department of Justice, Office of Victims of Crime.

Murrie, D. C., & Boccaccini, M. T. (2015). Adversarial allegiance among expert witnesses. *Annual Review of Law and Social Science, 11*, 37–55.

Murrie, D. C., Boccaccini, M. T., Guarnera, L. A., & Rufino, K. A. (2013). Are forensic experts biased by the side that retained them? *Psychological Science, 24*, 1889–1897.

Murrie, D. C., & Cornell, D. G. (2002). Psychopathy screening of incarcerated juveniles: A comparison of measures. *Psychological Assessment, 14*, 390–396.

Murrie, D. C., & Zelle, H. (2015). Criminal competencies. In B. L. Cutler & P. A. Zapf (Eds.), *APA handbook of forensic psychology: Vol. 1. Individual and situational influences in criminal and civil courts* (pp. 115–157). Washington, DC: American Psychological Association.

Musliner, K. L., & Singer, J. B. (2014). Emotional support and adult depression in survivors of childhood sexual abuse. *Child Abuse & Neglect, 38*, 1331–1340.

Myers, B., & Arena, M. P. (2001). Trial consultation: A new direction in applied psychology. *Professional Psychology: Research and Practice, 32*, 386–391.

Myers, B., Latter, R., & Abdollahi-Arena, M. K. (2006). The court of public opinion: Lay perceptions of polygraph testing. *Law and Human Behavior, 30,* 509–523.

Myers, J. E. B. (1991). Psychologists' involvement in cases of child maltreatment: Limits of role and expertise. *American Psychologist, 46,* 81–82.

Nadal, K., Davidoff, K. C., Davis, L. S., Wong, Y., Marshall, D., & McKenzie, U. (2015). A qualitative approach to intersectional microaggression: Understanding influences of race, ethnicity, gender, sexuality, and religion. *Qualitative Psychology, 2,* 147–163.

Nagayama-Hall, G. (1992, November/December). Inside the mind of the rapist. *Psychology Today, 25,* 12.

Nagin, D. S., Farrington, D. P., & Moffitt, T. (1995). Life-course trajectories of different types of offenders. *Criminology, 33,* 111–139.

Nagin, D. S., & Land, K. C. (1993). Age, criminal careers, and population heterogeneity: Specification and estimation of a nonparametric mixed Poisson model. *Criminology, 31,* 163–189.

Narag, R. E., Pizarro, J., & Gibbs, C. (2009). Lead exposure and its implications for criminological theory. *Criminal Justice and Behavior, 36,* 954–973.

National Center for Victims of Crime. (1999). *The NCVC does not support the current language of the proposed crime victims' rights constitutional amendment.* Arlington, VA: Author.

National Center on Elder Abuse. (1999). *Types of elder abuse in domestic settings.* Washington, DC: Author.

National Center for Women & Policing. (2002). *Equality denied: The status of women in policing: 2001.* Los Angeles: Author.

National Center on Elder Abuse. (2013). *Statistics/data.* Washington, DC: Author.

National College of Probate Judges. (2013). *National Probate Court Standards.* Williamsburg, VA: National Center for State Courts.

National Commission on Correctional Health Care. (2008). *Standards for health services in prisons.* Chicago, IL: Author.

National Council of Juvenile and Family Court Judges. (1993). The revised report from the National Task Force on Juvenile Sexual Offending. *Juvenile and Family Court Journal, 44,* 1–120.

National Council on Crime and Delinquency (2013). *What is restorative justice?* Retrieved from http://www.nnndglobal.org/what-we-do/restorative-justice-project

National Institutes of Mental Health. (1982). *Television and behavior: Ten years of scientific progress and implications for the eighties. Summary report.* Washington, DC: U.S. Government Printing Office.

National Organization for Victim Assistance. (1998). *Community crisis response team training manual* (2nd ed.). Washington, DC: Author.

National Psychologist. (2017, March/April). Little change after Pennsylvania mental health ruling. *The National Psychologist, 26,* 20.

National Research Council. (2003). *The polygraph and lie detection.* Washington, DC: The National Academies Press.

National Resource Center on Child Sexual Abuse (NRC). (1996, March/April). *NRCCSA News.* Huntsville, AL: Author.

National Tactical Officers Association. (2015a). *Tactical response and operations standard in law enforcement agencies.* Doylestown, PA: Author.

National Tactical Officers Association & International Association of Police Chiefs. (2015b). *National special weapons and tactics (SWAT) study: A national assessment of critical trends and issues from 2009 to 2013.* Doylestown, PA: Authors.

Neal, T. M. S., & Brodsky, S. L. (2016). Forensic psychologists' perceptions of bias and potential correction strategies in forensic mental health evaluations. *Psychology, Public Policy, and Law, 22,* 58–76.

Neal, T. M. S., & Clements, C. B. (2010). Prison rape and psychological sequelae: A call for research. *Psychology, Public Policy, and Law, 16,* 284–299.

Neff, J. L., Patterson, M. M., & Johnson, S. (2012). Meeting the training needs of those who meet the needs of victims: Assessing service providers. *Violence and Victims, 27,* 609–631.

Neimeyer, R. A. (2000). Searching the meaning of meaning: Grief therapy and the process of reconstruction. *Death Studies, 24,* 541–558.

Neimeyer, R. A., Prigerson, H. G., & Davies, B. (2002). Mourning and meaning. *American Behavioral Scientist, 46,* 235–251.

Nekvasil, E. K., & Cornell, D. G. (2012). Student reports of peer threats of violence: Prevalence and outcomes. *Journal of School Violence, 11,* 357–375.

Nekvasil, E. K., & Cornell, D. G. (2015). Student threat assessment associated with safety in middle schools. *Journal of Threat Assessment and Management, 2,* 98–113.

Nesca, M., & Dalby, J. T. (2011). Maternal neonaticide following traumatic childbirth: A case study. *International Journal of Offender Therapy and Comparative Criminology, 55,* 1166–1178.

Neubauer, D. W. (1997). *Judicial process* (2nd ed.). Fort Worth, TX: Harcourt Brace.

Neubauer, D. W. (2002). *America's courts and the criminal justice system* (7th ed.). Belmont, CA: Wadsworth.

Neumann, C. S., Schmitt, D. S., Carter, R., Embley, I., & Hare, R. D. (2012). Psychopathic traits in females and males across the globe. *Behavioral Sciences & the Law, 30,* 557–574.

Newirth, K. A. (2016). An eye for the science: Evolving judicial treatment of eyewitness identification evidence. *Journal of Applied Research in Memory and Cognition, 5,* 314–317.

Newman, G. (1979). *Understanding violence.* New York, NY: J. B. Lippincott.

Newman, J. P., Curtin, J. J., Bertsch, J. D., & Baskin-Sommers, A. R. (2010). Attention moderates the fearlessness of psychopathic offenders. *Biological Psychiatry, 67,* 66–70.

Newman, K., Fox, C., Harding, D., Mehta, J., & Roth, W. (2004). *Rampage: The social roots of school shootings*. New York, NY: Basic Books.

Nicholls, T. L., Cruise, K. R., Greig, D., & Hinz, H. (2015). Female offenders. In B. L. Cutler & P. A. Zapf (Eds.), *APA handbook of forensic psychology: Vol. 2. Criminal investigation, adjudication, and sentencing outcomes* (pp. 79–123). Washington, DC: American Psychological Association.

Nicholls, T. L., & Petrila, J. (2005). Gender and psychopathy: An overview of important issues and introduction to the special issue. *Behavioral Sciences & the Law, 23*, 729–741.

Nicholson, R. (1999). Forensic assessment. In R. Roesch, S. D. Hart, & J. R. P. (Eds.), *Psychology and law: The state of the discipline*. New York, NY: Kluwer Academic/Plenum.

Nicholson, R., & Norwood, S. (2000). The quality of forensic psychological assessments, reports, and testimony: Acknowledging the gap between promise and practice. *Law and Human Behavior, 24*, 9–44.

Niederhoffer, A., & Niederhoffer, E. (1977). *The police family: From station house to ranch house*. Lexington, MA: Heath.

Nielsen, L. (2017). Re-examining the research on parental conflict, coparenting, and custody arrangements. *Psychology, Public Policy, and Law, 23*, 211–231.

Nietzel, M. T., McCarthy, D. M., & Kerr, M. J. (1999). Juries: The current state of the empirical literature. In R. Roesch, S. D. Hart, & J. R. P. Ogloff (Eds.), *Psychology and law: The state of the discipline* (pp. 23–52). New York, NY: Kluwer Academic.

Nigg, J. T. (2000). On inhibition/disinhibition in developmental psychopathology: Views from cognitive and personality psychology and a working inhibition taxonomy. *Psychological Bulletin, 126*, 220–246.

Nigg, J. T., Butler, K. M., Huang-Pollock, C. L., & Henderson, J. M. (2002). Inhibitory processes in adults with persistent childhood onset ADHD. *Journal of Consulting and Clinical Psychology, 70*, 153–157.

Nigg, J. T., & Huang-Pollock, C. L. (2003). An early-onset model of the role of executive functions and intelligence in conduct disorder/delinquency. In B. B. Lahey, T. E. Moffitt, & A. Caspi (Eds.), *Causes of conduct disorder and juvenile delinquency* (pp. 227–253). New York, NY: Guilford Press.

Nigg, J. T., John, O. P., Blaskey, L. G., Huang-Pollock, C., Willcutt, E. G., Hinshaw, S. P., . . . & Pennington, B. (2002). Big Five dimensions and ADHD symptoms: Links between personality traits and clinical symptoms. *Journal of Personality and Social Psychology, 83*, 451–469.

Nigg, J. T., Quamma, J. P., Greenberg, M. T., & Kusche, C. A. (1999). A two-year longitudinal study of neuropsychological and cognitive performance in relation to behavioral problems and competencies in elementary school children. *Journal of Abnormal Child Psychology, 27*, 51–63.

Norko, M. A., Wasser, T., Magro, H., Leavitt-Smith, E., Morton, F. J., & Hollis, T. (2016). Assessing insanity acquittee recidivism in Connecticut. *Behavioral Sciences & the Law, 34*, 423–443.

Norris, F. H., & Kaniasty, K. (1994). Psychological distress following criminal victimization in the general population: Cross-sectional, longitudinal, and prospective analysis. *Journal of Consulting and Clinical Psychology, 62*, 111–123.

Norris, F. H., Kaniasty, K., & Scheer, D. A. (1990). Use of mental health services among victims of crime: Frequency, correlates, and subsequent recovery. *Journal of Consulting and Clinical Psychology, 58*, 538–547.

Norris, R. J., & Redlich, A. (2010, Summer). Actual innocence research: Researching compensation policies and other reforms. *American Psychology-Law Society News, 30*, 6–7.

Novosad, D., Banfe, S., Britton, J., & Bloom, J. D. (2016). Conditional release placements of insanity acquittees in Oregon: 2012–2014. *Behavioral Sciences & the Law, 34*, 366–377.

Nunes, K. L., & Jung, S. (2012). Are cognitive distortions associated with denial and minimization among sex offenders? *Sexual Abuse: A Journal of Research and Treatment, 25*, 166–188.

Oberlander, L. B., Goldstein, N. E. S., & Ho, C. N. (2001). Preadolescent adjudicative competence: Methodological considerations and recommendations for standard practice standards. *Behavioral Sciences & the Law, 19*, 545–563.

Ochoa, K. C., Pleasants, G. L., Penn, J. V., & Stone, D. C. (2010). Disparities in justice and care: Persons with severe mental illnesses in the U.S. immigration detention system. *The Journal of the American Academy of Psychiatry and the Law, 38*, 392–399.

O'Connell, P., Pepler, D., & Craig, W. (1999). Peer involvement in bullying: Insights and challenges for intervention. *Journal of Adolescence, 22*, 437–452.

O'Connor, T. P., & Maher, T. M. (2009, October). False confessions. *The Police Chief, 76*, 26–29.

Odgers, C. L., Caspi, A., Russell, M. A., Sampson, R. J., Arseneault, L., & Moffitt, T. E. (2012). Supportive parenting mediates neighborhood socioeconomic disparities in children's antisocial behavior from ages 5 to 12. *Development and Psychopathology, 24*, 705–721.

Odgers, C. L., Moffitt, T. E., Broadbent, J. M., Dickson, N., Hancox, R. J., Harrington, H., . . . & Caspi, A. (2008). Female and male antisocial trajectories: From childhood origins to adult outcomes. *Development and Psychopathology, 20*, 673–716.

Office for Victims of Crime. (2009). *Victims with disabilities: Collaborative, multidisciplinary first response*. Washington, DC: U.S. Author.

Offord, D. R., Boyle, M. C., & Racine, Y. A. (1991). The epidemiology of antisocial behavior in childhood and adolescence. In D. J. Pepler & H. Rubin (Eds.), *The development and treatment of childhood aggression* (pp. 31–54). Hillsdale, NJ: Erlbaum.

Ogawa, B., & Belle, A. S. (2002). Respecting diversity: Responding to underserved victims of crime. In A. Seymour, M. Murray, J. Sigmon, M. Hook, C. Edwards, M. Gaboury, & G. Coleman (Eds.), *National Victim Assistance Academy textbook*. Washington, DC: U.S. Department of Justice, Office of Victims of Crime.

Ogden, D. (2017, January). Mobile device forensics: Beyond call logs and text messages. *U.S. Attorneys' Bulletin, 65,* 11–14.

Ogle, R. S. (2000). Battered women and self-defense, USA. In N. H. Rafter (Ed.), *Encyclopedia of women and crime.* Phoenix, AZ: Oryx.

Ogloff, J. R. P. (1999). Ethical and legal contours of forensic psychology. In R. Roesch, S. D. Hart, & J. R. P. Ogloff (Eds.), *Psychology and law: The state of the discipline* (pp. 405–422). New York, NY: Kluwer Academic.

Ogloff, J. R. P., & Douglas, K. S. (2013). Forensic psychological assessments. In J. R. Graham, J. A. Naglieri, & I. B. Weiner (Eds.), *Handbook of psychology: Vol. 10. Assessment psychology* (2nd ed., pp. 373–393). Hoboken, NJ: Wiley.

O'Hara, A. F., & Violanti, J. (2009). Police suicide—A comprehensive study of 2008 national data. *International Journal of Emergency of Mental Health, 11,* 17–23.

O'Hara, A. F., Violanti, J. M., Levenson, R. L., & Clark, R. G. (2013). National police suicide estimates: Web surveillance study III. *International Journal of Emergency Mental Health and Human Resilience, 15,* 31–38.

O'Keefe, M. L., Klebe, K. J., Stucker, A., Sturm, K., & Leggett, W. (2010). *One year longitudinal study of the psychological effects of administrative segregation.* Colorado Springs: Colorado Department of Corrections.

Olaya, B., Ezpeleta, L., de la Osa, N., Granero, R., & Doménech, J. M. (2010). Mental health needs of children exposed to intimate partner violence seeking help from mental health services. *Children and Youth Services Review, 32,* 1004–1011.

Oliver, M. E., Nicholaichuk, T. P., Gu, D., & Wong, S. C. P. (2012). Sex offender treatment outcome, actuarial risk, and the aging sex offender in Canadian corrections: A long-term follow-up. *Sexual Abuse: A Journal of Research and Treatment, 25*(4), 396–422.

Olkin, R., & Pledger, C. (2003). Can disability studies and psychology join hands? *American Psychologist, 58,* 296–304.

Olver, M. E., Lewis, K., & Wong, S. C. P. (2013). Risk reduction of high-risk psychopathic offender: The relationship of psychopathy and treatment change to violent recidivism. *Personal Disorder, 4,* 160–167.

Olver, M. E., Preston, D. L., Camilleri, J. A., Helmus, L., & Starzomski, A. (2011). A survey of clinical psychology training in Canadian federal corrections: Implications for psychologist recruitment and retention. *Canadian Psychology, 52,* 310–320.

Olver, M. E., Stockdale, K. C., & Wormith, J. S. (2014). Thirty years of research on the level of service sales: A meta-analytic examination of predictive accuracy and sources of variability. *Psychological Assessment, 26,* 156–176.

Olver, M. E., & Wong, S. C. P. (2009). Therapeutic response of psychopathic sexual offenders: Treatment attrition, therapeutic change, and long term recidivism. *Journal of Consulting and Clinical Psychology, 77,* 328–336.

Omestad, T. (1994, Summer). Psychology and the CIA: Leaders on the couch. *Foreign Policy, 94,* 104–122.

Orne, M. T. (1970). Hypnosis, motivation and the ecological validity of the psychological experiment. In W. J. Arnold & M. M. Page (Eds.), *Nebraska Symposium on Motivation.* Lincoln: University of Nebraska Press.

Orne, M. T., Dinges, D. F., & Orne, E. C. (1984). On the differential diagnosis of multiple personality in the forensic context. *International Journal of Clinical and Experimental Hypnosis, 32,* 118–169.

Orne, M. T., Whitehouse, W. G., Dinges, D. F., & Orne, E. C. (1988). Reconstructing memory through hypnosis: Forensic and clinical implications. In H. M. Pettinati (Ed.), *Hypnosis and memory* (pp. 21–63). New York, NY: Guilford Press.

Ornstein, P. A., Ceci, S. J., & Loftus, E. F. (1998a). Adult recollections of childhood abuse: Cognitive and developmental perspectives. *Psychology, Public Policy, and Law, 4,* 1025–1051.

Ornstein, P. A., Ceci, S. J., & Loftus, E. F. (1998b). Comment on Alpert, Brown, and Courtois (1998): The science of memory and the practice of psychotherapy. *Psychology, Public Policy, and Law, 4,* 996–1010.

Ortega, R., Elipe, P., Mora-Merchán, I. A., Genta, M. L., Bright, A., Tippet, N., . . & Tippett, N. (2012). The emotional impact of bullying and cyberbullying on victims: A European cross-national study. *Aggressive Behavior, 38,* 342–356.

Orth, U., Cahill, S. P., Foa, E. B., & Maercker, A. (2008). Anger and posttraumatic stress disorder symptoms in crime victims: A longitudinal analysis. *Journal of Consulting and Clinical Psychology, 76,* 208–218.

Otero, T. M., Podell, K., DeFina, P., & Goldberg, E. (2013). Assessment of neuropsychological functioning. In J. R. Graham, J. A. Naglier, & I. B. Weiner (Eds.), *Handbook of psychology: Vol. 10. Assessment psychology* (2nd ed., pp. 503–533). Hoboken, NJ: Wiley.

O'Toole, M. E. (2000). *The school shooter: A threat assessment perspective.* Quantico, VA: National Center for the Analysis of Violent Crime, Criminal Incident Response Group.

O'Toole, M. E. (2013). Jeffrey Weise and the shooting at Red Lake Minnesota High School: A behavioral perspective. In N. Böckler, P. Sitzer, & W. Heitmeyer (Eds.), *School shootings: International research, case studies, and concepts for prevention* (pp. 177–188). New York, NY: Springer.

Otto, R. K., & Heilbrun, K. (2002). The practice of forensic psychology: A look toward the future in light of the past. *American Psychologist, 57,* 5–18.

Otto, R. K., Kay, S. L., & Hess, A. K. (2014). Testifying in court. In I. B. Weiner & R. K. Otto (Eds.), *The handbook of forensic psychology* (4th ed., pp. 733–756). Hoboken, NJ: Wiley.

Otto, R. K., & Ogloff, J. R. P. (2014). Defining forensic psychology. In I. B. Weiner & R. K. Otto (Eds.), *The handbook of forensic psychology* (4th ed., pp. 35–55). Hoboken, NJ: Wiley.

Otto, R. K., Poythress, N. G., Nicholson, R. A., Edens, J. F., Monahan, J., . . . & Bonnie, R. I. (1998). Psychometric properties of the MacArthur Competence Assessment Tool–Criminal Adjudication. *Psychological Assessment, 10*, 435–443.

Owen, B. (2000). Prison security. In N. H. Rafter (Ed.), *Encyclopedia of women and crime*. Phoenix, AZ: Oryx.

Owens, J. N., Eakin, J. D., Hoffer, T., Muirhead, Y., & Shelton, J. E. (2016). Investigative aspects of crossover offending from a sample of FBI online child sexual exploitation cases. *Aggression and Violent Behavior, 30*, 3–14.

Owhe, J. (2013). Indicated reports of child abuse or maltreatment: When suspects become victims. *Family Court Review, 51*, 316–329.

Ozer, E. J., Best, S. R., Lipsey, T. L., & Weiss, D. S. (2003). Predictors of posttraumatic stress disorder and symptoms in adults: A meta-analysis. *Psychological Bulletin, 129*, 52–73.

Packer, I. K. (2009). *Evaluation of criminal responsibility*. New York, NY: Oxford University Press.

Packer, I. K., & Borum, R. (2013). Forensic training and practice. In R. K. Otto & I. B. Weiner (Eds.), *Handbook of psychology: Vol. 11. Forensic psychology* (2nd ed., pp. 16–36). Hoboken, NJ: Wiley.

Padela, A. I., & Heisler, M. (2010). The association of perceived abuse and discrimination after September 11, 2001, with psychological distress, level of happiness, and health status among Arab Americans. *American Journal of Public Health, 100*, 284–291.

Page, K. S., & Jacobs, S. C. (2011). Surviving the shift: Rural police stress and counseling services. *Psychological Services, 8*, 12–22.

Palarea, R. E., Gelles, M. G., & Rowe, K. L. (2012). Crisis and hostage negotiation. In C. H. Kennedy & E. A. Sillmer (Eds.), *Military psychology: Clinical and operational applications* (2nd ed., pp. 281–305). New York, NY: Guilford Press.

Palarea, R. E., Zona, M. A., Lane, J. C., & Langhinrichsen-Rohling, J. (1999). The dangerous nature of intimate relationship stalking: Threats, violence, and associated risk factors. *Behavioral Sciences & the Law, 17*, 269–283.

Palfrey, J. G., & Gasser, U. (2008). *Born digital: Understanding the first generation of digit natives*. New York, NY: Basic Books.

Palmer, E. J., & Hollin, C. R. (2007). The Level of Service Inventory–Revised with English women prisoners: A needs and reconviction analysis. *Criminal Justice and Behavior, 34*, 91–98.

Palmer, J. W., & Palmer, S. E. (1999). *Constitutional rights of prisoners* (6th ed.). Cincinnati, OH: Anderson.

Paoline, E. A., III. (2003). Taking stock: Toward a richer understanding of police culture. *Journal of Criminal Justice, 31*, 199–214.

Pardini, D., & Byrd, A. L. (2012). Perceptions of aggressive conflicts and other's distress in children with callous-unemotional traits: "I'll show you who's boss, even if you suffer and I get into trouble." *Journal of Child Psychology and Psychiatry, 53*, 283–291.

Parent, D. G., Leiter, V., Kennedy, S., Livens, L., Wentworth, D., & Wilcox, S. (1994). *Conditions of confinement: Juvenile detention and corrections facilities*. Washington, DC: U.S. Department of Justice, Office of Juvenile Justice and Delinquency Prevention.

Parkinson, P., & Cashmore, J. (2008). *The voice of a child in family law disputes*. Oxford, England: Oxford University Press.

Parry, J., & Drogan, E. Y. (2000). *Criminal law handbook on psychiatric and psychological evidence and testimony*. Washington, DC: American Bar Association.

Partlett, D. F., & Nurcombe, B. (1998). Recovered memories of child sexual abuse and liability: Society, science, and the law in a comparative setting. *Psychology, Public Policy, and Law, 4*, 1253–1306.

Patihis, L., Ho, L. Y., Tingern, I. W., Lilienfeld, S. O., & Loftus, E. F. (2014). Are the "memory wars" over? A scientist–practitioner gap in beliefs about repressed memory. *Psychological Science, 25*, 519–530.

Paton, D. (2006). Critical incident stress risk in police officers: Managing resilience and vulnerability. *Traumatology, 12*, 198–206.

Patrick, C. J., Drislane, L. E., & Strickland, C. D. (2012). Conceptualizing psychopathy in triarchic terms: Implications for treatment. *International Journal of Forensic Mental Health, 11*, 253–266.

Patrick, C. J., Fowles, D. C., & Krueger, R. F. (2009). Triarchic conceptualization of psychopathy: Developmental origins of disinhibition, boldness, and meanness. *Development and Psychopathology, 21*, 913–938.

Patterson, D. (2011). The linkage between secondary victimization by law enforcement and rape case outcomes. *Journal of Interpersonal Violence, 26*, 328–347.

Patterson, G. R. (1982). *Coercive family processes*. Eugene, OR: Castalia Press.

Payne, B. K. (2008). Elder physical abuse and failure to report cases: Similarities and differences in case type and the justice system's response. *Crime & Delinquency, 59*, 697–717.

Payscale.com. (2016, October 28).

Pearl, P. T. (1995). Identifying and responding to Munchausen syndrome by proxy. *Early Child Development and Care, 106*, 177–185.

Pearson, F. S., Lipton, D. S., Cleland, C. M., & Yee, D. S. (2002). The effects of behavior/cognitive-behavioral programs on recidivism. *Crime & Delinquency, 48*, 476–496.

Pease, T., & Frantz, B. (1994). *Your safety . . . your rights & personal safety and abuse prevention education program to empower adults with disabilities and train service providers*. Doylestown, PA: Network of Victim Assistance.

Pemment, J. (2013). Psychopathy versus sociopathy: Why the distinction has become crucial. *Aggression and Violent Behavior, 18*, 458–461.

Penrod, S., & Cutler, B. L. (1995). Witness confidence and witness accuracy: Assessing their forensic relation. *Psychology, Public Policy, and Law, 1*, 817–845.

Pepler, D. J., Byrd, W., & King, G. (1991). A social-cognitively based social skills training program for aggressive children. In D. J. Pepler & K. H. Rubin (Eds.), *The development and treatment of childhood aggression* (pp. 361–379). Hillsdale, NJ: Erlbaum.

Perez, S., Johnson, D. M., & Wright, C. V. (2012). The attenuating effect of empowerment of IPV-related PTSD symptoms in battered women in domestic violence shelters. *Violence Against Women, 18,* 102–117.

Pérez-Fuentes, G., Olfson, M., Villegas, L., Morcillo, C., Wang, S., & Blanco, C. (2013). Prevalence and correlates of child sexual abuse: A national study. *Comprehensive Psychiatry, 54,* 16–27.

Perlin, M. L. (1991). Power imbalances in therapeutic and forensic relationships. *Behavioral Sciences & the Law, 9,* 111–128.

Perlin, M. L. (1994). *The jurisprudence of the insanity defense.* Durham, NC: Carolina Academic Press.

Perlin, M. L. (1996). "Dignity was the first to leave": *Godinez v. Moran,* Colin Ferguson, and the trial of mentally disabled criminal defendants. *Behavioral Sciences & the Law, 14,* 61–81.

Perlin, M. L. (2003). Beyond *Dusky* and *Godinez:* Competency before and after trial. *Behavioral Sciences & the Law, 21,* 297–310.

Perlin, M. L., & Dorfman, D. A. (1996). Is it more than "dodging lions and wastin' time"? Adequacy of counsel, questions of competence, and the judicial process in individual right to refuse treatment cases. *Psychology, Public Policy, and Law, 2,* 114–136.

Petersen, I. T., Bates, J. E., D'Onofrio, B. M., Coyne, C. A., Lansford, J. E., Dodge, K. A., . . . &Van Hulle, C. A. (2013). Language ability predicts the development of behavior problems in children. *Journal of Abnormal Psychology, 122,* 542–557.

Peterson, C., Morris, G., Baker-Ward, L., & Flynn, S. (2014). Predicting which childhood memories persist: Contributions of memory characteristics. *Developmental Psychology, 50,* 439–448.

Peterson, D. R. (1968). The doctor of psychology program at the University of Illinois. *American Psychologist, 23,* 511–516.

Peterson-Badali, M., Skilling, T., & Haqanee, Z. (2015). Examining implementation of risk assessment in case management for youth in the justice system. *Criminal Justice and Behavior, 42,* 304–320.

Petretic-Jackson, P. A., Witte, T. H., & Jackson, T. L. (2002). Battered women: Treatment goals and treatment planning. In A. R. Roberts (Ed.), *Handbook of domestic violence intervention strategies: Policies, programs, and legal remedies.* (pp. 298–320) New York, NY: Oxford University Press.

Petrila, J. P. (2009). Finding common ground between scientific psychology and the law. In J. L. Skeem, K. S. Douglas, & S. O. Lilienfeld (Eds.), *Psychological science in the courtroom* (pp. 387–407). New York, NY: Guilford Press.

Pfeffer, A. (2008). Note: "Imminent danger" and inconsistency: The need for national reform of the "imminent danger" standard for involuntary civil commitment in the wake of the Virginia Tech tragedy. *Cardozo Law Review, 30,* 277–318.

Pfiffner, L. J., McBurnett, K., Lahey, B. B., Loeber, R., Green, S., Frick, P. J., . . . & Rathouz, P. J. (1999). Association of parental psychopathology to the comorbid disorders of boys with attention deficit–hyperactivity disorder. *Journal of Consulting and Clinical Psychology, 67,* 881–893.

Phenix, A., & Jackson, R. L. (2016). Evaluations for sexual offender civil commitment. In R. Jackson & R. Roesch (Eds.), *Learning forensic assessment: Research and Practice* (2nd ed., pp. 162–201). New York, NY: Routledge.

Piechowski, L. D. (2011). *Best practices in forensic mental health assessment: Evaluation of workplace disability.* New York, NY: Oxford University Press.

Piechowski, L. D., & Drukteinis, A. M. (2011). Fitness for duty. In E. Drogin, F. Dattilio, R. Sadoff, & T. Gutheil (Eds.), *Handbook of forensic assessment* (pp. 571–592). Hoboken, NJ: Wiley.

Pillemer, K., & Finkelhor, D. (1988). The prevalence of elder abuse: A random sample survey. *Gerontologist, 28,* 51–57.

Pinizzotto, A. J. (1984). Forensic psychology: Criminal personality profiling. *Journal of Police Science and Administration, 12,* 32–40.

Pinizzotto, A. J., & Finkel, N. J. (1990). Criminal personality profiling: An outcome and process study. *Law and Human Behavior, 14,* 215–234.

Piquero, N. L., Piquero, A. R., Craig, J. M., & Clipper, S. J. (2013). Assessing research on workplace violence, 2000–2012. *Aggression and Violent Behavior, 18,* 383–394.

Pirelli, G., Gottdiener, W. H., & Zapf, P. A. (2011). A meta-analytic review of competency to stand trial research. *Psychology, Public Policy, and Law, 17,* 1–53.

Pithers, W. D., Becker, J. V., Kafka, M., Morenz, B., Schlank, A., & Leombruno, P. (1995). Children with sexual behavior problems, adolescent sexual abusers, and adult sexual offenders: Assessment and treatment. *American Psychiatric Press Review of Psychiatry, 14,* 779–819.

Planty, M., Langton, L., Krebs, C., Berzofsky, M., & Smiley-McDonald, H. (2013, March). *Female victims of sexual assault, 1994–2010.* Washington, DC: Department of Justice, Bureau of Justice Statistics.

Planty, M., & Truman, J. L. (2013, May). *Firearm violence, 1993–2011. Special report.* Washington: U.S. Department of Justice, Bureau of Justice Statistics.

Podkopacz, M. R., & Feld, B. C. (1996). The end of the line: An empirical study of judicial waiver. *Journal of Criminal Law and Criminology, 86,* 449–492.

Polanczyk, G., Lima, M. S., Horta, B. L., Biederman, J., & Rohde, L. A. (2007). The worldwide prevalence of ADHD: A systematic review and meta-regression analyses. *American Journal of Psychiatry, 164,* 942–948.

Polaschek, D. L. L., & Daly, T. E (2013). Treatment and psychopathy in forensic settings. *Aggression and Violent Behavior, 18*, 592–603.

Police Executive Research Forum (PERF). (2013). *A national survey of eyewitness identification procedures in law enforcement agencies.* Washington, DC: Author.

Polizzi, D. M., MacKenzie, D. L., & Hickman, L. J. (1999). What works in adult sex offender treatment: A review of prison- and non-prison-based treatment programs. *International Journal of Offender Therapy and Comparative Criminology, 43*, 357–374.

Polusny, M., & Follette, V. (1996). Remembering childhood sexual abuse: A national survey of psychologists' clinical practices, beliefs, and personal experiences. *Professional Psychology: Research and Practice, 27*, 41–52.

Pope, K. S. (2012). Psychological evaluation of torture survivors: Essential steps, avoidable errors, and helpful resources. *International Journal of Law and Psychiatry, 35*, 418–426.

Pornari, C. D., & Wood, J. (2010). Peer and cyber aggression in secondary school students: The role of moral disengagement, hostile attribution bias, and outcome expectancies. *Aggressive Behavior, 36*, 81–94.

Porter, S., Fairweather, D., Drugge, J., Hervé, H., Birt, A., & Boer, D. P. (2000). Profiles of psychopathy in incarcerated sexual offenders. *Criminal Justice and Behavior, 27*, 216–233.

Porter, T., & Gavin, H. (2010). Infanticide and neonaticide: A review of 40 years of research literature on incidence and causes. *Trauma, Violence, & Abuse, 11*, 99–112.

Porter, S., Yuille, J. C., & Lehman, D. R. (1999). The nature of real, implanted, and fabricated memories for emotional childhood events: Implications for the recovered memory debate. *Law and Human Behavior, 23*, 517–537.

Portzky, G., Audenaert, K., & van Heeringen, K. (2009). Psychological and psychiatric factors associated with adolescent suicide: A case–control psychological autopsy study. *Journal of Adolescence, 32*, 849–862.

Post, L. A., Biroscak, B. J., & Barboza, G. (2011). Prevalence of sexual assault. In J. W. White, M. P. Koss, & A. F. Kazdin (Eds.), *Violence against women and children: Vol I. Mapping the terrain* (pp. 101–123). Washington, DC: American Psychological Association.

Potoczniak, M. J., Mourot, J. E., Crosbie-Burnett, M., & Potoczniak, D. J. (2003). Legal and psychological perspectives on same-sex domestic violence: A multisystematic approach. *Journal of Family Violence, 17*, 252–259.

Powers, R. A., & Kaukinen, C. E. (2012). Trends in intimate partner violence: 1980–2008. *Journal of Interpersonal Violence, 27*, 3072–3080.

Poythress, N. G., Otto, R. K., Darnes, J., & Starr, L. (1993). APA's expert panel in congressional review of the *USS Iowa* incident. *American Psychologist, 48*, 8–15.

Poythress, N. G., & Zapf, P. A. (2009). Controversies in evaluating competence to stand trial. In J. L. Skeem, K. S. Douglas, & S. O. Lilienfeld (Eds.), *Psychological science in the courtroom: Consensus and controversy* (pp. 309–329). New York, NY: Guilford Press.

Prendergast, M. L., Farabee, D., Cartier, J., & Henkin, S. (2002). Involuntary treatment within a prison setting. *Criminal Justice and Behavior, 29*, 5–26.

Prentky, R. A., Burgess, A. W., & Carter, D. L. (1986). Victim responses by rapist type: An empirical and clinical analysis. *Journal of Interpersonal Violence, 1*, 73–98.

Prentky, R. A., Burgess, A. W., Rokous, F., Lee, A., Hartman, C., Ressler, R., . . . & Douglas, J. (1989). The presumptive role of fantasy in serial sexual homicide. *American Journal of Psychiatry, 146*, 887–891.

Prentky, R. A., Harris, B., Frizzell, K., & Righthand, S. (2000). An actuarial procedure of assessing risk in juvenile sex offenders. *Sexual Abuse: A Journal of Research and Treatment, 12*, 71–93.

Prentky, R. A., & Knight, R. A. (1986). Impulsivity in the lifestyle and criminal behavior of sexual offenders. *Criminal Justice and Behavior, 13*, 141–164.

Prentky, R. A., & Knight, R. A. (1991). Identifying critical dimensions for discriminating among rapists. *Journal of Consulting and Clinical Psychology, 59*, 643–661.

Prentky, R. A., Knight, R. A., & Lee, A. F. S. (1997, June). *Child sexual molestation: Research issues.* Washington, DC: U.S. Department of Justice, Office of Justice Programs.

Prentky, R. A., & Righthand, S. (2003). *Juvenile Sex Offender Assessment Protocol–II (J-SOAP-II).* Washington, DC: U.S. Department of Justice, Office of Juvenile Justice and Delinquency Prevention.

Presser, L., & Van Voorhis, P. (2002). Values and evaluation: Assessing processes and outcomes of restorative justice programs. *Crime & Delinquency, 48*, 162–188.

Preston, J. (2017, July 30). Migrants in surge fare worse in immigration court than other groups. *The Washington Post.* Retrieved from https://www.washingtonpost.com/national/migrants-in-surge-fare-worse-in-immigration-court-than-other-groups/2017/07/30/e29eeacc-6e51-11e7-9c15-177740635e83_story.html?utm_term=.30738cef8abf

Pridham, K., Francombe Pridham, M., Berntson, A., Simpson, A. I. F., Law, S. F., Stergiopoulos, V., & Nakhost, A. (2016). Perception of coercion among patients with a psychiatric community treatment order: A literature review. *Psychiatric Services, 67*(1), 16–28.

ProCon.org. (2017). *29 Legal medical marijuana states and DC.* Retrieved from http://medicalmarijuana.procon.org/view.resource.php?resourceID=000881

Purcell, R., Moller, B., Flower, T., & Mullen, P. E. (2009). Stalking among juveniles. *British Journal of Psychiatry, 194*, 451–455.

Puritz, P., & Scali, M. A. (1998). *Beyond the walls: Improving conditions of confinement for youth in custody.* Washington, DC: U.S. Department of Justice, Office of Juvenile Justice and Delinquency Prevention.

Putnam, C. T., & Kirkpatrick, J. T. (2005, May). Juvenile firesetting: A research overview. *Juvenile Justice Bulletin* (NCJ 207606). Washington, DC: U.S. Department of Justice, Office of Juvenile Justice and Delinquency Prevention.

Puzzanchera, C. M. (2009, April). *Juvenile arrests 2007*. Washington, DC: U. S. Department of Justice, Office of Juvenile Justice and Delinquency Prevention.

Puzzanchera, C. M. (2013, December). *Juvenile arrests 2011*. Washington, DC: U.S. Department of Justice, Office of Juvenile Justice and Delinquency Prevention.

Puzzanchera, C. M., Adams, B., & Sickmund, M. (2010, March). *Juvenile court statistics, 2006–2007*. Pittsburgh, PA: National Center for Juvenile Justice.

Puzzanchera, C. M., & Addie, S. (2014, February). *Delinquency cases waived to criminal court, 2010*. Washington, DC: U.S. Department of Justice, Office of Juvenile Justice and Delinquency Prevention.

Puzzanchera, C. M., & Robson, C. (2014, February). *Delinquency cases in juvenile court, 2010*. Washington, DC: U.S. Department of Justice, Office of Juvenile Justice and Delinquency Prevention.

Quay, H. C. (1965). Psychopathic personality: Pathological stimulation-seeking. *American Journal of Psychiatry, 122*, 180–183.

Quickel, E. J. W., & Demakis, G. J. (2013). The Independent Living Scales in civil competency evaluation: Initial findings and prediction in competency adjudication. *Law and Human Behavior, 37*, 155–162.

Quickel, E. J. W., & Demakis, G. J. (2017). Forensic neuropsychology and the legal consumer. In S. S. Bush (Ed.), *APA handbook of forensic neuropsychology* (pp. 445–459). Washington, DC: American Psychological Association.

Quinsey, V. L. (1986). Men who have sex with children. In D. N. Weisstub (Ed.), *Law and mental health: International perspectives* (Vol. 2, pp. 140–172). New York, NY: Pergamon.

Quinsey, V. L., Harris, G. T., Rice, M. E., & Cormier, C. A. (1998). *Violent offenders: Appraising and managing risk*. Washington, DC: American Psychological Association

Quinsey, V. L., Harris, G. T., Rice, M. E., & Cormier, C. A. (2006). *Violent offenders: Appraising and managing risk* (2nd ed.). Washington, DC: American Psychological Association.

Quinsey, V. L., Rice, M. E., & Harris, G. T. (1995). Actuarial prediction of sexual recidivism. *Journal of Interpersonal Violence, 10*, 85–105.

Rabe-Hemp, C. E., & Schuck, A. M. (2007). Violence against police officers: Are female officers at greater risk? *Police Quarterly, 10*, 411–428.

Rafferty, Y. (2013). Child trafficking and commercial sexual exploitation: A review of promising prevention policies and programs. *American Journal of Orthopsychiatry, 83*, 559–575.

Rafferty, Y. (2017, April 10). Mental health services as a vital component of psychosocial recovery for victims of child trafficking for commercial sexual exploitation. *American Journal of Orthopsychiatry*. Advance online publication. doi:10.1037/ort0000268

Rainbow, L., & Gregory, A. (2011). What behavioral investigative advisers actually do. In L. Alison & L. Rainbow (Eds.), *Professionalizing offender profiling* (pp. 35–50). London, England: Routledge.

Raine, A. (1993). *The psychopathology of crime: Criminal behavior as a clinical disorder*. San Diego, CA: Academic Press.

Raine, A. (2013). *The anatomy of violence: The biological roots of crime*. New York, NY: Vintage Books.

Ramchand, R., Schell, T. L., Karney, B. R., Osilla, K. C., Burns, R. M., & Caldarone, L. B. (2010). Disparate prevalence estimates of PTSD among service members who served in Iraq and Afghanistan: Possible explanations. *Journal of Traumatic Stress, 23*, 59–68.

Ramirez, D., McDevitt, J., & Farrell, A. (2000, November). *A resource guide on racial profiling data collection systems: Promising practices and lessons learned*. Boston, MA: Northeastern University Press.

Ramos-Gonzalez, N. N., Weiss, R. A., Schweizer, J., & Rosinski, A. (2016). Fitness to stand trial evaluations in immigration proceedings. *Canadian Psychology, 57*, 284–290.

Ramsay, J. R. (2017). The relevance of cognitive distortions in the psychosocial treatment of adult ADHD. *Professional Psychology: Research and Practice, 48*, 62–69.

Rand, M. R. (2009, September). *Criminal victimization, 2008*. Washington, DC: U.S. Department of Justice, Office of Justice Programs.

Rand, M. R., & Harrell, E. (2009, October). *Crime against people with disabilities, 2007*. Washington, DC: U. S. Department of Justice, Office of Justice Programs.

Raney, R. F. (2017, April). Unseen victims of sex trafficking. *APA Monitor, 48*, 32.

Raspe, R. E. (1944). *The surprising adventures of Baron Munchausen*. New York, NY: Peter Pauper.

Reaves, B. A. (2012a). *Federal law enforcement officers, 2008*. Washington, DC: U.S. Department of Justice, Bureau of Justice Statistics.

Reaves, B. A. (2012b, October). *Hiring and retention of state and local law enforcement officers, 2008*. Washington, DC: U.S. Department of Justice, Bureau of Justice Statistics.

Reaves, B. A. (2015, January). *Campus law enforcement, 2011–2012*. Washington, DC: U.S. Department of Justice, Bureau of Justice Statistics.

Redding, R. E. (2010, June). *Juvenile transfer laws: An effective deterrent to delinquency?* Washington, DC: U.S. Department of Justice, Office of Juvenile Justice and Delinquency Prevention.

Redding, R. E., Floyd, M. Y., & Hawk, G. L. (2001). What judges and lawyers think about the testimony of mental health experts: A survey of the courts and bar. *Behavioral Sciences & the Law, 19*, 583–594.

Redlich, A. D. (2010). False confessions, false guilty pleas: Similarities and differences. In G. D. Lassiter & C. A. Meissner (Eds.), *Police* interrogation and false confessions: *Current research, practice, and policy recommendations* (pp. 49–66). Washington, DC: American Psychological Association.

Redlich, A. D., Bibas, S., Edkins, V. A., & Madon, S. (2017). The psychology of defendant pleas decision making. *American Psychologist, 72,* 339–352.

Redlich, A. D., & Goodman, G. S. (2003). Taking responsibility for an act not committed: The influence of age and suggestibility. *Law and Human Behavior, 27,* 141–156.

Redlich, A. D., Kulich, R., & Steadman, H. J. (2011). Comparing true and false confessions among persons with serious mental illness. *Psychology, Public Policy, and Law, 17,* 394–418.

Redlich, A. D., Silverman, M., & Steiner, H. (2003). Pre-adjudicative and adjudicative competence in juveniles and young adults. *Behavioral Sciences & the Law, 21,* 393–410.

Redlich, A. D., Summers, A., & Hoover, S. (2010). Self-reported false confessions and false guilty pleas among offenders with mental illness. *Law and Human Behavior, 34,* 79–90.

Reed, G. M., Levant, R. F., Stout, C. E., Murphy, M. J., & Phelps, R. (2001). Psychology in the current mental health marketplace. *Professional Psychology: Research and Practice, 32,* 65–70.

Reese, J. T. (1986). Foreword. In J. T. Reese & H. Goldstein (Eds.), *Psychological services for law enforcement.* Washington, DC: U.S. Government Printing Office.

Reese, J. T. (1987). *A history of police psychological services.* Washington, DC: U.S. Government Printing Office.

Regan, W. M., & Gordon, S. M. (1997). Assessing testamentary capacity in elderly people. *Southern Medical Journal, 90,* 13–15.

Reichert, J., Adams, S., & Bostwick, L. (2010, April). *Victimization and help-seeking behaviors among female prisoners in Illinois.* Chicago, IL: Illinois Criminal Justice Information Authority.

Reid, J. A. (2012). Exploratory review of route-specific, gendered, and age-graded dynamics of exploitation: Applying life course theory to victimization in sex trafficking in North America. *Aggression and Violent Behavior, 17,* 257–271.

Reid, J. B. (1993). Prevention of conduct disorders before and after school entry: Relating interventions to developmental findings. *Development and Psychopathology, 5,* 243–262.

Reidy, T. J., Sorensen, J. R., & Davidson, M. (2016). Testing the predictive validity of the Personality Assessment Inventory (PAI) in relation to inmate misconduct and violence. *Psychological Assessment, 28,* 871–884.

Reijntjes, A., Vermande, M., Olthof, T., Goossens, F. A., van de Schoot, R., Aleva, L., & vander Meulen, M. (2013). Costs and benefits of bullying in the context of the peer group: A three wave longitudinal analysis. *Journal of Abnormal Child Psychology, 41,* 1217–1229.

Reinert, J. A. (2006, Summer). Guardianship reform in Vermont. *Vermont Bar Journal,* 40–43.

Reiser, M. (1982). *Police psychology: Collected papers.* Los Angeles, CA: LEHI.

Reisner, R., Slobogin, C., & Rai, A. (2004). *Law and the mental health system: Civil and criminal aspects* (4th ed.). St. Paul, MN: West.

Reitzel, L. R. (2003, January). Sexual offender update: Juvenile sexual offender recidivism and treatment effectiveness. *Correctional Psychologist, 35,* 3–4.

Rennison, C. (2001, March). *Violent victimization and race, 1993–1998.* Washington, DC: U.S. Department of Justice, Bureau of Justice Statistics.

Rennison, C. M. (2002b, August). *Rape and sexual assault: Reporting to police and medical attention, 1992–2000.* Washington, DC: U.S. Department of Justice, Bureau of Justice Statistics.

Reno, J. (1999). Message from the attorney general. In Technical Working Group for Eyewitness Evidence (Ed.), *Eyewitness evidence: A guide for law enforcement.* Washington, DC: National Institute of Justice.

Renzetti, C. M. (1992). *Violent betrayal: Partner abuse in lesbian relationships.* Newbury Park, CA: Sage.

Reppucci, N. D., Meyer, J., & Kostelnik, J. (2010). Custodial interrogation of juveniles: Results of a national survey of police. In G. D. Lassiter & C. A. Meissner (Eds.), *Police interrogations and false confessions: Current research, practice, and police recommendations* (pp. 67–80). Washington, DC: American Psychological Association.

Reppucci, N. D., & Saunders, J. T. (1974). Social psychology of behavior modification: Problems of implementation in natural settings. *American Psychologist, 29,* 649–660.

Ressler, R. K., Burgess, A., & Douglas, J. E. (1988). *Sexual homicide: Patterns and motives.* Lexington, MA: Lexington Books.

Rice, M. E., & Harris, G. T. (2002). Men who molest their sexually immature daughters: Is a special explanation required? *Journal of Abnormal Psychology, 111,* 329–339.

Rice, M. E., Harris, G. T., & Cormier, C. A. (1992). An evaluation of a maximum security therapeutic community for psychopaths and other mentally disordered offenders. *Law and Human Behavior, 16,* 399–412.

Ricks, E. P., Louden, J. E., & Kennealy, P. J. (2016). Probation officer role emphases and use of risk assessment information before and after training. *Behavioral Sciences & the Law, 34*(2/3), 337–351.

Righthand, S., & Welch, C. (2001, March). *Juveniles who have sexually offended: A review of the professional literature.* Washington, DC: U.S. Department of Justice, Office of Juvenile Justice and Delinquency Prevention.

Riser, R. E., & Kosson, D. S. (2013). Criminal behavior and cognitive processing in male offenders with antisocial personality disorder with and without comorbid psychopathy. *Personality Disorders: Theory, Research, and Treatment, 4,* 332–340.

Risinger, D. M., & Loop, J. L. (2002). Three card monte, Monty Hall, modus operandi, and "offender profiling": Some lessons of modern cognitive science for the law of evidence. *Cardozo Law Review, 24*, 193–285.

Ritchie, E. C., & Gelles, M. G. (2002). Psychological autopsies: The current Department of Defense effort to standardize training and quality assurance. *Journal of Forensic Science, 47*, 1370–1372.

Ritvo, E., Shanok, S. S., & Lewis, D. O. (1983). Firesetting and non-firesetting delinquents. *Child Psychiatry and Human Development, 13*, 259–267.

Rivard, J. R., Fisher, R. P., Robertson, B., & Mueller, D. H. (2014). Testing the cognitive interview with professional interviewers: Enhancing recall of specific details of recurring events. *Applied Cognitive Psychology, 28*, 917–925.

Robbennolt, J. K., Groscup, J. L., & Penrod, S. (2014). Evaluating and assisting jury competence in civil cases. In I. B. Weiner & R. K. Otto (Eds.), *The handbook of forensic psychology* (4th ed., pp. 469–512). Hoboken, NJ: Wiley.

Robbins, E., & Robbins, L. (1964). Arson with special reference to pyromania. *New York State Journal of Medicine, 2*, 795–798.

Robers, S., Zhang, J., Truman, J., & Snyder, T. (2012). *Indicators of school crime and safety: 2011*. Washington, DC: U.S. Department of Education, National Center for Educational Statistics.

Robins, P. M., & Sesan, R. (1991). Munchausen syndrome by proxy: Another women's disorder. *Professional Psychology: Research and Practice, 22*, 285–290.

Robinson, R., & Acklin, M. W. (2010). Fitness in paradise: Quality of forensic reports submitted to the Hawaii judiciary. *International Journal of Law and Psychiatry, 33*, 131–137.

Rodriguez, N. (2007). Restorative justice at work: Examining the impact of restorative justice resolutions on juvenile recidivism. *Crime & Delinquency, 33*, 355–379.

Roediger, H. L. (2016). Varieties of fame in psychology. *Perspectives on Psychological Science, 11*, 882–887.

Roediger, H. L., & Bergman, E. T. (1998). The controversy over recovered memories. *Psychology, Public Policy, and Law, 4*, 1091–1109.

Roesch, R., Zapf, P. A., & Eaves, D. (2006). *Fitness Interview Test: A structured interview for assessing competency to stand trial*. Sarasota, FL: Professional Resource Press.

Roesch, R., Zapf, P. A., Golding, S. L., & Skeem, J. L. (1999). Defining and assessing competency to stand trial. In A. K. Hess & I. B. Weiner (Eds.), *The handbook of forensic psychology* (2nd ed., pp. 327–349). New York, NY: Wiley.

Rogers, R. (1984). *Rogers Criminal Responsibility Assessment Scales (R-CRAS) and test manual*. Odessa, FL: Psychological Assessment Resources.

Rogers, R. (1992). *Structured Interview of Reported Symptoms*. Odessa, FL: Psychological Assessment Resources.

Rogers, R. (1997). *Clinical assessment of malingering and deception* (2nd ed.). New York, NY: Guilford Press.

Rogers, R. (2011). Getting it wrong about *Miranda* rights: False beliefs, impaired reasoning, and professional neglect. *American Psychologist, 66*, 728–736.

Rogers, R. (Ed.). (2012). *Clinical assessment of malingering and deception* (3rd ed.). New York, NY: Guilford Press.

Rogers, R. (2016). An introduction to insanity evaluation. In R. Jackson & R. Roesch (Eds.), *Learning forensic assessment: Research and Practice* (2nd ed., pp. 97–115). New York, NY: Routledge.

Rogers, R., & Ewing, C. P. (1989). Ultimate issue proscriptions: A cosmetic fix and plea for empiricism. *Law and Human Behavior, 13*, 357–374.

Rogers, R., & Ewing, C. P. (2003). The prohibition of ultimate opinions: A misguided enterprise. *Journal of Forensic Psychology Practice, 3*, 65–75.

Rogers, R., Harrison, K. S., Shuman, D. W., Sewell, K. W., & Hazelwood, L. L. (2007). An analysis of *Miranda* warning and waivers: Comprehension and coverage. *Law and Human Behavior, 31*, 177–192.

Rogers, R., Hazelwood, L. L., Sewell, K. W., Blackwood, H. L., Rogstad, J. E., & Harrison, K. S. (2009). Development and initial validation of the Miranda Vocabulary Scale. *Law and Human Behavior, 33*, 381–392.

Rogers, R., Rogstad, J. E., Gillard, N. D., Drogin, E. Y., Blackwood, H. L., & Shuman, D. W. (2010). "Everyone knows their Miranda rights"; Implicit assumptions and countervailing evidence. *Psychology, Public Policy, and Law, 16*, 300–318.

Rogers, R., & Sewell, K. W. (1999). The R-CRAS and insanity evaluations: A re-examination of construct validity. *Behavioral Sciences & the Law, 17*, 181–194.

Rogers, R., & Shuman, D. W. (1999). *Conducting insanity evaluations* (2nd ed.). New York, NY: Guilford Press.

Rogers, R., Tillbrook, C. E., & Sewell, K. W. (2004). *Evaluation of Competency to Stand Trial–Revised (ECST-R) and professional manual*. Odessa, FL: Psychological Assessment Resources.

Rohde, L. A., Barbosa, G., Polanczyk, G., Eizirik, M., Rasmussen, R. R., Neuman, R. J., . . . & Todd, R. D. (2001). Factor and latent class analysis of DSM-IV ADHD symptoms in a school sample of Brazilian adolescents. *Journal of the American Academy of Child and Adolescent Psychiatry, 40*, 711–718.

Romani, C. J., Morgan, R. D., Gross, N. R., & McDonald B. R. (2012). Treating criminal behavior: Is the bang worth the buck? *Psychology, Public Policy, and Law, 18*, 144–165.

Romans, J. S. C., Hays, J. R., & White, T. K. (1996). Stalking and related behaviors experienced by counseling center staff members from current and former clients. *Professional Psychology: Research and Practice, 27*, 595–599.

Root, C., MacKay, S., Henderson, J., Del Bove, G., & Warling, D. (2008). The link between maltreatment and juvenile firesetting: Correlates and underlying mechanisms. *Child Abuse & Neglect, 32,* 161–176.

Root, R. W., & Resnick, R. J. (2003). An update on the diagnosis and treatment of attention deficit/hyperactivity disorder in children. *Professional Psychology: Research and Practice, 34,* 34–41.

Rosenfeld, B., & Harmon, R. (2002). Factors associated with violence in stalking and obsessional harassment cases. *Criminal Justice and Behavior, 29,* 671–691.

Rosenfeld, B., Howe, J., Pierson, A., & Foellmi, M. (2015). Mental health treatment of criminal offenders. In B. L. Cutler & P. A. Zapf, *APA handbook of forensic psychology: Vol. 1. Individual and situational influences in criminal and civil contexts* (pp. 159–190). Washington, DC: American Psychological Association.

Rosin, H. (2014, April 29). *When men are raped.* NPR's Doublex. Retrieved from www. Slate.com

Rossmo, D. K. (1997). Geographical profiling. In J. T. Jackson & D. A. Bekerain (Eds.), *Offender profiling: Theory, research and practice* (pp. 159–176). Chichester, England: Wiley.

Rothman, D. (1980). *Conscience and convenience.* Boston, MA: Little, Brown.

Rozalski, M., Katsiyannis, A., Ryan, J., Collins, T., & Stewart, A. (2010). Americans with Disabilities Act Amendments of 2008. *Journal of Disability Policy Studies, 21,* 22–28.

Rubin, K. H., Bukowski, W., & Parker, J. G. (1998). Peer interactions, relationships, and groups. In N. Eisenberg (Ed.), *Handbook of child psychology: Vol. 3. Social, emotional, and personality development* (5th ed., pp. 619–700). New York, NY: Wiley.

Rubinstein, M., Yeager, C. A., Goodstein, C., & Lewis, D. O. (1993). Sexually assaultive male juveniles: A follow-up. *American Journal of Psychiatry, 150,* 262–265.

Ruiz, M. A., Cox, J., Magyar, M. S., & Edens, J. F. (2014). Predictive validity of the Personality Assessment Inventory (PAI) for identifying criminal reoffending following completion of an in-jail addiction treatment program. *Psychological Assessment, 26,* 673–678.

Russano, M. B., Narchet, F. M., & Kleinmann, S. M. (2014). Analysts, interpreters, and intelligence interrogations: Perceptions and insights. *Applied Cognitive Psychology, 28,* 829–846.

Russell, B. S. (2010). Revisiting the measurement of shaken baby syndrome awareness. *Child Abuse & Neglect, 34,* 671–676.

Sadeh, N., Javdani, S., & Verona, E. (2013). Analysis of monoaminergic genes, childhood abuse, and dimensions of psychopathy. *Journal of Abnormal Psychology, 122,* 167–179.

Saks, M. J. (1993). Improving APA science translation amicus briefs. *Law and Human Behavior, 17,* 235–247.

Salekin, R. T. (2002). Psychopathy and therapeutic pessimism: Clinical lore or clinical reality? *Clinical Psychology Review, 22,* 79–112.

Salekin, R. T., Brannen, D. N., Zalot, A. A., Leistico, A.-M., & Neumann, C. S. (2006). Factor structure of psychopathy in youth: Testing the applicability of the new four-factor model. *Criminal Justice and Behavior, 33,* 135–157.

Salekin, R. T., Lee, Z., Schrum Dillard, C. L., & Kubak, F. A. (2010). Child psychopathy and protective factors: IQ and motivation to change. *Psychology, Public Policy, and Law, 16,* 158–176.

Salekin, R. T., Leistico, A.-M. R., Trobst, K. K., Schrum, C. L., & Lochman, J. E. (2005). Adolescent psychopathy and personality theory—the interpersonal circumplex: Expanding evidence of a nomological net. *Journal of Abnormal Child Psychology, 33,* 445–460.

Salekin, R. T., & Lochman, J. (Eds.). (2008). Child and adolescent psychopathy: The search for protective factors [Special issue]. *Criminal Justice and Behavior, 35,* 159–172.

Salekin, R. T., Rogers, R., & Sewell, K. W. (1997). Construct validity of psychopathy in a female offender sample: A multitrait-multimethod evaluation. *Journal of Abnormal Psychology, 106,* 576–585.

Salekin, R. T., Rogers, R., Ustad, K. L., & Sewell, K. W. (1998). Psychopathy and recidivism among female inmates. *Law and Human Behavior, 22,* 109–128.

Salekin, R. T., Rosenbaum, J., & Lee, Z. (2008). Child and adolescent psychopathy: Stability and change. *Psychiatry, Psychology, and Law, 15,* 224–236.

Salisbury, E. J., Dabney, J. D., Russell, K. (2015). Diverting victims of commercial sexual exploitation from juvenile detention: Development of the InterCSECt Screening Protocol. *Journal of Interpersonal Violence, 30*(7), 1247–1276.

Salmivalli, C., Voeten, M., & Poskiparta, E. (2011). Bystanders matter: Association between reinforcing, defending, and the frequency of bullying behavior in classrooms. *Journal of Clinical Child & Adolescent Psychology, 40,* 668–676.

Salter, D., McMillan, D., Richards, M., Talbot, T., Hodges, J., Arnon, B., . . . & Skuse, D. (2003). Development of sexually abusive behaviour in sexually victimised males: A longitudinal study. *The Lancet, 361,* 108–115.

Sammons, M. T., Gorny, S. W., Zinner, E. S., & Allen, R. P. (2000). Prescriptive authority of psychologists: A consensus of support. *Professional Psychology: Research and Practice, 31,* 604–609.

Sanders, M. J., & Bursch, B. (2002). Forensic assessment of illness falsification, Munchausen by proxy, and factitious disorder, NOS. *Child Maltreatment, 7,* 112–124.

Sandler, J. C., & Freeman, N. J. (2007). Typology of female sex offenders: A test of Vandiver and Kercher. *Sexual Abuse: Journal of Research and Treatment, 19,* 73–89.

Sandler, J., C., Letourneau, E. J., Vandiver, D. M., Shields, R. T., & Chaffin, M. (2017). Juvenile sexual crime reporting rates are not influenced by juvenile sex offender registration policies. *Psychology, Public Policy, and Law, 23,* 131–140.

Sangrigoli, S., Pallier, C., Argenti, A.-M., Ventureyra, V. A. G., & de Schonen, S. (2005). Reversibility of the other-race effect in face recognition during childhood. *Psychological Science, 16*, 440–444.

Saum, C. A., O'Connell, D. J., Martin, S. S., Hiller, M. L., Bacon, G. A., & Simpson, D. W. (2007). Tempest in a TC: Changing treatment providers for in-prison therapeutic communities. *Criminal Justice and Behavior, 34*, 1168–1178.

Saunders, B. E., Arata, C., & Kilpatrick, D. (1990). Development of a crime-related posttraumatic stress disorder scale for women within the Symptom Checklist-90–Revised. *Journal of Traumatic Stress, 3*, 439–448.

Schafer, J. A., Huebner, B. M., & Bynum, T. S. (2006). Fear of crime and criminal victimization: Gender-based contrasts. *Journal of Criminal Justice, 34*, 285–301.

Scheflin, A. W. (2014). Applying hypnosis in forensic contexts. In I. B. Weiner & R. K. Otto (Eds.), *Handbook of forensic psychology* (4th ed., pp. 659–708). New York, NY: Wiley.

Scheflin, A. W., Spiegel, H., & Spiegel, D. (1999). Forensic uses of hypnosis. In A. K. Hess & I. B. Weiner (Eds.), *The handbook of forensic psychology* (2nd ed., pp. 474–500). New York, NY: Wiley.

Schmidt, A. F., Mokros, A., & Banse, R. (2013). Is pedophilic sexual preference continuous? A taxometric analysis based on direct and indirect measures. *Psychological Assessment, 25*, 1146–1153.

Schmucker, M., & Losel, F. (2008). Does sexual offender treatment work? A systematic review of outcome evaluations. *Psichotherma, 20*, 10–19.

Schopp, R. F. (2003). Outpatient civil commitment: A dangerous charade or a component of a comprehensive institution of civil commitment? *Psychology, Public Policy, and Law, 9*, 33–69.

Schramke, C. J., & Bauer, R. M. (1997). State-dependent learning in older and younger adults. *Psychology and Aging, 12*, 255–262.

Schreier, H. (2004). Münchausen by proxy. *Current Problems in Pediatric and Adolescent Health Care, 34*, 126–143.

Schwalbe, C. S., Gearing, R. E., MacKenzie, M. J., Brewer, K. B., & Ibrahim, R. (2012). A meta-analysis of experimental studies of diversion programs for juvenile offenders. *Clinical Psychology Review, 32*, 26–33.

Schwartz, B. K. (1995). Characteristics and typologies of sex offenders. In B. K. Schwartz & H. R. Cellini (Eds.), *The sex offender: Corrections, treatment and legal practice* (Vol. 1, pp. 3-1–3-36). Kingston, NJ: Civic Research Institute.

Schwartz, I. M. (1989). *Justice for juveniles: Rethinking the best interests of the child.* Lexington, MA: Lexington Books.

Scott, E. S., Reppucci, N. D., & Woolard, J. L. (1995). Evaluating adolescent decision-making in legal contexts. *Law and Human Behavior, 19*, 221–244.

Scott, E. S., & Steinberg, L. (2008). Adolescent development and regulation of youth crime. *The Future of Children, 18*, 15–33.

Scrivner, E. M. (1994, April). *The role of police psychology in controlling excessive force.* Washington, DC: National Institute of Justice.

Scrivner, E. M., Corey, D. M., & Greene, L. W. (2014). Psychology and law enforcement. In I. B. Weiner & R. K. Otto (Eds.), *The handbook of forensic psychology* (4th ed., pp. 443–468). Hoboken, NJ: Wiley.

Seagrave, D., & Grisso, T. (2002). Adolescent development and measurement of juvenile psychopathy. *Law and Human Behavior, 26*, 219–239.

Sedlak, A. J., & McPherson, K. S. (2010a, May). *Conditions of confinement: Findings from the survey of youth in residential placement.* Washington, DC: U.S. Department of Justice, Office of Juvenile Justice and Delinquency Prevention.

Sedlak, A. J., & McPherson, K. S. (2010b, April). *Youth's needs and services: Findings from the survey of youth in residential placement.* Washington, DC: U.S. Department of Justice, Office of Juvenile Justice and Delinquency Prevention.

Séguin, J. R., & Zelazo, P. D. (2005). Executive function in early physical aggression. In R. E. Tremblay, W. W. Hartup, & J. Archer (Eds.), *Developmental origins of aggression* (pp. 307–329). New York, NY: Guilford Press.

Seklecki, R., & Paynich, R. (2007). A national survey of female police officers: An overview of findings. *Police Practice and Research, 8*, 17–30.

Seligman, M. E. (1975). *Helplessness: On depression, development, and death.* San Francisco, CA: W. H. Freeman.

Selkie, E. M., Fales, J. L., & Moreno, M. A. (2016). Cyberbullying prevalence among United States middle and high school aged adolescents: A systematic review and quality assessment. *Journal of Adolescent Health, 58*, 125–133.

Selkin, J. (1975). Rape. *Psychology Today, 8*, 70–73.

Selkin, J. (1987). *Psychological autopsy in the courtroom.* Denver, CO: Author.

Sellbom, M., Fischler, G. L., & Ben-Porath, Y. S. (2007). Identifying MMPI-2 predictors of police officer integrity and misconduct. *Criminal Justice and Behavior, 34*, 985–1004.

Semmler, C., Brewer, N., & Douglass, A. B. (2012). Jurors believe eyewitnesses. In B. L. Cutler (Ed.), *Conviction of the innocent: Lessons from psychological research* (pp. 185–209). Washington, DC: American Psychological Association.

Senter, A., Morgan, R. D., Serna-McDonald, C., & Bewley, M. (2010). Correctional psychologist burnout, job satisfaction, and life satisfaction. *Psychological Services, 7*, 190–201.

Serin, R. C., & Amos, N. L. (1995). The role of psychopathy in the assessment of dangerousness. *International Journal of Law & Psychiatry, 18*, 231–238.

Serin, R. C., Peters, R. D., & Barbaree, H. E. (1990). Predictors of psychopathy and release outcome in a criminal population. *Psychological Assessment, 2*, 419–422.

Serin, R. C., & Preston, D. L. (2001). Managing and treating violent offenders. In J. B. Ashford, B. D. Sales, & W. H. Reid (Eds.), *Treating adult and juvenile offenders with special needs* (pp. 249–271). Washington, DC: American Psychological Association.

Seto, M. C., Hanson, R. K., & Babchishin, K. M. (2011). Contact sexual offending with online sexual offenses. *Sexual Abuse: A Journal of Research and Treatment, 23,* 124–145.

Sevecke, K., Kosson, D. S., & Krischer, M. K. (2009). The relationship between attention deficit hyperactivity disorder, conduct disorder, and psychopathy in adolescent male and female detainees. *Behavioral Sciences & the Law, 27,* 577–598.

Sexton, T., & Turner, C. W. (2010). The effectiveness of functional family therapy for youth with behavior problems in a community practice setting. *Journal of Family Psychology, 24,* 339–348.

Shahinfar, A., Kupersmidt, J. B., & Matza, L. S. (2001). The relation between exposure to violence and social information processing among incarcerated adolescents. *Journal of Abnormal Psychology, 110,* 136–141.

Shannon, L. M., Jones, A. J., Perkins, E., Newell, J., & Neal, C. (2016). Examining individual factors and during-program performance to understand drug court completion. *Journal of Offender Rehabilitation, 55,* 271–292.

Shapiro, D. (2011). *Banking on bondage: Private prisons and mass incarceration* (American Civil Liberties Union Report). Retrieved from https://www.aclu.org/files/assets/bankingonbondage_20111102.pdf

Shapiro, D. L. (1999). *Criminal responsibility evaluations: A manual for practice.* Sarasota, FL: Professional Resource Press.

Sharif, I. (2004). Münchausen syndrome by proxy. *Pediatrics in Review, 25,* 215–216.

Shaw, J., Campbell, R., Cain, D., & Feeney, H. (2016, August). Beyond surveys and scales: How rape myths manifest in sexual assault police records. *Psychology of Violence.* Advance online publication. doi: 10.1037/vio0000072

Shaw, T., Dooley, J. J., Cross, D., Zubrick, S. R., & Waters, S. (2013). The Forms of Bullying Scale (FBS): Validity and reliability estimates for a measure of bullying victimization and perpetration in adolescence. *Psychological Assessment, 25,* 1045–1057.

Shelton, J., Eakin, J., Hoffer, T., Muirhead, Y., & Owens, J. (2016). Online child sexual exploitation: An investigative analysis of offender characteristics and offending behavior. *Aggression and Violent Behavior, 30,* 15–23.

Shelton, J., Hilts, M., & MacKizer, M. (2016). An exploratory study of residential child abduction: An examination of offender, victim and offense characteristics. *Aggression and Violent Behavior, 30,* 24–31.

Shepherd, J. W., & Ellis, H. D. (1973). The effect of attractiveness on recognition memory for faces. *American Journal of Psychology, 86,* 627–633.

Sheridan, L. P., North, A., & Scott, A. J. (2015). Experiences of stalking in same-sex and opposite-sex contexts. In R. D. Mairuo (Ed.), *Perspectives on stalking: Victims, perpetrators, and cyberstalking* (pp. 105–119). New York, NY: Springer.

Sheridan, M. S. (2003). The deceit continues: An updated literature review of Münchausen syndrome by proxy. *Child Abuse & Neglect, 27,* 431–451.

Shihadeh, E. S., & Barranco, R. E. (2010). Latino immigration, economic deprivation, and violence: Regional differences in the effect of linguistic isolation. *Homicide Studies, 14,* 336–355.

Shirtcliff, E. A., Vitacco, M. J., Gostisha, A. J., Merz, J. L., & Zahn-Waxler, C. (2009). Neurobiology of empathy and callousness: Implications for the development of antisocial behavior. *Behavioral Sciences & the Law, 27,* 137–171.

Shneidman, E. S. (1981). The psychological autopsy. *Suicide and Life-Threatening Behavior, 11,* 325–340.

Shneidman, E. S. (1994). The psychological autopsy. *American Psychologist, 49,* 75–76.

Showers, J. (1997). *Executive summary: The National Conference on Shaken Baby Syndrome.* Alexandria, VA: National Association of Children's Hospitals and Related Institutions.

Showers, J. (1999). *Never never never shake a baby: The challenges of shaken baby syndrome.* Alexandria, VA: National Association of Children's Hospitals and Related Institutions.

Shulman, K. I., Cohen, C. A., & Hull, I. (2005). Psychiatric issues in retrospective challenges of testamentary capacity. *International Journal of Geriatric Psychiatry, 20,* 63–69.

Shuman, D. W., & Sales, B. D. (2001). *Daubert's* wager. *Journal of Forensic Psychology Practice, 1,* 69–77.

Sickmund, M. (2003, June). *Juveniles in court (Juvenile Offenders and Victims National Report Series)* (NCJ 195420). Washington, DC: U.S. Department of Justice, Office of Juvenile Justice and Delinquency Prevention.

Sickmund, M. (2004, June). *Juveniles in corrections.* (NCJ 202885). Washington, DC: U.S. Department of Justice, Office of Juvenile Justice and Delinquency Prevention.

Siegel, A. M., & Elwork, A. (1990). Treating incompetence to stand trial. *Law and Human Behavior, 14,* 57–65.

Siegel, L., & Lane, I. M. (1987). *Personnel and organizational psychology* (2nd ed.). Homewood, IL: Irwin.

Silke, M. (2012). Why women stay: A theoretical examination of rational choice and moral reasoning in the context of intimate partner violence. *Australian and New Zealand Journal of Criminology, 45,* 179–193.

Sim, J. J., Correll, J., & Sadler, M. S. (2013). Understanding police and expert performance: When training attenuates (vs. exacerbates) stereotypic bias in the decision to shoot. *Personality and Social Psychology Bulletin, 39,* 291–304.

Simon, T., Mercy, J., & Perkins, C. (2001, June). *Injuries from violent crime, 1992–1998.* Washington, DC: U.S. Department of Justice, Bureau of Justice Statistics.

Simons, D. J., & Chabris, C. F. (2011). What people believe about how memory works: A representative survey of the U.S. population. *PLos One, 6*, e22757.

Simons, D. J., & Chabris, C. F. (2012). Common (mis)beliefs about memory: A replication and comparison of telephone and mechanical Turk survey methods. *PloS One, 7*, e51876.

Simourd, D. J., & Hoge, R. D. (2000). Criminal psychopathy: A risk–and–need perspective. *Criminal Justice and Behavior, 27*, 256–272.

Simourd, D. J., & Malcolm, P. B. (1998). Reliability and validity of the Level of Service Inventory–Revised among federally incarcerated offenders. *Journal of Interpersonal Violence, 13*, 261–274.

Simpson, D. W., & Knight, K. (Eds.). (2007). Offender needs and functioning assessments from a national cooperative research program. *Criminal Justice and Behavior, 34*, 1105–1112.

Sinclair, J. J., Pettit, G. S., Harrist, A. W., & Bates, J. E. (1994). Encounters with aggressive peers in early childhood: Frequency, age differences, and correlates of risk for behaviour problems. *International Journal of Behavioural Development, 17*, 675–696.

Singer, M. T., & Nievod, A. (1987). Consulting and testifying in court. In I. B. Weiner & A. K. Hess (Eds.), *Handbook of forensic psychology* (pp. 529–556). New York, NY: Wiley.

Sinozich, S., & Langton, L. (2014, December). *Rape and sexual assault victimization among college-age females, 1995–2013*. Washington, DC: U.S. Department of Justice, Bureau of Justice Statistics.

Sipe, R., Jensen, E. L., & Everett, R. S. (1998). Adolescent sexual offenders grown up: Recidivism in young adulthood. *Criminal Justice and Behavior, 25*, 109–124.

Skeem, J. L., Edens, J. F., & Colwell, L. H. (2003, April). *Are there racial differences in levels of psychopathy? A meta-analysis*. Paper presented at the third annual conference of the International Association of Forensic Mental Health Services, Miami, FL.

Skeem, J. L., Edens, J. F., Sanford, G. M., & Colwell, L. H. (2003). Psychopathic personality and racial/ethnic differences reconsidered: A reply to Lynn (2002). *Personality and Individual Differences, 34*, 1–24.

Skeem, J. L., Eno Louden, J., & Evans, J. (2004). Venireperson's attitudes toward the insanity defense: Developing, refining, and validating a scale. *Law and Human Behavior, 28*, 623–648.

Skeem, J. L., Golding, S. L., Berge, G., & Cohn, N. B. (1998). Logic and reliability of evaluations of competence to stand trial. *Law and Human Behavior, 22*, 519–547.

Skeem, J. L., & Monahan, J. (2011). Current directions in violence risk assessment. *Current Directions in Psychological Science, 20*, 38–42.

Skeem, J. L., Monahan, J., & Mulvey, E. P. (2002). Psychopathy, treatment involvement, and subsequent violence among civil psychiatric patients. *Law and Human Behavior, 26*, 577–603.

Skeem, J. L., Polaschek, D. L. L., & Manchak, S. (2009). Appropriate treatment works, but how? Rehabilitating general, psychopathic, and high-risk offenders. In J. L. Skeem, K. S. Douglas, & S. O. Lilienfeld

(Eds.), *Psychological science in the courtroom* (pp. 358–384). New York, NY: Guilford Press.

Skeem, J. L., Polaschek, D. L. L., Patrick, C. J., & Lilienfeld, S. O. (2011). Psychopathic personality: Bridging the gap between scientific evidence and public policy. *Psychological Science in the Public Interest, 12*, 95–162.

Skeem, J. L., Poythress, N., Edens, J., Lilienfeld, S., & Cale, E. (2003). Psychopathic personality or personalities? Exploring potential variants of psychopathy and their implications for risk assessment. *Aggression and Violent Behavior, 8*, 513–546.

Skilling, T. A., Quinsey, V. L., & Craig, W. M. (2001). Evidence of a taxon underlying serious antisocial behavior in boys. *Criminal Justice and Behavior, 28*, 450–470.

Skrapec, C. A. (1996). The sexual component of serial murder. In T. O'Reilly-Fleming (Ed.), *Serial and mass murder: Theory, research and policy* (pp. 155–179). Toronto, Canada: Canadian Scholars' Press.

Skrapec, C. A. (2001). Phenomenology and serial murder: Asking different questions. *Homicide Studies, 5*, 46–63.

Slavkin, M. L. (2001). Enuresis, firesetting, and cruelty to animals: Does the ego triad show predictive validity? *Adolescence, 36*, 461–467.

Slobogin, C. (1999). The admissibility of behavioral science information in criminal trials: From primitivism to *Daubert* to voice. *Psychology, Public Policy, and Law, 5*, 100–119.

Slobogin, C., & Mashburn, A. (2000). The criminal defense lawyer's fiduciary duty to clients with mental disability. *Fordham Law Review, 68*, 1581–1642.

Slobogin, C., Melton, G. B., & Showalter, C. C. (1984). The feasibility of a brief evaluation of mental state at the time of the offense. *Law and Human Behavior, 8*, 305–320.

Slot, L. A. B., & Colpaert, F. C. (1999). Recall rendered dependent on an opiate state. *Behavioral Neuroscience, 113*, 337–344.

Slovenko, R. (1999). Civil competency. In A. K. Hess & I. B. Weiner (Eds.), *Handbook of forensic psychology* (2nd ed., pp. 151–167). New York, NY: Wiley.

Small, M. H., & Otto, R. K. (1991). Evaluations of competency to be executed: Legal contours and implication for assessment. *Criminal Justice and Behavior, 18*, 146–158.

Smith, D. (2002, June). Where are recent grads getting jobs? *Monitor on Psychology, 33*, 28–29.

Smith, E. L., & Cooper, A. (2013, December). *Homicide in the U.S. known to law enforcement, 2011*. Washington, DC: U.S. Department of Justice, Bureau of Justice Statistics.

Smith, M., Wilkes, N., & Bouffard, L. A. (2016). Rape myth adherence among campus law enforcement officers. *Criminal Justice and Behavior, 43*, 539–556.

Smith, S. F., Watts, A. L., & Lilienfeld, S. O. (2014). On the trail of the elusive successful psychopath. *The Psychologist, 15*, 340–350.

Smithey, M. (1998). Infant homicide: Victim–offender relationship and causes of death. *Journal of Family Violence, 13*, 285–287.

Snider, J. F., Hane, S., & Berman, A. L. (2006). Standardizing the psychological autopsy: Addressing the *Daubert* standard. *Suicide and Life-Threatening Behavior, 36*, 511–518.

Snook, B., Cullen, R. M., Bennell, C., Taylor, P. J., & Gendreau, P. (2008). The criminal profiling illusion: What's behind the smoke and mirrors? *Criminal Justice and Behavior, 35*, 1257–1276.

Snyder, H. N. (2000, June). *Sexual assault of young children as reported to law enforcement: Victim, incident, and offender characteristics.* Washington, DC: U.S. Department of Justice, Bureau of Justice Statistics.

Snyder, H. N. (2008, August). *Juvenile arrests 2005.* Washington, DC: U.S. Department of Justice, Office of Juvenile Justice and Delinquency Prevention.

Snyder, H. N., & Sickmund, M. (1995). *Juvenile offenders and victims: A national report.* Washington, DC: Office of Juvenile Justice and Delinquency Prevention.

Snyder, H. N., & Sickmund, M. (1999). *Juvenile offenders and victims: 1999 national report.* Washington, DC: Office of Juvenile Justice and Delinquency Prevention.

Snyder, H. N., & Sickmund, M. (2006, March). *Juvenile offenders and victims: 2006 national report.* Pittsburgh, PA: National Center for Juvenile Justice.

Sorensen, S. B., & Bowie, P. (1994). Girls and young women. In L. D. Eron, J. H. Gentry, & P. Schlegel (Eds.), *Reason to hope: A psychosocial perspective on violence and youth* (pp. 167–176). Washington, DC: American Psychological Association.

Spaccarelli, S., Bowden, B., Coatsworth, J. D., & Kim, S. (1997). Psychosocial correlates of male sexual aggression in a chronic delinquent sample. *Criminal Justice and Behavior, 24*, 71–95.

Spiegel, D., & Spiegel, H. (1987). Forensic uses of hypnosis. In I. B. Weiner & A. K. Hess (Eds.), *Handbook of forensic psychology* (pp. 490–510). New York, NY: Wiley.

Spielberger, C. D. (Ed.). (1979). *Police selection and evaluation.* Washington, DC: Hemisphere.

Spielberger, C. D., Ward, J. C., & Spaulding, H. C. (1979). A model for the selection of law enforcement officers. In C. D. Spielberger (Ed.), *Police selection and evaluation: Issues and techniques* (pp. 11–29). Washington, DC: Hemisphere.

Sporer, S. L. (2001). The cross-race effect: Beyond recognition of faces in the laboratory. *Psychology, Public Policy, and Law, 7*, 170–200.

Sprang, M. V., McNeil, J. S., & Wright, R. (1989). Psychological changes after the murder of a significant other. *Social Casework: The Journal of Contemporary Social Work, 70*, 159–164.

Stahl, P. M. (2010). *Conducting child custody evaluations: From basic to complex issues.* Thousand Oaks, CA: Sage.

Stahl, P. M. (2014). Conducting child custody and parenting evaluations. In I. B. Weiner & R. K. Otto (Eds.), *The handbook of forensic psychology* (4th ed., pp. 137–169). Hoboken, NJ: Wiley.

Standards Committee, American Association for Correctional Psychology. (2000). Standards for psychology services in jails, prisons, correctional facilities, and agencies. *Criminal Justice and Behavior, 27*, 433–494.

Stark, E. (2002). Preparing for expert testimony in domestic violence cases. In A. R. Roberts (Ed.), *Handbook of domestic violence intervention strategies: Policies, programs, and legal remedies* (pp. 216–252). New York, NY: Oxford University Press.

Starr, D. (2013, December 9). The interview: Do police interrogation techniques produce false confessions? *The New Yorker*, 42–49.

Stattin, H., & Klackenberg-Larsson, I. (1993). Early language and intelligence development and their relationship to future criminal behavior. *Journal of Abnormal Psychology, 102*, 369–378.

Steadman, H. J., Davidson, S., & Brown, C. (2001). Mental health courts: Their promise and unanswered questions. *Psychiatric Services, 54*, 457–458.

Steadman, H. J., Gounis, K., & Dennis, D. (2001). Assessing the New York City involuntary outpatient commitment pilot program. *Psychiatric Services, 52*, 330–336.

Steadman, H. J., McCarty, D. W., & Morrissey, J. P. (1989). *The mentally ill in jail: Planning for essential services.* New York, NY: Guilford Press.

Steadman, H. J., Osher, F. C., Robbins, P. C., Case, B., & Samuels, S. (2009). Prevalence of serious mental illness among jail inmates. *Psychiatric Services, 60*, 761–765.

Steadman, H. J., & Veysey, B. M. (1997). *Providing services for jail inmates with mental disorders.* Washington, DC: U.S. Department of Justice, National Institute of Justice.

Steblay, N. K., Dietrich, H. L., Ryan, S. L., Raczynski, J. L., & James, K. A. (2011). Sequential lineup laps and eyewitness accuracy. *Law and Human Behavior, 35*, 262–274.

Steblay, N. K., Dysart, J. E., & Wells, G. L. (2011). Seventy-two test of the sequential lineup superiority effect: A meta-analysis and policy discussion. *Psychology, Public Policy, and Law, 17*, 99–139.

Stehlin, I. B. (1995, July/August). FDA's forensic center: Speedy, sophisticated sleuthing. *FDA Consumer Magazine*, 17–28.

Stein, B. D., Jaycox, L. H., Kataoka, S., Rhodes, H. J., & Vestal, K. D. (2003). Prevalence of child and adolescent exposure to community violence. *Clinical Child and Family Psychology Review, 6*, 247–264.

Steinberg, L. (2007). Risk taking in adolescence: New perspectives from brain and behavioral science. *Current Directions in Psychological Science, 16*, 55–59.

Steinberg, L. (2008). A social neuroscience perspective on adolescent risk taking. *Developmental Review, 28*, 78–106.

Steinberg, L. (2010a). A behavioral scientist looks at the science of adolescent brain development. *Brain and Cognition, 72*, 160–164.

Steinberg, L. (2010b). A dual systems model of adolescent risk-taking. *Developmental Psychobiology*, 216–224.

Steinberg, L. (2014a). *Age of opportunity: Lessons from the new science of adolescence*. New York, NY: Houghton Mifflin Harcourt.

Steinberg, L. (2014b). *Adolescence* (10th ed.). New York, NY: McGraw-Hill Higher Education.

Steinberg, L. (2016). Commentary on special issue on the adolescent brain: Redefining adolescence. *Neuroscience and Biobehavioral Reviews, 70*, 343–346.

Steinberg, L., Albert, D., Cauffman, E., Banich, M., Graham, S., & Woolard, J. (2008). Age differences in sensation seeking and impulsivity as indexed by behaviour and self–report: Evidence for a dual systems model. *Developmental Psychology, 44*, 1764–1778.

Steinberg, L., & Cauffman, E. (1996). Maturity of judgment in adolescence: Psychosocial factors in adolescent decision making. *Law and Human Behavior, 20*, 249–272.

Steinberg, L., Cauffman, E., Woolard, J., Graham, S., & Banich, M. (2009). Are adolescents less mature than adults? Minors' access to abortion, the juvenile death penalty, and the alleged APA "flip-flop." *American Psychologist, 64*, 583–594.

Steinberg, L., Graham, S., O'Brien, L., Woolard, J., Cauffman, E., & Banich, M. (2009). Age differences in future orientation and delay discounting. *Child Development, 80*, 28–44.

Steinberg, L., & Monahan, K. (2007). Age differences in resistance to peer influence. *Developmental Psychology, 43*, 1531–1543.

Steiner, C. (2017, January/February). Pre-employment evaluation for police and public safety. *The National Psychologist, 26*, 10.

Stemple, L., & Meyer, I. H. (2014, June). The sexual victimization of men in America: New data challenge old assumptions. *American Journal of Public Health, 104*, e19–e26.

Stewart, A. E., Lord, J. H., & Mercer, D. L. (2001). Death notification education: A needs assessment study. *Journal of Traumatic Stress, 14*, 221–227.

Stickle, T., & Blechman, E. (2002). Aggression and fire: Antisocial behavior in firesetting and nonfiresetting juvenile offenders. *Journal of Psychopathology and Behavioral Assessment, 24*, 177–193.

Stockdale, M. S., Logan, T. K., & Weston, R. (2009). Sexual harassment and posttraumatic stress disorder: Damages beyond prior abuse. *Law and Human Behavior, 33*, 405–418.

Stockdale, M. S., Sliter, K. A., & Ashburn-Nardo, L. (2015). Employment discrimination. In B. L. Cutler & P. A. Zapf (Eds.), *APA handbook of forensic psychology: Vol. 1. Individual and situational influences in criminal and civil contexts* (pp. 511–532). Washington, DC: American Psychological Association.

Stone, A. V. (1995). Law enforcement psychological fitness for duty: Clinical issues. In M. Kurke & E. Scrivner (Eds.), *Police psychology into the 21st century* (pp. 109–131). Hillsdale, NJ: Erlbaum.

Stone, M. H. (1998). Sadistic personality in murders. In T. Millon, E. Simonsen, M. Burket-Smith, & R. Davis (Eds.), *Psychopathy: Antisocial, criminal, and violent behavior*. New York, NY: Guilford Press.

Stotzer, R. L. (2010). Sexual orientation-based hate crimes on campus: The impact of policy on reporting rates. *Sexuality Research and Social Policy, 7*, 147–154.

Stowe, R. M., Arnold, D. H., & Ortiz, C. (2000). Gender differences in the relationship of language development to disruptive behavior and peer relationships in preschoolers. *Journal of Applied Developmental Psychology, 20*, 521–536.

Strange, D., & Takarangi, M. K. T. (2012). False memories for missing aspects of traumatic events. *Acta Psychologica, 141*, 322–326.

Strange, D., & Takarangi, M. K. T. (2015). Investigating the variability of memory distortion for an analogue trauma. *Memory, 23*, 991–1000.

Straus, M. A. (1979). Measuring intra family conflict and violence: The Conflict Tactics Scale. *Journal of Marriage and the Family, 41*, 75–88.

Straus, M. A., & Gelles, R. (1990). *Physical violence in American families*. New Brunswick, NJ: Transaction Press.

Stredny, R. V., Parker, A. L. S., & Dibble, A. E. (2012). Evaluator agreement in placement recommendations for insanity acquittees. *Behavioral Sciences & the Law, 30*, 297–307.

Strier, F. (1999). Whither trial consulting? Issues and projections. *Law and Human Behavior, 23*, 93–115.

Strom, K. J. (2001, September). *Hate crimes reported in NIBRS, 1997–1999*. Washington, DC: U.S. Department of Justice, Bureau of Justice Statistics.

Sue, D. W., Bingham, R. P., Porché-Burke, L., & Vasquez, M. (1999). The diversification of psychology: A multicultural revolution. *American Psychologist, 54*, 1061–1069.

Sullivan, M. L., & Guerette, R. T. (2003). The copycat factor: Mental illness, guns, and the shooting incident at Heritage High School, Rockdale County, Georgia. In H. M. Moore, C. V. Petrie, A. A. Braga, & B. L. McLaughlin (Eds.), *Deadly lessons: Understanding lethal school violence* (pp. 25–69). Washington, DC: National Academies Press.

Sullivan, T. N., Helms, S. W., Bettencourt, A. F., Sutherland, K., Lotze, G. M., Mays, S., . . . & Farrell, A. D. (2012). A qualitative study of individual and peer factors related to effective nonviolent versus aggressive responses in problem situations among adolescents with high incident disabilities. *Behavioral Disorders, 37*, 163–178.

Summit, R. C. (1983). The child sexual abuse accommodation syndrome. *Child Abuse & Neglect, 7*, 177–193.

Super, J. T. (1999). Forensic psychology and law enforcement. In A. K. Hess & I. B. Weiner (Eds.), *The handbook of forensic psychology* (2nd ed., pp. 409–439). New York, NY: Wiley.

Surgeon General's Scientific Advisory Committee on Television and Social Behavior. (1972). *Television and growing up: The impact of television violence.* Washington, DC: U.S. Government Printing Office.

Sutton, J. (2011). Influences on memory. *Memory Studies, 4,* 355–359.

Swanner, J. K., Meissner, C. A., Atkinson, D. J., & Dianiska, R. E. (2016). Developing diagnostic, evidence-based approaches to interrogation. *Journal of Applied Research in Memory and Cognition, 5,* 295–301.

Swanson, J. W., Van Dorn, R. A., Swartz, M. S., Robbins, P. C., Steadman, H. J., McGuire, T. G., . . . & Monahan, J. (2013, July). The cost of assisted outpatient treatment: Can it save states money? *American Journal of Psychiatry.* doi:10.1176/appi.ajp.2013.12091152

Swartz, M. S., Swanson, J. W., & Hiday, V. A. (2001). Randomized controlled trial of outpatient commitment in North Carolina. *Psychiatric Services, 52,* 325–329.

Swartz, M. S., Swanson, J. W., Steadman, H. J., Robbins, P. C., & Monahan, J. (2009). *New York State Assisted Outpatient Treatment Program evaluation.* Durham, NC: Duke University School of Medicine.

Swearer, S. M., Espelage, D. L., Vaillancourt, T., & Hymel, S. (2010). What can be done about school bullying? Linking research to educational practice. *Educational Researcher, 39,* 38–47.

Symons, D. K. (2013). A review of the practice and science of child custody and access assessment in the United States and Canada. *Professional Psychology: Research and Practice, 41,* 267–273.

Taft, C. T., Resick, P. A., Watkins, L. E., & Panuzio, J. (2009). An investigation of posttraumatic stress disorder and depressive symptomatology among female victims of interpersonal trauma. *Journal of Family Violence, 24,* 407–415.

Takarangi, M. K. T., Strange, D., & Lindsay, D. S. (2014). Self-report underestimates trauma intrusions. *Consciousness & Cognition, 27,* 297–305.

Tanaka, J. W., & Pierce, L. J. (2009). The neural plasticity of other-race face recognition. *Cognitive, Affective, and Behavioral Neuroscience, 9,* 122–131.

Tappan, P. W. (1947). Who is criminal? *American Sociological Review, 12,* 100–110.

Tarescavage, A. M., Corey, D. M., Ben-Porath, Y. F. (2015). Minnesota Multiphasic Personality-2-Restructured Form (MMPI-2-RF) predictors of police officer problem behavior. *Assessment, 22,* 116–132.

Tarescavage, A. M., Corey, D. M., & Ben-Porath, Y. F. (2016). A prorating method for estimating MMPI-2-RF scores from MMPI responses: Examination of score fidelity and illustration of empirical utility in the PERSEREC police integrity study sample. *Assessment, 23,* 173–190.

Tate, D. C., & Redding, R. E. (2005). Mental health and rehabilitative services in juvenile justice: System reforms and innovative approaches. In K. Heilbrun, N. E. S. Goldstein, & R. E. Reddings (Eds.), *Juvenile delinquency: Prevention, assessment, and intervention* (pp. 134–160). New York, NY: Oxford University Press.

Tate, D. C., Reppucci, N. D., & Mulvey, E. P. (1995). Violent juvenile delinquents: Treatment effectiveness and implications for future directions. *American Psychologist, 50,* 777–781.

Taylor, E. A., & Sonuga-Barke, E. J. S. (2008). Disorders of attention and activity. In M. Rutter, D. Bishop, D. Pine, S. Scott, J. S. Stevenson, E. A. Taylor, . . . & A. Thapar (Eds.), *Rutter's child and adolescent psychiatry* (5th ed., pp. 521–542). Oxford, England: Wiley–Blackwell.

Taylor, P. J., Snook, B., Bennell, C., & Porter, L. (2015). Investigative psychology. In B. L. Cutler & P. A. Zapf (Eds.), *Handbook of forensic psychology: Vol. 2. Criminal investigation, adjudication, and sentencing outcomes* (pp. 165–186). Washington, DC: American Psychological Association.

Teaching-Family Association. (1993). *Standards of ethical conduct of the Teaching-Family Association.* Asheville, NC: Author.

Teaching-Family Association. (1994). *Elements of the teaching-family model.* Asheville, NC: Author.

Teplin, L. A., Abram, K. M., McLelland, G. M., Dulcan, M. K., & Mericle, A. A. (2002). Psychiatric disorders in youth in juvenile detention. *Archives of General Psychiatry, 59,* 1133–1143.

Terestre, D. J. (2005, August 1). How to start a crisis negotiation team. *Police: The Law Enforcement Magazine,* 8–10.

Terr, L. (1991). Childhood traumas: An outline and overview. *American Journal of Psychiatry, 148,* 10–20.

Terr, L. (1994). *Unchained memories.* New York, NY: Basic Books.

Terrill, W., & Reisig, M. D. (2003). Neighborhood context and police use of force. *Journal of Research in Crime and Delinquency, 40,* 291–321.

Tiesman, H. M., Gurka, K. K., Konda, S., Coben, J. H., & Amandus, H. E. (2012). Workplace homicides in U.S. women: The role of intimate partner violence. *Annals of Epidemiology, 22,* 277–284.

Till, F. (1980). *Sexual harassment: A report on the sexual harassment of students.* Washington, DC: National Advisory Council on Women's Educational Programs.

Tippins, T. M., & Wittmann, J. P. (2005). Empirical and ethical problems with custody recommendation: A call for clinical humility and judicial vigilance. *Family Court Review, 43,* 193–222.

Tjaden, P. (1997, November). The crime of stalking: How big is the problem? *NIJ Research Preview.* Washington, DC: U.S. Department of Justice.

Tjaden, P., & Thoennes, N. (1998a, November). *Prevalence, incidence, and consequences of violence against women: Findings from the National Violence Against Women Survey* (Research in brief). Washington, DC: U.S. Department of Justice, National Institute of Justice.

Tjaden, P., & Thoennes, N. (1998b). *Stalking in America: Findings from the National Violence Against Women Survey* (NCJ 169592). Washington, DC: U.S. Department of Justice.

Tjaden, P., & Thoennes, N. (2006, January). *Extent, nature, and consequences of rape victimization: Findings from the National Violence*

Against Women Survey. Washington, DC: U.S. Department of Justice, National Institute of Justice.

Toch, H. (Ed.). (1980). *Therapeutic communities in corrections*. New York, NY: Praeger.

Toch, H. (Ed.). (1992). *Mosaic of despair: Human breakdown in prisons*. Washington, DC: American Psychological Association.

Toch, H. (2002). *Stress in policing*. Washington, DC: American Psychological Association.

Toch, H. (Ed.). (2008). Special issue: The disturbed offender in confinement. *Criminal Justice and Behavior, 35*, 1–3.

Toch, H. (2012). *COP WATCH: Spectators, social media, and police reform*. Washington, DC: American Psychological Association.

Toch, H., & Adams, K. (2002). *Acting out: Maladaptive behavior in confinement*. Washington, DC: American Psychological Association.

Tombaugh, T. N. (1997). *TOMM: Test of Memory Malingering manual*. Toronto, Canada: Multi-Health Systems.

Tonry, M. (1990). Stated and latent functions of ISP. *Crime & Delinquency, 36*, 174–190.

Topp, B. W., & Kardash, C. A. (1986). Personality, achievement, and attrition: Validation in a multiple-jurisdiction police academy. *Journal of Police Science and Administration, 14*, 234–241.

Topp-Manriquez, L. D., McQuiston, D., & Malpass, R. S. (2016). Facial composites and the misinformation effect: How composites distort memory. *Legal and Criminological Psychology, 21*, 372–389.

Torres, A. N., Boccaccini, M. T., & Miller, H. A. (2006). Perceptions of the validity and utility of criminal profiling among forensic psychologists and psychiatrists. *Professional Psychology: Research and Practice, 37*, 51–58.

Traube, D. E., Chasse, K. T., McKay, M. M., Bhorade, A. M., Paikoff, R., & Young, S. (2007). Urban African American pre-adolescent social problem solving skills. *Social Work in Mental Health, 5*, 101–119.

Tremblay, R. E. (2003). Why socialization fails: The case of chronic physical aggression. In B. B. Lahey, T. E. Moffitt, & A. Caspi (Eds.), *Causes of conduct disorder and juvenile delinquency* (pp. 182–226). New York, NY: Guilford Press.

Tremblay, R. E., Boulerice, B., Harden, P. W., McDuff, P., Pérusse, D., Pihl, R. O., . . . & Japel, C. (1996). Do children in Canada become more aggressive as they approach adolescence? In Human Resources Development Canada and Statistics Canada (Eds.), *Growing up in Canada: National Longitudinal Survey of Children and Youth*. Ottawa: Statistics Canada.

Tremblay, R. E., & Nagin, D. S. (2005). The developmental origins of physical aggression in humans. In R. E. Tremblay, W. W. Hartup, & J. Archer (Eds.), *Developmental origins of aggression* (pp. 83–106). New York, NY: Guilford Press.

Trompetter, P. S. (2011, August). Police psychologists: Roles and responsibilities in a law enforcement agency. *The Police Chief, 78*, 52.

Trompetter, P. S. (2017). A history of police psychology. In C. L. Mitchell & E. H. Dorian (Eds.), *Police psychology and its growing impact on modern law enforcement* (pp. 1–27). Hershey, PA: IGI Global.

Trompetter, P. S., Corey, D. M., Schmidt, W. W., & Tracy, D. (2011, January). Psychological factors after officer-involved shootings: Addressing officer needs and agency responsibilities. *The Police Chief, 78*, 28–33.

Troup-Leasure, K., & Snyder, H. N. (2005, August). *Statutory rape known to law enforcement*. Washington, DC: U.S. Department of Justice, Office of Juvenile Justice and Delinquency Prevention.

Truman, D. M., Tokar, D. M., & Fischer, A. R. (1996). Dimensions of masculinity: Relations to date-rape supportive attitudes and sexual aggression in dating situations. *Journal of Counseling and Development, 74*, 555–562.

Truman, J. L., & Morgan, R. E. (2016, October). *Criminal victimization, 2015*. Washington, DC: U.S. Department of Justice, Bureau of Justice Statistics.

Truman, J. L., & Planty, M. (2012, October). *Criminal victimization, 2011*. Washington, DC: U.S. Department of Justice, Bureau of Justice Statistics.

Ttofi, M. M., & Farrington, D. P. (2011). Effectiveness of school-based programs to reduce bullying: A systematic and meta-analytic review. *Journal of Experimental Criminology, 7*, 27–56.

Tucillo, J. A., DeFilippis, N. A., Denny, R. L., & Dsurney, J. (2002). Licensure requirements for interjurisdictional forensic evaluations. *Professional Psychology: Research and Practice, 33*, 377–383.

Tucker, H. S. (2002). Some seek attention by making pets sick. *Archives of Disease in Childhood, 87*, 263.

Turrell, S. C. (2000). A descriptive analysis of same-sex relationship violence for a diverse sample. *Journal of Family Violence, 15*, 281–293.

Turtle, J., & Want, S. C. (2008). Logic and research versus intuition and past practice as guides to gathering and evaluating eyewitness evidence. *Criminal Justice and Behavior, 35*, 1241–1256.

Turvey, B. (2002). *Criminal profiling: An introduction to behavioral evidence analysis* (2nd ed.). San Diego, CA: Academic Press.

Tyiska, C. G. (1998). *Working with victims of crime with disabilities*. Washington, DC: U.S. Department of Justice, Office of Victims of Crime.

Tyler, N., & Gannon, T. A. (2012). Explanations of firesetting in mentally disordered offenders: A review of the literature. *Psychiatry, 75*, 150–166.

Tyner, E. (2013, June). *Psychology internship program: United States Medical Center for Federal Prisoners, 2014–2015*. Springfield, MO: Federal Bureau of Prisons.

Ullman, S. E. (2007a). Mental health services seeking in sexual assault victims. *Women & Therapy, 30*, 61–84.

Ullman, S. E. (2007b). A 10-year update of "Review and critique of empirical studies of rape avoidance." *Criminal Justice and Behavior, 34*, 411–429.

Ullman, S. E., Filipas, H. H., Townsend, S. M., & Starzynski, L. L. (2006). The role of victim–offender relationship in women's sexual assault experiences. *Journal of Interpersonal Violence, 21,* 798–819.

Ullman, S. E., Karabatsos, G., & Koss, M. P. (1999). Risk recognition and trauma related symptoms among sexually re-victimized women. *Journal of Consulting and Clinical Psychology, 67,* 705–710.

Underwood, M. K., & Ehrenreich, S. E. (2017). The power and pain of adolescents' digit communication: Cyber victimization and the perils of lurking. *American Psychologist, 72,* 144–158.

United Nations Office on Drugs and Crime. (2012). *Global Report on Trafficking in Persons.* Retrieved from http://www.unodc.org/documents/data-and-analysis/glotip/Trafficking_in_Persons_2012_web.pdf

Unnever, J. D., & Cullen, F. T. (2012). White perceptions of whether African Americans and Hispanics are prone to violence and support for the death penalty. *Journal of Research in Crime and Delinquency, 49,* 519–544.

Uphold-Carrier, H., & Utz, R. (2012). Parental divorce among young and adult children: A long-term quantitative analysis of mental health and family solidarity. *Journal of Divorce & Remarriage, 53,* 247–266.

U.S. Advisory Board on Child Abuse and Neglect. (1995). *A national shame: Fatal child abuse and neglect in the U.S.* (5th report). Washington, DC: Government Printing Office.

U.S. Census Bureau. (2011a). *Statistical Abstract of the United States, 2010* (129th ed.) Washington, DC: Author.

U.S. Census Bureau. (2011b, December). *Custodial mothers and fathers and their child support: 2009.* Washington, DC: Author.

U.S. Census Bureau. (2016, June 23). *The Hispanic population.* Washington, DC: Author.

U.S. Department of Health and Human Services. (2010). *Child maltreatment 2008.* Washington, DC: Author, Administration for Children and Family, Childrens' Bureau. Retrieved from http://www.acf.hhs.gov/programs/cb/stats_research/index.htm#can

U.S. Department of Health and Human Services. (2012, March 22). *First marriages in the United States: Data from the 2006–2010 National Survey of Family Growth.* Washington, DC: Author.

U.S. Department of Health and Human Services. (2017). *Administration for Children and Families.* Retrieved from https://www.acf.hhs.gov/media/press/2017/child-abuse-neglect-data-released

U.S. Department of Justice, Civil Rights Division. (2011, October). *Confronting discrimination in the post-9/11 era: Challenges and opportunities ten years later: A report of the Civil Rights Division's Post-9/11 Civil Rights Summit.* Washington, DC: Author.

U.S. Department of Justice. (2010, May). *The crime of family abduction: A child's and parent's perspective.* Washington, DC: Author.

U.S. Department of State. (2010). *Trafficking in persons report* (Annual No. 10). Retrieved from http://www.state.gov/documents/organization/142979.pdf

U.S. Equal Employment Opportunity Commission. (2017, May). *Sexual harassment.* Washington, DC: Author.

U.S. Secret Service. (2002). *Safe School Initiative: An interim report on the prevention of targeted violence in schools.* Washington, DC: National Threat Assessment Center.

Vaillancourt, T. (2005). Indirect aggression among humans: Social construct or evolutionary adaptation? In R. E. Tremblay, W. W. Hartup, & J. Archer (Eds.), *Developmental origins of aggression* (pp. 158–177). New York, NY: Guilford Press.

Vaisman-Tzachor, R. (2012). Psychological evaluations in federal immigration courts: Fifteen years in the making—lessons learned. *Forensic Examiner, 21,* 42–53.

Van der Kolk, B. A., & Fisler, R. E. (1994). Childhood abuse & neglect and loss of self-regulation. *Bulletin of Menninger Clinic, 58,* 145–168.

Van der Kolk, B. A., & Fisler, R. E. (1995). Dissociation and the fragmentary nature of traumatic memories: Overview and exploratory study. *Journal of Traumatic Stress, 8,* 505–525.

van der Stouwe, T., Asscher, J. J., Stams, G. J., Dekovic´, M., & van der Laan, P. H. (2014). The effectiveness of multisystemic therapy (MST): A meta-analysis. *Clinical Psychology Review, 34,* 468–481.

Van Hasselt, V. B., Flood, J. J., Romano, S. J., Vecchi, G. M., de Fabrique, N., & Dalfonzo, V. A. (2005). Hostage-taking in the context of domestic violence: Some case examples. *Journal of Family Violence, 20,* 21–27.

van Koppen, P. J. (2012). Deception detection in police interrogations: Closing in on the context of criminal investigation. *Journal of Applied Research in Memory and Cognition, 1,* 124–125.

Van Maanen, J. (1975). Police socialization: A longitudinal examination of job attitudes in an urban police department. *Administrative Science Quarterly, 20,* 207–228.

Van Voorhis, P., Wright, E. M., Salisbury, E., & Bauman, A. (2010). Women's risk factors and their contributions to existing risk/needs assessment: The current status of a gender-responsive supplement. *Criminal Justice and Behavior, 37,* 261–288.

VandenBos, G. R. (2007). *APA dictionary of psychology.* Washington, DC: American Psychological Association.

Vanderbilt, D., & Augustyn, M. (2010). The effects of bullying. *Pediatrics and Child Health, 20,* 315–320.

Vandiver, D. M., & Kercher, F. (2004). Offender and victim characteristics of registered female sexual offenders in Texas: A proposed typology of female sexual offenders. *Sexual Abuse: Journal of Research and Treatment, 16,* 121–137.

Varela, J. G., Boccaccini, M. T., Scogin, F., Stump, J., & Caputo, A. (2004). Personality testing in law enforcement settings: A meta-analytic review. *Criminal Justice and Behavior, 31,* 649–675.

Vecchi, G. M., Van Hasselt, V. B., & Romano, S. J. (2005). Crisis (hostage) negotiation: Current strategies and issues in high-risk conflict resolution. *Aggression and Violent Behavior, 10,* 533–551.

Vermeiren, R. (2003). Psychopathology and delinquency in adolescents: A descriptive and developmental perspective. *Clinical Psychology Review, 23*, 277–318.

Vermeiren, R., De Clippele, A., Schwab-Stone, M., Ruchkin, V., & Deboutte, D. (2002). Neuropsychological characteristics of three subgroups of Flemish delinquent adolescents. *Neuropsychology, 16*, 49–55.

Vermont Humane Federation. (2017). Retrieved from http://www.vermonthumane.org

Verona, E., Bresin, K., & Patrick, C. J. (2013). Revisiting psychopathy in women: Cleckley/Hare conceptions and affective response. *Journal of Abnormal Psychology, 122*, 1088–1093.

Viding, E., & Larsson, H. (2010).Genetics of childhood and adolescent psychopathy. In A. T. Salekin & O. R. Lyman (Eds.), *Handbook of childhood and adolescent psychopathy* (pp. 113–134). New York, NY: Guilford Press.

Vila, B., & Kenney, D. J. (2002). Tired cops: The prevalence and potential consequences of police fatigue. *National Institute of Justice Journal, 248*, 16–21.

Viljoen, J. L., MacDougall, E. A. M., Gagnon, N. C., & Douglas, K. S. (2010). Psychopathy evidence in legal proceedings involving adolescent offenders. *Psychology, Public Policy, and Law, 16*, 254–283.

Viljoen, J. L., McLachlan, K., Wingrove, T., & Penner, E. (2010). Defense attorneys' concerns about the competence of adolescent defendants. *Behavioral Science & the Law, 28*, 630–646.

Viljoen, J. I., Shaffer, C. S., Gray, A. L., & Douglas, K. S. (2017). Are adolescent risk assessment tools sensitive to change? A framework and examination of the SAVRY and the YLS/CMI. *Law and Human Behavior, 41*, 244–257.

Viljoen, J. L., Zapf, P., & Roesch, R. (2007). Adjudicative competence and comprehension of *Miranda* rights in adolescent defendants: A comparison of legal standards. *Behavioral Sciences & the Law, 25*, 1–19.

Violanti, J. M. (1996). *Police suicide: Epidemic in blue*. Springfield, IL: Charles C Thomas.

Violanti, J. M., Fekedulegn, D., Charles, L. E., Andrew, M. E., Hartley, T. A., Mnatsakanova, A., . . . & Burchfiel, C. M. (2009). Suicide in police work: Exploring potential contributing influences. *American Journal of Criminal Justice, 34*, 41–53.

Vitacco, M. J., Erickson, S. K., Kurus, S., & Apple, B. N. (2012). The role of the Violence Risk Appraisal Guide and Historical, Clinical, Risk-20 in U.S. courts: A case law survey. *Psychology, Public Policy, and Law, 18*, 361–391.

Vitacco, M. J., Neumann, C. S., & Jackson, R. I. (2005). Testing a four-factor model of psychopathy and its association with ethnicity, gender, intelligence, and violence. *Journal of Consulting and Clinical Psychology, 73*, 466–476.

Vitale, J. E., Smith, S. S., Brinkley, C. A., & Newman, J. P. (2002). The reliability and validity of the Psychopathy Checklist–Revised in a sample of female offenders. *Criminal Justice and Behavior, 29*, 202–231.

Voltz, A. G. (1995). Nursing interventions in Munchausen syndrome by proxy. *Journal of Psychosocial Nursing, 10*, 93–97.

von Polier, G. G., Vloet, T. D., & Herpertz-Dahlmann, B. (2012). ADHD and delinquency—a developmental perspective. *Behavioral Sciences & the Law, 30*, 121–139.

Vossekuil, B., Fein, R. A., Reddy, M., Borum, R., & Mozeleski, W. (2002, May). *The final report and findings of the Safe School Initiative*. Washington, DC: U.S. Secret Service and the U.S. Department of Education.

Vrij, A. (2008). Nonverbal dominance versus verbal accuracy in lie detection: A plea to change police practice. *Criminal Justice and Behavior, 35*, 1323–1335.

Vrij, A., Akehurst, L., & Knight, S. (2006). Police officers', social workers', teachers' and the general public's beliefs about deception in children, adolescents, and adults. *Legal and Criminological Psychology, 11*, 297–312.

Vrij, A., & Fisher, R. P. (2016). Which lie detection tools are ready for use in the criminal justice system? *Journal of Applied Research in Memory and Cognition, 5*, 302–307.

Vrij, A., Fisher, R. P., & Blank, H. (2017). A cognitive approach to lie detection: A meta-analysis. *Legal and Criminological Psychology, 22*, 1–21.

Vrij, A., & Granhag, P. A. (2007). Interviewing to detect deception. In S. A. Christianson (Ed.), *Offenders' memories of violent crimes* (pp. 279–304). Chichester, England: Wiley.

Vrij, A., & Granhag, P. A. (2012). Eliciting cues to deception and truth: What matters are the questions asked. *Journal of Applied Research in Memory and Cognition, 1*, 110–117.

Vrij, A., & Granhag, P. A. (2014). Eliciting information and detecting lies in intelligence interviewing: An overview of recent research. *Applied Cognitive Psychology, 28*, 936–944.

Vrij, A., Granhag, P. A., & Mann, S. (2010). Good liars. *Journal of Psychiatry & Law, 38*, 77–98.

Vrij, A., Granhag, P. A., Mann, S., & Leal, S. (2011). Outsmarting the liars: Toward a cognitive lie detection approach. *Current Directions in Psychological Science, 20*, 28 –32.

Vrij, A., Mann, S. A., Fisher, R. P., Leal, S., Milne, R., & Bull, R. (2008). Increasing cognitive load to facilitate lie detection: The benefit of recalling an event in reverse order. *Law and Human Behavior, 32*, 253–265.

Vrij, A., Mann, S., Jundi, S., Hillman, J., & Hope, L. (2014). Detection of concealment in an information-gathering interview. *Applied Cognitive Psychology, 28*, 860–866.

Waasdorp, T. E., & Bradshaw, C. P. (2015). The overlap between cyberbullying and traditional bullying. *Journal of Adolescent Health, 56*, 483–488.

Waber, D. R., Bryce, C. P., Fitzmaurice, G. M., Zichlin, M. L., McGaughy, J., Girard, J. M., . . . & Galler, J. R. (2014). Neuropsychological outcomes at midlife following moderate to severe malnutrition in infancy. *Neuropsychology, 28,* 530–540.

Waschbusch, D. A. (2002). A meta-analytic examination of comorbid hyperactive–impulsive-attention problems and conduct problems. *Psychological Bulletin, 128,* 118–150.

Wagstaff, G. F. (2008). Hypnosis and the law: Examining the stereotypes. *Criminal Justice and Behavior, 35,* 1277–1294.

Waldron, H. B., & Turner, C. W. (2008). Evidence-based psychosocial treatments for adolescent substance abuse. *Journal of Clinical Child & Adolescent Psychology, 37,* 238–261.

Walker, L. E. (1979). *The battered woman.* New York, NY: Harper Colophone Books.

Walker, L. E. (1984). *The battered woman syndrome.* New York, NY: Springer.

Walker, L. E. (1989). *Terrifying love: Why battered women kill and how society responds.* New York, NY: HarperCollins.

Walker, L. E. (1999). Psychology and domestic violence around the world. *American Psychologist, 54,* 21–29.

Walker, L. E. (2009). *The battered woman syndrome* (3rd ed.). New York, NY: Springer.

Walker, S. D., & Kilpatrick, D. G. (2002). Scope of crime/historical review of the victims' rights discipline. In A. Seymour, M. Murray, J. Sigmon, M. Hook, C. Edwards, M. Gaboury, & G. Coleman. (Eds.), *National Victim Assistance Academy textbook.* Washington, DC: U.S. Department of Justice, Office of Victims of Crime.

Walker, S., Alpert, G. P., & Kenney, D. J. (2001, July). *Early warning systems: Responding to the problem police officer.* Washington, DC: U.S. Department of Justice, National Institute of Justice.

Wallerstein, J. S. (1989, January 23). Children after divorce: Wounds that don't heal. *New York Times Magazine,* pp. 19–21, 41–44.

Walsh, A. C., Brown, B., Kaye, K., & Grigsby, J. (1994). *Mental capacity: Legal and medical aspects of assessment and treatment.* Colorado Springs, CO: Shepard's/McGraw-Hill.

Walsh, T., & Walsh, Z. (2006). The evidentiary introduction of Psychopathy Checklist–Revised assessed psychopathy in U.S. courts: Extent and appropriateness. *Law and Human Behavior, 30,* 493–507.

Walters, G. D. (1996). The Psychological Inventory of Criminal Thinking Styles. Part III: Predictive validity. *International Journal of Offender Therapy and Comparative Criminology, 40,* 105–122.

Walters, G. D. (2006). *The Psychological Inventory of Criminal Thinking Styles (PICTS) professional manual.* Allentown, PA: Center for Lifestyles Studies.

Walters, G. D. (2014, March). Predicting self-reported total, aggressive, and income offending with the youth version of the Psychopathy Checklist: Gender- and factor-level interactions. *Psychological Assessment, 26,* 288–296,

Walters, G. D., & Heilbrun, K. (2010). Violence risk assessment and Facet 4 of the Psychopathy Checklist: Predicting institutional and community aggression in two forensic samples. *Assessment, 17,* 259–268.

Waltz, J., Babcock, J. C., Jacobson, N. S., & Gottman, J. M. (2000). Testing a typology of batterers. *Journal of Consulting and Clinical Psychology, 68,* 658–669.

Ward, T., & Birgden, A. (2009). Accountability and dignity: Ethical issues in forensic and correctional practice. *Aggression and Violent Behavior, 14,* 227–231.

Warr, M. (2002). *Companions in crime: The social aspects of criminal conduct.* New York, NY: Cambridge University Press.

Warren, J. I., Fitch, W. L., Dietz, P. E., & Rosenfeld, B. D. (1991). Criminal offense, psychiatric diagnosis, and psycholegal opinion: An analysis of 894 pretrial referrals. *Bulletin of the American Academy of Psychiatry and Law, 19,* 63–69.

Warren, J. I., Hazelwood, R. R., & Reboussin, R. (1991). Serial rape: The offender and his rape career. In A. Burgess (Ed.), *Rape and sexual assault III.* New York, NY: Garland.

Warren, J. I., Reboussin, R., Hazelwood, R. R., & Wright, J. A. (1989). Serial rape: Correlates of increased aggression and relationship of offender pleasure to victim resistance. *Journal of Interpersonal Violence, 4,* 65–78.

Warren, J. I., Wellbeloved-Stone, J. M., Hilts, M. A., Donaldson, W. H., Muirhead, Y. E., Craun, S. W., . . . & Millspaugh, S. B. (2016). An investigative analysis of 463 incidents of simple-victim child abduction identified through federal law enforcement. *Aggression and Violent Behavior, 30,* 59–67.

Wasserman, G. A., McReynolds, L. S., Schwalbe, C. S., Keating, J. M., & Jones, S. A. (2010). Psychiatric disorder, comorbidity, and suicidal behavior in juveniles justice youth. *Criminal Justice and Behavior, 37,* 1361–1376.

Watson, S., Harkins, L., & Palmer, M. (2016). The experience of deniers on a community sex offender group program. *Journal of Forensic Psychology Practice, 16*(5), 374–392.

Webster, C. D., Douglas, K. S., Eaves, D., & Hart, S. D. (1997). *The HCR-20 scheme: The assessment of dangerousness and risk (Version 2).* Burnaby, BC, Canada: Mental Health, Law, and Policy Institute, Simon Fraser University.

Webster, W. C., & Hammond, D. C. (2011). Solving crimes with hypnosis. *American Journal of Clinical Hypnosis, 53*(4), 255–269.

Weekes, J. R., Moser, A. E., & Langevin, C. M. (1999). Assessing substance-abusing offenders for treatment. In E. J. Latessa (Ed.), *Strategic solutions.* Lanham, MD: American Correctional Association.

Weiner, I. B., & Hess, A. K. (2014). Practicing ethical forensic psychology. In I. B. Weiner & R. K. Otto (Eds.), *The handbook of forensic psychology* (4th ed., pp. 85–110). Hoboken, NJ: Wiley.

Weiner, I. B., & Otto, R. (Eds.). (2014). *Handbook of forensic psychology* (4th ed.). Hoboken, NJ: Wiley.

Weingartner, H. J., Putnam, F., George, D. T., & Ragan, P. (1995). Drug state-dependent autobiographical knowledge. *Experimental and Clinical Psychopharmacology, 3*, 304–307.

Weinstock, R., Leong, G. B., & Silva, J. A. (2010). Competence to be executed: An ethical analysis post Panetti. *Behavioral Sciences & the Law, 28*, 690–706.

Weisheit, R., & Mahan, S. (1988). *Women, crime, and criminal justice.* Cincinnati, OH: Anderson.

Weiss, D. S., Marmar, C. R., Schlenger, W. E., Fairbank, J. A., Jordan, B. K., Hough, R. L., . . . & Kulka, R. A. (1992). The prevalence of lifetime and partial post-traumatic stress disorder in Vietnam theater veterans. *Journal of Traumatic Stress, 5*, 365–376.

Weiss, P. A., Vivian, J. E., Weiss, W. U., Davis, R. D., & Rostow, C. D. (2013). The MMPI-2 L scale, reporting uncommon virtue, and predicting police performance. *Psychological Services, 10*, 123–130.

Wells, G. L. (1993). What do we know about eyewitness identification? *American Psychologist, 48*, 553–571.

Wells, G. L. (2001). Police lineups: Data, theory, and policy. *Psychology, Public Policy, and Law, 1*, 791–801.

Wells, G. L., & Loftus, E. F. (2013). Eyewitness memory for people and events. In I. B. Weiner & R. K. Otto (Eds.), *Handbook of psychology. Vol. 11. Forensic psychology* (2nd ed., pp. 617–629). Hoboken, NJ: Wiley.

Wells, G. L., Small, M., Penrod, S., Malpass, R. S., Fulero, S. M., & Brimacombe, C. A. E. (1998). Eyewitness identification procedures: Recommendations for lineups and photospreads. *Law and Human Behavior, 22*, 603–647.

Welsh, W. (2007). A multisite evaluation of prison-based therapeutic community drug treatment. *Criminal Justice and Behavior, 34*, 1481–1498.

Werth, J. L., Benjamin, G. A. H., & Farrenkopf, T. (2000). Requests for physician-assisted death: Guidelines for assessing mental capacity and impaired judgment. *Psychology, Public Policy, and Law, 6*, 348–372.

Wessler, S., & Moss, M. (2001, October). *Hate crimes on campus: The problem and efforts to confront it.* Washington, DC: U.S. Department of Justice, Office of Justice Programs.

West, C. M. (1998). Leaving a second closet: Outing partner violence in same-sex couples. In J. L. Jasinski & L. M. Williams (Eds.), *Partner violence: A comprehensive review of 20 years of research* (pp. 163–183). Thousand Oaks, CA: Sage.

Weyandt, L. L., Oster, D. R., Gudmundsdottir, B. G., DuPaul, G. J., & Anastopoulos, A. D. (2017). Neuropsychological functioning in college students with and without ADHD. *Neuropsychology, 31*, 160–172.

Wherry, J. W., Baldwin, S., Junco, K., & Floyd, B. (2013). Suicidal thoughts/behaviors in sexually abused children. *Journal of Child Sexual Abuse, 26*, 534–551.

Whitcomb, D., Hook, M., & Alexander, E. (2002). Child victimization. In A. Seymour, M. Murray, J. Sigmon, M. Hook, C. Edwards, M. Gaboury, & G. Coleman (Eds.), *National Victim Assistance Academy textbook.* Washington, DC: U.S. Department of Justice, Office for Victims of Crime.

White, H. R., Bates, M. E., & Buyske, S. (2001). Adolescence-limited versus persistent delinquency: Extending Moffitt's hypothesis into adulthood. *Journal of Abnormal Psychology, 110*, 600–609.

White, N., & Lauritsen, J. L. (2012). *Violent crime against youth, 1994–2010.* Washington, DC: U.S. Department of Justice, Bureau of Justice Statistics.

Whitehead, J. T., & Lab, S. P. (1989). A meta-analysis of juvenile correctional treatment. *Journal of Research in Crime & Delinquency, 26*, 276–295.

Whittaker, J. K., Kinney, J., Tracy, E. N., & Booth, C. (1990). *Reaching high-risk families: Intensive family preservation in human services.* New York, NY: Aldine de Gruyter.

Wijkman, M. N., Bijleveld, C., & Hendriks, J. (2010). Women don't do such things! Characteristics of female sex offenders and offender types. *Sexual Abuse: A Journal of Research and Treatment, 22*, 135–156.

Williamson, S., Hare, R. D., & Wong, S. (1987). Violence: Criminal psychopaths and their victims. *Canadian Journal of Behavioral Science, 19*, 454–462.

Willoughby, T., Adachi, P. J. C., & Good, M. (2012). A longitudinal study of association between violent video game play and aggression among adolescents. *Developmental Psychology, 48*, 1044–1057.

Wills, T. A., & Stoolmiller, M. (2002). The role of self–control in early escalation of substance abuse: A time-varying analysis. *Journal of Consulting and Clinical Psychology, 70*, 986–997.

Wills, T. A., Walker, C., Mendoza, D., & Ainette, M. G. (2006). Behavioral and emotional self-control: Relations to substance use in samples of middle and high school students. *Psychology of Addictive Behaviors, 20*, 265–278.

Wilson, A., Prokop, N. H., & Robins, S. (2015). Addressing all heads of the hydra: Reframing safeguards for mentally impaired detainees in immigration removal proceedings. *NYU Review of Law and Social Change, 39*, 313–368.

Wilson, B., & Butler, L. D. (2014). Running a gauntlet: A review of victimization and violence in the pre-entry, post-entry, and peri-/post-exit periods of commercial sexual exploitation. *Psychological Trauma: Theory, Research, Practice, and Policy, 6*, 494–504.

Wilson, C. M., Nicholls, T. L., Charette, Y., Seto, M. C., & Crocker, A. G. (2016). Factors associated with review board dispositions following re-hospitalization among discharged persons found not criminally responsible. *Behavioral Sciences & The Law, 34*, 278–294.

Wilson, J. J. (2001, January). From the administrator. In J. R. Johnson & L. K. Girdner (Eds.), *Family abductors: Descriptive profiles and preventive interventions*. Washington, DC: U.S. Department of Justice, Office of Juvenile Justice and Delinquency.

Wilson, J. K., Brodsky, S. L., Neal, T. M. S., & Cramer, R. J. (2011). Prosecutor pretrial attitudes and plea-bargaining behavior toward veterans with posttraumatic stress disorder. *Psychological Services, 8,* 319–331.

Wilson, M. M. (2014, February). *Hate crime victimization, 2004–2012 statistical tables.* Washington, DC: U.S. Department of Justice, Bureau of Justice Statistics.

Wilson, M., & Daly, M. (1993). Spousal homicide risk and estrangement. *Violence and Victims, 8,* 3–16.

Winick, B. J. (1996). The MacArthur Treatment Competence Study: Legal and therapeutic implications. *Psychology, Public Policy, and Law, 2,* 137–166.

Winick, B. J. (2003). Outpatient commitment: A therapeutic jurisprudence analysis. *Psychology, Public Policy, and Law, 9,* 107–144.

Winick, B. J., & Kress, K. (2003a). Foreword: A symposium on outpatient commitment dedicated to Bruce Ennis, Alexander Brooks, and Stanley Herr. *Psychology, Public Policy, and Law, 9,* 3–7.

Winick, B. J., & Kress, K. (Eds.). (2003b). Preventive outpatient commitment for persons with serious mental illness [Special issue]. *Psychology, Public Policy, and Law, 9.*

Winters, G. M., Kaylor, L. E., & Jeglic, E. L. (2017). Sexual offenders contacting children online: An examination of transcripts of sexual grooming. *Journal of Sexual Aggression, 23,* 62–76.

Wise, R. A., Pawlenko, N. B., Meyer, D., & Safer, M. A. (2007). A survey of defense attorneys' knowledge and beliefs about eyewitness testimony. *The Champion, 33,* 18–27.

Wise, R. A., Pawlenko, N. B., Safer, M. A., & Meyer, D. (2009). What U.S. prosecutors and defense attorneys know and believe about eyewitness testimony. *Applied Cognitive Psychology, 23,* 1266–1281.

Wise, R. A., & Safer, M. A. (2010). A comparison of what U.S. judges and students know and believe about eyewitness testimony. *Journal of Applied Social Psychology, 40,* 1400–1422.

Wolak, J., Finkelhor, D., & Mitchell, K. J. (2004). Internet-initiated sex crimes against minors: Implications for prevention based on findings from a national sample. *Journal of Adolescent Health, 35,* 424. e11–424.e20.

Wolak, J., Finkelhor, D., Mitchell, K. J., & Ybarra, M. L. (2008). Online "predators" and their victims. *American Psychologist, 63,* 111–128.

Wolak, J., Mitchell, K. J., & Finkelhor, D. (2003). *Internet sex crimes against minors: The response of law enforcement* (NCMEC 10–03–022). Alexandria, VA: National Center for Missing & Exploited Children.

Wolf, M. M., Kirigin, K. A., Fixsen, D. L., Blasé, K. A., & Braukmann, C. J. (1995). The teaching-family model: A case study in data-based program development and refinement (and dragon wrestling). *Journal of Organizational Behavior Management, 15,* 11–68.

Wolfe, S. E., & Nix, J. (2016). The alleged "Ferguson effect" and police willingness to engage in community partnership. *Law and Human Behavior, 40,* 1–10.

Wong, S. (2000). Psychopathic offenders. In S. Hodgins & R. Muller-Isberner (Eds.), *Violence, crime and mentally disordered offenders: Concepts and methods for effective treatment and prevention* (pp. 87–112). New York, NY: Wiley.

Wong, S., & Hare, R. D. (2005). *Guidelines for a psychopathy treatment program.* Toronto, Canada: Multi-Health Systems.

Wood, R. M., Grossman, L. S., & Fichtner, C. G. (2000). Psychological assessment, treatment, and outcome with sex offenders. *Behavioral Sciences & the Law, 18,* 23–41.

Woodhams, J., Bull, R., & Hollin, C. R. (2010). Case linkage: Identifying crime committed by the same offender. In R. N. Kocsis (Ed.), *Criminal profiling: International theory, research, and practice* (pp. 177–133). Totowa, NJ: Humana Press.

Woodworth, M., & Porter, S. (2002). In cold blood: Characteristics of criminal homicides as a function of psychopathy. *Journal of Abnormal Psychology, 111,* 436–445.

Woody, R. H. (2005). The police culture: Research implications for psychological services. *Professional Psychology: Research and Practice, 36,* 525–529.

Worden, A. P. (1993). The attitudes of women and men in policing: Testing conventional and contemporary wisdom. *Criminology, 31,* 203–242.

Worling, J. R., & Curwen, T. (2001). Estimate of Risk of Adolescent Sexual Offense Recidivism (ERASOR), Version 2.0. In M. C. Calder (Ed.), *Juveniles and children who sexually abuse: Frameworks for assessment.* Lyme Regis, Dorset, England: Russell House.

Worling, J. R., & Langton, C. M. (2012). Assessment and treatment of adolescents who sexually offend: Clinical issues and implications for secure settings. *Criminal Justice and Behavior, 39,* 814–841.

Wormith, J. S., Althouse, R., Simpson, M., Reitzel, L. R., Fagan, T. J., & Morgan, R. D. (2007). The rehabilitation and reintegration of offenders: The current landscape and some future directions for correctional psychology. *Criminal Justice and Behavior, 34,* 879–892.

Wormith, J. S., & Luong, D. (2007). Legal and psychological contributions to the development of corrections in Canada. In R. K. Ax & T. J. Fagan (Eds.), *Corrections, mental health, and social policy: International perspectives* (pp. 129–173). Springfield, IL: Charles C Thomas.

Wurtele, S. K., Simons, D. A., & Moreno, T. (2014). Sexual interest in children among an online sample of men and women: Prevalence and correlates. *Sexual Abuse: A Journal of Research and Treatment, 26,* 546–548.

Yarmey, A. D. (1979). *The psychology of eyewitness testimony*. New York, NY: Free Press.

Yates, G., & Bass, C. (2017). The perpetrators of medical child abuse (Munchausen Syndrome by Proxy)–A systematic review of 796 cases. *Child Abuse & Neglect, 72*, 45–53.

Ybarra, M. L. E., & Mitchell, K. J. (2007). Prevalence and frequency of Internet harassment instigation: Implications for adolescent health. *Journal of Adolescent Health, 41*, 189–195.

Yeater, E. A., Treat, T. A., Viken, R. J., & McFall, R. M. (2010). Cognitive processes underlying women's risk judgments: Associations with sexual victimization history and rape myth acceptance. *Journal of Consulting and Clinical Psychology, 78*, 375–386.

Yochelson, S., & Samenow, S. E. (1976). *The criminal personality* (Vol. 1). New York, NY: Jason Aronson.

Young, A. T. (2016). Police hostage (crisis) negotiators in the U.S.: A national survey. *Journal of Police and Criminal Psychology, 31*, 310–321.

Young, A. T., Fuller, J., & Riley, B. (2008). On-scene mental health counseling provided through police departments. *Journal of Mental Health Counseling, 30*, 345–361.

Young, S., Gudjonsson, G., Misch, P., Collins, P., Carter, P., Redfern, J., . . . & Goodwin, E. (2010). Prevalence of ADHD symptoms among youth in a secure facility: The consistency and accuracy of self- and informant-report ratings. *Journal of Forensic Psychiatry & Psychology, 21*, 238–246.

Young, T. J. (1992). Procedures and problems in conducting a psychological autopsy. *International Journal of Offender Therapy and Comparative Criminology, 36*, 43–52.

Zajac, R., Dickson, J., Munn, R., & O'Neill, S. (2016). Trussht me, I know what I sshaw: The acceptance of misinformation from an apparently unreliable co-witness. *Legal and Criminological Psychology, 21*, 127–140.

Zapf, P. A. (2015). Competency for execution. In R. Jackson & R. Roesch (Eds.), *Learning forensic assessment: Research and practice* (2nd ed., pp. 229–243). New York, NY: Routledge.

Zapf, P. A., Golding, S. L., & Roesch, R. (2006). Criminal responsibility and the insanity defense. In I. B. Weiner & A. K. Hess (Eds.), *The handbook of forensic psychology* (3rd ed., pp. 332–363). Hoboken, NJ: Wiley.

Zapf, P. A., Golding, S. L., Roesch, R., & Pirelli, G. (2014). Assessing criminal responsibility. In I. B. Weiner & R. K. Otto (Eds.), *The handbook of forensic psychology* (4th ed., pp. 315–351). Hoboken, NJ: Wiley.

Zapf, P. A., Hubbard, K. L., Galloway, V. A., Cox, M., & Ronan, K. A. (2002). *An investigation of discrepancies between forensic examiners and the courts in decisions about competency*. Manuscript submitted for publication.

Zapf, P. A., & Roesch, R. (2006). Competency to stand trial: A guide for evaluators. In I. B. Weiner & A. K. Hess (Eds.), *The handbook of forensic psychology* (3rd ed., pp. 305–331). Hoboken, NJ: Wiley.

Zapf, P. A., & Roesch, R. (2011). Future directions in the restoration of competency to stand trial. *Current Directions in Psychological Science, 20*, 43–47.

Zapf, P. A., Roesch, R., & Pirelli, G. (2014). Assessing competency to stand trial. In I. B. Weiner & R. K. Otto (Eds.), *The handbook of forensic psychology* (4th ed., pp. 281–314). Hoboken, NJ: Wiley.

Zapf, P. A., & Viljoen, J. L. (2003). Issues and considerations regarding the use of assessment instruments in the evaluation of competency to stand trial. *Behavioral Sciences & the Law, 21*, 351–367.

Zeier, J. D., Baskin-Sommers, A. R., Racer, K. D. H., & Newman, J. P. (2012). Cognitive control deficits associated with antisocial personality disorder and psychopathy. *Personality Disorders: Theory, Research, and Treatment, 3*, 283–293.

Zelazo, P. D., Carter, A., Reznick, J. S., & Frye, D. (1997). Early development of executive functions: A problem-solving framework. *Review of General Psychology, 1*, 198–226.

Zervopoulos, J. A. (2010). Drafting the parenting evaluation court order: A conceptual and practical approach. *Behavioral Sciences & the Law, 28*, 480–491.

Zhang, K., Frumkin, L. A., Stedmon, A., & Lawson, G. (2013). Deception in context: Coding nonverbal cues, situational variables and risk of detection. *Journal of Police and Criminal Psychology, 28*, 150–161.

Zibbell, R. A., & Fuhrmann, G. (2016). Child custody evaluations. In R. Jackson & R. Roesch (Eds.), *Learning forensic assessment: Research and practice* (2nd ed., pp. 391–412). New York, NY: Routledge.

Zimring, F. (1998). *American youth violence*. New York, NY: Oxford University Press.

Zipper, P., & Wilcox, D. K. (2005, April). The importance of early intervention. *FBI Law Enforcement Bulletin, 74*, 3–9.

Zona, M. A., Sharma, K. K., & Lane, J. A. (1993). A comparative study of erotomanic and obsessional subjects in a forensic sample. *Journal of Forensic Sciences, 38*, 894–903.

AUTHOR INDEX

Coyne, S. M., 323
Craig, J. M., 297, 300
Craig, L. A., 137
Craig, W., 321
Craig, W. M., 273
Cramer, R. J., 185, 311
Craun, S. W., 443
Crawford, M., 406
Crawford, N., 26
Crellin, K., 523
Crespi, T. D., 27
Crocker, A. G., 184
Cromwell, P. F., 87, 500
Crooks, C. V., 411
Crosbie-Burnett, M., 416–417
Crosnoe, R., 245
Cross, D., 320
Crossman, M. K., 252
Croy, C. D., 184
Crozier, W. E., 91, 92, 94, 110
Cruise, K., 167, 169, 510, 519
Cruise, K. R., 272, 358, 362, 513
Cullen, F. T., 284, 315, 335, 473–474, 491, 492
Cullen, R. M., 80, 81, 86–87
Culotta, M. C., 68
Cumming, G. F., 106
Cummings, E. M., 417
Cunliffe, C., 343
Cunningham, M. D., 188
Curtin, J. J., 273
Curtis, N. M., 523
Curwen, T., 364, 366
Cutler, B. L., 115, 142, 147, 149
Cuttler, M. J., 37
Cyterski, T. D., 250, 265, 267, 268, 273

Dabney, J. D., 407
Daggett, D., 463, 471
Dahlberg, L. L., 241
Daire, A. P., 411
Dalby, J. T., 425–427
Daley, K., 384
Dalfonzo, V. A., 61, 63
Daly, M., 412
Dana, R. Q., 504
Dancu, C. V., 421
Dane, H. E., 253
Daneshvar, D. H., 214–215
Daniels, J. A., 62, 293, 294, 296–297
Dansie, E. J., 388
Dargis, M., 417
Darnes, J., 85
Darrow, C., 191

Davidoff, K. C., 313
Davidshofer, C. O., 46, 48
Davidson, M., 47
Davidson, S., 127
Davies, B., 394
Davies, G., 433, 436
Davis, E., 67, 68
Davis, K. M., 266
Davis, L. S., 313
Davis, R. D., 45
Day, A., 14
Day, D. M., 400
Day, K., 513, 518
Day, N. L., 256
Dean, K. E., 340
DeBernardo, C., 295
Deboutte, D., 256
DeBurger, J., 304, 308
De Clippele, A., 256
DeClue, G., 98, 99
DeCoster, J., 272
De Fabrique, N., 61, 63
DeFilippis, N. A., 17
DeFina, P., 214, 215
DeGarmo, D. S., 417, 523
DeGloria, P., 424
De Graaf, R., 251
Dekovic´, M., 519, 523
De la Osa, N., 417, 418
Del Bove, G., 260
Del Carmen, R. V., 503
De Leon, G., 481
Delprino, R. P., 57
Demakis, G. J., 216, 217, 220, 221
Deming, A., 109
Demler, O., 389
Dempster, R. J., 264, 267
Dennis, D., 226–227
Dennison, S., 361
Denny, R. L., 17
Dern, C., 90
Dern, H., 90
Desari, R. A., 516
De Schonen, S., 114
DeShazo, T. M., 271
DeSmet, O., 417
Detrick, P., 40, 45, 47
Devine, P. G., 69
Dewaele, A., 417
DeWitt, J., 364, 366

Dexter, H. R., 149
Diamond, P. M., 463, 471
Dianiska, R. E., 92
Dibble, A. E., 184
Dickson, J., 147
Dickson, N., 242, 243, 252
Dietrich, H. L., 116
Dietz, A. S., 57, 60
Dietz, E. F., 463
Dietz, P. E., 181
DiLeone, B. A., 68
Dinero, T. E., 341
Dinges, D. F., 107, 108
Dinos, S., 343
Dionne, G., 256, 257
Dirks-Linhorst, P. A., 184
Dishion, T. J., 259
DiTomasso, N. D., 68
Dixon, L., 212, 400
Dobash, R. E., 413
Dobash, R. P., 413
Dobolyi, D. G., 114
Dobson, V., 426–427
Dodge, K., 242
Dodge, K. A., 243, 251, 256, 258–259, 291, 342
Dodson, C. S., 114
Doll, H., 517–518
Doménech, J. M., 417, 418
Domhardt, M., 400
Donaldson, W. H., 443
Donn, J. E., 16
Donnellan, M. B., 243
D'Onofrio, B. M., 256
Dooley, J. J., 320
Dorfman, D. A., 225
Dorken, S. K., 490
Dornbusch, S. M., 245
Dornsbusch, S., 209
Dougher, M. J., 364
Douglas, A.-J., 443
Douglas, J. E., 304
Douglas, K. S., 135, 136, 137, 138, 139, 148, 266, 268, 270, 273, 364, 419, 505, 513, 529
Douglass, A. B., 110
Dowdell, E. B., 427
Dowling, F. G., 54
Drasgow, F., 230
Drislane, L. E., 265, 268
Drizin, S., 91, 94, 97, 98, 99, 507
Drogan, E. Y., 146
Drogin, E. Y., 91, 210–211, 213, 216–217, 219, 221, 505, 506

Drugge, J., 262, 264, 482
Drukteinis, A. M., 216
Dsurney, J., 17
Dubowitz, H., 429
Dudycha, G. J., 436
Dudycha, M. M., 436
Duhaime, A., 429
Dulcan, M. K., 517, 521
Dunford, T. W., 240
D'Unger, A. V., 243
Dunham, R. G., 68, 70
DuPaul, G. J., 250, 251
Durand, V. M., 426
Durham, M. L., 227
Durham, T. W., 15–16
Dutton, D., 413
Dutton, M. A., 374, 394, 395, 413, 416, 420
Duwe, G., 309–310
Dysart, J. E., 115

Eaglesfield, G. D., 286
Eakin, J. D., 352, 358, 359–360
Eastman, O., 89–90
Eastwood, J., 63, 94, 95, 96, 502, 506
Eaves, D., 169, 419
Ebert, B. W., 85, 86
Eckstein, J. J., 413
Edens, J., 264
Edens, J. E., 268
Edens, J. F., 44, 47, 261, 266, 268, 270, 272, 274–275, 275, 276, 513
Edmunds, C., 330, 332–333, 335, 382, 383, 398, 401–402
Edwards, D. L., 522, 524
Ehlers, A., 60, 389
Ehrenreich, S. E., 321, 322, 323
Ehrlichman, H., 436
Einhorn, J., 201
Eisen, K., 405
Eke, A. W., 317, 318–319, 419
Ekman, P., 83–84
Elipe, P., 322
Elklit, A., 402
Elliot, G., 209
Elliott, D. S., 240
Ellis, C. A., 392–394, 429
Ellis, H. D., 113
Ellis, M., 271
Ellsworth, P. C., 146
El-Sheikh, M., 417
Elwork, A., 173
Emanuel, K. M., 516
Embley, I., 261, 267, 274

Emerson, R. M., 315
Emery, R. E., 425
Englert, H., 352
Eninger, L., 258
Eno Louden, J., 183
Ensley, D. T., 455, 489
Epperson, D., 364, 366
Epperson, D. L., 364
Equal Employment Opportunity Commission, 301
Erickson, C. D., 376
Erickson, K., 245
Erickson, S. K., 139, 204
Eron, L., 255, 342, 413, 503, 520
Eron, L. D., 289–290
Erskine, H. E., 252
Eshelman, L., 398–399, 421
Espelage, D. L., 320
Estepp, M. H., 259
Evans, C., 290
Evans, G. D., 294
Evans, J., 183
Evans, J. R., 91, 92, 93, 436
Evces, M., 59
Eve, P. M., 204, 205
Everett, R. S., 363
Everly, G., 56
Ewens, S., 102
Ewing, C. P., 153, 203
Eyler, V., 56
Eyssel, F., 341
Ezpeleta, L., 417, 418

Fagan, T. J., 463, 479, 481
Fairbank, J. A., 390
Fairweather, D., 262, 264, 482
Fales, J. L., 323
Falzer, P. R., 516
Fan, M.-Y., 320
Fan, X., 297, 320
Farabee, D., 481, 488, 490
Faravelli, C., 402
Fargo, J. D., 388
Faris, R., 320–321
Farrell, A., 83
Farrell, A. D., 321, 323
Farrell, H. M., 217, 218, 222
Farrenkopf, T., 223
Farrington, D. P., 240, 243, 275, 321
Faust, E., 463, 464, 471
Faw, L., 522
Fay, J., 39
Fayyad, J., 251
Fazel, S., 517–518

Federal Bureau of Investigation, 58, 65, 240, 281, 283, 312, 313, 337, 360, 362, 391, 396, 410
Federle, K. H., 503
Feeney, H., 334, 343
Fegert, J. M., 400
Fehrenbach, P. A., 362
Fein, R., 136, 294
Fein, R. A., 294–295, 296
Feindler, E. L., 285
Fekedulegn, D., 67
Feld, B. C., 94, 502, 503, 511
Felix, E. D., 441
Felmlee, D., 320–321
Felson, R. B., 401
Fernandez Smith, K., 266
Ferrar, A. J., 252
Ferrara, P., 428
Ferrell, S. W., 478, 488
Ferris, K. O., 315
Fichtner, C. G., 191
Fico, J. M., 37
Figueredo, A. J., 361
Filipas, H. H., 402
Filone, S., 14, 15, 19, 162
Findling, R. L., 272
Fineran, S., 301
Finkel, N. J., 76
Finkelhor, D., 28, 353, 358–360, 374, 387, 391, 396, 400, 402, 403, 404, 422, 423, 442, 443, 444, 446, 528
Finkelman, J. M., 142
Finn, P., 52, 53, 54, 56, 57
Fischer, A. R., 336, 341
Fischler, G. L., 45
Fishbein, D., 526
Fisher, B. S., 315, 335
Fisher, J., 306
Fisher, R. P., 93, 103, 105, 111, 112
Fisher, W., 190
Fisler, R. E., 434, 435–436
Fitch, W. L., 181
Fitzgerald, L. F., 229–230, 230, 334, 341
Fitzmaurice, G., 286
Fitzmaurice, G. M., 286
Fixsen, D. L., 520
Flaherty, C. V., 306
Flannery, R., 56
Fletcher, K., 221
Flood, J. J., 61, 63
Flora, D. B., 29
Flory, K., 250, 252
Flowe, H. D., 114

Flower, T., 319
Floyd, B., 400
Floyd, M. Y., 153
Flynn, S., 437
Foa, E. B., 390, 402, 421
Foellmi, M., 454, 478, 479, 490
Fogel, M. H., 508
Follette, V., 431
Folsom, J., 474, 486
Fon, D. L., 98, 99
Fontaine, N., 243
Foote, W. E., 182, 211, 380
Forehand, R., 260
Forsman, M., 273
Forth, A., 366, 505
Forth, A. E., 138, 263, 264, 266, 271, 327, 513
Foster, E., 19
Foster, K. L., 427
Fournier, L. R., 146, 148
Fowers, D., 364, 366
Fowles, D. C., 265, 268
Fox, C., 293
Fox, J. A., 304, 306, 307, 310, 391
Frame, C. L., 260
Francis, A., 238
Francoeur, E., 441
Francombe Pridham, M., 227
Franklin, C. L., 389
Frantz, B., 380
Fraser, J., 112
Frederick, R. I., 172
Freedman, S., 94, 95, 502, 506
Freeman, N., 189
Freeman, N. J., 358
Freeman, W. C., 169
Fremouw, W. J., 361
Frenda, S. J., 110
Freud, S., 430
Frick, P. J., 241, 252, 253, 256, 267, 270, 271–272, 275–276
Frie, A., 337
Friedman, T. L., 6, 290
Friedrich, W. N., 441
Frizzell, K., 361, 366
Frosina, P., 102
Frost, L. E., 173
Frumkin, L. A., 102–103
Fruzzetti, A. E., 420
Fry, D., 403, 405
Frye, D., 257
Fuhrmann, G., 199, 203
Fulero, S. M., 116, 181
Fuller, J., 56

Furby, L., 484
Furton, K. G., 436
Fuselier, G. D., 61, 62, 63
Fyfe, J. J., 69

Gaboury, M., 382, 383
Gacono, C. B., 264, 275
Gagliardi, C. R., 204, 205
Gagnon, N. C., 266, 270, 273, 513
Gallagher, C. A., 488
Gallagher, R. W., 474, 484
Galler, J. R., 286
Gallili, N., 5
Galloway, M., 266
Galloway, V. A., 167
Galvan, A., 246
Gannon, T. A., 260, 358
Garafalo, R., 338
Garcia-Moreno, C., 399
Gardner, C. B., 315
Gardner, H., 47, 254–255
Gardner, M., 249, 387
Garland, B. E., 470–471
Garland, J. T., 479
Garner, J. H., 68, 70
Garrett, B. L., 98
Garrett, E., 246, 247
Garthe, R. C., 335
Gasser, U., 290
Gates, M. A., 185
Gatto, A., 428
Gavin, H., 427
Gay, J. G., 173
Ge, X., 243
Gearing, M. L., 484
Gearing, R. E., 523, 527
Geiselman, R. E., 93, 111, 112
Gelles, M. G., 39–40, 61, 62, 63, 85
Gelles, R., 410
Gelles, R. J., 417
Gendrau, P., 463, 490
Gendreau, P., 80, 81, 86–87, 127, 455, 469, 473–474, 474, 475, 478, 488, 489, 490, 491, 492
Genet, B., 54
Genta, M. L., 322
Gentile, D. A., 322
Gentile, S. R., 315
Gentry, J. H., 413, 503, 520
Gentz, D., 59
George, D. T., 436
George, J. A., 87
George, M. J., 322
George, W. H., 485

Geraerts, E., 439
Gershon, R. R. M., 57
Getz, S., 246
Giallella, C., 519
Gianesini, J., 172
Gibas, A. L., 419
Gibbs, C., 259
Gibbs, J. C., 525
Giebels, E., 63, 92
Gies, D., 169
Gill, B., 212
Gill, C. J., 378, 380
Gillard, N. D., 91, 505, 506
Gillespie, C. E., 364
Gillis, J. W., 392
Girard, J. M., 286
Girdner, L. K., 444
Glass, C., 260
Glaze, L., 29, 451, 454
Glaze, L. E., 453, 454, 463–464
Glew, G. M., 320
Glick, B., 527–528
Glisson, C., 523
Godboldt, S. M., 410, 411
Goddard, C., 410, 417–418
Goddard, M., 492
Goff, P. A., 68, 69
Goggin, C., 455, 469, 473, 474, 478, 488, 490
Gohm, C. L., 335
Golant, S. K., 413
Goldbeck, L., 400
Goldberg, E., 214, 215
Golding, S. L., 161, 166, 167, 168, 169, 170, 172, 173, 179, 181, 182, 183, 184
Goldkamp, J. S., 127
Goldman, R., 364
Goldman, V. J., 15–16
Goldschmidt, L., 256
Goldstein, A. M., 167, 177, 181, 182, 184, 190, 506, 526
Goldstein, A. P., 527–528
Goldstein, C. G., 25
Goldstein, N. E., 508
Goldstein, N. E. S., 506, 519
Golinelli, D., 454, 484, 486
Gongola, J., 102
Good, G. E., 341
Goodling, M. M., 146
Goodman, G. S., 441, 507–508
Goodman, L. A., 413, 415
Goodman-Delahunty, J., 380
Goodstein, C., 363
Goodwill, A. J., 338, 339

Morrissey, J. P., 460, 473, 474, 487
Morry, M. M., 335
Morse, S. J., 177, 181, 182, 184
Morton, F. J., 184
Morton, J., 433, 436
Morton-Bourgon, K. E., 337, 362, 363, 364, 365–366
Moser, A. E., 524
Mosher, D. L., 341
Moss, M., 313
Mossman, D., 173, 216, 217, 218, 222, 475
Mount, M. K., 47
Mourot, J. E., 416–417
Moynihan, G., 54
Mozeleski, W., 294–295, 296
Mueller, D. H., 93
Muirhead, Y., 352, 358, 359–360
Muirhead, Y. E., 443
Mulder, R, T., 274
Mullen, P. E., 314, 317, 319
Mullins, W. C., 62
Mulvey, E., 221
Mulvey, E. P., 264, 276, 474, 483, 520, 527, 528
Mumcuoglu, K. Y., 5
Mumley, D., 508
Mumley, D. L., 161, 166
Mundt, I. A., 352
Munn, R., 147
Muñoz, L. C., 256
Munsch, C. L., 336
Münzer, A., 400
Muraya, D. N., 403, 405
Murdock, T. B., 402
Murphy, B., 268
Murphy, E. A., 306
Murphy, K. R., 46, 48
Murphy, M., 519
Murphy, M. J., 15
Murphy, S. A., 394, 395
Murphy, W. D., 342
Murray, J. B., 427
Murray, K., 256
Murray, M., 381, 390
Murrie, D. C., 14, 153, 166, 167, 172, 173, 174–175, 175, 182, 215, 268, 273
Musliner, K. L., 400
Muzzy, W., 445–446
Myers, B., 104, 140, 142, 146, 470–471
Myers, W. C., 337

Nachlis, L. S., 195, 197
Nadal, K., 313
Nafpaktitis, M. K., 400

Nagayama-Hall, G., 338
Nagin, D. S., 243
Nagle, J., 311
Naik-Polan, A. T., 441
Nakamura, E., 390
Nakhost, A., 227
Narag, R. E., 259
Narchet, F. M., 93, 101
Nater, U., 300
Nation, J. R., 286
National Center for Victims of Crime, 383
National Center for Women & Policing, 66
National Center on Elder Abuse, 445
National College of Probate Judges, 196
National Council of Juvenile and Family Court Judges, 361
National Council on Crime and Delinquency, 384–385
National Research Council, 105, 405
National Resource Center on Child Sexual Abuse, 422–423
Neal, C., 127
Neal, T. M. S., 14, 153, 185, 202, 215, 341, 455, 489
Neeb, A. A., 523
Neff, J. L., 373
Neimeyer, R. A., 394
Nekvasil, E. K., 293, 294
Nelson, C. B., 389
Nelson, L. D., 45, 379
Nesca, M., 425–427
Neubauer, D. W., 132, 133
Neumann, C. S., 250, 261, 265, 267, 268, 273, 274
Newell, J., 127
Newirth, K. A., 147
Newman, G., 279
Newman, J. P., 248, 257, 258, 273–274
Newman, K., 293
Newman, R. A., 470–471
Nguyen, Q. X., 488
Nicholaichuk, T. P., 484
Nicholls, T. L., 184, 261, 274, 358, 362
Nichols, R. M., 110
Nichols-Lopez, K., 436
Nicholson, R., 161, 169
Nicholson, R. A., 44
Nieberding, R. J., 264, 275
Niederhoffer, A., 37
Niederhoffer, E., 37
Nielsen, L., 209
Nietzel, M. T., 147, 153
Nievod, A., 155

Nigg, J., 250, 258
Nigg, J. T., 251
Nikolova, N. L., 268
Nix, J., 52
Noelanders, S., 63
Noesner, G. W., 61
Norcross, J. C., 8, 19, 28–29, 470, 471
Norgard, K., 187
Norko, M. A., 184
Norman, R. E., 252
Norris, F. H., 28
Norris, R. J., 100
Northam, E., 259
Norwood, S., 161
Norwood, W. D., 388
Novosad, D., 184
Nunes, K. L., 352
Nunn, R., 259
Nurcombe, B., 430, 440
Nussbaum, D., 463

Oberlander, L. B., 508
O'Brien, B. S., 271
O'Brien, L., 249
Ochoa, K. C., 162
O'Connell, D. J., 481, 489
O'Connell, P., 321
O'Connor, T. P., 90, 98, 99
Odgers, C. L., 243, 252, 322
Odgers, C L., 242
Offord, D. R., 252
Ofshe, R. J., 98–99
Ogawa, B., 376, 377
Ogden, D., 6
Ogloff, J. R. P., 6–7, 8, 136, 148, 150, 317
O'Hara, A. F., 60
Ohlin, L. E., 240
O'Keefe, M. L., 469
Okun, B. F., 25–26, 198, 200, 201
Olaya, B., 417, 418
Olfson, M., 399, 400
Oliver, M. E., 484
Olkin, R., 380
Olson, J. F., 87
Olson, N. D., 516
Olthof, T., 321
Olver, M. E., 15, 20, 267, 275–276
Omestad, T., 84
O'Neill, S., 147
O'Ran, S., 381
Ormerod, D., 86, 439
Ormrod, R., 374, 387, 391, 396, 442, 443
Orne, E. C., 107, 108
Orne, M. T., 107, 108, 109

Rosenfeld, B., 317, 454, 478, 479, 490
Rosenfeld, B. D., 181
Rosengren, K., 155–156
Rosin, H., 396
Rosinski, A., 161, 162–163
Ross, A. B., 91, 92
Ross, A. M., 93
Ross, D. F., 435
Ross, R., 259
Ross, R. R., 489
Rossmo, D. K., 82
Rosso, M., 45
Rostow, C. D., 45
Roth, W., 293
Rothbaum, B. O., 402, 421
Rothman, D., 500
Routh, D. K., 16
Rowe, K. L., 61, 62
Royster, T. E., 62
Rozalski, M., 42, 380
Rubel, J., 264, 275
Rubin, K. H., 258
Rubinstein, M., 363
Ruchkin, V., 256
Rufino, K. A., 153
Ruggerio, K., 396
Ruiz, M. A., 47
Russano, M. B., 91, 92, 93, 101, 149
Russell, K., 407
Russell, M. A., 242
Ruzek, J. I., 58
Ryan, J., 42, 380
Ryan, S. L., 116

Sabalis, R. F., 484
Sacco, D. F., 113
Sadeh, N., 273, 274
Sadler, M. S., 68, 69
Safer, M. A., 111
Saks, M. J., 133
Salekin, R., 272
Salekin, R. T., 264, 267, 270, 273–274,
    276, 483, 513
Sales, B., 426–427
Sales, B. D., 16, 147, 149, 199, 204, 210
Salisbury, E., 474, 486
Salisbury, E. J., 407
Salmivalli, C., 321
Salter, D., 361
Salvatori, S., 402
Samenow, S. E., 527
Sammons, M. T., 14
Sampson, R. J., 242
Samuels, S., 463
Sanders, M. J., 428–429

Sandler, J., 189
Sandler, J. C., 190, 358, 365
Sanford, G. M., 274–275, 275
Sangrigoli, S., 114
Santos, A. B., 522
Santtila, P., 87
Saum, C., 127
Saum, C. A., 481, 489
Saunders, B. E., 335, 402, 421
Saunders, J. T., 520
Savigné, K. C., 268
Savitsky, K., 25
Scali, M. A., 503
Scalora, M. J., 191
Schaefer, G. S., 352
Schaeffer, C. M., 522
Schafer, J. A., 388
Scheepers, F. E., 265
Scheer, D. A., 28
Scheflin, A. W., 106, 109–110, 438
Schell, T. L., 390
Schiffman, W., 508
Schlank, A., 529
Schlegel, P., 413, 503, 520
Schlenger, W. E., 390
Schmidt, A. F., 352
Schmidt, W. W., 55–56, 59
Schmitt, D. S., 261, 267, 274
Schmucker, M., 484
Schneider, B. A., 353
Schoenwald, S. K., 522, 524
Schopp, R. F., 226
Schramke, C. J., 436
Schreier, H., 428
Schrum, C. L., 513
Schrum Dillard, C. L., 273
Schuck, A. M., 67
Schwab-Stone, M., 256
Schwalbe, C. S., 518, 523, 527
Schwartz, B., 361, 528
Schwartz, B. K., 338
Schwartz, I. M., 503, 525
Schwartz, L. L., 69
Schwartz, R. G., 505
Schwarz, R., 509
Schweizer, J., 161, 162–163
Scogin, F., 43, 46
Scott, E., 509
Scott, E. S., 245
Scott, J. G., 252
Scovern, A. W., 484
Scrivner, E. M., 24, 36, 37, 39, 42, 43, 45,
    49, 50, 56, 60, 61, 63, 70, 71
Scurich, N., 102
Seagrave, D., 271, 272, 513

Sebanz, N., 103
Sedlak, A., 444
Sedlak, A. J., 404, 514, 516, 517, 518,
    520–521
Seeger, T., 293, 295
Segal, D. L., 251, 252
Seghorn, T., 338, 353
Séguin, J. R., 251, 258
Seklecki, R., 67
Seligman, M. E., 415
Selkie, E. M., 323
Selkin, J., 338
Sellbom, M., 45, 261
Semmler, C., 110
Senter, A., 471
Serin, R. C., 264, 339, 481–482
Serna-McDonald, C., 471
Serrano, S. D., 418
Sesan, R., 427, 428
Seto, M. C., 184, 339, 360, 402
Sevecke, K., 250
Sewell, K. W., 91, 94, 95, 169, 170, 182,
    216, 273–274, 506
Sexton, T., 523
Seymour, A., 335, 411–413, 415
Seymour, F., 260
Shaffer, C. S., 138, 505, 529
Shah, S., 19, 127, 487
Shahinfar, A., 388
Shakespeare-Finch, J., 59
Shannon, L. M., 127
Shanok, S. S., 260
Shapiro, D., 455, 489
Shapiro, D. L., 181
Sharif, I., 428
Sharma, K. K., 315, 316
Sharrón-Del-Río, M. R., 377
Shattock, A., 353, 396
Shaw, D., 102, 256
Shaw, J., 334, 343
Shaw, T., 320
Sheeran, T., 389
Shelden, R. G., 503, 521
Shelton, J., 443
Shelton, J. E., 352, 358, 359–360
Shepherd, J. W., 113
Sheras, P. L., 297
Sheridan, M. S., 319, 427, 428
Shields, R. T., 190, 365
Shields-Fletcher, E., 520
Shihadeh, E. S., 284
Shirtcliff, E. A., 273
Shneidman, E. S., 85
Shore, J. H., 184
Showers, J., 429

SUBJECT INDEX